THE *unofficial* GUIDE®
ᵀᴼCruises

11TH EDITION

THE *unofficial* GUIDE®

ᵀᴼCruises

11TH EDITION

KAY SHOWKER *with* BOB SEHLINGER

WILEY

Published by:
John Wiley & Sons, Inc.
111 River Street
Hoboken, NJ 07030-5774

Produced by Menasha Ridge Press

Cover design by Michael J. Freeland

Interior design by Michele Laseau

For information on our other products and services or to obtain technical support, please contact our Customer Care Department within the United States at 877-762-2974, outside the United States at 317-572-3993, or by fax at 317-572-4002.

John Wiley & Sons, Inc., also publishes its books in a variety of electronic formats. Some content that appears in print may not be available in electronic formats.

ISBN 978-0-470-46033-7

Manufactured in the United States of America

5 4 3 2 1

CONTENTS

MAPS *and* ILLUSTRATIONS

LAURELS
for the
LABORERS

THIS EDITION MARKS the 14th year and 11th edition for the *Unofficial Guide to Cruises*. It goes almost without saying that a book of this scope—covering more than 100 cruise lines with upward of 400 ships sailing to destinations from the North Pole to the South Pole and around the world—is the work of many people. Over the years it has required extensive research, interviews with passengers, seemingly endless discussions with specialized travel agents and other knowledgeable people about cruises, not to mention the incredible amount of follow-up due to the constantly changing nature of the cruise industry.

So many people have been tireless in their effort to help that it would take another book to name them all, but we would be remiss not to mention some.

Alan Wilson, editor/publisher of *Cruise News Daily,* an online newsletter; Mike Driscoll's online newsletter, *Cruise Week;* The World Ocean & Cruise Liner Society; Tom Cassidy's monthly publication, *Ocean Cruise News,* and its online version by cruise historian Bill Miller; *Cruisemates;* and *Travel Agent* and *Travel Weekly* magazines' online editions have been steady sources of information helping us keep abreast of the constantly changing cruise industry.

Lloyd Cole of Valerie Wilson Travel, Dr. Bradley Feuer of Pace Travel, and Lisa Haber of Cruise Professionals have given us plentiful insights and never seemed to tire of our endless questions.

We are grateful to all our public-relations friends at the cruise lines who helped us check the nitty-gritty details and who have been our hosts over the years without any obligation.

TEXT CONTRIBUTIONS

TIME CONSTRAINTS IN WRITING A BOOK such as this make it impossible for two people to visit and revisit every ship prior to our deadlines, as we would want to do. Throughout the years, we have called on colleagues for help, particularly writers who specialize in cruising and are as qualified as we to write this book.

Some of these folks contributed material written specifically for the book, others shared their knowledge from recent cruises or allowed us to use material from recently published research, while still others reviewed or helped with the updating of information we had already written. Specifically for Part Two, sections were written by Larry Miller (Azamara Club Cruises); Michael Bennett (Bahamas Celebration); Dave Houser (Cruise West); Ted Scull (American Safari Cruises; Saga Cruises); and Susan Young (Oceania Cruises); and Ann Kalosh, Marcia Levin, and Susan Milne, who not only wrote parts of this book but also generously contributed their insights and information to many of the cruise lines and ships profiled in Part Two. For Part Three, sections were written by Ted Scull (Hurtigruten and European Cruise Ferries); Dave Houser (Freighter Cruises); Ted Scull and P. J. Mooney (Hapag-Lloyd Cruises); Shann Davies (Yangtze River Cruises in China); and Carla Hunt (Cruceros Australis). Mary Brennan had the difficult task of preparing the complex and constantly changing cruise ship itineraries. Many other writing colleagues shared their firsthand experience with us, too. We particularly want to thank Arlene and Sam Bleecker, Anne Campbell, Michael Driscoll, Marilyn Green, Mary Ann Hemphill, and Molly Staub.

Many, many friends, friends of friends, travel agents, and cruise passengers along the way willingly gave us their time for interviews, helped with ship ratings, and phoned and sent us letters about their latest cruise, and to them we express our heartfelt thanks.

Last but not least, we thank the staff of Menasha Ridge Press, who worked tirelessly on the manuscript every step of the way.

—Kay Showker
and *Bob Sehlinger*

INTRODUCTION

◼ ABOUT *This* GUIDE

HOW COME "UNOFFICIAL"?

THE MATERIAL IN THIS GUIDE has not been edited or directed by the cruise lines profiled. In this "unofficial" guide we represent and serve you, the consumer. If a ship serves mediocre food, has cramped cabins, or offers poor shore excursions, we will say so. Through our independence, we hope we can make selecting a cruise efficient and economical and your cruise experience on-target and fun.

MAKING IT EASY

IN THE NEARLY TWO YEARS it took to write the first edition of this book, Kay had pinned on a wall in front of her a note that read: "This book has one purpose: To help readers select the right cruise—i.e., the cruise that's right for them." She kept it there to make sure we never lost sight of that goal.

Most guides to cruising approach their subject on a ship-by-ship basis, giving only the briefest attention to the cruise line and emphasizing ships—the hardware. But people don't buy ships, they buy cruises, and those cruises—the software—have been designed according to cruise lines' business plans, which define the types of cruises they offer. The cruise lines are challenged daily by their competitors and all the other leisure products vying for your attention to make their cruises irresistible. Yet they freely admit that although there's a cruise for everyone, not every cruise is for everyone. What it boils down to is that you can listen to Beethoven's Ninth Symphony played by the Boston Symphony Orchestra, or you can hear it played by the New York Philharmonic. It's the same music, but it's going to come out differently.

This book is designed to help you recognize the differences. By understanding the cruise lines and the experiences they offer, you will be able to recognize the different types of cruises available and identify the ones likely to appeal to you. Each line offers cruises with features that distinguish them from the others. It is these features—or "style" as we call it—that are the essence of the cruise experience.

A Carnival cruise is a Carnival cruise, for example. Each Carnival ship offers a "Fun Ship" vacation, and, except for the cruise's length and destinations, the experience varies little among their ships. Carnival has designed it that way. However, a Carnival cruise is as different from a Princess, Holland America, or Seabourn cruise as night is from day.

As cruise lines continue to standardize their operations to keep costs down and distinguish themselves from their competition, it becomes more important for you (or your travel agent), as you select a cruise, to understand the line and the type of cruises it offers. With that goal in mind, this guidebook is organized in three parts:

Part One, Planning Your Cruise Vacation, covers basic information on what cruises contain, tips on finding the best values, and preparing for your cruise.

Part Two, Cruise Lines and Their Ships, profiles all major "mainstream" cruise lines that sell primarily to U.S. and Canadian travelers. At the end of Part Two are cruise lines—some small, some also in the mainstream—but not necessarily on this side of the Atlantic. Most, but not all, are based in Europe and cruise less-traveled routes.

Part Three, Cruising Alternatives, describes other options, such as river cruises, adventure and expedition cruises, plus freighters, coastal ships, cruise ferries, and sailing ships.

COMMENTS AND QUESTIONS FROM READERS

MANY WHO USE THE *Unofficial Guides* write to us with questions, comments, or their own strategies for planning and enjoying travel. We appreciate all such input, both positive and critical. Readers' comments are frequently incorporated into revised editions and have contributed immeasurably to their improvement. Please write to:

Kay and Bob
The Unofficial Guide to Cruises
P.O. Box 43673
Birmingham, AL 35243

Please put your return address on both your letter and envelope; the two sometimes become separated. Also, include your phone number if you are available for a possible interview. And remember, our work often requires that we be out of the office for long periods, so forgive us if our response is slow. If you'd like a faster response, you can also try e-mailing us at unofficialguides@menasharidge.com.

A Reader Survey is included at the end of the book. We urge you to copy or clip it out, add your impressions, and send it in.

CRUISING:
A Look Back, A Look Ahead

DECEMBER 19, 1966, IS RECOGNIZED AS A LANDMARK because on that date a series of cruises was launched that, for the first time, had been created and packaged as a mass-market product and sold on a year-round basis. The ship, the *Sunward* of the Norwegian Caribbean Line (later renamed the Norwegian Cruise Line), sailed from Miami to Nassau with 540 passengers on the first three- and four-day cruises to be offered year-round between Miami and the Bahamas. No one, including the creators, imagined where that small step would lead. Indeed, many in the steamship business dismissed the idea as crazy, declaring there was not enough of a market to support such cruises.

Cruising, of course, did not actually start in 1966; it evolved over a span of 170 years. But it's true that until the 1960s the closest most people got to a big ship was on the big screen, either in movies about glamorous people living romantic lives, or in newsreels of the Duke and Duchess of Windsor arriving on the *Queen Mary,* or F. Scott and Zelda, the Astors, the Vanderbilts, and other celebrities sailing stylishly to Europe aboard an elegant ocean liner.

From the start of the first regular transatlantic steamship service by Samuel Cunard in 1840, a voyage on a great liner became the ultimate dream shared by people worldwide. In the early days, a sea voyage was more of an expedition, requiring passengers to endure hardships with few amenities on board ship or at ports. Passenger comfort, even in first class, was not a priority. But as competition developed and steamship travel gained popularity, each generation of ships brought enhanced comfort.

Then, too, throughout the late 19th century and up to World War I, ships carrying passengers had other purposes. Among them was transporting thousands of immigrants to the New World and a new life. To meet the demand—and reap large profits—many steamship companies were born and ships built, and, except for the war years when the vessels transported troops, ocean liners paraded across the Atlantic and Pacific in an endless stream, with the world's elite in their top decks and the huddled masses below.

Then in 1921, passage of the Immigration Act, intended to slow the torrent of new arrivals, forced steamship companies to change course. To make up for lost revenue from steerage, companies created cabin or tourist class in the several decks below first class and unwittingly took the next step toward modern cruising. Although a voyage remained a means of getting from one continent to another, it was no longer a pastime only for the privileged. Cabin class did not have the elegance and panache of first class, but it wasn't bad. It found a ready market in the GIs who had fought in Europe and wanted to return with their families, immigrants who had made good and wanted to visit relatives in their homelands, and America's growing middle class, who wanted to emulate the celebrities and aristocrats in first class.

THE GOLDEN AGE

THE ROARING TWENTIES WAS A GOLDEN AGE for steamship travel. It was a time of new prosperity, blithe spirits—and Prohibition in America. With alcoholic beverages legal at sea, ship companies offered a new type of short cruise—the party, or booze cruise—that made getting there half the fun.

In the dining room, passengers sat at long tables on chairs bolted to the floor (ships did not have stabilizers). In 1910, Ritz restaurants, replicating the setting of their shoreside operations, introduced round tables and carpeted floors in first class on ships of Hapag-Lloyd of Germany. The style soon became the standard for other ships. Private bathrooms were available in first class on the grandest liners, but in cabin class, passengers shared bath facilities until the 1950s. Air-conditioning was introduced by P&O Lines in the 1930s but did not become common until the 1950s.

The first indoor swimming pool appeared in 1910 on the *Olympic* of White Star Line. (It was the first of the line's three superliners; the others were the *Titanic* and the *Gigantic,* later renamed *Britannic.*) Known as a plunge bath, it had a balcony where others could watch the bathers. The first permanent outdoor pool was introduced in 1926 on the *Roma* of Italian Lines. Until the late 1950s, the top deck was fitted with machinery and was off-limits to passengers. Today, it's usually a sports deck.

A NEW ERA

AFTER WEATHERING THE GREAT DEPRESSION and another war, ocean liners resumed their traditional role, and by the 1950s were conveying hordes of students to Europe and masses of refugees to U.S. shores. The glamour returned with the comings and goings of a young Liz Taylor and the sailing of Grace Kelly to her fairyland prince. After World War II, the addition of radar and improved navigational equipment made passenger ships safer and more accurate in regard to arrival times, enabling operators to plan reliable itineraries. By the mid-1950s, most ocean liners had stabilizers. Radios were added in staterooms. The tradition to separate first class and tourist class on transatlantic service continued, but in 1958, Holland America launched the *Rotterdam,* which could be converted to one class. However, by decade's end, most elite passengers had taken flight—literally.

The final blow came in 1958, when the first commercial jets streaked across the Atlantic, cutting travel time from five days to just over five hours. Instead of dying out, however, the ships changed course and became part of the revolution that took place on the sea as well as in the sky.

THE CRUISE REVOLUTION

THE TURNAROUND OF THE 1960S brought radical changes. New cruise lines, untethered to the past, exchanged formality for fun and brought a new atmosphere to shipboard life. The barriers of separate classes were removed, and the space was used for sports, recreation, and entertainment, turning the ships into floating resorts. Getting there was no longer half the fun—it *was* the fun. Passengers no longer bundled under blankets in deck chairs. Instead, they bounced in aerobics classes, swung at golf and tennis balls, plunged into the sea with masks and fins, soaked in hot tubs, and luxuriated in shipboard spas. Bingo survived, but it now competed with jazzy casinos, Broadway shows and discos, wine and piano bars, comics and cabarets. New and younger passengers were attracted by the activity and informality. Families with children, too, were finding cruises to be ideal vacations.

The 1970s began with Royal Caribbean Cruise Lines making its debut with a fleet of ships built specifically for Caribbean cruising. It was followed two years later by Carnival Cruise Lines, which developed the "Fun Ship" concept to scuttle the elitist traditions of ocean liners and appeal to a mass market of younger, first-time passengers from all walks of life.

As the revolution's final irony, the spectacular growth in cruise vacations really took off in the 1970s, when cruise lines joined forces with airlines, which had almost put the steamship companies out of business. The union created air/sea programs that combined air transportation and ground transfers with a cruise in one package at one price. The programs enhanced the value of cruise vacations, simplified their purchase, and eliminated hassles for travelers. With the packages, cruise lines virtually brought their ships to people's doorsteps, regardless of where they lived. The marriage enabled cruise lines to base their ships in warm-weather ports from where they could cruise year-round and to fly passengers from faraway places to begin their cruises.

A relaxed, informal holiday in the sun—and available year-round—became the essence of modern cruising. Flying passengers to their ships saved time and enabled cruise lines to offer shorter, less expensive cruises that fit into the national trend toward shorter vacations. People who might never have considered taking a cruise booked them. It also allowed cruise lines to open new parts of the world to cruising; itineraries multiplied. No matter how many cruises a person took, new ones remained. Or so it seemed, until the oil crisis of the early 1970s, when dark clouds again threatened the future of vacations at sea.

Then, in 1978, despite skyrocketing fuel prices and predictions that cruising was doomed, Carnival Cruise Lines ordered a large, technologically advanced passenger ship. It became the forerunner of the

1980s superliners. Two years later, Norwegian Cruise Line shocked the cruise world by buying the fabulous *France* and transforming her into the *Norway*. The floating resort set cruise trends for the decade, introducing innovations, including a variety of entertainment lounges, a theater for Broadway-scale productions, a shopping plaza, and a "sidewalk" cafe. Holland America followed with *Nieuw Amsterdam* and *Noordam,* twin ships with square sterns that allowed over 20 percent more deck space for recreation, including two swimming pools. The ships also introduced computer keys to open cabin doors and other innovations.

Princess Cruises' stylish *Royal Princess,* which debuted in 1984, set new standards of comfort with all outside cabins fitted with minibars, television, and baths with tubs in every category. About the same time, the *QE2* introduced the first Golden Door spa at sea, the first computer learning center, and the first satellite-delivered newspaper.

Among the most interesting entries in the 1980s was the *Windstar,* a cruise ship with computerized sails. *Windstar* married the romance of sailing under canvas with the comforts of a cruise ship and the electronic age. At the same time, Carnival's superliners, *Holiday, Jubilee,* and *Celebration,* were introduced. Their madcap design totally changed the look of ship interiors and the use of public space.

Yet nothing since the *Norway* caused as much excitement as the 1988 debut of Royal Caribbean Cruise Line's *Sovereign of the Seas.* The world's largest cruise ship at the time, she became the pacesetter for the 1990s. Among her features was the first shipboard atrium, rising through five decks and creating a new environment. The ship offered such numerous and varied entertainment and recreation options that passengers needed several cruises to experience them all. Well-equipped gyms, elaborate spas, VCRs, cable television, and worldwide direct-dial telephones were rapidly becoming standard amenities. Small boutique ships, including those of the Seabourn and Silversea lines, brought new levels of luxury to cruising. Special-interest lines were finding their niche. Increased interest in adventure and nature cruises caused some traditional cruise lines to add them.

IN THE NEW MILLENNIUM

NOW INTO ITS FIFTH DECADE, the cruise boom shows no signs of slowing down. In that time, the number of passengers has swelled from under 500,000 annually to more than 13.5 million in 2009. Thirteen of the twenty-three members of the Cruise Lines International Association, the major cruise trade association, did not exist 20 years ago.

The 1990s were a blockbuster decade, with more than three dozen new ships costing billions making their debut; and followed by a similar launch in the new century with no letup. From 2007 to 2009, 38 ships were delivered at a pace of about a dozen ships each year. Throughout the decades, the new vessels have reflected the wide range of cruise-ship size and style—accommodating from 82 passengers on small riverboats to 6,000 passengers on the monstrous *Oasis of the Seas*—as well as the broad range of cruise experiences they offer.

By the new millennium, ships of 100,000 tons and more represented the new generation of megaliners. Most had new design features and facilities—such as the18-hole miniature golf course on Royal Caribbean's *Legend of the Seas,* and cruising's first rock-climbing wall and ice rink on 142,000-ton *Voyager of the Seas.*

In December 2003, Cunard's *Queen Mary 2* assumed the title as the biggest, widest, longest, and most expensive ship ever built, and at 150,000 tons she dwarfed all predecessors. The much-anticipated *QM2* came with the first and only spa at sea operated by the world-famous Canyon Ranch health resorts; the world's first and only planetarium at sea; the largest ballroom at sea; the largest library at sea; the largest wine cellar at sea; ten dining venues, including the first and only shipboard restaurant by popular American chef Todd English; and a learning center with guest lecturers from Oxford University.

However, *QM2* lost her "biggest" status in 2006 to RCCL's 162,000-ton *Freedom of the Seas,* and now the contest may have finally come to an end with Royal Caribbean's 220,000-ton *Oasis of the Seas,* delivered in November 2009. Stretching more than four football fields and costing $1.5 billion, she is capable of carrying up to 6,300 passengers.

Among other innovations, the new ships brought the first bowling alley at sea on Norwegian Cruise Line's *Norwegian Pearl,* the first Grand Prix (Formula One) race car simulator on *Costa Concordia,* and the first boxing ring at sea on Royal Caribbean's *Freedom of the Seas.*

Along with innovations, the new ships have enhanced the cruise experience. Standard cabins on most new ships are larger, and there are many more verandas across the price spectrum. More dining options have become standard, with Norwegian Cruise Lines setting the pace with 11 dining venues. There are also more entertainment choices, more sports opportunities, greatly expanded children's facilities, more elaborate spas, Internet cafes, in-cabin Internet access, wireless facilities, and cell phones that work at sea.

Other ways the cruise experience is being enhanced are through innovative enrichment programs, such as Crystal Cruises' Creative Learning Center, offering courses in cooking, art, business, technology, and health, and even piano lessons in an arrangement with Yamaha that provides instructors. Another such program is Princess Cruises' Scholarship Sea (which Princess calls "edutainment"), introduced on the *Coral Princess* with topics ranging from cooking taught in a demonstration kitchen like those seen on television, to pottery classes with the first shipboard kiln; and Holland America's Culinary Arts Institute, which is part of the line's ambitious $525 million Signature of Excellence, a multifaceted program that has upgraded and expanded all the shipboard facilities and amenities to appeal to maturing baby boomers, the growing family, and multi-generation vacationer market.

There has also been a vast improvement in the variety and number of shore excursions (although not an improvement in price), particularly in the Caribbean, for passengers to enjoy hiking, biking, kayaking, golf, swimming with dolphins, and much more. Now, too, many cruise lines enable passengers to book shore excursions online. Cruise lines faced with intense competition—again, particularly in the Caribbean—have looked for new and more varied itineraries, but the biggest shift, particularly after 9/11, and again with the economic downturn in 2008, has been a new emphasis on "homeland" cruising. This has resulted in more ships based in new U.S. ports and many more itineraries along the East and West coasts of the United States, Mexico, and Central America. By 2009, cruise lines were offering cruises from more than 30 domestic home ports where, collectively, more than half the U.S. population is within driving distance of a cruise departure port. In addition to attracting travelers who do not want to stray far from home, it has stimulated a market of drivers who do not want to fly out of fear or who prefer not to deal with the security hassles and delays at airports. Frequently, too, it results in significant savings to passengers by eliminating the cost of airfare.

Although innovation and product refinement is common throughout the cruise industry, Princess Cruises and Norwegian Cruise Lines have led the way. Most of the innovations address longstanding complaints of cruise passengers (they really do read all those survey forms). For cruisers who disliked being relegated to a specific seating for dinner, or for that matter, eating in the same restaurant each night, many vessels, particularly the newest ones, now offer multiple dining venues that operate like shoreside restaurants. Make a reservation or just show up at the restaurant of your choice.

Specialties at these stand-alone eateries cover a wide variety of cuisines, from Japanese to Mexican and Italian to Chinese. Carnival, Princess and Holland America, for example, have installed steakhouses on their fleets. The Princess Personal Choice Dining program also includes an Italian trattoria, a Southwestern restaurant, and a 24-hour buffet and bistro. Norwegian Cruise Line's Freestyle Cruising, which began the trend, will offer 14 restaurants, each with its own identity and area of specialization, on its new *Norwegian Epic*, set to launch in July 2010. On the Disney Cruise Line, passengers rotate to a different restaurant each night. The line also features a reservations- and adults-only Italian restaurant on each ship.

Carnival introduced "Total Choice" dining, enabling passengers to choose from four seating times in the main dining room instead of the usual two. Four seatings stagger the arrival of diners, preventing the galley from being inundated and allowing the waitstaff to concentrate on a smaller number of passengers at any given time. Carnival has also added a supper club with gourmet cuisine on some of its new ships, which has proven enormously popular.

Although more choice in dining sounds like a definite perk, there's a downside, particularly on large ships. A great number of singles and couples depend on meeting new friends at their assigned table in the main dining room. For many, their assigned dinner companions become their social circle for the duration of the cruise. Each night, they meet over dinner and discuss the day's activities. Some coordinate shore tours or enjoy each other's company outside the dining room, and it is a common occurrence for tablemates to become close friends and keep in touch once they return home. Needless to say, it's much harder to get acquainted and form friendships when your assigned dinner companions are off trying the alternative dining venues each night.

Among other notable initiatives is the Princess Flight-Choice program that confirms air itineraries purchased through Princess 60 days prior to the cruise date, allowing passengers ample time to make changes if desired. In a related program, Princess and other cruise lines have established an express check-in, where passengers can avoid the hassle of dockside check-in by completing boarding documents online or mailing them to Princess in advance.

More and more cruise lines enable passengers to "stay connected" by providing Internet access, including wireless connection. Staying connected can also mean using your cell phone as more and more cruise lines have installed enabling equipment.

Another bow to the electronic age: When you sail with Carnival, Holland America, MSC, Norwegian Cruise Line, or Princess Cruises, you will receive your tickets and other documentation via email unless you or your travel agent tell the cruise line otherwise. Other cruise lines are quickly following suit.

THE BIG TWO

ALTHOUGH NOT MANY CRUISERS KNOW IT, two companies control the lion's share of the American cruise market. These companies set the pace and establish norms for the mass-market cruise industry. Then, too, when there's a depressed travel market, as there was after 9/11, and again in 2008–2009, their discounts impact even the luxury end of the market.

Largest of the two is Carnival Corporation, which owns Carnival, Holland America, Cunard, Seabourn, Costa Cruises, P&O (which includes P&O Australia), Princess Cruises, and several small lines created to serve specific markets, such as Germany.

The other is Royal Caribbean International (RCI), which operates Royal Caribbean Cruise Line, Azamara Club Cruises, Celebrity Cruises, and Pullamtur, a major Spanish tour and cruise operator.

A new Number Three, Apollo International, a private equity firm, acquired Oceania Cruises, Regent Seven Seas Cruises, and half interest of Norwegian Cruise Line/NCL America in 2007.

Cruise lines big and small got off to a rough start in 2007–2008. First, there was the soaring price of fuel, followed by a serious dip in the economy. With new ships with thousands of extra berths to fill, the fight for passengers was running at full tilt. By the 2009 Christmas season, cruising had begun its comeback, but prices are still at an all-time low. Indeed, there has never been a better time than now to take a cruise for their unprecedented value.

Rather than cut prices further, however, lines are responding to the economic crisis with hard-to-resist promotions, such as kids sail free, shipboard credit offers, special prices on selected itineraries, lay-away and other payment plans, free airfare and/or shore excursions, adjusted deposit requirements, and relaxed cancellation policies.

Nonetheless, between the impact of 9/11 and the devastated economy of 2008–2009, six cruise lines—Premier, Commodore, American Classic Voyages (parent company of American Hawaii and Delta Queen Steamboat Company), Renaissance, Regal Cruises, and World Explorer Cruises—went out of business. The loss of these lines was especially sad because they were small, moderately priced operators serving areas that the big lines had ignored or could not serve with their huge ships.

On the bright side, two new cruise lines were launched in summer 2003: Oceania Cruise Lines, using two of Renaissance Cruises' former vessels and modeling itself, more or less, after that now-defunct line, and Voyages of Discovery, sailing on less-traveled routes. Despite the soft travel market, Oceania did well, added a third ship, and is building two new ships. Other former Renaissance ships have found their way to exploration and cultural cruise lines, and as a result, set a new deluxe standard for these types of cruises.

The loss of each small or medium cruise line is important because it diminishes competition and concentrates more power in the larger lines, especially in the American market. Interestingly, some of the ships of these defunct cruise lines have found their way to small European cruise lines, particularly British-based lines, such as Fred Olsen Cruise Lines and Saga Cruises, to name a few.

THE FUTURE

THE TWO OVERRIDING FACTORS that will influence all travel, and particularly cruises, for years to come will be the Internet and the maturing of the baby boomer generation. With someone in the United States turning 50 every seven seconds, it's easy to see who the cruise lines' passengers will be and why so many trends already in place or developing are a result, directly or indirectly, of these elements.

With regard to new ships, the numbers have slowed considerably. Those in the pipeline will have features designed to attract and satisfy the growing market of family and multi-generation vacationers and will further develop the concept of the ship as the destination.

Look also for ships more than eight years old to undergo major modifications and conversions that go beyond the required refurbishing to cater to the changing tastes of consumers and the maturing baby boomers. Examples include Holland America's $525 million investment in its "Signature of Excellence" program, Seabourn Cruises' doubling the size of its gyms, and Costa Cruises' adding balconies to one of its newest ships, which did not have them.

Even as ships continue to get larger, we are likely to see the entry of more small ships, tailored to specific markets and specific segments of the market. It's already happened in Europe—German ships for German speakers, British ships for Brits and Anglophiles, French ships for a French-speaking audience.

Average price of cruises will remain low for cruise lines to remain competitive and continue broadening the market—all the more so as long as the economy remains in the doldrums. At the same time, lines continue to be under the constant pressure of rising operating costs for food, labor, shipbuilding, fuel, amenities, and entertainment. Thus, they must look for ways, particularly through onboard revenue, to offset these increased costs, since there is little elasticity in prices and a limit to reducing operating costs without weakening the product.

Already labor cutbacks can be seen on the large, mass-market ships. In the past, cabin attendants might have been assigned 12 cabins, but now they care for 20. In the dining rooms, headwaiters and waitstaff might have had a dozen tables to serve, but now they have 20 and the wine steward is gone. There have been cutbacks in food quantity (and in some cases quality) as reflected in fewer courses at breakfast and lunch and/or fewer selections for each course.

New cruisers may not be aware of these changes and experienced ones may not care if it helps keep down prices. Then, too, there has always been too much food and too many choices served on most ships. What's more, people's interests and lifestyles have changed. As a result, cruise lines are switching their emphasis to activities and amenities, rather than food, as in the past. Food is still important but changing.

Look for a wider range of amenities and dining options with more venues, more types of food, and specialty restaurants onboard. We've seen the beginning of a trend—restaurants run by well-known chefs or shoreside restaurants. Todd English on the QM2 is an example.

Another trend to watch: ships staying overnight in port, giving passengers the opportunity to explore ports in more depth. This could be particularly appropriate for destination-oriented cruise lines and be a result of a maturing cruise market. It also reflects a shift from the old formula of more ports being seen as value to experienced cruisers understanding the value of overnight port stays.

Now that The World/ResidenSea has shown the way, look for new lines to try a variety of new ideas, such as cruise ships with apartments for sale as time-shares, or cabins booked for one to four months at a time or even a year.

One of the most significant trends has been the fundamental change in the cruise lines' sources of cruise passengers. Up to 30% year over year cruise passengers are coming from countries other than the United States and Canada. While it varies by line, the leading source is Europe, particularly the UK, Germany, Italy, and Spain. This is due largely to the cruise lines' expanded presence with more ships in Europe, as well as the overall trend toward globalization.

Another trend is the cruise lines' effort to go green. As new ships are introduced, lines are incorporating the latest technology to help produce environmentally friendly vessels. These include wastewater purification, air-emission reductions, LED lighting, solar power, high-efficiency appliances, low-sulfur fuels, and other initiatives.

The availability of Internet access on cruise ships has grown by leaps and bounds as has the availability of wireless connection and cell phone use. At the same time, the acceptance of personal computers as part of our lives and the ease of using them to book travel will have more and more people booking cruises on the Internet and the number of mom-and-pop travel agencies shrinking. Already those agencies dropped from 33,000 in 2001 to about 17,000 in 2004, and some predict there will be fewer than 5,000 by the end of the decade. Meanwhile, the number of home-based travel agents has skyrocketed and now account for one-third of all cruise sales. And the Internet may even force cruise lines to simplify their pricing, including, we hope, brochure prices that today have no relation to reality.

Despite setbacks and uncertainties, cruising as a vacation choice continues to attract new travelers by the thousands and has devotees returning year after year. That's because the fundamental attraction of cruising—value for money—has not and is not likely to change.

PART ONE

PLANNING *Your* CRUISE

▌█ UNDERSTANDING CRUISES

THE INCLUSIVE CRUISE VACATION

MOST CRUISES ARE INCLUSIVE—that is, their basic components are typically purchased together rather than à la carte. In general, a cruise—or what a travel agency or cruise line might describe as a "cruise-only" product—includes:

1. Shipboard accommodations.
2. Three full-service dining room meals daily (breakfast, lunch, and dinner), plus alternative breakfast, lunch, evening buffets, and late-night snacks. On most ships, room service meals do not cost extra. Many ships also offer options, such as early-bird breakfast and afternoon events, including tea, pizza snacks, ice-cream parties, and cookouts.
3. Most shipboard entertainment, including music, dancing, and shows in the lounges, discos, live bands, Las Vegas–style productions, nightclubs, karaoke, and movies.
4. Most shipboard sports and recreational facilities, including swimming pools, health club or exercise room, promenade or jogging track, whirlpool, sauna, library, game room, and child-care facilities. (Spa and beauty treatments, some specialized exercise classes such as Pilates, and sports equipment normally cost extra.)
5. Most shipboard activities, including casino entry, onboard games and contests, lectures, demonstrations, and most children's programs (where applicable, babysitting services are extra).
6. Stops at ports of call on the itinerary.

The features listed above are almost universally a part of any cruise vacation, and an inclusive cruise vacation is often a very good value, particularly when compared with the cost of similar pieces booked on a resort vacation. That said, other inclusions or lack of inclusion are line specific. Some cruise lines do include transfers—basically a bus or van ride from the airport to ship and ship to airport. Other lines charge for those transfers, unless you buy your air tickets through the cruise line in what is called an air/sea package.

Port charges (usually noted in the bottom fine print of any cruise advertising or brochure) are usually included in the cruise price. Still, it pays to check carefully or ask your travel agent, as port charges can range from $120 to $200 or even more on a seven-day Caribbean cruise, depending on the itinerary.

Taxes, optional shore excursions, alcoholic beverages and soft drinks, casino play, onboard shopping, some computer classes, use of Internet connection, and tips are not included in most cases. On a few very upscale lines, gratuities and wine and alcoholic beverages are included in the cruise price. On some, tips are pooled (you are asked to contribute a suggested amount per day to be divided among all staff except officers and senior staff) and now, more and more cruise lines are adding a service charge to your shipboard account in lieu of tipping. With most lines you have the option of paying it or having it removed and handling the tipping yourself. We include a section on tipping further in this chapter and in Part Two.

CRUISING'S UNFORTUNATE STEREOTYPES

YOU HAVE PROBABLY HEARD THAT "cruising is not for everyone." But that's like saying travel is not for everyone. If you like to travel, you will almost certainly enjoy cruising. It's that simple. Cruising, however, has accumulated unfortunate stereotypes, which continue to recycle.

MYTH NO. 1: I'LL BE BORED Many people, particularly men and younger, active folks, believe cruising is dull and sedentary. They picture bulk loaders crowding buffets while active folks sit bored and unstimulated. Sorry, not so.

Today, to appeal to a younger audience and changing lifestyles, most cruises offer around-the-clock activities. Ships have workout rooms with high-quality equipment, jogging tracks, pools, and daily exercise classes. Some larger ships have volleyball courts, basketball and squash courts, bowling alleys, and even climbing walls, golf simulators, and ice rinks. At ports of call, a variety of sports—from golf to cycling, snorkeling to kayaking—are offered. There are far more opportunities for sports and athletics than most of us have at home. Some lines now even offer extreme adventures like off-road vehicle trips or mountain biking. If you go on a cruise and sit on your butt, that's your decision.

For the active but less athletic, most ships offer swimming, shuffle-board, table tennis, walking areas, and spa amenities, including hot tubs and saunas. Many ships offer yoga or stretching classes. At night, for the energetic, there's dancing in many forms, from ballroom to reggae to line dancing to salsa.

A range of organized activities targets gregarious and fun-loving people. Versions of television game shows are popular, as are more traditional events, such as bridge tournaments, arts and crafts classes, and dancing lessons. Most cruise ships have casinos, and almost all have bingo.

If learning is your goal, dozens of cruises specialize in providing educational experiences and exploration of a region accompanied by experts. Like floating graduate schools, these cruises may focus on political and natural history, or may even offer lectures on topics unrelated to the ship's destinations.

Finally, there is no place better than a cruise ship to relax. The favorite cruise activity for many people is curling up in a comfortable deck chaise with a good book.

MYTH NO. 2: CRUISING IS FOR RICH PEOPLE; I CAN'T AFFORD A CRUISE If you take a vacation of three or more days during which you stay in hotels and eat in restaurants, you can afford a cruise. In fact, a cruise may be cheaper than a deluxe resort vacation.

Let's compare cruising with a modest vacation: Vic and Edna's one-week trip to Gatlinburg, Tennessee, and the Smoky Mountains. Driving from their home near Cleveland, Ohio, Vic and Edna spent about $400 on gas for the Chevy. They averaged $75 a night plus tax for motels, or $577 for the week. For breakfast and lunch, it was Shoney's- or Denny's-type restaurants. They'd go more upscale for dinner, and they liked beer or wine with their meal. Total for seven days' food: $588. In the mountains, they mostly hiked and drove around. One day, however, they played golf; on another they visited a museum and a theme park. On the Friday before heading home, they rented horses for half a day. Golf, admissions, and horses came to approximately $260. Recapping:

VIC AND EDNA'S SPLENDID VACATION	
Lodging	$577
Gas	$400
Meals	$588
Admissions	$260
Total	$1,825

During the same period, a good middle-of-the-market cruise line (not super-budget or super-luxury) offered a seven-night Caribbean cruise for $899 per person, including round-trip airfare. The cruise visited San Juan, St. Thomas, Martinique, Tortola, the British Virgin Islands, Antigua, and St. Maarten. Even better values could have been had with promotional fares, which were as low as $579.

These were promotional rates, not the "rack" rates listed in the brochures. The point is, on the seven-night cruise, Vic and Edna could have enjoyed the amenities of a full resort, dined in grand style, danced to live music, visited six beautiful tropical islands, and soaked in a whirlpool under the Caribbean moon for about the same amount they spent on their road trip. We are not suggesting Vic and Edna should swap the Smokies for the Caribbean, only that they could afford to do so if they are inclined.

MYTH NO. 3: CRUISES ARE STUFFY, ELITIST, AND FORMAL Most cruises are none of the above, though the description might fit some passengers. Cruises cover a broad range of dress and social protocols. You can choose a cruise at whatever level of formality or casualness feels right for you. Overall, cruises have become very casual and informal. Even on "formal" nights—such as the captain's welcome-aboard party and/or farewell party—only half of the men wear business suits, and women don cocktail or party dresses. Newer ships offering alternative (to the main dining room) dining options make it possible to avoid formal events entirely. Yet, on the most informal ships, like Carnival, some people dress to the nines—and it's often the men more so than the women. And they love it.

MYTH NO. 4: CRUISES ARE TOO REGIMENTED FOR ME Granted, it takes organization to get everyone on board a cruise ship. It takes similar regimentation to get everyone off at the end of the cruise. At ports, you need only get back on board before the ship sails.

Some folks lump cruises into the same category as whirlwind bus tours—eight countries in five days and that sort of thing. A cruise might visit eight countries in five days, but you will have to check in and unpack only once. That's the beauty of cruising—you can hang out on the ship and just enjoy the ride, or you can get off at each port and pursue your own agenda.

Also, the trend toward more relaxed dining hours and alternative (to the main dining room) dining venues has resulted in notably less regimentation aboard ship.

MYTH NO. 5: I'M AFRAID I'LL GET SEASICK Well, you might, but the vast majority of people don't, particularly on a Caribbean cruise. Even those who get queasy in a car can usually handle a cruise. Over-the-counter antinausea medications like **Bonine** (doesn't make you drowsy) or **Dramamine** get most folks over the acclimatization period of the first few hours at sea. Bring some: you may never need it, but having it is comforting. Usually, Dramamine or Bonine is available from the purser's desk or the ship's medical unit.

Some guests swear by **Sea Bands**—a pair of elasticized wristbands (similar to tennis bands), each with a small plastic disk that applies pressure to the inside wrist, according to acupressure principles. They are particularly useful for people who have difficulty taking medication. Sea Bands are sold in drug, toiletry, and health-care stores (sometimes on board ships as well) and can be ordered from **On the Go Travel Accessories** (5603 NW 159th Street, Miami, FL 33014; ☎ 888-303-3039; **www.onthegoaccessories.com**). If you take precautions and become seasick anyway, the ship's doctor can administer more powerful medication.

In regard to seasickness, remember: don't dwell on your fear, and if you become queasy, take medicine immediately. When you deal with symptoms quickly, relief is quick.

Minimize the probability of getting seasick by choosing an itinerary in calmer waters: Alaska's Inside Passage, the Caribbean, the Mediterranean, and the Gulf of Mexico. Less smooth are voyages on the Atlantic, Pacific, or Indian oceans or the South China Sea. And remember the time of year may also matter.

MYTH NO. 6: I'M APPREHENSIVE ABOUT WALKING ON A MOVING SHIP If you are not agile or fit on land, you might envision tortuous trips down narrow gangways or climbing ladders through tiny hatches while the ship rolls and pitches. But those images are really in the past. Generally, if you can handle a hotel, you can handle a cruise ship. Large vessels have wide, carpeted halls with hand railings, and slip-resistant outside decks. Elevators serve all passenger decks, so using the stairs may not even be necessary. Passengers use no tricky ladders or tiny hatches.

Modern cruise ships have state-of-the-art stabilizers, and even in bad weather and heavy seas they are amazingly stable. Small ships, depending on their draft and build, may be more subject to the motion of the ocean and are a little more challenging to get around. Being smaller, however, there's less territory to cover. Most ships launched in the last ten years were built with consideration for passengers with ambulatory disabilities. Most new ships offer wheelchair-accessible cabins and ramps.

A TYPICAL DAY ON A CRUISE

LET'S SAY YOU'RE CRUISING THE CARIBBEAN. You can start your morning with an early-bird breakfast or a walk or jog around deck, or you can have breakfast from the menu in the dining room. Late sleepers can order breakfast from room service or catch the breakfast buffet, which stays open later than the dining room. It may be served on the "lido" deck—a casual indoor/outdoor dining facility on the same deck as the swimming pool or sports facilities. The lido buffet has longer and more flexible hours, enabling you to come and go at will.

Days at sea are the most relaxing of the cruise itinerary. The casino, shopping arcade, spa, exercise room, and shore-excursion desk are open. Programs and activities are virtually nonstop on large ships; many folks, however, hang out by the pool or on deck to enjoy the beauty of the sea and the relaxing movement of being underway. The captain normally updates passengers over the public-address system on the ship's progress toward the next port. The captain or cruise director may also point out interesting sights.

Lunch works much like breakfast: you can eat in the dining room and order from the menu, or you can stay in your swimsuit and eat burgers or pizza by the pool, where there is likely to be a music combo playing upbeat rhythms. You can join the pool games—always a good way to meet people—or just watch or ignore them. You then might work out, read, nap, play bridge, learn the latest dance steps, or attend orientation lectures about the next port. Recently released movies are shown in the ship's movie theater or on cabin television in the afternoon. On some ships, afternoon tea is a big deal—white gloves and all. At cocktail hour, there is usually live music by the pool, often with special drinks or appetizers, or happy hour in one of the bars.

As dinner approaches, it's time to dress for the evening. The dress code generally is specified on the daily agenda slipped under your door every evening. It is also spelled out in the cruise line's brochure, so you can pack accordingly. (More information on dress codes is available under "Preparing for Your Cruise" later in this chapter.)

Some passengers stroll the deck before dinner, particularly at sunset, a beautiful time at sea. Others have a drink in one of the lounges. Dinner in the dining room is a social culmination of the day's activity. Spirits are always high.

After lingering over several well-prepared courses, it's off to the showroom, where live entertainment, ranging from Las Vegas–style variety shows to Broadway musicals, is offered nightly. After the show, early risers and those who had a long day of touring retire to their cabins. The more active or party-minded guests head for the casino, disco, or a lounge with entertainment. Midnight buffets are about gone these days. On select nights there may be a special late-night buffet or light snack fare. Now, too, on many ships, you have another option—a 24- (or almost 24-) hour alternative restaurant, often dressed up for the evening with table service and music. Before turning in, stretch out in a chaise lounge on deck with a glass of wine. Breathe in the balmy salt-sea air and be caressed by the warm breeze.

Usually, cruise ships sail through the night and arrive at the next port early in the morning. If you have risen in time to enjoy the early morning—another gorgeous time at sea—you can watch your ship dock. It's interesting and fun. After breakfast, the captain announces that the ship has been cleared by local officials and that passengers

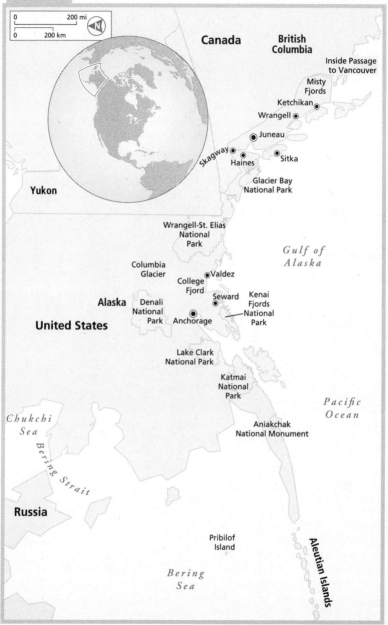

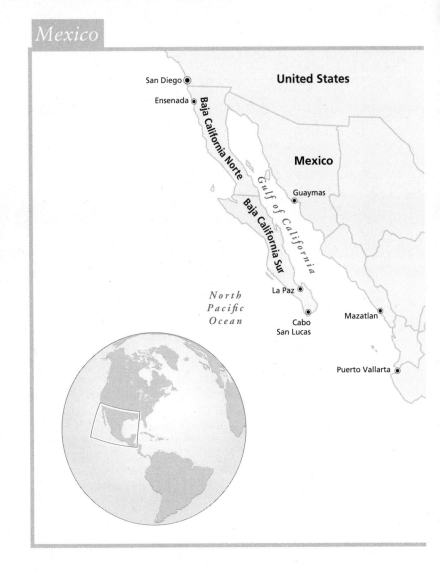

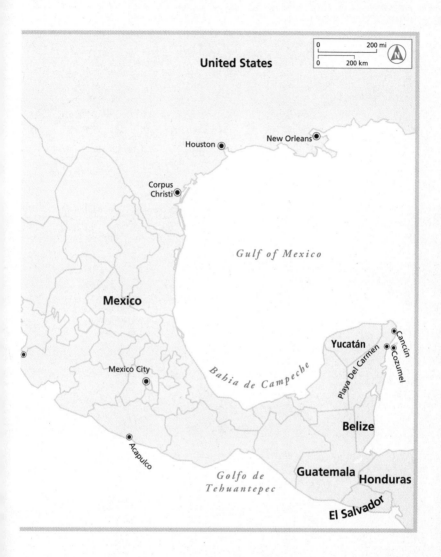

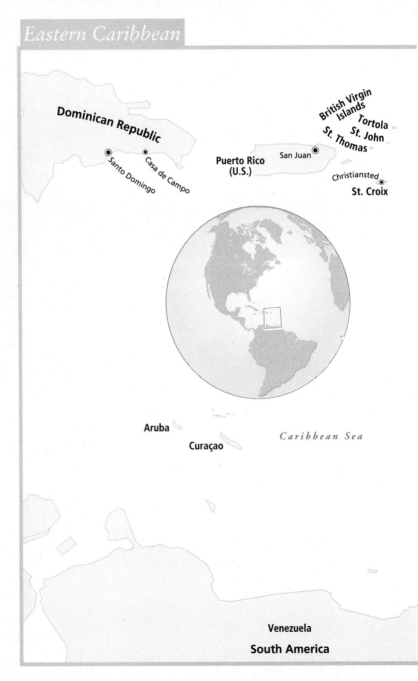

Eastern Caribbean

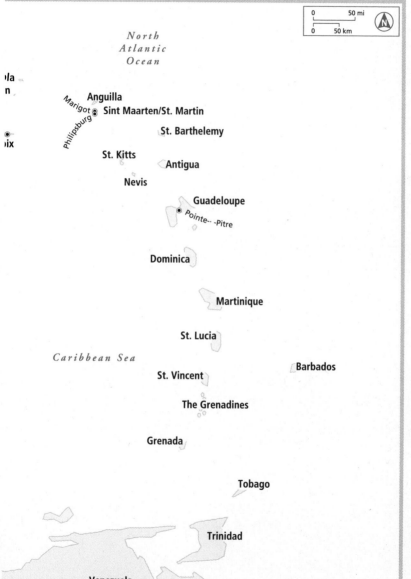

Western Caribbean

United States
Florida

Grand Bahama

Freeport ◉ ◉ Port Lucaya

Abaco

Miami ◉

Gulf of Mexico

Straits of Florida

Bahama Islands

Nassau ◉ **Eleuthera**

Andros

Exuma

Cuba

Cayman Islands (U.K.)

Grand Cayman
George Town ◉

Montego Bay ◉ Ocho Rios ◉ Port Antonio ◉

Jamaica

Caribbean Sea

Panama Canal

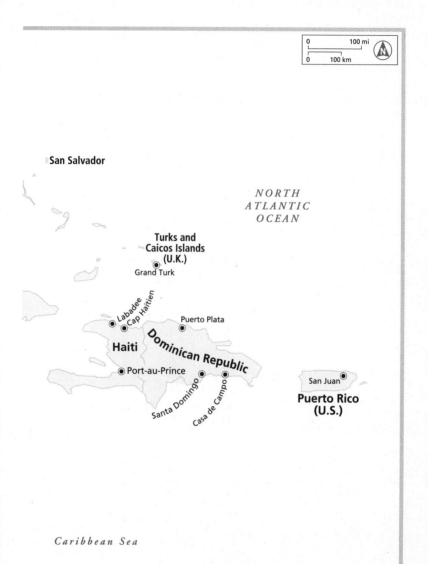

San Salvador

*NORTH
ATLANTIC
OCEAN*

Turks and
Caicos Islands
(U.K.)
Grand Turk

Labadee
Cap Haitien
Puerto Plata

Haiti

Dominican Republic

Port-au-Prince

San Juan

Puerto Rico
(U.S.)

Santa Domingo

Casa de Campo

Caribbean Sea

Aruba
Oranjestad

Curaçao

Bonaire

Willemstad Kralendijk

0   100 mi
0   100 km

South America

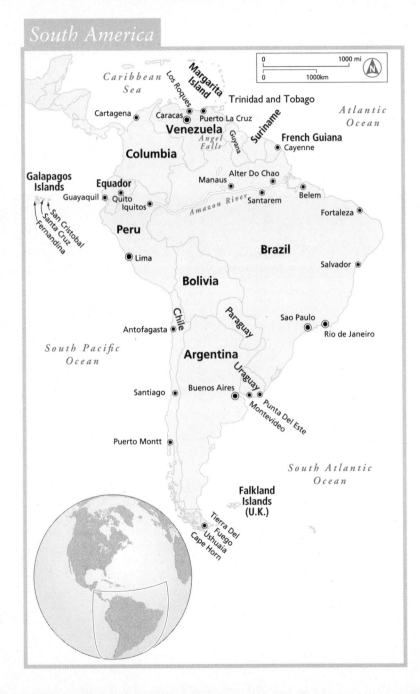

The Orient

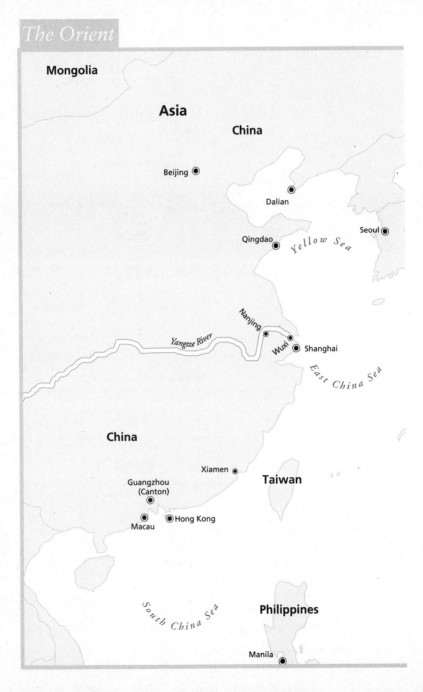

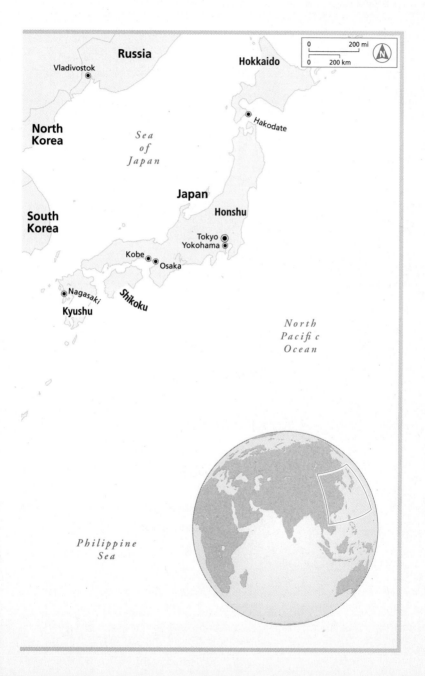

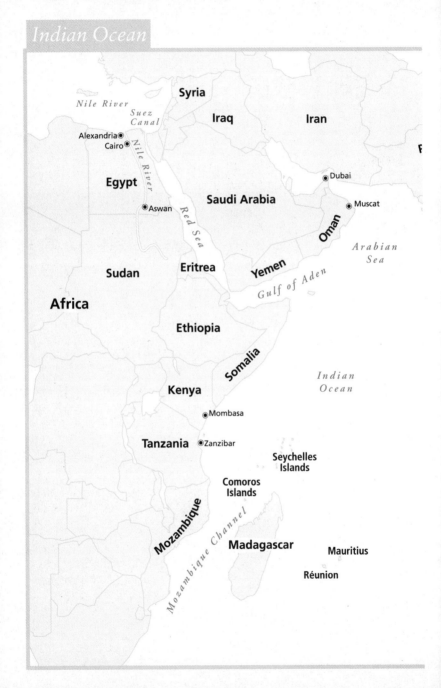

Indian Ocean

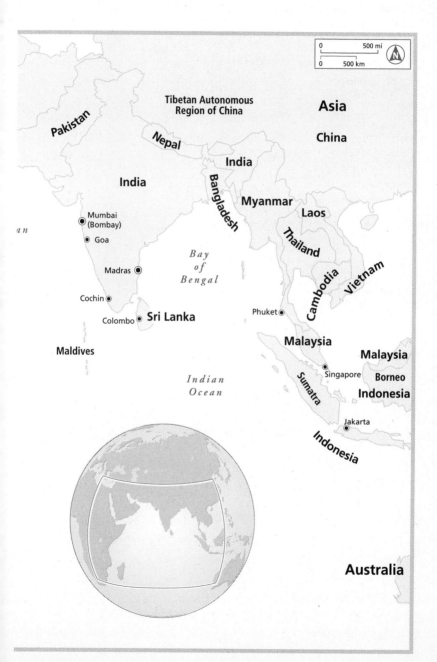

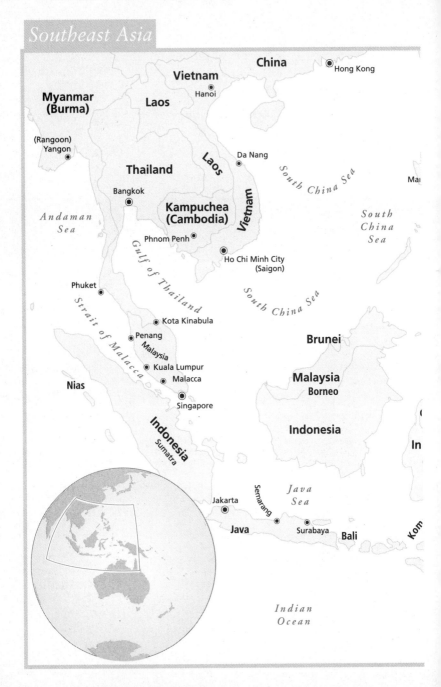

Southeast Asia

Eastern Mediterranean

Western Mediterranean

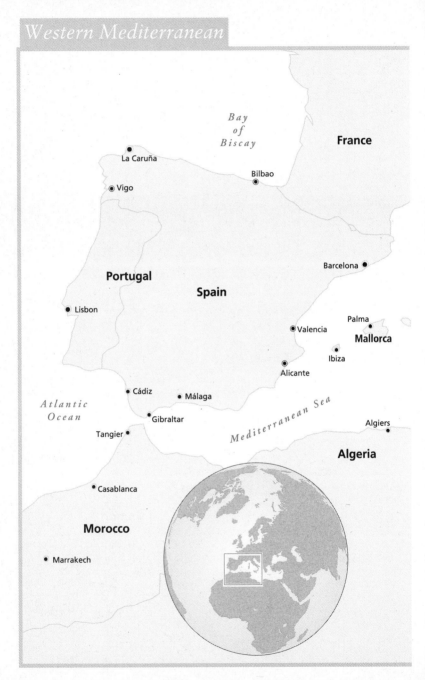

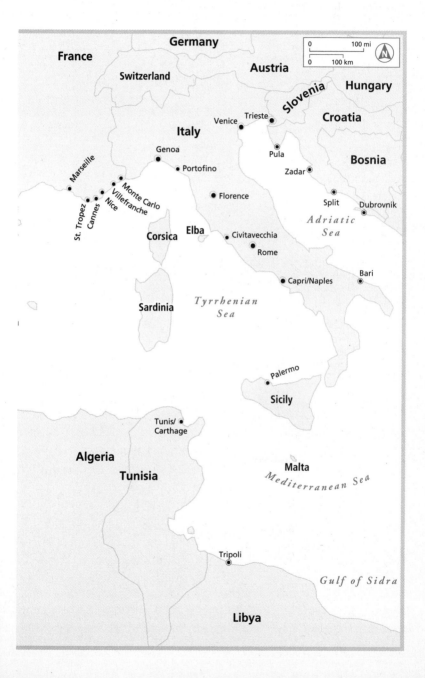

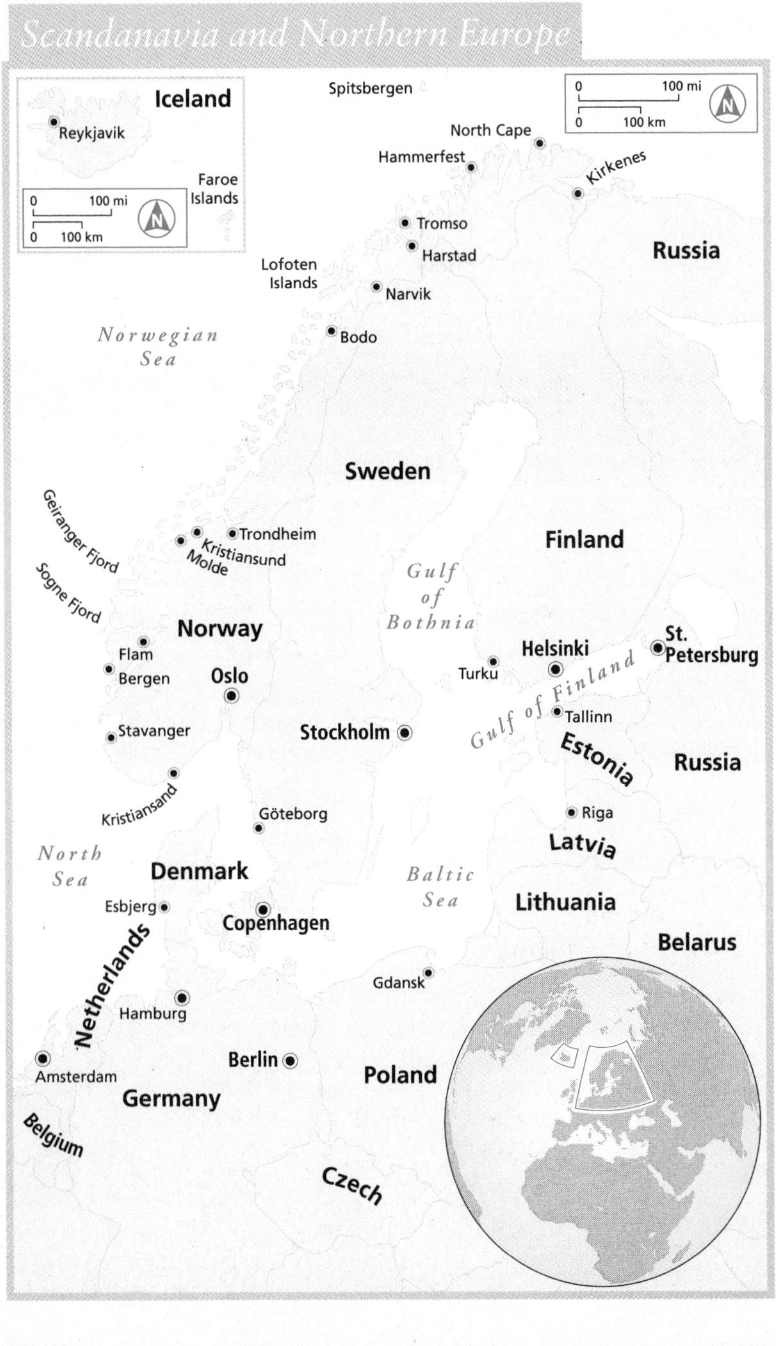
Scandanavia and Northern Europe
Iceland
Reykjavik
0 100 mi
0 100 km
N
Faroe Islands
Spitsbergen
0 100 mi
0 100 km
N
North Cape
Hammerfest
Kirkenes
Tromso
Harstad
Russia
Lofoten Islands
Narvik
Bodo
Norwegian Sea
Sweden
Geiranger Fjord
Trondheim
Kristiansund
Molde
Finland
Sogne Fjord
Gulf of Bothnia
Norway
Flam
Bergen
Oslo
Helsinki
St. Petersburg
Turku
Gulf of Finland
Tallinn
Stavanger
Stockholm
Estonia
Russia
Kristiansand
Göteborg
Riga
Latvia
North Sea
Denmark
Baltic Sea
Lithuania
Esbjerg
Copenhagen
Belarus
Netherlands
Gdansk
Hamburg
Amsterdam
Berlin
Poland
Germany
Belgium
Czech

may disembark. Those signed up for shore excursions are given last-minute instructions about when and where to meet and are normally first to go ashore.

Although port calls range from two hours to two days (with an overnight at dock), most are four to ten hours—enough time to get a taste of an island or city. As you disembark, crew members remind you of the sailing time and make sure you are carrying your cruise identification, which you must present to reboard. Once ashore, some people explore on foot on their own, take walking tours, shop, and perhaps try a shoreside restaurant. Others hire a cab for a driving tour, and most take shore excursions purchased aboard ship.

Shore excursions take many forms. Some are passive (bus tour), but others are active (snorkeling, sailing, hiking, biking, or fishing). Surprisingly, many folks, particularly repeat cruisers, stay aboard ship. It's quiet—almost empty of passengers—but it's in full operation, except for casinos and shops. Lunch is served on schedule in the dining room.

About an hour before sailing, you reboard the ship. Don't be late. The ship will not wait for you! Just before castoff, go topside to watch the crew prepare for departure. Leaving port is always interesting, and a ship's higher decks offer a great viewing platform. Once at sea, the ship settles into its normal nighttime routine, and so do you.

SO MANY CRUISES TO CHOOSE FROM

TO THE FIRST-TIME CRUISER and even many veterans, the number of cruise lines, ships, and itineraries is staggering. Travel agencies that sell only cruises ease their customers into the array of choices by comparing cruise lines with well-known hotel chains, and such comparisons are useful. They might see Carnival, for example, as the Holiday Inn of cruises. Holland America and Celebrity Cruise Line are up a notch, perhaps at the Hyatt level.

Ritz-Carlton–type cruises might appeal to the most discriminating cruisers and are at the upper end of price, service, and amenities. Large and medium ships in this class include those of Crystal Cruises and Regent Seven Seas Cruises. Boutique cruises overlap the luxury category and include the smaller, all-suite ships of Silversea and Seabourn, as well as the cruise/sail ships of Windstar.

Be aware that none of the hotel chains mentioned (except Hyatt) have anything to do with cruising, and these are only a handful of the lines available. Although the foregoing comparison may help you see where you fit into the general scheme, you must dig much deeper to find your perfect cruise.

GETTING YOUR ACT TOGETHER

CRUISES VARY WIDELY. To pinpoint your requirements and preferences in a cruise, you need to ask yourself dozens of questions. Once you settle on what you want, it's easier to match your demands and budget with the appropriate line and ship.

1. What Is My Vacation Budget?

Unless price is no object, one place to start planning is your general budget. How much can you afford, and what are you willing to spend for your cruise? Consider what you must or may add to the cruise price: port charges and taxes, shore excursions, shopping, drinks and dinner wine (on most ships), gambling in the casino, spa services, laundry, and tips for crew members. Once you figure a range within your uppermost limit for all costs, you can begin to explore what kind of cruise you can buy. A good travel agent may tell you about a special promotion that provides value or added perks on a cruise

unofficial **TIP**
Have flexibility and an open mind.

you may think is beyond your price range. In the end, it may cost less, and if it does cost more, you may decide it is the best choice due to "extras" you receive. In other words, use your budget as a starting point.

Although we will revisit this issue in "How to Get the Best Deal on a Cruise," let's say three-day cruises start at about $295 a person, assuming two people to a cabin. Seven-day cruises begin at about $650, and ten-day cruises are about $920 and up. These prices are discounted and represent what you might expect to pay, usually for an inside cabin (one without windows).

2. How Many Days Do I Want to Cruise?

Your available vacation time and budget are among the factors in your ultimate cruise selection. Generally, the larger your budget, the more cruise days you can buy. That is, the longer the cruise, the more it will cost. If your budget isn't up to the number of days you have your heart set on, you still have options. First, trade luxury for cruise days; consider a cruise on a less-luxurious ship. The fee for a week on an upscale ship will easily buy two weeks on a midrange vessel. Second, cruise during the off-season, when prices are lowest. Third, consider the least expensive cabin. Once aboard, all passengers have the same privileges, eat the same meals, and enjoy the same entertainment.

unofficial **TIP**
Don't veer too far from your lifestyle or interests, or you will be disappointed with your cruise.

Unless you plan to spend an extraordinary amount of time in your cabin, you might select less-expensive accommodations. We're not talking about special suites, just the difference between the highest deck outside cabin (with a window or veranda) and the lowest deck inside cabin (no window). For example, on a seven-day itinerary from New York to Bermuda on some ships, the upper-deck outside cabin costs more than twice as much as the lower-deck inside cabin.

3. Where Do I Want to Go?

You can cruise just about anywhere there is enough water to float a ship. This includes all of the world's oceans and seas and many rivers. Where you want to cruise depends primarily on your own interests and what's important to you. It also hinges on your preferred style of cruising and whether you enjoy visiting different destinations or the ship more.

Some destinations, including Alaska and Europe, are seasonal. Others, like the Caribbean and Mexico, are year-round. Almost all cruises worldwide are tailored to the market and the weather. Many to the Caribbean and Mexico, for example, are festive and high-spirited, emphasizing activity and fun. Mild temperatures allow time outdoors, and passengers tend to be younger. By contrast, Alaskan, Canadian, North Atlantic, Scandinavian, and Baltic Sea cruises are more passive, focusing on the beauty of the scenery, islands, fjords, and glaciers. Still, Alaska cruises can have very active shore trips. For these northerly venues, longer cruises and colder temperatures contribute to a more sedate experience and attract families or older passengers. Mediterranean itineraries generally revolve around antiquities and port cities of southern Europe, northern Africa, and the Middle East. Most ships visit a port each day, and sightseeing is the backbone of the vacation.

Hawaiian cruises occupy the middle, emphasizing both festivity and scenery, though passengers are, at times, older on average than those in the Caribbean. For other North Pacific, South Pacific, Indian Ocean, and South China Sea settings, the distance of the cruise areas and home ports from the United States ensures an older, wealthier market.

Though a great way to see exotic places without shuffling among hotels, cruises allow only a cursory glimpse of the countries visited. Ten hours in Venice on a cruise is no substitute for visiting Italy. Even in the Caribbean, short stopovers on small islands leave much undiscovered. Yet, many guests will enjoy seeing something new and may never travel to all these destinations on their own.

If you are interested in further exploring a destination, consider the add-ons most lines offer at the beginning and end of cruises. Two- or three-night packages include a hotel and some sightseeing. They are usually well priced and can be booked at the time you buy your cruise. Also consider picking an itinerary that offers "overnights" in certain high-profile ports such as St. Petersburg, Russia, or Venice, Italy. These cruises offer more intense destination time ashore.

DEFINING THE CARIBBEAN On a map with the arm of the compass pointing north, the islands closest to the United States are the Greater Antilles; they include Cuba, the Caymans, Jamaica, Haiti, the Dominican Republic, and Puerto Rico. All but Cuba (although this could change in the near future) are visited by ships from U.S. ports and have daily, direct air service from major U.S. cities.

unofficial **TIP**
Some travelers use cruising to sample cities and countries to determine whether they might want to return later for a more prolonged visit.

The Bahamas and the British colony of the Turks and Caicos lie north of the Greater Antilles and southeast of Florida. They are entirely in the Atlantic Ocean, but because their tropical environment is similar to that of the Caribbean, they are viewed as part of the region. The Bahamas and the Turks and Caicos are cruise stops; both have direct air service from the United States mainland.

In the eastern Caribbean are the Lesser Antilles, starting with the Virgin Islands in the north and curving south to Grenada. The northern of these many small islands are called the Leewards and comprise the U.S. and British Virgin Islands, Anguilla, St. Maarten, St. Barts, Saba, St. Eustatius, St. Kitts, Nevis, Antigua, Barbuda, Montserrat, and Guadeloupe. The south islands, called the Windwards, include Dominica, Martinique, St. Lucia, Barbados, St. Vincent and the Grenadines, and Grenada.

The Virgin Islands, St. Maarten, Antigua, Barbados, and to a lesser extent Martinique, St. Kitts, and St. Lucia, are frequent cruise stops and have direct air service from the United States mainland or via Puerto Rico. The others are reached through local airlines, and most are stops for small ships, particularly during winter cruise season. In the south are Aruba, Bonaire, Curaçao, and Trinidad and Tobago, which lie off Venezuela. Aruba and Curaçao are major ports on southern Caribbean and Panama Canal cruises. In the western Caribbean are Jamaica and the Cayman Islands, and off the Yucatán Peninsula are the Mexican islands of Cancún and Cozumel. All are major cruise destinations.

Along the 2,000-mile Caribbean chain, nature has been extravagant with its color, variety, and beauty. Verdant mountains rise from sun-bleached shores. Between towering peaks and the sea, rivers and streams cascade over rocks and hillsides and disappear into mangrove swamps and deserts. Fields of flowers, trees with brilliant blossoms, and a multitude of birds and butterflies fill the landscape. The air, refreshed by tropical showers, is scented with spices and fruit.

Yet what makes the Caribbean islands unique is their combination of exotic scenery and the kaleidoscope of diverse cultures. The cultures have evolved from traditions, music, dance, art, architecture, and religions from around the world.

We should warn you that the exponential growth of cruising in the Caribbean has had a tremendous, and many would say negative, impact on some islands. Cruise ships disgorging thousands of passengers a day on a tiny island disrupt the normal rhythms, changing a quaint, sleepy, laid-back port into a frenetic, artificial tourist attraction. Sprawling malls have sprung up like ragweed around the docks, and whole local populations have abandoned their lifelong vocations to cater to tourists. Some Caribbean islands have become the equivalent of private islands owned by several cruise lines: artificial, idealized versions more familiar to fans of *Gilligan's Island* than to veteran Caribbean travelers.

4. When Do I Want to Go?

Cruises follow the sun, visiting destinations during their best weather. Hence, for some exotic destinations and such seasonal cruise areas as Alaska, the British Isles, Canada, and Antarctica, you have only a two- to five-month window of opportunity. For the Caribbean, Mexico, Hawaii, and Asia, among others, cruises are available all year.

Below is a sampling of popular destinations and cruising seasons.

For every area, periods of peak demand are called high season; moderate demand, shoulder season; and low demand, low season or value season. Usually high season occurs when good weather in the cruise area coincides with times when people want to take vacations. In the Caribbean, that's between Christmas and the middle of April, and from June 15 to August 15. But in the Caribbean, for example, immediately after the Christmas–New Year holiday, demand drops and the first two weeks in January offer value-season rates. If you can be flexible, shifting cruise dates a week or two may offer big savings.

Africa	Year-round, but mostly May–October for north Africa; November–April for eastern and southern Africa
Alaska	May–September
Asia and the Orient	Mainly October–March
Baltic	May–October
Bermuda	May–October
Black Sea	April–October
Canada	May–October
Caribbean	Year-round
Hawaii	Year-round
India and Southeast Asia	Year-round, but mostly November–April
Mediterranean	Year-round, but mostly March–November
Mexico	Year-round
New England	May–October
Panama Canal	Year-round, but mostly September–May
South America	North coast, year-round; other areas, September–April
South Pacific	Year-round, but mainly November–April

Ask your travel agent to compare pricing on a week-to-week basis before you book. Always check the period immediately before or after your selected dates to find out your options.

unofficial **TIP**
Within high season, there are often valleys when prices are likely to be their lowest for the year, offering you an opportunity to save a bundle.

The January to April market targets seniors and Northerners seeking a respite from the winter. Although weather in summer is not generally as good as between January and April, families create high demand during midsummer. When demand tapers off, shoulder season follows, giving way to low season as cruise demand continues to decline.

During high season, ships generally are full and cruises are more expensive (because demand is high). If your plans are flexible, it is usually possible to identify several times in the year when your destination's weather is predictably good but cruise demand is moderate or low. Cruising during these periods provides lower prices, less-crowded ships, and good weather. Caribbean cruises in November and early December, before Christmas, are good examples. Hurricane season is over, prices are lower, and ships are less crowded. Early May for Alaska is another excellent time.

5. What Sort of Lifestyle or Activity Level Am I Seeking?

As baby boomers enter middle age and relative affluence, and as younger couples and families discover the economy of cruise vacations, cruising's demographics are changing. On most midmarket cruises of two weeks or less, passengers are amazingly diverse. Responding to a widening range of energy and interests among these passengers, lines have developed activities that offer something for almost everyone.

Even so, lines continue to fine-tune their product for their primary markets. Thus, although Celebrity Cruises might develop programs and activities for younger clients, these cruisers continue to be a secondary market. The line's real focus is the 45-to-65 age group. That means a younger person can have a good time on Celebrity, but an over-40 person will probably have a better time because the cruise is built around the latter's preferences.

How cruise lines serve their primary, secondary, and even tertiary markets makes relevant the question, "What sort of lifestyle or activity level am I seeking?"

In each of our cruise-line and ship profiles in Part Two, we pinpoint the style, tenor, and activity level of the cruises offered. Look for an activity and social mix that seems right for you, but don't get bogged down in demographics. Many older people are active, athletic, and like to party, and many young people appreciate a sedate cruise and may spend their days doing nothing more than reading in a lounge chair.

The choice to participate in activities or party all night is entirely yours. Do, however, pay attention to the ship's size. A small ship carrying 250 or fewer passengers may have only one or two lounges and limited deck space. If you don't care for a full day or evening of shipboard activity, you'll enjoy its low-key ambience. Large ships have the resources to offer considerable variety. Carnival Cruise Lines, for example, pretty much wrote the book on party cruising, but even on a Carnival ship it is possible to find quiet corners to relax.

Cruise lines design their promotional brochures to appeal to their target markets. If you identify with the people and activities depicted in the brochure, you probably will feel at home on one of that line's ships. Lines that do not cater to families, for instance, do not feature them in their literature. Study the brochures from your travel agent. Are the passengers pictured your age or of varied ages? Is the emphasis on shipboard activities or ports and scenery? Does shipboard life look like a 24-hour party, or do photos show a more laid-back experience? Onboard facilities need no interpretation. They're spelled out.

6. What Level of Formality Do I Prefer?

Most cruises give passengers an opportunity to play dress-up. On certain evenings in the main dining room, men may be requested to wear jackets, tuxedos, or dark suits, and women to wear cocktail dresses or gowns. Most ships have a dress protocol that passengers are expected to observe, and it varies widely by line. (See "Dress Codes" under "Preparing for Your Cruise.")

unofficial **TIP**
Even an informal ship might ask passengers not to wear shorts and tank tops in the dining room and be strict about it.

Formality (or lack thereof) is a way cruise lines set themselves apart. A luxury line targeting highly affluent passengers may be more formal than a midmarket line. Family and budget lines are less formal, but even the "fun ships" of Carnival have some formal nights. Adventure cruises are usually the most informal.

The bottom line is how much formality you want. The great majority of cruises vary attire from night to night and won't punish someone who breaks the dress code. If, for example, a man wears a dark suit instead of a tuxedo for the captain's party, it's likely no one will notice. Check the ship's dress code before you book. The information is usually detailed in the cruise line's brochures.

7. What Standards Do I Require for Dining and Food Quality?

Food—its quality and the overall dining experience—is cited by most passengers as a critical element of their cruise. The fare on cruise ships is generally very good—impressive considering that shipboard meals represent the ultimate extension of catered banquet dining.

Feeding 300 to 1,600 persons at a sitting is challenging under any circumstances. Doing it at sea with attention to detail, quality ingredients and preparation, multiple courses, and beautiful presentation is one of cruising's miracles. Ships have made an art of serving palatable food to crowds of diners. Hotel food and beverage managers could learn a lot from cruise ship chefs.

However, you can't expect the same excellence from a galley serving hundreds of dinners as you can from an upscale restaurant cooking to order for a small number of guests. A few small ships have cuisine rivaling better land-based restaurants, and small alternative or specialty restaurants on newer large ships can hold their own with the best of them.

The quality of meals and sophistication of the dining experience vary considerably among ships. Although luxury ships serving fewer passengers in single seatings have the greatest potential for serving memorable meals, midmarket lines like Celebrity, Holland America, and Princess have shown they can approach similar standards of excellence serving larger numbers.

If you have a refined palate and eat exclusively in the finest restaurants, you may meet your dining requirements only in the high-end group of cruise ships. If, however, you dine regularly in restaurants of varying quality, are acquainted with the world's major cuisines, and understand the limitations of cruise food service, you will find numerous ships capable of meeting or exceeding your expectations.

Cruise lines have tended to offer good dining-room meals or good buffets, but seldom both. Almost all lines have eliminated the midnight buffet, except for one special late-night extravaganza on some ships when chefs go all out to show off their culinary skills.

Under Norwegian Cruise Line's "Freestyle Cruising" program, you can eat in one of two main dining rooms, at whatever time you choose during normal hours of operation, or you can make reservations at any of ten alternative restaurants. On the *Norwegian Sun,* for example, Le Bistro serves French cuisine; East Meets West offers Pacific Rim and Asian fusion fare; Las Ramblas offers tapas bar fare; Il Adagio offers Italian cuisine; Pacific Heights specializes in healthy, light California cuisine; and Ginza offers sushi, sashimi, and teppan-yaki dining. If none of that works for you, the Garden Café operates a buffet around the clock, or alternatively there's 24-hour room service. The reservations-only alternative restaurants impose a surcharge of $10 to $30 per person, but it's worth it. The restaurants are elegant, quiet, and intimate, and often the food rivals that of good onshore restaurants—or perhaps more relevant, the fare served on ships in the luxury market. Boomers love the flexibility these multiple restaurants provide. Aside from the surcharge, the main downside is that you don't have the opportunity to meet people and form friendships as you would in a conventional dining arrangement, where you eat in the same place, at the same assigned table, and with the same people, every night—a feature important to more "traditional cruisers."

Among other cruise-dining innovators, Princess's Personal Choice Dining program offers multiple restaurants and no assigned seating; or alternatively, passengers can opt for the traditional dining arrangement. Disney Cruise Line ships feature several dining venues, but their system is unique. Passengers rotate among three different themed restaurants according to a prearranged schedule. And, in a concession to those passengers who develop a fondness for their waitstaff, their waiter and assistant rotate right along with them. Carnival, with yet another approach, offers "total choice" dining, where passengers can choose from four seating times in the main dining room, instead of the usual two; a number of other cruise lines have similar options. The four seatings stagger the arrival of diners, preventing the galley from being inundated, and allow both chefs and wait-staff to concentrate on a smaller number of diners at a given time.

Weather and lifestyle have clearly affected cruise dining. Because most ships spend all or part of the year in the Caribbean and Mexico, where passengers remain in their bathing suits most of the day, the lines found that it makes sense and saves money to expand the lido breakfast and lunch. Lido dining also gives passengers relief from the regimentation of dining-room hours.

8. How Gregarious Am I (Are We)?

Generally, it's easier to meet folks on a small ship if that is one of your prime goals on board. There are fewer passengers, and you see the same people more often. Conversely, on a large ship, the only folks you see regularly may be your dinner-table companions (hope you like them!). On larger ships, if you meet somebody you would like to see again, get their name and cabin number. We once met a nice woman checking in on the 2,300-passenger *Monarch of the Seas*. In a week aboard, we never again saw her. Then again, many people who are frazzled in their daily work life come aboard for escapism and personal pampering. Some don't need or want this socializing.

Large ships offer many social settings. It's possible to meet people in bars, lounges, and nightclubs; on shore excursions; in the health club; around the pool; and in the casino. But the easiest time to meet them is at planned activities. Whether it's aerobics and line dancing or bridge and wine tasting, such activities help people with similar interests come together.

The style of a cruise is important. If you are gregarious, you might prefer a ship that promotes a party atmosphere. If you are more solitary or are taking a romantic cruise with your significant other, you may prefer a less-frenetic social agenda.

Most cruisers solve the problem of companionship by taking significant others, friends, relatives, or all of the above with them. As on Noah's ark, the majority of passengers arrive already paired up. This is attributable in part to the double-occupancy norm for cabins.

On most ships, solo passengers pay a hefty "singles supplement" for the privilege of having a cabin to themselves. Ships schedule gatherings where singles can meet, and some try to seat singles at the same dining tables, but singles generally have to scout around to find other people who are sailing solo.

9. The Other Passengers: What Kind of People Am I Most Comfortable With?

The less expensive the cruise, the more varied the passengers. Aboard a recent, affordable, four-day cruise were retired seniors, middle-aged professionals, 20-something newlyweds, a bowling team from Pennsylvania, families with young children, a group of pipe fitters, and college students on spring break.

On upscale cruises of two weeks or longer, the cost ensures that passengers are somewhat more affluent and perhaps less diverse. On a seven-day Caribbean or Mexico cruise with midmarket lines, such as Princess, Celebrity, and Holland America, you will find more seniors, more professionals, fewer tradespeople, fewer families with children (except during summer), and fewer people younger than age 25. Passengers are even less varied on the same lines' seven-day or longer cruises to the more expensive destinations of Alaska and the Mediterranean.

On the most upscale lines, including Seabourn, Regent Seven Seas, and Silversea, the average passenger is older than age 50 and affluent. Passengers younger than age 20 are likely traveling with parents or grandparents. Some lines don't take children or discourage their presence because they do not have the facilities or atmosphere for them. Couples account for 80% of those on board. Singles are likely to be widows, widowers, or mature travelers able to afford the lifestyle. Many lines get a fair number of mother-daughter pairings.

In our profiles of cruise lines and ships in Part Two, we carefully scrutinized their passengers so you'll know what to expect. We believe the inclusion of this information is one element that makes this book different from other guidebooks on cruises. If you have strong feelings about who your fellow passengers will be, pay close attention to these descriptions.

WARNING: CHILDREN ABOARD One person's darling can be another person's pain in the neck. We have received a surprising number of complaints from readers about children on their cruises. However, most referred to cruises during holidays, spring break, and summer, when there can be 400 or more children aboard a ship. On Disney Cruise Line, the number could be much greater. In such cases, even people who adore children might find their patience wearing thin if the children are rowdy and ill-behaved, or if the cruise lines fail to supervise them adequately. As cruise popularity and family travel increase, the two converge with greater frequency.

If you do not want to cruise with children, avoid holiday periods, particularly on mass-market lines that promote family travel and cruise to the most popular Caribbean, Mexican, and Alaskan destinations. If, however, these are the only times you can travel (if you are a teacher, for example), search for ships that sail off the beaten track or focus on enrichment rather than entertainment. Finally, an experienced travel agent should be able to help you find the right ship—or the ones to avoid.

unofficial **TIP**
The simple fact is that cruising can be a wonderful family vacation.

10. What Kind of Itinerary Do I Prefer?

Among itineraries, there's a world to choose from. You can have mostly days at sea, mostly days in port, or a balance of the two. Your cruise can be educational or just fun. There are theme cruises where entertainment or education is the focus, such as a jazz festival, and cruises where specific activities are emphasized, such as scuba diving, golf, sailing, or viewing wildlife.

Start by deciding how much time at sea versus time in port you prefer. If you are more interested in visiting ports, seek an itinerary with many of them. (Be aware that when a ship visits more than five ports on a seven-day cruise, some stops will be half-day.) Port-intensive itineraries are most plentiful on Mediterranean, Baltic, and eastern Caribbean cruises. Compare itineraries for different lines listing the same ports. When figuring your time in each port, remember that your ship must clear customs on arrival before passengers are allowed to disembark. A ship making port at 8 a.m. may not put passengers ashore before 9 or 9:30 a.m. Most ships require passengers to be aboard 30 minutes or more before leaving port. Thus your time in port could be trimmed by an hour or more coming and going.

Another important consideration, if you want to maximize your time in port, is whether your ship ties up at the dock or anchors offshore. Having to use a tender (a small commuting boat) to reach shore can take a big bite out of your port time. The larger the ship, the more likely the need to use a tender. The published itinerary or your travel agent will provide information on tendering.

Many passengers, particularly older, experienced cruisers who have "been there, done that" relish the serenity of being at sea. In recent years, they have been very vocal in opposing cruise lines' cramming ports into their itineraries to attract first-time cruisers who commonly perceive value in the number of ports visited. Some itineraries offer "overnights" in highly desirable ports like St. Petersburg, Russia, or Venice, or China. Most three-, four-, and seven-day cruises spend more daylight hours in port than at sea. Longer cruises typically feature more time at sea. Itineraries list days spent under way as "cruising" or "at sea."

A map highlighting ports of call in the world's cruise areas shows the hundreds of ports ships can add to their itineraries. With the possible exception of the Atlantic coast of Africa, most ports are close enough to one another to allow a port visit every day. Fortunately, most itineraries of seven or more days strike a balance. A typical seven-day itinerary includes two days at sea. Three or four days of cruising is typical of ten-day itineraries; four to five days on 12- to 14-day itineraries.

Repositioning cruises occur at the end of the season in a cruise area when lines reposition their ship(s) by dispatching them to other areas where new seasons are beginning. Thus, Princess, Holland America, and many other lines reposition some of their Caribbean fleet in late April (the end of Caribbean high season) to the Pacific Northwest for summer cruises to Alaska. At the same time, Costa, Celebrity, Holland America, MSC Cruises, Princess, and others might dispatch ships from the Caribbean to Europe or the Mediterranean. Repositioning cruises stop at some ports, but there usually is a high ratio of sea days to days in port. Because such voyages occur only twice a year, they are difficult for lines to promote, and passage usually is discounted significantly.

unofficial **TIP**
Repositioning cruises are the best buys for those who crave more days at sea. They are also the best bargains.

11. Specialized Itineraries and Specialized Ships

Passengers aboard most large ships determine for themselves how they will use their time. Specialty cruises, by contrast, focus on a specific activity or pursuit. Some may specialize in whale-watching, others in exploring ancient ruins. Sometimes the vessel sets the focus. Smaller (20- to 200-passenger) ships can dock in small ports and anchor in secluded coves. This facilitates fishing, swimming, snorkeling, scuba diving, and water skiing (participants sometimes carry their own sports equipment) and makes a difference in the way passengers use their time.

Traditional ships sometimes offer theme cruises. For example, professional football players may be aboard and reruns of famous games are shown. Passengers should inquire about themes and book the cruise only if they're interested. A cruise ship can be the medium for countless activities and themes. For additional information on specialty cruises, see Part Three, "Cruising Alternatives."

Big Ships versus Small Ships

Hardly a week passes that some cruise line doesn't announce plans for another ship—bigger and, of course, better than the last. But bigger isn't necessarily better for a cruise.

New words have crept into the cruise lexicon. Not everyone agrees on their definitions, but for the purpose of comparison, these are the parameters we will use:

Ultraliner A cruise ship over 140,000 tons and with a basic capacity (that is, 2 people per cabin) of over 2,500 passengers. There's a substantial range within this category, with the larger ships accommodating as many 6,000 passengers.

Megaliner A cruise ship with a basic capacity of more than 2,000 passengers.

Superliner A cruise ship with a basic capacity of about 1,000 to 2,000 passengers.

Midsize A cruise ship with a basic capacity of 400 to 900 passengers.

Small ship A cruise ship with a basic capacity of under 400 passengers.

Boutique ship A luxury cruise or expedition ship with a basic capacity of under 300 passengers.

Ocean liner Generally, any oceangoing passenger vessel, but tends to be used for ships that provided transatlantic and worldwide service and have since been converted into cruise ships. Although the *QM2* could be called an ocean liner, she's also an ultraliner since she holds 2,800 passengers and offers transatlantic service on a regular basis.

Until you sail on small ships, you may not realize their special pleasures. Small ships are fewer but more diverse in style than larger ones. They range from traditional sailing ships, such as Star Clipper's tall ships, to computer-driven ones like Windstar Cruises' ships, and in the degree of comfort and service from the modest vessels of American Canadian Caribbean Lines to Silversea's ultraluxurious fleet. Prices likewise vary from the moderate to *très cher*.

It's difficult to generalize, but all small ships are cozy, imparting warmth never felt on a superliner. The smallest ones, such as American Safari's 12- to 36-passenger ships, are like private yachts—yet affordable. The congenial atmosphere also enhances interaction between passengers and crew, who are likely to call you by name from the first day. If you covet privacy and personal space, though, this type of cruise may not be your best bet.

Small ships with their shallow drafts, turn-on-a-dime maneuverability, and fewer passengers can gain access and acceptability in places where large ships simply cannot go. Their size makes them welcome at private islands and exclusive resorts and allows them to nudge into shallow bays and hidden coves. Their ports tend to be offbeat and uncommercialized.

Some small cruisers have bow or stern ramps, enabling them to disembark passengers directly onto beaches or into remote villages. Others carry Zodiacs and/or sea kayaks to transport passengers into wilderness. Some have retractable marinas, enabling passengers to water ski or swim from the ship.

A small ship offers exclusivity, even if it is unintended. Seating is unassigned at single seatings for meals. (On luxury ships, dining may be at the time of your choosing.) There are no crowds, no long lines, almost no regimentation. Best of all, on shore, you don't feel like part of a herd, unless you book a bus tour.

Today's superliners, megaliners, and ultraliners are self-contained floating resorts with facilities that operate almost around the clock. The bigger the vessel, the more the ship becomes the focus, although itineraries and ports are still important.

For small ships, destinations are key, and sightseeing is the main activity. These ships offer more varied and unusual itineraries than larger ships can, and often carry experts to discuss destinations and accompany passengers on shore excursions.

Small ships draw experienced, discriminating, and independent travelers who enjoy low-key ambience and often appreciate what is *not* available as much as what is. Many neither want nor need nonstop activities. Still, check with your travel agent, as some small ships are also great for active pursuits like diving, hiking, or hefty nature activities. A few small vessels have tiny casinos and small-scale entertainment, but most substitute conversation and companionship, or lectures by various experts, for chorus lines and cabarets.

The smaller size attracts all age groups. Sailing ships, particularly schooners, draw the young and adventuresome, attracted by the lower price and the opportunity to work alongside the crew. Deluxe ships and those with longer itineraries attract older travelers, many of whom are young in spirit and intellectually curious. They appreciate an island's culture and are eager to interact with the locals.

Sound appealing? Then consider one of the three basic types of small ships: Ultraluxurious liners offer privacy and pampering, exclusivity and elegance, tastefully opulent suites, gourmet dining, and often formal evenings. In sharp contrast are adventure-oriented ships, whose destinations are chosen for their natural beauty, wildlife, or cultural interest. Activities include hiking, kayaking, and birding. Cabins usually are modest, service minimal, and cooking down-home. They appeal to many people who spurn luxurious pampering but are keenly interested in participatory travel. A third type strikes a middle ground, offering comfortable (but not lavish) accommodations, good food, and attentive service. There is some adventure, some history and wildlife, and some time for sports. Evening entertainment includes games, movies, local talent, and guest speakers.

Even with these choices, small-ship cruising is not for everyone. Some would find it boring or confining. But if you abhor lines or regimentation, can operate on your own juices, yearn for a more intimate environment, or want to try trimming the sails or floating in luxury, small ships might be right for you.

Old Ships versus New Ships

Poets praise the beauty of sailing ships. But observers of classic cruise ships have been equally captivated by noble grace that is both massive and subtle. Unfortunately, great ocean liners like the *Norway* have been scrapped. Alas, such ships will never be built again.

Are old or new vessels better? The debate rages. Classic ships still in service, as opposed to those merely old, offer ambience that no newer ship can duplicate. But the newest cruise vessels have advantages only dreamed of in 1960. Because there still are well-maintained older ships in service, you have a choice between the old and the new afloat. Find your preference by surveying what each type of ship has to offer.

Notice first the appearance of any vessel, old or new. The newest ships are designed from the inside out to provide more and better public rooms and the most amount of usable deck space. These vessels spend most of their days in calm seas. None but Queen Mary 2 will cut through the North Atlantic at full speed to maintain a schedule, so the fine lines and razor-sharp bow of the old ocean liners aren't needed. Instead, new ships have squared sterns and chunky superstructures that provide many benefits internally but none externally.

As with some prima donnas, most new ships have one or two good angles. Publicity materials show profile shots and aerials of raked stems and funnels and broad decks for recreation.

Once inside your cabin, however, you may forget your ship's outward appearance. The space available to modern designers has generally made possible standard, usually larger, cabins for everyone. Some older ships offer comfortable space in every cabin, but they can't match the improved bathrooms and lighting of newer ships.

Luxury versus Midprice and Economy Cruises

Some of the most extraordinary spas, gyms, pools, lounges, and showrooms are found on the megaships of affordable midmarket lines such as Carnival and Princess. Likewise, dropping big bucks will not ensure that your ship is newer, nicer, or more competently and courteously staffed. (Check the ratio of passengers to crew. The lower the ratio, the more service you should get.) Booking a luxury cruise may get you a larger cabin (suites aboard Silversea or Seabourn Cruise Line) and almost certainly buys a roomier bath with tub and shower.

Regarding food, luxury lines have the edge. Usually they feed fewer passengers at a single seating spanning a couple of hours. Passengers arrive at the dining room a few at a time, like at a restaurant ashore. The staggered arrivals allow the galley the flexibility to provide more choice and cook dishes to order.

Most midmarket and economy cruises have two seatings for each meal. However, with the increase of dining venues on new large ships, like NCL's *Norwegian Epic*,

unofficial **TIP**
Spending more on a cruise does not necessarily get you more or better facilities.

which has 17 restaurants, and Royal Caribbean's new giant *Oasis of the Seas,* with 24 dining outlets, this situation has lessened. Surprisingly, however, the quality of meals on some luxury ships is only marginally better than that of better midmarket lines. A number of midmarket cruise lines such as Princess, Norwegian, and Disney offer exclusive, stand-alone specialty restaurants in addition to their main dining rooms. These restaurants require reservations, and passengers usually must pay a surcharge (between $10 and $30), but some serve fare that rivals the cuisine served in dining rooms aboard luxury vessels.

SPECIAL PEOPLE WITH SPECIAL NEEDS

SOME PASSENGERS REQUIRE SPECIAL SERVICES or accommodations. If you are a honeymooner, single, disabled, require a special diet, or plan to travel with young children or teens, read on.

Singles

Safety and security, comfort, convenience, companionship, fun, and freedom—all are reasons that cruises are among the fastest-growing options available to travelers who want to go it alone.

A cruise ship is about the safest, most secure environment a traveler can find. A woman might hesitate to talk with someone in a hotel bar, dine alone in a fancy restaurant, or walk alone into a nightclub, but such barriers don't exist on a ship. As always, though, for female travelers, common sense remains a good attribute.

The fun is at your fingertips. The nightclub, disco, casino, and theater are walking distance from your cabin. Relieved of the need for an escort and with ready-made companions for dinner or activities, single people—men and women—vacation on their own terms.

Cruise prices are based on two people sharing a cabin. For one person to occupy a cabin alone, cruise lines impose an extra charge over the per-person double-occupancy rate. This "single supplement" varies from 10% to 100% (expressed as 110–200%), depending on the line, ship, itinerary, season, and cabin category. The most frequent charge is 150% except for suites, which usually go for 200%. Brochures always publish the rate. Your choices are to pay it, bring a friend, or take one of these options:

GUARANTEED SINGLE RATE You pay a set price published in the brochure, which is comparable to the low end of a per-person double-occupancy rate. The line assigns your cabin at embarkation. You don't have a choice, but you do have a guarantee of price and privacy.

You are likely to be assigned an inside cabin. If you select low season (October in the Caribbean), the start of a new season (May in Alaska), or a repositioning cruise when the ship is unlikely to be full, you might get a nice outside cabin. When ships are sailing at full occupancy, these upgrades are less likely. Some lines do not show a

Cruising for Singles

S = Single cabins available   **GSP** = Guaranteed share program available

Single Supplement = Percentage of fare based on per-person double-occupancy rate

CRUISE LINE	S	GSP	SINGLE SUPPLEMENT
American Canadian Caribbean	Yes	Yes	175%
American Safari Cruises	Yes	No	175%
Azamara Club Cruises	No	No	150–175%
Carnival Cruise Lines	Yes	Yes	150–200%
Celebrity Cruises	Yes	No	200%
Costa Cruise Lines	Yes	No	180–200%
Cruise West	Yes	Yes	150%
Crystal Cruises	No	No	125–150%
Cunard Line	No	No	175–200%
Disney Cruise Line	No	No	175–200%
Fred Olsen Cruises	Yes	NA	inquire
Holland America Line	Yes	Yes	150–190%
Lindblad Expeditions	Yes	NA	NA
MSC Cruises	No	No	150–200%
Norwegian Cruise Line	On 1 ship	No	150–200%
Oceania Cruises	No	No	125–200%
Princess Cruises	No	No	150–200%
Quark Expeditions	Yes	NA	NA
Regent Seven Seas Cruises	No	No	30–100%
Royal Caribbean International	No	No	200%
Saga Holidays & Cruises	Yes	NA	NA
Seabourn Cruise Line	Yes	No	125–175%
Silversea Cruises	No	No	110–200%
Star Clippers	No	No	150%
Windstar Cruises	No	No	175%
Voyages of Discovery	Yes	No	150–185%

guaranteed single rate in their brochure but will accept a reservation when bookings are light. Be sure to ask.

LOW SINGLE SUPPLEMENT Some lines have single supplements of 115% or less. Seabourn offers 110% on some cruises; Silversea has a few at 110%, though most are at 150%. In all cases, you pay slightly more than the per-person double rate, but you get privacy, and in the case of Seabourn and Silversea, all accommodations are deluxe suites.

FLAT RATE Star Clipper and some other lines charge a flat rate for single occupancy. You pay more but are ensured privacy and choice.

GUARANTEED SHARE The line plays travel matchmaker. You pay the per-person double-occupancy price, and the line matches you with a cabin mate (same gender and smoking preference). If the line does not find a suitable mate, you get the cabin to yourself at no extra charge. The savings—and drawbacks—are obvious. It's a bit of Russian roulette. You stand a better chance of having a cabin to yourself during low season or on a repositioning cruise. Some lines don't publicize a guaranteed share program but will accept a reservation. Be sure to ask.

SINGLE CABIN Some older ships have single cabins. The price is set but not necessarily comparable to a per-person double rate. More likely, a surcharge has been built into the price. Also, some lines charge singles minimal or no surcharge for less desirable cabins, such as inside rooms, particularly when bookings are slow. Norwegian Cruise Line is introducing new singles accommodations on the new *Norwegian Epic* (see the line's profile in Part Two for more information).

Helpful Hands

Golden Age Travellers (Pier 27, The Embarcadero, San Francisco, CA 94111; ☎ 800-258-8880 or 415-296-0151; **www.gatclub.com**), offers about 300 cruises a year and provides a cabin-mate matching service and lower supplements based on bargaining clout. Limited to those age 50 and up. Annual fee is $10 per person; $15 per couple.

SinglesCruise (2929 East Commercial Boulevard, Suite 305; Fort Lauderdale, FL 33308; ☎ 800-393-5000; **www.SinglesCruise.com**) claims to be the largest singles cruise operator in the United States. Part of Minneapolis-based Travel Leaders Leisure Group, SinglesCruise has been booking singles cruises since 1991. SinglesCruise offers its clients private meet-and-greet singles events, cocktail mixers, lectures, theme parties, a separate dining area for its group, and ongoing activities organized by a dedicated cruise director. Singles can choose from a variety of itineraries planned throughout the year with 100–400 singles on board. Its singles, the company says, "are not all necessarily looking for love—some are looking for new friends to travel with."

Singles Travel Company (☎ 888-286-8687 or 408-354-6531; fax 408-354-3871; **www.singlestravelcompany.com**; cruisestoursinfo@ aol.com) is one of the country's largest travel organizations for singles and offers a variety of age-appropriate vacations. It also offers a free roommate matching if you sign up before final payment. You can sign up for its monthly e-mail newsletter. Ann Thomas, director of Singles Travel Company, has been conducting vacation trips and cruises for more than 15 years for singles from all over the United

States to every corner of the world. She has lectured extensively on single travel.

About.com (**seniortravel.about.com**) has one of the largest travel sites on the web and offers a section devoted to single travel and a list of specialized companies, including **Connecting: Solo Travel Network (CSTN),** a Canadian not-for-profit organization that specializes in finding information for single senior travelers, including cruises; **SoloCruiser,** which links single cruisers of all ages to cruises with low single supplements, as well as topical and themed cruises; **Singles Travel International,** which offers cruises for all ages; and **All Singles Travel (www.allsinglestravel.com),** which is part of Travel Services Worldwide and occasionally offers senior singles cruises. Their trips are supplement-free when you book more than 60 days in advance, or you can request a roommate to avoid the single supplement.

Escapade Cruises & Tours (7850 Nine Mile Road NE, Rockford, Michigan 49341; ☎ 888-775-0288 or 616-874-2594; fax 616-874-0126; **www.singlescruises-tours.com;** jeanne@singlescruises-tours.com) specializes in singles and/or solo travel. It was begun in 1998 and is owned and managed by Jeanne Steinberg, who has been in the travel business for more than 20 years. She has worked on cruise ships and has had extensive travel-agent training as a cruise specialist.

Finally, watch for specials and find a knowledgeable travel agent to help you. A smart, experienced agent knows which, when, and how cruise lines make special deals for singles, and she can often unearth ways to apply purchase and special promotional fares, even though based on double occupancy, to single travelers.

OTHER TIPS FOR SAILING SOLO The cruise industry has a long way to go in handling the singles market. The probability of finding love at sea varies according to age group. Twenty-somethings should look to the Caribbean on cruise lines that target a younger market, though the average passenger age remains above age 35.

Singles wanting to meet people should participate in activities, shore excursions, and sports. On a small ship, the chances of meeting many singles of the opposite sex are slim, particularly on high-end luxury ships. Among small ships, adventure and educational cruises are singles' best choices; camaraderie quickly develops among passengers. Also, the number of unattached men is likely to be higher than on traditional cruises. Big ships are considered better for meeting a wide range of people and also often have a get-acquainted session or other event for singles.

If you're a 40-something or older single woman who loves to dance, book a ship that employs gentlemen hosts—single males, age 50 or older, who dine and dance with all unattached women—no favoritism or hanky-panky allowed. Crystal, Cunard, and Holland America have them.

A common complaint we hear from singles concerns table assignment for dining. Some singles are unhappy because they're seated with married folks. Others are annoyed because they're seated with other singles and resent the cruise line playing matchmaker. Response varies, but your best bet is to submit a written request in advance outlining your preference in dining companionship. Aboard, if you are disenchanted with your table mates, ask the maître d'hôtel to move you; talk with the maître d' before the first night at a table, to state your preferences.

Honeymooners

If there is a better honeymoon option than a cruise, we can't think of it. There is nothing more romantic than balmy nights and sunny days under a Caribbean or Mediterranean sky. Your cabin is your honeymoon suite; room service usually is complimentary, so you never have to leave unless you want to. Forget the car, unpack only once, and still visit exotic places. Many lines (with advance notice) will provide a cozy table for two in the dining room. Regardless, tell the cruise line you are newlyweds. You will probably get preferential treatment, a bottle of Champagne, flowers in the room, a souvenir photo, or even a cabin upgrade.

If you are contemplating a cruise honeymoon, consider: if you marry on Saturday, then Sunday or Monday departures are most convenient. Check on the availability of bathtubs versus showers if that is important to you. Ask whether room service is available at all three meals and whether you can choose from the regular menu (room service menus are often limited).

Nonambulatory Disabled Passengers

Many people who use a wheelchair or other mobility aids have discovered the pleasures of cruising firsthand. However, you need to be very direct and specific when exploring your options. Dining rooms, showrooms, or public restrooms are not wheelchair accessible on many older or smaller ships. A few small ships have no elevators; on others, particularly older ships, elevators do not serve every deck. Most ships require that you bring your own wheelchair, often one that is collapsible or narrow-gauge. Do not count on a lot of wheelchair-accessible facilities or cabins. On the most wheelchair-accessible ships, no more than two dozen cabins will have wheelchair-accessible bathrooms, and there usually is no way to get a wheelchair into a regular cabin's bathroom. If you need an accessible cabin, book well in advance. We list the number of wheelchair-accessible cabins available under each line's Standard Features and each ship's Cabin Specifications. Look for a ship with a lot of elevators relative to its complement of passengers. Divide the number of passengers by the number of elevators. Generally, the lower the calculated number, the less time you will spend waiting for elevators.

It is important that you book your cruise through an agency specializing or experienced in travel for physically challenged guests.

If you power your own wheelchair, unaided by a companion, bring something to extend your reach. A rubber-tipped teacher's pointer is good, a collapsible one is ideal. You need the pointer to reach elevator buttons, some light switches, and the closet rod and higher storage space in your cabin, even in some wheelchair-accessible rooms.

Make sure that dining rooms, restrooms, showrooms, lounges, promenade decks, and the pool areas are wheelchair accessible. Determine whether gangways are accessible at ports. If tenders are used, will you be able to board in a wheelchair? In the dining room, will your table accommodate your wheelchair, or must you shift to a regular chair? If you cannot shift yourself, will you need a companion to help or are crew members allowed to assist? Can crew members help in your cabin and elsewhere aboard ship? Must you sign a medical waiver or produce documentation from your physician to obtain a wheelchair-accessible cabin? No matter how dependable your travel agent is, call the cruise line and double-check all important arrangements yourself.

Partially Ambulatory Disabled

If you use a wheelchair sometimes but can walk a little, you will do fine on most ships large enough to have elevators. You will be able to get around your cabin and into the bathroom on foot. A collapsible wheelchair will enable you to cover longer distances. Crutches are iffy on ships, walkers better, but the safest way for the partially ambulatory to get around is in a wheelchair.

Larger ships have wide passageways, spacious public areas, and, most likely, an adequate number of elevators. Smaller ships may have tight passageways, steep stairs, and no elevators. Older vessels may have bulkhead doors with raised thresholds, blocked passageways with steps to the next level, and no elevator access to some decks.

Choose a cabin near the elevators. Book one with a shower (with metal chair or stool); many ships' bathtubs are higher and/or deeper than yours at home. Ask whether the cabin's bath has sturdy handgrips.

Consider booking an itinerary on calmer water, such as Alaska's Inside Passage. If you cruise on the open sea, choose a cabin on a lower deck in the vessel's center; this area is least susceptible to motion.

Passengers with Sight and/or Hearing Impairments

Many people with sight or hearing impairments travel with a nondisabled companion. Regardless, be sure to inform your cabin steward of your disability. In the event of an emergency, he should know to check your cabin immediately to make sure your companion is with you and to assist you if not. If you are hearing-impaired, your steward should be given permission to enter your cabin in an emergency if there is no response to a knock.

Passengers with Diet Restrictions

Diet restrictions normally pose no problem on cruise ships. The galley will prepare meals to your specification and serve them at regular seatings in the dining room. Orthodox religious practitioners who must verify that a meal is prepared in a certain way should ask whether such verification will be possible. All lines request advance notice—either at the time of booking for some lines, or no less than 30 days prior to departure for others—for specific needs. We provide this information under cruise lines' Standard Features. Also, cruise line brochures detail procedures for diet requests.

Families with Younger Children

Although some lines are equipped to handle younger children, we do not recommend cruising for kids younger than age 5 on most lines, and ages 3 and up on lines such as Carnival, Disney, and Royal Caribbean, which have a special program for toddlers and their families. Lines that really want family business advertise that fact. If you have young children and want them to enjoy the cruise, but do not necessarily want to tend to them 24 hours a day yourself, book with a line specializing in family cruises. Its ships will have play areas, supervised activities, and sometimes a separate swimming pool for children. Best of all, the chaperoned children's program provides a respite from constant parenting. If, however, your rich Aunt Hattie wants to treat you and your little nippers to a luxury cruise, don't decline because the ship's brochure doesn't picture kids. Little ones on essentially adult cruises fare reasonably well. Although planned activities may be few or none, globally astute kids who relish history, culture, new sights, and meeting new people will get along fine. Kids who need constant entertainment and attention should not be brought along.

Usually, the children's center will be a sort of seagoing day-care facility. Group babysitting in the children's center is available on most ships in the evening. A few ships offer in-cabin babysitting. If the latter and all-meal room service are available, you've got it made. Sign up for second seating in the dining room, or go late if there is only one. Let the kids enjoy room service in the cabin, or take them to the buffet or informal dining area. Then turn the fed-and-scrubbed munchkins over to the sitter and head for the dining room. Of course, you can take your children to the dining room, but if they are age 6 or younger, once may be enough. If you prefer to dine with your children in the dining room, you should sign up for the early seating.

If your ship has a supervised children's program, your kids will be on the go all the time. However, we've seen children who scarcely countenance their parents at home refuse to leave them and go to the

Cruising for Children

This chart includes only those cruise lines with facilities for children; for details, see the line's profile in Part Two. Many lines not included on this chart accept children and offer cruises appropriate for them but have no special facilities for children. Also, note that age limits vary; always check with the cruise line before making plans.

KEY

A = All ships   S = Some ships and/or destinations

H = Only seasonal, usually Christmas, Easter, or summer holiday periods.

Source: *Cruise Line International Association (CLIA)*

CARNIVAL CRUISE LINES

REDUCED CRUISE RATE *(with 2 full-fare adults)*[1]	A
AIR/SEA RATE *(same as or less than full-fare passengers)*	A
BABYSITTING AVAILABLE[2]	A
CRIBS AVAILABLE[3]	A
QUAD/FAMILY CABINS AVAILABLE	A
ESCORTED SHORE TOURS	S
MENUS	A
MOVIES	A
PARTIES	A
POOL (JUST FOR KIDS)	A
TEEN CENTER OR DISCO	S
TEEN COUNSELOR	A
VIDEO GAMES	A
YOUTH CENTER/PLAYROOM	A
YOUTH COUNSELOR	A

CELEBRITY CRUISES

REDUCED CRUISE RATE *(with 2 full-fare adults)*[1]	A
AIR/SEA RATE *(same as or less than full-fare passengers)*	—
BABYSITTING AVAILABLE[2]	AH
CRIBS AVAILABLE[3]	A
QUAD/FAMILY CABINS	A
ESCORTED SHORE TOURS	—
MENUS	A
MOVIES	A
PARTIES	A
POOL (JUST FOR KIDS)	S
TEEN CENTER OR DISCO	S
TEEN COUNSELOR	A
VIDEO GAMES	A
YOUTH CENTER/PLAYROOM	A
YOUTH COUNSELOR	A

COSTA CRUISES

REDUCED CRUISE RATE *(with 2 full-fare adults)*[1]	S
AIR/SEA RATE *(same as or less than full-fare passengers)*	A
BABYSITTING AVAILABLE[2]	A
CRIBS AVAILABLE[3]	A
QUAD/FAMILY CABINS AVAILABLE	A
ESCORTED SHORE TOURS	—
MENUS	A
MOVIES	A
PARTIES	A
POOL (JUST FOR KIDS)	S
TEEN CENTER OR DISCO	S
TEEN COUNSELOR	S
VIDEO GAMES	A
YOUTH CENTER/PLAYROOM	A
YOUTH COUNSELOR	A

CRYSTAL CRUISES

REDUCED CRUISE RATE *(with 2 full-fare adults)*[1]	A
AIR/SEA RATE *(same as or less than full-fare passengers)*	A
BABYSITTING AVAILABLE[2]	A
CRIBS AVAILABLE[3]	A
QUAD/FAMILY CABINS AVAILABLE	—
ESCORTED SHORE TOURS	AH
MENUS	AH
MOVIES	A
PARTIES	AH
POOL (JUST FOR KIDS)	AH
TEEN CENTER OR DISCO	S
TEEN COUNSELOR	AH
VIDEO GAMES	AH
YOUTH CENTER/PLAYROOM	A
YOUTH COUNSELOR	AH

CUNARD LINES

REDUCED CRUISE RATE *(with 2 full-fare adults)*[1]	A
AIR/SEA RATE *(same as or less than full-fare passengers)*	A
BABYSITTING AVAILABLE[2]	S
CRIBS AVAILABLE[3]	A
QUAD/FAMILY CABINS AVAILABLE	A
ESCORTED SHORE TOURS	—
MENUS	A
MOVIES	A
PARTIES	S
POOL (JUST FOR KIDS)	—
TEEN CENTER OR DISCO	S
TEEN COUNSELOR	H
VIDEO GAMES	A
YOUTH CENTER/PLAYROOM	S
YOUTH COUNSELOR	H

HOLLAND AMERICA LINE

REDUCED CRUISE RATE *(with 2 full-fare adults)*[1]	A
AIR/SEA RATE *(same as or less than full-fare passengers)*	A
BABYSITTING AVAILABLE[2]	A
CRIBS AVAILABLE[3]	A
QUAD/FAMILY CABINS AVAILABLE	A
ESCORTED SHORE TOURS	S
MENUS	A
MOVIES	A
PARTIES	A
POOL (JUST FOR KIDS)	S
TEEN CENTER OR DISCO	A
TEEN COUNSELOR	A
VIDEO GAMES	A
YOUTH CENTER/PLAYROOM	A
YOUTH COUNSELOR	A

MSC CRUISES

REDUCED CRUISE RATE *(with 2 full-fare adults)*[1]	A
AIR/SEA RATE *(same as or less than full-fare passengers)*	A
BABYSITTING AVAILABLE[2]	A
CRIBS AVAILABLE[3]	S
QUAD/FAMILY CABINS AVAILABLE	S
ESCORTED SHORE TOURS	—
MENUS	A
MOVIES	A
PARTIES	A
POOL (JUST FOR KIDS)	S
TEEN CENTER OR DISCO	S
TEEN COUNSELOR	S
VIDEO GAMES	S
YOUTH CENTER/PLAYROOM	S
YOUTH COUNSELOR	S

NORWEGIAN CRUISE LINE

REDUCED CRUISE RATE *(with 2 full-fare adults)*[1]	A
AIR/SEA RATE *(same as or less than full-fare passengers)*	A
BABYSITTING AVAILABLE[2]	A
CRIBS AVAILABLE[3]	A
QUAD/FAMILY CABINS AVAILABLE	A
ESCORTED SHORE TOURS	S
MENUS	A
MOVIES	S
PARTIES	S
POOL (JUST FOR KIDS)	S
TEEN CENTER OR DISCO	SH
TEEN COUNSELOR	AH
VIDEO GAMES	A
YOUTH CENTER/PLAYROOM	S
YOUTH COUNSELOR	AH

ROYAL CARIBBEAN INTERNATIONAL

REDUCED CRUISE RATE *(with 2 full-fare adults)*[1]	A
AIR/SEA RATE *(same as or less than full-fare passengers)*	—
BABYSITTING AVAILABLE[2]	H
CRIBS AVAILABLE[3]	A
QUAD/FAMILY CABINS AVAILABLE	A
ESCORTED SHORE TOURS	—
MENUS	A
MOVIES	A
PARTIES	A
POOL (JUST FOR KIDS)	S
TEEN CENTER OR DISCO	S
TEEN COUNSELOR	A
VIDEO GAMES	A
YOUTH CENTER/PLAYROOM	A
YOUTH COUNSELOR	A

footnotes

1. On most cruises, infants travel free. Where applicable, maximum age is 1 to 3 years.
2. Where available, babysitting is arranged on board and not guaranteed.
3. Where available, cribs arranged for at time of booking.

children's center aboard ship. To avoid this issue, before you leave home, explain how things work and negotiate what time you will spend together and apart. If your children are too young to negotiate such deals, save the family cruise for another year or put the kids into the children's center and deal with any fallout.

Consider accommodations: Cabins are much more confining than children's homes or bedrooms. Your kids will size up your cabin in about ten seconds and figure there is not much to do there. From that point, they will be obsessed with running loose around the ship. Anticipate this response. Set limits in advance about bedtime, naps, meals, and parental private time, and plan for each day. Television, when available, is usually limited to a news channel, movies, and information about the ship and shore excursions. While family-focused lines may offer a cartoon channel or Nickelodeon, it's still good to bring games, books, and toys to keep the children reasonably content in the cabin.

If you can afford it, putting the children in an adjoining cabin is best, if the line's policy permits. If you buy kids their own cabin, the cruise line will sometimes include airfare in the deal. If you bunk the young ones in your cabin, you have to buy their airfare as an add-on. A few cruise lines offer a discount on a connecting cabin, where available, especially during low seasons.

Families with Teens

Teens do pretty well on cruises. They are old enough not to need constant supervision, will definitely eat their money's worth of food, and collect new experiences they can talk about back home. Teens are allowed to enjoy everything aboard except the casino and some lounges. On some ships, teens accompanied by parents are allowed in the disco and other adult areas. Family and midmarket ships often have clubs where teens can dance, and arcades with Ping-Pong, pool, or electronic games. These are noted in each cruise line's profile in Part Two under "Children's Facilities."

A cruise is a totally new environment for children—some embrace it with gusto, eager to learn, to find every nook and cranny, but others are intimidated and need help. For the right kids, it's a fabulous, fun, learning experience. With teens, as with younger kids, negotiate and set your limits before you leave home. Because teens can be messy and monopolize the bathroom, we stress our recommendation that you get them an adjoining cabin, again, if the line's policy permits. Finally, though we believe teens on their own are safe aboard ship, we suggest you keep them under tight rein ashore. If this is your first cruise and you have qualms about taking children, go without them and size up the situation. All of you might enjoy it more if you know the territory.

Additional Information

In both the cruise lines' Standard Features and the cruise ship profiles, we include a section on children's facilities. These references are a start. Also consult **Family Travel Times** (40 Fifth Avenue, New York, NY 10011; ☎ 212-477-5524; **www.familytraveltimes.com**), an online publication of TWYCH (Travel With Your Children) that frequently reports on family cruises, down to the last playpen and high chair. Annual subscriptions are $39, which buys you access to six online issues.

SHOPPING *for and*
BOOKING YOUR CRUISE

GATHERING INFORMATION

NOW THAT YOU HAVE OUTLINED YOUR REQUIREMENTS and preferences, compare them against the profiles of the cruise lines and ships described in this book. After you, or you and your travel agent, identify several lines that seem to meet your needs, obtain promotional brochures either through the agent or by contacting the lines directly, using phone numbers and addresses in the profiles.

A travel agent specializing in cruises or selling them routinely can be a tremendous source of information. Many agents who have sailed repeatedly can provide firsthand information about ships and lines. Also, many will put you in touch with clients willing to share thoughts and opinions. However, always understand from a self-interest perspective that cruise lines pay the agent a commission on every cruise the agent sells.

Finally, here are some helpful Internet sites: **www.cruisecritic.com, www.cruisemates.com, cruises.about.com, www.avidcruiser.com, www .shipsandcruises.com, www.southerncruising.com,** and **www.cruisediva .com** are written by veteran cruise writers. Their generally candid ship reviews are based on firsthand experience. They also have cruise line information, news updates, information on promotions, and deals.

Another Web site, **www.cruiseopinion.com,** offers more than 4,800 cruise evaluations written by passengers who submit monthly reviews, however, far too many are very old and the site is not maintained well. Another Web site to check out is found at **www.i-cruise.com,** which has a "guaranteed lowest price" feature. Both of these sites sell cruises in addition to providing comparative information. Also check **www .cruise.com** and **www.cruises.com.** All provide reviews, deck plans, tips for singles, and, of course, hot deals.

For those with an interest in the cruise industry as well as cruises, we recommend **www.cruisenewsdaily.com,** which publishes a daily newsletter that costs $47.95 for a semiannual subscription for new subscribers and well worth it.

Cruise Travel magazine (P.O. Box 342, Mount Morris, IL 61054; ☎800-877-5893; **www.cruisetravelmag.com**) is unabashedly rah-rah cruising and contains no critical content, but it's a good source of information. Its six issues a year contain ads from dozens of cruise discounters, consolidators, and cruise-specialty travel agents. Subscriptions are listed at $44.95 a year in the United States, $50 in Canada; however, the magazine frequently has a half-price promotional offer.

Cruise Week (Lehman Publishing, 3619 Hollywood Avenue, Brookfield, Il 60513; ☎ 800-593-8252; fax 775-402-7614; cruiseweek@aol.com; **www.cruise-week.com**), a two-page weekly industry newsletter available by fax or e-mail, is produced by an editor who has reported on the industry for many years. It's directed to the travel industry, but consumers interested in tracking news about cruising will find it a timely resource. Subscriptions are $125 annually.

Ocean & Cruise News (P.O. Box 4850, Stamford, CT 06907; ☎ 203-329-2787; **www.oceancruise.com**) reports on the industry and reviews a different ship in each issue. A much-publicized annual evaluation of lines and ships in the February issue is based on subscribers' votes, which tend to reflect seasoned cruisers' preferences for established lines. Subscriptions are $35 annually for 12 issues for U.S. readers ($40 elsewhere).

Porthole (P.O. Box 469066, Escondido, CA 92046-9066; ☎ 800-776-port; **www.porthole.com**) is by far the most attractive and lively magazine on cruises. It offers a range of interesting articles by knowledgeable writers, although criticism is rare. Subscriptions are $19.95, one year (six issues), U.S.A.; US $24.95, Canada; all other countries: first-class mail US $39.95, airmail US $79.95. **TravLtips** magazine (P.O. Box 580188, Flushing, NY 11358-0218; ☎ 800-872-8584; info@travltips.com; **www.travltips.com**) is a good bet if you are interested in freighter cruising, expedition cruising, or bargain around-the-world cruising on conventional cruise ships; it's published bimonthly. Subscriptions are $20 for introductory U.S. membership for one year, $35 for two years and include a special edition of *TravLtips: Roam the World by Freighter & Small Ship*. Canadian membership, $30 for one year, and $45 for two years. Call for overseas membership rates.

HOW TO READ A CRUISE LINE BROCHURE

CRUISE BROCHURES ARE VERY ELABORATE. Because they contain so much information, we offer a systematic approach to evaluating and understanding their contents.

Look at the Pictures

All photos in the brochures have been carefully chosen to excite the people for whom the cruise line tailors its product. If you identify with the activities depicted, this may be a good cruise line for you. Pay attention to ages of the people shown. Do you see yourself in the activities?

Sizing up the Ships

Look at the ships. Are they too big, too small, about right, or you don't care as long as they float? Talk to a travel agent about your vacation style. A good agent can help you make the right fit with a line and ship. Most brochures also contain a deck-by-deck schematic of the ship. Concentrate first on the ship's layout, looking for features important to you. If you work out, look at the relative size of the exercise room and try to find a photo of it so you can check the equipment. Ask about exercise classes, the spa, and such features as a jogging track or lap pool. If you have mobility problems, look for elevators.

Itineraries

Read the itineraries, making preliminary selections on where and how long you want to cruise. On what days and at what times does the cruise begin and end? Do these work for you? Focus on a couple of cruises. Read the itineraries, observing how much time the ship spends at sea and in port, how much cruising is during waking hours, and whether the number of ports and the time allowed to see them suits you.

For practice, let's look at a ten-day itinerary from Copenhagen to London/Tilbury.

The cruise sails at 6 p.m. Sunday, allowing several options. Because most flights from the United States to Europe depart in the late afternoon and evening, a person living in the eastern United States could work most or all of Friday and catch an evening flight to Copenhagen, arriving Saturday morning. He would have until about 3:30 p.m. Sunday to rest and see Copenhagen. Alternately, he could fly out Saturday

DAY	DATE	PORT	ARRIVE	DEPART
Sunday	June 4	Copenhagen		6 p.m.
Monday	June 5	Cruising		
Tuesday	June 6	Helsinki	8 a.m.	6 p.m.
Wednesday	June 7	St. Petersburg	8 a.m.	
Thursday	June 8	St. Petersburg		6 p.m.
Friday	June 9	Stockholm	4 p.m.	
Saturday	June 10	Stockholm		3 p.m.
Sunday	June 11	Cruising		
Monday	June 12	Oslo	8 a.m.	5 p.m.
Tuesday	June 13	Cruising		
Wednesday	June 14	London/Tilbury	7 a.m.	

evening and arrive in Copenhagen on Sunday morning with four or five hours at his disposal before boarding, although we do not recommend this. Remember, flights do cancel or have serious delays at times. Come in the day before. Why take a chance of missing your ship?

This cruise calls on four ports, not counting ports of origination and termination. This is fewer than average for a ten-day cruise, but all are major cities. The itinerary gives lots of time in each port. In St. Petersburg and Stockholm, the ship anchors overnight. If you're interested in St. Petersburg and Stockholm and a lot of sightseeing, this works well. If not, it's a long time in port. Full days (8 a.m. to 5 or 6 p.m.) are planned in Helsinki and Oslo.

Rates

Check published rates to determine whether the cruises you like fall roughly within your budget. Though some cruise lines publish rates in their brochures, others do not. Having a published brochure rate inhibits the cruise line from responding in a timely manner to market conditions. An alternative is for cruise lines to simply describe ships and itineraries in their brochures and to send interested parties to their Web site or to travel agents for price quotes.

When checking for rates online look for a link on the cruise line's or Internet seller's homepage that says, "How To Book," "Booking Your Cruise," or something similar. Clicking on this takes you to a page where you're asked to supply some preliminary information such as preferred destination (Caribbean, Alaska, etc.), how many days you want to cruise, and when approximately you'd like to go. Answering these queries will bring up a screen showing all the cruises offered in your selected time frame that meet your destination and length of cruise criteria. For each cruise listed, rates will be shown for each category of cabin. On most sites, no personal information is required to this point so you can shop to your heart's content without obligation or divulging personal information. The process is similar to that of shopping for airfares online and will be familiar to most travelers. Predictably, if you shop on a cruise line's site, only that line's cruises will appear. If you shop the site of an Internet seller, cruises from any cruise line meeting your requirements will be displayed.

unofficial **TIP**
Almost no one pays the brochure rates. Brochure rates are helpful only in providing a base for calculating discounts.

If you don't have a cruise line's printed brochure, be sure to avail yourself of deck plans, cabin photos and diagrams, and virtual tours on the cruise line's Web site

The fares are per-person, based on two persons sharing a cabin (double occupancy). If the per-person fare for a balcony cabin is $1,569, you and your traveling companion would pay $3,138 ($1,569 x 2) for the cabin. For singles supplement, see "Singles" in this chapter for a rate explanation.

All cruise lines sell cabins by category (suite, mini-suite, balcony, ocean view, obstructed ocean view, inside cabin) and by location on the ship. Traditionally, you select a deck and even a particular location on that deck, or even specify a specific stateroom. While most cruise lines continue to make these cabin selection options available on their Web sites and through travel agents, other cruise lines select your cabin for you from their inventory of available cabins in your chosen category.

As many as four persons may share a cabin, depending on its configuration. Rates for the third, fourth, and fifth persons are deeply discounted, sometimes as much as 66% off the double-occupancy fare. Let's say Tom, Ed, John, and Earl are willing to share a cabin that goes for $1,749 per person double occupancy. The line charges the double-occupancy price ($1,749) for two of the four men, and the third/fourth person rate of $399 for the remaining two. Thus, the tab for all four:

PERSON 1	$1,749	Cruise Only
PERSON 2	$1,749	Cruise Only
PERSON 3	$399	Cruise Only
PERSON 4	$399	Cruise Only
TOTAL	$4,296	

Usually, for cruise lines that bundle airfare to the port into the total price of the cruise (as part of an air/sea package), the airfare is normally included only for the two persons paying the double-occupancy rate. The cruise line will arrange airfare, often at a discounted rate, for the third and fourth persons.

If Tom, Ed, John, and Earl want to split the cost of their cruise equally, here's the way the finances average out:

Cruise fare for all four guys	$4,296
Final cost per person	$1,074

Because standard cabins (as opposed to suites) on almost all cruise ships are small with tiny bathrooms and little storage, we do not recommend cruising with more than two persons in a cabin unless, for budgetary reasons, there's no other choice. If you do elect to cruise with extra people in your cabin, select your roommates with care. Make sure everyone is compatible regarding smoking, snoring, and sleeping hours. Most of all, be tolerant and bring your sense of humor. Start with a cruise in a warm clime, when you can spend more time on deck than in your cabin. In the Caribbean, you might find yourself doing little more than sleeping and changing clothes there.

Most newer cruise ships are distinguished by the number of cabins with private balconies. These cabins become more affordable year by year and are highly recommended for those who want a quiet, private space to relax.

Sailing Dates

Check the sailing dates of cruises that interest you, looking for those compatible with your schedule. Check dates around these to see if a slight shift nets you a better fare.

Cabin Category and Ship Deck Plans

Now look at the types of cabins available. Many brochures and Web sites include floor plans for several types of cabins showing their size, configuration, and placement of furniture and fixtures. All cruise line Web sites and most brochures include color photographs of cabins.

Although some upscale lines offer only suites, most ships provide a choice of cabins. The top of the line—usually on the top decks—are the palatial owner's suite or royal suite, comparable to the presidential suite in a good hotel. Next are a small number of one- or two-bedroom suites, followed by a larger number of minisuites. After these deluxe accommodations come standard cabins, which account for about 85% of accommodations on most ships. Now, on more of the new, large ships, many standard cabins have verandas. In fact, on some ships 60% to 80% of all accommodations feature these balconies, which are becoming a must-have amenity for many guests. Outside standard cabins with a window are generally preferred to inside standard cabins without windows, but they are more expensive. Usually, the higher the deck, the higher the cabin's price. For outside standard cabins with windows, many cruise lines offer different categories and rates for windows with an unencumbered view, versus windows that are mostly or partially blocked, by a lifeboat for example.

Standard cabins on ships built since 1988 generally are the same throughout the ship. Windows may decrease in size as you descend from deck to deck. If the window view is obstructed, this information should be indicated on the rate charts. If not, ask.

Cabins toward the middle of the ship are considered more desirable than cabins on either end, because center cabins are closer to stairs and elevators and are less affected by the ship's back-and-forward motion (pitching). The side-to-side motion (rolling) is more pronounced the higher you go and is felt least on lower decks. But the fact is, on large cruise ships, you will feel very little motion of the sea, except perhaps on the highest decks.

unofficial **TIP**
The most stable cabins are at the waterline near the center of the lower passenger decks—the best cabins for travelers prone to motion sickness.

Before selecting a cabin category, study the ship's deck plan. Normally, the schematic is near scale and is color-coded for cabin category. Checking the Princess Cruise ship schematic for the *Grand Princess,* the

PRINCESS CRUISES

**MINISUITE WITH
PRIVATE BALCONY**

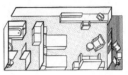

Large bedroom with twin beds, which make up into a queen bed. Sitting area with sofa bed and desk. 2 TVs, walk-in closet, refrigerator. Bath with tub and shower.

**OUTSIDE DOUBLE WITH
PRIVATE BALCONY**

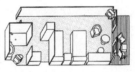

Two lower beds, which make up into a queen bed. TV, closet, refrigerator. Bath with shower.

**OUTSIDE OR
INSIDE DOUBLE**

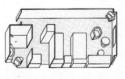

Outside staterooms have a picture window. Two lower beds, which make up into a queen bed. Many staterooms with two upper berths. Television, closet, refrigerator. Bath with shower.

PRINCESS CRUISES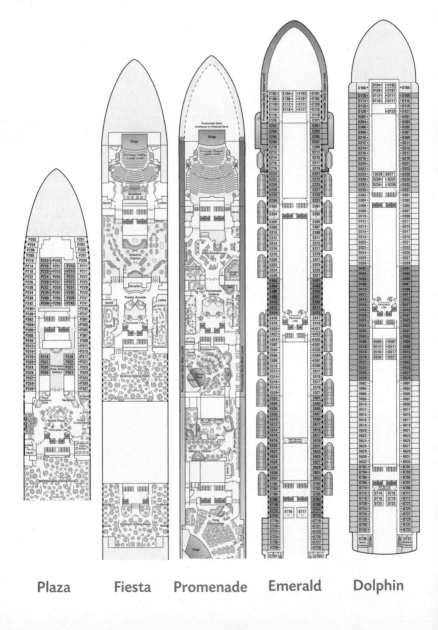

GRAND PRINCESS

Plaza   Fiesta   Promenade   Emerald   Dolphin

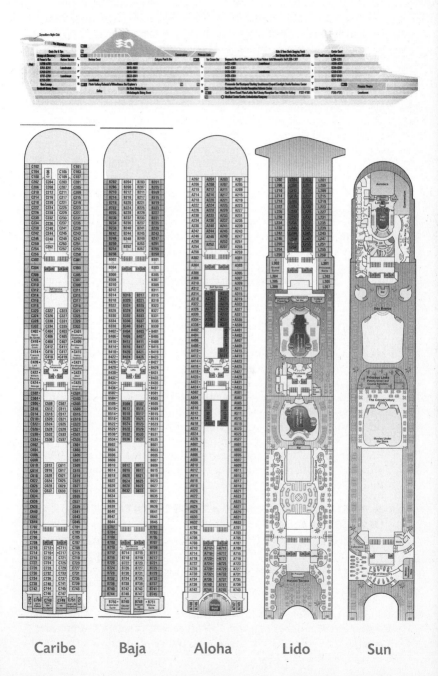

Caribe   Baja   Aloha   Lido   Sun

most expensive accommodations are on the Lido, Baja, and Caribe Decks, the first, third, and fourth highest decks respectively with passenger accommodations. All three decks are removed from noise of the galley, engines, lounges, pool area, and showroom.

Check the drawing for decks where passengers walk or jog. Avoid cabins beneath jogging tracks or promenades. Similarly, avoid cabins where the window overlooks a track or walkway. Pinpoint lounges, showrooms, the casino, discos, and other potentially noisy, late-night areas. Avoid cabins directly above or below them. Engine noise may be audible in lower-deck cabins toward the stern.

Although private verandas, or balconies, have become increasingly popular and affordable, not all balconies are created equal. When shopping, always ask about balcony size and configuration. Some are barely large enough for a chair, while others can accommodate a chaise lounge, a couple of chairs, and a table. Some balconies are covered, providing both shade and privacy, but others are open to the weather, perfect for sun bathing, but also subject to the nosy gaze of passengers on higher decks. Balconies on the bow face forward and are often subject to a great deal of wind when the ship is under way. Stern balconies, on the other hand, offer more protection and additionally provide sweeping views to either side of the ship.

Even veteran cruisers have difficulty gleaning this information from a deck plan, but a knowledgeable travel agent knows how to check out these details when you ask. Analyze what you get for a few dollars more or less. For example, a balcony cabin on Baja Deck is only $20 more than an ocean-view (no balcony) cabin on the higher Lido Deck.

Be aware that the newer megaships are very long indeed. *Allure of the Seas,* Royal Caribbean's newest ship, is 1,184 feet long, almost the length of four football fields. If you have a cabin toward the stern, it's quite a trek to the ship's main theater near the bow. One round-trip would be roughly a half mile. With the way the public areas are distributed throughout the ship, it's easy to log upward of four miles of walking on an average day.

A PRELIMINARY LOOK AT DISCOUNTS AND INCENTIVES

YOU SHOULD NOW KNOW WHETHER you are interested in a cruise offered in the brochure you are reading or the Web site you're browsing. If you are, the next step is to check the line's price incentives and discounts.

After three decades of steady growth, with dozens of new ships coming onstream, the supply of cabins sometimes has outstripped demand (the number of people to fill them). Competition put pressure on cruise lines to cut deals to keep their ships filled, and then a buyer's market prevailed.

When the most recent recession hit, the Caribbean felt it along with Europe and Asia. However, price and proximity helped the Caribbean; people could rationalize a quick vacation from U.S. ports, but they had to think twice about faraway places. Another destination where there were deep discounts on cruises was Hawaii.

In 2010, 11 new cruise ships with a total 27,263 berths are entering service. All of the 11 were ordered before the recent recession. Following 2010 there will be fewer new ships debuting than in the preceding three years, bringing supply more in line with demand. However, because the new ships entering service are so large (several carrying more than 6,000 passengers), we're unlikely to see anything approaching a real seller's market. So, until the economy makes a strong turn-around, there will still be bargains—a lot of them.

Incentives and discounts offered in the lines' brochures or on their Web sites are varied. First, the line sets prices according to times of greatest demand. High season is most expensive, followed by shoulder season, then low season. Savings may not be spectacular, judging from the brochure prices.

Remember: fares in the brochure or on the Web site are base prices to which discounts are applied. Also, ships are less crowded and cabin upgrades somewhat more available during low and shoulder seasons.

After studying seasonal discounts, check early-booking discounts. Lines offer substantial discounts to travelers willing to book six months to a year ahead. The line has use of your money in advance and gets critical information on whether a particular cruise is filling. Early-booking discounts commonly are 15% to 50% off the seasonal rate, or may be expressed as a two-for-one deal. Either way, early-booking incentives are generally the largest discounts given directly by the lines, and once they're gone, they're gone. You get other benefits, too: your choice of cabin, often the most direct air routing, and your dining-room seating preference (if the line bases seating on first come, first served). That's the kind of information available in fine print or from an experienced travel agent.

Cruise lines also may offer cabin upgrades, credit for shipboard purchases, receptions with the captain, or a couple of nights at a hotel at the originating or terminating port. In addition to an early-booking discount, almost all lines offer other discounts (often up to 50%) to repeat passengers. Some discounts from cruise lines, travel agents, wholesalers, and consolidators never appear in the cruise lines' basic brochures. For help in finding them, read the section "How to Get the Best Deal on a Cruise."

ROUND-TRIP AIRFARE

UNLESS YOU LIVE WITHIN DRIVING DISTANCE of your cruise's originating port, you will require transportation to it. Until a few years ago, most lines included air transportation in the cruise cost and promoted it as "free air." But times have changed.

What Happened to "Free Air"?

First, check the cruise brochure or Web site to determine whether prices include air transportation. When lines include air transportation in their packages (for a higher cruise cost, of course), they agree to fly you round-trip from specific "gateway" cities. These gateway cities vary among cruise lines, but usually include all major U.S. and Canadian cities and many smaller cities. If air transportation is part of the cruise package but your gateway city is especially far from the port, an air supplement—an extra charge—may be levied.

Until the late 1990s, air/sea packages were touted as all-inclusive, with "free" airfare. Nothing, of course, was ever free. Cruise lines built air transportation into the cruise cost and called it free. By buying in advance and in large volume, lines could negotiate big discounts on airfares. These discounts enabled the cruise lines to offer complete vacation packages—the cruise with airfare—for a good price. Since 1997, however, cruise lines have increasingly published their rates as "cruise-only" fares and sell the air transportation as an add-on. The reason for the change is that as demand for air travel increased, airlines radically reduced the availability and size of discounts for cruise lines. Even in the post-9/11 world, airlines could fill their planes without offering reduced fares to major ports, particularly for weekend flights when cruise lines need them most. Today, cruise lines can obtain the discounts required for a good air/sea package only by buying airlines' least desirable flights, including late-night flights, circuitous routes, and multiple stops. Luxury cruise lines are the exceptions, as they continue to offer air-inclusive packages to ensure that their customers get the most direct and convenient flights and often offer business class at a greatly reduced price as a further incentive.

At the same time, passengers often discover they can get better airfares and routing on their own or by using their frequent-flier points. Plus, they receive their tickets well in advance. Often with air/sea packages, airlines issue tickets only at the last minute (to distribute passengers equally among available flights). The practice panics cruise passengers near departure who wonder where their tickets are. Cruise lines accumulate reservations for several months before contacting the airlines and nailing down flight itineraries and seats. Standard practice is to advise you of your air itinerary 30 to 45 days prior to sailing (Princess has a program called Flight Choice, in which flight notification is made 60 days in advance). Understand, however, that we're only talking about flight

unofficial **TIP**
Flights arranged by the cruise lines are often not eligible for frequent-flier mileage. Plan to call the airline directly after the ticket has been issued to try to get proper credit.

information. Actual ticketing does not begin until about 30 days from your sailing date, and your tickets might not arrive until a week or two before you walk out of the door. The process affords the cruise line maximum flexibility but vastly increases the probability of your receiving an inconvenient itinerary with multiple connecting flights, and with little time left to make changes. As a kicker, you may be surprised to discover that making your reservations well in advance doesn't necessarily mean that you'll get one of the better flight itineraries. A few lines give priority to early bookers, with flight itineraries based on the "seniority" of cruise reservations that are paid in full. With many other lines, it matters not whether you booked eight months or eight weeks ahead—you'll get what's available at the time the cruise line finally books the air travel. That's where it really pays to have a good travel agent who will insist that you get the best routing and receive your flight information in a timely manner. Also, the use of e-tickets throughout the airline industry has made it much easier for customers to get their flight information in a timely manner.

If the air itinerary provided by the cruise line is not acceptable, you can request a change or a particular routing through your travel agent. Many cruise lines maintain "Air Deviation" desks to handle requests from passengers who want to change their assigned routing. Changes can cost $35 to more than $100 (as if you changed a ticket directly with an airline), and an additional air supplement may be charged if no seats are available in your designated airfare category. So, you ask, how bad can flight itineraries arranged by the cruise line be? A California couple was ushered off their ship and shuttled to the San Juan, Puerto Rico, airport at 9:30 a.m. for a flight home that departed at 6 p.m. Following a cruise, a family of six was split up with four of the party scheduled for an early flight and the other two reserved for a flight that arrived eight hours later.

If you purchase an air-inclusive cruise vacation but elect to arrange (and pay for) your own air transportation, the cruise fare will be decreased because you are not using the air-travel part of the package. The amount to be lopped off your package price is shown as "Cruise-Only Travel Allowance." The allowance, for example, is about $250 on one-week Caribbean air/sea packages.

Price and itineraries, however, are not the only considerations in buying air from the cruise line. When you buy the line's air add-on or an air-inclusive cruise, transfers are almost always included. The cruise line will meet you at the airport and transfer you to the ship. Likewise, at the end of the cruise, the line will return you to the airport.

When you purchase your air transportation independently or if you use frequent-flier awards, you can usually buy airport transfers from the cruise lines. Carnival, for example, offers one-way and round-trip transfers, which must be booked 14 days in advance; price varies with location. Without such an arrangement, you must set up your own transfers. This seems complicated, but travel agents can handle such details for you—and we advise you to let them. Be aware that at cruise's end only, some lines provide this transportation service regardless of whether you bought your air through them.

When arriving at the embarkation airport, you will claim your baggage. Those on an air/sea package or with transfers will board a bus and their luggage will be transported with them to the pier. There, luggage will be taken by porters, and you will see it several hours later, after it is delivered directly to your cabin. If the airline booked by the cruise line loses your luggage, the cruise line will do its best to get it to you (once it's recovered), even if the ship has sailed.

During busier times, cruise lines may fly you to the port city a day in advance and provide hotel accommodations. If you live in the western United States and are sailing from an eastern port, the cruise line may fly you to the port city on a late-night flight with arrival between midnight and 9 a.m. More considerate lines arrange hotel day rooms where you can rest before boarding your ship later in the day. Similar arrangements are sometimes made for East Coast passengers embarking on the West Coast, and passengers on European or Asian cruises.

The line, when it puts you in a hotel, assumes responsibility for transporting you to the pier. If you are to be accommodated in a hotel before embarkation, pack an overnight bag; you may not have access to your luggage until you're aboard ship.

Most air transportation purchased through cruise lines is coach class. Your travel agent can arrange seat assignments, boarding passes, and upgrades (when available).

If you are cruising during autumn (excluding holiday periods) or when airfares are discounted in your city, or if you can reach the port on a discount airline (like Southwest), you may want to book your own air travel to save money. If you can book your flights at or near the cruise line's air allowance, you will be able to choose your airline, ensure a good flight itinerary, accrue frequent-flier miles, and receive your tickets or e-tickets well before your departure date.

If you choose the air-inclusive package or buy air transportation as an add-on, take these precautions:

1. **DO YOUR HOMEWORK.** Ask the cruise line if preferred air itineraries are allocated according to reservations seniority (that is, those who book earliest get the best itineraries). Also ask when your booked flight itinerary will be available. If the cruise line does not give priority to those who book early or does not provide flight information far enough in advance to make changes, book your own air.

2. **CALL EARLY TO RESERVE.** Remember that cruise lines contract for a specific number of seats for every cruise—when they're filled, the line has to scramble for additional ones. That's when you're likely to get

a circuitous routing. But, to put this in perspective: the airline crunch comes at holiday times—Memorial Day, July 4th, Labor Day, Thanksgiving, Christmas, spring break through Easter—and can be exacerbated by bad weather. So, if you plan a cruise during a holiday period, arrange it early and save yourself a pile of headaches. As a veteran travel agent advised, "Passengers should seriously consider taking the air/sea package from the cruise line during the winter months, especially if they are flying from a cold-weather gateway. If there are weather- or equipment-related delays, the cruise line will help air/sea passengers get to the ship. If passengers have booked their own air, they are on their own if they miss the ship. Passengers who book their own air would also be well advised to purchase third-party travel insurance that covers trip interruption, delay, or cancellation due to weather- or equipment-related problems."

The travel agent's advice is valid, but only up to a point. The cruise line sees itself as merely an airline ticketing agent. As a matter of customer relations, many cruise lines will step in and assist a passenger who is delayed or misses the boat because of problems with flights that the cruise line booked. The salient point, however, is that the cruise line is under no obligation to help. If you read the terms and conditions of your passage contract, you'll almost immediately bump into language like the following: "Under no circumstances does [X Cruise Line's] responsibility extend beyond the ship. All arrangements made for the guests with independent contractors [such as airlines] are made solely for the convenience of the guest and are at the guest's risk." We'll explore the ramifications of this and related issues later under "When Things Go Wrong." For now, let us add that we recommend third-party travel insurance whether you book air through the cruise line or not.

3. **ASK YOUR TRAVEL AGENT WHEN YOU CAN EXPECT YOUR TICKETS.**
Most cruise brochures tell this in the fine print, and Internet booking sites usually have a Terms and Conditions page that contains the same information. Normally, paper tickets arrive two to three weeks before departure. E-tickets are generally e-mailed at the time the flight itinerary is booked, usually farther in advance than paper tickets. Smaller cruise lines frequently deliver earlier than the big lines do.

4. **PLAN YOUR ROUTE.** If you have a specific route you want to fly to your departure port, tell your travel agent when you book or as soon as possible, so that your plane tickets can be issued properly. If you receive tickets requiring layovers and a change of planes, have your agent contact the cruise line's Air Deviation desk.

HOW TO GET THE BEST DEAL ON A CRUISE

TO GET A GOOD DEAL ON A CRUISE, know the players and how the game is played. In the case of cruising, game rules pivot on the unalterable reality that a cruise is a time-sensitive product. If a cabin is not sold by sailing time, it loses all of its value. This makes selling cruises like playing *Beat the Clock*. From the time a cruise is announced, the line is on a countdown to sell all the cabins. The immense expense of operating a cruise ship makes the selling a high-pressure, big-stakes endeavor. For consumers, the time sensitivity is a major plus. Any time a dealer must make a sale or write off the inventory (empty cabins, in this case), wheeling and dealing are likely, and this almost always benefits the buyer. However, we emphasize that there's more to buying a cruise than its price. If you allow yourself to be influenced only by "getting the best deal," you are likely to end up on the wrong cruise. Talk to your agent and evaluate all factors.

Note that in American ports, it is no longer possible to show up at the dock, suitcase in hand, and negotiate a last-minute fare with the purser. For security reasons, cruise ships must submit passenger manifests to the FBI about a week prior to departure.

The Players: Cruise Lines

Lines have sales offices and, more and more, Web sites that sell cruises directly to consumers. But as many as 95% of all cruises are sold through travel agents or other players, and you usually get a better price by buying from them. To their credit, cruise lines are loyal to those who sell their product and usually won't undercut the prices available to them. Practically, the lines don't want the bother, and until the Internet came along, it wasn't cost-effective. It costs cruise lines far more to maintain sales offices to serve the general public than it does to maintain a sales network through travel agencies and Internet sellers. Note, however, that sales directly to consumers on the Internet are not necessarily at a discount. Many cruise lines have a flat rate policy that forbids travel agents and Internet sellers to advertise fares below those published in the line's brochure and on its Web site. The operational word here is "advertise." Once you make contact with a live agent, there may be additional discounts and other goodies that the agent wasn't allowed to advertise.

Many lines will penalize and even ban agencies from selling their products if they advertise a lower price. Carnival Cruise Lines, saying that it "would rather have thirty-five thousand people selling Carnival than ten," closed ranks with the little guys by offering the same prices to all of its accounts. Royal Caribbean has gone even farther: whether small agencies or giants, it says it would no longer deal with any agency that is found undercutting prices by rebating commissions. In addition, Celebrity, Oceania Cruises, and Norwegian Cruise Lines now have similar anti-rebating practices. Some lines still offer large operators preferential pricing. To gain an even greater advantage, the big sellers also use their extensive resources to gobble up blocks of cabins at group rates and then resell the cabins one at a time to individual travelers. That too may eventually become passé as major lines are beginning to forbid this practice as well. They hope to stabilize prices and avoid abuse of their policies. (We should note, however, that during the present economic downturn, even the best of intentions and determination often go out the window when cruise lines need to fill their ships. Deep discounts have become the norm.)

The smaller agencies are also smacked by the way the cruise lines handle "distressed inventory," for example, cabins yet unsold as the sailing date for a cruise approaches. Once again, not unexpectedly, these bargain-basement goodies are sometimes handed over to the line's big-volume brick-and-mortar and Internet accounts to move. Although most of us like to root for the underdog, it's tough to walk away from the great prices offered by larger sellers. It's worth remembering, however, that the big guys usually can't compete with a good hometown travel agent when it comes to service, accessibility, and peace of mind.

The Players: Wholesalers and Megasellers

Wal-Mart founder Sam Walton taught Americans that the more of something you buy, the lower the price should be. Businesspeople call it buying in quantity or volume discounting. In cruising, travel wholesalers and megasellers are volume buyers. Booking well in advance, they buy large numbers of cabins on specific cruises with the intention of reselling the cabins at a profit. Advance purchasing and volume discounts, coupled with the fact that the cruise lines do not have to pay commissions, allow them to buy at prices substantially below what an individual could obtain. Some cabins that go unsold can be returned to the cruise company by a certain date; others are bought on a non-returnable basis. In the latter case, the wholesaler or megaseller absorbs the costs of any cabins that aren't sold. The biggest cruise discounts available to any player go to those who buy cabins in bulk on a non-returnable basis. Wholesalers sell to travel agents and, often, like megasellers, directly to consumers. If the wholesaler sells a cruise through a travel agency, then the wholesaler pays the agent a commission.

Note that these players generally deal with lines having large ships, or they offer the best deals on a limited number of ships and lines. If they spread themselves too thinly over the spectrum of cruises, they diminish their clout with specific lines. Remember: it's in the wholesaler's or megaseller's interest to steer you to ships where they get the best deal. That may or may not be in your best interest.

The Players: Travel Agents

Travel agents act as sales representatives of the cruise lines. Unlike wholesalers and consolidators, they don't buy cabins. Instead, they sell from the line's inventory, on commission. Like cruise lines and wholesalers, however, agents earn the most when they sell in volume.

Some full-service travel agencies specialize in cruises, whereas others are cruise-only agencies, selling nothing but cruises and cruise-related travel. The latter sell so many cabins for certain lines that they earn "override commissions"—a higher percentage level of commission over the norm. There is usually a volume threshold where the override kicks in. Some general travel agencies and independent agencies cash in on override commissions by joining a consortium—a group of agencies that pool their sales to receive the overrides. Several consortiums are made up of many individual travel agencies—such as Virtuoso, Ensemble, Signature, and American Express—and with their greater buying power can offer lower rates on specific cruises. Normally, a representative from the consortium is on board to help their passengers and host a cocktail party and/or a special dinner or shore excursion for them.

To make the most in commissions and overrides, some agents push selected cruise lines, known in the industry as preferred suppliers. If the line that interests you is among your agent's preferred suppliers, great. If not, your agent may try to interest you in a line with which the agency has such an arrangement. However, a good agent who wants to stay in business will never put a customer on an inappropriate cruise just to earn one commission check. Remember, agents rely heavily on good word of mouth for their business. Their goal is to satisfy you, so you will come back. Because most cruises are sold by travel agents, it is critically important for cruise lines to develop extensive systems of loyal travel agents. Competition among cruise lines to influence agents is so heated that consumers sometimes become pawns in a marketing chess game.

Over the years, for example, Holland America has awarded its agencies bonus points redeemable for chocolate, picnic lunches, dinners in local restaurants, or any number of other choice perks. Such incentives may influence agents' recommendations and narrow consumers' choices. All cruise lines are not necessarily a good fit for all of an agent's customers. Good agents place their clients' needs and preferences first, but some agents go for the largest commissions and the most goodies.

As we noted earlier, in the past, many agents sacrificed part of their commission or override to make a cruise more affordable to a good customer and to compete with large-volume discount agencies. Some agencies selling cruises in volume still take lower commissions to undercut other agencies. But again, some cruise-line policy changes have decreased these practices but have not eliminated them. In many locations, competition among agencies for cruise business is as keen as it is among cruise lines, particularly with the proliferation of cruise-only agencies and large Internet sellers. And with airlines having decreased agents' commissions, the competition for cruise business has grown even hotter.

In the final analysis, buyer beware. Protect yourself best by developing a long-term relationship with a knowledgeable travel agent who works to put you on the cruise that's right for you.

HELPING YOUR TRAVEL AGENT HELP YOU When you call a travel agent, ask whether he or she has cruised, how many times, and on what lines. Firsthand knowledge is invaluable. If the answer is no, find another agent or be prepared to give your agent a lot of direction. Ask who your agent's preferred vendors are. Just asking that question will tell the agent you are a savvy buyer. A good agent will ask you many questions, such as your age, preferences, tastes, and so on to better recommend a particular line or ship. Compare the agent's questions and recommendations with information in this guide. Request permission to contact other clients who have been on the cruise line recommended, and ask your friends. Someone you know may have sailed on the line. Also check the independent cruise Web sites listed earlier under "Gathering Information." These sites feature cruise reviews from both travel writers and the general public.

To help your travel agent obtain the best possible deal, do the following things:

1. Determine from brochures, friends' recommendations, the Internet, and this book a general idea of where and when you want to cruise, which lines offer the kind of cruise that most appeals to you, and how much you can spend. Remember that your cruise tickets are only a part of your costs. Budget also for air travel and shore excursions, alcoholic beverages, tips, and shopping.

2. Shop the Internet for deals. Because the Internet operates in real time, new deals are posted continuously. Shop only sites that publish a phone number where you can access a live representative.

3. Phone consolidators or retailers (including Internet sites) whose ads you have collected. Ask about their offers, but do not book your trip with them directly.

5. Tell your travel agent about cruises you find, and ask if he or she can match or beat the price or provide any "added value." Some producers may offer a bottle of wine, a fluffy robe, or another perk. Be aware that promotional ads are often bait to get your attention. The "lead" price probably applies to a limited number of cabins on a specific sailing. This element is probably the trickiest part of obtaining the best deal. Every ship has 6–30 categories of cabins. Often, unless you can pinpoint the date, itinerary, and cabin category being advertised, it may be hard to know whether you are getting a good deal. Nobody said this was easy.

6. Choose among options uncovered by you and your travel agent. Whatever option you elect, have your agent book it. It may be commissionable (at no additional cost to you) and will provide the agent some return on the time invested on your behalf. Also, your agent should be able to help you verify the quality and integrity of the deal, and be there to assist if any glitches arise. As discounts have become so pervasive and airlines have dropped or greatly reduced travel-agency commissions, more and more travel agents have had to charge a fee for booking and planning your trip in order to stay in business. A good agent will have earned every penny.

HOW THE GAME IS PLAYED: THE SALES COUNTDOWN

CRUISE LINES WORK WELL IN ADVANCE to schedule cruises and develop promotional brochures. It is essential to roll out marketing campaigns quickly to avoid "fire sales" as sailing dates near.

Most itineraries and dates are announced 10 to 18 months in advance. Particularly attractive dates on popular ships and itineraries sell out quickly. Likewise, cruises to popular seasonal destinations fill fast. The highest- and lowest-priced cabins sell out first. Usually the last cruises to fill are low- and shoulder-season cruises to year-round areas. Many consumers wait for last-minute discounts when cruise lines hit the panic button. Although distress selling continues, cruise lines have learned to control the inventory more efficiently.

Breakthrough Pricing

Pioneered by Brian Rice, Royal Caribbean's chief financial officer, breakthrough pricing seeks through the analysis of many variables (season, weather, price- sensitivity data, competitive pressures, and the like) to determine a minimum floor price for each type of cabin on a particular sailing month before the sailing date. The floor price is theoretically the lowest price to be offered for a particular cruise and is predicated to stimulate early demand and cash flow in the form of deposits. If the ship fills according to expectations, demand for the sailing will increase as the number of available cabins decreases as they're sold. This puts the cruise line in a position to raise fares for passengers who book later rather than earlier. As it's communicated to the public, the cruise line is essentially saying that you'll get a better deal by buying now than if you wait. Therefore, a consumer who books a November cruise in the preceding April would pay less than a passenger who books in June. That passenger, in turn, would pay less than someone booking in August, and so on. The line can maintain the discounted rate if the ship is filling slowly, or raise it incrementally as the cruise approaches being sold out. (Needless to say, since the economy slowed down, much has changed; there have been more fire sales in the last year than at anytime in the past that we can remember.)

Cruise lines operate two pricing systems. Primary is breakthrough pricing. If the cruise sells to near capacity, only that model will be employed. If sales lag behind expectations, however, the line goes to its separate and collateral model: the special-situations system.

Special-Situations System

Special-situations initiatives—usually time-limited and tightly targeted efforts for boosting sales—run concurrently with, and independently of, the escalating base-rate system. Examples of such initiatives include a deeply discounted senior citizen's rate, a direct mailing to previous customers offering a big discount, a regional campaign, advertising last-minute bargains on the Internet, or a heavily discounted group-sales overture to a large company for their executives or employees.

Each special-situation initiative targets a carefully selected market segment. Initiatives may run sequentially or concurrently but usually are short-lived and end when the cruise sells out. What is really important about special-situation initiatives is that the price offered might be less than the breakthrough pricing minimum floor. If you can locate such an initiative, you may have found the lowest possible fare. If the special is advertised in Atlanta and you live in Buffalo, the package's air component will be useless to you. However, if you can buy the cruise-only part of the special and arrange affordable airfare from Atlanta, you've got a deal. Be aware, however, that cruise lines offering such promotions sometimes ask for proof of residence.

A common special-situations approach is for the cruise line to join forces with specific travel agents or Internet sellers. Like travel agents who have preferred suppliers, cruise lines have preferred retailers. When a cruise is not selling to expectations, some lines have policies permitting them to enlist favorite big-volume agencies to help move the remaining cabins; other lines' policies may prohibit this, in an effort to give all retailers equal opportunities for sales. When this tactic is used, it develops promotions with these agents featuring extra-deep discounts and special incentives, such as cabin upgrades or discounted air add-ons. Many preferred agencies and Web sites sell cruises only and field hundreds of calls daily. If they have an especially juicy deal to offer, they can sell lots of cabins fast. Big-volume, cruise-only agencies advertise in magazines, including *Cruise Travel, Travel & Leisure, Budget Travel,* and *Condé Nast Traveler,* and in large-market newspapers.

The Dump Zone

In the cruise marketplace, anything can happen. Sometimes, lines expert in special-situations initiatives don't fill their cruises. The upshot is that a goodly number of empty cabins may be sold at distress prices during the final eight weeks before sailing, especially in the off-season.

When time is short, agents and cruise lines know it is much easier and less complicated to sell a cruise to someone who doesn't require air transportation to the port. Florida is a huge market for late-breaking deals because of its large population of retirees and its proximity to ports. Major ports on the Pacific Coast and Northeast likewise enjoy distress sales. If you live within easy driving distance of a major cruise-ship port, you live in a dump zone. You are well situated to benefit from last-minute discounts.

Discount Alphabet Soup

Before you shop for discounts, pick the cruise type that appeals to you. Once you start looking, don't get sidetracked by price alone. Instead, stay doggedly on the trail of the cruise that meets your needs and will satisfy and exceed your vacation expectations. Never equate cheapest with best, but don't equate it with worst, either.

More than a dozen types of cruise discounts are commonly offered, other than seasonal discounts. As you encounter them, be aware that catchy marketing come-ons, like "two-for-one" or "sail three days free," aren't always what they seem. For example, a promotion advertising 50% off the second person in the cabin (a frequent gimmick) is nothing more than 25% off for both (you probably could have done better with an early-booking discount). The best method for comparing rates, with or without discounts, is to calculate the per diem (cost per day) of your cruise vacation. Add the cruise cost and the airfare cost if it isn't included, plus taxes, port charges, and other applicable fees (transfers, etc.). Divide the total by the number of nights you will stay on the ship or in hotels included in the package.

Always compare apples to apples. Some cruising areas are more expensive. For example, Caribbean cruises should be compared with Caribbean cruises, not with Alaskan or Mediterranean cruises. Remember also that cruise lines are not created equal. Comparing a seven-day Carnival (Holiday Inn–type) cruise with a seven-day Silversea (Ritz-Carlton–type) cruise is meaningless. The cruise line profiles in Part Two describe the differences.

Early-Booking Discounts

The more common of two kinds of early-booking discounts, the breakthrough pricing model, was described earlier. Minimum floor rates are capacity-controlled and can be withdrawn or escalated without notice. Most of the major lines employ capacity-control pricing. A similar type of early-booking discount is the flat cutoff date. If you book before the specified date, you get the discount. This, too, is common practice on selected itineraries. Passengers who pay in full by a specified date (as much as six to nine months before the cruise) receive a 10–20% discount. This discount is popular with Crystal, Silversea, and others in the luxury market.

Free Days

Passengers are offered 7 days' cruising for the price of 6, or 12 for the price of 10. Variations include complimentary days (with hotel) in the port city before and/or after the cruise, or "book a seven-day cruise and receive a free two- or three-day land package." Divide the double occupancy price by the number of days in the package to get a per-diem cost for comparative purposes.

Two-for-One and Second Passenger Cruises Free

The deal is that two passengers cruise for the price of one, but some tricky math is involved. Pick your cruise and cabin category and find the double-occupancy price per person, air included, on the brochure's rate chart. The two-for-one price is this rate less the cruise line's air cost for one person from your gateway city.

Let's say the brochure's air-inclusive double-occupancy rate is $2,000. If the brochure does not give it, ask your travel agent to call the cruise line to learn the round-trip airfare cost from your gateway city. This amount is subtracted from $2,000, and the remainder is your cruise-only cost for two persons. You must then make your own air arrangements or buy airfare from the cruise line as an add-on. Celebrity, Oceania, Princess, Costa, and Holland America are among the lines frequently offering two-for-one promotional fares. These fares work well if you can travel to and from the port on frequent-flier miles or by car. If you have to pay for air, however, comparative math might demonstrate that a discounted air/sea package is a better deal.

unofficial **TIP**
Normally, two-for-one fares are offered far in advance, with a cutoff date to secure early bookings.

Two-for-one offers come and go with supply and demand. It's difficult to keep up with them. They also might pop up on short notice. Such fire-sale fares aim to boost short-term sales and can be withdrawn at any time.

Flat Rates

This is an early-booking program in which every cabin in the ship, except probably the luxury accommodations, is sold for the same flat rates (one for inside cabins and one for outside cabins) on a first-come, first-served basis. The earlier you book, the nicer your cabin. Flat rates are usually cruise only, but airfare may be purchased as an add-on. Flat rates are frequently offered by Princess, Crystal, and Norwegian Cruise Lines.

X Percent Off Second Passenger in a Cabin

In this very common discount offered by many cruise lines: The first passenger pays the double-occupancy brochure rate and the second passenger gets 40% to 70% off. Some simple averaging demonstrates that this works out to a discount of 20% to 35% per passenger.

Reduced Rate Air Add-ons

If you purchase airfare from the cruise line separately (as opposed to included in the cruise price), that is an air add-on. Sometimes cruise lines will couple a discounted cruise-only rate (no airfare) with a very attractive air add-on. This usually occurs when the cruise line is able to negotiate an exceptionally good bulk airfare purchase with an airline from a specific gateway city. In essence, the cruise line is passing some of their savings along to the consumer. Typically, this kind of deal applies only to specific cities and is offered only for a short time. It often results from an airline's slow sales and its need to stimulate air travel from a particular area, as opposed to being a cruise-line initiative.

Senior Citizen Discounts

Because seniors have traditionally been the backbone of the cruise market, they are often one of the first groups targeted for a discount program if a line is having difficulty filling a cruise. Usually the discount requires that one person sharing the cabin must be at least 55 years old (although the age can vary). The discount size varies, as does the inclusion of airfare. Also, Carnival and some other cruise lines have year-round discounts for members of AARP (anyone age 50 or older can join), the American Association of Retired Persons.

Kids or Third/Fourth Passengers Go Free or at Reduced Rate

This discount is fairly common for lines like Carnival, Disney, and MSC that target families and younger cruisers. Third and fourth persons or children sharing a cabin cruise free or at a substantial discount. Airfare for the third/fourth person or children is usually not included. Third-fourth-person rates are generally part of a cruise line's basic rate structure (rather than promotional fares). They normally appear in the cruise line's brochure and are applicable year-round. Their promotional use might come into play seasonally by being reduced or waived altogether, perhaps in summer to stimulate family travel or in the shoulder season to stimulate first-timers to buy a cruise when three or four friends can share the cost.

Back-to-Back or Contiguous Segments Discounts

The seven-day cruise is the most popular product offered by any cruise line, as it suits the vast majority of people in terms of time and cost. However, there are people who have both the time and means for longer cruises. To satisfy both groups, the cruise lines have several choices. They may break longer cruises into seven-day segments, enabling a passenger to board in one port and depart from another. Or, they may offer two 7-day segments with different itineraries as one 14-day cruise, offering the second week at a greatly reduced price. For example, a ship departing from Miami sails one week to the eastern Caribbean and the next week to the western Caribbean. In combining the two, the only port repeated in 14 days is Miami, the departure port. Throughout our cruise line profiles, we highlight ships whose itineraries lend themselves to this sort of coupling and offer attractive discounts for the second segment.

Repositioning Cruises

Rather than dispatch a ship empty, lines sell their repositioning cruises; to attract as many passengers as possible, they offer them at cut-rate prices. The majority of repositioning cruises are in spring and fall when the great "migration" of ships occurs—mostly when ships that have spent the winter on Caribbean, Panama Canal, and Mexico cruises are dispatched to Alaska or to New England/Canada and/or Europe for the summer; and again in autumn, when these ships return.

unofficial **TIP**
When a cruise line moves a ship from one cruise area to another, this is called a repositioning cruise—and it represents one of the year's biggest bargains.

Repositioning cruises with interesting and unusual itineraries, such as from the Caribbean to New England via the Eastern Sea-board, are unlikely to have as much of a discount as those with few ports of call, such as transatlantic crossings. Those with more days at sea, however, appeal to folks who really love to cruise and cherish having uninterrupted days or weeks at sea. However, *Queen Mary 2,* for example, has a wealth of onboard activities designed for every type of traveler.

Group Discounts

Persons traveling together can almost always negotiate a group rate. The larger the group, the better the rate. For a big group, at least one free berth or cabin is customarily provided for the organizer. What constitutes a group varies among cruise lines, but eight or more persons traveling together and occupying at least four cabins generally can obtain a discount, extra amenities, or a cabin upgrade.

Standby Rates

Lines may offer deeply discounted standby rates for specific itineraries and sailing dates. Normally, you rank your ship, departure, and cabin preferences and submit them to the line with a deposit. If your preferred date is available, the line notifies your travel agent at least

30 days in advance. If you are offered your first choice, the deposit is nonrefundable. Airfare is additional.

Cabin Upgrades

Four basic ways to get a cabin upgrade are:

1. ADVERTISED OR UNADVERTISED SPECIALS Usually publicized primarily (some are in press releases to media) to travel agents, upgrade programs give them a powerful selling tool. Upgrades apply to specific sailings and can be guaranteed by the agent and line at time of booking. Such specials allow consumers to buy the cheapest fare and be upgraded from one to five cabin levels.

2. SOFT SAILING UPGRADES A soft sailing refers to a cruise that is likely to depart at substantially less than full capacity. Booking the least expensive cabin category on a low- or shoulder-season cruise offers the best opportunity for receiving an upgrade. Early booking an inside cabin on a ship with few inside cabins (study the ship's deck plans) might result in upgrading to an outside cabin. Nothing is guaranteed, however, and you might be stuck with the inside cabin. Just be prepared to accept it if you are not upgraded.

3. GUARANTEES If a cruise is sold out of the cabin category you request when booking, the line will offer a guarantee, promising a cabin in your preferred category or better. You pay the same rate as for the cabin you requested, including early-booking or other applicable discounts. Because guarantees are offered only when a cruise is sold out or oversold in a requested category, chances of getting the upgrade are good. Cabin location is up to the cruise line.

4. PAID UPGRADES A number of lines, particularly on soft sailings, sell upgrades. Sometimes the upgrades are as little as $15 per person per cabin category.

Confusion among passengers regarding cabin-upgrade availability often leads to frustration and disappointment. A travel agent wrote us:

> *PLEASE, PLEASE tell your readers that cabin upgrades are a privilege and not a right. . . . When ships sail at or near capacity, most people have a slim-to-none chance of getting upgraded—and almost certainly not from an inside cabin to an outside cabin. Many cabin upgrades are given at the time of booking, but "guaranteed cabin categories" do not mean guaranteed upgrades—these are based solely on availability. The only thing that is guaranteed is that they will get a cabin in at least the category they are booked in! Former passengers and people who book the earliest are the most likely to get upgrades, if they become available. If a certain cabin category is that important to someone, they should book it and pay for it, and not hope to be*

upgraded to it. . . . Plus, any travel agent that tells [clients] to take a "guaranteed" or "run of ship" rate to increase their chances of being upgraded is setting up their clients for disaster. The agent may say one thing, but the client hears the word "upgrade" and thinks this is a given. Then when it doesn't happen, the client gets angry with the travel agent and the cruise line.

Organizational Discounts

Cruise lines commonly develop relationships with organizations like the American Automobile Association or AARP. Check for discounts available through organizations to which you belong.

Credit Card Programs

Some cruise lines have credit card programs. Whenever you use the credit card, you accrue points or "cruise dollars." These can be applied toward a cruise or taken as a credit to spend aboard. Cardholders receive mailings promoting discounts, and charging a cruise on the card may result in cabin upgrades. Similarly, miles accrued on the American Express program offering one mile for every dollar charged are redeemable for cruises.

Travel Agents' Discounts

We have found that agents selling the same discount program for a cruise may quote different prices. Usually the difference is small, 2% to 5%. What's going on is that a few retailers are sacrificing part of their override commissions to lowball the competition. Big-volume, cruise-only agencies routinely do this, but local agents frequently will knock a few dollars off their commission to retain a good customer. Ads that claim, "We will beat or match your best offer," usually mean an agent is rebating some commission to his or her clients. But beware of this practice. Commissions represent an agent's costs and profit. As any businessperson knows, if you give away your profit, you will end up with red ink. In addition, cruise lines—including Carnival, Oceania, Norwegian Cruise Line, Royal Caribbean, and Celebrity— have cracked down on agencies that rebate an advertised price. So the number of agencies rebating has been reduced.

Cruise Loan Programs

Pioneered by Princess, cruise loan programs are seen by the lines and travel agents as "a tool for taking away one of the clients' biggest stumbling blocks: paying in full for a cruise before sailing." Loans may also help sellers trade the customer up. Basically, you borrow your cruise's cost on a revolving line of credit (like most credit cards) and pay off the loan in 24, 36, or 48 installments, like a mortgage or car loan. The main difference between a mortgage or car loan and a cruise loan is that the former are secured by pledging your home or car as collateral. Because there is nothing to pledge as collateral on a cruise loan, interest rates are much higher. Generally, the lowest annual percentage rate for a cruise loan is about 9%; the highest, 31%. Loans are administered by participating banks that are unaffiliated with the cruise lines. If you obtain the lowest interest rate for cruise loans on a 36-installment loan, the monthly payment for a seven-day cruise costing $5,000 per couple is $161 per month. Multiply the $161 by 36 months to see you'll actually be paying $5,796 for your cruise. Most people would do better taking out a loan on their own.

Lost in the Information Haze

Deals come and go so rapidly that a travel agency has to be knowledgeable, well staffed, and computerized to keep on top of the action. Although big cruise-only agencies are the best equipped to handle the information flood, even they occasionally lag.

unofficial **TIP**
Never fall into the trap of buying a cruise simply because it sounds like a great deal—especially if you are buying your first cruise.

The National Association of Cruise-Only Agencies (NACOA) can provide a list of member agencies in your area. Check out **www .cruising.org** for a list of member agencies of Cruise Lines International Association (CLIA). Discount agencies usually advertise widely. Always check the reliability of any agency with whom you do business.

CRUISING THE INTERNET FOR CRUISES

OVER THE PAST DECADE, cruise information on the Internet has increased so much, it's nearly impossible to keep track. There are thousands of Web sites to investigate. The majority are travel agencies, large and small. Even if you're a whiz at searches, you'll still need a great deal of time and infinite patience to find the facts you need. Despite Google and Yahoo and other useful search engines, cyberspace remains chaotic. We can't organize it for you, but here are facts that can help you navigate the ocean of information on your own.

Essentially, cruise-related information on the Internet is precisely that—information. You can ask questions and order brochures, and most major cruise lines have taken the next step, enabling you to buy a cruise directly from them on the Internet. The best way to find out if a particular cruise line is selling online is to check out its Web site. The Web addresses for all cruise lines with Web sites are included in this book.

The Internet has become a particularly handy tool for advertising last-minute specials. There are a number of sites that, after you sign up, will automatically send you an e-mail advertising deeply discounted cruises. Many sites specialize in cruises, while others offer air, hotels, rental cars, and a range of other travel products.

Many sites will provide a form for you to complete listing the kind of deals (cruises, air, hotels, etc.) that you're interested in. When they send out their weekly e-mail, they limit the message to those products. Some of the best deals we've seen are on these Web sites, but buyer beware. Some Web sites have sold cruises without advising the customer of required passport and visa requirements or other pertinent information.

A useful Web site is **www.CruiseCompete.com,** which calls itself "the world's exclusive competitive cruise vacation pricing Web site." It has an advanced search tool to help travelers find their ideal cruise at the best available price, enabling travelers to find multiple cruise itineraries based on a preferred port of call or country. Cruisers also can narrow their search by departure port, date range, cruise length, and cruise line at the same time. After selecting a cruise based on destination, you can then click on a sail date to request competing quotes from nearly 100 member travel agencies across the country, potentially helping consumers save substantially on their cruise vacations. If, for example, you want to take a cruise to St. Kitts in the Caribbean, you type "St. Kitts" in the search tool, and in a few seconds, CruiseCompete.com finds all of the cruises that go there. Next, set up an account for quotes (no charge). Another click and you'll get the best prices. We are not aware of any other site on the Internet offering this type of function and ease of use.

Though not as versatile as CruiseCompete when looking for a cruise, **Kayak.com** is the best all-around travel search engine on the Internet. In addition to cruises, you can comparison shop for hotels, flights, rental cars, and packaged vacations.

Information is also available from these sources:

- **Cruise associations** Trade organizations, including Cruise Lines International Association, that have their own Web sites (**www.cruising.org**).
- **Travel agencies** Hundreds of agencies have Web sites, and others participate through their trade organizations. Most take bookings online or via e-mail.
- **Travel publications** Major travel magazines, such as *Travel & Leisure* and *Travel Weekly,* and book publishers, including John Wiley & Sons (which publishes this book), have Web sites.
- **Individuals** Recognized travel experts and some people who consider themselves cruise experts or are interested in cruises have created their own sites.
- **Subscriber services** Many, such as AOL and **cruises@about.com,** have specialized programs on cruises and most feature special deals.

The typical cruise-line Web site offers about the same information available in a cruise brochure. However, fares are likely to be sample or lead prices only. Cabin sizes or configurations aren't always specific, although more and more lines are providing diagrams of cabin layouts in different categories. You usually can request a brochure by e-mail or on the Web (you will probably be required to give a phone number or e-mail address), but such sites are most useful when you know where and when you plan to cruise. Information, of course, covers the host cruise line only.

Some sites are well done, fun, clever, and even amusing, and they have gotten much, much better in the last few years. The best sites have special features, such as itineraries with links to maps and port information, or the facility to search by ZIP code for travel agencies near you. On most major cruise lines' Web sites, you can take a virtual tour of each of their ships. Often, the site is linked to other cruise-related information.

The range of information is as broad as it is voluminous—Princess Cruises' Web site is huge! But it is also one of the best. Among other things, it enables you to book shore excursions in advance—a service that is becoming available from more and more cruise lines. There is no uniformity in presentation, style, or amount of detail between cruise lines. On Windstar Cruises' Web site, you can go through a typical day on board, see a sample dinner menu, review itineraries with sailing dates, and read about special fares and onboard credits for Internet users. Carnival Cruise Lines, with one of the most extensive sites, offers pictures and descriptions of each cabin category, including drawings and pictures of cabin layouts. Some of the smallest cruise lines have the best Web sites; of course, with fewer or smaller ships, it easier to provide information and easier for consumers to navigate the site.

Some cruise lines, particularly the largest ones like Carnival, Norwegian Cruise Lines, and MSC Cruises, post their deals weekly on their Web sites. Usually, you can sign up with these lines to receive this information directly via e-mail.

For news, guidance, and evaluations, **www.cruisecritic.com** is maintained by a team of cruise specialists and knowledgeable persons. Included are generally candid updated ship reviews and evaluations on more than 150 ships, with detailed descriptions on facilities, activities, amenities, itineraries, and fellow passengers; news on industry developments; and features ranging from seasickness to bargains. The Cruise Critic library contains trip reports and travel tips.

Similar information is available from **www.cruisemates.com, cruises.about.com, www.shipsandcruises.com, www.avidcruiser.com,** and **www.southerncruising.com,** sites by established writers who specialize in cruises. In addition to constantly updated information on special deals, Cruisemates promotes several specially priced cruises throughout the year. The site has message boards where people can ask questions or post their opinions on cruises, ports, and related matters. Its ship reviews are timely and in-depth.

Cruise Opinion (**www.cruiseopinion.com**) claims to have the largest database of cruise ship reviews on the Web, but many are very old. Each reviewer, based on personal experiences, evaluates the ship in 42 categories using a rating of 0 to 100 and describes the cruise experience. A recent check showed more than 4,500 reviews on file.

CruiseReviews (**www.cruisereviews.com**) is limited but more current than Cruise Opinion. The site lists about 20 major cruise lines and another 20 smaller lines and all their ships. About a third had been reviewed recently. Those we checked were short but pointed.

Other sites you might want to check out include:

- **www.expedia.com, www.orbitz.com,** and **www.travelocity.com.** The three big players in Internet travel sales. Besides offering copious content, each post weekly discounts on a broad range of travel products.
- **www.lastminutetravel.com** offers a full range of travel products, including cruises and air.
- **www.lowestfare.com** sells all travel products but limits its e-mails to a small number or particularly hot deals.
- **www.cheaptickets.com** posts a weekly newsletter advertising mostly air and hotel deals.
- **www.bestfares.com** is a good all-purpose travel discount site.

Additional Web sites specializing in cruise information and discounts include **www.seasaver.com** or **www.cruiseonly.com, www .cruise.com, www.i-cruise.com, www.cruiseplanners.com, www.cruise-holidays.com, www.cruisebrothers.com,** and **www.cruise411.com.**

Many of these Web sites offer deck plans; ship descriptions and reviews; tips on insurance; advice for couples, singles, seniors, and the disabled; and of course, hot deals. Last-minute specials and bargain rates can be found on all the sites.

Buying on the Internet

If you want to purchase a cruise from an Internet company, first try to run the transaction through your travel agent. If your travel agent can't match or beat the deal, make the booking through the site's phone number as opposed to purchasing electronically. If this isn't an option, find another site. Because many online sites specialize in last-minute deals, you probably won't have much time to resolve a problem should one occur, so not being able to communicate with a live person is a risk too great to take. Before you book, ask the seller when your reservation will be

unofficial **TIP**
If the deal is available only through the Internet direct to the consumer, make sure before you buy that the site provides a phone number so that you can get a real person on the line if something goes amiss.

unofficial **TIP**
Be cautious about comments on message boards, forums, and chat rooms from unidentified sources whose reliability you can't check.

recorded as fully paid in the cruise line's system. Repeat the process with the airline if you buy air from the cruise line. On the date provided by the seller, call the cruise line and airline directly to confirm that everything is in order. If time is short when you make your reservations, you should request overnight delivery; it's worth the cost for the peace of mind. Regarding air travel purchased through the cruise line, you are likely to get electronic ticketing. At least it saves you from having to worry about paper tickets being delivered on time. By the way, your travel agent and the cruise line will ask for your date of birth (which is required by TSA) and your name exactly as it appears on your driver's license or passport.

Online Auctions

A twist in discounting is auctioning cruises online at such sites as **www .allcruiseauction.com.** If ever there were a need for "buyer beware," it is here. We know that some people have scored true bargains, but we also hear of people bidding more for a cruise than they would have paid through their travel agent. The bottom line: If you want information, cruising the Internet can be useful and fun. It can also be frustrating and time-consuming. You will learn quickly which sites are worthwhile.

We believe that this book—we say in all modesty—together with cruise lines' compendiums and a knowledgeable travel agent, remains the most efficient and effective way to help you select the right cruise—that is, the cruise right for you.

Price Protection

The airlines and cruise lines encourage you to book early to obtain the lowest fares. But what if you plunk down $1,200 for a cruise and discover a few months later that the same class of cabin on the same cruise is selling for $800? Getting a refund for the difference or being able to cancel and rebook at the lower rate is known as price protection. The cruise lines claim to be flexible and cooperative in this regard, but when it comes to giving back money already in their pocket, things usually get sticky. Sometimes customers must "qualify" for deals offered at lower prices. These qualifications sometimes make sense, as when a deal is offered to persons over 65 years of age, or to a promotional fare offered on a strictly regional basis, for ex-ample to residents of Dade County, Florida. Often, however, the qualifications for obtaining the lower rate are specious in the extreme. A common practice among cruise lines is to reject requests to rebook after the passenger has made his final payment. If you have been a good little passenger and paid on time, you're rewarded for your punctuality by being prohibited from taking advantage of lower fares available to most everyone else. Another way cruise lines accomplish the same thing is to limit the lower fare to "new bookings only." In other words, if the right fist doesn't get you, the left will.

Almost all cruise lines assess penalties for canceling within a certain number of days from the sailing date. If you cancel before the applicable penalty date, you're free to rebook at the lower promotional fare. Problem is, cruise lines usually time the announcement of cut-rate deals to fall well inside the penalty period. Because 2009 was such a free-for-all, "normal" doesn't always apply.

The most straightforward and consumer-friendly policy we were able to uncover is offered by Royal Caribbean and Celebrity. These lines will allow a passenger to rebook at any lower rate for which they qualify until the "sailing closes" (usually one or two days prior to departure). If you're age 50 and try to take advantage of a senior deal, you won't qualify, but for deals offered to the broader market, you'll be allowed to rebook without penalty.

Finally, the best price protector you'll ever have is a good travel agent. A good agent can often use her influence and clout to beat some of the silly arbitrariness out of the cruise lines. If the agent can't arrange an actual rebate, she frequently can get you compensated through other concessions such as cabin upgrades, shipboard credit, and the like. Remember that your agent will probably have dozens, if not hundreds, of clients booked on various cruises at any one time. Thus, it's unrealistic to expect her to monitor discount deals circulated by the cruise lines. It's your job to check for lower prices periodically, and if you find something, bring it to her attention.

PULLING IT ALL TOGETHER

YOU KNOW THE PLAYERS and how the game is played. Now it's time to put your knowledge into action.

Step 1. To Agent or Not to Agent

Your first big decision is whether to use a travel agent. This guide, cruise lines' brochures, Sunday newspaper travel sections, cruise specialty magazines, and the Internet will enable you to narrow your choices. Even so, a reliable travel agent can contribute immeasurably in offering advice and facilitating the process. If you have a travel agent who has served you well, particularly if you're a volume customer, you should use him or her.

unofficial **TIP**
Try to select a travel agent near your age or one who shares your interests and lifestyle.

If you don't have a regular agent, ask your friends for recommendations. Make sure the agency has a good reputation and that the agent with whom you are dealing is experienced in selling cruises.

Step 2. Narrow Down

Using this book and the other material, make a priority list of four lines, ships, and cruises. Be flexible. Also be alert to the possibility of travel agents' pushing their preferred suppliers, who may not be on your list. If so, ask why the agent feels the supplier might meet your needs better than those you have selected. You might be surprised at the response. Sometimes consumers are not the best judge of the right cruise fit for themselves.

Step 3. Scout the Discounts

Using information collected from newspaper travel sections, Internet, and other sources, ask your agent if she can meet or top any special deals you have found or provide extra "value" in some way. Call a few high-volume, cruise-only agencies on your own. Ask about cruises on your priority list, then ask what's the best deal the agency is selling. Always ask for the bottom-line cost in dollars rather than the percentage discount. Repeat the quote to the agent and verify what is included (airfare, accommodations, transfers, and so on). Take notes.

Your top priority is to determine which cruise is right for you. Only then is it time to scout deals. The best way to ruin your cruise vacation is to book the wrong ship or the wrong cabin in an effort to save a few dollars.

Step 4. Buy Early or Buy Late

As we said, the biggest discounts are usually given for buying early (four to eight months before sailing) or late (during the last six weeks). First-time cruisers have greater choice and peace of mind taking the early-bird route. Experienced cruisers are in a better position to play the best-deal game. But any time you hold out for a deal, you decrease your options for getting the cabin, dining room seating, and airline routing you prefer. In the long run, these factors are much more important to the quality of your cruise than saving $50 or $100.

Step 5. Give the Seller a Price to Beat

When you've narrowed the field to one or two cruises and you're ready to buy, call the three or so agents who quoted the best prices in your first round of inquiries. Say, "I've been quoted a price of X dollars for this particular cruise; can you beat it?" Give your travel agent a chance to match it. If he can't, he may be able to verify the deal's integrity or uncover hidden problems. If the deal is commissionable, have your agent book it, or if the agent has invested a lot of time on your behalf, offer a $50 or $100 consultation fee.

Step 6. Check It Out

If you decide to buy from an agency outside your city or state, try to determine whether it's bonded and a member of its local Better Business Bureau and/or Chamber of Commerce or a well-established consortium such as Virtuoso, Ensemble, Signature, or American Express. Also check whether it's a member of the American Society of Travel Agents (ASTA), the Association of Retail Travel Agents (ARTA), the National Association of Cruise-Only Agencies (NACOA), or Cruise Line International Association (CLIA). Membership isn't a guarantee of ethical business practices, but the organizations have a vested interest in maintaining the good reputation of cruising and try to attract only upstanding members.

American Society of Travel Agents ☎ 703-739-2782 **www.astanet.com**

Association of Retail Travel Agents ☎ 800-969-6069 **www.artonline.com**

Cruise Line International Association ☎ 212-921-0066 **www.cruising.org**

National Association of Cruise-Only Agencies ☎ 305-663-5626 **www.nacoaonline.com**

Virtuoso ☎ 866-401-7974 or 817-870-0300 **www.virtuoso.com**

To find out how consolidators and wholesalers respond to questions about their affiliations and accreditations, we called all of the cruise discounters advertising in *Cruise Travel* and *Condé Nast Traveler* magazines. Some agencies were gracious and seemed to understand that customers have a right to check their credentials. An amazing number, however, were surly and uninformative. "Who are you?" and "What do you need to know that for?" were typical responses. Representatives from four agencies said they didn't know the answers to our questions but would call us back. Of course, we never heard from them. When you call to check an agency, accept nothing less than complete courtesy, openness, and cooperation. Life's too short, and your cruise is too important, to deal with rude salespeople. Remember to show the same respect. Good travel agents will work hard for you, but they can spot someone on a fishing expedition. Just be prepared. Some agents will not put quotes in writing if they feel you are only "shopping around" and will buy on price alone and not on price *and* service.

Step 7. Protect Yourself

When you pay for your cruise, use a credit card and insist that the charge be run through the cruise line's account, not the agency's account. This precaution is important. Financially shaky agencies sometimes use their customers' payments to settle agency debts instead of to secure the customer's booking. If these agencies fold, the customer is often left with no cruise and no refund. Paying with a credit card allows you to cancel payment if the cruise is not provided as promised. Reputable travel agents and other sellers are more than happy to run the charge through the cruise line's account and will absolutely not be offended by your request. Financially sound sellers make a practice of running credit card charges through the cruise line's account anyway. This is done so that the cruise line will have to pay the credit-card merchant fees. If you purchase your cruise from any seller other than your usual travel agent, ask the seller when the paid reservation will be posted in the cruise line's system. On the date provided, call the cruise line directly to confirm the reservation.

Protect your cruise investment with travel insurance. Most comes with lots of bells and whistles, but three things should concern you: (1) loss of your paid fare if you must cancel or if your cruise is interrupted, (2) the potentially huge costs of emergency medical evacuation, and (3) major medical expenses while traveling that your primary health insurance doesn't cover.

Although overpriced at about $5 to $8 per every $100 of coverage, travel insurance nevertheless is a prudent expenditure. You never know when you might become ill, have a death in the family, or miss your sailing because of a flight cancellation or delay.

Although travel insurance coverages can be purchased separately, they are usually "bundled." We recommend you purchase good coverage for trip cancellation/interruption and emergency medical evacuation. Trip cancellation/interruption insurance covers the insured traveler and traveling companion(s) against losses caused by illness, injury, or death. Most policies cover losses resulting from the interruption of your trip by the death, serious injury, or serious illness of a close family member back home. **Access America (www.accessamerica.com)** and **Travel Guard (www.travel-guard.com)** also offer coverage for the illness, injury, or death of a business partner.

unofficial **TIP**
If you buy a cruise at the double-occupancy rate and your companion must cancel, your policy should cover the single supplement if you want to continue alone.

If you must cancel your cruise before departure, most cancellation/interruption insurance plans will reimburse you for the cruise's full cost, less any refund you receive from the cruise line. Although cancellation and refund policies vary, most lines provide a full refund if you cancel 61 or more days before your departure date. Remember that these policies generally cover only the extent of your investment. If you are buying a $1,500 cruise, you don't need $10,000 in insurance.

Ideally, insurance will allow you to cancel your trip for any reason. Most policies, however, stipulate situations that qualify for coverage. At a minimum, insist on being covered for death, injury, illness, jury duty, court appearances, accidents en route to the airport or pier, and disasters at home, including fire or flood. The same coverage applies to your traveling companion(s).

Policies usually cover airline or ship worker strikes, but not earthquakes or other disasters at scheduled ports of call. Cruise lines reserve the right to alter the itinerary once under way to avoid bad weather or other problems. Also, please keep in mind that some insurance companies may only allow you to cancel *for any reason* up to 24 or 48 hours *prior* to scheduled departure.

The fine print in many policies can be tricky, and seemingly innocuous loopholes limit the carrier's obligation. One essential question regarding cancellation/interruption insurance is whether it covers preexisting conditions: any for which you were treated by a physician in the 60 days (90 days in Maryland) before the policy was purchased. In better policies, if the preexisting condition is controlled by medication, it is covered. In insurance company language, however, "controlled" is very different from "treated." If you have high blood pressure and medication maintains it at normal, safe levels, your condition is controlled. If you have a tumor and are receiving radiation, carriers would say you are being treated, but that your condition is not controlled. If your tumor caused you to cancel your cruise, the policy would not reimburse you. The same stipulations regarding preexisting conditions apply to your family back home. If, for example, your mother dies while you're traveling, your trip interruption coverage would be void if her death was related to a preexisting condition. We recommend that you question the insurance carrier directly about any health problems, obtaining written confirmation of coverage if necessary. One reputable travel agency advised us that you stand a better chance of having preexisting conditions covered with private insurance than with many cruise-line insurance plans.

Pregnancy is covered by most policies if you cruise during your first two trimesters. If a complication arises, the policy will pay. Amazingly, if you deliver your baby normally while on a cruise, you are not covered. Many cruise lines won't accept a pregnant passenger in her third trimester.

Another potential land mine in cancellation/interruption insurance is operator failure. What if your travel agent, airline, or cruise line goes belly-up? Although brochures and most policies say they will pay in the event of operator failure or default, fine print sometimes defines *failure* and *default* as bankruptcy. Because many businesses fail without declaring bankruptcy, this is an important distinction. Note that most policies exclude the failure of the company that sold the cruise (usually a travel agent) or the company that sold the insurance. If you buy insurance from a travel agency, you're covered if the cruise line or airline fails, but not if the agency fails. This is yet another reason you should pay for your cruise with a credit card and insist that the charge be run directly through the cruise line's account, not the travel agent's. It's also a good reason to buy travel insurance directly from the insurance company, something easily done on the Internet. If all of this sounds far-fetched, think again. Established cruise lines that went under in the past decade include Delta Queen, Commodore, Premier, Renaissance, and American Hawaii.

Trip interruption coverage, sold with trip cancellation policies, supplements what you recover from the cruise line if something goes wrong during your trip. If a family member dies, for example, and you must fly home from a port midcruise, the interruption coverage will pay for your plane ticket home plus reimburse you for the unused portion of your cruise (less any refund you receive from the cruise line). The policy also would pay the single supplement of your cabin companion if he or she remains on the cruise. Some insurance companies also place a certain dollar limit on their trip interruption coverage and normally list the amount in their policy. Try to find a company with the highest percentage—say 150% of the trip cost rather than just 100%. Remember, when plans change, you may incur additional air or hotel charges.

Trip interruption insurance covers fire, flood, vandalism, burglary, and natural disaster as it affects your home, but does not cover similar catastrophic events if they occur at your place of business. In our estimation this is a huge gap in travel insurance coverage. As it turns out, it's also a gap in standard business-casualty insurance. If your office building burns down while you're cruising in Alaska, chances are about 99 to 1 that your business insurance will decline to reimburse you for the cost of returning home or for the unused portion of your cruise.

Something much less likely than a fire at your office, however, is now covered. As a consequence of the September 11, 2001, terrorist attacks, most travel insurance policies offer coverage for cancellation or interruption occasioned by an act of terrorism. Coverage varies from policy to policy.

A common but very important coverage exclusion relates to "travel arrangements canceled or changed by an airline, cruise line, or tour operator, unless the cancellation is the result of bad weather or financial default." What this means is that your trip cancellation/interruption insurance doesn't cover you if, say, your flight is cancelled for reasons other than weather, and you miss the boat. Logically, one would think, this is exactly the sort of circumstance for which you need travel insurance. When we asked the insurance companies why such events are excluded, their response, to quote one company representative, was, "Oh, we couldn't cover that. It happens too often." Isn't that reassuring?

Bundled with trip cancellation/interruption is emergency medical evacuation insurance. This pays to transport you to a place where you can obtain high-quality medical care. In some areas of the Caribbean and even more remote cruise areas in Africa, Asia, or Latin America, you might prefer not to entrust your care to local doctors. The insurer in conjunction with a qualified physician usually must verify your condition and authorize the evacuation. Once authorized, the insurer usually selects the means of transportation.

As a rule, evacuation insurance does not cover hospital stays, doctors, diagnostic procedures, treatments, or medications, though medical coverage sometimes is bundled with a comprehensive policy covering trip cancellation/interruption. Ask your primary health insurer, Medicare, or HMO whether you are covered for medical attention required when traveling abroad. If you are not covered, buy supplemental insurance.

If you book an upscale cruise and pack Rolex watches, gems, and other valuables, check your homeowner's policy to determine what's covered when you travel. If you aren't covered, take out a rider. When you travel, carry your valuables on your person, not in checked luggage. Even better, leave them at home.

Cruises today cover the world. Before purchasing travel insurance, check the State Department's official travel warning list at **http:// travel.state.gov/travel/cis_pa_tw/tw/tw_1764.html.** State Department warnings are sometimes a bit overblown, but we can tell you that insurance companies generally cancel or restrict benefits to countries that are on the warning list when you buy your policy. Bluntly put, if you travel to a country on the list, you're on your own for evacuations, medical emergencies, costs or prepaid reservations, baggage loss, and a number of other coverages. Among countries on the list at press time were Philippines, Sri Lanka, Kenya, Haiti (where Royal Caribbean has its own private beach), and Israel. If your cruise makes ports of call in these countries, you are at risk of not being covered while ashore.

Another consideration in these difficult economic times is employment layoff coverage. This coverage kicks in as part of trip-cancellation coverage if you're fired or laid off. Most insurers require employment with the same company for one, two, or three years, depending on the specific policy. The coverage also includes the person you share your cabin with.

Cruise lines and travel agencies, as a rule, do not self-insure. In other words, the policy they sell is an off-the-shelf or customized product of an independent travel insurance company. This is true even when the policy has the cruise line's name in the title, for example, "Happy Sea Cruise Line Total Protection." As mentioned earlier, any third party selling a policy is automatically excluded from "supplier default" coverage. Thus, if you buy that Happy Sea travel insurance and Happy Sea Cruise Line goes belly- up, you could get caught holding the bag. Because of many cruise lines, wholesalers, and travel agencies defaulting (going out of business) in the wake of 9/11 and the recent recession, most travel insurance companies now maintain a list of travel suppliers, including cruise lines and cruise retailers, that they will not cover. Most of the failed cruise lines were on those lists *prior* to their ultimate collapse.

A number of travel insurance companies require that you buy your policy within 15 days of making your initial payment to be covered for supplier default. In other words, buy the insurance when you first make a deposit on a cruise—not when you pay the balance weeks or months later. With most policies, the 15-day rule doesn't apply to other policy coverage. An exception, and it's a big one, is preexisting medical conditions that might force you to interrupt or cancel a trip.

Finally, most travel insurance companies post their policies, as well as their list of excluded travel suppliers, on the Internet. Read the policies before you buy, and call the company's customer service representative if you have any questions. The best Web site for comparing policies and insurance companies is **www.squaremouth.com. Insuremytrip.com** is also a good resource.

Here are several major insurers and their phone numbers and Internet sites:

Access America Travel Insurance ☎ 800 284-8300
   www.accessamerica.com

CSA Travel Protection ☎ 800-711-1197 **www.csatravelprotection.com**

Travelex ☎ 800-228-9792 **www.travelex-insurance.com**

Travel Guard ☎ 800-826-4919 **www.travelguard.com**

Travel Insured ☎ 800-243-3174 **www.travelinsured.com**

There are also other smaller firms that may have good plans as well; ask your agent. When shopping for travel insurance, remember that language in the brochure is marketing language. The language in the policy legally defines the carrier's obligations.

If your cruise line underwrites its own policy, compare it with one or more of the policies listed above. If the cruise policy is comparable and the line's in good shape financially, consider it. The line has a greater interest in your satisfaction than an insurance company does and may be more helpful in a crisis. Be aware, however, that there is some risk involved with buying your insurance from the cruise line. If the line goes out of business, as Delta Queen, Commodore, Renaissance, American Hawaii, and Premier did, your claim will be thrown in with claims of all the cruise line's creditors waiting to be reimbursed, and you may get back only pennies on the dollar, if anything.

When you buy travel insurance, make sure the policy covers you *from the date of purchase until the day you arrive home from your vacation.* This is extremely important: you can't imagine the problems some folks have had with policies that did not take effect until departure time or that didn't cover the travelers' whole time away from home. In one example, a couple from Texas bought travel insurance from a cruise company. On their own, they scheduled a two-night hotel stay at their originating port and another two-night stay at their port of disembarkation. When the husband became ill on the second day after the cruise, they tried to invoke the medical coverage on their travel insurance. Much to their chagrin, they were told that their policy covered only the days of the cruise, not the extra precruise and postcruise days the couple had arranged themselves. This is yet another example of why it's usually preferable to purchase your policy directly from the travel insurance company.

Finally, be aware before you leave home that if you need to make a claim, the travel insurance companies will hold you to an exacting standard of documentation. From the time you book your cruise, hang onto every correspondence, invoice, statement, canceled check, and receipt. For trip cancellation/interruption, travel delay, and/or medical claims, you will need some or all of the following:

1. Proof of complete trip payment.
2. Proof of insurance payment.
3. Invoice from your travel agent or tour operator showing complete trip costs and cancellation penalties.
4. If your situation involves illness, accident, or death, you'll need to produce doctor's medical records, hospital records, and/or a death certificate.
5. Paid receipts for all expenses incurred.
6. Original travel documents.

A final note: If you have made the decision to forgo travel insurance, consider a few important points before declining. Understand the serious financial and personal difficulties you could find yourself in should an unexpected illness or family emergency develop. First, most travelers decline because they say, "Oh, I have insurance with my company or Medicare." Understand that these plans generally only cover you while you are within the United States, not overseas. If a serious illness develops, you will be taken off the ship and deposited in a foreign land. In fact, many cruise lines, fearing Norwalk virus, will boot you off the ship at the nearest port of call if you are treated on board for vomiting, diarrhea, or other Norwalk-like symptoms.

Travel insurance almost always comes with resources, such as a 24-hour help line to provide support while you are dealing with medical problems in a foreign land. Yes, travel insurance may not immediately pay the bills on site at a foreign hospital, but it will reimburse you later for those fees so you don't forfeit your kids' college fund or your own retirement nest egg unnecessarily. Understand as well that treatment while on board a ship is not free and not necessarily inexpensive. For example, one travel agent reports she had a 29-year-old customer who was in excellent health prior to his cruise. He took no travel insurance, then suffered a massive heart attack; his bill for one day in the ship's medical center until he could be evacuated was $6,000. That didn't count the charges from the land-based hospital. Travel insurance is not really a nicety, but a necessity.

WHEN THINGS GO WRONG

AS YOU'VE ASCERTAINED FROM THE DISCUSSION of travel insurance above, there are a number of things that can go wrong between the time you book your cruise and the day you arrive back home. Long-range planning minimizes surprises and generally allows sufficient time to work out any snags. Last-minute deals can sometimes save a ton of money, but cramming all of your planning and arrangements into a few short weeks or days before departure increases the probability of a problem arising with little or no time to resolve it.

unofficial **TIP**
If you bought your cruise through the Internet or from a nonlocal seller, call the cruise line first to make sure your reservation is in their system and that full payment has been received.

Eliminating problems should be an integral part of your long-term planning. Begin by analyzing your risks. Take a look at your health and the health of your family and business associates. There may be foreseeable risks that suggest it's not really the best time to take a cruise. Before you book your cruise, get a handle on the financial stability of your intended cruise line. *Make sure you pay with a credit card and have the charges run through the cruise line's account as opposed to the travel agent's or other third-party sellers.* Buy travel insurance that takes effect on the date of purchase and provides coverage until you get home. Buy it directly from the insurance company. If you are traveling to a part of the world where you'd prefer not to be treated by the local health-care industry, make sure emergency medical-evacuation coverage is included in your policy. Go over all preexisting medical conditions with the insurance carrier before you buy. Make sure you have already acquired trip cancellation/interruption coverage. If you have special concerns, such as the possible death of an aging parent or business partner, make sure those situations are covered by the policy. Realize that there are a number of circumstances besides death that may require your unexpected return home. We have readers whose cruises were interrupted by a fire at their place of business, a tree falling on their home, a burglary, and an unexpected lawsuit, to name a few. In short, the broader and more inclusive your trip cancellation/interruption coverage, the better. Medical care shipboard is not free; there are insurance policies available to cover these costs.

Problem 1: Missing Flight Information
If you purchased your air from the cruise line, or if air was included in the price of your cruise, you should receive your flight *itinerary* 30

to 45 days prior to departure. If fewer than 30 days remain prior to departure and you haven't received your information, call your travel agent and have him or her find out what's going on. If everything checks out, phone the seller. Work your way from reservationist to supervisor to manager to owner as required until you get a satisfactory explanation. Take the same approach with the seller if the cruise line has no record of your reservation.

Problem 2: Missing Cruise Documents or Airline Tickets

Your date of departure is looming, but you haven't received your airline tickets and/or cruise documents. If you have a good travel agent, you are virtually assured that everything will get sorted out in plenty of time. If you purchased on your own through a print ad, the Internet, or from a seller with whom you do not ordinarily do business, the situation is much iffier. In that case, start by calling the cruise line directly and making sure that your reservation is in order and *that full payment has been received*. If you purchased air with your cruise, and you know your flight itinerary, go through the same process with the airline. If everything is properly recorded, next call the seller. You'll probably be told that late delivery of documents, especially airline tickets, is standard practice (unfortunately true) and not to worry. Most of the time this will be valid advice, but if something is actually screwed up (documents lost in mail, misplaced, etc.), you won't have much time, once the seller acknowledges a problem, to resolve it. The one thing you can count on is that the cruise line and airline are going to refer you back to the seller for resolution.

More and more cruise lines are issuing electronic instead of paper documents. If your airline reservation is in the system and fully paid, and if you have an electronic ticket, you're home free. Just go to the airport and produce your government-issued photo ID document and confirmation. If paper tickets are lost, you're back to dealing with the seller. If it's a weekend or holiday and you can't contact the seller, call the airline and ask for a customer-service representative. All airlines have different policies, but the representative will usually try to help if the reservation is in the airline's system and fully paid.

If your reservations, either air or cruise, are not in the cruise line's or airline's system, you've got a big problem. It could be a simple as a transmission error between the seller and the cruise line, or it could mean that the seller lost your reservations, failed to record your payments, erroneously cancelled your reservations, or is about to, or has, gone out of business. Assuming the seller is still in business, call the seller, explain your situation, and then start working your way up the chain of command until you get someone on the phone with the knowledge and authority to address your problem.

Most of these situations can be avoided, of course, by doing business with a brick-and-mortar travel agent in your hometown, by a reputable Internet seller affiliated with a reliable travel consortium, and by arranging your air itinerary through the travel agent (or on your own) rather than through the cruise line. Buying your own air, unfortunately, puts you at some risk for a couple of other unpleasant eventualities having to do with missing the ship and losing your luggage, but we'll deal with those problems later. Finally, on the topic of arranging your own flight itinerary, we don't want to overstate the case. While working on this section of the guide, we received a direct-mail promo from an excellent European cruise line offering outside cabins at half price with air to Europe included. Would we hesitate to buy because the cruise line is providing air? Not for a second.

Problem 3: Bad Weather or Air-Traffic Delays on Departure Day

When you book your air, either on your own or through the cruise line, give some thought to what weather and air-traffic conditions are likely to be on your day of departure. If you're traveling the same day as your cruise departure, over a holiday period, or at a time of year when bad weather is likely, you might want to take some precautions. Begin analyzing your airport choices. In the New York area, for example, be aware that Newark and Kennedy have longer runways, more de-icing equipment, and electronic traffic-control systems that often allow them to function when La Guardia is shut down. New Yorkers can also take a Washington-bound train directly to the Baltimore–Washington Airport (BWI) from Penn Station in under three hours. (Washingtonians can do the same on a northbound train.) BWI has a better track record than any of the three New York airports for on-time departures.

During holiday periods or bad weather, the chance of a serious snafu increases exponentially with every flight connection you have to make. If, with a little inconvenience, you can eliminate a connection, it's usually worthwhile to do so. Let's say you live in Louisville, Kentucky; Columbus, Ohio; or Charleston, West Virginia, and you're flying to Fort Lauderdale, Florida, for a cruise out of Port Everglades. If there's no direct flight, you might be better off driving to the Cincinnati airport (located in northern Kentucky) and taking a direct flight from there to Fort Lauderdale, thereby eliminating the connecting flight.

Early morning flights have a much better on-time record than do flights later in the day. Plus, if there's an equipment problem or a cancellation, the airline can put you on a later flight. *For maximum peace of mind, travel to the port of departure one or two days prior to your sailing date. If things go awry on your travel day, you've still got sufficient time to make alternative arrangements.* Why risk jeopardizing a cherished vacation? Arrive a day early at minimum.

You've probably heard the ongoing debate regarding electronic versus paper airline tickets. Generally speaking, we prefer electronic tickets with the proviso that you double-check with the airline to insure that your correct itinerary is in their system and that your reservations are shown as fully paid. The one situation where paper tickets are preferable is when your flight is cancelled and your airline cannot book you on another flight. In this case, you'll want to make arrangements with an alternative carrier. Most carriers will honor the tickets of another airline in the event of cancellations or labor actions, but they will require paper tickets or some form of documentation as proof of purchase.

unofficial **TIP**
Always book the earliest flight of the day on an airline that offers a number of flights throughout the day to your destination.

Problem 4: Missing the Boat

This is the nightmare scenario that haunts all cruisers. If you're savvy in your travel planning, and especially if you plan to arrive at your departure port a day or so ahead of time, you'll almost eliminate the likelihood of missing the boat. We all know, however, that travel, like life, can get mixed up in ways that we never anticipate.

If you purchase your air from the cruise line, the cruise line will do its utmost to get you on the ship. There are many, many documented cases of ship departures being delayed while awaiting the arrival of a delinquent flight full of cruise passengers. Likewise, cruise lines have flown passengers who actually missed the boat to rendezvous with the ship at the first port of call. The more passengers that are affected by late flights, the more likely the cruise line is to hold the ship. The most important thing to understand, however, is that the cruise line is absolutely not under any legal obligation to hold the ship or to assist in any other manner. If you read the terms and conditions of your passage contract, you'll almost immediately encounter language like the following: "Under no circumstances does [X Cruise Line's] responsibility extend beyond the ship. All arrangements made for the guests with independent contractors [such as airlines] are made solely for the convenience of the guest and are at the guest's risk." What you *can* count on, exclusively as a matter of customer relations, is for the cruise line to do what is practicable. Do 30 late-arriving guests on a weather-delayed flight from Cleveland justify delaying the departure of a 3,000-passenger cruise ship? Perhaps, but don't count on it. We know of at least one situation when the ship sailed while two bus-loads of flight-delayed passengers waited at the airport to be driven to the port, 20 minutes away.

Sometimes, when air is arranged through the cruise line, and passengers miss the boat owing to flight delays, the airline will help out. Assistance usually comes in the form of a meal and perhaps a hotel room. If the airline flies to your first port of call, it will try to book you on a flight so that you can meet the ship. Because the airline is not responsible for weather or air-traffic delays, it has no legal obligation to help. Like the cruise line, any assistance rendered is primarily a matter of customer relations.

If you book your own travel arrangements to the departure port, you're on your own. As far as the cruise line is concerned, you're totally responsible for getting to the ship, though sometimes you can purchase transfers from airport to ship from the cruise line. If you miss the ship through no fault of your own, however, as in the case of a delayed flight, you will have that travel insurance we recommended to fall back on. Travel insurance is also your safety net if you miss the boat because of sickness, or because of bankruptcy of the cruise line. Missing the boat because of an airline strike is also usually covered by travel insurance, though the conditions for coverage vary from policy to policy. If you or your cruise line book you on an airline involved in a labor dispute, discuss the situation with your insurance carrier to determine under what circumstances you're covered. When it comes to travel insurance, don't, as the saying goes, leave home without it. Also, ask a ton of questions and compare plans carefully.

Problem 5: Lost Luggage

If you book air through the cruise line, the cruise line will make every effort to get your luggage to you (once it's recovered), including flying it to meet you at a port of call. Once again, this assistance is purely voluntary as opposed to obligatory. If you handle your own air, you must depend on the airline (generally without any assistance from the cruise line) to get your recovered luggage to you. In such situations, the probability of your luggage catching up with you while on your cruise is slim. Minimize the chances of your luggage being lost by arriving in port a day early and/or eliminating connecting flights where possible. Buy travel insurance, and make sure it pays if your bags are delayed more than 24 hours. The possibility of lost luggage is a good reason to pack essentials for an overnight in your carry-on luggage. It's a good idea to list your name, address, ship/cabin number, and itinerary inside your suitcases. Be sure to have a photocopy of your passport and any credit cards you will be carrying with you.

Problem 6: You Get Sick during Your Cruise

Although most cruise ships carry a physician and usually one registered nurse, only the new large ships are equipped to handle serious problems; and some, such as Princess's ships, maintain satellite contact with stateside hospitals when serious diagnosis is needed. Nonetheless, the majority of cruise ships fly under foreign flags, and hence their physicians are not required to be licensed to practice in the United States. From the cruise physician's perspective, shore-based facilities are better equipped to handle serious illness and emergencies. In practical terms, this means the cruise physician will want to transfer you to a hospital on shore at the first opportunity if he anticipates your illness taxing the limitations of his clinic. Also, you should know that according to the fine print in your passage contract, the cruise line is not responsible for medical care you receive while on board. As with the problems discussed earlier, travel insurance is a must. When you purchase your policy, make sure any preexisting condition is covered and understand the policy's medical-evacuation coverage.

In the last several years a media circus has swirled around the periodic occurrence of gastrointestinal viruses aboard cruise ships. Referred to in the media as "outbreaks" and "epidemics," these cases of viruses have been so sensationalized that they have become known as the "cruise ship disease." The facts, however, tell a different story. The viruses, known as Norwalk virus, Norwalk-like virus, and norovirus (collectively known as NLV) occur everywhere, ranking second only to the common cold in the number of cases reported. Because of the extraordinary sanitation practices aboard cruise ships (operated and monitored in partnership with the U.S. Centers for Disease Control and Prevention[CDC]), these NLV occur far less frequently on cruise ships than among the general population. NLV is a very common ailment, and incidents occur far more often in the home, office, and at school than on cruise ships. Most cruise ship outbreaks are not caused by a "sick ship" but by sick people who bring it on board.

Symptoms can include vomiting, diarrhea, abdominal cramps, and a low-grade fever. NLV is not an upper respiratory virus such as the flu, and is usually not life-threatening, unless someone has other, more serious, medical problems.

NLV is transmitted from person to person through direct contact, and indirectly from surfaces that are then touched by another person. NLV can also be transmitted through a food or water source; the CDC has concluded that person-to-person transmission has been the means of transmission on almost all cases reported on cruise ships.

"We continue to work very closely with the cruise lines," said David Forney, chief of Vessel Sanitation Program of the CDC. "These ships are maintaining the highest standard of sanitation in the world."

If cases of a gastrointestinal virus are reported, cruise lines take extensive precautions to contain the spread through aggressive sanitation measures and open communication with their guests prior to boarding and while on board the ship. Some of the measures employed when responding to reported cases may include:

- Passengers with obvious symptoms may not be allowed to board.
- To avoid the risk of spreading the virus, passengers who experience typical gastrointestinal symptoms are sometimes told to remain in their cabins until they are non-contagious. The current trend, however, is to summarily expel passengers with symptoms from the ship at the next port of call. The CDC endorses this procedure. The problem, of course, is that the onboard clinic doesn't have the capability to make a confirmed diagnosis. Therefore, passengers are expelled based solely on their symptoms, which can be caused by any number of

different things, the majority being non-contagious. The same policy is followed for passengers suspected of being infected with the well-known H1N1, so-called swine flu, virus.

- Crew with symptoms may be similarly quarantined until they are non-contagious but may also be disembarked at the next available port.
- An aggressive onboard communications effort to encourage guests to frequently wash their hands. Washing one's hands regularly (each hour or two) is a very good way to reduce the spread of contact viruses.
- Aboard ship, staterooms and public areas are cleaned and disinfected daily. Some lines also offer hand sanitizers at the entrance to the gangway or at a buffet line.
- On turn-around days, extra crew are brought on board to disinfect the ship with the CDC-recommended chlorine-based solution from top to bottom before additional passengers board.
- Onboard medical facilities and staff are always available to prescribe medication for symptomatic treatment of gastrointestinal symptoms. There is a charge for medical services aboard most ships. Insurance policies are available and may be purchased prior to your cruise.

Be aware that the cruise lines are so sensitive to bad press surrounding NLV and the need to assure that as many guests as possible remain well that some have enacted rather draconian policies, endorsed by the CDC. A man from Maryland on a Caribbean cruise sought care for gastrointestinal symptoms and was notified that he would be involuntarily disembarked at the next port of call. Although there were any number of alternative explanations for the symptoms, and no diagnostic testing was done, the man and his wife were ordered ashore the next day. Quarantined until time of disembarkation, his symptoms completely resolved after about ten hours. Onboard medical staff, realizing then that the symptoms could not be attributed to NLV, apologized but informed the couple that the decision was made by the line's home office and could not be reversed. After the man's return home, laboratory tests ordered by his doctor showed no evidence of a viral infection. The cruise line was so intent on getting the man off the ship that it evidently failed to clear the couple's entry into the port. Later, when they went to the airport for their flight home, they were detained by immigration for supposedly entering the country illegally. In case you're wondering, the cruise line did pay the couple's travel expenses home. Granted, this is a worst-case scenario, but it always helps to know what could happen.

Problem 7: Onboard Complaints

If your stateroom toilet backs up, the air conditioner conks out, or the showroom performers quit, don't expect a refund. If it's not resolved on board when it happens, the best you are likely to get is a discount on a subsequent cruise. Once again, it's that pesky passage contract that purports to absolve the cruise line from all responsibility, anytime, anywhere. In point of law, however (as any attorney who specializes in travel will tell you), some of the language is nothing but smoke, totally unenforceable and made part of the contract as a bluff to inhibit you from taking legal action. Understand, however, if you decide to sue, that cruise lines operate under maritime law, and you might have to file the lawsuit in the country where the ship is registered. It's not an accident that so many cruise ships fly under the so-called flags of convenience, particularly those of Liberia and Panama.

Legalities aside, it's always preferable to settle problems on the spot. Usually, you will direct your complaint to the chief purser or to the hotel manager, and usually they will be quite responsive. Be polite and friendly, and keep your anger under control. As a last resort, if your complaint is not addressed, fax the president of the cruise line. Resend each day until your problem is resolved. Keep copies of your faxes in case the complaint goes unremedied for the entire cruise. As of this writing, Carnival is the only cruise line that will allow you to cancel your cruise and disembark at the first available port of call once under way if things are not satisfactory. You can get a refund for the *unused* portion of your cruise fare.

If you are really unlucky, like when your cabin is for some reason uninhabitable and the ship is completely full, your only option is to negotiate the best deal you can or leave the ship on your own initiative at a port of call. If you jump ship, regardless of the reason, you're on your own. Consequently, we recommending contacting your travel-insurance carrier for advice about how to best proceed before taking action.

Problem 8: Credit Hold

It has become common practice for cruise lines to ask passengers to complete a form prior to leaving home authorizing the cruise line to hold X dollars in credit per day for each day of the cruise. On a Holland American cruise, for example, the line held $60 per day. The same credit card covered both husband and wife, so the credit hold amounted to a not insignificant $2,160. In practicality, if the card had a $3,000 credit limit, the credit hold would leave only $840 of available credit on that card for the couple to use for onshore shopping, restaurants, etc.

Cruise lines use credit holds to make sure a passenger's onboard charges are covered. On land, each transaction on your card is approved and processed individually. On a cruise it doesn't make sense for the line to pay $10 or so in satellite telecommunications to process that $4 beer you enjoyed on the Lido Deck. Consequently, charges are recorded but not processed until the end of the cruise. At that time they are totaled and the ship runs through a single transaction. To make sure you have the credit available to pay your onboard charges, the line puts a credit hold on what it estimates you'll charge. Among other things, the practice largely eliminates messy credit problems at the time of disembarkation. Actually, it's a good idea to check your bill often so that any errors may be corrected immediately.

Although using credit holds addresses a legitimate problem (passengers without sufficient funds or credit to pay their onboard tabs), there are a couple of problems. First, the cruise lines do not communicate what they are doing very well, and some of the credit-hold preauthorization forms are confusing. Because many passengers don't realize what's going on, they are surprised and embarrassed when their credit card is subsequently rejected when they attempt to purchase something ashore.

The second problem is that the cruise line may hold much more per day that you'll actually charge on board. The solution to these problems is to carefully review any form the cruise line sends, particularly one that requires your signature. If the credit amount the cruise line holds is out of line with your normal onboard spending habits, negotiate with the purser a lower per-day amount when you board the ship. Remember, however, those spa treatments and shore excursions are expensive. Your onboard spending may very likely exceed your bar bill and a couple of T-shirts for the grandchildren.

Be aware that cruise lines that do not send preauthorization forms for credit holds will probably put a similarly calculated credit hold on your card when you present it during embarkation. The salient point in the latter case is to ask the amount of the credit hold. Finally, remember that a credit hold is not a charge on your credit card. The credit hold is an amount reserved, and nothing is actually charged to your card until your total onboard bill is processed at the end of the cruise.

Problem 9: Itinerary Changes/Cancelled Ports of Call

The cruise line has complete discretion in regard to changing the itinerary or canceling a scheduled port stop. This discretion is necessary to ensure the safety of the passengers, ship, and crew. It is this flexibility that permits a ship to circumvent storms or offload a passenger at a nonscheduled port for medical reasons or other emergencies.

Problem 10: Shore Excursion Problems

Because shore excursions are conducted off the ship and produced by local tour companies, the cruise line will decline responsibility for any problem you have, however serious. Sometimes, however, as a matter of customer relations, a cruise ship might offer you a refund or assist you in obtaining satisfaction from the tour operator. Nevertheless, you should always register your complaint with the cruise line immediately after the tour. Although of little comfort to you, so doing may result in the cruise line forcing an errant tour operator to clean up its act.

WHAT'S THE REAL COST OF A CRUISE?

SOME READERS REPORT BEING SURPRISED by all the extras that are not covered by their cruise fare: items like beverages on board, spa services, photos taken by the ship's photographer, shore excursions, wine tastings, specialized cooking, exercise or computer classes, and even designer ice-cream treats. Although all these things add up to a hefty sum, we don't consider them to be "hidden" charges. Except for port charges (if the cruise line doesn't include them in the fare), such purchases are optional. Any travel provider will try to sell you stuff; it's like the popcorn or beer vendors at the ballpark. You know they'll be there and that what they sell will be expensive. Buy or not as you see fit, but don't be surprised by their presence. The cruise lines find these services to be very lucrative profit centers, which help them keep basic cruise prices down. Also, these multiple options increase guest choices on board, which attracts different types of customers to cruise ships. Because most folks don't like to scrimp on their vacation, however, it's wise to anticipate these expenditures. Even the little stuff can tack on $200 to $400 to a weeklong cruise. So be forewarned.

Concerning port charges, after some lawsuits in Florida seeking to redress the less-than-forthright ways that certain cruise lines represented port charges, almost all cruises from Florida to the Caribbean now include port charges in the cost of the cruise rather than tack them on as a separate charge. Still, watch out for port charges, particularly for Europe and Asia.

PREPARING *for* YOUR CRUISE

A CRUISE MAY BE ABOUT THE EASIEST VACATION you can take when it comes to making preparations, because so much is done for you, particularly when you buy an air/sea package. During the cruise, entry formalities are handled by the ship for its passengers in most cases, sparing you the need to fill out immigration forms or clear customs in each port of call.

In most ports you can simply walk off your ship after it has been cleared by local authorities, spend the day sightseeing, shopping, enjoying a sport or other pleasant pursuits, and return to your ship without having to do anything more than pass through metal detectors and put your purchases through an X-ray machine for security reasons, and show your boarding pass.

The destination of your cruise will make some difference—the more exotic the location, the more you may have need for planning, perhaps for inoculations, visas, and the like. And of course, the weather during your cruise will determine the wardrobe you select.

Such advice may seem obvious to those who have traveled, and if it does, let this information serve simply as a reminder or checklist. Even the most seasoned travelers have been known to pack their cruise tickets and passports in their checked luggage or leave their traveler's checks at home.

CRUISE LINE BROCHURES

THE EASIEST PLACE TO START YOUR PREPARATION is by reading the brochures from the cruise line you selected for your cruise. Similar information is available on the cruise line's Web site. These have a wealth of useful information. To be sure, much of it is evocative photos and promotional puff to entice you to take a cruise, but almost all materials contain several pages, usually toward the back, aimed at answering the questions people ask most often.

These include the specifics about dining hours, smoking/nonsmoking provisions, paying for incidentals on board, embarkation and sailing times, and similar tips. In this book, too, each of the major cruise line profiles in Part Two includes a chart entitled Standard Features, which will answer similar questions pertaining to a specific cruise line and its ships.

CRUISE LINE VIDEOS/DVDS

MOST CRUISE LINES HAVE VIDEOTAPES OR DVDS of the cruise you are taking that they would be happy to send you—for a fee. Most cost about $15 to $20. Essentially, it is a promotional video, but it will give you an idea of what to expect, particularly if your cruise is to an area of the world in which you have not traveled previously. You will probably receive a flyer from the cruise line to order the tape directly from a distributor. Some cruise line Web sites allow for purchasing the video online; some sites feature virtual ship tours and shore excursions.

TRAVEL DOCUMENTS

IN 2005, THE U.S. STATE DEPARTMENT began phasing in a new border-control program that will ultimately require a valid passport to both enter and leave the country. The Western Hemisphere Travel Initiative (WHTI) brings an end to decades of travel to Mexico, Canada, and the majority of Caribbean nations with only a birth certificate as proof of citizenship.

- As of **January 23, 2007** ALL persons, except as described below, including U.S. citizens, traveling by air between the United States and Canada, Mexico, Central and South America, the Caribbean, and Bermuda are required to present a valid passport, Air NEXUS card, or U.S. Coast Guard Merchant Mariner Document, or an Alien Registration Card, Form I-551, if applicable.

- Since **June 2009** ALL persons, except as described below, including U.S. citizens, traveling between the U.S. and Canada, Mexico, Central and South America, the Caribbean, and Bermuda by land or sea (including ferries), are required to present a valid passport or other documents as determined by the Department of Homeland Security. Your travel agent and cruise line will require your name exactly as it appears on your passport, as well as your date of birth—day/month/year.

Exceptions

- **U.S. Territories** The passport requirement does NOT apply to U.S. citizens traveling to or returning directly from a U.S. territory. U.S. citizens returning directly from a U.S. territory are not considered to have left the United States and do not need to present a passport. U.S. territories include the following: Guam, Puerto Rico, the U.S. Virgin Islands, American Samoa, Swains Island, and the Commonwealth of the Northern Mariana Islands.

- **Youth Travel** Under a Department of Homeland Security proposed rule, U.S. and Canadian children ages 15 and younger, with parental consent, would be permitted to enter the United States with a certified copy of their birth certificates. The same would be true for U.S and Canadian citizens ages 16 through 18 traveling with public or private school groups, religious groups, social or cultural organizations, or youth athletic teams. The proposed rule notwithstanding, some cruise lines may require that passengers under 18 years of age have a passport in order to board.

Aliens residing in the United States need to have valid alien registration cards and passports. All non-U.S. citizens must have valid passports and necessary visas when boarding any cruise ship departing from and returning to U.S. ports.

Passengers on some cruises visiting Europe, former Soviet bloc countries, Asia, Africa, and South America may also be required to have a visa. *A valid passport usually means one that will not expire for at least six months.* If yours has less than six months left, it will most likely be rejected by either the cruise line or ports of call.

Often, on cruises to these destinations, ship authorities will ask you to surrender your passport when you check in and will keep it until the end of your cruise. This enables them to clear the ship more quickly in foreign ports. In such cases, you do not need to worry about giving over your passport to the ship. The passports are locked away securely and are taken out only if local authorities ask to see them. Finally, never pack your passport in your suitcase; carry it with you at all times.

TRAVEL REQUIREMENTS

SPECIFIC REQUIREMENTS FOR PASSPORTS, VISAS, and vaccinations will be provided by your cruise line or travel agent. However, obtaining the necessary visas and any other documentation required for embarkation, debarkation, and reentry into the United States is your responsibility; if you do not have the proper documents, you will be denied boarding. If you buy your cruise on the Internet or from a seller not located in your city, the seller may neglect to inform you of required travel documents and other pertinent information. Even when you purchase from a travel agent, however, it's a good idea to independently confirm document, visa, and vaccination requirements for the countries you'll be visiting. Nobody likes a last-minute surprise.

Documents that will be accepted as proof of identification vary with each cruise line. You will need to inquire in advance if the information is not provided in the cruise line's brochure (which it usually is—in the fine print) or on the cruse line's Web site.

Children traveling with anyone other than their parents or legal guardian must have notarized permission in writing from both parents for the child to travel. Failure to comply with this requirement can also result in denial of boarding.

DRESS CODES AND PACKING

WHAT TO PACK WILL BE DETERMINED BY YOUR SHIP, its destinations, and, to some extent, the itinerary. An adventure cruise might be three weeks long, but not a single night will be formal or even very dressy. The dress code is usually explained in the cruise line's brochure; we also note it in the Standard Features in each cruise line's profile in Part Two.

There are no limits on the amount of luggage you can bring on board, but most cabins do not have much closet and storage space. More importantly, because you are likely to be flying to your departure port, you need to be guided by airline regulations regarding excess baggage. All airlines have weight restrictions. Buy too many souvenirs and you will pay. So pack light on the outbound journey with that in mind.

As a consequence of the 9/11 terrorist attacks, all checked and carry-on luggage is carefully screened before being allowed on board. Even if you pack something in your checked baggage as seemingly innocuous as a corkscrew, knitting needles, or a pair of small scissors, these items might possibly be confiscated and not returned until you disembark. Moreover, none of your checked luggage will be delivered in the normal fashion to your cabin. After an hour or two of panic, thinking your baggage is lost, you'll be summoned to ship security. There, you will be asked to identify the offending luggage and objects and to sign forms acknowledging that you brought such items aboard, and that they have been impounded for the duration of the cruise. While on your cruise, be aware also that purses, bags, and packs that you carried ashore will be searched before you're allowed back on board. Ditto for anything you purchased while ashore.

Despite the image you may have about fancy parties and clothes, the reality is that shipboard life is very casual. You will spend your days in slacks, shorts, T-shirts, and bathing suits. Lightweight mix-and-match ensembles with skirts, shirts, blouses, shorts, and slacks are practical. For women, colorful scarves are another way to change the look of an outfit. Cocktail dresses or dressy pantsuits are appropriate for evening wear.

Men usually are asked to wear a jacket at dinner in the dining room. A dark suit and white shirt work fine in place of a tuxedo if the evening is black tie. Add a selection of slacks and sport shirts, and one or two sports jackets. If you are heading for a warm-weather cruise (Caribbean, Mexico, Hawaii, Tahiti), pack as you would for any resort destination. Lightweight, loose-fitting clothing is ideal, and cotton or cotton blends are more comfortable than synthetic fabrics for the tropics. Include two bathing suits if you are likely to be spending much time in the sun and at the beach. Don't forget a cover-up and flip-flops for the short jaunt between your cabin and the pool or other outside decks, as cruise ships ask passengers not to wear bathing suits or go barefoot in the public rooms.

Bring cosmetics and suntan lotion, but don't worry if you forget something. It will most likely be available on board or in portside duty-free shops. Sunglasses and a hat or sun visor for protection against the sun are essential. A tote bag comes in handy for carrying odds and ends, as do plastic bags for wet towels and bathing suits on returning from a visit to an island beach. You might also want to keep camera equipment in plastic bags as protection against the salt air, water, and sand.

unofficial **TIP**
For a one-week or shorter cruise, you should be able to fit everything you need into one suitcase.

The first and last nights of your cruise are usually casual, and the nights your ship is in port almost always call for informal dress. At least one night will be the captain's gala party, where tuxedos for men and long dresses for women are the norm, but a jacket and tie for men and a cocktail dress for women are also just fine.

Bring your most comfortable walking shoes for shore excursions. Tennis, deck, or other low-heeled rubber or nonskid shoes are recommended for walking about the ship, up and down gangways, getting in and out of the ship's tenders, and for sightseeing. And you will need a sweater for breezy nights at sea or for the air-conditioning in the dining room or shore-excursion bus. A small flashlight, a fold-up umbrella, and a light jacket are often handy.

Pack lightly. But most of all, be comfortable. You do not need to rush out and buy an expensive wardrobe. Obviously, if your cruise is in a cool or cold climate, you will need to plan accordingly. A Baltic or Scandinavian cruise in summer is likely to encounter colder temperatures than you might think—similar to a New England fall—but then can quickly turn to a hot summer day. Plan for layers when the weather is uncertain.

As we mention elsewhere, it's a sound practice to have a small carry-on bag for your medications and cosmetics and to include a change of clothing for your first afternoon aboard your ship, in the event of a delay in the delivery of your luggage. Also, bring a foldaway bag to carry all those souvenirs, gifts, and duty-free bargains that probably won't fit in your suitcase.

Every evening, an agenda for the following day is delivered to your room; it states the dress code for the following evening. It may be:

CASUAL Comfortable day wear, such as slacks, shorts, or jeans, but some cruise lines will state specifically that T-shirts, tank tops, or shorts are not allowed in the dining room for dinner.

Informal Dresses and pantsuits are suggested for the ladies; jackets for the men, but ties are optional.

FORMAL Cocktail dresses or gowns for the ladies, and tuxedo, dinner jacket, or dark business suit for men; jacket and tie are requested but not always required.

It varies greatly by line, but as a general rule, the lineup might be like this:

3- to 4-night cruises One formal, one informal, and one or two casual; or there might be only one or two informal and one or two casual.

7- to 8-night cruises One or two formal, two informal, two or three casual.

10- to 14-night cruises Two to four formal; four or six informal; four or five casual.

You are asked to comply with the ship's stated dress code, if for no other reason than out of respect for your fellow passengers. Generally, the suggested attire is respected throughout the evening or at least until after the shows in the main showroom and the late-night buffet, when it is a gala event. Often, those who want to stay up late for the disco or casino change to more comfortable dress, if they prefer.

COSTUMES

A FEW SHIPS STILL HAVE ONE NIGHT as a masquerade party, and others have theme nights for which some people bring an outfit—a 1950s and 1960s night or a country-and-western night, for example. It's entirely up to you whether or not to participate. The cruise line's brochure usually tells you about theme nights, or you can ask your travel agent for theme nights featured on your cruise, if you want to join in. If you don't have space for a costume, the cruise staff often can help you make one.

SPORTS EQUIPMENT

IF YOU PLAN TO PLAY GOLF OR TENNIS FREQUENTLY, you might want to bring your own equipment, and of course, you'll need the appropriate clothes and shoes. Ships that have golf practice facilities and shoreside golf programs sometimes supply the equipment for a nominal fee. Inquire.

Fins and a snorkeling mask (particularly if you have one fitted with your eyeglass prescription) are bulky, but might save you a $10 to $20 fee each time you go snorkeling on your own. If you buy the ship's shore excursions, the snorkeling equipment is included. Scuba gear is usually included in dive packages, too, and except for your regulator, is impractical to bring on a cruise.

Hiking boots, jogging shoes, riding attire, and other sporting gear will depend entirely on you and the nature of your cruise. For adventure or expedition cruises, such as to Antarctica, your cruise line will give you ample information about dress and the equipment you need; some supply guests with winter parkas and boots.

MONEY MATTERS

DOLLARS ARE READILY ACCEPTED throughout the Caribbean and in some other regions, as are traveler's checks and major credit cards. In Europe or Asia, the ship's purser or front office usually offers foreign currency exchange facilities, or the ship brings someone aboard to provide the facility in each port of call.

If you do exchange money (it's a great opportunity to teach kids about other currencies—euros in Martinique, Dutch guilders in Curaçao, pesos in Mexico), exchange only small amounts for your immediate use. Seldom will you have time to exchange the money back before returning to your ship, and you lose money every time you make the exchange. An exception is a European cruise. If you are visiting multiple European countries, say France, Italy, Spain and Greece, simply exchange a lot of dollars in advance for euros, which can be used in many countries.

Even with U.S. dollars, always carry small denominations—ones, fives, tens. Chances are, if you are owed change, it will be returned in the local currency. Incidentally, U.S. coins are seldom accepted in foreign countries and are impossible to exchange except in quantity at foreign-exchange banks. Likewise with foreign coins when you want to exchange them back into U.S. currency. Most become souvenirs.

Some travelers report problems cashing traveler's checks in foreign cruise ports, especially on the weekend. Major credit cards have become the currency of travelers worldwide and are accepted in most places. On a cruise, you will often find them the most convenient method of payment for settling your account aboard ship, for shopping at duty-free shops, and for payment of local

Who's Who on the Cruise Ship

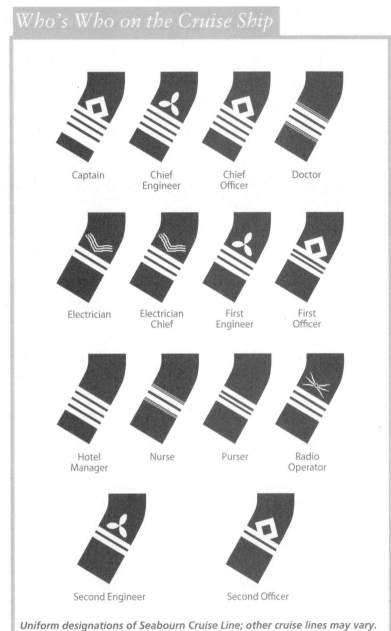

Uniform designations of Seabourn Cruise Line; other cruise lines may vary.
Courtesy of Seabourn Cruise Line.

restaurant or hotel bills. However, do not expect to use them in select off-the-beaten-track locations. The Cuna Indians of the San Blas Islands—an exotic stop on Panama Canal cruises—want your greenbacks. After you return home and receive your credit card bills, review them carefully. The theft of credit card numbers is a worldwide problem and cruise passengers, who are normally in for only a day, are easy prey.

PRESCRIPTION MEDICINE AND OTHER MEDICAL REQUIREMENTS

AS WITH ANY TRIP, WHETHER ON LAND OR SEA, you should have all your required medicine with you and carry it in original bottles and in your hand luggage, not packed in your suitcase. As a further precaution, bring copies of your medicine prescriptions—and for your eyeglasses, too.

If you have dietary requirements, you or your travel agent should communicate them to your cruise line at the time you book your cruise. Most ships can accommodate normal requirements of low salt and low fat, but more complex ones that require special stores be carried aboard require planning. Do not take anything for granted. Inquire. For example, many ships do not normally stock skim milk. In each of the cruise line profiles in Part Two under Standard Features, the amount of advance notice a cruise line requires to handle special diets is indicated.

Cruise ships that travel beyond coastal waters are required to have a doctor on board; most large ships have nurses and adequate medical facilities for normal circumstances. The doctor and nursing staff have limited daily office hours, which are printed in the ship's daily agenda, and they are always on call for emergencies. There are charges for most medical services.

SUNBURNS

YOU WILL NEED TO TAKE PRECAUTIONS against the sun when you are on a Caribbean, Mexican, Antarctic, southern European, or southeast Asian cruise. The sun in these regions is much, much stronger than the sun to which most people are accustomed. Always use a sunscreen with an SPF of 15 or higher, preferably 30 and above, and do not stay in the direct sun for long stretches at a time. Nothing can spoil a vacation faster than a sunburn.

LEARNING THE LINGO

CRUISE SHIPS HAVE A LANGUAGE ALL THEIR OWN. Although it is not necessary to enroll in a Berlitz course to learn it, becoming familiar with a few terms will be worthwhile so you won't feel lost at sea, if you will forgive the pun.

Cruise Lingo

Add-on A supplementary charge added to the cruise fare, usually applied to cor-related airfare and/or postcruise land tours.

Aft Near, toward, or in the rear (stern) of the ship.

Air/sea A package consisting of the two forms of travel, that is, air to and from the port of embarkation, transfers to and from the port, as well as the cruise itself.

Astern Beyond the ship's stern.

Batten down To secure all open hatches or equipment for seaworthiness while the ship is under way.

Beam Width of the ship (amidships) between its two sides at its widest point.

Berth Dock, pier, or quay (pronounced "key"); also, the bed in the passenger cabins.

Bow Front or forward portion of the ship.

Bridge Navigational and command control center of the ship.

Bulkhead Upright partition (wall) dividing the ship into cabins or compartments.

Category The price level of a cabin, based on location on the ship, dimensions, and amenities.

Colors A national flag or ensign flown from the mast or stern post.

Course Direction in which the ship is headed, usually expressed in compass degrees.

Crow's nest Partially enclosed platform at the top of the mast, used as a lookout.

Deck plan An overhead deck-by-deck diagram illustrating cabin and public room locations in relation to each other.

Disembark Depart from the ship.

Dock Berth, pier, or quay (pronounced "key").

Draft Measurement in feet from waterline to lowest point of ship's keel.

Even keel The ship in a true vertical position with respect to its vertical axis.

Fathom Measurement of distance equal to six feet.

First seating The earlier of several meal times in the ship's main dining rooms.

Fore The forward mast or the front (bow) of the ship.

Forward Toward the fore or bow of the ship.

Funnel The smokestack or "chimney" of the ship.

Galley The ship's kitchen.

Gangway The opening through the ship's bulwarks (or through the ship's side) and the ramp by which passengers embark and disembark.

Gross registered ton A measurement of 100 cubic feet of enclosed revenue-earning space within a ship (see "Space ratio").

Hatch The covering over an opening in a ship's deck, leading to a hold.

Helm Commonly the ship's steering wheel, but more correctly the entire steering apparatus consisting of the wheel, the rudder, and their connecting cables or hydraulic systems.

Hold Interior space(s) below the main deck for storage of cargo.

House flag The flag denoting the company to which the ship belongs.

Hull The frame and body (shell) of the ship exclusive of masts, superstructure, or rigging.

Knot A unit of speed equal to 1 nautical mile per hour (6,080.2 feet), as compared with a land mile of 5,280 feet.

League A measure of distance approximating 3.45 nautical miles.

Leeward In the direction of that side of the ship opposite from which the wind blows.

Manifest A list or invoice of a ship's passengers, crew, and cargo.

Midship In or toward the middle of the ship; the longitudinal center portion of the ship.

Nautical mile 6,080.2 feet, as compared with a land mile of 5,280 feet.

Open seating Seating in the main dining room(s) is not assigned. You eat where and with whom you wish.

Paddlewheel A wheel with boards around its circumference, and, commonly, the source of propulsion for traditional American riverboats.

Pitch The rocking back and forth (bow to stern) motion of a ship that may be felt in heavy seas when the ship is under way.

Port The left side of the ship when facing toward the bow.

Port charge Port taxes, collected by the line and paid to a local government authority; it may include other miscellaneous charges, such as gasoline surcharge and fees, as well as fees to dock in a particular port.

Port tax A charge levied by the local government authority to be paid by the passenger.

Prow The bow or the stem (the front) of the ship.

Cruise Lingo (continued)

Purser A senior management position on board ship. In most cases, the purser is like the general manager of a hotel, but in some cases, he or she is more the financial or administration officer.

Quay (pronounced "key") A dock, berth, or pier.

Registry The country under whose flag the ship is registered and with whose laws the ship and its owners must comply, in addition to compliance with the laws of the countries at which the ship calls and/or embarks/disembarks passengers/cargo.

Rigging The ropes, chains, and cables that support a sailing ship's masts, spars, kingposts, cranes, and the like.

Roll The alternate sway of a ship from side to side.

Running lights Three lights (green on the starboard side, red on the port side, and white at the top of the mast) required by international law to be lighted when the ship is in motion between the times of sunset and sunrise.

Second, third, or fourth seating The later meal times in the ship's dining room(s).

Space ratio A measurement of cubic space per passenger. Gross registered ton divided by the number of passengers (basis two) equals space ratio.

Stabilizer A gyroscopically operated finlike device extending from both sides of the ship below the waterline to steady the ship and reduce its roll.

Stack The funnel or chimney from which the ship's gases of combustion are released into the atmosphere.

Passengers don't reserve rooms on a ship, they book **cabins,** which cruise lines sometimes call by a fancier name, **staterooms.** The price level of a cabin is known as its **category.**

When you reach your ship, you will **board** or **embark;** when it's time to leave the ship, passengers **disembark.** If the ship arrives at a port where it cannot pull into the dock, the ship will anchor and passengers are taken ashore in a **tender,** one of the small ancillary vessels or lifeboats that travel on board the ship.

Several terms will assist you in finding your way around the ship. The **bow** is the front of the ship, the **aft** is the rear, and the center portion is **midship.**

Heading forward, toward the bow, the right side of the ship is known as the **starboard side;** the left side of the ship is called the **port side.** Ships have **decks,** never floors. Decks are named after such things as precious stones (Emerald Deck), activities (Sports Deck), places (Monte Carlo Deck), and planets (Venus Deck).

Starboard The right side of the ship when facing toward the bow.

Stateroom Cabin or suite.

Steward Personnel on board ship.

Stem The extreme bow or prow of the ship.

Stern The extreme rear of the ship.

Suite Upscale accommodations with more space, more in-room amenities, a bigger balcony and, at times, more rooms than standard or balcony cabins.

Superstructure The structure of the ship above the main deck or waterline.

Tender A small vessel, sometimes the ship's lifeboat, used to move passengers to and from the shore when the ship is at anchor.

Transfers A bus or van ride between the ship and other locations, such as airports, hotels, or departure points for shore excursions.

Upper berth A single-size bed higher from the floor than usual (similar to a bunk bed), usually folded or recessed into the wall or ceiling by day.

Wake The track of agitated water behind a ship in motion.

Waterline The line at the side of the ship's hull that corresponds to the surface of the water.

Weigh To raise; for example, to weigh the anchor.

Windward Toward the wind, to the direction from which the wind blows.

If you've built up an appetite from all this exploring, you can go to the **main seating** (or sitting) and eat early, or the **second seating** and dine late. Both times are assigned by the line. Some lines also offer two early and two late seatings. Some ships have **single seating,** which means that all passengers eat at the same time for all three meals. Some ships also have **open seating,** in which case you may sit anywhere—at any unoccupied table or join others. By invitation, you may even find yourself at the **captain's table.**

On board, there are people to help you decode ship lingo. The **purser's office** is the information center, similar to a check-in desk at a hotel. The **hotel manager** is in charge of all passenger-related shipboard services, such as dining, housekeeping, and so on. The **chief steward** is responsible for cabin services, and **cabin stewards** or **stewardesses** take care of cabins; the **dining steward** is your waiter. The **cruise director** functions as the emcee, and the **cruise staff,** who are his assistants, run all activities and entertainment and make sure you are having a good time. Finally, there's the **captain,** who is in charge of everything. Cruise lingo is part of the fun, so don't take it too seriously.

TIME *to* GO

IF YOU PURCHASE AN AIR/SEA PACKAGE, your cruise begins from the moment you arrive at the airport. Here's how.

CRUISE DOCUMENTS

NORMALLY, YOU RECEIVE YOUR TRAVEL DOCUMENTS—including tickets, transfer vouchers, boarding forms, and luggage tags—about two weeks before departure. Some cruise lines, particularly deluxe and smaller ones going to offbeat destinations, begin sending material a month or more in advance, and often include information on ports of call and on shore excursions sold on board ship. A "Welcome Aboard" brochure is intended to familiarize you with your ship. Read it.

The final documents will include your airline and cruise tickets. Your agent should have checked them before sending them to you. Check them yourself. If you buy your cruise late, documents may come directly to you from the cruise line. Check them, too. Remember that you must show your cruise ticket when you check in at the dock.

unofficial **TIP**
Be sure to carry all documents and essential literature you receive from your cruise line or travel agent with you. Do not pack them in your luggage.

In 2007, Princess Cruises and Norwegian Cruise Lines began sending cruise tickets and other documentation to passengers via e-mail, unless you or your travel agent request otherwise. Gradually, other cruise lines have followed suit. Actually, it's better for you as you will receive the tickets earlier and you will have a chance to examine them sooner to correct any errors that might have occurred.

Luggage tags show the cruise line's name and logo. They have spaces for your name and address and the name of your ship, cruise and cabin numbers, and departure date and port. Complete the luggage tags using information contained in your cruise ticket. Attach at least one tag to every piece of your luggage, including your handbags. (An amazing number of people, in their excitement, leave hand luggage behind on an airplane, in the airport, or on a motorcoach. If it's tagged, airline or port personnel will know immediately what to do with it.)

When you arrive at the airport, you will claim luggage and it will ride on the transfer bus with you for the drive to the pier. There, it will be taken by baggage handlers and will show up in your cabin in a few hours. If not, do not panic. Cruise ships, especially large ones, have thousands of bags to load and sort as passengers arrive. In our experience, luggage is moved from the airport to your cabin with amazing speed.

AIRPORT ARRIVAL AND TRANSFERS

AS YOU LEAVE YOUR AIRPLANE IN MIAMI, Fort Lauderdale, San Juan, Vancouver, or any major departure city, you will be met by uniformed cruise line representatives, usually holding a placard showing your ship's name. The representatives gather their charges and escort or direct them to a waiting motorcoach. Keep your transfer voucher handy; you must show it to board the bus.

If you do not spot your cruise line representative, ask airline personnel or other cruise lines' reps for help. Or go to an airport "red" phone and ask that your line's representative be paged. Or proceed to where motorcoaches pick up passengers for transfer to the pier.

ADVANCE ARRIVALS OR DELAYED RETURNS

ALMOST ALL LINES HAVE HOTEL AND SIGHTSEEING PACKAGES for people who choose to arrive at their port of departure in advance of their cruise or linger there afterward. Packages are described in your cruise brochure. If your cruise begins after a long flight, lines normally schedule the first day for cruising to give passengers time to overcome jet lag. If the itinerary calls for immediate ports of call, you might consider arriving a day before departure.

Give the most serious consideration to a day-in-advance arrival when you buy the cruise by itself, are arranging your own transportation to the departure port, or your travel falls during busy travel periods when weather in the northern United States often turns bad and flights are delayed (such as Thanksgiving, Christmas, New Year's, and Presidents' Day weekend).

If you're on an air/sea program, your line has a greater incentive—although not necessarily a legal one—to get you to the ship when you've been delayed, either by postponing the sailing or by arranging a hotel room and transporting you to the first port of call. In such instances, you're likely to be one of many stranded passengers.

Your name is on a passenger list, and the cruise line representative at the airport expects you. He or she is in touch with the airline and your ship and probably is setting strategy before you arrive. If you're traveling on your own and are delayed, your cruise ship has no record of your flight and no obligation to help, although most will try. If you arrive at least a day early, you can avoid this hassle.

This is highly recommended whenever possible. Why risk missing the ship due to a flight snafu? Some people advise arriving early to avoid standing in line for check-in. We view this as the least valid reason unless you want to be on as early as physically possible to enjoy onboard amenities. Queues at the airport and dockside departure gates are a fact of life in mass-market travel. If you're so impatient that you cannot stand in a check-in line—even if it takes an hour—without having your blood pressure skyrocket, then you're probably on the wrong cruise. Megaships have megapassengers, and they must be individually processed. (It would speed the process if everyone arrived with all their documents completed properly.)

AT THE PIER

IF YOU'RE LUCKY, YOU WILL BE AMONG the first to arrive from the airport and the first in line for check-in. More likely, you'll be among several hundred others, and, depending on the cruise line, day of the week, size of the ship, and other contingencies, you will stand in line ten minutes to two hours. Pull out a magazine or travel book and start reading.

Large ships have a check-in system, asking you to line up behind your letter in the alphabet. Despite occasional glitches, this works well. You often have until 60 minutes before departure to board the ship. Some lines let you board until 15 to 30 minutes before departure, but we don't suggest cutting it that close.

Normally, lines begin processing passengers at noon or 1 p.m. for a 4 or 5 p.m. departure. But they seldom allow passengers to embark sooner than two or three hours before departure, because time is needed for previous passengers to disembark and the crew to clean the ship and prepare your cabin. Some luxury or premium lines will let you come aboard sooner, but you must remain in public areas, as your cabin will probably not be ready.

VISITORS

FOR SECURITY REASONS, cruise lines do not allow visitors. If your friends or family want to send you off in style, they can contact your travel agent to arrange a party for you in your cabin, complete with flowers, wine, and Champagne, or a birthday cake or anniversary surprise in the dining room when the ship is at sea.

SETTLING IN

BOARDING YOUR SHIP

SOME SHIPS, PARTICULARLY THE MOST LUXURIOUS ONES, have uniformed cabin stewards and stewardesses at the gangway to take you to your cabin and carry your hand luggage. Your escort may offer a quick orientation or ask you to wait for your regular steward, whose name is probably on a small tent card on your dresser. Also in your cabin is ship's literature, including an agenda for the day's events, a deck plan, and possibly stationery.

CHECKING OUT YOUR CABIN

TAKE A QUICK LOOK AROUND THE CABIN to be sure everything is working—it usually is on new ships, not necessarily on old ones. Check how to operate air- conditioning, lights, and the hot-water faucets—some fancy new ones are tricky, and the water can scald you. Check the location of life preservers, blankets, and pillows—do you have enough? If anything is missing or not as you requested—twin beds instead of a double—report it now. If you cannot locate your steward, go to the purser or front desk. If you do not get satisfaction, work your way up to the hotel manager.

TELEPHONES AND OTHER COMMUNICATIONS

ALL BUT A FEW SHIPS HAVE TELEPHONES in cabins with instructions for using them. Most phones have direct-dial to the United States 24 hours a day, but be aware of the price. Usually, you are charged $6 to $10 per minute for a ship-to-shore call. Receiving a call or a fax may cost $5 to $7 or more per minute. Policies vary. Some allow you to call collect or charge your call to your shipboard account. Shore to Ship has technology enabling passengers to dial toll-free numbers in the United States directly from their cabins. The price is $6.95 per minute, maximum ten minutes per call. Crystal Cruises was among the first to enable passengers to send and receive e-mail with relative ease. Now, most cruise ships, including even small adventure ships, have e-mail facilities and more and more are adding wireless access.

If someone wants to reach you at sea, they can telephone the ship by calling ☎ 800-SEA-CALL, asking for the ship by name, and giving its approximate location. The specific phone number for your ship is often included in the documents you receive from the cruise line in advance of your cruise. Charges for this call will appear on the caller's long-distance telephone bill. Ship-to-shore telephone and fax services are normally available only at sea. When the ship is in port, onshore communications must be used.

Until recently, cell phones worked locally in ports and up to about two miles at sea, depending on the phone and the location. But now, cruise ships, especially new ones, have technology that enables passengers to use their own cell phones at sea with the cost being charged to the passengers' cell phone account. Be warned: it's expensive. With e-mail becoming so readily available on cruise ships, it is the best, least costly means to stay in touch with family and friends, or to tend to business during a cruise.

*un**official* TIP**

If assigned arrangements are not what you requested, make a beeline for the maître d'hôtel.

Almost all new ships have an Internet cafe with a dozen or more computer terminals, and older ships and many small ones have installed at least one or two terminals for passengers' use. Many older ships have also been retrofitted with these cafes. Charges range from 25 cents to 75 cents per minute, including dial-up time, which can often take five minutes or more at sea. On weeklong or longer cruises, many ships offer weekly rates. Wi-Fi access is rapidly becoming the norm on large ships; cards usually cost $10 per day. Internet cafes in ports of call are now available around the world and are usually very inexpensive to use to send and retrieve mail—certainly much less costly than shipboard facilities.

CHECKING OUT YOUR SHIP

AFTER YOU CHECK OUT YOUR CABIN, you might want to tour the ship or, alternatively, relax in a lounge or visit the spa. The ship will be your home for a while, and it's nice to feel at home as quickly as possible.

CHECKING ON YOUR DINING RESERVATIONS

WHEN YOU BOOK YOUR CRUISE, your travel agent should state your dining preference and request reservations. On ships with assigned seating times, you may request first or second seating, or on ships with four seating times, any of those. Tables for two, four, six, or eight are available; and guests can ask for smoking or nonsmoking areas, although most ships departing from U.S. ports now have smokeless dining rooms. Most lines say they honor requests on a first-come, first-served basis, yet few confirm them in advance. On older ships, dining reservations are confirmed by the maître d'hôtel on board, but on new ships you often can reserve in advance on the cruise line's Web site.

Royal Caribbean International is among the few lines that print passengers' dining reservations on their cruise tickets. Why, in this computer age, all can't do the same is a mystery—unless it's to allow the maître d'hôtel to control last-minute shuffling and to ensure he gets his tips.

You may receive confirmation of your dining arrangements on check-in, or it may be in your cabin. If not, check on it. Even lines that give you a dining reservation in advance may ask you to confirm it with the maître d'hôtel. If you have a problem with your dining arrangements, know that most cruise lines will accommodate your change request, though not necessarily on the first night. Rest assured, you won't be the only one. No other item causes more consternation than dining-room reservations.

If you let the cruise line or maître d'hôtel place you randomly at a table and you are unhappy with your companions, do not hesitate to ask the maître d'hôtel to move you. Nothing is worse than spending a week dining with people with whom you have nothing in common and no basis for conversation. And you don't need to.

Now, with new ships having so many dining venues, many of the problems of the past regarding reservations and seating in the dining room are less likely to be matters of concern.

DINING HOURS

CONSUMERS OFTEN ASK ABOUT DINING HOURS before they cruise. They vary so much that it is difficult, if not impossible, to give an accurate generic overview. Keep in mind that each line, each itinerary, and sometimes each ship may have varied hours. You will get a complete list of hours on board, and some general information before boarding about dining times and seatings. Ask your travel agent or cruise line.

But before booking, it is more important to assess how you will dine and to pick a line that meets your needs. Do your homework up front. What type of dining do you prefer? Are you more structured or flexible in dining times? Do you like to socialize with other passengers every night or do your own thing? Check brochures, Web sites, consumer cruise bulletin boards, and ask questions of your agent or friends. Find out exactly what the dining policies and dining style are on every ship you are thinking of sailing on (see our descriptions in Part II).

For those seeking the most flexibility, some luxury lines offer open seating and anytime dining programs, as well as dining alternatives. On the mass-market side, Norwegian Cruise Line offers the highly flexible Freestyle Dining—guests eat where, when, and with whom they want; and guests can also access a host of onboard alternative restaurant choices in addition to the main dining room. Some are free, some come with a charge. Expedition and small ship lines may have open seating but set very specific times for their dining service.

Princess, in another twist, offers both a flexible dining experience and a more traditional fixed one; guests choose which so they can have the best of both worlds. Some lines also have open seating for breakfast and lunch, yet more structured, assigned seating times and tables for dinner. That means you are assigned a table with other guests and you dine at that same table, at that same time, every evening; of course you don't have to dine there every night. Guests often take a break and have room service one night, or visit an alternative restaurant or the buffet restaurant on another. But if you do dine in the dining room on any evening you will eat at that table and with those people each night.

Generally, there are two fixed dinner seatings between 5:30 and 7:30 p.m. and between 8 and 10 p.m. But even those times can vary. Carnival and Holland America have both adopted four seatings within the same period to offer more flexibility for guests. Carnival also offers anytime dining similar to Princess. We expect other cruise lines will follow their lead. So if you have strong preferences, tell your travel agent, who can explain what the dining hours and choices are on individual lines.

Whichever line you pick, you won't go hungry. In addition to the regular meals, most lines offer a host of other options. In addition to room service, these might include ice cream on deck, pizza parlors (some 24 hours), a late-night snack or buffet, afternoon tea, barbecues on deck, early-bird coffee and continental breakfast in a lounge, cocktail canapés, and a host of alternative dining options.

ESTABLISHING SHIPBOARD CREDIT

MOST LINES USE A CASHLESS SYSTEM ABOARD SHIP. At check-in, you receive a card—like a credit card—which will be your identification card and probably your cabin door key. If you want to establish credit for purchases on board, drinks at the bar, wine in the dining room, and so forth, you must present a major credit card at check-in or the purser's office (you will be told at check-in) to have an imprint made and signed.

On the last night of the cruise, you receive a printout of your charges for review. You can pay the amount with cash or traveler's checks or have it billed to your credit card. In profiles in Standard Features in Part Two, we list credit cards each cruise line accepts. Also see our discussion of credit holds on pages 111–112.

PREPARING *for* TIME ASHORE

PORT TALKS AND SHOPPING GUIDELINES

ALL SHIPS OFFER "PORT TALKS"—briefings on the country or island and port where the ship will dock. The quality of these talks varies enormously among lines and ships, depending largely on the cruise director's knowledge and the importance the line puts on such programs.

Most mainstream lines with large ships do a lousy job with port talks. On the other hand, adventure and expedition cruises offer superb talks. Small ships generally have a better track record than large ones.

Avoid being misled. If, during a port talk, the cruise director or anyone else recommends one store over another, shop around before buying. The store recommended may be the best place to buy—or it may not.

Also, be cautious of advice that fabulous buys are available in duty-free shops on board and in ports. Most often, you can do as well or better at discount stores and factory outlets at home. If you are considering sizable purchases of jewelry, cameras, china, or crystal, bring a list of prices from home and comparison shop. Be sure you are comparing similar products. Prices in shipboard shops are a good gauge; they usually are competitive with those in ports.

In the Caribbean, expect to save up to 20% on such well-known brands as Gucci, Fendi, and Vuitton, and on French perfumes, which must be sold at prices set by the makers. Any store caught undercutting the price will be dropped from distribution. The biggest savings are on cigarettes and liquor, not because the price is so much less, but because you save the hefty U.S. taxes imposed on them.

When preparing for your day ashore, be aware also that purses, bags, and packs that you carry along will be searched before you're allowed back on board. Purchases you make while shopping will likewise be inspected.

Some cruise lines do not allow passengers to bring liquor or beer on board for consumption during your cruise (they want you to patronize their bars) and will confiscate it if you try to slip it in. They usually store it and return it to you at the end of your cruise.

SHORE EXCURSIONS:
SOME PITFALLS AND COSTS

ALTHOUGH THERE HAS BEEN MUCH IMPROVEMENT recently, "shore excursions"—the tours passengers buy from the cruise line to take at ports—are often the weakest element of the cruise vacation. Cruise lines are finally recognizing the needs of younger, more active passengers by providing more adventurous excursions featuring horseback riding, hiking, mountain biking, scuba diving, snorkeling, sailing, and even a MiG flight over Moscow. But the core product—large to medium group sightseeing tours—needs more work, given the shore excursion's importance to the cruise experience.

All the latest cruise lines' research indicates that what attracts customers to buy a particular cruise are the specific ports of call on the itinerary. Travelers often view their shore trips as one of the more important aspects of the cruise. In response, major cruise lines have beefed up their shore excursion departments to offer more compelling tours, which often include exploring a destination on foot as well as by bus, van, or boat.

Shore excursions are available at every stop on a ship's itinerary, almost always at

unofficial **TIP**
More and more, cruise lines are enabling passengers to purchase shore excursions in advance on the line's Web site, and some even by phone or mail.

additional cost. The exceptions are adventure and expedition cruises, where shore visits are an integral part of the experience (and one reason these cruises appear to be more costly than mainstream ones). Also, cruises in China usually include the cost of shore excursions, not because cruise lines are altruistic, but because the Chinese want it that way.

Shore excursions have traditionally been sold aboard ship either by a shore excursion office or, rarely, from the purser or cruise director. It has been assumed that people prefer to buy excursions on board because their interests and plans change once the cruise begins. However, that assumption may have no foundation in fact. After you have been subjected to the way shore excursions are sold aboard many ships, you might say as we do: there must be a better way. And now, there is. More and more cruise lines list their shore excursions on their Web sites where you can read information about them and book and pay for your choices. Be aware of the line's cancellation and refund policies. Often they are strict and even punitive.

Often you must choose your excursions on the first night of the cruise, especially for the first port of call. Unless you have done your homework in advance of your cruise, you will be buying blind. The shore excursion office usually has limited hours. For the first few days of a cruise, particularly on large ships, ticket lines are long. Therefore, it really pays to read your cruise literature plus books and magazine articles about your destinations in advance.

If possible, take advantage of the opportunity to book shore excursions in advance. In addition to significantly increasing your chances of getting the excursion you want, you also avoid the hassle of booking on board. Usually, a pamphlet on shore excursions is included in the literature sent prior to your cruise. Not all brochures list prices, but they are listed on those cruise lines' Web sites that provide a booking facility. Absent that convenience, you can request prices through your travel agent, if you need them for budgeting purposes. We are happy to report that more lines are including prices in their literature. Also, more often pamphlets are specific to cruise itineraries, making it easier to select tours of interest.

Shore excursions normally are operated by local tour companies. Motorcoaches seating 30 to 50 passengers are the most common form of transportation, particularly on general sightseeing tours offered by large ships. Minibuses and vans are common for smaller groups; location and terrain are also factors in the choice of conveyance. Most tours assume that passengers are on their first visit to the locale—one reason shore excursions are a weak link.

Standard shore excursions vary little among cruise lines and are, for the most part, passive and unimaginative city and/or countryside tours to the best-known sights. There are exceptions, however, like the excursions on Greek Isles cruises, where escorts are university graduates who must pass stiff examinations to qualify as guides, and customized tours offered by smaller ships and luxury liners. Happily, many cruise lines have added a variety of sports activities and tours that emphasis nature and culture in an effort to appeal to younger travelers and in response to passengers' requests.

After years of being bad to awful, shore excursions available on Caribbean cruises have shown a great improvement, as cruise lines have worked with local operators to be more creative, provide greater variety of tour offerings, and enhance the tour experience with more substance and better-trained guides.

As a rule of thumb, most standard half-day tours cost $25 to $35 in the Caribbean, but they can cost twice that in Alaska and Europe. Adventure excursions run $50 and up, mainly because the groups are small and hence cost more per person to operate. Full-day tours can run as much as $70 to $150, and some, like helicopter tours, might cost $200 or more. Often the most expensive are the first to sell out. That's usually because the number of participants is limited, or they are perceived as a great value or a once-in-a-lifetime experience, or it's an excursion that would be difficult to arrange on one's own. Variables that affect price include the locale, the number of participants, local costs, and mode of transport.

As you study excursions offered by your line, look for options that keep things simple. Excursions that involve multiple activities, sights, and stops could drive some people nuts. It's on the bus, off the bus, back on the bus, head counts. "Wait, Thelma's in the restroom!" "Where are Harry and Louise?" "I left my credit card in the stuffed parrot shop! I'll be right back." With few exceptions, you'll spend more time driving among sites and loading and unloading the bus than you will touring or doing something interesting.

When you read descriptions of available excursions, check how long the primary activity or event is. If the written material doesn't say, ask the cruise director. You'll sometimes discover that the half-day "riverboat excursion" spends only an hour on the water. The remainder of the time is spent commuting and waiting for fellow passengers to shop.

In ports where most attractions you want to see are clustered in a small area, you may save time by taking a cab or walking. Rental cars are another option. By forgoing a $48-per-person half-day shore excursion, two people can apply the $96 toward cab fares, rental cars, and admissions to attractions. In most ports, you can see and do a lot for $96.

Ask probing questions about each port. Is it a good and safe place to explore on foot? What are the local people like? At some ports, tourists are subjected to swarms of in-your-face hucksters and peddlers. In such places, escorted tours, though regimented and inefficient, can be a less stressful way to visit.

When the ship arrives in port, people who have purchased shore excursions are allowed to disembark first and are usually asked to follow a departure schedule to avert a traffic jam at the gangway. This is seldom a problem when the ship docks and passengers can disembark quickly. It can be a problem when the ship must tender, because it cuts an hour or more (depending on ship size) from the time you have in port if you plan to tour on your own.

At the END of YOUR CRUISE

TIPPING

THERE ARE NO DEFINITIVE RULES ABOUT TIPPING, but because it causes so much consternation for passengers, cruise lines offer guidelines, distributing them aboard ship. Some even publish them in their cruise brochures, which is helpful if you want to budget for tipping in advance. In Part Two, the cruise ship profiles' Standard Features includes Suggested Tipping. The guidelines are similar: Tip slightly less on budget cruises, slightly more on luxury cruises. Lines will also tell you if gratuities are included or if they are automatically added to your bill. Follow guidelines or your inclinations. Ship officers and senior management are never tipped. For all service personnel, tips are their main source of compensation. Only a few deluxe ships include tipping in the cruise cost (noted in the cruise line profiles in Part Two).

In a session at voyage's end, the cruise director will discuss disembarkation procedures and outline tipping guidelines. There no longer is anything subtle about tipping. Either the line will automatically add the tips or it won't; if not, on the final cruise day, your cabin steward will leave a supply of envelopes for distributing your tips, possibly with guidelines. Lately, the envelopes are crassly stamped with titles—Cabin Steward, Dining Steward, Waiter—in case you did not know whom to tip!

On ships without "automatic" tipping, tips are usually given to individuals—your cabin stewards and dining room waiters. On ships with Greek crews and on many small vessels, tips are pooled for distribution to include those behind the scenes, such as kitchen staff.

The advent of alternative dining venues has confused tipping customs in recent years. Passengers sometimes were deducting from the amount given to their dining room waitstaff to compensate for gratuities rendered at the alternative restaurants. To create a more uniform approach, a number of cruise lines add gratuities directly to your shipboard bill. Most of these offer the option of decreasing or increasing the amount on your bill depending on how you felt about the service. Whatever the tipping protocol on your cruise, you can be sure it will be explained to you in detail, probably several times.

If tips are not added to your shipboard bill, custom dictates that you distribute tips the last night of the cruise. Some lines, particularly deluxe ones, will arrange prepayment of tips. Check the Standard Features section in our cruise line profiles for each line's "Suggested Tipping" information.

DEPARTING

TO SMOOTH DISEMBARKATION, your captain and cruise director will ask you to follow procedures outlined in the cruise director's final talk and repeated on closed-circuit television in your cabin and in the daily agenda. On the last day, your cabin steward will give you luggage tags to be completed and attached to your bags. You are asked to place your bags (except hand luggage) outside your cabin door before you retire. Times vary; some lines want them out by 8 or 10 p.m.— an unreasonable hour for passengers dining at the late seating. Such requests are for the ship's convenience, because no luggage can be unloaded until the ship docks. Do what's convenient for you and tell your cabin steward what to expect.

The last night of a cruise is almost always casual; plan your packing accordingly. And don't pack everything. Remember you still need to dress the next day. It's not unheard of for people to pack shoes, underwear, and even needed travel documents in their exuberance to put their bags out.

Luggage tags use a color-coded, alphabetic system that enables the ship to disembark passengers by cabin locations and airline departure times for those on air/sea packages. (Passengers on the earliest flights disembark first.) Tags also identify your airline so that your bags will go to the correct place at the airport.

Ships normally dock about 7 or 8 a.m. the last day and require about an hour to unload luggage, meaning no passengers are likely to disembark before 8:30 or 9 a.m. The ship is very eager to unload passengers as quickly as possible. Some people find disembarkation so abrupt that it's unpleasant. Try to remember that the next group of passengers will arrive soon, and staff and crew have only about four hours to prepare the ship and be all smiles for them.

Breakfast is served either at normal hours with the full menu or at abbreviated hours with a short menu. Room service usually isn't available. You will be called to depart by the color of your luggage tags. After leaving the ship, you encounter chaos that varies depending on the port. Usually, you proceed first to immigration and then to the baggage holding area, where your luggage has been placed according to the color of your tags or under large signs with letters of the alphabet. You are responsible for finding it and taking it to customs. In Miami, for example, baggage handlers help you, and the customs official stands by the exit to take the declaration form you completed aboard ship. He or she may check your passport, so have it handy.

After clearing customs, your luggage will go with you to the air-port on the transfer bus. Find the motorcoach going to your airline's departure area, show your transfer voucher, give the driver your lug-gage, and climb aboard. If you aren't on an air/sea package, you may be allowed aboard the motorcoach unless you have lots of luggage. Otherwise, taxis are nearby.

CRUISE LINES
and THEIR SHIPS

The **HEART** *of the* **MATTER**

PART TWO CONSISTS OF IN-DEPTH CRUISE LINE and ship profiles—the heart of this guide—serving the U.S. and Canadian markets. Listed alphabetically by cruise line, each line has three parts: A company profile, its ships' standard features, and ship descriptions. Cruise lines profiled in this section are listed in the Table of Contents. For listings of specific ships, itineraries, destinations, or for a general subject index, refer to the respective indexes at the end of this book.

CRUISE LINE PROFILES

THE FIRST THREE TO FOUR PAGES focus on the cruise line and the type of cruises it offers. At-a-glance summaries—**Type of Ships, Type of Cruises, Cruise Line's Strengths, Cruise Line's Shortcomings, Fellow Passengers, Recommended for, Not Recommended for**—help you select cruise lines of potential interest.

Summaries are followed by background on the line, its fleet, and cruise areas to reveal the company behind the cruise. The **Style** section defines the experience you can expect on any ship of that cruise line. **Distinctive Features** highlights amenities or facilities that are innovative or unusual. The **Rates** section explains discounts, special fares, and packages. **Past Passengers** tells what repeat customers can expect, and **The Last Word** is our summary of the line—the big picture.

Standard Features

Information on elements common to all ships of a line—including officers, staff, dining facilities, dress code, cabin amenities, and electricity—is listed in one chart for handy reference.

Cruise Ship Profiles

The cruise line's fleet, starting with its flagship (or the most representative) vessel, is covered in-depth. Sister ships with identical design are clustered. Other ships that vary only in degree receive shorter treatment. We recommend that readers review the entire section for a given cruise line to have a complete picture of the cruise experience offered.

QUALITY RATINGS To differentiate ships by overall quality of the cruise experience and to allow comparison of ships from different lines, we give ships a rating of 1–10, with 10 being the best. The numerical rating is based on the quality and diversity of the ship's features and service, taking into consideration its state of repair, maintenance, and cleanliness; the design, comfort, decor, and furnishing of public areas; recreational and fitness facilities; meal quality and dining room service; entertainment, activities, and shore excursions; cabin comfort, decor, furnishings, and spaciousness; and hospitality, courtesy, and responsiveness of officers and crew.

We have opted for numerical ratings because some of our colleagues in the travel press have hopelessly muddled the more familiar star ratings. Traditionally, ships have been rated one to five stars. This system was easily understood by the cruising public and provided a quick way to compare critics' opinions. Several years ago, however, some writers changed the scale to one to six stars, precluding meaningful comparison. Although those guidebooks are no longer published and the writers are deceased, the practice continues, mainly because the cruise lines perpetuate it. We believe a standardized rating system helps consumers. But so long as the star system remains corrupted, we elect to abandon the star business.

VALUE RATINGS There is no consideration of cost in the quality ratings. If you want the finest cruise available and cost is no issue, look no further than the quality ratings. If, however, you seek both quality and value, consult the value rating, expressed in letters. All value ratings are based on brochure rates. Any discount you obtain will improve the value rating for a ship. Value ratings are defined as follows:

A	Exceptional value, a real bargain.
B	Good value.
C	Absolutely fair. You get exactly what you pay for.
D	Somewhat overpriced.
F	Significantly overpriced.

A WORD ABOUT NEW SHIPS

WE DO NOT EVALUATE OR RATE NEW SHIPS until they have been in service for at least one year. This allows the new ship to work out any kinks and settle into normal operation. If you are considering a cruise on a new ship, check our ratings and descriptions of other ships in the same line for a good idea of what to expect. If a ship has not completed a year of service at press time, it will be marked as a "preview" in the ship's ratings box.

American Canadian Caribbean Line

461 Water Street
Warren, RI 02885
☎ 401-247-0955 or 800-556-7450
FAX 401-247-2350
www.accl-smallships.com

TYPE OF SHIPS Small, no-frills, budget.

TYPE OF CRUISES Light adventure, destination-oriented, unhurried pace.

CRUISE LINE'S STRENGTHS
- innovative, small ships
- imaginative itineraries
- homey ambience
- friendly, diligent staff
- moderate prices

CRUISE LINE'S SHORTCOMINGS
- minimal service
- spartan cabins with small bathrooms
- limited shipboard facilities

FELLOW PASSENGERS Mature, experienced travelers ages 55-85; retired couples, seniors; teachers. Not all are sporty, but all are good sports; friendly and unpretentious, most with moderate means, college-educated, well-traveled. Even affluent passengers who care little for luxury and ostentation, are keenly interested in history, wildlife, and ecology. They are avid readers and play bridge and Scrabble.

Recommended for Travelers seeking friendship, companionship, light adventure in unusual destinations; budget-conscious travelers favoring a small ship with family atmosphere. Those who abhor large ships.

Not recommended for Swingers, super-achievers, snobs, or night owls.

CRUISE AREAS AND SEASONS Spring–fall, U.S. coastal and intercoastal waterways between New England and Florida; Hudson River, Erie Canal, Maine, New England, Canada; Mississippi River, small mid-America rivers and Great Lakes from Chicago. Winter, Belize, Guatemala, Honduras' Bay Islands.

THE LINE Shipbuilder and adventurer Luther Blount designed and built his first small ship in 1964 for cruising the Hudson River, Erie Canal, and Canada's inland waterways with his friends. A loyal following developed, and his hobby became a business that pioneered innovative itineraries and ship design.

With slightly larger ships, he expanded to the Bahamas and Virgin Islands, added "Caribbean" to the line's name, and pioneered unusual itineraries in Central America and other U.S. waterways.

Each vessel, built at Blount's shipyard in Warren, Rhode Island, had design improvements, larger cabins, and better public space. Blount was a hands-on

THE FLEET	BUILT/RENOVATED	TONNAGE	PASSENGERS
Grande Caribe	1997/2009	94	100
Grande Mariner	1998	97	100
Niagara Prince	1994/05/09	N.A.	90

president, designing every aspect of the ships (with design concepts adopted by many small cruise ships), supervising the building, and scouting new itineraries until his retirement at the age of 84 in 2001 and his death in 2006 at age 90.

ACCL remains a family enterprise. Daughter Nancy Blount, who took over when her father retired, is company president.

STYLE Adventure at budget prices. Leave your Guccis at home—no one here would be impressed. Since its inception, ACCL has maintained an informal, unpretentious atmosphere with limited service and planned entertainment. Passengers receive an intimate look at places they visit. The ships' shallow drafts enable them to cruise small tributaries. Bow ramps, a Blount innovation, allow access to inaccessible places. The ships carry a glass-bottom boat, small sailboats, kayaks, and snorkeling equipment for use in warm climates.

ACCL cruises, staffed by American officers and crew, are run like a family outing. Surprisingly good food is served family style in a folksy atmosphere conducive to friendships. Limited table service is provided by cheerful, hard-working staff who are always ready to bring beverages or second helpings and deal with special requests.

New itineraries are offered every year, tapping pristine areas strong in natural beauty and history and providing frequent opportunities for exploring, particularly in ports where large ships cannot go.

DISTINCTIVE FEATURES Bow ramps; retractable pilothouse, allowing vessels to sail the length of the Erie Canal; stair lifts, glass-bottom launch, kayaks.

RATES Port charges are additional.

Special fares and discounts 10% discount on certain cruises when two cruises are booked back to back; up to 15% discounts or more periodically on special promotions. Also offered is a "bring-a-friend" discount.

- **THIRD PASSENGER:** 15% discount for each occupant of cabin.
- **SINGLE SUPPLEMENT:** 175% for certain cabins, depending on season and time of booking. On select cruises, a single's willing-to-share program offers double-occupancy rates.

PAST PASSENGERS Loyalty is rewarded; after ten cruises, a passenger gets one free. Advanced mailings on new itineraries and special discounts.

THE LAST WORD Up to 68% of passengers are repeat, suggesting that ACCL has found the right formula for a certain type of passenger: one who doesn't want or need pampering and appreciates small-ship cruising, preferring conversation and friendship to chorus lines and casinos. New itineraries usually sell out quickly. ACCL reflects the owners' hands-on philosophy and personal touch

ACCL Standard Features

Officers American.

Staff *Dining, Cabin, Cruise:* American.

Dining facilities One dining room with open seating; meals served at specific hours: breakfast, 8 a.m.; lunch, noon; dinner, 6 p.m.

Special diets Notice at booking; chefs can accommodate basic requests.

Room service None.

Dress code Casual at all times; men never need a tie. Gentlemen might bring a jacket and women a dress in case they want to try a fancy place in a port.

Cabin amenities Air-conditioning/heat; upper-deck cabins have windows that can be opened. Very small bathroom. Reading light; plug for hair dryers. Limited drawer and closet space.

Electrical outlets 110 AC.

Wheelchair access No designated cabins; motorized chair between Main and Sun Decks.

Recreation and entertainment Lounge with bar setup, books, and videos; informal entertainment, occasional lectures; bridge and parlor games.

Sports and other activities Glass-bottom boat, Sunfish, kayaks, and snorkeling equipment on board for warm-weather charter.

Beauty and fitness No facilities. On request, cruise director will provide information about beauty/barber salons in ports.

Other facilities Ships have no doctors; "BYOB" policy.

Children's facilities None. Children under age 14 not accepted.

Theme cruises Fall foliage.

Smoking No smoking inside ships; allowed only in outside open areas.

ACCL suggested tipping $10–$15 per person per day. All tips are pooled and shared.

Credit cards None on board. Passengers may use traveler's checks or personal checks. Visa or MasterCard to book a cruise.

---

with customers. Passengers who understand the limitations of a small ship and the nature of these cruises enjoy themselves immensely; those who do not may discover they're on the wrong ship.

The only thing missing is information on shore excursions sent to passengers before their cruise, particularly when its cruises and passengers are destination-focused. It's even more puzzling when you know that ACCL is one of the few cruise lines that does not profit on shore excursions. They're sold at cost—one of many reasons ACCL cruises are a truly good value.

Grande Caribe	QUALITY 2	VALUE A
Grande Mariner	QUALITY 2	VALUE A
Niagara Prince	QUALITY 2	VALUE A
REGISTRY United States	LENGTH 183/182/175 feet	BEAM 40 feet
CABINS 50/40	DRAFT 6.6/6.3 feet	SPEED 12 knots
MAXIMUM PASSENGERS	PASSENGER DECKS 3	ELEVATORS Chairlift
100/96/90	CREW 15/17	SPACE RATIO NA

THE SHIPS Built at Blount Marine in Warren, Rhode Island, the *Grande Caribe* and her near twin, *Grande Mariner,* are designed for coastal cruises. Like ACCL ships of the past, they have shallow drafts and bow ramps to guarantee access to areas large cruise ships cannot reach. They also have a retractable pilothouse for passage under low bridges and a chairlift for passengers who have trouble negotiating stairs. On warm-weather cruises, the ships can carry a Blount-designed glass-bottom boat, kayaks, snorkel equipment, and Sunfish.

The U.S.-flagged *Niagara Prince,* smaller than her sister, was ACCL's most innovative ship when she debuted in 1994. She was designed to navigate the length of the Erie Canal and sail on coastal waters. The comfortable but basic ship has two passenger decks with low ceilings. After a two-year absence, she returned to the ACCL fleet with new nautical decor among her recent renovations. The lounge and dining room are located forward on the top or Sun Deck and have windows at the bow and along the sides, providing enhanced views. The lounge, shaped by the bow, has books, newspapers (updated as available in ports), and the ship's only television set. The dining room is an all-purpose room between meals. The Sun Deck has cabins and a wraparound promenade with small sitting areas at each end. A flight of steps at the bow accesses the patented bow ramp, used when a site of interest has no dock. Extensions lengthen the ramp and allow for dry-shore landings. The ship has a motorized chairlift for passengers who have difficulty negotiating stairs and hallway railings to improve capabilities for disabled passengers.

The *Niagara Prince's* profile can be made lower with a hull feature Blount likened to letting the air out of a tire. It enables the ship to pass under the Erie Canal's lowest bridges and traverse the waterway from Troy to Buffalo, the first boat to do so in more than 120 years. (Previous ACCL ships traveled about three-quarters of the way.) The feature also allows the *Niagara Prince* to navigate Lake Champlain and the Chicago River through the heart of the Windy City, passing under its bridges.

Although *Grande Caribe* is only slightly larger than earlier ACCL ships, her layout varies in several ways. The dining room is on the main deck; the lounge, with wraparound windows, is on the top deck; and the ship has a stern swimming platform. *Grande Caribe* gained nautical decor in her 2009 renovation. *Grand Mariner* is slated to be renovated in 2010.

All three ships have a retractable pilothouse, which is lowered to pass under bridges by lifting off its roof, folding down its sides, and disconnecting all the equipment. The captain's chair, console, steering mechanism, and equipment are then lowered to the Promenade Deck and reconnected so the ship can resume operation. It's quite a scene to watch, leaving you with an I-had-to-see-it-to-believe-it feeling.

Grande Mariner, which made her debut in 1998, has more comfortable cabins than *Grande Caribe* or *Niagara Prince,* as well as unique features such as an acoustical "floating deck" between the engine room and main-deck cabins. This special deck is meant to reduce engine noise, along with sound-deadening enclosures for the ship's main generators. (We did not find the ship quieter than her earlier sisters. In fact, our cabin, 44A, was actually noisier from the sound of the generators.)

In another first for ACCL, the hull of *Grande Mariner* is ice-strengthened for cruising in the Canadian subarctic waters of Labrador, Newfoundland, and parts of the St. Lawrence River. Incidentally, the ship's 24-passenger glass-bottom boat and shore launch are built with the same foam-based materials found in a life raft.

The *Grande Mariner's* "vista view" lounge, a multifunctional room located forward on the upper deck, has wraparound windows to showcase passing scenery. The room has a bar, piano, and large projection screen; it can be used for lectures by visiting experts, historians, and naturalists, or for business seminars. A self-service bar has storage shelves for passengers' liquor and a fridge for chilling wine and beer. Nightly, the chef prepares hors d'oeuvres for the cocktail hour.

ITINERARIES *See* Itinerary Index.

CABINS Small, spartan but functional cabins have twin beds on metal frames. Storage space is limited to four drawers, about one square foot of counter space, and a cabinet for hanging clothes; luggage goes under the beds.

Bathrooms, ingeniously designed by Blount, are small but utilitarian; they're a deluxe version of a "head" on a sailboat or RV. A small sink with spring taps lets water run for only a few seconds at a time. The handheld shower is very efficient and can be left in its wall mount when showering. The toilet has a fill-and-flush system that works very well.

Grande Caribe has a third, lower deck with six cabins fitted with upper and lower berths and no windows. There are three similar inside cabins on the main deck. These nine are the least expensive of *Grande Caribe's* 50 cabins. All other cabins are on the main and Sun decks and have two beds, either side by side or in an L shape. Two cabins have double beds. Six cabins on the Sun Deck have doors that open to the outside promenade; others have large sliding windows—a pleasant feature when fresh air fills the room. Cabins are cleaned daily; linens are changed weekly. Bath towels are replaced every second day or as needed. (The ship does not have laundry facilities.) There is no room service.

On *Grande Mariner,* each cabin has its own air conditioner with air circulated outside through ducts. Unlike many other ships where air is recirculated, the Blount-designed system supplies fresh air continuously to the cabins, and stale air is removed. *Grande Mariner's* cabins are ACCL's most comfortable. Bathrooms, particularly, show marked improvement over earlier ships in the fleet. Cabin doors can be locked from the inside. However, passengers are not issued keys and don't need them.

Specifications 50 cabins (*Caribe* 9, *Mariner* 7 inside/no window; *Caribe* 8, *Mariner* 9 open onto promenade); all have private facilities and twin lower beds (except *Mariner* has 2 cabins with double beds); some convert to doubles. *Caribe* 8, *Mariner* 10 have upper/lower berths. Standard dimensions, 80–110 square feet. *Niagara Prince* 40 outside cabins (14 open onto promenade); 2 inside; all have private facilities, twin lower beds; 4 with upper/lower berths.

DINING A big advantage of a small ship is its fresh food and homemade bread and pastries. Aboard these ships, well-prepared American fare is much better than expected for the ship's category and better than on more expensive lines. Menus are posted daily. One of two entrées available is lighter, healthful fare. This reflects past passengers' criticism of the ship's tendency to serve high-cholesterol foods.

Meals are family-style with the staff serving dessert, beverages, and second helpings. The main course of the hearty breakfast—eggs, pancakes, and so on—varies daily. Lunch usually includes a freshly made soup (the best we've had on any ship), salad, and dessert. Dinner features fish, chicken, or other meat; vegetables; and dessert. Coffee, tea, and cookies are always available.

The dining room, which has an open kitchen, has tables for four, six, eight, and ten. Square tables for four are also used for card games. Passengers bring their own liquor and wine, and ACCL provides storage, setups, and ice. For the captain's dinners, ACCL supplies wine and an open bar. Likewise, for Celebration Night, when passengers collectively celebrate birthdays, anniversaries, and so on.

SERVICE The young and energetic crew members, most from Rhode Island and neighboring states, are outstanding. They are hardworking, smiling, and unfailingly polite. The same teams that clean the cabins also attend the dining room. They are particularly accommodating to older passengers.

FACILITIES AND ACTIVITIES There is no evening entertainment of the usual cruise variety. Passengers gather in the lounge for informal, predinner cocktails. After dinner, some may linger for card or parlor games or to watch a film. The lounge has a television monitor for videotapes, and visiting lecturers or local talent may appear at ports of call. Most passengers are in bed by 10 p.m. Although the ships have some paperbacks, avid readers should bring their own books. ACCL's captains are very knowledgeable about places the ships visit and often provide running commentary.

SPORTS AND FITNESS On board, a mile walk on the Promenade Deck usually starts the morning fitness activity for most passengers. Ashore, sports activities depend on the itinerary.

SHORE EXCURSIONS On the cruise's first day, the cruise director distributes descriptions of tours. Excursions vary with itineraries, cost $4–$45 each, and often are subject to demand and weather conditions. ACCL uses local operators specializing in small special-interest groups. The line says it continuously checks tours and books the most appealing choices.

Azamara Club Cruises

1050 Caribbean Way
Miami, FL 33132
☎ 305-539-6000 or 877-999-9553
FAX 305-536-0140
www.azamaraclubcruises.com

TYPE OF SHIPS Stylish, small- to medium-size ships.

TYPE OF CRUISES Moderately priced, upscale cruises; emphasis on quality and destinations. Some seven-night, but mostly ten-night-and-longer cruises.

CRUISE LINE'S STRENGTHS
- cuisine
- well-designed, stylish ships
- two specialty restaurants and sushi bar
- open seating in main restaurant
- value for money
- frequent overnight stays in port
- quiet, relaxing atmosphere
- imaginative itineraries

CRUISE LINE'S SHORTCOMINGS
- lack of outside, wraparound promenade deck
- service is a work in progress
- small bathrooms
- limited U.S. mainland departures

FELLOW PASSENGERS Moderately affluent, typical passenger is age 50 or older, married, with a combined income of $150,000+. He/she tends to be an educated, experienced traveler who understands quality and owns a house in an affluent suburb. Many have cruised before, most likely with Celebrity. They are active travelers looking for value and new ways to see the world. They want a refined, intimate, and upscale experience and may be buying up from mainstream cruising or buying down from luxury ones.

Recommended for Small-ship devotees; middle- to upper-middle-income travelers in their 40s and older; first-timers or experienced cruisers who appreciate fine furnishings, cuisine, an easy pace, and care minimally about onboard recreation and entertainment.

Not recommended for Big-ship enthusiasts and party seekers.

CRUISE AREAS AND SEASONS Winter, Caribbean; Panama Canal/Mexico; Asia. Transatlantic fall and spring, Europe/Mediterranean, Baltic. Spring, summer, fall, Middle East/North Africa.

THE LINE When Royal Caribbean International acquired the Spanish tour and cruise operator Pullmantur in 2006, it also got two of the latter's ships, *Blue Dream* (originally Renaissance's *R6*) and *Blue Moon* (Renaissance's *R7*). Both were moved to Celebrity Cruises, and during a month-long dry dock, some

THE FLEET	BUILT/RENOVATED	TONNAGE	PASSENGERS
Azamara Journey	2000/2006	30,277	710
Azamara Quest	2000/2007	30,277	710

facilities and attractions were added to make the ships more consistent with the Celebrity fleet, including a wine bar, junior suites, and a variety of Celebrity's most popular signature elements. But soon after, Royal Caribbean decided to create a new brand, Azamara Club Cruises, to be operated by Celebrity Cruises, and a new category, "deluxe," meant to fill the gap between the premium (such as Celebrity and Holland America) and luxury-category (Seabourn and Silverseas) cruises.

Azamara Club Cruises are designed mainly for experienced travelers who seek an affordable alternative to big cruise ships and are intended to compete specifically with the popular Oceania Cruises (which operates three of the "R" ships). The two newly acquired ships were renamed *Azamara Journey* and *Azamara Quest*. The name, Azamara, was created for elements of two words—aza from the Italian *azzurro*, meaning blue, and mar or *mare*, meaning sea in Italian.

Now, after two years in operation, Azamara has found that as good as the product was, its focus needed to be sharpened, first by adding "Club" to its name to convey the clublike ambience of its ships, and then by refining its identity for a more upmarket audience in four aspects. Azamara's primary focus has been and will continue to be destination-oriented, but enhanced with longer port stays that range from late-night departures to three overnights. In addition to having more time to explore a destination, shore excursions will provide deeper and more unusual perspectives.

A second new spotlight is on food and wine. From its start, Azamara has emphasized fine dining, but this will be enhanced with guest chefs and partnerships with known culinary organizations. A series of food-and-culture Festivals at Sea will be unveiled later in 2010. There will also be greater stress on wine, highlighting, for example, boutique wineries from around the world and providing the featured wines complimentary at lunch and dinner. The third new focus is onboard service, which is being reorganized. Concierge services will be available to all passengers, while butlers (who are being given more training to upgrade their skills) will be available in suites only. The final focus is on health and wellness so that passengers can come away looking and feeling healthier and more youthful. In addition to new onboard spa and fitness programs, these experiences are to be extended ashore.

With these new features, Azamara is making the cruise more inclusive (and thus, more expensive). For example, in addition to the complimentary wines with meals, there no longer is a charge for bottled water, specialty coffees and teas, and self-service laundries. Free shuttle buses will be provided, where available, between the port and town. The charge for dining in specialty restaurants is waived for suite passengers. Gratuities for the cabin and restaurant staffs are now included in the price of the cruises; prices are no longer shown in the line's brochures but are available on Azamara's Web site only.

STYLE Azamara ships have style, combining the glamour of traditional cruising with opulent decor, yet they are comfortable with a relaxing atmosphere. For example, dress is usually resort-casual, and no evenings require formal attire.

DISTINCTIVE FEATURES Butler service in suites; concierge amenities in all cabins; robes and slippers. Specialty restaurants. Internet access, Wi-Fi. Advance bookings for Astral Spa. Onboard check-in and luggage valet for some ports.

RATES Rates do not include airport or port fees or alcoholic beverages.

Special fares and discounts Advance-purchase fares offer up to 50% discounts on cruise-only rates (suites excluded).

- **THIRD/FOURTH PASSENGER:** Yes.
- **CHILDREN'S FARE:** None.
- **SINGLE SUPPLEMENT:** 150% available on select sailings. Inquire for details.

PAST PASSENGERS The Captain's Club, Azamara's loyalty program, is similar to that of Celebrity's and is open to all passengers after their first Azamara Club cruise. Passengers can enroll on Azamara Club's Web site. The program has three levels, determined by the number of cruises you take. Azamara is planning to launch a new loyalty program called Le Club Voyage. Details have not been announced, but it is expected to be an enhanced version of the Captain's Club, its current program.

THE LAST WORD Azamara Club Cruises has had only two seasons of operation and is still a work in progress. Its formula is right for a certain, growing segment of the market. If the line can maintain high standards for its price range, despite the economy, it should fair well, especially with those turned off by bigger ships. Almost anyone with cultivated tastes would enjoy an Azamara Club cruise. For those who crave the shipboard intimacy that used to be a common feature of cruising, and who are not averse to sometimes providing their own activities, these are just the ships.

Look for Azamara Club to offer more shorter itineraries and more overnights, including an increase in two- to three-night overnights.

THE SHIPS In 2007, Royal Caribbean created Azamara Club Cruises as a new deluxe brand—between premium and luxury—meant to be a competitor to Oceania Cruises. In dry dock, 34 junior suites were created (by taking three cabins and making them two), as well as a wine bar where fine wines by the glass are offered and tastings, seminars, and food and wine mini-pairings are held. Its two specialty restaurants were refurbished and some popular Celebrity signature elements were added. Concierge services were expanded as well.

The highly regarded "R ships," as the eight former Renaissance Cruises vessels were called, were unusual not only because of their compact size but

Azamara Journey	QUALITY 6	VALUE B
Azamara Quest	QUALITY 6	VALUE B
REGISTRY Malta	LENGTH 593 feet	BEAM 95 feet
CABINS 348	DRAFT 20 feet	SPEED 22 knots
MAXIMUM PASSENGERS	PASSENGER DECKS 9	ELEVATORS 4
804	CREW 390	SPACE RATIO 43.5

Azamara Club Cruises Standard Features

Officers European Union.

Staff *Dining:* European; *Cabin:* Philippines, India, international; *Cruise:* European and South American.

Dining facilities One main dining room with open seating for breakfast, lunch, and dinner; indoor/outdoor Lido buffet breakfast and lunch; alternative restaurants. Alcoholic beverages and some menu items (such as Prime C's kobe beef and Aqualina's wine–food pairings menu) are extra.

Special diets Request at time of booking.

Room service 24-hour menu; butler service in all cabins.

Dress code Country-club casual but not sloppy during the day; informal in evening. No formal evenings.

Cabin amenities Direct-dial phone; bath with shower, suites with tubs; robes, slippers, television with CNN when satellite reception permits, music channels. Hair dryers, safes, minibars, umbrellas, binoculars, fresh flowers, pillow menu, tote bags. Butler service and concierge amenities in all cabins and suites.

Electrical outlets 110/220 AC.

Wheelchair access 6 cabins.

Recreation and entertainment Card room, library, casino, show lounge, bars/lounges. Bingo, lotto, culinary demonstrations, wine tastings.

Sports and other activities Outside swimming pools, exercise classes, table tennis, deck games, Jacuzzi, BAGGO (popular bean bag sport), Blongo, basic golf.

Beauty and fitness Barber, beauty salon; health club, gym, and sauna; spa with beauty treatments; exercise classes, personal training for a fee.

Other facilities Boutiques, laundry and dry-cleaning services, meeting facilities, Internet access, passenger-operated washers and dryers.

Children's facilities None.

Theme cruises None.

Smoking Not permitted in dining room or theater, cabins, or cabin verandas. Smoking is not permitted except in two designated areas: one indoor (part of one lounge) and one outdoor (near pool).

Azamara Club suggested tipping $12.25 per person per day added to passenger's bill at end of cruise; additional $4 per person per day for butler service in suites. 15% service charge added to beverage checks.

Credit cards Cruise/onboard charges: American Express, MasterCard, Visa, Discover.

because of their opulent period decor. Stairwells and corridors resemble those found in first class aboard transatlantic Cunard Line vessels of the 1920s. Some areas, including the main staircase, were inspired by the movie *Titanic*. The ships have an intimate, upscale feel. (In addition to Oceania's three R's, three R's sail for Princess Cruises.)

The ships' shallow draft and their comparatively short length enable them to dock at most ports and to call at out-of-the-way places where large ships often cannot go. Due to their limited number of passengers, the vessels never give the impression that they are taking over a destination. Although Azamara's activities and entertainment options are less varied or extensive as those on large ships, Azamara does a better job at entertaining passengers than most other companies operating ships this size.

Azamara Journey and *Azamara Quest* are largely smoke-free. Smoking is only permitted in the port side aft section of the Looking Glass Lounge (Deck 10) and outdoors, on the starboard forward section of the pool deck (Deck 9).

CABINS The 15 categories of accommodations comprise 7 basic types: inside, ocean view, sunset veranda, deluxe ocean view with veranda, Sky Suite, Royal Suite, and Penthouse Suite. Of the 348 cabins and suites, 93% are outside; of these, 62% have a balcony or larger veranda. While compact (depending on the category), the cabins are comfortable and attractively furnished. All accommodations have such amenities as fresh-cut flowers, fresh fruit, Elemis toiletries, Frette cotton robes, slippers, plasma televisions, and plush bedding. Six cabins (two inside, four outside) are wheelchair accessible. The four outside units are fully accessible with all doors 32 inches wide, no doorsills to the cabins, ramped bathroom thresholds, bathroom grab bars, lowered sinks and vanities, roll-in showers, fold-down shower benches, handheld shower heads, and other amenities.

The cabins are furnished with a minibar, safe, 23-inch plasma television (32 inches in Sky Suites; 42 inches in Royal Suites), phone with voice mail, hair dryer, an umbrella, personalized stationery, and complimentary use of binoculars. Passengers enjoy 24-hour room service, afternoon canapés, and complimentary shoeshine service. Passengers in suites get free garment pressing (limit two items per person on embarkation days), complimentary sodas and bottled water, as well as specialty coffees and other amenities.

Specifications 322 outside, 26 inside cabins; 4 Royal, 6 Penthouse, and 32 Sky Suites. Cabins range from 158 square feet inside to the more typical outside and veranda rooms at 170–175 square feet. Category 8 on Deck 6 are smaller outside cabins with obstructed views at 146 square feet.

DINING The ships have open seating in **Discoveries,** the main dining room; formal attire is not required. The venue provides an elegant and sophisticated setting for all three meals. With windows on three sides and the vessel's limited dimensions, the passing scene is visible from almost anywhere in the room. Recesses in the ceiling contain fresco-like paintings that add to the air of soft elegance that pervades this room. Menus offer an extensive variety of conventional choices and always include salad, pasta, and a vegetarian entree at dinner. Presentation is excellent.

The specialty restaurants are **Prime C** and **Aqualina.** Prime C is a steak house *par excellence,* featuring not only steak but lobster, lamb chops, and other selections. Entree of choice has to be the steak. Aqualina focuses on Mediterranean cuisine usually expressed in its variety of fish and preparation. However, it's not a typical Mediterranean restaurant as might be conceived stateside. A tasting menu is offered ($60 per person) with wine pairings for each course.

Passengers in standard cabins get two dinners in either of the specialty restaurants; those in suites have three. Thereafter, passengers may continue to dine in these venues on a space-available basis, with an extra charge for alcohol and gratuities. Both specialty venues provide highly personal service and great views of the sea through floor-to-ceiling windows. Indeed, the views make dining here worth booking, especially when there's something scenic to enjoy.

The specialty restaurants have their own wine lists with selections not available elsewhere on the ship. Vintage wines are pricey, a fact that received some comment from passengers; however, there are several reasonably priced, good choices for $25–$32 per bottle. An 18% gratuity is automatically added to your bill. Wine in all venues is provided by servers under the supervision of a wine specialist who serves as a resource for those less knowledgeable about wine. Although there is no charge for dining in the specialty restaurants, a $5 per person gratuity is recommended, and passengers are presented a charge form for this purpose, in spite of the per diem gratuity paid by all passengers for service throughout the ship.

The casual **Windows Café** is a delightful setting for breakfast, lunch, and a quick dinner. Breakfast includes such offerings as freshly squeezed orange juice, freshly baked bread, fresh and frozen fruit, an egg station, plus the standard cruise ship buffet. Lunch offers a range of salads in unusual presentations, a carved roast, pastas, a dessert table, and coffee. Dinner includes selections from the Discoveries Restaurant as well as a fresh sushi table and desserts. The Café has a sheltered outdoor deck at the stern. When weather conditions are right, it's a perfect dining spot.

The **Pool Grill,** open noon–6 p.m., serves the usual grill fare. On the main public room deck, **Mosaic Café** offers gourmet coffees, pastries, and, during lunch, sandwiches and wines are available for purchase.

SERVICE Although *Azamara Journey* and *Azamara Quest* have been in service for more than a year, the cruise experience is still a work in progress. Nonetheless, service by almost all individuals was professional, attentive, and caring. Where there was a shortfall, it was most often due to not having enough staff at the right place at the right time. To a greater-than-usual extent, management solicited passenger comments, including a special mid-cruise questionnaire that was immediately transcribed and followed up.

Service in the main dining room was always attentive and professional, but often slow, with as much as 40 minutes passing between the time of arrival and delivery of the appetizer. Service was better at tables for two, four, and six than at tables for eight. In the buffet restaurant, you carry your own tray, but once seated, the service is attentive in such matters as offering beverages and clearing away used dishes.

FACILITIES AND ACTIVITIES Shipboard activities are fairly traditional—quizzes, trivia, bingo, computer classes, seminars relating to spa and art auctions, and deck game competitions. There are a variety of lectures, some rather specialized. Cooking demonstrations were popular and well attended. Wine tastings are offered, one free for repeaters, others at nominal cost for all passengers. A good shipboard orchestra provides music for dancing. In the evenings, music in bars may be provided by a vocalist or harpist, and an assortment of other music is offered in venues throughout the vessel. The overall tone of these ships is quiet, with announcements confined to the once-a-day captain's navigational information, followed by a single summary of the day's activities by the cruise director.

The **Drawing Room,** with its illuminated old-fashioned glass dome and comfortable armchairs, is a popular and relaxing place for reading and offers views of the sea from large windows facing forward. The library collection is lackluster, so bring your own reading materials. **The Looking Glass** (Observation Lounge high on Deck 10 and forward) is the venue for daytime activities such as dance classes, evening receptions, and late-night disco. Predinner cocktails are served in the Discoveries Lounge, an intimate bar adjoining the main dining room. The casino at midship on Deck 5 was expanded to occupy most of the floor and seating area, but it was patronized little during our cruise.

Despite the ship's limited size, a great effort is made to offer many of the entertainment advantages of a larger vessel. Three musical reviews are staged by a fresh, highly talented Broadway-bound troupe. Comedians, magicians, and vocalists join the ship at various points along the way and provide high-quality entertainment. **Cabaret Lounge,** the showroom, has a true club-like atmosphere with good sightlines and an intimate ambience. No matter how popular the evening's show, there was never a problem getting a seat with a good view of the entertainment.

SPORTS, FITNESS, AND BEAUTY The ships' spas offer treatments not available on any Celebrity ships. Passengers in suites can have certain spa services in their rooms. The ships also have an outdoor spa—relaxation lounge and an aesthetics suite offering acupuncture at sea, laser hair removal, and microdermabrasion. Spa services are quite pricey, ranging from $125 for a body-sculpting session to $225 for a derma new hydralift facial.

A complete fitness schedule issued on the first day of the cruise includes such activities as walk-a-mile, Pilates, aerobics, stretch, and spin. There are also lectures on nutrition, metabolism, posture, and such. A physical program consultant is available by appointment. The gym is part of the spa complex and is in an attractive room with great sea views through floor-to-ceiling windows and a range of up-to-date equipment.

Carnival Cruise Lines

3655 NW 87th Avenue
Miami, FL 33178-2428
☎ 305-599-2600, 800-438-6744
or 800-CARNIVAL
www.carnival.com

TYPE OF SHIPS New, mod superliners and megaliners.

TYPE OF CRUISES Casual, contemporary, mass market. "Fun Ships" hallmark makes the ship the destination—as central to the cruise experience as the ports of call.

CRUISE LINE'S STRENGTHS
- lavish recreational and entertainment facilities
- fleet with unusual, innovative interiors
- value
- extensive shore excursions
- variety of dining venues
- quality of cuisine for price category

CRUISE LINE'S SHORTCOMINGS
- megaliner size
- little relief from crowds and glitz
- lack of outdoor promenade deck on some ships
- long lines for facilities and services

FELLOW PASSENGERS From all walks of life, ages 3–93. Although Carnival's image has been that of a shipload of young swingers partying day and night (an image Carnival once cultivated to attract young people to cruising), the mix now is more likely to range from Joe Sixpack and his Nike-shod kids to Lester and Alice celebrating their 50th wedding anniversary. The cruises lend themselves to families with or without kids, honeymooners, married couples, singles, and seniors. Average age: 43. On a typical cruise, 40% are ages 35–55; 30% younger than 35 (including 575,000 kids annually); 30% older than 55. Fifty percent are repeat cruisers, and of those, 70% are Carnival repeaters. Most have middle to upper-middle income.

Recommended for First-time cruisers who want an active, high-energy, party atmosphere; families, young singles, and couples; young-at-heart of any age; those who enjoy Las Vegas glitz or similar ambience.

Not recommended for Small-ship devotees; sophisticated travelers who prefer ultraluxury and individual travel; anyone seeking a quiet or cerebral travel experience; those who consider Martha's Vineyard their ideal vacation spot.

CRUISE AREAS AND SEASONS Bahamas, Caribbean, Mexican Riviera, and West Coast, year-round. Alaska, Bermuda, Hawaii, and New England/Canada, seasonally.

THE LINE In 38 years, Carnival Cruise Lines went from one ship that ran aground on its maiden voyage to becoming the largest, most influential company in the cruise business, having revolutionized the nature of cruises along the way. Its story is the stuff of legends.

The late Ted Arison, a cruise executive in Florida, and a maverick travel company in Boston bought the *Mardi Gras* (formerly the *Empress of Canada*) in 1972. After three years of losses and near bankruptcy, Arison took over the company, assumed its $5 million debt, bought the assets—*Mardi Gras*—for $1, and created the "Fun Ship" concept, turning a profit in his first year and adding two more ships.

THE FLEET	BUILT/RENOVATED	TONNAGE	PASSENGERS
Carnival Conquest	2002/08	110,000	2,974
Carnival Destiny	1996/05	101,353	2,642
Carnival Dream	2009	130,000	3,646
Carnival Ecstasy	1991/2000/06/09	70,367	2,052
Carnival Elation	1998/2009	70,367	2,052
Carnival Fantasy	1990/2000/03/09	70,367	2,056
Carnival Fascination	1994/06/08	70,367	2,052
Carnival Freedom	2007	110,000	2,974
Carnival Glory	2003	110,000	2,974
Carnival Imagination	1995/2008	70,367	2,052
Carnival Inspiration	1996/2008	70,367	2,052
Carnival Legend	2002	88,500	2,124
Carnival Liberty	2005	110,000	2,974
Carnival Magic	2011	130,000	3,652
Carnival Miracle	2004	88,500	2,124
Carnival Paradise	1998/2009	70,367	2,052
Carnival Pride	2002	88,500	2,124
Carnival Sensation	1993/2009	70,367	2,052
Carnival Spirit	2001	88,500	2,124
Carnival Splendor	2008	113,000	3,006
Carnival Triumph	1999	102,000	2,758
Carnival Valor	2004	110,000	2,974
Carnival Victory	2000	102,000	2,758
Unnamed	2012	130,000	3,690

Arison's aim was to take the stuffiness out of cruising, abandon the elitist image on which classic ocean liners had thrived, and make cruises fun and available to everyone, particularly to middle America, who never dreamed of a holiday at sea. Through the 1970s, Carnival ships broke occupancy records, while traditional companies were sinking all around.

Carnival continued to defy conventional wisdom. In the late 1970s, with spiraling shipbuilding costs and the oil crisis putting the future of cruising in doubt, Carnival ordered a new ship, *Tropicale,* whose technology set new industry standards, changed ship profiles, and enhanced Carnival's Fun Ship concept. Then, a decade after its inauspicious beginning, Carnival added three radically new ships—*Holiday, Jubilee,* and *Celebration*—which became trendsetters of the 1980s and beyond. Their design and madcap decor were profoundly different from ocean liners of the past.

To prepare for the 21st century, Carnival added eight megaliners, each for more than 2,600 passengers, and lifted eyebrows with such names as *Fantasy* and *Ecstasy*. They were followed in 1996 with 101,000-ton, 3,400-passenger *Carnival Destiny,* the world's largest ship at the time. Carnival was so pleased with her performance and passenger response it ordered four more.

From 2001 to 2009, Carnival added three new classes of ships for a total of 12 ships. Carnival's new ship investment in the 1990s exceeded $5 billion; those so far for the 21st century added more than $4 billion, bringing the fleet total to 22 ships. When the new ships for its sister companies—a total of 15—are added in, the expenditure reached more than $8 billion by 2009.

Under Arison's son Micky—Carnival Corp.'s chairman since 1990—Carnival Cruise Lines' young, aggressive team has marketed cruises as the universal dream vacation for everyone. The line carries about 3.6 million passengers a year. A publicly held company since 1987, Carnival Corp. broadened its base (and buffed its image) by acquiring the classic Holland America Line in 1989. In the 1990s, it acquired ownership of ultraluxurious Seabourn Cruise Line, Costa Cruises (Europe's largest line), and Cunard Line. More recently, it out-maneuvered Royal Caribbean for the purchase of P&O Princess Cruises, adding six brands to its inventory. These acquisitions give Carnival a total of 85 ships and a huge share of the world cruise market. All 11 lines operate as separate companies, each with a sharp focus; together, they give Carnival Corp. tremendous clout. By 2010, the companies under the Carnival umbrella will have a total of 99 cruise ships.

In 1999, Carnival became the first major cruise line to launch direct booking on its Web site. In recent years, the line has introduced departures from new gateways, particularly new U.S. ports, such as Baltimore, Maryland; Jacksonville, Florida; and Mobile, Alabama advancing the "close-to-home" trend following the 9/11 attacks. For 2010, the line is using 18 North American home ports and will have year-round departures from Charleston, South Carolina, for the first time. It launched its first Mediterranean cruise in 2005 and got even more involved in Europe with a joint venture with the Spanish cruise line Iberojet Cruceros, in which Carnival Corp. owns 75% and Orizonia Corp., Iberojet Cruceros' owning company, has a 25% stake. Iberojet operates the 834-passenger *Grand Voyager* and the 1,196-passenger *Grand Mistral.* After a three-year absence, Carnival is returning to Europe with its newest ship, the 3,690-passenger

Carnival Magic, sailing on 7- to 12-day Mediterranean cruises round-trip from her homeport, Barcelona, from May to October 2011.

At the same time, Carnival has expanded its focus on families, adding extensive children's facilities to all its ships. The line carries about 625,000 children a year, and its children's program, Camp Carnival, employs one of the cruise industry's largest staffs of trained personnel—more than 100 child counselors spread over 22 ships on a full-time basis, with additional personnel hired during peak periods. Available fleetwide is the Club O2 teen program, developed with The Coca-Cola Company. More recently, the Circle "C" program for kids ages 12–14 has been added fleetwide.

Vacation Guarantee, a Carnival innovation, allows a dissatisfied passenger, after notifying the purser's office, to leave a cruise at the first non-U.S. port of call and get a prorated refund. Another Carnival first is a 24-hour, toll-free hotline—☎ 877-TVL-HTLN (885-4856)—for passengers who encounter a travel emergency (such as severe weather or an airline strike) en route to or returning from their cruise. Passengers outside the United States can call collect: ☎ 305-406-4779.

The ships offer passengers Internet access and Wi-Fi in the public areas; the newest ships have Wi-Fi from stem to stern, including in cabins. In a joint venture with Wireless Maritime Services, Carnival has outfitted its fleet with technology that enables guests with any cell phone service to make or receive calls as they do on land, no matter how far out to sea they are. Calls are charged at international roaming rates as determined by the carrier and billed directly to passengers' cell phone bills. The technology also enables passengers to send and receive text messages on their phone and wireless devices such as Blackberrys.

Not to be outdone by its competitors in the fun-and-games category, Carnival is the first cruise line to offer Water Wars, a popular attraction found in amusement parks in 22 countries. Created by Minnesota-based Water Wars, the units consist of two custom-built "battle stations," in which participants propel water balloons through the air via catapults in an effort to splash their opponents. Located adjacent to the main pool area, the feature has been installed fleetwide. The recent redesign of the pool deck, upgrading, and refurbishing of the eight *Fantasy*-class ships was part of an ambitious $250 million program completed in 2009.

Carnival can be found on Twitter at **www.twitter.com/carnivalcruise**; Facebook **at www.facebook.com/carnival**; and Flickr at **www.flickr.com/ photos/carnivalcruiselines.** Also, the line's Web site now has a new community and social-media hub called "Funville."

STYLE Youthful and casual, Fun Ships have so much action and diversions that the ship itself is the cruise experience. The emphasis on fun aims to get people out of their cabins and into public spaces to become part of the action. The variety of activity and entertainment attracts a range of passengers, but the basic appeal is to the young and young at heart—at reasonable prices.

An important part of creating Carnival has been Joe Farcus, an interior architect and decorator. He believes people go on vacation to have fun, and his job is to create the surroundings and atmosphere for it. If you accept his flamboyant decor as entertaining, you will find it ingenious. But sometimes, so much bombards the senses that the impact is more exhausting than exhilarating.

Another characteristic: Carnival has standardized features on its ships. If you see a waterslide on one ship, you can count on it being on the others. A menu with four desserts on one ship will be on others. Even deck names are the same. The uniformity helps keep down costs, and consistency is reassuring to passengers—and to their travel agents.

Carnival cabins are furnished with the Comfort Bed sleep system with plush mattresses, luxurious duvets, high-quality linens, and comfortable pillows, including a "suite pillow" menu for guests in suites. The items can be ordered on a special Web site, **www.carnivalcomfortbed.com.** Other new features on the ships are children's water parks and Serenity adults-only deck areas. Carnival has continued to improve its cuisine by hiring renowned French master chef Georges Blanc to create gourmet menus for the line's restaurants fleetwide. Blanc has also trained Carnival chefs at his restaurants in France and aboard the line's ships. Passengers now have three dining options with Your Choice Dining: first and second seating or "Your Choice." Generally, there is open seating in the upper seating area of the dining room and traditional fixed seating in the lower area. Dining assignments can be confirmed at the time of booking.

Carnival's revamped and enhanced Web site has new and expanded features, including an interactive destination map, virtual tours, a close-to-home cruise locator, and **www.carnivalconnections.com,** an online community where family and friends can meet to plan and manage their cruise. Shore excursions and spa treatments can also be purchased on the Web site. Also revised were the cabin categories to define them more clearly. The reclassification is now based on location: midship, aft, and forward, along with proximity to public areas and specific decks.

In 2009, Carnival introduced some important changes fleetwide: With FunPass, passengers can register online up to the day prior to sailing and get a printable document allowing them to "fast track" through embarkation when they arrive at the cruise terminal. Carnival is testing a new service to speed embarking at the port of Miami with a self-service kiosk to complete the registration process. To use it, passengers must have pre-registered online and be a U.S. or Canadian citizen or from a visa-waiver country.

Among other new features, "Behind the Fun" is a guided tour of the inner workings of a Carnival ship. The three-and-a-half-hour tour costs $95 per person, is available on seven-day itineraries, and can be booked at the shore excursion desk. Each tour is limited to 16 participants who must be age 13 or older. Carnival's travel insurance now includes severe weather watch and warning protection, as well as job loss protection. The plan must be purchased at least 14 days prior to the cruise departure date; prices begin at $49 per person and vary by cruise length. For passengers who purchase their air transportation from Carnival, the line's FlyAweigh air-sea program now provides full protection (at no cost) when a passenger encounters a trip disruption en route to their cruise. To receive the service, passengers should contact Carnival's 24/7 Travel Hotline to rebook their reservation.

DISTINCTIVE FEATURES Ships' design and decor, children's programs, 24-hour pizzerias, miniature golf, free ice-cream and yogurt stations, sushi bars fleetwide, steak-house supper clubs, fitness centers, tuxedo rentals, vacation guarantee, golf program, travelers' hotline, self-service digital photo printing kiosks, Internet cafes, wireless Internet access, cell phone facilitation, water parks fleetwide.

RATES All include port fees.

Special fares and Super Savers Early-bird program provides a range of discounts.

- **CHILDREN'S FARE:** Same as deeply discounted third-/fourth-person rates. Passengers younger than age 21 must be accompanied by a parent, grandparent, or legal guardian 25 years old or older in the cabin. Exceptions apply to married couples and to children traveling with parents in a separate cabin.
- **SINGLE SUPPLEMENT:** 150% or 200%, depending on category.

PAST PASSENGERS Carnival Concierge Club is the line's loyalty program, exclusively for "platinum" cardholders—that is, passengers who have sailed on Carnival ten or more times. The program provides cardholders with a staffed concierge desk at the purser's station; dedicated phone line on all Carnival ships; priority embarkation, debarkation, and tender boarding; guaranteed supper club reservations and dining times; personalized stationery and custom-designed Carnival logo items; canapés one evening delivered to cabin; $20 entry fee into blackjack tournament; spa priority reservations and complimentary treatment upgrade; complimentary wash-and-fold laundry service; special luggage tags; and welcome letter from Carnival's president. After their first cruise, all passengers receive a two-year subscription to *Currents,* the line's onboard magazine, which includes discounts. A repeater's party is offered on five-day or longer cruises.

THE LAST WORD Carnival has had an enormous impact on cruises, particularly those aimed at the mass market. Despite its success, a Carnival cruise isn't for everybody. The ships have more glitter than glamour. Some people love them; others think they redefine tacky. For the generation that grew up with shopping malls and Las Vegas–style glitz, Carnival's gargantuan, flashy ships may feel like home. But if big and boisterous is not your style, Carnival is probably not for you. However, even the most buttoned-down party poopers are often turned on by the Carnival neon and end up having the time of their lives.

Note: Carnival Cruise Lines prohibits passengers from bringing alcoholic and nonalcoholic beverages on board, including bottles of water. Carnival's policy allows passengers to bring one bottle of wine or Champagne per person (21 years and older) on board only during embarkation at the beginning of the cruise. Any additional quantity of wine, Champagne, alcoholic, and non-alcoholic beverages will be confiscated and discarded without compensation.

THE SHIPS Launched between 1990 and 1998, the eight, 70,367-ton *Fantasy*-class superliners went a long way to define the Carnival experience. With their exhuberant, flashy, often zany, decor and nonstop activity and entertainment, they were the very essence of Carnival's "Fun Ships," driving the line's phenomenal growth and enabling it to become the industry powerhouse that it is. Now, after almost two decades of service, the *Fantasy*-class ships were recently given a stem-to-stern $250 million renovation, appropriately dubbed the "Evolution of Fun," to change their image and redirect their goal to make them "Fun Ships" for the whole family.

Carnival Standard Features

Officers Italian.

Staff International.

Dining facilities Two main dining rooms with four seatings (except *Spirit* class, one dining room). Breakfast and lunch cafeteria-style and Seaview Bistro dinner service in Lido restaurant; midnight buffet. Lido restaurant is four-in-one: pizzeria, Asian, trattoria, American grill. New York–style deli, sushi bars; steak-house restaurant ($30 surcharge) on newest ships. Your Choice Dining offers three options.

Special diets Low-salt, diabetic, vegetarian.

Room service 24 hours, upgraded menu.

Dress code Casual; no shorts in evening; two formal nights on 7-day; tuxedos not required, semiformal dress is acceptable.

Cabin amenities Closed-circuit television; safe. Bath with shower; international direct-dial phones. Hair dryers on *Destiny, Conquest, Spirit*, and *Carnival Splendor* class; other ships on request. Terry robes fleetwide.

Electrical outlets 110 AC.

Wheelchair access 14–28 cabins, depending on ship.

Recreation and entertainment Casino, bingo, dance club, library; 10 bar/lounges (16 on *Spirit* class; 18 *Destiny* class; 22 *Conquest* class); two-deck show lounges (three-deck on *Destiny, Conquest,* and *Spirit* classes).

Sports and other activities Three or four outside swimming pools, shuffleboard, jogging tracks (*Fantasy, Destiny, Spirit* classes), table tennis, volleyball, and basketball on some ships.

The extensive makeover included such new attractions as an expansive water park on the Verandah Deck at the top of the ship, with a dizzyingly circuitous, 300-foot-long, four-story-high waterslide—the largest slide at sea. This slide sits alongside twin-lane, 82-foot-long racing waterslides—all certain to please most of the 625,000 kids Carnival carries yearly—and probably even some of their parents.

The main pool area, located midship, has been given a resort-style look with umbrellas to shade the lounging and seating area at the pool's edge. A thatched roof covers one of the two whirlpools at either end of the swimming pool, and faux palm trees further enhance the tropical ambience.

Inside the ships, walls were knocked down to create 50 new interconnecting cabins, designed specifically for families. At the same time, the Circle "C" program for 12–14-year-olds was created to complement Camp Carnival for younger kids and Club O2 for older teens. The facility replaces a large space formerly used as a meeting room.

Adults weren't forgotten in the refurbishment. They have Serenity, an exclusive adults-only outdoor retreat on Deck 11 aft. Designed as an oasis of

Beauty and fitness Beauty salon, sauna. Spas on all ships; full gym, exercise classes, body treatments. Spa fare on menus. Spa treatments can be booked online in advance of cruise.

Other facilities Boutiques, tuxedo rentals, infirmary, DVD of cruise souvenir ($9.95–$29.95), and coin-operated laundry facilities; Internet cafes, Wi-Fi fleetwide.

Children's facilities Year-round, with supervised activities for four age levels from toddlers to teens. Video arcades, waterslides, playroom, teen club/ disco, children's menus, high chairs. Babysitting, 10 p.m.–3 a.m., $6 per hour for first child, $4 for each additional child in same family; children under age 2 also welcome. Passengers under age 21 must be accompanied by an adult older than age 25 staying in the same cabin.

Theme cruises Some.

Smoking Smoke-free dining room, main show lounge, selected lounges, and certain areas of the ships.

Carnival suggested tipping $10 per person per day added automatically to passenger's onboard account, which can also be prepaid when booking the cruise; 15% added to wine and bar bill.

Credit cards Cruise and shipboard charges: American Express, MasterCard, Visa, Discover, Optima.

comfort and tranquility where adults can get away from the kids, the retreat is furnished with plush chaise lounges and chairs, colorful oversize umbrellas, two whirlpools, and a separate shaded area. Bar service is provided.

Other enhancements and upgrades include completely renovated cabins and suites, including new bathrooms; flat-panel televisions in cabins; and other amenities such as a nine-hole miniature golf course, a renovated 12,000-square-foot spa, updated dining rooms, a New York–style deli, an atrium lobby bar, a new purpose-built conference facility, a patisserie serving specialty coffees and sweets, and new photo and art galleries. High-tech sound and lighting systems for live music and entertainment venues also were incorporated into the revamp.

Extensive cosmetic enhancements were made to virtually all public rooms and areas, with new upholstery, furniture, and wall coverings in the main show lounge, piano bar, dance club, and main dining rooms. The Internet cafe was relocated to the Empress Deck, and new workstations were added. Overall, the ships now sport a contemporary, more sophisticated look.

ITINERARIES *See* Itinerary Index. Designed to appeal to families, particularly in today's economic climate, are short three-, four-, and five-day cruises, which are the specialty of *Fantasy*-class ships. Several ships also have seven-day cruises occasionally.

Carnival Ecstasy / *Carnival Fantasy*	**QUALITY 4**	**VALUE B**
Carnival Elation	**QUALITY 5**	**VALUE B**
Carnival Fascination / *Carnival Imagination*	**QUALITY 6**	**VALUE A**
Carnival Inspiration	**QUALITY 6**	**VALUE A**
Carnival Paradise	**QUALITY 6**	**VALUE A**
Carnival Sensation	**QUALITY 4**	**VALUE B**
REGISTRY *Ecstasy/Elation/* *Fantasy/Paradise* Panama; *Fascination/Imagination/Inspiration/Sensation* Bahamas	**LENGTH** 855 feet	**BEAM** 118 feet
CABINS 1,026/1,028	**DRAFT** 26 feet	**SPEED** 21 knots
MAXIMUM PASSENGERS	**PASSENGER DECKS** 10	**ELEVATORS** 14
2,610/2,606	**CREW** 920	**SPACE RATIO** 34

CABINS The *Fantasy*-class ships have some of the largest standard cabins and junior suites of any ships in their price category. They are finished in light oak, and although color schemes vary, the furniture and decor are essentially the same: basic and comfortable. Recent renovations brought a contemporary minimalist look to the decor with white bedding topped with a colorful throw. Verandas were added to 98 of the outside cabins on *Carnival Ecstasy*, *Carnival Fascination*, and *Carnival Sensation*. Sixty-two of the veranda cabins are located aft, 24 are midship, and 12 near the stern. Particularly attractive for families are the 50 new interconnecting cabins, created by combining cabins. The ship's 54 suites were remodeled with updated wall coverings, carpeting, tile work, lighting fixtures, and newly installed bathrooms. Several suites were modified to create larger, extended balconies.

Almost all cabins have twin beds that convert to king-size—a Carnival innovation quickly copied by other cruise lines. All have Comfort Beds, which have upgraded bed linens, duvets, and a pillow menu (in suites only). In the recent refurbishment, cabins and suites got flat-panel televisions with channels for movies, cartoons, and satellite programs (depending on the ship's location); remodeled bathrooms have roomy shower stalls, but they lack shelf space for toiletries. Bathrooms contain soap and some toiletries; hair dryers are available on request. Closet space is adequate for short, warm-weather cruises. Cabins have international direct-dial phones, a desk/dressing table, and wall safes. Outside cabins have picture windows. All ships have self-service laundry rooms with washers, dryers, irons, and ironing boards—a big plus for families traveling with children.

Specifications 389 inside cabins, 514 outside (98 newly added verandas on *Sensation* and *Ecstasy* and 50 connecting family cabins); 54 suites with verandas (28 suites with bathtub Jacuzzis). Standard dimensions, 183–190 square feet; 953 with twins convertible to doubles; 19 inside with upper and lower berths; no singles. All ships have wheelchair-accessible cabins.

DINING Each ship has two dining rooms with two seatings for breakfast and lunch, and four seatings for dinner at 5:45 p.m., 6:15 p.m., 8 p.m., and 8:30 p.m. In 2009, Carnival introduced the "Your Choice Dining" program, offering passengers three dining options: early or late assigned seats and open seating, especially appealing to those who prefer less regimentation. There has been some reconfiguration of the dining rooms and incorporation of entertainment into the schedule (Carnival's waiters normally dance in the dining room between the main course service and dessert) as the program is being implemented gradually, but it should be available on all the ships by summer 2010. Generally, on ships with bi-level dining rooms, open seating is available in the upper seating area, and traditional fixed seating is found in the lower area. Dining assignments can be confirmed at time of booking.

When booking, passengers are asked to choose either Early dining at 6 p.m., Late dining at 8:15 p.m., or Your Time dining, any time between 5:45 p.m. and 9:30 p.m. (depending on the ship and sailing date). Assignments are accommodated on a first-come, first-served basis. If your choice is not available, you can confirm an alternate choice and be wait-listed for your first preference. Waiting lists are cleared prior to sailing, and passengers are notified via email. Your Choice passengers may request any table size or waiter and are normally seated upon arrival at the dining room. But if there's a wait time, passengers are given a pager and are free to relax elsewhere.

Restaurants have round tables for eight people in the center of the room; the sides are lined with rectangular tables, which are sometimes difficult to get in and out of. All earn criticism for high noise levels.

Breakfast, lunch, and midnight buffet are served cafeteria-style in **Windows on the Sea** on the Lido Deck. The restaurant, with its handsome, newly renovated interior, has independent food stations, including a new Mongolian wok where you select your choice of meat or shrimp, vegetables, and noodles and have the dish prepared as you watch. A rotisserie has been added as well. **Seaview Bistro,** an alternative casual dinner service available fleetwide, offers specialty salads, pastas, steaks, and desserts in a cafe setting. It operates each evening 6–9:30 in the Lido restaurant. Service is buffet style, but waiters refill drink orders and serve food requests. Another winner is the around-the-clock pizzeria, offering delicious pizzas with varied toppings, fresh Caesar salads, and warm garlic rolls. All ships have sushi bars.

In recent years, Carnival has made a real effort to upgrade the quality, selection, and variety of the cuisine served throughout the ships. The line has further improved its cuisine by adding gourmet selections created by French master chef Georges Blanc to restaurant menus fleetwide and training its chefs at Blanc's restaurants in France. The line also offers menus with lighter, more contemporary cuisine and an expanded wine list.

SERVICE Dining staff generally earn good marks, but cabin attendants get mixed reviews. Cruise directors and their staff are very professional, but the cruise director on ships of this size is in little evidence except when he or she is on stage. Recent passengers have reported that contacting their room steward or the purser's desk by phone was nearly impossible during their cruise; it appears to be an ongoing problem that Carnival still has not corrected. In addition, boarding passengers are not escorted to their cabins but instead are given a ship diagram and directed to find their cabins on their own, which often results in disorientation for new-to-cruising passengers. The bottom line: Megaliners offer many wonderful facilities and options, but personal service is not among them.

FACILITIES AND ACTIVITIES   The ships' array of activities include bingo, a singles party, a newlywed game, a passenger talent show, horse racing, ballroom and country line dance classes, masquerades, wine and cheese parties, and sing-alongs. There are also daily showings of first-run movies and abundant boutiques. Some ships have a library/lounge, but I suggest you bring your own books and reading material.

Most evening entertainment on *Fantasy* ships takes place on Decks 8 and 9, where many of the bars, lounges, disco, and nightclubs are located, as well as a casino with more than 200 slot machines, blackjack tables, roulette, and other games.

At the forward end of the ship is the spectacular two-deck show lounge where nightly entertainment is staged on the scale of a Las Vegas extravaganza; it's outstanding. At the stern is the opulent Majestic Bar, with a king's ransom in marble and onyx. At the stern, you will find another bar and large lounge, where you can catch a cabaret or the naughty comedy act.

SPORTS, FITNESS, AND BEAUTY   The biggest change in the makeover of the *Fantasy* ship is on Deck 11, the Verandah Deck, where the aft third has been converted into an expansive water park dominated by the largest slide at sea—a winding 300-foot-long, four-story-high waterslide—and twin-lane, 82-foot-long racing waterslides, plus a variety of water spouts.

The main pool area, midship, now has a resort-style look with umbrellas to shade the lounging and seating area at the pool's edge. A thatched roof covers one of the two whirlpools at either end of the swimming pool, and faux palm trees further enhance the tropical ambience. Adults aren't forgotten here. They have Serenity, an exclusive adults-only outdoor retreat on Deck 11 aft. Designed as an oasis of comfort and tranquility where adults can get away from the kids, the retreat is furnished with plush chaise lounges and chairs, colorful oversize umbrellas, two whirlpools, and a separate shaded area. Bar service is provided there as well. Most Carnival ships also have a secluded deck area for topless sunbathing.

In addition to great water recreation, there's mini-golf, Ping-Pong, shuffleboard, and volleyball too. On Caribbean and Mexican cruises, depending on their ports, you can play golf, sail, ride horseback, bike, hike, snorkel, scuba dive, and windsurf.

The Sports Deck has a fully equipped gym with trained instructors, separate locker rooms, dressing rooms, showers for men and women, whirlpools, saunas, steam rooms, and a 500-foot outside jogging track. Or one can choose from an array of exercise and aerobics classes. Instructors will also create a fitness regimen for you to follow at home.

Carnival's golf program provides play at 50 courses in the Bahamas, Caribbean, Hawaii, Europe, and Mexico. It offers one-on-one, 30- or 60-minute instruction from PGA teaching pros aboard ship and on golf excursions. Golf packages include greens fees, instruction, cart rental or caddie, and transportation to and from courses. Prices range from $50 for onboard lessons to

$225 for golf excursions. Equipment rentals include Nike-brand clubs, golf shoes, and apparel.

The beauty salon and spa, operated by the Steiner Group, a British-based company, offer a variety of body and facial treatments for women and men in private rooms. The popular gentle touch tooth whitening is $199 for 40 minutes. Carnival's Web site lists more than 30 different spa treatments, which can be booked online prior to your cruise. The spa and gym on all *Fantasy* ships have been expanded with new facilities on the Sports Deck. The fitness center has new equipment, along with a full-body workout circuit and an aerobics studio with yoga, Pilates, or spinning classes. The facility is staffed 7 a.m.–8 p.m.

CHILDREN'S FACILITIES Camp Carnival, which handles 600,000 kids fleetwide annually, is a year-round program with a wide array of activities supervised by trained counselors for children in different age groups: toddlers (ages 2–5), juniors (ages 6–8), intermediate (ages 9–11), Circle "C" for teens (ages 12–14), and Club O2 for older teens (ages 15–17). Young children enjoy puppet making, finger painting, and learning the alphabet and numbers; older kids have pizza parties, scavenger hunts, and lip-synch contests and play bingo, charades, and Twister. Teens can participate in the Club O2 program with activities ranging from disco parties and star-search contests to evening deck parties. All ships have video arcades, wading pools, playrooms, teens' club/discos, children's menus, and high chairs. One playroom is geared toward toddlers; another is designed for kids ages 6–11 and is stocked with age-appropriate toys, games, and puzzles, including such popular pastimes as air hockey, foosball, and "pop-a-shot" basketball, along with the latest video games. For older kids, there's an educational computer lab on board with computer games. Teens have **Virtual World,** photography workshops, late-night movies, and disco parties. The new Circle "C" facility for 12- to 14-year-old teens has been incorporated into Atlantic Deck forward. The center features a high-tech sound and lighting system, plasma-screen televisions displaying movies and music videos, a touch-screen jukebox, and gaming pods with the latest video games and consoles.

A youth fitness and spa program, introduced originally on *Carnival Miracle* and now available fleetwide, allows kids ages 12–14 and their parents to have body and beauty treatments together on port days at discounted rates. Also featured is ExerSeas, a recreational fitness program designed to encourage kids to enjoy a diversity of fun physical activity from obstacle courses and basketball to popular games. A-B-Seas is a reading program in which youth counselors read popular children's books to parents and kids in the ships' libraries, and then parents and kids present their own creative interpretations of the stories through puppet shows, skits, and other group activities. A science program, H2Ocean, offers a variety of fun, hands-on science projects, allowing kids to make their own ice cream or miniature hovercrafts. The EduCruise program has been expanded to include more interactive projects focusing on the cultures, landmarks, history, and geography of the ships' destinations. Kid-friendly dining options include special children's menus in the main dining rooms and a program that enables kids to dine with the youth counselors on the Lido Deck. Carnival also offers teen shore excursions and Club O2 teen clubs.

Camp Carnival operates from 9 a.m. until 10 p.m. At 10 p.m., babysitting is available in the form of slumber parties for $6 per hour for the first child, $4 for each additional child. Carnival has a Fountain Fun Card for those younger than age 18, which is good for unlimited sodas from the bars and costs $13.75 on a three-day cruise and $32.25 on a seven-day cruise. For those who are 18 years old and older, the card costs $19 and $44.25, respectively.

SHORE EXCURSIONS   Passengers can review shore excursions and make reservations online at **www.carnivalcruises.com** after paying for their cruise. Carnival has greatly expanded the quality and variety of shore excursions it offers. Nonetheless, dockside in almost all Caribbean ports, there are plenty of vans with drivers/guides eager for your business and ready to design a tour to your liking. Prices depend on your ability to bargain and the driver's eagerness, but always agree on a fee before the tour begins.

An air/sea package is recommended for cruises departing from Port Canaveral combined with Orlando attractions because the Orlando International Airport, where most passengers arrive, is about an hour's drive from Port Canaveral, where the ships depart. There is no public transportation between the two; those traveling on their own must hire a taxi or rent a car. Or, those booking cruise-only can buy Carnival's transfer package. Also, if you buy the Orlando package, plan to take the Spaceport USA bus tour on the day you sail. That way, the full morning can be spent at Spaceport USA, about 20 minutes from Port Canaveral. Lunch is available aboard ship until 3:30 p.m.

THE SHIPS   *Carnival Destiny* was the largest cruise ship ever built when she made her debut in 1996 and was the first Carnival ship too wide to transit the Panama Canal. When the ship was being planned six years earlier, Carnival employees were asked to submit their wish lists for enhancing the new vessel. Apparently, they got most of their wishes.

The *Destiny* had Carnival's first double-deck dining room; a show lounge spanning three decks; a double-width promenade lined with lounges and bars; a mall-style shopping area; a 9,000-square-foot casino; 18 bars and lounges; four swimming pools and an expansive spa; a retractable glass dome over the pool area; and sports and recreation facilities similar to the *Fantasy*-class ships. The pool area has a stage for entertainment and teak decks cantilevered in an amphitheater. **Virtual World** is a high-tech virtual reality

Carnival Destiny	QUALITY 8	VALUE A
Carnival Triumph	QUALITY 8	VALUE A
Carnival Victory	QUALITY 8	VALUE A
REGISTRY *Destiny/ Triumph* Bahamas; *Victory* Panama	LENGTH 893 feet	BEAM 125 feet
CABINS 1,321/1,379	DRAFT 27 feet	SPEED 22.5 knots
MAXIMUM PASSENGERS 3,400/3,470	PASSENGER DECKS 12 CREW 1,050/1,100	ELEVATORS 18 SPACE RATIO 37/38

game center. In 2005, after a multimillion-dollar renovation, an expansive teen club was added, and suites were upgraded. In late 2008, private balconies were added to 14 cabins on *Carnival Destiny* and *Carnival Triumph* that previously had floor-to-ceiling windows.

Destiny's configuration was a departure for Carnival at the time. Entertainment and recreation decks are between the accommodations decks. The two lowest passenger decks have only cabins, followed by three decks of public rooms, then five decks of cabins and suites with balconies. To avoid big rooms and long corridors that would make the ship's huge size obvious, public rooms span two or three levels. The layout is often confusing, however.

Despite her size—nearly three football fields in length—*Destiny* does not seem as large from the inside as some of her *Fantasy*-class cousins. This is primarily because of the layout and decor, which is softer and toned down—sometimes even tony.

The Rotunda (**Capital Lobby** on *Triumph;* **Seven Seas Atrium** on *Victory*), a nine-deck atrium with four glass elevators and a glass dome, is the ship's focal point. An enormous marble and onyx mural of geometric forms suggesting skyscrapers decorates the walls. The atrium has an attractive lobby bar at its base, creating a meeting place that helps humanize the huge space.

The *Carnival Triumph,* which debuted in 1999, built on *Destiny's* success but incorporated new features, including an extra deck of cabins. Sixty percent of cabins have ocean views with a sitting area, and more than 60% of those have verandas. The ship celebrates the world's great cities, with such venues as **Underground Tokyo** video arcade, the **Rome Theater, Vienna Café** coffee bar, and **Oxford Bar.** A huge golden globe dominates the atrium; it's inlaid with glittering fiber optics that mark the world's metropolises. Smaller globes are part of the decor shipwide. The new Panorama Deck, one level above the Lido Deck, has 42 ocean-view cabins, most with verandas, and 24 inside ones, adding capacity for 132 guests. *Carnival Victory,* whose theme is the seven seas, arrived in August 2000.

ITINERARIES *See* Itinerary Index.

CABINS The group's standard cabins are among the largest and the most attractively furnished in the Carnival fleet. All have hair dryers and safes; some have interactive television. Cabin numbers pinpoint your deck and location (forward, aft, or midship). Each section has its own elevators. Sixty percent of standard outside cabins have small balconies, all with clear panels for unobstructed ocean views. Unfortunately, they do nothing to absorb sound. This and insufficient soundproofing make the cabins noisy. Particularly to be avoided are cabins on Deck 6 forward, which are directly above lounges that operate most of the night. Ocean-view cabins have a sitting area with a sofa and coffee table. Family cabins are near the children's play facilities. In late 2008, a set of 14 cabins on Deck 10 or 11 on *Carnival Destiny* and *Carnival Triumph* that had floor-to-ceiling windows were retrofitted with private balconies, creating 230-square-foot veranda cabins. Their in-room amenities were also upgraded to match those of other existing balcony cabins.

Specifications 515 inside cabins, 446 outside with verandas; 48 suites with verandas, some with bathtub whirlpools. Standard dimensions, 220–260 square feet; all cabins with twins convertible to kings; 4 inside with upper and lower berths; no singles; 25 *Destiny,* 27 *Triumph, Victory* wheelchair-accessible cabins.

DINING Carnival's first bi-level dining rooms feel roomy, and the additional space allows wider separation between tables. Nonetheless, the restaurants are noisy. Both dining rooms enjoy ocean views.

The two-deck **Sun & Sea** (**South Beach Club** on *Triumph;* **Mediterranean** on *Victory*), the casual Lido restaurant, is dressed in shades of green with yellow, hand-blown Murano glass and hand-painted ceramic tile decorating walls and countertops. Different settings create dining options: Trattoria for pasta and made-to-order Italian dishes; Happy Valley for Chinese cuisine, stir-fried to order; and The Grille for hamburgers and hot dogs. Service has also been upgraded; waiters carry dishes and beverages to tables. The **Seaview Bistro** alternative dinner service in the Lido restaurant offers specialty salads, pastas, steaks, and desserts—plus a daily special—in a cafe setting. The bistro operates from 6–9:30 each evening. Also open are a 24-hour pizzeria and a patisserie. *Carnival Victory* has a New York–style deli. Open-seating dinners have become an option to traditional, fixed-time early or late seatings for dinner. (See *Fantasy*-class ships for details.)

FACILITIES AND ACTIVITIES In the evening, you are likely to run out of energy before you run out of choices. The flashy **Millionaire's Club** (**Club Monaco** on *Triumph;* **South China Sea Club** on *Victory*), one of the largest casinos afloat, has more than 200 slot machines and 23 table games. In the lavishly decorated **Apollo Bar,** the piano revolves, enabling the pianist to shine a spotlight on anyone eager to test the microphone on each table.

In the **Point After Dance Club,** tricolor neon lights snake across the ceiling above a bi-level floor, and more than 500 video monitors flash pictures and computer-generated graphics around the room. A staircase by the dance floor leads to the elegant **Onyx Room,** a more sedate club where back-lit alabaster panels glow softly beside a neon-and-glass dance floor.

The three-deck **Palladium** show lounge, the venue for Vegas-style production shows, is one of the most technologically sophisticated afloat. The additional deck below seating levels allows the orchestra pit to be retracted, and the space above enables backdrops, lighting equipment, and performers to be "flown" offstage via cables. A Venetian glass chandelier hangs from the dome; at show time, it goes high-tech with fiber optics.

To achieve three decks of seats for 1,400 people, some sacrifices were made. The main floor is almost level, making viewing more difficult the farther back one sits. Also, balcony rails partially block some views. Big production shows are top-notch.

Yet more entertainment is offered in **Virtual World,** a game center with virtual-reality and electronic games, and at **All Star Bar,** decorated with celebrity memorabilia, including tables bearing autographs of sports stars, and featuring seven big-screen televisions broadcasting sporting events.

SPORTS, FITNESS, AND BEAUTY *Destiny* has four pools, including a children's pool, and seven whirlpools. One has Carnival's trademark waterslide—but here, it is three decks tall and 214 feet long. A retractable dome covers the aft pool.

The 14,500-square-foot spa and health club is on two levels, one with a beauty salon, massage rooms, whirlpools, and sauna and steam rooms, the other with an aerobics room. The spa offers hydrotherapy baths, aromatherapy, and other body treatments. There is also a "Nouveau Yu Health Environment Capsule," an egglike temperature-controlled capsule designed to induce relaxation. The gym has an array of equipment, including 16 Keiser or Life-Fitness machines. Instructors lead exercise classes and can be hired as personal trainers. An eighth-mile jogging track is on the Sun Deck. On *Triumph,* more open space was provided on the Lido Deck for deck chairs, and the forward and aft pools were enlarged.

CHILDREN'S FACILITIES The two-deck-tall, 1,300-square-foot indoor and outdoor play center includes a jungle gym and pool. See the *Fantasy* profile for information on Carnival's children's program.

THE SHIPS *Carnival Spirit,* the first of a new class of ships for Carnival, entered service in 2001, followed by triplets: *Carnival Pride* and *Carnival Legend* in 2002, and *Carnival Miracle* in 2004. They are among the longest ships in the Carnival fleet, but they still can pass through the Panama Canal. The ships have a number of environmentally friendly technical enhancements, and their technologically advanced Azipod propulsion system enables them to reach a maximum speed of 24 knots and thus sail on innovative itineraries. The ships boast an exceptional space ratio of 40 (the *Fantasy* class is 34, *Destiny* class, 37) with the usual array of Carnival amenities and facilities, as well as some new ones, such as the first Carnival ships with a wedding chapel and, more recently, self-service digital-photo printing kiosks, now available fleetwide.

The theme of *Carnival Spirit* is design, particularly architectural design (which makes for an eclectic mix of decor), while that of *Carnival Pride* is icons of beauty, which gave Farcus's active mind never-ending inspiration—from architecture and artistic masterpieces to athletic achievement and the human body. The beauty icons start with Renaissance inspiration in the atrium lobby, elevator, and stairwell areas, where huge reproductions of murals by Botticelli, Raphäel, and other Italian painters adorn the walls. Here, too, the craftsmanship of the Italian Renaissance is reflected in rich details of wood and bronze moldings, and it's dominated by gold, sienna, and burnt-red tones.

Carnival Legend's motif is inspired by great legends of history, from the ancient Greeks in the atrium, to modern jazz in the New Orleans design of **Satchmo's Club,** and the Art Deco of **Billie's Piano Bar,** named for blues legend Billie Holiday. *Carnival Miracle* has fictional characters as its theme.

Carnival Legend	QUALITY 8	VALUE A
Carnival Miracle	QUALITY 8	VALUE A
Carnival Pride	QUALITY 8	VALUE A
Carnival Spirit	QUALITY 8	VALUE A
REGISTRY Panama	LENGTH 963 feet	BEAM 105.7 feet
CABINS 1,062	DRAFT 25.7 feet	SPEED 22 knots
MAXIMUM PASSENGERS	PASSENGER DECKS 12	ELEVATORS 15
2,667	CREW 930	SPACE RATIO 40

The ships' interior promenade meanders through public rooms on two consecutive decks, linking the ship's two atriums with its dining rooms, more than a dozen bars, lounges, and entertainment venues, and a shopping arcade that includes a tuxedo rental and flower shop. The ships also have a wraparound outdoor promenade on Atlantic Deck—the first for a Carnival ship in two decades. All the *Spirit-* and *Conquest*-class ships have an upscale supper club located atop a towering 11-deck-high atrium, plus a large percentage of balconied cabins. They have a two-level dining room; large poolside food courts offering casual breakfast, lunch, and dinner; a 24-hour pizzeria; and a sushi bar. *Spirit*-class ships have 16 lounges, ranging from an elaborate, multilevel showroom for Vegas-style revues, to an intimate piano bar, a casino, shopping mall, wedding chapel, video game room, and Internet cafe. There are several swimming pools—including one with a spiral waterslide—a spa and gym, a Camp Carnival program for kids ages 2–15.

CABINS Ships have several levels of suites with private balconies and set a new standard for outside cabins, 80% of which have private balconies. Many cabins can accommodate up to four guests; other connect and are ideal for large families.

Specifications 213 inside cabins, 99 outside, 624 outside with balconies, 68 with French doors; 52 suites, 6 penthouses, 16 wheelchair accessible.

DINING Each ship has three restaurants. *Pride*'s main dining room, the **Normandie Restaurant,** (**Empire** on *Spirit;* **Golden Fleece** on *Legend*), spanning two decks with wraparound windows, has elegant decor based on the famous ocean liner *Normandie,* one of the most beautiful passenger vessels ever built. Open-seating dinner is an option to a traditional, fixed-time early or late seating for dinner. (See *Fantasy*-class ships for details.)

Spirit's unusual **Nouveau Supper Club,** Carnival's first alternative restaurant (reservations only; $30 charge), is situated topside, with one end bordering the ship's huge red-glass smokestack and the other extending out over the top of the ship's multideck atrium. Menu specialties are prime aged beef, seafood, and other gourmet selections. The restaurant's counterpart on the *Pride* is **David's Supper Club,** with a full-size replica of the famous Michelangelo sculpture, *David,* celebrating the beauty of the human body.

The **Mermaids' Grille,** the ship's Lido restaurant, has a variety of food stations, each offering a different type of cuisine and including a 24-hour pizzeria.

FACILITIES AND ACTIVITIES The ships seem to have a dance floor at every turn. From the **Beauties Dance Club** to the **Starry Night** jazz club and the grand **Taj Mahal** show lounge. On the *Pride,* a famous Van Gogh painting was the inspiration for the Starry Night jazz club (**Club Cool** on *Spirit*). The beauty of ideas and intellectual achievement is enshrined in the **Nobel Library,** with a portrait of Alfred Nobel, who created the famous prize. The room also houses the Internet cafe. The beauty of experience is represented in the **Perfect Game** sports bar and the **Winner's Club** casino. **Butterflies Lounge** draws on natural beauty with faux windows decorated with colorful transparent fabrics that resemble butterfly wings. The fabrics disappear under special lights that illuminate the flocks of butterflies behind. Four different butterfly patterns are seen in the upholstery. Architectural beauty is celebrated in the Taj Mahal show lounge (**Pharaoh's Palace** on *Spirit*), filled with intricate Indian designs and stonework sparkling with small jewels pressed into decorative elements. Infrared listening devices for hearing-impaired passengers are available in the main lounge on most *Spirit*-class ships.

Other highlights include a chapel suitable for weddings or religious services, ice-cream/frozen yogurt bar, and a large conference center.

SPORTS, FITNESS, AND BEAUTY The ships' **Spa Carnival** is a two-level health and fitness facility, along with huge open decks and three swimming pools, one with a two-deck-high waterslide plus a children's wading pool. One of the pools is heated and has a sliding glass roof, known as a magrodome—ideal for chilly climates. A golf program includes private lessons, digital teaching technology, and packages for shoreside play with priority tee times; it's $45 for excursions or $50 for a half-hour lesson and video. Equipment rental is available for an additional fee. Advance tee times can be made at ☎ 800-324-1106.

CHILDREN'S FACILITIES A variety of new and expanded family-friendly amenities have been added fleetwide to the Camp Carnival and include choices from fun, educational geography classes and candy-making machines to special family activities on a private island, teens-only shore excursions, and "just-for-kids" port lectures. **Fun Club,** located forward on upper Deck 5 and decorated with a colorful undersea motif, is divided into three areas. The first area houses an arts and crafts center, the second has a computer lab, and the third has a playroom stocked with toys and games, a video wall displaying movies and cartoons, and kid-size tables and chairs. An outdoor play area has a mini-basketball hoop and other playground equipment. **Real Virtuality,** a high-tech game room housing video and arcade games, is one deck below Camp Carnival.

A turndown service offering freshly baked chocolate chip cookies on formal nights is available. So, too, is the fleetwide Fountain Fun Card, a soft drink program for unlimited sodas, that costs from $13.95 for three-day cruises to $32.25 for seven-day cruises for those under age 18 (18 years and over, $19 and $44.25, respectively); there are kids' menus. Babysitting is available 10 p.m.–3 a.m. in the children's playroom for $6 per hour for the first child and $4 for each additional child in the same family. Strollers are available for rent at $6 per day and $25 for the week.

THE SHIPS *Carnival Conquest,* which made her debut in New Orleans in 2002, kicked off delivery of the largest class of vessels in the fleet at the time. She also was the first to have her interior decor tied directly to her home port. Using the ship's interiors as a huge canvas, designer Joe Farcus created something of an ode to Impressionist and Postimpressionist art and the Big Easy's French legacy.

The main atrium, called the **Atelier,** has Impressionist paintings on the central ceiling dome and wall; the **Artists' Lobby** is dominated by a large hand-painted mural collage of famous paintings. The collage effect is picked up on the promenade and in other public areas throughout the ship. In 2009, during an extensive, multimillion-dollar renovation, Carnival modified ocean-view cabins with 18 balconies, added a new Circle "C" club for 12- to 14-year-old teens, updated the Camp Carnival facilities for children and Club O2 for teens, and installed a gigantic LED screen on the Lido Deck.

Carnival Conquest	QUALITY 8	VALUE A
Carnival Freedom	QUALITY 8	VALUE A
Carnival Glory	QUALITY 8	VALUE A
Carnival Liberty	QUALITY 8	VALUE A
Carnival Valor	QUALITY 8	VALUE A
REGISTRY Panama	LENGTH 952 feet	BEAM 116 feet
CABINS 1,486	DRAFT 27 feet	SPEED 22.5 knots
MAXIMUM PASSENGERS	PASSENGER DECKS 13	ELEVATORS 15
3,700	CREW 1,160	SPACE RATIO 37

Her sister ship, *Carnival Glory,* which arrived in 2003, takes colors as a theme, with public rooms done in different shades of the rainbow and reflected in their name and decor. The kaleidoscope of colors begins in the Colors lobby, **Color Bar,** and the main atrium, named **Old Glory** after the United States flag. Each deck was given a different color; looking up through the atrium, it's easy to see the color definition of each deck. **Kaleidoscope Boulevard** has one-square-meter light fixtures subdivided into geometric modules that are back-lit with strips of color. The result is thousands of tones in a slow-moving kaleidoscope.

Carnival Valor, inspired by its name, has heroes and heroism—real and imagined—as its theme. *Carnival Liberty,* launched in 2005, celebrates artisans and their crafts. She was the first cruise ship to offer 100% stem-to-stern wireless Internet access, enabling passengers to surf the net from every public room, pool decks, and any cabin. Her sister ships have this technology as well.

Carnival Freedom, launched in Europe in 2007, has design as her theme and takes passengers on a journey of styles through the centuries—from ancient Babylon to the heyday of disco, from the 19th-century Victorian era to the contemporary style of the 1990s. In an unprecedented promotion, nine watercolors and pencil murals by Massachusetts-based artist Joan Barber, commissioned for *Carnival Freedom* and part of the ship's multimillion-dollar art collection, were on display at Flomenhaft Gallery in Manhattan four months prior to the ship's debut.

The ships of the *Conquest* group have 22 lounges and bars, four swimming pools, a 214-foot-long waterslide, an Internet cafe, a 13,300-square-foot health club, a comprehensive golf program, and four restaurants, including an upscale reservations-only supper club, two bi-level main dining rooms, a sushi bar, a patisserie, and a 1,200-seat casual poolside restaurant.

ITINERARIES *See* Itinerary Index

CABINS By Carnival standards, the cabins are exceptionally low-key and understated, dressed in soft pastels and rich wood that blends with the soft colors. They are also large for ships in this category, ranging from 185 square feet for a standard inside cabin to 220 square feet for a deluxe balcony cabin. A wall unit has a dresser/desk with drawers and cabinets; safe; minifridge; television;

and three closets that should be ample for most people on a week's cruise. All outside cabins have a sofa; most are sofa beds. The bathroom with a rather tight shower stall has a dispenser for shampoo and shower gel. All outside cabins get terry robes. A larger number of cabins have small balconies with space for two chairs—and that's about all. In her recent renovations, 18 cabins on *Conquest* and on *Liberty* that previously had floor-to-ceiling windows have been retrofitted with private balconies, creating 230-square-foot veranda cabins and bringing the ship's number of balcony cabins to 573. *Carnival Liberty* has also been fitted with two new "deluxe penthouse suites" at the forward end of Deck 9, above the bridge. The 750-square-foot suites are almost double the size of the largest cabins in the fleet.

> *Specifications* 10 penthouse suites, 42 suites, 2 deluxe penthouse suites on Liberty; 575 outside with balcony, 343 standard outside without balcony, 570 inside cabins, 28 wheelchair accessible.

DINING Each ship has two bi-level dining rooms. On *Conquest,* the **Monet** and **Renoir** dining rooms (**Platinum** and **Golden** on *Glory*) are identical architecturally and have panels of wood-veneered images of the Eiffel Tower in the walls and ceiling. The fabrics and colors are based on works by the two painters. *Glory*'s dining rooms take their decor from their colors and are elegant in their simplicity—resembling, somewhat, the uncluttered lines of Japanese decor, with only a touch of color from a few hand-painted bonsai and cherry-blossom trees on the walls and ceiling. The rooms are the most crowded of any dining rooms we've experienced on any Carnival ship. Off to each side of *Glory*'s Golden dining room is a private dining room, **Copper** (for 28 people) and **Silver** (for 36 people), which are among the most handsome rooms on the ship. *Conquest*'s Renoir Restaurant was inspired by *Lunch at the Restaurant Fournaise,* a tranquil scene of boaters relaxing at a cafe overlooking the Seine, featured in the wall-covering fabric. In the Monet Restaurant, one of the artist's famous *Water Lilies* series sets the motif. Open-seating dinner has become an option to traditional, fixed-time early or late seatings for dinner. (See *Fantasy*-class ships for details.)

Freedom's **Chic** and **Posh** dining rooms reflect the styles of the 1990s. The mood of the restaurants can be changed dramatically through innovative lighting strips that meander around the rooms and create a sparkling effect through the use of embedded color-changing lightbulbs. Poolside **Freedom Restaurant** incorporates the style of the 1980s with various replications of the Statue of Liberty in the decor. The bi-level **Restaurant Cezanne** (**Red Sail** on *Glory*, **Rosie's** on *Valor*) on the Lido Deck has the atmosphere of a 19th-century French cafe. In addition to Carnival's standard variety of Italian, Chinese, and other food stations, there are hamburgers and hot dogs, a 24-hour pizzeria, and a self-service ice-cream and frozen yogurt station. The restaurant is also the venue for an upscale seafood station on the second level of the Lido restaurant. **Café Fans** (**Creams** on *Glory*) on the Promenade Deck is a patisserie serving a variety of coffees and rather pricey desserts; next door is a sushi bar. And there's 24-hour room service with new, expanded menus.

The Point, high on Panorama Deck, is *Conquest*'s reservations-only supper club, named for the style of Georges Seurat, known as pointillism, which renders images through thousands of individual dots, or points, of color. *Glory*'s

Emerald Room has light fixtures resembling giant emeralds and a huge medallion on the wall made up of hundreds of these light fixtures. *Liberty*'s **Harry's,** named for famed jeweler Harry Winston, is bedecked with jeweled decor; *Freedom*'s **Sun King Supper Club,** named after Louis XIV, reflects the opulence of the 18th century with elaborate tapestries, antique mirrors, an impressive chandelier, and a large mural depicting the royal court. For structural reasons, the club is divided into two separate rooms (rather than the large open space by the funnel as on the line's *Spirit* class). **Scarlett's,** inspired by *Gone With the Wind,* is *Carnival Valor*'s alternative restaurant, with a small combo that plays music for dancing. Cost is $30 per person. In our experience, Carnival's alternative restaurants are excellent, with food and service top-notch and well worth the extra charge. Reserve early, as they are very popular and fill up fast.

FACILITIES AND ACTIVITIES The **Toulouse-Lautrec Lounge,** the main show lounge, takes its inspiration from the painter's sketches, which were drawn from the subjects he saw in the cabarets, circuses, and brothels of Paris's Montmartre. To the sides of the stage are the famous windmill signs of the Moulin Rouge cabaret; the windmill motif is repeated in the carpet. *Glory*'s **Amber Palace,** the most extravagant room on the ship, is named after Russia's famous Amber Room (now reconstructed and open to the public) in the palace of Peter the Great. The wall covering, for example, replicates the mosaics of amber as they are on the palace walls; hanging from the ceiling is an enormous crystal chandelier, with smaller ones at the sides of the room. The Russian eagle is designed into the room's carpet, and the cut velvet covering on the seats would suit any czar's palace. *Freedom*'s **Victoriana** show lounge, named after Britain's Queen Victoria, is designed to evoke theaters in London's West End, with ornate moldings, fancy marble, and gold leaf. For those who take a backstage tour, the state-of-the-art stage and equipment is on par with the latest of Broadway.

The two shows on *Glory, Livin' in America* and *Rock Down Broadway,* are in keeping with the Carnival tradition of fast-paced Vegas-style revues that blend choreography with elaborate sets and costumes. *Rock Down Broadway* is one of the best shows we have ever seen on any cruise ship—or on Broadway, for that matter. *Carnival Valor* has *Far From Over: the 80s,* a tribute to the music and the movies of the 1980s, and *Nightclub Express,* a rollicking tour—hosted by a talking, singing sofa!—of ten famous cabarets and nightspots (with different sets, costumes, and music appropriate to each). The shows were produced by Carnival Productions, the line's in-house entertainment group. The show lounges of this group boast the latest in shipboard technology, such as "fly-in" scenery capabilities and a turntable stage with built-in lifts.

Conquest's **Tahiti Casino** and **Gauguin's Bar,** a sports bar, recall Postimpressionist Paul Gauguin's paintings of Polynesia. **Henri's Dance Club** takes its theme from the exotic jungle paintings of Henri Rousseau. Painted metal cutouts, meant to look like the coarse grass of Rousseau's paintings, are mounted on the wall, with occasional three-dimensional animal heads, similar to those lurking in the artist's works. *Glory*'s **Camel Club Casino** is a bit incongruous. The camel color inspired Farcus to install statues of reclining camels (which kids love to climb, despite a sign reading "No one under 18 years of age is allowed in the Casino"), but from the camels it's a stretch to the main decor, meant to reflect the age of European rediscovery of ancient

Egypt and the Orient. *Freedom*'s **Babylon Casino** takes its theme from the famed Hanging Gardens of ancient Babylon.

On *Glory*, the **White Heat Dance Club** has gigantic white candles, 12–18 inches in diameter, in silver candelabra bases from two to five feet tall and giving off imaginary white heat. One deck below, the multipurpose **Ivory Club** has an Indian theme set off with elephant tusk replicas, and the bar stools and table bases replicate elephant feet. Across the way, the **Burgundy Bar** is a wine bar; **Cinn-a-Bar,** a piano bar; and the **Bar Blue,** taking its "blue" from giant peacock feathers in the motif, is the ship's jazz bar. The **Ebony Cabaret,** a multifunction showroom with African decor, is one of *Glory*'s most successful rooms, using ebony wood, African textiles, and handsome authentic wooden masks in the decor. **On the Green,** the sports bar, celebrates golf with memorabilia from the game's legends

Carnival Liberty's **Seaside Theatre** has one of the largest LED screens (12 feet by 22 feet) ever installed on a cruise ship. Utilizing the same technology featured in large stadiums and New York's Times Square, this state-of-the-art entertainment system includes a 70,000-watt sound system that provides concert quality sound, even outdoors. Located poolside on the Lido Deck, the facility shows movies, sporting events, concerts, and other programs, including the ship's "Morning Show," hosted by the cruise director. The Seaside Theatre was recently added to *Conquest*, as well as to other ships in the fleet.

On *Freedom*, **Player's Sport Bar,** with giant plasma screen televisions, shines with chrome, sports medallions, and memorabilia highlighting the 1950s, often referred to as the "golden era of sports"; **Studio 70** is an updated version of the famed Studio 54 disco in New York; **Bar Nouveau** on the promenade is a step back in time to the 1890s with its Art Nouveau style. There's also the 1940s **Habana Cigar Bar;** the 1770s **Monticello Library;** the 1910s **Scott's** piano bar, named for ragtime piano master Scott Joplin; and the 1930s **Swingtime** jazz club.

Daytime activities range from a Jazz & Bloody Mary Party to a Sing-Along or a Men's Hairy Chest Contest; art auctions, trivia quizzes, game shows, and adult comedy shows in the evening round out the offerings. They also have libraries, multipurpose conference centers, boutiques, infirmaries, and Internet cafes—$0.75 per minute, or packages of 30 and 60 minutes for slight savings. Cruise e-mail is available for a one-time activation fee of $3.95. Local calls from passengers' cabins are $6.99 per minute within the United States; international calls, $9.99. Cell phone service is available fleetwide; international roaming fees apply.

SPORTS, FITNESS, AND BEAUTY Each ship has a spa with a large variety of treatments, sauna and steam rooms, a very small indoor pool with a most unusual half-moon-shaped Jacuzzi, a gym with state-of-the-art equipment, and a beauty salon. There are four swimming pools, including one with Carnival's signature slide; seven whirlpools (although that number is often halved because of all the kids in them, even though they're not supposed to be); and a jogging track. You can start your day in the gym as early as 6 a.m. and be treated to classes in aerobics or abs or (for $10 extra per session) yoga, Pilates, or seminars on body care, diet, or cellulite. Sports include basketball, volleyball, and golf.

CHILDREN'S FACILITIES The *Conquest*-class ships introduced an expanded teen recreation center called Club O2 that houses a large, high-tech video-game room and teen dance club with a DJ spinning the latest hits, a bar serving nonalcoholic specialty drinks, and a video wall, along with new activities and shore excursions for teen groups. More recently, *Carnival Conquest* got a Circle "C" facility, the line's fleetwide program for 12–14-year-old kids. Situated on Deck 8, the center includes a high-tech sound and lighting system, plasma-screen televisions displaying movies and music videos, a touch-screen jukebox, and gaming pods with the latest video games and consoles.

For younger children, the *Conquest* group has the largest play areas in the Carnival fleet. Camp Carnival offers an arts and crafts center with spin and sand art and candy-making machines; an all-ages playroom; a video room showing kids' movies and cartoons; and a children's library, along with the latest PlayStation games. Babysitting is available nightly in the playroom 10 p.m.–3 a.m. for $6 per hour for the first child and $4 per hour for the second child in the same family. There is also an outdoor play area and a wading pool and access to Carnival's trademark waterslide. Strollers rent for $6 per day and $25 per week and are available fleetwide.

Kids can make their own culinary creations through cake-decorating and pizza-making sessions, part of a full schedule of morning-to-night activities for children ages 2–14. Children receive their own printed activities program daily. Sample activities include storytelling, sing-alongs, and Play-Doh Fun for younger cruisers, and disco parties, scavenger hunts, and pool parties for older kids. The ships offer a variety of kid-friendly dining choices and a daily junior special in the main dining rooms. Kids are also provided with freshly baked chocolate chip cookies on formal nights; youth counselors host children's-only meals poolside with a different cuisine featured each night. WaterColors, which debuted on *Carnival Valor,* is an art program that has been expanded fleetwide, teaching kids the techniques employed by professional artists in papier-mâché, oil paintings, and watercolors. SeaNotes is a music program that introduces kids to different musical instruments and genres.

THE SHIP Launched in July 2008, in Dover, England, the 113,300-ton *Carnival Splendor* was Carnival Cruise Lines' largest ship at the time. Prior to arriving in her permanent home port of Long Beach, California, she sailed on the line's first-ever Northern Europe cruise, followed by a series of cruises in the Mediterranean before heading to Florida and around South America. In anticipation of *Carnival Splendor*'s arrival, the Long Beach cruise terminal, owned and operated by Carnival's parent company, Carnival Corporation, underwent an $8 million upgrade.

Although she is a new ship class for Carnival and comes with new features, *Splendor*'s layout will be familiar to Carnival fans, as will her decor by designer Joe Farcus, who was heard to say that *Splendor* has "less kitsch than Las Vegas." Pink is an overall color with lots of pink circles and swirls in the atrium's stainless steel and pink-stained wood walls that follow you all the way up through the ship.

Actually, *Splendor* is only marginally larger than the *Conquest*-class ships, and the differences are most notable at the top of the ship in the innovative area, dubbed "Cloud 9," with a bi-level 21,000-square-foot spa and health club and Carnival's first spa suites and cabins. Also at the top are expansive children's

Carnival Splendor	**PREVIEW**	
REGISTRY Panama	**LENGTH** 952 feet	**BEAM** 116 feet
CABINS 1,503	**DRAFT** 27 feet	**SPEED** 21 knots
MAXIMUM PASSENGERS	**PASSENGER DECKS** 13	**ELEVATORS** NA
3,006	**CREW** 1,160	**SPACE RATIO** 37.7

facilities; the Seaside Theatre for movies, concerts, and other programming; a midship pool with a retractable dome that can be closed during inclement weather; and the adults-only Serenity area. Four restaurants, a 24-hour pizzeria, and an elegant reservations-only supper club are the ship's dining highlights. For diversions, *Carnival Splendor* has 22 lounges and bars, a duty-free shopping mall, casino, ship-wide Internet access, and cell phone service.

ITINERARIES *See* Itinerary Index. She is currently sailing on seven-day Mexican Riviera cruises year-round.

CABINS Of the ship's 1,503 cabins and suites, 60% are outside, and 60% of those have balconies. There are several levels of suites; nearly 200 cabins are interconnecting, and more than 350 accommodate up to three and four passengers, which is ideal for families. Adjacent to the Cloud 9 spa are 68 spa suites and cabins—Carnival's first. All accommodations feature the Carnival Comfort Bed sleep system with plush mattresses, luxurious duvets, and high-quality linens and pillows.

DINING The ship's four restaurants include two bi-level main dining rooms; a large poolside casual restaurant with multi-food stations and 24-hour pizzeria; and **The Pinnacle,** an elegant reservations-only supper club. The main dining rooms, **Black Pearl** and **Gold Pearl,** topped by ceiling decorations of pearls in shells with pearl-encased chandeliers and pearl-filled horns of plenty, offer diverse menus with a choice of six appetizers and soups, two salads, six entrees, and desserts (particularly chocolate melting cake) daily. Broiled lobster tail is served once each cruise. A fleetwide custom at dinner has the waiters—on cue from the maître d'—in colorful costumes, climbing up on platforms and performing a dance routine while camera-toting passengers click away.

The Pinnacle, the ship's elegant, reservations-only supper club, modeled after New York's famous steak houses, serves dry-aged U.S.D.A. prime steaks and other specialties on fine china in an intimate, sophisticated ambience with polished, leisurely paced service. Charge is $30 per person. The venue has a skylight and a glass dance floor suspended over a mini-atrium.

Carnival Splendor's poolside restaurant, **The Lido,** offers a wide range of breakfast, lunch, and dinner choices at food stations. In addition, it has a tandoor-oven station offering Indian-style chicken, fish kebabs, breads, and other delicacies, and a Mongolian wok where passengers select vegetables, seafood, meat, and spices and have their combination prepared while they watch. There's also a New York–style deli for sandwiches and popular sides, a 35-item salad bar, pasta and meat-carving stations, and a grill serving hot dogs and hamburgers. After arriving on the West Coast and marking the ship's year-round Mexican Riviera itinerary, a burrito bar was added.

Carnival Splendor's other choices are **The Coffee Shop** for espressos, lattes, cappuccinos, and decadent sweets; and **California Roll,** a sushi bar offering Asian specialties prior to dinner each evening. There are late-night buffets with a different theme each night, highlighted by the Gala Midnight Buffet and Chocolate Extravaganza, and if you're still hungry, there's no-charge, 24-hour room service.

FACILITIES AND ACTIVITIES Three high-energy revues—"The Beat," "Vroom," and "Fiesta Latina"—are presented in Spectacular Spectacular, the 1,500-seat, three-deck-high main show lounge where sight lines are good. Other entertainment options are the popular "Midnight Special" comedy show and the outdoor Seaside Theatre, with a 270-square-foot LED screen on the Lido Deck where movies are shown and concerts and other programming are held. The popular El Morocco, the aft lounge on the Promenade Deck, is the most colorful room, with black-and-white zebra-patterned leather sofas and plush red chairs, a red carpet, and gold palm trees, and colored mosaics in the ceiling—all meant to evoke the famous New York club of the 1930s. The Cool Jazz Bar has Miles Davis–inspired artwork with photos of the famed trumpeter and his sheet music. Revelers are greeted by a line of mannequins outside the nightclub, supposedly representing the "beautiful" people, and flashing lights (paparazzi cameras, according to Farcus) at the nightclub entrance. Most of the ship and its lounges are nonsmoking, except for the Sports Bar and Cuban-style Rubusto Bar.

SPORTS, FITNESS, AND BEAUTY The two-deck-high central pool area, decorated with colorful hanging flower baskets, is the largest on any Carnival ship and features the Seaside Theatre. A retractable roof over the pool is new. Two hot tubs on the upper level enjoy unobstructed sea views. The ship has four swimming pools and minigolf.

Forward on Deck 11 is the expansive two-level spa and health club, Cloud 9, with lovely Asian-themed decor. It has a thalassotherapy pool, a thermal suite, indoor and outdoor quiet rooms, and 17 private treatment rooms, including some for couples, a sea-view sauna and steam room, and a well-equipped gym. The facility's 68 spa cabins and suites have private access to the spa area via a glass-walled elevator and have priority spa reservations.

CHILDREN'S FACILITIES *Splendor* boasts Carnival's most elaborate and extensive children's facilities, with a 5,500-square-foot children's play area—the largest in the fleet at roughly 30% bigger than the others—along with a fun-filled water park and dedicated facilities and activities for tweens, teens, and kids of all ages. The water park, dominated by the line's signature 214-foot-long "Twister Waterslide," has various water-spray apparatus for splashing fun.

As with other Carnival ships, *Carnival Splendor* offers age-specific programs and facilities for children: Camp Carnival (ages 2–11), Circle "C" (ages 12–14), and Club O2 (ages 15–17). Located midship on the Panorama Deck, a two-level children's facility is divided into separate areas with each focusing on a different activity or function. One area is an all-ages playroom with a variety of toys, games, and puzzles. Another is a computer game room with the latest computer-gaming consoles, while a third area is a dance floor with plasma-screen televisions displaying music videos and children's movies.

Carnival Splendor is the first to have a purpose-built Circle "C" facility. Located midship on the Atlantic Deck, the sleek, modern complex has a dance floor with a high-tech sound and lighting system, along with 42-inch plasma-screen televisions displaying movies and music videos, and a touch-screen jukebox stocked with the latest hits. Other features include gaming pods with the latest video games and consoles, with 20-inch plasma screens positioned throughout the room and used exclusively for video gaming. Activities include basketball, volleyball, Ping-Pong, water games, late-night movies, and pool parties.

Continuing Carnival's emphasis on providing older kids with their own spaces and activities, *Carnival Splendor* has its own version of the line's Club O2, located midship on the Promenade Deck. The 2,365-square-foot facility has a dance floor, DJ, a state-of-the-art sound and lighting system, and a lounge where teens can relax and enjoy nonalcoholic specialty drinks.

Carnival Splendor also offers educational programs geared toward the ship's various destinations and a library with popular teen-oriented books and magazines. Special shore excursions offer older kids an opportunity to visit historic destinations as a group, and Carnival's Y Spa teen spa treatment program is another age-specific option.

Children's menus in the main dining rooms, 24-hour pizza, and ice cream at the poolside restaurant are sure to please every kid. Popular too are a meal with the youth staff, a turndown service with freshly baked cookies at bedtime, and a Fountain Fun Card, for unlimited soft drinks throughout the cruise for a one-time fee. Fee-based nightly babysitting services and stroller rentals are also available.

THE SHIP The 130,000-ton *Carnival Dream* is Carnival's most family-oriented ship to date. She made her debut in September 2009 with a short Mediterranean series followed by a transatlantic crossing to New York before beginning her regular pattern from Port Canaveral. Constructed in Italy at the Fincantieri Monfalcone yard and spanning 1,004 feet in length, she is the largest, longest ship Carnival has ever built and makes maximum use of her size. Her sister ship, *Carnival Magic*, will arrive in June 2011, and a third sister ship is scheduled to debut in spring 2012.

The first of a new class, *Carnival Dream* has a new layout, distinctive profile, and new features for Carnival. The Piazza, located midship on the Promenade Deck, is a new concept in entertainment with an indoor-outdoor cafe and live music venues, similar to the Piazza on new Princess ships. Designed as an oasis for relaxing during the day and a bustling entertainment complex at night, the venue is a large space spanning the width of the ship and opening onto the

Carnival Dream	PREVIEW	
REGISTRY Panama	LENGTH 1,004 feet	BEAM 122 feet
CABINS 1,823	DRAFT 27 feet	SPEED 21 knots
MAXIMUM PASSENGERS	PASSENGER DECKS 13	ELEVATORS NA
4,631	CREW 1,367	SPACE RATIO NA

promenade, thus making both outdoor sides of the ship part of a cafe. A massive floor-to-ceiling curved glass wall separates the room, creating spacious indoor and outdoor seating areas with great ocean views. The Piazza has a large circular dance floor and a bandstand where a variety of musical genres are showcased. It offers full bar service and an espresso bar for gelato and decadent pastries, along with high-speed Internet access.

Taking a page from Royal Caribbean, along the expansive Promenade Deck are four "scenic whirlpools" that cantilever over the sea to provide wide sea views. The Promenade itself is a return to the tradition of an outdoor thoroughfare that encircles the ship and is wide enough to have classic deck chairs, as in the olden days of fashionable steamship travel.

Other new features are Carnival's first 18-hole miniature golf course, new cabin categories (some designed especially for families), and the most elaborate children's facilities on any Carnival ship. The Lido (Deck 10) houses the line's most elaborate and expansive open-deck area with a tropical, resort-style main pool complete with a Seaside Theatre LED screen and a Serenity adults-only retreat. Both have proven to be very popular on the recently refurbished *Fantasy*-class ships. *Dream* has basketball and volleyball courts with stadium-style seating; a variety of lounges, bars, and nightspots; and an expansive 23,750-square-foot Cloud 9 Spa—Carnival's largest and most elaborate health-and-wellness center to date.

ITINERARIES *See* Itinerary Index. During her maiden year *Carnival Dream* is sailing on Saturdays from Port Canaveral on alternating seven-night eastern and western Caribbean itineraries.

CABINS *Carnival Dream* introduced several new types of accommodations, which are particularly attractive for families. These include cabins configured for five passengers and larger, more deluxe outside cabins without balconies but with two bathrooms (a full bathroom and a second one with a junior tub, shower, and sink) that sleep up to four. In addition, many cabins are interconnecting. Adjacent to the Cloud 9 Spa are 65 spa cabins and suites, which offer a number of exclusive amenities and privileges.

Carnival Dream has the line's first balcony cabins down low in the ship close to the water line and dubbed "cove balcony" cabins. (Other lines call them "hull balconies" because the balconies fit into the hull rather than protrude like the ones on higher decks.) All the accommodations feature the Carnival Comfort Bed sleep system with plush mattresses and deluxe duvets.

DINING *Carnival Dream*'s dining choices range from a casual two-level eatery with a new Italian pasta station, Indian tandoor, and burrito bar to an elegant steak house and Ocean Plaza's indoor-outdoor cafe. All are available free of charge, except the steak house menu items, specialty coffees, and select patisserie items.

The Gathering, a casual buffet on two levels, offers breakfast, lunch, and dinner alternatives and a 24-hour pizzeria. New on *Dream* is a pasta bar where passengers select a pasta, sauce, and ingredients to create a custom-made dish. At the burrito bar, patrons can create their own wraps; at the Mongolian wok, they can get made-to-order stir-fries. The Gathering also has Taste of the Nations, where a different international cuisine is featured each day; a New

York–style deli; a tandoor oven offering Indian-style dishes; a grille serving hot dogs, hamburgers, and grilled chicken sandwiches; an extensive salad bar; and frozen yogurt available 24 hours a day.

In the two-level **Scarlet** and **Crimson** main dining rooms, passengers can select from six different appetizers and soups, two salads, and six entrees each night, including pasta dishes, along with a decadent dessert menu with six different selections. Not to be missed is the warm chocolate melting cake offered nightly. For the health-conscious, dining room menus list Spa Fare selections; there are vegetarian choices and children's menus. **Chef's Art Steakhouse** (Deck 12) features prime dry-aged U.S.D.A. beef along with lobster tails, lamb chops, Chilean sea bass, Maine lobster ravioli, and more. Reservations are recommended; cost is $30 per person.

Along the Promenade Deck is Wasabi, a sushi and sake bar. The new Ocean Plaza, the ideal spot for people watching, has the Plaza Café, a patisserie and espresso bar, as well as full bar service for mojitos and other popular cocktails. In addition to a dance floor and a stage with live entertainment, Ocean Plaza offers Wi-Fi access, along with 12 stand-alone kiosks where passengers can access the FunHub, *Carnival Dream*'s comprehensive portal and onboard social network. FunHub access is also available 24/7 via 24 more stations on Decks 3, 4, and 5. Passengers can use their own laptops or ten-inch netbooks that are available for rent and usable anywhere on board. And if you are still hungry, the 24-hour room-service menu—with delivery anytime day or night at no charge—has been expanded to include new choices.

FACILITIES AND ACTIVITIES *Carnival Dream*'s massive size, along with technical advances and the imagination of the line's entertainment team, has made possible the creation of spectacular shows. All three of the ship's production numbers feature advanced video technology, sophisticated special effects, and elaborate sets and costumes.

A gritty, urban scene with brick walls, streetlights, and the latest in special effects is the backdrop for *Dancin' in the Street*, which showcases recognizable songs that run the gamut from pop and R&B to hip-hop and hard rock. The show uses *Dream*'s "Fun Force" team that performs break-dancing numbers, acrobatic Chinese-pole routines, and a high-flying trampoline segment. The second show, *Get Ready*, takes a musical look at various professions through Motown classics, R&B hits, and songs of great vocal artists. For example, "Midnight Train to Georgia" and "Mustang Sally" playfully highlight the job of transportation workers, while "Rescue Me" and "Hold On, I'm Coming" is a high-energy number focusing on rescue workers. *Xtreme Country* is, as the name implies, a toe-tapping salute to country and western music.

Carnival Dream debuted Carnival's first comedy club with six 35-minute shows on four different nights during each voyage. Presented in the Burgundy Lounge, the club highlights a variety of comedians and offers both family-friendly and adult-only performances each night (the last two performances being the adult-only shows). But perhaps the most exciting entertainment and the first ever for a North America–based cruise ship are Carnival's outdoor laser shows, which combine the latest laser technology with rock music by such popular artists as Styx, Rush, Pink Floyd, and others. Four all-weather LaserNet ScannerPro lasers are positioned high atop the Lido Deck. Each laser is independently computer controlled using software that synchronizes the lasers with the music.

In addition, *Carnival Dream* offers a diversity of entertainment venues: Ocean Plaza stages a variety of entertainment throughout the day and night; there are also singers along the Promenade, a karaoke lounge, sing-alongs in Sam's piano bar, calypso bands on the Lido Deck, live bands ranging from country to disco, plus the casino and casino bar.

CHILDREN'S FACILITIES As with all Carnival ships, *Carnival Dream* offers a wide variety of activities specifically geared toward children. Camp Carnival, with more than 19,000 square feet of space catering to children, tweens, and teens, is the line's most elaborate facility to date. WaterWorks, the biggest and best water park in the fleet, offers expansive indoor and outdoor play areas and a sprawling aqua park housing a 303-foot-long, four-deck-high corkscrew waterslide—the longest in cruising; twin 80-foot-long racing slides; and various water-spray apparatus. The water park's newest attraction is the DrainPipe, a 104-foot-long enclosed spiral waterslide attached to a giant funnel that provides riders with a fun conclusion to their trip "down the drain."

Camp Carnival (Deck 11) is divided into three distinct sections, each catering to a different age group. The area designed for children ages 2–5 has an arts and crafts center and a variety of age-appropriate toys and games; a second area, aimed at 6–9-year-olds, offers video-game consoles such as PlayStation 2 and Wii linked to the latest plasma television screens; and the third area for kids ages 9–11 includes a karaoke machine, air hockey and foosball tables, PlayStation 2, and Wii video-game consoles.

Celebrity Cruises

1050 Caribbean Way
Miami, FL 33132-2096
☎ 305-539-6000 or 800-646-1456
FAX 800-437-511
www.celebritycruises.com

TYPE OF SHIPS Stylish superliners and megaliners.

TYPE OF CRUISES Moderately priced deluxe, ample activity at comfortable pace, emphasis on quality.

CRUISE LINE'S STRENGTHS
- cuisine
- well-designed, stylish, spacious ships
- dining room service
- children's program
- value for money

CRUISE LINE'S SHORTCOMINGS
- lack of outside, wraparound promenade deck
- excessive promotion of onboard shopping
- loud deck music on some ships

FELLOW PASSENGERS Moderately affluent, ages range from late 30s to 60s in high season; ages lower in off-season. Typical passenger is age 48, married, with a household income of $50,000+. He/she tends to be an educated, experienced traveler who understands quality, owns a house in a relatively affluent suburb,

THE FLEET	BUILT/RENOVATED	TONNAGE	PASSENGERS
Celebrity Century	1995/2006	71,545	1,814
Celebrity Constellation	2002	91,000	1,950
Celebrity Eclipse	2010	122,000	2,850
Celebrity Equinox	2009	122,000	2,850
Celebrity Infinity	2001	91,000	1,950
Celebrity Mercury	1997	77,713	1,870
Celebrity Millennium	2000	91,000	1,950
Celebrity Silhouette	2011	122,000	2,850
Celebrity Solstice	2008	122,000	2,850
Celebrity Summit	2001	91,000	1,950
Celebrity Xpedition	2001	2,842	94
Unnamed	2012	122,000	2,850

and has college-age children. Fifty percent have cruised before, and of this group, 20-30% are repeaters with Celebrity. Due to the line's regular departures from the northeast United States in summer, a majority of passengers live on the East Coast; the balance come from the Midwest and West Coast.

Recommended for Middle- to upper-middle-income travelers in their 40s and older, whether first-timers or experienced cruisers, who appreciate good service and cuisine and want the recreation and entertainment of a large ship at an easy pace. Those with children during the holidays.

Not recommended for Small-ship devotees (except *Celebrity Xpedition*), those seeking a party atmosphere.

CRUISE AREAS AND SEASONS Caribbean in fall and winter; Alaska, West Coast, Baltic, Bermuda, Canada and New England, Europe, spring to fall; Hawaii, Mexico, Panama Canal, South America, winter and spring; Galápagos, year-round; Australia and New Zealand, winter.

THE LINE From its inception in 1989, Celebrity Cruises' objective has been to offer deluxe cruises for experienced travelers at affordable prices. The plan was greeted with skepticism, but in less than three years, Celebrity achieved its goal and did better than anyone imagined.

Quickly, it became apparent that Celebrity Cruises was more than just a new cruise line. It was a completely new product with a new generation of ships designed for today's travelers and new standards of service and cuisine in its price category. To their admirers, Celebrity's first vessels defined the ideal size of a cruise ship and balanced contemporary design and decor with traditional cruising.

Starting in 1992, Celebrity built a new class of cruise ships for the 21st century. Once again, Celebrity's ships were winners. The *Century* series of ships accommodated 26% more passengers in 48% more space than Celebrity's first generation of ships and had the latest in entertainment and interactive communications systems. The addition of these ships enabled Celebrity to expand beyond the Caribbean to Alaska and Europe. Celebrity was purchased by Royal Caribbean in June 1997 but operates as a separate brand.

No sooner were the *Century* ships in service than Celebrity added another new class of ships, the 91,000-ton *Millennium* group. The first of the French-built ships, *Millennium,* made her debut in 2000, followed by three more in 2001 and 2002. Then in 2006, it announced construction of five ships in yet another new class. The first, *Celebrity Solstice,* was launched in 2008, the second, *Celebrity Equinox,* in 2009, and the other three will launch at a pace of one per year to 2012.

In 2004, Celebrity took a big leap into adventure cruises with cruises in the Galápagos on board the 296-foot *Celebrity Xpedition.* As a result of Royal Caribbean Cruises' 2006 acquisition of Pullmantur (the Spanish tour and cruise operator), a ship switch took place. Pullmantur's *Blue Dream* (originally Renaissance's R6) and *Blue Moon* (originally Renaissance's R7) moved to the Celebrity Expedition's brand, while Celebrity's *Zenith* went to Pullmantur.

If this is not confusing enough, in May 2007, Royal Caribbean announced the creation of a new brand and a new category, Azamara Club Cruises, to be operated by Celebrity Cruises. Its category is meant to be "deluxe," that is, between premium and luxury, and it will be a specific competitor to the popular Oceania Cruises. Two Celebrity ships were renamed *Azamara Journey* and *Azamara Quest*. The short-lived Celebrity Expeditions brand has been retired, and its ship, *Xpedition*, has rejoined the Celebrity fleet.

STYLE From the handsome, deep-blue-and-white exteriors with their signature stacks to the elegant interiors, Celebrity ships have style, combining the glamour of traditional cruising with a contemporary look. An example: Famous contemporary artists, such as David Hockney and Roy Lichtenstein, are displayed alongside ancient Greek artifacts. On its first ships, introduced when atriums were becoming standard on cruise ships, Celebrity chose instead to make more space for public rooms, giving passengers entertainment and recreation options similar to those on megaliners but without the glitz. Small lounges, each with its own ambience and entertainment, appeal to a broad range of tastes. The ships were also designed for passenger comfort and flow. For example, the **Rendezvous Lounge** midship provides a place where passengers can mingle before and after dinner, reducing crowds waiting for the restaurant or show lounge to open.

Celebrity distinguished itself from competitors by giving top priority to superior cuisine, hiring as food consultant Michel Roux, an award-winning master French chef who operates a Michelin three-star restaurant and other food enterprises in England. Roux helped design the ships' kitchens, trained its chefs, and guided food suppliers to ensure year-round quality. He created a sophisticated but unpretentious cuisine for refined palates, emphasized quality over quantity (although quantity is there too), and established a new standard for competitors. Celebrity and Roux parted ways in 2006.

Celebrity is the first cruise line to offer Acupuncture at Sea, now available fleetwide. Celebrity Discoveries, the line's enrichment program, has been expanded with up to four lecturers on every cruise. The number of Concierge Class cabins increased from 100 to 228 on all *Millennium*-class ships.

In late 2008, Celebrity tightened its smoking policy, and now passengers cannot smoke in cabins or verandas; smoking is allowed only in specific public areas such as the port side of one lounge per ship and in a designated slot-machine area and designated locations on open decks. On *Celebrity Xpedition,* smoking is allowed only in designated outdoor areas. Violators are fined a $250 cleaning fee, charged to their onboard account, and can be off-loaded.

Celebrity launched a new program in July 2009 called "Celebrity Life," a new series of palate-pleasing, intellectually enriching, and life-enhancing programs designed to provide passengers with the most unusual, sophisticated onboard experience in premium cruising. Celebrity Life encompasses three categories. "Savor" takes its much-lauded culinary experience to new levels, with eight new wine enrichment events, six spirits and mixology tastings, and more than seven different interactive programs for guests, hosted by the ship's executive chef and team. "Discover" provides an opportunity to do or learn what one has always wanted to try, whether it's learning a new language through Celebrity's cruise-first alliance with Rosetta Stone or attending enrichment lectures through the line's new association with Smithsonian Journeys. "Renew" is the line's new health and wellness program, which offers goal-oriented classes, seminars, and treatments designed to help participants look younger, feel better, and live longer. As part of its new program called "Designed for You" launched in January 2010, the line plans a $200-million upgrade of its four Millennium-class ships with features found on the newer Solstice-class vessels.

In August 2009, Celebrity—one of the last holdouts—finally launched a flexible dining program with "Select Dining," it's name for anytime dining in the main dining room on a day-by-day basis. When choosing this option, a prepaid gratuity is added to the passenger's bill. Traditional dining is still available. Up to four days prior to boarding, passengers can go online to select their dining time for each day of their cruise; they will be accommodated on a first-come, first-served basis. Or passengers can reserve on board with the main dining room's maitre d'. The new program is available on all ships except *Celebrity Xpedition*. Another dining change for Celebrity is its replacement of the midnight gala buffet with a once-per-cruise brunch in the main dining room. The line has also upgraded casual dining in the Lido Café and added 200 new selections to dining-room menus. Passengers on a 14-day itinerary do not see the same menu twice.

DISTINCTIVE FEATURES Computer room, shipboard passenger-service manager. Children's program and specially priced shore excursions. Martini bars; ice bar. Advance bookings for **AquaSpa** and dining. Robes in all cabins. Butler service in suites. Alternative restaurant for casual dining; sushi cafes, made-to-order pasta and pizza bars; Internet cafes. Unique restaurants, music libraries, and concierge service. LeapFrog SchoolHouse programs.

RATES All published rates include port fees.

Special fares and discounts Early-bird discounts, called Five Star rates, represent some of cruising's best values. Advance-purchase fares offer up to 50% discounts on cruise-only rates (deluxe cabins and suites excluded). Base rates for seven-day cruises offer upgrades for a low fee. Two itineraries—such as Eastern and Western Caribbean—can be combined at a special rate.

- **THIRD/FOURTH PASSENGER:** Yes.
- **CHILDREN'S FARE:** None
- **SINGLE SUPPLEMENT:** 150%-200%, depending on category. Guaranteed single rate.

PAST PASSENGERS The Captain's Club, the three-tiered past-passenger recognition and benefits program, was recently redesigned with member-inspired improvements and new features. Tier credits (rather than number of cruises) are earned with each cruise, and additional awards are gained for cruises of 12 or more nights and for booking certain cabin and suite categories. New features include the Captain's Club Celebration, a social and entertainment event for all members; improved Internet and laundry benefits for Select and Elite tier members; and a new onboard lounge for Elite members. The Captain's Club Celebration, available across the fleet except on *Celebrity Xpedition,* is held once per sailing and provides the opportunity to meet fellow members, the Captain, and senior shipboard officers and to enjoy interactive cooking demonstrations and a "CC Jams" performance by shipboard musicians. The Captain's Club Lounge at Michael's Club is exclusively for Elite members 8–10 a.m. and 4–6 p.m. Elite members now receive complimentary, 90-minute Internet packages, while Select members receive a 25% discount on Internet packages.

Select- and Elite-level members also enjoy new laundry, dry cleaning, and pressing benefits, based on the length of their cruise. Members are asked to join the Captain's Club Advisory Board on a rotating basis.

Benefits for Classic members (with one to four tier credits) include access to the loyalty desk and host, a premium onboard discount booklet, the Captain's Club Celebration event, complimentary custom air request, precruise specialty restaurant reservations, member reunion cruises, one-category upgrades (when available), and an online newsletter. Select members (with five to nine tier credits) receive: all Classic benefits plus priority embarkation, a complimentary wine seminar, priority status on the shore excursion waitlist, an invitation to the senior officers' cocktail party, 25% off any Internet package, complimentary pressing of two clothing items, and discounted laundry services on cruises of 12 nights or more. Benefits for Elite members (with ten or more tier credits) include: all Select benefits plus availability of a private shipboard departure lounge with continental breakfast; priority tender service; priority waitlist for dining-room seating; elegant tea service; complimentary use of thalassotherapy pool on *Celebrity Mercury* in the Persian Garden (port days); Captain's Club Lounge at Michael's Club; 90 free Internet minutes; one free item of dry cleaning; complimentary wash, dry, and fold of one bag of laundry; and additional discounted laundry service on cruises of 12 nights or more.

THE LAST WORD Celebrity Cruises has been one of the industry's true success stories. It created the right formula at the right time: classic cruising updated for contemporary lifestyles and available at reasonable prices. Its immediate success resulted from exceeding everyone's expectations and reflected the extensive planning and testing that went into the ships. The line has maintained high standards for its price range and continues to enhance the product by adding new deluxe amenities as well as value items like reduced rates for children. Almost anyone would enjoy a Celebrity cruise, but first-timers with cultivated tastes and experienced cruisers who seek greater comfort and service than is common in this price range will most appreciate the value.

THE SHIPS Celebrity got a jump on the millennium with the 1995 debut of the *Celebrity Century*, first of a new fleet designed for 21st-century cruising. Two sister ships followed in 1996 and 1997 (one of the sisters, *Celebrity Galaxy*, was transferred in March 2009 to TUI Cruises, Royal Caribbean's joint venture in Germany). More than ten teams worked with Century's builders to achieve a comfortable, inviting, integrated design. With 48% more space than the first ships but only 26% more passengers, this spacious trio has one

Celebrity Century	QUALITY 8	VALUE B
Celebrity Mercury	QUALITY 8	VALUE B
REGISTRY Malta	LENGTH 815/866 feet	BEAM 105/105.6 feet
CABINS 907/935	DRAFT 25/25.5 feet	SPEED 21.5 knots
MAXIMUM PASSENGERS	PASSENGER DECKS 10	ELEVATORS 9/10
1,750/1,870	CREW 860/909	SPACE RATIO 40

Celebrity Cruises Standard Features

Officers Greek.

Staff *Dining:* European; *Cabin:* International; *Cruise:* European and American.

Dining facilities One main dining room with two seatings for breakfast and lunch; midnight buffet; indoor/outdoor Lido buffet breakfast and lunch. *Century* and *Millennium* classes, two-level dining room. Alternative restaurants. AquaSpa cafe on *Millennium* class and *Century*. Two dining venues on *Celebrity Expedition* ships.

Special diets Request at time of booking.

Room service 24-hour menu; butler service in suites.

Dress code Casual but not sloppy during the day; informal in evening, with two nights formal or semiformal.

Cabin amenities Direct-dial phone; bath with shower; suites with marble bathrooms. Robes in all cabins. Television with CNN and music channels. Hair dryers, safes, minibars on *Century* and *Millennium* classes.

Electrical outlets 110/220 AC; 110 AC only on *Horizon* and *Zenith*.

Wheelchair access See Cabin section for each ship.

Recreation and entertainment Card room/library, casino, three-deck show lounge, bars/lounges, disco, video game room. Bingo, lotto, horse racing, culinary demonstrations, wine tasting, fashion show, dance lessons, art auctions, floral demonstrations on *Millennium*. High-tech entertainment center on *Century* class.

Sports and other activities Two outside swimming pools; exercise classes, walks, golf putting, table tennis, deck and pool games. Golf simulators on *Century* and *Millennium* classes; volleyball, basketball on *Millennium* class.

Beauty and fitness Barber/beauty salon; health club, gym, and sauna; jogging track on sun deck; elaborate spa with beauty treatments.

Other facilities Boutiques, hospital, laundry and dry cleaning services, meeting facilities on *Century, Millennium* classes; Internet on all ships. No passenger-operated washers or dryers.

Children's facilities Playroom; teen disco; babysitters; age-specific programs with counselors year-round.

Theme cruises Occasionally.

Smoking Not permitted in dining room, theater, cabins, or verandas. Smoking permitted only in designated areas of one lounge per ship, a designated slot-machine area in the casino, and designated locations on open decks. On *Celebrity Xpedition* smoking allowed only in designated outdoor areas. Violators fined $250 cleaning fee and can be off-loaded.

Celebrity suggested tipping Per person per day: waiter, butlers (suites only), $3.50; assistant waiter, $2; restaurant, 15% service charge added to all beverage checks.

Credit cards Cruise/onboard charges: American Express, MasterCard, Visa, Discover.

of cruising's highest passenger-to-space ratios in their category. Public rooms range in style from an elegant wood-paneled bar to a futuristic disco. Sony Corporation of America designed a sophisticated, interactive communications and entertainment system, and the company's music, pictures, and electronic publishing divisions provide products and expertise.

Century's focal point is a three-deck **Grand Foyer** encircled by a staircase and topped with a painted glass dome lit as if by sunlight during the day and as a starlit sky at night. The piazza has marble floors, burled woods, brass trim, suede furniture, and a waterfall with changing fiber-optic images. Nearby are boutiques and the **COVA Café de Milano,** a floating version of Pasticceria Confetteria COVA, the Milan-based pastry shop famous for its exquisitely packaged chocolates, pastries, and signature coffees.

The atrium on *Mercury* was improved with a spiral staircase leading to the Promenade Deck, where the port side has the COVA Café.

Mercury's best new feature was a retractable glass dome covering a swimming pool and the surrounding deck. The **Oasis,** one of the ship's most popular areas, has an indoor/outdoor grill and bar that in the evening offers alternative casual dining, now available fleetwide.

The ships have multilevel, multipurpose observation lounges that become discos in the evening. One of the ships' two atriums, positioned aft and spanning three decks, opens onto the casino, **Rendezvous Lounge,** the dining room's foyer, and a Champagne bar.

Century-class vessels, like their predecessors, have multimillion-dollar art collections that are virtually contemporary art museums at sea. The focus for *Century* is contemporary masters and for *Mercury* works by artists who emerged after pop art in the 1960s and 1970s. The collections were assembled by Christina Chandris, the ships' curator and former fine art adviser, in collaboration with the Marlborough Gallery of New York. The line provides information for a self-guided art tour.

In spring 2006, *Century* emerged from a $55 million remake that transformed the decade-old ship into one closer to the line's newer *Millennium* class. The most important changes are the addition of 314 large balconies to cabins throughout the ship and 24 new cabins and suites (2 wheelchair accessible) on the stern of Deck 12. A sushi cafe and an alfresco dining area were added on Deck 12. Another big addition is a specialty restaurant with tableside cooking. The spa was expanded and a cafe added. A new Sports Deck was added on Deck 14—complete with basketball court and table tennis. Cabins were given new decor, new mattresses, duvets, and luxurious Egyptian cotton linens, accented with colorful throws and shams, and flat-panel televisions.

On Deck 7, the sports bar became a martini bar. The computer station became a High Seas Computing learning center with newly dedicated space for courses ranging from basic computer use to Web site creation to digital photography. On Deck 4, six cabins were removed to enlarge the children's area and add a new teen area and video arcade.

In spring 2007, *Mercury* was the next to get a makeover that included the addition of 14 new verandas to aft cabins and a transformation of the ship's shopping area. Among the additions were **Boutique C,** an appointment-only jewelry store; a destinations store featuring merchandise reflective of the region in which the ship is sailing; and Celebrity's **Blue Collection,** a line of upscale, casual apparel. It also has **Beauty,** Celebrity's first "cosmeceutical" (pairing science with cosmetics) store, offering brands such as Dr. Brandt, DermaNew, Freeze 24/7, L'Occitane, and others. A skin-care specialist is available by appointment. Other improvements included upgraded gym equipment, each with individual televisions; new bedding similar to that of *Century;* and refurbished pool deck, bars, and other public areas.

ITINERARIES *See* Itinerary Index.

CABINS Each deck has its own color scheme, with cabins on each using complementary colors for carpeting and bedspreads. Windows in the spacious cabins are framed in rosewood, conveying luxury and comfort. All cabins in *Century* class have built-in vanities; generous closet and drawer space; large bathrooms with showers, hair dryers, and terry robes; telephones, safes, and minibars; radios and flat-panel televisions; and Internet access and wireless facilities. Interactive cabin television enables passengers to order breakfast or room service, book spa appointments, buy shore excursions, gamble (charged to the room), order merchandise from shops, and watch pay-per-view movies (including adult selections). Interactive televisions located throughout the ship provide information and entertainment.

All cabins have minibars. The ships have penthouse and royal suites, and all suites have marble bathrooms, whirlpool tubs, verandas, and butler service. The number of Concierge Class cabins and suites was expanded to 178.

Specifications *Celebrity Century*, 304 inside cabins, 581 outside; 66 suites, 314 suites and deluxe cabins with verandas. 806 with twin beds; 10 wheelchair accessible. *Celebrity Mercury*, 305 inside cabins, 615 outside; 48 suites and 170 (184 *Mercury*) mini-suites with verandas; 877 with twin beds; 10 wheelchair-accessible. Standard dimensions, 172 square feet; all twins convertible to doubles; third/fourth persons available; no singles.

DINING *Century's* stylish **Grand Restaurant,** the main dining room, was Celebrity's first two-tiered dining room; a majestic staircase leads to a colonnaded center aisle reminiscent of the Karnak Temple in Egypt. Each of two galleys prepares food for half of the dining room, thus providing speedier service, consistent temperatures, and freshness. The *Mercury's* **Manhattan Restaurant,** with a backdrop depicting the Big Apple skyline, is completely different from those of its sisters. Food, however, is the same on all three ships and meets the line's high standards. Celebrity eschews themed nights for dinner—common on other lines. Rather, themes are given to the lunchtime buffets, when chefs are better able to do justice to ethnic cuisine. A popular nightly feature is the presentation of Gourmet Bites, a chef's sampling provided in public rooms and available fleetwide.

In its remake, *Century* got a luxurious specialty restaurant, **Murano,** offering elegant dining in the style similar to reservations-only restaurants on the *Millennium*-class ships, and with a special menu. The venue offers tableside cooking, carving, and flambéing. There is a surcharge.

The **Casual Dining Boulevard** on the Lido Deck was expanded to include a sushi cafe, a made-to-order pasta and pizza bar, and a small ice-cream parlor. The venue also serves buffet breakfasts, themed lunches, and dinner service with a casual dress code. Here, too, an afternoon tea buffet is served in addition to Celebrity's traditional **Elegant Tea. Palm Springs Grill** on *Mercury* is a casual-dining alternative restaurant. The outdoor section has a small swimming pool in a garden setting and is covered by a dome. Celebrity was the first line to offer complimentary pizza delivered to cabins—a service now available on many cruise ships.

SERVICE European-style service distinguishes Celebrity from other midprice cruise lines and has been one of the ships' best and most rewarding features.

FACILITIES AND ACTIVITIES The two-deck **Celebrity Theater** used for Broadway-style revues and cabaret shows has a sloping orchestra section and cantilevered balconies providing unobstructed sight lines. The venue has a revolving stage, the ability to handle multiple backdrops, an orchestra pit with adjustable height, sophisticated lighting, and other special effects.

The Art Deco **Crystal Room** on the *Century* (**Pavilion** on *Mercury*), a low-key nightclub for evening dancing, has etched-glass panels, a luminous alabaster dome ceiling, rotating bronze globe, and a chic color scheme of red, black, and gold that recalls 1930s New York. The **Savoy** employs a jungle motif in its late-night cabaret, and **Fortune's Casino** has the full roster of games. **Rendezvous Square,** next to the dining room, is a lively place for cocktails or socializing before and after dinner.

High atop *Century,* **Hemisphere** (Navigator Club on *Mercury*) is an airy, sunlit observation lounge by day transformed into a futuristic "disco under the dome" at night, when window blinds lower automatically, etched-glass room dividers illuminate one by one, and a special table "glows." The hemisphere then rises—casting light from within—and the dance floor appears. Telescopes are placed around the room's edge for stargazing.

Century's **Martini Bar** has the first "ice bar" at sea with a liquid wall that freezes to form a sparkling crystalline surface and a bar counter that freezes into ice-cold stone, while a solid block of ice displays bottles of liquor behind the bar. To complement the cool design, kinetic lighting was installed throughout the room and regularly changes the venue's color and appearance. The bar offers Celebrity's menu of more than 30 versions of martinis. The sister ships have martini bars too. *Century's* outdoor **Sunset Bar** on the top deck aft is a tapas bar dressed in teak, stone, and stainless steel, topped with an arched-glass canopy. There also is a bandstand with live music, offering a romantic setting at sunset. *Century's* other clubs and lounges include the fleetwide favorite, COVA Café, serving pastries and a menu of coffees, teas, and other beverages by day. At night, the cafe is transformed into a romantic, lamp-lit wine bar with live music. All other clubs and lounges on *Century*—**Crystal Lounge, Michael's Club** jazz/piano bar, **Rendezvous Lounge,** and **Hemispheres**—were refurbished. Flexible walls fold into pillars in a conference center, allowing it also to serve as a cinema, meeting room, library, or card room. Keypads in the armchairs can be used for responses to questions or for interactive movies.

Activities are numerous and varied to appeal to a range of passengers and include exercise and dance classes, contests, singles' parties, honeymooners' Champagne party, and karaoke. Informational seminars also may be scheduled. First-run movies, older films, and adult pay-per-view movies are shown daily on cabin televisions; a schedule is provided in your cabin. High Seas Computing has a new home in a dedicated space and offers Internet access and courses ranging from basic computer use to Web site creation to digital photography.

SPORTS, FITNESS, AND BEAUTY The spacious ships have 62,000 square feet of open decks that allow for a variety of sports, including simulated golf, Ping-Pong, volleyball, basketball, darts, and jogging. The *Century*'s two swimming pools have cylindrical waterfalls and are rimmed with teak benches.

AquaSpa, the ships' health and fitness center, is among the most popular features on the ships. It's one of the best-equipped gyms at sea, with a hydropool, saunas, steam rooms, cardiovascular machines, and weight stations. Personal trainers are available to create individualized training programs. Aerobics classes are ongoing. The spa offers a variety of beauty and health treatments. The most unusual is rasul, based on an Asian ceremony, with a seaweed soap shower, medicinal mud pack, herbal steam bath, and massage. Not to be missed on *Mercury* is the tranquilizing thalassotherapy treatment taken in a 115,000-gallon pool with water-jet massage stations. Spa treatments are expensive; they may be booked in advance of your cruise. During her renovation, *Century*'s AquaSpa was expanded, and a Spa Café was added. *Celebrity*'s Acupuncture at Sea program is available fleetwide.

CHILDREN'S FACILITIES With every new ship, Celebrity's children's facilities have been improved. The **Fun Factory** on *Mercury* is a 1,600-square-foot playroom, and there's also a kids' splash pool. *Century*'s Fun Factory area was expanded, adding a teen room and offering a variety of activities geared exclusively to teenagers. During summer and major holidays, Celebrity ships offer supervised daily programs for four age groups: Ship Mates (ages 3–6), Celebrity Cadets (ages 7–9), Ensigns (ages 10–12), and Admiral T's (ages 13–17). Younger children enjoy painting, drawing, songs, dances, movies, and other age-appropriate activities.

Celebrity Summer Stock lets young actors participate in theatrical shows with dances and costumes. The Young Mariners program showcases the operations of the ship and provides the opportunity to meet the captain and learn navigation by the stars. Junior Olympics offers water volleyball and basketball, golf putting, Ping-Pong, and other games. At meals, kids can join their peers at the Celebrity Breakfast Club and at dinner, order from their own or the regular menu. The program also has family activities and a masquerade parade. Century's **X-Treme,** the teen lounge and video arcade, is a dedicated space with a dance floor, juice bar, jukebox, and karaoke, along with computers offering Internet access.

Celebrity, working with LeapFrog SchoolHouse, has enhanced the onboard activities for kids of all ages by providing multisensory learning tools and instruction that align with Celebrity's travel itineraries around the world. Recognized for its interactive, electronic education programs and products for pre-kindergarten through eighth grade, LeapFrog has created on board a variety of its most popular products, plus six exclusive educational modules for children ages 3 through 9. The programs focus on such subjects as dinosaurs, science and space, sports, art and music, and wildlife. Also developed were activities tailored to specific Celebrity itineraries.

SHORE EXCURSIONS Passengers can review and make reservations online at **www.celebritycruises.com.**

THE SHIPS When the *Celebrity Millennium* debuted in 2000, she launched a new class of ships for Celebrity—somewhat larger than her sister ships and with many of the same facilities, but even more spacious and with contemporary refinements sure to please maturing baby boomers. These included the line's largest spa, a unique specialty restaurant with a dine-in wine cellar, a large boutique of designer fashions, a music library, floral conservatories with full-service florists, and huge suites.

The *Millennium,* the first of four sister ships, also enabled Celebrity to expand its cruise horizons. *Celebrity Infinity,* which debuted in 2001, offered the line's first cruises to Hawaii; *Celebrity Constellation* entered service in Europe in 2002.

The interiors, created by some of the same design teams that worked on other Celebrity ships, are the line's most sophisticated and elegant to date. They have something of a back-to-the-future decor, blending the glamour and grandeur of turn-of-the-19th-century luxury liners with the amenities and state-of-the-art technology that passengers in the new millennium expect. The ships also boast Celebrity's signature features: museum-quality contemporary art collections, an enormous **AquaSpa, COVA Café, Michael's Club** piano bar, and martini and Champagne bars.

Passengers are introduced to the *Millennium* via the **Grand Foyer,** which has a translucent, back-lit onyx staircase. Opposite the shore excursion desk is a bank of four glass elevators—the first external-facing ones ever built on a cruise ship—that capture panoramic views as they rise. One passenger, enjoying her elevator ride with Amsterdam views, said, "It was almost as good as a shore excursion." Next to the elevators, a paneled wall of wood and metallic vinyl rises from the entry to the top of the ship through a series of atriums. In October 2009, *Celebrity Millennium* was given a $10 million "refreshment" while the ship was in service, intended to make the ship sparkling rather than undergo major renovations.

The *Millennium*-class ships also have **Online@Celebrity Cruises** Internet cafe, a computer training and education program, Acupuncture at Sea, and meeting space with a business center.

With the $200-million upgrade of the *Millennium*-class ships announced in January 2009, intended to bring the ships closer in line with the newer *Solstice* class, the ships will get the **Tuscan Grille, Bistro on Five,** and an ice-topped **Martini Bar and Crush**—all popular *Solstice* features. **Café al Bacio** and **Gelateria**

Celebrity Constellation	QUALITY 8	VALUE B
Celebrity Infinity	QUALITY 8	VALUE B
Celebrity Millennium	QUALITY 7	VALUE B
Celebrity Summit	QUALITY 8	VALUE B
REGISTRY Malta	LENGTH 965 feet	BEAM 105 feet
CABINS 1,059	DRAFT 26 feet	SPEED 24 knots
MAXIMUM PASSENGERS	PASSENGER DECKS 11	ELEVATORS 10
2,038	CREW 999	SPACE RATIO 46.6

will replace the former Cova Café, and an Enomatic wine bar (the Italian wine serving system that enables guests to select wine by the glass at the touch of a button) will be added. Accommodations get new furniture, flat-panel televisions, upholstery, bedding, and carpeting. Public rooms with have new upholstery, carpeting, and color schemes reflective of the *Solstice* class. *Celebrity Constellation* is the first to receive the new enhancements, scheduled for April. Other *Millennium*-class ships will be upgraded too.

ITINERARIES *See* Itinerary Index. In summer 2010, Celebrity Summit sails every Sunday from its Cape Liberty (Bayonne, New Jersey) cruise port to Bermuda, marking Celebrity's return to that destination after four years. Celebrity Cruises has been closely identified with Bermuda since the line's founding.

CABINS Of the 1,059 cabins, 80% are outside, and of those, 74% (or 56% of the total) have verandas. All cabins have air-conditioning, minibar, safe, telephone with voice mail, shower, hair dryer, and multifunction interactive television. Standard cabins are furnished with twin beds that are convertible to queen size. *Infinity, Summit,* and *Constellation* have Connect@Sea and in-cabin Internet access. The spacious cabins are well appointed and beautifully finished. Added touches, such as a silver carafe of fresh water replenished regularly, heighten the level of service. However, there are no self-service launderettes—particularly missed on long sailings.

The Penthouse suites, measuring 1,690 square feet with veranda, have marble-floor foyers, separate living and dining rooms, baby grand piano, butler's pantry, master bedroom with generous closets, exercise equipment, dressing room with vanity, marble master bath with twin sinks, whirlpool tub, separate shower, toilet and bidet area, powder room, lights and security system, two interactive audio/visual entertainment systems with flat-panel TV, fax machine, veranda with whirlpool, wet bar, and lounges.

The Royal suites have floor-to-ceiling glass doors, separate living room with dining and sitting area, two entertainment centers with flat-panel TVs and VCRs, walk-in closet, bath with whirlpool tub and stall shower, and a veranda with whirlpool tub. There are also Celebrity suites, each with themed decor and floor-to-ceiling windows; and Sky suites (including six wheelchair accessible) also with floor-to-ceiling glass doors, sitting area with sofa bed and lounge chair, entertainment center, minibar, walk-in closet, and bathroom with whirlpool tub. All but a few suites have verandas, and all have butler service.

Celebrity Concierge Class is an enhanced level of accommodations with upgraded amenities and priority services with the notion that little extras make a big difference. The amenities include a bottle of chilled Champagne on arrival, fresh flowers and fruit, afternoon canapés, a leather key holder, personalized stationery, an oversize tote bag, and an umbrella to use during the cruise. In 2005, the number of cabins in the Concierge Class was more than doubled from 100 to 228.

Sleeping comfort is enhanced with pillow-top mattresses, lush duvets, pillow selections (such as goose down, Isotonic, and others), and a new room-service breakfast menu. In the bathroom, Concierge Class passengers find oversize Egyptian cotton towels, Frette bathrobes, two hair dryers, a Hansgrohe showerhead, and a selection of fine toiletries. On the veranda, they have a table for alfresco dining, cushioned chairs, and binoculars.

Priority service gives them priority luggage delivery, dining-time and seating preferences, shoeshine service, VIP invitations to exclusive shipboard events, priority shore excursion bookings, early embarkation and debarkation privileges, and a one-touch phone button that connects directly to a Concierge Class desk representative.

Specifications 853 outside; 206 inside. 2 Penthouse suites; 8 Celebrity suites; 8 Royal suites; 32 Sky suites (6 wheelchair accessible)—all with verandas. 5 inside and 4 outside cabins are wheelchair accessible and have flat floor entrances and 35-inch-wide cabin bathroom doorways. Public elevator doorways are 39 inches wide.

DINING The **Metropolitan Restaurant,** the main dining room spanning two levels, features bold, geometric motifs in reds, blues, and golds based on French designs from the late 1940s and early 1950s, which the designers describe as "restrained exuberance." At night, panels with dramatic architectural scenes are lowered onto the room's expansive windows, with a quintet providing quiet, elegant accompaniment. It's called **The Trellis** on *Infinity* and has an 18th-century-garden theme.

The **Olympic,** Celebrity's first specialty restaurant, is the *Millennium's* showstopper. It takes its name from a rare maritime treasure—a section of the original Edwardian carved-wood paneling from the *Olympic,* sister ship of the *Titanic.* First discovered in a private English residence, the exquisite French walnut paneling ornamented with gold leaf in Louis XVI–style was bought at auction at Sotheby's. Seating only 134 people, the intimate dining room uses an Edwardian decorating theme to convey nostalgia for the elegant golden days of steamship travel. The Olympic restaurant had the cruise industry's first demonstration galley (an open kitchen where guests can see their meals being prepared). The reservations-only restaurant (surcharge, $30 per person) has its own menu of gourmet cuisine, and to make the dining experience even more memorable, some dishes are finished and presented tableside. One treat is Waldorf pudding—a re-creation of an original dessert from the *Olympic.* There is piano and violin entertainment. Memorabilia from the *Olympic* includes White Star Line china and the ship's bell, which is on exhibit in the foyer.

Adjoining the room is a separate wine cellar, which can be used as a private dining room for small groups of eight persons or so. The wine list has almost 200 international selections, some of them quite prestigious. Passengers may also order recommended wines by the glass with each of the four courses. Wine and after-dinner espressos can increase the tab to $100 or more for a couple.

The same theme of honoring a different liner from the past, with superb design and decor re-creating the first-class dining experience of a past era, is found on *Millennium's* sister ships. *Infinity's* **S.S. United States** restaurant has etched-glass panels from the famous American liner's first-class ballroom. The French liner *Normandie* is featured in *Summit's* alternative restaurant; **Ocean Liners** on *Constellation* salutes the classic ships of the past with memorabilia and paintings of famed liners and original lacquered panels from the *Ile de France.*

At the entrance to each restaurant, glass cases containing memorabilia from the famous ships invite a close look. The ambience of the great liner era is enhanced by cutlery and china reproduced from classic ship designs as well

as the style of music performed throughout the evening. The three-hour dining experience is a unique opportunity to enjoy fine dining in the style of a
bygone age. It is certainly worth the $30-per-person service charge added to
your shipboard account when booking these restaurants.

The **Ocean Café** (**Seaside Café** on *Constellation*), an indoor/outdoor restaurant designed to resemble a Portuguese outdoor cafe, is the casual dining
venue for breakfast and lunch buffet, while the **Ocean Grill,** with a separate
entrance, is an alternative dining venue featuring steak, fish, rotisserie
chicken, pizza, and pasta. There is no fee for this by-reservation, partial-
waiter-service restaurant. Fleetwide, Celebrity's Casual Dining Boulevard on
the Lido Deck, with its sushi cafe and pizza-and-pasta bar, is a nightly alternative to the more formal atmosphere in the main dining rooms. Savvy travelers
discover the **AquaSpa Café,** where they can select light, healthy food, including fruit plates, whole-grain cereals and breads, and yogurt at breakfast, plus
cold poached salmon and chicken and crudités at lunch. Smoothies and fresh
vegetable and fruit juices are available for an extra charge.

SERVICE Service in the main dining rooms is very attentive and up to Celebrity's high standards. In the buffet-style cafe, you never have to carry your
tray; waiters are ready to assist you. The alternative dining rooms have the
highest level of service of any ship of this category and price range.

FACILITIES AND ACTIVITIES The Celebrity Theater is the line's first three-tiered
show lounge, seating 900 passengers in a classically inspired but contemporary setting with a full circular balcony. Designed by premier theater
designers, the stage, orchestra pits, and lighting can accommodate most any
Broadway-style show at sea. Sight lines are excellent, and seats are extremely
comfortable with room between rows. The use of dazzling laser and lighting
effects, movable stage levels, and the big-screen video is stunning, but they
are frequently more remarkable than the quality of entertainers.

The ever-popular **Rendezvous Lounge,** an elegant cocktail lounge that
leads to the dining room, has music for dancing, and the **Platinum Club,** on a
balcony overlooking the lounge, is a martini and Champagne bar. **Michael's
Club,** another Celebrity tradition, is a richly appointed piano bar with traditional English Georgian decor and natural cherry paneling. **Extremes,** at the
top of the ship overlooking the pool deck, was Celebrity's first sports bar.

High above the ship on Sunrise Deck is a glass-sheathed observation lounge
for panoramic viewing by day. It is transformed into an early evening cabaret
and piano bar with a dance floor and a late-night disco. The richly decorated
Fortune's Casino has 228 slot machines, 23 game tables, and a huge selection
of video casino games. Overlooking the Grand Foyer is a card and games area;
the **COVA Café,** with a separate tearoom and well-attended classical music
performances each evening; The cafe quickly becomes a favorite hangout for
many, especially non-American travelers who enjoy the European flair of this
onboard version of the classic Milan coffeehouse. Passengers are served a variety of coffee drinks, Champagne cocktails, and morning and afternoon pastries,
often accompanied by music from a harpist or pianist.

Words is a two-level library where passengers can check out books and
rent iPods. **Online@CelebrityCruises,** the line's Internet cafe, has 18 individual stations enabling passengers to check e-mail and other services. The

charge is a flat $2 per message, incoming or outgoing, or $0.75 per minute. There are reduced-rate packages of $70 for 100 minutes, $120 for 200 minutes, and $250 for 500 minutes. If you want to use your laptop, there is a $10 daily charge for rental of the Connect@Sea kit, plus the above charges for minutes. Computer classes are available for $20 an hour. Similar facilities have been added fleetwide.

SPORTS, FITNESS, AND BEAUTY The Resort Deck has the Riviera pool with four freshwater whirlpools and plenty of areas for sunbathing, as well as shaded spots. The deck also houses an entertainment area with a canopied stage and bandstand, a teakwood dance floor, two outdoor bars, and the **Grill.** Forward is the **AquaSpa, Aqua Dome,** and fitness area. The Sunrise Deck overlooking the pool area has a running track and golf simulator (reserve at the Purser's Deck), and the Sports Deck holds a full-size basketball court, paddle tennis, volleyball, and quoits, a game similar to horseshoes.

The 25,000-square-foot AquaSpa is an impressive facility that includes a large fitness area; a gym with an enormous array of equipment (rowers, exercise bikes, recumbent bikes, treadmills, steppers) and an aerobics area; and an indoor hydropool with air beds, whirlpools, sauna, steam, and tropical showers. The Persian Garden is a tranquil aromatherapy oasis that can be booked by the hour. The AquaSpa has a beauty parlor and 16 treatment rooms, including a dry float room with shower, Alpha Massage Capsule, a disabled-accessible, full-body treatment room, and other specialty rooms.

The spa offers Celebrity's water-oriented treatments of Middle Eastern, Asian, and European origin, as well as such specialties as thalassotherapy, hydrotherapy, a new aromatic bath, and first-at-sea treatments such as hot-stone therapy. Fitness consultants are on hand to assist with programs and assessments. In addition to the equipment in the fitness area, there are four daily classes, two of which, such as yoga and spinning, carry a $10 fee. Four decks down, the promenade does not completely circle the ship, as the lower level of the main dining room takes up the aft portion of Promenade Deck. Still, the long and wide promenade is a fine place for walkers and passengers for whom being on deck, close to the sea, is one of the great joys of cruising.

CHILDREN'S FACILITIES The **Fun Factory,** for children ages 3–12, offers a variety of activities with an ocean-travel and exploration theme. Children enjoy a puzzle wall, movie room, and colorful play area under the supervision of experienced counselors. A separate arts and crafts room is available for younger children, while older kids have their own broadcast room (though sometimes used by the younger children), video game arcade, dance floor, and CD jukebox.

SHORE EXCURSIONS A variety of tours from adventure activities to cultural experiences can be reviewed and booked on Celebrity's Web site.

THE SHIPS The much-anticipated debut of *Celebrity Solstice* in November 2008 was worth waiting for. She is elegant, sophisticated, and innovative in her architecture, decor, and facilities. But most of all, she has style. Photographs don't do her justice.

Celebrity Solstice's spacious interiors are stunning with a very cool, modern look. Glass walls everywhere create a light and airy ambience and offer

Celebrity Eclipse	2010	
Celebrity Equinox	PREVIEW	
Celebrity Silhouette	2011	
Celebrity Solstice	QUALITY 9	VALUE A
Unnamed	2012	
REGISTRY Malta	LENGTH 1,033 feet	BEAM 121 feet
CABINS 1,525	DRAFT 27	SPEED 24 kts
MAXIMUM PASSENGERS	PASSENGER DECKS 13	ELEVATORS 12
3,679	CREW 1,253	SPACE RATIO NA

marvelous ocean views, so you really know you are at sea. While keeping the Celebrity Cruises tradition of contemporary refinement with clean, pure lines, display of a multimillion-dollar art collection, and attention to detail, *Celebrity Solstice* departs from the past in that she does not have an overarching theme. Rather, each lounge, restaurant, and feature of the ship is meant to be distinctive, and it is. If there's a common thread, it's in the use of white—white walls, white marble columns, white leather furniture, white bed coverings, white canvas over the Lawn Club, white lounges in the solarium.

A new class of ships for Celebrity, the *Solstice* is the new pacemaker and the first of five, 118,000-ton ships being built in Germany by the well-known shipbuilder Meyer Werft, who built most of Celebrity's previous ships. The second *Solstice*-class ship, *Celebrity Equinox*, arrived in summer 2009; the third, *Celebrity Eclipse*, will enter service in spring 2010, the others in 2011 and 2012.

The ships are identical in measurements with slight modifications in some lounges and decor. For example, the art collection on *Celebrity Equinox* came from the former *Celebrity Galaxy* (now sailing for a German company). The new ships' larger size has allowed for larger standard cabins and a range of new services and amenities inspired by input from past passengers and travel agents. Approximately 90% of the accommodations are outside; 85% of those have balconies. Enlivening the walls and spaces throughout the ship is an unusual art collection created by 98 artists from 26 countries. Purchasing, producing, and installing the collection took more than two years and a $5 million investment. *Celebrity Solstice* cost about $245,000 per berth.

Prior to the launch of the *Solstice*, her great curiosity and heavily promoted feature was the Lawn Club with real grass, but equally innovative is her glass-blowing facility presented by the famous Corning Museum of Glass in New York—both firsts for a cruise ship. The more significant innovations, however, are the result of new technology often not seen. There are too many to detail here, but for starters, *Celebrity Solstice* is the cruise industry's first ship to use solar energy, with 216 solar panels in five areas on the ship. Indeed, Celebrity's effort to make its *Solstice*-class ships energy efficient and environmentally responsible would warm the heart of any environmentalist.

High overhead the gorgeous, contemporary indoor pool area of the Solarium is a glass-covered ceiling that incorporates solar panels. They produce only a fraction of the power needed to operate the ship, but they can be upgraded as technology improves. More importantly, being in the forefront of such developments for ships is one of several efforts Celebrity is making to lower its costs of energy, dependent as they are on oil, and reduce its ships' environmental impact.

For example, the hull's breakthrough design achieves both energy and environmental benefits. More than 90 tests were conducted to improve the hull's design and to optimize the ship's center of buoyancy to reduce resistance and burn less fuel, resulting in fewer emissions. Even the coating on the hull is a special nontoxic silicon that reduces frictional resistance and trims fuel consumption. It also inhibits marine growth such as barnacles and algae on the hull, among other features. Then, too, all major openings on the ship were analyzed to further minimize drag and improve efficiency, as well as lower levels of vibration and noise. Energy-efficient lighting was installed in *Solstice*-class ships as well as *Millennium*-class ships. The high-quality glazed glass of *Celebrity Solstice*'s windows reduces heat transfer into cabins and public areas, in turn reducing energy required for air-conditioning while protecting the ship's interiors and furnishings from sun damage.

Did you ever think river rocks could reduce water and energy consumption? Apparently they can when substituted for ice beds in the ship's buffet areas—enough that Celebrity is using them across the fleet. The line has also installed a new type of showerhead that conserves water. *Celebrity Solstice*'s advanced wastewater purification systems are capable of treating all wastewater streams on board—including gray and black water—and restoring it to drinking-water quality before discharging. The ship houses low-energy reverse osmosis water makers to produce fresh drinking water, reduced-flow dishwashers, and low-consumption laundry equipment, and the line is making improvements to its engines, turbines, and air-conditioning systems.

ITINERARIES *See* Itinerary Index. For the first time, Celebrity placed its newest ship, *Celebrity Solstice,* on seven-day alternating Eastern and Western cruises. The two itineraries, which will be continued in 2011, can be combined into a 14-day cruise that does not repeat any ports except Fort Lauderdale.

CABINS So much publicity about the 130 AquaClass cabins preceded the ship's inauguration, it would have been easy to overlook the other accommodations. Deluxe and standard cabins are 15% larger than those on other Celebrity ships and have larger bathrooms, expanded safes, and digital entertainment. In a deluxe cabin with a balcony—which represents more than half of the ship's accommodations—standard features include two beds convertible to queen, individual nightstand reading lights, a bedside shelf for personal items, a vanity, a sitting area with sofa (trundle bed in some cabins), a shower with footrest, a flat-panel television, Wi-Fi (fee), and a floor-to-ceiling glass door that opens onto the veranda. Features are the same in ocean-view cabins, except there is no veranda.

AquaClass cabins, located near the AquaSpa on Deck 11, are handsome and comfortable with very modern decor. The new category for a new style of cruising was "expressly designed to provide . . . a balance between indulgence and wellness," according to Celebrity. The AquaClass experience is meant to embody five pillars related to health and wellness: renew—sleep, replenish–nutrition, refresh–body, restore–spirit, revive–fitness. Well, maybe. Basically, these cabins are the same as Concierge, Sunset, and Deluxe ocean class, but with a slightly different decor and amenities.

A team of five women from outside Celebrity Cruises was asked for its input on cabin design, but how much these ladies had to say about the final layout is unknown. For example, the cabin has a large, comfortable couch, but it's placed directly in front of the closet, making access to the closet difficult. A set of drawers, too small to be very useful, gets hot air from the adjacent refrigerator. A flat-panel television mounted on a flexible arm can be viewed from almost anywhere in the cabin, but its remote control—a small computer keyboard—is too large to fit on the nightstand.

In AquaClass cabins, patrons get a special color-coded SeaPass card; a welcome kit with a teeth-whitening sample, slippers, a spa-oriented amenities kit, and shower gel; European-style bedding, pillow menu, and sound and aromatic elements for relaxation; nightly turndown ritual; and a carafe of flavor-infused iced tea. One of the cabin's best features is its roomy bathroom with a large shower and footrest, a five-head Hansgrohe "shower tower" designed to invigorate, oversize bath towels, and Frette robes. AquaClass room service offers healthy menu options. Other amenities include daily canapés, a dedicated television channel with special programming, music recommended by music therapists, and a "conscious dream enhancer" to increase mental awareness during waking hours. To enhance further a spa lifestyle at sea, AquaClass patrons enjoy exclusive dining in Blu; use of the Persian Garden, aromatherapy steam room, and AquaSpa relaxation room; spa concierge services; and a library of wellness books on yoga, aging, herbology, healthy cooking, nutrition, and more.

Family veranda suites are large and have a master bedroom with two beds convertible to queen size, a second bedroom with one twin bed, a sitting area with a sofa convertible to a trundle bed, a vanity, a privacy partition, a 32-inch LCD television, and wireless Internet access (fee).

In the Penthouse suites, the master bedroom has a king-size bed, flat-panel television, vanity, and walk-in closet; a marble master bath with whirlpool tub, shower stall with dual showerheads, double sinks, and small television; and floor-to-ceiling sliding glass doors opening onto a large veranda. These suites also have a separate living room with a dining area and are furnished with a baby grand piano, queen sofa sleeper, full bar, surround sound entertainment system with a 52-inch flat-panel television, wireless connection, and a full guest bath.

Specifications Suites: 2 Penthouse (1,291 square feet; veranda 385 square feet); 8 Royal/4 Family (590/575 square feet; veranda 153/53–106 square feet); 44 Sky/12 Celebrity (300/394 square feet; veranda 77/105 square feet). Junior suites: 130 Aqua Class/273 Concierge/24 Sunset/719 Deluxe (192 square feet; veranda 53 square feet). Standard: 70 outside (176 square feet); 140 inside (183–200 square feet). 30 wheelchair accessible: 4 Sky (344 square feet; veranda 102 square feet); 4 AquaClass/4 Concierge/8 Deluxe (299 square feet; veranda 80 square feet); 4 outside (289 square feet); 6 inside (245 square feet). 418 third- and fourth-passenger cabins; 121 connecting.

DINING From its inception, Celebrity Cruises made its reputation on its fine cuisine. So naturally, *Celebrity Solstice's* debut was met with high culinary expectations. She does the company proud. The ship has 10 dining venues—the most for Celebrity—ranging from a casual bistro to Asian fare in elegant surroundings. The cruise line partnered with some famous restaurant designers, like Adam Tihany, creator of such well-known New York restaurants as Per Se, Jean Georges, and Le Cirque, as well as top restaurants in Las Vegas and London. In his first design on board a cruise ship, Tihany created the spectacular main dining room, a classic steak house described as Napa-meets-Old-World-Italy, and the casual but stylish Lido buffet.

The Grand Epernay, the two-level main dining room with a white and bone decor is stunning. Touches of Old Hollywood glamour blend with a refined contemporary design that is highlighted by a dramatic, two-story glass wine tower. Open for breakfast, lunch, and dinner, it has a Champagne collection from the region that inspired its name and includes Perrier-Jouet Grand Brut, Moet & Chandon, and other famous bubbles.

The ship's four alternative restaurants (with surcharges) are clustered aft on Deck 5. On seven nights or less itineraries, passengers get two complimentary evenings; on eight nights or more itineraries, three evenings ($5 per person, per dinner recommended for gratuity). The reservations-only Murano ($30 per person), Tuscan Grille ($25 per person), and Silk Harvest ($20 per person) fill quickly; reservations should be made prior to boarding. Murano, a beautiful, intimate wood-paneled room with fine furniture and soft lighting, is reflective of specialty restaurants on *Millennium*-class ships. Classic and modern continental cuisine is served in an elegant setting with fine china, silver tableware, and Riedel stemware. Its wine cellar stocks selections from around the world, including limited-production vintages. At Tuscan Grille, patrons enter through an archway reminiscent of a Napa Valley wine cellar. Here, they enjoy Caesar salad prepared tableside, an antipasti bar, Kobe beef, and a variety of steaks, paired with fine Italian wines. Silk Harvest serves fusion Thai, Vietnamese, Japanese, and Chinese cuisine in an exotic Asian decor. A selection of sakes, Asian beers, and cocktails created with ginger root and acai berries are also available.

Blu, with a white rose–sculptured wall, is intended exclusively for passengers booked in AquaClass. It's open to suite guests, based on availability ($5 per person gratuity). The menu, in keeping with the wellness program of Aqua-Class, features "clean cuisine" with such items as roasted beet salad with goat cheese, blackened ahi tuna, and herb-crusted rack of lamb. AquaClass and suite patrons can also enjoy continental breakfast here in the morning. The Bistro on Five, where the specialty is crepes, has sandwiches, soups, and salads and is proving to be very popular ($5 per person gratuity). Café al Bacio & Gelateria, an upscale coffeehouse and patisserie reminiscent of a popular European cafe, features traditional gelatos and Italian ices, specialty coffees, and fresh-baked pastries. AquaSpa Café is a good option for light fare in the quiet setting of the Solarium at tables or relaxing on a lounge chair. Mast Grill & Bar, a poolside eatery, offers burgers, tacos, nachos, hot dogs, and other comfort food.

Oceanview Café and Grill is the prettiest Lido buffet I've ever seen. Designed as a chic but casual marketplace, the large, bright room has a great layout with a dozen or so food-station islands separated by plenty of space for easy passenger flow, even during the busiest hours. Open for breakfast, lunch, and dinner, it has indoor-outdoor seating. In the evening, a section of linen-draped tables provides a casual dining option ($2 per person gratuity); one area is open 24/7.

FACILITIES AND ACTIVITIES The ship's spaciousness is evident throughout, but particularly in the white-dressed Sky Lounge, the multipurpose, topside observation lounge with wonderful views; the glass-enclosed Solarium; and the huge Solstice Theater with comfy seats tiered to provide good sight lines from every direction. Three new 45-minute shows, written by Poet Theatricals, are playing: *Ghost Light* is a celebration of Broadway favorites, past and present, with a young, energetic cast; *Pulse,* with the central character Rhythm Man, ignites a motion and vocal spectacle driven by widely varied music and instruments that create the beat; and *Solstice,* a European-style theatrical circus.

The *Solstice* show is built around the clash of day and night and includes vocalists, physical comedy, spectacular acrobatic and aerial performances, and other specialty acts. As well-known cruise lecturer, Bill Miller, describes it: "The music soared, steam sprayed, laser lights darted, and all while the likes of trim, handsome Rumanians and chiseled, beautiful Russians were suspended from steel cables, some of which travel on tracks . . . there were trampolines, huge spinning wheels, and a poised figure dangling by a single leg from a long silk strand. Characters, including the sparklingly dressed, golden ray–crowned Sun Queen, worked their interwoven magic . . . singing, dancing, floating above the audience. Afterward, standing ovations!"

Complementing the three shows are a variety of specialty acts, also created with Poet Theatricals, that include still performers, ring jugglers, fairy characters, and a variety of acrobatic artists. *Celebrity Solstice* has numerous lounges and bars with decor ranging from the traditional in Michael's Bar to the retro, funky decor of the high-energy Quasar Nightclub, where wild looking white leather chairs are suspended from the ceiling. There are quiet corners like the Passport Bar or Cellar Masters for wine enthusiasts, as well as the lively Martini Bar and Crush—another place bathed in white.

On the Boulevard (Deck 4) and at the Galleria Boutiques (Deck 5) are 18 shops. Topping the list for serious shopping is the high-end jewelry store, Boutique C, featuring the newly patented "Solstice Cut" diamond, an 86-faceted, 10-sided stone, available only on *Solstice*-class ships.

But the ship's showstopper is The Lawn Club on Deck 15. There is nothing like it on any cruise ship, past or present. If you are skeptical, as I was, you'll be pleasantly surprised. It's very pretty with something of a country club ambience and is more functional than I had imagined, with a three-hole putting course, croquet, and a grassy area for picnicking or relaxing. Alas, Keep Off the Grass signs went up in areas with brown patches after only three days of use. The half acre of Bermuda grass, cut like a putting green, has a full-time groundskeeper.

The Lawn Club shares its forward area with the Hot Glass Show—another cruise ship first—which draws huge crowds, day and night. Called the 2300 Show, referring to the heat of the oven, demonstrations in the art of glass-blowing by master glassblowers ("gaffers") from the Corning Museum of Glass, are given three times during the day and once at night. As an enriching entertainment option, you have to say, it's original. Aft of the Lawn Club is the Patio on the Lawn and the quiet Sunset Bar, which is the most pleasant, least-talked-about, quiet spot on the ship. It offers fabulous views of the ocean and just enough soft breezes for a true "wow!" at sunset, especially with a Eureka, the club's signature cocktail, in hand.

SPORTS, BEAUTY, FITNESS An advantage of a large cruise ship like the *Solstice* is that it has enough space for three swimming pools: two outdoors, a family pool with an adjacent fun fountain called the Wet Zone and a sports pool; and the third, the indoor, adults-only Solarium, which is not only quiet but beautiful, with luxurious lounges and a waterfall fountain that changes colors at night. There is no charge to use any of the 12 cabanas that line the main pool; they are taken on a first-come, first-served basis.

Forward on Resort Deck (11), the AquaSpa with its cool blue-and-white colors offers the usual massages, facials, manicures, and pedicures. But you can also have your teeth whitened in a 30-minute session for $199, a Botox treatment for $300, or work on what ails you in a 50-minute acupuncture session for $150. Further forward is the fitness center, with ladies' and gents' changing rooms, and a gym fully stocked with exercise equipment; an hour with a personal trainer is $85. An aerobics area offers a variety of exercise classes, usually with a small charge. The new indoor cycling workout ($30) consists of three sessions, which are 45 minutes each.

THE SHIP Celebrity's *Xpedition,* added in 2004, is completely different from the rest of the fleet. Small and deluxe, it is used for year-round sailing in the Galápagos Islands. But even eco-focused travelers appreciate fine cuisine, wine, and modern amenities, and indeed, Celebrity Cruises uses as a tag line for *Celebrity Xpedition*'s Galápagos cruises: "Where the untamed meets the indulged."

Celebrity is able to offer these cruises by having purchased an Ecuadorian tour operator that held the necessary government permits for Galápagos sailings and ensuring that the 100-passenger *Xpedition* (formerly the *Sun Bay*) was Ecuadorian-flagged and crewed. The German-built vessel is headed by an experienced Royal Caribbean or Celebrity captain, assisted by Ecuadorian and international officers. Most of the staff are experienced in cruise service but have been retrained by Celebrity.

The cruise includes all meals, naturalist guides, folkloric entertainment, enrichment program, shore excursions, gratuities, and Zodiac rides, as well as bottled water, soft drinks, and alcoholic beverages (except premium brands) on board. On cruise-tour packages, passengers fly to Quito for a two-night stay at the luxurious J. W. Marriott hotel and a city tour by bus and on foot. In addition, the package includes airport transfers, round-trip flights between

Celebrity Xpedition	QUALITY 7	VALUE B
REGISTRY Ecuador	LENGTH 296 feet	BEAM 49 feet
CABINS 50	DRAFT 25 feet	SPEED 15 knots
MAXIMUM PASSENGERS 94	PASSENGER DECKS 10	ELEVATORS none
	CREW 64	SPACE RATIO NA

Quito and Baltra via Guayaquil, Galápagos entry fee, one or two nights' hotel stay in Quito on return, and some meals in Quito.

Despite its small size, *Xpedition* feels spacious. The **Discovery Lounge** includes a large bar, comfortable seating, and a library with books and games. Here, passengers attend folkloric presentations, lectures, and naturalist discussions about each day's program. The ship also has a small exercise room with sauna, several bars, outdoor deck lounging space, and a small boutique.

The open seating **Darwin Dining Room** is elegant but not stuffy. It serves breakfast and luncheon buffets with cooked-to-order dishes, including omelets and pastas, and full-service dinner. Waiters eagerly bring drinks and special sandwiches or entrées beyond the regular menu choices. Guests can also dine alfresco on many occasions at the **Beagle Grill.**

Cabins and suites have television, telephone, fluffy cotton bathrobes, Egyptian cotton towels, safe, and hair dryer. Standard cabins (145 square feet) have a large rectangular window and are furnished with two twin beds or one queen bed, a small sofa, desk area with minifridge, and mirror. There is ample closet space and a well-appointed bathroom. The one penthouse suite (460 square feet) has two single beds and one double bed, as well as two verandas. Other suites measure 230 square feet.

Xpedition does not have a passenger elevator and is not equipped to accommodate wheelchair passengers or those who can't climb two or three flights of stairs. The ship has a doctor on board for every voyage.

Passengers enter and leave the ship via a platform incorporated into the vessel's structure. To explore ashore, they are tendered via Zodiac craft and proceed on foot. The ship stops at several islands for wildlife viewing. Snorkeling and swimming are included on several excursions; a dive trip can be booked for an additional charge. As on all Galápagos cruises, naturalist guides or the ship's staff accompany all excursions, providing commentary and discussions.

Costa Cruise Lines

Venture Corporate Center II
200 South Park Road, Suite 200
Hollywood, FL 33021-8541
☎ **954-266-5600 or 800-462-6782**
FAX **954-266-2100**
www.costacruises.com

TYPE OF SHIPS New, modern superliners.

TYPE OF CRUISES Mass market, designed for Europeans as much as North Americans—hence, more European in service and ambience.

CRUISE LINE'S STRENGTHS
- Italian style and service
- friendly, attentive crew
- itineraries
- innovative, new ships

CRUISE LINE'S SHORTCOMINGS
- noise level in dining rooms
- excessive announcements on European-based ships
- language problems

FELLOW PASSENGERS Costa has two seasons: Caribbean (and South America for its European clients), from late fall to early spring, and Europe, mainly from spring through fall, although some European cruises are now year-round. This results in two sets of passengers. In the Caribbean, up to 70% of passengers are North Americans, depending on the cruise; average age is 54 years, with annual household income of $50,000+. A bevy of Italian-American fans and newly-weds are attracted by the line's Italian style. Most have cruised before.

In Europe, 80% or more are Europeans likely to have traveled abroad, probably even cruised before. Among North Americans, average age is about the same as Caribbean cruisers, but they would be inclined to rent a car and drive through Europe on their own instead of taking an escorted tour. They enjoy traveling with and meeting people from other countries. Yet another profile is emerging from Costa's new commitment for sailing from Dubai and from basing two of its ships in Asia.

Recommended for Italophiles; first-time cruisers and less experienced travelers who want to sample European ambience, but with facilities typical of a large ship; and repeat cruisers who want to try something different.

Not recommended for Those who like small ships as well as an all-American atmosphere, or those who prefer to travel with Americans.

CRUISE AREAS AND SEASONS Baltic Sea, Black Sea, Caribbean, New England and Canada, Egypt and Dubai, Indian Ocean and Mauritius, Far East, Greek islands, the Holy Land, Mediterranean, northern Europe, Norwegian fjords, Russia, South America, and transatlantic cruises.

THE LINE Genoa, Italy-based Costa Crociere, parent company of Costa Cruise Lines, had been in the shipping business for more than 100 years and in the passenger business for almost 60 years when it was bought jointly by Carnival Corporation and Airtours, a European tour company, in 1997. (Three years later, Carnival acquired Airtours' shares as well.)

Costa, Europe's largest cruise line, was among the earliest lines to offer one-week Caribbean cruises from Miami (1959) and the first to introduce an air/sea program (late 1960s). Despite its long Florida-Caribbean association, Costa changed course in the 1990s to become more Europe focused. Of its 14 ships, only 2 sail from U.S. ports, and they sail only in winter. The others are positioned in Europe, Dubai, and Asia.

In the 1990s, Costa launched five new ships that cost more than $1 billion and were intended to serve a broad spectrum of passengers. The ships combined modern and classic qualities with new design features. The line added the larger *Costa Victoria* in 1996, followed by six more even larger ships between 2000 and 2007, which more than tripled the line's passenger capacity.

But Costa wasn't finished. In 2009, in a duel ceremony in Italy, the line launched its largest ship to date, the 114,500-ton *Costa Pacifica*, and the 92,700-ton *Costa Luminosa*, with another three ships scheduled for delivery in the next three years. These additional ships will bring the Costa fleet to a total of 18 ships by 2012. Meanwhile, all the other ships in the fleet have been renovated and upgraded.

THE FLEET	BUILT/RENOVATED	TONNAGE	PASSENGERS
Costa Allegra	1990/2001	28,430	1,000
Costa Atlantica	2000/09	85,619	2,114
Costa Classica	1991/2001/07	52,926	1,356
Costa Concordia	2006/09	114,500	3,000
Costa Deliziosa	2010	92,700	2,260
Costa Fascinosa	2012	114,500	3,000
Costa Favolosa	2011	114,500	3,000
Costa Fortuna	2003	102,600	2,720
Costa Luminosa	2009	92,700	2,260
Costa Magica	2004	102,600	2,720
Costa Marina	1990/02/07	25,600	1,000
Costa Mediterranea	2003	86,000	2,114
Costa Pacifica	2009	114,500	2,260
Costa Romantica	1993/2003/09	53,049	1,356
Costa Serena	2007/09	114,500	3,000
Costa Victoria	1996/2004/07	75,166	1,928

Costa's trailblazing move in 2006 as the first European mass-market line to base ships in Asia and Dubai has proven to be so successful that the line has added further capacity in both locations in 2010. Also in 2010, Costa launched a groundbreaking program for mainland Chinese passengers with four-night cross-straits cruises from Hong Kong to Taiwan.

Costa passengers sailing on all of Costa's itineraries worldwide may now check in online and print their boarding documents up until the day prior to departure. Since 2008, Costa passengers departing on Caribbean routes from Port Everglades have been able to check in at its electronic kiosks—the first to offer this service.

Costa is on Facebook at **www.facebook.com/costacruises.na** and Twitter at **www.twitter.com/CruiseCosta.**

STYLE In the early 1980s, Costa coined the phrase "Cruising Italian Style" to celebrate its Italian basis in everything from design to cuisine. Its fleet is designed and built in Italy by Italians, with floors and walls of Italian marble, splendid wood cabinetry, designer fabrics and linens, and Italian art through-out. The ships reflect the sophisticated architecture and decor of modern Italian designers rather than the classic Italian look. Indeed, Costa sees its ships as ambassadors of Italian excellence and its mission as a modern-day patron of the arts and design, promoting contemporary cultural and artistic forms of expression and focusing on the central role of art and architecture as added value in the design of its ships.

Life on board is made to seem *molto Italiano*, from the pasta and espresso to Italian language lessons, Italian cooking classes, Italian ice cream, pizzas in the pizzerias, and toga parties. Theme nights such as Festa Italiana feature an Italian street festival with boccie ball games, tarantella dance lessons, pizza dough–tossing contests, and more. Yet for all the trimmings, the Italian ambience has been diluted, mainly because Costa ships no longer have all-Italian crews.

Ships are modern, with gyms, spas, and fitness programs, and Costa's Caribbean shore excursions emphasize outdoor activities. One of Costa's most popular attractions is its private beach on Isla Catalina off the Domini-can Republic. The island is near the sprawling resort of Casa de Campo, which, among its many facilities, has a tennis village, four of the Caribbean's best golf courses, and a marina village with restaurants and shops, enabling Costa's ships on Eastern Caribbean cruises to spend the day at the island and the evenings at the marina.

All dining and public rooms on Costa ships are nonsmoking, but that doesn't mean passengers, especially European ones, don't light up. Ships do not have self-service launderettes, a much-appreciated amenity available on most new large ships. Costly laundry and pressing services are available from the ships' facilities.

DISTINCTIVE FEATURES Free hot pizza throughout the day. On Caribbean cruises, couples can renew their wedding vows in a shipboard ceremony. Alternative dining on the newest ships, unusual private Caribbean island, fiesta nights, toga party. Grand Prix driving simulator and spa cabins and suites on the newest ships, beginning with *Concordia/Serena*.

RATES Port charges are included.

Special fares and discounts Early booking fares offer up to 45% savings. Ask about ProntoPrice, the line's pricing policy for early bookers.

- **CHILDREN'S FARE:** Same as third/fourth passenger fares (works for single parents too); also $199 or "Kids Sail Free" for children ages 17 and younger on some cruises.
- **SINGLE SUPPLEMENT:** 180%–200%.

PAST PASSENGERS Costa Club is the line's passenger club, which passengers can join after their first cruise. With each subsequent Costa cruise, you receive points based on the number of days of the cruise and expenditures charged to your cruise card. The Costa Club card is valid for three years. Depending on your category, members receive discounts in the beauty salon, fruit basket, free dinner in an alternative restaurant that has a charge; and discounts on cruise fares, ranging from 5–18%, among others. Members also receive mailings announcing new itineraries and a Costa magazine.

THE LAST WORD Costa prefers to be number one in Europe, where it has a strong base and years of experience, rather than struggle in the fierce competition of the Caribbean. The strategy virtually guarantees that when you take a Costa cruise in Europe, the experience will be European rather than one catering to American tastes. Some Americans welcome the opportunity to take a European vacation with Europeans. Others are turned off by cliques in lounges and bars and the steady stream of announcements—for bingo, shopping talks, and shore excursions—in five languages, even though English-speaking hostesses are aboard to cater to North Americans. Fortunately, the multilingual announcements on Caribbean cruises are kept to a minimum and normally are used when matters of safety are being broadcast.

In sum, Americans who want to cruise Europe or the Caribbean on a large ship with the latest amenities will find the facilities, activities, and entertainment on Costa to be similar to those on mainstream U.S. lines like Carnival. There's plenty of action for children, teens, and adults, from games and sports contests to classes, shopping, and shows—plus, an international flair and nightlife centered around dancing and dining—and cruising Italian style.

Areas are designated as smoking or nonsmoking on Costa ships, but some European smokers flout the restrictions—defiantly.

THE SHIPS *Costa Atlantica* and her twin, *Costa Mediterranea,* were the largest, fastest ships in the fleet when they entered service in 2000 and 2003. After Costa came under the Carnival umbrella, and with interior design in the hands of architect Joe Farcus, who is known for creating the flamboyant decor of

Costa Atlantica	**QUALITY** 7	**VALUE** C
Costa Mediterranea	**QUALITY** 7	**VALUE** C
REGISTRY Italy	**LENGTH** 960 feet	**BEAM** 106 feet
CABINS 1,057	**DRAFT** 19.5 feet	**SPEED** 24 knots
MAXIMUM PASSENGERS	**PASSENGER DECKS** 12	**ELEVATORS** 12
2,680	**CREW** 920	**SPACE RATIO** NA

Costa Cruise Lines Standard Features

Officers Italian.

Staff *Dining*: Italian, European, Asian, and others; *Cabin*: International; *Cruise*: International.

Dining facilities One main dining room (two on *Costa Victoria*; five restaurants on *Concordia* class), two seatings for breakfast and dinner, one for lunch, midnight buffet featuring Italian cuisine; indoor and outdoor buffet breakfast and lunch. Alternative dining (extra charge) on newest ships. Pizzerias and pastry cafes on most ships.

Special diets Should be requested four weeks in advance.

Room service 24 hours, limited menu; butler service in suites with full service for meals from dining room menus.

Dress code Casual; informal, evenings; two nights formal/semiformal.

Cabin amenities Phone, radio, private shower, hair dryer, safe, television; suites have whirlpool bath, minibar, and veranda.

Electrical outlets 110/220 AC; adapters available on board.

Wheelchair access 6 cabins on *Classica, Romantica, Victoria*; 8 on *Allegra, Atlantica, Mediterranea*; 24 on *Magica, Fortuna*; 29 on *Concordia* class.

Recreation and entertainment Casino, bars, and lounges with nightly entertainment, showrooms, disco, dance, Italian language lessons, bingo, bridge, horse racing, library, card room. *Concordia/Serena*: Grand Prix driving simulator, giant video screen on Pool Deck.

Sports and other activities Three swimming pools, *Atlantica, Concordia class, Fortuna* (one for children); *Mediterranea, Magica, Serena*; two, *Classica, Romantica, Victoria* (plus one inside); one, *Allegra, Marina, Riviera*. Exercise classes, snorkeling lessons, paddle tennis, table tennis, deck and pool games. *Victoria, Atlantica, Mediterranea, Magica, Fortuna*, tennis and basketball.

Beauty and fitness Barber shop and beauty salon, spa, sauna, European beauty treatments, fitness centers, jogging track, whirlpools.

Other facilities Boutiques, medical facility, laundry and dry cleaning services, meeting room, chapel. Internet access on all ships.

Children's facilities Costa Kids year-round; babysitters. (No babysitting service in cabins.) Concordia class, computer games for kids.

Theme cruises Golf, food and wine, health, music, others.

Smoking Smoking in designated public areas; all dining and public rooms are nonsmoking.

Costa suggested tipping Costa debits passenger shipboard account as follows: $3 per person per day each for cabin steward/stewardess, waiter; $1.50 per person per day for waiter's assistant and $1 per person per day for head waiter. Passengers may change the amounts by contacting Guest Relations desk; 15% gratuity added to all beverage bills (including mineral water in dining room).

Credit cards For cruise payment and onboard charges: American Express, Carte Blanche, Diners Club, Discover, MasterCard, Visa.

Carnival ships, there was considerable concern that he would "Carnivalize" these Costa ships. Farcus's imprint is unmistakable, but he has combined touches of his trademark fantasy and glitter with European elegance that seems to work and delight most—but not all—of the North Americans and Europeans who have sailed on them. It's safe to say that Farcus's decor is the antithesis of the modern, spare interiors created by Italian designers for some of Costa's other ships.

Atlantica, because of her balconies and large windows, has a more open, lighter appearance than *Costa Victoria*, which subsequently had balconies added to 246 of her cabins. During *Atlantica*'s recent renovation, 44 new spa cabins were added. Most of the public rooms are on Decks 2 and 3, anchored by a spectacular glass-ceiling atrium. The decor of *Atlantica*, including the use of Murano glass and inlaid mosaic, is flamboyant, with such features as the *Alice in Wonderland*–style red-leather chairs with extremely high backs. The Farcus touches are everywhere—the red-leather benches near the theatrical, multilevel fitness room have little boots on them. Whimsical or fantastic motifs are worked into the carpets, the banquettes, and the tables with subtlety and taste.

Atlantica is dedicated to Federico Fellini, the great Italian filmmaker, with her 12 passenger decks named for movies directed by him and huge blow-ups from his work placed in public rooms. (Although, as one passenger pointed out to us on a recent cruise, none of Fellini's movies are to be found among the ship's movie selections.) Besides the impressive large public spaces, there are intimate quiet areas, like the small Italian garden by the chapel. The ship also pays homage to Venice with Caffe Florian, a replica of the 18th-century landmark in St. Mark's Square, with a menu and music taken from the original. Traditionalists will probably find these rooms to be the ship's most attractive areas. *Costa Mediterranea* is dedicated to the history, art, and architecture of Italy and the Mediterranean. The decks, for example, are named for mythic and historic figures—Medea, Pandora, Cleopatra, etc. Recently, *Costa Mediterranea* completed a multimillion-dollar refurbishing.

Atlantica was the first Costa ship to offer Internet access, available in a center that doubles as the library and in some cabins and suites, where guests can bring their own laptop computer or rent one. The cost is $0.50 per minute.

The ships have received the Green Star from the Italian Register of Shipping for innovative environmental protection design.

ITINERARIES *See* Itinerary Index.

CABINS The ships have 13 categories of cabins, most on Decks 1 and 4 through 8. Of the total 1,057 cabins, 78% are outside. The 678 cabins, or almost 65% of cabins and suites, have verandas with clear acrylic barriers in front, enabling passengers to lie in bed and look out at the port of call or the sea. Another 68 cabins have French balconies, but these have views obstructed by the lifeboats, as noted in the deck plan.

Cabins are stylish in decor and very well designed, with an unusual amount of polished hardwood floors, as well as carpets and fine leather. All cabins have direct-dial telephone, television, minibar, safe, hair dryer, amenities, and ample storage. In the suites, the bedside lamps have exceptionally attractive Murano glass shades with smaller, concentrated lights attached for nighttime reading. The suites also have plush robes, marble baths, double sinks, and Jacuzzi tubs. In standard cabins, showers are much larger than on the line's previous vessels.

Passengers booked in the new spa suites receive extra treats, including three spa treatments, two fitness or meditation classes, access to the Wellness restaurant with spa cuisine, and priority spa reservation times. The spa cabins feature special showers and minibars stocked with healthy food and beverages.

Specifications 824 outside cabins; 233 inside; 678 cabins (including 58 suites and 44 spa cabins) with verandas. Cabins with verandas measure 210 square feet; inside cabins, 162 square feet; suites with verandas, 360 square feet. 8 are wheelchair accessible.

DINING The ships have several dining venues. The two-level **Tiziano Restaurant** (**Degli Argentieri** on *Costa Mediterranea*) is the main dining room serving undistinguished continental cuisine with some Italian specialties; the **Botticelli Buffet** offers breakfast and lunch in an informal setting with a rather limited, repetitive selection; and the **Napoli Pizzeria** serves a variety of fresh, hot pizzas throughout the day. Surprisingly, there are no pasta stations in either the dining room or the Lido buffet, as on Costa's other ships.

The dining rooms are comfortable, but the noise level is high, depending on where you sit. Healthful menus with low-fat, low-carb, low-calorie, and low-cholesterol courses are available in the dining rooms for lunch, dinner, and at the informal breakfast. A generous number of vegetarian dishes is offered, and there is a separate children's menu.

Club Atlantica by Marchesi (**Club Medusa** on *Mediterranea*), the alternative, by-reservation restaurant, is located at the top of the ship, above the Lido restaurant. It is modeled after its namesake in Venice and has an extra charge of $25 a person—and it's worth every penny. It offers two appetizing single-choice menus and wines served amid candles, flowers, and live musical entertainment. If you come only once, you might want to mix and match selections from both menus. The cuisine here is so outstanding that it shows up the dining room's mediocre results and makes one wonder why there is such a marked difference.

SERVICE Not everyone agrees about the service. Some say it's excellent, warm, and efficient; others say it's often haphazard. But for sure, longtime Costa fans will miss the verve of an Italian crew, as now the only Italians in the restaurants are the maître d'hôtel and his assistant. On a recent cruise, we found service throughout the *Costa Atlantica* to be excellent and its top attraction. There are no wine stewards in the dining room.

FACILITIES AND ACTIVITIES Daytime diversions include dance, gaming, and golf lessons; port and shopping talks; the ubiquitous art auctions; health and beauty workshops; bridge; handwriting analysis; tennis singles; arts and crafts; and quizzes. The cruise staff is one of the most active this writer has ever encountered, keeping passengers busy with games, dancing, and other activities, and creating an atmosphere that reminded me of traditional cruises of the past. The library and card room are handsome and well used, but the multinational nature of the passengers means a somewhat limited number of books in English. The Internet center, which is part of the library, has five terminals. **Via della Spiga** is the ship's shopping promenade, and there's a full-service conference center.

Evening entertainment is designed for the multinational nature of the passengers, with more dance, music, and magic than comic routines. The **Caruso Theater** (**Osiris** on *Mediterranea*), the impressive three-level main show lounge at the front of the ship, has very few columns to interrupt sight lines. En route to the theater, passengers pass the **Paparazzi Lounge** with bigger-than-life, black-and-white photographs of celebrities, such as Joe DiMaggio.

Caffe Florian, replicating the famous St. Mark's Square landmark, serves afternoon tea, coffees, liqueurs, and aperitifs with background music evoking the romance of the Venetian legend that captivated such luminaries as Vivaldi, Dickens, Stravinsky, and others. The **Madama Butterfly Grand Lounge** is a large multifunction room and bar used for activities throughout the day and evening. The **Coral Lounge,** used for seminars and special entertainment, has an underwater quality, with blue walls and huge white coral trees behind etched glass.

The glittering **Fortuna Casino** (**Grand Canal Casino** on *Mediterranea*) is well laid out, with comfortable access to slots, roulette, and blackjack tables. It has its own bar—one of 12 on the ship—and is adjacent to the Madama Butterfly Grand Lounge.

Dancing in the evenings ranges from disco to swing, and bands playing for guests waiting to enter the dining room inspire impromptu dance sessions in the lounges. The bi-level **Dante's Disco,** with an outstanding sound system, is positioned on the bottom two passenger decks—a good choice because the action tends to go to the wee hours of the night.

Theme nights are offered in the Costa tradition and include Fiesta Italiana and Notte Mediterranea, street festivals at sea with boccie ball and tarantella dance lessons, costumes, music, and finger food from Spain, France, Greece, and Turkey. Then, too, the last night is the always popular Toga Party-at-Sea, when passengers show their ingenuity—or lack thereof—creating a toga out of a bedsheet that the ship supplies.

SPORTS, FITNESS, AND BEAUTY Each ship has three outdoor pools plus Jacuzzis. One pool has a retractable roof that converts the central pool deck into an 11,000-square-foot solarium, thus providing all-weather swimming. At the top of the ship is a stand-alone waterslide that does not empty into a pool. The **Aurora Pool,** the third pool located in the rear of the ship, is a quiet hideaway. It adjoins the dramatic two-level **Ischia Spa and Gym,** which has thalassotherapy and a broad range of other treatments, as well as well-used sauna, steam, and whirlpools. Costa has full- and half-day spa packages, as well as à la carte, all of them pricey. Above the spa is a tennis court, where undersize racquets are used; it converts to a basketball or volleyball court.

The workout area is theater style, with a main floor and balcony; it has an array of Technogym equipment like that found in a major health club, plus sophisticated electronic aerobic monitoring equipment. Exercise classes are offered for all fitness levels, including children's jogging and aerobics.

CHILDREN'S FACILITIES The large and well-fitted **Pinocchio's Children's Room** is the center of children's activities. Costa Kids, a year-round program available on Caribbean and European cruises, offers daily activities geared to two age groups: Costa Kids Club, ages 3–12, and Costa Teens Club, ages 13–17. Two youth counselors are aboard each ship year-round; counselors are added when there are more than 12 children on a cruise. Youth Center activities include video game competitions, bridge and galley tours, arts and crafts, a treasure hunt, Italian lessons, bingo, board games, karaoke contests, pizza parties, ice-cream socials, movies, and more.

At sea, Kids Club hours generally are 9–11:30 a.m., 2–5:30 p.m., and 8–11 p.m. On Caribbean cruises, group babysitting for ages 3 and up (children must be out of diapers) is available on request 6:30–11 p.m. In port, hours are 8:30 a.m.–12:30 p.m. and 2:30–6:30 p.m. There is a charge. Costa also offers Parents Night Out. On two different nights, parents can enjoy evenings alone while their children have the evening with their peers at a supervised buffet or pizza party with activities designed especially for them.

European cruises have three clubs: Baby Club, ages 3–6 years; Junior Club, ages 7–12; and Teens Club, ages 13–17 years. Baby Club offers a story hour, crafts, games, and ice-cream parties. Junior Club has aerobics, a puppet theater, mini-Olympics, and team treasure hunts. Teens Club offers sports and fitness programs, guitar lessons, video productions, and a rock-and-roll hour. In Europe, free group babysitting for children ages 3–6 is available, subject to staff availability. A disco and teen club offer a dance floor, large TV, video games, and four computer stations.

SHORE EXCURSIONS On Eastern Caribbean cruises, the ship stops at Isla Catalina, where Costa developed facilities for a fun day at the beach with games and water sports. The ship also offers tours to **Casa de Campo,** one of the Caribbean's largest resorts, for tennis, horseback riding, and golf on world-famous Pete Dye courses. You must buy the ship's shore excursion to go to Casa de Campo; cruise passengers are not allowed to venture there on their own during the day. The ship docks at Isla Catalina for the day and the Casa de Campo marina for the evening, enabling passengers to enjoy the resort's elegant dining and nightlife. The ship offers diving and snorkeling at selected ports.

In Europe, shore excursions generally are as varied as the cruises and range from a glacier walk in Norway to a visit to Egyptian pyramids. Itineraries are port-intensive, rarely with more than one or two days at sea in a week.

THE SHIPS If the name is any indication, then good fortune showered Costa with the *Fortuna*, launched in late 2003, followed by her twin, *Magica*, in 2004, as part of the line's enormous expansion program that added four big ships in four years. *Costa Fortuna* and *Costa Magica* were the largest ships in Costa's history and the largest ships in Italian maritime history when they were launched. They were also the first post-Panamax ships (ships too wide

Costa Fortuna	**QUALITY 8**	**VALUE C**
Costa Magica	**QUALITY 8**	**VALUE C**
REGISTRY Italy	**LENGTH** 890 feet	**BEAM** 124 feet
CABINS 1,358	**DRAFT** NA	**SPEED** 20 knots
MAXIMUM PASSENGERS	**PASSENGER DECKS** 13	**ELEVATORS** 18
3,470	**CREW** 1,068	**SPACE RATIO** NA

to transit the Panama Canal) for a European cruise line and the first post-Panamax ships to sail in Europe year-round.

Although the ships are not quite as large, their "footprints" are similar to *Carnival Destiny*'s, with a three-story show lounge, two main dining rooms, a casual Lido restaurant, large spa and fitness center, three swimming pools, shops, a chapel, Internet cafe, and children's and teen's areas. But there are differences too. For example, the casino was made smaller to accommodate the **Grand Bar** with a large dance floor because Costa's Italian and European passengers like to dance more than gamble. Also, in place of the sports bar on the Carnival ships, the ships have cigar bars.

Costa Fortuna's interiors pay tribute to the great Italian liners of yesteryear; public rooms are named for these classic ships and the year they entered service. **Michelangelo 1965 Restaurant** has a 20-foot-long model of the liner *Michelangelo* in its foyer. Exhibited for years in Milan's central railway station, it is believed to be the second-largest ship model in the world.

Inverted scale models of Costa vessels, past and present, glide across a blue ceiling over the bar of the *Costa Fortuna*'s nine-deck atrium. The models are among 38 found on the vessel, which is awash in art and memorabilia, including a collection of antique nautical objects and antique globes. *Costa Magica*'s theme is the magic of Italy's enchanting small villages.

ITINERARIES *See* Itinerary Index.

CABINS More than half (853) of the 1,358 cabins are outside. Of those, 522 cabins and 64 mini-suites and suites have balconies. All come with hair dryer, safe, and stocked minibar. Standard cabins have showers only, but mini-suites have bathtubs, and suites are equipped with whirlpool tubs. Mini-suites and suites also have butler service.

Specifications 474 inside cabins (160 square feet); 335 outside standard (174–190 square feet); 458 outside with balcony (210 square feet); 64 suites (360–650 square feet); 27 wheelchair accessible (220 square feet).

DINING Italian specialties are highlights in the bi-level main restaurant, **Michelangelo 1965** (with big windows in the stern), and Raffaello 1965 at midship (**Costa Emerald** and **Portofino** on *Costa Magica*). Casual meals and pizza are served in the spacious **Cristoforo Columbo 1954** buffet restaurant; and perched high on Deck 11 is the **Conte Grande 1927** supper club (**Vicenza Club** on *Magica*), a reservation-only venue where you dine on dinnerware by Versace and eat Italian cuisine by Zeffirino, the famous Genoa restaurant with a branch in Las Vegas. The cover charge is $25. When the ship is in the Caribbean, the alternative restaurant becomes the Tuscan Steak House.

FACILITIES AND ACTIVITIES The ships' main gathering spot, morning and night, is the centrally located **Conte di Savoia 1932 Grand Bar** named for Italy's most elegant ocean liner (**Grand Bar Salento** on *Magica*). People gather here from early morning for cappuccino until late into the night, when a live band plays for dancing. The room has a huge parquet dance floor, sweeping black granite bar, and gilded fabrics in yellow, blue, and green. At 11,000 square feet, it may be the largest bar afloat.

In the **Vulcania 1927 Disco,** a glass wall surrounds the upper level, enabling gamblers in the casino one deck up to look down on the dancers.

Named after the liner *Vulcania,* the disco has a large mechanized figure of Vulcan, the mythical god of fire, who pounds out fiber-optic sparks on an anvil in time to the music.

Other appealing rooms are the **Leonardo da Vinci 1960 Lounge,** displaying reproductions of masterpieces like the *Mona Lisa* etched onto large glass canvases. The room has a combo for dance music and becomes the venue for late-night cabaret. A more intimate bar/dance venue is **Conte Verde 1923 Lounge.** Inspired by the grand ballroom of the *Conte Verde* liner, the room sports an emerald green ceiling and large malachite vases of Murano glass that sprout topiary trees ("verde" means *green* in Italian). The **Conte Rosso 1921 Piano Bar** pays tribute to *Conte Verde*'s sister ship and is colored red ("rosso" means *red* in Italian).

Rex Theater 1932 (**Urbino Theater** on *Magica*), where big production shows are staged, is an enormous room stretching over three decks and seating 1,100 passengers. The stage is flanked by towering funnels to recall the powerful *Rex*, which held the transatlantic speed record from 1933 to 1935. The *Rex* was Italy's fastest and most famous ocean liner.

THE SHIP Costa's flagship, *Concordia*—a symbolic name connoting concord or peace—was the largest cruise ship built for an Italian company when she was launched in 2006 and the European cruise ship with the largest passenger capacity. Built in Italy and costing €450 million, she usually sails the Mediterranean year-round. *Costa Concordia* was the first of five sister ships. The second ship, *Costa Serena*, made her debut in 2007, and the third, *Costa Pacifica*, in 2009. Two more are scheduled for 2011 and 2012.

Among *Concordia*'s special features are the **Samsara Spa,** one of the largest spas at sea, extending over two decks, with cruising's first spa accommodations (55 cabins and 12 suites) that come with special and exclusive privileges for passengers who reserve them. It also has the **Ponte Francia** pool deck—spanning two decks and including two swimming pools with retractable glass roofs—making it the largest enclosable pool area on any cruise ship, according to Costa. The deck has a huge movie screen and a multilingual audio system for watching movies day and night. But the ship's most unusual feature of all is the Grand Prix (Formula One) race car simulator, identical to the cars in which real champions train. Race car aficionados can drive like the

Costa Concordia	QUALITY 8	VALUE C
Costa Fascinosa	2012	
Costa Favolosa	2011	
Costa Pacifica	PREVIEW	
Costa Serena	QUALITY 8	VALUE C
REGISTRY Italy	LENGTH 951 feet	BEAM 116 feet
CABINS 1,500	DRAFT 24 feet	SPEED 20.5 knots
MAXIMUM PASSENGERS	PASSENGER DECKS 11	ELEVATORS 13
3,780	CREW 1,110	SPACE RATIO NA

pros and even get a recording of their performance. *Costa Serena* and *Costa Pacifica* have these special features too.

Concordia was the fifth Costa ship to be designed by Joe Farcus, the well-known interior designer for Carnival Cruises. For this ship, he drew inspiration from European architectural styles up to the 1900s, such as Irish Gothic, Belgian Art Deco, Austrian Baroque, and Italian postmodern, among others. The public areas on the ship are named after some of Europe's most beautiful and famous cities—Dublin, Lisbon, London, Paris, Prague, Stockholm, Vienna. In 2009, *Concordia* became the first Costa ship to install telemedicine on board, which enables ship staff to enhance passenger care in the seagoing environment with the use of advanced medical technology available around the clock. The new service allows for diagnosis and consultation at a distance for first aid, toxicology, cardiology, radiology, dermatology, and ophthalmology in collaboration with Genoa's Galliera Hospital.

Costa Pacifica's theme is the "Ship of Sound," with songs, music, musical symbols, artwork, and instruments played out visually and audibly throughout the ship. Twenty-nine musical selections—including variations on new and established numbers arranged by Italian composer Mauro Pagani—are heard throughout the ship. Corridors on the ship have their own music by masters from Chopin to Beethoven, while each lounge has its own international music, chosen by Pagani. More than ten singers perform live in the lounges. The musical theme plays further in the high-tech recording studio, where passengers can record a song, have it edited and enhanced by an expert, and take home a CD of it for €35 (for an hour's worth of singing). You also can take individual drum, piano, and guitar lessons for €35 per hour.

Costa Pacifica is a beautiful ship with a lively, casual lifestyle that is definitely Italian. Most passengers will be European; many will be family groups.

ITINERARIES *See* Itinerary Index.

CABINS The ultra-comfortable Samsara cabins and suites, adjacent to the spa or nearby, have an Asian atmosphere typical of Samsara and were designed specifically for passengers who want to immerse themselves in the spa and wellness program. Samsara passengers have direct access to the spa via private elevators and stairs not available to other guests, and such exclusive amenities as flat-panel televisions, Elemis bath products, and exclusive access to the **Ristorante Samsara,** with a full menu of wellness cuisine.

Passengers staying in Samsara accommodations receive a Welcome Ritual package (included in the cruise price), which allows unlimited access to the spa and thalassotherapy pool, two complimentary fitness classes, a personalized consultation with a spa expert, two treatments, two sun-lamp sessions in the solarium, and an invitation to a special spa tea ceremony.

Other passengers have free access to the fitness center, but for access to some spa amenities, they must purchase a day pass for €35 or a weekly pass for €199. Spa accommodations have been so popular on *Costa Concordia* that their number on *Serena* was increased from 66 to 99 (87 cabins and 12 suites); *Costa Pacifica* has 103 spa accommodations (91 cabins, 12 suites).

Specifications 586 inside cabins, 343 outside; 70 suites; 501 cabins with balconies; 29 wheelchair accessible.

DINING The Concordia group has five restaurants each—two main restaurants, a buffet, a spa restaurant for the spa cabin guests, and a specialty (reservations-only and extra-fee) restaurant. The main dining rooms are elegant in decor, with beautiful table settings. The cuisine is mostly Mediterranean with an Italian flair. Costa prides itself on its use of Italian products. The reservations-only specialty restaurant, **Club Concordia,** features cuisine by renowned chef and creator of Italian molecular cuisine, Ettore Bocchia, executive chef of the Michelin-star restaurant of Villa Serbelloni in Bellagio, Italy. *Costa Pacifica* offers exclusively Amarone Aneri Stella 2003, an extraordinary red wine reserved especially for Costa (only 133 bottles are available on the ship).

FACILITIES AND ACTIVITIES These ships have 13 bars, including one Cognac and one cigar bar; a show lounge spanning three decks; a casino and nightclub, an Internet cafe and library, shops, and a giant movie screen on the Pool Deck. For kids, the Children Squok Club has its own splash pool; teenagers have **Mondovirtuale,** a computer game area. As noted earlier, those who are musically inclined can take guitar, piano, or drum lessons on board *Costa Pacifica* and rent the recording studio to produce his or her own CDs.

On the Grand Prix race car simulator, passengers 16 years of age and older can learn how to drive like the pros. Located on one of the top decks, the simulator has real-time vehicle modeling (the same technology used by Grand Prix champion drivers in training). Passengers can compete virtually in a Grand Prix race at speeds of more than 200 miles per hour and can record their performances throughout the week to compete with other guests.

Costa Pacifica was the first of the *Concordia* group to have PlayStation3 and PlayStation2 consoles in certain public areas and cabins through a recent agreement between Costa Cruises and Sony Computer Entertainment Italia. There also are PlayStations in the children's and teens' clubs and in the area overlooking the Lido decks. The program is gradually being installed across the Costa fleet.

SPORTS, FITNESS, AND BEAUTY *Concordia* and her sisters each have three pools, of which two are under retractable magrodomes, enabling their use in any weather, even in midwinter. A fourth pool is for kids, and there are five Jacuzzis and an outdoor jogging track. One of the pools has a giant video screen with movies and programs shown both day and night.

The ships' pride is their 20,500-square-foot **Samsara Spa,** which extends over two decks. Elements in the spa's design and treatments were inspired by the meaning of "Samsara," which is associated with the path to spiritual enlightenment and balancing of life energies. The spa offers a full menu of treatments based on Ayurvedic principles, an ancient Indian holistic healing method. The spa is centered by an indoor pool where passengers can enjoy thalassotherapy sessions; other facilities include a state-of-the-art fitness center, sauna, Turkish bath, solarium, and a treatment room for couples.

THE SHIP Costa's first megaship, *Costa Victoria* made her debut in 1996 and was renovated in 2009. Designed by well-known naval architect Robert Tillberg, she was the largest passenger liner built in Germany when she was launched. Despite her large size, her shallow draft provides exceptional maneuverability and gives the ship access to smaller ports and the Suez Canal.

Costa Victoria	QUALITY 5	VALUE C
REGISTRY Italy	LENGTH 828 feet	BEAM 105 feet
CABINS 964	DRAFT 24 feet	SPEED 23 knots
MAXIMUM PASSENGERS	PASSENGER DECKS 10	ELEVATORS 12
2,394	CREW 800	SPACE RATIO 38.9

Ultramodern and sophisticated, the circular **Planetarium Atrium** spans seven decks and has four glass elevators connecting the lobby with the pool deck above. It's capped by a large glass dome, admitting sunlight that reflects off a colored glass sculpture by Milanese artist Gianfranco Pardi on the Boheme Deck (Deck 5). Deck 5 also has the purser's office, shore excursion desk, and a piano bar. Nine of the ten passenger decks are named after Italian operas.

The most dramatic room is the **Concorde Plaza,** an observation lounge at the bow. It spans four decks; a floor-to-ceiling glass wall provides spectacular ocean views. Opposite the windows is a marble dance floor adjoining a center stage; its backdrop is a waterfall inspired by Leonardo da Vinci's drawings of the moon eclipsing the sun. Decorated in blues, silver, and gold, the lounge serves as an elegant area for socializing, special events, and evening entertainment, including cabaret shows, games, bingo, and port lectures.

ITINERARIES *See* Itinerary Index. The ship sails in Europe year-round.

CABINS The majority of cabins are on the upper decks. Sixty percent are outside cabins with a porthole or large, square window. Cabins are small compared with those on *Costa Romantica*. Originally, the ship had no cabins with balconies, which was definitely a drawback for the ship, but in 2004, full balconies were fitted to 246 cabins. *Victoria* was the line's first ship to have a minibar, safe, hair dryer, and interactive television in every cabin. All cabins have direct-dial telephones and sliding doors that separate the living area and bathroom. Circular bathrooms have rounded showers and vanity areas.

The six top suites and 14 mini-suites, forward on the pool and sports decks, have sitting areas, whirlpool baths, walk-in closets, and queen beds, plus one upper berth and a Murphy bed, accommodating up to four people. Butler service is provided.

The *Victoria*'s unique fan coil system allows each cabin to be refreshed with its own recycled air or outside air. Thus, nonsmokers' air isn't mixed with smokers'. The ship does not have self-service laundries for passenger use.

Specifications 391 inside cabins, 553 outside; 20 suites; 250 cabins with balconies; 6 wheelchair accessible. Standard cabins are 120–150 square feet.

DINING *Costa Victoria* was the first Costa vessel to have two dining rooms: **Sinfonia Restaurant,** aft, and **Fantasia Restaurant,** midship. Both are decorated with marble and pine walls and glass chandeliers from Murano. Their picture windows are transformed from ocean views by day to Italian scenes by night with murals that drop in place like window shades.

Dinner menus have fewer selections than are offered on some ships in Costa's price group, but choices are ample and of good quality, balancing Italian and European dishes with American favorites. A different pasta is featured at lunch and dinner; American audiences rave over them. The presentation is always attractive.

Ristorante Magnifico by Zefferino, the ship's reservations-only alternative restaurant, is modeled after the famous Zefferino's in Genoa. Passengers pay an extra charge of $25 per person, but it's worth it and has proven to be popular. Walls are hung with ten paintings of earlier Costa passenger ships by artist Stephen Card and contribute to the cozy atmosphere created by the addition of candlelight, flowers, soft music, and excellent service.

Passengers dine informally at an indoor/outdoor buffet serving breakfast and lunch. **Bolero,** the indoor buffet, is surrounded by glass windows and furnished with rattan chairs and marble tables. The outdoor **Terraza Café,** similar to one on *Romantica* but much larger, is protected by a large white canopy made by Canobbio, an Italian firm specializing in circus tents and sports arena coverings. Other dining options include two buffets, a pizzeria, ice-cream bar, and grill.

FACILITIES AND ACTIVITIES Daytime diversions include lessons in dance, Italian, and gaming; bingo; bridge; backgammon; culinary demonstrations; port and shopping talks; horse racing; and the Not-So-Newlywed Game. The teen center has a video game room, and there's a library, card room, and Internet center. Movies are shown on the in-cabin televisions.

The two-deck **Festival Show Lounge** is decorated in rich reds with Tivoli lights twinkling in the ceiling. The stage can be raised for variety and production shows or lowered for dancing. **Grand Bar Orpheus** is popular for cocktails and after-dinner espresso. It's connected by a curved glass stairway to the big, bright **Monte Carlo Casino.** Just outside the casino is **Capriccio Lounge,** an intimate piano bar decorated with floor-to-ceiling mosaics by Italian painter Emilio Tadini.

The full-service conference center offers meeting space, audiovisual equipment, movable leather chairs equipped with flip-top desks, and a board room for 20.

SPORTS, FITNESS, AND BEAUTY The **Solarium,** a top-deck viewing and sunning area, has pipes that continuously emit mists of cool water. The two outdoor pools are surrounded by six whirlpools and two shuffleboard courts. Nearby is the **Wimbledon Tennis Court,** a miniature court using smaller racquets and balls. It can be converted to a basketball or volleyball court.

In addition to the beauty salon, the **Pompei Spa** has an indoor swimming pool centered with a large mosaic and surrounded by Roman columns and teak lounge chairs. The spa offers a Turkish bath, saunas, massage, thalassotherapy, hydrotherapy, and other beauty treatments. A 1,312-foot jogging track connects the spa to the gymnasium, which is equipped with weight-training equipment and an aerobics room. This is the first ship to carry products from Tuscany's chic Terme di Saturnia.

CHILDREN'S FACILITIES Costa Kids Club for children ages 3–12 is further divided by age group depending on the number of children on a particular sailing. See *Costa Atlantica* for details on the children's program.

Costa Classica	QUALITY 7	VALUE C
Costa Romantica	QUALITY 7	VALUE B
REGISTRY Italy	LENGTH 722/610 feet	BEAM 102 feet
CABINS 654/678	DRAFT 24 feet	SPEED 18 knots
MAXIMUM PASSENGERS	PASSENGER DECKS 11	ELEVATORS 10/8
1,680/1,697	CREW 650/722	SPACE RATIO 41.5/40

THE SHIPS *Costa Romantica* and *Costa Classica* are almost identical. These spacious ships with public rooms on the upper four decks have ultramodern Italian interiors using a king's ransom in marble, dramatic window walls, futuristic sculptures, clean lines, angular shapes, and fine art. The result reflects modern Italian design and is a radical departure from traditional Italian ocean liners.

Passengers are introduced to the ship in its dramatic **Grand Lobby,** set low on the Copenhagen Deck, which is dedicated entirely to cabins, as are the deck below and the two decks above. White-gloved room stewards escort passengers to their cabins. The background music of Vivaldi and other Italian composers is meant to underscore the start of a week of "Cruising Italian Style." The ships' layouts are easy to follow, with one lounge or public space flowing to the next, creating openness and harmony. Decks are named after European cities.

Romantica's heart and social center is the **Piazza Italia** on the Verona Deck—an atrium furnished as a lounge, with a small bandstand and dance floor on one side and a bar on the other. The lounge is the favorite gathering spot for prelunch and predinner drinks, as it's a short walk from the dining room. Forward are meeting rooms, the library, chapel, card room, and the ground floor of **L'Opera,** the bi-level show lounge. From the Piazza, a double stairway leads up to the Vienna Deck and the popular **Romeo's Pizzeria** and **Juliet's Patisserie.** Forward are shops on the Via Condotti, named for Rome's fashionable shopping street.

ITINERARIES *See* Itinerary Index. Both ships are now based in Asia, catering primarily to the Chinese market.

CABINS Spacious and well designed, cabins are these ships' best feature. Standard cabins are fitted in cherry furnishings, including a dresser and desk unit with large mirror; bedside tables; a control panel for lights by the bed; ample closet space; and two chairs, one of which opens into a bed suitable for a child.

Elegant touches are the white curtain spanning the room, which can be raised and lowered to cover the oversize porthole; designer amenities; and high-quality bed and bath linens. All cabins have television, radio, safe, direct-dial satellite phone, and hair dryer. The 24-hour room service offers sandwiches and beverages.

Specifications Costa Romantica, 216 inside cabins, 428 outside, no singles, 16 suites, 18 mini-suites. Standard dimensions, 175 square feet inside, 200 square feet outside. 242 take third and fourth persons. Costa Classica, 216 inside cabins, 688 outside; 4 grand suites, 16 with verandas. Standard dimensions, 175–200 square feet. 359 cabins take third and fourth persons. 6 singles. 6 wheelchair accessible.

DINING *Romantica's* **Botticelli Restaurant,** similar to *Classica's* counterpart, **Tivoli,** is beautifully laid out almost entirely in off-white and brown Carrara marble with coffered ceilings. Elegantly designed wicker-backed chairs encircle round tables, most seating eight, dressed in starched white cloths, fine china, glassware, and flowers. Movable side panels faced with a variety of scenes—a European city, landscapes, or Italian gardens—are changed each evening. They were designed by Giorgio Cristini, set designer for Milan's famous La Scala opera house.

The lovely room lacks carpeting or wall coverings, causing an extraordinarily high noise level that hinders conversation. Acoustical material was added, particularly in the ceiling, which helped—but not enough. Side tables toward the back of the room get less noise.

Il Giardino, the Lido cafe for indoor breakfast and lunch buffets, is among the ship's prettiest informal settings; its rattan chairs are dressed in English country fabrics against aquamarine glass walls and wood floors. At least two evenings per cruise, a dinner buffet is offered. The midnight buffet's setting changes depending on weather and the theme.

Adjacent to the Lido cafe, the **Terrazza Café** reproduces the *Classica's* popular **Al Fresco Café,** the ship's most pleasant location from dawn to dusk. Set with wicker chairs and tables under a high-peaked canvas canopy, it provides a cool, inviting outdoor setting for breakfast and lunch.

The other big hit is **Romeo's Pizzeria,** where pizza is served throughout the day. It's free, but you might want to buy a glass of wine or beer to wash it down. Romeo's neighbor, **Juliet's Patisserie,** open 9 a.m.–midnight, serves pastries (without charge) and espresso. It's also the **Martini Bar.**

FACILITIES AND ACTIVITIES Lessons in dance, Italian, and gaming; bingo. Bridge, backgammon, and culinary demonstrations are some of the daytime diversions. Evening entertainment is designed to appeal to the multinational passenger mix. *Romantica's* main show lounge, **L'Opera Theater** (**Colosseo** on *Classica*), is a modern interpretation of a classic, horseshoe-shaped concert hall. Creating a glamorous setting are red and royal-blue carpets, blue-velvet seats against a wall of blue mosaics, and brass accents. Most seats have good sight lines, and back-pain sufferers will like the hard, stiff balcony seats. L'Opera has shows nightly.

Romantica's casino is spectacular, with stucco walls inlaid with gold accents and a large crystal chandelier. **The Tango Ballroom,** a multipurpose lounge with a large dance floor, becomes a high-energy nightclub with live music. The room has window walls and is a lovely daytime retreat. The **Diva Disco** atop the ship, a daytime observation and cocktail lounge with floor-to-ceiling windows, is the late-night hot spot.

SPORTS, FITNESS, AND BEAUTY Two outdoor pools are separated by Costa's distinctive yellow stacks. One has four Jacuzzis and is surrounded by three terraces of teak decks with lounge chairs. The second is inlaid with ceramic tiles; suspended above it is a Susumu sculpture in red metal, which changes shape in the wind.

The **Caracalla Spa** on the *Classica* has floor-to-ceiling windows. *Romantica*'s smaller spa is beside the stack. In addition to weights, life cycles, and treadmills, the spa has sauna, steam, and massage rooms, plus a beauty salon offering personalized hair and body treatments. A partial deck above the swimming pools has a jogging track and sunbathing space.

THE SHIP Stylish *Costa Luminosa,* launched in June 2009, is the first of a new class of ships. Built by Fincantieri for €450 million as the most exclusive and innovative ship in the Costa fleet, the *Costa Luminosa* is the company's new flagship and a true symbol of Italian workmanship. She was christened together with the *Costa Pacifica*—the first time two ships built by the same shipyard for one company were ever christened in the same place at the same time. Her sister ship, *Costa Deliziosa,* is scheduled to be delivered in February 2010.

Costa Luminosa, as the name implies, is the "Ship of Light." The beautiful interiors, designed by architect/interior designer Joseph Farcus, were inspired by the concept of light in all its forms. The ultra-contemporary design lavishly uses 20 different types of high-quality marble, wood, mother-of-pearl, and granite; 120 Murano glass lamps and chandeliers filled with iridescent colors and LED lights; and world-class art, such as a sculpture commissioned by artist Fernando Botero, entitled *Reclining Woman 2004,* which is on display in the ship's atrium. Beyond the atrium, passengers will find 288 original works of art and more than 4,700 reproductions throughout the ship. The high quality is meant to attract and appeal to a high-end clientele.

CABINS Of her total 1,130 cabins, 772 or 68% have verandas—the most for a Costa ship—and 23 wheelchair-accessible cabins. Standard accommodations are furnished with flat-panel televisions, phones, safes, and hair dryers, while suites get robes, slippers, and pillow menus, among other amenities.

DINING In addition to the main dining room and Lido restaurant, the ship has a specialty restaurant, Club Luminosa, featuring cuisine by Ettore Bocchia, executive chef at the Michelin-star restaurant Mistral at the Grand Hotel Villa Serbelloni in Bellagio, Italy.

FACILITIES AND ACTIVITIES As on all Costa ships, the *Costa Luminosa* theater features Costa's own "in-house" musicals. These Broadway-scale productions are based on a central theme with specially designed stage sets and costumes and a cast of up to 14 singers and dancers, all meant to appeal to Costa's international clientele. Each cruise offers two or three original, 45-minute shows with two performances daily. There are also short "variety acts" that precede and follow each performance. And then there's the ship's new 4-D cinema, a 20-seat room where sight, sound, touch, and scent come together to form a multisensory experience. Unique in the cruise ship industry, attendees use special glasses to view three-dimensional images and sit in vibrating seats, while jets of water, wind, and smells impact all the senses.

The ship has a casino, eight bars including a piano bar, shopping center, conference room, library, and Internet access. It also has a solarium and three pools, as well as a pool for thalassotherapy. Like the Concorde group, *Costa Luminosa* has a Grand Prix race car driving simulator. Sony PlayStation has exclusive dedicated areas on the ship equipped with PS3 consoles and the

Costa Deliziosa	2010	
Costa Luminosa	PREVIEW	
REGISTRY Italy	LENGTH 965 feet	BEAM 106 feet
CABINS 1,300	DRAFT 24 feet	SPEED 21.6 knots
MAXIMUM PASSENGERS	PASSENGER DECKS 12	ELEVATORS 13
2,826	CREW 921	SPACE RATIO NA

latest-generation video games, as well as on-demand PS3 games available in cabins. A roller-skating track on one of the ship's top decks enables passengers (minimum age is 8 years old) to skate with strap-and-go "Skorpion" skates that attach to one's shoes. Golfers have an 18-hole golf simulator for 37 virtual courses and a putting green—both Costa firsts.

The ship has the line's popular Samsara Spa, with its accompanying 52 spa cabins and four suites that have direct access to the spa via private elevator and stairway, and a Samsara restaurant. The fitness center features a new kinesis circuit by Technogym, a system based on natural movements through a patented system of pulleys for resistance training.

On the technical side, Costa Luminosa is the first Italian ship (and one of the first in the world) to be fitted for "cold ironing"—a special system that allows the ship to be berthed at a dock to receive power from shore without having to keep its engines running to feed the onboard generators.

Cruise West

2301 Fifth Avenue, Suite 401
Seattle, WA 98121-1856
☎ 888-851-8133; FAX 206-441-8687
www.cruisewest.com

TYPE OF SHIPS Small, informal, coastal cruising vessels; small, deluxe ocean-going ships.

TYPE OF CRUISES Casual, close-up, light adventure, with emphasis on scenery and wildlife in coastal areas.

CRUISE LINE'S STRENGTHS
- innovative itineraries
- enthusiastic crew
- itinerary flexibility allows extra time for wildlife viewing
- small-ship experience
- exploration leaders on board; presentations by local experts

CRUISE LINE'S SHORTCOMINGS
- small cabins; noisy lower-deck cabins on older ships
- small bathrooms with handheld showers on older ships
- limited shipboard facilities and evening activities

FELLOW PASSENGERS Mature, physically active; mid-40s to mid-80s. Retired couples and seniors. Passengers somewhat older on Columbia River cruises; younger on Alaskan cruises. Up to 70% have college degrees or some college education; passengers are well traveled and more curious about nature, history, and ecology than typical passengers on mainstream cruise ships.

Passengers are outgoing; most would rather rise early to catch the sunrise than party late. Most are from California, Florida, New York, the Great Lakes region, Pacific Northwest, and Texas; some are from Canada. About 40% are repeaters. Regardless of age, they like the intimacy of a casual cruise to places larger liners cannot reach.

Recommended for Small-ship devotees; people looking for light adventure, to experience a region up close; those preferring wildlife to nightlife.

Not recommended for Travelers who need to be entertained; seek a lavish, resortlike experience with emphasis on nightlife; prefer facilities and activities of large ships; or gamblers.

CRUISE AREAS AND SEASONS Alaska and western Canada, spring and summer; Europe, summer and fall; Columbia and Snake rivers, Pacific Northwest, spring and fall; Costa Rica and Panama, Gulf of California, Galapagos, Antarctic, winter; Round-the-World, March 2010–February 2011.

THE LINE After flying "The Hump" in the China-Burma-India theater in World War II, Charles B. "Chuck" West moved to Alaska to become a bush pilot. Flying over the northern wilderness, he recognized Alaska's great tourism potential. In 1946, he organized, sold, and piloted the first all-tourist air excursion north of the Arctic Circle. From that, he built the

THE FLEET	BUILT/RENOVATED	TONNAGE	PASSENGERS
Pacific Explorer	1995/98/08	575	100
Spirit of Alaska	1980/95	97	78
Spirit of Columbia	1979/95	95	78
Spirit of Discovery	1976/92	94	84
Spirit of Endeavour	1983/99	95	102
Spirit of Glacier Bay	1984/95/06	95.8	102
Spirit of '98	1984/95	96	96
Spirit of Oceanus	1991/2001/05	1,263	120
Spirit of Yorktown	1988/97/07	97	138

largest tour company in Alaska—Westours—which he sold to Holland America Line in 1971.

Starting over again at age 60, West built the tour company that became Cruise West, beginning in 1986 with a luxury cruiser for day tours on Prince William Sound. In 1990, adding its first overnight coastal cruising vessel sailing from Juneau to Glacier Bay, and six vessels in seven years, the line became America's largest small-ship cruise company. Other ships followed as the company expanded its operations. In 1997, *Spirit of Endeavour*, the line's first four-star ship, began offering more upscale cruises. In 1998, the line took another major step, sending one ship to cruise Mexico's Gulf of California for the winter, thus becoming a year-round operator. The line's American-built and -flagged vessels are subject to Federal Maritime Commission bonding and strict U.S. Coast Guard inspections.

In 2001, Cruise West added *Spirit of Oceanus* and launched a new era for the line, enabling it to develop new worldwide itineraries and attract new audiences. The all-suite ship, formerly *Renaissance V*, was the line's first oceangoing vessel and the most luxurious ship in the fleet. In the same year, it added the *Pacific Explorer* (formerly *Temptress Explorer*), offering cruises in Costa Rica and Panama. One of its biggest moves was the purchase in 2006 of two former Clipper Cruises ships, which were more upscale than the line's oldest ships. Also in 2006, Cruise West introduced cruises to Japan, the South Pacific, and the Kuril Islands, and the following year expanded in Asia by adding Vietnam. Meanwhile, the cruise line was awarded nearly 80% more entries into Glacier Bay National Park, further enhancing its role as the leading small-ship line in Alaska.

More recently, Cruise West has expanded in new directions by chartering a variety of vessels for cruises of the Galapagos (*Galapagos Explorer II, Isabella II*), river cruises in Europe (*Amadeus Diamond*), and Antarctica (*Corinthian II*, whose maiden voyage was in February 2010). Information and deck plans on these chartered ships are available on Cruise West's Web site.

Yet, the most ambitious expansion of all is the line's 335-day world cruise on the *Spirit of Oceanus*, which departs in March 2010 and returns a year later. Titled "Voyages of the Great Explorers," the circumnavigation of the world is divided into six parts, each with a focus on the great explorers of the area where the ship is sailing, and, for booking purposes, is divided into 24 segments of 9–18 nights.

In late 2009, in a bid for the family market, Cruise West introduced a child fare: travelers ages 18 and under will now pay only 50% of the adult rate, and those age 2 or younger will travel for free on all voyages.

STYLE Cruise West believes that responsible travel means having enriching experiences that cause minimal impact on the environment. The company encourages environmental education and understanding through unusual, up-close experiences, while respecting wildlife and natural habitats.

The small, shallow-draft vessels can nose into shore for close views of scenery and wildlife and navigate intricate waterways, narrow locks, and small marinas inaccessible to larger ships. Their size and casual atmosphere inspire instant friendships not always possible on larger ships.

Two of the vessels, *Spirit of Alaska* and *Spirit of Columbia*, have bow-landing capabilities, enabling them to pull up to wilderness beaches or shoreside parks. En route, narration and occasional talks by park rangers, historians, and other specialists inform passengers of the history, geology, and wildlife of areas they're visiting. Otherwise, onboard style is unstructured. Passengers entertain themselves by immersion in the scenery and wildlife, reading, playing cards and games, or socializing with other passengers and the crew. From time to time, the line offers cruises with a theme, such as food and wine and photography.

In spring 2009, Cruise West launched Spirit of Distinction, an enhancement program intended to add value to its product and comprised of three parts: Compass, an enrichment program; Palate, with a wine and food focus; and Explorer Class, a new upgraded cabin category being added to three ships.

Like the points on a compass, the enrichment program has four categories: science, culture, history, and immersion. Guided by a Board of Advisors including renowned oceanographer Dr. Don Walsh and naturalist Brent Nixon, the program has guest expert lecturers to complement onboard exploration leaders, while Zodiac excursions on select itineraries are being increased. Compass has an Exploration Academy to train the line's exploration leaders in the culture, history, wildlife, and geology of regions visited.

Palate is designed to help diners discover the synergy between wine and food. All Cruise West ships now feature food and wine pairings with menu selections that highlight the cuisine of the Pacific Northwest. The updated wine list with selections by the line's chairman, Dick West, will include wines from *Wine Spectator's* "Top 100 Wines of the World." In affiliation with the U.S. Sommelier Association, onboard servers are participating in a certificate course to ensure high standards. Generally, Cruise West's cuisine is more sophisticated than is normally associated with small-ship, adventure cruising.

On *Spirit of Oceanus, Spirit of Yorktown, Spirit of Endeavour*, and *Spirit of '98*, passengers have three dining options at lunchtime: alfresco dining, weather permitting; regularly scheduled lunch in the dining room; or a light-fare luncheon served in the lounge. Menus include fresh grilled favorites, salads, and a carving or taco bar.

New Explorer Class cabins (formerly AAA cabins) on *Spirit of '98, Spirit of Endeavour*, and *Spirit of Yorktown* are intended for guests accustomed to a higher level of comforts. "Ecofriendly" amenities of Explorer Class include linens and towels of ultrasoft bamboo fiber (a sustainable resource), hypo-allergenic down duvets, cotton bathrobes, and water-conserving Speakman easy-jet showerheads. Passengers on Alaska itineraries receive a copy of Cruise West's founder's book, *Mr. Alaska*.

Cruise West's young, mostly college-age crew on Alaska to Gulf of California cruises is recruited primarily from the Pacific Northwest and Alaska. Their caring attitude and enthusiasm are some of the line's strengths.

DISTINCTIVE FEATURES Bow ramp on *Spirit of Columbia;* bow stairs on *Spirit of Alaska.* Open bridge. Dib launches (inflatable, Zodiac-like motorized launches with covers, seats, and railings) and Zodiacs for adventure cruises. Spirit of Distinction enhancements.

RATES Port charges included.

Special fares and discounts Look for early-bird discounts and refund-able/changeable air on seven-day or longer cruises when booked by specific deadlines. New child fares allow passengers ages 18 and under to pay 50% of the adult rate, and those age 2 or younger travel for free on all voyages.

- **SINGLE SUPPLEMENT:** Varies from 125% to 200%; single cabins on *Spirit of '98* and *Spirit of Discovery.* A twin rate is available for singles on select cruises and all inside "B" and "C" cabins.

PAST PASSENGERS The Quyana Club (the name means "thank you" in Yu'pik Eskimo) offers passengers newsletters, shipboard credits, and 5% savings on all cruises and pre/post packages.

THE LAST WORD The company remains faithful to its founder's vision that small groups maximize travelers' enjoyment without overwhelming villages, small ports, and wilderness areas they visit, and that the focus should be outward, on nature and culture, rather than inward, on nightclubs and gambling. By focusing on wildlife—passengers are likely to see whales, bears, seals, and eagles—and the wilderness, Cruise West says it is increasing awareness and support for protection of natural treasures. And now, Cruise West has a whale of a guarantee: On any of its Wilderness Inside Passage Cruises, you are given a guarantee that whales will be sighted—if not, Cruise West will extend a $250 future cruise credit.

Cruise West's Web site is particularly useful regarding cabins. It has diagrams with precise measurements of each cabin category and readable deck plans. Most passengers try an Alaskan cruise first. If they like it, they graduate to cruises elsewhere. Costa Rica and Panama or Mexico cruises give Cruise West alumni a complete contrast to Alaska or the Northwest itineraries. Yet, the Gulf of California offers similar attractions—wildlife, beautiful scenery, and interesting culture—and much the same appeal. With the addition of Asia and the Galapagos, and now Antarctica and a world cruise, Cruise West has come a long way and offers a wide range of choices—a very long way from the day of cruises on Prince William Sound where the line began.

THE SHIP Built in 1991 as the *Renaissance V,* the *Spirit of Oceanus* was acquired by Cruise West in 2001 and named the line's flagship. Prior to that she had been the *Sun Viva* of Sun Cruises, and *MegaStar Sagittarius* under Star Cruises, from which Cruise West purchased her.

Cruise West Standard Features

Officers American.

Staff *Dining, Cabin, Cruise:* American.

Dining facilities One dining room with open seating; meals served at specific hours. Early continental breakfast and 6 p.m. appetizers in forward lounge. Coffee, tea, fresh fruit available throughout day. Occasional buffet on open deck or picnic on shore. *Spirit of Oceanus, Spirit of Yorktown, Spirit of Endeavour,* and *Spirit of '98,* three options at lunch: alfresco, weather permitting; dining room; and light fare in lounge.

Special diets Vegetarian, low-fat, low-salt, and other heart-healthy requests accommodated; notice required at time of booking.

Room service Only on *Spirit of Oceanus* and owner's suite on *Spirit of '98.*

Dress code Casual at all times. Most passengers wear jeans, chinos, and layer with shirts, sweaters, and light jackets in cooler climates.

Cabin amenities Air-conditioning/thermostat; upper-deck cabins on oldest ships have windows that open. Most bathrooms on older ships are small, some with handheld showers; some have sink and vanity in room, separate from bathroom. Reading lights over bed; limited closets, storage on older ships. *Spirit of Endeavour, Spirit of '98,* and *Spirit of Oceanus* have televisions, Internet access, minifridges, safes, hair dryers. *Spirit of Yorktown* balcony cabins: teak-floored balconies, each with a cafe table and two chairs; queen beds; minifridges. *Spirit of '98, Endeavour, Yorktown Explorer Class* cabins: eco-friendly linens, robes, and water-conserving showerheads. All ships have satellite phones.

The deluxe, all-suite *Spirit of Oceanus* was Cruise West's first oceangoing vessel and, as such, opened up new horizons for the line, from new destinations worldwide to newer, more upscale cruises that would appeal to a completely new market. She introduced long voyages to the Bering Sea from Anchorage, the South Pacific and Japan, Vietnam, and China. Now, she will launch a completely new venture, sailing westward, following the sun, circumnavigating the globe from March 2010 to February 2011. Among the lectures and presentations, some will feature noted travel experts from Smithsonian Journeys (the Smithsonian Institution's educational travel program) on select segments.

Registered in the Bahamas—another first for Cruise West—the ship has American officers, an onboard expedition leader and exploration guide, and

Spirit of Oceanus	QUALITY 6	VALUE C
REGISTRY Bahamas	LENGTH 295 feet	BEAM 50 feet
CABINS 57	DRAFT 13.25 feet	SPEED 14.5 knots
MAXIMUM PASSENGERS	PASSENGER DECKS 5	ELEVATORS 1
120	CREW 64	SPACE RATIO NA

Electrical outlets 110 AC.

Wheelchair access Inquire. *Spirit of '98* and *Spirit of Oceanus* have elevators.

Recreation and entertainment Forward lounge with bar setup, television, small library with reference books of area, informational videos, movies; informal entertainment by crew; briefings by exploration leaders, occasional talks by historians, park rangers, and other experts. Bridge, other card and board games. All cabins have binoculars, but it's wise to bring your own.

Beauty and fitness Some fitness equipment; *Spirit of Oceanus* has stair steppers and exercise bicycles. No beauty or barber shop.

Other facilities Doctor on Sea of Cortes cruises and on *Spirit of Oceanus*; at least one crew member on each vessel is trained in First Response. Satellite phone, e-mail, and Internet access on *Spirit of '98, Spirit of Oceanus, Spirit of Endeavour.*

Children's facilities None.

Theme cruises Occasionally on culinary and wine, photography.

Smoking Not allowed in public rooms or cabins; smoking allowed only in designated outside area.

Cruise West suggested tipping No tipping is expected or required for either cruise or land-based service. Any tips offered are pooled and shared by nonofficer staff.

Credit cards For cruise payment and onboard charges: American Express, Visa, MasterCard.

an English-speaking crew whose numbers constitute the highest crew-to-guests ratio in the line's fleet. In 2005, the ship was refurbished with two additional suites, new carpeting, mattresses, upholstery, window treatments, and passenger phone and Internet access. *Corinthian II*, with which Cruise West launched its Antarctica voyage, is a sister ship to the *Spirit of Oceanus.*

ITINERARIES *See* Itinerary Index for details on the "Voyages of the Great Explorers," a global circumnavigation divided into 24 segments of 9–18 nights.

CABINS *Spirit of Oceanus* has spacious (215–550 square feet), all-outside suites, each with a large picture window or porthole. The 15 suites on the Sun and Sports decks have private teak balconies—another first for Cruise West ships. Other cabin amenities include a walk-in closet, marble-topped vanity, and a lounge area separated from the bedroom by a curtain. All suites can be configured with two twin beds or a queen-size bed and have a television, safe, minibar with nonalcoholic beverages, satellite telephone, and private bathroom with a marble sink and shower and hair dryers.

The ship also has a posh 550-square-foot Owner's Suite, which has a foyer with Italian limestone tile; a spacious bathroom with jetted whirlpool tub; a state-of-the-art living room with a flat-panel television, Bose stereo system, and dining, gaming, meeting, and library areas; a teak sun deck. The master bedroom is furnished with a king-size bed and decor details from Ireland and Italy.

Specifications 57 cabins, 215–550 square feet; 15 suites with balconies.

DINING Cruise West's new Spirit of Distinction program has benefited from the Palate segment, which features food and wine pairings with menu selections that highlight the cuisine in the area of the cruise.

On *Spirit of Oceanus,* passengers have a choice of two dining options at lunch: alfresco dining, weather permitting, and full-service lunch in the dining room. Menus include fresh grilled favorites and salads.

FACILITIES AND ACTIVITIES The handsomely appointed *Spirit of Oceanus* has marble and polished hardwood interiors, sumptuous fabrics, and fine art. There are two large lounges (one with a baby grand piano) and several elegant bars, providing havens for conversation, reading, or playing board games. Among other features passengers enjoy on a Cruise West ship for the first time are a hot tub on the aft Sports Deck, a health facility, and a patio bar.

The ship has a library, an elevator providing access to all five passenger decks, and spacious outside viewing areas and walkways on four of the five guest decks. The elegant dining room accommodates all guests at a single seating. Among the changes in the latest renovations, the casino was removed to make room for more public space, and a small room with exercise equipment was added. The ship has a small clinic staffed by a doctor.

THE SHIP Built in 1983 in Jeffersonville, Indiana, *Spirit of Endeavour* (formerly *Newport Clipper* of Clipper Cruise Lines) was launched for Cruise West in 1996 after a $5 million refurbishing. She was Cruise West's most luxurious ship at the time and added a new level of comfort to the line's fleet until *Spirit of Oceanus* was acquired. One of the more deluxe small vessels sailing in Alaska and the Gulf of California, *Endeavour* has teak decks, a wide companionway, and comfortable lounges.

In the renovations, passenger phone and Internet access were added; safety features were updated, and new engines and bridge electronics were installed. New bow and stern designs increase the ship's fuel efficiency by more than 22%. A bulbous underwater bow extension reduces the bow wake and water resistance. A stern fairing forces water to flow closer to the surface, reducing drag.

Spirit of Endeavour's clean lines and raked bow make it look most like a small cruise ship. Viewing breathtaking scenery in Alaska is a major activity on this ship, which appeals to those looking for quiet social life and a relaxed itinerary; in the Gulf of California, there are daily excursions that appeal to those eager for light adventure.

Spirit of Endeavour	QUALITY 3	VALUE C
REGISTRY United States	LENGTH 217 feet	BEAM 37 feet
CABINS 51	DRAFT 8.5 feet	SPEED 12 knots
MAXIMUM PASSENGERS	PASSENGER DECKS 4	ELEVATORS None
102	CREW 28	SPACE RATIO NA

Passengers give high marks to the ship's educational programs, and they appreciate finding two pairs of high-powered binoculars and umbrellas in their cabins. The ship does not have an elevator. The decor throughout is understated and pleasing. *Endeavour* does not have a promenade deck completely surrounding the ship.

ITINERARIES *See* Itinerary Index.

CABINS Cabins are large compared with the line's older sister ships and have wide picture windows. Refurbishment in 1999 added new closets, lighting, window treatments, wall coverings, artwork, and furniture; bathrooms were upgraded as well.

Cabins are on three decks and of four types: The 100 series on the Main Deck includes eight of the AAA category, measuring 109 square feet, and four A cabins of about the same size. The Lounge Deck has As that open onto the outside deck, 12 AAAs, and 2 deluxe cabins measuring 155 square feet. Upper Deck has 20 AAs and one deluxe cabin, all opening to an outside veranda. The A and AA have twin or double beds, and some cabins accommodate three passengers; most have large picture windows.

Specifications 51 cabins. The cruise line's brochures show precise layouts of each category.

DINING The **Resolution Dining Room** accommodates all passengers at a single open seating; most tables seat six or eight persons, none are for two. Mealtimes may vary depending on the itinerary, but generally, breakfast is served at 7 a.m., lunch at 12:30 p.m., and dinner at 7 p.m. The food gets high praise from passengers, and there's a good selection on the updated wine list. An unusual custom on board: the chef personally introduces the evening menu and invites passengers to dinner. As with most small ships, there is a great deal of camaraderie among passengers and friendly interaction with the ship's staff. Endeavour is benefiting from the Palate program that features food and wine pairings. Passengers have three dining options at lunch: alfresco dining, weather permitting; lunch in the dining room; or a light fare luncheon in the lounge.

FACILITIES AND ACTIVITIES The spacious **Explorer Lounge** is a multipurpose room and the heart of the ship's activity, beginning with continental breakfast in the morning and coffee, tea, and cocoa available 24 hours a day. It is also used for most of the lectures. A wide selection of videos and magazines is available in the library, along with a good selection of books and reference works pertaining to the area of the cruise.

The main activity on an Alaska cruise is sightseeing, which Alaska offers like no other place in the country. A Baja California and Gulf of California cruise during the winter months offers more sports activities, such as hiking, swimming, snorkeling, and kayaking, as well as sightseeing and spotting wildlife. Among the highlights are an opportunity to swim with sea lions, watching dolphins play, and photographing a colony of blue-footed boobies, but the most anticipated activity of all is whale watching. From about mid-January to mid-March, large numbers of California gray whales assemble in the lagoons of Bahia Magdalena, which passengers visit.

Spirit of Glacier Bay	QUALITY 5	VALUE C
Spirit of Yorktown	QUALITY 5	VALUE C
REGISTRY United States	LENGTH 207/257 feet	BEAM 37/43 feet
CABINS 51/69	DRAFT 11.5/12.5 feet	SPEED 7/10 knots
MAXIMUM PASSENGERS	PASSENGER DECKS 4	ELEVATORS None
102/138	CREW 29/42	SPACE RATIO NA

THE SHIPS United States-built and flying the American flag, the *Spirit of Glacier Bay* and the slightly larger *Spirit of Yorktown* are sister ships—similar but not identical. They were acquired by Cruise West from Clipper Cruises in early 2006; the ships' staff were rehired by Cruise West.

Spirit of Glacier Bay has three passenger decks and *Spirit of Yorktown* four, including a spacious top Sun Deck aft of the bridge—a comfortable place for watching the passing scene. With shallow drafts, the ships glide into small places as easily as they tie up in small ports, sailboat-filled harbors, and coves. Lounges and cabins are decorated with high-quality furnishings. No glitter, no glitz.

Both ships have a single forward observation lounge and bar on the center deck that serves as a social center. Three sides of the cheerful room have large windows trimmed with light wood. Textured fabric and neutral colors give the lounge a warm, contemporary look. During cruises, the room has the air of a club, with passengers conversing, reading, writing postcards, or simply watching scenery. It is also the scene for lectures, early breakfast buffet, afternoon cookies, and hors d'oeuvres at cocktail time.

In late 2007, the *Spirit of Yorktown* was given a $2 million refurbishment and upgrade, creating four balcony-category cabins. Other upgrades included renovation of public corridors, the lobby, and the observation lounge—passengers' favorite gathering spot for lectures and conversation—with renewed furniture, new carpeting, bookcases, and lighting.

ITINERARIES *See* Itinerary Index.

CABINS All six categories of cabins are outside, and all but the lowest category have picture windows. Cabins on the promenade deck open onto an outdoor, wraparound deck (as on river steamboats). Although these have an airy feel, some passengers might prefer cabins that open onto a central corridor.

On the *Spirit of Yorktown*, four cabins were converted into a new category. Located on the Sun Deck, the new balcony cabins underwent extensive remodeling with a new layout and teak-floored balconies, large enough for a cafe table and two chairs. The cabins are furnished with queen beds and minirefrigerators, along with new cabinetry, fixtures, carpet, and lighting. All cabins received new bedspreads and window treatments, and beautiful, original watercolor paintings by artist Marilynne Bradley were reframed and better displayed. Bradley's work has been recognized in museum exhibitions and major competitions.

Cabins are small but adequate and well lighted, offer ample storage, and appear more spacious because of a large wall mirror. Beds are parallel or at right angles; the latter provides more floor space. The furnishings have a clean, modern look, with closets and dressers in light wood and landscape paintings on the wall. Bathrooms have showers only and are small, with limited shelf space. In an effort to let passengers get away from it all, cabins have neither telephones nor televisions. Radios, however, provide wake-up calls, ship information, and music. Some cabins get noise from the hydraulic lift that raises and lowers the gangplank in port.

There is no room service. Laundry, beauty shop, and barber shop are usually available in port. The ships carry no nurses or doctors except on specific cruises. However, the vessels are almost always near shore in case of medical emergency. Lack of medical staff and the difficulty of walking on steep gangways make the ships unsuitable for many physically disabled persons.

Specifications All outside cabins; no suites. Standard dimensions are 122–139 square feet on *Yorktown*, 106–123 square feet on *Glacier Bay*. *Yorktown* balcony cabins have queen beds; all others have two lower beds, some with a pull-down third bunk; no singles. None are wheelchair accessible.

DINING The dining room, on the lower deck, has large windows and pleasant decor reflecting fine quality. Passengers dine at a single, open seating at round or square marble-topped tables, which are covered with cloths for dinner. The food is American cuisine overseen by a chef trained at a prestigious culinary school. Meals feature excellent soups, good-quality beef, fresh seafood, vegetables, and fruit. They're presented in a straightforward manner by the young, cheerful staff. Selections are not as extensive as on larger ships—dinner menus offer four entrees—but all menus include a regional specialty. A small but moderately priced selection of wines is available.

An early light breakfast is served in the lounge. For lunch, passengers have three options: alfresco dining on the Sun Deck, weather permitting; regularly scheduled lunch in the dining room; or light fare served in the lounge. Snacks, including fresh fruit, are available throughout the day. In the afternoon, freshly baked chocolate chip cookies are in the lounge, welcomed by passengers who have gathered in anticipation. The bar is open 11 a.m.–midnight.

SERVICE The clean-cut staff of young American men and women are cheerful, attentive, friendly, and unfailingly polite. Most are college students from the U.S. heartland. They take care of the restaurant, bar, and cabins, working 12 hours a day, seven days a week, and smile through it all.

FACILITIES AND ACTIVITIES The cruise director briefs passengers daily about upcoming adventures. Daily seminars by naturalists, historians, or other experts on places visited on the cruise precede follow-up discussions after the visits. The naturalist also acts as a guide for nature walks, bird-watching, and study of the local environment. Afternoons at sea, a movie plays in the dining room. A local folklorist or other interesting characters may come on board for a lecture, discussion, or entertainment. Activity centers on the destination, whether it's a tour of a historic town, a golf game, or a forest hike. There are no organized fun and games. Deck space is adequate for a destination-oriented ship, and most people use it to sunbathe, read, or watch the scenery—often through binoculars. Otherwise, passengers gather in the lounge after dinner to visit, or they retire to the dining room to watch movies. Most are in their cabins by 10 p.m.

SPORTS AND FITNESS Walkers can circumnavigate the Promenade Deck. The ships have no pools, whirlpools, exercise equipment, or fitness centers.

SHORE EXCURSIONS Cruises usually call at ports seldom visited by other ships and often tie up at small, out-of-the-way marinas and yacht harbors, enabling passengers to explore remote islands and coastlines on foot. Where *Spirit of Glacier Bay* cannot dock, passengers go ashore by Zodiac boat; *Yorktown* has dib launches. In urban areas, ships often tie up within walking distance of cultural attractions and offer above-average tours at reasonable costs.

THE SHIP Added to Cruise West's fleet in 1993, *Spirit of '98* previously sailed as the *Pilgrim Belle, Colonial Explorer*, and *Victorian Empress*. The handsome vessel has the profile and interior of a turn-of-the-19th-century riverboat (she had a role in the 1994 movie *Wyatt Earp*).

Built in 1984, *Spirit of '98* has decor that recalls a Victorian country hotel. Accenting a handsome mahogany and mirrored bar in the forward observation lounge are fanciful wall lamps and wood columns trimmed with strip mirrors. Continuing the theme on her four decks are extensive use of wood, wingback chairs, leaded glass, and old-fashioned brass lamps. The ship has one elevator operating between Main and Upper decks.

ITINERARIES *See* Itinerary Index.

CABINS All cabins are outside and have varied arrangements. They're roomy, with closet and storage space adequate for a casual cruise. All are decorated in rich Victorian-style colors and fabrics. All are air-conditioned and have windows that open—a welcome feature.

Cabins on Lounge and Upper decks open onto promenades. On Main Deck, lower-priced cabins have windows on the outside hull, a benefit for those who like privacy but want to keep their curtains open.

The ship has an amazingly large, two-room owner's suite on the top deck with picture windows on both sides. The only cabin on the deck, just behind the bridge, it has a sitting area, a game and meeting area, complimentary bar, television, DVD player, king-size bed, and bathroom with full-size tub. Occupants may have their meals served en suite.

The new Explorer Class cabins (formerly AAA cabins) on *Spirit of '98* are intended for passengers accustomed to a higher level of comfort. The "ecofriendly" amenities of these cabins include linens and towels of ultra-soft bamboo fiber (a sustainable resource), hypoallergenic down duvets, cotton bathrobes, and water-conserving Speakman easy-jet showerheads. Passengers on Alaska itineraries receive a copy of Cruise West's founder's book, *Mr. Alaska*.

Spirit of '98	QUALITY 3	VALUE C
REGISTRY United States	LENGTH 192 feet	BEAM 40 feet
CABINS 49	DRAFT 9.3 feet	SPEED 13 knots
MAXIMUM PASSENGERS	PASSENGER DECKS 4	ELEVATORS 1
96	CREW 26	SPACE RATIO NA

Specifications 48 outside cabins; 1 suite. Standard dimensions, 100–120 square feet. 40 with twins; 2 with upper/lower bunks; 4 with queens, 6 with doubles. 2 singles.

DINING The **Klondike Dining Room** provides seating at a variety of table configurations, including booths next to the picture windows. One open seating is offered at each of three meals. Cuisine is better than expected for this type of cruise. It's mostly Pacific Northwest fare encompassing fresh seafood, local produce, and Northwest wines and local specialty beers. In Mexico, meals have Mexican choices. Bread and pastries are baked on board. Coffee, tea, cocoa, and fruit are available all day.

An early continental breakfast is available in the forward lounge; full breakfast is at 7:30 a.m. in the dining room. Lunch features soups, salads, and sandwiches. Appetizers are served between 6 and 7 p.m.

SERVICE The young, enthusiastic crew are friendly, caring, and especially considerate of older passengers. These "guest service representatives" perform a variety of duties, including cleaning cabins and serving in the dining room.

FACILITIES AND ACTIVITIES Unusual in coastal cruise ships, **Soapy's Parlor** is a second, quiet lounge with wraparound windows at the stern, a good spot for watching the vessel's wake. Coffee, tea, and cocoa are served in the afternoon. The Bridge Deck has ample space for sunning, viewing scenery, or lounging. A barbecue lunch is offered in good weather. A small area serves as a gift shop, where caps, mugs, and similar items are sold.

The forward lounge is the ship's social center at night. Most entertainment is provided by the passengers interacting with each other in conversation, cards, or board games in the lounge or dining room. Absent are a pool, casino, aerobics classes, bingo, midnight buffet, or napkin-folding classes. The crew provides informal talent and lively entertainment on crew nights. Guest lectures, talks by the cruise coordinator-naturalist, and entertainment from the old-style player piano are offered.

THE SHIP Built in 1976, the vessel (formerly the *Independence* and renamed *Columbia*) was acquired by Cruise West in 1992 and renamed *Spirit of Discovery*. The forward lounge of this three-deck vessel is the ship's social center. Nicely decorated in blues, soft grays, teals, and mauves, it has a bar with standard spirits plus Pacific Northwest wines and specialty brews. Furniture is arranged in groupings. These features, along with a mirrored ceiling and chrome accents, give the ship the look of a private yacht or small, European-style hotel.

The *Spirit of Discovery's* lounge offers good views on both sides and over the bow through vertical windows at the front. Passengers at the bow can

Spirit of Discovery	QUALITY 2	VALUE D
REGISTRY United States	LENGTH 166 feet	BEAM 37 feet
CABINS 43	DRAFT 7.5 feet	SPEED 13 knots
MAXIMUM PASSENGERS	PASSENGER DECKS 3	ELEVATORS None
84	CREW 21	SPACE RATIO NA

almost touch the vegetation when the ship noses up to shore. The bridge has a wraparound viewing area and is open to passengers at most times. A stair stepper, exercise bicycle, and rowing machine are available.

ITINERARIES *See* Itinerary Index.

CABINS Cabins on all three decks are outside with large windows. Most are small but adequate enough and furnished with a vanity, desk, and chair. Bathrooms have showers. Two smaller cabins, sold as singles, are midship on the Bridge Deck.

Each of the four spacious, deluxe cabins on the top level have a queen-size bed, desk and chair, television, and fridge/minibar. All Bridge Deck cabins and most Lounge Deck cabins open onto a promenade. The two lowest-priced cabins are on the lower Main Deck forward, reduced in size to fit the hull's curvature.

Specifications 43 outside cabins; no suites. Standard dimensions, 64 square feet (single cabin) to 127 square feet. 34 with twins, 1 with double, 4 queens, 2 with upper/lower berths, 2 singles.

DINING The **Grand Pacific Dining Room,** aft on the main deck, is pleasant and airy but a bit noisy because it's over the engine room. The food is imaginative and quite good, encompassing Pacific Northwest versions of classic American fare with fresh local produce and seafood. All passengers dine in one open seating; table configurations vary.

A continental breakfast is available for early risers. Sit-down breakfast, lunch, and 6 p.m. appetizers are served. Two entrees are offered at dinner; they may include lingcod baked in parchment or a superb rack of Ellensburg lamb roasted with Dijon rosemary crust.

SERVICE Customer service, galley and engine crew, and deckhands are young Americans, most from the Pacific Northwest. They're attentive, enthusiastic, and outgoing. Friendships form between crew and passengers, and many crew members receive holiday greetings from passengers for years after they meet.

THE SHIPS *Spirit of Alaska* and *Spirit of Columbia* are identical in size, similar in layout, and are smaller versions of their sister ships. *Spirit of Alaska,* built in 1980 as the *Pacific Northwest Explorer*, was extensively renovated when acquired by Cruise West in 1991, and then renovated again in 1995. *Spirit of Columbia* (formerly *New Shoreham II* of American Canadian Caribbean Line) joined in 1994 after being refitted in a Western national park lodge theme.

Spirit of Alaska	QUALITY 2	VALUE D
Spirit of Columbia	QUALITY 2	VALUE D
REGISTRY United States	LENGTH 143 feet	BEAM 28 feet
CABINS 39/38	DRAFT 7.5/6.5 feet	SPEED 12/10 knots
MAXIMUM PASSENGERS	PASSENGER DECKS 4	ELEVATORS None
78	CREW 21	SPACE RATIO NA

Both ships have four decks, with most cabins on the lower and upper decks and a forward lounge and dining room midship on the Main Deck. The lounge is the center of social life and site of briefings. It has a small bar, gift shop, reference library focused on the cruise area, television, and movies. The upper deck has an unobstructed walking and jogging circuit and several exercise machines.

On *Spirit of Alaska*, the Bridge Deck provides open and covered seating and a good-weather venue for buffet lunches. Bow ramp stairs enable passengers to walk directly onto shore; some complain the stairs are steep and difficult to negotiate.

Besides decor, *Spirit of Columbia* differs in having a large owner's suite with windows overlooking the bow, three additional suites, a raised wheelhouse with 360-degree viewing, and an unusual bow ramp. A hinged, V-shaped segment of the bow can be lowered to form a ramp, giving direct access to shore from the forward lounge.

ITINERARIES *See* Itinerary Index.

CABINS Cabins on both ships range from roomy—for ships of this size—to very small. *Spirit of Alaska*'s suites and deluxe cabins have small sitting areas and are open to promenades. Three Bridge Deck suites have oversize double beds and windows on two sides and accommodate a third person.

Spirit of Columbia's 11 suites and deluxe cabins have a television/VCR, refrigerator, side tables, and a chair. Suites have a double bed; deluxe rooms, twins. The owner's suite has a queen-size bed, tub/shower, and complimentary bar. Upper and Bridge deck cabins open directly onto promenades.

On both ships, Main Deck cabins are on the short passage between the dining room and forward lounge, a high-traffic area but convenient for those who want easy access to activities and facilities. Windows in these cabins are on the outside hull, ensuring privacy. Lower-deck cabins have portlights high on the bulkhead and not for viewing. Baths are small units with handheld showers and curtains on tracks. Most cabins have twin beds; all have reading lights, closets, and under-bed storage. They're just above the engine room and can be noisy when the ship is under way, but they are a good buy for budget watchers.

Specifications Alaska, 12 inside cabins; 24 outside; 3 suites. Dimensions range from 81 to 130.5 square feet. 26 with twins; 13 with doubles; 7 cabins accommodate third persons; no singles. *Columbia*, 12 inside cabins; 20 outside; 7 suites. Dimensions range from 73.5 to 176 square feet.

DINING Meals are served at a single open seating. Cuisine is good American fare, emphasizing fresh Pacific Northwest and Alaskan seafood and local produce. The *Spirit of Alaska*'s Grand Pacific Dining Room has small round and square tables with upholstered banquettes running bow to stern underneath side windows.

SERVICE The young American staff helps set the friendly ambience and, despite the considerable workload, remains courteous, enthusiastic, and helpful, especially to seniors. Most retain a sense of awe about the magnificent region the vessel sails, often sharing passengers' excitement for wildlife sightings or glacier calvings, when enormous pieces of a glacier break off and crash into the sea.

Pacific Explorer	QUALITY 3	VALUE C
REGISTRY Honduras	LENGTH 185	BEAM NA
CABINS 50	DRAFT 12 feet	SPEED 12 knots
MAXIMUM PASSENGERS	PASSENGER DECKS 4	ELEVATORS None
100	CREW 33	SPACE RATIO NA

THE SHIP Built in 1995, remodeled in 1998, and renovated in 2008, *Pacific Explorer* specializes in cruises of Costa Rica and Panama. The historic Panamanian port of Portobello, dating from 1502, is on its itinerary. The ship is staffed with English-speaking Costa Ricans and guides. A lounge and dining room are on the lower of four decks; cabins and a forward lounge are on Main and Upper decks. The bridge, sunning area, and outdoor bar are on the Sun Deck.

All cabins have picture windows and are air-conditioned. They have private baths with showers. There are three types of cabins—deluxe (152 square feet), AAA/AA (122 square feet), and A (107 square feet)—and they are furnished with either twin or double beds. International cuisine and Central American specialties are served, along with breads and desserts made on board by the pastry chef.

Crystal Cruises

2049 Century Park East, Suite 1400
Los Angeles, CA 90067
☎ 310-785-9300 or 888-799-4625
FAX 310-785-3891
www.crystalcruises.com

TYPE OF SHIPS Modern, luxury superliners.

TYPE OF CRUISES Modern version of glamorous, traditional cruising with a touch of California glitz, for upscale, sophisticated travelers.

CRUISE LINE'S STRENGTHS
- service
- beautifully designed ships
- alternative restaurants
- globe-roaming itineraries
- interesting, unusual, and varied shore excursions
- enrichment program

CRUISE LINE'S SHORTCOMINGS
- two seatings in main dining room
- some cabins with restricted views on *Symphony*

FELLOW PASSENGERS Professional, retired or semiretired, experienced travelers; likely to be business owners, entrepreneurs, and executives rather than staff; ages 45–70. Typical passenger is affluent, active, friendly, fashion-conscious, and often a 55- to 60-year-old couple or mature single. Seventy-five percent come from the U.S., and the balance are Europeans and other affluent travelers. Approximately 53% are repeaters.

Recommended for Quality-conscious travelers who appreciate style with flash and attention to detail and want large-ship facilities; urbane first-time cruisers who can afford it.

Not recommended for Anyone uncomfortable with or uninterested in sophisticated ambience.

CRUISE AREAS AND SEASONS Caribbean, Central America, Mexico, Panama Canal, fall and winter; South America and world cruise, January to March; Asia, Middle East, spring; Alaska, Arctic Circle, Baltic, Europe, Mediterranean, and North Cape, summer; New York, New England, Canada, fall. Antarctic, South Africa, winter.

THE LINE Two years before her first ship debuted in 1990, Crystal Cruises promised it would return grand ocean liner elegance and personalized service to modern cruises for the "upscale mass market"—an apparently inconsistent term. The line not only delivered on its promise, but its first ship was even better than its advance billing. Crystal quickly became the cruise line by which others in her class—or aspiring to be in her class—were measured.

And therein lies the tale. There were no other ships in her class. Crystal Cruises created a niche all its own with a ship the size of a superliner that carries a third fewer passengers (some comparably sized ships carry twice as many passengers) and offers the best of all worlds—the facilities of a large, spacious ship with the personalized service of a small vessel.

Crystal Cruises' first ship was built in Japan by its owners, Mitsubishi Heavy Industries, a subsidiary of Nippon Yusen Kaisha, the Japanese ship-building giant known for its technologically advanced ships. The ship incorporated state-of-the-art engines, radar, and navigational equipment. Comfort and amenities went far beyond the norm. (*Crystal Harmony* left Crystal Cruises in late 2005 to join the new cruise line created by its owners for the Japanese market.)

Ironically, Crystal's second ship, *Crystal Symphony,* was built in Finland, for cost-saving reasons. *Crystal Serenity,* a third ship that debuted in summer 2003, was built in France. Somewhat larger than her sister ships, *Serenity* set a new direction for Crystal Cruises, with facilities for greater focus on enrichment programs and enhanced onboard amenities. Between 2004 and 2006, in a two-stage effort, *Crystal Symphony* was given a major makeover that brought her facilities closer to *Crystal Serenity*. In 2008, the latter ship was renovated, and eight new suites were added.

STYLE Exceptionally spacious ships with superliner facilities and Rodeo Drive style are designed for affluent travelers willing to pay for luxury and personal attention and who appreciate high quality in details. The cruises provide fine food and service in a gracious atmosphere, stimulating enrichment programs, a year-round roster of celebrity and expert speakers, and varied itineraries with more structure than ultraluxurious lines but less formality than luxury ships of old. Itineraries generally include more days at sea than is the norm, so passengers have time to fully enjoy the luxury and pampering that Crystal offers. In recent years, the ships have been remaining in ports overnight, a trend that is growing more and more in popularity. Every year, the line seeks out new ports to visit—with six maiden calls in 2009 and another six in 2010.

Not one to rest on its laurels—Crystal consistently sweeps the awards ratings—the line continues to add enhancements and interesting options and, thus, value to its cruise experience. Crystal has an incredible range of interesting and unusual shore excursions, enabling passengers to go canoeing in Croatia, explore Italy in a Ferrari, climb Kilimanjaro in Africa, or hike steep Mount Huashan in China. There are more and more adventure-type shore excursions—with 150 new ones added for the Mediterranean and Baltic itineraries in 2009 alone; additional programs in the onboard Creative Learning Institute; an expanded roster of theme cruises, plus a new Science and Technology theme in 2010, focusing on the world's latest scientific developments; and a series of extended land programs. On board, there are such added attractions as wine tastings, Pilates and yoga classes, and shuttles to town in ports free of charge.

THE FLEET	BUILT/RENOVATED	TONNAGE	PASSENGERS
Crystal Serenity	2003/08	68,000	1,080
Crystal Symphony	1995/2004/06	51,044	922

Following installation of wireless service aboard its ships, Crystal offers cell phone service in partnership with SeaMobile. The wireless service allows text messaging and the use of such equipment as a Blackberry. International roaming fees apply to all shipboard cell phone calls or messages and appear on the passenger's home cell phone bill. Passengers can also get their news from no less than 370 international newspapers for $6.50 each.

In response to the growing trend in multigenerational travel, Crystal has created a special area on its Web site to offer advice and guidance for families seeking to design a family reunion vacation. Responding to another trend, in 2007, Crystal became the first line to remove trans fats from its ships' galleys and replaced them with trans fat–free oils, incorporating the changes in all ships' menus and restaurants. In an effort to attract new as well as younger passengers, for 2010, the line has almost doubled the number of cruises that are ten days or less.

In 2009, Crystal introduced the cruise industry's first Technology Concierges to instruct passengers on the latest gadgets from iPods to iPhones, from BlackBerrys to GPS devices. In autumn, Crystal began offering classes based on Microsoft's Windows 7 a month before the operating system was available to the public. Passengers on *Crystal Serenity*'s 2010 World Cruise are able to earn three transferable college credits for various computer courses using both Microsoft and Apple systems. In another industry first, Crystal Cruises is partnering with the Travel Channel Academy to teach its guests how to produce, direct, and edit professional travel films.

Luggage Concierge, Crystal Cruises' exclusive partner in door-to-door luggage delivery service, is offering passengers the convenience of shipping their luggage to and from every Crystal cruise in 2010 at reduced two-for-one pricing. In fact, the new prices for shipping two bags in 2010 are even less than shipping one bag in 2009. Crystal has expanded its Mind, Body, and Spirit cruises in a new partnership with the UCLA Center for East-West Medicine, whose wellness mission blends the best of Eastern and Western medicines. Other wellness programs include the Cleveland Clinic, with lectures on the latest trends and treatments, and the Tai Chi Cultural Center.

DISTINCTIVE FEATURES Computer University@Sea, Creative Learning Institute. Two specialty restaurants at no extra cost; gentlemen hosts; close-captioned television for hearing-impaired passengers; free self-service laundry on each deck; business center with audiovisual equipment, fax machines, and office equipment; secretarial, translation, and e-mail services; takeout laptops; air-conditioned tenders with toilets. Wireless and cell phone service. Luggage Concierge.

RATES Port charges additional.

Special fares and discounts Normally, Crystal has promotional discounts ranging from 10% to 30% and more, depending on the cruise, but in September 2009, it introduced exceptionally attractive promotional rates with two-for-one savings on all its cruises in all cabin categories in 2010. Other new features are As You Wish spending credits for all destinations, up to $2,000 per couple; free round-trip air with most cruises; business-class air for Penthouse categories in Europe; and price guarantee, meaning passengers get Crystal's lowest published fares, even if the line reduces fares.

Introduced in 2009 and available in 2010 for all cruises, the Crystal Memories promotion addresses reunion and multigenerational travelers, enabling as few as six full-fare guests traveling together (three staterooms!) to receive prepaid gratuities, a $100 per person shipboard credit (in addition to the As You Wish spending credit), a group family photo, and a $500 credit toward a Crystal Private Adventure, and to allow kids under age 17 to sail free in a third berth. For ten full-fare guests, the group will get all of the above, plus a free cruise berth (no air).

- **THIRD PASSENGER:** Ages 12 and older: minimum fare for cruise.
- **CHILDREN'S FARE:** Younger than age 12, half-fare with two full-paying adults and free on certain cruises.
- **SINGLE SUPPLEMENT:** Crystal's single's fare begins at 125% of the double-occupancy rate for the lowest categories and is applicable to advance-purchase discount rates (130% for World Cruises).

PAST PASSENGERS Crystal Society past-passenger club offers amenities that increase with the number of cruises. These include business- and first-class air upgrades, confirmed stateroom and penthouse upgrades, shipboard credits, free cruises in staterooms and penthouses, limousine transfers, prepaid gratuities, and private luncheon and dinner parties.

Passengers are automatically enrolled after their first Crystal cruise and receive financial bonuses with every subsequent cruise. The higher reward levels are 5–30 cruises, 50, 70, and 100 cruises, but all members receive a 5% cruise discount, an additional 5% savings for reservations made while on a cruise, priority check-in, a Crystal Society travel bag, membership card, recognition pin, quarterly newsletter, and, beginning with the tenth cruise, a complimentary bottle of wine and fresh flowers on every cruise. Several cruises, including the annual president's cruise, are Crystal Society Sailings (marked with a C in the compendium) and feature a personal escort, exclusive events, and special gifts.

THE LAST WORD Crystal Cruises identified a market of experienced travelers (but not necessarily experienced cruise passengers) who weren't being served by other cruise lines and created a product that set new standards of luxury for large ships. Those who can afford the cruises get quality all the way. Compare Crystal's quality and extra amenities with those of other lines in the same price bracket, and you find that Crystal's cruises are among cruising's best values. And now, with the two-for-one promotion for all cruises in 2010 and free air transportation and other amenities, Crystal has become a fantastic value.

THE SHIPS Gleaming white inside and out, Crystal Cruises' ships are a symphony of Japanese technology and artistry, European service and tradition, and American flair for fun and entertainment. The elegance is in their simplicity, clean lines, and extraordinary attention to details. The line's quality, luxury, and spaciousness—one of the highest ratios of passenger-to-space of any ships—are immediately evident. The decor—a bit glitzy but always in good taste—was created by Swedish, Italian, and British designers and influenced by an understated Japanese aesthetic. Quiet colors and well-made furnishings harmonize. Fine fabrics and textures set off marble and woods accented with brass and stainless steel. The generous use of glass gives interiors an airy ambience.

Crystal Cruises Standard Features

Officers Norwegian captains and international officers

Staff *Dining:* European; *Cabin:* International; *Cruise:* American.

Dining facilities One main dining room, two seatings for dinner with open seating for breakfast and lunch; buffet breakfast and lunch on the Lido Deck, plus a new casual dinner on the *Crystal Symphony;* two alternative dinner restaurants; cocktail hour; tea.

Special diets Requests should be made when reservations are confirmed (or at least one month in advance). Kosher, 90 days advance notice. Low-carb selections are available on menus in all dining venues.

Room service 24-hour menu; butler service on Penthouse Deck.

Dress code Casual by day; casually elegant in the evening, with two formal evenings per week of cruising.

Cabin amenities Direct-dial phone with voice mail; television with CNN and ESPN, DVD; stocked minibar; safe; bathroom with tub, two hair dryers, robes; suites with marble bathrooms and whirlpool tubs. Wi-Fi, cell phone access.

Electrical outlets 110/220 AC.

Wheelchair access 8 *Serenity;* 4 cabins on *Symphony*.

Recreation and entertainment Casino, disco, nightclub, show lounge, piano bar, coffee and wine bar, cinema/theater, six lounges, observation lounge, card game and meeting room, video game room, smoking room. Guest lecturers, area specialists, celebrities. Bingo, bridge, dancing, computer, and crafts classes.

Sports and other activities Two outdoor swimming pools, one with retractable roof; two Jacuzzis; teak deck for walking or jogging; paddle tennis; table tennis, golf clinics, and practice corner; deck and pool games.

Beauty and fitness See text.

Other facilities Boutiques, concierge, hospital, laundry and dry cleaning, valet service, launderettes, photo processing center, video camera rentals, meeting facilities, business service center, e-mail facilities.

Children's facilities Playroom, babysitters, youth programs.

Theme cruises Food and wine; Fashion and Style; Golf; Film and Theater; Crystal Comedy Club at Sea; Big Band; Ballroom Dancing; Jazz; Cabaret at Sea; Mind, Body, and Spirit; Sotheby's; Smithsonian Journeys; Tennis; Photography; and others.

Smoking Dining rooms, main entertainment lounges, most bars, and cabin balconies, nonsmoking; public rooms, smoking in designated areas.

Crystal suggested tipping Per passenger per day: cabin stewardess, $5 ($6 for single travelers); butler, $4; senior waiter, $5; waiter, $3; $7 per person per dinner in specialty restaurants; 15% added to bar bills.

Credit cards For cruise payment and onboard charges: all major credit cards and traveler's checks. Ship uses a charge system, with the bill settled at end of cruise.

Crystal Symphony	QUALITY 9	VALUE B
REGISTRY Bahamas	LENGTH 781 feet	BEAM 99 feet
CABINS 461	DRAFT 25 feet	SPEED 20 knots
MAXIMUM PASSENGERS	PASSENGER DECKS 8	ELEVATORS 9
940	CREW 545	SPACE RATIO 55.3

Passengers' introduction to *Crystal Symphony*, which debuted in 1995, is the **Crystal Plaza,** an atrium lobby with a spiral waterfall and cascades of Lucite lights, stairways, and railings that appear to float in space. They're outlined with brass fixtures against white marble walls. Fresh greenery, hand-cut glass sculpture, and a waterfall provide accents. Summing up the feeling of opulence is—what else?—a crystal piano. The beautiful vessel has lounges for many purposes and moods.

The **Palm Court,** one of the most handsome lounges afloat, is an airy space in white and mint green with graceful palms under skylights. It wears the atmosphere of a traditional palm court in the afternoon when tables are set for tea with crisp linens and gleaming silver, and a harpist strums. Forward of the Palm Court is the fabulous **Vista Lounge,** a tri-level observation room with white leather chairs on sky-blue carpets and floor-to-ceiling windows that frame a 270-degree view. The lounge is designed in accordance with the principles of feng shui, the ancient practice of balance and harmony. All cabins are outside—about half have verandas, and all have large, well-designed bathrooms.

From 2004 to 2006, Crystal invested $45 million in two stages to renovate the *Crystal Symphony*, bringing her more in line with the *Crystal Serenity*. The work included a completely new feng shui–minded spa and fitness center, an expanded Computer University@Sea, redesigned specialty restaurants, a Vintage Room, as well as a refurbished dining room, library, and penthouse suites and cabins. With a sophisticated, contemporary style, the comprehensive undertaking transformed all staterooms and much of the Tiffany Deck, the ship's main entertainment area, with boutiques, shops, and a cafe, as well as a new casino, new nightclub, and dozens of behind-the-scenes improvements. *Crystal Symphony* spent two weeks at the Atlantic Marine Boston shipyard in 2009 to undergo a $25+ million makeover to redesign its penthouses, pool areas, Prego Italian restaurant, and Lido Café, among other upgrades.

ITINERARIES *See* Itinerary Index.

CABINS Large, comfortable, and handsomely appointed with fine fabrics and high-quality furnishings, the well-equipped cabins have sitting areas. *Symphony's* standard cabins are roomy. All are outside, and 214 have verandas and overall dimensions of 246 square feet. Other standard cabins cover 202 square feet and have large windows. All have a sitting area with two chairs, large bathrooms with two sinks in a six-foot counter, bathtubs plus showers, and large closets.

In the 2006 renovations, all of *Symphony's* deluxe and standard cabins were completely redesigned with the minimalist look of today's boutique hotel. Ultra-luxury notes are found in the new Murano glass bedside lamps,

Rubelli fabrics, and handsome leather headboard, along with special LED reading lights and new 20-inch flat-panel televisions that carry CNN and ESPN (when available). Bathrooms also have a new look, with oval glass sinks atop granite countertops. Large down pillows (there's a pillow menu) and comforters on beds, plush robes, fluffy towels, fine toiletries, and voice mail on the direct-dial telephone reflect attention to detail. All cabins have fresh flowers, two hair dryers, and Internet access.

More than half of all cabins have private verandas. Lifeboats obstruct views from some cabins, but Crystal's literature notes them as "limited" or "extremely limited" views and prices the cabins accordingly.

The ship's ultimate luxury is on the all-suite, concierge-attended Penthouse Deck. The two 982-square-foot Crystal penthouses with large verandas were stripped and completely transformed into spaces with the feel of elegant residential apartments with luxurious fabrics, details, and finishes. Internal space was extended to enlarge the living spaces and bedroom. Both the master and guest bathrooms feature rare marbles and designer fittings, but the master bathroom has a sunken Philippe Stark Duravit Jacuzzi bathtub with 90-degree ocean views, glass mosaics, and a recessed television, among other features.

Crystal Symphony's 61 butler-serviced penthouses and penthouse suites were also refurbished in soothing taupe and sand tones, accented by either citrus or icy blue colors. Updates include new custom cabinetry that sports stone countertops and flat-panel televisions, as well as new bedding, end tables, and bedside reading lights framed by new headboards, carpeting, and window treatments. All bathrooms were retiled with mosaic accents and fitted with glass showers, contemporary hardware, lighting, and fresh white and neutral colors. All Penthouse Deck suites have verandas.

The suites are attended by European-trained, white-gloved butlers and Scandinavian stewardesses. The young men, dressed in formal attire (some find this pretentious) are as competent as they are eager to serve. They will unpack your bags (and repack them at cruise's end), arrange a party or a dinner in your suite, and attend to other special requests. Nightly at cocktail time, they serve hors d'oeuvres and pour drinks from your fully stocked bar.

Specifications **Symphony,** 411 outside cabins, including 2 Crystal penthouses; 61 penthouse suites with verandas and 214 deluxe cabins (246 square feet) with verandas; 182 deluxe cabins (202 square feet) without verandas; 4 wheelchair accessible. Eight connecting cabins; 89 cabins with third berth. No singles. All twins convert to queens or kings.

DINING Super in quality and stunning in presentation, cuisine is one of Crystal ships' best features, on par with top restaurants in New York and Los Angeles. Food is served on fine china by waiters who are as polished as the silver. The spacious dining rooms with floor-to-ceiling windows and modern chandeliers are elegant and well designed. More space than usual is allowed between tables, helping keep noise down. Tables for two are numerous.

The redesigned *Symphony's* **Crystal Dining Room** has rich, dark paneling that offsets a bronze, maroon, and peach color palette. Along with the new decor came new lighting, window treatments, and an acoustically designed, elegant ceiling. **The Vintage Room,** a classic boardroom with access to the ship's extensive wine cellar, is a copy of the one on *Crystal Serenity*. It is located at the heart of the ship's entertainment area on Deck 6. Designed for the line's exclusive winemaker's dinners, The Vintage Room accommodates 12 in a luxurious setting of deep green colors and rich polished woods. The charge is $200 per person for the special menu paired with fine wines; however, for the "Ultimate" lavish dinner with rare wines, the price can go to $1,250 per person. For another "ultimate," Crystal has professional, certified cheese sommeliers.

Dinner menus, placed in cabins in advance, are greatly varied during a cruise. Typically, they include a choice of four appetizers; three soups; two salads; pasta; five entrees of fish, poultry, and meat; vegetables; and an array of desserts. Low-salt, low-fat, low-carb, and low-sugar choices are available. Since 2007, all trans fats have been removed from galleys on both ships and replaced with trans fat–free oils.

The maître d'hôtel often asks passengers for their favorite dishes, which the kitchen will prepare with advance notice. The wine list has more than 250 varieties. The ships' most innovative features—the first for cruising and starting the trend—are the intimate, alternative dinner restaurants, available at no extra cost to all passengers. The alternative restaurants have a hidden charm: Dining in the same surroundings on a long cruise can sometimes become boring. The two additional restaurants offer a change of ambience and cuisine.

One alternative is **Silk Road and Sushi Bar,** a duplicate of the popular Asian restaurant on *Crystal Serenity*, created by the famous master chef and Crystal consultant Nobuyuki "Nobu" Matsuhisa. The new design of the Italian restaurant **Prego** retains elements of its traditional Venetian architecture and portraiture presented in a fresh and modern way. Luxuriously padded, dark-chocolate fabric walls frame delicate chandeliers, art by famed Venetian artists, and richly upholstered seating. Each restaurant has its own kitchen; dishes are cooked to order and are outstanding. Reservations are required. Make yours early because both are enormously popular and have a waiting list almost every night.

The level of service and cuisine in the dining room and alternative restaurants is meant to compensate for the lack of the single-seating dining room traditionally found on luxury ships. (Diehards and some self-styled cruise critics consider this Crystal's unforgivable sin. I don't agree. The two seatings accommodate the many passengers who like to eat early. What's more, it has had no adverse effect on Crystal's success.)

The indoor-outdoor **Lido Café,** popular for breakfast and lunch, has been transformed into an upscale dining spot with a completely new Crystal dining experience, designed to showcase Crystal's freshly cooked fare as well as add intimate seating and improve flow. Inspired by the Hamptons seashore, the room is infused with light through a new glazed indoor-outdoor extension and expansive floor-to-ceiling windows. Natural tones of sand and weathered timber provide a backdrop for polished metal accents and sea-grass screens. New food and drink service islands, each with different choices, enable diners to make their selections. A new bread oven, grill, woks, and other culinary equipment provide a great array of freshly cooked-to-order choices. The **Trident Bar,** an extension of the Neptune Pool swim-up bar, offers hot dogs, hamburgers, and other snacks, and there's a bar for ice cream and frozen yogurt.

Crystal ships serve a late-risers breakfast from 10 a.m. to noon, as well as a Sunday brunch in the **Crystal Cove** on Sundays at sea. The line also offers casual dining with an informal menu on deck on select evenings, usually after a day in port; passengers dress as they like in slacks, jeans, or shorts, and they eat when they wish.

A sumptuous tea is served daily in the **Palm Court,** and the Crystal Plaza is the setting for a weekly dessert extravaganza set to the music of Mozart. Should you still suffer hunger pangs, the fruit basket in your cabin will have been replenished, or your cabin attendant will bring any item on the extensive 24-hour room service menu. You also may dine in your cabin, with courses served one by one.

The attractive **Bistro Café** serves coffee and pastries for late risers and wine and cheese, coffees, teas, and desserts during the day. Annually on a series of sailings, Crystal offers a wine and food festival featuring guest chefs and wine experts.

SERVICE The ships have among the highest crew-to-passenger ratios in cruising. The well-trained staff is young, cheerful, and eager to please; service is thoroughly professional and consistently excellent. Dining room staff primarily are European; cabin attendants, European and Filipino; and the cruise and entertainment staff, American. A European-style concierge and purser service are available around-the-clock.

FACILITIES AND ACTIVITIES Cultural and destination-oriented lectures by experts, political figures, and diplomats are a regular afternoon or after-dinner feature. Daytime pursuits include cards and other games, dancing classes, golf clinics, and arts and crafts. The well-stocked library has videos, DVDs, books, and periodicals.

The **Computer University@Sea** is outfitted with new equipment and a wireless facility, including cell phone service. Depending on cruise length, classes range from PC Basics to Digital Video Editing. The newest courses and a cruising first are offered by Technology Concierges on each ship, who instruct passengers on the latest gadgets from iPods to iPhones, from Black-Berrys to GPS devices.

The classroom aboard *Symphony* has 25 computer workstations and hands-on lab sessions. Passengers may also schedule private instruction in their cabins. Rental laptop computers are available. Crystal was among the first to introduce e-mail service on its ships. Passengers have their own e-mail address, which they receive with their cruise ticket. There is an initial $5 set-up fee and a range of charges thereafter, depending on use. The line also offers a selection of packages based on the number of days used. Internet access is available in all cabins. The **library,** with more than 3,000 titles, is located in the ship's atrium midship.

The **Hollywood Theatre,** with high-definition video projection and hearing-aid headsets, runs films each afternoon and evening. Films and other programs also are available on cabin televisions. For further diversion, pricey temptations with designer names are sold in the pretty shops on **Avenue of the Stars.** The elegant space is dressed with dramatic white marble, black accents, clean stone finishes, and stunning chandeliers. **Facets** has a private area for passengers to consider high-end jewelry purchases, and **Apropos** offers the line's logo items and resort wear.

Pre-dinner options include cocktails in the **Vista Lounge** or wood-paneled **Avenue Saloon** or a classical concert by a harpist or trio. The **Connoisseur Club,** adjacent to the Avenue Saloon, is a cigar and Cognac lounge with private club atmosphere.

Two Broadway-style, full-scale, high-quality productions in the **Galaxy** show lounge are offered at night. Local entertainers may perform at ports of call. One evening is a masquerade party.

Repertory Theatre at Sea is a delightful innovation for entertainment. It includes well-known comedy and light drama performed by professional actors on every cruise. The diverse roster offers up to 91 scenes, excerpts, or reading from larger works as varied as Shakespeare, Edgar Allan Poe, and Henry James. The Starlite Club, centrally located midship on Tiffany Deck, has a dramatic round bar as its centerpiece. With window walls sparkling with Swarovski crystals, the Starlite Club provides a stylish, open environment with panoramic sea views where lectures are featured by day and dancing by night.

Galaxy Lounge, the main show lounge, offers an array of first-rate productions that might range from classical ballet to a Broadway revue. Crystal has its own production team of Gretchen Goertz and Kathy Orme, who create all the production shows, which are original and very good. The talented show troupe includes former dancers from the Bolshoi Ballet and London's West End. The shows usually have spectacular costumes—some valued at $10,000 apiece—and sets by award-winning designers. The ship's redesigned casino with black flooring and a sophisticated black and silver color palette offers blackjack, roulette, and baccarat, plus Ultimate Texas Hold-'em and state-of-the-art slot machines. Before sailing, passengers receive an application for credit at the casino, if they care to have it. The late-night nightclub, Luxe, with the sophisticated contemporary look of polished aluminum, Philippe Starck bar stools, and glass Bizzaro mosaics, has a dazzling lighting system that flashes electric color off shimmering finishes and shades of black, silver, and white.

During the recent renovations, the elevators were upgraded and the medical center improved with digital x-ray equipment, enabling doctors to share x-rays with passengers' personal physicians and other specialists. Other behind-the-scenes projects included a major upgrade of the ship's onboard broadcast production studio, enhancing its extensive television programming.

SPORTS, FITNESS, AND BEAUTY A lap pool has adjacent whirlpools, and an indoor-outdoor swimming pool has a swim-up bar and a retractable roof. The pool areas were redefined with new spaces and water features and provide more indoor and alfresco dining and varied sunbathing options. Sophisticated limestone tile offsets the azure pool and the new, larger whirlpool, while deck furniture offers a harmonious combination of antique white and taupe accented with tropical elements. The Neptune Pool was given teak decking and alfresco dining and lounging options around the Trident Bar. There's generous sunning space on deck, plus table tennis, shuffleboard, pool games, golf, and the only full-scale paddle tennis court at sea. Deck 7 offers a wraparound, unobstructed route for walking or jogging.

The enlarged spa was constructed following the design principles of feng shui. The facility, with sweeping ocean views, houses eight treatment rooms, a relaxation area, a private canopied teak sun deck, a state-of-the-art steam shower and sauna area, and custom-designed manicure/pedicure areas with sunken foot bowls. A dry float-bed suite, appropriate for singles or couples, has a sensory bed to create a feeling of weightlessness, ideal for Aroma Spa and other treatments. The **Fitness Center** has a separate room for yoga, Pilates, aerobic and personal training instruction, and a gym with state-of-the-art fitness equipment, all with heart-rate sensors.

Crystal has expanded its Mind, Body, and Spirit cruises in a new partnership with the UCLA Center for East-West Medicine, whose wellness mission is blending the best of Eastern and Western medicines. Other wellness programs include the Cleveland Clinic with lectures on the latest trends and treatments; the Tai Chi Cultural Center with experts leading classes; the Walk on Water program utilizing the Walkvest training system for walking with weight resistance; kinesis equipment using cable resistance to improve strength, flexibility, and balance; Tour de Spin indoor cycling classes that mirror three stages of the Tour de France; acupuncture; and healthy culinary options on virtually every menu. Always on the cutting edge of wellness, Crystal recently introduced Nordic walking poles for use at no charge. The poles are said to help distribute stress evenly while walking, increase stability, improve balance, and alleviate the impact of running and jogging.

Crystal's alliance with TaylorMade showcases its prestigious r7 superquad driver and other TaylorMade equipment. Crystal's golf program includes right- and left-handed clubs for men and women, golf clinics, instruction by PGA golf pros, a putting green, practice cage, and driving ranges aboard the ships. A golf pro is generally on board, offering lessons and tips, and the line schedules several golf cruises during the year. Usually, Crystal can arrange play at golf courses in many ports.

CHILDREN'S FACILITIES Supervised youth programs are provided only when the line knows in advance that a sizable number of children will be aboard. **Fantasia,** a children's playroom, is more of an entertainment center, with video games for children ages 3–16. In-room babysitting can be arranged with crew members for $7.50 per hour for one child, $10 per hour for two children, and $12.50 per hour for three children.

SHORE EXCURSIONS The line has an incredible array of shore excursions. They are sold on board, but they can also be booked in advance online. Crystal's efficient tenders have air-conditioning—a much-appreciated amenity. Crystal provides good maps and information about each port. The concierge and excursion desk helpfully suggest and arrange independent port programs.

Crystal continues to add interesting and ambitious excursions. They range from hiking and kayaking to rafting, horseback riding, and wildlife viewing. One exotic option is a wildlife tour in dugout canoes on a Botswana safari offered on the occasional Africa cruises. The Florence and Pisa by Private Ferrari excursion, available on three Mediterranean sailings, puts you in the driver's seat of a Ferrari for a day to explore Italy, complete with an expert Ferrari driver and lead car guiding the way. Often excursions are timed to special events such as the annual Fiesta of San Fermin in Pamplona—more familiarly known as the Running of the Bulls.

Crystal Serenity	QUALITY **10**	VALUE **C**
REGISTRY Bahamas	LENGTH 820 feet	BEAM 105.6 feet
CABINS 535	DRAFT 25 feet	SPEED 22 knots
MAXIMUM PASSENGERS	PASSENGER DECKS 13	ELEVATORS 8
1,235	CREW 655	SPACE RATIO 64.4

THE SHIP *Crystal Serenity*, built at Alstom Chantiers de L'Atlantique in France, made her debut in July 2003. The ship combines the best features of her sister ship with new ones, including more dining venues, more penthouse suites, more cabins with verandas and butler service, more entertainment lounges, and more fitness options, among others. The new ship is almost 20% roomier and is richly decorated in refined taste, incorporating soft, muted colors that complement the beautiful crystal-glass signature touches throughout the vessel.

The new features introduced on *Serenity*, and now on *Sympathy*, were the Asian restaurant by Nobu and sushi bar, and a boardroom with a wine cellar for special dinners and wine tastings (at an extra charge). She also gained a second paddle tennis court, a new learning center for creative and educational hands-on classes, and a club lounge off the atrium for Crystal Society members, making *Serenity* one of the first ships to have a room dedicated specifically to its past passengers.

The familiar favorites from previous Crystal ships include a contemporary rendition of the **Palm Court,** a spacious observation lounge with potted palms set into hexagonal skylights, the clubby **Avenue Saloon,** and the **Connoisseur Club.** The large **Computer University@Sea** classroom has a 24-hour Internet center, plus a private area for one-on-one computer instruction. The *Serenity*'s spa and fitness center, approximately 40% larger than the one on her sister ship, are quite lavish. Located high up and aft, the two sections have separate entrances and good soundproofing—hence the thumping of exercise machines does not intrude upon the serenity of the treatment room or the **Lido Café** below.

Crystal Serenity has an even greater space ratio (64) than her sister ship, with 34% more public space and one deck more than *Crystal Symphony*. The ship was designed by an international team headed by well-known Swedish naval architect Robert Tillberg, who worked on Crystal's other ship. Tillberg says *Serenity* is a sister, not a twin, to *Symphony*. His team was responsible for most of the public rooms and all passenger and staff accommodations. Other firms designed the specialty lounges and restaurants, spa, and retail shops.

ITINERARIES *See* Itinerary Index

CABINS Like *Crystal Symphony*, the ship has no inside cabins, and approximately 85% of the outside cabins and suites have private verandas. None have obstructed views, as the lifeboats are stowed below the cabin decks. One and a half decks of *Serenity* are devoted to penthouse accommodations with verandas (56% greater than on *Crystal Symphony*). Of those, the most lavish are four Crystal penthouses, each measuring 1,345 square feet. In 2008, due to high demand, the number of penthouse accommodations was increased by converting 12 deluxe cabins with verandas on Deck 10 into eight penthouses with 403 square feet. Four new penthouses can connect with the penthouse suites. The richly appointed penthouses enjoy butler service, a large private veranda, sizable living area, bar stocked with complimentary wine and choice of liquor, Jacuzzi tub and separate shower, walk-in closet, flat-panel television, DVD and CD player, Riedel glassware, and complimentary pressing. In addition to 24-hour in-stateroom dining from the dining room, penthouse patrons can order from the specialty restaurants during dinner hours.

In addition to the suites, there are 456 outside cabins with verandas and 80 outside staterooms with large picture windows. The eight wheelchair-accessible cabins are found in various categories: two penthouses, two veranda cabins, and four cabins with picture windows.

The deluxe cabins with verandas (Categories A and B) are virtually identical to the penthouse cabins with verandas (Category PH), all being 269 square feet, but the former do not have butler service. The cabins are each furnished with a comfortable sofa with a pop-up coffee table for in-cabin dining, queen or twin beds with two night tables, and lamps rather than reading lights. The entertainment center has a remote-control television and DVD player. The minibar and refrigerator are stocked with complimentary soft drinks and bottled water. All cabins have a data port for laptop computer hookup.

All accommodatons have 100% Egyptian cotton sheets, down pillows (and a pillow menu), duvets, two hair dryers, fresh fruit, and flowers, as well as Frette bathrobes, kimonos, slippers, an umbrella, and English mohair lap blankets. Double sinks, makeup mirrors, a shower, and a bathtub are standard with every bathroom. Other amenities include laundry and dry cleaning service, twice-daily housekeeping, and 24-hour in-stateroom dining. The veranda is furnished with two white plastic chairs and a table; chaise lounges can be requested.

Specifications Serenity, 465 outside cabins, including 4 Crystal penthouses; 32 penthouse suites and 72 penthouses with verandas (403–538 square feet); and 356 deluxe cabins (269 square feet) with verandas; 182 deluxe cabins (226 square feet) without verandas; 8 wheelchair accessible; 46 connecting cabins; 165 cabins with third berth. No singles. All twins convert to queens or kings.

DINING Passengers on *Serenity* have the choice of five evening dining venues: the main **Crystal Dining Room** (two seatings); **Tastes,** an indoor-outdoor poolside area for casual evening dining; and three specialty restaurants, including **Prego** for Italian fare; a sushi bar, a first for Crystal; and **Silk Road** for Pan-Asian cuisine. The latter features eclectic creations by famous master chef and Crystal consultant Nobuyuki "Nobu" Matsuhisa, known for his innovative blend of classic Japanese dishes with Peruvian and European influences. Two of the alternative restaurants operate on a reservations-only basis for no extra charge. No reservations are needed on the sushi bar. In general, service seems better and a bit less harried in Silk Road, perhaps because the menu is less extensive. Among the Nobu selections on Silk Road's Pan-Asian menu are lobster with truffle yuzu sauce, black cod with miso, and chicken with teriyaki balsamic. The airy portside setting is executed in lime green with soft blue lighting and the sushi bar at the entrance.

Serenity's Prego is entirely different in style than on her sister ship. It is a long, two-level room located aft on the starboard side, decorated in white and gold with bas-relief urns filled with fruit on the bulkhead pilasters. The decorative panels show Tuscan city scenes using two-dimensional depictions: the front panel low in height and the rear one in full height, with indirect lighting between to brighten the settings and create depth. Two Italian favorites on the menu are pumpkin ravioli flavored with apricot and filet of Angus beef topped with Gorgonzola. The restaurant also offers mouthwatering blends of seafood and pasta.

During the day, passengers have choices similar to her sister ship, plus some new ones. Permanent hot-food stations aft of the ship's second pool serve luncheon buffets with a theme. The ship also offers stylish versions of its popular **Bistro**, a coffee and wine bar for morning and afternoon snacks such as cold meats, salads, cheeses, and desserts; the **Lido Café** for breakfast and lunch; the **Trident Grill** for casual, poolside lunches throughout the afternoon; an ice-cream/frozen yogurt bar; and 24-hour room service. Crystal expanded its healthy breakfast options at **Tastes** with gluten-free, lactose-free, sugar-free, fat-free, and whole-grain selections.

FACILITIES AND ACTIVITIES   The **Galaxy Show Lounge** is the main entertainment venue for production shows and has improved sight lines and state-of-the-art sound and lighting systems. It's truly a showroom for the 21st century. Several shows are offered. A second cabaret lounge, the **Stardust Club,** provides a venue for daytime activities, such as dance classes and wine tasting, as well as for evening dancing and cabaret entertainment.

The **Palm Court,** with floor-to-ceiling 270-degree panoramic windows, is a splendid, roomy top-deck lounge in blue-gray with rattan seating, used for afternoon tea with a menu of about a dozen regular and herbal teas. It's also a good spot for evening dancing and entertainment, special events, and for simply enjoying the changing scenery. Room extensions offer unusual views of the glass-enclosed bridge wings one deck below. Other public facilities include the **Crystal Plaza** and **Crystal Cove,** the lobby area with a two-story atrium and **Crystal Piano Bar;** the **Avenue Saloon,** Crystal's clubby signature piano bar; the **Connoisseur Club,** a cigar lounge for after-dinner drinks; a casino; **Pulse,** a disco/nightclub for late-night dancing and karaoke; **Hollywood Theater,** a cinema-conference center with theater-style seating for day and evening movies, lectures, and religious services; a staffed library with books and DVDs—and even a great selection for kids—and comfy reading bays; a card room for Crystal's avid bridge players; and a gallery of high-end retail shops.

Passport to Music is a partnership with Yamaha to offer a program of music instruction as part of the line's new **Creative Learning Institute** (CLI), perhaps the most original experiential and interactive "edutainment," as Crystal calls it, offered at sea. Music instruction is offered in **The Studio,** *Crystal Serenity's* handsome, high-tech facility created expressly for CLI programs.

The Studio is outfitted with 15 portable grand-piano keyboards—Yamaha's newest state-of-the-art model—and supported with the Clavinova digital piano. Certified Yamaha music teachers are aboard to teach groups of 12–15 guests. Depending on the length of the cruise, the average curriculum offers six

60-minute sessions; guests receive a certificate at the program's completion. A selection of software created by Yamaha enables guests to continue their musical journey at home.

Other Crystal partnerships for the Creative Learning Institute allow well-known organizations and schools, such as Berlitz, the Cleveland Clinic, Society of Wine Educators, Pepperdine University, and Tai Chi Cultural Center, among others, to bring experts aboard to share their knowledge in a classroom setting. The CLI curriculum offers progressive levels of instruction on a single subject or several one-class sessions of related topics. The main categories are Arts and Entertainment, ranging from Asian woodblock printing to acting workshops; Business and Technology, covering estate planning to fundraising to patent applications; Lifestyle, dealing with topics such as book clubs, candle making, or menu planning; Wellness, with health and fitness topics and serious medical subjects, such as prostate cancer, led by an expert from the Cleveland Clinic; and Wine and Food. The CLI is very popular—a kind of Elderhostel at sea. Thus, when the ship is full, it's wise to sign up early. There is no charge for any of the courses.

Repertory Theatre at Sea, similar to that on *Crystal Symphony*, features well-known comedy and light drama performed by professional actors. The diverse roster offers scenes, excerpts, or reading from larger works as varied as Shakespeare, Edgar Allan Poe, and Henry James.

SPORTS, FITNESS, AND BEAUTY *Serenity*'s 8,500-square-foot spa and fitness centers are approximately 40% larger, with more treatment rooms and a larger gym and aerobics studio than her sister ship, with state-of-the-art equipment. In response to passenger feedback, the ship has a second paddle-tennis court; an outdoor lap pool flanked by two whirlpools; a second indoor/outdoor pool covered by a sliding roof; a full promenade around the exterior of the ship for walking, jogging, and shuffleboard; and a Sports Deck with two golf driving ranges, putting green, and table tennis.

CHILDREN'S FACILITIES *Crystal Serenity* has a **Fantasia** children's and teen center with video games, both small and located high up and aft of the Palm Court foyer. Programs apply when there are children aboard, which is not often on long cruises. Holiday cruises bring out families. Then, too, Crystal, like most cruise lines, is seeing a steady increase in multigenerational as well as family cruising.

Cunard Line

24303 Town Center Drive, Suite 200
Valencia, CA 91355-0908
☎ 661-753-1035 or 800-7-CUNARD
www.cunard.com

TYPE OF SHIPS Large, traditional ships; deluxe megaship.

TYPE OF CRUISES Wide range of destinations and durations, from warm-weather vacations to transatlantic spring-to-fall service for affluent, demanding travelers; distinctively British pedigree.

CRUISE LINE'S STRENGTHS
- name recognition
- distinctive ships
- itineraries
- accommodations and service

CRUISE LINE'S SHORTCOMINGS
- mixed products on ships

FELLOW PASSENGERS Cunard attracts a broad spectrum of passengers—from first-timers eager to visit many ports to veterans who seldom leave the ship—but most are upscale, mature, experienced travelers. Depending on the time of year, American and British travelers make up (about 50-50) the majority of the line's passengers, with large contingents of European and repeat customers. Cunard's world cruises attract a very different crowd—affluent and older, taking long winter vacations—from that on other itineraries. *QM2* passengers may be all ages, incomes, and professions, as well as families with children, and people eager to take an ocean voyage on the famous ship.

> *Recommended for* Those who enjoy a certain amount of formality and tradition and are accustomed to luxury and willing to pay for it.

> *Not recommended for* Those uncomfortable with elegance, who prefer a casual or nonstop party atmosphere.

CRUISE AREAS AND SEASONS Around the world in winter; transatlantic, April to November; Europe, spring to fall; Baltic, Caribbean, Mediterranean, New England, Canada, Panama Canal, and South America, seasonally.

THE LINE Cunard Line, with a history stretching back to 1840, sailed into the 21st century with new owners, new management, and a new direction. But reinventing itself is nothing new for Cunard. With the postwar birth of the jet age and the demise of transatlantic passenger service, traditional steamship companies like Cunard had to adapt to the new realities to survive. Some converted their ships for modern cruising, some built new ships, and some bought or merged with other cruise lines. Cunard took all these steps and more.

During the era of the grand ocean liners, Cunard Line was best known for its queens—the *Queen Mary* and *Queen Elizabeth*—which set the standard of elegance at sea for decades. The new *Queen Elizabeth 2* made her debut in 1969 when the future of transatlantic service was uncertain, and doubts persisted throughout the next decade as to whether the line would survive. Having the only ocean liner on regular transatlantic service helped keep her going. In 1982, the *QE2* was pressed into Her Majesty's service during the Falkland Islands War. For Cunard it was a blessing in disguise, giving the *QE2* a new lease on life with publicity and a much-needed refurbishment by the British government before her return to passenger service.

In 1998, Cunard was sold to Carnival Corporation. The new owners spent millions renovating the *QE2* and rebuilding Cunard with new ships. The first, *Queen Mary 2*, christened by Her Majesty Queen Elizabeth II in 2004, was billed by Cunard as the "grandest and largest passenger liner ever built." She was intended to evoke a bygone era of seagoing luxury while representing the next era of ocean liner evolution to create "a new golden age of sea travel for those who missed the first." *Queen Victoria* arrived in 2007, and the new *Queen Elizabeth* will debut in 2010. Cunard's blog can be found at **www.wearecunard.com.** The line is also on Twitter and Facebook.

STYLE The legendary and distinctive style of the *Queen Elizabeth 2* continues to have an enduring impact on Cunard's style, which the *QM2* and Queen Victoria have followed, each similar yet different too. Today, *QM2* is the only passenger ship sailing the Atlantic on a regular schedule, from April to November, with three levels of service. She offers shorter cruises, usually in the Caribbean and Europe, to fill the weeks between.

To many, the *Queens* are the ultimate cruise experience. They are proud, elegant, formal, and as British as—well, yes—the queen. Throughout its history, Cunard has been an innovator in response to changing lifestyles. *QE2* was the first ship to have a full-fledged spa, and now *QM2* has Canyon Ranch's first spa at sea. Recognizing the impact of the electronic revolution, Cunard has the first computer learning center, satellite editions of world news, and an electronic library on its ships.

DISTINCTIVE FEATURES Year-round gentlemen hosts, computer learning centers, British nannies, driving range and putting green, florist, tuxedo rental, electronic library, bookshop. *QM2:* **Canyon Ranch SpaClub,** Royal Academy of Dramatic Art performances, and **Illuminations,** the only planetarium at sea, largest ballroom and largest library at sea.

RATES Most port charges are included.

Special fares and discounts
- Early-booking discounts: Approximately 20% off brochure fares with extra 5% off for past passengers.
- **THIRD/FOURTH PASSENGER:** Specific fares listed in chart in brochure.
- **CHILDREN'S FARE:** If the child is the third or fourth person, third/fourth person fare applies.

THE FLEET	BUILT/RENOVATED	TONNAGE	PASSENGERS
Queen Elizabeth	2010	90,140	2,000
Queen Mary 2	2004	150,000	2,592
Queen Victoria	2007	90,000	2,014

- **SINGLE FARES:** Single-occupancy cabins listed in brochure. Supplement for single occupancy of double cabin is 140%–200%, depending on cabin.

PAST PASSENGERS Cunard World Club, the past passenger program, has four levels: Silver, after one cruise; Gold, third through sixth voyage or 20 days on board; Platinum, seven cruises or completion of 70 days on board; and Diamond, 15 voyages or 150 days on board. Each level has all the benefits of previously achieved levels, including savings on sailings, an onboard club representative, special mailings with savings offers, preferred reservations, and more. Gold members get two hours of free Internet service. Platinum members get two hours of free Internet, a 20% discount off laundry and dry cleaning services, and an onboard invitation to a Senior Officers' Party. Diamond members get four hours of free Internet, priority check-in, complimentary lunch at Todd English, and priority luggage delivery.

THE LAST WORD Cunard has long been known for luxury, but if you don't understand the differences in the levels of luxury, it can be somewhat misleading. For example, the line's popular image is associated with glamour, grand luxury, and haute cuisine. For those who buy the highest-priced suites and deluxe cabins and dine in the grills, this picture is accurate—but that segment of travelers makes up less than 15% of passengers. On her transatlantic run, QM2 has four levels of service, including the Britannia Club, determined by cabin category, which is a polite way of saying four classes based on price. Each category is assigned specific restaurants, and entry by the others is restricted accordingly. The redeeming factor is that all entertainment, sports, recreational facilities, and shops are available to everyone, regardless of their cabin location.

Cunard's White Star Service is a training program for officers and staff that focuses on three pillars: the legendary, the elegant, and the memorable. Each member of the ship's crew wears a black enamel pin on which the three words are inscribed. Named for the White Star Line with which Cunard merged back in 1934, the service is intended to acquaint the crew with Cunard's long history, and through it instill in them the pride and high level of service that is the Cunard tradition.

THE SHIP *Queen Mary 2*, Cunard's flagship, was not only the biggest, widest, longest, and most expensive ship ever built when she was launched, but her debut gave birth to a new Cunard cruise line.

The ocean liner is meant to be reminiscent of great transatlantic steamships and, in Cunard's words, "relaunch the golden age of travel for those who missed the first one." Designed as an ocean liner for the 21st century and intended to appeal to baby boomers who Cunard sees as the ship's main market, the overall impression is one of quiet grace, conservative and a bit

Queen Mary 2	QUALITY **8**	VALUE **B**
REGISTRY Great Britain	LENGTH 1,132 feet	BEAM 135 feet
CABINS 1,296	DRAFT 32 feet	SPEED 30 knots
MAXIMUM PASSENGERS	PASSENGER DECKS 14	ELEVATORS 22
3,090	CREW 1,253	SPACE RATIO 57.25

Cunard Line Standard Features

Officers British and international.

Staff British and international.

Dining facilities *QE2*, single seating in grills for three meals; two seatings in Britannia; informal Lido cafe for three meals and midnight buffet; snack bar. *QM2, Queen Victoria*, Todd English restaurant; pub; and a Lido-style King's Court with distinct sections offering four types of food: Asian, Italian, carved meats, and salads and such.

Special diets Diabetic, low-calorie, low-cholesterol, low-salt, and vegetarian.

Room service 24-hour room service.

Dress code Formal/informal for dining, depending on evening.

Cabin amenities Radio, direct-dial telephone, 20-channel television with CNN. Bathroom with tub and shower in suites. Refrigerator, walk-in closet, bathrobes, hair dryer, safe, fruit baskets, nightly turndown service, and verandas.

Electrical outlets 220/110 AC.

Wheelchair access *QM2*, 30 cabins; *Queen Victoria*, 20 cabins.

Recreation and entertainment Casino, cabaret, revues, enrichment seminars, guest lectures. Lounges, bars, disco, bingo, dance lessons, gentlemen hosts, computer learning center, planetarium (*QM2*).

Sports and other activities Indoor/outdoor pools, deck sports, putting and driving net, jogging track, paddle tennis, table tennis.

Beauty and fitness Spa, fitness center, gym, barber/beauty salon, exercise class. See text for details.

Other facilities Cinema/theater, launderette, laundry/dry cleaning service, library, bookshop, shops, hospital. *QE2*, tuxedo rental shop, foreign exchange, Harrods, florist, boardroom, synagogue. *QM2*, Hermès, Chopard, kennels.

Children's facilities Teen center, video, supervised children's playrooms, nursery, British nannies, babysitting; special children's evening meal served daily in the Lido at 5:30 p.m.

Theme cruises None.

Smoking Designated areas in public rooms.

Cunard suggested tipping $11–$13 per day added to bill, depending on cabin category. Both ships include 10–15% gratuity for bar and salon services.

Credit cards For cruise payment and onboard charges: American Express, Diners Club, Discover, MasterCard, Visa.

formal in a British manner without being stuffy. The refined interiors successfully combine contemporary elegance with a classic liner look.

The spacious *QM2*, which cost more than $800 million and was constructed at STX Europe (formerly Alstom Chantiers de L'Atlantique) in Saint-Nazaire, France, was christened by Her Majesty Queen Elizabeth II in 2004. The slick-hulled 150,000-ton vessel, with a height of 237 feet from keel to funnel top, travels at speeds of up to 30 knots, making her one of the fastest cruise ships and able to undertake unusual itineraries. She can carry up to 3,090 passengers in a quasi-class system, with the cabin category determining restaurant assignments.

QM2 has the first spa-at-sea operated by the world-famous Canyon Ranch health resorts; the world's first and only planetarium at sea; the largest ballroom at sea; the largest library at sea; the largest wine cellar at sea; and ten dining venues, including the first shipboard restaurant by popular American chef Todd English.

There are 14 lounges and bars; a two-story theater; a casino; five indoor and outdoor swimming pools, including a children's pool, an adults-only pool, and another pool with a magrodome; hot tubs; boutiques; and a children's facility complete with British nannies. The learning center offers a variety of lecturers from a range of industries, disciplines, and academic backgrounds. The ship's $5 million art collection includes more than 300 original works of art.

QM2 is the only cruise ship sailing on regularly scheduled transatlantic crossings between New York and Southampton from spring to November.

ITINERARIES *See* Itinerary Index.

CABINS The main cabin categories correspond to the ship's dining rooms—**Britannia, Princess,** and **Queen.** Britannia offers 17 cabin levels ranging from standard (about 194 square feet) to deluxe (248 square feet). Princess accommodations are 381-square-foot junior suites, while Queen encompasses five levels of suites, ranging from 506 square feet to two-story Grand Duplex apartments at 2,249 square feet each.

Seventy-five percent of the 1,296 cabins have eight-foot-deep balconies. Thirty cabins for disabled passengers are available in various categories. The cabins are well laid out and very comfortable. The decor throughout has a quiet, tony quality, using light apricot, beige, and other soft pastels. All have interactive television with multilingual film and music channels, direct-dial phone, hair dryer, 110/220-volt outlets, and bathroom with tub and/or shower.

The five duplex apartments (**Balmoral, Windsor, Holyrood, Buckingham,** and **Sandringham** suites) are two stories high and cover 1,500–2,250 square feet. They have two-story glass walls at the ship's stern, providing great sea views. The lavish suites have their own exercise area, veranda, two full bathrooms with tub and shower, a walk-in closet, a separate sitting area, and refrigerator. Occupants in duplex apartments are pampered by butler service and room-service dining prepared by chefs from the **Queen's Grill.**

Four deluxe penthouses (Queen Mary, Queen Anne, Queen Elizabeth, and Queen Victoria suites) overlooking the ship's bow measure between 861 and 1,076 square feet. Each features a marble bathroom with tub and shower, walk-in closet, refrigerator, separate dining area, and sitting area with large picture windows.

Suite amenities include two plasma flat-panel televisions, an entertainment system, a bon voyage bottle of Champagne, personalized stationery, a bar with selected spirits or wine and soft drinks, plush terry cloth bathrobes, slippers, and daily fresh fruit and predinner canapés. Penthouses can also be connected with two of the suites to create more than 5,000 square feet of living space. In addition to dining at the Queen's Grill restaurant, suite passengers have an exclusive lounge for afternoon tea, cocktails, and an after-dinner aperitif. Several suites have a private elevator entrance.

Specifications Duplex apartments, 5; deluxe penthouses, 4; penthouses, 6; suites, 82; outside standards with veranda, 782; outside standards, 138; inside standards with atrium view, 12; inside standards, 281; wheelchair accessible, 30.

DINING Seating in the main restaurants corresponds to the category of the passenger's accommodation. The elegant Queen's Grill is reserved exclusively for luxury penthouses, duplexes, and suites, and the **Princess Grill** for passengers in junior suites. Both have single-seating dining and operate much like an upscale à la carte restaurant.

The **Britannia Restaurant** accommodates all other cabin categories with 1,347 seats and offers open seating for breakfast and lunch and two seatings for dinner. The three-deck-high room spans the width of the ship, with a dramatic central staircase meant to recall the grand dining rooms of past Cunard liners. Despite the large number of passengers being served at one time, the food and service get high marks. The Britannia Club, a private room within the restaurant, is for the exclusive use of passengers booked in the 46 AA deluxe accommodations. This single-seating clublike restaurant offers the Britannia Restaurant menu, plus à la carte options and table-side flambé service.

Another vast space is the **King's Court,** the Lido restaurant serving buffet breakfast and lunch and four casual dining alternatives for dinner. At lunch, there are regional specialties and carved meats. In the evening, King's Court is transformed into sit-down restaurants: **La Piazza** for Italian specialties, **Lotus,** offering Chinese and Asian cuisine, the **Carvery,** serving carved meats, and **Chef's Galley** for chef's selections. Here, passengers can watch and learn the preparation of their meal from Cunard or guest chefs.

Other dining options include **Todd English,** featuring the innovative Mediterranean cuisine of its renowned namesake, open for lunch (surcharge, $20) and dinner (surcharge, $30) with indoor seating overlooking the aft pool terrace. Reservations are required. The cuisine is outstanding, and indeed the restaurant was so popular that Cunard added the surcharge in order to handle the demand. The **Golden Lion** and **Boardwalk Café** are casual venues for pub grub or fast food, offering hot dogs, hamburgers, and other grills, a daily specialty, soups, and salads. Afternoon tea is served in the **Queens Room** or in the Queens Grill Lounge.

FACILITIES AND ACTIVITIES During a transatlantic crossing, the QM2 offers a roster of more than 200 activities. Some are traditional cruise-ship fun and games, but many are designed especially for this ship. For example, Cunard has partnered with The Juilliard School to present classic and contemporary jazz performances by Juilliard students and faculty in the Royal Court Theatre on select 2010 eastbound transatlantic crossings. The **Royal Court Theatre,** the main showroom with tiered seating for 1,100 passengers, boasts concert-hall acoustics, a hydraulic proscenium stage, and sophisticated lighting and sound equipment. The theater is the venue for full-scale West End- or Broadway-type productions and other entertainers. The **Empire Casino** offers blackjack, roulette, and slot machines. The **Queen's Room** is truly the most elegant ballroom at sea.

Illuminations, the first-of-its-kind planetarium at sea, has stadium-type seating where passengers are entertained with celestial shows, movies, lectures, and other programs. In 2007, in partnership with the American Museum of Natural History's Hayden Planetarium, Cunard added two space shows in Illuminations. Four shows are presented daily, including the Hayden Planetarium's productions, *Cosmic Collisions*, narrated by Robert Redford, and *Passport to the Universe*, narrated by Tom Hanks. A third show, *The Search for Life: Are We Alone?* is narrated by Harrison Ford. It was developed by the AMNH in collaboration with NASA.

In 2009, Cunard partnered with Oxford University Press to introduce the Science Club, a multifaceted membership program with Science at Sea lectures on *QM2* by prominent science writers. Cunard guests can join the Science Club by completing a membership card on board. Membership entitles them to quarterly e-mails from Oxford University Press and invitations to book launches, promotional offers, competitions, and information on speakers.

ConneXions, with the latest electronic equipment and Internet access, has seven function rooms to use as classrooms or meeting rooms; they can be separated or joined to adjust for class sizes. The ship's enrichment programs range from wine appreciation and cooking to seamanship and navigation; they are taught by expert guest instructors, some from Oxford University. Computer classes and business services are also available. The facility has the latest electronic equipment and Internet access. Also on tap are the plays and workshops being presented by members of England's famous Royal Academy of Dramatic Art, which supplies the actors and conducts the workshops.

The *QM2*'s 8,000-volume library, the largest at sea, and the **Bookshop,** similar to those on the *QE2*, are furnished with comfortable leather sofas and armchairs and directed by a full-time librarian. The library also has books on CD. Mayfair Shops, a shopping gallery, offers a myriad of items from sundries to fine leather goods and formal wear for sale and rental. Also in this area is the elegant **Champagne Bar,** created by the famous Champagne house Veuve Clicquot Ponsardin, its first and only venture on a cruise line.

SPORTS, FITNESS, AND BEAUTY *QM2* boasts one of the largest spas afloat, designed by the famous Canyon Ranch, which also operates it. The **Canyon Ranch SpaClub,** covering 20,000 square feet on two decks, has a staff of 50 to provide treatments and lead classes in yoga and tai chi, as well as health-related workshops. The spa has 24 treatment rooms, an aqua-therapy center, whirlpool, saunas, reflexology, an aromatic steam room, a gym with state-of-the-art equipment, a juice bar, and men's and women's locker rooms. Now into its sixth year, Canyon Ranch is offering a new VOYA seaweed treatment (seaweed freeze-dried in Ireland), Japanese detoxifying and revitalizing rituals utilizing Red Flower products, and performance orthotics services where service providers will measure gait and foot force and fit guests with customized orthotic shoe inserts utilizing specialty equipment. The spa is very popular. You should book your treatments early, as it fills up fast.

The *QM2* proves that passengers are willing to pay extra for many shipboard amenities—in this case, *QM2*'s fitness facilities and Canyon Ranch Spa. The spa issues a Canyon Ranch SpaClub Passport, covering the locker rooms and aquatic center for these charges: one-day Passport, $35; three consecutive days, $55; five consecutive days, $85. The fee is the same for at-sea or in-port days. The Passport is issued free with the booking of a spa treatment. Appointments can be made 21 days or more prior to sailing. To book, call ☎ 866-860-4662 for U.S. residents; +1-(702) 414-6279 for all other nationalities, who can call collect or e-mail the ship at **qmhspa2@cunard.com.**

CHILDREN'S FACILITIES The **Play Zone** for small children and **The Zone** are located all by themselves on Deck 6 aft. The area has a small splash pool, and toddlers are supervised by nannies. Older children have a separate facility with computer terminals and activities.

PET FACILITIES Cunard has a long tradition of carrying and caring for passengers' pets aboard its ships. To our knowledge, *QM2* is currently the only ship that has kennels. The ocean liner has 12 kennels and a full-time kennel master who manages the kennel program and daily pet care such as feeding, walking, and cleaning. The Pets on Deck program has been enhanced by adding amenities such as fresh-baked biscuits at turndown and a choice of beds and blankets. Kennel reservations may be made at time of booking and are based on availability; fee is $300–$500.

THE SHIP Past Cunard passengers will feel at home on *Queen Victoria*, which keeps Cunard traditions, reinforcing Cunard's commitment to its British heritage, and borrows from her sister ships—even public rooms mostly carry the same names as on *QM2*. The elegant ship presents an inviting, gracious ambience of yesteryear, with a grand lobby three stories high with a sweeping staircase, mosaics and marble floors, sparkling chandeliers, plush carpets, large artworks, and rich fabrics. Designers incorporated the latest technology in her contemporary interiors elsewhere.

Launched in 2007, she was first seen on America's shores in January 2008, at the start of her maiden world cruise. Departing Southampton, *Queen Victoria* was joined by *QE2,* sailing in tandem for a historic transatlantic crossing and arriving in New York on January 13. There, they were met by *QM2* for a three-*Queens* landmark event.

ITINERARIES *See* Itinerary Index.

Queen Victoria	PREVIEW	
REGISTRY Great Britain	LENGTH 964.5 feet	BEAM 106 feet
CABINS 1,007	DRAFT 26.2 feet	SPEED 23.7 knots
MAXIMUM PASSENGERS	PASSENGER DECKS 12	ELEVATORS 12
2,206	CREW 900	SPACE RATIO NA

CABINS Of *Victoria's* 1,007 cabins and suites, approximately 86% are outside, and 71% of them have balconies. In Cunard tradition, the choice of accommodation determines your dining venue. Passengers of the high-end suites with marble bathrooms and butler service dine exclusively in the **Queen's Grill.** Those one level down dine in the **Princess Grill** at a reserved table in a single seating. All other passengers dine in the **Britannia Restaurant.**

The standard amenities for all passengers include 24-hour room service, satellite television, direct-dial telephone, refrigerator, safe, and hair dryer, bathrobe and slippers, nightly turndown service with pillow chocolate, shoe-shine service; daily fresh fruit (on request); and daily shipboard newspaper (additional charge).

The top categories—Princess, Queen, Penthouse, Master, and Grand—of suites range in size from 342 to 2,131 square feet (measurements include balcony). In addition to the standard amenities for all passengers, those exclusive to Queen's Grill suites include priority embarkation and luggage delivery; pillow menu; fresh fruit daily; Champagne and strawberries on embarkation; butler and concierge service; personalized stationery, atlas, and books; whirlpool bathtubs; refrigerators stocked to passengers' preferences; complimentary bottled water; bar stocked with spirits, wines, and soft drinks; access to the Queen's Lounge and private deck area; in-suite dining; flower arrangement; board games and computer games console; and DVD player. Princess Suites have most, but not all, of these amenities; butler service, priority embarkation, and luggage delivery, for example, are not included.

Britannia category includes balcony, ocean view, and inside cabins that measure 242–472 square feet including balcony; ocean-view cabins, 180–201 square feet; and standard inside cabins, 152–243 square feet. Passengers dine at a reserved table for either early or late seating in the Britannia restaurant. Sparkling wine awaits them at embarkation.

Specifications 864 outside cabins, 143 inside; 718 with balconies. Queens Grill suites: Grand 4, Master 2, Penthouse 25, Queens 35; Princess suites 61; Britannia cabins: balcony 591, ocean view 146, inside 143; wheelchair accessible 20.

DINING The Queens Grill and Princess Grill, limited to passengers booked in the Queen and Princess suites, offer à la carte menus and service meant to be the ultimate dining experience of the ship. Both restaurants have one seating. These passengers have exclusive use of the Grills Lounge, accessed by a private elevator. It opens onto the **Grills Terrace,** where predinner cocktails, canapés, and Champagne are served. They also have exclusive use of the Courtyard for afternoon tea and dining alfresco, as well as the Grills Terrace and **Grills Upper Terrace,** outdoor areas that offer deck service.

The two-tiered Britannia restaurant on Decks 2 and 3 serves early and late dining with assigned seating. Next door, the **Chart Room** is an elegant predinner cocktail lounge and bar with a nautical theme.

Dining alternatives include the ever popular **Todd English Restaurant.** The reservations-only restaurant has a surcharge ($20 for lunch, $30 for dinner). The **Lido,** the venue for casual eating, has a bright and airy ambience by day and night. The **Golden Lion** offers an impressive selection of beer and cider and a hearty pub menu. **Café Carinthia** specialties are teas, coffees, and pastries. Then, too, room service is available around the clock.

FACILITIES, ENTERTAINMENT, AND ACTIVITIES *Queen Victoria*'s elegant public rooms offer a variety of lounges to cater to the different interests and moods of passengers. These include the **Midships Lounge,** a wine bar; **Churchill's Cigar Lounge,** featuring a worldwide selection of cigars; a casino; the **Commodore Club,** an observation lounge on Deck 10, which should be popular for watching sunsets as the ship travels around the world; and **Hemispheres,** the nightclub with contemporary decor and a spectacular setting.

The ship's main show lounge, the splendid **Royal Court Theatre,** rises three levels and has the first private boxes at sea. The boxes are open to anyone on the ship and can be reserved. If there's space at the start of the show, boxes will be available on a first-come, first-served basis ($50 per couple; reservations can be made at Purser's desk or Grills Concierge). For passengers using the boxes, there's a private lounge where they can have after-dinner or preshow drinks with items such as Champagne and chocolates. The theatre features star performances and West End–style productions.

Cunardia is a museum at sea with maritime memorabilia and artifacts from the company's former grand liners. The museum has rotating exhibitions featuring a particular period of the company's history, complete with "amusing anecdotes." Nearby, the stylish **Royal Arcade,** with its wood paneling, wrought iron, green marble, and white stone, was inspired by London's Burlington and Royal arcades.

ConneXions Conference Centre hosts guest lecturers, celebrity speakers, and other enrichment programs. **ConneXions Internet Centre,** just off the **Grand Lobby,** offers Internet and e-mail access and classes to improve your computer skills. Charges apply for Internet and e-mail access. The library, with 6,000 titles, is set on two levels connected by an ornate spiral staircase. Its warm mahogany interiors, leather sofas, and huge windows that face the sea make an inviting quiet corner for reading or daydreaming. The **Winter Garden,** a sun-dappled conservatory filled with greenery, has a retractable glass roof.

The **Queens Room** is meant to evoke an ambience reminiscent of that enjoyed by Queen Victoria in her much-loved home. Here, passengers are treated to a white-glove service for a traditional afternoon tea. Cantilevered balconies, ornate frescoes, and back-lit glass panels rising two decks in height create an unmistakable sense of occasion. In the evening, the elegant room becomes the setting for another fine Cunard tradition—ballroom dancing. It also makes an ideal setting for the captain's cocktail parties, themed balls, and a host of social occasions.

SPORTS, FITNESS, AND BEAUTY The **Cunard Royal Spa and Fitness Club** offers aerobics classes and a gym with state-of-the-art cardiovascular fitness equipment, including treadmills and bikes complete with their own personal LCD television screens. The spa, which has a hydropool and thermal suite, offers a range of therapies and beauty treatments. Spa appointments can be made online up to 21 days in advance of the voyage. The ship has two outdoor pools.

CHILDREN'S FACILITIES *Queen Victoria* has dedicated facilities inside, as well as outside areas, for children ages 1–12.

THE SHIP The launch of the new *Queen Elizabeth* was so widely anticipated by Cunard fans that in April 2009, when Cunard put her October 2010 maiden voyage on sale, it sold out in a record 29 minutes. Her first world cruise, scheduled for January 2011, also broke first-day booking records.

Named for the original *Queen Elizabeth*, launched in 1938 as the world's largest liner, the new ship is 964.5 feet long, which is the equivalent of 36 London buses laid end to end. She will be the third new ocean liner to be introduced by Cunard in six years and the second largest Cunard ship ever built.

The new ship will reflect her predecessor in grandeur, decor, and style, but with a modern twist. She also will be filled with reminders of Cunard's heritage, particularly the line's links with royalty and notables, in a photographic display in the Cunarder's Gallery on Deck 3 and in a separate collection of Cunard memorabilia and exhibits at Cunard Place on Deck 2.

Passengers will be introduced to the gracious new liner in the dramatic Grand Lobby with its marble floors, stunning chandelier, curved staircases, Art Deco–inspired patterns, and spectacular artwork. Overlooking the grandeur is the two-tier library, a calm haven of warm wood tones bathed in natural reading light and crowned with a fabulous leaded-glass ceiling. Throughout, *Queen Elizabeth*'s public rooms will be impressive with marble, fine wood, mosaics, plush fabrics and furnishings, and Art Deco flourishes paying homage to the original *Queen Elizabeth*.

Some public rooms that will be familiar to Cunard patrons are the two-deck-high Queen's Room Ballroom, the Commodore Club, the Midships Bar (named after the one on the original *Queen Elizabeth*), and the Yacht Club (named for the one on *QE2*)—all with reminiscent decor.

ITINERARIES *See* Itinerary Index. In her maiden year, *Queen Elizabeth* will sail in tandem with *Queen Victoria* before all three Queens will rendezvous in New York on January 13, 2011; later she will meet *Queen Mary 2* in Sydney and Civitavecchia and *Queen Victoria* in Aruba.

CABINS Approximately 85% of the cabins are outside, and 71% have balconies; 12% are Queen and Princess Grill suites. The ship will also have Britannia Club balcony cabins. As with other Cunard ships, the cabin category determines a passenger's dining venue.

The standard Britannia cabins are the most numerous and will have bathrobes, slippers, nightly turndown service with a pillow chocolate, a half bottle of wine at embarkation, Wi-Fi access, interactive television with multilingual film and music channels, a safe, telephone, refrigerator, hair dryer, shipboard newspaper, daily fresh fruit (on request), and 24-hour room service. Britannia Club balcony (AA) cabins (242–472 square feet including balcony) will enjoy single-seating dining in the Britannia Club restaurant, a pillow menu, a

Queen Elizabeth	PREVIEW	
REGISTRY Great Britain	LENGTH 964.5 feet	BEAM 106 feet
CABINS 950	DRAFT 25.9 feet	SPEED 18 knots
MAXIMUM PASSENGERS	PASSENGER DECKS 12	ELEVATORS NA
2,092	CREW NA	SPACE RATIO NA

bon voyage bottle of wine, and similar furnishings and amenities as Britannia cabins, plus some special amenities.

Princess Grill suites (P1 through P4) (335–513 square feet including balcony) get priority embarkation, a bottle of wine and fresh strawberries, daily fresh fruit, and personalized stationery. Pre-dinner Champagne and canapés in a separate living area can be arranged by your concierge. The exclusive Princess Grill amenities include priority luggage delivery, concierge service, access to the Queens Lounge, single-seating dining in the Princess Grill, in-suite dining, choice of pillows and duvets, atlas and books, and complimentary bottled water. The suites will be furnished with all the standard amenities as well.

Queen's Grill accommodations include Grand suites (Q1) (1,375–1,493 square feet), Master suites (Q2) (1,100 square feet), Penthouse suites (Q3 and Q4) (520–707 square feet), and Queen suites (Q5 to Q7) (508–771 square feet). Measurements include the balcony. The six Master and Grand suites will be named in honor of past Cunard commodores who have received knighthoods. Each sumptuous suite will be decorated in light woods and luxurious furnishings and have a full bathroom. In addition to butler and concierge services, suites will have priority embarkation/disembarkation; priority luggage delivery; and exclusive amenities such as a bon voyage bottle of Champagne and strawberries, single-seating dining in the Queen's Grill and in-suite dining from the Queen's Grill menu; access to the Queen's Lounge and private deck; flower arrangement in suite; bar stocked with spirits, wines, and soft drinks; predinner canapés; all standard amenities; as well as the exclusive amenities of Princess suites.

DINING The Britannia restaurant, the elegant two-tier dining room with a grand staircase under an eye-catching Art Deco chandelier and other Art Deco accents, will serve three meals daily in two seatings for passengers in Britannia cabins. Britannia Club passengers (AA category balcony accommodations) will dine in the Britannia Club restaurant, an intimate venue with a patterned-glass ceiling with gold and silver leaf.

Princess Grill on Deck 11 is the single-seating restaurant for passengers in Princess Grill suites. The Queen's Grill, also on Deck 11, for Queen's Grill passengers, is expected to be the top gourmet experience on the new *Queen Elizabeth*. The Courtyard will serve afternoon tea and provide evening dining alfresco for Grill passengers. From the Courtyard, steps will lead up to the Grills Terrace, a secluded retreat where suite passengers can enjoy luxurious lounges and dedicated waiter service. Passengers in these categories also have exclusive access to the adjacent Queen's Grill Lounge, with a private bar next to the Grills restaurants, complete with a resident concierge. Exclusive to Grills guests, this refined, comfortable, and relaxed haven is perfect for predinner drinks or afternoon tea.

The ship's other dining options are the Lido restaurant on Deck 9, where casual buffet dining is available throughout the day and evening in a bright and airy ambience. It will serve breakfast and lunch buffets, but in the evening, one section will continue offering an extensive buffet, while the other two sections convert to more formal restaurants serving different styles of regional cuisine. The Golden Lion, a Cunard passenger favorite, will offer a wide selection of beer, cider, and wine to complement its pub-style lunch in a comfortable, traditional setting.

FACILITIES, ENTERTAINMENT, AND ACTIVITIES The Queen's Room, the traditional Cunard Grand Ballroom, reflects the line's royal links with its artwork and murals, cantilevered balconies, ornate frescos, and back-lit glass panels. Here, passengers will sip afternoon tea served by white-gloved waiters, offering teas from around the world, cucumber sandwiches, and scones with jam and clotted cream; or they may waltz across the intricate wooden dance floor, illuminated by a magnificent chandelier. The room will also be the venue for Royal Nights–themed balls and the Captain's cocktail parties. The intimate Yacht Club with the compass-shaped dance floor will have 270-degree views in all directions and will be the setting for activities and gatherings during the day, lively evenings with the resident DJ, and dancing until the small hours.

The three-tier Royal Court Theatre with private boxes and regal blue and gold decor creates a sumptuous setting for dramatic performances and Cunard Insights, featuring renowned guest speakers. The Garden Lounge on Deck 9, named after a similar lounge on the original *Queen Elizabeth*, boasts a beautiful conservatory roof inspired by the glass houses at Kew Gardens and will provide a wonderfully atmospheric venue for occasional "Supper Clubs" with dining and dancing under the stars. The lounge will also set the stage for Country House Soirees, where passengers will join friends for Champagne at a black-tie ball and relive the glamour of the golden age of ocean travel. ConneXions Internet Centre, located off the Grand Lobby, will provide classes to allow passengers to improve their computer skills and keep up-to-date on e-mail. Charges will apply for Internet and e-mail access. The library, similar to those on other Cunard ships, will have 6,000 titles. The ship will also have a casino, a Royal Arcade with designer boutiques set on two decks, Café Carinthia overlooking the Grand Lobby for speciality teas and pastries, and will show films from the golden era as well as contemporary ones.

SPORTS, FITNESS, AND BEAUTY The Cunard Royal Spa and Fitness Centre will have a 30- by 15-foot thalassotherapy pool with airbed recliner lounges, neck fountains, air tub, and body-massage jet benches. Adjacent is the fully-equipped thermal suite with an herbal sauna, Finnish sauna, reflexology basins, and steam room. The SpaClub also features 24 private treatment rooms and a fitness center with 50 pieces of cardio and weight-training equipment. There's an outdoor swimming pool and two whirlpools as well.

The new Games Deck forward on Deck 11, named after a similar deck on the original *Queen Elizabeth* and with an English country garden ambience, will offer paddle tennis, croquet, and traditional British bowls in the welcome shade of its canopy. The de rigueur striped blazers will be sold on board.

CHILDREN'S FACILITIES A children's program and facilities feature both inside and outside areas dedicated to children ages 1–12.

Disney Cruise Line

P.O. Box 10210
Lake Buena Vista, FL 32830
☎ 407-566-3500 or 800-DCL-2500
FAX 407-566-7417
www.disneycruise.com

TYPE OF SHIPS Modern ocean liners with classic steamship lines.

TYPE OF CRUISES Family-oriented mainstream cruises combined with a Walt Disney World vacation, designed for all ages.

CRUISE LINE'S STRENGTHS
- Disney name recognition
- innovative ships
- dining venue variety and presentation
- friendly, conscientious staff
- outstanding private island
- children's facilities
- family cabins

CRUISE LINE'S SHORTCOMINGS
- intrusive, loud public announcements
- Disney overdose
- over-regimentation of children's programs
- uneven cuisine
- unnecessary pressure to vacate ship on disembarkation

FELLOW PASSENGERS A cross-section of the nation—similar to patrons at Disney theme parks.

Recommended for Families with children or grandchildren. But, like the Disney parks, a Disney product for kids of all ages.

Not recommended for Anyone who isn't enraptured by Disney.

CRUISE AREAS AND SEASONS Bahamas and Caribbean, year-round; Europe, summer; Mexican Riviera, summer; Alaska, summer (2011).

THE LINE When Disney does something, it does it big, in a spare-no-expenses way. So we were ready for the Disney Cruise Line to make a huge splash when its first ship, *Disney Magic*, was launched in 1998. What you see here and on her twin, *Disney Wonder*, is the result of three years of intensive planning by cruise industry veterans, Disney creative talent, and dozens of the world's best-known ship designers. Their task was to design a product that makes every adult feel the vacation is intended for them, while at the same time giving every child the same impression. The results may surprise people, including adults without children.

The ships are both classic and innovative. Exteriors have traditional lines, reminiscent of great ocean liners. Inside, they're up-to-the-minute technologically and full of novel ideas in dining, entertainment, and cabin design. Even

THE FLEET	BUILT/RENOVATED	TONNAGE	PASSENGERS
Disney Magic	1998/2003/05	83,000	2,700
Disney Wonder	1999/2004/06	83,000	2,700
Disney Dream	2011	128,000	2,500
Disney Fantasy	2012	128,000	2,500

Disney's exclusive cruise terminal at Port Canaveral, Florida, is part of the overall strategy, aiming to make even embarkation and disembarkation enjoyable.

Disney offers a "seamless vacation package," that enables you to combine a three- or four-day stay at Walt Disney World with a three- or four-day cruise on *Disney Wonder*, or seven-day cruises on *Disney Magic*. Disney Cruise Line passengers are met at the airport by Disney staff and transported to the terminal in easily identifiable buses. During the hour's ride, they watch a cruise video. When your cruise is packaged with a stay at most Disney hotels, you check in once. The key that unlocks your hotel room door also opens the door to your cruise cabin.

The major innovation is in dining. Each evening on board, you dine in a different restaurant with a different motif, but your waiters and dining companions move with you.

To cater to varied constituencies, some facilities, services, activities, and programs were designed specifically for adults without children, seniors, and honeymooning couples. For example, in addition to the themed restaurants, each ship has an alternative restaurant, swimming pool, and nightclub for use by adults only, as well as entertainment for all the family. Disney continues trying to enhance the adult experience with such facilities as an adults-only cafe, an adults-oriented sports bar, and an area for teens. The line also has kept up with technology by providing advanced online check-in for passengers and wireless access (at a cost) for those who bring their computers. Cell phone service is available only in cabins and while the ship is at sea. Passengers are billed by their cell phone provider. Passengers can also book shore excursions and register children for youth activities; adults can make spa appointments and restaurant reservations for Palo.

Overcoming the hassle of tendering passengers was an important consideration when Disney selected its private Bahamian island visited on all its cruises departing from Port Canaveral; deep water enables ships to pull dockside.

In 2005, *Disney Magic* ventured to the West Coast, in conjunction with Disneyland's 50th anniversary celebrations, sailing from Los Angeles to Mexico, and returned in 2008. Disney's biggest leap to date—a series of European cruises in 2007. Recently, the line announced it will return to Europe in 2010, and beginning in 2011, *Disney Wonder* will homeport at Los Angeles and during the summer will offer Disney's first-ever seven-night Alaskan cruises.

Disney is building two ships to be launched in 2011 and 2012, more than doubling the line's capacity. The 128,000-ton ships will be two decks taller than the line's present ships and have 1,250 cabins. The post-Panamax ships (too large to transit the Panama Canal) are being built at Meyer Werft yard in Germany. Disney has released some details about the ships, indicating they will be a modern interpretation of classic ocean liners, much like the present fleet, and will feature many innovative ideas.

DISTINCTIVE FEATURES Three themed restaurants with "rotation" dining, sports bar in a funnel, children's facilities, cabin design, port terminal. Pagers for adults with children participating in youth activities. Online check-in.

RATES Price includes port charges.

Special fares and discounts Early booking can save on three-, four-, and seven-night cruises and packages; consult Disney's brochure or its Web site for details.

- **CHILDREN'S FARES:** Prices vary depending on the length of the cruise. Consult Disney's brochure or its Web site for details.
- **SINGLE SUPPLEMENT:** 175%.

PAST PASSENGERS You become a member of the Castaway Club, the line's loyalty awards program, after you take your first cruise. On your next cruise, you will get priority planning privileges for early online shore excursions, Palo reservations, the spa and salon reservations, youth activities, and Flounder's Reef nursery bookings. The program has a dedicated toll-free phone number: 800-449-3380; you will need a Castaway Club identification number when calling and, for guests under 18 years of age, a parent or guardian's permission to dial the number. Other program benefits are an exclusive check-in area at the Club desk in the port terminal; and on board, a complimentary Castaway Club lanyard, a gift in your cabin (one per cabin), an invitation to the Castaway Clubhouse party (where you can meet some of the ship's officers and crew and other Club members), offers if booking your next cruise on board (subject to availability), and access to exclusive Club merchandise (unavailable elsewhere). After the cruise, you will have access to a members-only area at **www.disneycruise.com/castawayclub** for news, special offers, and behind-the-scenes information.

THE LAST WORD The vessels are complex and innovative, breaking the mold of traditional cruise ships. Initially, cruise experts questioned whether Disney could fill its ships when kids are in school, but Disney estimated that if 1% to 2% of the estimated 40 million annual visitors to Disney's resorts and parks bought a Disney cruise vacation, the ships would sell out. Disney was right; now, after more than a decade of success, no one is questioning them.

THE SHIPS *Disney Magic* and *Disney Wonder* are modern cruise ships with long, sleek lines, twin smokestacks, and styling that recalls classic liners but with instantly recognizable Disney signatures. Colors—black, white, red, and yellow—and the face-and-ears silhouette on the stacks are clearly those of Mickey Mouse. Look closely and you'll see that *Magic*'s figurehead is a 15-foot Goofy (Donald Duck on *Wonder*) swinging upside down from a boatswain's chair, "painting" the stern.

Interiors combine nautical themes and Art Deco inspiration, but Disney images are everywhere, from Mickey's profile in the wrought-iron balustrades to the bronze statue of Helmsman Mickey (Ariel on *Wonder*) at the center of the three-deck Grand Atrium. Disney art is on every wall, stairwell, and corridor. Some works are valuable old prints of Disney cartoon characters. A grand staircase sweeps from the atrium lobby to Deck 4, where there

Disney Cruise Line Standard Features

Officers European, American, and international.

Staff *Cabin and Dining:* International; *Cruise:* American and International.

Dining facilities Three themed family restaurants with "rotation" dining; alternative adults-only restaurant; indoor/outdoor cafe for breakfast, lunch; pool bar and grill for burgers, pizza, and sandwiches; ice-cream bar.

Special diets Request at the time of booking for low-sodium, kosher, and other dietary requirements.

Room service 24 hours.

Dress code Casual by day; resort casual and informal in the evenings. Jacket requested for men in Palo, Lumiere's, Triton's in evening; one formal and one semiformal night on *Magic* seven-night cruises.

Cabin amenities Direct-dial telephone with voice mail; tub and shower, two-in-one bathrooms; television, safe, hair dryer. Beachside massages on private island for a fee.

Electrical outlets 110 AC.

Wheelchair access Yes.

Recreation and entertainment Theater with Broadway-style musicals, movie theater, family nightclub, adult nightclub, pub, lounges.

Sports and other activities Sports Deck, basketball, paddle tennis, family sports, adult, family and kids' pools, table tennis, shuffleboard, biking and water sports on Castaway Cay (extra charge).

Beauty and fitness Spa with sauna, steam rooms; beauty salon, newly expanded fitness center.

Other facilities Self-service launderettes; digital photographic services; dry cleaning; satellite phone services; medical facilities; guest services desk; 24-hour front-desk service; fax conference facilities on *Disney Wonder*.

Children's facilities Age-specific supervised children's program, year-round youth counselors; teen club; nursery for ages 12 weeks to 3 years.

Smoking Smoking not allowed, except in designated areas.

Disney suggested tipping Per guest per length of cruise from 3 to 14 nights: dining room server, $12–$56; assistant server, $9–$42; head server, $3–$14; cabin host/hostess, $12–$56. 15% service charge added automatically to bar, beverages, wine, and deck-service bills.

Credit cards For cruise payment and onboard charges: all major credit cards.

are shops selling Disney Cruise-themed clothing, collectibles, jewelry, and sundries, classic Disney toys, and souvenirs. (The shops are always full of buyers; some people speculate that the cruise line derives as much revenue here as other lines do from their casinos, which the Disney ships do not have.)

Disney Magic	QUALITY 8	VALUE C
Disney Wonder	QUALITY 8	VALUE C
REGISTRY Bahamas	LENGTH 964 feet	BEAM 106 feet
CABINS 875	DRAFT 25 feet	SPEED 21.5 knots
MAXIMUM PASSENGERS	PASSENGER DECKS 11	ELEVATORS 12
2,700	CREW 950	SPACE RATIO 35.4

The ships have two lower decks with cabins, three decks with dining rooms and showrooms, then three decks of cabins, and two Sports and Sun decks with separate pools and facilities for families and for adults without kids. Signs with arrows point the way to lounges and facilities, and all elevators are clearly marked forward, aft, or midship. (More deck plans mounted on walls would help newcomers get their bearings.) Daily in your cabin, you receive Your Personal Navigator, listing onboard entertainment and activities separated into options for teens, children, adults, and families, plus shore excursions. The ships also have age-specific venues to appeal to adults and older teenagers—**Aloft** (**The Stack** on *Magic*), a teen haven; **Cove Café;** and **Diversions,** a sports bar.

ITINERARIES *See* Itinerary Index.

CABINS Cabins and suites are spacious with generous wood paneling throughout. About three-fourths are outside, almost half with verandas. The 12 cabin categories range from standard to deluxe, deluxe with veranda, family suite, one- and two-bedroom suite, and royal suite. Categories are similar to those at Walt Disney World hotels. The cruise cabin category passengers select are matched with a comparable category for their three or four days' stay at a Disney hotel.

Note: If you're staying at a Disney resort before your cruise, be sure to complete and return your cruise forms at the hotel. By showing your shore-side room key card at the cruise terminal, you can bypass lines and board directly. Cruise-only passengers may encounter a wait at check-in.

Cabin design reveals Disney's finely tuned understanding of the needs of families and offers a cruise-industry first: a split bathroom with bathtub/shower and sink in one room and toilet, sink, and vanity in another. This configuration, found in all but standard inside cabins, allows any member of the family to use the bathroom without monopolizing it entirely. All bathrooms have both tub and shower. *Note:* For added convenience, couples or families should pack two of essentials like toothpaste, providing one for each sink.

All cabins sleep at least three; many accommodate four or five and some up to seven. In some, pull-down Murphy beds provide additional daytime floor space. Storage space is generous. Bureaus are designed to look like steamer trunks.

Cabins have direct-dial telephones with voice mail; flat-panel, 22-inch LCD televisions mounted on swivel arms (*Disney Magic*); hair dryers; and coolers. The room key also opens the safe. All cabins on both ships have Sealy Posturepedic Premium Plush Euro-top mattresses and fine linens. The concierge-level suites are dressed with duvets, and their occupants have a choice of pillows. In the bathrooms, passengers will find deluxe bath towels and bath sheets and upgraded products—all in specially designed bottles with the Disney logo and Mickey's picture.

Specifications 256 inside cabins, 621 outside. Two Walt/Roy Disney suites (sleeps up to seven); 2 two-bedroom suites, 18 one-bedroom suites, 80 family cabins—all sleep up to five; 282 deluxe cabins with verandas (up to three or four); 237 deluxe outside cabins (up to four), 96 deluxe inside cabins (up to four), and 160 standard inside cabins (up to four). 16 wheelchair accessible, including 4 one-bedroom suites, 6 deluxe cabins with verandas, 2 deluxe outside cabins, and 4 standard inside cabins.

DINING Disney's most innovative area is dining. Ships have three different family restaurants, plus an alternative restaurant for adults only. Each night, passengers move to a different family restaurant, each with a different theme and menu, taking along their table companions and waitstaff. In each restaurant, tableware, linens, menu covers, and waiters' uniforms fit the theme.

On *Magic*, **Lumiere's**—named for the candlestick character in *Beauty and the Beast*—is a handsome venue serving continental cuisine. A mural depicts Beauty and the Beast (the equivalent restaurant on *Wonder* is called **Triton**, themed after *The Little Mermaid*). **Parrot Cay** dishes up Caribbean-accented food in a fun, tropical setting and seems to be the most popular for breakfast. But it's **Animator's Palate** that reflects the creative genius of Disney animation. Diners are given the impression they have entered a black-and-white sketchbook. Over the course of the meal, the sketches on the walls are transformed into a full-color extravaganza. Waiters change their costumes from black and white to color. The first course is a montage of appetizers served on a palette-shaped plate, and one of the desserts—a Mickey-shaped tasteless mousse—comes with a parade by waiters bearing trays of colorful syrups—mango, chocolate, and strawberry—used to decorate it. It's entertaining, but the food is, at times, less than inspired, and hot dishes are likely to arrive cold, but no ones seems to care—they are too absorbed in watching Disney perform its magic.

Palo, the Italian restaurant named for the pole gondoliers use to navigate Venetian canals, is the intimate, adults-only restaurant. It's the best aboard. The lovely, semicircular room has a sophisticated ambience with soft lighting, Venetian glass, inlaid wood, and a back-lit bar. Northern Italian cuisine is featured. Food and presentation are excellent. More than two dozen kinds of wine are available by the glass at reasonable prices. There's a $15 per person cover charge for both dinner and the Champagne brunch. Palo also serves a high tea on all seven-night or longer sailings; fee is $5. Reservations are required and can be booked in advance online. Otherwise, make them as soon as you board, as the restaurant is very popular and reservations go fast.

Other dining options include **Topsiders** (**Beach Blanket Buffet** on *Wonder*), an indoor/outdoor cafe serving breakfast and lunch; a pool bar and grill for hamburgers and hot dogs; **Goofy's Galley** for sandwiches, wraps, paninis, and ice cream; **Pinocchio's Pizzeria** for brick-oven pizza. In the adults-only Cove Cafe, located next to the Quiet Cove Pool, passengers can enjoy gourmet coffees, specialty drinks, and lighter fare, along with a supply of popular magazines. The ships also have 24-hour room service.

On seven-night cruises, the dining options are expanded. They include a Captain's Gala dinner with wine and French continental cuisine, and a Til We Meet Again dinner as a final-night farewell, featuring some of the best dishes of the cruise. On four- and seven-night cruises, there's also a Champagne brunch ($10 per person) on sea days, high tea, and character breakfasts hosted by Chip and Dale, the latter offering kids a chance to meet and pose for pictures with popular Disney characters in Caribbean attire.

A new feature, "Dine and Play," should be a winner for both parents and kids. It is offered during the second seating in all main dining rooms and is open to children ages 3–12. Upon arrival, parents tell their server that their children want to participate in "Dine and Play." Kids get their meals expedited, and youth counselors arrive in about 45 minutes to take the children to their evening activities. Parents can then enjoy their meal at a more leisurely pace.

SERVICE Passengers lavishly praise Disney cast members, as cruise and park staff are called. Staff are among the most accommodating you will encounter in travel, and they try hard to smooth your way. More than once when I stopped to get my bearings, a staff member was beside me in seconds to help.

FACILITIES AND ACTIVITIES Disney diversions are geared to children, families, and adults. A day at **Castaway Cay,** Disney's 1,000-acre private island, is meant to be the ultimate escape. The natural environment has been preserved. Miles of white-sand beaches are surrounded by beautiful water. A pier allows access without tendering. A four-car open tram (like those at Disney World) conveys passengers from the ship to **Scuttle's Cove** family beach. The shuttle runs every five minutes. (Bring sunblock and wear a hat.) Strollers are available, as are rental bikes, floats, and kayaks. Lounge chairs under pastel umbrellas are plentiful.

Disney Imagineers have created shops, restrooms, and pavilions that give the impression they have been there for years. A supervised children's area includes a "dig" at a half-buried whale skeleton replica. Water sports are offered in a protected lagoon. One snorkeling course is near shore; the other, farther out, requires more endurance. Lifeguards watch snorkelers all around the courses. The cruise line has also planted several "shipwrecks." There's also a treasure chest, its contents guarded by large fish. Snorkel equipment rents for a pricey $25 for adults and children 10 years and older, $10 for ages 5–9. The Gateway Package, a combination of snorkel equipment and float for the day, plus a one-hour bicycle rental, is also available for $16 for children 5–9 years old; $32 for children age 10 and older and for adults. Nature trails and bike paths are provided. The main beach offers kids' activities, live Bahamian music or DJ, and shops. **Cookie's BBQ** serves a buffet lunch of burgers, pork ribs, hot dogs, baked beans, slaw, corn on the cob, fruit, and chips.

A second tram connects to **Serenity Bay,** the adult beach on the island's opposite side. The adult beach is a long sweep of sugary sand. A bar serves drinks, and passengers can enjoy a massage in one of the private cabanas with shuttered doors opening on the sea. At Castaway Cay, you can see the *Flying Dutchman,* the pirate ship in the film *Pirates of the Caribbean: Dead Man's Chest.* The 175-foot "ghost ship," anchored off the island, provides a scenic photo op; passengers who rent boats on Castaway can get a closer look at the ship.

Castaway Cay is getting an extra dose of pixie dust with enhancements to be completed by summer 2010. To accommodate Disney's new ships, additional mooring dolphins will be installed to lengthen the dock. The family beach will be extended by more than 700 feet, and a new lunch buffet in a covered pavilion will be added, as will a new beach bar and shop for Castaway Cay–exclusive items. Da Shade Game Pavilion near the family beach will provide a place to take a break out of the sun and play games such as table tennis, billiards, and basketball. On the far side of the family beach, 20 new private cabanas will be added, and three more will be added on Serenity Bay Beach. At a brand-new water play area called Spring-a-Leak guests can cool off while immersing themselves in what appears to be the remnants of a washed-away beach dwelling. Scuttle's Cove will have a new water play area for the youngest passengers. Hide Out is a new secluded area for teens.

Nightly entertainment is unlike any other cruise line's and features high-quality, Disney-produced shows. The 977-seat **Walt Disney Theater** stages a different musical production each night, with talented actors, singers, and dancers. These family musicals are on the level of Disney theme parks' live entertainment rather than Broadway.

Disney Dreams has about every Disney character and song ever heard and offers a light plot wherein Peter Pan visits a girl who dreams of Disney's famous characters. Recently, the show got a sprinkling of its own pixie dust with laser effects that give the impression of real pixie dust falling from the ceiling of the theater. It's pure schmaltz, but audiences give it a standing ovation. Another night on *Disney Wonder* passengers see *Toy Story–The Musical*, one of the most beloved animated features of all time transformed into a stage spectacular. The show represents one of the largest productions ever developed for a cruise ship and only the second time a Pixar animated feature has been adapted for the stage. Preserving the humor and heart of the original *Toy Story* film, the show explores the meaning of friendship as Buzz Lightyear and Woody transform from jealous adversaries to best friends. (Pixar Animation Studios is a wholly owned subsidiary of The Walt Disney Company.)

In the smaller **Buena Vista Theater** with full-screen cinema, passengers watch first-run movies and classic Disney films. Movies are also playing poolside on a state-of-the-art, giant 24-by-14-foot LED screen affixed to the forward funnel on Deck 9 in the Goofy Pool area. One of the latest innovations is Disney Digital 3-D, a one-of-a-kind cinematic experience exclusively on board the *Disney Magic* and *Disney Wonder*.

Another fun evening is the "Pirates IN the Caribbean" deck party, when passengers are transformed into pirates for the night and treated to a special dinner with selections presented on a parchment menu. This is followed by a deck party with classic Disney characters in pirate garb, stage performances, fireworks, and the original *Pirates* movie airing on the jumbo screen. Passengers join a conga line with the cruise staff, Goofy, and his seafaring friends to learn special dance steps. Then suddenly, the mood of the party changes as Captain Hook, Mr. Smee, and a gang of "bad" pirates take over the party with special effects including black lighting, skull-and-crossbone projections, and an invasion of pirates rappelling from the funnel. Just in time, and before Captain Hook can enlist audience dads to join his gang of pirates, Captain Mickey appears and saves the day.

The seven-night cruises also have a show that includes variety acts, musical performances, and a cavalcade of Disney characters. The show tells the story of a young cruise passenger trying to achieve his dream of becoming a seafaring captain. Mickey, Minnie, and the rest of the Disney characters help the boy realize that if he believes in his dream, it can come true.

Another show on both ships is *The Golden Mickeys*, a character-filled musical using all the glitz and glamour of an awards show to honor the great animated films and characters that Disney has produced for more than 75 years.

Twice Charmed: An Original Twist on the Cinderella Story is seen on *Magic* only. **Studio Sea,** modeled after a television- or film-production set, is a family-oriented nightclub offering dance music, cabaret acts, passenger game shows, and multimedia entertainment. The Art Deco **Promenade Lounge** is a daytime haven for reading and relaxation and a nightspot for cocktails and piano music.

Beat Street on *Magic* (**Route 66** on *Wonder*) is an adult-oriented evening entertainment district with shops and themed nightclubs: **Rockin' Bar D,** (**Wavebands** on *Wonder*) with live bands or DJ playing rock and roll, top 40, and country music; **Diversions**, a sports pub and casual hangout with flat-panel plasma televisions where passengers can watch sports or play games; and **Sessions** on Magic (**Cadillac Lounge** on *Wonder*), a casual yet sophisticated place to enjoy easy music. Disney ships have no casinos or libraries.

Unlike *Disney Magic, Disney Wonder* has three conference rooms on Deck 2 with state-of-the-art presentation tools and LED flat-panel televisions. The meeting space has a business center, individual computer stations, and a refreshment bar. Both ships provide wireless connections for passengers who come with wireless-ready laptops. The hot spots are in several public areas and lounges and all open areas on Decks 9 and 10. Rates for wireless access start at $0.75 per minute, or $27.50 for a 50-minute plan, $40 for 100 minutes, and $75 for 250 minutes. Those without laptops can use computers in the ship's Internet cafes.

SPORTS, FITNESS, AND BEAUTY Of three top-deck pools, one has a Mickey Mouse motif and waterslide and is intended for kids. Another is set aside for families; the third is for adults. At night, the family pool area can be transformed for deck parties and dancing.

The ocean-view **Vista Spa and Salon,** above the bridge, is an area reserved exclusively for adults. The spa has three specifically designed, ocean-view spa villas, complete with an indoor spa treatment suite connected to a private outdoor veranda with a hot tub, open-air shower, and chaise lounge. The fitness center offers Life Fitness exercise equipment, exercise instruction, thermal-bath area, saunas, and steam rooms. It's supervised by a qualified fitness director. Along with the spa expansion, the fitness center was doubled in size, providing space for more exercise equipment, spinning classes and Pilates instruction, and personal beauty and fitness consultations. The spa, run by the British-based Steiner group, offers pricey beauty treatments along with a sales pitch for Steiner products. Despite high prices, the spa is very popular; it's generally booked for the entire cruise within hours of embarkation. Adult passengers can make spa appointments on the Disney Cruises Web site. The Sports Deck has paddle tennis and a basketball court. The expanded fitness center provides preloaded iPod Shuffles, programmed with

67 upbeat tracks ranging from pop to techno to hip-hop, designed to help participants with their workouts.

CHILDREN'S FACILITIES Playrooms and other kids' facilities occupy more than 15,000 square feet. Programs of age-specific activities are among the most extensive in cruising. They include challenging interactive activities and play areas supervised by trained counselors. Also offered is a children's drop-off service in the evening at the **Oceaneer Club,** a Neverland-themed play space for 3- to 7-year-olds. This service is available from 9 a.m. until midnight or 1 a.m. and is included in the cost of the cruise. Children in the drop-off program are taken to dinner at Topsiders or Beach Blanket Buffet.

The Oceaneer Club and the Oceaneer Lab, a whacky and interactive laboratory exclusively for 8- to 12-year-olds, have new registration areas that make the checking-in process more efficient. Radio Frequency Identification (RFID) technology in the youth activity areas has further streamlined the check-in process. RFID tags embedded on wristbands allow children to simply tap a sensor to check in and out of the clubs.

The ships' expanded **Flounder's Reef nursery** was improved with enhanced lighting that creates the look of being under the sea. The toddler area, doubled in size, has toys from Hasbro, Disney's partner, and a special porthole for parents to check on their kids without the little ones seeing them. The ships provide parents with pagers. Passengers can register their children for the nursery online at Disney's Web site up to three days prior to vacation, and in the nursery on sailing day between 1:30 p.m. and 3:30 p.m. Availability is limited and on a first-come, first-served basis. The nursery holds up to 30 children (10 infants and 20 toddlers). The child/counselor ratio is one babysitter to four children (ages 12 weeks–1 year); one babysitter to six children (ages 1–2 years); and one babysitter to 11 children (2–3 years). On embarkation day, the nursery is open 1:30–3:30 p.m. to take reservations for the cruise. In *Wonder*'s most recent renovations, the Mickey Pool on Deck 9 was extended to provide a pool with interactive fountains and splash zones for children not yet toilet trained and in swim diapers.

For children not yet toilet trained and in swim diapers, Mickey's Splash Zone, a 385-square-foot extension to the Mickey Pool on Deck 9, is a new toddler water playground inspired by *Fantasia's* Sorcerer's Apprentice. It has star- and moon-shaped interactive fountains, a soft play surface, and whimsical splash zones. Disney's newest amenity enables families preparing to sail with little ones to order baby supplies from an online service in advance and have them delivered to their cabin. The service, exclusive for Disney Cruise Line passengers, is provided by Babies Travel Lite, an online retailer offering more than 1,000 brand-name baby products.

Group babysitting in Flounder's Reef nursery is available for select hours every day. (Passengers should check with programming once on board for the exact times, as the hours change daily in accordance with daily activities, ports of call, and the like.) Cost is $6 per child per hour; $5 per hour for each additional child. A one-hour minimum is required; maximum ten hours per child, based on demand and availability.

The Oceaneer Adventure program encompasses the Oceaneer Club (ages 3–7), resembling Captain Hook's pirate ship, with plenty of places for activity. Its Neverland theme has been expanded and the Captain's Closet dress-up area revamped. **Oceaneer Lab** (ages 8–12) offers high-tech play, including video games, computers, lab equipment, and a small room for listening to CDs.

On *Wonder*, Oceaneer Lab has a computer simulator enabling children to try their hand at steering the ship in and out of ports. The simulator, fashioned as a replica of the ship's bridge, has giant video screens that provide a panoramic view of the ports similar to the actual view from the ship's bridge. Kids wear ID bracelets, and parents receive pagers for staying in touch with their playing children. Both parents and children give the youth programs high marks.

Aloft (The Stack on *Magic*) sits high on Deck 11 in the ornamental smoke-stack with lots of space and nooks and crannies. The program also has organized activities, including volleyball at Castaway Cay. The teen program seems to be a hit, as teens enjoy having an area to themselves in the evenings, as well as having their own area apart from the kids. Aloft, with eclectic decor that's a cross between a college dormitory and a trendy coffee shop, features beanbags and a soda bar. It's a teen haven for socializing with newfound friends and offers high-tech diversions such as a big-screen television, MP3 players, computers, and video-game systems, some of which have wireless controllers. While the room succeeds in its hardware, the activities—apparently too juvenile for teens—appear to need some work; on a recent cruise, one passenger reported that only a handful of teens hang out at any one time there, often munching on snacks, sometimes watching movies. Passengers can register their children for youth activities on Disney Cruise's Web site.

SHORE EXCURSIONS On some itineraries, the ships dock in Nassau for 15 hours—ample time to explore the island, enjoy a sport, visit Atlantis Resort on Paradise Island, shop, and take in a show and casino. The ship offers more than 20 excursions to Nassau, most of them fairly standard tours. Among choices (prices are for passengers age 10 and older/children under age 10 or as noted) are the Glass Bottom Boat Tour, $26 /$17 ; Snorkel Tour, $37/$27 (ages 6–9); Discover Atlantis, $52/$35 (ages 3–9); eSegway "Off Road" Back to Nature $75 (ages 14 and up). Scuba diving, dolphin trainer for a day, dolphin encounter, sea lion encounter, and stingray interactions tours are also available. The new Disney Cruise Line Signature Adventures include Graycliff Hotel Wine and Cheese Pairing, and Graycliff Cigar and Rum Experience (for guests age 21 and older, $189 each). Shore excursion descriptions are available on the line's Web site, and can be booked in advance.

THE SHIPS Inside cabins with ocean views (?!), a roller coaster at sea (?!!), and a talking sea turtle (?!!!)—these are just a few of the innovations that the Disney Imagineers have created for the 128,000-ton *Disney Dream*, set to debut in January 2011.

Disney's first new ship in 12 years (to be followed by her twin, *Disney Fantasy*, in 2012), *Disney Dream* is approximately 40% larger than her predecessors. Similar to them with Art Deco interiors and exteriors inspired by the great ocean liners of ole with a sleek bow and circular portholes, she will elevate family cruising to a new level with innovations on almost every deck.

At the top, sure to thrill kids of all ages, is cruising's first water coaster—the 765-foot-long, four-deck-high combination slide and roller coaster dubbed AquaDuck. (Donald Duck will be in command of the *Dream* with his five-foot statue in the atrium to greet passengers.) The coaster employs the

Disney Dream	2011	
Disney Fantasy	2012	
REGISTRY Bahamas	LENGTH 1,114 feet	BEAM 121 feet
CABINS 1,250	DRAFT 26 feet	SPEED 22 knots
MAXIMUM PASSENGERS	PASSENGER DECKS 14	ELEVATORS NA
4,000	CREW 1,458	SPACE RATIO NA

Master Blaster technology found at the Disney theme parks. A rider starts the journey by boarding an inflated raft, which is then propelled by high-powered water jets up and forward at 20 feet per second into a clear acrylic tube. The rider then careens around the twin stacks on the upper decks of the ship and through a series of twists, turns, and drops, including a 13-foot "swing out" loop to view the ocean 150 feet below and a 335-foot stretch of river rapids, to splash down to the end of the ride two decks below.

ITINERARIES *See* Itinerary Index.

CABINS Almost nine out of ten of the 1,250 cabins are outside cabins, and of those, 90% have a private veranda. Clearly designed for families, including multigenerational ones, *Dream* has a high percentage of cabins for four or five people, along with 500 connecting cabins. The partition between connecting veranda cabins can be opened to create a larger shared balcony.

Disney's signature "bath-and-a-half" design is being retained; most cabins have a bathroom with a vanity, sink, and full tub/shower and a second half bath with a vanity, sink, and toilet. One important change: Bed frames are higher from the floor to create more under-bed storage space. Pull-down beds open to reveal a celestial scene overhead, and every cabin will have a 22-inch LCD flat-panel television on a swivel arm and an iPod docking station.

Another innovation is the 21 suites near the top of the ship that enjoy access to a private concierge lounge and sun deck. Each of the lavish suites will come with a living room, master bedroom, walk-in closet, Blu-ray disc player, large veranda, and two bathrooms designed with granite and marble finishes. The master bathroom has a whirlpool tub, rain shower, double sinks, and a television built seamlessly into the mirror. Both the living area and master bedroom have a 42-inch, high-definition LCD television. Most suites connect to another stateroom, creating a spacious living area for families or groups.

But of all the new-to-cruising features, the one that shows the genius of Disney innovators is found in the inside cabins. For the first time, occupants of inside cabins will have a view of the outside. Yes, the outside. A large "virtual" porthole on the back wall of the cabin is connected to high-definition cameras placed on the exterior of the ship that feed live video to each porthole for real-time outside views.

Specifications 150 inside cabins; 1,100 outside cabins, 199 with ocean views and 860 with verandas; 21 suites with verandas.

DINING *Disney Dream* retains the "rotational dining" concept introduced on the earlier ships but with new themes: **The Enchanted Garden,** a whimsical, casual restaurant inspired by the gardens of Versailles, will offer a dining environment that transforms from day to night as light fixtures "bloom" and change colors and the "sky" on the ceiling experiences a sunset. In **The Royal Palace,** featuring classic Disney films, passengers will be in the company of Cinderella, Snow White and the Seven Dwarfs, Beauty and the Beast, and Sleeping Beauty. The third dining room, **Animator's Palate,** will be similar to the venue on the first ships but with a new look meant to be a more realistic representation of an animator's studio. Another carryover will be **Palo,** the line's adults-only specialty restaurant, where all patrons will enjoy ocean views while soft piano music plays in the background.

FACILITIES AND ACTIVITIES The **Walt Disney Theatre,** seating 1,340 passengers, will be the main show lounge and will feature a new Broadway-style show based around the villains of Disney lore. A smaller, 399-seat theater will show first-run and classic Disney films.

Disney Dream will have an adults-only playground called **The District** (not to be confused with a neighborhood). The nighttime entertainment enclave away from kids will have five different venues, including Palo. Its most innovative area is **Skyline,** a stylish lounge with "windows" that look out over the ever-changing skylines of famous cities. Large LCD screens along the walls give patrons the illusion of sitting in a sky-high venue in such cities as Paris, London, and Tokyo. Other sections of The District include **Pink,** an upscale, Art Nouveau–inspired Champagne bar lined with back-lit inset glass "bubbles"; **Evolution,** a hip nightclub with a butterfly motif; **Metro Pub,** a modern interpretation of a traditional pub, and the **District Lounge,** a piano bar.

SPORTS, FITNESS, AND BEAUTY **Senses Spa & Salon,** the ship's bi-level facility located at the front of the ship, will boast 17 treatment rooms in lavish spa villas with indoor treatment rooms and private outdoor verandas, and the **Rainforest,** a special section of the spa offering the benefits of steam, heat, and hydrotherapy.

CHILDREN'S FACILITIES *Disney Dream* will have five distinct, age-specific youth areas. Disney's **Oceaneer Club,** for 3- to-10-year-olds, will offer everything from a stage for child-produced theatrical performances and storytelling sessions to a *Toy Story*-themed play area with larger-than-life characters from the popular film. Animated characters such as Crush, the sea turtle from *Finding Nemo,* and Stitch, the mischievous alien from *Lilo and Stitch,* will chat, play, and joke with children in live, unrehearsed conversations from their digital undersea and intergalactic environments via 103-inch plasma screens. The **Oceaneer Lab,** also for 3- to-10-year-olds, will have an amazing range of activities, from an arts-focused Animator's Studio to a sound studio where kids can create their own original tunes using song-making software.

The Edge, a dedicated tween club for ages 11–13, will be located in the forward funnel of the ship overlooking the pool deck. **Vibe,** the 9,000-square-foot teen club for ages 14–17, is a much larger teen area than on Disney's earlier ships. Accessible by teens' own special key cards, the club will have its own exclusive indoor/outdoor area near the bow. Designed with a contemporary feel with trendy furniture, it will have a fountain bar, a media room with games and movies, a dance club area, iPod chairs, video walls, and outside, lounge chairs for sunbathing, fountains, pop jets, and outdoor deck games.

Holland America Line

300 Elliott Avenue West
Seattle, WA 98119
☎ 206-281-3535 or 877-SAILHAL (724-5425)
FAX 800-628-4855
www.hollandamerica.com

TYPE OF SHIPS Modern superliners.

TYPE OF CRUISES Traditional yet modern, high-quality premium cruises.

CRUISE LINE'S STRENGTHS
- tradition and experience
- easy-to-like ships
- consistent quality and style
- worldwide itineraries
- impeccable condition of ships

CRUISE LINE'S SHORTCOMINGS
- show lounge entertainment
- shore excursion cancellation policy
- communication problems with dining staff due to language

FELLOW PASSENGERS Experienced travelers and families who seek comfort and consistency, quality, a refined environment, and those who choose cruises by their destinations. Many are retired business owners with some college education and professionals, but the range includes secretaries on their first cruise, affluent seniors who cruise often, honeymooners, young families, multigenerational families, and some disabled travelers. They're social-minded, well mannered, and outgoing, but not loud. They enjoy traveling with old friends and making new ones. They're conservative and seek good value. They often cruise to celebrate a special occasion, such as an anniversary or a family reunion.

The average age varies by cruise length and itinerary. A seven-day Alaska and seven-day Caribbean cruise on the same ship attract different ages and incomes. More than 55% are couples; 50% are groups—as different as business or tour groups, or square-dancing and stamp-collecting clubs.

Recommended for Those who enjoy cruise traditions and want a high-quality experience in a refined environment but like the facilities of superliners. Small-ship devotees open to trying a larger ship. Budget cruisers able to move up to higher quality; families and multigenerational vacationers.

Not recommended for Swingers, party seekers, late-night revelers, trend seekers, or pacesetters.

CRUISE AREAS AND SEASONS Africa, Asia, Caribbean, Mexico, Pacific Coast, Panama Canal, fall to spring; Alaska, Canada and New England, Europe transatlantic, summer and fall; Antarctica, South America, Australia and New Zealand, world cruise, winter.

THE LINE Holland America has carried passengers since 1872. It's among the few lines to make a successful transition from a classic steamship company to a modern cruise line, and it did so better than most, managing to keep its identity and traditions intact while developing a fine mainstream product.

One turning point came in the early 1980s when the line introduced the *Nieuw Amsterdam* (sold in 2000), a forerunner of today's superliners. She was revolutionary because of such features as a square stern that provided 20% more open deck; two outdoor heated pools; a fully equipped gym, spa, and whirlpool; coded cards rather than keys for cabins; and cabin television—all features that quickly became standard on new ships.

In 1988, HAL acquired the unusual Windstar Cruises, and the following year, Holland America, Windstar, and Seattle-based Westours, which pioneered Alaska tours and cruises, were acquired by Carnival Corp. The marriage proved to be brilliant, enabling Holland America to continue its expansion (four stunning new ships in the 1990s, and another four early in the new millennium) and allowing the line to expand in Alaska, return to Europe after nearly two decades, and increase its number of longer cruises. All were factors critical to HAL's retaining its many loyal fans.

The *Statendam*-class ships, the first HAL ships to have private verandas, combine classic elegance with state-of-the-art technology, offering such features as multideck atriums, fountains, whirlpools, and treadmills. The faster *Rotterdam* and her sister ship, *Amsterdam*, with top cruising speeds of 25 knots, gave the line new flexibility in creating itineraries. They were followed by slightly larger twins, *Volendam* and *Zaandam*, and another new class of 82,000-ton cruise ships, dubbed the Vista series, arrived between 2002 and 2006. Altogether, the line introduced ten new ships in ten years—a challenge for any cruise line. And then in 2008, the first of two 2,044-passenger Signature-class ships, *Eurodam*, was launched; her sister, *Nieuw Amsterdam*, the line's 15th ship, is scheduled to debut in summer 2010.

In 2001, the line introduced wheelchair-accessible tenders and Internet access for passengers fleetwide. More recently, the line has added wireless connection and cell phone service fleetwide, plus a shore-excursion booking facility on its Web site. But these enhancements pale compared with the extensive, $525 million Signature of Excellence program carried out over the last five years, updating the line for the modern traveler while continuing to uphold the traditions that are Holland America's signature. Holland America Line is on Twitter, Facebook, and the Holland America blog. Social media outlets can be accessed via the Online Communities quick link on **www.hollandamerica.com.**

STYLE HAL cruises are classic but contemporary, blending Old World traditions with modern lifestyles. They offer the full range of activities expected on large, mass-market ships. The pace is leisurely, designed for experienced, mature travelers and families.

To attract younger passengers, the line has progressively expanded onboard sports and fitness facilities; added sports bars with ESPN programming, alternative dining, Internet access, sports and adventure shore excursions for active passengers on Alaska and Caribbean cruises; and beefed up its children's program, with special teens-only areas as well.

In 1997, Holland America bought the uninhabited 2,400-acre Bahamian island of Little San Salvador, renamed it Half Moon Cay, and developed it as

HAL's private island destination on Caribbean itineraries. Located between Eleuthera and Cat Island, less than 100 miles southeast of Nassau, the 45-acre facility fronts a gorgeous white-sand beach. Three areas, connected by walkways and a tram, are an arrival marina and plaza built to resemble ruins of a Spanish fort, a shopping area styled as a West Indian village, and a food pavilion.

The market has shops, an ice-cream parlor, coffee shop, bar, and art gallery. There is a playground, wedding chapel, and post office selling Bahamian stamps—including one issued to commemorate the island. Passengers get a barbecue lunch of West Indian selections. The sports center offers snorkeling and diving on nearby reefs, Sunfish sailing, other water sports, volleyball, and basketball, and there's horseback riding and swimming with dolphins. Nature trails feature a bird sanctuary designated by the Bahaman National Trust. Passengers can debit the cost of all services and sports to their cabins; cash is required for island stamps; craft vendors take credit cards.

Holland America's vessels feel like ships, not floating hotels. The fleet shares characteristics that reinforce the line's traditions: art and antiques reflecting Holland's association with trade and exploration in the Americas; Dutch officers and Indonesian crews, linking Holland's historical ties to Asia; and the **Crow's Nest,** an observation bar inspired by the lookout on the main mast of the company's old sailing ships. Passengers can view the multimillion-dollar collections with a free self-guided tour using an iPod.

With the Signature of Excellence program, the line has aimed for an even more youthful look and ambience with enhancements to cabins, dining, spa, and children's facilities, and the introduction of new features throughout the

THE FLEET	BUILT/RENOVATED	TONNAGE	PASSENGERS
Amsterdam	2000/06	61,000	1,380
Eurodam	2008	86,7000	2,104
Maasdam	1994/2006	55,451	1,258
Nieuw Amsterdam	2010	86,7000	2,104
Noordam	2006	85,000	1,848
Oosterdam	2003/06	81,769	1,848
Prinsendam	1988/99//04/07/09	38,000	793
Rotterdam	1997/2005	59,652	1,316
Ryndam	1994/2004	55,451	1,258
Statendam	1993/2005	55,451	1,258
Veendam	1996/2006/09	55,451	1,258
Volendam	1999/2006	60,906	1,432
Westerdam	2004/05	81,769	1,848
Zaandam	2000/04	60,906	1,432
Zuiderdam	2002/06	81,769	1,848

fleet, such as early boarding from 11:30 a.m. on the day of departure, four evening dining times, and the addition of the **Pinnacle Grill,** a steak and seafood specialty restaurant, and the Culinary Arts Center. New activities and shore excursions stress active sports. The goal has been to make the HAL experience more relevant to today's and tomorrow's traveler (read baby boomers).

The programs of the Culinary Arts Center have proven to be one of the most popular innovations. In partnership with *Food and Wine* magazine, Holland America offers a series with celebrated chefs and wine experts who give culinary demonstrations, tastings, and hands-on cooking classes to passengers. On cruises without a guest chef, classes and demonstrations in the show kitchen are conducted by the line's own chefs. A youth program to teach kids to cook is also offered. Another new feature are sommelier options in the Pinnacle Grill on sailings of ten days or longer. The Sommelier Dinner ($75 per person) pairs at least four glasses of wine with a six-course menu. A culinary team of six, including the executive chef and cellar master, collaborate to produce the dinner. Prior to the event, participants meet for Champagne or Kir Royal in the Explorer's Lounge or Pinnacle Grill Wine Bar. A Sommelier Wine Package, available throughout a cruise, consists of two wine-tasting events, a Pinnacle Grill dinner, five vintage bottles of wine, a Holland America commemorative bottle, and a wine gift. Cost of the package is $251 per person or $308 per couple.

The line's latest innovation is a book club on cruises of 14 days or longer. The lively book discussions are hosted by the shipboard librarian in the Explorations Café. The chosen title is posted online prior to each sailing. Generally, books chosen relate to the cruise destination either by author or topic. Another new program, Cruise with a Purpose, is a series of shore excursions during which participants can engage in a public service project. Developed with a selection of tour operators and nonprofit organizations in different parts of the world, the first excursion-project was readied for the 2009 summer season in Alaska. At the end of the tour, participants receive a pin and can track their project(s) on the Cruise with a Purpose program page on the Holland America Web site. And, yes, even though you are volunteering to do good, there's a charge.

Ever-mindful of their longtime loyal fans, Holland America has worked to strike a balance between the pace and nature of the changes needed to attract a broader, younger audience, while keeping the traditions that older passengers cherish.

One of Holland America's most important initiatives has been On-Deck for the Cure, an onboard, noncompetitive 5K fitness walk to raise money for the Susan G. Komen Breast Cancer Foundation. Offered fleetwide, the program invites passengers to participate, suggesting a $15 donation. Up to 250 passengers per cruise are participating.

With its latest innovation, Holland America's passengers will receive their cruise documents electronically and can print their boarding passes to use at check-in. Those booking suites receive a distinctive boarding pass to use at the Suite Check-in Desk at the pier. Passengers may still request the old-fashioned paper documents to be sent by mail.

If you would like to have the amenities that usually come with a suite, but not the suite, Holland America will sell you a Suite Amenities Package. The price varies, depending on the length of the cruise, but starts at $285 per person (double occupancy) for cruises up to ten days. Each day you receive your choice of high tea or cold canapés in your cabin, complimentary laundry and pressing service throughout the cruise, fresh flowers, pillow menu, two souvenir monogrammed bathrobes, and a beverage setup with two bottles of wine and two bottles of liquor. You also receive a coffee card for ten cups of premium or specialty coffee in the Explorations Café, a daily DVD selection from the ship's library along with fresh hot popcorn, and one dinner at the Pinnacle Grill. On departure, you get access to a disembarkation lounge with refreshments and luggage pickup, and your departure is at your leisure. Now, that's a suite deal.

DISTINCTIVE FEATURES Escalators; self-service laundries on some ships, good libraries, fresh flowers shipwide; fruit basket, robes in cabins, hot hors d'oeuvres at cocktails, private Bahamian island, alternative dining, Internet centers, cell phone capability; Culinary Arts program, Explorations Café powered by the *New York Times*. Self-guided art tour with iPod; Greenhouse Spa.

RATES Port charges are included.

Special fares and discounts Save up to 45% for early booking under the Caribbean Savings program. A similar Alaska program offers 25% off. Membership Rewards, a program with American Express, offers mileage redeemable for upgrades and discount dollars.

- **THIRD/FOURTH PASSENGER:** Low rates.
- **CHILDREN'S FARE:** Reduced rates for ages 2–18; specific rates for younger than age 2. Ages 19 and older are billed as third/fourth persons sharing parents' room.
- **SINGLE SUPPLEMENT:** 150% to 190% of double rate or specific rate on certain cruises; guaranteed share program.

PAST PASSENGERS Holland America recently redesigned its Mariner Society Rewards Program with benefits tiered on four levels and based on the number of cruise sailing days, and credits based on onboard spending or purchase of suite options. All who sail with Holland America are automatically enrolled. With Star Mariner, the first level, passengers earn cruise days towards future cruises and a gift, special offers, and a 50% discount for third and fourth passengers on select sailings, hosted cruises with Holland America ambassadors, a welcome-back embarkation brunch on future cruises, *Mariner* magazine, and a Mariner Champagne brunch on future cruises.

With Two-star Mariner, after 30 cruise day credits, passengers receive all Star Mariner amenities plus a 15% discount on merchandise from **www .ShopHollandAmerica.com** and 10% off logo apparel on board, a complimentary ship photo, an annual cruise planner, and a recognition pin. With Three-star Mariner, after 75 cruise days, passengers get all Two-star amenities plus discounts, including 10% off select spa treatments; 25% off all wine packages, minibar purchases, Explorations Café drinks, and alternative restaurant surcharges; advanced notice of new itineraries; and air deviation fee waiver. Four-star Mariners, with 200 cruise days, enjoy the benefits of Star levels One, Two, and Three, as well as free third/fourth passengers on select sailings; complimentary wine tasting and laundry/pressing; a 50% discount on all wine packages, minibar purchases, Explorations Café drinks, and alternative restaurant surcharges; a 15% discount on logo apparel on board; priority tender service and check-in; priority shore excursion prebooking; and a subscription to *Food and Wine* or *Travel and Leisure* magazine.

THE LAST WORD Holland America puts itself in the premium category, between luxury and economy, but it's at the high end of premium, a hair's breadth from luxury, and deluxe by any standard. The refinements and thoughtful touches it offers are unavailable on many comparably priced ships. HAL's consistency—even the names of most public rooms are the same fleetwide—has built a large, loyal following that doesn't find the predictability boring—rather, it's reassuring.

THE SHIPS The *Statendam* and her sisters introduced a new class of ships in the 1990s that set the style and standard for Holland America into the next century. They combined Old World tradition with state-of-the-art technology and provided an imposing yet inviting ambience. The spacious ships differ in decor but are identical in layout and offer almost identical facilities and activities.

Interiors of the Italian-built ships were designed by De Vlaming, Fenns, and Dingemans (VFD), the Dutch firm responsible for earlier HAL ships, which helped establish the line's signature look. In the group's public areas, designers drew from Holland America's history to capture the golden age of Dutch shipping but in a contemporary context. Multimillion-dollar collections of art and artifacts from the 17th to 19th centuries are integrated into the decor. These combine with contemporary art to enhance the ships' modern image. Together, they make the ships floating art galleries. In materials, the world was VFD's emporium. Designers used woolen fabrics from Holland; leathers from Germany, France, and England; glass from Italy. Cabins were made in Finland, a Danish company supplied teak, and furniture was built in Slovenia. Galley equipment came from the United States. Public rooms span two decks on the Promenade and Upper Promenade in an asymmetrical pattern, allowing for bars and lounges of different sizes.

The *Statendam*-class ships are being upgraded with Signature of Excellence enhancements in two stages. *Ryndam* was the first to receive a makeover and now sports new public rooms with brighter decor, cabin improvements, dining enhancements, and children's facilities, among other additions. In the second phase, the ships will add 32 veranda cabins to their aft portion and install verandas on 12 cabins on Deck 9 forward. In addition, 46 new lanai

Maasdam	QUALITY 8	VALUE B
Ryndam	QUALITY 8	VALUE B
Statendam	QUALITY 8	VALUE B
Veendam	QUALITY 8	VALUE B
REGISTRY Netherlands	LENGTH 720 feet	BEAM 101 feet
CABINS 675	DRAFT 24.6 feet	SPEED 22 knots
MAXIMUM PASSENGERS	PASSENGER DECKS 10	ELEVATORS 8
1,350	CREW 557	SPACE RATIO 44

Holland America Line Standard Features

Officers Dutch, British, Norwegian.

Staff *Dining:* Dutch and Indonesian supervisors, Indonesian and Filipino; *Cabin:* Indonesian and Filipino; *Cruise:* American, others.

Dining facilities One dining room, four seatings. Indoor/outdoor Lido restaurants for casual buffet breakfast, lunch, and alternative dining; taco, pasta, and ice-cream bars. Pinnacle Grill.

Special diets Kosher; low-sodium, low-cholesterol, low-fat; vegetarian; sugar-free desserts; baby foods. Request 30 days in advance.

Room service hours; dining room menu during dining hours.

Dress code Casual with two formal/semiformal nights per week of cruise. Tuxedo rental service available.

Cabin amenities Television with CNN, ESPN, TCM, Discovery, children's channel, and others; multichannel music system, hair dryers, and direct-dial telephone. Suites and deluxe cabins have DVD players, whirlpool bath, and minibar.

Electrical outlets 110 AC.

Wheelchair access 21 cabins on *Amsterdam, Rotterdam*; 22 on *Volendam, Zaandam*; 28 on Vista class; 4–6 on others; 30 on *Eurodam*.

Recreation and entertainment Theater for movies and lectures, show lounge, nightclub, casino, bars, lounges, karaoke, masquerades, crew show, culinary demonstrations, kitchen tours, bingo, card games, bridge, pool games, dance classes, library. Sports bars with ESPN.

Sports and other activities Two outdoor pools, tennis, golf putting, volleyball, table tennis, shuffleboard.

Beauty and fitness Beauty/barber shop, saunas, massage, fitness program, gym with professional instructors, treadmills, bikes, stair climbers, practice tennis. Spa treatments and fitness programs.

Other facilities Religious services, medical facilities, laundry/dry cleaning service, self-service launderettes on some ships, meeting room. Credit-card phones. Wedding ceremony and amenity packages for vows renewal, honeymoons, and anniversaries at additional charge. Internet centers or Exploration Cafés.

Children's facilities Club HAL year-round youth program with counselors and age-specific activities for three age groups. Teens ages 13–18 have their own areas with sun deck, waterfall, lounge, and other features.

Theme cruises See specific ships.

Smoking Designated smoking areas in public rooms; some, such as dining rooms, card room, library, and theater, are designated nonsmoking.

Holland America suggested tipping An $11 per person per day gratuity is added to passenger's shipboard account; 15% added to bar bills.

Credit cards Cruise and onboard charges: American Express, Discover, MasterCard, Visa; no cash.

cabins on the Lower Promenade Deck will allow direct access to the Promenade. Fifteen new spa cabins, near the Greenhouse Spa, will be created from existing cabins and have special in-room spa amenities and exclusive in-cabin spa treatments. The ships also will add a number of inside cabins.

In spring 2009, the *Veendam* got her Signature of Excellence makeover and emerged with a new, contemporary look and renovated cabins and bathrooms. She gained new lanai cabins (created by replacing cabin windows with sliding glass doors that open directly onto the Promenade) and spa cabins near the Greenhouse Spa. Topside, The Retreat, the resort-style pool amenity, was added, as was Canaletto, the casual Italian dinner venue in the Lido restaurant introduced in 2008 on the *Eurodam*. The Lido restaurant has a new canopy and windscreens, providing additional covered seating. There's a new pool bar, a giant LED screen for evening movies, and a pizzeria called Slice.

The casino and piano bars were reconfigured into Mix, a new socializing venue with three separate bars: Champagne, for midday mimosas or anytime celebrations, with electronic tables for playing video checkers and chess; Martinis, for Grey Goose cocktails and martinis and enjoying piano and guitar music in the stylish setting; and Spirits & Ales, a sports bar for microbrews and single malts. Next door, the casino was redesigned, and the main show lounge, located forward, was transformed into the "Showroom at Sea" with the ambience of a glamorous nightclub and the addition of new shows. At midship, the Merabella luxury jewelry shop was added.

The upgrade program also includes significant enhancements to the ship's crew area, including a new fitness facility and Internet center. In 2010, the *Ryndam* gets the same treatment in January and February; *Statendam* in March and April; and *Maasdam* late in the year.

The *Maasdam*, fifth ship in the company's history with that name, is a far cry from the first *Maasdam*—a double-masted iron steamship that carried eight first-class and 288 steerage passengers. It sailed the Atlantic monthly from 1872 to 1884 at a speed of ten knots. Today's computer-piloted *Maasdam* has only one class and moves at more than twice that speed.

Passengers are introduced to the *Maasdam* by a three-deck atrium on the Lower Promenade Deck. Under a ceiling of mirrors and fiber-optic lights, the atrium sparkles with a 30-foot glass sculpture, *Totem*, by Italian artist Luciano Vistosi. The sculpture contains thousands of pieces of glass that catch the light and cast specks of color on nearby surfaces.

ITINERARIES   *See* Itinerary Index.

CABINS   Comfortable, contemporary furnishings in light wood are combined with continental touches. Standard cabins are almost 30% larger than comparable ones on ships of similar category. Large mirrors lighten the rooms, and in many, curtains separate the sleeping and sitting areas. Seventy-seven percent are outside cabins.

All cabins in all categories fleetwide have custom-designed Sealy Posturepedic Premium Euro-top mattresses (called Mariner Dream Beds) and a pillow menu. All have been given a modern, very different look for HAL, with a light bed cover and a display of pillows. The cabins also have upgraded linens, towels, and terry robes, flat-panel televisions with DVD players, massage showerheads, and lighted magnifying mirrors. The cabins come with hair dryers, direct-dial telephones with automated wake-up service, and multi-channel music systems. Full-length double closets and deep chests of drawers—nice features for long cruises—provide ample storage.

Standard cabins have sofas, of which 70% are sofa beds. All outside cabins have a bathtub and shower. Suites and deluxe cabins have a veranda, minibar, DVD player, and whirlpool bath. Each suite also has a small private dining area; laundry and dry cleaning are free.

Passengers in suites have a concierge to assist with appointments and other needs, plus the comfortable **Neptune Lounge** for the private use of Penthouse and Deluxe suite passengers only. It has its own library, television, and bar.

As part of the Signature of Excellence's second phase, all cabins and bathrooms were renewed with new bedding and carpets, and desks and vanities resurfaced. Highlights of the new decor are rich earth hues with sienna and gold accents, olive-colored sofas with decorative pillows, and chairs in gold chenille, while decorative wall sconces, curtains, and accent pillows add a touch of modern elegance. Suites have a contemporary color scheme with a traditional twist. A rich, dark carpet and chocolate-colored leather sofa contrast with the light golden tones of soft goods and maple casework. Accents of reddish-orange punctuate sofa pillows, chairs, and the bed runner.

Specifications 144 inside cabins, 575 outside (including 120 deluxe cabins, 15 spa suites, and 29 suites with verandas). All with twin beds convertible to queen. Standard dimensions are 186 square feet, inside cabin; 196 square feet, outside cabin. 16 deluxe/36 standard outside have connecting doors for family suites. Some upper/lower berths and single cabins; 6 wheelchair-accessible cabins.

DINING The ships' crowning glories are their dazzling **Rotterdam Dining Rooms.** Surrounded on three sides by floor-to-ceiling windows that embrace the scenery and span the Promenade and Upper Promenade decks, the rooms are a harmony of elegant tradition and modern technology. An impressive curved staircase connects the two levels.

On the *Maasdam,* a fountain of antique Argentine marble is the lower level's centerpiece. A ceiling canopy of a thousand morning glories is made of blown glass from Murano, Italy. Between the decks is a border of fiber-optic florets programmed to change color, altering the room's mood. Four large, colorful linen screens depicting day and night cover the walls on both decks.

One passenger's verdict: "The room is so beautiful, it takes your breath away." The room is large but remarkably quiet; diners can converse in normal voices and hear chamber music playing on the balcony. The secret: glass ceilings look spectacular—and absorb sound.

Dining here and on all Holland America ships is more elegant, and menu choices more extensive, than on most mainstream cruise ships. Tables are set with white Rosenthal china bearing a gold HAL logo, silver tableware, wine coolers, and fresh flowers on starched tablecloths. Many tables have either window or balcony seats.

An important element of the Signature of Excellence program has been the fleetwide addition of the **Pinnacle Grill.** Sterling beef is the grill's major draw; you choose your cut from the display tray, including a 20-ounce porterhouse steak. The food is superbly prepared, presented, and served. Reservations are required, and there is a charge: $10 for lunch (served usually on sea days only) and $20 for dinner.

Responding to passengers' preference for casual, flexibly timed breakfast and lunch—and alternative dining in the evening—Holland America has worked to perfect the Lido buffet, outdoing competitors in quality, choice, and presentation. More lunch choices—hot dogs, hamburgers, pasta, satay, and tacos—are available by the Lido pool. A free ice-cream bar is open daily. Sandwiches, desserts, coffee, and tea are available here around the clock. Hot hors d'oeuvres with Indonesian tidbits are served in public rooms before dinner, and a weekly Indonesian Lido buffet is popular. And should you still be hungry, the 24-hour room service menu has been expanded, and your cabin's fruit basket is freshened daily.

On all ships now, the Lido restaurant has been reconfigured into food stations, replacing the cafeteria design. Entrées from the dining room are served as part of the casual dinner option—a nice alternative after a busy day ashore.

One of the main ingredients that Signature of Excellence added to the fleet is the Culinary Arts program and **Culinary Arts Center,** presented by *Food and Wine* magazine. It has a state-of-the-art show kitchen where cooking demonstrations, tasting events, and cooking classes take place. Some cruises offer presentations by guest chefs. Passengers in the audience get an up-close view of the cooking action on large plasma screens, while broadcast capabilities provide all guests the opportunity to watch from their cabins. In addition to the onstage kitchen, the centers have portable cooking stations where up to 16 guests can participate in hands-on classes that often feature regional cuisine reflecting the ship's itinerary.

The one-hour demonstrations by the executive or guest chefs are free. The daily classes, limited to a dozen or so participants sharing six cooking stations, run one-and-a-half hours, during which an appetizer, entree, and dessert are prepared. There is a charge of $29 per person for Holland America chefs and $39 per person for guest chefs. A set of recipes is included, plus a 10% discount at the Pinnacle Grill or complimentary admission to a wine-tasting event.

Integral to the program is Holland America's culinary adviser, master chef Rudi Sodamin, who has been instrumental in developing the centers and instructional programs. The **Gourmet Shop** sells culinary items, china, and silverware from the Pinnacle Grill, as well as Rudi Sodamin's cookbooks.

SERVICE HAL's efficient Dutch officers and the friendly Indonesian and Filipino crew are a good combination. Unobtrusive service by a gracious and attentive staff is a hallmark—and a reason the line has so many loyal fans. Dining room supervisory personnel are officers; many crew members have been with Holland America for many years.

Unlike most cruise ships, HAL has retained a tradition its fans love: a uniformed steward passes through the ship playing chimes to summon passengers to dine.

FACILITIES AND ACTIVITIES The *Maasdam* and her sisters each have five lounges, often with the same names and similar entertainment. The Promenade Deck is anchored by the two-deck main show lounge designed by Joe Farcus, who is known for his innovative, flamboyant ship interiors for Carnival Cruise Lines. Daytime activities include lectures, bridge tournaments, dance lessons, bingo, putting contests, kite flying, movies (with popcorn), religious services, and—the most unusual—guided tours of the ship's art and antiquities.

The ships have large, comfortable card and puzzle rooms, a shopping arcade, and libraries with floor-to-ceiling windows. The ships hold auctions of contemporary art. Be wary of the sales pitch. If the bargain sounds too good to be true, it probably is.

"Showroom at Sea," which debuted on the *Veendam* in May 2009, is a new concept in shipboard entertainment for Holland America. Its centerpiece is an innovative musical repertory company made up of seasoned Broadway performers. Created in partnership with Stiletto Entertainment, producers of Emmy-winning television shows and concert tours, the repertory company is made up of four pop/rock and two classical vocalists backed by a 14-piece orchestra and a comedian. Meant to be a modern-day take on the classic nightclub, Showroom at Sea, with state-of-the-art technology, offers a different show and themed environment nightly. Cast members come with such credits as *Les Miserables* and *Rent* on Broadway and the national tour of *Mamma Mia*, among others. The venue's main stage was completely redesigned to provide a seamless transition between the room and the stage. The room has all new seating and an enlarged dance floor, enabling guests to combine cocktails, dancing, and a show. Each evening also features unique drink menus and table settings. The similar attraction will be installed in the other *Statendam*-class ships in 2010.

The casino offers blackjack, Caribbean poker, roulette, dice, and slot machines. Outside, kinetic artist Yaacov Agam created a computer display wall that shows thousands of constantly changing images. The Explorer's Lounge has traditionally been passengers' favorite spot for after-dinner drinks.

Another Signature of Excellence initiative is **Explorations Café**, powered by the *New York Times*, a new concept not only for Holland America, but also for the cruise world. The venue is a combination 2,000-book library, puzzle corner, Internet center, music-listening area, DVD library, and Torrefazione coffee bar. Located on Upper Promenade Deck 8, it replaced the card room, which was moved to the former Queen's Room section of the dining room.

Designed to replicate the comfort of a living room, it is operated in cooperation with the *New York Times* and has *Times* crossword-puzzle tables with write-on, wipe-off tops, plus cases of memorabilia from the *Times* archives. The electronic edition of the *New York Times* is downloaded to the room's computers. The daily quiz and crossword puzzle can be picked up at the desk. The area also includes a huge globe, educational programs on interactive flat screens, and Discovery Channel programming on a larger screen. There's a DVD library in the Explorations Café, where passengers can choose from 1,000 titles for $3 per day. Internet access is $0.75 per minute; wireless hot spots are located in various lounges around the ship for use with your own laptop. Wireless card rentals are $10 per day.

The **Crow's Nest**, traditionally a sedate observation lounge by day and disco by night, got a big Signature of Excellence makeover and has lively nightlife, thanks largely to the venue's design changes. *Ryndam*'s lounge is outfitted in shocking pink and other bold colors, and private seating areas are cordoned off by soft curtains. There are disco lights, a dance floor, a high-tech video wall, and a striking bar of back-lit onyx.

SPORTS, FITNESS, AND BEAUTY The ships' upper decks cater to active passengers. At the center of a teak expanse on the Navigation Deck is one of two outdoor swimming pools. On the Lido, a second swimming pool, with whirlpools and wading pool, has a retractable glass roof for use in cool weather—a great asset on Alaskan cruises. A tiled wall with a bronze sculpture of dolphins frames the area.

The topside Sports Deck has two practice tennis courts (on *Statendam*, the space is a jogging track). A teak deck encircling the Lower Promenade Deck has space for deck chairs, walkers, and joggers (four laps equal one mile). The fleetwide Passport to Fitness program awards points for daily exercises and activities that can be redeemed for prizes, such as a belt pack or T-shirt.

The **Greenhouse Spa and Salon,** a brand exclusive to Holland America, is available fleetwide. It has features developed in the Texas-based Greenhouse Spa chain, such as a Strawberry Herbal Back Cleanse, a hydrotherapy pool (day use, $20), and a thermal suite ($20 for the day). Operated by Steiner, the larger, more sophisticated facility has more treatment rooms, a steam and aromatic room, a relaxation room with heated ceramic lounges, and a wide range of skin, body, and hair treatments, as well as couples' massage rooms, reflecting a change in the demands of today's passengers. The ocean-view gym is equipped with treadmills, step machines, rowing machines, stationary bikes, and a Hydra fitness circuit with ten resistance machines. In front of the spa is an outside deck for exercise classes.

At **Half Moon Cay,** HAL's private island, which is a stop on most Caribbean itineraries and Panama Canal cruises, passengers have a great variety of activities to enjoy as a result of the Signature of Excellence program. These include a horseback riding and swimming excursion, a stingray adventure, a guided personal watercraft tour, and an aqua park with large water toys in the shapes of whales, octopuses, sharks, and dolphins. Other recreation includes scuba diving, catch-and-release deep-sea fishing, eco-tours by glass-bottom boat, kayaking, and parasailing. The island has a water-sports center, a playground, volleyball, basketball, nature trails, and a bird reserve. Passengers can have a beachside massage or rent a private, air-conditioned beachfront cabana for the day ($249).

CHILDREN'S FACILITIES All ships have year-round, full-time youth coordinators (one for every 30 children, more during holidays and summer). They organize and supervise programs for three age groups: generally, 5–8 years, 9–12 years, and teens. On some ships, Club HAL accepts children as young as 3 years old.

Daily activities for children ages 5–8 may include storytelling, candy-bar bingo, games, arts and crafts, charades, and ice-cream parties. Those ages 9–12 might learn to putt, have dance lessons or theme parties, or participate in deck sports or scavenger hunts, table tennis, or karaoke. Older children have a teen disco, dance lessons, arcade games, sports, card games, trivia contests, bingo, and movies. All have pizza and Coke-tail parties and ship tours. The ships have wading pools, activity rooms with video games, and children's menus listing such favorites as hamburgers, hot dogs, fish and chips, chicken fingers, and pizza.

On the first night of each cruise, kids and their parents meet the youth coordinator, who outlines the program. At sea, there is at least one activity in the morning, afternoon, and evening; none are scheduled on port days. Babysitting by staff volunteers (availability isn't guaranteed) costs $8 per hour for the first child and $5 more per hour for additional children from the same family.

One of the main objectives of the Signature of Excellence program—to appeal to the growing market of multigenerational vacationers—can be seen in the expanded Club HAL facilities. Teens have their own area, which is supervised but off-limits to adults. The **Loft** lounge has a dance floor, lights, music videos, and DVDs. Upstairs is the **Oasis,** the teens' private sun deck, complete with its own waterfall, covered snack areas, and hammocks. Two rooms loaded with games and toys for kids ages 3–7 accommodate 20 children each, with additional areas available as needed. For the 8- to 12-year-olds, entertainment includes PlayStations, Internet access, arcade games, and karaoke. Among other enhancements is a Port Day program, allowing parents to place kids in Club HAL 8 a.m.–5 p.m., including a boxed lunch. Mom and Dad are then free to go off the ship and enjoy the destination. From 10 p.m. to midnight, parents can take advantage of Club HAL's After Hours program, which runs $5 per child per hour.

SHORE EXCURSIONS It's almost hard to believe, but Holland America offers more than 2,500 shore excursions in 296 ports of call in 60 countries. They range from active, exotic, cultural, and historic to nature and adventure tours, and from a few hours to a full day, and include those suitable for families, as well as unusual experiences like Formula One racing in Barcelona. The 106 Medallion Collection, intended for those who want something more than a typical tour, offers extraordinary adventures and exclusive events; group size is limited. Part of the Medallion series is the Signature Collection, personalized tours with private luxury vehicle, professional driver, and English-speaking guide. The custom-designed tours are available in four- and eight-hour segments and best for parties of two to eight.

Holland America has been a leader in Alaska travel and offers programs ranging from cruising near glaciers on day boats to rail travel on the domed McKinley Explorer. In Ketchikan, you can have a half-day sightseeing/flightseeing combination, or you can kayak, fish, or pan for gold. Every Glacier Route cruise visits Sitka's Alaska Raptor Rehabilitation Center, dedicated to returning injured bald eagles to the wild. Noting the trend for wilderness expeditions, Holland America recently added new adventure excursions to its Alaska program to now offer more than 250 options throughout Alaska and the Yukon.

In the Caribbean, in addition to standard offerings, there are environmentally sensitive eco-tours focusing on the islands' nature, history, and culture, which are designed to help passengers better understand the islands. They range from guided rain forest hikes to air tours to view archaeological sites. European shore excursions can be expensive on any cruise line, but HAL's seem to cost more than its closest competitor. Save money by taking standard city tours on your own and buying the cruise line's excursions that are unique or that visit attractions difficult to reach.

Note: Shore excursions can be booked on Holland America's Web site. Be very sure of your tour choices before you buy. In addition to the industry's standard policy of no refunds for cancellations 24 hours before a tour, Holland America charges a 10% fee for any cancellation made ten days prior to the cruise sailing. There are other, rather complicated cancellation fees and credits for such items as a private car or minivan; you should inquire before making a commitment.

THE SHIPS The *Rotterdam*, the line's sixth ship bearing that name, upholds Holland America's tradition in contemporary style but little resembles *Rotterdam V*. She's more like the *Statendam* quartet, with almost the same layout and with many of their most popular features. Both she and her slightly larger sister, *Amsterdam*, were designated as the line's flagships and introduced new features. Their speed gives HAL more flexibility in designing itineraries. Each has more deluxe cabins with verandas, an alternative restaurant, extensive facilities for the disabled, and a private lounge and concierge desk for suite passengers.

In late 2009, the *Rotterdam* got the same upgrade and increase in the number of cabins as the *Statendam* group, including 32 veranda cabins added to her aft portion and 39 new lanai cabins on the Lower Promenade Deck with direct access to the Promenade. Twenty-three spa cabins, near the Greenhouse Spa, were created from existing cabins and have special in-room spa amenities and exclusive in-cabin spa treatments. In dry dock, the aft deck was expanded to create The Retreat, the resort pool concept, and Mix, the bar with three separate areas—Martinis, Champagne, and Spirits & Ales. She also was fitted for the casual Canaletto restaurant and for the Showroom at Sea.

The *Volendam* and *Zaandam*, built in Italy, created a new generation of luxury cruise ships that combined features from the *Statendam* group and the *Rotterdam*. The twins are about as long and wide as *Rotterdam*, but their tonnage is greater because they have more passenger cabins—1,432 compared with *Rotterdam*'s 1,404 passengers.

The principal architect for all four ships, Frans Dingemans, created interiors in keeping with HAL's tradition and passenger preferences. He describes *Rotterdam*'s interiors as an evolution from the *Statendam* group. The enhancements are a three-story atrium (oval instead of octagonal), a larger Lido restaurant, and a dome over the Lido pool. But *Rotterdam* differs from *Statendam*-class ships in other ways too: She's longer, wider, and more spacious, as well as faster. Because she's designed to be speedier, the hull is longer and more tapered. Like *Rotterdam V*, she has two funnels aft. Three stairwells put passengers never farther than about 125 feet from access to the public rooms. The layout of the public rooms on the *Volendam* and *Zaandam* is the same as that of *Rotterdam*. *Rotterdam*'s interior was inspired by (not a replica of) her predecessor, though some of her namesake's rich interiors

Amsterdam	QUALITY 8	VALUE C
Rotterdam	QUALITY 9	VALUE C
Volendam/Zaandam	QUALITY 8	VALUE C
REGISTRY Netherlands	LENGTH 780/781 feet	BEAM 105.8 feet
CABINS 690/702/716	DRAFT 29.8/24 feet	SPEED 25/23 knots
MAXIMUM PASSENGERS	PASSENGER DECKS 10	ELEVATORS 12
1,380/1,404/1,432	CREW 647	SPACE RATIO 44/47/42

and 1930s Art Deco style have been incorporated. More woods and darker colors were used to achieve a classy as well as classic ambience.

A huge sculpture fills the *Rotterdam*'s three-deck atrium. More a curiosity than a work of art, it represents a Flemish clock tower with 14 timepieces and is embellished with mermaids, dolphins, and snakes. All HAL ships have valuable art collections, but *Rotterdam*'s is the most varied, with museum-quality antiques that evoke the Dutch maritime tradition. The most memorable are life-size replicas of the terra-cotta warriors found at Xi'an, China.

In the *Volendam*'s three-deck-tall atrium is a monumental crystal sculpture by Luciano Vistosi, one of Italy's leading contemporary glass artists. He also created the towering atrium sculptures of the *Maasdam* and *Veendam*. The centerpiece of the *Zaandam*'s atrium is an impressive pipe organ with mechanical figures of dancing musicians. The organ may be played by hand or operated automatically. Both ships showcase multimillion-dollar art collections, including works created specifically for the vessels by world-class artists.

HAL invested $1 million to add a closed-loop system for the hearing impaired, Braille directories and directional buttons in the elevators, and large-print menus for the visually impaired. In cabins, light-flashing telephones and bed-shaker alarm systems are available.

The atrium centerpiece of *Amsterdam* is an ornate astrolabe clock tower with a carillon in its base and four faces: an astrolabe, world clock, planetary clock, and astrological clock. On display near the **Crow's Nest Lounge** is *Four Seasons*, a gold-plated sculpture of four pieces, originally created for the *Nieuw Amsterdam* of 1938 and bought from a private collector. At the Lido pool, passengers will see a trio by British sculptor Susanna Holt—two brown bears fishing, their cub nearby.

ITINERARIES *See* Itinerary Index.

CABINS Standard cabins, a roomy 185–195 square feet, are similar to those in the *Statendam* group. On the *Rotterdam*, another 120 deluxe cabins at 245 square feet have whirlpool baths, DVD players, minibars, refrigerators, and verandas with chaise lounges.

Navigation Deck 7 has 40 suites, all with verandas, a private lounge, and concierge station where passengers may settle accounts, book shore excursions, and make special requests. The area's glass walls overlook the corridor, but when privacy is wanted, an electric current makes the high-tech glass opaque. Each of four penthouse suites offers living room, dining area and kitchen, bedroom, dressing areas, and steward's entrance. Two suites are wheelchair accessible. The *Amsterdam* has 15 more suites than her sibling.

The *Volendam* and *Zaandam* have more deluxe veranda cabins than their sister ships. The penthouse, 28 deluxe suites, and 168 Verandah mini-suites and deluxe cabins have large verandas, DVD players, whirlpool bath, and minibar. All cabins have a sofa, hair dryer, telephone with voice mail and automated wake-up service, music system, and television. They are furnished with twin beds, convertible to a queen size.

Specifications Rotterdam/Amsterdam, 139/135 inside cabins, 358/383 outside, 36/50 suites, 161/172 cabins with verandas, some adjoining cabins. *Rotterdam*, 39 lanai cabins; 23 spa cabins; 498 standard cabins with twin beds; 618 with convertible twins or queen beds; 284 with third and fourth berths. No singles. 21 wheelchair accessible (*Amsterdam*, 23); four have connecting doors for accompanying companions. *Volendam/Zaandam*, 1 penthouse and 28 suites with verandas, 168 deluxe cabins (120 deluxe mini-suites) with verandas, 383 standard outside cabins, 136 standard inside, 21 wheelchair-accessible cabins.

DINING   *Rotterdam*'s elegant, bi-level **La Fontaine Dining Room** spans the Promenade and Upper Promenade decks. Decor mingles Venetian, contemporary, and baroque designs. Panoramic windows overlook the stern. The ceiling represents a star-filled night sky broken by circles of colored glass. Around the balcony are hundreds of individually lighted Venetian-glass morning glories. On the back wall are two giant murals of waterbirds, recalling *Rotterdam V*'s famous Ritz-Carlton room.

In the large, informal **Lido restaurant,** passengers can enjoy a full breakfast and lunch, including hot dogs and hamburgers grilled to order or make-it-yourself tacos. An ice-cream-sundae bar, tea, and coffee are available all day. Alternative evening dining is offered several days of every cruise.

The *Volendam*'s impressive, bi-level **Rotterdam Dining Room** at the stern has huge windows and an elegant staircase connecting the two levels. Overhead, six large wrought-iron chandeliers designed by Italian artist Gilbert Lebigre hang from the ceiling; they are lighted by fiber optics.

FACILITIES AND ACTIVITIES   The *Rotterdam*'s **Ambassador Lounge and Tropic Bar** (Upper Promenade Deck) has a movable wall allowing different configurations. After dinner, the lounge is a large room for dancing; in late evening, it's an intimate piano bar with the piano on a turntable.

Repeat passengers will recognize the ships' traditional collection of small public rooms. The adjoining **Half Moon** and **Hudson** rooms accommodate up to 115 people for meetings or parties. **Ocean Bar** has replicas of items from the old Holland America building in Rotterdam; a copy of the sculpture of Henry Hudson's ship, *Halve Maen* ("half moon"), crowns the roof. The larger **Explorers' Lounge** focuses on the maritime heritages of Italy and Holland in a large mural of Renaissance Venice. The dance floor is made of Italian marble in a floral pattern.

The Crow's Nest Lounge has floor-to-ceiling windows around three quarters of this delightful daytime observation lounge. The room has three sections. To one side is a **Tea Area** decorated with porcelain and silver. To the other is a **Captain's Area,** with leather chairs and old ship models. At center is a circular bar and dance floor that become the nighttime disco.

Queen's Lounge, the bi-level main show lounge, has state-of-the-art sound and lighting equipment, a rotating stage, hydraulic lifts, and a dance floor. Deep red, burgundy, and orange decor reflects the opulent age of sea travel. Huge, gold-etched Murano glass chandeliers resemble upside-down umbrellas. The theater curtain is hand-painted satin in maroon, gold, and black.

Volendam's main show lounge, the two-level **Frans Hals Lounge** in Art Deco design, was inspired by the city of Amsterdam's famous Tuschinski Theater. The multicolored ceiling and colonnades contrast with dark wood walls and huge, colorful ceramic vases. The **Casino Bar,** the ship's sports bar, showcases cinematic memorabilia. On *Zaandam*, the **Casino Bar** spotlights music. The ship also has the cruise line's traditional **Explorer's Lounge, Ocean**

Bar, Piano Bar, Library, Half Moon Room, and **Hudson Room,** the last of which serves as a card or meeting room, and **Crow's Nest,** which doubles as an observation lounge and nightclub. The **Wajang Theater,** equipped with writing tables and headphones for meetings, has become the venue for the **Culinary Arts Institute** as part of the Signature of Excellence program.

On *Volendam*, the Navigation Deck was extended aft to accommodate additional cabins, and the outdoor swimming pool moved to the Lido Deck. The arrangement provides direct access between indoor and outdoor swimming pools and the **Lido restaurant.** For *Volendam*'s Lido pool area, British artist Susanna Holt created a bronze sculpture of arcing dolphins, similar to those found on other HAL ships.

Volendam was the first of the fleet to have an Internet center with eight computer terminals and a printer. (It's now part of the Explorations Café powered by the *New York Times*.) Open 24 hours, it is staffed 9 a.m.–noon, 2–6 p.m., and 9 p.m.–midnight. There is a one-time activation fee of $3.95 and basic charge of $0.75 per minute with a five-minute minimum; bulk pricing packages start at 100 minutes for $55. Instructions for use are posted on each computer terminal. Internet centers and wireless Internet service are available fleetwide. Laptop rental is $20 per day or free with purchase of a time plan; wireless card, $10 per day. CruisE-mail offers passengers an e-mail address, if they are unable to access their own. There is a $3.95 charge to send a CruisE-mail (in addition to the basic time charges), but passengers only pay the time charge to receive incoming messages.

SPORTS, FITNESS, AND BEAUTY The ships have a **Greenhouse Spa.** (See *Statendam* group for details.) The Lower Promenade Deck is a wraparound teak deck, ideal for walking or cooling off in the line's traditional wooden deck chairs.

All Holland America ships that call at the line's private island, Half Moon Cay, benefit from Signature of Excellence enhancements, such as horseback riding and swimming excursion, the stingray adventure, and aqua park with large water toys in the shapes of whales, octopuses, sharks, and dolphins. The new activities augment the cay's array of excursions—scuba diving, fishing, eco-tours, kayaking, and its water-sports center, playground, volleyball, basketball, nature trails, and bird reserve.

CHILDREN'S FACILITIES The Sports Deck has a playroom with craft-making areas, video games, and a teen disco. As part of the Signature of Excellence program, they have Club HAL facilities. (See "Children's Facilities" under the Statendam group for details.)

THE SHIP The *Prinsendam* comes to the line with an illustrious history as the *Seabourn Sun* and *Royal Viking Sun*, having been the prize of Cunard's purchase of Royal Viking Line in 1994. The *Sun* was given a $15 million renovation, renamed, and moved to Seabourn, which turned out to be a mismatch.

When the ship was transferred to Holland America Line in 2002, Swedish architect Thomas Tillberg, the vessel's original interior designer, and Frans Dingemans, HAL's main architect, were engaged to oversee major renovations that transformed her into a HAL ship. The ship emerged with a redesigned interior, new decor, and renamed decks and public rooms to correspond with the other ships in the HAL fleet. Artwork was added, including a frosted and sculptured glass cylinder and wall murals by Bolae for the circu-

Prinsendam	QUALITY 7	VALUE C
REGISTRY Netherlands	LENGTH 669 feet	BEAM 95 feet
CABINS 398	DRAFT 23.5 feet	SPEED 21.8 knots
MAXIMUM PASSENGERS	PASSENGER DECKS 9	ELEVATORS 4
837	CREW 443	SPACE RATIO 48

lar atrium. The *Prinsendam* was named for a sentimental favorite that was lost after an accident in Alaskan waters several years ago.

The sleek vessel has a sharply raked bow and a beautiful profile, which distinguishes her from the rectangular shape of newer ships. The Finnish-built *Prinsendam* is a spacious ship. Penthouse and deluxe veranda suites are palatial; standard cabins are as large as other ships' suites. Treats include walk-in closets, comfortable lounges, a swim-up bar in the main pool, a lap pool, a spa, and a golf simulator of famous courses, plus some unusual features like a same-level gangway for easy access to docks or tenders; air-conditioned tenders with lavatories and catamaran hulls for stability; and two high-speed man-overboard boats. Fine wood and high-quality fabrics are used throughout. Public rooms and facilities are on three center and two top decks.

Prinsendam has received Signature of Excellence enhancements, including a Culinary Arts Center and flat-panel televisions in all cabins and suites. The ship operates a Greenhouse Spa and a Pinnacle Grill. Since *Prinsendam* sails longer voyages around the globe and attracts a mature audience, it did not receive expanded youth facilities. Due to space limitations (she is half the size of the Vista-class ships), *Prinsendam* also does not have the Explorations Café.

ITINERARIES *See* Itinerary Index.

CABINS Cabins are spread over eight decks. Seventeen categories offer four accommodation types: suites, deluxe veranda outside, outside with a large window, and standard inside cabins. All suites and deluxe cabins (more than a third of accommodations) have verandas. HAL spent millions of dollars upgrading cabins and giving them a new, more modern look in the Signature of Excellence style. Bathrooms received new sinks, tile, and plumbing repairs, while verandas got new doors, teak decks, and rattan furniture. All the ship's bathrooms have been renovated and upgraded.

All cabins have flat-panel televisions with CNN, TNT, ESPN, TCM, Discovery, and ship's programming, phone, minifridge, locking drawers, safe, hair dryer, refrigerator, and walk-in closets (cruising's first, but not found in wheelchair-accessible cabins). Most bathrooms have tub and shower. All but a few have twin beds convertible to kings, and most have a small sitting area with love seat, table, and chair. Two decks have launderettes. Room service is available 24 hours a day.

The largest, most luxurious suites are on the top two decks. Dividers separate the bedroom and sitting areas. Additional amenities for deluxe cabins and suites include bathrobes, extra-luxurious towels, DVD and video library access, personalized stationery, veranda, and floor-to-ceiling windows. In addition, penthouse and deluxe veranda suites have the private Neptune Lounge, staffed by a concierge, for their exclusive use. They receive afternoon tea and hors d'oeuvres before dinner upon request; a private cocktail party with the captain; an exclusive Indonesian rijsttafel luncheon hosted by the captain and hotel manager; and complimentary corsages and boutonnieres on the first formal night, among other amenities. The sole penthouse veranda suite was one of the first on a cruise ship to have a whirlpool bath surrounded by picture windows facing the sea. Promenade Deck has lanai cabins, each complete with private deck area and whirlpool—a new concept for HAL.

In early 2010, as part of the continuing Signature of Excellence enhancement program, 21 cabins, most with verandas, were added to the *Prinsendam*. With the addition of cabins aft, the pool deck was expanded with more space and more deck chairs and a new sea-view bar. Sixteen of the new cabins are deluxe with verandas, and two are slightly smaller. Four are standard inside staterooms. As is customary on *Prinsendam*, the new cabin bathrooms were given elegant appointments. Other amenities include Mariner Dream Beds, Elemis spa toiletries, a large vanity mirror, fruit basket, flat-panel television and DVD player, quality showerhead, and more.

Specifications   25 inside cabins, 373 outside, including suites; 68 suites; 1 penthouse suite; 151 with verandas; 82 deluxe. Standard dimensions, 191 square feet. 344 outside cabins and suites with two lower beds, convertible to kings; 19 suites with two lower beds convertible to kings and a sofa bed; 3 single cabins (2 outside, 1 inside); 8 wheelchair accessible.

DINING *Prinsendam*'s dining room on Lower Promenade Deck has large windows on three sides, providing a panorama of sea and scenery. Passengers are served in two seatings, with assigned tables for dinner and in open seatings for breakfast and lunch. Tables seating two, four, six, or eight are set with fresh flowers, fine china, crystal, and silverware.

A major change that HAL made with her acquisition was the switch from one- to two-seating dining, which means the main dining room no longer needs to seat all passengers at once. However, the Lido restaurant required expansion. The **Pinnacle Grill at the Odyssey,** the handsome alternative restaurant, features steaks, seafood, and Pacific Northwest wines. Entrees are prepared on a hot grill to guarantee tenderness and taste. Reservations are required, and the service carries a charge of $20 for dinner and $10 for lunch (sea days only).

The **Lido restaurant** is the venue for casual buffet breakfast, lunch, dinner, and late-night snacks. The variety of food here is impressive and includes a salad bar, soups, hot entrees, carvery, pizzeria, cafe, taco bar, ice-cream bar, and dessert area; 24-hour coffee and tea are available. The restaurant, located aft on Lido Deck, has been expanded to both sides of the ship with two service lines. A wall of windows overlooks the deck and sea. There's outdoor seating on the terrace, which resembles a sidewalk cafe with a teak floor. The **Terrace Grill** serves hot dogs and hamburgers poolside.

FACILITIES AND ACTIVITIES Promenade Deck holds most of the public rooms, including a casino, the **Explorer's Lounge,** a movie theater showing first-run films, a card room, the library, boutiques, shore excursions office, the 24-hour front desk, and the show lounge. *Prinsendam* offers a program of port and theme lectures similar to those on other HAL ships and has Signature of Excellence's new **Culinary Arts Center** (see *Ryndam* for details).

The redesigned **Queen's Lounge** showroom was given a new stage and state-of-the-art sound and light to bring the facility up to par with newer HAL ships. Production shows feature a cast of seven top-notch entertainers. In front of the stage is a sizable dance floor. Typical of ships built in the 1980s, the lounge has a low ceiling and poor sight lines from seats in the rear. The Ocean Bar, with bandstand and dance floor, is action central in the evening. Forward of the Ocean Bar is the **Internet Center** with 11 flat-panel computer stations and an art gallery.

The casino offers slot machines and roulette, craps, and blackjack tables. Just outside the casino is the **Java Bar and Café,** one of the ship's most popular spots. It leads to the handsome **Oak Room,** reminiscent of a men's club, with leather chairs in a wood-paneled setting. It's a cozy daytime retreat and popular for after-dinner drinks.

The busy Explorer's Lounge, opposite the casino, is one of the *Prinsendam*'s loveliest rooms. It has a wall of windows with sea views and is decorated with Dutch etchings. In keeping with the Holland America fleet, there is a massive painting of 17th-century Dutch ships—in this case, being given a royal send-off on a voyage of exploration. Classical music is piped in during the day, and a trio plays classical favorites every evening. The lounge's comfortable leather chairs are popular with passengers who want to read, because the nearby **Erasmus Library** seats only four. Stairs lead to the dining room below. Above the bridge is an observation lounge with 180 degrees of wraparound windows facing the bow. It's a favorite perch for watching the world go by wherever the ship may roam. A pianist plays here in the evenings.

SPORTS, FITNESS, AND BEAUTY A wind-sheltered swimming pool on Lido Deck has a whirlpool and swim-up bar and is ringed by a sunning area. Outdoors are shuffleboard, table tennis, and quoits. A teak deck for walking wraps the Lower Promenade Deck, and an Astroturf jogging track encircles the Sports Deck. The wood-paneled **Golf Club and Pro Shop** on Deck 5 is a cozy hangout for golfers, with comfortable seating and magazines. It has a sophisticated golf simulator of 22 courses, including many on the PGA tour (similar to the high-tech simulator on the *Zuiderdam*). A large golf cage is found on the Sports Deck (12), as well as a versatile sports court for volleyball, basketball, and tennis.

The **Greenhouse Spa** has a lap pool with two whirlpools and a glass-enclosed fitness facility with toning and cardiovascular equipment. The spa boasts nine treatment rooms and an array of treatment choices. Also available are a sauna and beauty salon.

THE SHIPS With the arrival of the *Noordam* in 2006, Holland America completed the Vista-class 84,000-ton cruise ships. The ships take their names from the "vista" points of the compass: *Zuiderdam*, south; *Oosterdam*, east; *Westerdam*, west; and *Noordam*, north. The "-dam" suffix follows the line's century-old tradition for its passenger ships.

The Vista-class name, selected from an employee contest, is meant to represent the ships' forward-looking design and HAL's future direction with ships that are the most advanced and most luxurious Holland America has ever built. Constructed at the Italian shipyard Fincantieri Cantieri Navali, these ships more than doubled Holland America's passenger capacity in less than four years. *Noordam* came with Signature of Excellence facilities and

Noordam	QUALITY 9	VALUE B
Oosterdam	QUALITY 8	VALUE C
Westerdam	QUALITY 8	VALUE B
Zuiderdam	QUALITY 8	VALUE C
REGISTRY Netherlands	LENGTH 935 feet	BEAM 105.8 feet
CABINS 958	DRAFT 24 feet	SPEED 22 knots
MAXIMUM PASSENGERS	PASSENGER DECKS 12	ELEVATORS 14
1,848/1,916	CREW 800	SPACE RATIO 46

amenities, and *Oosterdam* got its first makeover in late 2006. *Westerdam* and *Zuiderdam*, which already have some of the amenities, such as the Pinnacle Grill, the Greenhouse Spa, and the Euro-top mattresses, have added others. Those ships also will receive new aft cabins, increasing their passenger capacity to 1,918, matching that of *Noordam*. In early summer 2009, in the second phase of the Signature of Excellence program, 34 new cabins, a larger Pinnacle Grill, the Pinnacle Bar, a specialty wine bar, and the Canaletto Italian restaurant were added to *Oosterdam*. Other changes included a new location for the Explorations Café—powered by *The New York Times*—by the Crow's Nest, and the addition of Digital Workshops led by Microsoft-trained "techsperts," who teach computer skills, digital photography, and social media applications in a dedicated space with laptops. HAL expanded and updated *Oosterdam's* shopping arcade and added the exclusive jewelry shop Merabella. The *Oosterdam* also received a new home theatre–style screening room for small-group audio-visual presentations, video and DVD viewing, and private parties.

Zuiderdam was the line's determined effort to attract younger passengers, broaden its base, and lower the average age of its customers. The ship offers a more contemporary image—with the use of bright colors (orange, purple, and magenta), suede walls, and jazzy patterns in Holland America's first disco—and such 21st-century amenities as data ports in cabins and a high-tech golf simulator. *Zuiderdam* definitely is a departure from past Holland America ships. Some people see in it the influence of Carnival Cruises and say it was time for updating the HAL look; others prefer the line's traditional style. Yet, there's no mistaking the ship is a Holland America product.

Traditional fresh flowers are everywhere, and so is the multimillion-dollar art collection and signature HAL rooms like the Explorer's Lounge, Half Moon, Hudson Room, and Ocean Bar. There's also a three-deck-high atrium with Art Deco styling and a fascinating Waterford crystal sea horse suspended from the ceiling. In a cruise-ship first, Holland America offers a free self-guided tour of the ship's outstanding art and antiques collection using an iPod—now available on all its ships.

Before the introduction of the larger *Eurodam*, this quartet were HAL's largest ships. Passengers benefit by having bigger cabins and more (but not necessarily larger) lounges and other public areas in an asymmetrical layout that reduces the impression of an immense ship.

Other new features include a cabaret-style show lounge, as well as a new three-deck main show lounge, a casual around-the-clock cafe, an Internet cafe, data ports in all cabins, the largest spa facilities in the fleet, an extensive **Club HAL** children's facility with inside and outside play areas, two interior promenade decks, an exterior covered promenade deck encircling the entire ship, a large Lido pool with a retractable dome, and the signature Crow's Nest observation lounge.

CABINS One of the most significant differences in the Vista ships is their large number of veranda cabins. Eighty-five percent of the accommodations are outside, and two-thirds have balconies. The deluxe veranda outside cabins—the largest category of accommodations—have 200 square feet, plus a roomy, 54-square-foot veranda. All cabins are furnished with sofas, minibars, hair dryer, safe, and telephone with voice mail and data port. Most cabins have tubs, an amenity normally found in more costly suites on other lines. There is a Neptune Lounge with a concierge for the exclusive use of penthouse and deluxe veranda suite passengers. In addition to 28 wheelchair-accessible cabins, there is a dedicated elevator for wheelchair users, assistance with tender embarkation, and two tenders equipped with wheelchair-accessible platforms.

Oosterdam's recent refurbishment included the addition of Elemis toiletries, Euro-top Mariner's Dream Beds, deluxe waffle–terry cloth robes, Egyptian cotton towels, flat-panel televisions and DVD players, makeup mirrors, massage showerheads, hair dryers, fresh flowers, and complimentary fruit baskets. The other Vista-class ships will have similar amenities when their makeovers are completed.

Specifications 958 cabins, 623 with verandas. 2 penthouse suites (1,318 square feet), 60 deluxe suites (510–700 square feet), 100 superior suites (398 square feet), 461 deluxe outside (254 square feet), 165 standard outside cabins (185 square feet), 136 inside (170–200 square feet), 28 wheelchair accessible cabins.

DINING The two-story **Vista Dining Room,** the main restaurant, has floor-to-ceiling windows on three sides and two grand staircases. Each level has its own galley, which makes for faster service. On the *Westerdam*, the dining room ceiling is made up of colorful Chihuly-designed glass around the light fixtures. The large, bright **Lido restaurant** is designed in food-court style, with specialty areas offering made-to-order omelets, deli sandwiches, Italian and Asian specialties, salads, etc. Outside, the large Lido pool area is covered by a retractable dome; a sculpture of polar bears is a reminder of Holland America's role in Alaska cruising.

The **Pinnacle Grill** is the ship's specialty, reservations-only restaurant and is twice the size of those on her sister ships, but the decor with elaborate silver chairs and overhead lights is in keeping with their rococo style. The tables are set with Bulgari china for displaying the featured Pacific Northwest cuisine. There is a $20 per-person charge for dinner; $10 for lunch (sea days).

SERVICE The *Noordam* has received especially good reviews, particularly for the friendly and gracious Indonesian and Filipino crew for their unobtrusive, attentive service.

FACILITIES AND ACTIVITIES **Queen's Lounge** is a versatile venue where cabaret-style shows are staged and movies shown; the **Windstar Café,** which is open 20 hours a day, offers specialty coffees, smoothies, pastries, and snacks; and HAL has its first disco. The three-tier, bright red **Vista Lounge,** with a bar near the entrance, an orchestra pit, and $10 million of the latest sound and light equipment, is where big production shows are staged. Currently playing are *Stage & Screen* (based on movie musicals) and *Under the Boardwalk*.

Passengers on the *Oosterdam* see *Tommy Tune's Paparazzi*, a multimillion-dollar musical extravaganza created by the nine-time Tony award-winning director, choreographer, dancer, and singer Tommy Tune; it was the first show he created specifically for a cruise ship. The show, which pays homage to our fascination with celebrities and the photographers who chase them, was first seen on the *Westerdam*. As popular as ever is the Crow's Nest, the topside observation lounge, where passengers escape for quiet by day and dancing by night.

SPORTS, FITNESS, AND BEAUTY The **Greenhouse Spa,** operated by the Steiner Group, is more than twice the size of the spas on the original *Statendam*-class ships. It has 11 treatment rooms (including one for couples), a large hydro-therapy pool, and offers features such as a unisex thermal suite with aromatic steam and sauna chambers.

As noted earlier, all Holland America ships that call at Half Moon Cay already benefit from some Signature of Excellence initiatives, such as the horseback riding and swimming excursion and the stingray adventure. The new activities augment the island's array of excursions—scuba diving, fishing, eco-tours, kayaking, and its water sports center, playground, volleyball, basketball, nature trails, and bird reserve.

CHILDREN'S FACILITIES **Club HAL,** enhanced with Signature of Excellence features, has new and expanded facilities like those on the *Ryndam* and other ships in the fleet. See "Children's Facilities" in the *Statendam* group for details.

THE SHIPS Holland America's newest ship, the 86,000-ton *Eurodam*, a Panamax passenger ship, is the first of two vessels designated as Signature class and part of its Signature of Excellence program. Costing $450 million, *Eurodam* was launched in 2008; her sister will arrive in 2010. The name *Eurodam* breaks with the Holland America tradition of reusing the name of a previous vessel (there has never been a *Eurodam*), but "Euro" certainly reflects the line's heritage and "-dam" retains the suffix used for all its vessels.

Eurodam is the same length and width as the Vista-class ships, but she has one more deck, which enabled the designers to add 63 more cabins, a new

Eurodam	QUALITY **9**	VALUE **B**
Nieuw Amsterdam	2010	
REGISTRY Netherlands	LENGTH 936 feet	BEAM 105.8 feet
CABINS 1,052	DRAFT 24 feet	SPEED 22 knots
MAXIMUM PASSENGERS	PASSENGER DECKS 13	ELEVATORS 14
2,044	CREW 929	SPACE RATIO 44

topside Pan-Asian restaurant and lounge, an Explorer's Lounge Bar, a premium wine-tasting lounge, a new Italian specialty restaurant in the Lido area, a luxury jewelry boutique, a new atrium bar, an enhanced and reconfigured show lounge, and a new photographic and imaging center. The Explorations Café has been relocated to the starboard side of the Crow's Nest Lounge, providing a new venue for passengers who want to relax, read, listen to music, or simply watch the world go by.

The *Eurodam* also has Signature of Excellence upgraded amenities and facilities, including a Culinary Arts Center (presented by *Food and Wine* magazine), an expanded Greenhouse Spa with a thermal suite and hydropool, HAL's largest gym, and extensive youth facilities. Like all Holland America ships, *Eurodam* showcases a multimillion-dollar art collection ranging from the Dutch Golden Age to dramatic, contemporary sculpture. The collection can be viewed on a self-guided tour with an iPod free of charge.

The *Nieuw Amsterdam, Eurodam*'s twin, will debut in 2010, on a 12-day Mediterranean voyage. The ship reflects her name—the one early Dutch explorers gave to New York City—with interiors following a New York theme featuring a Manhattan restaurant and a skyscraper theme for starters.

CABINS More than 67% of *Eurodam*'s cabins have verandas, and 86% have ocean views. Ten are a new style of cabin with floor-to-ceiling, wall-to-wall panoramic windows. As the first Signature-class ship, *Eurodam*'s cabins and suites are distinctly different in decor with a calm, monochromatic design accented with bursts of color, replacing the line's floral schemes of the past. The stylish, elegantly simple design by NB Design Group of Seattle is enhanced with rich wood tones and burnished nickel fixtures. Passenger corridors leading to the cabins are treated in the same contemporary theme. For the first time on a Holland America ship, cabins were added to the top decks. Just off the Crow's Nest on Deck 11 are ten French balcony–style veranda cabins; below on Deck 10 are 28 cabins with verandas and four forward-facing "panorama" rooms.

All accommodations enjoy Signature of Excellence premium amenities: Euro-top Mariner's Dream Beds, deluxe waffle–terry cloth robes, Egyptian cotton towels, flat-panel televisions, DVD players, makeup mirrors, massage showerheads, hair dryers, fresh flowers, complimentary fruit baskets, and a much-appreciated new feature—bright gooseneck lamps on each side of the bed so that you can read without disturbing your roommate or spouse. The Neptune Lounge is a private lounge for passengers in suites. *Eurodam* offers 56 luxury spa cabins and suites—the first ship in Holland America's fleet to have them—located on the two highest decks near the Greenhouse Spa. Special in-room spa amenities include organic cotton bathrobes and slippers, a Burmese teak mat for bath and shower, and an invigorating showerhead, as well as a body buff loofah mitt and aromatherapy bath salts. The cabins also have an iPod docking station, a yoga mat, a pedometer for use aboard ship, fitness DVD, a no-host minibar stocked with specialty waters, a cut-fruit tray at embarkation, and a spa concierge to book treatments. Each cabin reflects a nature theme, with walls of soft earth tones, fresh green accents, and a water feature in each.

Guests booking a spa cabin may order packages for spa services in advance or during the cruise. For example, the Body of Indulgence Package offers a hot stone massage and facial bamboo massage for $256; His Sanctuary includes a grooming treatment, shave, and deep-tissue massage for $189. Another amenity is in-room breakfast with spa selections, as well as an all-day room-service menu with spa selections.

Specifications Suites: 2 penthouse veranda (1,318 square feet); 60 deluxe veranda (510–700 square feet); 50 (2 spa) superior veranda (389 square feet). Outside: 586 (36 spa) deluxe veranda (254 square feet); 10 deluxe curved veranda (222 square feet); 189 (4 spa) standard (185 square feet). Inside: 155 (4 spa) standard (175–200 square feet). 30 wheelchair accessible (170–200 square feet).

DINING In addition to its elegant main dining room, Lido buffets, and Pacific Northwest–themed **Pinnacle Grill,** *Eurodam* has three new venues: **Tamarind,** a reservations-only Pan-Asian restaurant ($15 per person) on Deck 11; **Canaletto,** an Italian restaurant in a section of the Lido restaurant; and Slice, an all-day pizza eatery. **Silk Den,** a new quiet, elegant lounge adjacent to Tamarind, has wonderful views of the pool and the ocean.

The **Rembrandt** dining room has a new look with a ceiling that has a "wave effect" that can be lit with different colors. The menu ranges from steak and lobster to vegetarian and entrees from the region of the itinerary. "As You Wish" dining enables passengers to choose either the traditional preset seating and dining times or a flexible dining schedule that allows them to make reservations or simply walk up anytime during dining hours. The lower dining room is used for "As You Wish" dining, and the upper level has two fixed seatings.

Reservations-only Pinnacle Grill ($20 per person for dinner and $10 for lunch) features Sterling Silver beef and seafood, along with select wines from renowned Pacific Northwest vineyards. Canaletto features casual dining with waiter service, available each evening 5:30–9:30 p.m. It offers seven different menus from the various regions of Italy. Reservations are required, but there is no charge. Be sure to make your reservations early, as the restaurant is very popular. Indeed, Canaletto has been so popular that Holland America is adding it to most of its other ships. During dining hours, room service includes selections from the Rembrandt dining room menu as well as 24/7 pizza.

FACILITIES AND ACTIVITIES Among the familiar Holland America facilities found on the *Eurodam* are the **Crow's Nest,** the **Culinary Arts Center, Explorer's Lounge and Bar, Ocean Bar, Piano Bar, Sports Bar, Half Moon** and **Hudson** rooms, casino, show lounge, and **Northern Lights Nightclub.** Having one more deck than Vista-class ships enabled the line to move the *Eurodam's* Explorations Café–powered by *The New York Times*–to a new location on Deck 11 on the starboard side of the Crow's Nest. The **Atrium Bar** is new, as is the **Microsoft Digital Workshop.** Digital Workshops began in conjunction with Microsoft in 2008 on four ships, but they proved to be so popular that *Eurodam* and a dozen other ships have them now. The curriculum consists of 11 hour-long courses (free of charge) that teach various skills, such as how to transfer photos from camera to computer and send them via e-mail, turn photos and videos into a movie, and blog about your cruise. Each class is limited to 15 participants and is presented multiple times throughout the cruise by a Microsoft-trained "techspert."

SPORTS, FITNESS, AND BEAUTY   The enlarged **Greenhouse Spa and Salon** has saunas, massage rooms (including couple's massage rooms), a dry-float suite with massage option, thermal suites with a hydrotherapy pool, steam and aromatic rooms, heated ceramic lounges and in-suite showers, accessible treatment rooms, Tui Na relaxation area, a fitness center, and a beauty salon/barber shop with manicure and pedicure area.

Cabanas were introduced on Signature-class vessels; the *Eurodam* has 8 on the Lido deck around the midship pool and 14 on the Observation Deck in an area called **The Retreat.** The tented cabanas are furnished with modern woven chaises, ottomans, and upholstered settees. They come stocked with bathrobes and plush towels, handheld fans, an Evian spray mister, and iPods preloaded with great music. Chilled waters are available, and iced fruit skewers are served midmorning; frozen grapes, chocolate-covered strawberries, and a glass of Champagne are served in the afternoon. Lunch can be ordered from the **Terrace Grill** or Lido restaurant. Children up to the age of 16 are allowed in the cabanas, when accompanied by two adults. Discounted select services from the Greenhouse Spa are available on port days to passengers who book the cabanas. The cabanas may be rented for the day or for an entire cruise. The Retreat cabanas are $45 on port days and $75 on sea days; Lido cabanas are $30 and $50, respectively.

CHILDREN'S FACILITIES   The ship has Club HAL with features similar to such programs on other Holland America ships (see the *Statendam* class for descriptions). Holland America's youth Culinary Arts Center program teaches kids and teens how to cook and incorporates dishes from breakfast, lunch, dinner, and snacks into complimentary 45-minute-long classes.

MSC Cruises

6750 North Andrews Avenue
Fort Lauderdale, FL 33309
☎ **800-666-9333 or 954-772-6262**
FAX **908-605-2600**
www.msccruises.com

TYPE OF SHIPS New, modern superliners and megaliners; classic ocean liners.

TYPE OF CRUISES Mass market, designed for Europeans as much as North Americans—hence, more European in service and ambience.

CRUISE LINE'S STRENGTHS
- Italian style and service
- friendly, attentive crew
- itineraries
- value for money
- entertainment
- new, spacious ships

CRUISE LINE'S SHORTCOMINGS
- uneven cuisine
- language problems, especially on European cruises

FELLOW PASSENGERS MSC has two itineraries—New England/Canada and the Caribbean from late fall to early spring, and Europe year-round—which results in two sets of passengers. On our side of the Atlantic, up to 75% of passengers are North Americans, depending on the cruise; the average age of guests is 50 years and older, with an annual household income of $50,000 or more. Italian American fans and newlyweds are attracted by the line's Italian style. Most passengers have cruised before.

In Europe, up to 95% of passengers are Europeans, including Eastern Europeans, in a wide range of ages; a large number are families with children.

Recommended for Italophiles, less experienced travelers who want to sample European ambience with large-ship facilities; those looking for a real bargain; repeat cruisers who want to try something different.

Not recommended for Anyone who prefers small ships, an all-American atmosphere, or prefers to travel with Americans only; or people who have not traveled in foreign countries.

CRUISE AREAS AND SEASONS Caribbean, Mediterranean, northern Europe, South Africa, South America, and transatlantic seasonal positioning cruises.

THE LINE Starting in 1995, a Swiss group operating a global fleet of 325 container ships and 36 fast ferries, Mediterranean Shipping Company (MSC), acquired three cruise ships in less than four years. In 2005, the new line added another four ships, increasing its fleet from three to seven ships almost overnight and launching the line's bid to be a major player in Europe and North America. To underscore its intentions, MSC expanded its presence in North America with new offices in Fort Lauderdale, Florida, and hired one of the cruise industry's best-known executives, Rick Sasso, to head up the operation.

MSC continued to expand at a breathtaking pace. The 89,600-ton, 3,013-passenger *MSC Musica* was added in 2006. Her twin debuted in 2007, followed in 2008 by another sister, and the fourth in March 2010. MSC also built two larger, post-Panamax ships (too large to transit the Panama Canal) delivered in 2008 and 2009. These builds bring MSC Cruises' fleet to 12 ships—one of the youngest fleets in the industry. All the new ships have been christened by film star Sophia Loren, who has also served as the cruise line's spokesperson. And MSC has not finished building. The 93,000-ton, 2,550-passenger *MSC Meraviglia* is scheduled to be launched in 2011 and her sister, *MSC Favolosa*, in 2012. The total expansion investment exceeds $5.5 billion.

One of the largest cruise lines in the Mediterranean and still privately owned, MSC also sails to northern Europe, South Africa, and South America. In autumn 2010, the new *MSC Magnifica* arrives in New York to launch the line's first New England–Canada cruises. MSC Express allows for online check-in at all of MSC's major European ports and Fort Lauderdale, Florida. Passengers with completed forms are fast-tracked to the MSC Express Desk at the cruise terminal. Also, you can follow MSC on Twitter@MscCruisesUSA or **www.twitter.com/MSCCruisesUSA**, **www.Facebook.com/MSCCruises USA**, and **www.youtube.com/user/MSCCruiseLines**.

STYLE MSC Cruises is Italian in heart and spirit, from design to cuisine to personnel. It's tagline "Beautiful. Passionate. Italian." suits it well. The ships reflect classic cruising updated for today's travelers and are very much "today," with

THE FLEET	BUILT/RENOVATED	TONNAGE	PASSENGERS
MSC Armonia	2003	58,625	1,556
MSC Fantasia	2009	133,500	3,300
MSC Favolosa	2012	93,000	2,550
MSC Lirica	2003	59,058	1,560
MSC Magnifica	2010	89,600	2,550
MSC Melody	1982/92/97	35,143	1,062
MSC Meraviglia	2011	93,000	2,550
MSC Musica	2006	89,600	2,550
MSC Opera	2004	59,058	1,712
MSC Orchestra	2007	92,409	2,550
MSC Splendida	2009	137,936	3,300
MSC Poesia	2008	94,600	2,550
MSC Sinfonia	2002	58,625	1,556

gyms, spas, and fitness programs. In the Caribbean, MSC makes some changes to accommodate Americans. For example, prices are in dollars rather than euros; cabin television carries American movies; announcements are given first in English; and breakfast and lunch buffets offer choices that American passengers prefer. But, make no mistake. MSC cruises Italian style. For example, the Italian cuisine is prepared as it might be in a restaurant or at home in Florence or Rome. It's not the Olive Garden. As one passenger commented recently, "When I stepped onto the ship, I felt like I had landed in Italy."

All dining and theaters on MSC ships are nonsmoking, but don't be surprised to see some passengers, especially European ones, light up. Laundry and pressing services are available from the ships' facilities, but ships do not have self-service launderettes. Throughout the season, MSC has promotions—for baby boomers, seniors, baseball fans, golfers—with substantial reductions and Kids Sail Free, and it offers more theme cruises than almost any cruise line.

DISTINCTIVE FEATURES Sophia Loren is spokesperson and godmother for all the newest MSC ships, which have pizzerias and sushi bars, golf simulators, Internet cafes, and Wi-Fi access. Children age 17 and under cruise for free year-round when sharing a cabin with two full-fare adults. There is a Formula 1 simulator and 4-D cinema on *Fantasia*-class ships.

To enhance onboard service, MSC recently added Guest Relations Managers who speak several languages fluently. They are available throughout every cruise and provide a single point of contact and the reassurance of being empowered to handle any issue immediately. On the new *MSC Fantasia* and her sister ship *MSC Splendida,* guests have the services of a concierge.

RATES Port charges are included.

Special fares and discounts
- **CHILDREN'S FARE:** Age 17 and younger sharing a cabin with two full-fare-paying adults are free year-round.
- **SINGLE SUPPLEMENT:** Varies with sailing; consult MSC brochure for details.

PAST PASSENGERS MSC Club, the past-passenger program, has three levels based on one point accrued for each night sailed on any MSC Cruise worldwide and for purchases made on board. Passengers may join by completing the form in their cabin and can begin accumulating points on their current cruise. They may also write to the club at **www.mscclub.org.** Passengers begin at the Classic level; at 22 points they move to the Silver level (22–42 points); and at 43 points they reach the Gold level. The rewards include a welcome cocktail and discounts on shore excursions, in onboard boutiques, and on future cruises. As a passenger's level increases, so do the benefits.

Recently, the rewards program was enhanced. Silver and Gold levels are now rewarded with a complimentary dinner for two in a ship's specialty restaurant, a complimentary one-hour thermal suite (both sauna and Turkish bath) in its spa, and discounts on a variety of spa-related services from massages and facials to manicures and pedicures. All MSC Club members, including Classic, will receive complimentary laundry service for up to ten garments per cruise, fresh fruit delivered twice weekly in cabin, and substantial Internet and MSC logo item discounts. Discounts for cruise fare, spa treatments, Internet usage, and MSC logo items vary by membership level, with those in the upper tiers earning greater discounts.

THE LAST WORD   MSC Cruises is basically a European product for Europeans. In Europe, when the ships make announcements (in five languages), English is not the first language or even the second or third one you'll hear. (In the Caribbean, English is the first language.) The crew will speak English, you'll get menus and daily programs in English, but don't expect other passengers to speak English. Television will not be in English, except CNN International and, perhaps, one or two other news programs. Movies (pay-per-view) are available for a fee, and there's a charge for each item on the room-service menu. (However, in the Caribbean, room-service charges are dropped.) MSC cruise fares are attractively low, but be prepared for onboard charges. Prices are reasonable—and to incur them or not is your option.

THE SHIPS   *MSC Musica*, constructed at STX Shipyard (formerly Aker Shipyard and Chantiers de l'Atlantique) in France, debuted in 2006. The Panamax vessel was part of the line's $3 billion expansion program launched in 2003. She was followed by two sisters in 2007 and 2008. In September 2010, the brand-new *MSC Magnifica* arrives in New York for the line's inaugural season of Canada– New England itineraries, round-trip from New York City and Quebec City.

The *Musica* members were the largest of the MSC Cruises' fleet at the time of their debut (the newer *MSC Fantasia* and *MSC Splendida* are larger), and they came with plenty of wow. If Sophia Loren as godmother isn't enough of a wow, then *MSC Musica's* three-deck atrium with a waterfall and a see-through piano suspended over a transparent floor above the waterfall provides plenty more. The atrium is normally filled throughout the day and into the night with passengers enjoying a mariachi band or a classical string quartet, while sipping specialty coffees and drinks. Then there's the three-deck show lounge with red walls, red carpets, and red seats—there's even red (and black) in the cabins—plus four restaurants, a wine bar, and a sushi bar.

MSC Musica's interiors blend Art Nouveau and Art Deco geometric 1930s designs with high-tech and contemporary styles, along with Italian touches.

ITINERARIES   *See* Itinerary Index.

MSC Favolosa	2012	
MSC Magnifica	2010	
MSC Meraviglia	2011	
MSC Musica	QUALITY 7	VALUE B
MSC Orchestra	QUALITY 7	VALUE B
MSC Poesia	PREVIEW	
REGISTRY Panama	LENGTH 964/961 feet	BEAM 106/108 feet
CABINS 1,275	DRAFT NA	SPEED 23 knots
MAXIMUM PASSENGERS	PASSENGER DECKS 13	ELEVATORS 13
3,013	CREW 987	SPACE RATIO 35

MSC Cruises Standard Features

Officers Italian.

Staff *Dining:* Italian, other European, Asian, Central American; *Cabin:* international; *Cruise:* international.

Dining facilities Two main dining rooms on newest ships; one on older ships; open seating for lunch, fixed dinner; Lido buffet restaurant for breakfast, lunch, casual dinner. *Musica*-class have four restaurants, sushi bar, and alternative dining (extra charge); *Orchestra* has four specialty restaurants (two require reservations and charge). *Fantasia* and *Splendida* have six restaurants. Pizzerias on most ships.

Special diets Should be requested at time of reservations.

Room service 24 hours.

Dress code Casual, informal; formal/semiformal—one night on 4- to 6-night cruise, two nights on 7- to 10-night cruise, three nights on 11- to 14-night cruise, and four nights on 15-night or longer cruise.

Cabin amenities Phone, radio, private shower or bathtub, hair dryer, safe, television; minibar and veranda in higher categories. *Fantasia* and *Splendida*, MSC Yacht Club.

Electrical outlets 110/220 AC; adapters available on board.

Wheelchair access *MSC Musica, MSC Orchestra* 17 (2 outside, 3 with balcony, 12 inside); *MSC Opera* 5; *MSC Lirica, MSC Sinfonia, MSC Armonia* 4 inside; *MSC Melody* 4; *Fantasia* and *Splendida*, 43 cabins, including 2 in Yacht Club.

Recreation and entertainment Casino, bars, lounges with nightly entertainment, showrooms, disco, dance lessons, bingo, library, card room, video arcade. Cigar room on *MSC Musica* and *MSC Orchestra*. *Fantasia* and *Splendida,* 18 bars. *Splendida,* sports bar with two bowling alleys.

CABINS In response to passengers' preferences for outside cabins, more than 80% of the cabins are ocean-view accommodations, and 65% of them have balconies. Cabins are elegant and restful, with the line's signature royal blue and rose against light woods. All have hair dryers, bath amenities, safes, minibars, flat-panel televisions, 110/220-volt electrical outlets, and ample drawer and closet space. Bar-service choices in cabins are priced the same as in the bar, and the small room-service menu (nominal fee in Europe, free in the Caribbean) is very good. There are connecting cabins, triples, and suites, and charming children's activity rooms. Cabin television has interactive capability for shore excursions, reservations for the alternative restaurants and spa appointments, as well as television stations in several languages and movies (pay-per-view in Europe, free in the Caribbean). *Musica*-class ships have 17 wheelchair-accessible cabins (3 ocean view with balcony, 2 ocean view without balcony, 12 inside).

Sports and other activities Two swimming pools, five on *Fantasia* and *Splendida*. Exercise classes. Golf simulators, volleyball, shuffleboard, table tennis.

Beauty and fitness Beauty salon, spa, sauna, fitness centers, jogging track.

Other facilities Boutiques, medical facility, laundry and dry cleaning services, meeting room, Internet access on all ships. Internet cafes, Wi-Fi in select public areas on newest ships.

Children's facilities Supervised Mini Club Kids program year-round; babysitters; children's pools. Juniors Club on newest ships.

Theme cruises Art, Well-being, Golf, Culinary, Hobby, Dance, Singles, Astrology, Bridge, Baseball, Big Band, Polka, Presidents, Latin Music, Comedy, Country Music, Oldies Music, Festa Italiana.

Smoking Smoking in designated public areas; no smoking in dining rooms and main show lounges. Some of the bars and sections of others are non-smoking, as are elevators, stateroom balconies, and the spa; smoking is discouraged in staterooms.

MSC Cruises suggested tipping Gratuities, which may be adjusted, added to passenger onboard accounts. Normally, €6 per person per day in Europe, €3 per day for children ages 4–17; $12 per person per day in the Caribbean, $6 per child per day. Gratuities are included in the price of beverages on bar bills.

Credit cards For cruise payment and onboard charges: American Express, MasterCard, Visa.

DINING Dining venues on *Magica* include the elegant **Garden Restaurant,** with columns and fresco ceilings, a sushi bar with a Zen garden, a self-service pizzeria, and a large grill cafeteria. The Grille offers hamburgers, hot dogs, and the like at lunchtime, while the pizzeria (open evenings in Europe) has longer hours in the Caribbean and no fee.

Orchestra's main dining rooms are found on Deck 5 and Deck 6 with layout and menus the same, but the decor is very different. Only one is open daily for breakfast and lunch, except on sea days when both are open; both serve dinner at the traditional two seatings. Menus offer ample choices and variety and always include a pasta dish, seafood, vegetarian entree, and a lighter option. There's an extensive wine list and a separate children's menu. Some passengers give the food high marks, but others call it bland. The "always available" section on dinner menus is very much appreciated.

The buffet on Deck 13 serves three meals as well. This attractive area is divided into forward and aft sections, each with four stations and distinctive decor. At lunchtime, one station serves hamburgers, hot dogs, and pizza; one is a salad bar; another, a dessert station. Dress is casual, which makes the buffet particularly popular as a dinner option for families with children.

Orchestra has three specialty dinner restaurants, all with charges. **Shanghai,** which gets high marks, is a reasonably-priced Chinese restaurant where most items are $6–$11. **Four Seasons,** the upscale restaurant, is situated in a small area of the aft buffet and serves mostly steaks, chops, and fish, but passengers say that neither the steaks nor the service are up to the quality they expect in this type of restaurant and that are available on MSC's competitors; price is $25. Reservations must be made for these restaurants at the front desk. **The Pizzeria,** where pizzas are cooked to order, is located on one side of the forward buffet. Set up with checkered tablecloths and waiter service, it's open 7:30–10:30 p.m.; price: $4–$6.

SERVICE Cultural differences seem to show up most in service, particularly in the dining venues. For Italians (and most Europeans), a meal is an event and the time to enjoy food and friends leisurely. Too often, Americans want the meal to be served quickly so they can move on to other activities; thus, they complain that service is slow. Alas, neither the waiter nor the kitchen is likely to move faster. One result of the MSC's rapid expansion is that dining staff and crew are now mostly Asian, while Italians have been moved into supervisory positions. As a result, the Italian ambience of earlier ships has lessened. Generally, passengers find the Asian crew eager to please but in need of more training; in some cases, language is a problem, particularly with impatient Americans who fail to explain their needs carefully.

FACILITIES AND ACTIVITIES Ships have a lounge that can be used as a theater, concert, or conference room; a music hall equipped for orchestras, cabaret performances, and dancing; a panoramic disco with plasma screens; and a well-equipped stage in the pool area.

Orchestra's **Covent Garden Theatre,** the showroom, accommodates about half the passengers at one time with good sight lines from most seats. Its decor is stunning and has walls covered with neon-like lights that change color and intensity and, thus, change the mood of the room. *Orchestra* passengers rave about the entertainment, which has included acts from *Cirque du Soleil*–influenced acrobats and dancers to magic, all with wonderful costumes. *Orchestra* has jazz, dance music, and singers for entertainment throughout the ship. A 21- by 12-foot outdoor LED screen airs movies on the pool deck, and a disco at the ship's stern, a high-tech space with plasma screens in the floor, rocks after 11 p.m.

MSC Poesia, which debuted in spring 2008, has a somewhat different interior design from her sisters, especially in the entertainment areas. The ship has the Kaito Sushi Bar with a Zen garden that serves Japanese fare; Aurea Spa; 12 bars and lounges—a cigar room, piano bar, and a 46-foot-long bar in the casino; a wellness bar in the spa; and a **Cozy Bar** for after-dinner drinks or cappuccino. A sports bar has replaced the wine bar, and, instead of a Chinese restaurant, passengers will find a Mediterranean-themed specialty restaurant with menus that change nightly.

The ships also have a card room, library, art gallery, virtual games room, and a shopping mall. *Orchestra* shops include an electronics shop; a perfumery with cosmetics; a jewelry store; and a duty-free wine, spirits, and cigarettes shop. Madison Avenue carries traditional adults' and children's clothing. The 24-hour Internet cafe offers ten-minute time blocks for about $6. For those planning to be online frequently, it's probably worth it to bring a laptop, since Wi-Fi packages are available: 60 minutes, $30; 250 minutes $80.

SPORTS, FITNESS, AND BEAUTY **Mind and Body Spa,** at the forward end of the Pool Deck, offers aerobics, yoga, and such treatments as aromatherapy, thalassotherapy, hot stone, reflexology, shiatsu, acupuncture, and a purifying Turkish bath, which is very popular. Dressed in an Asian decor, the handsome spa has a specialty coffee bar that serves smoothies and herbal infusions. Its large exercise room, situated at the front of the spa, has floor-to-ceiling windows overlooking the bow. The center is equipped with treadmills, free weights, bicycles, and resistance equipment and offers classes from aerobics to Pilates.

In addition to the spa, the Sports Deck has two large swimming pools, a kids' wading pool, four hot tubs, tennis and volleyball court, golf simulator, minigolf and golf training, and a jogging track. Equipment is available at the front desk.

CHILDREN'S FACILITIES The ships have cheerful and colorful play areas and can cater to the specific needs of all ages. Special activity leaders organize age-appropriate activities for children ages 3–9 in the Mini Club, 9–13 in the Junior Club, and 14–17 in the Teenager Club. The ships also offer a Teen's Card, a personalized card for children ages 12–17, which can be used on board like a credit card. Each card comes with a bonus amount: in the Caribbean, a $30 card comes with a $5 bonus; $50 card with a $10 bonus. In the Mediterranean and northern Europe, a €30 card comes with a €5 bonus, €50 card with a €10 bonus. The ships offer children's menus and a 30% discount on shore excursions for children under age 14.

THE SHIPS The launch of *MSC Fantasia* in December 2008 and *MSC Splendida* in July 2009, with Sophia Loren serving as godmother, brought a new class of ships for the line. Built at STX Europe in Saint-Nazaire, France, these 133,500-ton vessels were the largest ships to be built by a European shipowner to date. Each ship represents an investment of $1 billion. Designed by the Italian naval architectural firm De Jorio Design International, which has been the designer for most of MSC Cruises' ships, this duet combines traditional Italian elegance with leading-edge technology, particularly in its environmental protection features.

The new *Fantasia* (pronounced, Fanta-SEE-a) class also gave birth to a new concept for the line: the MSC Yacht Club, a VIP area of 99 cabins and suites, with private access, butler service, and a host of amenities. The exclusive ship-within-a-ship has a Club concierge, bar, solarium, small pool with sky dome, two Jacuzzis, plus an observation lounge with its own bar and panoramic view overlooking the bow.

MSC Fantasia	PREVIEW	
MSC Splendida	PREVIEW	
REGISTRY Panama	LENGTH 1,092 feet	BEAM 124 feet
CABINS 1,637	DRAFT NA	SPEED 23 knots
MAXIMUM PASSENGERS	PASSENGER DECKS NA	ELEVATORS 15
3,959	CREW 1,325	SPACE RATIO 40

MSC Splendida also has the line's first bowling alleys, and among the ships' other features are five restaurants (six on *Splendida*), five swimming pools, a water park, and 18 lounges and bars—we said these are big ships.

ITINERARIES *See* Itinerary Index.

CABINS On *MSC Fantasia*, 1,266 cabins (including 107 suites) have private balconies; 77 cabins have windows; and 294 are inside cabins. Accommodations range from 193 to 571 square feet. The cabins with balconies are roomy and well arranged, but the decor might take some getting use to. On one deck, the color is red—red bedspread, red sofa, red draperies, red wall behind the bed, red carpet; on another deck, the color is green, and so on. There are a large number of connecting cabins, but these have been reported to have inadequate soundproofing.

The most prevalent cabin type with a balcony measures about 208 square feet and is furnished with twin-size beds that can be converted to a queen, a sofa that can be converted into a bed, a chair and writing table, a rather small closet, and a bathroom with a shower. It also has a safe, minibar, and flat-panel interactive television, which offers pay-per-view movies. Passengers can view their onboard account and watch real-time information from the bridge with maps and navigational details.

MSC Yacht Club is located on the upper foredecks, offering these passengers great views from their own private balconies—or, for those without a balcony, full-height panoramic windows (you can understand why those passengers complain). Non-Yacht Club passengers complained about the Yacht Club's location. Club suites and a private lounge occupy the forward areas of four different decks. Thus, there are almost no forward views available anywhere for regular passengers, including the forward part of the Sun Deck, which has the Club's private pool reserved exclusively for the Yacht Club and accessible only with a key card.

MSC Yacht Club interiors are elegant and refined, with oak wood walls and parquet and Siena marble floors. Swarovski crystal stairs—a cruise-ship first—connect the deck between the MSC Yacht Club concierge area and Deck 16. The spacious Club suites are fitted with a full bath and shower with marble accents, interactive television, Wi-Fi, Nintendo Wii, plush linens by Mascioni Italy, ergonomic mattresses, pillow menu, complimentary minibars, and have laundry and dry-cleaning service. MSC Yacht Club offers a choice of 88 deluxe suites (sleeping two to four adults), 9 family suites, and 2 royal suites. Two of the deluxe suites are fully equipped for people with disabilities.

Other MSC Yacht Club exclusive features include priority boarding at check-in and butler assistance with unpacking; complimentary dining and special menus at L'Etoile, the gourmet French restaurant, as well as a special reserved section in Il Cerchio D'Oro, the main dining room; 24-hour dedicated room-service menu; daylong complimentary drinks, pastries, and appetizers; daily English high tea in the Top Sail Lounge, a private lounge with panoramic views; and a VIP reserved area in Liquid Disco. Club passengers also enjoy a private library. One of the ship's 15 passenger elevators is reserved exclusively for Yacht Club passengers and provides easy access to the spa. Each suite is served by a butler providing everything from daily newspapers to valet services, booking spa treatments, arranging a private party in the suite, priority booking for shore excursions, front-row seats in the ship's theater, and private shopping visits.

DINING *Fantasia* has five restaurants (*Splendida,* six restaurants), including **El Sombrero** (**Santa Fe** on *Splendida*), a Tex-Mex eatery with an open kitchen that serves tacos, margaritas, and other Mexican specialties; and **La Cantina Toscana** (L'Enoteca on *Splendida*), a wine bar serving fine Italian wines plus antipasto and light food at lunch and dinner. The **Sports Bar** has burgers and kebabs for a small charge. The ship's main dining rooms, **Red Velvet** and **Cerchio d'Oro,** offer fixed two-seating dining for three meals and tend to be crowded; meals here are included in the price of the cruise. However, in the specialty restaurants, MSC charges à la carte for each item on the menu—as in a stateside restaurant (including pizza and kebabs in the buffet area)—and the same holds true for room service. The ship's Lido buffet is actually two restaurants, **Zanzibar** and **i'Africana,** with several counters. They are particularly crowded for breakfast and lunchtime but have outdoor seating for overflow. Also, two of the alternative restaurants serve lunch.

New to MSC ships is *Fantasia*'s **L'Etoile** French restaurant, located aft on Deck 15 and overlooking the Gaudi adult pool area. Meant to be the gourmet restaurant, it's the priciest of the options. Its counterpart, **L'Olivo,** on *Splendida*, named for the olive tree as a symbol of the Mediterranean basin, offers selections from 14 different Mediterranean countries. Yacht Club passengers dine here free of charge; this perk, and complimentary wines in the main dining room, make the Yacht Club a good value.

FACILITIES AND ACTIVITIES **Piazza San Giorgio,** like the Venice original, is a popular meeting place, particularly in the evening to enjoy music and dancing. During the day, it's the place for pastries and gelato treats. Passengers can choose from the ship's 18 bars and lounges, such as the **Manhattan Jazz Bar,** to gather with friends. *MSC Splendida*'s Sports Bar has two innovative mini-bowling alleys—the first for MSC Cruises and the first on a European cruise ship. The ten-pin bowling alleys have a traditional-looking bowling surface that is actually made of a tough phenol compound, which allows guests to bowl without having to wear special bowling shoes. The alleys are scaled down to work in a bar environment and to encourage people to mix and mingle. The bowling balls are slightly smaller than usual, so they are manageable for youngsters, while still challenging for older players. There are also two large LCD electronic screens with interactive video game animations, and surrounding the bowling alleys are big-screen televisions and interactive sports games for solo and group play.

MSC Cruises has teamed up with Nintendo to bring cutting-edge interactive play to its entertainment programs and facilities. *MSC Fantasia* is equipped with 114 Wii consoles, including 9 Wii Sport consoles in the Sports Bar, 4 Wii Fit stations with balance boards in the Fitness Center, a competition console on the Sport Deck, and an additional console in the main pool area that's connected to a massive 23- by 9-foot screen for competitions and activities.

L'Avanguardia is the ship's large theater, which offers nightly shows. There's also a coffee bar, casino, disco, interactive 4-D cinema, Formula 1 simulator, and specialty shops.

SPORTS, FITNESS, BEAUTY The ships have four outside pools and one, **I Tropici,** with a magrodome (a retractable roof)—the first on an MSC ship—and a dozen hydro-massage tubs. The retractable roof will be especially appreciated when the ships are cruising in the Mediterranean in the winter. Also new on an MSC ship is the **Acqua Park,** or water park, with 150 fountains and water jets that light up at night to the rhythm of music. The ships also have shuffleboard, a jogging track, squash and tennis courts, and a sports center.

The large **Aurea Spa** on Deck 14 is billed as an authentic Balinese wellness center offering innovative treatments. The center is divided into four areas: thalassotherapy room, thermal area, gymnasium, and relaxation area. The thalassotherapy room has three treatment rooms facing the sea where Balinese massages, as well as reflexology, lava stones, infrared massage, and shiatsu, are given by Balinese attendants. This area also houses the latest generation of Q-Age therapies that combine technology with the ancient Balinese art of massage and offers sauna, vapor, infrared, thalassotherapy, and vichy shower. In the same area, three advanced technologies are also offered under medical supervision: Q-Frequency, to combat the slackening of muscle tone in both face and body; Mya Advance, the nonsurgical alternative to liposculpture; and Active-Press, for lymphatic drainage to combat cellulite. The thermal area has four saunas plus two Turkish baths.

CHILDREN'S FACILITIES A children's area with a waterslide that straddles two decks is found on the side of the disco. There are three age-specific areas. See "Children's Facilities" in the *MSC Musica* section for details.

THE SHIPS The first of MSC's new ships, the *Lirica* (or "Lyric" in English) debuted in 2003, with Sophia Loren doing the christening honors. *Lirica* was followed by a sister ship, *MSC Opera*, in 2004, the first phase of the line's expansion plans. The ships are powered by an advanced propulsion system to reduce engine noise and increase comfort levels.

The *Lirica*'s decor is more subdued than the *Opera*'s, with her public rooms in quieter colors and low lighting but with lots of windows to connect passengers to the sea and keep the atmosphere cheerful. The *Lirica* has eight bars and lounges and a disco that doubles as an observation lounge during the day.

ITINERARIES *See* Itinerary Index.

CABINS All cabins are furnished with twins that convert to queens, vanity and chair, satellite television, minibar, safe, radio, hair dryer, and 24-hour room service. The bathrooms are small but provide adequate storage space. Some have with upper bunks for triples or quads. Only suites have private balconies, bath with tub, a sitting area with a love seat that converts to a third bed, coffee table, and chair. There are two two-room family suites (237 square feet).

MSC Lirica	QUALITY7	VALUEB
MSC Opera	QUALITY7	VALUEB
REGISTRYPanama	LENGTH824 feet	BEAM94 feet
CABINS795	DRAFT25 feet	SPEED19 knots
MAXIMUM PASSENGERS	PASSENGER DECKS9	ELEVATORS9
1,756	CREW800	SPACE RATIONA

Specifications *Lirica/Opera*, 795 cabins, 387 standard outside, 272 inside (140 square feet); 132 suites with verandas (250 square feet); *Lirica* 4, *Opera* 5, inside cabins for disabled passengers (226 square feet).

DINING Each of the sister ships has two dining rooms—**La Bussola** and **L'Ippocampo**—that serve authentic Italian cuisine as well as international selections. Both restaurants have two seatings for dinner with assigned seating. Breakfast and lunch are open seating.

Le Bistrot Cafeteria is another option, and hot dogs, hamburgers, and pizza are available at the poolside grill for lunch and in the evening. The *Lirica* serves afternoon tea and the traditional midnight buffet. There's an ice-cream bar (extra cost) on Lido deck and a 24-hour room service menu. The **Coffee Bar** serves real Italian espresso ($1.60), which is also available at most of the ship's bars.

Wines are reasonably priced, with house wine costing about $4 per glass. Wine, beer, and soda packages are available for purchase.

FACILITIES AND ACTIVITIES Typical of MSC's ships is lots of activity during the day and evening. Throughout the ship, one of the "animators" (entertainers dressed in various costumes) is likely to surprise you with some lighthearted antics. **The Lyric Lounge** is the setting for games and contests, when the cruise staff manages to get passengers to participate—Europeans seem to get with the fun more readily than American passengers do. There's music nightly in the various lounges, especially for dancing, which, again, Europeans seem to enjoy most. The **Broadway Theater,** the main show lounge, stages two Las Vegas–type shows or dance productions, magicians, and comics every evening.

Each ship has two swimming pools separated by two hot tubs. There and on the sun decks, you can relax on a lounger with its own shade attached. The ships have spas, fully equipped gyms, saunas, and jogging tracks. They are equipped with a **Virtual Reality Center** and an Internet cafe with 16 terminals and Wi-Fi hot spots on the pool decks and in select bars, cafes, lounges, and a shopping gallery. Internet access costs $5 for the first ten minutes and $0.50 each additional minute. For those with their own wireless laptop, prepaid packages for Internet access cost from $15 for 30 minutes.

Passengers can pass their time inside with Italian cooking and language lessons, trivia, bingo, dance lessons, and arts and crafts—or outside with minigolf, Ping-Pong, and shuffleboard tournaments.

CHILDREN'S FACILITIES The I Pirati Mini-Club, open for three hours in the morning and afternoon and two hours in the evening, has a full-time staff. Children under age 3, when accompanied by an adult, may use the space. Babysitting is available for a fee. An MSC Junior Card for kids for sodas costs $28.

THE SHIPS *MSC Sinfonia*, the former *European Stars*, was launched in 2002 by the now-bankrupt First European (Festival) Cruises and began sailing for MSC in 2005, after she had been purchased at auction in 2004 for €220 million. *MSC Sinfonia*, as the name indicates, has been inspired by the great symphonies of classical composers from Beethoven and Mozart to Debussy and Tchaikovsky. Both *Sinfonia* and her sister ship, *Armonia* (the former *European Vision*), were constructed at Aker Shipyard in France. The *Armonia* has most of the same facilities as her sister ship, but her interior architecture is different.

MSC Armonia	QUALITY 7	VALUE B
MSC Sinfonia	QUALITY 7	VALUE B
REGISTRY Panama	LENGTH 824 feet	BEAM 94 feet
CABINS 777	DRAFT 22 feet	SPEED 21 knots
MAXIMUM PASSENGERS	PASSENGER DECKS 9	ELEVATORS 9
2,087	CREW 700	SPACE RATIO NA

Each ship has six bars, a showroom, dining room, indoor/outdoor restaurant, pizzeria, grill, spa and fitness center with gym and sauna, beauty salon, disco, cabaret, casino, Internet cafe with 16 terminals, two outdoor swimming pools, jogging area, two whirlpools, children's club, minigolf, golf simulator, video arcade, shops, and conference room.

ITINERARIES *See* Itinerary Index.

CABINS All accommodations have air-conditioning, satellite television, phone, minibar, safe, radio, bath, hair dryer, and 24-hour room service. Suites feature a bedroom with a king-size bed, bath with bathtub and shower, private veranda, sofa bed, Internet (extra fee), and floor-to-ceiling windows. Standard cabins have a convertible king-size bed and bath with shower.

Specifications 371 outside, 272 inside cabins (140 square feet); 132 suites with private balcony (237 square feet); 2 family suites without balcony (140 square feet); 4 inside cabins for disabled passengers (226 square feet).

Norwegian Cruise Line/ NCL America

7665 Corporate Center Drive
Miami, FL 33126
☎ 305-436-4000 or 866-234-0292
FAX 305-436-4120
www.ncl.com

TYPE OF SHIPS Modern superliners and new megaliners.

TYPE OF CRUISES Contemporary, mainstream, "Freestyle Cruising."

CRUISE LINE'S STRENGTHS
- new, innovative ships
- sports activities
- Freestyle Cruising options and flexibility
- large number and variety of dining venues
- nonsmoking cabins
- value
- entertainment
- unusual luxury accommodations

CRUISE LINE'S SHORTCOMINGS
- loud deck music
- small bathrooms on some ships
- megaliner size

FELLOW PASSENGERS Norwegian Cruise Line is the everyman's cruise line, with attractive ships where anyone can feel comfortable. Passengers, mostly from the United States and Canada, represent all walks of life, including young professionals, families, and seniors. Average household income is $50,000–$70,000.

Recommended for First-time cruisers, active travelers of all ages who want a fun vacation and like a large ship. Middle-income travelers and multigenerational vacationers. Those who seek an unstructured atmosphere.

Not recommended for Snobs with five-star pretensions. Seasoned or sedentary travelers who want to be catered to for every whim.

CRUISE AREAS AND SEASONS Bahamas, Caribbean, Hawaii, New York–Caribbean, year-round; Mexico, South America, winter to spring; Alaska, Bermuda, Europe, Mediterranean, spring to fall; New England-Canada, fall; Panama Canal, April and September to October.

THE LINE On December 19, 1966, the *Sunward* sailed from Miami with 540 passengers on the first three- and four-day cruises to be offered year-round by Norwegian Caribbean Line between Miami and the Bahamas. With this voyage, NCL was born and so was modern cruising. Those cruises—the first packaged for the mass market—are credited with launching cruising as we know it today. Since then, NCL, renamed Norwegian Cruise Line, has played a major role in shaping today's cruises. Within five years of start-up, NCL had acquired three brand-new ships, pioneered weekly cruises to many Caribbean destinations, and introduced a day on a private island in its itineraries.

Yet for all these innovations, nothing equaled in excitement and impact NCL's purchase of the *Norway* in 1980. After buying her as the *France* for $18 million, NCL spent $100 million to transform her from a great ocean liner to a Caribbean cruise ship, setting in motion trends that transformed cruising completely.

Later in the decade, a series of costly expansions, including the acquisition of Royal Viking Line and Royal Cruise Line, weakened NCL's debt-encumbered parent company, opening the way for more aggressive lines to take over NCL's pacesetting role. However, by the 1990s, NCL had reinvented itself with a fleet of new, innovative ships that made NCL a trendsetter once again. Among the most notable were alternative dining and separate sitting areas in standard cabins—an amenity that usually had been reserved for deluxe accommodations. These innovations became standard on new ships.

In 1997, NCL became the first line to base a ship in Houston for year-round cruises to the western Caribbean. The following year, it became the first mainstream cruise line to base a ship in southern South America for the winter season, sailing between Chile and Argentina. NCL took over two ships of the defunct Majesty Cruise Line, then ordered a 2,000-passenger ship, bought an unfinished hull intended for Costa Cruises (completed as the *Norwegian Sky*), stretched three ships, and streamlined the fleet with new names.

At the dawn of the new millennium, a bidding war between Carnival Cruises and Star Cruises (Asia's major cruise line) ended with Star Cruises as the sole owner of NCL. By 2001, NCL's new owners had launched Freestyle Cruising, an innovative concept providing passengers with flexibility and

THE FLEET	BUILT/RENOVATED	TONNAGE	PASSENGERS
Norwegian Dawn	2002/05	92,250	2,244
Norwegian Epic	2010	150,000	4,200
Norwegian Gem	2007	93,000	2,380
Norwegian Jade	2006/08	93,000	2,466
Norwegian Jewel	2005	92,502	2,376
Norwegian Majesty	1992/99/2004	40,876	1,462
Norwegian Pearl	2006	93,530	2,394
Norwegian Sky	1999/2004/08	77,104	2,002
Norwegian Spirit	2000/05	75,338	1,966
Norwegian Star	2001	91,000	2,240
Norwegian Sun	2001	78,309	1,936
NCL AMERICA FLEET			
Pride of America	2005	81,000	2,138

challenging many cruise traditions; added a series of megaships; and started new, year-round cruises of Hawaii.

NCL once again astonished the cruise world by acquiring Project America's unfinished ships (left abandoned by the bankruptcy of American Classic Voyages Co. in 2001), agreeing to finish their construction. With the help of Hawaii's powerful Senator Daniel Inouye, NCL gained congressional exemption to reflag NCL's foreign-flagged *Norwegian Sky* to the U.S. ship registry and sail it and the two Project America vessels year-round in Hawaii under the American flag. After an auspicious beginning, NCL America ran into heavy competition from other cruise lines and soaring fuel prices that had a major impact on travel to Hawaii. By 2008, NCL had pulled two ships out of Hawaii, leaving only one ship to sail the Hawaiian itineraries.

Meanwhile, NCL expanded its Homeland Cruising program with more new U.S. departure ports, such as seasonal cruises from Philadelphia; Baltimore; and Charleston, South Carolina; and year-round cruises from New York. Between 2001 and 2007, the cruise line added seven new ships—all with the Freestyle Cruising concept and innovations that have been picked up by their competition and added to their ships. These are just a few examples: NCL was the first cruise line to offer wireless Internet access fleetwide; the first to have bowling alleys; and now, almost every new ship built by any cruise line has several alternative restaurants and a flexible dining system.

Even with all these developments, NCL has not finished. In 2006, NCL marked its 40th anniversary by ordering a a 150,000-ton megaship, *Norwegian Epic*, as the third generation of Freestyle Cruising ships. Costing more than $1 billion, the ship is being built at STX Europe in France, to be delivered in summer 2010. Based on a new design with a host of new features and innovations, the Freestyle Cruising megaship carrying 4,200 passengers will be NCL's first post-Panamax ship. Among her most significant new amenity will be all outside cabins with private balconies.

NCL passengers can now check in online, print their cruise tickets, and make shore excursion reservations at the NCL Web site. You can also find NCL on Facebook (**www.ncl.com/facebook**); Twitter @NCLFreestyle (**www.ncl.com/twitter**), **www.twitter.com/NCLFreestyle;** Flickr at **www.flickrcom/groups/nclfreestylefans/;** and YouTube at **www.youtube.com/user/NCL Freestyle.** In August 2009, NCL launched Freestyle Voices, **www.ncl.com/FreestyleVoices,** an online social media forum.

STYLE NCL has always been at the heart of mainstream cruising, with attractive ships reflecting contemporary lifestyles and offering a variety of activities for all ages almost around the clock. NCL ships have thoughtful amenities and signature items, including a full luncheon buffet served on embarkation, expanded room-service menus, ice-cream parlors, and alternative restaurants; the Chocoholic Buffet, a weekly dessert extravaganza. In some casinos, some blackjack tables are reserved for nonsmokers. On the newest ships, facilities for disabled passengers have been substantially enhanced, including cabins and show lounges equipped for the hearing-impaired and for wheelchairs.

Fitness centers—open 24 hours/7 days a week fleetwide—offer fully equipped exercise facilities, aerobics classes, basketball/volleyball courts, and golf practice facilities. Water sports instruction is combined with experiences

Norwegian Cruise Line Standard Features

Officers Norwegian.

Staff *Dining and Cabin:* international; *Cruise:* American and British.

Dining facilities *Dream*, 6; *Star* and *Sun*, 11; *Spirit*, 9; *Dawn*, 11; *Jewel, Pearl, Gem*, 10; *Pride of America*, 9; *Norwegian Sky*, 6; *Norwegian Jade*, 14—all with open seating, some with a charge ($10–$25). Embarkation lunch; choco-holic, midnight buffets; Sports Bar & Grill; ice-cream parlors; pizzerias; French, Italian, Spanish, Asian, and steak house specialty restaurants. *Norwegian Epic*, 20 restaurants.

Special diets Vegetarian, low-salt/calorie, kosher; must be requested 14–30 days in advance.

Room service 24 hours.

Dress code Casual by day, informal in evening. Optional formal/semiformal attire one night on short cruises, two on seven-day cruises.

Cabin amenities Phone, refrigerator, some bathrooms with tub, sitting areas in standard cabins on newest ships, television with CNN and ESPN, safe, hair dryers. Jewel-class ships, coffeemakers, espresso in suites, terry robes.

Electrical outlets 110 AC.

Wheelchair access *Dream*, 7 cabins; *Spirit*, 4; *Sun, Star*, 20; *Dawn*, 24; *Jewel, Pearl, Gem, Jade*, 27; *Norwegian Epic*, 42 cabins. All have cabins with bathtubs with grab bars. Newer ships: Braille indicators for elevator buttons and cabin numbers, electrical hoists for pools and Jacuzzis, tender boats accessible via wheelchair. Older ships: barriers to wheelchairs removed, ramps built. For details on each ship's facilities, contact NCL.

Recreation and entertainment Up to 11 lounges, sports bars; Broadway shows, Las Vegas-style revues, comedy, nightclub, disco, casino, library. Wine tastings, singles, honeymooner parties, video arcade. Martini, wine-tasting bars on newest ships.

in ports. All ships have a Dive-In snorkeling program and can arrange scuba excursions for certified divers—even in Alaska. Great Stirrup Cay, NCL's private Bahamian island, offers varied activities.

Freestyle Cruising's goal has been to broaden cruising's appeal. Gone are rigid dining hours, assigned seating, and dress codes. Instead, NCL ships' dining venues (the newest ships offer ten or more restaurants) have open seating and open dining with continuous service as in a restaurant. Passengers can dine when, where, and with whom they want. The dress code is also optional, from casual to formal, depending on the venue. Other elements of Freestyle Cruising include increased service, with a ratio of almost one crew member per cabin; upgraded cabins; more relaxed disembarkation at the end of a cruise; enhanced enrichment, from computer classes to yoga and moun-

Sports and other activities Sports Afloat program with golf practice, basketball, volleyball, table tennis. Snorkeling; scuba for certified divers. Private island with water sports rental equipment. Most ships, two swimming pools (*Jewel*, three pools); jogging track. *Pearl* and *Gem*, four bowling alleys ($5 with shoes), climbing wall and full-dimension tennis court and viewing stand. *Norwegian Epic*, mixed-use sports deck, climbing and rappelling walls, 6 bowling lanes, squash court, Aqua Park with 3 slides and 4 pools.

Beauty and fitness Aerobics, fitness center, sauna, jogging track, barber/beauty salon. Spa on *Dream, Spirit, Jewel*-class, *Sun*.

Other facilities Medical, dry cleaning/laundry. Meeting facilities; 24-hour Internet cafe and wireless access fleetwide—$0.75 per minute, packages available; laptop rental, $20 per day; Wi-Fi network card, $10 per day.

Children's facilities New and enhanced year-round program for ages 2–17 in four age-specific levels with youth counselors. Children's menus, fares, babysitting. *Dawn, Star, Spirit*, kids' splash pool, playroom; *Dream, Majesty, Spirit, Jewel*-class, unlimited soda packages, $16, backpack with unlimited soda program, $39.50; teen passport, $34.50.

Theme cruises See text.

Smoking Nonsmoking dining rooms; nonsmoking sections in public rooms.

NCL suggested tipping NCL automatically applies a service charge to passenger's shipboard account: $12 per passenger per day for those ages 13 and older, $5 per day for children ages 3–12; no charge for children under age 3. Charges can be adjusted; 15% added to bar tabs and spa services.

Credit cards For cruise payment and onboard charges: American Express, Visa, MasterCard, Discover.

tain biking; and a simplified gratuity system. Wireless access and cell phone service are available fleetwide.

One of NCL's best innovations, available on all the newest ships, makes selecting a dining venue easier and more convenient. Flat-panel televisions situated in easy-to-see locations around the ship list all the restaurants and indicate availability and waiting time for dinner. If passengers prefer not to wait, the staff at each restaurant can make reservations in another restaurant, or passengers can be given a pager to be buzzed when space becomes available. Another bow to the electronic age, NCL has gone to e-tickets. Passengers now receive their tickets and other documents via e-mail, unless they or their travel agents request otherwise.

In January 2010, NCL entered a three-year partnership with Nickelodeon to feature Nickelodeon-themed family entertainment and programming all year on select NCL ships. The program began in April on *Norwegian Jewel* and in summer on the new *Norwegian Epic*.

NCL's latest innovation is for solo travelers on *Norwegian Epic*, when she is launched in July 2010. The ship's Studios, a new category and style of cabin, will be priced for single occupancy with no single supplement and begin from $799 for a seven-day Eastern or Western Caribbean cruise.

DISTINCTIVE FEATURES Freestyle Cruising, chocoholic buffets, dive program and offbeat excursions in Alaska, open seating for many meals, alternative dining and dining-availability monitoring screens, full-scale Broadway shows, and sports bars. Galley and backstage tours. Nonsmoking cabins; cabins for the hearing-impaired. 24/7 fitness centers, Internet centers, wireless access. Bowling and climbing walls on *Norwegian Pearl*, *Norwegian Gem*, and *Norwegian Epic*. Studio cabins and ship-within-a-ship luxury suites; a "big top" at sea.

RATES Port charges are included.

Special fares and discounts NCL's LeaderShip fares, available through travel agents, are capacity-controlled with discounts up to 50%. Other early-booking fares are available. NCL's Premium Air Service handles requests for upgrades, stopovers, and flights on specific airlines and air/sea bookings. Requests for deviations must be written or faxed 60 days in advance and carry a nonrefundable service fee, plus fare differential.

- **CHILDREN'S FARE:** Children under age 2 free, charged only taxes and port charges. At certain times of the year, NCL offers family fares that provide a 10% discount on the cruise fare for the second stateroom when booking a mini-suite (second can be in any category); inquire.
- **SINGLE SUPPLEMENT:** Based on double occupancy rate.

PAST PASSENGERS Latitudes, NCL's past passenger program, was recently enhanced with benefits based on the number of cruises passengers have taken. The program is divided into four tiers: Bronze (1–4 completed cruises), Silver (5–8), Gold (9–13), and Platinum (14 or more). All levels have access to a Latitudes customer service desk, subscription to *Latitudes*, a quarterly members-only magazine, exclusive pricing on all sailings, Polo Club benefits when sailing on Orient Lines, Latitudes check-in desk at pier, Latitudes ship pin, members-only cocktail party hosted by Captain, and Latitudes onboard liaison.

Additionally, Silver members receive treats delivered to their cabin twice during the cruise; Gold receives VIP service, including priority boarding, a welcome-aboard basket, priority restaurant reservations, tender tickets and disembarkation, and an invitation to the Captain's VIP cocktail party. Platinum gets all of the above plus complimentary dinner in Le Bistro restaurant. Membership is automatic and free. Members can call ☎ 800-343-0098 or 305-436-4872 or visit **www.ncl.com.**

THE LAST WORD In the 1990s, NCL had a litany of problems and financial woes that caused its competitors to outpace it in expansion and innovations. But thanks to Star Cruises' deep pockets, NCL was able to reinvent itself and can look ahead to a bright future once again, as a trendsetter with its new direction and new ships with many innovative features.

THE SHIPS The $400-million, 91,000-ton megaliner *Norwegian Star* was a prototype for future NCL ships. In 2001, she joined the *Norwegian Sun* for the first-ever dual cruise ship christening in Miami. By 2007, *Star*'s five sister ships had been launched.

Norwegian Dawn	QUALITY 8	VALUE B
Norwegian Gem	QUALITY 8	VALUE B
Norwegian Jade	PREVIEW	
Norwegian Jewel	QUALITY 9	VALUE B
Norwegian Pearl	QUALITY 9	VALUE B
Norwegian Star	QUALITY 8	VALUE B
REGISTRY Panama	LENGTH 965/935 feet	BEAM 105 feet
CABINS 1,112–1,233	DRAFT 27/28 feet	SPEED 22.5–25 knots
MAXIMUM PASSENGERS	PASSENGER DECKS 10–15	ELEVATORS 10–12
2,224/2,376/2,240	CREW 1,100–1,154	SPACE RATIO 38.3–40.5

Built at the maximum size still possible to pass through the Panama Canal, these ships were NCL's largest and fastest ships until the debut of *Norwegian Epic*. They have been fitted with pod drives, which greatly improve maneuverability. While all the ships are meant to be similar, each has introduced new features that subsequent sister ships have enhanced or expanded. The trend-setting *Star* was the first to have NCL's trademark of decorative artwork splashed along her hull—a burst of colorful stars and streamers in green, red, yellow, purple, and aqua running from bow to midship. The design is meant to evoke the longtime cruise tradition of passengers throwing streamers from the bow of the ship as the vessel pulls away from the dock to embark on its voyage. Other *Jewel*-class ships have similar artwork.

However, no ship took her innovative role quite as far as the *Norwegian Pearl*, which is loaded with wow! For starters, she has cruising's first bowling alley, NCL's first climbing wall, a full tennis court, a Chihuly sculpture in the **Crystal Atrium,** buffet "action stations" for *à la minute* food preparation, new "romance" suites, three spa treatment rooms for couples, and sexy, wide lounging beds in quiet corners around the ship.

ITINERARIES *See* Itinerary Index.

CABINS The ships have set new cruise industry standards in their cabins, with rich cherrywood finishing, tea- and coffeemakers in every cabin, and larger bathrooms than in the line's other ships, with toilet, shower, and washstand compartments separated by sliding doors, television, safe, and hair dryer. Sixty-five percent of cabins are outside, and more than 70% of these have balconies. Cabins are furnished with two beds that convert to queen, and most cabins have a sofa bed or pop-up trundle bed for a third lower bed; some have a fourth pull-down berth. A large number of cabins (including suites and mini-suites) interconnect to create a two-, three-, four-, or five-bedroom area suitable for families.

A steel-and-glass structure on top of the ships, aft from the main sun deck, is a fantasy world, unlike anything on any other vessel today. Meant to create a ship within a ship, two six-room Garden Villas on *Star* and *Dawn* each cover 5,750 square feet (*Pearl* and *Jade*, 4,390 square feet), and each have a roof terrace and private garden and offer open-air dining, Jacuzzis, and totally private sunning and relaxing areas—all yours for a mere $26,000 per week. In addition, these ships have two Owner's Suites, two Honeymoon Suites, 30 Penthouse Suites, and an entire deck of spacious mini-suites with balconies; and on *Pearl*, a new category of Romance Suites at the stern with floor-to-ceiling glass doors to enjoy sea and sunset views. Cabins for disabled passengers are available in various categories.

The ship-within-a-ship concept on *Norwegian Jewel* and *Norwegian Pearl* has somewhat different configurations, demonstrating the enhancement and expansion of earlier NCL innovations. On Deck 14, a block of ten suites (which NCL calls villas) is grouped around an open courtyard with a small swim-against-the-current lap pool at the center. It also has a hot tub, men's and women's steam rooms, and a small fitness area. Eight of the villa suites have separate children's bedrooms. Both ships have two large three-bedroom garden villas with ultramodern decor. Each bedroom is furnished with a king- or queen-size bed and a luxury bath.

The *Pearl* has even more Owner's Suites and, at the very top of the ship on Deck 15, two new Deluxe Owner's Suites with private patios and fabulous views. All the top category suites have butler service and access to an exclusive concierge. Accommodations throughout the *Pearl* are brightly decorated in orange, fuchsia, and teal, and if you have trouble remembering the direction of fore and aft, the corridor carpeting has fish swimming forward.

Both *Jewel*'s and *Pearl*'s facilities for the disabled are particularly outstanding. The 27 wheelchair-accessible cabins are available in various categories, including suites; all have collapsible shower stools mounted on shower walls and toilets with collapsible arm guards and lowered wash basins. Hearing-impaired kits are available on request. Cabin equipment includes such items as vibrating alarm clock, a light that flashes when there's a knock on the door, television with closed captioning, fire alarm flashing light, and permanently lit emergency lights. Cabins and elevators have Braille text. In public rooms, there are dedicated wheelchair positions in the Stardust Theater, which is equipped with hearing-impaired induction systems, and an electrical hoist for access to the pools and hot tubs. An NCL crew member will tour the ship with passengers on the first day to help them get oriented.

Specifications Dawn/Star 360 standard cabins with balconies; 242 outside, 355 inside; 107 mini-suites with balconies; 4 Owner's Suites, 4 Romance Suites, 30 Penthouse Suites on *Dawn*, 26 on *Star*; 2 multiroom Garden Villas; 20 wheelchair accessible on *Star*, 24 on *Spirit. Jewel/Pearl/ Gem*: 360 standard cabins with balconies (205 square feet); 243 outside (161 square feet), 412 inside (143 square feet); 134 mini-suites with balconies (284 square feet); 2 Garden Villas with 3 bedrooms (4,390 square feet); 2 Deluxe Owner's Suites (928 square feet); 5 Owner's Suites (750 square feet); 24 Penthouse Suites (572 square feet); 4 Romance Suites (288 square feet); 10 Courtyard Villas (572 square feet); 27 wheelchair accessible. *Jade:* 784 outside cabins, 360 with balconies; 417 inside; 27 wheelchair accessible. 134 mini-suites with balconies (up to 340 square feet); 2 Garden Villas with three bedrooms (4,390 square feet); 1 Deluxe Owner's Suite (928 square feet), 4 Owner's Suites (up to 928 square feet);

26 Penthouse Suites (up to 600 square feet); 4 Romance Suites (288 square feet); 10 Courtyard Villas (up to 660 square feet).

DINING In keeping with the line's trendsetting Freestyle Cruising, enabling passengers to dine where, when, and with whom they wish, the ships have up to 11 (*Pearl*, 11 or 14, depending on how they're counted) different restaurants offering different menus every night.

Versailles (**Venetian** on *Dawn*) is an ornate main dining room with floor-to-ceiling windows, offering the traditional five-course cruise dining experience with the same waitstaff for the cruise or opening seating. *Jewel*'s **Tsar's Palace** and *Pearl*'s **Summer Palace,** inspired by palaces of the Russian czars, have white and gold ceilings, green marbled pillars, and 24-karat-gold-coated chandeliers. **Aqua** (**Indigo** on *Pearl*) is a contemporary-styled second dining room with a lighter menu. Both rooms are open 5:30–10 p.m. On *Star*, **Endless Summer** (**Salsa** on *Dawn*), set around the second level of the central atrium, is a Tex-Mex and tapas-style restaurant. On *Dawn*, it's **Impressions,** with a 1900s French bistro style. These restaurants do not have a surcharge.

Pearl's Tex-Mex cafe ($10) faces a 24-hour bistro on the atrium's second level. The *Star*'s **Soho** (*Jewel*'s **Chin Chin** and *Pearl*'s **Lotus Garden**)—a high-end Pacific Rim group of restaurants—features California fusion and Asian cuisine with such specialties as Mongolian Hot Pot. **Ginza,** the Japanese restaurant ($15), has an à la carte section, a sushi bar (all you can eat for $15), and a teppanyaki room ($25; reservations required). On *Dawn*, the Japanese-Chinese-Thai complex is called **Bamboo,** with similar outlets.

The handsome **Cagney's Steakhouse,** with a 1930s theme, has become the line's signature restaurant and is featured on all *Jewel*-class ships ($25 per-person cover charge; reservations required). **Le Bistro,** a French restaurant, serves nouvelle cuisine and French classics ($15 per person; reservations required).

For restaurants that require reservations, it's wise to reserve early. Cagney's is particularly popular. Checking availability has been made easy with NCL's new electronic system. Seventeen screens, placed strategically around the ship, show the status of seat availability and/or waiting time in each restaurant. Passengers who select a specific restaurant are given a beeper that buzzes them when their table is ready.

Market Café on *Star* (**Garden Cafe** on *Jewel*; redesigned **Garden Café** on *Pearl* and *Gem*) offers "action stations" preparing made-to-order omelets, waffles, fruit soups, ethnic specialties, and pasta, as well as an extensive buffet and grills, including hamburgers, fish and chips, potpies, and wok dishes. On *Pearl*, the indoor/outdoor buffet has a new layout and extends over a third of the deck, with a large area of outdoor seating at the stern. To one side in the Garden Café is the kids' cafe, with small seats and low tables. In another corner, **La Trattoria** (**La Cucina** on *Pearl*) opens in the evening, provides table service, and offers popular Italian fare, including an antipasto cart for passengers to make their own selections ($10 per person, wine or margarita included). The ships also have an outdoor grill, an ice-cream bar, and a coffee shop, plus 24-hour room service.

SERVICE The downside of NCL's otherwise terrific ships is service in the dining room and Le Bistro and in some bars, which is often very slow and haphazard. In contrast, cabin attendants are good, often very good.

FACILITIES AND ACTIVITIES One of the ships' most distinctive attractions is the show lounge, spanning three decks without obstruction and seating up to 1,042 people. One of the *Pearl*'s several new shows, entitled *Tubez*, is an edgy (some might say over the edge) musical interspersed with daredevil stunts on bikes, skateboards, and in-line skates against a hip-hop set.

The **Star Club Casino** (**Pearl Club** on *Pearl*) offers blackjack, baby baccarat, roulette, three-card poker, Caribbean stud poker, and craps, as well as some games other lines don't have, such as pai-gow poker, pai-gow tiles, and even a big baccarat table (available only by special request prior to sailing). Also available is a new electronic player tracking system that logs each passenger's play and rewards him for it. The card records players' earnings and offers various rewards, including onboard amenities, credit applied to their onboard account, reduced rates for future cruises, and even a complimentary cruise if the level of play is high enough.

On *Dawn*, passengers are treated to two shows. *South Beach Rave!*, meant to reflect the energy and excitement of Miami's hot South Beach, has DJs from the popular Miami television show *Deco Drive* manning the controls, plus red-hot radio personality Nikki Night from Miami's Y-100 FM. *Rave!* rocks as musicians appear from every corner of the theater, together with horn players, guitarists, and drummers, combining for a pastiche of Latin sounds. *Bollywood* is a celebration of India's traditional film culture, founded on spontaneous song and dance. Bombay nights come alive when the audience enters the theater as the scents of spices, incense, and perfumes fill the air. Bright sarongs and turbans combine to create a tapestry of color as stilt walkers, magicians, and jugglers assemble to present the story. The Broadway-type shows that passengers enjoy on *Jewel* are *Band on the Run* and *Cirque Bijou*.

Under an exclusive partnership with the famed Second City improv troupe, six performers stage a comedy revue aboard *Norwegian Dawn* on each of her round-trip sailings from New York City. In addition to performing one night each sailing, the inventive and hilarious Second City ensemble hosts onboard workshops introducing the art of improvisation to *Dawn* passengers, exploring their artistic voices and providing the techniques needed to express those voices. The troupe also gives workshops designed especially for children. Second City also appears on *Norwegian Jewel*, *Norwegian Spirit*, and *Norwegian Pearl* when the ships are in the Caribbean.

Star has a cabaret lounge, karaoke bar with a large screen, a cigar lounge, wine cellar, Champagne bar, a beer garden, an atrium cafe for coffee and pastries, an English pub, an attractive card room and library, and an Internet cafe with 17 stations. There is also a cinema/auditorium, four adjoining meeting rooms, gift shop and department store, and a wedding chapel.

Norwegian Dawn has these attractions, too, but its most distinctive feature is the high-quality art on loan from Star Cruises Chairman Tan Sri Lim Kok Thay's personal collection. These include paintings by Henri Matisse, Claude Monet, and Pierre-Auguste Renoir—all of which have been exhibited in such famous museums as the National Gallery of Art in Washington, D.C.

Pearl's (*Gem* and *Jade*) Deck 7 is action central for the ship, centered by the colorful **Crystal Atrium,** which is dominated by a floor-to-ceiling big-screen television and bright, cheerful decor of aqua and strawberry. It houses the reception, concierge, cruise consultant, shore excursions offices, and to one side, Java Café. Nearby stands a large Dale Chihuly glass sculpture, and overhead, the crystal ceiling by this artist resembles hundreds of icicles. Off to one side of the atrium is **Bar Central**—actually three connected but very different bars—a martini bar, a Champagne and wine bar, and a beer and whiskey pub. A circular stairway from the atrium leads to Deck 8, where there are two casual restaurants: **Blue Lagoon,** serving snacks, burgers, and a variety of light fare around the clock, and **Mambo's Latin,** offering tapas and Tex-Mex specialties.

On your way aft on Deck 7, you pass the Internet cafe on the port side and the photo gallery on starboard, to reach the *Pearl*'s (*Gem*'s) most distinctive feature—**Bliss Ultra Lounge & Nightclub.** During the day, Bliss is a sports bar with the cruise world's first shipboard bowling alley ($5 including shoes for a ten-frame game) with flat-panel televisions tuned to the day's top games or sports events and foosball and other arcade games. In the evening, Bliss is completely transformed into a hip, high-energy ultralounge, complete with plush turquoise, purple, and red velvet banquettes and sexy daybeds. The plasma screens blare with hot music videos spun by the ship's Vibe Master, the bar and dance floor gather crowds, and mood-lit bowling adds to the unusual experience—all decadent enough that you might imagine walking into Hugh Hefner's bedroom or Paris Hilton's playpen.

While it may be surprising to find a four-lane, ten-pin bowling alley on a cruise ship, placing it in a sports bar and nightclub was brilliant. Bowling immediately creates camaraderie and fun. It's a great place to meet people, and it sure beats just going to a bar. The bowling alley also gives NCL a leg up on other cruise ships' breakthroughs, such as climbing walls, because bowling can be enjoyed by all ages.

Among the *Pearl*'s other 11 bars and lounges is the **Corona Cigar Club,** offering hand-rolled cigars, cognacs, and spirits, and a small **Sake Bar** with a selection of sake and Asian beers. On Deck 13, the **Spinnaker Lounge** is a large observation lounge with horizontal windows in the floor, allowing views of the bridge. The lounge has a dance floor and stage for entertainment, with colorful decor and unusual mod chairs and sculpted settees. It's the venue for bingo, dance lessons, and similar activities by day and cabaret in the evening.

NCL was the first cruise line to offer wireless Internet access fleetwide. Passengers who bring their laptops can rent a wireless network card for $10 a day; laptops can be rented for $20 a day. Wireless Internet access costs $0.75 per minute, though buying minutes in bulk—100- or 250-minute packages—can bring the cost down to $0.40 per minute. Now, too, NCL offers the use of cell phones at sea. The *Pearl* has meeting facilities with three breakout rooms, including a boardroom, a library, card room, and chapel.

NCL's galley and backstage tour takes passengers into many areas that are generally off-limits to the public. Tours are now available fleetwide once per cruise on a sea day and limited to eight to ten participants. Price is $55 for the basic two-hour tour, $150 for the extended version.

SPORTS, FITNESS, AND BEAUTY The *Star*'s main pool is located midship on Deck 12. Aft is the bi-level spa and fitness center, with a waterfall in its reception area and an indoor pool, said to be the longest on any cruise ship. The fitness center has state-of-the-art cardiovascular workout equipment, aerobic and boxercise area with a sprung wooden floor, steam and sauna rooms, a jet-current exercise pool, whirlpool, and hydrotherapy facilities.

On the *Dawn*, the 11,302-square-foot **El Dorado Spa** (**South Pacific** on *Pearl*) has 15 treatment rooms, with one designed exclusively for couples. There are private hydrotherapy baths, a lap pool, a Jacuzzi, two Japanese pools, sauna, and a steam room in both the men's and women's areas. The *Pearl* has NCL's first thalassotherapy pool and 17 treatment rooms, of which three are designed for couples. Passengers may also have spa treatments in their cabins, poolside and on-deck massages on port days, and massage and de-stress treatments on secluded beaches during private island visits. Deck 12 of the *Jewel* and *Pearl* has two swimming pools, a three-tiered slide, and a kid's wading pool.

The Sports Deck has an outside jogging track, golf driving range, and volleyball, tennis, or basketball court. This deck on the *Pearl* sports NCL's first climbing wall and a large sports area that includes a multifunction court for regulation tennis, volleyball, and basketball, complete with a spectator stand. To complement the ships' sports facilities, NCL offers an array of active shore excursions, including mountain biking, sailing, and scuba diving.

CHILDREN'S FACILITIES The ships have huge children's centers, complete with a playroom, outdoor pool, movie theater, computer rooms, teen center, video arcade, a nursery, and toddlers' nap room. There is even a special children's area in the buffet restaurant, where kids have their own low-level serving counter and kid-size tables and chairs. *Norwegian Dawn*, constructed with families in mind, also has the **T-Rex Kid's Center**, a supervised facility with a jungle gym, a playroom, **Flicks theater, Clicks,** a computer learning center equipped with five terminals, **Doodles** arts and crafts area, and **Snoozes** sleeping area. A highlight is the **T-Rex Pool,** a Jurassic-themed children's pool with dino-riffic waterslides, a kids-only Jacuzzi, and a paddling and wading pool for the little ones.

The **Teen Club** is a disco strictly for teens, with a video wall showing the latest music video hits, a cinema, and **Video Zone,** a huge arcade with 23 of the latest video games. On the *Pearl*, teens get the New York–inspired **Metro Center** teen's club, complete with graffiti. NCL has a special kids' menu, including kid-size hamburgers, hot dogs, spaghetti, chicken fingers, and ice-cream sundaes.

In NCL's year-round Kid's Crew, program coordinators plan and supervise daily activities for four age groups: Juniors (ages 2–5), First Mates (ages 6–9), Navigators (ages 10–12), and Teens (ages 13–17). At sea, hours are 9 a.m.–noon, 2–5 p.m., and 7–10 p.m.; first evening of cruise, 8–10 p.m.; port days, 7–10 p.m. Group-sitting in port is available 9 a.m.–5 p.m. for a nominal charge. Children under age 2 sail at a substantially reduced fare. For babysitting, inquire with the line prior to departure.

Activities include dances and arts and crafts. There are races, treasure hunts, and games planned for the day at the beach. The ship publishes *Kids' Cruise News* and *Teen Cruise News* daily. Also available are an ice-cream bar and children's menus. The Kids' Soda package gives unlimited soda-fountain access for $28 ($4 per day) for seven days. Teen Passport for teens ages 13–17 enables them to purchase a coupon book for $34.50 to be used for up to 20 nonalcoholic specialty drinks, as well as enjoying exclusive dance and pizza parties and a farewell Frat Party.

SHORE EXCURSIONS NCL's Web site lists the shore excursions, together with prices. The excursions can be booked online. Frequently, the ships on Caribbean itineraries stop at Great Stirrup Cay, NCL's private island in the

Bahamas—an idea originated by NCL in 1977 and copied by many other cruise lines. The island has two main beaches and several others that are not maintained. It has two bars, food service, restrooms, beach chairs and umbrellas, and a straw market. A wide variety of water sports is available, including snorkeling, sailing, and kayaking, as well as volleyball, table tennis, and walking and jogging paths. A live calypso band provides music for listening and dancing.

THE SHIPS *Norwegian Sun's* handsome interior, created by Swedish marine architects Tillberg Design, is one of cool elegance. In the glass-domed, eight-deck atrium and throughout the ship, there is no glitz or bright lights but rather an airy, refined setting with a multimillion-dollar art collection integrated into the decor.

The reception and purser's desks, concierge, and shore excursion offices are on Atlantic Deck. **Neptune's Court,** a second atrium, has a grand staircase just outside the **Seven Seas Dining Room,** connecting the Atlantic Deck to the Promenade and International decks with the main show lounge.

The *Norwegian Sun* was the first of the fleet to have NCL's Freestyle Cruising elements included during the construction. Among them are more dining options—11 restaurants (some with surcharge or pay as you go). They include three dining rooms, an outdoor buffet, an indoor garden buffet, pizzeria, and wine bar, the NCL signature **Sports Bar & Grill, Le Bistro,** an ice-cream bar, and Champagne and cigar bars.

Among other features, *Norwegian Sun* has a "lifestyle area" for classes in computers, financial planning, yoga, and so on; a wedding chapel; a larger gym and spa than NCL's earlier ships; and larger cabins. She was the first to have the new cabin category of mini-suites with balconies, now available on all the newest *Jewel*-class ships.

At the **Internet cafe,** passengers can go online 24 hours a day. Ship's photographers have digital cameras, enabling passengers to e-mail photos home (for an additional fee). A Skycam on the bridge is downloaded onto a Web site so family members ashore can track the voyage. Other facilities include the Atrium Room, available for small private functions, and a medical center.

In a joint venture, **www.dutyfree.com** and Colombian Emeralds International manage *Norwegian Sun's* gift shops. Passengers view jewelry patterns and designs at a kiosk, with home delivery available. Liquor selections, displayed in the shopping arcade, can be ordered through room service.

Norwegian Spirit (formerly Star Cruises' *SuperStar Leo*), added to the fleet in 2004, is not a twin of the *Sun* but a close relative in her features and facilities.

Norwegian Sky	QUALITY 8	VALUE B
Norwegian Spirit	QUALITY 8	VALUE B
Norwegian Sun	QUALITY 8	VALUE B
REGISTRY Panama/Bahamas	LENGTH 882/853 feet	BEAM 105 feet
CABINS 1001/998/968	DRAFT NA/26 feet	SPEED 24/23 knots
MAXIMUM PASSENGERS	PASSENGER DECKS 12/11	ELEVATORS 13/12
2138/1,966/1,936	CREW 920/882/968	SPACE RATIO 38.3/40

She has similar Freestyle Cruising elements, such as nine restaurants, a large spa and fitness center, and a 24/7 Internet cafe, among others.

In October 2006, *Norwegian Sun* was the first cruise ship to homeport in New Orleans after Hurricane Katrina, at the city's new $37 million Erato Street Terminal, designed to accommodate larger cruise ships. After being the first ship to launch NCL America as *Pride of Aloha,* she returned to the NCL fleet in 2008, took back her original name, *Norwegian Sky,* and has been sailing from Miami on very successful short cruises to the Bahamas. In June 2009, *Norwegian Sky* emerged from dry dock after having a complete refurbishment and an addition of three new cabins. Improvements were made in the Atrium, the Stardust Theater, Il Adagio (the Italian specialty restaurant), and Dazzles bar and nightclub. The Garden Café got new food stations, and 14 suites received new wall treatments and new marble tiles in their bathrooms, while the woodwork and teak decking around the whirlpools on the suite balconies were also refinished.

ITINERARIES *See* Itinerary Index.

CABINS Cabins are similar to those on other NCL ships and are furnished with two lower beds that convert to a queen, a sitting area, dressing table, refrigerator, safe, television, radio, and telephone. Those on the *Sun* have bathrooms with bidets. Other than the Penthouses and Owner Suites, all cabins are uniform in size and efficiently laid out. Closet space is adequate. All cabins have Internet hookups. Sixteen penthouses with teakwood-furnished balconies have butler service and an exclusive room service menu for breakfast, lunch, and dinner.

The *Sun,* with more outside cabins (64% total) than NCL's earlier ships, has larger cabins and 52 suites, including 30 mini-suites with balconies, measuring 267–301 square feet. Four Owner's Suites, located forward above the ship's bridge, have 828 square feet each.

All of *Sky's* cabins have a refrigerator, small desk, telephone, coffeemaker, in-room safe, and television. Bathrooms have nice storage nooks, but, except for suites, all are shower-only. There are several suite categories, including ten Penthouse Suites, at 364 square feet and up, and four Owner's Suites at 650 square feet.

Specifications Norwegian Spirit, 591 outside cabins, 374 with balconies; 374 inside; 16 Penthouse Suites; 4 wheelchair accessible. *Norwegian Sun,* 675 outside (145–221 square feet), 325 inside (167–176 square feet); 52 suites with balconies (436 square feet); 16 doubles, 185 triples, 779 quads; 20 wheelchair accessible. Norwegian Sky, 986 cabins, including 572 outside, of which 243 have balconies; 10 Penthouse Suites; 4 Owner's Suites.

DINING All three ships reflect the Freestyle Cruising's concept with their dining options. On a seven-day cruise, passengers never need to eat dinner in the same restaurant more than once if they care to pay extra in some of the eateries. Among their choices, they can enjoy either of two main dining rooms, **Four Seasons** and **Seven Seas** on the *Sun,* with open seating 5:30–10 p.m. every evening; a more formal Italian restaurant, **Il Adagio** (on *Sun* and *Sky;* La Trattoria on *Spirit*) ($10), by reservation; French fare at **Le Bistro** ($15); a Pacific Rim restaurant complex with a sushi bar and teppanyaki (except *Sky*) room ($15–$20); an Asian restaurant on *Sun* and *Spirit* ($10); and a 24-hour indoor/outdoor cafe with food stations serving hamburgers, hot dogs, soups, and salads. *Norwegian Sun* has a "healthy living" restaurant with a lighter, more contemporary menu, including selections from *Cooking Light* magazine and spa menus. *Spirit* also has **Cagney's,** a traditional steak house ($20), where patrons can enjoy certified Angus beef, veal, pork, lamb, seafood, and grilled chicken.

The casual **Great Outdoor Café** and **Garden Café (Raffles Terrace and Buffet** on *Spirit*) have "food action stations," serving up paella, sushi, Norwegian waffles, pasta, and more, intended to eliminate long buffet lines. Both cafes offer breakfast, lunch, and snack specialties that vary daily. There is a pizzeria and **Sprinkles Ice Cream Bar.** The 24-hour room-service menu offers pizza too. **Blue Lagoon Café** on *Spirit* is a 24-hour food court serving hamburgers, fish and chips, potpies, and wok dishes and includes a buffet for kids with small seats and tables.

Passengers give the ship's cuisine, especially the alternative dining options, good reviews. The only dining disappointment is breakfast and lunch in the Pool Deck cafe for the lack of variety.

On *Norwegian Sky*, Freestyle dining gives passengers the option of two open-seating main dining rooms, Crossings and the Palace Restaurant, as well as the 24-hour buffet in the Lido Cafe and other casual venues for no charge. The three excellent specialty restaurants—one for Asian fusion, another for Italian fare, and the third, Le Bistro, for French-Mediterranean cuisine—have a charge. Room service is available around the clock.

FACILITIES AND ACTIVITIES The ships have similar bars, including a **Champagne Bar,** by the atrium with large glass windows and a view of the lobby area, serving Champagne and premium vodkas. Nonsmoking guests can select from the martini menu in the **Windjammer Bar** on *Sun*, and cigar connoisseurs enjoy freshly hand-rolled stogies and premium brandy behind the glass walls of the adjoining but segregated **Cigar Club** with humidor. The **Java Bar** (*Sun*) and **The Café** (*Spirit*) coffee bar have a great selection of coffees, teas, and liqueurs at fair prices and serve pastries and cookies. *Spirit* also has the **Bier Garten Grill,** offering beer and cocktails and Bavarian food, such as weisswurst and pretzels.

Sun Club Casino offers blackjack, roulette, Caribbean poker, and slot machines. The golden, two-deck **Stardust Lounge** with a proscenium stage features Broadway-style shows. Brand-new shows premiered recently on *Norwegian Sun* and *Norwegian Spirit*. With the venue's sound, lighting, and audiovisual facilities, the lounge can be easily transformed into a disco.

Dazzles Lounge has what NCL claims is the longest bar at sea. Passengers can see cabaret acts, illusionists, and comedians. The entertainment is uniformly of high standard, in keeping with the NCL tradition.

Sun also has a wedding chapel for ceremonies in port, a library, and **East Indies Conference Center,** which seats 100 and can be divided into three smaller rooms.

On the Pool Deck, **Topsider's Bar** is a long poolside bar with stools and outdoor tables; on the Sports Deck, the **Sports Bar** offers televisions with videotaped and live broadcasts of sporting events. The **Observation Lounge** has floor-to-ceiling windows overlooking the bow. Roaming the decks is a

Skymobile beverage cart making drink deliveries to passengers. When the ships sail in the Caribbean, pool attendants provide Evian water, suntan lotion, cold face towels, and fresh fruit.

NCL racked up another first in 2004 when it began offering onboard cell-phone service on *Norwegian Sun*. The technology is now available fleetwide. Consumers are charged by their cellular wireless providers at the roaming rates set by their carriers.

SPORTS, FITNESS, AND BEAUTY The two swimming pools are connected by steps and a central wading platform to four hot tubs and set off by dark-wood decks and dark-green lounge chairs. Also on the enormous Sun Deck is a spa with therapists trained in a wide range of treatments. It has a unisex beauty salon and a gym/aerobics area with exercise equipment; exercisers can enjoy ocean views through floor-to-ceiling glass walls.

On *Sun*'s Sports Deck, passengers will find a golf driving net, a full-size basketball/volleyball court, a batting cage, and shuffleboard. A walking and jogging track circles the Promenade Deck. *Spirit*'s Sports Deck is similar, with four golf driving nets. *Norwegian Sky*'s Body Waves Fitness Center has a good selection of machines and a spacious aerobics studio. As with NCL's other ships, the spa offers facials, massages, manicures, and hairstyling services. The ship also has two golf driving nets and a kids' pool.

CHILDREN'S FACILITIES Kids Korner playroom on International Deck offers Kid's Crew, a year-round, supervised program divided into four age groups. (See "Children's Facilities" in the *Norwegian Dawn* section for details.)

SHORE EXCURSIONS In Alaska, NCL offers some of mainstream cruising's best offbeat excursions, such as glacier hiking, mountain biking, forest trekking, a six-hour hike outside Skagway, and three hours of sea kayaking and flight-seeing from Juneau to a remote lodge. The more exotic tours have few slots; book early. Among the most popular is Dive Into Adventure—few people can say they have been diving in Alaska.

Note: Alaska shore excursions are expensive on every cruise line because of the very short season in which operators have to make money and the very high costs of operating tours in Alaska.

THE SHIPS The 153,000-ton *Norwegian Epic,* the third generation of a Freestyle Cruising ship and NCL's largest ship to date, is slated for delivery in May 2010 and its inauguration in July. This ship will embody NCL's commitment to innovation and incorporate a wide range of new features, such as cabins with curved walls, the only "big top" at sea, and a host of other cruise ship "firsts," and so many options you'll need more than one cruise to try them all.

Typical of NCL ships, *Norwegian Epic* has artwork on its hull, but, unlike the others whose art is inspired by the ship's name or its destinations, *Norwegian Epic*'s hull design takes its inspiration from the ship's interior. Designed by the company's own marketing team, the motifs are sophisticated, sleek, and color-ful, reflecting everything from the curved cabin walls to the contemporary notes of the ship's public rooms. Painted on both sides with free-form rolling waves of varying sizes, the design runs through a color spectrum of lime, aqua, red, and purple dotted by silver circles.

In addition, the ship features cabins dubbed New Wave standard, New Wave balcony, New Wave deluxe, and a new category of inside studios

Norwegian Epic	SUMMER 2010	
REGISTRY Panama	LENGTH 1,068 feet	BEAM 133 feet
CABINS 2,000	DRAFT 28.5 feet	SPEED knots 22
MAXIMUM PASSENGERS	PASSENGER DECKS 19	ELEVATORS 16
5,186	CREW 1,730	SPACE RATIO NA

designed for budget and single travelers. There's also a fresh take on maximized open living space and bathroom design with a separate shower stall, separate toilet, and a modern vanity top sink. The cabins' decor is a sophisticated earth-tone palette accented with splashes of color and dark wood. Concealed contour LED lighting and back-lit domed ceilings set a relaxing mood.

ITINERARIES *See* Itinerary Index.

CABINS *Norwegian Epic*'s innovative accommodations with groundbreaking design offer something for everyone—travelers on a budget, singles, families, as well as those seeking a spa experience or luxury. The most interesting are the New Wave cabins with curved walls and a new model of inside cabin—the studio—that shares a common space, called the Living Room. There are spa accommodations in the spa area and family cabins next to the children's area. The luxurious ship-within-a-ship, first seen on *Norwegian Jewel,* is larger, even more private, and loaded with amenities. All outside cabins have balconies. All cabin categories (except studios and top-deck villas) have unusual bathrooms with a separate shower stall, separate toilet, and a modern vanity top sink. The sink is on the living side of the privacy curtain that separates the shower and toilet from the living area.

The Studios and Living Room: 128 studios on Decks 11 and 12. At 100 square feet, a studio is slightly smaller than a standard inside cabin (128 square feet); it sleeps two and has unusual—even funky—features: a large, round window that looks out into the corridor (yes, there's a curtain), along with a control panel that enables guests to select their own color of lighting, depending on the time of day and their mood, including a love setting for romantic nights at sea. Occupants have exclusive key-card access to the Living Room, a two-story private lounge with a concierge, private bar, two large-screen televisions, room service, and comfy chairs with lamps for reading; the Living Room is also a place to enjoy a cocktail before dinner or just hang out.

Designed for budget-conscious travelers, the innovative inside-cabin category and its design are a first in the cruise industry. One drawback: The shower, toilet, and wash basin are directly in the cabin, with only the toilet walled off. The price for two people sharing a studio is about the same as a standard inside cabin; thus, the attraction has less to do with price and more to do with lifestyle. The 1,000-square-foot Living Room is a shared social space that might appeal to budget seekers and singles, but not to everyone.

Family Staterooms: 225 family deluxe balcony and 146 family balcony cabins, with triples and quads and many connecting, are on Decks 13 and 14, near the Kids Crew, the expanded children's area. The cabins maximize living space and have the New Wave design with contemporary curved walls and ceilings, as well as the unusual bathrooms described earlier.

Spa Suites and Cabins: 39 spa suites, deluxe balcony, and balcony cabins. Located on Deck 14, these accommodations adjacent to the spa's thermal suite and fitness center have a private key-card entry. For an added indulgence, eight of the spa suites have an in-room whirlpool. *Epic* will be the first NCL ship to have spa accommodations.

Villas and Suites: 60 Courtyard Villas, Penthouse Suites, and Deluxe Owner's Suites. Located on two private decks (16 and 17) high at the top, these accommodations are a ship-within-a-ship and three times larger than similar complexes on other NCL ships. All have exclusive access to a private pool, two whirlpools, saunas, sun deck, fitness facility, private indoor/outdoor dining, bar, and concierge lounge. The 46 luxurious Courtyard Villas come with two bedrooms and two bathrooms. The six Penthouses and eight Deluxe Owner's Suites have a bedroom with separate living and dining area, while Owner's Suites have all-around floor-to-ceiling windows. Seven more Penthouse Suites are located in other areas of the ship.

Deluxe Balcony, 98 cabins; New Wave Balcony, 851 standard cabins; inside, 560 cabins. Located on Decks 8–14, all these accommodations feature the New Wave design, with contemporary curved architecture, open living space, and bathrooms described previously. *Norwegian Epic* will have 42 wheelchair-accessible cabins in various categories.

DINING *Norwegian Epic* will offer Freestyle Dining in a choice of 17 restaurants. These include **Taste,** by the ship's atrium on Deck 5, that serves a selection of traditional and contemporary cuisine in a setting of off-white, free-form plastered walls with European retro-chic furnishings, brick details, and floor-to-ceiling velvet curtains. **O'Sheehan's Neighborhood Bar & Grill,** a classic neighborhood sports bar and restaurant to be open 24 hours, will serve American favorites and comfort food. The atrium's two-story high LCD screen will be visible from inside the restaurant, and additional flat-panel televisions will show sporting events while patrons enjoy such activities as dartboards, pool tables, foosball, arcade games, and three lanes of bowling. The two-story-high **Manhattan Room** on Deck 6, reminiscent of an elegant Art Deco supper club, has a dance floor and floor-to-ceiling panoramic windows looking aft; it will offer live music and dancing in the evening and elegant cuisine reflecting the romantic nature of the room. These three venues will not have a cover charge.

Café Jardin and **The Great Outdoors,** with decor modeled after a traditional English country garden conservatory, is the casual Lido restaurant with action stations where chefs cook fresh, prepared-to-order food. Selections include seafood, pizza, fruit, soups, pasta, ethnic specialties, burgers, and desserts. A section of the Café includes a kid's corner with child-friendly seats and tables. The Great Outdoors, the Café extension, will have a view of the Aqua Park. **La Cucina,** a Tuscan-style eatery that opens to Café Jardin above, will serve regional Italian specialties such as pizza and pasta, as well as meat, chicken, and fish dishes. Its traditional Italian decor reflects two distinct areas: a Tuscan farmhouse and an Italian courtyard.

Cagney's Steakhouse and Churrascaria is NCL's traditional American steak house with a twist—the addition of Argentinean churrasco. In addition to premium steaks, diners will be able to sample a variety of skewered meats presented tableside by *passadors*. A large salad bar has also been added. The upscale **Le Bistro** serves classic French cuisine with an American flair. Its elegant decor will be highlighted with contemporary and traditional paintings and sculptures. **Shanghai's,** another new addition to the specialty dining options, will have an open kitchen where traditional Chinese cuisine, noodles, wok-fried dishes, and dim sum are prepared. Decor is meant to reflect Old Shanghai in the 1930s and the China Club in Hong Kong. As the largest teppanyaki restaurant at sea, the expanded restaurant will feature up to 24 knife-wielding chefs cooking exhibition-style Japanese cuisine on flat-top grills. **Wasabi** is the expanded sushi and sake bar serving sushi, sashimi, and Japanese yakitori dishes. With clean lines and modern decor, Wasabi is located outside the teppanyaki restaurant. Prices for these specialty restaurants are expected to be about the same as on other NCL ships.

The Epic Club and Courtyard Grill: Located high atop the ship in The Villas complex, this modern, elegant dinner restaurant is reserved exclusively for *Norwegian Epic*'s suite and villa guests. Decor reflects a private-club ambience with contemporary furnishings and a large wine display. The Courtyard Grill is the more casual, outdoor area serving breakfast and lunch. Villa passengers have another restaurant, which the cruise line has not yet detailed. *Norwegian Epic* will offer 24-hour room service for all passengers.

FACILITIES AND ACTIVITIES   NCL believes that *Norwegian Epic* will change the face of cruise line entertainment. Instead of the traditional two nightly shows in one large main theater, *Norwegian Epic* will have multiple, specially designed entertainment venues throughout the ship so that passengers can choose from a variety of entertainment each evening, some offered for the first time ever at sea. Like the selection of cabins and variety of dining options, there's something for everyone among the entertainment options—and there are new ones that might appeal to people who never thought a cruise was for them.

Headlining the list is another cruise-industry first: The famous Blue Man Group—an entertainment staple in Las Vegas, Orlando, and New York—will perform in the ship's 685-seat **Epic Theater.** The group with blue-painted bodies is known for its unique theatrical shows and concerts, which combine music, comedy, and multimedia theatrics. The group will present the same show eight times on four nights of a seven-night cruise; there will be no cover charge or entrance fee for the show.

In another first, *Norwegian Epic* boasts the only "big top" at sea. In a 265-seat theater-in-the-round, famed producer-director Neil Goldberg will present *Cirque Dreams* and Dinner. The one-of-a-kind interactive theatrical-acrobatic dinner show with music, mayhem, and acrobatics will be performed twice nightly under a Spiegeltent ($15 per person). NCL says it's an experience unlike anything else at sea, and they are probably right!

To date, the company has revealed five nightlife venues meant to reflect Las Vegas, Ibiza, the Riviera, and South Beach. **Posh Beach Club,** a first-of-its-kind beach club at sea, offers an exclusive, adults-only setting at the top of the ship, and **Spice H20** is an adults-only aft pool deck. **Bliss Ultra Lounge,** NCL's all-day entertainment and nightclub complex, has a four-lane bowling alley. **Headliners Comedy Club** will highlight troupes from Chicago's famous Second City comedy club, which have long been popular on NCL ships. They will perform in a custom-designed venue with a show-lounge format of a small, raised stage, bringing the audience close to the performers. **Fat Cats Jazz Club,** the place for cool jazz and blues, is a small club featuring world-class performers in an urban setting with comfortable leather sofas and chairs. Ice Bar and Spice H20 offer nonstop entertainment day and night.

The **Epic Casino** will have a more upscale, Monte Carlo-like atmosphere than most of NCL's ships. The casino will open to Taste, the atrium restaurant above, and Bar Central below. Throughout the ship, there will be a total of 18 bars and lounges; among them will be the **Atrium Bar; O'Sheehan's; Cascades,** the casino bar; **Cagney's Bar; Sake Bar; Malting's Whiskey Bar; Shaker's Martini Bar; Humidor Cigar Lounge; Waves Bar; Epic Club;** and **Ice Bar,** a first-at-sea beach club.

SPORTS, FITNESS, AND BEAUTY *Epic*'s seven decks of Freestyle family fun will be highlighted by a 33-foot-high, 64-foot-wide rock-climbing wall and the first-ever rappelling wall at sea; six bowling lanes in two venues (Bliss Ultra Lounge and O'Sheehan's Neighborhood Bar *&* Grill); and the expansive Aqua Park with three waterslides. One slide, specifically designed for children, zips straight through the rock-climbing wall; a more adventurous slide twists and turns down three stories; and The Epic Plunge, the only tube slide at sea, blasts riders on inner tubes into the core of a bowl slide before a thrilling drop through a 200-foot-long tube. Riders are then launched into the vortex of The Epic Plunge, where centrifugal forces keep them high on a wall for several turns, before ending in an exciting transition to a splashdown lane.

The Aqua Park also includes two main pools with water effects that illuminate at night; five whirlpools; as well as a wading pool and a kid's pool in the children's Splash and Play Zone, which has whimsical sculptures, water sprays, and effects, along with a kiddie slide.

The mixed-use Sports Deck has eight different athletic activities for passengers to try, in addition to three separate kids' and teen activity areas. The ship has a basketball court, the first squash court at sea, volleyball, soccer, dodge ball, batting cage, bungee trampoline, rope adventure course, and a 24-foot-high enclosed climbing cage called the spider web. The 33-foot-high extreme rock-climbing wall, accessible on two levels with varying degrees of difficulty, is rated according to official U.S. climbing grades.

CHILDREN'S FACILITIES *Norwegian Epic* will have NCL's largest Kid's Crew facility, centrally located on Deck 14 and easily accessible to the family cabins. Two separate areas are specifically designed for kids ages 2–9 and tweens ages 10–12. The kid's area includes a space-themed play area, air-hockey table, an interactive light-up dance floor, Wii gaming areas, and an arts-and-crafts area, along with a state-of-the-art surround-sound cinema. The Tween Zone has a futuristic feel and includes multiple Wii and PlayStation areas, in addition to a private karaoke performance stage that doubles as a cinema.

Entourage, at the top of the ship on Deck 16, is *Norwegian Epic's* high-energy, exclusive teen zone for kids ages 13–17. This funky space includes air hockey; pinball; foosball; a video jukebox; and nine large flat-panel televisions, five of which are located around a central video game console featuring PlayStation3. In the evening, Entourage becomes a hip nightclub with comfy couches and a space for dancing or just hanging out.

NCL AMERICA

In May 2003, NCL Corp. surprised the cruise world when it announced that it would have a U.S.-flagged ship in Hawaii by summer 2004, employing an all-American crew and subject to all American laws. The announcement came soon after Congress passed a federal spending bill that included an exemption to the Passenger Services Act. As a result, NCL, in exchange for completing two former Project America vessels to sail in Hawaii under the U.S. flag, was also given an exemption to reflag one existing, foreign-flagged NCL ship that would sail under the U.S. flag within Hawaii (but not Alaska or the Caribbean). Under the exemption, NCL's *Norwegian Sky* was reflagged to U.S. ship registry in 2004. Renamed *Pride of Aloha*, she launched NCL America's first Hawaii cruises with all-American crews on July 4, 2004. (She has since returned to the NCL's fleet, resumed her original name, and sails on short cruises between Florida and the Bahamas.)

In February 2008, NCL withdrew *Pride of Hawaii* from Hawaii cruising and deployed her in Europe as a result of the steep increase in competition in Hawaii and the soaring price of gasoline, which adversely impacted travel to Hawaii. Her name was changed to *Norwegian Jade*.

Pride of America, constructed at the Lloyd Werft shipyard in Germany, was the first new oceangoing passenger ship built in nearly 50 years to sail under the American flag. She began service in Hawaii in 2005, offering seven-night, inter-island cruises round-trip from Honolulu.

THE SHIP *Pride of America* has as her theme the "Best of America," reflected in the decor and names of public rooms—you can't miss it, starting with the design of the atrium, called the **Capitol Atrium,** inspired by the U.S. Capitol and the White House. The nine dining outlets and many lounges have such names as **Liberty Restaurant, Lazy J Steakhouse, Cadillac Diner,** and **Napa Wine Bar,** among others. In keeping with NCL's new signature, painted on the hull of *Pride of America* is a vibrant, artistic interpretation of the Stars and Stripes and the bald eagle.

In addition to an abundance of public rooms, the ship has state-of-the-art entertainment venues, two pools, extensive children's facilities, and large meeting facilities. It also sports several NCL firsts, including a conservatory, a new category of family suites, a tennis court, and an art gallery—all named and decorated to reflect America's diversity.

ITINERARIES *See* Itinerary Index.

CABINS *Pride of America*'s extensive choice of cabins is highlighted by a Grand Suite, as well as NCL's new concept—Family Suites. The six Owner's Suites,

Pride of America	QUALITY 8	VALUE B
REGISTRY United States	LENGTH 921 feet	BEAM 105 feet
CABINS 1,069	DRAFT 26 feet	SPEED 23/22/25 knots
MAXIMUM PASSENGERS	PASSENGER DECKS 10	ELEVATORS 10
2,002	CREW 921	SPACE RATIO 38

each with 870 square feet, are named after Hawaiian flowers; each of six deluxe Penthouse Suites covers 735 square feet, and 28 Penthouse Suites range from 504 to 585 square feet. The suites are furnished with a king-size bed and walk-in closet, a bathroom with a separate shower and Jacuzzi bath, dressing area, and flat-panel television; a separate living room has a Bang & Olufsen entertainment center, television with a DVD player and CD/DVD library, and computer access with Internet connection.

Each of the eight new family suites covers 360 square feet and has a living room furnished with a double sofa bed and entertainment center, separate den with a single sofa bed, a private bedroom with twin beds convertible to a queen, and a private balcony. Four additional family suites (330–356 square feet) are interconnecting cabins sleeping up to eight people. The larger of the two cabins is an oversize outside cabin with two single beds that can be combined for a queen-size bed, plus a sitting area with a double sofa bed. The cabin interconnects with another outside cabin that has two single beds and two upper berths. The eight-person family suites have two bathrooms.

The 1,400-square-foot Grand Suite, positioned high atop the ship forward of the main sundeck, offers sweeping views of the ocean and an impressive assortment of amenities. It has a large living room with a Bang & Olufsen entertainment center with television, CD, stereo, DVD player, CD/DVD library, computer access with Internet connection, and a wet bar. The suite also has a dining room with a polished teak table seating six, plus a private butler. The master bedroom has a king-size bed and bathroom with separate shower and Jacuzzi bath, a dressing area with a flat-panel television and a large walk-in closet, and a separate powder room. On the large wraparound veranda, suite occupants and their guests can enjoy open-air dining, a Jacuzzi for up to six people, and private areas for sunbathing and for entertaining up to 50 visitors.

Specifications *Pride of America*, 1,069 cabins, of which 660 have balconies; 250 family accommodations; 1 Grand Suite; 34 Penthouse Suites; 6 Owner's Suites; 12 Family Suites.

DINING *Pride of America* offers nine restaurants and nine different menus every night. These include two main restaurants and alternative gourmet, ethnic, and casual eateries. Chefs are out of the galley and positioned at the serving islands to prepare items such as pasta, sushi, and stir-fry *à la minute* or carving to order.

Pride of America's **Skyline,** a main restaurant, has decor inspired by the architecture and skyscrapers of the 1930s; **Liberty,** the second main restaurant one deck up, has Colonial design featuring America's Founding Fathers and large paintings depicting important moments in American history. Both offer traditional dining.

Also on Deck 5, **East Meets West,** an elegant Pacific Rim/Asian fusion restaurant, has a sushi and sashimi bar and a teppanyaki room with two tables accommodating 32 people. **Jefferson's Bistro,** NCL's signature restaurant, has an à la carte menu of nouvelle and classic French cuisine and decor inspired by Thomas Jefferson's home, Monticello. (Jefferson was the U.S. ambassador to France from 1785 to 1789.)

On Deck 6, **Lazy Jay Steakhouse** is an upscale steak house with Texas decor and art depicting the Houston Space Center, Texas Rangers, and Dallas

Cowboys. It serves Angus beef and other grilled meat, seafood, and chicken. The indoor/outdoor **Cadillac Diner,** a 24-hour diner, has decor of 1950s pop stars, complete with Cadillac seats and a video jukebox. The fare includes hamburgers, fish and chips, potpie, and wok dishes.

On Deck 11, **Little Italy,** a casual Italian eatery inspired by New York's Little Italy, serves pasta, pizza, and other Italian specialties. **Aloha Café/Kids Café,** the indoor/outdoor buffet with a Hawaiian theme, has food stations for prepared-to-order omelets, waffles, fruit, soups, and ethnic specialties. It also includes a buffet with small chairs and tables to accommodate 36 kids.

SERVICE When NCL America started its Hawaii operation, it was bombarded with complaints about service. However, the cruise line tackled the problems and worked hard to correct them with an extensive crew training program and other measures. Approximately 65% of the crew is from Hawaii; after they had proper training, the service complaints dropped considerably.

FACILITIES AND ACTIVITIES **Capitol Atrium,** the heart of *Pride of America*, carries her all-American theme with a decorative stone floor, water feature, and a stunning back-lit glass dome. Her nine lounges and bars are designed to reflect the diversity of the country, such as **Mardi Gras Cabaret,** the ship's nightclub, **Gold Rush Saloon,** and two outdoor pool bars, **Key West Bar & Grill** and **Waikiki Bar.**

The **Soho Art Gallery** offers original works of art, while Newbury Street resembles New England shops in the early 1900s. There is NCL's first conservatory, with a tropical landscaped garden and live exotic birds; the **S.S. America Library,** honoring the famous ship; and the **Hollywood Theater,** with large golden statues adorning the walls. The ship has Wi-Fi capability and an Internet cafe. Passengers can obtain an Internet access card for their laptops or rent a laptop with wireless Internet capability.

Pride of America's meeting facilities—among the largest at sea—encompass six meeting rooms, ranging from boardrooms for 10 people to an auditorium that can accommodate more than 250 people. Five of the meeting rooms—named for Hawaii and her islands—can be used individually or combined. The **Diamond Head Auditorium** is a multilevel circular room that boasts a state-of-the-art audiovisual system with multiple screens that lower from the ceiling to be viewed by all participants. The auditorium also splits into two amphitheater-style presentation rooms. The conference area has a business center, a separate large gathering and break area, and the **Lanai Bar and Lounge** for group cocktail parties and other purposes.

Pride of America's meeting facilities should appeal to the business market on several accounts. Meetings on board the only large U.S.-flagged ships regularly sailing the Hawaiian islands and visiting only U.S. ports qualify for corporate and individual tax deductions for meetings expenses.

SPORTS, FITNESS, AND BEAUTY *Pride of America*'s **Santa Fe Spa and Fitness Center,** a tranquil area decorated with natural elements such as stone, wood, and artifacts from New Mexico, offers an exotic menu of spa and beauty treatments. The fitness center has Cybex exercise equipment and Life Fitness cardiovascular machines, each with its own flat-panel television, an aerobics room for yoga, power walking, and other fitness classes, and saunas and steam room.

The Sports Deck has a basketball and volleyball court. The large South Beach sunning and swimming area, inspired by Miami's Art Deco district, has some novel distractions and activities capturing the energy and fun of Ocean Drive and Lincoln Road.

CHILDREN'S FACILITIES On *Pride of America*, **Rascal's Kids Center** and pool offers supervised facilities designed around an animal theme. The ship has NCL's age-specific children's program to keep little ones busy throughout their cruise. (See *Norwegian Dawn* for details.)

SHORE EXCURSIONS The ship offers dozens of shore excursions, as varied as golf and rain forest walks to kayaking and helicopter rides over lava flows. All are listed on the cruise line's Web site, together with their prices. For the night the ship spends at Kauai, the highlight is a luau and show that NCL America created in partnership with the 35-acre Kilohana Plantation, NH Productions, and Gaylord's Restaurant, one of the island's top restaurants. Kilohana Plantation also offers additional activities for passengers, including a train ride on the Kauai Plantation Railway or a vintage carriage ride through the estate. They can play traditional Hawaiian games or have a Hawaiian arts and crafts lesson. The show, produced by a local company and entitled *Kalamaku*, tells the story of one family's journey from Tahiti to Kauai and is performed by a cast of 40. It is staged on Monday, Thursday, and Saturday evenings to coincide with the ship being in port.

Another feature gives passengers a taste of the real Hawaii in *Ho'okipa Aloha*, a 45-minute show with real Hawaiian students of hula performing as they would for each other. The show is staged on embarkation day from Honolulu. NCL America has partnered with several halau, a hula school for young and old, to present the hula in a form most visitors never see. To NCL's credit, it is an ongoing effort to give passengers an authentic look at the Hawaiian culture and heritage.

Oceania Cruises

8300 NW 33rd Street, Suite 308
Miami, FL 33122
☎ **305-514-2300 or 800-531-5658**
FAX **305-514-2222**
www.oceaniacruises.com

TYPE OF SHIPS Midsize and large deluxe ships.

TYPE OF CRUISES Upscale cruises with a casual ambience on worldwide, destination-oriented itineraries, usually ten days or longer.

CRUISE LINE'S STRENGTHS
- medium-size ships
- diverse foreign home ports and itineraries
- overnights in interesting ports
- gourmet dining in specialty restaurants
- choices of four open-seating restaurants
- casual onboard atmosphere; no formal dress code
- affordable fares, value-added deals

CRUISE LINE'S SHORTCOMINGS
- lack of facilities for children
- few cruise departures from U.S. ports
- no short cruises to sample the product
- limited nightlife
- crowded tables in main dining room

FELLOW PASSENGERS Oceania Cruises attracts a mix of first-time cruisers eager to try a premium cruise line and experienced travelers who simply enjoy the line's longer, destination-focused itineraries. Average passenger age is 55. Many are former Renaissance Cruises fans; others are likely to be experienced travelers who have sailed on other premium and luxury lines attracted by the value Oceania's prices represent. Oceania passengers prefer smaller ships and savor international travel.

Recommended for Travelers who want to visit far-flung lands; those who appreciate extra time in ports. Intellectually curious couples and mature singles who appreciate a good value and enjoy touches of luxury cruising. Those who prefer medium-size ships.

Not recommended for Families with children; those who seek the party atmosphere of some large cruise ships or seek lots of nightlife and entertainment.

CRUISE AREAS AND SEASONS Europe, spring, summer, fall; Asia, Caribbean, South America, winter and spring; transatlantic, spring and fall.

THE LINE A privately held company built from scratch, Oceania Cruises was founded in 2003 by two cruise industry veterans—Frank Del Rio, former president and CEO of now-defunct Renaissance Cruises, and Joe Watters, former president of Crystal Cruises—who brought complementary talents to the new cruise line. Del Rio, who knows the ships well, having previously operated them with Renaissance, had been running Oceania's day-to-day operations until he took over as chairman; Watters, until his retirement, focused on developing the onboard product, designated as premium with luxury touches—an effort to set the line apart from its competitors in the premium cruise category.

Oceania Cruises was launched with the 684-passenger *Regatta*, the former *R2*. Her identical sister, *Insignia*, the former *R1*, was added the following year, and a third copy, *Nautica*, the former *R5*, debuted in 2005. Oceania selected these three specific ships because they had the most high-end suites, an important asset in attracting sophisticated travelers. In addition, Oceania got a great deal for leasing the vessels from the banks that repossessed the ships after Renaissance's collapse, thus avoiding incurring a big debt and enabling the new cruise line to provide its product at very competitive prices.

In 2006, Oceania was able to purchase the three ships for $375 million—the cost to build even one ship today. Then in early 2007, Apollo Management, a New York-based multibillion-dollar private equity firm, acquired majority interest in Oceania Cruises for approximately $850 million.

Soon thereafter, Oceania placed a billion-dollar order with Italy's Fincantieri shipyard for two 1,260-passenger, 65,000-ton ships to be delivered in the fall of 2010 and summer of 2011, and an option for a third vessel to be delivered in 2012. The new midsize vessels represent a new class of ships for the line, dubbed Oceania class, and defined as upper-premium cruising. Among their many new features, the ships will have six open-seating restaurants and larger, more luxurious cabins and suites with more amenities than the present fleet.

Oceania's destination focus first centered on Europe, South America, and the Caribbean; new destinations such as North Africa, Australia, and New Zealand have been added as the line builds its passenger base. Many itineraries have been tailored to include overnight port stays to allow passengers more time to enjoy particular destinations, such as St. Petersburg, Russia, on the Northern Europe cruises, and Venice on Mediterranean ones. With the arrival of *Nautica*, Oceania was able to chart a different course, with winter and spring in the Far East, and include overnight stays in such cities as Beijing, Dubai, Hong Kong, and Mumbai (Bombay), to name a few.

STYLE Oceania's goal has been to create a fine product focused on cuisine, service, and destination-oriented itineraries, and to offer it at reasonable prices. The line's relaxed onboard atmosphere resembles the casual elegance of a country club, neither stuffy nor pretentious. Formal wear is never a require-

THE FLEET	BUILT/RENOVATED	TONNAGE	PASSENGERS
Insignia	1998/2004/05/07	30,277	684
Nautica	2000/05/07	30,277	684
Regatta	1998/2003/05/07	30,277	684
Marina	2010	65,000	1,260
Oceania II	2011	65,000	1,260

ment for dinner; passengers dress stylishly but comfortably to enjoy their evenings. Oceania's *Regatta*-class ships—small compared with today's more typical megaships—provide the intimate atmosphere of a small ship, and at the same time have many of the facilities of larger ships. For example, each ship has several lounges, a spa, and four restaurants with open seating, enabling passengers to dine when, where, and with whom they choose. The new Marina, while double the size and accommodating almost double the number of passengers, will still be a moderate-size ship compared with most new ships today, and it will introduce a number of new features, sure to please Oceania fans, such as ten restaurants and a culinary center for hands-on workshops.

Oceania's innovations—Cruise Planner and Guest Referral Network—to its Web site, **www.oceaniacruises.com,** enable passengers to plan and book a cruise online 24/7 with complete access to live inventory and prices. They can also customize their vacation with regard to pre- and postcruise hotel options, shore excursions, and insurance. With the Cruise Planner, passengers can plan and save information on their cruise and build a day-by-day planning journal to take on their cruise.

Prior to its debut on the *Marina* in the winter of 2010, Oceania introduced the Canyon Ranch Spa Club on the three *Regatta*-class ships in September 2009.

For 2010, Oceania's European cruises are its most extensive to date, with 34 different itineraries, nearly three-quarters of which are brand-new.

DISTINCTIVE FEATURES Medium-size ships. An upper-end premium product with deluxe touches. Tranquility Beds. Four restaurants, open-seating dining, destination-focused itineraries. Affordable pricing; many special deals. Canyon Ranch spa. Ten restaurants and a culinary center on *Marina*.

RATES Gratuities and port charges are additional. Complimentary, unlimited bottled water and soft drinks for all passengers.

Special fares and discounts Oceania's early-booking policy is to open most new itineraries with two-for-one pricing or free economy air, and then close on the promotions as the ships fill. Guests who book early can realize tremendous savings.

- **THIRD PASSENGER:** Fares vary by individual sailing.
- **CHILDREN'S FARES:** None.
- **SINGLE SUPPLEMENT:** 200%.

PAST PASSENGERS After passengers sail once, they automatically become a member of the Oceania Club, the line's past-passenger club. The more they sail, the higher their level of rewards. All members receive an *Oceania Club Journal* and an invitation to the captain's cocktail party for members. Other awards, depending on level of membership, might include complimentary gratuities, spa or onboard credits, and discounts on future cruises. A dedicated page for the club at **www.oceaniacruises.com** includes information, news, and fun behind-the-scenes information.

THE LAST WORD Oceania Cruises has developed a substantial following in less than six years. The line is well run, and passengers have favorably responded to its consistent product. They like the line's midsize ships, their country-club-casual atmosphere, the cuisine, and unusual itineraries.

Oceania Cruises Standard Features

Officers Italian, Croatian, and other Europeans.

Staff *Dining and Cabin:* European and international; *Cruise:* British, North American, and European.

Dining facilities Four restaurants include a main dining room, two alternative restaurants, and a casual buffet-style eatery. *Marina,* six restaurants.

Special diets Request at booking or no later than 30 days prior to sailing.

Room service 24 hours with cabin menu. Top suites may order from any of the four restaurant menus.

Dress code By day, resort-casual attire. Evenings are business casual or smart casual. No jackets, ties, or fancy dress. Each cruise has two gala evenings, but formal wear is not required.

Cabin amenities Direct-dial telephone, television with CNN and ESPN, cabin music, hair dryer, safe, deluxe toiletries, and bathrobes. Concierge-level and higher cabins and suites: DVD players and minifridge; Owner's and Vista suites: full entertainment system. *Insignia:* Concierge Level, Veranda and Penthouse suites, flat-panel televisions.

Electrical outlets 110/220 AC

Wheelchair access *Regatta* class, two inside cabins; *Marina,* two ocean-view balcony and two penthouse suites.

Recreation and entertainment Several lounges have live music by ship's orchestra or musical trio. Entertainment, typically low key, features cabaret acts, soloists, jugglers, comedians, and dance music. One to two small production shows staged on every cruise.

THE SHIPS Because the *Regatta*-class ships are practically identical, the line has been able to create a consistent product across its fleet. Each of the former Renaissance ships were given a major renovation prior to entering them into service. These included new teak decks on the Pool Deck, the aft dining terrace, and private balconies. The patio has classy-looking lounges, and the pool and whirlpool area were resurfaced with an attractive marble-and-tile look.

Oceania also revamped the decor and use of the interior public spaces, such as the observation lounge, martini bar, atrium and grand staircase area, and the alternative restaurants. Decor remains traditional but toned down with a more elegant, muted look and the addition of a $2 million contemporary art collection.

More enhancements were completed when all wooden furniture was replaced, brass handles added to cabin doors, and teak decks on balconies were replaced. Public areas, cabins, and the spa were refurbished.

The reception desk, destination services, the concierge, medical center, and an imposing grand staircase are found on Deck 4. One deck above, Deck 5, is totally dedicated to public spaces, including the casino, **Martini's Lounge,**

Sports and other activities Outdoor pool, golf cage, shuffleboard, deck sports, and jogging track.

Beauty and fitness Men's and women's steam rooms, full-service Mandara Spa with treatment rooms, beauty salon, exercise facility, aerobics, and fitness classes. Massages on deck in private cabana.

Other facilities Library with 1,000 books, card room, two boutiques, Oceania@Sea 24-hour Internet cafe, medical center, self-service laundry, dry cleaning and laundry services, four elevators. Nondenominational Sunday services; Jewish Sabbath observance led by crew member or passenger.

Children's facilities None.

Theme cruises None.

Smoking Smoking is permitted only in two designated areas of the ship: forward starboard on the Pool Deck and aft port corner on Horizon Deck. Smoking is prohibited in all other areas, including within cabins and on cabin or suite balconies.

Oceania suggested tipping $12.50 per person per day; and $4 per person per day gratuity for private butlers in Penthouse, Owner's, and Vista suites added automatically to onboard account. It may be adjusted at the passenger's discretion. Also, 18% added to spa services and bar purchases.

Credit cards For cruise payment and onboard charges: American Express, Diners Club, Discover, MasterCard, and Visa.

the **Regatta** (or **Insignia**) **Lounge,** the **Grand Bar,** photo gallery, two boutiques, and the main dining room.

In 2006, *Insignia* was given a multimillion-dollar refurbishment from stem to stern with stylish new furnishings and new amenities, as well as a behind-the-scenes mechanical and technical upgrade. Among the enhancements, all teak decking and railings and all cabin doors and hardware were reconditioned. Throughout the ship, its rich wood paneling was restored, and new carpeting was installed. **Horizons,** the ship's observation lounge and nightclub,

Insignia	QUALITY9	VALUEA
Nautica	QUALITY9	VALUEA
Regatta	QUALITY9	VALUEA
REGISTRYMarshall Islands	LENGTH593.7 feet	BEAM83.5
CABINS342	DRAFT19.5 feet	SPEED18 knots
MAXIMUM PASSENGERS	PASSENGER DECKS9	ELEVATORS4
684	CREW410	SPACE RATIONA

got a new bar with a handcrafted granite top and a front of crackled, back-lit Murano glass.

At the top of the ship on Deck 11, eight new private cabanas were added, along with teak decking. The luxury cabanas offer sweeping sea views through walls of glass and are furnished with a custom-made teak Balinese daybed, chic white privacy drapes, and a roll-back Roman-shade roof that affords optimum amounts of sun and shade. Cabanas may be reserved for a day or the full cruise and include the services of a dedicated attendant who provides drinks, snacks, and chilled towels. Passengers may also get meal service and spa treatments in their cabana. Cabanas cost $50 per day for port days and $100 per day for sea days. Passengers can book full-cruise packages and receive a discount and special amenities; discount varies from cruise to cruise based on length and number of port and sea days.

Insignia also got new state-of-the-art communication equipment to facilitate faster Internet speeds and the use of cell phones at sea. The ship has a new multimillion-dollar art collection, comprising antique nautical paintings and models, along with contemporary and traditional pieces from renowned artists and masters.

ITINERARIES *See* Itinerary Index.

CABINS Prior to entering service for Oceania, all cabins were upgraded with deluxe appointments: fine linens and bedding, including Tranquility Bed mattresses, silk-cut duvets and fluffy goose-down pillows, French-milled toiletries, and teak verandas. Passengers also enjoy plush cotton robes and slippers.

The roomy Owner's (aft) and Vista (forward) suites on Decks 6 through 8 have floor-to-ceiling glass doors with spectacular views from the living room, dining room, and master bedroom and lead to a private wraparound teak veranda. The suites have a separate guest bathroom and butler service. These suites are furnished with queen-size bed, whirlpool, two color TVs, and an entertainment center with DVD and CD players. DVDs are available from the reception desk.

On Deck 8, the Penthouse Suites offer a large living area with sliding glass doors, stylish furniture, and either twin or queen beds, space for in-suite dining, minibar, vanity desk, bath with tub, ample closet space, and butler service that includes arranging priority restaurant reservations and complimentary shoeshine, among other services.

To fill the gap between the more pricey suites and standard cabins, Oceania created a new category called Concierge Level. These 216-square-foot cabins with verandas occupy preferred locations on Deck 7. They have amenities similar to a Penthouse Suite, but the space is much smaller. Concierge Level passengers, however, get many perks, including priority embarkation with a dedicated check-in desk and priority luggage delivery, welcome bottle of Champagne, minibar, 20-inch color television and DVD player, personalized stationery, Hansgrohe massaging showerheads, and Caswell-Massey toiletries.

All cabins and suites fleetwide have new third-generation Tranquility Beds with Imperial mattresses. They were redecorated in warm jewel tones of gold and deep sapphire. Sleek new glass-topped cocktail tables custom-made in Italy lend a chic yet functional element. The Owner's and Vista suites have been completely rebuilt from the bottom up under the direction of renowned shipboard architect Petter Yran. The suites were lavishly fitted with new Empire-style furnishings and couture fabrics of claret and gold, a wide-screen plasma television, a Bose surround-sound audio system, and wide-screen laptop computers. The Vista Suites, using a palette of gold, meadow, and sage, project an ambience of understated elegance. All Concierge Level Veranda and Penthouse suites have flat-panel televisions.

Specifications 342 cabins and suites, of which 314, or 92%, are outside and almost 70% have verandas. Six Owner's Suites (962 square feet); 4 Vista Suites (786 square feet); 52 Penthouse Suites (322 square feet); 171 cabins (216 square feet), all with balconies; 83 ocean-view cabins (150–165 square feet) and 26 inside cabins (158 square feet); 3 inside wheelchair-accessible cabins.

DINING The **Grand Dining Room**—open for breakfast, lunch, and dinner—is elegantly appointed with a domed ceiling adorned with hand-painted frescoes, soft lighting, and dramatic ocean views. The decor is similar to the room's look during its Renaissance days. Unfortunately, tables are crowded next to each other, often making it difficult for waiters to serve.

While the service is decidedly white glove—and in the evening, waiters wear tuxedos—passengers dine in a relaxing atmosphere in casual attire. The dress code never requires jacket and tie, although many gentlemen do wear jackets with a sport shirt for dinner. On gala nights, passengers might dress more elegantly, if they choose to do so. A classical string quartet or concert pianist usually provides background music during dinner.

The ship's menus have been crafted by master chef Jacques Pepin, the line's executive culinary director and one of America's best-known chefs via his numerous television appearances, food columns, and cookbooks. He has also served as the personal chef to three French heads of state, including Charles de Gaulle. The line offers a selection of more than 150 wines.

The ships have two alternative dining venues, **Polo Grill** and **Toscana;** both are very good and outshine the main dining room in cuisine and service. Reservations are required, but there is no extra charge. Resplendent with rich, dark woods and elegant furnishings, they have floor-to-ceiling windows affording views of the seascapes. Polo Grill is a classic steak house with an extensive menu of aged prime beef, lamb, pork, and fresh seafood. Desserts might include New Orleans pecan pie or a traditional New York cheesecake.

In Toscana, diners enjoy an Italian ambience and may select from such Italian specialties as gnocchi in creamy pesto sauce, risotto with porcini mushrooms, caramelized shallots and fresh thyme, or sautéed medallions of veal tenderloin with roasted bell peppers in Gorgonzola cheese and Marsala wine sauce—all served on fine china and crystal. Great service enhances the ambience.

According to Oceania's policy, all suite and Concierge Level passengers may make two reservations at each of the alternative dining venues (total of four nights), while standard-cabin passengers may make one reservation in each venue (total of two nights). After that, the venues are open to more reservations as space permits.

For a more casual dining experience, the buffet-style **Terrace Café**—where breakfast and lunch are available—is transformed at dinner into **Tapas on the Terrace.** Passengers serve themselves at a buffet, but the atmosphere is enhanced by linens and upgraded dinnerware and glassware on the table, and service by waiters who often carry plates to the tables and bring drinks. Menus vary but are decidedly Mediterranean in flair, along with different chef's specials nightly.

Waves, the poolside bar and grill, is a lunchtime option offering grilled meats, seafood, salads, and made-to-order deli sandwiches. All passengers can order room service from a cabin menu 24 hours a day. Those in Penthouse Suites and above may also order room service from the four restaurant menus.

In the restaurants, you will dine on tableware of Versace china, Reidel crystal, and Christofle silver, which Oceania has dubbed the Perfect Table.

SERVICE Passengers praise the service as warm and attentive. The high staff-to-guest ratio of more than one crew member per cabin facilitates a high degree of personalized service.

FACILITIES AND ACTIVITIES The **Regatta** (**Insignia** or **Nautica**) **Lounge** is furnished with curved couches, upholstered chairs, and cocktail tables. During the day, enrichment lectures might be held here. When the sun goes down, the lounge features entertainment that might include a soloist, comedian, or juggler, and a revue-style production show once or twice during a cruise.

Martini's, reminiscent of a private gentlemen's club, is the place to relax with friends for martinis and live piano music. In the **Grand Bar,** just outside the main restaurant, you can enjoy a rare vintage or a grappa. **Horizons**, a convivial bar on Deck 10, offers live entertainment and sweeping views to enjoy along with your favorite cocktail. Later in the evening, it becomes the venue for dancing.

Before the ship visits a port, the cruise director provides a talk with historical background and information on the culture, traditions, and language of that destination. The line also offers culinary demonstrations by its executive chef and his staff. Passengers might take a dance lesson, an arts and crafts class, a golf or bridge lesson, or enjoy bingo or a wine-tasting session. The **library** is stocked with more than 1,000 volumes. Oceania@Sea is the line's 24-hour Internet center.

SPORTS, FITNESS, AND BEAUTY The **Canyon Ranch SpaClub** debuted on the three *Regatta*-class ships in September 2009, prior to its installation on the *Marina*. Heretofore, Cunard's *Queen Mary 2* was the only cruise ship with a famous health resort operating a spa-at-sea. Canyon Ranch's healthy spa cuisine will be available in April and May 2010, for all three meals in the Grand Dining Room and Terrace Café.

Located on Deck 9, the spa also has a hair salon, fitness center, an outdoor pool, and two whirlpools. The large, airy fitness center has exercise equipment, a large aerobics area, and offers a variety of fitness classes led by personal trainers. One deck up, on Deck 10, passengers can walk, jog, or run along the fitness track (13 laps equal one mile). The Deck 11 Sun Deck is the place for a tranquil respite on a cozy lounge chair. Here, golfers can practice their swing in a golf cage.

CHILDREN'S FACILITIES Oceania cruises are not designed for families with children. The ships have no children's facilities.

SHORE EXCURSIONS Oceania offers two sets of shore excursion packages online: Discovery, for those new to the ports of call, and Explorers, for experienced cruisers who may have already visited the ports. Prebooking a shore package can bring peace of mind for some, saving having to stand in line at the shore excursion office onboard ship. Others prefer to wait until they get on board to book shore excursions individually. Prearranged packages provide a 10% discount—a good value. However, these packages are nonrefundable and cannot be changed nor substitutions made. Purchasing excursions on board costs more, but there's often a wider selection from which to choose. Also, booking on board offers greater flexibility, as passengers often change their minds about excursions after they board the ship.

Also to be considered in making a selection are the ports where the ships overnight. For example, when *Nautica* sails in Asia, her itineraries feature overnight stays in such cities as Bangkok, Beijing, Dubai, Hanoi, Ho Chi Minh City, Hong Kong, Kyoto, Luxor, Mumbai (Bombay), and Shanghai. Passengers are able to enjoy two full days and an evening in each of these ports.

Oceania has also developed pre- and postcruise hotel stays and extended land tours of three to nine days to such locales as Beijing and the Great Wall, Chiangmai, Guilin, Myanmar, Siem Reap, Xian, and the Yangtze River.

THE SHIPS Oceania Cruises is building two 1,260-passenger, 65,000-ton ships, with the first, *Marina,* to be delivered in winter of 2010 and the second, *Oceania II,* in summer of 2011, with an option for a third vessel. The new midsize vessels, being built at Italy's Fincantieri shipyard and costing a half-billion dollars each, represent a new class of ships for the line. Dubbed Oceania class and being defined as upper-premium cruising, the ships will have ten restaurants (six with open-seating) and larger, more luxurious cabins and suites with more amenities than the present fleet, a CanyonRanch SpaClub, and state-of-the-art fitness center, among other new features.

Designed by renowned marine architectural firm Yran & Storbratten, public areas and cabins will be dressed with rich wood paneling, granite accents, marble, opulent furnishings, and a museum-quality art collection. Facilities include an array of elegant bars and lounges, an outdoor swimming pool and hot tubs, suites with butler service, and laptop computers in all cabins.

These "green ships," employing the most advanced environmental systems and technology, are powered by diesel-electric engines and operate with twin screw propellers. With a service speed of 20 knots, they're designed to cruise the world, boasting a cruising speed that is 20% faster than the present *Regatta* class. They are equipped with two bow thrusters to enhance maneuverability.

Marina	**2010**	
Oceania II	**2011**	
REGISTRY TBA	**LENGTH** 782 feet	**BEAM** 105
CABINS 629	**DRAFT** 24 feet	**SPEED** 20 knots
MAXIMUM PASSENGERS	**PASSENGER DECKS** 15	**ELEVATORS** 6
1,258	**CREW** 787	**SPACE RATIO** NA

ITINERARIES *See* Itinerary Index. The ship's maiden winter will be spent in the Caribbean and Latin America and summer in Europe.

CABINS The Oceania-class vessels' 629 cabins and suites—almost double the number on the *Regatta* fleet—are, on average, 50% larger than the *Regatta* class. Approximately 96% of all accommodations come with large, private teak verandas and all have Oceania's exclusive Tranquility Bed. They also come with flat-panel televisions, direct-dial phones, laptop computers with wireless access, minibars, safes, writing desks and stationery, bathrooms with hairdryers, French-milled toiletries, cotton robes and slippers, and nightly turndown service. Suites have a sitting area and the additional amenities of Champagne upon arrival, 1,000-thread-count linens, 42-inch plasma televisions, Hermès and Clarins toiletries, and butler service. Guests in Owner's, Vista, and Oceania suites get the added luxury of ordering from any of the ship's restaurants for in-suite dining. Room service and self-service laundry are available.

Specifications: 3 Owner's, 8 Vista, 12 Oceania, 124 Penthouse Suites, and 200 concierge, 244 veranda, 20 ocean view, and 18 inside cabins.

DINING The new *Marina* is being hailed as "*the* ship for food lovers" and with ten dining venues, including six open-seating, gourmet restaurants—all at no additional charge—it could be a tagline well earned. Topping the list is **Jacques,** the first restaurant at sea by renowned master chef Jacques Pépin, executive culinary director for Oceania Cruises. Pépin says Jacques will draw inspiration from bistros in his hometown of Lyon and Paris with "freshly prepared, simple dishes that are as visually pleasing on the plate as they are on the palate." The restaurant will have a grand rotisserie. Overhead, chandeliers fashioned from crystal decanters add a whimsical note. Some of Pépin's personal art collection and original works that Pépin created especially for *Marina* will add a personal touch to the room. Highlights will be freshly baked French baguettes, the chef's daily "specialités de la maison" based on selections from local markets in the ports *Marina* visits, and a choice of nine classic French desserts and a tray of French cheeses. Sample menus and reservations should be available on Oceania Cruises' Web site several months prior to the ship's inaugural.

Red Ginger, a Pan-Asian specialty restaurant featuring Thai, Japanese, and Vietnamese cuisine, will offer a five-course *menu de gustacion* (tasting menu) designed to be an Asian culinary adventure—all at no supplement or surcharge. On the à la carte menu, patrons will find fresh interpretations of Asian classics, as well as new creations and fusion dishes. Set amid a comfortable, stylish, contemporary decor with ebony, bronze, and glass light fixtures and eclectic, modern Asian artwork, Red Ginger has as a centerpiece three Buddha heads, carved from a single piece of glass and lit with multiple colors from within. Among the other restaurants are two popular transplants from the *Regatta* fleet, **Polo Grill** and **Toscana.**

Marina will have a state-of-the-art culinary studio with fully equipped individual work stations, each with induction cooktops—a first at sea—affording passengers the opportunity for a hands-on learning experience cooking side-by-side with a master chef. The multimillion-dollar, groundbreaking culinary center will have *Bon Appétit* magazine as its culinary partner, which will assist in creating the center's curriculum. Depending on the itinerary, classes may range from 45 minutes to three hours and cater to all levels of skill from beginner to master chef. The culinary experience will also be brought ashore, with market tours where guests will shop for local ingredients with the chef. Guest chefs may also arrange for students to have private tastings at wineries and access to famous shoreside kitchens.

FACILITIES AND ACTIVITIES **Marina Lounge** is the ship's main performance venue, with nightly headline acts, comedians, magicians, classic movies, enrichment lectures by guest experts, and folkloric shows by local performers on select sailings. **Martinis,** with an atmosphere reminiscent of a private gentleman's club, will have nightly piano entertainment. **Horizons,** the forward observation lounge with floor-to-ceiling windows on three sides, is the ideal spot to watch the passing scenery and enjoy afternoon tea. In the evenings, Horizons becomes a center for action with lively swing and jazz ensembles, disco dancing, and karaoke. **Grand Bar** is a prime location for predinner drinks or Cognac after dinner. **The Patio,** overlooking the pool, is a place to gather with friends at sunset or to relax after dinner. The ship also has a cabaret, casino, disco, boutiques, library/bookshop, card room, photo gallery/shop, tour office, medical center, dry cleaning/valet, and an Internet corner.

In the **Studio,** passengers can learn from the ship's artists-in-residence about painting with watercolors, needlepoint, scrapbook making, and more. **The Library** is an English-style reading room with book-lined, wood-paneled walls. In the **Card Room,** passengers can enjoy popular board games, and on select voyages, guest instructors will host duplicate bridge. **The Galleria** has four duty-free boutiques selling logo wear, gifts, accessories, fragrances, cosmetics, jewelry, and sundries.

SPORTS, FITNESS, AND BEAUTY Canyon Ranch is designing and will operate the spa, beauty salon, and wellness and fitness facilities on board *Marina.* Heretofore, the operator's only spa-at-sea was on Cunard's *Queen Mary 2.* The facility is a Canyon Ranch SpaClub and has 16 massage, body, and skin-care treatment rooms, two whirlpools, a gym and weight room with more than 50 pieces of cardio and weight-training equipment, a juice bar, and men's and women's locker rooms. Canyon Ranch spa cuisine will also be available in late 2010.

The facility has a thalassotherapy pool with airbed recliner lounges, neck fountains, deluge waterfall, air tub, and body-massage jet benches. Adjacent to the pool is a coed thermal suite with an herbal sauna, Finnish sauna, reflexology basins, and an aromatic steam room. Also available will be the Rasul Ceremony, a Canyon Ranch SpaClub signature treatment. Canyon Ranch–certified fitness instructors will conduct daily group and private fitness, Pilates, yoga, and tai chi classes; on select voyages, Canyon Ranch healthy living experts will offer presentations and workshops on lifestyle change, stress management, and other topics. The beauty salon will offer complete beauty services for women and men.

Recreational facilities include an outdoor swimming pool, table tennis, shuffleboard, bocce ball court, a golf putting green and driving range, jogging track, and a chess set with extra-large pieces for fun match play.

Princess Cruises

24305 Town Center Drive
Santa Clarita, CA 91355-4999
☎ 661-753-0000 or 800-PRINCESS
FAX 661-753-1535
www.princess.com

TYPE OF SHIPS New superliners and megaliners.

TYPE OF CRUISES Modern, mainstream, worldwide, moderately upscale.

CRUISE LINE'S STRENGTHS
- worldwide itineraries
- Caribbean private island
- ScholarShip@Sea enrichment program
- spacious cabins, many with verandas
- traditional or anytime dining
- scuba certification
- excellent dining room and specialty restaurant cuisine

CRUISE LINE'S SHORTCOMINGS
- congestion in 24-hour restaurants
- uneven cuisine in 24-hour restaurants

FELLOW PASSENGERS Princess passengers are difficult to characterize because their ages and incomes vary with the ships, seasons, and destinations. Basically, passengers are age 45 and older with annual incomes of $50,000 and up. They tend to be experienced travelers who cruise frequently and enjoy Princess's mainstream vacations. They can range from a California schoolteacher or a midwestern computer systems analyst on a first cruise to affluent retirees on their 20th cruise. On longer cruises and those to "exotic" destinations, the average age is 55 or older; on one-week Caribbean cruises, the average age is younger.

Recommended for Modestly affluent first-timers, frequent cruisers who want easy-paced travel and prefer a balance between sea and land time, and those who understand *The Love Boat* was only a TV show.

Not recommended for Swingers or first-time cruisers in search of The Love Boat; small-ship devotees.

CRUISE AREAS AND SEASONS Caribbean, year-round; Africa, Amazon, Antarctica, Australia and South Pacific, Hawaii and Tahiti, Holy Land, Mexico, Orient, Panama Canal, Southeast Asia, winter; Alaska, Baltic, Bermuda, Canada and New England, Europe, Mediterranean, Scandinavia, summer.

THE LINE Princess marks its beginning as 1965, when a small, one-ship line called Princess Cruises sailed to the Mexican Riviera, using a 6,000-ton ferry vessel named *Princess Patricia*. In the intervening years, the company has grown from a pioneer of modern-day cruising with a focus on the West Coast to a worldwide fleet of 17 modern ships sailing to all seven continents.

From its inception, Princess Cruises helped create the relaxed, casual atmosphere that typifies today's cruises.

In 1974, P&O (Peninsular and Orient Steam Navigation Company), a British firm and one of the world's oldest and largest steamship companies (in the cruise business since August 1844), bought Princess Cruises. It acquired its first *Island Princess*, and the following year, P&O bought *Island Princess*'s sister, *Sea Venture*, and renamed her *Pacific Princess*, better known to TV viewers as *The Love Boat*.

In the early 1980s, Princess became a trendsetter for modern mainstream cruising when it launched the first *Royal Princess*. She was hailed as the most stylish ship of the day, setting new standards in comfort and amenities. (Much to the sorrow of her loyal fans, *Royal Princess* was transferred to P&O Cruises in 2005.) In 1988, Princess almost doubled its capacity when it acquired Los Angeles-based Sitmar Cruises, another cruise pioneer. The line continued to benefit from its involvement in *The Love Boat* television series, which had an incalculable impact on modern cruising, popularizing it for a generation of television viewers and helping dispel cruising's elitist image.

In the 1990s, Princess launched $3 billion worth of dazzling megaships. *Sun Princess* ushered in the *Grand*-class concept and the line's largest vessel when it entered service in 1995. She was followed by triplets over the following four years—all with the architect, Njal Eide, who designed the *Royal*

THE FLEET	BUILT/RENOVATED	TONNAGE	PASSENGERS
Caribbean Princess	2004	113,000	3,100
Coral Princess	2003	92,000	1,970
Crown Princess	2006	113,000	3,080
Dawn Princess	1997/2009	77,000	1,990
Diamond Princess	2004	116,000	2,670
Emerald Princess	2007	116,000	3,070
Golden Princess	2001	109,000	2,600
Grand Princess	1998	109,000	2,600
Island Princess	2003	92,000	1,970
Ocean Princess	1999/2002	30,277	670
Pacific Princess	1999/2002	30,277	670
Royal Princess (until 2011)	2001/2007	30,277	710
Ruby Princess	2008	113,000	3,080
Sapphire Princess	2004	116,000	2,670
Sea Princess	1998/2005	77,000	1,950
Star Princess	2002	109,000	2,600
Sun Princess	1995	77,000	1,990

Princess, and, like her, with significant new features, including cruising's first 24-hour restaurant, two atrium lobbies, and two show lounges.

The 109,000-ton, $400 million *Grand Princess*, the largest cruise ship ever built when she debuted in 1998, was the first of the Princess fleet too large to transit the Panama Canal. The expansion tripled the line's capacity. Two more like her followed in 2001 and 2002.

That was only the beginning. Two more ships, the 92,000-ton *Coral Princess* and *Island Princess*, made their debut in 2003 and ushered in a new class of ship. They were the best yet, combining the best features of the *Sun-* and *Grand*-class ships. They came with innovative power generation technology, combining diesel engines and gas turbines (the latter placed in the ship's funnel), and only 10% inside cabins and 80% of outside ones with balconies. From 2004 to 2008, Princess saw its largest expansion, adding its five largest ships.

In spring 2007, Princess added the 710-passenger *Royal Princess* (formerly *Minerva II* of Swan Hellenic) for a series of European cruises to new destinations and new ports. More new ports were added when Princess returned to world cruising for the first time in more than five years with a 102-day voyage on *Pacific Princess* in 2008.

Already a major player in Alaska and the Panama Canal, in the last few years, Princess has greatly increased its Caribbean presence, added itineraries throughout Asia and the Pacific, expanded in Europe, added safaris in Kenya and South Africa, sailed on its first Antarctic cruise, expanded its Scholar-Ship@Sea program, and opened Internet cafes fleetwide.

Princess's Alaska role was enhanced in 1997 with the opening of the handsome Mount McKinley Princess Lodge, featured on the line's cruise tours. The lodge sits on 146 acres inside Denali State Park and has a spectacular view of 20,320-foot Mount McKinley and the Alaska Range. Princess has four other Alaskan properties.

On Caribbean cruises, the line offers Princess Cay, its private island in the Bahamas. Princess has one of the industry's best and most extensive selections of shore excursions. Almost all can be booked in advance of your cruise. Just about everything you ever wanted to know about Princess Cruises is available on its Web site, one of the most extensive of any cruise line.

In 2003, the hard-fought battle between Carnival Corp. and Royal Caribbean to buy Princess/P&O Cruises ended in Carnival's favor. All of Carnival's cruise lines continue to operate separately under their own brands.

Princess fans can find the line on Facebook at **http://www.facebook.com/pages/Princess-Cruises/19788524059;** Twitter at **http://twitter.com/PrincessCruises;** and Flickr at **http://www.flickr.com/photos/princesscruises.**

STYLE California modern in the mainstream, sedate but not staid, a Princess cruise is the essence of mass-market cruising: warm, inviting, and comfortable, suitable for a broad spectrum of people. The fleet has British officers, with their steamship tradition; Italian officers, with their natural charm; and a multicultural dining and hotel staff. Often trendsetters in facilities and amenities, the ships have the look of a well-bred, middle- to upper-middle-class environment (that is, nothing too flashy or exaggerated) where almost anyone can feel at home. The line has worked hard to improve its entertainment and food, with menus featuring fresh, contemporary selections, and now offers some of the best cuisine in its category and superior to most in its alternative Italian restaurant. Shipboard activities are varied and numerous. Ships fleetwide have gyms, saunas, and spa services and offer fitness and sports programs on board and in port. Princess's newest ships have telemedicine technology, giving ships' doctors worldwide access to medical specialists.

The New Waves scuba diving program, associated with PADI (Professional Association of Diving Instructors), offers snorkeling and scuba certification. All Princess ships have Internet and wireless access, cell phone use, and alternative dining options. Personal Choice Dining and Anytime Dining are flexible dining room options, available on *Sun*- and *Grand*-class ships. With it, an automatic gratuity system for the staffs is in effect on board, adding $10.50 per person per day for balcony cabins and categories below, $11 for mini-suites and above to a passenger's shipboard account. FlightChoice provides passengers with information on their flight schedule 60 days prior to sailing with the option to choose a customized air schedule. Cruise Personalizers is an online service that enables passengers to book shore excursions, make special occasion arrangements, and tell staff about dietary requirements before their cruise.

One of Princess's newest facilities, which the line dubbed Direct to the Wilderness, enables passengers to extend their cruise to tour Alaska, to board their train right at the new Princess terminal in Whittier. From there, they are whisked off to one of Princess' two Denali lodges, arriving the same afternoon. The new facility slashes travel time and the number of transfers, and thus gives passengers more time at Denali.

A new amenity, **The Sanctuary,** an adults-only retreat in a secluded area of the top deck, provides tranquility and comfort with plush, padded lounge chairs and the services of dedicated Serenity stewards. Patrons can arrange to have spa treatments here too. Another amenity, available on most ships, is **Movie under the Stars**—the first on a cruise ship—in which the top deck becomes an open-air theater, showing popular films and major sporting events on a huge screen. Those ships also have **Engagement under the Stars** by video—a new way to pop *the* question. All *Grand*-class ships, plus *Coral* and *Island*, have wedding chapels with Webcams. As we said, Princess is *The Love Boat*.

Princess's innovation, Chef's Table, launched on *Emerald Princess* in 2007, is now available fleetwide, except on *Sun* and *Dawn*. It's an opportunity to join the executive chef in the ship's galley for predinner cocktails and hors d'oeuvres with Champagne, followed by a multicourse tasting dinner especially created for participants by the chef at their special table in the dining room. For the dessert course, the chef rejoins the group. Each couple receives an autographed copy of Princess's cookbook, *Courses, A Culinary Journey*, and a complimentary photo with the chef. *Chef's Table* can be reserved for up to ten passengers on select nights at a cost of $75 per person.

In spring 2007, Princess Cruises debuted a series of enhancements to its food service meant to reflect changing trends and passenger preferences. Available fleetwide, it includes new menus and presentations in dining rooms, alternative restaurants and buffets, as well as an afternoon "cookies and milk break" and cabin delivery ($3 service charge) of homemade pizza.

Princess has been among the first to offer Luggage Valet, an advance home-to-cabin shipping service (provided by DHL Worldwide Express). First available for Europe-bound travelers on four Princess ships in summer 2007,

Princess Cruises Standard Features

Officers British and Italian.

Staff *Dining:* Italian, European, Filipino; *Cabin:* Filipino; *Cruise:* American, British.

Dining facilities One main dining room, two seatings for three meals; *Sun* and *Coral* groups, two dining rooms; *Grand* group, three; *Diamond, Sapphire,* five. Personal Choice/Anytime Dining on *Sun, Coral,* and *Grand* groups; alternative bistro on *Sun, Grand* group; *Coral,* Italian and New Orleans. Informal buffet breakfast, lunch in Lido restaurant, pizzeria, patisserie, 24-hour dining, balcony breakfast or dinner, all ships in *Grand, Coral,* and *Sun* groups.

Special diets Diabetic, low-calorie/cholesterol/salt, vegetarian.

Room service 24-hour room service with light menu.

Dress code Casual during day, evenings vary; usually there are two smart casual, three informal, and two formal in week's cruise.

Cabin amenities CNN, ESPN, Discovery/Learning channels, and movies on television, fresh fruit daily and terry robes in cabins on request, direct-dial telephone, minifridges, hair dryers.

Electrical outlets 110/220 AC.

Wheelchair access 25–31 cabins on *Grand* group; 20 on *Coral* group; 19 on *Sun* group; 3 on *Pacific, Tahitian.*

Recreation and entertainment Las Vegas- and Broadway-style revues, music and dancing, casino, disco, wine and caviar bar, karaoke, theater, dance classes, bingo, bridge. *Grand* group, virtual reality center, three show lounges. *Coral* group, two show lounges, one with three revolving stages; demonstration kitchen. ScholarShip@ Sea courses.

the program is being expanded to other destinations. Prices start at $90 per bag one way for domestic shipments and vary internationally depending on weight and destination. Bags are insured up to $2,000; additional insurance is available for purchase. Reservations can be made up to 30 days prior to sailing date. Package Valet, enabling passengers to ship home items purchased at the ship's boutiques, is also available.

DISTINCTIVE FEATURES Scuba certification, 24-hour restaurants, terry robes and fresh fruit in cabins on request, fresh flowers in suites, self-service launderettes. Private Bahamian island, Alaska lodges. Telemedicine technology, wedding chapels, wedding Webcam on *Grand* class, Personal Choice and Anytime Dining on *Sun* and *Grand* classes, balcony breakfast and dinner, wireless Internet, cell phone use fleetwide, Movie under the Stars, Chef's Table, Luggage Valet, Ultimate Ship Tour, kilns.

RATES Port charges included.

Special fares and discounts Frequent two-for-one fares; savings and upgrades on combining consecutive cruises.

Sports and other activities Two or three outdoor pools on all ships; *Grand* group, five. Paddle tennis, jogging, scuba program, golf practice. *Grand* group, swim-against-current lap pool.

Beauty and fitness Spa, saunas, beauty/barber salon, fitness program.

Other facilities Library, hospital, boutiques, self-service laundry, meeting facilities, religious services; *Grand* group, wedding chapel, wedding Webcam, Internet cafe.

Children's facilities Princess Kids, Princess's youth program on all ships, has special facilities and full-time youth coordinators: *Grand Coral* and *Sun* groups. *Royal, Pacific,* and *Tahitian,* no dedicated spaces, but youth counselor runs planned activities when there are 20 or more kids. Group babysitting available 10 p.m.–1 a.m. for children ages 3–12 for a $5 per hour charge. No in-cabin babysitting. See text.

Smoking No smoking in dining rooms and main showrooms; other public rooms have designated areas.

Princess suggested tipping Gratuities automatically added to passenger's account at $10.50 for balcony cabin and below, $11 for mini-suite and above, per person per day for dining and cabin service. Passengers can add or reduce amount at pursers' desk; 15% is added to bar bills.

Credit cards For cruise payment and onboard charges (settled at the end of the cruise): American Express/Optima, Carte Blanche, Diners Club, Master-Card, Visa, Discover; traveler's and personal checks; U.S., Canadian, and British currency.

- **THIRD/FOURTH PASSENGER:** 50% of fare for suites to 30% of fare for inside cabins.
- **CHILDREN'S FARE:** Same as third/fourth passenger.
- **SINGLE SUPPLEMENT:** 150% to 200%, Love Boat Savers discounts.

PAST PASSENGERS Captain's Circle, the Princess loyalty program, gives members the ability to qualify for awards either by the number of cruises completed or the total number of days sailed. Captain's Circle offers three membership levels: Gold (one cruise), Platinum (five cruises or 50 cruise days), and Elite (15 completed cruises or 150 cruise days). Some of the other perks, depending on the passenger's level, are a free minibar setup, free Internet access, free laundry services, priority tender embarkation, complimentary wine tasting, a boutiques discount, upgraded stateroom amenities, and priority embarkation and disembarkation, which enables Elite passengers to choose the time they prefer to leave the ship. Captain's Circle past-passenger club members are invited to a captain-hosted cocktail party and to participate in activities, such as a photo contest with prizes. Members receive a membership number to use when booking a cruise or corresponding with Princess, ensuring that they receive club benefits. Recognition pins are given and fine-quality gifts are presented at onboard parties to passengers who have sailed the most days with Princess. Members receive newsletters reporting new itineraries, new ship plans, staff profiles, chef's recipes, special discounts, and coupons for specific sailings and members-only sailings.

THE LAST WORD For millions of Americans, the popular image of cruising is a Princess cruise. It's perhaps not as luxurious or glamorous as the television image, but it's apparently close enough for the line to attract more than 1.3 million passengers a year. Princess's strength is in its consistency, new fleet, itineraries, and well-executed shore excursions. Little changes from ship to ship. Your ship will be comfortable, your cruise enjoyable, and you will get a lot for your money, if you have realistic expectations.

THE SHIPS Before its launch, *Sun Princess*—at the time, the largest cruise ship ever built—was described by Princess as offering an intimate feel. Skeptics scoffed.

But guess what? Princess did it. Well, "intimate" is perhaps a stretch, but it certainly managed to diminish the interiors of this big ship to a human scale. The Italian-built ship made her debut in December 1995, the first of Princess's new class of ships. Her mates, *Dawn Princess, Sea Princess*, and *Ocean Princess*, arrived between 1997 and 2000. (*Ocean Princess* left the fleet in September 2002 to join P&O Cruises.) From the outside, the gleaming white liners look colossal, towering 14 decks and stretching nearly three football fields in length. But inside, clever design has created a welcoming, accessible ambience.

Ships are spacious without being overwhelming. Warm colors and refined decor enhance the inviting atmosphere. The group set new standards for megaliners. Their layout is innovative in many ways. Rather than one cavernous atrium, these ships offer two. Instead of one enormous show lounge, there are two main show lounges. Two dining rooms are on different decks, and their layout, decor, and table arrangements help create an intimate ambience. Five dining outlets, including cruising's first 24-hour restaurant, provide options. Small bars and lounges capture the intimacy of a small ship while giving passengers choices. Although other ships offer multiple lounges and dining alternatives, few developed the concept to the extent of Princess's *Sun-* and *Grand*-class ships. Whatever you choose to do, you can do, and whatever you miss one night, you can catch the next night.

The four-deck **Grand Plaza** is the ships' main atrium and social hub. It's a showcase of the exquisite Italian craftsmanship evident throughout the vessels and sets the tone for each ship. On the *Sun Princess*, in the elegant space, golden marble suggests the sun, and beige, bronze, and brown accents hint

Dawn Princess	QUALITY 8	VALUE C
Sea Princess	QUALITY 8	VALUE C
Sun Princess	QUALITY 9	VALUE B
REGISTRY Bermuda	LENGTH 856 feet	BEAM 106 feet
CABINS 975	DRAFT 26 feet	SPEED 21 knots
MAXIMUM PASSENGERS	PASSENGER DECKS 14	ELEVATORS 9
1,950	CREW 830	SPACE RATIO 39.5

at shade. Sunbursts are set in the marble floors at every level of the atrium, and a back-lit stained-glass dome overhead conveys an abstract underwater scene in aqua and turquoise. Glass elevators and a circular, floating staircase connect the decks and provide a stunning setting for the captain's parties.

Among the amenities are five swimming pools, a huge health center and spa, children's and teen rooms, a shopping arcade, computerized golf simulator, library and reading room with "audio chairs," each with its own bay window looking out to sea, and a business and conference center for up to 300 people. Each ship has a $2.5 million collection of paintings, sculptures, ceramic tiles, and Murano glass.

Another significant feature of the ships is their connection with the sea. A wraparound teak promenade lined with canopied steamer chairs provides a peaceful setting. *Sea Princess* was renovated in September 2009, when she received a refresh similar to *Dawn Princess,* and The Sanctuary was added.

ITINERARIES *See* Itinerary Index. *Dawn Princess* and *Sun Princess* will spend all of 2010 sailing from Australia.

CABINS About two-thirds of cabins are outside; 70% of those have private balconies. There are 28 cabin categories. Nineteen cabins were designed to Americans with Disabilities Act specifications. Lifeboats obstruct views from 28 outside cabins on Promenade Deck. All standard cabins have a queen-size bed convertible to two singles, refrigerator, safe, ample closet, and bath with shower, terry robes, and hair dryers. All are well appointed and decorated in light, eye-pleasing colors.

Category A mini-suite with a private balcony is lavish in comfort, decor, and size—at almost 400 square feet, plus the balcony. A marble-floored foyer with a mirror gives the illusion of a large apartment. Tastefully decorated in beige and butter tones accented by light woods and fine fabrics, each has a separate sitting area with leather chairs and a sofa that converts to a queen-size bed, plus an entertainment console with television and music channels. A bar includes a refrigerator.

The bedroom, separated by a curtained archway, has a queen-size bed, vanity/desk, and second television. Drawer space is ample, and the small walk-in closet has a safe. Sliding doors in the sitting area and bedroom lead to a balcony extending the length of the suite. Two lounge chairs and a table make it ideal for breakfast or napping. Etched glass divides the whirlpool tub from a shower stall, and a door separates the toilet and washbasin.

As on all new Princess ships, there are self-service launderettes with washers, dryers, irons, and ironing boards at no charge. You pay for soap, bleach, and dryer sheets from a dispensing machine.

Specifications 372 inside cabins, 603 outside (410 with verandas); 32 mini-suites and 6 suites with verandas. Standard dimensions, 135–173 square feet. All with two lower beds, convertible to queen; 300 with third berths; no singles; 19 wheelchair accessible.

DINING Here are the choices: two dining rooms, cruising's first 24-hour restaurant, pizzeria, grill, patisserie, ice-cream bar (there's a charge), 24-hour room service, and a steak house ($15 surcharge). And now passengers have the option to dine where and when they want with Personal Choice and Anytime Dining.

The two main dining rooms are on Emerald Deck and Plaza Deck. They have an asymmetrical seating layout and small table groups in various sizes separated by etched-glass dividers. The design gives each group of tables a certain privacy. Separate galleys and service stations in every corner reduce traffic and help ensure that food reaches tables at the proper temperature. Lunch and dinner menus offer a selection of appetizers, soups, salads, entrees, and desserts. A pasta special is offered every evening, although it is no longer prepared tableside. Healthy Choice selections are included on the regular menu. Wine list choices are reasonably priced, some under $20; wines are also available by the glass.

Horizon Court on Lido Deck is an innovative 24-hour cafe with 270-degree ocean views through floor-to-ceiling windows, with seating on a trio of terraces. By day, buffets are served at two stations; at night, the center of the room becomes a restaurant with table service and a dance band. Reservations aren't needed, and there's no extra charge.

The pizzeria offers a sidewalk cafe setting with marble-top tables and wrought-iron chairs on the balcony overlooking the atrium. It's open for lunch, and 6 p.m.–2 a.m. it serves pizza hot from the ovens. Waiters take orders for drinks and pizzas. There's no charge for the pizza, but diners usually tip the waiters. The outdoor **Grill** serves cooked-to-order hamburgers and hot dogs; the patisserie on the Plaza Deck has espresso, cappuccino, and pastries. **Sundaes** is a poolside ice-cream parlor; there's a charge per scoop.

SERVICE Officers are British and Italian, dining staff European, bar and cabin stewards Filipino, and reception and cruise staff American and British. Most of the crew are friendly and well trained, especially the dining staff, which consistently garners high praise. Service at the reception desk is uneven and sometimes brisk; individual cabin stewards, ever smiling and eager to please, occasionally get mixed reviews, often the result of insufficient training.

FACILITIES AND ACTIVITIES The cruise staff presents an enormous variety of entertainment. You might start your day's activities with bridge or dance lessons, or a craft demonstration. In the afternoon you might play golf or table tennis, take a lesson in the casino, join a trivia game, or watch a culinary demonstration or horse races. Movies are shown three or four times daily. And then there's bingo.

The wood-paneled library has a large selection of books, plus audio chairs with built-in headsets that are set by large bay windows overlooking the water. The **Card Room** is also used as a meeting room or for private parties. Internet cafes with 20 or more computers are available on all ships; access costs 35¢ per minute.

Note: Art auctions have become ubiquitous on major cruise ships. Most of the art is terrible and terribly overpriced, despite claims to the contrary. One *Sea Princess* passenger recently wrote:

> . . . *the tacky, in-your-face display of art for auction [is] everywhere on the ship from embarkation to disembarkation—and it grew day by day. Frankly, Princess has too much class to be using this sort of revenue-generating scheme in the first place, but the carnival hawker's atmosphere and the total lack of knowledge or finesse exhibited by the auctioneer were almost comical. Sea Princess, like her sisters, is an elegant ship with*

lovely decor, but even the "legitimate" artwork in many passageways and some elevator lobbies was obscured by the easels and announcements of art for sale.

We couldn't agree more.

The Grand Plaza is the ship's hub. The Promenade Deck contains only public rooms and is anchored by the two showrooms. Forward is the **Princess Theatre,** with an enormous stage for Broadway-style productions. Graduated theater seating and an absence of pillars ensure fine sight lines.

Aft is the marble-walled **Vista Lounge** with tiered seating and floor-to-ceiling ocean views. Dancing and cabaret-style entertainment are offered. To one side, a large, free-form bar encourages mingling. Shows in both lounges are repeated—four performances each for early and late seating over consecutive days.

The **Grand Casino** has slot machines, video poker, blackjack, roulette, and craps. The stained-glass ceiling, lighted to simulate a spinning roulette wheel, is visible on the deck below, from where passengers access the casino via a staircase in the second atrium.

Flanking the ships' second atrium are the disco and romantic **Rendezvous Lounge.** The disco's entrance glitters with fiber-optic lights and a video dance floor, rather than video wall. Rendezvous Lounge, an elegant refuge, serves caviar, imported wines, and Champagnes by the glass. The **Atrium Lounge,** with a white baby grand piano and dance floor, is particularly popular for predinner cocktails and late-night sing-alongs. Afternoon tea is also served there as well as in the **Horizon Lounge.**

The **Wheelhouse Bar** near the Princess Theatre is one of the ship's most attractive, inviting rooms. Resembling a British men's club, it's decorated in rosewood and dark burgundy with sumptuous, spruce-green leather chairs. Ship models and P&O memorabilia adorn the walls. Passengers pack the room at lunch for the new pub lunch, recently introduced on *Ruby Princess* and now available fleetwide. They also enjoy the room's lively atmosphere at cocktails packing the dance floor before dinner and late into the night.

SPORTS, FITNESS, AND BEAUTY Some of the most innovative architectural designs benefit sports and fitness activities. One of the ship's pools is open to the sky, though set between two decks. On Riviera Deck are the main pools and the ocean-view spa. Half of this large area is a well-equipped gym; the other half is a mirrored room where aerobics classes are held. The spa has 11 massage and beauty treatment rooms, saunas, showers, changing facilities, and an ocean-view beauty salon. Next door, a computerized golf center simulates play on a half-dozen top courses ($20 per half hour for up to four players).

The **Lotus Spa** program features daily exercise and well-being classes as well as traditional and exotic spa and salon services. Start your day with a Lotus Walk on Promenade Deck, followed by a spinning class or aerobics and stretch classes. More leisurely classes include Aqua Aerobics, Pathway to Yoga, and the use of visualization, meditation, and relaxation techniques in the Mind, Body, and Soul classes.

Sunbathing areas are spread across three top decks with a pool and bar (live band during daytime) on one; another pool, whirlpool, and grill on another; and a splash pool, bar, and paddle tennis, volleyball, and basketball court on the third. A one-sixth-mile jogging track girdles the top deck; a broad teak promenade encircles the ship. (Three times around equals a mile.)

Another amenity added to *Dawn Princess* during her recent renovation was The Sanctuary, the adults-only retreat in a secluded area of the top deck, that provides a quiet and comfortable setting with plush, padded lounge chairs and service by dedicated Serenity stewards. Price is $10 for a half day. Spa treatments can be arranged here.

CHILDREN'S FACILITIES Princess Kids, Princess's fleetwide youth program, provides age-specific activities for three groups: Princess Pelicans (ages 3–7), Shockwaves (ages 8–12), and Remix (ages 13–17). It also includes in-port programs with lunch, running 8 a.m.–5 p.m. at no charge, and learning opportunities through a partnership with the California Science Center and the use of National Wildlife Federation educational materials on wildlife and conservation. The program includes studies of the stars, oceans, and coral reefs, and building and racing sailboats, among others, and complements Princess's junior ranger program in Alaska and the fleetwide Save our Seas environmental program. Participants take home a "Pete's Pals" booklet reflecting endangered species, including white pelicans, manatees, sea turtles, and panda bears in areas Princess sails. Group babysitting for ages 3–12 is available 10 p.m.–1 a.m. for $5 per hour per child. Children can now travel on most itineraries at six months.

Sun Princess's **Fun Zone** is one of the most enchanting playrooms at sea. Here, kids romp in a splash pool, play in a castle and big-as-life doll's house, and perform in a little theater. Next door, **Cyberspace** (**Wired** on *Sea Princess*), the teen club, offers video games, a disco, and refreshments.

THE SHIPS Saying the 109,000-ton, $450 million *Grand Princess* was the largest, most expensive cruise ship built when she debuted doesn't say much. But comparisons clarify the image: *Grand Princess* is about four times the length

Caribbean Princess	QUALITY **8**	VALUE **B**
Crown Princess	QUALITY **9**	VALUE **A**
Diamond Princess	QUALITY **8**	VALUE **B**
Emerald Princess	QUALITY **8**	VALUE **B**
Golden Princess	QUALITY **8**	VALUE **B**
Grand Princess	QUALITY **8**	VALUE **B**
Ruby Princess	QUALITY **8**	VALUE **B**
Sapphire Princess	QUALITY **8**	VALUE **B**
Star Princess	QUALITY **8**	VALUE **C**
REGISTRY Bermuda/Britain	LENGTH 951 feet	BEAM 118/159
CABINS 1,300–1,557	DRAFT 26 feet	SPEED 22 knots
MAXIMUM PASSENGERS	PASSENGER DECKS 13	ELEVATORS 16/15
2,600-3,100	CREW 1,225/1,110	SPACE RATIO 37/42

of New York's Grand Central Station. She's 28 feet taller than Niagara Falls, 49 feet taller than the Statue of Liberty, and too wide by 43 feet to transit the Panama Canal.

Grand Princess's price tag was almost twice the cost of the Pathfinder mission to Mars. Happily, there's plenty on this ship to suggest that Princess got its money's worth. Of the ship's 928 outside cabins, 710 have balconies—the most on any cruise ship at the time she was launched. She was the first with three main dining rooms and three main show lounges, each with a different show nightly. Her 13,500-square-foot casino was the largest afloat.

Get the picture? She's big, expensive, and has plenty of wow! But Grand Princess also comes with innovations even more exciting than those of the Sun group. For starters, she had cruising's first wedding chapel; the first virtual-reality arcade with a motion-based ride for up to 18 people, car races, and skiing; a blue-screen video production facility that lets passengers star in their own videos; and the first swim-against-the-current lap pool at sea. She was the first cruise ship to have 28 wheelchair-accessible cabins. At the time she debuted, Grand Princess was one of a few cruise ships with duplicate operational and technical systems to ensure continued operation in emergencies. Her sisters have similar features.

Grand Princess's most unusual and noticeable design feature is **Skywalkers Nightclub,** an aluminum structure suspended 18 decks above the water at the stern like a skybox at a stadium. Accessed by a glass-enclosed moving walkway, it's an observation lounge by day and a disco by night. On Crown Princess, Skywalkers was moved forward, freeing up space for **The Sanctuary,** a premium amenity for adults only and a nonsmoking outside area with lounges for sunning and pampering ($10 for a half-day pass). There are two private cabanas for spa treatments. The Sanctuary is now available on all Grand-class ships, except Diamond and Sapphire.

The ship's enormous interior is diminished by being divided into many small spaces offering dozens of activities—so many choices that a week of cruising isn't enough time to try them all. The myriad options should be a comfort to first-time cruisers fearful of feeling confined or having nothing to do.

Among other distinctive features is the bridge, which extends beyond both sides of the ship. It's glass-enclosed to protect the computerized navigational instruments. A bow observation area gives passengers nearly the same view that officers have from the bridge. Balconies, outlined in blue glass, are built out from the ship's body in stair-stepped tiers. The design opens all balconies to the sun, but the negatives are a loss of privacy (cabins above overlook lower spaces) and noise traveling upward.

In spring 2004, the Grand class more than doubled in cabin count when three more megaliners were added: the 113,000-ton Caribbean Princess in April, the 116,000-ton Diamond Princess in May, and the 116,000-ton Sapphire Princess in June. The count jumped again when three more ships similar to the Caribbean Princess were added—Crown Princess in 2006, Emerald Princess in 2007, and Ruby Princess in 2008. Each of the last three ships introduced significant changes, such as La Piazza, which is meant to resemble a town square with cafes and entertainment and is now the ships' focal point. It was added to Caribbean, Golden, and Star Princess during their recent renovations.

Crown Princess introduced a new itinerary for Princess Cruises, sailing from the new Brooklyn, New York, Terminal Port facility on alternating nine-day eastern and western Caribbean cruises, including Grand Turk in the Turks and Caicos islands. Pre- and post-cruise motor coach transfer service is available from all major metropolitan areas, including Baltimore–Washington, D.C.; eastern Pennsylvania; Massachusetts; and Connecticut–Providence, Rhode Island. *Crown Princess* was one of the first cruise ships to call at Grand Turk at the island's new port and terminal.

Caribbean Princess introduced Movie under the Stars, a great way for passengers to enjoy the latest movies under the heavens as they relax on deck. The movies and special sports events play on a giant, Times Square–style screen built into the superstructure of the vessel at the midship pool. The feature has been so popular that Princess installed it on all *Grand*-class ships, except *Diamond Princess* and *Sapphire Princess*. (It's another Princess innovation copied by other cruise lines.) True to any movie-watching venue, popcorn and other snacks are available.

As noted before, Princess is the line of *The Love Boat*, and now *Crown Princess* and all other Princess ships that have Movies under the Stars provide an opportunity for an "Engagement under the Stars by video." Just before the outdoor evening movie, a guest can pop the question by video, while passengers watch the big screen in anticipation of the answer. The pricey package includes a special romantic dinner, amenities, and the creation of keepsakes to remember the occasion long after they return home. If the couple wants to marry aboard ship, Princess has a complete program for that also.

ITINERARIES *See* Itinerary Index.

CABINS These Princesses each have 35 cabin categories! (*Crown Princess* has only 13 cabin categories.) Most cabins are on Decks 8 through 12, with a few on Decks 5 and 14, and of the outside cabins, 80% have verandas. The majority range from 215 to 255 square feet, a spaciousness generally available only in deluxe suites. The pastel decor renders a pleasant ambience. Closet and shelf space is generous; drawers are limited but adequate.

The ships' balconies offer several benefits. First, they entice passengers to spend more time in their cabins, reducing crowds in public areas. Second, with so many available in standard cabin, the amenity is affordable for a wider audience. The ships' wheelchair-accessible cabins are also available in all main categories.

Cabins are more traditional in layout than those on the *Sun* group. Suites have tiled (not marbled) bathrooms and do not have Jacuzzi tubs. The two 800-square-foot Grand Suites (one on *Golden*) are aptly named. Each has a large balcony with whirlpool, living room with fireplace, wet bar, three televisions, and walk-in closets.

Passengers in suites get expedited embarkation and disembarkation, packing and unpacking service upon request, free Internet access, dry cleaning, laundry, and even shoe polishing. On formal nights, they receive a complimentary corsage and boutonniere. They can enjoy tea served in their suites and schedule a private portrait sitting with a shipboard photographer.

Specifications Caribbean/Crown, 1,557 cabins, 1,105 outside, 452 inside; 25/28 suites with balconies; 2 interconnecting family suites; 180/186 mini-suites with balconies; 674/532 standard with balcony; 25 wheel-chair accessible. *Golden, Star/Grand,* 1,301 cabins, 935/928 outside, 366/372 inside (160 square feet); 205/208 suites with balconies (325–800 square feet); 502 outside with balconies (215–255 square feet); 228/218 standard outside (165–210 square feet); 28 wheelchair acces-sible, including 18 outside/10 inside (240–385 square feet); 609 with upper berths. *Diamond, Sapphire,* 1,337 cabins, 960 outside, 377 inside; 28 suites with balconies; 2 interconnecting family suites; 186 mini-suites with balconies; 532 standard with balcony.

DINING Each ship has eight dining venues and offers the line's Personal Choice dining options. This enables passengers to choose between Traditional Fixed Seating dining with assigned seats and Anytime Dining, thus providing pas-sengers more flexibility in deciding when, where, and with whom they dine, as in a restaurant.

The main dining rooms, named for famous Italian artists—**Botticelli, Da Vinci,** and **Michelangelo** (on *Star,* rooms are named for famous Italian places: **Portofino, Amalfi,** and **Capri**)—have low ceilings and clusters of tables in a ser-pentine layout that breaks the space, so guests don't feel they're dining in a large room with many people. At least one of the three dining rooms is desig-nated for traditional dining; one for Anytime Dining; and the third for either arrangement, depending on demand. Generally, it is wise to make a reservation if you want to dine at a specific time. Otherwise, you can just show up.

Horizon Court, the 24-hour Lido cafe, has its own galley and a terrace for outdoor dining. The layout is different from that on *Sun Princess* and causes crowding and confusion. Open for brunch (on sea days only) and dinner by reservation are the popular **Sabatini's Trattoria,** an Italian specialty restau-rant ($20 surcharge), and **Sterling Steakhouse** ($15 surcharge). *Crown Princess's* Sabatini's was moved to Deck 16, expanded in size and menu, and made more elegant. The ship's steak house is now **Crown Grill** on Deck 7 and is much larger ($25 surcharge). All the fleet, except *Sun*-class, now has a Saba-tini's, and the Crown Grill is available on the *Emerald, Ruby, Caribbean,* and *Golden Princesses.* Another new feature on *Crown Princess* is **Vines,** a wine bar where sushi, finger foods, and artisan cheeses are served. Vines is available on all the ships with La Piazza, the entertainment square.

Sapphire Princess expanded the Personal Choice dining concept with a new twist—five main dining rooms, four with a different decor and theme, along with a dish to go with the theme. Passengers on the Anytime Dining plan can choose the one traditional seating dining room or smaller restaurants, each with its own menu—**Vivaldi** (Italian cuisine), **Sterling** (steak house), **Santa Fe** (southwestern), and **Pacific Moon** (Asian). They also have the option of order-ing from each restaurant's themed dishes in addition to each day's menu. Those in the traditional dining room also have changing menu options, includ-ing items from the themed restaurants.

Another popular feature is Balcony Dinner, $50 per person, and Balcony Breakfast, $28 per couple, with cocktails, fresh flowers, Champagne, special menus, and in-room service. (The breakfast is a terrific indulgence and offers a vast amount of delicious food; at $28 for two it is a real bargain. Try it. You'll love it.) The breakfast is served on sea days and is available fleetwide, but the dinner is an amenity on *Grand*-class ships only. A new version of the idea—a special breakfast for suite passengers—came with the *Ruby Princess* in its relocated, fancier Sabatini's and is available fleetwide.

Outdoors are **Prego,** where pizza is served all day; **Trident Grill,** providing hot dogs and burgers; and an ice-cream bar where a scoop costs $2. As noted earlier, *Crown Princess* introduced a somewhat different take on its atrium called **La Piazza,** which is used for daytime entertainment, such as a mime or stilt walkers, and can be enjoyed by the whole family. On the sides of La Piazza are **Crooner's,** the lobby bar; **International Café,** a patisserie and coffee bar; and Vines, the wine bar. Room service is available 24 hours. Because dining is available at all times, passengers do not need to plan shore time around mealtimes. The many dining options also reduce lines and crowds.

FACILITIES AND ACTIVITIES The *Grand Princess*'s **Voyage of Discovery,** the $2.5 million virtual reality center, is an eye-popper. The room has interactive games and a cyber bar, but its main attraction is a wild, motion-based virtual-reality ride that seats 18 people. Passengers buy a Voyager card for $20, which they use to start machines, and the cost of play ($0.75–$3) is deducted. At the blue-screen **Limelight Studio,** passengers can star in their own video, inserted into an existing scene from a popular movie or historical event. Neither the virtual-reality center or blue-screen studio are found on *Golden Princess* or *Star Princess.* Rather, *Golden* has a digital studio that provides a face-replacement computer program. *Star* (and other ships) have a blue-screen-portrait type of computer with which subjects can be photographed against a variety of backgrounds (similar to the Limelight system). It's a portable system operated off a laptop computer.

Standard diversions are plentiful: bingo, karaoke, cards, board games, spelling bees, and dance classes. The small business center has phone, fax, and computer facilities. (There's a charge to use the equipment.) In the 36-seat wedding chapel, couples can be married or renew their vows with the captain presiding. All nine ships have Webcams in their chapels, enabling folks at home to watch an onboard wedding live.

Shops sell sundries, clothing, jewelry, perfumes, and souvenirs. All are convenient to the **Grand Atrium,** the heart of the ship. In the **Art Gallery,** reproduction and original prints are for sale; the ubiquitous auctions are held almost daily. The ship's library, **A Quiet Corner,** boasts an extensive book collection and the ever-popular private reading and listening chairs. The **Internet Café** is open 24 hours daily, and the florist prepares fresh floral arrangements for purchase. Introduced on *Coral Princess,* Princess Cruises has extended the innovative ScholarShip@Sea fleetwide, offering a a wide range of courses, such as the Art of Entertaining, Navigation@Sea, and Astronomy@Sea, along with a variety of computer courses. There is a small fee, usually about $10, for some classes.

Ships offer a great variety of entertainment. Each of three showrooms has its own shows nightly. **Vista Show Lounge,** the midsize theater, presents cabaret-style entertainment that's quite varied. On Deck 16, across from Sabatini's, *Crown Princess* has a delightful, living room–style piano bar, **Adagio Lounge,** that has proven to be very popular, particularly when Sammy Goldstein is tickling the ivories.

Princess Theatre, a two-deck showroom, stages large-scale production shows and revues and has the best sight lines and most comfortable seats of any shipboard theater we have experienced. Shows, all created by Princess's production department, are outstanding. Now playing on *Ruby Princess* are *Broadway Ballroom* and *Once upon a Dream*. The **Explorer's Lounge** nightclub features soloists and bands playing a variety of music. The **Casino,** designed by the architects who created Caesars Palace Forum in Las Vegas, has one of the world's largest examples of holographic art, plus 260 slot machines, 17 black-jack/poker tables, roulette, and craps.

The ships have many other small entertainment venues, some with music and dancing. The **Wheelhouse Bar,** with the ambience of a private club, offers music for dancing and the popular pub grub at lunchtime; **Snookers** sports bar (although not on *Crown*) has a bank of television monitors that broadcast sports programs, also available in cabins (the system can show events on Princess Theatre's big screen too). **Calypso Bar** and **Oasis Bar,** outdoors and poolside, are frequently the scene of special events, including the Captain's Party. A retractable dome can be closed in bad weather. **Center Court Bar** is near the sports facilities; **Sea Breeze** and the **Mermaid's Tail** are middeck bars. **Alfresco's** bar overlooks the aft pool, which can be covered and converted into a stage for live concerts.

On *Sapphire Princess*, the signature **Skywalkers Lounge** has been moved a bit farther forward than on other *Grand*-class ships, providing 35% more space and a new 125-foot balcony. **Club Fusion,** a multipurpose, high-tech venue, is ideal for dancing or for use as a theater with its 42 high-definition television screens. On *Crown Princess*, this balcony was given over to **The Sanctuary.**

SPORTS, FITNESS, AND BEAUTY Each of the *Grand*-class ships has five swimming pools—including one for children and one for crew—and nine whirlpools. The **Princess Links** computerized golf simulator lets passengers try some of the world's top courses. A landscaped putting green is available, as are paddle tennis, basketball, and volleyball courts. A swim-against-the-current lap pool is the centerpiece of the **Lotus Spa.** The gym has treadmills, Stairmasters, Lifecycles, weight machines, an area for exercise and aerobics classes, and trainer-led options (for a charge) such as yoga, kickbox press, pulse group cycling, and Pilates. There are changing rooms and saunas (no charge) for men and women and an outside jogging track. The spa, operated by Steiner, has 11 massage rooms offering a range of pricey treatments. On *Star Princess*, the Lotus Spa is even larger than on her sister ships, with more treatment rooms and a thermal suite with steam rooms, heated lounge chairs, cool showers, and an ice bath for use by spa clients only. A teak promenade encircles the ship; five and a half laps is just shy of a mile.

CHILDREN'S FACILITIES The two-level **Shockwaves** offers a whale-shaped splash pool, life-size dollhouse, children's theater, ball jump, and more. Programs are age-specific and supervised. **Remix Teen Center,** also bi-level, has a video disco, refreshment bar, video games, and private whirlpool. See "Children's Facilities" in the *Sun* group for Princess Kids' expanded program. *Crown Princess* and other ships have the Youth Security Patrol—specially trained young adults wearing easily identifiable bright yellow shirts walk around the ship to help keep an eye on kids. Among the latest additions are Wizards Academy, Yoga for Kids, and projects from the well-known arts and crafts company, Klutz.

SHORE EXCURSIONS Princess shore excursions are well organized, given the size of ship and number of people touring. Excursions on Mediterranean cruises cover the most important attractions; we recommend them, especially for first-timers. Passengers familiar with the ports may want to arrange their own activities. During calls in Mexico, Princess has a variety of adventure-type tours, such as Dolphin Encounters and kayaking, certified scuba diving, and excursions in all-terrain vehicles, at a range of prices. Descriptions of shore excursions and prices are available on the Princess Web site; once you have booked your cruise, you can also book shore excursions online.

Princess's Web site has an interactive eBrochure, said to be the cruise industry's first. It offers a clickable table of contents, interactive deck plans, a built-in search function, custom printing of selected pages, the ability to zoom in on maps and deck plans, and direct links to detailed content on **www.princess .com.** The site also enables passengers to access their boarding passes and review information on their cruise, air, transfers, pre- and post-hotel packages, shore excursion reservations, and spa appointments in one place.

THE SHIPS In 2003, the 92,000-ton *Coral Princess* made her maiden voyage and was christened in the Panama Canal by the president of Panama—the first cruise ship ever to have such an honor; and her sister, *Island Princess,* debuted in Vancouver, marking a milestone as the first cruise ship christened in that city.

These twins were a new class of ships for Princess, built specifically to transit the Panama Canal, and they reverse the line's recent trend of building megaships of more than 100,000 tons. Despite their smaller size, they are very spacious and include most amenities and services found on Princess's largest vessels, such as a wedding chapel, alternative dining options, a 24-hour restaurant, **Internet cafe,** and a substantial number of balcony cabins. Indeed, the duo appear to combine the best features of the *Sun* and *Grand* classes, plus they have some great attractions that even the bigger ships can't boast.

Constructed at Chantiers de l'Atlantique, the ships were Princess's first French-built vessels. They are very well laid out, making it easy for passengers to get oriented quickly. Their refined and pleasing decor is sophisticated yet comfortable, interesting in detail, and easy on the eyes. Among their newest features are the unusual high-tech facilities in the aft show lounge and their innovative power-generation technology. The configuration not only has environmental advantages but also allows for additional space inside the ships used for enhanced passenger facilities. Then there are the unique features: the first-ever cruise ship kiln—yes, a kiln—and a television-style demonstration kitchen.

ITINERARIES *See* Itinerary Index.

CABINS Nearly 90% of the ships' cabins are outside, and most of these—83%— have private balconies. Although there are 33 price levels, mostly resulting

Coral Princess	QUALITY **9**	VALUE **B**
Island Princess	PREVIEW	
REGISTRY Bermuda	LENGTH 964 feet	BEAM 106 feet
CABINS 987	DRAFT 26 feet	SPEED 21.5 knots
MAXIMUM PASSENGERS	PASSENGER DECKS 16	ELEVATORS 12
2,566	CREW 900	SPACE RATIO 44.6

from location, season, and length of cruise, essentially there are only five types of cabins: suites with balconies (468–591 square feet), mini-suites with balconies (323 square feet), outside standard with balconies (214–257 square feet), outside standard (168 square feet), and inside standard (160 square feet). The best value for the money are the outside standards with balconies, rightly called affordable balconies. The wheelchair-accessible cabins range from 217 to 374 square feet and are available in most categories.

Throughout, the cabins are decorated in easy-to-live-with warm colors and mellow wood. All cabins have twin beds that can be converted to a queen; television with CNN, CNBC, ESPN, TNT, Discovery Channel, movies, and several radio channels; minifridge; ample closet and drawer space; two hair dryers; safe; telephone with voice mail; and bathroom with shower. Further amenities are added in the pricier categories: mini-suites have a queen-size bed, separate sitting area with sofa bed, balcony, two televisions, bathroom with tub and shower, and robes (can be requested in standard cabins). Suites enjoy a larger balcony, walk-in closet, a wet bar, and bath with whirlpool tub. The pebbly nonslip surface of the bathroom floor is a welcome safety feature. There's a self-serve laundry on every cabin deck—another appreciated amenity.

Specifications 879 outside cabins (527 with balconies), 108 inside; 16 suites and 184 mini-suites with balconies; 8 mini-suites; 616 upper berths; 20 (16 outside/4 inside) wheelchair accessible.

DINING The ships' Personal Choice Dining lineup offers two main dining rooms, **Provence** and **Bordeaux,** which passengers can choose for either Traditional Fixed Seating (Provence Dining Room at either first or second seating each evening) or Anytime Dining (Bordeaux Dining Room, 5:30–10 p.m., or by reserving a specific time). Passengers may change from Traditional to Anytime Dining during the cruise, if they prefer. Further options are the 24-hour **Horizon Court** for breakfast, lunch, and bistro dinner for casual evening dining; the **Pizza Bar,** where the specialties are varied and excellent; and the patisserie.

Two alternative restaurants carry a surcharge. **Bayou Café and Steakhouse,** the first New Orleans–style dinner restaurant at sea ($15 per person, which includes a hurricane cocktail), offers Cajun specialties and live jazz. Reviews on this eatery are mixed. Some thought the food was excellent; I did not, and considering that New Orleans is noted for fabulous cuisine and some of the best restaurants in the country, I was disappointed with the Bayou's menu. The best aspect of the cafe is the jazz music in the evening, but be sure to avoid the seating at the side tables behind the orchestra; the sound level there is deafening.

Sabatini's ($20 surcharge), the popular Princess signature Italian restaurant, is open for dinner only except on sea days, when it serves brunch. Dinner has a set menu of so many courses—all excellent—that it's almost too much food. The outstanding service is as good as the food. And if you are still suffering hunger pangs, there's a poolside hamburger grill, an ice-cream bar (extra charge) near the pool, and 24-hour room service.

SERVICE Service throughout the ship is excellent. The friendly staff greets passengers at all times of day in all parts of the ship and are eager to help. The **Sabatini** staff is wonderful, and our Filipino room steward was superb, going out of his way to be helpful. We have never had a more cheerful, attentive, and professional room steward on any ship, including the most luxurious ones. Other passengers have reported enthusiastically the same kudos for the staff of *Island Princess*.

FACILITIES AND ACTIVITIES   The ship's design maximizes the public space for passenger activities, with some lounges spanning the ship from port to starboard. Most of the public rooms are on Decks 6 and 7. Just as on the larger vessels, this duo has three show lounges but with an added dimension—the two-story interactive high-tech aft lounge. Known as the **Universe Lounge,** the decor was inspired by Jules Verne's classic *20,000 Leagues Under the Sea* and sports three revolving stages with integrated lifts, giant projection screens, and the latest in lighting technology, digital sound, and video systems. Stages are designed for a diverse slate of entertainment, from Vegas-style shows to movie screenings and small classroom-style demonstrations.

Universal Lounge is also home to Princess Cruises' fleetwide enrichment program, ScholarShip@Sea, which Princess calls "edutainment." Considering the courses available—cooking, photography, ceramic painting, decorating, visual arts, computers, health, finance, and lectures on a wide variety of topics—the term is accurate. Introduced on *Coral Princess*, the lounge's demonstration kitchen can be moved into place for cooking classes by the ship's chef or visiting culinary experts. The room has network plug-ins for up to 50 laptop computers and an infrared headset system for the hearing impaired. Each cruise offers a slate of up to 20 courses, with 6 options offered each sea day. For some there is a small fee, usually about $10–$25. Other daytime activities are standard cruise-ship fare (which pale by comparison to the edutainment).

Evening entertainment is as varied as the venues. *Coral Princess* has musical shows performed by a cast of 17 lively and very professional singers and dancers in the bi-level **Princess Theatre,** the main show lounge, or the multipurpose Universal Lounge. There is also a variety of music, comedians, and novelty acts in other lounges and bars, as well as classical concerts on some days. **Wheelhouse Bar,** which spans Deck 7, is one of the most handsome rooms on any cruise ship and is very popular with passengers at lunchtime for the newly available pub grub and for cocktails and dancing before and after dinner. Farther along the deck are some new gathering places, such as the **Churchill Lounge,** a cigar and spirits lounge with its own humidor, and the **Rat Pack Bar,** a 1960s retro martini bar. One deck down is the casino, with London-style decor, and the Explorer's Lounge, which becomes the disco in the late evening. There's also a wedding chapel, an Internet cafe, a library and card room, duty-free shops, and an art gallery.

SPORTS, FITNESS, AND BEAUTY   The Lido Deck (14) has a swimming pool, three whirlpools, and a poolside bar. In the **Lotus Spa,** meant to reflect the soothing aura of Bali, there is a swim-against-the-current pool, covered by a retractable glass magrodrome, and two whirlpools. Farther aft is the aerobics room and gym. The vessels offer a nine-hole putting course and golf simulator.

CHILDREN'S FACILITIES   See "Children's Facilities" in the *Grand* group for details.

THE SHIPS   *Tahitian Princess* and *Pacific Princess*, which joined the Princess fleet in late 2002, and the later-acquired *Royal Princess* were the former *R3, R4,* and *R8* of the now-defunct Renaissance Cruises. *Royal Princess*, formerly *Minerva II* of Swan Hellenic Cruises, is named for a beloved former Princess ship. She

Ocean Princess	QUALITY 8	VALUE C
Pacific Princess	QUALITY 8	VALUE C
Royal Princess	QUALITY 8	VALUE C
REGISTRY Gibraltar	LENGTH 594 feet	BEAM 83.5 feet
CABINS 344	DRAFT 19.5 feet	SPEED 20 knots
MAXIMUM PASSENGERS	PASSENGER DECKS 9	ELEVATORS 4
680/710	CREW 373	SPACE RATIO 44

joined the fleet in April 2007 after a refit that transformed her into a Princess. *Tahitian Princess* spent several weeks in a Singapore dry dock in November 2009, where she had a general refurbishment and emerged as the renamed *Ocean Princess. Royal Princess* will be leaving the fleet in the spring of 2011 to join Princess Cruises' sister company, P&O Cruises.

The triplets are tiny compared with the other ships in the Princess fleet, but many of the line's passengers who lamented the departure of the former *Pacific Princess* have been pleased with these ships. In addition to their more intimate cruise environment, the ships come with many modern features.

The ships offer many of the Personal Choice Cruising options that have become Princess trademarks. These include four restaurant choices: the main dining room, **Sabatini's Trattoria, Sterling Steakhouse,** and the 24-hour **Lido cafe,** plus a poolside barbecue grill.

The ships each have a show lounge, eight bars, an observation lounge, casino, a library and card room, two shops, and a medical center. There is a swimming pool, a spa with two whirlpools and beauty salon, a fitness center, and jogging track.

Ninety-two percent of the cabins are outside, and more than two-thirds of these come with a private balcony. All have television, DVD player, safe, refrigerator, and hair dryer. Passengers have a self-service launderette.

Specifications 344 cabins, including 10 suites, 52 mini-suites; 317 outside, 27 inside; 232 have balconies; 3 wheelchair accessible.

Regent Seven Seas Cruises

1000 Corporate Drive, Suite 500
Fort Lauderdale, FL 33334
☎ 954-776-6123, 800-477-7500
or 800-285-1835
FAX 954-772-3763
www.theregentexperience.com

TYPE OF SHIPS Small and midsize luxury vessels with big-ship facilities.

TYPE OF CRUISES Quiet, luxurious, destination-oriented cruises with personal service and sophisticated amenities.

CRUISE LINE'S STRENGTHS
- service
- itineraries
- cuisine
- single, flex-time/open-seating dining
- all-inclusive prices
- all-outside deluxe accommodations and amenities

CRUISE LINE'S SHORTCOMINGS
- limited, staid shipboard activities

FELLOW PASSENGERS Affluent, well educated, well traveled, 45 years and older, $150,000+ annual income; more than 75% are Americans. They cherish their individuality and shun group travel. Most are senior executives, professionals, and high-end resort vacationers. They usually have cruised before on luxury liners, have sophisticated tastes, and care about elegance and service. Some are likely to be special-occasion celebrators and incentive awards winners.

Recommended for Upscale, independent, active, seasoned travelers accustomed to luxury and quality. Small-ship devotees who appreciate the advantages and accept the limitations of such vessels.

Not recommended for Joiners; people who need to be entertained, want a full day of shipboard activity, or thrive in a Vegas atmosphere.

CRUISE AREAS AND SEASONS World cruise, Asia, Australia, Middle East, New Zealand, winter; Canada, Caribbean, Central and South America, Mexico, transcanal, U.S. East Coast, fall, winter, spring; Alaska, Bermuda, Europe, Mediterranean, spring and summer; Northern Europe, summer.

THE LINE Launched in 1990 by a wealthy Japanese businesswoman who established its high standards, Seven Seas Cruise Line quickly made its mark by offering deluxe cruises at rates considerably lower than its competitors and winning accolades and awards after only its first year. In 1995, Radisson Diamond Cruises and Seven Seas Cruise Line merged to form Radisson Seven Seas Cruises. The deal represented an expansion into cruising by Radisson Hotels International, owned by Carlson Hospitality Worldwide. Radisson Seven Seas, in a joint venture with Monte Carlo–based V. Ships, debuted the all-suite luxury *Seven Seas Navigator* in 1999, the larger, all-suite, all-balcony *Seven Seas Mariner* in 2001, and her sister ship, *Seven Seas Voyager*, in 2003. Each ship can boast some of cruising's highest space-to-passenger and crew-to-passenger ratios.

In a major reorganization of its hotel division in 2006, Carlson Hospitality brought Radisson Seven Seas Cruises into the Regent brand and changed the cruise line's name to Regent Seven Seas Cruises. Following the name change, RSSC began a multimillion-dollar investment to upgrade and refit all cabins and suites and public areas fleetwide. Then in 2007, Apollo Management bought controlling interest in Regent Seven Seas Cruises and Oceania Cruises and soon after formed Prestige Cruise Holdings (PCH) as the parent company to manage Apollo Management's cruise investment portfolio.

In 2009, RSSC completed the first phase of its ambitious refurbishment program for *Seven Seas Voyager* and *Seven Seas Mariner*, in time for their 2009 World Cruises. In the second phase, *Seven Seas Navigator* was given a similar makeover. The $40 million refurbishment program was overseen by RSSC's Operations team with the marine architectural firm of Yran and Storbraaten of Oslo, Norway, the ships' original architects, who gave the ships a fresh, new, elegant, and luxurious feel.

In 2010, *Seven Seas Voyager* left San Diego in January for a 119-night world cruise, which will mark Regent's tenth world cruise.

STYLE The size of the ships, their relatively small number of passengers, and price ensure the cruises a certain exclusivity. They also help define the high level of service and personal attention passengers expect—and receive.

Shipboard life is informal during the day but formal in style (though not necessarily in dress) in the evening. Surroundings are spacious and luxurious, the ambience sophisticated. The ships have loyal fans.

The affluent passengers on these ships are accustomed to a high level of service and comfort, and the ships deliver in their spaciousness, luxurious surroundings, and attentive staff. There is the usual array of shipboard staples—exercise classes, word and board games, bingo, the ubiquitous art auctions—but nothing too taxing. In fact, if there's a criticism to be made, it would be the need to provide passengers with more imaginative shipboard activities. All-inclusive prices include select complimentary wine and spirits at all bars and restaurants fleetwide on every sailing.

RSSC offers NewspaperDirect across the fleet. With this service, passengers may receive daily printed editions of their favorite national or international newspapers, including *USA Today, Financial Times*, the *Wall Street Journal, Frankfurter Allgemeine Zeitung*, and *Le Monde*, among others. The line offers Internet access and digital satellite-fed television, Wi-Fi hot spots in select public areas, shipboard cell phone service, and additional online capabilities. Internet access has a one-time setup fee of $3.95 and costs $0.35 per

THE FLEET	BUILT/RENOVATED	TONNAGE	PASSENGERS
Seven Seas Mariner	2001/06/09	50,000	700
Seven Seas Navigator	1999/07/10	33,000	490
Seven Seas Voyager	2003/06/09	46,000	700

minute or $62.50 for a package of 250 minutes. Now, too, passengers with deposited reservations can prereserve a table for dining at one of the line's reservations-only restaurants, as well as spa treatments.

RSSC has a series of programs and amenities called The Regent Experience. It includes Destination Services, meant to give passengers the tools to customize their travel based on their personal interests and preferences. Special à la carte tour and hotel arrangements can be prebooked through a dedicated toll-free number, or passengers may select from an array of shore excursions and pre-register on RSSC's Web site. Passengers confirmed in suites with butler service can e-mail their special requests in advance.

Regent offers iJourneys, which are downloadable, personal iPod walking tours available for purchase for a variety of European ports such as Barcelona. Each one-and-a-half-hour tour, compatible with iPod or MP3 players, comes with a map, commentary, historical context, a touch of humor, and tips.

DISTINCTIVE FEATURES No-tipping policy. Extensive book/DVD libraries. Cordon Bleu–directed venues on *Mariner* and *Voyager*. Wi-Fi hot spots. iPod music systems with Bose speakers preset with music in upper-category suites. Selection of free shore excursions for 2010. Inclusive prices (see Rates below).

RATES Gratuities and wine with lunch and dinner included. Select complimentary wine and spirits at all bars and restaurants fleetwide on every sailing. Soft drinks and room bar setup included; nonalcoholic drinks restocked daily, depending on ship. Government fees and taxes and a selection of shore excursons included in standard cruise prices for 2010.

Special fares and discounts
- Between 25% and 50% savings on select voyages. Second-passenger savings of 50% savings off standard fares.
- **SINGLE SUPPLEMENT:** Specific amounts per cruise in brochure.

PAST PASSENGERS Regent Seven Seas Society for repeat passengers offers members' sailings with incentives and special prices. Some sailings are hosted by the line's president. Members receive gifts based on the number of days they cruise. The program has five tiers: Bronze (4–20 nights), Silver (21–74 nights), Gold (75–199 nights), Platinum (200–399 nights), and Titanium (400+ nights). Details on the benefits for each tier are available on Regent's Web site.

THE LAST WORD RSSC has been able to maintain the lead it has enjoyed for several years, despite the fact that the line has been bought, sold, and merged several times and the intense competition in luxury cruises, not only from the established luxury lines but also from new entries. In early 2009, in the face of an economic downturn, RSSC unveiled its "ultra-inclusive" cruises, adding a selection of free shore excursions in every port on all sailings in 2010, rather than discount those prices. More recently, RSSC announced it would fold government fees and taxes into the standard cruise prices for 2010. Both of these moves represent a truly value-added cruise option for passengers. The moves have attracted a lot of attention and enough business for the line to add more free excursions to the list, but the jury is still out on its success or how long the line will continue these offers. Stay tuned.

Regent Seven Seas Standard Features

Officers *Mariner*: French and European; *Navigator, Voyager*: European, international, Italian.

Staff *Dining and Cabin:* European and international; *Cruise:* American and British.

Dining facilities Two dining rooms on *Navigator*; four on *Mariner, Voyager* with open seating for three meals; informal indoor/outdoor cafe for buffet breakfast and lunch. Reservations-only alternative dining on *Navigator, Mariner, Voyager*; four choices.

Special diets Accommodated with advance notice.

Room service 24-hour service with full-meal, in-cabin dining.

Dress code Casual by day; smart casual most evenings; some evenings, jackets required for men. Formal or semiformal for Captain's parties. Visits in some ports of call may require women to cover heads, legs, and arms.

Cabin amenities Direct-dial phone, hair dryer, television, CD/DVD, radio, stocked minibar, marble bathroom with tub and shower, CNN, *Navigator*, all suites; *Mariner, Voyager* all suites, all verandas, robes, safe. Butler service in select cabins, iPod and Bose speakers in Butler Suites.

Electrical outlets 110 AC.

Wheelchair access *Mariner*, 6; *Navigator, Voyager*, 4.

Recreation and entertainment Nightly shows, nightclub, cabaret, and piano entertainment in two lounges, small casino, dancing, card games, backgammon, book/DVD library, lecture program.

Sports and other activities One outside pool. See text.

Beauty and fitness Beauty salon, small gym. Carita spas on all ships; see text.

Other facilities Boutique, hospital; *Mariner, Voyager*, Internet cafe, launderettes; *Navigator*, Internet access in library. Meeting space and business facilities.

Children's facilities Club Mariner children's program on select cruises.

Theme cruises Yes.

Smoking Smoking sections designated in public areas; no cigar or pipe smoking in dining room.

Regent Seven Seas suggested tipping Gratuities are included in cruise fare; therefore, no-tipping policy.

Credit cards For cruise payment and onboard charges: American Express, Diners Club, MasterCard, Visa, Discover.

Seven Seas Navigator	QUALITY 8	VALUE B
REGISTRY Bahamas	LENGTH 560 feet	BEAM 81 feet
CABINS 251	DRAFT 21 feet	SPEED 20 knots
MAXIMUM PASSENGERS	PASSENGER DECKS 8	ELEVATORS 5
490	CREW 345	SPACE RATIO 67.3

THE SHIP In a joint venture with Monte Carlo-based V. Ships, Regent Seven Seas Cruises launched its all-suite luxury ship, *Seven Seas Navigator*, in 1999 and renovated her in 2007 and again in November 2009. The Italian-built vessel, the fastest in the Regent fleet at the time, has an ice-strengthened hull, giving her the ability to operate virtually anywhere in the world. V. Ships, established in 1984, is part of the Vlasov Group, one of the world's largest providers of ship management and related services.

A small, spacious ship with a big-ship feel, the *Navigator* (with one of the industry's highest space ratios) has half a dozen lounges, superbly appointed outside suites (90% with balconies, walk-in closets, and well-appointed bathrooms), single-seating dining, alternative restaurants, a wide teak deck surrounding the pool, and a Canyon Ranch spa.

Norwegian architects, Yran & Storbraaten, were in charge of the design of the *Navigator*'s recent renovations, which have enhanced the ship's elegance and sophistication with rich fabrics, textures, and furnishings. A bank of glass elevators offers a bird's-eye view of the gracefully designed ship and a panoramic view of the pool area.

ITINERARIES *See* Itinerary Index. At the end of her 2010 Alaska season, *Seven Seas Navigator* will embark on her longest, most exotic voyage to date: a 96-night Grand Asia Pacific cruise.

CABINS Particular attention was lavished on the accommodations. They range from roomy standard suites of 301 square feet plus veranda to Master Suites with 1,067 square feet plus a 106-square-foot balcony. Standard suites are identical; price varies by location. Ten suites are interconnected. Four suites are wheelchair accessible.

Suites, like the rest of the elegant ship, are decorated in subdued colors with cherrywood accents. They have sitting areas, twin beds convertible to a queen, marble bathrooms with separate tub and shower, and a walk-in closet with safe. Other amenities include a minibar with liquor setup, bathrobes, hair dryer, new flat-panel television, DVD players, and clocks. In the 2007 renovations, the layout of some suites was changed, and big cabinets that had been built to hold televisions were replaced with flat screens, which allowed for more room in the suites. All accommodations fleetwide have new mattresses, down comforters, Egyptian cotton percale Anichini linens with satin-stitch embroidery, cashmere throws, and new linens and Regent luxury amenities in bathrooms. Upper category suites also have iPod music systems with Bose speakers preset with music content.

In standard suites, a coffee table rises to dining-table height with the touch of a button, and upper-level suites have proper dining room tables. Passengers can dine en suite, ordering from the dining room menu during meal hours, with dishes served course by course. The ship offers 24-hour room service.

Master and Grand suites, which come with butler service, have a foyer with a powder room, living/dining area, and a separate bedroom with bathroom that has a bidet. Two other top suite categories (A and B) also offer butler service—a posh touch that includes cocktails served daily.

Specifications 251 outside suites, 90% have balconies. Standard balcony suites, 301 square feet plus balconies; 10 Grand Suites, 538 square feet plus balconies; 4 Master Suites, 1,067 square feet plus balconies; 4 wheelchair accessible.

DINING The open, single-seating **Compass Rose Restaurant,** the main dining room, provides a gracious setting, with a small dance floor for occasional dinner dances. After the most recent renovations, the room appears dramatically different with new armchairs in jewel tones of cranberry and opal atop plush carpets of russet and cocoa, creating a regal setting where the widely spaced tables are set with new china, silver, and glassware.

Fine service, gracious ambience, and generous space between tables add to the luxury. Seating is open; neither times nor tables are assigned. Gourmet cuisine is the ship's most outstanding feature. Selections change daily; preparation and presentation are varied and sophisticated.

The newest addition is Prime 7, a contemporary interpretation of a classic American steak house, with an innovative menu of prime-aged steaks and chops, along with fresh seafood and poultry. Rivaling elegant restaurants ashore, a rich palette of green and golden hues creates an ambience of glamour and intimacy. Supple leather, polished granite, and burnished woods create a stage for tables set with custom-designed china, flatware, and crystal.

Passengers stroll across a parquet floor to enter **La Veranda,** which has replaced Portofino's. The new indoor/outdoor restaurant serves breakfast and lunch in a casual atmosphere and, in the evening, features regionally themed specialty dinners. There is no service charge here or elsewhere on this gratuities-included ship. Complimentary wine is served.

High atop the ship on Deck 10, a new pool grill with a barbecue grill offers a hot and cold buffet, panini sandwich station, and coffee and dessert area for a casual, alfresco dining option open throughout the day.

FACILITIES AND ACTIVITIES The two-tiered **Seven Seas** show lounge hosts varied entertainment, ranging from Broadway revues to concert pianists. The **Stars Lounge** is the disco/after-hours club, where sleek, deep-blue leather chairs backed in wood line up along a glass-topped bar.

A few steps away, cigar lovers gather in the **Connoisseur Club's** tobacco-colored leather armchairs near a granite-topped faux fireplace. Next door, the small **Navigator Lounge** has a new decor in hues of cappuccino, camel, and navy accented by apple green and lemon, creating a vibrant, urbane feel; here coffee and cocktails are served throughout the day. At the large library stocked with books, periodicals, and DVDs, there is a bank of nine computers where passengers can check their e-mail. Two boutiques sell designer wares.

A dark, rich-looking casino has tables for blackjack, stud poker, roulette, and craps; slots and poker machines are found in an adjacent room. High on

Deck 11, passengers walk through a hall of marble and carpet to emerge in the attractive **Galileo's,** a piano bar and lounge with indoor/outdoor seating and a dance floor. Galileo's now sports bold new interiors of burgundy and gold offset with accents of soft lavender, sky blue, and moss; a sleek new bar area was added as well. One deck higher, forward, the **Vista Lounge** provides a hideaway.

SPORTS, FITNESS, AND BEAUTY As part of the most recent renovation, the Canyon Ranch SpaClub has made its debut. The state-of-the-art spa and fitness facility has a gym and weight room with cardio and weight-training equipment, a juice bar, men's and women's locker rooms, thalassotherapy, a sauna, and steam rooms. Spa treatments, some created specifically for RSSC patrons, include massages and therapeutic bodywork, mud, aromatherapy, ayurvedic and seaweed treatments, body scrubs, therapeutic body cocoons, facials, and masks featuring Canyon Ranch's award-winning Your Transformation skin-care products.

In addition to the grill, the large midship pool area offers two whirlpools and is a venue for moonlight barbecues and dancing. Two driving cages and a putting green are available for golfers.

CHILDREN'S FACILITIES **Club Mariner** children's program is available on select cruises. The program has two tiers: one for ages 6–11 and the other for ages 12–17. Activities focus on the destination's nature, heritage, and crafts. Special tours and a children's menu are offered.

SHORE EXCURSIONS RSSC's new policy of free shore excursions for guests on all its ships in 2010 represents genuine value. The number of excursions available varies by the destination and its ports and goes well beyond the basic city tour. For example, in Europe, there are almost 300 free tours; in Asia, up to 200 free tours; and in Alaska, more than 30 tours. As a general rule, if a tour previously cost up to $200 per person, it is now free. Those that used to cost more than $200 are now offered at a greatly reduced rate. For example, in Juneau, Alaska, the Mendenhall Glacier and Whale Quest used to cost $189 per person; now it's free. The Helicopter Glacier Walkabout used to cost $449 per person; now it costs $159 per person.

THE SHIPS In another joint venture, Monte Carlo–based V. Ships and Regent Seven Seas built cruising's first all-balcony, all-suite luxury cruise ship. The *Seven Seas Mariner*, delivered in 2001, and her sister, *Seven Seas Voyager*, delivered in 2003, had the same architect and interior designer, Petter Yran and Bjorn Storbraaten, who have designed many luxury cruise ships. The stylish sisters are

Seven Seas Mariner	**QUALITY 8**	**VALUE B**
Seven Seas Voyager	**QUALITY 9**	**VALUE B**
REGISTRY Wallis and Futuna/ Bahamas	**LENGTH 709/670 feet**	**BEAM 93/94.5 feet**
CABINS 328/353	**DRAFT 21/23 feet**	**SPEED 20 knots**
MAXIMUM PASSENGERS	**PASSENGER DECKS 8/9**	**ELEVATORS 8**
700	**CREW 445/447**	**SPACE RATIO 71.4/70**

the largest ships in the RSSC fleet, with the greatest space ratio of any cruise ships to date. Both ships were renovated and upgraded in 2006 and 2007, and in January 2009, both were given their most extensive makeover to date.

Highlights of the makeover include the addition of Prime 7, a contemporary rendering of a traditional grill restaurant; the redesign of lounges and public rooms; the creation of new lounge and dining areas around the Pool Grill; new decor and soft goods in most public areas and suites; installation of a pizza oven and ice-cream bar; and an extension of the coffee and snack bar area on *Seven Seas Voyager*, similar to the popular Coffee Connection on *Seven Seas Mariner*.

The two ships, which were built at different shipyards—*Mariner* in France, *Voyager* in Italy—are sisters rather than twins, with some major differences. The latter ship improved over her sister ship by taking some of the best features from *Navigator*, particularly the larger size of its suites and the full bathtub and separate glass-enclosed shower stall, along with some extra marble touches in the bathroom. *Voyager*'s hull is wider than *Mariner*'s, and she has one additional deck. Two of the alternative restaurants, **Signatures** and the new **Prime 7,** on Deck 5 are serviced by a single galley.

On both ships, most of the public rooms are located on the first three and top two passenger decks and have as their focal point an eight-deck-high atrium with three glass-enclosed elevators and stairways curving up through the atrium. For some, the lounges on *Mariner* were so spacious that they lacked atmosphere; for others, the spaciousness of her public areas was the very essence of the ship's luxury. Significantly, the area of the public rooms on *Voyager* was reduced by 23%. With the latest renovations, lounges and public rooms on both ships have been redesigned and now, resplendent with new furnishings, are inviting and sophisticated.

The ships' spaciousness and sparseness are immediately evident in the atrium, where the sculpture decor and visible elevator machinery give it a raw, unfinished look. The starboard side gallery leading off the atrium on Deck 6 serves as a wide connecting boulevard running fore and aft past the open-plan library. The Promenade Deck windows provide natural light, and the generously proportioned space features wicker chairs, planters, and greenery. Art auctions take place here.

The ships' facilities include a spa, a bi-level main show lounge, a small nightclub lounge with a dance floor, a large forward observation lounge, a library, and an Internet cafe. There is a Club Mariner for children on select cruises. The ship has the standard RSSC features, such as all gratuities included in the fare, port-intensive itineraries, and single, open-seating dining with complimentary wine at dinner, but it's the choice of four restaurants that makes these ships different. The newest and very meaningful amenity are free shore excursions, which further validate RSSC's all-inclusive claim and make RSSC more inclusive in many ways than almost any other cruise line.

Voyager was the first ship to have two independent propulsion and power-generation systems in two separate areas of the ship—a significantly enhanced safety measure. Also, the duo's innovative pod propulsion system eliminates the traditional shaft-and-rudder system, making the vessel up to 15% more efficient and reducing noise and vibration. The pods have forward-facing propellers that can be turned 360 degrees, which optimizes maneuverability, fuel efficiency, and speed.

ITINERARIES *See* Itinerary Index.

CABINS Cabins are spread over five center decks and come in 12 or 13 categories of outside suites, all with balconies. *Mariner* suites range from 301 square feet to 1,580 square feet, including the veranda (*Voyager*, 356–1,403 feet). *Voyager* suites are paneled in light wood with fabrics in gold, orange-rust, and light green. The deluxe suites are the most numerous and have a slightly partitioned and curtained bedroom with king-size bed (convertible to twins) and lounge, walk-in closet, and marble bathroom with a full tub and shower. Curiously, the bath and closet on *Mariner* are smaller than on the *Navigator*, something that was rectified on the *Seven Seas Voyager*. The ships now have new furnishings and linens. Some 47 of *Mariner*'s suites have new deluxe shower stalls, with rain showers and tile seating.

The Penthouse Suites, somewhat misnamed, are larger than the deluxe category at 449 square feet on *Mariner* (370 square feet on *Voyager*), but not all are located on the top deck as the name might imply. They feature a roomy, partitioned lounge with L-shaped couch, two lounge chairs, and a glass-top table. The 73-square-foot teak deck balcony on *Mariner* (50 square feet on *Voyager*) has rather ordinary white plastic chairs and a low table. Accommodations increase in spaciousness in the higher categories, which also offer butler service. Some suites will take a third person, and the two-bedroom master suites accommodate up to five. The suites are attended by European stewardesses.

All accommodations have safes; bathrobes; hair dryers; in-suite bar setup upon embarkation; complimentary replenished bottled water, soft drinks, and beer; satellite telephones; and flat-panel televisions with 13 channels, including CNN and ESPN; CD/DVD players for American and European systems; and hookups for personal video cameras. A large selection of complimentary movies-on-demand through the interactive television system is available on all three ships.

An expandable tabletop makes in-cabin dining a pleasure and is very popular, especially at the end of a busy day ashore. A full meal may be ordered from the **Compass Rose Restaurant** or from an in-suite menu 24 hours a day. Valet dry cleaning, laundry service, and tailor service for minor repairs and small alterations are available. The self-service launderettes on cabin decks are complimentary.

Bose Wave music systems have been installed on *Voyager, Mariner*, and *Navigator*. In addition, all suites on *Mariner* and *Navigator* have DVD players and an extensive DVD movie library. *Voyager* has a DVD library and players in all suites. The Butler Suites (categories C and above) also have an iPod dock (with an iPod provided for the duration of the cruise, preloaded with a wide range of music).

Specifications Mariner 328/*Voyager* 353 suites; 80 deluxe suites (356–1,403 square feet). Limited number of suites accommodate 3 persons; *Mariner*, 6/*Voyager*, 4 wheelchair accessible. On *Voyager*, 24 suites are interconnecting.

DINING The choice of four dining venues gives the *Mariner* and *Voyager* their most distinctive quality, and all the venues offer a wide variety of high-quality cuisine. Two restaurants have open seating with no reservations necessary; two take reservations for specific tables; none have an additional charge. Complimentary wines are served with dinner in all four restaurants.

The spacious **Compass Rose Restaurant,** the main restaurant and the largest of the four, accommodates most passengers in open-seating dining for three meals. The attractive room, now with a lovely gold- and wine-colored decor, has a recessed arched ceiling and faux light-wood columns topped with a band of stainless steel capitals. The menu, changed daily, might offer homemade crab cakes as an appetizer, cream of asparagus soup, two salad selections, pasta dish, and main courses, such as sautéed jumbo prawns and Black Angus beef. The choices also include vegetarian dishes and a menu degustation (a sampler of dishes appropriate to the cruising region).

La Veranda, an indoor/outdoor venue, serves a buffet with sheltered outdoor seating aft at wooden tables and chairs set under an awning. There is also an outdoor grill here. Inside the room's etched glass doors, the stylish highback wooden chairs are set around tables under a coffered ceiling; the walls are hung with alluring black-framed Cote d'Azur travel posters. The unusual chairs have vertical double rows of hollow squares cut into the high backs, reminiscent of the work of Scottish designer Charles Rennie Macintosh. In the evening, a portion of La Veranda becomes a Mediterranean bistro for casual dining, offering a tapas, mezze, or antipasti buffet, followed by table service for the soup of the day, salad, pasta, main course, and dessert.

The former Asian restaurant, Latitudes, has been transformed into **Prime 7,** a steak house with an extensive menu that ranges from 12-ounce New York strip and 32-ounce porterhouse steaks carved tableside, to lamb, lobster, and seafood. Each meal is accompanied by pairings of fine California wines, and there is an extensive list of extraordinary American wines available for purchase by the glass. The smallest of the four, the elegant, reservations-only dinner restaurant is decked out in rich green and golden hues with supple leather furniture, polished granite, and burnished woods.

Signatures, the first permanent dining venue aboard a cruise ship directed by chefs from Le Cordon Bleu, the famed French culinary institute, is newly dressed in bold, jewel-colored decor. The reserved-table restaurant is repeated on *Voyager*, offering a wide choice of entrees and main courses and worth several visits on a long cruise. Marinated fillet of red snapper and roast breast of quail with turnips in a morel sauce are two examples from the list of six choices. The appetizing dessert list may include warm chocolate tart with cinnamon ice cream. The sophisticated setting features rust-red chairs with gold tassels, an etched-glass divider between the serving and dining area, and black glass against the aft wall. The chefs take their talents a step further by offering Le Cordon Bleu *Classe Culinaire des Croisieres* on certain voyages. Workshops, conducted by Le Cordon Bleu-trained chefs, provide a hands-on introduction to the art of French cooking. Classes are limited to 16 guests in three two-hour sessions and cost $499 per person. Upon graduation, participants receive their own chef's apron and short toque, a tea towel, and a Le Cordon Bleu cookbook of classic recipes, as well as a certificate of participation. Inquire from the cruise line for future schedules. Both *Mariner* and *Voyager* have this program on select sailings.

With the latest renovations, the Pool Grill gained new lounge and dining areas. To one side is the new pizza oven and to the other side, the new ice-cream bar.

FACILITIES AND ACTIVITIES Public rooms are varied in location from high up and forward to down low and aft. The **Observation Lounge,** located two decks above the bridge, offers comfy seating in the soothing colors of sand and sea to enjoy hot hors d'oeuvres and soothing piano music before dinner, while taking in a grand 180-degree view. From a perch along the horseshoe-shaped bar, the space takes on a magical quality at night.

The semicircular, newly redesigned **Horizon Lounge,** facing aft on one of the lowest passenger decks, is the handsome setting for afternoon tea, with music and light after-dinner entertainment and the new "Dinner and a Show" option introduced in early 2009. Additional covered outdoor seating provides a quiet spot for daytime reading. Nearby, the **Connoisseur Club,** with tan leather chairs and an electric fireplace, makes a sophisticated setting for smoking Cuban and Dominican cigars and sipping liqueurs and wines.

"Dinner and a Show," a new entertainment concept on *Seven Seas Voyager* and *Seven Seas Mariner,* offered on the long winter cruises, begins with a cocktail party with French canapés, followed by a gourmet meal with fine wines at Signatures with such highlights as Sicilian lobster salad to start, Tournedos Rossini or Branzino al Ferri for the main course, topped off with a yummy dessert. Patrons then adjourn to the Horizon Lounge for the evening's entertainment. Florence Henderson was scheduled to appear on the 2010 Circle South America cruise and Clint Holmes for the 2010 World Cruise. On tap for the future are Broadway star KT Sullivan; Australian Mo award-winning singer Rhonda Burchmore; cabaret star Jeff Hamar; actress and singing star Susan Anton; and from Buenos Aires, "Tango e Tango." There is no additional charge for "Dinner and a Show," but reservations are required. This event is limited to around 90 guests (the capacity of Signatures) per evening and repeats on several evenings during the cruise.

The liveliest venue is the **Mariner Lounge** (**Voyager Lounge** on *Voyager*), drawing a crowd before dining in the adjacent Compass Rose or Prime 7 restaurants. **Stars** nightclub-cum-disco, decorated with black-and-white photos of Fred Astaire, Ingrid Bergman, Katharine Hepburn, and other movie stars, is an oddly designed space with a spiral staircase in its midst that links to the midsize casino above. The semicircular two-level **Constellation Lounge,** with continuous banquette seating, is joined by staircases flanking the stage. Here, full shows and cabaret acts are presented under a starlit ceiling of changing colors.

In the past, production shows have not been a strength of this line, but to their credit, that changed with shows that debuted on *Voyager,* performed by four primary singers plus a production cast of six. The shows change from time to time but offer a wide repertoire from classical to jazz, rock, and Broadway favorites. The four lead singers have a real opportunity to shine, especially when three different Gilbert and Sullivan operettas were staged in one production. Both ships stage other enjoyable shows as well. The ships also bring aboard local entertainment from destinations the ships visit, such as (on a South American cruise) a tango and folkloric show in Argentina and a troupe of Chilean folk singers and dancers in Valparaiso.

The open-shelf library offers a generous selection of hardbacks, reference books, and DVDs, with tables to spread out an atlas and comfortable seating for reading newspapers and magazines. The adjacent **Club.com** is the plainly decorated Internet center with more than a dozen terminals (three more in the library) and offers very low charges for sending and checking e-mail. Passengers may also browse and enjoy computer games. Computer instruction, free and very popular, is excellent. A long, rectangular card room also serves as a conference center.

Midship on the same deck is a gallery of high-end shops, plus two specialty boutiques placed at two corners of the atrium landings.

SPORTS, FITNESS, AND BEAUTY The ships' spas are operated by Carita of Paris, with trained therapists available for a variety of treatments that include thalassotherapy, aromatherapy, seaweed and mud wraps, and a variety of massages. Adjoining the spa is an indoor/outdoor fitness center with treadmills, aerobic benches, Nautilus machine, Lifecycles, Stairmasters, free weights, and other exercise equipment. The center also has a beauty salon.

Deck space centers on the Lido pool and three whirlpools, an outdoor bar, and a mezzanine/jogging track above. Outdoor sports include paddle tennis, shuffleboard, and golf nets.

CHILDREN'S FACILITIES See "Children's Facilities in the *Navigator* section for details.

SHORE EXCURSIONS See "Shore Excursions" at the end of *Seven Seas Navigator*.

Royal Caribbean International

1050 Caribbean Way
Miami, FL 33132
☎ **305-539-6000 or 800-327-6700**
FAX **800-722-5329**
www.royalcaribbean.com

TYPE OF SHIPS Superliners and megaliners.

TYPE OF CRUISES Mainstream, mass market, modestly upscale, wholesome ambience.

CRUISE LINE'S STRENGTHS
- new, innovative ships
- outstanding sport facilities and activities
- unique entertainment
- value

CRUISE LINE'S SHORTCOMINGS
- limited storage in cabins on older fleet
- impersonal nature of big ships

FELLOW PASSENGERS Moderately upscale couples, singles, and families with household income of $40,000+ looking for wide variety in shipboard activities and destinations. Average age is 40s, slightly lower on three- and four-night cruises and slightly higher on ten-night or longer trips. In summer, the age drops because of the large number of families traveling with children. About half have cruised at least once, and a quarter are Royal Caribbean repeaters. Genders split evenly, and nine in ten are North Americans on those ships based in North America, but European-based ships have a different mix. Up to 73% of men and 65% of women are married; 36% are professional, managerial, or proprietors. Educational level, occupations, and age differ on three- and four-night cruises, which are less expensive, shorter cruises appealing to younger people and first-timers.

> *Recommended for* Almost anyone taking a first cruise. Those who like large ships, want an array of options, want to be active, sociable, and don't mind large crowds. Ideal for families, particularly several generations traveling together, because there's something for every age.

> *Not recommended for* Small-ship devotees; those who seek a quiet or intellectual milieu, hate crowds, and have no patience for long lines.

CRUISE AREAS AND SEASONS Caribbean, year-round; Costa Rica, Mexico, Panama Canal, fall to spring; Alaska, Bermuda, Europe, Mediterranean, northeastern United States, spring to fall; Asia, Australia, New Zealand, South America, South Pacific, fall.

THE LINE Founded in 1969 as a partnership of three prominent Norwegian shipping companies, Royal Caribbean Cruises Ltd. was the first company to launch ships designed for year-round Caribbean cruising. The vessels proved to be so popular that within five years more capacity was needed. Two vessels were stretched—cut in half, then lengthened by inserting prefabricated midsections, and more superliners with unique designs were added. In 1988, *Sovereign of the Seas* was the first of a new generation of megaliners and the largest cruise ship ever built at the time. On *Sovereign's* arrival in Miami, traffic backed up for miles as people on shore tried to glimpse her. In 1997, Royal Caribbean changed its name to Royal Caribbean International to reflect its global expansion. However, RCCL and RCI are used interchangeably.

The line got a jump on the 21st century with a new generation of six megaliners. The first, *Legend of the Seas*, debuted in 1995 with cruising's first 18-hole miniature golf course. In 1999, RCCL launched *Voyager of the Seas*, another new ship class and the industry's first 142,000-ton cruise ship. It

THE FLEET	BUILT/RENOVATED	TONNAGE	PASSENGERS
Adventure of the Seas	2001	142,000	3,114
Allure of the Seas	2010	225,282	5,400
Brilliance of the Seas	2002	90,090	2,100
Enchantment of the Seas	1997/99/2005	80,700	2,252
Explorer of the Seas	2000	142,000	3,114
Freedom of the Seas	2006	154,407	3,634
Grandeur of the Seas	1996/98	74,140	1,950
Independence of the Seas	2008	154,407	3,634
Jewel of the Seas	2004	90,060	2,100
Legend of the Seas	1995	69,130	1,800
Liberty of the Seas	2007	154,407	3,634
Majesty of the Seas	1992/97/2006	73,941	2,350
Mariner of the Seas	2003	142,000	3,114
Monarch of the Seas	1991/99	73,941	2,350
Navigator of the Seas	2002	142,000	3,114
Oasis of the Seas	2009	225,282	5,400
Radiance of the Seas	2001	90,090	2,100
Rhapsody of the Seas	1997	78,491	2,000
Serenade of the Seas	2003	90,060	2,100
Splendour of the Seas	1996/98	69,130	1,800
Vision of the Seas	1998	78,491	2,000
Voyager of the Seas	1999	142,000	3,114

came with cruising's first climbing wall and ice rink. The climbing walls proved to be so popular that they have been installed fleetwide.

In 2001, the *Radiance* group, another new class, was introduced with the 2,100-passenger, 90,060-ton *Radiance of the Seas*; she was followed by three more sister ships. Then, not to let any other cruise line get ahead of it in the "largest ship" category, the cruise line introduced the 160,000-ton, 3,600-passenger *Freedom of the Seas*, dubbed an ultra-voyager, in 2006; her sister, *Liberty of the Seas*, in 2007; and the third, *Independence of the Seas*, in 2008. But RCI wasn't finished. Its largest ship yet, the 5,400-passenger, 220,000-ton ship, *Oasis of the Sea*, was delivered in November 2009 at an estimated cost of $230,000 *per berth* or $1.5 billion per ship. A sister ship, *Allure of the Seas*, is scheduled to launch in 2010.

In a surprise move in 1997, RCI bought Celebrity Cruises—a deal worth $1.3 billion. Celebrity operates as a separate brand. In 2002, RCI's attempt to buy Princess Cruises, one of its main competitors, was thwarted by Carnival, which won out in the end after a heavy bidding war. After two decades of focusing solely on the Caribbean, RCI expanded to other parts of the world, such as Canada, Europe, Asia, Australia and New Zealand, and Latin America. It also added more U.S. departure cities and built a cruise departure port in New Jersey named Cape Liberty Cruise Port.

In 2006, RCI made a major investment in Europe by buying Pullmantur, a well-established Spanish tour and cruise operator. As further evidence of RCI's expansion and diversification, the line will have eight ships in Europe in 2010, will homeport *Independence of the Sea* in Southampton year-round, base *Brilliance of the Seas* in Dubai, and *Legend of the Seas* in Shanghai. Meanwhile, Royal Caribbean is helping Jamaica build a new cruise terminal at Falmouth to accommodate *Oasis of the Seas* and improve berthing and other facilities at Ocho Rios and Montego Bay.

RCI provides fleetwide cell phone service for passengers in international waters. Wi-Fi hot spots are also available fleetwide, and *Freedom*-class ships have wireless capability in cabins and throughout the ship.

Express Departure is an option available on all Royal Caribbean and Celebrity ships in their arrival ports in North and South America and Europe. The program enables passengers who are willing to carry their own luggage off the ship to keep their luggage in their cabin the night before departure. Luggage Valet also facilitates your journey's end. You pay $10 per person (for up to two bags per person) for the service to the participating airlines—American, Continental, Delta, and United—and receive your airline boarding pass and luggage tags before you disembark the ship. After you clear Customs, you leave your luggage with the airline representative. At the airport, you can proceed directly to the security checkpoint. The service must be booked on board the ship and is offered at Los Angeles, Miami, Port Canaveral, Port Everglades, San Diego, San Juan, Seattle, Tampa, and Vancouver. The service is particularly convenient if you have a flight later in the day.

For all its firsts and innovative designs, RCI is still a conservative company that built its success on a solid, consistent product. Royal Caribbean is a public company, traded on the New York Stock Exchange.

STYLE   RCI ships are big ships that hum with activities almost around the clock and are designed for high-volume, year-round, warm-weather cruises. That C in RCI could just as well stand for *consistency*. Whether you take a Royal Caribbean cruise in Europe or the Caribbean, the activities are many and varied and designed primarily for U.S. and Canadian passengers.

The ships have acres of sun decks, large pools, and lots of outdoor activity: games, competitions, the Vitality fitness program, and sports, like golf, that often combine with sports in port. The ships have contemporary decor with such themes as Broadway hits, operas, and the circus. All vessels have extensive programs for children, catering to the 400,000 kids that RCI carries annually.

Royal Caribbean was one of the first cruise lines to remove trans fat from its menus fleetwide. Its program catering to today's lifestyles is called Vitality, which is meant to bring together many elements—the onboard spa and fitness classes, shoreside activities, special menus, take-home workout plans, virtual personal trainers, and healthy cooking recipes—to create a total experience for passengers who participate in it.

In spring 2009, after a year's testing, RCI extended My Time Dining, its flexible dining program, fleetwide. This program enables passengers to eat in any main restaurant at any time during dining hours. They can make daily reservations for specific seating times or simply walk in, request to be seated with other passengers, or dine alone; they do not have a preassigned table. My Time Dining passengers must prepay gratuities and enroll in the program on board or in advance at RCI's Web site or reservations department.

At the same time, the new My Family Time Dining program offers families with kids ages 3–11, enrolled in the Adventure Ocean youth program, an expedited 40-minute dinner during the first seating in the main dining room. A youth counselor escorts children from the main dining room to the Adventure Ocean area for evening activities, enabling parents to spend the rest of dinner at their leisure. Another new kids' option is Lunch and Play ($7.95 per child), providing kids in Adventure Ocean with lunch, movies, cartoons, and free-play time between noon and 2 p.m. under the supervision of Adventure Ocean counselors.

Passengers can have meals in their cabins and select from RCI's new Dine In Delights menu—in addition to room-service menus—available 24/7 for an additional charge. It offers such well-known options as The Original Johnny Rockets hamburger, Eli's Cheesecake Company's original cheesecake, and more. A service charge of $3.95 is added to room deliveries between midnight and 5 a.m. Passengers can also make dinner reservations in the specialty restaurants and preorder wine, juices, and other beverages online.

Also in 2009, RCI added new services and amenities for passengers in suites, including a dedicated security line (where available), check-in desk in the arrival terminal, and a distinctive gold SeaPass card, recognized by crew and staff members as a sign to provide personalized service. The SeaPass card is also a key to the Concierge Club. Some of the suites' new amenities are enhanced bathroom toiletries and complimentary pressing service on formal nights, and guests in suites enjoy new services such as reserved seating for ice shows, priority disembarkation, and complimentary valet luggage transfers to the airport.

DISTINCTIVE FEATURES **Viking Crown Lounge,** climbing wall, golf program, Labadee (RCI's private beach), and Coco Cay in the Bahamas, **Crown & Anchor** lounges in San Juan and St. Thomas. Room service from dining room menus during lunch and dinner; children's program. Internet centers.

Miniature golf course on *Legend, Splendour, Radiance, Voyager*, and *Freedom* class; ice rink, *Voyager* and *Freedom* class; *Explorer*'s Oceanography Center, *Freedom, Liberty*'s surfing, boxing ring. FlowRider, *Freedom* class.

RATES   Port charges are included.

Special fares and discounts

- **BREAKTHROUGH FARES:** Capacity-controlled discounts (up to 40% and more) that change daily; the earlier you buy, the better the discount. RCI's Best Price Guarantee program means that if a passenger who booked early finds a lower fare advertised by Royal Caribbean for the same ship, sail date, and cabin category, they can receive the difference in price as an onboard credit; any dollars not spent will be refunded at the conclusion of the cruise. The price guarantee is available from the time of booking up to 72 hours prior to sailing by contacting Royal Caribbean or your travel agent.
- **THIRD/FOURTH PASSENGER:** Yes.
- **CHILDREN'S FARE:** Third/fourth person rates.
- **SINGLE SUPPLEMENT:** 200%
- **SINGLE GUARANTEE:** Category and cabin assigned by RCI.

PAST PASSENGERS   The Crown *&* Anchor Society has four membership levels based on how many cruises you take: Gold membership, one to four cruises; Platinum, five to nine; Diamond, ten or more; and Diamond Plus, 24 cruises or more. They receive a cruise credit each time they sail, as well as extra cruise credits when they sail on a cruise/cruise-tour of 12 nights or longer and book a suite. The biggest benefit is personalized attention by shipboard personnel. Members get *Crown & Anchor,* a quarterly magazine with information on new programs, itineraries, and ships; special offers and coupons; a color-coded landing card sticker; wine tasting; members-only Web page, sweepstakes, and shoreside events; and on cruises of seven or more nights, a cocktail party. Gold members also receive special offers on future cruises. Platinum members get terry robes for use during the cruise, custom air arrangements, private departure lounge, special 800 number for reservations, and more.

Diamond customers can count on exclusive coupons, boarding privileges, concierge service on select ships, party in the Concierge Lounge, and priority dining room seating, shore excursions, spa services, and disembarkation. The Diamond Plus level, in addition to the benefits of other levels, gets behind-the-scenes tours, a personalized amenity delivered to their cabin, and a cabin upgrade. After 49 cruise credits, a member gets dinner with a ship's officer and a VIP theater experience. When one reaches 100 cruise credits, the member is treated to a free seven-night cruise in a balcony stateroom.

In 2007, Royal Caribbean introduced the first loyalty program specifically designed for passengers under the age of 18. Members automatically attain their parents' membership level—Gold, Platinum, Diamond, or Diamond Plus— when they enroll. Some of the program's benefits include onboard specials at venues like Ben *&* Jerry's and Y-spa, Royal Caribbean's teen spa. Parents can enroll their children in the program at **www.royalcaribbean.com/youth.**

THE LAST WORD   RCI is a cruise line of megaliners. It targets 80% of people buying cruises; only budget and luxury customers are excluded. There's no denying that the huge ships are big and impersonal, and they have blurred and narrowed the quality that once separated RCI from the pack. If you don't like big ships, this isn't the line for you. But if you want a cruise vacation on ships that have everything, RCI offers good value.

THE SHIPS *Legend of the Seas*, the first of six megaliners in the Project Vision series, arrived in 1995, and her five sisters followed over the next four years. Constructed in France and Finland, the megaliners were quickly labeled the ships of glass. Each has two acres of windows, glass windbreaks, skylights, and walls of windows in public spaces. The **Centrum,** the centerpiece atrium, rises seven decks—two more than on the *Sovereign*-class vessels—and is topped by the **Viking Crown Lounge.** Bubble elevators whisk passengers to the lounge. The ships embrace the sea and vistas through windows and glass. Natural light sparkles, and open space is abundant.

Each ship has distinguishing features. At the Centrum's base is the **Champagne Terrace and Bar,** where fine wines and Champagne are served by the glass. The elegant setting sets the tone for the ships. *Grandeur*'s **Champagne Bar** covers the Centrum's entire lower level. A white baby grand piano stands next to a stairway to the second level. Decorative screens create conversation corners.

Works of art on *Splendour* were created by more than 50 artists and studios. The ship's atrium sculpture is the fleet's most dramatic. The work consists of three elements symbolizing the solar system. The dominant component, an 18-foot gilded disk representing the sun, hangs on a diagonal, silhouetted by rays from the skylight. Iridescent bulbs around the disk transmit and reflect colored light throughout the atrium. Hundreds of steel cords attached to the upper, outer rim of the disk gather at the top of the atrium and are illuminated, creating a glow.

On the Sun Deck is the Solarium, a landscaped indoor/outdoor area with a second swimming pool, whirlpools, and a cafe. Its Crystal Canopy provides cover in inclement weather. Unlike glass roofs on other ships, this one doesn't fold onto itself; instead, it moves intact. The design uses much more glass, admitting maximum light into the Solarium when the roof is closed. The most celebrated features on *Legend* and *Splendour* were the world's first full-scale floating miniature golf courses. The station where equipment and tee times can be obtained resembles a miniature clubhouse.

Enchantment/Grandeur	QUALITY 7	VALUE A
Legend of the Seas	QUALITY 7	VALUE C
Splendour/Rhapsody	QUALITY 7	VALUE A
Vision of the Seas	QUALITY 8	VALUE A
REGISTRY Bahamas	LENGTH 867–990 feet	BEAM 105–106 feet
CABINS 902–1,126	DRAFT 24–25 feet	SPEED 22–24 knots
MAXIMUM PASSENGERS	PASSENGER DECKS 10	ELEVATORS 9–11
1,804–2,435	CREW 735–784	SPACE RATIO 38.32

Royal Caribbean International

Officers Norwegian, international.

Staff *Dining, Cabin:* international; *Cruise:* American and British.

Dining facilities Two seatings for dinner; Chocolate Extravaganza one night; indoor/outdoor cafe with breakfast and lunch buffet; alternative dining for dinner with table service on all ships. *Voyager* and *Freedom* classes, three-level dining room; five alternative venues; *Radiance, Freedom* class, six venues. **Johnny Rockets,** *Freedom* and *Voyager* classes, *Majesty. Oasis of the Seas,* 24 dining venues. My Time Dining and My Family Time Dining fleetwide. $3.95 charge for room-service delivery between midnight and 5 a.m.

Special diets Low-fat, low-cholesterol, lean cuisine. Full vegetarian menus. Request kosher at time of booking.

Room service 24 hours with light menu; dining room menus for lunch/dinner.

Dress code Casual but neat by day, informal in evening; one or two nights formal/semiformal. Tuxedo rental available.

Cabin amenities Direct-dial telephone, radio, television, daily world news update, bathtubs in suites, suites with marble baths on *Majesty, Monarch*; Family Suites; *Voyager, Radiance, Freedom* classes: cyber-cabins.

Electrical outlets 110 AC.

Wheelchair access Ramps on all ships; 4 cabins on *Majesty, Monarch*; 17 on *Legend, Splendour*; 15 on *Vision* and *Radiance* class; 26 on *Voyager* class; 32 on *Freedom* class; 46 on *Oasis of the Seas*.

Recreation and entertainment Show lounge with entertainment nightly, disco, bingo, movies, wine tastings, dance lessons. **Viking Crown Lounge,** bars/lounges, card room, library, Internet cafe.

Enchantment of the Seas had major surgery in 2005 when the ship was cut in two in Rotterdam, and a 73-foot midship section constructed in Finland was inserted. It brought her overall length to 990 feet, displacement to 80,700 tons, and her cabin total to 1,126 with the addition of 151 new accommodations. But lengthening the ship was more than an engineering feat. It was a complete makeover, with some unusual features added, such as an ondeck trampoline complete with bungee cords.

One of the most striking additions to *Enchantment* were two suspension bridges on Deck 10, raising the walkway/jogging track and spanning more than 75 feet on each side of the Pool Deck below. Supported by dramatic arches, the bridges cross over two new areas of the Pool Deck, which jut out past lower decks to overhang the water. Each area is edged with 14-foot-high sheets of glass, offering great views. They also have peekaboo windows in the floor to see the water below. The overhanging space on the port side has a bar; the starboard side houses a band shell that opens like an orange for poolside musical entertainment.

Standard Features

Sports and other activities Two outdoor pools; sports deck with basketball, table tennis, shuffleboard. Miniature golf course on *Legend, Radiance, Freedom, Oasis,* and *Voyager* classes. Climbing walls fleetwide. Ice rink on *Voyager, Oasis,* and *Freedom* classes. Trampoline, three pools, *Enchantment.* Boxing ring, FlowRider surf simulator, H20 Zone aqua park, three (six *Oasis*) swimming pools, *Freedom, Oasis* class.

Beauty and fitness Beauty and barber shop, massage, sauna, Vitality fitness program, jogging track, health club. Solarium, elaborate spa on *Vision, Voyager, Radiance, Freedom,* and *Oasis* classes; cantilevered whirlpools, *Freedom* class.

Other facilities Boutiques, medical facilities, laundry and dry cleaning services, meeting rooms, Internet and e-mail service, fleetwide; cinema/theater on *Monarch, Freedom,* and *Voyager* classes; florist, chapel, ice-cream parlor (on *Majesty, Oasis*), karate room on *Freedom* class.

Children's facilities Year-round youth programs, playrooms, and teen centers on all ships. Fisher-Price program for infants and their parents. Lunch and Play, $7.95.

Theme cruises Usually organized by travel agency or affinity group.

Smoking Public rooms are nonsmoking except in designated areas.

RCI suggested tipping Per person per day, cabin steward $3.50; dining room waiter, $3.50; assistant waiter, $2; 75¢, head waiter. 15% added to bar/wine bill.

Credit cards For cruise payment and onboard charges: American Express, Carte Blanche, Diners Club, Discover, MasterCard, Visa, JCB.

In total, the main pool area was expanded by nearly 50%, with two pools, four whirlpools, and a circular, kid-focused Splash Deck with 64 water jets. Forty of the jets are connected to an interactive touch-pad system, letting kids spray each other or create their own fountain effects. At night, the area closes to become a decorative fountain with a fiber-optic light show.

In addition to the signature climbing wall at the stern, *Enchantment* has four bungee trampolines at the stern on Deck 10. Participants strap into a harness connected to two bungee cords that help them head skyward, while keeping them safely centered when they come in for a landing on the trampolines. The jogging track offers a "vitality course" with four fitness stops. In between laps on the quarter-mile track, runners can pause to jump rope, work their arms, back, and stomach at the sit-up/push-up bars, strengthen their legs at a step-up station, and cool down with a series of suggested stretches. Another addition was **Grab and Go,** a fast-food restaurant on deck. The deck also has two ball zones, each with three basketball hoops of different heights to accommodate youth, teen, and adults.

Enchantment's expanded fitness center and the **Day Spa,** with five more treatment rooms, including a couple's massage room, is one deck below.

Boleros Latin Club, a bar with a glass dome ceiling, serves specialty drinks such as mojitos and caipirinhas and features live Latin jazz in the evenings. **Latte'tudes** coffee and ice-cream shop has espresso drinks from Seattle's Best Coffee and Ben & Jerry's ice cream. The area also has computer terminals for Internet access. Next door, **Casino Royale** was expanded with more slot machines, while more boutiques were added in the shopping area. Accessibility features were added throughout the ship, including ramps, pool and Jacuzzi lifts, access to the Splash Deck, and a lift to the bungee trampoline area.

ITINERARIES *See* Itinerary Index. In March 2009, with the official approval of Chinese authorities, *Legend of the Seas* operated six chartered cruises from Shanghai to Taiwan for Amway China, making Royal Caribbean the first international cruise company to provide cruises within China's territory.

CABINS A major improvement in the *Vision* class was the size of standard cabins—153 square feet compared with 122 square feet in comparable *Sovereign*-class cabins. For two decades, Royal Caribbean said cabin size was unimportant because passengers spend so little time in their rooms, but in the *Vision* class, cabins are larger and more comfortable, with sitting areas and, for the first time, many balconies—one in four. Many more have bathrooms with tubs and showers too. The Royal Suite has a baby grand piano, whirlpool tub, and veranda. Two family cabins sleep six.

> *Specifications* 327 inside cabins, 575 outside; 83 suites; 4 Family Suites; 231 with balconies; 388 third/fourth persons; no singles; 17 wheelchair accessible. *Grandeur/Enchantment*: 399/463 inside cabins, 576/663 outside, 18 suites; 4 Family Suites; 72 deluxe outside; 212/248 with balconies; 403 third/fourth persons; no singles; 14/20 wheelchair accessible. *Rhapsody/Vision*: 407 inside cabins, 593 outside; 18 suites; 72 deluxe; 4 Family Suites; 229 with balconies; 287 third/fourth persons; no singles; 14 wheelchair accessible.

DINING *Legend*'s Romeo and Juliet Dining Room (the King and I on *Splendour*) spans two decks and has 20-foot-tall glass walls on each side, offering spectacular views from every table. The walls are virtually all glass—the load-bearing function is handled by interior columns. On the other, slightly larger *Vision*-class, the lower-level windows are circular. A revolving platform with a grand piano is framed by curving stairways to the balcony. Recently, RCI added Chops Grille signature restaurant's ten-ounce filet mignon entree as a dinner option for $14.95 per person on its dining room menus fleetwide. The idea is to give all passengers a chance to enjoy the specialty restaurant's steak and to provide an alternative to those unable to dine at Chops (such as travelers on the ships that do not have an alternative restaurant or groups too large to be accommodated in the more intimate restaurant).

The restaurants utilize My Time Dining, RCI's flexible dining program, that enables passengers to dine at the time of their choosing (during dining hours), and the new My Family Time Dining, which offers an expedited 40-minute dinner to families with kids ages 3–11 who are enrolled in the Adventure Ocean program. My Time Dining passengers must prepay gratuities and can enroll in the program in advance at RCI's Web site or on board. Passengers can have meals in their cabins and select from RCI's new Dine In

Delights menu, available 24/7 for an additional charge—in addition to room-service menus. The Dine In Delights menu offers such well-known options as The Original Johnny Rockets hamburger, Eli's Cheesecake Company's original cheesecake, and more. A service charge of $3.95 is added to room deliveries between midnight and 5 a.m. Passengers can also make dinner reservations in the specialty restaurants and preorder wine, juices, and other beverages online.

Decor in *Splendour*'s King and I is noteworthy. A Thai temple facade has been replicated, and 16 historical paintings plus two epic murals were created by artists of Thailand's royal family. Each painting tells a story.

The nautical-motif **Windjammer Café** on Sun Deck is the indoor/outdoor area for breakfast and lunch buffets and alternative evening dining. Glass walls on three sides and a sloping skylight brighten the room. Each lunch has a theme, and ethnic food joins the regular array of hot dishes, salads, and sandwiches. Dinner, served 6:30–10:30 p.m., offers full table service. The cafe is a popular spot for reading, playing cards, and watching the water.

SERVICE Recent experience indicated that past mixed reviews and complaints about language problems of dining-room service personnel and room stewards appear to have been addressed, and reports indicate improvement.

FACILITIES AND ACTIVITIES *Vision*-class ships are state-of-the-art at every turn. Computers helped design the bi-level theater to ensure good sight lines for nightly, full-scale Broadway productions. The venue has a computerized system to move scenery, a device commonly used on Broadway, as well as an orchestra pit that can be raised and lowered.

The **Schooner Bar** is a piano lounge popular for its sing-along sessions. Decor includes authentic rigging and an aroma of tar. **Casino Royale** is next door. On *Grandeur*, passengers enter across a glass floor strewn with "sunken treasure" of jewels and gold coins. The cruise line has a beverage program for adults and kids for unlimited fountain soda for $4 per day for ages 17 and under and $6 per day for over 18 plus 15% gratuity.

The spacious **Anchor's Away Lounge** on *Legend* and **Top Hat Lounge** on *Splendour* span the ship's stern. It's a second showroom, used for parlor games, art auctions, daytime dance activities, and late-night shows and dancing. (Aboard the other *Vision* ship, this area became the upper level of the main show lounge, while the secondary show lounge spans the ship's stern.) Topside, the glass-sheathed **Viking Crown Lounge** is an observation lounge by day and a nightclub and disco at night. Nightclub action is away from the room's quieter piano bar. On all the ships, the lounge is accessible from the atrium by glass elevators. Aft of the show lounge (to entice you coming and going!) is a mall with varied shops in attractive settings. For example, the **Harbour Shop,** selling liquor and sundries, recalls an old English vintner's shop through aged timber, antique barrels, and stone floors. The casino offers blackjack, Caribbean poker, roulette, craps, and 178 slot machines.

The conference center can be divided into four rooms, each with full audiovisual support. Adjoining is an attractive lounge that also can be divided. A card room can be divided into two sections, and there is a 2,000-volume library that on the *Grandeur* has an amusing lifelike sculpture entitled *Snoozin*.

SPORTS, FITNESS, AND BEAUTY The Sun Deck has an outdoor pool. Contrasting is the quiet Solarium, the second pool area. When the Windjammer Café and main dining room are closed, the Solarium's cafe serves snacks, alcoholic beverages, sodas, and juices. The area can be covered by a glass canopy. Beyond the Solarium, the **Fitness Center and Day Spa** contains a beauty salon, aerobics area, gym, changing rooms, saunas, steam baths, and seven massage rooms (treatments are pricey). A Sports Deck is at the stern. Each ship has a padded promenade circling most of the ship. A climbing wall was added to all ships.

Legend's much-publicized 17-hole golf course, **Legend of the Links** (12 holes called **Splendour of the Greens** on *Splendour*), is above the spa. Each hole of the 6,000-square-foot links is surrounded by rough to simulate a shoreside layout. Courses range in size from 155 to 230 square feet, tees are 5 feet wide, and the longest hole is 32 feet. There is no charge for play. The glass dome over the aft swimming pool can slide to the golf course, where it can be raised to provide almost ten feet of vertical clearance for golfers. A walkway along one edge of the course has benches to encourage spectators.

CHILDREN'S FACILITIES Outstanding *Vision*-class facilities for children complement RCI's supervised youth program, Adventure Ocean, available year-round, day and evening, and in port. Activities target ages 3–17, split into five age groups. Daily schedules are delivered to cabins. Among the most distinctive activities is Adventure Science, which aims to make science entertaining and amusing. Group babysitting ($5 an hour per child) is available 10 p.m.–1 a.m. In-room babysitting is also available for $10 an hour per room for two children, $15 for three children (minimum age, 1 year old). Family Suites have separate bedrooms for children.

Club Ocean is the children's center. On *Grandeur*, it's submarine themed and includes a tunnel, slide, pool of colored balls, and writing wall. Nearby is the teen center, a lounge with a futuristic design for games, parties, and contests. The ships also have video arcades. A new kids' option is Lunch and Play ($7.95 per child), which provides kids in the Adventure Ocean program with lunch, movies, cartoons, and free-play time between noon and 2 p.m. under the supervision of Adventure Ocean counselors.

Note: If you or your children consume a lot of soft drinks, consider buying the unlimited soda and juice package detailed earlier in this section.

THE SHIPS The $500-million *Voyager of the Seas* was the largest cruise ship ever built—142,000 tons—when she made her debut in 1999 and also the first of five similar ships launched over the following five years.

Voyager is awesome. She's twice the size of the largest aircraft carrier ever built, twice as wide as Broadway in New York, and taller than a 20-story building. She has six diesel engines, each the size of a locomotive, and they produce 15,000 horsepower—the equivalent of 150 cars.

A crew of 10,000 people worked 21 million hours to cut, shape, bend, and weld more than 300,000 pieces of steel into the vessel's hull. Her 14 passenger decks cover 646,000 square feet. Furnishings include 538,000 square feet of carpeting, 15,000 chairs, and a $12 million art collection.

Voyager is cruise ship as entertainment. In contrast to other megaliners, where the goal has been to reduce the behemoth to human scale, RCI has made a virtue of *Voyager's* enormous size, touting her many options and features that

Adventure of the Seas	QUALITY **8**	VALUE **C**
Explorer of the Seas	QUALITY **8**	VALUE **C**
Mariner of the Seas	QUALITY **8**	VALUE **C**
Navigator of the Seas	QUALITY **8**	VALUE **C**
Voyager of the Seas	QUALITY **8**	VALUE **C**
REGISTRY Bahamas	LENGTH 1,020 feet	BEAM 157.5 feet
CABINS 1,900	DRAFT 29 feet	SPEED 23.7 knots
MAXIMUM PASSENGERS	PASSENGER DECKS 15	ELEVATORS 14
3,114	CREW 1,185	SPACE RATIO NA

only a ship of this size could offer. These include an ice rink, climbing wall, inline skating track, five-story theater, and tri-level dining room.

Voyager also has a television studio, wedding chapel, and the largest youth facilities, largest spa and fitness center afloat at the time of her debut (since overtaken by *Freedom*-class ships). Fifty percent of cabins have balconies.

At the heart of the ship, the **Royal Promenade** stretches the length of one-and-a-half football fields between a 10-story atrium at one end and an 11-story grand atrium at the other. Stores, an ice-cream parlor, Champagne bar, and pub border the tree-lined boulevard. Around-the-clock entertainment, including jugglers, magicians, and mimes, brings a street-fair atmosphere to the Promenade. Overhead lighting simulates day-to-night conditions outside. Three decks of inside cabins "with a view" overlook the boulevard. The rooms have window seats to watch the scene below, but the idea has not worked as RCI planned because the line failed to put one-way glass on the windows; hence, passengers in these cabins can see and be seen. To avoid being part of the peep show, they must keep their curtains closed.

Studio B is *Voyager's* pièce de résistance. It has a 40-by-60-foot ice rink with arena-style seating for 900 spectators and is available for passenger use during the day (skates may be rented at no additional cost) and for ice shows at night. Fifty television monitors and a broadcast studio are adjacent to the area, which can also serve as a show lounge or conference facility or be used for game and variety shows and musical concerts.

When we first heard about the ice rink for a ship cruising the Caribbean, we were puzzled, to say the least. But we were pleasantly surprised. The entertainment is wholesome, high-quality, and a welcome alternative, particularly for families.

Explorer of the Seas, Adventure of the Seas, Navigator, and *Mariner* are almost identical to *Voyager* and have the same unusual attractions, including the ice rink and climbing wall, as well as the RCI standard features. *Explorer* was the first ship to boast an interactive, state-of-the-art atmospheric and oceanography laboratory.

ITINERARIES *See* Itinerary Index. In February 2009, *Mariner of the Seas,* the largest ship ever to offer cruises from the West Coast, began sailing year-round from Los Angeles on a seven-night Mexican Riviera itinerary.

CABINS Large by RCI standards, cabins are similar in size and decor to those aboard *Vision*-class ships. Enhancements include larger closets and beds with rounded corners to leave more floor space. All cabins offer telephone, television, electronic minibar, hair dryers, and twin beds convertible to queen.

Specifications Standard inside cabins, including the 138 Category G with atrium views, 150 square feet. 757 cabins with private verandas (50% of the total) have 180-square-foot interiors plus 4.5-by-8.8-foot balconies; 26 wheelchair accessible.

DINING *Voyager*'s main dining room is actually three: the **Carmen, La Boheme,** and **Magic Flute** (**Mozart, Strauss,** and **Vivaldi** on *Adventure*; **Columbus, De Gama,** and **Magellan** on *Explorer*) restaurants connected by a grand staircase. Decor includes a 15-foot crystal chandelier, an antique harp, and gilded marble pillars. Seats—enough for almost 2,000 people—offer views of the staircase and main floor or the ocean. Recently, RCI added a charge of $15 for steak in the dining room. The restaurants utilize My Time Dining, RCI's flexible dining program, that enables passengers to dine at the time of their choosing (during dining hours), and the new My Family Time Dining, which offers an expedited 40-minute dinner to families with kids ages 3–11 who are enrolled in the Adventure Ocean program. My Time Dining passengers must prepay gratuities and enroll in the program on board or in advance at RCI's Web site or reservations department.

Other dining venues are **Portofino,** an upscale Italian restaurant for dinner (reservations only; $20 service charge); **Windjammer Café,** the Lido restaurant for breakfast, lunch, and dinner; **Café Promenade,** for continental breakfast, all-day pizzas, and specialty coffees; **Island Grill,** with a display kitchen, for casual dinner; **SeaSide Diner,** a 1950s, 24-hour eatery with indoor/outdoor seating and jukebox music; and **Sprinkles,** with around-the-clock ice cream and yogurt. There's a **Johnny Rockets,** a wildly popular seagoing version of the fast-food chain. *Mariner* and *Navigator* also have RCI's steak house, **Chops Grille,** specializing in grilled steaks and other meats ($25 service charge).

Passengers can have meals in their cabins and select from RCI's new Dine In Delights menu—in addition to room-service menus—available 24/7 for an additional charge. The Dine In Delights menu offers such well-known options as The Original Johnny Rockets hamburger, Eli's Cheesecake Company's original cheesecake, and more. A service charge of $3.95 is added to room deliveries between midnight and 5 a.m.

FACILITIES AND ACTIVITIES In addition to the ice rink and television studio, *Voyager* has one of the most impressive showrooms afloat. The 1,347-seat **La Scala Theater,** inspired by Milan's famous opera house, rises through five decks and has a stage trimmed with gold leaf, a dome with hand-painted murals, and boxes with satin bunting.

Voyager also offers the $1 million **Aquarium Bar,** with 50 tons of water in four huge saltwater aquariums; **Spinners,** a revolving gambling arcade with an interactive roulette wheel that players sit in to play; and **Casino Royale,** one of cruising's largest casinos. Also aboard are a cigar and brandy lounge, Champagne bar, English pub, **Schooner Bar,** and a two-deck-tall library. The **Scoreboard** sports bar carries events live on large monitors. Alongside the glass bridge spanning the Royal Promenade is the **Vault,** a two-deck-high late-night disco. **Jesters,** the adults-only nightclub on *Adventure* (the **Chamber** on *Explorer*) is made to look like a gothic castle, with suits of armor, bats, and gargoyles. Sitting atop of *Voyager* is **High Notes,** a jazz club, and a chapel where weddings are performed.

Voyager's conference center seats up to 400 people and can be converted into six smaller rooms and a boardroom. Also available are a multimedia screening room, video conferencing, classrooms, and space for exhibition and trade shows. Business services provide typing, copying, and computer access.

SPORTS, FITNESS, AND BEAUTY The 15,000-square-foot health center offers exercise equipment. The Solarium and spa occupy 10,000 square feet. On the ship's funnel is cruising's first climbing wall. Novices and experienced climbers alike are well briefed in advance, and participants work in teams. For most passengers, it's their first rock-climbing experience, and they love it! Other facilities include a nine-hole golf course, golf simulators ($25 an hour), inline skating track, and basketball/volleyball court. Also available are **Sea Quest** dive and snorkel shop and the **19th Hole** golf bar. Little wonder that one passenger upon touring *Voyager* remarked, "This sure is a guy's ship."

CHILDREN'S FACILITIES See *Legend of the Seas* section (page 396) for details.

THE SHIPS When *Sovereign of the Seas* and her two sister ships were introduced between 1988 and 1992, they were the largest cruise ships ever built and stirred unprecedented excitement and publicity. More importantly, they came with innovations that influenced the design of all superliners and megaliners that followed.

Their dramatic atrium, the **Centrum,** was a cruise-ship first. Located midship and spanning five decks, the atrium opens the space to create a light and inviting environment. Stairs and balconies around the atrium and its glass-enclosed elevators seem suspended in air. A white piano set amid tropical foliage at the atrium's base plays soft music that carries to upper decks and sets the harmonious tone found shipwide. The atrium, similar to a hotel's lobby, provides a friendly focal point. Passengers are dazzled but not intimidated, and the notion of entering a behemoth dissipates. The atrium also separates the forward section of the ships, which contains the cabins, from the aft, with all public rooms and dining, sports, entertainment, and recreation facilities.

The arrangement has several advantages. Cabins are quieter, distances among public areas are shorter, and the ship doesn't seem so enormous. The ship looks outward—few areas lack natural light or a view to the outdoors— a feature absent on many new ships. Together with an incredible array of

Majesty of the Seas	**QUALITY 5**	**VALUE C**
Monarch of the Seas	**QUALITY 5**	**VALUE C**
REGISTRY Bahamas	LENGTH 880 feet	BEAM 106 feet
CABINS 1,127–1,193	DRAFT 25 feet	SPEED 19 knots
MAXIMUM PASSENGERS	PASSENGER DECKS 11	ELEVATORS 11
2,744–2,852	CREW 833	SPACE RATIO 32.3/30.8

facilities, they explain passengers' immediate acceptance of the megaliner. *Monarch of the Seas* and *Majesty of the Seas* arrived with a few more cabins, a Family Suite, and a redesigned **Windjammer Café** (which was later redesigned on *Majesty* into Windjammer Marketplace). Many public rooms carry the same names. Throughout, contemporary elegance creates an inviting ambience.

The ships are floating resorts, making the most of their size by providing spaces for varying tastes. These include the signature **Viking Crown Lounge** perched high on the stack; wide, outdoor promenades encircling the vessels; and sunny and shaded areas on three decks. They offer so many facilities and activities that even the most frantically active person can't participate in all the options.

ITINERARIES *See* Itinerary Index.

CABINS Each of the duet has 16 categories of cabins. Designed to make the most out of every inch of space, they're fitted with a vanity table, chair, and twin beds convertible to daytime couches. *Monarch*'s and *Majesty*'s cabins came with major enhancements—verandas on 50 deluxe outside cabins, plus suites and Family Suites sleeping up to six. Later, balconies were added to 62 suites and junior suites on Deck 10, and bathrooms in these accommodations were completely renewed.

Family Suites have two bedrooms, a sitting room, two bathrooms, and veranda. *Majesty* has 146 cabins in the larger outside category, more comfortable than those on *Sovereign*, and the Bridge Deck contains only suites and deluxe cabins with private verandas. Bathrooms, though not large, are well designed with ample space for toiletries, thick towels, hair dryers, and excellent water pressure.

> *Specifications Majesty* and *Monarch*, 444 inside cabins, 721 outside; 12 suites; 62 deluxe cabins and suites with verandas. Standard dimensions, 120 square feet; 917 with twin beds (convertible to queen); 299 third/fourth persons; no singles; 4 wheelchair accessible.

DINING RCI ships don't serve gourmet fare and don't intend to. Rather, galleys produce ordinary food that's plentiful but not excessive, with ample variety. All ships have the same menus (consistency at work), although longer European and Asian cruises may feature local dishes. A typical menu offers five juices and appetizers, three soups, two salads, five entrees with a choice of pasta, fish, chicken, veal, and beef; three desserts, and a selection of cheeses and ice cream.

In keeping with its Vitality program, all menus have light selections annotated with nutritional information. You can also select vegetarian dishes or request the full vegetarian menu for an entire cruise. Wine lists include California, French, and other vintages. Prices are moderate.

Each ship has two dining rooms serving three meals, all with assigned seating. *Monarch*'s Brigadoon Dining Room has a Scottish tartan motif; the **Flower Drum Song Dining Room** has sophisticated Asian decor. Lunch and dinner can be ordered from dining-room menus through room service. Recently, RCI added a charge of $15 for steak in the dining room. The restaurants offer My Time Dining, RCI's flexible dining program, which enables passengers to dine at the time of their choosing (during dining hours), and the new My Family Time Dining, which offers an expedited 40-minute dinner to families with kids ages 3–11 who are enrolled in the Adventure Ocean program. My Time Dining passengers must prepay gratuities and enroll in the program on board or in advance at RCI's Web site or reservations department.

Windjammer Marketplace offers breakfast, lunch, and a casual alternative dinner in the evening with full table service and a menu that changes daily. **Johnny Rockets** on *Majesty* is similar to the popular *Voyager*-class venue, as is **Sorrento's** pizza parlor and **Compass Deli.** On the *Monarch*, the **Windjammer Café** spans the ship's width and is wrapped on three sides by windows. The Café also has a mini-atrium with a winter garden, waterfalls, and a skylight. Passengers can have meals in their cabins and select from RCI's new Dine In Delights menu—in addition to room-service menus—available 24/7 for an additional charge. The Dine In Delights menu offers such well-known options as The Original Johnny Rockets hamburger, Eli's Cheesecake Company's original cheesecake, and more. A service charge of $3.95 is added to room deliveries between midnight and 5 a.m. Passengers can also make dinner reservations in the specialty restaurants and preorder wine, juices, and other beverages online.

SERVICE RCI's crews, from the Norwegian captains to the mini-United Nations of the cabin and dining-room staff, are courteous and eager to please. An affable, largely Filipino group of stewards tidies rooms twice daily and provides evening turndown service. Dining staff is so conscious of the constant evaluation of their work, as reflected in passengers' comment cards, that they sometimes overdo their attention. And it's likely that your waiter, when his supervisors aren't around, will all but beg you to praise him in your comments—his job may depend on it.

FACILITIES AND ACTIVITIES Among activities may be bingo; napkin folding; wine tasting; parlor games; dance classes; bridge; ice carving; parties for singles, children, and teens; a costume party; religious services; and a passenger talent show. The wood-paneled library resembles an English club; it can also be used for meetings. Two levels of sun decks provide privacy and a place to read.

Almost 24 hours a day, there's music to suit every mood. **Follies Lounge,** the richly decorated bi-level showroom, stages two shows nightly. Rooms have video walls with 50 television monitors on movable banks of 25 screens each. Comfortable seats have excellent sight lines, with a few exceptions. **Boleros Nightclub** is the hot Latin-flavored nightspot.

Cantilevered from the funnel and encircling it is the extraordinary **Viking Crown Lounge.** The room, 12 stories above the water, provides a fabulous 360-degree view of the sea and sunset. Among small lounges is the nautical-motif **Schooner Bar,** a favorite casual bar by day and a lively piano bar at night. **Casino Royale** next door offers blackjack, 170 slot machines, and American roulette. **Touch of Class** is a chic Champagne bar where 50 people can clink flutes and scoop caviar. Decor lives up to the lounge's name with two lifelike bronze statues of 1920s flappers. Other options include **Flashes** (the teen nightclub), karaoke, a shopping boulevard, and a movie theater.

SPORTS, FITNESS, AND BEAUTY Fitness enthusiasts have a one-third-mile outside deck encircling the vessel and a second jogging track. The well-equipped health club offers saunas and locker rooms, a large exercise room with ballet barres, an array of exercise equipment, and a high-energy staff. The Sports Deck has twin swimming pools, two whirlpools, and a basketball court. Vitality fitness activities start with a sunrise stretch class or water exercises, low-impact aerobics, and walkathons, basketball, and table tennis tournaments. Participants earn "dollars" for each activity, redeemable for T-shirts and visors. Vitality Unlimited is designed for senior citizens. All menus offer low-fat, low-calorie entrees, prepared to American Heart Association guidelines. The beauty salon/barber shop offers massage and beauty treatments at an additional cost.

On *Majesty*, the spa and fitness center were moved to Deck 9 and redesigned and enlarged with 11 treatment rooms, including a couples massage room. There are also new state-of-the-art cardiovascular and resistance machines, free weights, and an aerobics center with free classes; yoga, Pilates, and spinning classes are available for $10 per session.

CHILDREN'S FACILITIES *Majesty* has **Adventure Ocean and Teen Club** with learning and play areas. **Fuel** is the teen's own disco, and the **Living Room** is their place to chill out, watch large-screen televisions, or surf the Web. Teens also have a no-adults-allowed area, the **Back Deck**—a sun deck with an outdoor dance floor. See *Legend of the Seas* section (page 396) for more details.

SHORE EXCURSIONS Except for its golf programs and cruises that include Labadee in their itinerary, RCI's shore excursions are similar to those of other lines cruising the Caribbean. They include island tours, beach trips, and snorkeling and diving. RCI's private resort, **Labadee,** created in 1987 on the north coast of Haiti, offers one of the best days at the beach of any line. Its setting is beautiful—lush mountains rise behind a lovely cove with a series of crescent-shaped beaches. There are pavilions for dining, entertainment, water sports equipment, and a marketplace with Haitian crafts, which are the Caribbean's best. Music, dancing, and performances by a local folklore group are provided.

Labadee has a pirate-themed water playground, sponsored by the Coca-Cola Company, featuring a "sunken" pirate ship and a mascot, Labadee Luc, who appears on signage throughout the peninsula. The **Splash Bash,** a special play area for kids ages 3–5, has a central pipe that sends water into three play areas with dams, water wheels, and other fun activities. Volleyball courts and the Dragon's Flight, a 4,000-foot-long zip line, have been added. The line glides participants 200 feet above the ground, offering great views of the water and scenery around them. The newest thrill-maker is the Dragon's Tail Coaster, a single "cart" that holds up to two people and rushes at breakneck speed (you have to sign a waiver) down the forested mountainside with no brakes. To get ready for the gigantic *Oasis of the Seas*, RCI expanded Labadee and redesigned some parts. The most significant addition is the new 1,300-foot pier, enabling passengers to walk ashore instead of using a tender. Dining facilities were more than doubled, and spa facilities at Barefoot Beach were upgraded, among other enhancements.

Some itineraries call for a day at **Coco Cay,** a small Bahamian island. Diversions for a range of ages include beach games, pedal boats, shopping, steel-band music, visits to a shipwreck led by snorkeling instructors, a barbecue, palm-shaded trails, six sandy beaches for swimming, and hammocks and beach chairs for lounging. Children's programs are available.

THE SHIPS With sunshine shimmering through walls of glass, Royal Caribbean's *Radiance of the Seas* lives up to her name. The ship is so bright and airy you'll want to keep your sunglasses on when you come in from an outside deck.

Launched in 2001, *Radiance* has floor-to-ceiling windows on all levels of its nine-deck atrium and in 16 public areas, plus exterior glass elevators spanning 12 decks. Passengers never have to miss a minute of the beauty of Alaska and the Caribbean or the connection with the sea.

First of the new class of ships for Royal Caribbean, *Radiance of the Seas* is a classy lady—smaller than the giant *Voyager* class and larger than the *Vision* group. She incorporates the best of her predecessors: the many entertainment and activity options of *Voyager* (including the famous climbing wall), and glass galore. Her twin, *Brilliance of the Seas*, debuted in 2002. *Serenade of the Seas* arrived in 2003 and *Jewel of the Seas* in 2004. The ships are Panamax class, meaning they are narrow enough—just barely—to pass through the Panama Canal.

And these ships have highlights of their own: the most balconies of any RCI ships when they were built; Internet ports in every cabin; a bookstore/coffeehouse; and gas and steam turbines said to reduce emissions, noise, and vibration. The ships reflect RCI's resortlike style, with the purser's desk called Guest Relations, its staff outfitted in resort wear, and a general manager and vacation experience director intended to foster guest satisfaction.

Radiance also boasts a first at sea: self-leveling pool tables. These high-tech tables are the big attraction in the **Bombay Billiard Club,** one of four lounges clustered in the **Colony Club.** The others are the **Calcutta Card Club; Jakarta Lounge,** an intimate bar with gaming tables; and **Singapore Sling,** a piano bar with floor-to-ceiling windows offering spectacular views aft. The **Centrum,** a dramatic, airy atrium and an RCI signature, is decorated in light woods and soft tones of sand, coral, and aqua, set off with greenery, a waterfall, and colossal abstract sculpture—all part of the ship's $6 million-plus art collection.

Another memorable area is the African-themed **Solarium,** with three life-size stone elephants, a bronze of a lion cub, a waterfall, stone relief art panels depicting gazelles and antelopes, greenery, and piped-in sounds of chirping birds. It also has a raised pool (with a countercurrent), two whirlpools, a bar, and pizzeria, all under a retractable glass roof.

Brilliance of the Seas	QUALITY 8	VALUE C
Jewel of the Seas	QUALITY 8	VALUE C
Radiance of the Seas	QUALITY 8	VALUE C
Serenade of the Seas	QUALITY 8	VALUE C
REGISTRY Bahamas	LENGTH 962 feet	BEAM 106 feet
CABINS 1,050	DRAFT 26.7 feet	SPEED 25 knots
MAXIMUM PASSENGERS	PASSENGER DECKS 12	ELEVATORS 9
2,501	CREW 859	SPACE RATIO NA

On the *Jewel of the Seas*, passengers enjoy unobstructed views of the sea and landscapes afforded by the ship's nearly three acres of exterior glass in the dining rooms, lounges, ocean-facing glass elevators, and floor-to-ceiling windows in most public areas. The ship has an eclectic, $5.3-million art collection with themes of landscape and light in paintings, sculptures, textiles, ceramics, and mosaics throughout the ship.

ITINERARIES *See* Itinerary Index.

CABINS Accommodations are spacious and attractively decorated; 70% have verandas. The most lavish, the Royal Suite, is a palatial 1,035 square feet, with 173 square feet of balcony and such amenities as a baby grand piano, wet bar, entertainment center with a 42-inch flat-panel television, CD/DVD player, and bath with whirlpool, bidet, and steam shower. Veranda cabins measuring 179 square feet with a 41-square-foot balcony are situated on Decks 7, 8, 9, and 10, with the ones on Deck 10 closest to the pools and other outdoor amenities. The lowest-priced cabins are inside cabins measuring 166 square feet.

All cabins are equipped with an interactive television, telephone, computer jack, vanity table with an extendable working surface for a laptop computer, refrigerator/minibar, hair dryer, 110/220 electrical outlets, two single beds convertible to double, and reading lights by the beds.

Wheelchair-accessible cabins are available in most categories. The needs of passengers with disabilities are addressed not only in the cabins and oversize hallways, but also with special devices to aid the hearing-impaired. Listening devices are available, as well as telephone amplifiers and strobe-light door knockers and telephone ringers. For the visually impaired, cabin doors, service directories, and even elevator buttons and dining menus are written in Braille. The personalized service sometimes extends to extra assistance at the pier, early-boarding orientation, sign language interpreter, special diet accommodation, or onboard medical services.

Specifications 1,055 cabins; 238 inside, 817 outside (577 with balconies); 62 suites; 62 deluxe suites; 6 Family Suites; 65 third/fourth persons; no singles; 15 wheelchair accessible.

DINING **Cascades,** the elegant, two-level main dining room, has a grand staircase, etched-glass mural, and a cascading waterfall. The upper level has floor-to-ceiling windows; the lower level, large windows. Two smaller dining rooms, **Breakers** and **Tides,** are ideal for private parties. Breakfast and lunch are open seating; dinner is served in two seatings. Vitality (or low-fat) selections are offered for lunch and dinner. Recently, RCI added a charge of $15 for steak in the dining room. The restaurants offer My Time Dining, RCI's flexible dining program, which enables passengers to dine at the time of their choosing (during dining hours), and the new My Family Time Dining, which offers an expedited 40-minute dinner for families with kids ages 3–11 who are enrolled in the Adventure Ocean program. My Time Dining passengers must prepay gratuities and enroll in the program on board or in advance at RCI's Web site or reservations department.

The casual **Windjammer Café** serves buffet-style breakfast and lunch with a choice of indoor and outdoor seating. The **Seaview Café** cooks up burgers, hot dogs, and nachos. The food ranges from mediocre to delicious. Passengers can have meals in their cabins and select from RCI's new Dine In Delights menu—in addition to room-service menus—available 24/7 for an additional charge. The Dine In Delights menu offers such well-known options as The Original Johnny Rockets hamburger, Eli's Cheesecake Company's original cheesecake, and more. A service charge of $3.95 is added to room deliveries between midnight and 5 a.m. Passengers can also make dinner reservations in specialty restaurants and order wine and other beverages online.

Alternative eateries include **Chops Grille** ($25 per person service charge), serving steaks and other grills from an open kitchen, and **Portofino** ($20 per person service charge), an upscale Euro-Italian restaurant with Tuscany-inspired decor. Service charges cover gratuities; reservations required.

FACILITIES AND ACTIVITIES The three-level **Aurora Theatre,** the setting for Broadway-style revues, has Arctic-themed decor with sculptured balconies, sidewalls, and parterre divisions resembling glacial landscapes. The futuristic **Starquest** (with a revolving bar) and **Hollywood Odyssey** are two nightspots housed in RCI's hallmark Viking Crown Lounge, perched high over the sea. The latter features jazz ensembles, comedians, pianists, and vocalists. The ship has a large casino, several bars, and a library reminiscent of a traditional English study, as well as **Royal Caribbean Online,** the Internet center with 12 stations.

SPORTS, FITNESS, AND BEAUTY The ocean-view spa, the beauty and health center, has 12 treatment rooms, including rasul and a thermal suite, gym with 18 treadmills and an array of equipment, and fitness activities and exercise classes. Out on deck, passengers have more challenges at the climbing wall, with five separate climbing tracks, golf simulator ($20 per hour), nine-hole miniature golf course, basketball court, and jogging track.

CHILDREN'S FACILITIES See *Legend of the Seas* section (page 396) for details.

THE SHIPS Back in 1999, when I said *Voyager of the Seas* was cruise ship as entertainment, I could not have imagined *Freedom of the Seas*. It's a wow! and then some. Many of her features—and those of her sister ships—are the same as those found on *Voyager*-class ships, including bars with the same names, but many other features are innovations appearing on a cruise ship for the first time.

At 154,407 tons, with a maximum capacity of 4,370 passengers, *Freedom of the Seas*, constructed in Finland, was the largest cruise ship in the world when she debuted in May 2006, and she represented a new class of ships for RCI. She and her two sisters were also the most innovative ships the company had built when they were launched.

Freedom of the Seas	QUALITY 9	VALUE B
Independence of the Seas	QUALITY 9	VALUE B
Liberty of the Seas	QUALITY 9	VALUE B
REGISTRY Bahamas	LENGTH 1,112 feet	BEAM 184 feet
CABINS 1,800	DRAFT 28 feet	SPEED 21.6 knots
MAXIMUM PASSENGERS	PASSENGER DECKS 15	ELEVATORS NA
4,370	CREW 1,360	SPACE RATIO NA

Among the most noteworthy innovations found on *Freedom* are the first boxing ring, a FlowRider (the first surf simulator at sea), and an unusual top-deck aquatic playground with three massive pool areas, including an interactive water park, two dramatically situated whirlpools, and a dedicated sports pool—each with a different audience appeal.

The most interesting space is the **H20 Zone,** a colorful wonderland of large, bright sculptures doubling as interactive fountains that spray and spurt water in every direction. The oversize sculptures are in all shapes and sizes, giving passengers numerous playful opportunities—by turning wheels, setting off sensors, and dodging dumping buckets—to get soaked or to soak others.

In one corner of the water playground, a circular pool shoots a current of water in a river around a central island. Passengers can float with the flow as they are misted by one of the fountain sculptures. A shallow pool area, fed by a flamingo-shaped fountain, is a secluded space for the youngest kids. At the back of the park, a rectangular swimming pool is flanked by wading areas and fed by a waterfall cascading from an overhanging bridge. At night, the water park becomes a dramatically lit sculpture garden.

The **Solarium,** an adults-only oasis, offers another cruise ship first. Two hot tubs, large enough for the neighborhood, are cantilevered out 12 feet from the sides of the ship and suspended 112 feet above the ocean. The panoramic views from here are definitely not for those with acrophobia. But interestingly enough, every time I passed by the pools, no one was looking out at the views—they were too busy talking to each other. The Solarium's jungle decor has tropical foliage, rain forest–inspired mosaics and murals, tall metal palm trees, hammocks, and seven-foot-tall parrot sculptures.

Another first for RCI is its two parallel pools in the main pool area at the center of the ship. One of the pools is designated as a sports pool for activities ranging from pool volleyball to synchronized swimming competitions. The sports pool has lane markers for lap swimming. At night, the main pool area can be transformed into an open-air nightclub, with a large dance floor situated between the two pools. The ship's combined pool areas—the family pool area, adults-only Solarium, and the main pool area—are 43% larger than on *Voyager*-class ships.

ITINERARIES *See* Itinerary Index. In April 2010, *Independence of the Seas* becomes the first RCI ship to be based in the United Kingdom year-round, with Southampton as her homeport from where she sails to the Mediterranean.

CABINS Other innovations on *Freedom of the Seas* are flat-panel televisions in all cabins and six categories of family cabins designed especially for large families and groups of friends. These accommodations come in several new configurations, sizes, and price ranges.

The largest is the 14-person Presidential Suite, with a 1,215-square-foot interior and an 810-square-foot balcony equipped with a whirlpool, wet bar, eight lounge chairs, and a 14-person table for dining alfresco. The oversize suite has dual entryways, two master bedrooms with 30-inch flat-panel televisions, and bathrooms with bathtubs. Two other bedrooms will accommodate four people each, with convertible twin/queen and Pullman beds. Both rooms have a 23-inch flat-panel television. The suite's common area includes two additional bathrooms with showers, a living room with a sectional sofa that sleeps two, a card/dining table, and an entertainment center with a 42-inch plasma television.

The five other types of family accommodations are in addition to the ship's standard triples and quads. Each category includes twin beds, convertible to a queen bed and bunks. Four, eight-person Royal Family Suites (600 square feet with a 270-square-foot balcony), each with two bedrooms, include a master bedroom with a bathroom with bathtub, a second bathroom with shower, and a living area with a sectional sofa and an entertainment center with a 30-inch flat-panel television, and an alfresco dining table for eight. Each suite can be expanded to accommodate up to ten people via a connecting cabin.

Three categories with a total of 15 cabins, each for six persons, have a curtained-off sleeping alcove with bunk beds, sleeper sofa, a bathroom and shower or tub; some with walk-in closets; 1 Accessible Family (400 square feet with a 120-square-foot balcony); 8 Family Ocean view (up to 495 square feet with windows); 4 Promenade Family (335 square feet, two windows with window seats overlooking Royal Promenade); and 2 Inside Family (330 square feet).

Specifications 1,084 outside cabins, 844 with balconies; 732 inside (558/561 with no window, 168/172 overlook Promenade; 855 have third and fourth berths); 21 Family Suites (1 for 14 persons, 4 for 8 persons, 15 for 6 persons, 1 wheelchair accessible); 32 wheelchair accessible.

DINING *Freedom* has a very large main dining room that spans three levels. There are two seatings in this nonsmoking room. Tables are available for 4–12 persons. Recently, RCI added a charge of $15 for steak in the dining room. The restaurant utilizes My Time Dining, RCI's flexible dining program, that enables passengers to dine at the time of their choosing (during dining hours), and the new My Family Time Dining, which offers an expedited 40-minute dinner for families with kids ages 3–11 who are enrolled in the Adventure Ocean program. My Time Dining passengers must prepay gratuities and enroll in the program on board or in advance at RCI's Web site or reservations department.

The ship has many other dining options: the casual **Windjammer Café,** serving buffet breakfast, lunch, and table-service dinner; **Jade,** an Asian-fusion specialty restaurant in the Windjammer Café; a **Johnny Rockets** diner; and several eateries along the Promenade, including the **Portofino,** an upscale Italian restaurant ($20) requiring reservations, and **Chops Grille,** ($25 per person) a specialty restaurant for steaks. Passengers can also make dinner reservations in the specialty restaurants and preorder wine, juices, and other beverages online. The Royal Promenade has a coffee shop serving sandwiches, pizza, and pastries; **Latte'tudes,** a coffee bar; **Sorrento's,** a pizza parlor and Italian restaurant; and **Bull and Bear Pub,** an English pub. In addition to room-service menus, passengers can select from RCI's new Dine In Delights menu, available 24/7 for an additional charge. The Dine In Delights menu offers such well-known options as The Original Johnny Rockets hamburger, Eli's Cheesecake Company's original cheesecake, and more. A service charge of $3.95 is added to room deliveries between midnight and 5 a.m.

FACILITIES AND ACTIVITIES The *Freedom* class has RCI's standard features, such as the ever-popular ice-skating rink with nightly shows, and three production shows in the main theater. The disco is crowded until the wee hours, but the best action is on the **Royal Promenade,** which spans three decks at the heart of the ship. The 445-foot-long shopping, dining, and entertainment boulevard brims with activities throughout the day and special ones at night, including festive circus parades with bright costumes and colorful characters. Among the shops on the Promenade are **A Clean Shave** barber shop, **Book Nook** (a bookstore with French cafe seating), and **Ben & Jerry's** ice-cream parlor.

Some of the ship's 20 bars include **Olive or Twist,** which is part of RCI's signature, glass-enclosed Viking Crown Lounge on Deck 14 and a private club for Crown & Anchor members. The bar has live jazz shows nightly. **Cloud Nine,** a quiet corner, is also part of the Viking Crown Lounge. **Bolero's** offers mojitos and Latin music; **On Air Club** is the venue for karaoke. **Wipe Out!,** on Deck 13, offers draft beer, wine, and fruit ice drinks. The **Champagne Bar,** with a wide Champagne selection, and **Vintages,** a wine bar, are on the Promenade. The always-popular **Schooner Bar,** RCI's signature cocktail lounge and piano bar, is on Deck 4, the same deck as the lower level of the main dining room.

SPORTS, FITNESS, AND BEAUTY *Freedom* class's **Fitness Center,** the largest at sea, is incredible and, to my thinking, the ship's biggest wow! It should be called No Excuses. The huge gym has every type of exercise equipment and instruction imaginable, with special studios for Pilates ($10 per person), spinning, yoga (including classes on the beach in Labadee), and others, but the biggest attraction is the full-size 18-by-8-foot Everlast boxing ring. For the first time ever on a cruise ship, novices can test their chops in a variety of boxing-related activities—groups of three people in sparring sessions with freestanding Body Masters bags, supervised by a coach ($10), or Rocky wannabes can have three one-hour training sessions with a coach inside the ring. The workout includes a warm-up, bag work, mirror boxing, footwork, and pad work.

Some of the many novel programs are Boot Camp X-Treme circuit training for seasoned exercisers; Salsamania, a Latin-inspired exercise class incorporating dance moves and energetic music for a lively workout; and the Night Klub indoor cycling program, held in a high-tech studio outfitted with enhanced lighting features to create a nightclub-style light show throughout the class. To help familiarize passengers with all of the fitness activities available, the Center has two 65-inch interactive plasma televisions where classes and equipment are reviewed and class schedules are available.

And not to be forgotten are the climbing wall; the eight-hole minigolf course; and the much-publicized, first-on-a-cruise-ship FlowRider, a surf simulator that accommodates only two people at one time. It is surrounded by viewing stands for some to watch and even get splashed. The climbing wall (43 feet high and 44 feet wide) is 30% larger than the original on *Voyager*-class ships. The freestanding wall has a central spire, adding a new dimension to the experience. Passengers have 11 routes to choose, from easy to expert.

In addition to the large fitness and spa facility spread over two levels, the *Freedom* class has an adults-only solarium and two outdoor pools. To some, another wow! are the two semicircular whirlpools (port and starboard in the solarium area), which are cantilevered from the ship, giving patrons sweeping views of the sea as they soak in the bubbling water—but when we took a look on *Independence,* the bathers were so busy talking to each other, they could have been in the middle of the ship.

CHILDREN'S FACILITIES   **Adventure Ocean Program** is RCI's program for kids ages 3–17. On *Freedom,* teens particularly are catered to with three areas just for them: **Fuel** nightclub, the **Living Room** hangout, and the **Back Deck** sun deck. For tiny tots ages 6–36 months and their parents, *Freedom* offers the line's Aqua Babies and Aqua Tots playtime programs developed by partner Fisher-Price (available fleetwide). Lunch and Play ($7.95 per child), a new kids' option for lunch, movies, cartoons, and free-play time, is available between noon and 2 p.m. under the supervision of Adventure Ocean counselors.

THE SHIPS   Launched in November 2009, the much-anticipated, 225,282-ton *Oasis of the Seas* set the record as the largest and most revolutionary cruise ship at sea. Something of an architectural and maritime marvel, she spans 1,187 feet in length (imagine four football fields laid end-to-end) and has 2,700 cabins for up to 6,296 passengers when all the berths are filled, plus a crew of 2,165 and 24 dining venues. In other words, *Oasis of the Seas* and her sister, *Allure of the Seas,* coming in December 2010, are very, very big ships.

Indeed, *Oasis of the Seas* is so large and has so many facilities, activities, and options that passengers are likely to be overwhelmed. To bring her 225,282 tons down to human scale, the ship was designed with seven "neighbor-hoods," each with a focus and special architectural features—many never seen on a cruise ship. The neighborhoods are The Broadwalk with AquaThe-ater, Central Park, Royal Promenade, Entertainment Place, Pool and Sports Zone, Vitality at Sea Spa and Fitness Center, and The Youth Zone.

The **Boardwalk,** inspired by seaside piers along the coast of England or those of yesteryear like Atlantic City and Coney Island, is a family area with attractions to be enjoyed together. At the stern is the AquaTheater, an outdoor amphithe-ater and pool where water shows by professional divers, ballet shows, and theatrical performances are staged day and night. The first of its kind at sea, RCI says the AquaTheater is the most technologically-advanced area of the ship.

Boardwalk's centerpiece is a full-size carousel—a first ever at sea and one of a kind. Handcrafted for Royal Caribbean, the traditional carousel has 21 animal figures such as zebras and lions alongside hand-painted horses and a chariot for two. The frame, with a red and gold facade, has turn-of-the-century artwork panels and LED lights that twinkle day and night. Other Boardwalk diversions include cruising's first psychic and tattoo parlors, carnival games, a candy store, an ice-cream parlor, a Johnny Rockets restaurant, a doughnut shop, bar, and seafood shack.

Allure of the Seas	PREVIEW	
Oasis of the Seas	PREVIEW	
REGISTRY Bahamas	LENGTH 1,187 feet	BEAM 208 feet
CABINS 2,706	DRAFT 30 feet	SPEED 24 knots
MAXIMUM PASSENGERS	PASSENGER DECKS 16	ELEVATORS 24
6,296	CREW 2,165	SPACE RATIO NA

Central Park, a tropical expanse longer than a football field and open to the sky, occupies the center of the ship and is meant to be the ship's central piazza or town square. This public space has quiet pathways and reading corners, canopy trees and seasonal flower gardens, along with an art gallery, portrait studio, and six of the ship's main restaurants and bars. The Park has a chess garden with large-scale pieces; pergola garden, an interpretive garden of Caribbean flora; and a sculpture garden with work by international artists. The Park's tranquil atmosphere during the day becomes a lively gathering spot for alfresco dining and entertainment, such as concerts and street performances, in the evening. Located on Deck 8, the Park is lined with 334 cabins (254 with balconies) that rise through six decks and overlook the Park.

The **Royal Promenade** neighborhood, familiar to RCI fans from *Voyager*- and *Freedom*-class ships, has a new design that connects it to Central Park. Moving between the Promenade and the Park is the Rising Tide Bar—the first moving bar at sea and an amazing engineering feat—that spans three decks (think gigantic elevator). Directly on the Royal Promenade, the façade of the Globe and Atlas Pub has a giant copper globe, which "cracks open" to unfurl a bridge on hinged hydraulics that extends over the Promenade, creating a platform approximately ten feet above the deck and adjacent to the entertainment area. Other features include 18 Promenade View cabins; a barber; photo, fine jewelry, liquor, perfume, leather, and apparel stores, including the first ship shops for Coach and Eileen Fisher, and logo shops; pizzeria; coffee, Champagne, and karaoke bars; and Boleros, the Latin dance club. On the mezzanine level are RCI's signature Schooner Bar and the members-only Crown & Anchor Society lounge.

In a first for Royal Caribbean, passengers board *Oasis of the Seas* directly into the Royal Promenade, rather than on a lower deck. Welcoming them is a large tree sculpture by international artist Larry Kirkland.

ITINERARIES *See* Itinerary Index.

CABINS *Oasis of the Seas'* 2,700 cabins come in 37 categories. The newest category, billed as urban living on the high seas, has 28 Loft Suites. The two-level ultramodern suites sit at the top of the ship on Decks 17 and 18 and enjoy spacious ocean views with floor-to-ceiling windows. Each loft measures 545 square feet or larger and is outfitted in contemporary decor. The upper-level bedroom overlooks a spacious living area and balcony on the lower level. Beds are dressed in white, luxurious duvets complemented by tropical blue and green accents. Downstairs, the lofts have LCD televisions, separate vanity areas, and guest bathrooms; upstairs, the master bathrooms have his and her showerheads and limestone mosaic tiles.

In addition to the 25 Crown Loft Suites, one Royal Loft Suite, the largest of the group with 1,524 square feet, accommodates six. It is furnished with a baby grand piano, indoor/outdoor dining rooms seating eight, a wet bar, library, and an 843-square-foot balcony with its own LCD television, entertainment area, and Jacuzzi. Sky Loft Suites (Corner A, 722 square feet and Corner B, 770 square feet) are larger than standard lofts with more living room space, separate dining rooms with tables seating four. The Crown Accessible Loft Suite has the same amenities as standard Crown Loft Suites but measures slightly larger (737 square feet) and has an elevator for passengers with special needs.

Oasis also has a variety of suites offering additional space and amenities that exceed those at the standard cabin level. All have private balconies, televisions, and more. The one-of-a-kind Royal Suite sleeps four. It has one bedroom, two baths, a separate living area with a baby grand piano, full bar, 52-inch LCD television, and floor-to-ceiling glass windows and doors leading to a large balcony. Its alternative sitting area has a large jetted tub and windows facing the sea. The Presidential Family Suite, another one of a kind, has four bedrooms, four baths, and can sleep 14.

Six AquaTheater Suites overlook the Boardwalk and AquaTheater and have wraparound balconies and an outdoor oceanfront dining area for six. Each of ten Owner's Suites has one bedroom, a living room with a convertible queen sleeper sofa, a balcony with an outdoor dining table, and accommodates four people. Four Family Suites with balcony each have a master bedroom and bath, a guest room with private bath, an outdoor dining and lounge area, and each sleeps eight. The 30 Grand Suites have one bedroom, a full bath, a living area, and balcony with jetted tub.

In other cabins—interior or ocean view, with or without balconies—the bedroom has underbed storage, expansive closets that include retractable clothing and shoe shelves, and flip-up bedside tables to provide more space as needed. The bathrooms have a fresh design that provides a feeling of open space with clear-glass shower enclosures and additional shelves and ledges.

Specifications   254 outside cabins, 1,956 with balconies; 406 inside (683 have third and fourth berths); 46 wheelchair accessible.

DINING With 24 distinct dining venues, there's little chance anyone will go hungry or want for places to eat on the *Oasis*. Options range from the traditional dining room to a gourmet restaurant, a steak house, and themed eateries. In **Central Park, 150 Central Park,** with a trendy upscale ambience, combines gourmet cuisine with modern design ($35 cover charge). Its internationally acclaimed chef de cuisine, Keriann Von Raesfeld, was the first American and first woman to be named Best Young Cook in the World by the 2008 World Association of Chefs Societies Congress, among many other awards.

Giovanni's Table, a Tuscan-influenced trattoria with indoor and alfresco seating, features rustic dishes with a contemporary flair, served family-style; $10 lunch, $15 dinner service charge. **Chops Grille,** RCI's signature steak house, has an indoor contemporary setting and alfresco dining; dinner only, $25 service charge. **Central Park Café,** an indoor/outdoor gourmet market with walk-up counters, offers salads, crepes, made-to-order sandwiches, paninis, soups, and pastries. Patrons order directly from chefs behind food stations. Open from breakfast to late night. **Vintage,** a wine bar, has a selection of cheeses and tapas; open for lunch and dinner with à la carte prices.

On the **Boardwalk, Seafood Shack** is an indoor/outdoor family restaurant serving a variety of seafood and oversize desserts; $7.95 lunch, $9.95 dinner cover charge. **Boardwalk Bar** has on-the-go snacks, prepackaged sandwiches, fruit, and salads; open for breakfast, lunch, and dinner. **Donut Shop,** an anytime stop for a snack at breakfast, lunch, and dinner. **Ice Cream Parlor** is a 1950s-style ice-cream venue with à la carte prices. **Johnny Rockets,** the popular diner, has a new breakfast menu; $3.95 breakfast, $4.95 lunch and dinner cover.

On the **Royal Promenade, Mondo Café,** a new addition open 24/7, offers sandwiches, pastries, and coffee native to such countries as Italy, Spain, and Cuba. At the opposite end from Mondo Café is **Café Promenade,** the popular 24-hour cafe serving Seattle's Best Coffee, fruit shakes, pastries, and sandwiches; à la carte prices. **Sorrento's Pizzeria,** a New York–style pizzeria, is open for lunch, dinner, and late-night snacks. Another new addition is **The Cupcake Cupboard,** a 1940s-style shop with an array of goodies. It hosts daily hands-on classes.

In the **Pool and Sports Zone, Solarium Bistro,** a casual, contemporary bistro, serves healthy breakfasts and lunches. In the evening, it is transformed into a romantic setting for dinner ($20 cover) and dancing. **Wipe Out Café,** a buffet with pizza, hamburgers, sandwiches, and salads is great for a quick snack and dessert and for young cruisers on the go. At the **Vitality at Sea Spa and Fitness Center,** the **Vitality Café** features a spa menu of snacks, wraps, fruit, juices, and smoothies for the calorie conscious; open for breakfast, lunch, and dinner.

Fleet fixtures include the three-level **Opus Dining Room,** the main dining room with Art Deco design evoking the grandeur of the 1920s. Open for all meals, it offers My Time Dining and My Family Time Dining, as well as traditional main- and late-seating options. My Time Dining passengers can make daily reservations for specific dining times or walk in (during dinner hours). My Family Time Dining provides an expedited 45-minute dining service for young cruisers, ages 3–11. **Windjammer Marketplace** is open for breakfast, lunch, and dinner for buffet fare. **Izumi** for Asian cuisine has a sushi bar and features hot-rock cooking, as well as other Asian fare in a more formal setting. Open for lunch and dinner; à la carte prices. Room-service menus and the newly introduced Dine In Delights menu (à la carte prices) are available 24/7. A service charge of $3.95 is added for deliveries between midnight and 5 a.m.

FACILITIES AND ACTIVITIES **Entertainment Place,** the nightlife neighborhood, includes **Blaze** nightclub, with doors "burning" with hot flames to indicate it's the hottest spot on the ship; **Jazz on 4;** and **Comedy Live,** with decor suggesting a New York subway station, including a ceiling map of the subway system. The **Opal Theater,** the 1,380-seat main theater, normally stages shows created by the Royal Caribbean Productions team; however, for the next three years, Royal Caribbean has the exclusive rights to perform the award-winning Broadway favorite *Hairspray,* featured four times on every *Oasis* seven-night cruise. The theater's other two shows, *Come Fly with Me,* also performed four times, takes audiences on a journey of soaring heights, with interactive video and singing, dancing, aerial stunts, and gymnastics; and *Headliner Showtime,* offered three times each cruise, includes world-class singers, musicians, and magic and juggling acts.

In **Studio B,** with its popular ice-skating rink, passengers continue to be awed by spectacular ice shows. There are theatrical street performances in Central Park and street parades and aerial acrobatics in the Royal Promenade. **Casino Royale** has a bar and lounge, a poker room, and player's club.

Dazzles, a dance lounge offering dance lessons and competitions, spans two decks with expansive floor-to-ceiling windows overlooking the Boardwalk below.

By day passengers can swim in the **AquaTheater's** kidney-shaped pool, relax on sun lounges on tiered platforms, and even take scuba lessons. In the evening they can watch water ballet, synchronized swimming, and heart-pounding aerial and aquatic acrobatic performances by professional divers. Fitted with stage machinery devices, the pool's depth can rise or fall to meet the needs of its various daytime functions and evening performances. Underwater cameras film performers and project images onto two giant Barco LED screens that flank the stage.

For water shows, a giant trampoline centered between two diving towers enables gymnasts and aerialists to flip and dismount into the pool. The diving towers have two springboards and two 33-foot-high platforms. A bridge connects the two high boards, which can support a row of divers. On the bridge's underbelly are lights and nozzles that allow water to fall like a curtain into the pool below. A trapeze hangs behind the high-dive boards giving the appearance that trapeze artists are climbing the curtain of water. There are fountain shows choreographed to music and lights.

SPORTS, FITNESS, AND BEAUTY   The **Pool and Sports Zone** neighborhood, located above Central Park, runs the length of the ship and has a solarium; multiple pools, including a zero-entry one; an **H20 Zone** with a huge octopus with long tentacles spouting water; private cabanas with attendants; two FlowRiders; rock-climbing walls; a sports court; miniature golf; and the first zip line at sea. The FlowRider surf simulators are situated at the rear of Deck 15. On the starboard side is the sports court; on port, Oasis Dunes, a nine-hole miniature golf course. Nine decks above the Boardwalk, Deck 16 is the starting place for the zip line.

Farther along on Deck 15 is a pool for lap swimming in the mornings and team water sports, such as badminton and water polo, in the afternoon. On starboard, across the wide canyon that looks down to Central Park, is the H2O Zone with water sprays and pools for infants and toddlers. Farther on is the zero (sloped)-entry Beach Pool with whirlpools. Across the seven-deck canyon on port is the main pool with its own twin whirlpools.

The glass-paneled, two-deck-high solarium, designed for adults only, is situated at the front of the ship and enjoys commanding views over the bow. It has a swimming pool, relaxation area, and six whirlpools, including four cantilevered 136 feet above the sea. By day, **Solarium Bistro** serves healthy fare from the Vitality Spa menu. At night, it becomes Club 20, a romantic specialty restaurant for casual dining and dancing.

The **Vitality at Sea Spa and Fitness Center,** another neighborhood, is intended to soothe the mind, body, and soul with its spa services and fitness lineup. The spa has a beauty salon, thermal suite with heated tile loungers, saunas and steam rooms, three couples massage suites, and seven treatment rooms; in-cabin massages are also offered. There are Kinesis group classes and a dedicated children's and teen spa. The Fitness Center is fitted with the latest cardio and resistance equipment and offers classes for spinning, kickboxing, Pilates, yoga, and more. The jogging track is partially covered. Vitality Café is a convenient stop for healthy snacks and juices.

CHILDREN'S FACILITIES   **Youth Zone,** the children's and teens' neighborhood, covers more than 28,700 square feet. It includes Kids Avenue, a central boulevard connecting the various Adventure Ocean and themed play areas; a nursery for infants and toddlers (age 6 months or older); and dedicated teen areas. Oasis' Adventure Ocean, RCI's fleetwide children's program, offers the curriculum of the other ships but with enhancements. Crayola arts and crafts, scavenger hunts, talent shows, and other age-specific activities are available to three age groups, each with its own area: Aquanauts, ages 3–5; Explorers, ages 6–8; and Voyagers, ages 9–11.

There are common play areas, such as the **Kid's Arcade** for video games; the **Workshop,** where families can learn scrapbooking or jewelry-making skills; **Imagination Studio,** where kids explore the world of color; **Adventure Science Lab** that houses a fully equipped lab; **Play,** a circular area where children participate in sports and games; and **Adventure Ocean Theater**—complete with a stage, audience seating, and state-of-the-art equipment—where children can learn about theatrical productions and take part in talent shows.

The teen-only spaces are located one deck above the Adventure Ocean areas and adjacent to the Sports Deck. Teens have their favorite **Fuel** disco and **The Living Room** lounge, with an adjacent outdoor deck. The physical separation of the teen-only area from areas for younger cruisers came from a recommendation by Royal Caribbean's Teen Advisory Board, recruited to identify what passengers ages 12–17 years old would want on future RCI ships.

The Royal Babies and Tots nursery, a first for Royal Caribbean, is fully staffed by professionals and has various playgroups created by Fisher-Price and Crayola for babies and tots. Open daily, the nursery offers childcare drop-off options for parents in the daytime and evening.

Seabourn Cruise Line

6100 Blue Lagoon Drive, Suite 400
Miami, FL 33126
☎ 305-463-3000 or 800-929-9391
FAX 305-463-3010
www.seabourn.com

TYPE OF SHIPS Small, modern, ultraluxurious ocean liners.

TYPE OF CRUISES Top-shelf luxury cruises on worldwide itineraries.

CRUISE LINE'S STRENGTHS
- impeccable service
- luxurious accommodations
- exclusivity
- ship size/maneuverability
- open-seating dining
- cuisine
- worldwide itineraries

CRUISE LINE'S SHORTCOMINGS
- limited activities
- limitations on use of water sports facilities

FELLOW PASSENGERS Sophisticated, discriminating, well-heeled, experienced travelers; 80% from North America; others are from Europe and elsewhere. Age varies, depending on season and destinations. Most are age 50 and older; active business owners and professionals as well as honeymooners and some semi-retired. They come mainly from the Northeast, Florida, California, and the Chicago area. Fifty percent or more are repeaters. Passengers are likely to have sailed on other luxury vessels and stayed in five-star hotels. They know and understand quality; their expectations are high and their judgment tough.

Recommended for Sophisticated, seasoned travelers accustomed to the best; affluent passengers whose first priority is service; those who seek exclusivity; yacht owners who want to leave the driving to others; those who shun big-ship, glitzy cruises; first-timers who seek and can afford small-ship ambience; honeymooners with rich parents; lottery winners.

Not recommended for Those unaccustomed to luxury or a sophisticated environment; anyone uncomfortable in a fancy restaurant or five-star European hotel; flashy dressers; late-night revelers; inexperienced travelers; children.

CRUISE AREAS AND SEASONS Australia and New Zealand, Caribbean, Panama Canal, South America, Southeast Asia, winter. Baltic, Black Sea, British Isles, Europe, Mediterranean, Norwegian fjords, spring and summer; Egypt, Canada, Caribbean, New England, Red Sea, autumn; transatlantic, spring and fall.

THE LINE Founded in 1987 by Norwegian industrialist Atle Brynestad, Seabourn Cruise Line's goal has always been to offer the world's most luxurious cruises on the most elegant ships afloat for the most discriminating travelers.

THE FLEET	BUILT/RENOVATED	TONNAGE	PASSENGERS
Seabourn Legend	1991/96/03/05	10,000	208
Seabourn Odyssey	2009	32,000	450
Seabourn Pride	1988/97/03/05	10,000	208
Seabourn Quest	2011	32,000	450
Seabourn Sojourn	2010	32,000	450
Seabourn Spirit	1989/99/03/06	10,000	208

Seabourn's posh ships with sleek, yachtlike profiles are small enough to be exclusive yet large enough to be spacious and offer most facilities of a large ship. The ambience is carefree elegance. Cruises follow the sun on worldwide itineraries that circle the globe in a year's time.

In 1999, Carnival, which had owned 50% of Seabourn Cruises, acquired 100% ownership. Seabourn remains a separate brand. With the purchase, Carnival became a major player in the luxury market, and its deep pockets enabled Seabourn to increase its fleet. In June 2009, the first of three new 32,000-ton ships, *Seabourn Odyssey*, made her debut. The second ship, *Seabourn Sojourn*, is scheduled to launch in 2010; the third, *Seabourn Quest*, is planned for a 2011 entry. Although the ships are more than three times the size of the older vessels, the hotel-staff-to-guest ratio is similar to the smaller ships, and many traditional features have been retained but with enhancements and the addition of new features.

Every year Seabourn adds new ports of call and new itineraries. In 2010 and 2011, the cruise line will have a first-ever, year-round presence in Asia and a return to Indonesia after a lengthy hiatus. Seabourn is also offering new destination services with land safaris, journeys to Bhutan, and more. In January 2010, *Seabourn Odyssey* departed on the line's first world cruise.

STYLE Elegant but not stuffy, glamorous but not glitzy, Seabourn ships are like tony private clubs. Quality is key, starting with a nearly effortless embarkation and a white-gloved attendant to escort you to your suite (as luxurious as the brochure promises), where fruit and Champagne await you. Decor exudes understated elegance. Service—always attentive, never intrusive—is as polished as the silver with which you dine. You will be addressed by name by the staff after your first appearance.

Seabourn attracts both old-money travelers who disdain mainstream cruise ships and newly rich who appreciate the line's status symbolism. It also caters to stressed-out professionals and others seeking privacy. Whatever their background, they're affluent enough to be accustomed to a high level of service and style without excessive fuss.

Days at sea are for relaxing. Dress and atmosphere are informal, and time is unstructured. The usual announcements, pool games, and contests are absent. In fact, a Seabourn cruise is so low-key, you may need to read your daily agenda to know what's happening. Each cruise has one or two special events meant to be highlights. It might be a special concert in an unusual location for Seabourn passengers only; a visit to a private island, marina, or estate; or a sporting event. Evenings aboard ship are more formal; fine dining is the day's highlight. On evenings when you prefer to relax, a full-course dinner will be served en suite.

All the ships are wired for Wi-Fi access, enabling passengers with suitable laptop computers to receive and send e-mail and Web-surf from all suites and most public areas on board. Internet access costs $0.50 per minute, with lower bulk rates available. Phone service is $4.95 per minute. The ships offer an expanded menu of television channels, with sports, news, and entertainment. Cell-phone capability is available fleetwide.

Seabourn offers the ultimate in vacation flexibility by enabling passengers to choose from varied options. These include tailoring their cruise with separate and independently priced cruise fares, air-travel options, pre- and post-cruise tours, hotel, and transfers. For air, the choices are Seabourn's air program with preselected carriers (economy, business, or first class); the cruise line's independent air program, booked through Seabourn; or a chartered Gulfstream to and from the ship anywhere in the world.

One of Seabourn's most useful innovations has been Personal Valet Luggage Shipping. By teaming up with DHL Worldwide Express, Seabourn enables passengers to ship their luggage directly from their home to their ship. The service prepares all the shipping and customs paperwork, picks up the luggage, maintains 24-hour online tracking, provides insurance, and delivers the shipment. The cost is based on weight. Luggage traveling from the United States to Europe that weighs 30 pounds or less costs about $240 to ship; the cost is $420 for 70 pounds, which includes $2,000 insurance per suitcase. After passengers have booked their cruise, they can order the luggage service, shore excursions, spa appointments, pre- and post-cruise hotel extensions, and fully-escorted land programs, on Seabourn's Web site.

DISTINCTIVE FEATURES Unusual care for solo passengers. Foldout water sports marina. Walk-in closets, complimentary self-service laundry. Computer learning centers. Luggage shipping. Visiting chefs. Wi-Fi access in suites. Personal-shopper services in many ports. Ipods and netbooks on *Odyssey* and *Sojourn*.

RATES Tips are included; government fees and taxes are additional. Prestocked minibar in cabins; wine with meals; open-bar policy throughout ships.

Special fares and discounts Advance-purchase, capacity-controlled discounts, known as EBS (Early Booking Savings), reward early birds with up to 65% savings. Combo savings of 10% are added for booking consecutive cruises totaling up to 17 days. Longer combinations of 18 days or more get 50% or more Grand Voyage savings. Future cruises booked aboard a cruise earn an extra 5% savings. For the line's other special fares, consult its brochures and its Web site. Those who have sailed on Seabourn or any of the other Carnival member lines qualify for Club Signature Savings of 50% on an array of cruises throughout the world. Club Signature Value Sailings are clearly marked in Seabourn's cruise catalog and on the Web site.

- **THIRD PASSENGER:** 50% of per-person published tariff.
- **CHILDREN'S FARE:** Same as third-person rate. No infants under one year; children ages 1–2 sail free.

- **SINGLE SUPPLEMENT:** 125% to 200% of per-person double-occupancy basic suite, depending on cruise, and capacity controlled.

PAST PASSENGERS Members receive up to 50% savings on selected cruises and 140 days earn a 7-day cruise, 250 days earn a 14-day one. Passengers who book while still on board a cruise get an extra 5% savings on top of whatever other savings are available. They can make an "open booking" and have two years to pick a cruise and apply the extra 5%. There are also savings for early bookings.

THE LAST WORD To compete in the ultra-deluxe market, Seabourn widened its price range and offered much more flexibility. The per diems on some sampler and promotional cruises are no more than those of mainstream cruises. If you can afford the price, you're unlikely to find any finer cruising—even on your own yacht.

THE SHIPS In this age of glitzy ships, the Seabourn triplets (they are nearly identical) epitomize understatement. Clean lines, fine fabrics, and subtle styling are meant to soothe. Passengers board through a lobby that instantly reveals the ships' character. Quietly elegant, the small atrium spans five decks with a double circular stairway accented by brass railings and etched glass. A glass dome above illuminates the stairs and adjacent hallways with diffused natural light. The sense of space and serenity is immediate and is among the ships' most appealing features.

Seabourn has embarked upon a multimillion-dollar renovation of the original trio. *Seabourn Spirit* was the first of the trio to have her makeover, followed by *Pride* in January (just in time to begin a new year-round schedule of cruises in Asia), and *Legend* in fall 2010. The look and feel of each vessel is being transformed with open, airy interiors, modern embellishments, contemporary furnishings, and areas that resemble the new *Seabourn Odyssey*.

Public rooms occupy all of the two top levels and are aft on the two center decks. The dining room is on the lowest passenger level. In 2000, all three ships were given stem-to-stern multimillion-dollar renovations, along with the addition of French balconies to 36 suites, a computer learning center, a cigar humidor, and an expanded gym, among other improvements.

The main showroom, **Magellan Lounge** (**King Olav** on *Legend*; **Amundsen Lounge** on *Spirit*), has a stage and dance floor. It is used for daytime lectures and evening entertainment. In the lobby area are the purser's and tour desk, cruise director's office, writing room, and computer center.

Seabourn Legend	**QUALITY 9**	**VALUE C**
Seabourn Pride	**QUALITY 9**	**VALUE C**
Seabourn Spirit	**QUALITY 9**	**VALUE C**
REGISTRY Bahamas	**LENGTH** 439 feet	**BEAM** 63 feet
CABINS 104	**DRAFT** 16 feet	**SPEED** 18 knots
MAXIMUM PASSENGERS	**PASSENGER DECKS** 6	**ELEVATORS** 3
208	**CREW** 165	**SPACE RATIO** 49

Seabourn Cruise Line Standard Features

Officers Norwegian, international

Staff *Dining, Cabin, Cruise:* international

Dining facilities Two open-seating restaurants; one more formal, the other a casual indoor/outdoor cafe. Alfresco grill on deck some nights. In-suite dining. Complimentary wine. *Odyssey* and *Sojourn,* four restaurants.

Special diets On request, four weeks prior to sailing.

Room service 24 hours, cabin menu and full service.

Dress code By day, casual but conservative, comfortable. Dinner is a dressier affair some nights, casual (no jacket required) other nights; informal (jacket but no tie for men) or formal (black-tie optional one evening in the dining room on one-week cruise; two on two-week cruise); there are casual alternatives for dinner every night.

Cabin amenities Flat-panel television with DVD player, CNN, ESPN, and Discovery channels; financial fax service, Bose Wave CD/stereo, direct-dial telephone, marble bathroom with twin sinks (one on *Legend*), tub and shower, deluxe toiletries, hair dryer, bathrobes, walk-in closet, minifridge, safe. Stocked bar; umbrella, atlas, personalized stationery. Wi-Fi in all suites. Ipod and netbooks on *Odyssey* and *Sojourn*.

Electrical outlets 110/220 AC.

Wheelchair access 4 suites; *Odyssey* and *Sojourn* 7.

Recreation and entertainment 3 lounges with entertainment/dance music nightly, cabaret, classical music concerts, folkloric performances in ports of call, weekly dinner dance, casino, cruise-related lectures, bridge instructor and lessons, enrichment programs.

Sports and other activities Water sports marina, outdoor pool, deck sports; parlor games. *Odyssey* and *Sojourn* 2 outside pools

Beauty and fitness Several saunas, outdoor whirlpools, gym, exercise classes, beauty salon, spa with massage, beauty treatments.

Other facilities Self-service laundry, laundry/dry cleaning, library, boutique, hospital, nondenominational religious services. Wi-Fi access, medical facilities, and computer center.

Children's facilities None; children under age 18 must be accompanied by parent or adult with written permission.

Theme cruises Classical music, food and wine, others.

Smoking Dining venues and areas of lounges are designated as nonsmoking. Cigar, pipes on open decks only.

Seabourn suggested tipping No-tipping-expected policy.

Credit cards For cruise payment and onboard charges: American Express, Diners Club, Discover, MasterCard, Visa.

One flight up is a second entertainment lounge, which is cleverly glass-partitioned in three sections: a small casino, an informal bar, and a piano lounge used for activities, socializing, daytime parties, and predinner cocktails. After dinner, it's a nightclub. There's also a small library.

The first of the two top levels contains the Sports and Spa Deck and indoor/outdoor **Veranda Café.** Another flight up is the **Observation Lounge,** a beautiful room with sloping floor-to-ceiling windows. Early-bird continental breakfast and afternoon tea are served here—both stellar times for ocean panoramas.

ITINERARIES *See* Itinerary Index.

CABINS Accommodations—all spacious, outside suites—are among the ships' finest features. Even standard Seabourn Suites are large. Their practical design maximizes space, and appointments—wall coverings, carpets, draperies, bedcovers of fine, lightly textured fabrics—enhance harmony and elegance.

They have well-defined sitting and sleeping sections. The roomy conversation area has a sofa, two chairs, and a coffee table that can be transformed into a dining table. Two cushioned stools provide extra seating for guests. The sitting area is next to a five-foot-wide picture window placed low enough that you can lie in bed and watch the passing scenery. The window has a mechanical shade operated by a switch near the desk and a device to clean the outside automatically.

In 36 of each ship's 104 suites French balconies have replaceed the five-foot picture window. The balconies consist of two full-length sliding glass doors opening onto a narrow Riviera-style balcony with a waist-high glass balustrade. The sliding doors can be opened to enjoy sea breezes without cutting into the interior space of the room. In the ships' tariff, these suites are designated by categories B2 and B3, and their locations are shown on deck plans.

A curtain separating the sitting and sleeping areas can be drawn to put sleepers in darkness. Beds can be configured as twins or a queen. The bedroom section has a long dresser/desk and a large, lighted mirror. A wall-mounted minifridge and bar is stocked with two bottles of spirits or wine that you select when you book. Replenishments cost extra. Mineral water and soft drinks are free. The bar contains Norwegian crystal glassware. On the opposite wall is a pullout writing desk, containing your personalized stationery and a small sewing kit. On a shelf opposite the bed is a flat-panel television and DVD player. CNN and other channels are available, depending on the location of the ship. The suites also have a Bose Wave stereo radio and CD player. The walk-in closet contains extra shelf space and a safe.

The marble bathroom has twin sinks (*Legend*, one sink), mirrored storage shelves, a large tub, and a shower. Thick terry robes, a hair dryer, and toiletries are supplied. Fine bed and bath linens are used throughout.

A hall-side door can be used to convert adjacent standard suites into doubles. Twenty suites on each ship can be joined, by opening a movable wall, and made into double suites, with a total of 554 square feet, two baths, one queen bed, and a separate dining area. Six larger suites are in three configurations. Classic suites have queen beds only, a larger sitting area, and a small veranda. Two Owner's Suites have a separate bedroom and living room, a master bath with shower and tub and guest bath, a table with four chairs, one walk-in and one alcove closet, two sofas, and a private veranda. Two other Owner's Suites are the largest and have large living rooms and forward-facing private verandas.

Specifications All suites: 88 are standard Seabourn Suites; 2 larger Classic Suites and 4 Owner's Suites—all with verandas, 36 with French balconies. Standard dimensions, 277 square feet; 102 suites with twins (convertible to queen); no singles; 4 wheelchair accessible.

DINING Fine dining is central to a Seabourn cruise, and the choices are diverse. For any meal, you dine when and with whom you like in the **Restaurant** dining room or the casual **Veranda Café,** an indoor/outdoor venue for buffet breakfast and lunch. In the evening, this venue becomes a second restaurant, serving tasting menus and theme dinners by reservation. On sea days, lunch and some evenings feature alfresco dining at the **Sky Bar Grill**. Or one can dine en suite, choosing from the 24-hour cabin menu or the dining room menu, served course by course. Morning bouillon is served in the Sky Bar, and afternoon tea with cucumber sandwiches can be enjoyed in the Observation Lounge. Weather permitting, a lavish deck barbecue dinner is offered on one evening of the cruise.

With Seabourn, the emphasis is on fresh ingredients, such as seafood, fruits, and vegetables, obtained in ports. Breads, pastries, and ice cream are prepared on board. Menus, changed daily and repeated on a 21-day cycle, are created by celebrity chef Charlie Palmer and offer three appetizers, two soups, two salads, five entrees, three desserts, cheese, and ice cream. Generally, dishes are innovative and sophisticated. Vegetarian and lean specialties are available daily, as are classic steak, chicken, and fish.

Menu entrees are cooked to order, and presentation is outstanding. Compatible wines are complimentary. Suggested wines are usually moderately priced; the wine list is more elaborate and offers attractive prices on rare and unusual wines bought as a package in advance. Wine is also available by the glass. Caviar available by request.

The Restaurant is a pretty room dressed in pastels where tables are set with Porsgrund china, fine crystal, silverware, and fresh flowers. Most tables seat four or six, but two, eight, and tens are available.

Breakfast and lunch appeal most to those who prefer a quiet environment and full service. Dinner is a lavish, somewhat formal affair. One evening each week calls for black tie or optional dark suit, and for all but casual nights, dress suitable for fine dining in New York or Paris is expected. Seabourn has expanded its passengers' choices by offering a more casual dining alternative in the Veranda Café on evenings when the suggested attire for the Restaurant is black tie.

Seabourn ships now have two more dining options: **Sky Grill** is created by turning the Sky Bar area into an alfresco dining venue, complete with candlelight and table service for grilled steak and seafood, along with a great buffet. Sky Grill can accommodate about two dozen passengers and is available one or two nights of the cruise, depending on the weather. **Tasting @ 2,** the daytime casual restaurant, is transformed nightly into a romantic yet casual spot for up to 50 passengers. The three tasting menus alternate with themed dinners such as Asian or Mediterranean cuisine, very different from those being served in the main restaurant.

Service is unfailingly superb. In fact, service in the Restaurant is the best and most professional we have encountered on any cruise ship. Unlike on other cruise ships, singles are invited to join an officer's table or one hosted by management or a social-staff member. An invitation will be clipped to your door almost daily, and the maître d' will seat singles with other guests, unless you indicate that you prefer to dine alone. At least once each cruise, a dinner dance is held in the Restaurant.

The informal, convivial atmosphere of the Veranda Café makes it the most popular choice for breakfast and lunch or for dinner after a long shore excursion. In the ships' most recent refurbishing, the Café got fresh new decor and new contemporary menus. The lively cafe bustles with people and conversation indoors. Outside, tables are set under protective awnings. In fair weather, the deck is one of the most delightful dining places anywhere.

Seabourn's popular "Shopping with the Chef" excursions allow passengers in some ports to accompany the ship's chef to local markets to buy fresh local ingredients and then enjoy them for dinner.

SERVICE Most passengers rate service as the single best feature—and with good reason: it's impeccable. Shipwide, the thoroughly professional staff is gracious and attentive, but never intrusive. The Norwegian captain and officers, European hotel staff and stewardesses, and British and American cruise and social staff work harmoniously and are visibly proud of their ship. The ships' small size lends them to personalized service impossible on larger ships. The luxury setting offers more opportunities to provide good service, and the high crew-to-passenger ratio enables staff to deliver it.

The ship's no-tipping policy appeared to work very well, but we've recently been told that it's being modified to allow staff to accept tips for unusual service. We thought it was the result of the line's lowering its cruise prices (20% or more), but we were wrong. Gratuities are still included in the cruise price. We hope the change won't impact service. Also, to note, some guests give donations to a crew fund through the purser's office; it pays for crew parties and other activities during their free time.

FACILITIES AND ACTIVITIES The daily agenda isn't taxing but might include a cooking demonstration; afternoon lecture by a well-known person from the arts, academia, politics, or show business; port talks; bridge lessons or play; art class; galley tour; wine-and-cheese party; ice-cream social; parlor games and quizzes; or folkloric show. A movie about one of Seabourn's other cruises—and a not-too-subtle sales pitch—may be presented. Not on the schedule are bingo, horse racing, pool games, or costume parties.

The library has music and books, including CDs. Also, cabin stewardesses will deliver DVDs to suites, upon request. The boutique beckons to shoppers. The **Computer Learning Center,** with four computers, offers classes for a fee. Or you can do nothing at all. If the weather is fair, you'll probably be out on deck, relaxing, snoozing, soaking in the Jacuzzi, or enjoying a "massage moment" (complimentary from the spa staff). Some places offer protection in hot or cool weather.

Evening entertainment is tony, designed for sophisticated people. The ship's quartet plays easy listening and dance music in the **Club,** or a pianist/

vocalist performs at the cocktail hour. Evening cabaret and variety shows staged in the **Magellan Lounge** are usually very good. They feature the cruise director and three or four social-staff members. Lounge seats are slightly tiered, providing excellent sight lines. A classical concert or program by a young artist may be offered, or the Restaurant becomes a supper club with dancing. The casino offers roulette, blackjack, slot machines, and gaming lessons.

SPORTS, FITNESS, AND BEAUTY Decks have ample space for sunning and a teak promenade for walking or jogging. Whirlpools and a small, deep swimming pool are in a peculiar spot near the Veranda Café—the pool is often shaded by the ship's superstructure, inhibiting swimmers.

The ships have a water sports platform with a 30-by-30-foot steel-meshed cage that drops into the sea, creating a protected saltwater pool. A teak border provides a launch area for paddleboats, windsurfers, kayaks, and sailboats in warm-weather ports. Two high-speed boats pull water-skiers or banana boats and also transport snorkelers and divers to choice locations. Although the ships try to use these marinas at least once a week, rough water may preclude it.

In earlier renovations, fitness facilities were upgraded substantially, with the gym doubled in size and more state-of-the-art equipment added, along with new cabinets and lockers. Daily stretch and exercise classes at varied workout levels, individual training, sauna, and steam rooms are available. The **Spa at Seabourn** has a wide selection of beauty treatments and services, along with fitness classes in yoga, Pilates, and cardio tae bo circuit training.

Seabourn does not have a golf program; however, the line can make arrangements for tee times on request. Seabourn's ships visit 90 ports around the world where passengers have access to more than 100 golf courses, including most of the major and famous ones.

CHILDREN'S FACILITIES Seabourn doesn't offer the ideal family vacation.

SHORE EXCURSIONS Excursions are well organized and orchestrated by an experienced, knowledgeable staff. On a Norwegian fjord cruise, the briefing was the most thorough heard on any but expedition-type cruises accompanied by specialists. There's no push to sell excursions, and even off-the-shelf motor coach tours tend to be pricey. Information on excursions is available on Seabourn's Web site; excursions can be booked online.

Each cruise offers one event designated as an Exclusively Seabourn excursion for all passengers. These often are a cruise highlight and may be visits to private homes or local sites off the tourist track. Refreshments and entertainment are provided, and guests may be introduced to local dignitaries. For example, a Norwegian voyage offered a concert of Edvard Grieg's music at his lakeside home near Bergen, presented by Norway's foremost pianist.

In addition, the line has more than 75 unusual shore excursions created exclusively for Seabourn passengers. These excursions include special entry to sites of interest, meetings with famous personalities, and a variety of special-interest pursuits such as car racing, yacht racing, photography, and river rafting. There's a visit to Hong Kong's Cantonese Opera to watch artists apply their makeup; a ride in a horse-drawn carriage to a winery in the Medoc; and shopping in Florence markets for an Italian Cordon Bleu Cooking School class, to name a few.

THE SHIPS *Seabourn Odyssey*, Seabourn's new, $250 million flagship, made her debut in June 2009. She is the first vessel in the luxury category to be built since Regent's *Seven Seas Voyager* in 2003 and Seabourn's first new ship in almost two decades. Her duplicate, *Seabourn Sojourn,* will be launched in June 2010, and a third ship, *Seabourn Quest,* is scheduled for 2011.

Designed by architects Yran & Storbraaten of Norway and built in Italy by T. Mariotti, the new ship mirrors the silhouette and general interior layout of her smaller Seabourn sisters but with new facilities and amenities, such as more dining options, more types of suites, more verandas, more entertainment venues, and enhanced spa and recreational facilities. And at 32,000 tons, she is three times their size. Yet, she carries only twice as many guests, boasting a 71.1 space ratio—among the highest in cruising. For this and other reasons, the handsome vessel is setting a new standard in luxury cruising.

Seabourn has kept its signature yacht-like ambience, despite the ship's larger size, by creating intimate spaces and maintaining an understated decor of soft colors, light wood, and an abundance of glass in the interior. In other words, the ship is *cool*. As one recent cruiser described her, she's "where South Beach meets Palm Beach."

Seabourn's aim to appeal to a potential audience of younger upscale travelers seems to be working. *Seabourn Odyssey*'s early voyages carried nearly 40% more first-time passengers than the cruise line's average, and they were, on average, 10% younger than the line's longtime loyal following. Those under 45 years of age exceeded the norm by 64%.

According to the builders, *Seabourn Odyssey* features the "highest levels of sophistication and innovation in the cruise industry, blending luxury and elegance with advanced technologies and new materials." They note, too, that she has been awarded the Green Star designation, the highest rating for ships employing advanced wastewater treatment technology to minimize pollution and protect the environment. The ship is powered by two fully independent propulsion systems and complies with the latest safety standards that came into effect in 2009.

ITINERARIES *See* Itinerary Index. *Seabourn Odyssey* will depart from Fort Lauderdale in January 2010, on Seabourn Cruise Line's first world cruise, a 108-day voyage visiting 42 ports with special exclusive events along the way.

CABINS The *Odyssey*'s 225 beautifully appointed ocean-view suites come in 13 categories and are located on 7 of the 11 passenger decks. Ninety percent

Seabourn Odyssey	PREVIEW	
Seabourn Quest	2011	
Seabourn Sojourn	2010	
REGISTRY Bahamas	LENGTH 650 feet	BEAM 84 feet
CABINS 225	DRAFT 21 feet	SPEED 19 knots
MAXIMUM PASSENGERS	PASSENGER DECKS 11	ELEVATORS 6
462	CREW 335	SPACE RATIO 71.1

(197) of the suites have verandas—an enormous asset over Seabourn's smaller fleet, which was built long before verandas became *de rigueur*. The spacious suites range in size from 295 to 1,682 square feet indoors; verandas add 65–505 square feet of outdoor space, large enough for alfresco dining.

All suites have granite bathrooms with a separate tub and shower, twin sinks, a handsome glass vanity, hair dryer, terry robes and slippers, fine soaps by Hermès and L'Occitane, and a new line of plant-based bath products by Molton Brown. They also have a full-length window or glass door to a veranda, living area, queen-size bed, or two twin beds; walk-in closet with a safe; interactive flat-panel television; Wi-Fi access; cell phone service; refrigerator and bar stocked with your preferences prior to arrival; and a writing desk with personalized stationery. Other amenities include complimentary Champagne upon arrival, 24-hour room service, fruit basket replenished daily, nightly turndown service, daily newspaper, world atlas, umbrella, and clock/barometer/thermometer. The suites are attended by stewardesses who will welcome you with such touches as preparing a warm-scented bath upon request. A self-service launderette and laundry/dry-cleaning services are available.

Specifications 4 Grand Suites (1,097–1,682 square feet); 5 Owner's Suites (760–1,062 square feet); 22 Penthouse Suites (436 square feet plus veranda 98 square feet); 166 Veranda (standard) Suites, 365 square feet; 28 Seabourn Suites, 295 square feet. 12 suites can accommodate a third person; 7 suites are wheelchair accessible.

DINING *Seabourn Odyssey* has four dining venues, of which three offer casual dining alternatives nightly. All venues are overseen by celebrity chef Charlie Palmer. Complimentary wine and spirits are served throughout the voyage.

The Restaurant on Deck 4 is an open-seating gourmet dining room with tables set with fine china and crystal. The room is paneled in marble, and sheer white draperies hang at intervals to separate the room and buffer sounds. This room's standout feature is a large crystal chandelier in its double-height center section. The Restaurant serves breakfast, lunch, and dinner and has tables for two, four, six, and eight, as well as raised tables with bar stools for 18. Most evenings, attire is "jacket required," except on special nights when the venue becomes a sophisticated supper club with dancing after dinner, and a black tie is requested but optional. For The Restaurant, Palmer introduced new menus to reflect the flavors of the Mediterranean destinations *Seabourn Odyssey* visited during her inaugural summer and fall.

The Colonnade, also on Deck 8, is a casual eatery for three meals and table service with indoor seating, as well as a larger outdoor seating area. The venue has an open kitchen and food stations, where you can watch the chefs. Each evening has a different theme. Also on Deck 8, **Restaurant 2** is an avant-garde dining space that offers tasting menus of innovative cuisine and wine pairings. The chef prepares dishes individually in tasting portions of small plates, which are served with selected wine. Occasionally there are themed dinners.

The poolside **Patio Grill** serves breakfast, lunch, and dinner, weather permitting. Favorites at Patio Grill are freshly baked cinnamon buns in the morning and gourmet pizzas in the afternoon. The grill also has hamburgers, hot dogs, and salads. In-suite dining offers an extensive menu of gourmet breakfast, lunch, and dinner items available around the clock.

FACILITIES AND ACTIVITIES *Seabourn Odyssey* has a showroom, library, business center, and three boutiques. Six lounges and bars invite patrons to gather throughout the day and evening to mingle, and an open-bar policy eliminates any bills to sign.

Aft on Deck 7, a new feature, Seabourn Square, is a concierge lounge, an inviting space where guests may access every shipboard service in a living-room atmosphere designed to encourage sociability. The Square has a library, upscale shops, an outdoor terrace, and a coffee bar, as well as concierges. During the day, there may be a game of bridge to join or a cooking demonstration with the chef to enjoy. Seabourn's famous advertisement of a waiter bringing Champagne to a passenger relaxing in beautiful aqua water has led to the ritual of Caviar in the Surf, delivered with Champagne on a surfboard. More simply, you can cool off poolside with a chilled towel and a sorbet. In the evening, you can enjoy cabaret in the Grand Salon and dancing by the music of the ship's six-piece band, a game in the casino, classical guitar in the Observation Bar, and dancing in The Club. The ship shows classic and first-run movies during Movies under the Stars, complete with popcorn. Then there's Dessert under the Stars, with yummy treats from the chef, and, on special nights, a romantic evening of Dancing under the Stars.

Seabourn Odyssey passengers can borrow iPods on board for yoga or Pilates classes, or for listening to music. The ship also has netbook computers for loan (and for purchase) for those who haven't brought their own laptop so that guests can take advantage of the ship's Wi-Fi access in all suites and nearly all public areas. Interactive television in suites makes it easy for guests to book shore excursions and access movies- and music-on-demand.

Among the duty-free shops on board is **The Collection,** featuring fine jewelry and watches from luxury designers including Hermès, Chanel, and Dior, as well as a private diamond showroom—a first for the Seabourn fleet.

SPORTS, FITNESS, AND BEAUTY The main Pool Patio, midship on Deck 8 and much larger than other Seabourn ships, has a pool and two whirlpools, as well as cabanas. On Deck 5, there's a more secluded, well-shaded pool and two whirlpools. If those don't appeal, another option is one of 18 double sun-beds on the Sun Terrace on Deck 11 near the bow, where drinks and cold towel service are available. Aft of the Sun Terrace is **The Retreat,** a multi-diversion plaza and a first for Seabourn. It has a contoured nine-hole, minigolf course; chess on a giant board; and shuffleboard. The Retreat is also the place to be for sunsets and stargazing after dark. Another spot for sunsets or tranquility is the whirlpool at the very front of Deck 6, similar to ones on Deck 5 of *Odyssey*'s smaller sister.

The **Spa at Seabourn** spans two decks and at 11,400 square feet claims to be the largest spa on any luxury ship. The spa has seven treatment rooms on Deck 9 and two 750-square-foot Spa Villas on Deck 10, which passengers can book for a half day of shamelessly sybaritic indulgence. The pricey villas have a treatment area for two, complete with shower; a bathtub big enough for two; a double daybed on a private wraparound balcony for sunbathing; a full living-room area; and a dining area where healthy snacks can be enjoyed.

The spa has a thalassotherapy pool, a relaxation room with heated loungers, two unisex herbal steam/sauna rooms (as well as separate men's and women's steam rooms and saunas), and an outdoor deck space for patrons to relax in the sun. *Seabourn Odyssey* is the only cruise ship to offer SkinCeuticals products in its spa, with a range of treatments, including a regenerating facial, firming facial, and gel peel by SkinCeuticals.

Patrons can indulge in a collection of treatments, ranging from Chinese reflexology and aromatherapy to warm stones or seaweed wraps, gleaned from ten Asian cultures. Certified massage therapists can design a spa package based on your preferences. The full-service beauty salon offers manicures, full makeovers, and a "nail buff bar," which serves as a social area that offers manicures and pedicures, along with smoothies and other drinks. A popular amenity is a complimentary "massage moment," poolside.

The fitness center comes with cardio, strength, and weight-training equipment; a studio for fitness classes; and a Kinesis wall, a new pulley-and-cable system that offers low-resistance exercise. Personal trainers are available to develop a customized workout plan.

Water sports from the ship's marina include kayaking, waterskiing, snorkeling, and, weather permitting, beach parties ashore on select cruises.

Silversea Cruises

110 East Broward Boulevard
Fort Lauderdale, FL 33301
☎ 954-522-4477 or 800-722-9955
FAX 954-522-4499
www.silversea.com

TYPE OF SHIPS Ultraluxury, all-suite small ships.

TYPE OF CRUISES Luxury cruises on worldwide itineraries.

CRUISE LINE'S STRENGTHS
- luxurious all-suite accommodations, most with verandas
- open-seating dining
- cuisine
- impeccable service
- worldwide itineraries
- comprehensive, all-inclusive prices

CRUISE LINE'S SHORTCOMINGS
- somewhat staid evening activities and entertainment
- shallow draft in rough seas

FELLOW PASSENGERS Diverse demographically, experienced cruisers. Many have made the rounds of the luxury ships. Well traveled and outgoing, passengers range from young professionals in their 30s to lively 80-year-olds. The majority are older than 50; couples are the rule. Passengers come from throughout the United States, but Silversea also has a sizable European following. A high number of passengers are repeaters.

Recommended for Sophisticated, knowledgeable travelers who prefer a finely crafted ship and low-key atmosphere to the glitz and games of big ships; those who appreciate exacting service in casual elegance.

Not recommended for Those for whom subtle luxury and attention to detail are unimportant; anyone uncomfortable among non-Americans. Late-night revelers or children.

CRUISE AREAS AND SEASONS Africa, Alaska, Amazon, Australia, Baltic, Canada, Caribbean, China, Far East, India, Madagascar, Mediterranean, New England, New Zealand, Northern Europe, Seychelles, South America, South Pacific, seasonally. World cruise, winter.

THE LINE Silversea Cruises was created in the early 1990s by the Lefebvre family of Rome with the Vlasov Group of Monaco, commercial and passenger shipping families that previously owned Sitmar Cruises.

When the Italian-built fleet of identical twins was launched in 1994 and 1995, Silversea took the luxury market by storm with reasonable pricing, uncompromising service, outstanding accommodations, and a space ratio of 55.74, among the highest of any cruise ship. The ultradeluxe six-deck ships were substantially larger than most of their direct competitors, offering big-ship facilities and all-suite accommodations in a comfortable small-ship atmosphere. Their biggest advantage was their high number of cabins with verandas. Prices cover beverage service throughout the ship (wine, liquors, and nonalcoholic drinks), stocked in-suite beverage cabinet, in-suite hors d'oeuvres and full meals, a special shoreside event on some sailings, baggage handling, gratuities, and butler service for accommodations fleetwide. The ratio of crew to passengers is 1 to 1.34.

Encouraged by its initial success, the line added another set of larger twins: *Silver Shadow* in 2000 and *Silver Whisper* in 2001. They are about a third bigger and carry about a third more passengers than the line's first twins. The design is similar but with enhancements based on passengers' comments: larger bathrooms and closets, more top-grade suites, 80% of cabins with verandas, a poolside dining venue, computer center, cigar lounge, and larger spa and fitness center. The ships were built at the T. Marrotti Shipyard in Italy, where the first two ships were built.

In 2007, *Silver Shadow* sailed on her first world cruise. Launched in late 2009, *Silver Spirit*, a 36,000-ton luxury ship, carries 540 passengers and represents a 40% increase in the line's capacity. In 2008, *Silver Wind* underwent a major renovation and redesign, and Silversea took the unusual step of adding an expedition ship (*World Discoverer II*), which it renamed *HSH Prince Albert II* in tribute to Prince Albert of Monaco.

STYLE Sparkling clean, impeccably maintained, and luxurious in an understated way consistent with fine yachts, the ships offer elegance undisturbed by pretense or formality. From boarding to disembarking, passengers are attended by a crew that makes a genuine effort to know each individual and anticipate every need. This attention is direct and friendly, but never obsequious.

Suites are exceptionally comfortable and exceed their representation in the line's brochure. Public areas are inviting and elegant. Structured activities are available, but they tend toward the relaxing and cerebral. Announcements, games, and contests are the exception rather than the rule.

At sea and in port, days are casual. Evenings are low-key but dressier. Most cruises include a Silversea Experience signature event—usually an excursion with dining and drinks in a beautiful setting, perhaps a private island, private club, or secluded coast.

Through Silversea's exclusive partnership with the National Trust for Italy (*Fondo per l'Ambiente Italiano*), passengers enjoy an enhanced program of shore excursions, cultural events, and access to some of Italy's most historic sites. FAI protects and maintains some of Italy's most beautiful architectural

THE FLEET	BUILT/RENOVATED	TONNAGE	PASSENGERS
HSH Prince Albert II	1989/2008	6,072	132
Silver Cloud	1994/01/04/08	16,800	296
Silver Shadow	2000	28,258	382
Silver Spirit	2009	36,000	540
Silver Whisper	2001	28,258	382
Silver Wind	1995/03/08	16,800	296

and cultural treasures, including ancient castles, villas, a monastery, gardens, and stretches of pristine countryside and coastline.

Silverseas ships have Wi-Fi hot spots and cell-phones-at-sea access enabling passengers to use their own cell phones in international waters. Recently, too, Silversea enhanced their suites with the installation of custom-designed Sealy Posturepedic Plush Euro-top mattresses fleetwide. The top suites—Owner's, Grand, Royal, and Rossellini—got Stearns & Foster Plush ultraluxury mattresses that are 10% larger than a conventional mattress.

Silversea expanded its guest lecturer program with a series called The Spirit of Exploration. On select voyages, an internationally acclaimed adventurer serves as the ship's Resident Explorer, hosting a series of presentations and accompanying passengers on selected shore excursions.

Silversea's Silver Links golf program is available, on 12 itineraries aboard *Silver Shadow* and *Silver Whisper* in 2010, for play on 30 beautiful and challenging courses in 15 countries, ranging from the Caribbean and Europe to Australia. Nike golf clubs are available for rental or purchase. Golfers can further hone their skills aboard ship with sophisticated split-screen swing analysis utilizing the most advanced V1 digital-coaching system. The cost for private swing analysis starts at just $30. More information is available at **www.silversea.com.**

Silversea's new Silver Shore Concierge service aims to arrange whatever you want to do ashore before, during, or after your cruise. Once you have a deposited booking, the concierge desk will go to work for you up to 120 days before sailing. Payment is required in advance and includes a service fee. For those who can't plan that far ahead, the concierge desk also provides support for the concierge aboard your cruise. The dedicated toll-free phone line is 800-968-9518, or e-mail **concierge@silversea.com.**

In 2010, through its partnership with Relais & Châteaux, Silversea Cruises introduced **L'École des Chefs,** a new interactive cooking school featured on 11 voyages. The program offers passengers a special culinary curriculum and entertaining events hosted by Silversea executive chef David Bilsland, who was educated in classic French cooking. The curriculum for each cruise is designed to celebrate the cultural flavor of the ship's itinerary. Highlights include workshops ranging from basic knife skills and kitchen terminology to sauces and baking; cooking demonstrations with wine pairings and interactive Q&A sessions; a "Lunch and Learn" event offering small groups a chance to sample a meal of specially prepared dishes; and "Take It Home" recipes. Certain voyages provide an escorted tour of a local market followed by a cooking class, and an instructor-escorted excursion to a local restaurant or other venue. Select L'École des Chefs voyages will feature Silversea's wine consultant, Lyn Farmer.

DISTINCTIVE FEATURES   All-suite accommodations; comprehensive air and sea travel with personalized service at intermediate travel stops; all-inclusive prices. Silversea Experience on most sailings; moderate single supplements; golf program; Internet access; Personalized Voyage program; personal e-mail; Silver Shore Concierge; butlers in all categories fleetwide.

RATES   Tips and onboard beverages, including select wine and spirits, in cruise-only rate; an optional air/hotel program includes round-trip airfare (with upgrades to business class available), one-night precruise deluxe hotel, transfers, and baggage handling.

Special fares and discounts Early-booking incentive savings range from 5% to 20%; they are capacity-controlled and subject to availability. An additional advanced payment savings of 5% may be combined with the early-booking savings when payment is made in full by a specified date.

Silver Sailing savings program enables passengers to save up to 50% off cruise-only fares on Vista, Veranda, and Midship Veranda suites and higher categories (Medallion to Owner's suites), up to 35% and more on certain cruises. The Silver Sailing offers are subject to availability; they are valid only for new cruise bookings and do not apply to land, hotel, and air programs.

- **THIRD PASSENGER:** Approximately 50% of the Vista or Veranda Suite per-person published rate.
- **SINGLE SUPPLEMENT:** 110% to 175% of per-person double-occupancy basic suite, depending on cruise.

PAST PASSENGERS Past passengers automatically become members of the Venetian Society, named to reflect the line's Italian ownership. On their second voyage, members receive a silver pin bearing the society's winged-lion emblem, a symbol of Venice. After they have sailed for 100-, 200-, and 500-plus days, they receive sapphire, emerald, and diamond pins, respectively. Members also receive a newsletter three times yearly containing information on special discounts. Other benefits include shipboard events hosted by the captain. Members get fare reductions of 5%, 10%, and 15%, combinable with early-booking incentives, advance-payment bonus, and consecutive-cruise savings. Members may bring friends in an additional suite at some savings. They also receive $250 or $500 shipboard credits and a credit to their Society account for the days their friends cruise.

THE LAST WORD Silversea got off to a great start with its first two ships, setting exceptionally high standards for itself and the industry. The second two larger ships did not draw the same level of praise initially, and the line fell into a slump. Now, after a determined effort to improve the product across the board, Silversea has made a comeback. The new food, entertainment, and enrichment programs are innovative, and itineraries are creative. Officers and crew are actively involved in providing highly personalized service.

Silversea Cruises remains a good value for those who can afford it, and competition keeps a constant pressure on price. The cruise line's Personalized Voyages program provides prospective passengers with the utmost flexibility and convenience to customize a cruise to suit their needs.

THE SHIPS Styled to soothe, the first Silversea twins are the antithesis of the huge floating hotels that dominate cruising. Elegance is anchored in simplicity, clean lines, earth-tone fabrics, and polished wood and brass. The entry lobby surprises with its modest proportions. No six-story atrium here.

In late 2008, a multimillion-dollar renovation of *Silver Wind* involved virtually every aspect of the ship, giving her an Observation Lounge, an expansive new spa, and eight new suites. The investment exceeded the usual refurbishment budget, but it set the line's future to bring *Silver Wind* up to the standard

Silversea Cruises Standard Features

Officers Italian.

Staff *Dining and Cabin:* European; Cruise: British and American.

Dining facilities All meals served at one seating in restaurant; indoor/outdoor cafe for casual breakfast and lunch. Alternative dining specialty dinners on most evenings. In-suite dining.

Special diets Available on request.

Room service 24 hours, cabin menu and full-service dining room menu.

Dress code By day, casual but conservative and comfortable. Dinner is more dressy. Informal (jacket, tie optional for men) or formal (two black-tie or dark-suit nights on one-week cruise; four on two-week cruise).

Cabin amenities Stocked bar, minifridge, interactive television with CNN, CD/DVD player, direct-dial telephone, marble bathroom with sink, tub, and shower, hair dryer, bathrobes, walk-in closet, safe.

Electrical outlets 110/220 AC.

Wheelchair access Limited.

Recreation and entertainment Three lounges with entertainment/dance music nightly, cabaret, classical music concerts, folkloric performances in ports of call, nightly dancing, casino, cruise-related lectures, Internet access.

Sports and other activities Outdoor pool, deck sports, bridge instructor and lessons, enrichment programs.

Beauty and fitness Two saunas, two outdoor whirlpools, small gym, exercise classes, beauty salon, spa with massage, beauty treatments.

Other facilities Self-service laundry, laundry and dry cleaning, library with books and video, hospital, cigar lounge, computer center, nondenominational religious services, Internet access.

Children's facilities None; children under age 18 must be accompanied by parent or adult with written permission.

Theme cruises Cuisine, wine, golf, music, and others.

Smoking Dining and public rooms nonsmoking except designated areas in lounges and bars.

Silversea suggested tipping No-tipping policy.

Credit cards For cruise payment and onboard charges: American Express, Diners Club, MasterCard, Visa.

of the new *Silver Spirit*. In spring 2009, *Silver Cloud* got refurbished, but not as extensively as her twin.

Sophisticated and contemporary in style, *Silver Wind* is still warm and inviting with natural cherrywood and russet and golden tones. The addition of an Observation Lounge, the enlarged new spa, beauty salon, and fitness center on the forward section of Deck 9, with floor-to-ceiling windows that wrap

Silver Cloud/Silver Wind	QUALITY 8	VALUE C
REGISTRY Bahamas	LENGTH 514 feet	BEAM 70 feet
CABINS 148	DRAFT 18 feet	SPEED 20.5 knots
MAXIMUM PASSENGERS	PASSENGER DECKS 6	ELEVATORS 4
296	CREW 210	SPACE RATIO 56.8

around the new space, altered the ship's exterior appearance. A new two-floor, glass-enclosed elevator was installed that connects Decks 8 and 9. Other enhancements include new upholstery, curtains, wall treatments, and carpets or flooring in the restaurants, public lounges, lobbies, stairs, and corridors.

The ships' layout is simple. Below the redesigned Deck 9 are the pool and pool bar on Deck 8, which also contains the bridge, twin whirlpools, **Panorama Lounge** with indoor and outdoor seating, **Connoisseur's Corner,** an elegant wine and cigar lounge, plus four new Medallion Suites.

On Decks 4 through 7, all cabins are forward, all public areas aft. Elevators and a circular stairwell are aft of midship. Deck 7 offers the library (on *Silver Cloud*) and **Terrace Café** for informal dining and breakfast and lunch buffets. Deck 6 has the main lobby, travel desk, reception desk, card and conference room, and showroom, which is large enough for small production shows but small enough to be intimate. Deck 5 has a sundries shop, casino, and the Bar, where the showroom audience gathers. The **Library** (on *Silver Wind*) and **Restaurant** are on Deck 4. Public areas are extensive for ships of this size. Dozens of quiet places throughout the ship invite reading or watching the world go by.

ITINERARIES *See* Itinerary Index.

CABINS The spacious, all-outside suites are among the ships' signature features. Suites provide twin beds convertible to a queen, walk-in closet, sitting area with love seat, coffee table and side chairs, writing desk, dressing table with hair dryer, marble bathroom with full-size tub and shower, stocked refrigerator and cocktail bar, entertainment center with satellite interactive television and CD/DVD player, and direct-dial telephone. A curtain separates the sleeping and living areas.

Eighty percent of the suites have private teak verandas; the remainder have picture windows. All suites are decorated in light earth tones or pastel blues with nautical trim of polished wood and brass. Other extras are fine bed linens and robes, down pillows, personalized stationery, fresh fruit, large umbrellas, complimentary shoeshine, and 24-hour room service.

Acqua di Parma, the century-old Italian fragrance house and maker of luxury bath amenities, supplies the in-suite toiletries characterized by natural ingredients, delicate production processes, and meticulous attention to detail; most products are still packaged and bottled by hand. All suites have Sealy Posturepedic Plush Euro-top mattresses; in the top suites—Owner's, Grand, Royal, and Rossellini—there are Stearns & Foster Plush ultra-luxury beds.

During *Silver Wind*'s renovations, the queen beds in larger suites were replaced with convertible twin-to-queen beds, and custom-built television cabinets and flat-panel televisions were added to all Vista and Veranda suites.

Also added were new sofas, armchairs, desks, vanities, night tables, head-boards, and soft furnishings. The bathrooms were updated with new fixtures and bathtubs and new marble countertops, walls, and flooring.

In addition to the four new Medallion Suites on Deck 8, an Owner's Suite with a connecting second-bedroom suite, a Medallion Suite, and a Vista Suite were added on Deck 7.

Specifications All suites: 102 Veranda Suites (295 square feet); 27 Vista Suites (240 square feet, no veranda); 5 Medallion Suites (490–667 square feet); 3 Silver Suites (541 square feet); 1 Rossellini Suite (1,314 square feet with two bedrooms); 2 Royal Suites (1,031 square feet in the two-bedroom configuration); 2 Grand Suites (1,314 square feet with two bedrooms); and 2 Owner's Suites (827 square feet). No singles; 2 wheelchair accessible.

DINING The main dining room, the **Restaurant,** is reminiscent of an exclusive club. Tables are set with Eschenbach china, Christofle silver, linen, and Schott crystal. Draped picture windows flank the elegant room, and a domed center section adds to its spaciousness. A small marble dance floor allows for occasional dinner dances. Although formal, the Restaurant is also comfortable, relaxed, and unpretentious.

Passengers aren't assigned seating times or tables; they may eat any time during published hours. Lunch and breakfast buffets in the Terrace Café provide an informal option. No late-night buffet is offered. Room service is available 24 hours and is delivered with the same attention to detail characteristic of the dining room. Service is outstanding.

Carrying fewer passengers enables Silversea ships to cook dishes to order, as in a restaurant. (However, we have received complaints from some passengers that the kitchen isn't as accommodating as the line claims or as it should be for this price, or as some competitors are.)

Silversea also provides for picky eaters, health-conscious diners, and the meat-and-potatoes set. Only the finest ingredients are used, regardless of how simple or complex the dish. Meat eaters in search of a cruise ship that can prepare a good steak, chop, or prime rib will find nirvana here. There are light and vegetarian entrees too. The dessert menu is separate. Wines are included in the cruise price.

The food is excellent in quality and presentation. Freshness of ingredients is not a problem. One day, returning to ship aboard the tender, we were assaulted by an unexpected smell. Peering around the bulkhead, we discovered a grinning chef with a huge string of fish just purchased from local fishermen—a luxury that could never be provided on a large ship.

The casual **Terrace Café** high on the stern offers a commanding view of the sea. A wall of windows faces the sheltered outside dining area. Tables are always set with china, crystal, and silver. Buffet waiters take orders for drinks and hot entrees. On most evenings the cafe is transformed into **La Terrazza,** offering an à la carte experience with fine Italian cooking. Reservations may be made on board.

Silver Cloud and *Silver Wind* have a **Connoisseur's Corner,** similar to those on *Silver Shadow* and *Silver Whisper.* The Connoiseur's Corner, located on Deck 8 and adjacent to the Panorama Lounge, is a wine and cigar room offering guests a cozy venue where they can relax and settle back into sumptuous leather chairs to enjoy a select vintage or fine cigar.

Saletta, an alternative gourmet dining venue, is one of Silversea's Wine Restaurants by Relais *&* Châteaux and features some of the world's rarest vintages, chosen by Relais *&* Châteaux–trained sommeliers. The fee is about $200 per person to dine, and advance reservations may be made on board.

SERVICE Passengers rate service in a dead heat with accommodations as these twins' best feature. Without exception, the staff is professional and attentive but never intrusive, friendly without being familiar, and thoroughly gracious in the European manner. Working harmoniously, officers and crew form a highly effective and responsive team. A concierge is available for special services. These ships' size lends itself to more personalized service than larger ships can offer. There's no tipping. Period.

FACILITIES AND ACTIVITIES The next day's programs, delivered nightly to your suite, are more mainstream than you might expect on an ultra-luxury cruise, but they prove that even the pampered and sophisticated play bingo! A typical day might include an early power walk with the fitness instructor, a visit to the bridge, a lesson about computers or multimedia, aerobics, wine tasting by the sommelier, a bridge lecture, bingo, backgammon, shuffleboard competition, water volleyball, golf-putting competition, afternoon tea, team trivia, and line-dancing lessons.

Experts lecture on the cruise area, and a folkloric show might be staged by a local group. A morning port talk will include a sales pitch for tours. Doing nothing is an option. In fair weather, you'll probably be on deck, relaxing in a lounge chair or soaking in the Jacuzzi. There are ample places in shade or sheltered from wind. In foul weather, the library stocks books, magazines, periodicals, and videos; it's open around the clock and sports computer terminals with Internet access. Also available are daily printed news and market-wrap reports.

In the evening, there's music for dancing before and after dinner, as well as evening entertainment—a variety show, comedy, and magic. The ship's small orchestra plays easy listening and dance music in the **Bar,** and a pianist or vocalist duo performs in the **Panorama Lounge.** The casino offers roulette, blackjack, slot machines, and gaming lessons. Entertainment in the **Main Lounge** spotlights individual entertainers and production shows by a six-member group. All passengers can be accommodated in the steeply tiered, two-level room. Murals of sinuous women add an Art Deco touch. Most sight lines are good. Late-night diversions consist of audience-participation games, dancing, and piano music in the Panorama Lounge.

SPORTS, FITNESS, AND BEAUTY The Pool Deck has a large swimming pool, plentiful sunbathing space, two whirlpools, and a pool bar. Blue-and-white-striped chair cushions create a nautical atmosphere. The new, enlarged spa, the Spa at Silversea, a beauty salon and fitness center at the top of the ship, commands spectacular panoramic ocean views. Now operated by Steiner, the spa has four massage rooms, one body treatment room, one dry sauna, and one steam sauna, while the new fitness center has a body-building room and separate aerobics room, as well as ample exercise equipment and free weights. One or more daily stretch and exercise classes for various workout levels are offered; individual training is available.

The spa offers a comprehensive program of fitness, beauty, and spa treatments. It uses naturally blended treatments and Balinese techniques, incorporating its signature blend of exotic, traditional, and cutting-edge health and beauty programs, offering such unusual indulgences as a hot lava-rock massage and a Japanese honey steam wrap. Spa treatments can now be booked on Silversea's Web site.

CHILDREN'S FACILITIES Children are rare on Silversea cruises, and no children's facilities or programs are offered.

SHORE EXCURSIONS Shore excursions are administered efficiently on board, and the line has a good batting average with them. Silversea passengers' expectations that excursion operators will provide the same level of service they receive aboard ship may be unrealistic in some regions of the world, no matter how hard the cruise line tries. This problem is, of course, not unique to Silversea; only that the contrast from the ship to the land operation is sometimes sharper.

Excursion sales are low-key, and some cruise directors do an excellent job of matching passengers with the tours most suited to their tastes. Even off-the-shelf motor coach tours tend to be pricey. Shore excursions can now be booked online. Many cruises include one Silversea Experience, a special shore excursion showcasing an area's culture. This may be a private tour or dinner in an extraordinary location. For example, the line has hosted wine tastings at a private château and dinner at a palace in St. Petersburg, Russia.

THE SHIPS *Silver Shadow*, launched in 2000, was followed by her twin, *Silver Whisper*, in 2001. The noted Norwegian architectural team of Petter Yran and Bjorn Storbraaten, designers of *Silver Cloud* and *Silver Wind*, created the ships, which are slightly larger and accommodate 100 more passengers than the line's first ships. Otherwise, they are similar, more or less, to their sister ships in layout and contemporary decor. Throughout the ships, mellow wood furnishings and fine fabrics combine with marble floors and crystal chandeliers to create an elegant, stylish setting. Their passenger space ratio of 73.9 may be the highest of any cruise ship.

Silversea's hallmarks—Veranda Suites, open-seating dining, in-suite dining, Christofle silverware, fine linens, down pillows—are found aboard these ships. Among the new features were a casual poolside dining venue, a computer center, and a conference center. The ships also have an observation lounge, show lounge, boutique, a larger spa, swimming pool, and whirlpools.

ITINERARIES *See* Itinerary Index.

Silver Shadow	**QUALITY 8**	**VALUE C**
Silver Whisper	**QUALITY 8**	**VALUE C**
REGISTRY Bahamas	LENGTH 610 feet	BEAM 82 feet
CABINS 194	DRAFT 19.6 feet	SPEED 21 knots
MAXIMUM PASSENGERS	PASSENGER DECKS 7	ELEVATORS 5
382	CREW 295	SPACE RATIO 73.9

CABINS More than 80% of the suites have teak verandas. A standard Veranda Suite measures a spacious 345 square feet, including veranda. The smallest cabins measure 287 square feet. All cabins have a walk-in closet and large Italian marble bathroom with telephone, double-basin vanity, full bath and shower, and separate toilet, and are equipped with small refrigerators and cocktail bar, entertainment center with interactive television and CD/DVD player, and fresh fruit and flowers.

The largest suites are 701–1,435 square feet and include the Owner's, Grand, and Royal suites in six variations. They have enlarged balconies, separate bedrooms and living rooms, large-screen televisions, and private bars. Owner's Suites also have a guest powder room and CD stereo system. Two Medallion Suites, 501 square feet each, are extremely comfortable, with enough storage space for a family of five.

All suites have Sealy Posturepedic Plush Euro-top mattresses, and the top suites—Owner's, Grand, Royal, and Rossellini—have Stearns & Foster Plush ultra-luxury mattresses.

Room service, available 24 hours a day, offers a full menu. Passengers can order from the Restaurant's menu and have their meal served course by course in their staterooms. Self-service laundry facilities are available.

Specifications: 186 outside suites; 2 Owner's Suites (1,264 square feet with two bedrooms); 3 Grand Suites (1,286–1,435 square feet with two bedrooms); 13 Silver Suites (653–701 square feet); 2 Medallion Suites (521 square feet); 128 Veranda Suites (345 square feet); 35 Vista Suites (287 square feet, no veranda); 2 Royal Suites (1,312–1,352 square feet); 1 Rossellini Suite (1,286–1,435 square feet with two bedrooms); 2 wheelchair accessible with verandas.

DINING The **Restaurant,** the main dining room, has an elegant ambience with tables set with fine linens and Christofle silverware. It offers open seating and a variety of table configurations for two to six people. The popular bistro-style **Terrace Café,** with floor-to-ceiling windows opening onto panoramic views off the ship's aft deck, serves buffet breakfast and lunch and makes a charming setting in the evening, when it is transformed into La Terrazza, serving Italian fare with fresh and flavorful ingredients.

Another dining alternative is the gourmet restaurant, **Le Champagne,** one of Silversea's Wine Restaurants by Relais & Châteaux, which features some of the world's rarest vintages, chosen by Relais & Châteaux–trained sommeliers to highlight the culinary experience. The fee is about $200 per person to dine, and advance reservations may be made on board.

FACILITIES AND ACTIVITIES The **Humidor,** an elegant wine and cigar bar, adjoins Le Champagne. Designed in the style of a traditional English smoking club with rich wood floors and deep galley chairs, it has a walk-in humidor stocked with Davidoff products, a Swiss-based purveyor of fine cigars and luxury merchandise, and a selection of Dominican, Honduran, and Cuban cigars. The lounge seats 25 and offers complimentary Cognacs and cordials, along with cigars.

Of the ship's four bars, the **Casino Bar,** a small nook adjoining the casino, seems to be the most popular. Simply furnished with a semicircular cherry-wood bar with ebony leather stools, it has two small leather sofas and modern-style halogen lamps and fixtures.

The ships have a shopping arcade, a library with books in various languages, videos, and seven computer terminals with Internet access. Silversea has an unusual way of charging for their use: The $0.75 per minute is charged only for as long as it takes a Web page to download and come into view. The charges then stop until another Web page is requested.

SERVICE These ships do not have as high a crew-to-passenger ratio as the smaller twins; nonetheless, they continue to receive high marks for service.

SPORTS, FITNESS, AND BEAUTY The ships have large health clubs and spas that occupy most of Deck 10. Decorated in a soothing combination of aqua and blue tiles and blonde carpets, the facility has a beauty salon and an aerobic and fitness center with weights, treadmills, stationary bikes, and other equipment. There are separate steam rooms, saunas, and changing facilities for men and women. The ships also have a heated outdoor pool and two whirlpools.

In 2007, Silversea Cruises launched a new spa concept fleetwide, starting with *Silver Shadow*. Dubbed The Spa at Silversea, it replaced Mandara spas and features new treatments and ceremonies designed to offer passengers a more personalized and holistic spa experience. The Spa has been refurbished with new artwork and contemporary furnishings. The program, part of the line's Wellness Program, offers cutting-edge body-age assessment technology that gauges body fat, cardiovascular health, strength, and flexibility to see how one's body age compares with his or her actual chronological age. Based on the results, The Spa's personal trainers design a lifestyle program for a participant and recommend a fitness regimen as well as dining options developed specifically for the Wellness Program. The program is available also for men and for couples. Elemis aromatherapy products are used, and the facility is operated by Steiner.

On many cruises, the Silver Links golf program provides the opportunity for passengers to improve their game with the help of an onboard PGA-class golf professional. The program also offers golf excursions, arranged and escorted by the ships' golf pros, to such challenging courses as Shanghai's Silport Golf Club.

THE SHIP Although she is twice the size of the first Silversea twins and a third larger than the second duet, *Silver Spirit* has the same elegant, soothing style and is the last word in ultimate luxury. The ship has an expansion of the *Silver Whisper* and *Silver Shadow* profile, with new features, larger suites than any other Silversea ship, six restaurants, as well as several new dining concepts, and the largest spa of the Silversea fleet. All of *Silver Spirit*'s accommodations are outside suites, and all but 12 of the 270 suites have verandas.

The layout of the spacious ship is easy to follow, with all accommodations forward and public rooms aft on all the passenger decks. Three of the six restaurants are on Deck 4; the main lobby with the reception desk, travel desk, conference room, and showroom are on Deck 5; the spa and fitness center on Deck 6; another restaurant, supper club, card room, and library/Internet cafe on Deck 7; the casino, shops, and The Humidor on Deck 8; the pool and two whirlpools, pool grill, and Panorama Lounge on Deck 9; and the Observation Lounge on Deck 11, the top deck. Dozens of quiet places throughout the ship invite reading or watching the world go by.

ITINERARIES *See* Itinerary Index. In late January 2010, *Silver Spirit* departed

Silver Spirit	PREVIEW	
REGISTRY Bahamas	LENGTH 642 feet	BEAM 86 feet
CABINS 270	DRAFT 20.3 feet	SPEED 20.3 knots
MAXIMUM PASSENGERS	PASSENGER DECKS 8	ELEVATORS NA
608	CREW 376	SPACE RATIO 67

from Fort Lauderdale on her maiden 91-day world cruise.

CABINS Accommodations on the all-suite *Silver Spirit* are the largest in the Silversea fleet, and 95 suites have floor-to-ceiling glass doors leading to a private teak veranda with patio furniture. All suites have a separate sitting area, a walk-in closet with personal safe, writing desk, telephone, flat-panel television with DVD, and a marbled bathroom with a double vanity with hair dryer, full-size tub, and separate shower. They are furnished with twin beds or queen-size beds, fresh fruit and flowers, a beverage cabinet stocked to your preference, European bath amenities, fine bed linens and your pillow choice, plush robes and slippers, personalized stationery, and a daily news summary. Pommery Champagne awaits your arrival, and with Silversea's in-suite dining option, you can enjoy breakfast in bed, a late lunch, or a romantic dinner served course by course. Room service is available 24 hours. The suites are attended by stewardesses or butlers with twice-daily service plus turndown nightly.

Vista Suites, the smallest of the accommodations, have a large picture window (no veranda). The slightly bigger Veranda and Midship Veranda suites, the largest category, have floor-to-ceiling glass doors that open onto a teak veranda with patio furniture. Some Vista, Veranda, and Midship Veranda suites accommodate three persons. The considerably larger Silver Suites have a living room with a convertible sofa to accommodate an additional person, sitting and dining area, CD player, and complimentary laundry service (not dry cleaning or press only).

The Grand Suites, which have two teak verandas, are available as a one-bedroom suite or as two bedrooms by adjoining it with a Veranda Suite. The Grand Suite has a living room with sitting area (the two-bedroom unit has an additional sitting area) and a separate dining area; the marbled bathroom has a full-size Jacuzzi as well as a double vanity and separate shower (the two-bedroom suite has an additional full bathroom). The largest accommodations are the two Owner's Suites, also available as a one-bedroom suite or as two bedrooms by adjoining it with a Vista Suite. Each Owner's Suite has a large teak veranda, living room with sitting area (the two-bedroom unit has an additional sitting area), CD player, separate dining area, marbled bathroom with Jacuzzi, and a powder room. The Grand and Owner's suites have butler service, laundry service, and a daily newspaper of your choice.

Specifications: 12 Vista Suites (312 square feet); 50 Veranda and 166 Midship Veranda Suites (376 square feet, veranda 65 square feet); 26 Silver Suites (742 square feet, veranda 118 square feet); 6 Grand Suites, one bedroom (990 square feet, veranda 125 square feet), two bedroom (1,302 square feet, veranda 190 square feet); 2 Owner's Suites, one bedroom (1,292 square feet, veranda 190 square feet); two bedrooms

(1,668 square feet, veranda 190 square feet). 16 suites are connecting; 4 wheelchair accessible.

DINING *Silver Spirit* offers a choice of six dining venues—**The Restaurant, La Terrazza, Le Champagne, Seishin Restaurant, Stars Supper Club,** and **Pool Grill**—that live up to Silversea's reputation as an innovator in the luxury segment. All venues have open seating. An extensive selection of fine wines, Champagne, spirits, bottled water, and soft drinks are served throughout the ship at no additional charge.

The ambience of The Restaurant, the main dining room on Deck 4, can be described as sophisticated elegance, yet comfortable and unpretentious. Contemporary international cuisine is served for breakfast, lunch, and dinner with exclusive menus by Relais & Châteaux. Silversea's partnership with the Grands Chefs Relais & Châteaux provides a signature series of innovative dishes, "La Collection du Monde," featured nightly in The Restaurant. Like its sister ships, tables are set with Eschenbach china, Christofle silver, linen, and Schott crystal. The 24-hour room service provides selections from The Restaurant menu served course by course.

La Terrazza, at the stern on Deck 7, provides 180-degree views of the seascape. It is open for casual, buffet-style breakfast and lunch with indoor/ outdoor seating available. For dinner, La Terrazza becomes an à la carte eatery for fine Italian cooking. Reservations are required for dinner.

Le Champagne, situated aft of The Restaurant on Deck 4, provides an intimate atmosphere where guests can savor Champagne and wines paired in a tasting menu with regionally inspired gourmet fare. This innovative wine restaurant by Relais & Châteaux, its only one at sea, offers some of the world's rarest vintages, carefully chosen to make the culinary experience memorable. There is a fee to dine; reservations may be made on board.

Seishin Restaurant, located aft of The Restaurant on Deck 4, is one of the new dining concepts for Silversea. Taking its name from the Japanese word for "spirit," this intimate, stylish restaurant specializing in Asian fusion cuisine, has a large, round chef's table as its centerpiece. Patrons at surrounding tables can watch the chef at work preparing fresh sushi and sashimi. The varied menu ranges from *bento* (boxed meal) lunches and à la carte Asian seafood specialties to lobster, Kobe beef, and a nine-course degustation dinner. There is a fee to dine; reservations may be made on board.

Stars Supper Club, located forward of La Terrazza on Deck 7, is another new nightly dining concept for Silverseas. The warm and inviting Art Deco–inspired decor of this restaurant is meant to recall the supper clubs of the 1930s, but Stars offers a modern twist with trendy menus of regional and seasonal selections to be enjoyed in a succession of small courses. Evenings start early with cocktails and go late as the venue's mood is transformed by live music, dancing, and nightclub-style entertainment. Reservations are required for dinner.

The Pool Grill, on Deck 9 adjacent to the pool area, is a casual outdoor venue for lunch, offering grilled meats and fresh-from-the-oven pizzas, sandwiches, salads, hamburgers, and hot dogs. The Pool Grill on *Silver Spirit* introduced a wellness breakfast designed to complement morning poolside fitness classes. It serves such nutrition-packed selections as fresh fruit smoothies, organic cereals, egg-white omelets, and spinach and artichoke frittatas. For dinner, the Pool Grill introduced an unusual cooking concept that lets guests cook healthy fare on their own heated volcanic-rock plate.

FACILITIES AND ACTIVITIES Like other Silversea ships, *Silver Spirit* offers an enrichment program led by destination specialists, authorities on world affairs, famous authors, celebrity chefs, wine experts, and other knowledgeable staff. The well-stocked library and Internet cafe on Deck 7 neighbor the card room where there's likely to be a bridge game in progress. When you are ready to splurge, there are opportunities aplenty one deck up in the three shops with designer collections. Perhaps you prefer a quiet place to watch the sunset in the Observation Lounge, high atop the ship. In the evening, you can try your luck in the casino, take in a show at the show lounge, or relax with an after-dinner Cognac and fine cigar in The Humidor. You might choose to whirl around the dance floor in the Panorama Lounge or stroll on deck to take in the starry sky and the evening breeze. Some nights, there might be movies on deck or a show of traditional dances by local folkloric troupes.

SPORTS, FITNESS, AND BEAUTY The Pool Deck has a large swimming pool (heated for cooler weather), two whirlpools, and a pool bar with plenty of teak lounging and sunbathing space and attentive service. The **Spa at Silversea** on Deck 6 makes it easy to relax and rejuvenate from head to toe with a wide range of facials, body wraps, massages, and an exclusive selection of innovative treatments. The Spa features floor-to-ceiling windows and has nine treatment rooms, indoor/outdoor relaxation areas, sauna, steam rooms, and an outdoor whirlpool.

The Fitness Center has two aerobics studios and the latest cardio, strength, and weight-training equipment, including a Kinesis Wall that provides an innovative way to increase flexibility, strength, and balance through zero-impact resistance exercises. Daily sessions for aerobics, yoga, Pilates, and circuit training are led by an onboard fitness trainer. Special classes, private fitness instruction, and personalized fitness sessions are also available. Spa treatments can be booked on Silversea's Web site.

THE SHIP Silversea's new expedition ship, which made her debut in 2008, set a new level of luxury for expedition cruising. Originally acquired as *World Discoverer II*, she was renamed *HSH Prince Albert II*, in tribute to Prince Albert of Monaco—an appropriate name for a ship dedicated to worldwide exploration and conservation of the ocean, wildlife, and indigenous cultures. Monaco, in addition to being Silversea's headquarters and the home base of renowned marine explorer Jacques Cousteau, has long been a leader in marine research. In the early 1900s, Prince Albert I pioneered oceanographic science, founded the renowned Oceanographic Institute, and explored the Svalbard archipelago. In 2006, Prince Albert II, who christened his namesake in Monaco in June 2008, made a similar voyage to the North Pole to add to the scientific work started by his ancestor and to draw attention to the impact of global warming on the Arctic region. At the same time, the prince became the first incumbent head of state to reach the Earth's northernmost point.

Prior to entering service, the A1A ice-rated ship underwent extensive renovation at the Fincantieri shipyard in Italy to bring her up to Silversea's luxury standard. The refurbishment included a comprehensive upgrade of all accommodations and public rooms, as well as exterior design modifications

Prince Albert II	**PREVIEW**	
REGISTRY Bahamas	**LENGTH** 354 feet	**BEAM** 52 feet
CABINS 66	**DRAFT** 14 feet	**SPEED** 14 knots
MAXIMUM PASSENGERS	**PASSENGER DECKS** 5	**ELEVATORS** 2
132	**CREW** 111	**SPACE RATIO** NA

and technical enhancements. The ship is outfitted with eight, latest-model Zodiacs with the lowest possible emissions for up-close exploration and access to remote areas.

Prince Albert II offers the best of all possible worlds: adventure on a genuine expedition ship in the comfort of a luxury ship, plus an intellectually enriching experience from an expedition team of natural, cultural, and historical experts who share their knowledge and insights. Heading the program is Conrad Combrink, who was expedition leader on *World Discoverer I* and *II*. As director of expeditions for *Prince Albert II*, he is responsible for developing the ship's itinerary and recruiting expedition staff and lecturers.

ITINERARIES *See* Itinerary Index. *Prince Albert II*'s varied itineraries with much to explore make it possible to sail for up to 48 days on back-to-back voyages without repeating a Zodiac landing site.

CABINS Despite her small size, *Prince Albert II* claims to have the largest average size of accommodations of any expedition ship. They range from 175 to 675 square feet, with 18 premium suites measuring more than 400 square feet. All 66 cabins and suites have ocean views and offer spacious living areas in tasteful luxury, marble bathrooms with bathtubs, and butler service. Most suites have French balconies or verandas, while the largest suites have double French balconies or large verandas.

Accommodations are furnished with convertible twin-to-queen beds; sitting areas and writing desks; direct-dial telephones; safes; flat-panel televisions with DVD players, satellite news reception, music channels, and on-demand movies; Wi-Fi and cell phone service; fitted or walk-in closets; pillow menus; plush robes and slippers; hair dryers; Bvlgari or Neutrogena bath toiletries; personalized stationery; expedition binoculars; stocked beverage cabinets; 220 volt/60 Hz AC electric current; and Pommery Champagne upon arrival. Grand and Owner's suites have complimentary laundry service.

Specifications: 6 Adventurer-Class cabins (175–184 square feet); 4 Explorer-Class cabins (185–275 square feet). Suites: 12 View (230 square feet); 16 Vista (194–230 square feet); 8 Veranda (230 square feet with French balcony, 15 square feet); 4 Expedition (460 square feet); 2 Medallion (351 square feet, veranda 86 square feet); 4 Discoverer (460 square feet); 6 Silver (460 square feet, two French balconies 30 square feet); 2 Grand Suites (675 square feet, veranda 87 square feet); 2 Owner's (626 square feet).

DINING AND FACILITIES Passengers enjoy many amenities found on the larger ships, such as The Restaurant (Deck 4), the single-seating main dining room serving buffet breakfast and lunch and à la carte dinner, and Outdoor Grill (Deck 6), which offers a fitness breakfast, lunch, and bar service. The Panorama Lounge on Deck 5 aft—a cozy lounge spot for a smoke and a Cognac—is next door to Connoisseur's Corner and is similar to The Humidor found on the line's other ships. Also on Deck 5 is the well-stocked library and Internet cafe with four computer stations with Internet access. In the ship's lounges, the latest audiovisual equipment, complete with high-definition video screens, displays live lectures hosted by the ship's expedition staff and visiting destination experts.

The Observation Lounge, forward, shares Deck 6 with The Theater, midship, as well as a small spa with a massage room and sauna/steam room. The ship does not have a swimming pool, but it does have two whirlpools. There's a boutique, beauty salon, launderette, and fitness center with an elliptical stepper, treadmill, stationary bike, and multi-exerciser.

Star Clippers, Inc.

7200 NW 19th Street, Suite #206
Miami, FL 33126
☎ 800-442-0551 or 305-442-0550
FAX 305-442-1611
www.starclippers.com

TYPE OF SHIPS Replicas of 19th-century clipper sailing ships.

TYPE OF CRUISES Casual, active, sports-oriented, sailing under canvas to out-of-the-way places.

CRUISE LINE'S STRENGTHS
- traditional sailing with some cruise-ship comforts
- camaraderie
- ship size/maneuverability
- itineraries

CRUISE LINE'S SHORTCOMINGS
- meager port information
- potential language/cultural collisions among passengers
- small cabins

FELLOW PASSENGERS International mix. About half are American, Canadian, and Latin American; the other half are European, particularly Germans, including non-English speakers. Average age is 45, but some cruises have 20- and 30-year-olds. The majority are couples, usually including about a dozen newlyweds.

As many as 50% may be repeaters, attracted by sailing on a square-rigger. Many appreciate the beauty and authenticity of the clipper ships and have no interest in the nightclubs, casinos, and glitter aboard mainstream cruise ships, which they probably have shunned.

Recommended for Independent, active travelers who seek light adventure and off-the-beaten-track itineraries, small-ship devotees, stressed-out urbanites, honeymooners and romantics captivated by the notion of sailing on a tall ship. Also, avid sailors, water sports enthusiasts, experienced cruisers weary of crowded large ships, and conservationists who appreciate environmentally friendly travel aboard ships that use their engines only when necessary. It's a great experience for children ages 7 and older who mix well with adults.

Not recommended for Those seeking gourmet cuisine, pampering, around-the-clock activity, and resort facilities of a superliner. Physically impaired travelers.

CRUISE AREAS AND SEASONS Caribbean, Costa Rica, winter; Mediterranean, summer; transatlantic, April and October.

THE LINE Launched in 1991, Star Clippers was the dream come true of Swedish shipping entrepreneur Mikael Krafft, whose passion for sailing and building yachts and love of the clipper ship (one of America's greatest inventions, he says) led him to create an unusual cruise line with replicas of the sleek, mid-19th-century trading ships. Called greyhounds of the sea, they were the fastest ships afloat until the arrival of the steam age in the late 1860s.

About 100 feet longer than the original clippers and equipped with the latest marine technology, these clippers combine the romance of yesteryear's sailing with some modern amenities. They offer the excitement of manning an authentic square-rigger and cruising out-of-the-way waters of the Caribbean, Mediterranean, or South Asia.

The success of Star Clippers' twins led the line to build a third ship, which is reported to be the world's largest sailing vessel. She entered service in July 2000.

For 2010, Star Clippers has many new itineraries and will visit 40 ports for the first time, including Myanmar and Turkey's Turquoise Coast, as well as offer new round-trip Monte Carlo itineraries. After *Star Flyer* sailed in French Polynesia for two years, she is repositioning to the Mediterranean in spring 2010 for the summer months and then to Costa Rica for its inaugural season in that region.

In addition to its own Web site, Star Clippers can be found online at **www .starclippersblog.com,** Twitter, and Facebook.

STYLE Cruises have the freewheeling spirit of a private yacht and are intended to fit between budget-priced Windjammer cruises and pricey Windstar Cruises. They're designed for active, healthy folks who want their travel to be interesting, educational, and fun. Daytime dress is very casual (shorts and deck shoes); evenings are only a bit dressier. Cabins are of average size and public rooms few, but the teak decks are roomy.

Cruises offer island hopping in a laid-back atmosphere with varied options at each port of call. The clippers can anchor in bays where large cruise ships cannot go. Launches take passengers to isolated beaches and places for scuba diving, snorkeling, and other water sports.

After a week's cruise, you will know many passengers on a first-name basis and most of the crew, who are both deckhands and sports instructors. You can help hoist the sails or laze about on deck watching the canvas and the sea. Itineraries ensure daylight cruising under sail. The environment is great for families with children ages 7 and up.

In 2010, from spring to autumn, Star Clippers' fleet will offer its Signature Collection Host Series that includes distinguished experts in the culinary arts, wine, photography, and writing. Among the hosts are top chocolate artisan Fran Bigelow of Fran's Chocolates; winemakers Jay Schuppert of Cuvaison Estate Wines and Eric Dunham of Dunham Cellars; San Francisco–area restaurateur, author, national radio and television personality Narsai David;

THE FLEET	BUILT/RENOVATED	TONNAGE	PASSENGERS
Royal Clipper	2000	5,000	227
Star Clipper	1991	2,298	170
Star Flyer	1992	2,298	170

photographer Roger Paperno; author Joe Wolff of the *Cafe Life* series; restaurateurs Chef Don Curtiss and Michelle Quisenberry of Seattle's Volterra restaurant; and Chef Keith Luce of Northwest restaurant The Herbfarm.

DISTINCTIVE FEATURES The ship and helping sail it; captain's daily briefings; PADI certification for those interested in scuba diving.

RATES Port charges are additional.

Special fares and discounts 10% discount on published rates for booking 120 days in advance on selected cruises.

- **SINGLE FARE:** Guaranteed rate, depending on season, with cabin assigned two weeks before departure.
- **SINGLE SUPPLEMENT:** 150% for categories 2 through 6 (selected seasons) of published fare. 200% for highest-category cabins, deluxe suites, and Owner's Suites.

PAST PASSENGERS Members receive special discounts and a bottle of Champagne in their cabins on boarding and are placed on the ship's VIP list.

THE LAST WORD Star Clippers provides an unusual experience on unique ships that are modern and comfortable yet steeped in tradition. More affordable than Sea Cloud and more upscale than Windjammers, Star Clippers' ships are more authentic than those of Windstar. Yet they definitely aren't for everyone.

The ships cannot readily accommodate disabled passengers and aren't for people who want mainstream cruising's comforts and options. English is the ships' language, but announcements are likely to be in other languages, depending on passenger makeup. Language can become a problem when English speakers are outnumbered by non-Anglophones, and some may feel left out of activities. Onboard charges are in euros.

THE SHIPS *Star Clipper* and *Star Flyer* are identical, with four masts and square-rigged sails on the forward mast—a barkentine configuration—with a total of 16 sails (36,000 square feet of Dacron). They are manned, not computerized, and are capable of attaining speeds up to 19 knots. A diesel engine is in reserve for calms and maneuvering in harbors.

At 226 feet, they are among the tallest ships (the cruise line says *Royal Clipper* is the tallest) and the first true sailing vessels to be classified by Lloyd's Register of Shipping since 1911. Built in Belgium, they comply with the latest safety regulations for passenger vessels on worldwide service.

The ships have four passenger decks; all but eight cabins are on the lower two. Public spaces are on the top two decks. There, amid sails and rigging,

Star Clipper/Star Flyer	**QUALITY 7**	**VALUE A**
REGISTRY Luxembourg	LENGTH 360 feet	BEAM 50 feet
CABINS 85	DRAFT 18.5 feet	SPEED 17 knots
MAXIMUM PASSENGERS	PASSENGER DECKS 4	ELEVATORS None
170	CREW 72	SPACE RATIO 15

Star Clippers Standard Features

Officers European.

Staff *Dining, Cabin:* international; *Cruise:* Swedish, Australian, and Hungarian.

Dining facilities One dining room for three meals with open, unassigned seating. Light breakfast, occasional buffet lunch, hors d'oeuvres on deck at 5 p.m.

Special diets Inquire in advance. Vegetarian, low-calorie standard on menus.

Room service Only for top suites on *Royal Clipper.*

Dress code Relaxed and casual. Walking shorts, bathing attire with cover-up, skirts, slacks for daytime; slacks with polo or casual shirts, no jackets required for men in evening.

Cabin amenities DVD players, radio, hair dryer, safe, cellular-satellite phone, movies, ports-of-call videos and music, bathrooms with showers, upper category with whirlpool bath and minifridge.

Electrical outlets *Star Clipper/Flyer,* 110 AC; *Royal Clipper,* 220 AC, American adapter needed.

Wheelchair access None.

Recreation and entertainment Piano bar with entertainer, outdoor deck bar for dancing and local entertainment, library/writing room, backgammon, and bridge.

Sports and other activities Two small outdoor pools, water sports and equipment, sailing dinghies, windsurfers, waterskiing, underwater viewing craft, water-jet launches, and inflatables carried on board. Learn-to-sail and dive programs.

Beauty and fitness No beauty/barber service on *Star Clipper/Flyer;* spa, hair salon, gym on *Royal Clipper.* Exercise sessions.

Other facilities Dining room doubles as conference room with audiovisual equipment. Nurse on cruises; doctor and nurse on transatlantic. Ship's officers trained in emergency medicine.

Children's facilities None; younger than age 18 must be accompanied by adult.

Theme cruises None.

Smoking No smoking in cabins. At first briefing, captain emphasizes that smoking is allowed on deck or in rear of dining room.

Star Clippers suggested tipping $8 per person per day; 15% added to bar bills.

Credit cards For cruise payment and onboard charges: American Express, MasterCard, and Visa.

every Walter Mitty begins to salivate with anticipation. They can help hoist the sails or watch in wonder. The ships are generally under sail from late evening to the following midmorning. Under normal conditions, they use the engine only to maneuver in port. For true salts and romantics, balmy tropical air filling the white sails against a star-filled sky is the essence of bliss. Many stay up half the night savoring it.

ITINERARIES *See* Itinerary Index.

CABINS Small but comfortable, cabins are carpeted, air-conditioned, and tastefully furnished with a counter/desk and built-in seat, large mirror, wood paneling, brass lamps, and prints of sailing scenes. Two portholes admit light. Under-bed storage holds luggage or scuba gear, and closet and drawer space is adequate for informal cruising.

Most cabins are outside and have twin beds convertible to a double. They have multichannel radio, phone, DVD players, hair dryer, safe, ceiling-mounted television/video monitor (DVDs are available from the library in English and German), and 24-hour news prepared in British English, American English, Canadian English, and German. Each version includes news of interest to that group.

Bathrooms are very small. They have marble-trimmed fixtures and showers. Eight top-category cabins have a whirlpool bathtub, hair dryer, and minifridge stocked at cruise's start (occupants pay for restocks). These cabins open onto the deck; some people may feel that decreases their privacy. Cabin service is limited to cleaning. Aft cabins on lower decks are the least desirable due to engine noise.

Specifications 6 inside cabins, 78 outside; 1 suite. Standard dimensions, 120 square feet. 66 cabins with 2 lower beds (convertible to queen); 18 cabins with fixed double beds; 12 cabins accommodate third passenger; 6 inside cabins have uppers and lowers; no singles.

DINING The **Clipper Dining Room,** resplendent with shining brass and etched glass, is rather formal for such an informal ship. Seating is at tables for six among or around a forest of columns, and banquettes line the walls by portholes. All passengers and officers are accommodated at one open seating. When the ship is full, the room is crowded.

The buffet breakfast has made-to-order omelets; lunch has a different pasta daily and a self-service salad bar. A light early-morning breakfast and occasional lunch buffet are also served on deck.

Dinner selections include beef, chicken, and fish, vegetables, cheeses, and desserts. The food is plentiful but appeals mostly to those with minimal interest in epicurean delights. During a week, food can range from adequate to good, but not gourmet. The menu emphasizes fresh ingredients, fruit, salads, vegetables, and seafood. Wines are available at reasonable prices.

SERVICE Officers and deck crew are friendly, energetic, and easygoing. They mix freely and easily with passengers, helping create the ship's relaxed atmosphere. The dining and hotel staff is low-key and congenial. An easy camaraderie among officers, staff, and passengers is part of the ships' appeal.

FACILITIES AND ACTIVITIES Passengers might be found playing backgammon or bridge. The teak-paneled library/writing room resembles an English club, with large brass-framed windows, paintings of nautical scenes, and a non-working fireplace (snuffed out by the U.S. Coast Guard). Furnished with card tables and comfortable chairs, it's a reception desk at boarding and a small meeting room. A good selection of popular fiction, travel, and coffee-table books is stocked. A tiny shop sells film and souvenirs. The dining room converts to a meeting room with screen projectors and video monitors for port lectures. The captain and cruise director hold "story time," an informal briefing, on deck in late afternoon or the morning before arriving in port. Passengers congregate around the open bridge, where they can hear the captain and his mates at work and watch the sails being raised and lowered. Many lend a hand with the rigging, but few hang in for the full cruise.

A small, U-shaped piano lounge wraps the landing of the stairway between the Main Deck and dining room. It has brass-framed panoramic windows and small tables with cushioned banquettes that seat about two dozen people. The skylight overhead is actually the transparent bottom of a pool on the Sun Deck. A pianist or vocalist entertains before and after dinner. Swinging doors connect to the outdoor **Tropical Bar.** Depending on the hour, it's a social center, meeting area, stage (where the captain speaks daily), spot for light breakfast or buffet lunch, or dance floor (taped music or electronic keyboard). There's no casino.

SPORTS, FITNESS, AND BEAUTY There are two tiny outdoor pools, one filled with freshwater and one with seawater. Beginning scuba lessons are offered at the forward pool.

Exercisers can walk from the stern to the bow around the open parts of the Main and Sun decks. At 8 a.m. daily, one of the water sports teams leads a half-hour aerobics session.

In the Caribbean and South Asia, water sports are a more important element of the cruise than in the Mediterranean. The ships carry sailing dinghies, windsurfers, underwater viewing craft, boats for waterskiing and skis, snorkel gear (issued for cruise duration), scuba equipment for certified divers, volleyballs, and oversize, solid-surface Kadima paddles for beach sports. The ships might anchor in a remote cove or off a deserted beach and shuttle passengers to and from shore for snorkeling, sailing, windsurfing, and swimming.

The sports and recreational staff includes multilingual instructors. Snorkeling is organized almost daily in the Caribbean. Certified divers with C cards can join trips to reefs and underwater wrecks. A charge of €65 covers air tank refill, personal supervision, and transport by Zodiac.

Three dive programs are available: Discover Scuba Diving is open to all guests over the age of 12 and costs €96; PADI Open Water Dive Course, a full PADI certification course, costs €410. For the latter, the line requires that divers spread the course over a two-week cruise. Guests can also earn an Advanced Open Water Dive Certificate for €310.

SHORE EXCURSIONS Guided tours (usually $25–$85) focus on a destination's architectural, historical, and environmental points of interest and are likely to be more interesting than those offered by mainstream ships. Fewer passengers and unusual itineraries ensure stimulating, personalized tours for participants.

The ships tie up in port as seldom as possible. Patented stabilizing tanks keep the ship steady at anchor. Tender service is offered every half hour until sailing time, usually around 6 p.m.

Royal Clipper	QUALITY **9**	VALUE **A**
REGISTRY Luxembourg	LENGTH 439 feet	BEAM 54 feet
CABINS 114	DRAFT 18.5 feet	SPEED 20 knots
MAXIMUM PASSENGERS	PASSENGER DECKS 5	ELEVATORS None
227	CREW 106	SPACE RATIO NA

THE SHIP *Royal Clipper* made her debut in 2000 as the longest, largest sailing vessel ever built. Her gross tonnage of about 5,000 tons is more than twice that of *Star Clipper* or *Star Flyer*. Her appearance contrasts sharply with her running mates, which resemble large white-hull racing yachts. *Royal Clipper* is a full-rigged ship, with square sails on all five masts; the earlier four-masters are barkentine-rigged. *Royal Clipper* carries 56,000 square feet of Dacron sail, compared with 36,000 square feet on each of the small twins.

The vessel's interior, created by noted megayacht interior designer Donald Starkey of London, is more upscale than her sisters and has many new features. One of her three outdoor swimming pools—an oval center pool— has a glass bottom, which allows light into the three-deck atrium below. A circular staircase links the atrium with lounges, cabins, and public rooms. **Captain Nemo's Lounge,** on the lowest passenger deck, has 16-inch portholes looking out on marine life day and night.

On the Main Deck below the bridge is an observation lounge with wrap-around windows; it is used for meetings, informal talks, and Internet connections. The Main Deck also has the purser's office, a large piano lounge, an indoor/outdoor bar, and library.

The main lounge, located midship, is as comfortable as they come, with banquette, soft couch, and chair seating. It has a sit-up bar and a central well that looks down into the dining room two decks below. Leaving via the aft doors, the covered **Tropical Bar** recalls the earlier *Star Clipper* pair; so, too, does the paneled Edwardian library, though aboard *Royal Clipper* both rooms are on a much larger scale.

When there is no wind, the twin Caterpillar 2,500-horsepower diesel engines can drive the ship at up to 14 knots. When maneuvering in and out of port, the captain may put up most of the sails, then use a very quiet generator to turn the ship and drive it forward to leave the harbor.

ITINERARIES *See* Itinerary Index.

CABINS Standard cabins, each with 148 square feet, are 35% larger than those on sister ships; 32 have a third fold-down bed. There are two deck cabins of 125 square feet and six inside cabins of 100 square feet. The cabins are furnished in much the same style and vary mostly by location. They have marble bathrooms with shower, television, satellite telephone, radio channels, private safe, and hair dryers.

Outstanding deluxe suites are located along a narrow, central, mahogany-paneled companionway with a thick, sloping mast penetrating the corridor at the forward end. These luxurious cabins, measuring 215 square feet, are mahogany-paneled with rosewood framing and molding against an off-white ceiling and upper portion walls. Pale gold-framed mirrors enlarge the space, and brass-framed windows bring in light to bathe the far corner-sitting alcove. Brass wall lamps and sailing-ship prints round out the feel of an upward sloping ship's cabin, not a hotel-style room on a hull. One door opens to a huge marble bathroom with Jacuzzi bath—a nod to upscale cruise ship amenities. Another heavy wooden door leads to a private teak veranda with shrouds passing upward from the ship's side.

The two Owner's Suites at the stern are even larger at 355 square feet and have a private entrance and butler service. There are also two 226-square-foot deluxe cabins that open onto the aft deck.

> *Specifications* 114 cabins, 6 inside with double bed; 90 outside—all but 4
> have 2 lowers, convertible to doubles; 32 convertible to triples; 2 Owner's
> Suites; 14 Deck Suites with verandas; 2 Deck Suites.

DINING The handsome bi-level dining room accommodates all passengers at a single seating for all meals. The paneled room with brass wall lamps has rectangular, round, and banquette-style tables and is set low enough that in any kind of sea, the water splashes in, washing-machine fashion, over the portholes.

An omelet chef cooks to order at breakfast, and a carvery features roast beef, ham, and pork at lunch. The lunch buffets are the biggest hits on the menu for the first day at sea, providing such fare as jumbo shrimp, foie gras, artichoke hearts, herring, potato salad, lots of salad fixings, hot and cold salmon, meatballs, and sliced roast beef.

SERVICE The international crew provides friendly service, though the pace can be slow at dinner when passengers order from the menu.

SPORTS, FITNESS, AND BEAUTY At least once during the cruise, passengers with a Walter Mitty fantasy may climb (wearing safety belts) the steel mast to a crow's nest, 60 feet above the deck. They may also climb out on the netting that cascades from the bowsprit. Although passengers do not handle the sails as on Windjammers, they can enjoy being part of the navigation by helping the helmsmen on a raised platform above the bridge and chart room. They can also take lessons in sailing and rope tying.

The lower deck has an exercise room, spa, tiled Turkish bath, and beauty salon. A hydraulic platform stages the water sport activities, which include banana boats, waterskiing, diving, snorkeling, and swimming from the 16-foot inflatable raft. An interior stairway gives access to the marina. Two 60-passenger tenders, resembling military landing craft, take passengers for beach landings. Two 150-passenger fiberglass tenders ferry passengers between the anchored ship and pier.

POSTSCRIPT The ship has no special facilities for children, but when they are aboard, they are looked after well by the crew and staff, and there is much for them to observe, learn, and enjoy.

Although the overall experience and attraction of *Royal Clipper* is similar to the smaller clippers, comparisons are difficult. *Royal Clipper* is truly different. Her size, her 42 sails, the sheer amount of deck equipment, and her lavish Edwardian interiors are a sharp contrast to the smaller-scale, relatively simple sleek sisters. As one passenger saw it, "For an ocean crossing, I would want the full-rigged *Royal Clipper*; for sailing the Caribbean or Mediterranean, I would be happy with either."

Windstar Cruises

300 Elliott Avenue West
Seattle, WA 98119
☎ **206-281-3535 or 800-258-7245**
FAX **206-281-7110**
www.windstarcruises.com

TYPE OF SHIPS Deluxe sailing yacht/cruise ships.

TYPE OF CRUISES Low-key, laid-back, yet luxurious, for active, affluent travelers with cosmopolitan tastes for offbeat corners in sunny climes.

CRUISE LINE'S STRENGTHS
- appealing lifestyle
- private-yacht exclusivity on small ships
- cabins
- romantic escape
- water sports

CRUISE LINE'S SHORTCOMINGS
- evening activity
- port-intensive itineraries with minimal time under canvas

FELLOW PASSENGERS The mix is broader than generally perceived. Not all drive BMWs and Porsches: 40% have Jeeps and Fords, and 77% of those are the family version rather than sports model. Passengers range from 20 to 80 years in age, but the majority are 35–65 years old. Incomes differ, and they might be first-time or experienced cruisers. Despite many differences, they have one aspect in common—a lifestyle preference, even if they cannot enjoy it 365 days of the year. Passengers are likely to be well traveled, from the United States, Europe, and Latin America, and about 75% are professionals—lawyers, doctors, business executives—and probably work in high-pressure jobs. The remainder are apt to be retirees from similar pressure cookers, plus a few honeymooners. They are active and enjoy individual and low-energy sports, such as golfing, walking, and swimming.

Recommended for Active, affluent, type-A individualists, 25–75 years old, who really mean it when they say they want to chill out; those who abhor mainstream cruising; divers and others who enjoy water sports; experienced cruisers looking for something different; those attracted by the romance of sailing ships while wanting upscale luxury.

Not recommended for Anyone who prefers large ships, thrives on nightlife, or enjoys wearing fancy clothes; those who need to be entertained, don't relate to a sophisticated ambience; those who prefer a burger to brûlée.

CRUISE AREAS AND SEASONS Caribbean, Costa Rica, Panama, winter; Greek Isles, Mediterranean, spring through fall; transatlantic, March to April and November.

THE LINE Four masts in a row, each with enormous triangular sails and as tall as a 20-story building, tower above a deck one-and-a-half times the length of a football field and half as wide. The great sails are manned by computers designed to monitor the direction and velocity of the wind to keep the ship from heeling more than 40 degrees.

These ships are wind cruisers, which on their introduction in 1985 were called the most revolutionary vessels since the introduction of the steamship. The vessels use wind power alone up to 50% of the time at sea, depending on the itinerary; electrical power and backup propulsion are provided by diesel-electric engines. The ships marry the romance and tradition of sailing with the comfort and amenities of a cruise ship. Their all-outside cabins are larger, better designed, and better appointed than most standard cabins on mainstream cruise ships. The French-built vessels' shallow draft enables them to call at less-visited ports, private marinas, and secluded beaches.

Windstar Cruises was acquired by Holland America Line in 1988, and the next year both companies were purchased by Carnival Corporation. Windstar continues to operate as a separate entity. In 1998, Windstar bought the five-masted *Club Med 1*, a larger version of the Windstar ships, and after remodeling, renamed her *Wind Surf*. In early 2007, to the surprise of most cruise-watchers, Carnival sold Windstar Cruises for $100 million to Ambassadors International, Inc., which has been having financial difficulties stemming from its acquisition of the Delta Queen Steamship Company and other riverboats that it has not been able to sell.

A companion—"Degrees of Difference"—has been added to Windstar's tagline, "180 Degrees from Ordinary," to highlight the updating and upgrading of the features and amenities of all three Windstar ships, and the addition of wireless access and cell-phone capability fleetwide.

STYLE Laid-back, romantic, and informal, the cruises combine the atmosphere of a private yacht with the amenities and services of a cruise ship. From the outset, the ships have offered exclusivity because of their size, ambience, and the people they attract: upscale professionals who can afford a luxury cruise but want a less-structured environment and more unusual vacation than is available on today's typical cruises.

The ships are wonderfully quiet under sail; you can hear the ocean wash the hull and the sails snap as wind fills them. Passengers may visit the open bridge to see how everything works. The captains—their hands never far from the wheel—usually give eager passengers a few minutes at the helm.

There's a casual elegance and easygoing informality about the ship and its occupants. Regardless of age, passengers seem to blend easily; by week's end, they're good friends. Pressure to keep a schedule is nonexistent. You decide how to spend your day. Even ardent type-A personalities can unwind.

Monogram Valet Luggage Service enables passengers to travel luggage-free to their ship for a fee. Bags are picked up at their home and delivered to their

THE FLEET	BUILT/RENOVATED	TONNAGE	PASSENGERS
Wind Spirit	1988/2003/07	5,350	148
Wind Star	1986/2003/07	5,350	148
Wind Surf	1990/98/01/03/06	14,745	312

cabin on the ship, wherever it may be. The luggage is shipped via an air valet service and requires no boxing or extra packaging. At the end of the cruise, luggage can be shipped back home. Windstar uses Luggage Forward, a courier company based in Boston, Massachusetts, for the luggage express service. Charges are assessed by weight, destination, and type of service. For example, it costs $280 to ship a 45-pound suitcase from Florida to Barbados. Bags are insured up to $500. Supplemental insurance may be purchased in $500 increments at a rate of $10 per $500 of additional coverage during the booking process. The luggage service can be booked on Windstar's Web site, where details are available and a link connects to Monogram Valet Luggage Service.

The Concierge Collection of Shore Excursions, Windstar's newest feature, further enhances the exclusiveness of small-ship cruising with such offerings as a private tour of the Vatican, underground cave-trekking in Slovenia, a cooking class at Moulin de Mougins in Monte Carlo, and more.

DISTINCTIVE FEATURES The ship. Water sports platform; use of most sports gear is free. Wireless Internet access and cell phone capability. A passenger lucky enough to hook a fish on a deep-sea outing can have it cooked by the chef.

RATES Port charges are included; tips are extra.

Special fares and discounts Booking six months in advance saves up to 50%. Windstar frequently offers two-for-one promotions. Other discounts are on a quarterly basis.

- **SINGLE SUPPLEMENT:** 175% of the published per-person rate.

PAST PASSENGERS The Foremast Club is open to all who take a Windstar cruise. They receive a quarterly newsletter, e-mails, and other literature highlighting new itineraries and special discounts, including alumni savings on select cruises.

THE LAST WORD On our first Windstar cruise, having expected passengers on the level of royalty, the ones who seemed to be enjoying themselves most were a blue-collar couple from Massachusetts on their second honeymoon—and first cruise. A Windstar cruise is a relaxing, romantic escape, but the perception more than the reality seems to put it out of reach in price and ambience for many people. Although it's definitely a way to impress your friends, deciding whether this cruise is for you shouldn't be based on price (although you get a lot for your money), but on the type of cruise it offers. Those who relate to it think it's heaven; those who don't would probably be bored.

Our only complaint is that some itineraries are so port-intensive they leave little time for passengers to enjoy the ships, particularly under sail. Windstar recently added a day at sea to some Mediterranean cruises. We think two would have been better.

Windstar's new owners took over the cruise line in April 2007, indicating that they planned to continue with the upgrading of the vessels and maintain their staff and crew. Those commitments have been kept and we haven't heard of any significant changes for the future. Stay tuned.

THE SHIPS The ships are identical inside and out. If not for their itineraries, they would be difficult to tell apart. Throughout, the tasteful appointments are well designed and inviting. They have the feel of a sailing ship—wood and

Windstar Cruises Standard Features

Officers British

Staff *Dining, Cabin:* Indonesian and Filipino; *Cruise:* American, British, some European.

Dining facilities One open-seating restaurant, indoor/outdoor cafe for breakfast and lunch buffet featuring traditional and tropical specialties, occasional barbecues on the beach. *Wind Surf*, lunch, dinner in Degrees; espresso bar.

Special diets Sail Light menus with low-calorie, heart-smart, and vegetarian selections. Advance notice requested for others.

Room service 24 hours.

Dress code Casual and elegantly casual.

Cabin amenities Flat-panel television and DVD player, CD player, three-channel radio, international direct-dial telephone, safe, minibar and refrigerator, hair dryer, and terry robe.

Electrical outlets 110 AC (220 *Wind Surf*).

Wheelchair access None. Guide dogs have been permitted.

Recreation and entertainment Piano bar, casino, lounge with local musicians or ship's band, library, videocassette/CD library.

Sports and other activities Water sports platform for sailboats, windsurfers, motorized inflatables, waterskiing, scuba diving (extra charge); snorkeling equipment carried on board; saltwater pool.

Beauty and fitness Spa and beauty salon, hot tub, sauna, masseuse, fitness room with weight-training equipment.

Other facilities Laundry, doctor, infirmary, e-mail and Internet, Wi-Fi access, cell phone capability.

Children's facilities None. Children's videos.

Theme cruises None currently.

Smoking Allowed in designated areas but not in dining room.

Windstar suggested tipping A service change of $12 per person per day is added to passenger's onboard bill. A 15% service charge is added to bar bills.

Credit cards For cruise payment and onboard charges: American Express, Discover, MasterCard, Visa, traveler's checks.

leather, portholes, and nautical blue and white—yet they're modern, with expanses of windows creating spaciousness and space-station-white walls adorned with contemporary art.

Because the number of passengers is small, boarding is speedy. You're greeted with a glass of Champagne or chilled fruit drink and escorted to the main lounge to complete paperwork. Then you're escorted to your cabin, where your luggage should be waiting.

Wind Spirit	QUALITY **9**	VALUE **C**
Wind Star	QUALITY **9**	VALUE **C**
REGISTRY Netherlands	LENGTH 440 feet	BEAM 64 feet
CABINS 74	DRAFT 13.5 feet	SPEED 8–12 knots
MAXIMUM PASSENGERS	PASSENGER DECKS 4	ELEVATORS None
148	CREW 94	SPACE RATIO 36

The cabins, gym, and sauna are on the bottom two of four passenger decks. The third deck contains a main lounge and dining salon—both handsome. Through a lounge skylight, passengers have dramatic views of the majestic sails overhead. You'll also find a bar, a tiny casino, boutique, and a beauty salon and spa. The top deck offers a pool, bar, and veranda lounge. Under Windstar's Degrees of Difference enhancement program, both ships' public rooms and cabins were renovated and new features added in 2007.

ITINERARIES *See* Itinerary Index.

CABINS With the exception of the Owner's Suite, cabins are identical: large and outside. Larger than those on mainstream cruise ships, these well-designed, nicely appointed cabins make optimum use of space and are fitted with twin beds or a queen-size bed.

The marriage of tradition and technology is apparent in the ship's cabins. Each cabin has twin portholes with brass fittings and wood cabinetwork, including a foldout vanity with makeup mirror. Amenities include a flat-panel television and DVD player, international direct-dial telephone, Wi-Fi access, CD player, and safe. The newest additions to all cabins and suites are Bose Sound Dock speakers, Apple iPod Nanos preloaded with music available for complimentary checkout, and laptops available for rent. Minibars are stocked with beer, wine, spirits, and soft drinks. Note, however, that drinks are expensive. A beer, for example, costs about $5.

Bathrooms have showers, hair dryers, and terry robes. In the 2007 renovations, all cabin and suite bathrooms were remodeled for a more contemporary look with new fixtures, open glass shelves, new cabinets, granite countertops, porcelain sinks, a magnifying mirror, and their teak floors refinished. Egyptian cotton towels and bath amenities by L'Occitane were being added.

Specifications 74 outside cabins; 1 suite with queen-size bed. Standard dimensions, 185 square feet. 73 with twin beds (convertible to queen); 11 (20 on *Wind Star*) with third berths. No singles and no wheelchair accessible.

DINING The teak-lined dining room—nautical in design with rope-wrapped pillars—has low ceilings and subdued lighting, giving it an intimate atmosphere. Seating is open, restaurant style. Cuisine continues to be uneven, ranging from super to ordinary.

Fresh menus are prepared by Windstar's culinary team and cater to the varied lifestyles of the line's savvy travelers in The Restaurant on all three ships; alfresco dining is available (weather permitting) at the poolside grill, Candles. *Wind Surf* also has a seafood bar, Le Marché. To complement the cuisine, Windstar offers an extensive wine list.

Coffee, tea, juices, and breakfast rolls are served poolside for early risers. Breakfast in the glass-enclosed veranda offers tropical fruits and freshly baked breads. Afternoon tea on the Pool Deck with pastries and finger sandwiches is popular. Room service is available 24 hours a day. In the Caribbean, a highlight is the Pool Deck barbecue, serving grilled lobster tails, shrimp, and other seafood accompanied by local music.

SERVICE The captain and European officers are affable, accessible, and visible, inviting passengers to watch the ship in operation, visiting with them, and participating in activities when possible. They welcome questions. Cabin staff and most restaurant personnel are Indonesian; deck stewards, bar personnel, and section captains are Filipino. All get very high marks.

FACILITIES AND ACTIVITIES Windstar ships don't have scheduled daily activities. You set your own schedule and make your own activities, independently or with new friends. That's what this cruise is all about. Days are passed sunbathing, reading, deep-sea fishing, swimming, and watching the ship's operation. (Readers should bring books; selections aboard are limited.) Ship's television features two current movies daily, plus satellite news around the clock.

Nightlife is low-key and minimal. The tiny casino has blackjack tables, a Caribbean stud poker table, and slot machines. An easy-listening trio plays nightly for dancing in the lounge. You also can watch a movie in your cabin; a selection of DVDs is available at the reception desk. A Caribbean night showcases a reggae band, and passengers young and old dance on the Pool Deck.

SPORTS, FITNESS, AND BEAUTY Water sports from the ships' foldout platform more than compensate for the absence of onboard sports. Furthermore, the ships' shallow draft enables them to stop at less-visited ports and secluded beaches and coves. On Caribbean more than Mediterranean cruises, water sports are a main attraction. Carried aboard are sailboats, windsurfing boards, snorkeling and diving equipment (including tanks), and Zodiacs to take passengers snorkeling, waterskiing, and deep-sea fishing; gear is available free of charge.

Snorkeling, kayaking, and scuba-diving excursions are usually available for a fee and are provided by shore-excursion vendors in selected locales.

In recent renovations, the salon and spa was moved to the Main Deck and expanded to provide room for two treatment rooms and a pedicure chair. Each ship has a fitness room with some exercise equipment, sauna, and masseuse; health and exercise classes are offered. Jacuzzis are on the Pool Deck.

SHORE EXCURSIONS Most excursions are half-day tours with an emphasis on tropical gardens, national parks, and other natural attractions. Excursions at St. Kitts in the Caribbean, for example, include a rain forest hike and horseback riding. In the Mediterranean, sightseeing is emphasized. Passengers can book their shore excursions on the Windstar Web site in advance in conjunction with their cruise.

Wind Surf	QUALITY 7	VALUE C
REGISTRY Netherlands	LENGTH 617 feet	BEAM 66 feet
CABINS 156	DRAFT 16 feet	SPEED 12 knots
MAXIMUM PASSENGERS	PASSENGER DECKS 6	ELEVATORS 2
312	CREW 191	SPACE RATIO 48

THE SHIP *Wind Surf,* acquired by Windstar Cruises in 1997, is the former *Club Med 1,* a larger version of *Wind Star.* After extensive remodeling, the ship was rechristened *Wind Surf* and entered Windstar service in 1998. She has had several subsequent alterations, the most recent being a five-week, multimillion-dollar refit in 2006, when *Wind Surf* emerged with Degrees of Difference enhancements that updated her public rooms and cabins. More luxury amenities, a spa treatment room for couples, and two new luxury suites were added, and the technical operations of the ship were improved.

The Yacht Club, which replaced the library, is anchored by a flat-panel television and provides comfortable seating for relaxing and socializing. The new room is meant to be similar to today's coffeehouse, with an espresso bar offering gourmet coffee drinks, eight computers with Internet access, and a library of books, CDs, and DVDs for checkout. Wireless access and cell phone capability are available on all three ships.

The ship has a meeting room that is a fully equipped conference center with new audiovisual equipment and meeting facilities for up to 50 people.

The **Wind Surf Lounge & Casino** has a nautical design, color scheme, and furniture; a beautiful teak bar; and clear sight lines to the stage from every seat. Other public rooms include a signature shop and spa and fitness center. The captain maintains an open bridge while at sea. Also available are 24-hour room service, laundry service, and a doctor's office.

ITINERARIES *See* Itinerary Index.

CABINS The deluxe outside cabins encompass 188 square feet each and offer queen-size beds (convertible to twins) and a work/desk/vanity area. They are similar in layout and decor to standard cabins on Windstar's other ships. All have flat-panel television and DVD player, CD player, safe, minibar and refrigerator, and direct-dial telephone. The bathroom has a shower, hair dryer, toiletries, and terry robe.

After the most recent renovations, all cabin and suite bathrooms were remodeled for a more contemporary look, with new fixtures, open glass shelves, new cabinets, granite countertops, porcelain sinks, and a magnifying mirror. Refinished teak floors retain the popular nautical style. Egyptian cotton towels and bath amenities by L'Occitane have been added. Bose Sound Dock speakers were installed in all cabins and suites, while Apple iPod Nanos preloaded with music are available for complimentary checkout; laptops are for rent. Desks have granite surfaces, and full-length mirrors were added. Suites have a second flat-panel television and DVD player.

The two luxury suites on the Bridge Deck are approximately 500 square feet each and include a living and dining area, separate bedroom with walk-in closet, and a marble bathroom with whirlpool tub and separate shower. Bridge Suites come with extra amenities such as chilled Champagne upon arrival; an invitation to dine with the captain; unpacking, laundry, and pressing service; evening appetizers; high-tea service upon request; complimentary bottled water in the suite; and additional L'Occitane bath amenities.

The 31 ocean-view suites were created in selected areas of top decks by combining two cabins into one. Each measures 376 square feet and has decor accented by teak, linen wall coverings, and original art. Each suite has a queen bed convertible to twins and a sofa bed. A curtain can be pulled across the bedroom to separate it from the living room for dining or entertaining. In addition to standard amenities, suites boast his-and-her bathrooms with shower, teak flooring, plush towels and robes, and vanity lighting.

Specifications 33 deluxe outside suites; 123 outside cabins with queen beds (convertible to twins) and sitting area. Some cabins have third berth; some side-by-side cabins have an adjoining private door.

DINING The ship's two dining rooms—the **Restaurant** and the smaller **Degrees**—accommodate all passengers at one open seating. Passengers have the opportunity to dine in both during a cruise. Light and vegetarian menus are available. The **Verandah Café,** with covered outdoor seating where breakfast and lunch are served, was expanded. Degrees is *Wind Surf*'s alternative restaurant. Reservations are required, but there is no surcharge.

All three venues have been improved with increased capacity. Degrees' decor uses French- and Italian-inspired colors, fabrics, and furniture. The glassed-in Verandah had its aft wall pushed back to enclose a portion of the deck to allow for additional indoor seating, which is preferred by guests on hot or windy days. *Wind Surf*'s newest addition is a seafood bar, **Le Marché.**

SPORTS, FITNESS, AND BEAUTY The 10,000-square-foot **WindSpa,** operated by Steiner, has a staff of ten and offers three kinds of treatments. It has a pedicure chair and a couples massage room, and the gym was upgraded. Health and exercise classes are offered for aerobics, yoga, and Pilates. Pampering includes Swedish, deep tissue, sports, and other massage; aromatherapy; hair care, manicures, pedicures, and facials; and hand, foot, and spa bath treatments. Purification treatments include herbal wraps, body masks, and mineral baths. Treatments can be purchased in advance or on board. The Windstar brochure outlines options.

Wind Surf offers a complimentary water sports program. The ship has a water sports platform and equipment similar to that on the other Windstar vessels; two saltwater pools are located near them, as well as two hot tubs.

EUROPEAN, ASIAN, *and* SMALLER CRUISE LINES

IN ADDITION TO THE CRUISE LINES AND SHIPS in the American mainstream of cruising already profiled in this section, another group of lines, with ships based mostly in Europe, may be of interest to readers. Space doesn't allow the same in-depth treatment, but generally they have small to midsize ships operated in the European tradition. Their interesting itineraries often visit places many Americans would need an atlas to find. Ships have English-speaking staff, although the majority of passengers may be Europeans speaking other languages. A few ships operate from U.S. or Asian ports.

The degree of luxury varies widely. Some are luxury vessels launched only in the last few years; others are renovated vintage ships that form a flotilla of new cruise lines.

Cruises appeal particularly to those who have traveled the main routes often and are looking for new destinations or a new environment in which to return to places seen previously. They also appeal to those who might never consider a typical cruise ship, preferring to explore less-traveled waters.

Also described are a few lines and ships that cater mainly to the U.S. market but weren't profiled in-depth for other reasons, such as the fact that they're sold mainly through tour companies in combination with larger tour programs, they're under charter much of the year, or we had difficulty obtaining information.

Note: In parentheses after each ship name is information about the number of cabins and passengers; officers and crew; and the ship's length and tonnage (cabins/passengers; officers/crew; ship length/tonnage) when available.

Abercrombie & Kent USA
1411 Opus Place, Executive Towers West II, Suite 300;
Downers Grove, IL 60515;
☎ **800-652-7963 or 630-725-3400; fax 630-725-3401;**
www.abercrombiekent.com

Abercrombie & Kent is a prestigious international tour operator specializing in exotic journeys worldwide for affluent, sophisticated travelers with an avid interest in nature and wildlife. The cruise programs focus on Antarctica; barge and river cruises in Europe and on the Irrawady (Ayeyarwady), Nile, and Yangtze rivers; and a wide selection of other areas, such as the Galápagos, Tahiti, and Alaska. All emphasize culture and ecologically sound tourism. Most passengers are professionals, retired or semiretired, well educated, well traveled, usually ages 50 and older, in good health, and fit enough to enjoy hikes in Antarctic snows or snorkeling in the Galápagos. Singles make friends easily on these trips.

Marco Polo is a club for A&K veterans and offers a quarterly newsletter, members-only trips, a 5% discount on land arrangements on most tours, personalized luggage tags, priority on new destinations, tailored itineraries, a free lending library of A&K videotapes, and eligibility to compete in the annual Marco Polo Photo Contest. Annual membership is $95; five-year, $325; lifetime, $950; and children's memberships are available.

Le Boreal (108 CABINS/24 SUITES/264 OR 199; FRENCH/INTERNATIONAL/139; 466 FEET/10,700 TONS)

For its 2010–2011 Antarctic season, Abercrombie & Kent has chartered the brand new Le Boreal, an expedition ship of ultramodern design, which enables the operator to strike a balance between onboard luxury and wilderness adventure. Normally, the ship can carry up to 264 passengers, but in Antarctica A&K will limit her complement to 199 guests to ensure an outside cabin with private balcony for all passengers. The small size of the sleek ship with a 15.3-foot draft should allow A&K to offer a distinctly different adventure-cruise experience with access to bays and narrow fjords that big cruise ships cannot reach, as well as private balconies for all passengers from which they can view Antarctica's magnificent scenery. Built at the Italian Fincantieri shipyard, the language of the French-owned ship is English.

Le Boreal is laid out well on six decks. Highlights include a single-seating dining room, alfresco dining, an outdoor heated pool, and a modern lecture facility and theater, as well as a comfortable gathering area and library. There's a full-service salon, steam rooms, spa, and fitness center. Beautifully decorated by French designers, the 80 balcony cabins and 24 suites are among the most spacious and comfortable on any Antarctic cruise ship and come with king, queen, or two single beds. Cabin amenities include a minibar, safe, flat-screen television, DVD/CD player, iPod player, direct-dial telephone, individually-controlled heat and air-conditioning, and wireless Internet access, which is also available throughout the ship. Bathrooms are lined with marble and teak and are equipped with a shower, hair dryer, and bathrobes. Laundry service and 24-hour room service are available. The ship has three passenger elevators.

International cuisine is served in the ship's two restaurants: **The Restaurant** on Deck 2, offering gourmet, contemporary, and international cuisine, and the casual **Compass Grill** on Deck 6, with indoor-outdoor dining for breakfast, lunch, and themed dinners. A selection of lighter fare and vegetarian dishes is always available, and most special diets can be accommodated with advance notice. The ship is attended by a crew of 139 members.

Le Boreal sets high standards of comfort in her public areas. Forward on Deck 6 is the spacious **Panoramic Lounge and Terrace,** ideal for social gatherings, afternoon tea, or relaxing and enjoying magnificent views. **The Club** aft on Deck 3 provides an evening setting for live music and dancing. Aft on

Deck 4, **The Theatre,** a show lounge with unobstructed views for all, is the venue for nightly entertainment, enrichment lectures, and movies. The library offers a wide range of titles with generously sized reading areas.

The atmosphere on board is informal and unregimented with an easy camaraderie among the passengers and the experts (naturalists, geologists, zoologists, historians, photographers, and ornithologists) who accompany every cruise. Each day, passengers gather for informal pre-excursion briefings or post-trip wrap-ups in the ship's theatre. Throughout the trip, passengers interact with the experts to exchange ideas and ask questions at dinner, at the rail, or on a Zodiac. Staff and crew add to the experience with their informal talks and entertainment. Days are packed with intellectual and physical activities, and there is a recap of the day before dinner. Lectures are well attended but are also broadcast in cabins. Most talks are accompanied by audiovisuals.

In Antarctica, A&K's shore excursions are hosted by the team of experts. The December 2010 cruise will have Dr. James McClintock, Professor of Polar and Marine Biology at the University of Alabama, who has conducted research in Antarctic waters for more than 25 years and recently discovered an anti-cancer compound in a marine invertebrate.

In addition to accommodations and meals, A&K's all-inclusive cruise prices include all bar drinks and house wines, onboard gratuities, and sightseeing. You are given a backpack and parka for Antarctica cruises and very good precruise information; on board, you are provided with waterproof boots and binoculars.

Le Boreal has an ice rating that exceeds the requirement for Antarctica and is equipped with the latest navigation, communications, and safety equipment, including a GMDSS emergency communication system and a satellite weather system that receives real-time images of weather and ice conditions. A technologically advanced stabilizing system minimizes the effect of rough waters. In the event of an emergency, lifeboats are fully enclosed and equipped with survival gear, blankets, food, and water.

Designed to be environmentally responsible, *Le Boreal* will be one of the most environmentally friendly ships sailing in Antarctica. Her cutting-edge technology includes an up-to-date waste-water system that sorts, treats, and stores in a special refrigerated zone for proper discharge in port. No water (other than fully potable water), waste, or rubbish is discharged at sea. The ship's state-of-the-art computerized dynamic positioning eliminates the need for dropping anchor in fragile marine reserves, protecting corals and the environment. Thermal and phonic insulation in engines and the propulsion system reduces overall energy consumption. This insulation also minimizes noise and vibration for passenger comfort. Also, the ship's Zodiac boats are equipped with fuel-efficient four-stroke engines that meet the strictest environmental standard.

Le Boreal operates on the lightest- and cleanest-burning Marine Gas Oil fuel, in full compliance with new International Maritime Organization (IMO) standards. (The new IMO rules required of ships in Antarctic waters will take effect in July 2011.) The International Association of Antarctica Tour Operators (IAATO), of which A&K is an active member, was founded in 1991 to advocate, promote, and practice safe and environmentally responsible travel to Antarctica. The association anticipates that the new regulations will reduce the number of ships operating in Antarctica by 40%.

Antarctic cruises are intended for serious travelers who cherish unusual opportunities and draw intellectually curious people, among whom many lasting friendships are forged. If you don't have a similar thirst for knowledge or the flexibility to deal with frequent changes caused by weather and sea, you could find yourself on the wrong ship a long way from home. Gadabouts and tourists wanting to add exotic destinations to their tally should look elsewhere.

A&K also markets a variety of river cruises in Europe and on the Nile and Yangtze rivers. See Part Three, River Cruises.

American Canadian Caribbean Line

(*See* Part Two, Cruise Lines and Their Ships)

American Cruise Lines

741 Boston Port Road, Suite 200, Guilford, CT 06437; ☎ 800-814-6880 or 203-453-6800; fax 860-453-0417; www.americancruiselines.com

American Eagle **(31/49; AMERICAN; 165 FEET)**

American Glory **(31/49; AMERICAN; 168 FEET)**

American Spirit **(51/100; AMERICAN; 215 FEET)**

American Star **(52/100; AMERICAN; 215 FEET)**

Independence **(53/104; AMERICAN; 215 FEET)**

The small coastal ship *American Eagle,* completed in 2000 at the owner's Chesapeake shipyard in Salisbury, Maryland, takes only 49 passengers on close-to-shore trips from Maine and New England through the Chesapeake Bay to the Deep South and Florida via the Intracoastal Waterway from March to December. (For the eagle-eyed, some of the company ads and brochure photos might be familiar. American Cruise Lines first surfaced in 1974 with a previous *American Eagle,* and after operating six ships for 15 years, the company quietly went bust.)

In 2002, the *Eagle* was joined by *American Glory,* which is three feet longer and three feet wider at the beam and has 14 Veranda Suites. The larger *American Spirit,* which debuted in 2005, has 23 veranda cabins. The latest addition, *American Star,* made her debut in June 2007.

The *American Star,* which was launched in 2007, is similar in design to *American Spirit* but features more large cabins with private verandas. All cabins are fitted with flat-screen satellite television and DVD players, Internet access, hair dryer, and other amenities. The ship has an elevator to all four decks, four lounges, an Observation Deck, library, and a dining room with surrounding windows. The ship with its 6.5-foot draft, sails on 6-, 7-, and 14-night cruise itineraries along the East Coast from Maine to Florida.

The new *Independence* is scheduled to debut in June 2010. Similar to

American Spirit, the new ship is slightly wider on the beam, which allows for slightly larger staterooms, and 80% of the cabins and suites will have balconies. All accommodations have large opening picture windows, satellite television and DVD players, roomy bathrooms, and Internet access. The ship is equipped with Rolls Royce stabilizers, providing a more comfortable ride.

The ships' public spaces are roomy, considering they have only four decks. The forward-facing **Nantucket Lounge** (**Chesapeake Lounge** on *Spirit*) seats all passengers; and midship, a ship-wide foyer offers additional comfy couch seating. A library has television, DVD, and books. The decor is a bit plain, with utilitarian-looking walls and ceilings, but the carpets and fabrics help to dress it up. The ships have an elevator with access to each floor, and equipment for the disabled is available.

The dining room, glass-enclosed on three sides, has open seating at large, round tables. The ships do not have a liquor license; instead, there is a complimentary bar and sumptuous predinner hors d'oeuvres for the very popular cocktail hour, and there are carafes of wine on the dinner table. Each ship has chefs from the Culinary Institute of America and Johnson & Wales University. Their expertise shows in the delicious, creative meals. The food is uniformly excellent throughout the cruise. Lunch is light fare, such as crab cakes and chicken Caesar salad. The set dinner menus, with a choice of two entrees, might be grilled artichoke hearts, hearts of palm in balsamic vinegar, Cornish game hen with wild rice, grilled catfish, broiled lobster, and desserts such as pecan peanut butter pie.

The fourth or Sports Deck, open to the sky, has deck chairs for all passengers, plus tables and chairs and a putting green. Additional covered deck space faces aft, and the open deck forward of the lounge is excellent for viewing ahead.

There are five cabin categories, all with private bath and outside with windows that slide open to allow in fresh air. AA, the second grade up, measures 192 square feet and compares favorably to the line's competition. The six AAV cabins are 249 square feet, including veranda. The average size of *Glory*'s cabins is slightly larger at 220 square feet. All ships have five single cabins priced at about a 50% premium over the AA category. Cabins are furnished with comfortable couches.

The American Cruise Lines' ships offer a low-key cruising experience with itineraries from Maine and New England to Florida that celebrate Americana, sometimes with the help of an enrichment lecturer. There are ten itineraries in all, plus a new one for 2010, the Philadelphia and Potomac Cruise, which will sail between Philadelphia and the Washington, D.C., area. The passengers are mostly an amiable retired lot who like sailing in a small club setting. There may also be mothers, grandmothers, daughters, and sons. The all-American crew includes college-age men and women, some just out of high school, serving as deckhands, cleaning cabins, and waiting tables. The level of service is friendly, if sometimes haphazard. The line offers early-bird discounts to those who book six months in advance.

In late November 2009, American Cruise Lines acquired the 120-passenger, U.S.-flagged riverboat, *Queen of the West,* enabling the cruise line to expand to the West Coast for the first time. The paddlewheeler will sail on seven-night Pacific Northwest itineraries on the Columbia and Snake rivers, departing from Portland, Oregon, and Clarkston, Washington, in summer 2010. The line is making some modifications to the ship, including creating some larger cabins, thus decreasing her passenger capacity. American Cruise Lines also announced plans for further West Coast expansion in 2010.

ITINERARIES *See* Itinerary Index.

American Safari Cruises
3826 18th Avenue West, Seattle, WA 98119; ☎ 206-284-0300 or 888-862-8881; fax 206-283-9322; www.amsafari.com

Safari Explorer **(18/36; AMERICAN/16; 145 FEET)**

Safari Quest **(11/22; AMERICAN/9 TO 10; 120 FEET)**

Safari Spirit **(6/12; AMERICAN/6; 105 FEET)**

Formed in 1996, American Safari Cruises offers nature-oriented adventure cruises for affluent travelers on three small yachts. The Alaska itineraries are off-the-beaten-track, close-up experiences of wildlife, or scenery viewing at a leisurely pace with the pampering of a luxury cruise. The line's seven- and eight-night fall cruises sail in the Pacific Northwest on the Columbia and Snake rivers, and in the San Juan Islands and British Columbia Gulf Islands. There also is a winter series of weekly cruises of Baja California and the Gulf of California, departing from Loreto.

In early 2009, the line had a change of ownership when InnerSea Discoveries purchased American Safari Cruises' assets and assumed its operation. The line's management team and staff and its mission have remained essentially unchanged. Based at historic Fishermen's Terminal in Seattle, the new parent company plans to add several new brands to complement the American Safari experience of up-close exploration of routes less traveled.

All cabins on the vessels are outside, nicely appointed, and furnished with a king or queen bed or two twin beds (except for one single cabin with one twin on *Safari Explorer* and on *Safari Quest*), television with DVD, and private bathroom with a shower; suites have a tub. Amenities include evening turndown service and terry robes.

The main gathering spot is a salon furnished with comfortable couches and chairs. A self-service bar separates the dining area and salon. The salon opens onto the sports platform, where passengers can board a launch or a two-passenger kayak. A spiral staircase links all public decks, the library and lounge, and the bridge. A promenade circles the entire yacht. The yachts have a top-deck hot tub for an under-the-stars spa experience. Upon request, fishing charters can be arranged for an additional charge.

On Alaskan itineraries, binoculars, rain jackets and pants, and rubber boots are provided, as are wet suits, fins, snorkel gear, laser sailboats, water skis, knee boards, and other toys in the Gulf of California. A skilled and personable expedition leader accompanies each cruise and serves in lieu of a cruise director. A trained naturalist and usually university educated, the expedition leader(s) organizes hikes and biking excursions, leads kayak explorations, and identifies wildlife en route. In the evenings and when appropriate during the day, the expedition leaders lecture on the flora, fauna, geology, and the history of the areas visited. Praised by passengers as caring, enthusiastic, and knowledgeable, the expedition leaders elevate this cruise experience to a horizon-expanding voyage of discovery.

Food aboard American Safari Cruises is good but not gourmet. Each day, the chef joins the passengers to discuss the menu and to describe special dishes to be prepared. An early-bird breakfast of fresh fruit, pastries, cereal, juices, and hot beverages starts at 6 a.m., with a full-service, cooked-to-order breakfast available at 8 a.m. A full-course lunch is served at 1 p.m. Hors d'oeuvres (which are usually excellent and creative) are offered nightly during the cocktail hour preceding dinner at 7 p.m. Two entrees are offered each evening—usually fresh local seafood, as well as chicken, lamb, or beef. Wine with meals and all other alcoholic beverages are included in the price of the cruise. The wine selection is commendable, as are the better labels in the well-stocked bar. Beer drinkers will be pleased with the draft beers from a prize-winning Alaskan microbrewery.

The yachts travel in daytime for wildlife viewing and scenic exploration. In late afternoon, they anchor in a scenic, secluded cove or bay for the night, offering further discovery on foot or by Zodiacs. Sighting wildlife—whales, porpoises, harbor seals, black bears, brown bears, sea lions, bald eagles, cormorants, herons, sandhill cranes, oystercatchers, and gulls—is all but guaranteed. In the Gulf of California, sightings include the mammoth blue whale, the largest creature ever to exist, other whale species, manta rays, huge pods of up to 1,000 dolphins, giant sea turtles, sea lions, and 200 species of birds, including pelicans. The yachts are small enough that the captain can change course immediately to approach something for closer inspection. Long summer days in Alaska allow kayaking, up-close excursions to the face of glaciers, whale watching by Zodiacs, and hiking until evening.

All meals, excursions, and events on these cruises are strictly informal. Jeans, khakis, and shorts, along with outdoor gear appropriate to the cruise venue and time of year, are all you need. Although the expedition leader has lots of activities on tap each day, the decision to participate is yours. Soaking in the hot tub, reading, napping, and watching movies on your cabin DVD player are some of the alternatives available. Each ship also has at least two aerobic exercise machines. The Alaska itineraries explore remote areas and small villages. They range from 7 to 14 nights. Prices cover shore excursions, including unlimited use of kayaks, guided nature walks, all private transfers, open bar, and port charges. Tips are extra. Extensions to remote fly-in wilderness lodges—such as Winterlake for kayaking, canoeing, and fishing; the Iditarod Trail for world-class hiking; and Redoubt Bay for access to a creek where bears feed—are available. The Gulf of California seven-night itinerary operates from November to late March, while the seven-night cruises of the Pacific Northwest operate in September and October. A seven-night trip sails on the Columbia and Snake rivers, with some departures scheduled as wine and culinary theme cruises. Golf and spa packages are available in conjunction with the Gulf of California cruises; Kids in Nature programs are featured on some Alaska and Gulf of California cruises. All three vessels are available for private full-yacht charter. ASC expects to begin operating cruises in the Hawaiian Islands in either December 2010 or November 2011.

For those who have sailed in Alaska on a large or mid-size ship, ASC's small ships do offer a totally different experience, starting with the time spent in the wilderness and away from towns. *Safari Explorer*, the line's new flagship, which underwent a ten-month, $3.5-million renovation prior to her debut in May 2008, is more than a small ship. She's a very small ship on which passengers feel like they are sailing on their own yacht with some new friends. You cannot help but appreciate her benefits: the close-up views, the ship's ability to turn on a dime, the instant stops when there's something interesting to see.

Yet, from my experience on *Safari Explorer*, its number-one asset is its staff. From Captain Scott on down, I was deeply impressed with the staff's care, eagerness to please, friendliness, relaxed yet efficient matter by which they dispense their duties, humor and good nature, teamwork, and thoughtfulness. One simple example of the latter: On the coldest, dampest day when most passengers were on outside decks watching whales and chilled to the bone, the dining staff suddenly arrived with piping hot chocolate. What an easy way to warm the heart of every passenger! The ship's size and its staff together set the stage for another plus—the quick camaraderie among the passengers. I did not witness any prima donnas or grumblers; if they were on board, the staff quietly took care of them.

It's hard to beat Alaska as a destination, and it seemed to be the motivation for most passengers. They were not disappointed. Most passengers were on their first visit to Alaska, and judging from the "ahs" and "ohs," they were thrilled with every sighting of whales—some got very, very close to our DIBs (inflatable boats)—a glacier calving, sea lions lazing on the ice, bald eagles standing watch, and bears lumbering along the shore.

The DIBs (similar to Zodiacs but more comfortable and stable) and kayaks add a great deal to the adventure. By the end of the cruise, most passengers had tried their hand at kayaking in icy waters. The expedition leaders, Beth and Amy, both studying for advanced degrees in marine biology, were very good and their talks informative, usually given in the morning or early afternoon. I was a little disappointed that they did not offer an evening wrap-up about the day's activity, wildlife seen, birds spotted, and the like, which is a popular feature on expedition cruises.

The space on *Safari Explorer* is well utilized on the main deck, which is particularly attractive with a fine wood finish around the bar, library, and elsewhere. The library features books on Alaskan wildlife, but it would have been helpful to have had lists of birds, flowers, and animals we were likely to see available at the start of the cruise.

All of *Safari Explorer's* accommodations are outside and have large windows. Two suites are suitable for up to three persons and have small balconies. My cabin on Deck B was comfortable, but the layout left much to be desired, particularly the cramped position of the double bed. Drawer space is sufficient, but the closet is small. Particularly appreciated in cold Alaska are the heated tile floors in the bathroom and the terrific shower. Another nice feature is the promenade deck that wraps around the ship. The top deck has some exercise equipment and a hot tub, and stretch sessions are held each morning. The food is good but uneven, and not gourmet, except the hors d'oeuvres at cocktail time, which are excellent. Wines are outstanding.

Safari Explorer is a first-rate, well-run ship, but I would not call it luxurious, as ASC's promotional material claims. But perhaps it depends upon one's definition of "luxury." The highly personalized and intimate private-yacht experience offered by American Safari Cruises represents good value. Early-booking discounts and the inclusion of wine, liquor, a complimentary massage, and all shore excursions in the price of the cruise provide further value. After your first American Safari cruise, you'll receive a $150 per person savings on your next cruise; after your fifth cruise, you'll receive a $500 per person savings. Early-bird savings and promotional fares are available from time to time. American Safari passengers are typically over 40 years old, well-educated, and adventurous individuals who revel in learning and discovery and who enjoy making new friends. Life aboard these very small vessels is, after all, a very intimate experience, one that practically ensures you will become well acquainted with your fellow passengers.

ASC is developing a new brand of small-ship cruising with vessels for 65 to 78 passengers, to be operated in Alaska's Inside Passage beginning in summer 2011. The ships are being fully refurbished with new, updated decor. The cruises, aimed at a broader audience, will have much lower prices than American Safari Cruises but fewer of its inclusive amenities. The cruises will focus on adventure: kayaking, hiking, caving, birding, and such. Some specialized activities, like fishing with a fully-equipped fishing boat, will cost extra, as will premium spirits and massages. A Web site for the new brand is being developed. Stay tuned.

ITINERARIES *See* Itinerary Index.

Celebration Cruise Line
2419 East Commercial Boulevard, Suite 302, Fort Lauderdale, FL 33308;
☎ **800-314-7735 or 954-414-1336; fax 954-414-1321;**
www.celebrationcl.com; email info@celebrationcl.com

Bahamas Celebration **(650/1,500; 360 CREW; 35,855 TONS)**

The latest entrant into the Florida short-cruise market, *Bahamas Celebration* (formerly the Norwegian ferry *Prinsesse Ragnhild*) was purchased by Fort Lauderdale–based Celebration Cruise Holdings in 2008. Built in Germany in 1981, she was subsequently lengthened, substantially rebuilt, and transformed into a warm-weather cruiser in 2008. Initially weighing 15,000 tons, she now tips the scales at 35,855 tons and has capacity for 650 cars, although her vehicle decks are not in use. She sports a vibrant blue hull, and her ferry origins are readily apparent in her boxy design with bow and stern doors.

Highlights of her 2008 transformation include a unique raised pool with glass sides, twin whirlpools, an alfresco buffet, and two tiki bars. Aft on the same deck is the **Kids of The Caribbean** water park, a shallow basin with water features and a sinuous 180-foot slide.

Nine cabin categories run the gamut from deluxe suites (four feature semi-enclosed stern-facing balconies) to diminutive inside and outside "coach" cabins with upper and lower berths, a nod to the vessel's ferry origins. More typical are the larger Category 4 ocean-view cabins and Category 5 inside cabins. These offer two lower berths (some have additional upper berths). Most cabins have a flat-screen television. The Category 8 and 9 "coach" cabins have open closets, limited seating, and no television. Upper berths throughout the ship have a 200-pound weight limit. Electrical outlets require a converter.

Bahamas Celebration offers three dining venues. The **Crystal Restaurant** offers traditional table service and a continental menu. **Rio** is a Brazilian steak house, with waiters offering carved meats at dinner; other items are procured from a buffet. Both venues feature two or three nightly seatings. The cheerful **Trattoria di Gerry** serves pastas, pizzas, salads, plus items for purchase such as coffee and pastries. The extra-tariff **Cove Restaurant** ($25) has an upgraded menu. On some sailings, The Cove operates as an extension of the Crystal Restaurant with no surcharge.

The View, a 630-seat, two-level nightclub, overlooks the stern and is the largest public room. **Pub 437** recalls an English club ambience with a decor of leather, wood, and brass. Quieter types like the elegant, understated **Ocean Breeze Lounge** with its chandeliered ceiling. The cavernous **Wynmore Casino** impresses with a splashy entrance, Craftsman-style accents, and a double-height ceiling. Additional facilities include the **Fountain of Youth Spa, Mussel Beach Gym,** and **Treasure Chest Gift Shop.**

Age-appropriate kids' facilities on board include **Island Coconuts Club** for children ages 4–10, **Club Wave** for those ages 11–14, and **Open Water Club** for teens ages 15–17.

In early March 2010, Celebration Cruises moved *Bahamas Celebration* to Palm Beach (from Port Everglades), from where she sails every other day on two-night cruises to Grand Bahama Island. Passengers are offered the option to disembark and remain in the Bahamas with a hotel package at Our Lucaya Beach & Golf Resort. Celebration's move is considered a good fit for both the cruise line and the port. Palm Beach has wanted a cruise line to homeport there since it built an expensive terminal about ten years ago. At Port Everglades, Celebration was competing with larger, newer ships operated by much better-known lines. At Palm Beach, she is the only game in town.

Bahamas Celebration has made an ingenious transition from a Nordic workhorse to a Caribbean party girl. She offers a budget-minded option for new cruisers or a quick getaway for non-fussy types. For those wanting a longer vacation, two- and three-night stays at Atlantis or Comfort Suites Paradise Island in Nassau are available.

ITINERARIES *See* Itinerary Index.

Croceros Australis

(*See* Part Three, Adventure and Cultural Cruises)

Cruise North Expeditions

(*See* Part Three, Adventure and Cultural Cruises)

Discovery World Cruises

(*See* Voyages of Discovery, further in this chapter)

easyCruise

362, Syngrou Avenue, 176 74 Kallithea, Athens, Greece;
☎ U.S. and Canada (toll-free) 866 335 4975; U.K. 0871 210 0001;
Greece 211 211 6211; www.easycruise.com; email info@easyCruise.com

---

easyCruise Life **(231/574; GREEK/INTERNATIONAL/145; 452 FEET/12,637)**

Upstart easyCruise, launched in May 2005, was both a new cruise line and a new concept. Billed as no-frills cruising, the line "unbundled" the cruise package, selling cabins on board the ship on a night-by-night basis, for a two-night minimum, at low prices for a simply furnished cabin; passengers were charged for meals, housekeeping, and other onboard services. Initially, the line allowed passengers to hop on and off the ship, cruising for as many or as few nights as they wished, but that proved not to be practical. Now, passengers buy a specific number of days, as on other cruise ships, but still at a low cost and with some frills.

The venture was the brainchild of Stelios Haji-Ioannou, known to one and all simply as Stelios, the founder of easyGroup, which includes **easyJet.com,** the successful British no-frills airline, **easyHotel.com,** and other enterprises in the same low-cost, no-frills mode.

The first ship, *easyCruise One* (previously *Neptune*), was the former 114-passenger luxury *Renaissance II*, built in Italy in 1990. It was completely refitted with new interiors to carry 170 passengers in a no-frills style. The ship was retired in 2008 and, reportedly, was bought by a member of Dubai's ruling family to convert her into a super yacht.

The second ship, *easyCruise Life*, was given a complete renovation in 2008. The modern, more stylish, and comfortable ship has an attractive restaurant and bar, lounge, cabins showcasing a minimalist style, a spa and wellness zone, chill-out zone, and pool bar. The restaurant serves both Greek and international cuisine.

easyCruise Life, with more than double the capacity of the first ship, offers a wide range of air-conditioned suites and cabins. The one premium suite has floor-to-ceiling windows, while 14 panoramic and 14 junior suites have windows with a full view, and another six suites have a partial view. All are furnished with twin beds that convert to a double bed, a minibar, television, and bathroom with a shower. Bathrobes, slippers, and amenity kits are provided. All suites sleep up to four persons (the sofa bed sleeps one adult or two children).

Sixteen compact outside cabins have a window or porthole, twin beds, and sleep up to three persons. Eight compact outside cabins have a porthole, one lower and one upper bed, and sleep two persons. Sixty-five inside cabins have twin beds or one lower and one upper bed—some sleep up to four persons; all have a bathroom with a shower. The dining room serves breakfast, lunch, and dinner. The menu offers a variety of local specialties and international dishes as well as light meals and pizzas.

EasyCruise Life passengers range in age from the 20s and up, but to the surprise of the cruise line, the average age of passengers is 40. Tickets are sold via the Internet at **www.easyCruise.com.** The best prices are available to customers who book early. From its start, easyCruise calculated that its flexibility and low prices would attract a wider customer base of new travelers who have never cruised. That plan, apparently, has paid off.

easyCruise Life, which is managed by the well-known V Ships of Monaco, sails on three- and four-night cruises of the Aegean Islands and Turkey from April to mid-November.

In 2009, Hellenic Seaways, a Greek ferry line, purchased easyCruise and the rights to use the name in the Mediterranean, marking the giant Greek ferry line's first entry into cruise operations. The new owners are continuing to operate easyCruise in a similar way as the previous owner. Apparently Stelios, who owns a stake in Sea Star Capital, one of Hellenic Seaways' largest shareholders, still has an interest in easyCruise.

ITINERARIES *See* Itinerary Index.

Fred Olsen Cruise Lines

Fred Olsen House, White House Road, Ipswich IP1 5LL, United Kingdom;
☎ **01473-742434; fax 01473-292-410; www.fredolsencruises.co.uk;**
or c/o Borton Overseas, 5412 Lyndale Avenue South,
Minneapolis, MN 55419;
☎ **612-822-4640; fax 612-822-4755; www.bortonoverseas.com**

The family-operated cruise line, now in its 43rd year of operation, has acquired some of the best ships that main line cruise companies sold off in favor of big ships. Over the years, it has established a reputation for well-maintained, comfortable ships and the family's dedication to their operation. The British-based line offers a classic cruise experience with small-town friendliness and reasonable prices. It caters mostly to a British clientele, but their ships—the size and ambience—have found an American and Canadian audience who shun big ships. Aimed mainly at travelers over age 50, the line frequently promotes to this age group with special programs.

The line has a golf package available on selected cruises in the Baltic, Canary Islands, Caribbean, and Mediterranean. It consists of up to four rounds of golf ashore, the services of the resident PGA professional on board, competitions, and social activities for both players and nonplaying partners. The package must be booked in advance of one's cruise.

The Arts Club is a program of special-interest topics operating on selected cruises. The subjects, with expert lecturers and instruction, include music, dance, antiques, gardening, wine, photography, wildlife, bridge, and more. The programs are available to all passengers and at no additional cost (except wine tasting and painting materials). The cruise line provides a children's program with entertainment and activities on cruises over Easter, during July and August, and Christmas and New Year's on several ships. Smoking is now banned on all balconies and all restaurants on all Fred Olsen ships. It is also banned in all cabins and suites on *Boudicca* and in forward suites on Deck 9 on *Black Watch*. There are designated smoking areas in the lounges and bars.

Oceans is Olsen's past-passengers club and enables members to take advantage of some exclusive benefits with every booking. Members are awarded a Cruise Point for each night spent on board the line's ships since January 1, 2000; the more points one accrues, the more benefits to be enjoyed. The conditions and benefits are detailed on the line's Web site. Members are automatically enrolled upon return from their first cruise and are issued a membership number to be used when booking future cruises. The cruise line also publishes an online newsletter. British sterling is the currency of the fleet. Note: All passengers must have traveler's insurance, which Americans must purchase in the United States, and provide their policy number to the cruise line in advance of their cruise.

Black Watch (320/807; NORWEGIAN/INTERNATIONAL; 674 FEET/28,613 TONS)

Formerly the *Royal Viking Star*, the much-loved *Black Watch* was judged too small and too old to compete in the U.S. market and was sold to Fred Olsen Lines in 1996 and given an $8 million refurbishment. In 2005, the ship was given major surgery during a 63-day refit to install four new engines and renovate her cabins, as well as add 36 balconies to cabins on the Bridge Deck. In early December 2009, during an extensive refurbishment of her public areas, a new casual dining area was created.

The new, casual **Braemar Garden,** midship on Deck 6, was created in the space where the Braemar Lounge and Garden Cafe were situated, replacing the smaller Garden Cafe. Fresher and more contemporary, Braemar Garden has a new bar and buffet and offers a more spacious option for dining. One section is screened off as a 40-seat room that can be used for private dining.

The ship's public areas are exceptional. The library is among cruising's largest and most splendidly appointed. (Unfortunately, it's open only a couple of hours each day.) Equally impressive is the card and game room. Both rooms display artifacts from earlier ships in the Olsen fleet. During the 2009 face-lift, **Neptune Lounge, Piper's Bar,** and **Glentanar Restaurant** (the main dining room) got new furnishings.

The refurbished **Observation Lounge** overlooks the bow and **Lido Lounge,** the stern. Both provide live music well into the night. A third bar/lounge adjoining the main showroom honors the Scottish Black Watch Regiment in its decor. The ship also has a 170-seat auditorium that occasionally hosts classical concerts.

The ship's cabins come in a bewildering number of configurations. Thirty-nine cabins are singles. Although most are small, all are nicely appointed. Ninety percent are outside with portholes, a picture window, or a private veranda. Baths are well designed, and many were recently refitted. All cabins have televisions and phones, and many have refrigerators.

Well-designed public areas continue outside with a promenade that encircles the ship. Also available are pools, Jacuzzis, exercise pools, golf nets, bars, cafes, casino, an Internet center, and outdoor areas (some covered) for sunning or relaxing.

Entertainment is professional, varied, and appealing to a range of ages and backgrounds. It puts to shame the offerings aboard many superliner competitors. During a recent voyage, we enjoyed Las Vegas–style production shows, an incredibly talented opera company, an illusionist, a comic, a celebrity vocalist, and classical music concerts. Lounges and the casino bustle into the wee hours. Theme cruises are varied.

For an American, the greatest pleasure aboard *Black Watch* is meeting Britons—delightful, interested, and interesting. Many hours are spent with new English, Scottish, Welsh, and Irish friends exploring the subtleties that make our cultures so similar yet so different. Some misunderstandings of idiom and accent are uproarious: Announcement of a "folkloric presentation" was heard by the Americans as a "full colonic presentation.". . . We couldn't wait! Because the British are gracious and friendly, being the minority was a special pleasure.

In January 2011, the ship will depart on her fifth world cruise.

Boudicca (320/839; NORWEGIAN/INTERNATIONAL; 674 FEET/28,388 TONS)

The *Boudicca* began life as *Royal Viking Sky* and for a short while was the *Grand Latino* of Spanish tour operator Iberojet before being acquired by Olsen. As a sister to *Black Watch*, she is an ideal fit, further enhancing the line's style of worldwide itineraries on small, more intimate cruise ships. The purchase also gave Olsen an opportunity to expand its fleet quickly and to operate an even wider choice of itineraries for its repeat customers.

Boudicca underwent extensive, multimillion-dollar renovations prior to entering service in February 2006. In keeping with the cruise line's tradition, the refit included the creation of 44 single cabins, some with a veranda, making it an ideal choice for the solo traveler. The ship has a wide selection of cabins and suites, ranging in size from 140-square-foot inside cabins to 550-square-foot top suites with sitting room and veranda. All cabins have television, hair dryer, and luxury Molton Brown toiletries. The top suites also have a DVD/CD player, minibar, and refrigerator. All cabins are nonsmoking.

Boudicca has three dining rooms with open seating for breakfast and lunch and assigned seating for dinner. The informal **Secret Garden** is an option for breakfast, lunch, and dinner buffet and an outdoor grill for lunch, weather permitting. In the evening, musical and comedy shows are staged in the ship's show lounge. Music for dancing is available nightly. Other facilities include a fully equipped gym offering exercise classes, a spa, swimming pool, wading pool, hot tubs, and a swim-against-the-current pool; an Internet room with six computers; and two small shops. During summer and holidays, the ship has a supervised children's program.

Braemar (310/727; EUROPEAN/INTERNATIONAL; 537 FEET/19,089 TONS)

The former *Crown Dynasty* of Crown Cruise Line and *Norwegian Dynasty* of Norwegian Cruise Lines, she is one of the nicest ships in her size and price category in cruising. She is small enough to be cozy but large enough to offer modern cruise-ship amenities and facilities.

Elegant but not stuffy, *Braemar*'s decor communicates a sophistication that is apparent the moment you step on board. Expansive glass windows throughout the ship, large open decks and terraces, and a five-story atrium with walls of glass create a feeling of space and openness. Polished woods, gentle lighting, and soft hues contribute to the stylish comfort.

Built in Spain in 1993 and originally designed by Scandinavian architect Petter Yran, known for his work on many luxury ships, the pretty *Braemar* was given a face-lift in 2001, and a drastic one in 2008, when the ship was cut in half and a new section was put in place that provided for more accommodations, increasing the total passenger capacity from 727 to 968. Many accommodations have balconies, bringing the total number of cabins and suites with balconies to 70.

Significant additions to passenger facilities are seen on the Marquee Deck (Deck 8) with the brand-new **Observatory Lounge;** the **Grampian Restaurant,** a new dining facility; and a completely transformed pool area, with two swimming pools, a pool bar, and a dedicated children's pool. Another new enhancement is the **Morning Light Pub** next to the Neptune Lounge on the Lounge Deck (Deck 5), a popular place to relax with a drink and enjoy live evening entertainment. Aft on the Bridge Deck (Deck 7), close to the **Skylark Club,** is the new **Arts and Crafts Room,** which is used for talks and other events as part of Fred Olsen's Arts Club program.

Some of the existing facilities have a new location: the beauty salon and fitness center were moved to the Atlantic Deck (Deck 3) midship, and the Internet room is now on the Lounge Deck (Deck 5), along with the card room and library. Overall, many wonderful new spaces have been created.

From the beginning, the layout of the eight-deck ship was unusual, if not unique. The five-deck, greenery-filled atrium lobby is aft, rather than midship. Also, it's on the starboard side rather than at the center, with windows spanning Decks 4 to 8, admitting natural light and sea views, and helping connect passengers with the sea. Four of the main public rooms are stacked vertically at the stern, allowing for large windows in virtually every area. The decks are connected by outdoor stairways and open decks.

Deck 5 is devoted to public rooms. It's anchored at both ends by lounges oriented to the port side horizontally and facing large windows (rather than the usual arrangement of lounges facing the bow or stern). The multilevel show lounge, for example, is semicircular, with the stage and dance floor on the port side. Between the lounges are shops, the photo gallery and tours desk, and the elegant **Braemar Room**—a relaxing lounge with cocktail music and a bar.

Cabins are on five decks; about two-thirds are outside. They are nicely appointed in pastels with light wood furniture and brass fixtures. All have television, phone, safe, and card-key door lock. Closet space is good, but drawer space is minimal. Many cabins are fitted with twin beds that can be converted to a queen. Bathrooms are small but have large medicine cabinets, mirrored doors, and vanities. Deluxe cabins and suites have refrigerators and sitting areas with large windows. Four wheelchair-accessible cabins have large bathrooms with grab bars and wide doorways. There are four elevators.

The dining room has a skylight and panoramic windows on three sides, providing natural light and sea views for all diners. Although tables are close, noise is low. The room, decorated in muted colors with lively, contemporary art, has a variety of table configurations.

Above the dining room on Deck 5 is the **Coral Club,** a comfortable lounge with bar and a small stage for live music shows. The small dance floor comes into its own during the evening. Above on Deck 6 is the **Palms Café**—a casual indoor/outdoor cafe—more elegantly decorated than usual for a Lido cafe. Up on Deck 7 is the **Skylark Club**—two lounges with a full-service bar, which can be divided by screens or left as one large sitting and relaxing area. It's also used as the disco by night. The slot machine room is close by. The ship also has a cozy library with good sea views, a card room, an Internet center, a small casino, and a medical center.

The spa is equipped with state-of-the-art exercise equipment, an aerobics area, a juice bar, two saunas, and steam and massage rooms. Windscreens line the deck's perimeter. A wide, outside promenade circling Deck 5 provides an uninterrupted track for walking or jogging.

The 2010 Caribbean cruise features a Flagship Golf Package with access to an 18-hole course at ports of call. This package costs $660 per golfer and includes four rounds of golf (including fees and transportation), free practice facilities on board, a welcome party, up to five sessions with a resident PGA pro, onboard social gatherings, and fun competitions. For details, go to **www.fredolsencruises-flagshipgolf.co.uk.**

Balmoral **(710/1,350; NORWEGIAN/INTERNATIONAL/510; 720 FEET/43,537 TONS)**

Acquired from Star Cruises, one of the owners of Norwegian Cruise lines, the *Balmoral* was originally built in 1988 as the *Norwegian Crown* of NCL at the Meyer Werft shipyard in Germany. When she was transferred to Olsen in autumn 2007, she had a 90-foot section inserted at a Hamburg shipyard. It increased her capacity by 350 berths, including 79 single cabins and nine wheelchair-accessible ones. At the same time, she was given an extensive refurbishment prior to joining the fleet in January 2008, becoming the largest passenger ship in the Olsen fleet.

During the renovations, the public areas were redesigned, the accommodations altered by adding balconies to many suites and converting several cabins and suites into a single accommodation, and, in general, the ship was brought in line with *Black Watch*. Balmoral's facilities now include three restaurants with two seatings and assigned tables, an observation lounge and bar on the top deck, a show lounge, a pub, two swimming pools, a spa with six treatment rooms and two saunas, a fitness center, an Internet center with 14 computers, and one of the best libraries on any ship.

The *Balmoral* added a new dimension to the Olsen product, with its range of facilities and cabin sizes well suited for long-range cruising as well as shorter U.K.-based routes.

The itinerary of *Balmoral*'s 2010 world cruise was changed to avoid potential pirate danger when sailing through the Gulf of Aden. Instead, the 106-night cruise departed in early January from Dover to sail around Africa and is calling at South Africa and Mauritius instead of Dubai and Salalah. She returns to Dover in April.

In April 2012, the *Balmoral* will mark the 100th anniversary of the *Titanic* sinking on a *Titanic*-themed cruise that will include a memorial service in the early hours of April 15, 2012, above the *RMS Titanic* vessel that lies on the Atlantic floor. The ship will leave Southampton, England, on April 8, and sail to Cobh, Ireland, where the *Titanic* made its final port of call on April 11, 1912. The cruise will continue following the *Titanic*'s route and arrive over the spot where the ship sank on April 14. After the memorial service, the *Balmoral* will continue on to Halifax, Nova Scotia, where passengers can visit Fairview Lawn Cemetery, the resting place of 121 *Titanic* victims, along with Mount Olivet Catholic Cemetery and Hirsch Jewish Cemetery, which also have graves of *Titanic* victims. The cruise's final destination—as was planned for the original voyage—is New York City.

ITINERARIES *See* Itinerary Index.

Genting Hong Kong Limited (formerly Star Cruises)
Hong Kong Office, 1528 Ocean Centre, 5 Canton Road,
Tsimshatsui, Hong Kong SAR; ☎ 852-2317-7711; fax 852-2317-5551;
www.starcruises.com

A Malaysian-based cruise line, owned by Genting Group, a publicly traded investment group, recently changed its name from the widely recognized and snappy Star Cruises to the less-than-catchy Genting Hong Kong Limited. It appears that big changes are afoot with Genting, a powerful corporation in the region that runs the highly successful Genting Highlands Resort, a casino in Malaysia. Part owner of the Norwegian Cruise Line and Cruise Ferries brands, the company also has a hand in oil-palm plantations, property development, power generation, and oil- and gas-related business activities. Genting is scaling back its Asia cruise division, which was launched in 1993; at press time, several vessels in their Asia-based fleet were either laid-up, for sale, and/or offered for long-term charter. Currently, two ships operate out of Singapore and Hong Kong year-round. Although overall quality has slipped over the past few years, Star's strengths have always been its variety of restaurants serving a range of cuisine from Chinese to Indian, Italian, and Japanese, along with impressive entertainment, family-friendly features, and friendly (and patient) crew members, who know how to cater to a diverse mix of passengers.

SuperStar Virgo **(980/1,960; INTERNATIONAL/1,100; 879 FEET/76,800 TONS)**

SuperStar Virgo arrived in 1999. A classic megaliner on par with NCL's ships of the same vintage, she has multiple Vegas-style entertainment lounges, nine restaurants (four serving exclusively Asian fare), and excellent facilities for children. *SuperStar Virgo* does a good job catering to both Asian and non-Asian clientele, except on its two-night weekend cruises-to-nowhere that are heavily focused on gambling. These weekend cruises attract mostly gamblers, and the casino is so packed that passengers stand five and six deep around the card tables. We definitely recommend the three-, four-, or five-night itineraries, which offer a much more well-rounded cruise experience. Singaporean Chinese and Malays are in the majority on most cruises, followed by a sizable contingent of Indians from the Subcontinent, Australians, and a handful of Europeans, North Americans, and other Asians.

The ship offers a casino, spa, and fitness center, shops, library and Internet center, and an impressive indoor/outdoor children's space that includes a large outdoor play area with themed pool. Cabins are definitely on the small side—avoid the cramped inside cabins—but, for the most part, the other categories are comfortable and stylish and offer extras like tea- and coffeemakers.

The ship's cruising speed is a zippy 25.5 knots, enabling her to include more ports of call on her itineraries. She sails on one- to five-night cruises to Malaysia and Thailand, round-trip from Singapore.

SuperStar Aquarius **(765/1,529; SCANDINAVIAN/INTERNATIONAL; 754 FEET/51,039 TONS)**

The ship offers a multitude of cuisine (Asian and Chinese, Continental, Japanese, Indian, and more), unremarkable Vegas-style entertainment, and activities that appeal to families, honeymooners, senior citizens, and business and incentives groups that hail mostly from China and Hong Kong.

Oceana Barbecue, Spices, Mariner's Buffet, and **Dynasty** are all buffet restaurants whose names indicate their specialties. **Taipan** is the Chinese à la carte fine-dining venue for frequent cruisers who become part of the "Member's Club" and receive various perks. Other dining choices include **Blue Lagoon,** a 24-hour bistro offering local and international delicacies; **Champ's,** the pool bar; and **Aquarius Lounge,** offering cocktails, specialty coffees, and music.

The ship has an outdoor swimming pool and Jacuzzi, jogging track, basketball court, golf driving range, and a spa, beauty salon, sauna, and gym. The show lounge stages international entertainment, and there are also a karaoke lounge, casino, and several lounges with music. Shops, a card room, video arcade, meeting room, and a small children's playroom and nursery are available as well.

SuperStar Aquarius has been sailing from Hong Kong; but at press time, no future itineraries were available.

ITINERARIES *See* Itinerary Index.

Hapag-Lloyd Cruises
1640 Hempstead Turnpike, East Meadow, NY 11554,
☎ 800-334-0284; www.hl-cruises.com; www.eurolloyd.com

Hapag-Lloyd Cruises traces its origins back to the mid-19th century and two venerable German shipping companies, Hamburg America Line of Hamburg and North German Lloyd of Bremen. Until World War II, the two companies operated some of the world's largest and fastest liners and were pioneers in the operation of pleasure cruises. Today the company's cruising arm is only a very small part of a giant—the third largest in the world—Hamburg-based container-shipping operation.

The current fleet offers the very high standards of the past, and while the majority of its cruises are designed for the German market, the line aims to increase its numbers of North American passengers with a group of cruises that are designated "bilingual" on its Web site and in its literature. These cruises have bilingual menus, programs, entertainment, lectures, and video presentations, and announcements in English. Most of the crew, mainly German and Filipino, speak English. But some passengers report they have found that language continues to be a barrier for those who do not understand German.

The vessels boast high space-to-passenger and crew-to-passenger ratios. They are decidedly European, yet each has her own distinct character and distinctive features. Daytime usually has everyone in an adventure mode and dress; nighttime brings out conservative fineries. Hapag-Lloyd Cruises has three U.S. offices with toll-free booking numbers.

Europa (204/408; GERMAN/INTERNATIONAL/275;
652 FEET/28,600 TONS)

The flagship of Hapag-Lloyd Cruises, *Europa* is primarily a German ship, but to attract English-speaking travelers, Hapag-Lloyd has extended its bilingual sailings to attract more U.S. and Canadian passengers. However, the effort has not always been consistent. On a recent cruise specifically marketed as a bilingual one, all officers and crew spoke English, but the entertainment was in German only, with no translation. When we reported this to Hapag-Lloyd's U.S. representatives, they maintain that all dedicated bilingual cruises are now fully bilingual, no matter if 1 or 15 English-speaking people join. We'll keep checking.

To take one example, on the last night of a cruise, the captain traditionally holds an auction—the money goes to charity—of the chart for that cruise. The captain is good at the task and is very animated. For those who understand German, it must be hilarious, but for non-German speakers it's difficult, even when translation is offered. Fortunately, one cruise netted $150,000 for UNICEF.

The all-suite ship, known for its attention to detail, is designed for cruisers who have refined tastes and are interested in the music, food, and art of the places the ship visits. On board, there are wine masters, three-star Michelin guest chefs, and a PGA professional to help golfers improve their game. The line provides renowned lecturers; arranges excursions for passengers to view art, architecture, and nature; and looks for cruises that provide once-in-a-lifetime experiences. *Europa*'s size allows her to dock at smaller ports or anchor off remote beaches. She carries Zodiacs to reach remote areas.

Europa's spacious suites, ranging from 291 to 915 square feet, have large living and bedroom areas, a luxurious bathroom, and a minibar. All furnishings are top of the line. Marking her tenth birthday in 2009, the ship was given a face-lift; all accommodations received fresh new fabrics and colors, and the penthouse suites were fully renovated. She also gained Cruise Net, one of the finest infotainment systems at sea, which includes a television, music center, an information medium with which guests can send and receive personal e-mails free of charge, as well as movies, music on demand, cruise information, and the Internet. The e-mail system and the music choices are great. The exception is television, which carries Cubavision, DW, and the recently added BBC—the only English-language station. One DW radio station does report some English-language news. There are about a dozen English-language films offered, along with a choice of 150 German flicks (without subtitles). *Europa*'s Penthouse Deck has ten Deluxe Suites and two Grand Suites. Each Grand Suite has its own sauna, whirlpool, guest bathroom, and a dining table for six. Passengers on Penthouse Decks are served by personal butlers 24/7. In 2007, four spa suites were added. Most of the other 192 outer suites have balconies. Two suites are specially designed for disabled persons.

The *Europa*'s main restaurant, which can accommodate all passengers at one seating for all meals, serves haute cuisine. Two specialty restaurants, **Oriental** and **Venezia,** offer Asian and Italian cuisine. Europa Deck has a cigar bar, piano bar, the **Clipper Lounge** for cocktails and snacks, and a boutique. On the Lido Deck, an informal indoor/outdoor cafe serves a buffet and snacks three times a day. The Lido Deck also has a club and bar, a well-stocked library (including a shelf of left-behind English-language paperbacks), and an auditorium where lectures and films (in German and English on bilingual cruises) are presented frequently. The ship's entertainment ranges from classical musicians to well-known popular acts.

The newly designed **Ocean Spa** on the Sports Deck now has four enclosed spa treatment suites and an enlarged fitness loft with ocean views. The center is fitted with a sauna, steam bath, massage parlor, Japanese bath, and solarium. The fitness center covers three levels—all with ocean views. Top-of-the-line equipment for cardiovascular training and other exercises is available, as is a personal trainer for individual programs and fitness counseling. The golf-training unit has a golf simulator, video analysis, two tee-offs, and a putting green. The swimming pool, one of the longest on any cruise ship, has a magrodome for use as an indoor as well as an outdoor pool.

Sansibar at the stem, designed in cooperation with its namesake's creators on the island of Sylt, enjoys great ocean views. The sophisticated **Club Belvedere** is almost entirely glassed-in, providing another venue for sea views.

Families with children are welcome on the *Europa*, with a special children's program and staff during vacation periods. The ship has two children's areas—for younger and older children.

Europa also has a fully equipped hospital and two self-service launderettes.

For luxury and beauty, *Europa* is a wonderful cruise experience, particularly for those who understand some German, as she sails to exotic ports around the world. *Europa* is a ship for well-traveled English speakers, content to be on their own, not particularly interested in interacting with other passengers or who don't mind missing some of the action due to the language barrier. We are told that the mandatory fire drill is now conducted in English as well as German.

Europa—in cooperation with eight international opera houses, including New York's Metropolitan Opera—hosted its first annual classical music competition at sea named Stella Maris ("Stars of the High Seas") on board a sold-out European cruise in October 2009. Via an arrangement with Cruise Critic, online viewers could vote on the competition, which focused on up-and-coming young singers.

Note: The euro is the currency of the ship. When checking prices for spa treatments, shore excursions, or a bottle of wine, it's important to remember that you are reading euros, not U.S. dollars; thus, at the current rate of exchange, prices may be considerably higher than you might think at first glance.

Bremen (82/164; GERMAN/INTERNATIONAL; 366 FEET/6,752 TONS)

Described as a world-class private club aboard a first-class exploration cruise ship, the *Bremen* (formerly *Frontier Spirit*) was constructed at the Kobe Shipyard in Japan by Mitsubishi Heavy Industries in 1990. Slightly smaller than the *Hanseatic,* the *Bremen* is a fine expedition vessel with an ice-hardened hull, which means she can sail in places such as Antarctica. Her 16-foot draft enables her to sail to remote areas of the Amazon and Orinoco rivers, and her Zodiac landing craft allows her to take passengers even farther into areas where large ships cannot go.

Public rooms include a light-filled observation lounge that is used for lectures, a roomy main lounge and bar with a small dance floor and band, and a well-stocked library. The restaurant operates on an open-seating plan for breakfast and lunch and assigned seating for dinner. Meals are prepared with high-quality ingredients. Additional amenities include a sauna, small fitness room, and a heated outdoor swimming pool, usable for polar bear types in cold-weather conditions, with a pool bar and awnings covering 60% of the deck.

All cabins, arranged in four categories, are outside and measure a standard 149 square feet. They have a sitting and bedroom area, large panoramic windows or portholes, and private bath. Eighteen cabins have private verandas. All cabins are fitted with closed-circuit television, satellite telephone, writing desk, a moderate amount of closet space for a casual cruise, and a stocked minibar; bathrooms have a hair dryer and bathrobes. In addition to the cabin amenities, suites have a large, comfortable entertaining area and separate sleeping area with twin beds convertible to queen. All cabins have a special niche for storing personal expedition gear and a warming drawer for drying wet clothing.

The *Bremen* is often chartered for worldwide cruising by American special-interest and alumni groups, among whom her reputation is high.

Hanseatic **(92/184; GERMAN/INTERNATIONAL; 403 FEET/8,378 TONS)**

A small ship offering adventure-in-luxury cruises, *Hanseatic* was launched in 1993 as one of the most luxurious, technologically advanced adventure-cruise vessels afloat, and at the time set a new level of luxury for adventure cruises. The small ship offers a high crew-to-passenger ratio and amenities typical of small luxury ships. Her rich wood, brass interiors, and fine appointments create the atmosphere of a private yacht.

Hanseatic is said to be one of the most environmentally friendly cruise ships ever built, with a nonpolluting water disposal system, a pollution-filtered incinerator, and full biological treatment plant. The sleek vessel, designated 1A Super Ice class—the highest rating for a passenger vessel—can carry passengers into the far reaches of the Arctic and Antarctica, while her shallow draft, small size, and maneuverability enable her to penetrate deep into the Amazon and other areas inaccessible to most cruise ships.

The *Hanseatic* has six passenger decks with public rooms on all of them. The reception area and all-purpose **Explorer's Lounge** is on Explorer Deck, the dining room is one flight below on Marco Polo Deck, and the **Columbus Lounge** for casual dining is one flight up on Bridge Deck. **Darwin Hall,** the lecture hall, is located on the lowest deck.

Topside, the Observation Deck is a combination sports and sun deck with a small outdoor swimming pool and a glass-enclosed indoor hot tub. The ship has a small health club with exercise equipment, sauna, massage therapy, and a beauty salon. Forward, the **Observation Lounge,** with a 180-degree span of windows, is the ship's most popular room, where passengers socialize and relax while viewing the passing scene. The lounge has a library, ocean charts, maps, and a radar monitor to follow the progress of the ship. Essentially, the *Hanseatic* is a nonsmoking vessel, but passengers are allowed to smoke in certain clearly marked smoking areas.

Outside cabins come in six categories and are located on four of the ship's seven decks. All are large (standard average dimension, 236 square feet) with separate sitting areas and large windows. Recently, the ship's accommodations underwent major renovations to replace cabin windows, to gut and rebuild bathrooms with separate bathtubs and showers, and to add new marble walls and granite floors. Two suites received a new cabin design. The cabins are furnished with twin or queen beds, writing desk, spacious closets, a flat-screen television and DVD, radio, hair dryer, and a refrigerator restocked daily with soft drinks and water. Some cabins accommodate third and fourth persons. Four deluxe suites have a separate sleeping area, walk-in closets, and a large entertaining area. The suites and eight deluxe cabins on Bridge Deck have butler service. The ship also has a small boutique for gifts and clothing. In the recent renovations, the hair salon was transformed into a modern styling and cosmetics studio.

The **Marco Polo Dining Room,** an attractive setting with large windows on three sides at the stern, accommodates all passengers at a single, open seating for breakfast and lunch and assigned seating for dinner. Some passengers give the food high marks; most call it uneventful. Casual breakfast and lunch buffet are served in the airy Columbus Lounge with an indoor/outdoor seating—weather permitting. At night on select evenings, the Columbus Lounge is transformed into the intimate, reservations-only (no extra charge) **Ethno Restaurant** and serves a fixed menu with a regional theme related to the area of cruising. Daily in the Explorer's Lounge, an English tea is served with piano background music. Room service offers in-cabin dining.

Life aboard is casual, unregimented, and leisurely paced, with none of the organized activity that typifies mainstream cruise ships. Every cruise has lecturers, who might include naturalists, marine biologists, geologists, zoologists, research scientists, or anthropologists. They make daily presentations with films and slides and accompany shore excursions, acting as guides; and in the late afternoon, they recap the day's visit. Four tenders and 14 Zodiac landing craft take passengers ashore, from the Far North or the Galápagos to Antarctica. Parkas and rubberized boots are issued gratis to all passengers on Arctic and Antarctic voyages; snorkel equipment is provided in the tropics.

Hanseatic cruises are designed for passengers seeking off-the-beaten-path voyages in comfort. Her passengers are small-ship devotees, affluent, age 50 and older, adventurous, interested in natural history, and committed to preserving the environment. They are independent, active, seasoned travelers accustomed to luxury and quality. The ship globe-trots throughout the year. Although most of her cruises are light adventures, many entail considerable walking, wet landings, and climbing in and out of Zodiacs in remote areas. Anyone with physical limitations or health problems should not underestimate the difficulties they could encounter. The Antarctica itineraries involve traversing the Drake Passage, a notoriously rough stretch of water. Often, this ship is on charter to an American cruise line or group.

On August 16, 2010, the *Hanseatic* will sail on a Northwest Passage itinerary, on one of the most challenging sea routes in the world. The fully bilingual voyage departs Kangerlussuaq, Greenland, for a 24-day voyage around Greenland and the Arctic Circle, ending in Nome, Alaska, on September 9.

ITINERARIES *See* Itinerary Index.

Hebridean Island Cruises
Kintail House, Carleton New Road, Skipton, North Yorkshire,
United Kingdom BD23 2DE; ☎ 011-44-1756-704-700 or 800-659-2648;
fax 011-44-1756-704-794; www.hebridean.co.uk

Two weeks after *Hebridean Princess*'s parent company, Hebridean International Cruises, went into "administration" (a British term similar to receivership), All Leisure Group, which owns Swan Hellenic and Voyages of Discovery lines, and headed by Lord Sterling, bought *Hebridean Princess* for £1.4 million. Hebridean had already sold its larger ship, the 98-passenger *Hebridean Spirit* for $7 million. Lord Sterling, chairman of Swan Hellenic, became chairman of the renamed

Hebridean Island Cruises, and All Leisure indicated that it intended to continue the traditional itineraries of *Hebridean Princess*—famously chartered by Queen Elizabeth for her 80th birthday—and to increase her range.

Hebridean Princess **(30/49; ENGLISH/SCOTTISH/38; 235 FEET/2112 TONS)**

Built in 1964 to carry 600 passengers, Hebridean Island Cruises redesigned the ship in 1994 to carry only 49 passengers in the gracious style of a deluxe country inn. The well-appointed accommodations vary from 11 singles with shared facilities to suites. The ship has a lounge, restaurant, library of books and videos, and shop. She visits lochs, estuaries, and Scotland's Inner and Outer Hebrides islands on three- to eight-night cruises from March to November, usually departing from the West Highlands port of Oban.

A selection of "Footloose" cruises caters to most walking abilities and offers a range of guided walks in the hills and mountains, seashores, and lochs, with the promise of a nip of whiskey and a fine and hearty meal back on board. With a passenger-to-crew ratio of about one-to-one, you are almost guaranteed the excellent service for which the ship is known. It isn't often a cruise can be called unique, but this one is, and passengers often say there is no cruising experience quite like it.

All-inclusive prices start at about £800 for a four-night Highland cruise and include house wines and spirits, Champagne, beer, soft drinks, tea, and coffee throughout the cruise; up to three walking guides on each of the Footloose itineraries; use of the ship's bicycles, gym equipment, and fishing tackle; all gratuities (the line actively discourages tipping); and port and passenger taxes.

ITINERARIES *See* Itinerary Index.

Hurtigruten

(*See* Part Three, Cruising Alternatives: Norwegian Coastal Cruises and Cruise Ferries)

Kristina Cruises
**Kirkkokatu 16, 48100 Kotka, Finland; ☎ 358-5-211-4230;
fax 358-5-211-4500; www.kristinacruises.com**

Kristina Cruises, the Finland-based shipping company, has almost 60 years' experience in the cruise business. Today, the second generation of the Partanen family heads the company and operates two cruise ships.

Kristina Regina **(119/245; FINNISH/55; 327 FEET/4,295 TONS)**

The ship, which has a receptive audience among well-traveled Americans, sails on multi-length itineraries that visit the Baltic region, Iceland, the Mediterranean, and West Africa. In spring of 2001, she underwent a million-dollar renovation. She has an English-speaking staff, two dining rooms and one evening restaurant, a cafe, library, health center, sauna, laundry, and Sun Decks. Dining is at one seating; menus vary. Her small size enables her to dock within walking distance of town centers.

Kristina Brahe **(57/129; FINNISH/24; 186 FEET/1,105 TONS)**

Regina's sister ship, in summer of 2003, inaugurated cruises on the route of the Russian czars between the Finnish archipelago and Lake Saimaa, taking passengers to the destinations westbound from Helsinki through the Finnish Archipelago National Park and different outer islands. The eastbound cruise leads through the Saimaa canal to Lappeenranta and on the Saimaa to Savonlinna, a town noted for its opera festival. These cruises won the Scandinavian Travel Award in 2004.

Bookings in the United States can be made through the following agencies: Scantours, CA; ☎ 800-223-7226; **www.scantours.com;** Five Stars of Scandinavia, WA; ☎ 800-722-4126; **www.5stars-of-scandinavia.com;** Borton Overseas, MN; ☎ 800-843-0602; **www.bortonoverseas.com**. In Canada: Valhalla Travel, Ontario; ☎ 800-265-0459; **www.valhallatravel.com.**

ITINERARIES *See* Itinerary Index.

Lindblad Expeditions

(*See* Part Three, Cruising Alternatives, Adventure and Cultural Cruises)

Louis Cruises
8, Antoniou Ambatielou Street, Piraeus 185 36 , Greece;
☎ 011 30 210 458-3403; fax 011 30 210 458–3479;
e-mail sales@louiscruises.gr
U.S. (toll-free) ☎ 877-louis-us or 877-568-4787 or 305-682-0109;
fax 305-682-0963; www.louiscruises.com;
e-mail LCLUSA@louiscruises.com
Louis UK, Chesterfield House, 385-387 Euston Road, London, NW1 3AU;
☎ 0800-0183883; fax + 44-2073832992; e-mail cruise@louis-uk.co.uk

The Cyprus-based Louis Cruises, which markets its ships in North America through U.S. tour companies, stepped up its U.S. presence in early 2007 by joining the Niche Cruise Marketing Alliance (NCMA), a group of 14 small U.S. and foreign cruise lines whose purpose is to help its members penetrate the U.S. market. Louis Cruises, a well-established cruise and hotel company in the Eastern Mediterranean, began more than 30 years ago, operating short cruises from Cyprus to the Eastern Mediterranean. Today with a fleet of 12 small and midsize cruise ships, the company operates classic cruises of 3 to 16 days out of Genoa and Marseilles to the West Mediterranean and North Africa and from Cyprus and Piraeus to the Greek Islands and the Eastern Mediterranean. In December 2009, in a joint five-year venture with Kerala Tourism, Louis launched a new operation in India with the 1,200-passenger *Aquamarine,* departing from the southwestern port of Kochi to the Maldives, as well as between Kochi and Sri Lanka on two to three cruises.

The ships that the line sells directly—*Aegean Pearl, Aquamarine, The Calypso, Coral, Emerald, Louis Cristal, Louis Majesty, Orient Queen*—sail on a wide variety of itineraries to France, Gibraltar, Italy, Portugal, and Spain; to North Africa, visiting Morocco, Tunisia, Malta, and Libya; and to Greece, the Greek Isles, Turkey, Egypt, and Israel, plus short-term cruises from Cyprus to Israel and Egypt. Passengers on the Greek Island cruises have the option of embarking in Piraeus, Istanbul, Kusadasi, or Mykonos and disembarking in Santorini.

The cruise line's latest acquisition, *Louis Majesty* (formerly NCL's *Norwegian Majesty*), began sailing from Genoa and Marseilles in December 2009. Built in 1992, she was lengthened in 1999, with a 112-foot midsection that added 202 cabins, a second pool, a second dining room, casino, outdoor bar, restaurant, coffee bar, more elevators, and deck space, and increased the ship's capacity to a maximum of 1,790 passengers. The nine-deck ship has an understated elegance intended to appeal to affluent passengers. Stylish interiors create a harmonious environment of simplicity and clean lines. The ship is laid out well with many quiet corners; forward lounges have walls of sloped windows.

Cabins come in 14 categories that range from Owner's Suites to inside cabins with lower and upper berths. About 65% are outside cabins. Standard cabins, modest in size, have clean, uncluttered lines and are finished in natural wood. Most have twin beds separated by a chest of drawers, a desk unit with drawer space, and a dressing mirror; three closets add to storage. Bathrooms have showers and a large sink, with ample counter and shelf space and a hair dryer. Forward on Majesty Deck, a group of cabins spans an unusual half-moon contour overlooking the bow. The impressive main dining room has wraparound, full-length windows. The Palace Theater, the show lounge, is on one level with a steeply tiered floor. Sight lines to the circular stage are excellent from almost every seat. The ship has a fitness center, spa, small beauty parlor, and a jogging track circles the Promenade deck.

The seven-deck *Coral* (486 feet; 13,995 tons) has 344 air-conditioned cabins (231 outside; 113 inside), all equipped with bath with shower, phone, and radio. Most cabins have two lower beds; some have a third and/or fourth upper bed. The ship has a dining room, theater, nightclub, disco, casino, small pool, gym and sauna, jogging track, and two elevators.

The eight-deck *Orient Queen* (525 feet; 15,781 tons) has 364 air-conditioned cabins (199 outside; 165 inside), all equipped with bath with shower, phone, and plasma television. Most cabins have two lower beds or double; some have a third and/or fourth berth. All ten deluxe cabins have a minibar and a bathtub. The ship has a dining room, Lido buffet, disco, several bars, show lounge, casino, small pool, fitness center, beauty salon, card room, library, children's club, shops, and four elevators. The ship operates cruises from France and Italy.

The seven-deck *Aegean Pearl* (537 feet; 16,710 tons) has 395 air-conditioned cabins (261 outside; 134 inside), all equipped with bath with shower, phone, and radio. Most cabins have two lower beds; some have a third and/or fourth upper berth. The 52 suites and deluxe cabins have sofa and bathtub. The ship has two restaurants, show lounge, disco, several bars, casino, two swimming pools, spa and fitness center, ice-cream parlor, beauty salon, card room, minigolf course, children's club, shops, and four elevators.

Two Louis Cruises' ships, *Thomson Destiny* and *Thomson Spirit*, are chartered to Thomson Cruises of TUI AG. The NCMA Web site (**www .nichecruise.com**) has information on Louis Cruise Lines and a direct link to its Web site, as well as information on the alliance's 13 other members.

ITINERARIES   *See* Itinerary Index.

Nomade Yachting
P.O. Box 40186, Fare Tony–Vaiete, 98713 Papeete, Tahiti, French Polynesia; ☎ 689-544 505; fax 689-451 065; www.boraboracrusies.com

Tu Moana/Ti'a Moana **(37/74; FRENCH; 230 FEET)**

Nomade Yachting (formerly known as Bora Bora Cruises), launched in 2003, sails on weekly cruises of French Polynesia with its two custom-built luxury super-yachts. The boutique cruise yachts are aimed at a niche of customers who want exclusive, stylish voyages with great attention to detail, a high level of service, gourmet cuisine, and designer furnishings and amenities.

The twin vessels take their names from the native Tahitian language: *Moana* is the universal Polynesian word meaning "the sea," *Tu* and *Ti'a* carry similar meanings "to stand erect, to be upright" and "to fit, agree, answer the purpose." Thus, each ship's name literally means "comfortably upright in the sea."

Built in Australia by Austal Ships, with interiors by the well-known Swedish firm of Tillberg Design and technical oversight by V-Ships of Monaco, *Tu Moana* and *Ti'a Moana* have the sleek lines of private luxury yachts. The vessels are identical in all areas except interior decor. Their fine finishes combine exotic hardwood interiors, original Polynesian artwork, and glass staircases with the latest technologies.

All cabins are outside ones with large windows and lovely furnishings, located on three decks. They have three different layouts with an average size of about 170 square feet. Each cabin has a queen bed with an exclusive Kenzo throw, high-quality European bed and bath linens, flat-screen television and DVD/CD player, phone, safe, minibar and refrigerator, writing desk and stationery, handblown glass bowl with fresh fruit, bedside reading lamps, bathrobes, and BBC logo beach bag. In the glass-enclosed bathroom, there are Philippe Starck–designed bath fixtures, a hair dryer, an adjustable showerhead, a BBC bathrobe, and exclusive hypoallergenic bathroom toiletries.

The crew speaks several languages, and the French chef's creations have garnered rave reviews. Special touches include breakfast served on linen and china at tables in the warm waters of the lagoon, dinner under the moonlight on a beach, movies shown on a secluded island under the stars, and a kayak expedition for two up a tropical river. Passengers can snorkel, get a massage on the beach, or enjoy other options, including a romantic tête-à-tête dinner on a secluded *motu* or islet, a four-by-four island safari, horseback riding, mountain climbing, shark and manta ray feeding, aft-deck night fishing, and lagoon photo excursions.

The ships have an unusual flat-water design, which draws only 7.5 feet and allows for safe navigation in the lagoons inaccessible to larger vessels, providing passengers with a unique experience. The shallow draft enables the yachts to travel close to the shoreline and to the most beautiful coral reefs near these islands; at the same time, the ships' advanced stabilization technology provides smooth sailing in open water.

Both vessels depart Bora Bora on Monday mornings and return to Bora Bora Sunday evenings, gliding across the calm lagoons of Huahine, Raiatea, Taha'a, and Bora Bora on six-night, seven-day cruises. Travelers can book a 7-day cruise to the islands or a 10- or 14-day island-and-sea package, which combines a cruise with a stay at the Hotel Bora Bora or St. Regis in Bora Bora, and Taha'a private island resort and spa. For reservations, contact the U.S. representative, JoAnn Kurtz-Ahlers, joann@kurtzahlers.com; ☎ 949-487-0522. Most passengers are from Europe and the United States.

Nomade Yachting is the dream of its founder, owner, and chairman, Mehiti Degage, a young Polynesian woman whose love for the sea and lagoons of her country inspired her to provide visitors with an experience that captures the essence of these islands in a stylish, intimate manner.

ITINERARIES *See* Itinerary Index.

Orion Expedition Cruises
A.B.N. 88 456 259 434; 26 Alfred Street, Milsons Point,
Sydney N.S.W. 2061, Australia; ☎ +61-2-9033-8700 (international);
02-9033-8700 (local); fax +61-2-9033-8799 (international); fax 02-9033-
8799; www.orioncruises.com.au; e-mail info@orioncruises.com.au

Orion (53/106; GERMAN/EUROPEAN; 337 FEET/4,050 TONS)

Billed as a vessel for a new age of exploration cruising, the *Orion*, which made her maiden voyage in 2003, combines the latest advances in ship design and communication technology with the style and comfort of a luxury cruise ship. From her ice-strengthened hull (rated E3, the highest rating available) to the remote viewing cameras atop its mast, no expense was spared in *Orion's* construction.

Built at the Cassens Shipyard in Emden, Germany, *Orion* is a model of German craftsmanship and engineering, with such features as technologically advanced stabilizers, bow and stern thrusters for easy maneuverability, a surround-sound audio system in the lecture hall, and direct Internet access in every cabin.

But it's *Orion's* luxurious accommodations that distinguish her from older, more traditional expedition ships. Each of the 22 standard cabins measures between 175 and 180 square feet, while each of the 31 suites measures from 215 to 345 square feet; eight have French balconies. All cabins are outside; many suites and the Owner's Suites have a balcony. All cabins include a sitting area or living room, flat-screen television, DVD and CD player, minifridge, private marble bathroom, ample closet space, and twin beds that can be converted to a queen. Large oval, rectangular, or sliding glass floor-to-ceiling windows offer panoramic views.

Orion's facilities include a spa, sauna, whirlpool, massage services, hairdresser, boutique, several lounges, and a library equipped with Internet access. At the center of the ship is a glass atrium that wraps around the elevator and serves *Orion's* seven decks. The **Constellation Restaurant** accommodates all guests at a single unassigned seating; an open deck off the main lounge is available for dining alfresco. Dinner menus featuring fresh local produce are conceived by award-winning chef Serge Dansereau (of The Bathers' Pavilion, Balmoral). The ship offers 24-hour room service as well.

The spacious observation lounge on the top deck opens onto a wraparound deck for optimal viewing. The bridge also leads out to an open observation area. A mudroom on the lower deck stores parkas, boots, and other equipment used during and after a day of exploration. Ten heavy-duty Zodiac inflatable motorized boats are used for landing in shallow areas and to navigate small waterways. Several two-seater kayaks are available for individual exploration.

Onboard expedition leaders and lecturers include marine biologists, botanists, anthropologists, ornithologists, historians, and other specialists, depending on the voyage. *Orion* combines adventure through access to remote areas by Zodiac with five-star facilities on board. Each itinerary features a range of inclusive shore expeditions, as well as optional excursions such as helicopter or fixed-wing flights, scuba diving, and fishing, depending on each particular voyage.

Classified with Germanischer Lloyd, *Orion* meets the latest international safety rules and regulations. The ship is served by 75 European officers and crew. Permanently based in Australian waters, *Orion* sails on a wide range of expeditions that vary by season: the Kimberley (north to west Australia) between April and September; Papua New Guinea/Melanesia in March, April, and November; Antarctica in December and January. Most cruises are of 10 or 11 nights' duration, although there are some 6-night (Great Barrier Reef) and 7-night voyages (Hobart to Sydney); those to the Antarctic are 18 nights' duration.

In 2010, the ship continues on paths less traveled with expeditionary voyages to explore more Australian coastal marine parks, nature reserves, national parks, and World Heritage areas. Added, too, are a range of seven-night East Coast, South Australian, and Tasmanian explorations stretching from Cairns to Hobart. The Papua New Guinea itineraries have six new destinations, including new parts of the exotic Spice and Tanimbar islands and, for the first time, an expedition that includes Irian Jaya, world-famous for its Asmat Art.

In 2011, Orion Expedition will add a new ship to its fleet, effectively doubling its capacity, and sailing her on new Southeast Asian itineraries. The 50-suite vessel ship, to be called *Orion II,* is a long-term lease of the *Clelia II* from Travel Dynamics International. Approximately $21 million was spent recently to upgrade her technical and environmental systems; further cosmetic enhancements are planned by Orion after delivery. Orion plans to use the new ship on intensive Vietnam and Borneo itineraries, including circumnavigation of Borneo, and some areas heretofore inaccessible to other cruise ships.

ITINERARIES *See* Itinerary Index.

P&O Cruises
Richmond House, Terminus Terrace, Southampton S0143PN, England;
☎**08453-555; fax 023-8065-7409; www.pocruises.com**

P&O Cruises stems from the original steamship company founded in 1837, whose principal routes served the British Empire from India to New Zealand. In 1974, P&O Cruises purchased Princess Cruises, and through it had a big impact on modern cruising, particularly on the U.S. West Coast market.

The introduction of the *Oriana* in 1995, P&O Cruises' first brand-new ship in more than two decades, signaled the start of a modern era for the cruise line, replacing her old ships and building new ships designed primarily for British passengers. *Oriana's* sister, *Aurora,* was delivered in 2000 with even more new features. In 2003, the *Oceana,* formerly the *Ocean Princess* of Princess Cruises, joined the fleet. In 2005, the line added *Arcadia* as well as *Artemis* (formerly *Royal Princess*). In 2003, P&O Cruises, along with Princess Cruises and the company's other cruise lines, were bought by Carnival Corporation after an intensive bidding war with Royal Caribbean Cruises. The 115,000-ton *Ventura* was Britain's largest cruise ship when she entered service in 2008; her near sister, the 116,000-ton *Azura* will debut in 2010..

P&O Cruises offers moderately priced, classic cruises sailing on worldwide itineraries. P&O Cruises defines them as three different styles of cruise experience: original and authentic cruising on *Aurora* and *Oriana*; contemporary and innovative cruising on *Arcadia* and *Oceana*; and traditional and intimate cruising on *Artemis*. The line's multimillion-dollar Elevation program of refinements to its onboard experience was introduced in early 2007 and rolled out fleetwide over two years. It encompassed dining, accommodations, entertainment, shore excursions, and booking.

The ships' British style cannot be overemphasized; it's what P&O passengers want. The atmosphere is very social, helped by friendly British officers who mingle with passengers and host tables at dinner, a popular feature. The ships are well organized, aboard and ashore, with excellent programs that include outstanding lecturers on port history and culture, classical pianists, afternoon teas, Sunday religious services (Anglican) with a passenger-staff choir, and varied evening entertainment. The dress code tends to be dressier than on similar ships catering to Americans. Men wear jackets and ties on most nights at sea and on formal evenings they wear tuxedos or dinner jackets, and women don cocktail and long dresses.

P&O focuses generally on three programs: cruises departing from Southampton, those based in the Caribbean in winter, and annual around-the-world voyages. Most passengers are British, of all ages and incomes. Americans, Australians, and New Zealanders are a sizable minority on around-the-world voyages. Once-in-a- lifetime shore excursions are among the offerings fleetwide and include such adventures as an evening concert and after-hours evening visit of the Hermitage in St. Petersburg, Russia, or a Turkish bath experience in Istanbul. There are tours designed for families and others for teens, and gourmet tours such as wine tasting in Provence or a Greek gastronomy class in Corfu.

P&O Cruises has an unprecedented four world cruises scheduled for winter 2010–2011, with all four departing from Southampton: *Oriana* on an 84-night round-the-world voyage in September 2010; the others in early January 2011. *Artemis* will embark on a 98-night round-trip Grand Voyage through the Mediterranean, Middle East, India, Asia, and South Africa. *Arcadia*, making its third circumnavigation of the earth, sails westward on an 82-day cruise across the Atlantic to the Panama Canal, South Pacific, Asia, Suez Canal, and Mediterranean. *Aurora* will travel to South America and the South Pacific on her 95-night round-trip voyage and return via San Francisco, Acapulco, the Panama Canal, and the Caribbean. Recently, P&O Cruises changed the registry on the *Arcadia, Oceana, Oriana,* and *Artemis* from British to Bermudian to allow weddings at sea with a traditional ceremony conducted by the captain. (Weddings are not recognized aboard U.K.-registered vessels.) The *Ventura* uses Bermudian colors too.

Aurora **(939/1,874; BRITISH/INDIAN AND EUROPEAN;
886 FEET/76,000 TONS)**

Oriana **(914/2,016; BERMUDIAN/INDIAN AND EUROPEAN;
853 FEET/69,153 TONS)**

The *Oriana* is big and beautiful. Although she is modern, her design and decor is of a classic liner with traditional oil paintings, historic documents, and ship models on the walls. Interiors are as fine and refined as tea in a British parlor. No flashy neon or glitz here. The ship has an inviting calm and numerous nooks where it's easy to relax, read, write postcards, and let the world go by. It's cruising as it should be.

As part of the cruise line's new Elevation program, *Oriana* was given a multimillion-dollar refit that added **Oriana Rhodes,** a 96-seat restaurant created by well-known British chef Gary Rhodes and a new children's club; also, 914 cabins were refurbished with upgraded mattresses and deluxe Egyptian cotton bed linens, towels, and robes. Other cabin innovations were fitness facilities for passengers who prefer to exercise in private, improved tea- and coffeemakers in every cabin, and a Champagne-breakfast-in-bed option.

Gourmet tasting menus in select venues, two additional gala dinners in the main restaurants, including a Chaîne des Rôtisseurs culinary dinner, and nightly themed buffet menus in the food court offering Indian, French, Spanish, Italian, and British cuisines are dining highlights. A special children's tea at 5 p.m. is available on all the line's family-friendly ships, providing bibs, beakers, and children's cutlery, along with new, healthy menu options.

Entertainment options tailored to the three respective styles of cruising have been added. These include more celebrity speakers, sports heroes, and television personalities; more live broadcasts of sporting events; a golf pro on *Aurora* to give lessons on the golf simulator; and a family production show launched on *Oceana*.

Aurora, which debuted in 2000, came with new features and a bit more glitz, as well as some firsts for a ship dedicated primarily to the British market. These include two-deck Penthouse Suites, four decks of cabins with balconies, and interconnecting family cabins. She also had P&O Cruises's first 24-hour bistro-style restaurant, coffee and chocolate bar, Champagne bar, tea- and coffee-making facilities in all cabins, a retractable dome over one swimming pool, and a virtual-reality center. Her four-deck atrium has a waterfall and Lalique glass–style sculpture and is surrounded by shops and a tour desk.

The size and spaciousness of these ships allow for a variety of public rooms and entertainment facilities, as well as some larger public rooms enabling passengers of all types to find comfortable and familiar surroundings. Vast amounts of open deck call to British sun worshippers and those who take a daily constitutional walk.

Oriana's cabins are spacious and more luxurious than on previous P&O ships and come in a wide range of configurations with ample storage space. The ship has 114 singles—an unusual feature for today's superliner. Almost all cabins, including suites, are on the three middle decks. *Aurora*'s cabin choices are even wider and include interconnecting cabins suitable for families. More than 40% of the cabins, including some standard ones, have balconies. Cabins on both ships have tea- and coffeemakers, safe, refrigerator, television, direct-dial telephone, air-conditioning, and music system; some have bathtubs, hair dryers, and minibars.

Two main restaurants offer two sittings for three meals. The cuisine is very English: lots of meat and potatoes and sauces, excellent soups but few salads. The **Conservatory** on Lido Deck, with indoor/outdoor seating, serves a buffet breakfast and lunch. The area can become very crowded at peak lunch hours.

The ships' elaborate activities programs range from bingo and crafts to bridge and dance classes. Port lecturers are very knowledgeable and generally have a dry, British sense of humor. They wouldn't dream of giving the shopping sales pitch heard on many Caribbean cruise ships. The comfortable library is well supplied.

Public rooms spread over two Main Decks offer a variety of atmospheres catering to class-conscious Brits. Many reflect in name and style the company's 165-year history and range from cabaret in the **Pacific Lounge** to large production shows in **Theatre Royal.** There's **Lord's Tavern,** a cricket-themed pub, and the spacious **Crow's Nest** observation bar and lounge, with wraparound windows and a trio playing dance music before and after dinner. **Monte Carlo Casino** is small, compared with casinos on big ships sailing the Caribbean.

On *Aurora*, a West End–style theater has the latest production technology, and the new-concept main show lounge comes with a spacious bar, large dance floor, and retractable stage. Midship is an intimate, futuristic nightclub with a small dance floor and stage. One deck above, a large concert hall/cinema shows first-run films and stages concerts; there's also a business center with computers.

Activities on *Oriana*'s vast open decks include deck tennis, quoits, shuffleboard, golf nets, and trapshooting. Cricket matches between passengers and officers are popular. One of two adult pools is a generous 42 feet long. Passengers take daily walks on a wide promenade sprinkled with deck chairs shaded by lifeboats. A large spa offers aerobics, a gym, whirlpools, sauna, massage, beauty and therapy rooms, and a hair salon.

A pool between Decks 11 and 12 on *Aurora* has a waterfall and is surrounded by tiered decks. Another pool can be covered by a dome in inclement weather; still another is reserved for families at certain times of year. A netted deck area is adaptable for cricket, soccer, and tennis, and golfers can practice on the golf simulator. A well-equipped gym and aerobics studio overlook the forward pool. The spacious area is linked by stairs to health and beauty facilities.

P&O Cruises' children's program is highly praised. In peak times, four age-specific areas have separate, supervised, well-designed programs; two age groups are used at other times. Children have their own pool and Lido area, and they eat at an early sitting, with or without their parents. A staffed night nursery is available for children under age 5, and cabins have baby "listening" facilities.

Arcadia (984/1,952; BERMUDIAN/INTERNATIONAL; 952 FEET/83,000 TONS)

Arcadia, which joined the fleet in 2005, is children-free. Among her spacious public rooms, the 11-passenger-deck ship has an array of dining options, a three-tier theater, 12 bars, nightclub, coffee and chocolate bar, spa with a thermal suite and hydrotherapy pool, an outdoor pool, five Jacuzzis, and an indoor/outdoor swimming pool with retractable dome. Other facilities include shops, a casino, a library, an observation lounge with panoramic views, Cyb@ study, hair salon, art gallery, touch-screen photo gallery, and 14 passenger elevators, including two panoramic glass ones on the sides of the ship.

More than two-thirds of the cabins have balconies. **The Belvedere,** a food court so named because it commands fine views, offers informal dining around the clock with a wide choice of menus, from Asian and Italian to bistro-style dishes and a delicatessen counter. Light and airy, the decor has a soft, calm Japanese theme and is furnished with outside seating for dining alfresco. There is a two-tier main restaurant, and the ship's specialty restaurant, **Arcadian Rhodes,** is the creation of Gary Rhodes, one of Britain's best-known chefs who is noted for his innovative take on contemporary British cuisine. Rhodes created the menu and several signature dishes for the restaurant.

Oceana (1,008/2,016; BERMUDIAN/INTERNATIONAL; 856 FEET/77,000 TONS)

Oceana (formerly *Ocean Princess*) joined the P&O fleet in fall 2003. She was part of Princess Cruises' *Sun Princess* group. (For a description of these ships, see Princess Cruises earlier in Part Two.)

Artemis (520/1,196; BERMUDIAN/INTERNATIONAL; 757 FEET/45,000 TONS)

The *Artemis* (the former *Royal Princess*), which joined P&O Cruises in spring 2005, has been sold but leased back through April 2011. She was launched in 1984 and christened by Diana, Princess of Wales. Both made an indelible mark on the 1980s. At the time, *Artemis* was the most expensive passenger ship ever built. Her sleek lines and tapered bow looked traditional, but she had so many innovations inside that she was called revolutionary and set new standards in passenger comfort for the cruise ships that followed.

Artemis was the first cruise ship to have all outside cabins and television with remote control, minifridge, and full bathroom with tub and shower in all cabins. She was first to have verandas in all suites, deluxe cabins, and even in some lesser categories, and large windows instead of portholes in every category. The ship, with nine passenger decks, has two acres of open teak decks, three swimming pools, and a fully equipped spa. Her decor is refined. Interiors are defined less by walls than by art, sculpture, and glass with brass railings. Live plants and abundant windows create openness throughout the ship.

Artemis's layout is unusual. Most public rooms are on the two lower levels, and virtually all cabins are on upper decks. A large foyer on the lower Plaza Deck spans two decks—the first shipboard atrium, perhaps. This greenery-filled area is dominated by a large David Norris sculpture consisting of a bronze spiral with seagulls rising over rocks. A dramatic staircase with glass balustrade curves in two wings upward to a balcony with piano lounge over-looking the foyer; it is a gathering spot where passengers enjoy prelunch or predinner drinks, entertained by a pianist-vocalist. This deck also holds the main showroom, cabaret-style lounge, casino, boutique, card room, and a theater. The ship has six elevators.

Artemis's cabins are spacious, each with picture windows, a tiled bathroom with tub and shower, retractable clothesline, mirrored medicine-cabinet door, minifridge, safe, multifunction phone, television, and four-channel music radio. High-quality interiors and attention to detail are reflected in a large dressing table with makeup lights, an easy-to-reach hair dryer, ample drawers, and large closets. In many cabins, a twin bed folds into a wall, providing extra sitting space by day. Some cabins have obstructed views, indicated on the deck plan. Standard dimensions are 168 square feet. Some cabins accommodate a third person, and there are ten wheelchair-accessible cabins. Self-service launder-ettes offer washers, dryers, irons, and ironing boards at no charge.

Suites and cabins with verandas are very roomy. The two largest suites have separate sitting and dining rooms, Jacuzzi bathtub, separate bedroom with queen bed, and large veranda. Mini-suites are similar but without walls between bedrooms and sitting areas.

The warm, pleasant **Continental Dining Room** has a raised perimeter level delineated with brass railings. Small islands of round tables break up the space, provide privacy, and help lower the noise level and allow easy conver-sation. Senior dining staff is Italian and very attentive. The **Lido Café,** an indoor/outdoor cafe with tile-topped tables, serves an informal buffet breakfast, lunch, and snacks.

The show lounge has seats tiered in a semicircular fashion; sight lines are generally good, except from the back. There are several other lounges offering entertainment and playing dance music every evening, as well as a casino.

A cluster of five small pools is the centerpiece of the Lido Deck, the main outdoor recreation area. On Sun Deck, passengers sunbathe on a raised plat-form, play table tennis and shuffleboard, swim in one of cruising's largest lap pools, and exercise in the spa. The fitness complex has a gym with state-of-the-art equipment, sauna and massage rooms, and a large whirlpool. Joggers and walkers circle the wraparound teak promenade (four laps equal one mile).

Ventura **(1,550/3,597; BERMUDIAN; 957 FEET/115,000 TONS)**

Launched in April 2008, the £300 million *Ventura*, designed specifically for the British market, is 40% larger than the *Arcadia*. Three distinct elements of British culture are being brought together on the ship: fine dining, family entertainment, and modern and contemporary art.

Well-known British chef and three-star restaurateur Marco Pierre White created a signature restaurant, **The White Room,** and acts as a consultant to P&O Cruises. His culinary flair was also integrated into other areas of the dining experience, such as **The Beach House,** a family dining venue, said to be a cruise-ship first as a venue designed specifically for families to dine together.

Further emphasizing *Ventura*'s family-friendly facilities, the much-loved British Toyland character Noddy is featured in the children's area for 2- to 4-year-olds. Noddy is on board all cruises to delight youngsters at character breakfasts and during playtime. Older children are offered lessons in how to become a rock star and learn to play a guitar, keyboards, and drums. For the first time, P&O Cruises has designed an area specifically for parents to supervise their children under 2 years old.

Art and design are key themes for the *Ventura*, and she is a floating showcase for the best of British contemporary art, with 7,000 pieces from 55 artists. Art experts from the famous Tate Modern museum in London host Introduction to Modern Art cruises with seminars, presentations, and practical art classes throughout the year.

The *Ventura*'s design is embodied in the atrium—striking, contemporary, yet designed for purpose: the hub of the ship from which all public areas can be easily accessed. The 14-deck ship carries a maximum of 3,600 passengers. She has eight restaurants, six boutiques, five pools, and three show lounges, including the largest theater on a British ship; 900 cabins with private balconies; and 1,200 crew members. British designer Nick Munro, renowned for his unique furniture, ceramic, and home ware designs, created items designed specifically for contemporary British tastes.

Ventura's cabins are contemporary and stylish in decor with modern art on canvas, fashionable bed linens, and designer touches. Deluxe cabins have two lower beds convertible to a king-size bed; bathroom with full-size bath and separate shower; lounge sofa, chairs, and table; vanity/writing desk; flat-screen television and radio; safe, hair dryer, and refrigerator; tea- and coffee-making facilities; direct-dial telephone; and balcony furnished with teak furniture. Suites have all these features, plus butler service, a full-size Jacuzzi bath, a dressing area, DVD player and Hi-Fi, and trouser press and ironing board.

The ship's spa with alluring sea views is equipped with a thermal suite and a pool. It offers a blend of ancient traditions and alternative therapies and a wide range of treatments, from body wraps to a makeover and a massage.

Ventura's sister ship, the 3,100-passenger *Azura*, is scheduled to launch in April 2010. The 15- deck passenger ship has 11 restaurants and more than 900 cabins with private balconies and some single cabins. She comes with some "firsts" for P&O Cruises: an open-air cinema-at-sea and **The Retreat,** an open-air spa terrace; an Indian fine-dining restaurant, **Sindhu,** offering fine British and Indian fusion cuisine, with a menu designed by Atul Kochhar, one of London's top celebrity chefs and the first Indian chef to be awarded a Michelin star for his restaurant, Benares; and the **Glass House,** a wine bar and specialty restaurant, where British television wine expert Olly Smith lent his expertise to the pairing of fine wines with each dish.

ITINERARIES *See* Itinerary Index.

Paul Gauguin Cruises
11100 Main Street, Suite 300, Bellevue, WA 98004;
☎ **800-848-6172, 866-786-2009, or 425-440-6171; www.pgcruises.com**

Paul Gauguin (166/332; TAHITIAN/INTERNATIONAL; 513 FEET/19,200)

Named for the French artist whose life and work embodied the romance of French Polynesia, the *Paul Gauguin* is the most deluxe ship of its size to cruise the South Seas year-round. Its space ratio (59) is among cruising's highest, and its shallow draft (16.9 feet) allows access to small, rarely frequented ports.

The French-built vessel, which marked her 12th anniversary in 2010, is owned and managed by Pacific Beachcomber, a company with extensive hotel interests in French Polynesia, which took ownership in August 2009. (Pacific Beachcomber owns four InterContinental Resorts in French Polynesia, owns and manages the Maitai Hotel on Bora Bora, and is developing a luxury eco-resort, "The Brando" on the late actor's private island.)

Gauguin's clean lines, understated elegance, and attention to detail are immediately apparent. The yacht-like ship, with an airy ambience and stylish touches, underwent a $6-million refurbishment in 2006. It added a piano bar, five suites at the stern with private balconies, a remodeled casino, and new fabrics and carpeting throughout the public areas.

More recently in 2009, another multimillion-dollar enhancement converted 26 ocean-view cabins to balcony cabins, increasing the number of cabins with private balconies to nearly 70%. Le Grill, the casual poolside dining venue, was upgraded, and La Veranda restaurant's alfresco dining space was expanded. The Internet area and fitness center were improved, while water sports activities were upgraded with new sport boats. All public areas were extensively refurbished. The ship has four elevators and seven passenger decks.

All cabins are outside suites with separate sitting areas. Each is furnished with a queen- or twin-size bed (convertible to queen), closed-circuit television and CD/DVD, safe, direct-dial telephone, and refrigerator stocked with soft drinks, mineral water, and complimentary liquor on arrival. Interior decor is enriched by crown moldings and wood accents. Finely crafted furnishings include a love seat and vanity/desk; two closets and built-in drawers provide storage space. Marble bathrooms have a full-size bathtub and shower, plush towels and cotton robes, hair dryer, and assorted toiletries. Categories B and above have butler service, including a bar setup and a SoundDock for iPod. The minibar is replenished daily with soft drinks, beer, and bottled water. There's 24-hour room service and in-room dining.

The ship has 166 outside cabins and suites; 80 with balconies; and 1 wheelchair-accessible cabin. Accommodations range from 200 square feet with a picture window or portholes and 249 square feet with a 56-square-foot veranda to the 531-square-foot Owner's Suite with a 57-square-foot veranda. Pictures and diagrams showing the layout of each cabin type are available on the line's Web site. Some passengers report being able to hear conversations next door and cabins above the engine being noisy.

Two restaurants, with ocean views on three sides, offer a single open seating. **Restaurant L'Etoile** features French and Continental cuisine; the smaller **La Veranda,** with floor-to-ceiling windows, is a reservations-only dinner restaurant offering Italian cuisine and other selections. A small, outdoor bistro, **Le Grill,** serves a casual buffet breakfast and lunch by the pool. In the evening, it is transformed into a cozy restaurant. An espresso bar is another option.

Complimentary wine is served at lunch and dinner, and there's an excellent wine list. Evening attire is "country club elegant" (no ties). Les Gauguines, a local Tahitian group, serve as entertainers, storytellers, and share their local Tahitian culture with guests. Gratuities are included in the cruise fare.

In tribute to Gauguin and French Polynesia, the **Fare** (pronounced "faray") **Tahiti Gallery** is a small library with books, videos, and other materials on the artist and region. The ship has a card room and boutique stocked with Polynesian gifts.

Le Grand Salon, the main lounge, offers early-evening dancing, entertainment, and daily lectures. The indoor/outdoor **La Palette Lounge** is used for afternoon tea, cocktails, and late-night disco. The small casino has blackjack, roulette, and slot machines, but local regulations bar use of the slots. Nighttime entertainment is minimal. Movies are shown daily on the closed-circuit cabin system; the reception desk lends DVDs. A singer-pianist performs in La Palette before dinner, and the ship's Filipino band plays for dancing before dinner and afterward until 11:30 p.m., when the disco starts up.

The *Paul Gauguin* offers a joint program with Jean-Michel Cousteau's Ocean Futures Society, called Ambassadors of the Environment, promoting ocean responsibility. The program engages children ages 9–15 with fun activities to educate them about marine and island ecosystems and traditional Polynesian culture. The program includes a variety of onboard and shoreside activities. Adult family members are encouraged to participate in the program's optional shore excursion.

The ship's fitness center provides free weights and exercise machines. Aerobics, hydro-calisthenics, and a walkathon are held daily. The spa offers a steam room, massage, facials, and marine-based beauty treatments. The *Paul*

Gauguin has an outdoor pool and splash bar on an upper deck and a retractable marina at sea level, where windsurfing and kayaking equipment are available and snorkeling and diving (a major attraction) excursions depart. Snorkeling gear can be signed out at the start of the cruise. The ship provides PADI-certified instructors and dive boats, as well as courses for novices (PADI certification available), and excursions for certified divers.

Passengers concerned about seasickness should know that rough sailing isn't unusual for this ship, owing to her shallow draft and the sometimes rough Pacific waters. The redeeming feature: she travels mostly short distances between ports and is often at anchor in a sheltered bay at night.

In 2010, the *Paul Gauguin* is sailing on 38 itineraries, ranging from 7 to 15 nights, and visiting Tahiti, the Society Islands, Tuamotus, the Cook Islands, Marquesas, Tonga, Fiji, and New Zealand.

ITINERARIES *See* Itinerary Index.

Peter Deilmann Reederei
Amholm 25, Neustadt-in-Holstein, Germany, D 23730;
☎ **011-49-4561-396-135; www.deilmann-kreuzfahrten.de**

Peter Deilmann Cruises' *Deutschland*, launched in 1998, was built in the Art Nouveau and Art Deco style of ocean liners of the past, as a traditional luxury liner in the grand European style. She has three restaurants and a Promenade Deck and accommodates 513 passengers in a variety of mostly outside staterooms. The ship is renowned in Germany (it was the venue for filming the German television version of *The Love Boat*), and the majority of the passengers are from German-speaking countries. But it also attracts different nationalities, including some from England, Canada, and the United States. Not all sailings offer announcements in English; be sure to check in advance if you do not speak German. In late October 2009, the cruise line closed its U.S. office and may be de-emphasizing its English-speaking audience.

In addition to German food, the menu includes Italian, French, American, and international selections, while reflecting the cuisine of port of call. Grilled meats, fish, and shrimp are available on the open-air Lido Deck for lunch. Each day's menu also features vegetarian dishes, both at the indoor **Lido Buffet** restaurant and the **Berlin,** the ship's main restaurant, where breakfast, lunch, and dinner are served daily. There are two seatings for dinner in the Berlin Restaurant. The waitstaff are especially friendly, and the service is excellent in this plush dining venue. An alternative gourmet restaurant, **Four Seasons,** requires advance reservations. Both intimate and quiet, Four Seasons serves as many as six courses at a leisurely pace (dinner is routinely a two- to three-hour affair). A buffet on the Lido Deck offers breakfast, lunch, and dinner and frequently offers dishes from the menu of the main dining salon. In the **Lili Marleen** lounge, nightly musical trios perform for both listening and dancing. The **Old Fritz Pub,** a cozy wood-paneled bar, opens to additional seating outdoors. Entertainment here is low-key, consisting of a pianist playing European and American standards. The two-story **Emperor's Ballroom** serves as the ship's theater, with nightly revues and dancing. Shows include Las Vegas–style production shows, classical concerts, magicians, and stand-up comics who usually perform in German only, as does the MC. Cabins on the *Deutschland* feature polished burled walnut paneling and pastel yellow furnishings. Well-designed bathrooms in Italian marble are unusually spacious, but for the most part offer showers only. Amenities include a radio and color television with CNN and MSNBC and English-language films, a minifridge, two armchairs and a table, a desk, robes, slippers, a hair dryer, Molton Brown toiletries, and, for outside cabins, a medium to large picture window.

The *Deutschland* provides a small but adequate fitness center and a full-service spa that offers thalassotherapy, Cleopatra bath, a wide range of massages, and other beauty and health treatments. The fitness programs include daily classes in Pilates, Nordic walking, and aqua exercise. Fitness consulting sessions are also held. Deilmann has prebooked wellness packages for ladies' facials, special body baths, and classic back massages, as well as two-hour men's grooming and relaxation packages. Although a notable array of outdoor activities is available, there is no place on board to run or jog. There are two swimming pools: one indoors on Deck 3 and another outdoors (saltwater). Smoke-free areas on the *Deutschland* cover about 90% of the passenger areas. For a ship that caters mostly to older Germans and other Europeans, it's a notable change.

Announcements are conducted in German. When there are enough English-speaking passengers to warrant it, announcements are repeated in English. All staff members on board speak English, some much better than others. Cabin crews are often from Eastern Europe and speak English as a second language rather than German; waitstaff come mostly from eastern Germany. Menus and daily wellness and spa programs are available in English. English-language shore excursions are offered in a package at a discount when prepurchased. Theme cruises include a music, golf, garden, and equestrian focus.

ITINERARIES *See* Itinerary Index.

Ponant Cruises/Compagnie des Iles du Ponant
408 Avenue du Prado, 13008 Marseille, France; ☎ +33 (0)1 42.56.54.50; fax +33 (0)1 45 63 01 51; e-mail info@ponant.com

L'Austral **(2011) (132 CABINS, SUITES/264; FRENCH/139 CREW; 470 FEET/10,700 TONS)**

Le Boreal **(2010) (132 CABINS, SUITES/264; FRENCH/139 CREW; 470 FEET/10,700 TONS)**

Le Diamant **(113 CABINS, SUITES/226; FRENCH/120; 407 FEET)**

Le Levant **(45 CABINS/90; FRENCH/50; 330 FEET)**

Le Ponant **(32 CABINS/64; FRENCH/32; 290 FEET)**

Founded in 1988, Ponant Cruises, the French-flagged cruise line, is a subsidiary of CMA-CGM, the third largest container shipping company in the world. Since 2004, Ponant Cruises has offered worldwide luxury cruises on three ships, *Le Ponant, Le Levant,* and *Le Diamant,* and is known for offering unusual destinations and itineraries. At the Italian Fincantieri shipyard, the line is building two luxury ships in ice class 1C, *Le Boreal* and *L'Austral,* scheduled to debut in May 2010 and May 2011, respectively. The (French) ship names were chosen as points of the compass—*Le Levant* meaning the East; *Le Ponant,* the West; *Le Boreal,* the North; and *L'Austral,* the South—signifying the cruise line's global coverage. The onboard language is English.

Designed like private yachts, the architecture firm Stirling Design International (SDI) was responsible for the ships' exteriors and Jean-Philippe Nuel for the interiors, creating a subtle blend of relaxation and sophistication with a French touch. All accommodations are outside, and 95% of them have balconies. Each of the new ships has six passenger decks and a streamlined silhouette and is fitted with large, arched windows fore and aft to further enhance its style. With a 15.3-foot draft and capable of sailing at a speed of 16 knots, the new ships have dynamic positioning systems to avoid anchoring in protected marine areas.

The ships have fully equipped auditoriums, observation lounges, outside observation decks, and sun decks. Other facilities on each ship include **The Club** lounge for live music and dancing, an open bar (excluding premium wines, liquors, and Champagne), a theater with unobstructed views, an outside heated pool, a library with an extensive selection of books and DVDs, two restaurants, a panoramic lounge and terrace, three bars, a boutique, a fitness center with state-of-the-art equipment, a beauty salon, a spa with sauna and steam rooms, wireless Internet access throughout the ship, three passenger elevators, 24-hour onboard medical facilities with a certified doctor, and 24-hour room service. Onboard gratuities are included in the price.

Le Boreal will sail from South America to Antarctica as well as in the White Sea, toward Spitsbergen, Greenland, and the Canadian Arctic, while *L'Austral* is scheduled to call on southeast Asia, Japan, India, and the Mediterranean. Some of these destinations are already served by Ponant's other vessels, but the new ships will also explore new destinations. Ponant Cruises anticipates that the new ships will enable it to attract a more international clientele and respond to the demand for small luxury ships, both as charter and for individual passengers. That's in line with Ponant's ambition to become a key player in the international cruise business.

Le Diamant's spacious cabins, distributed on all five decks, have ocean views and air-conditioning; ten suites on the top deck have private balconies. The accommodations range from 183- to 200-square-foot cabins to 398-square-foot suites and are furnished with double or twin beds, minibars, flat-screen satellite televisions, radios with music channels, DVD players, telephones, bathrooms with bathtubs or showers, and bathrobes.

The Jade Deck, the lowest deck, has the **Îles de France Restaurant,** which serves French and international cuisine for breakfast, lunch, and dinner in an elegant and sophisticated environment. The deck also has a massage room and a beauty salon. Turquoise, the lobby deck, houses **Le Club,** a piano lounge; a boutique; and **L'Escapade,** a second restaurant for breakfast, buffet lunches, and themed dinners. Emeraude, the third deck, features a full-circle observation deck and promenade and the **Main Lounge,** which offers entertainment and is used for lectures. Rubis is the Sun Deck with the swimming pool, fitness room, bar, and buffet/grill. On *Diamant,* the **Observatory Lounge,** bar, and promenade are on the top deck. The ship is certified in ice class 1D.

Le Levant's sleek silhouette is likened to a thoroughbred. Her elegance provides a taste of a private yacht experience in a sophisticated and harmonious setting. Her main lounge with the latest audiovisual technology, the outdoor **Panoramic Restaurant,** and Sun Deck and swimming pool area can handle all the passengers at one time. Cabin furnishings and amenities are similar to *Le Diamant,* as are the cuisine and ambience of its two restaurants. The **Main Lounge,** with a dance floor and access to an outside terrace, offers tea in the afternoon and live music in the evening. The ship has a library, beauty salon, fitness room, and sauna.

The three-masted sailing ship *Le Ponant,* with her limited capacity of 64 passengers provides an intimate, convivial atmosphere. Her public rooms are flexible as lounges or for conferences or presentations. She has a restaurant that serves three meals, as well as an outside cafe for breakfast and buffet lunch. All cabins are outside and equipped with minibars, flat-screen televisions, and Hi-Fi radios. Under full sail with the ship gliding over the sea, passengers are almost guaranteed relaxation.

Saga Cruises
100 Cummings Center, Suite 120B, Beverly, MA 01915; ☎ 800-343-0273

Saga Cruises is part of the Saga Group, an English firm based in Folkestone that began operating tours in 1951 for British senior citizens ages 60 and older; then, in 1995, it dropped the minimum age to 50. Companions ages 40 and up may accompany the lead passenger. While Saga may be unfamiliar to North Americans, its ship, the *Saga Ruby,* was once well-known in the luxury market. A graceful ship with a classic ocean liner profile, she traces her heritage to Norwegian America Line when she sailed in 1973 as the *Vistafjord,* offering some of the most luxurious cruise experiences afloat. After a period with Cunard Line as the *Caronia,* she joined the Saga Group as the *Saga Ruby* in 2004; she was given a $30 million refit before starting to cruise in early 2005. (Her sister ship, *Saga Rose* [the former *Sagafjord*], was purchased by the Saga Group in 1996, and retired in December 2009. At press time, her fate had not been announced, but speculation in the British press is that Saga will convert her into a hotel based in Southampton.)

Meanwhile, the Saga Group has replaced *Saga Rose* with *Saga Pearl II* (the former *Astoria* built in Germany in 1980), which it purchased at auction in August 2009, and, after a multimillion-dollar renovation, will re-launch her in March 2010. Saga Cruises also markets the *Spirit of Adventure* (former *Berlin* of Deilmann) under the brand Voyages of Discovery. After a complete make-over in 2006, the 352-passenger ship has been sailing on exploratory cruises and offering strong enrichment programs.

Saga Pearl II **(253/446; EUROPEAN/FILIPINO/269; 5390 FEET/18,891 TONS)**

Saga Ruby **(376/655; EUROPEAN/FILIPINO/380; 627 FEET/24,492 TONS)**

After her multimillion-dollar refit, *Saga Pearl II* will be similar to *Saga Ruby* in her essence, providing one of the few traditional cruising experiences left on the high seas that is the antithesis of the mass-market mega-ship experience. Regular Saga cruise passengers will feel at home when they see the familiar faces of *Saga Rose* officers and crew who have transferred to the new ship. On both ships, the atmosphere is genteel and subdued inside and out on deck. You won't find art auctions, loud entertainment, inches of gold for sale, pool games, or even a casino. Rather, think about enjoying a good book in the library or a deck chair, an intense game of team trivia, serenaded afternoon tea, and a glass of port following the evening meal.

The vast majority of passengers will always be British, mostly ages 65 and older—people who have been successful financially and now have the time and money to travel. While Saga cruising is a highly social experience, some come for a quiet time and like to read and dine at a table for two. Anglophile North Americans who like a traditional but not stuffy atmosphere will enjoy the lifestyle of these two ships. Walking aboard, one enters a British-style boutique hotel with rich colors and handsome wood paneling.

The main dining rooms are designed to take the full complement of pas-sengers and top officers at one sitting, the later hosting tables on formal nights. Tables of two, four, six, and eight are reserved for dinner for the entire cruise, while breakfast and lunch provide open seating. Wine selec-tions and bar drinks are reasonably priced. The hotel staff is largely Filipino and many have worked with Saga Cruises since its beginning.

Because most passengers are British, the menu entrees include veal chop, chicken breast, grilled fillet of beef, and roast halibut with appetizers such as asparagus tips with Parma ham and curried carrot and parsnip soup. An inter-national cheese board is a popular alternative dessert. Preparation and presentation are consistently good.

The Lido buffet has inside and, in good weather, outside seating on the open deck under umbrellas. There are daily specials geared to the cruising regions and a delightful, and sometimes quite elaborate, dessert spread fol-lowing the evening show.

The most attractive public space on *Saga Ruby* is the semicircular **Britan-nia Lounge,** where the windows arc 180 degrees. The room sweeps upward toward the bow, and the perimeter seating is raised above the circular cen-ter section occupied by additional chairs, a dance floor, and bandstand. Readers who like a light airy space gravitate here during the day, and at

4 p.m. a popular (and proper) afternoon tea with scones and clotted cream and those English-style crustless sandwiches takes place to the accompaniment of live music. After dinner, the room takes on a restful glow from the bands of recessed ceiling lights as passengers gather for after-dinner drinks and classical concerts.

The high-ceilinged **Ballroom** is just that, a throwback to the day when the main evening entertainment was dancing to a good band. Gentlemen hosts are on hand before and after dinner to give the ladies a twirl. Passengers today expect to be entertained, so the room hosts vocalists, instrumentalists, small acts, and local groups who come aboard in port. In the afternoon, an informal buffet-style tea extravaganza takes place and—being a British ship—is extremely well attended.

South Cape Bar on *Saga Ruby*, located portside, provides a cozy setting for drinks and a pianist. Just around the corner, a traditional theater is used for screening first-run films and hosting special interest lectures and the Sunday interdenominational worship service. The library offers a very good collection with high-back chairs for reading along the starboard side gallery. Both ships have a card room and gift shop. On *Saga Ruby*, the upper level becomes a specialty restaurant in the evening.

Saga Ruby's cabins vary greatly even within the same category, so have a careful look at the deck plan, or ask someone who knows the ship well. One of her best features is the availability of 70 single cabins (small); hence, the line attracts many passengers who are on their own or with a friend but do not wish to share a cabin. The largest cabins and suites are located on the Promenade Deck and the two decks of cabins added during the Norwegian America Cruises era. Some of the two dozen balcony cabins look over, around, or between the lifeboats; they are marked in the brochures. Cabins are furnished with flat-screen television, DVD player, radio, direct-dial phone, hair dryer, 24-hour room service and fresh fruit, stocked refrigerator, and video in categories C and up. The great majority have bath with tub as well as shower. Originally designed for long-distance cruises, storage space is more than adequate.

Saga Pearl II's refit brings new features, including the addition of new balcony cabins, an upgraded show lounge, a spa and two swimming pools, an outstanding library, an elegant, alternative **Veranda Restaurant,** and new kitchens to support the gourmet dining experience in her stylish single-seating dining rooms. **Discovery Lounge** is the venue for afternoon tea and evening entertainment. The ship's 253 cabins include 126 twins, 42 doubles, 25 convertible twins or kings, and 60 singles—almost 25% of the total. Twenty cabins have balconies, and nine cabins have French balconies. A special coating has been applied to *Saga Pearl II*'s hull, which will enable her to travel with greater ease through the sea, significantly reduce fuel consumption, and reduce her carbon footprint.

The ships' daytime entertainment features individual quizzes and team trivia, dance classes, bridge instruction, computer sessions, cooking demonstrations, darts, bingo, special interest, enrichment and destination talks, and navigational bridge visits. Social gatherings are hosted for passengers traveling alone. In the evening, there are stage shows with a British-humor comedian (some jokes will translate and some won't), singers, dancers, classical concerts, ballroom dancing, sing-along, and game shows.

Outdoor deck space is more than adequate for passengers who do not take the sun for long stretches. The continuous Promenade Deck has shady recesses for reading and dozing, but the small aft-facing tiered decks are the most sought-after locations for reading or conversation while gazing down on the swimmers in the outdoor pool and over the stern to the ship's wake. Games include putting practice, table tennis, deck quoits, and shuffleboard.

As *Saga Ruby* was originally built to cruise in cool waters, the ship has an indoor pool (rare on ships today), sauna, and steam room deep down in the ship, two decks below the lowest passenger cabin level. The spa is relatively small but offers a generous number of treatments. The outdoor pool is located aft on the Veranda Deck.

Dress alternates between formal black tie, informal jacket and tie, and casual during in-port evenings. On formal nights, about 90% of the men will be wearing dinner jackets. During the day, unlike on American-oriented ships, you will see very few men in T-shirts or jeans or women wearing shorts during the day aboard or ashore.

Most Saga cruises begin and end at Southampton or Dover, from where the itineraries fan out to the Baltic, Greenland, Iceland, Norway, Scotland, and south to Iberia, Atlantic Isles, western Mediterranean, and the North African coast. A seasonal long transatlantic cruise visits the Canadian Maritimes, St. Lawrence River Seaway, and U.S. East Coast. *Saga Pearl II*'s inaugural cruise departs Southampton on March 15, 2010, for the Norwegian coast and the Arctic. Afterwards, she sails from either Dover or Southampton on 7- to 24-night cruises to the Canary Islands, Mediterranean, and Baltic. *Saga Ruby*'s deep 27-foot draft makes her a worthy sea vessel. The ships' reasonable fares are virtually all-inclusive, with all gratuities and a choice of two excursions in each port. Saga also offers European river cruises.

ITINERARIES *See* Itinerary Index.

SeaDream Yacht Club
601 Brickell Key Drive, Suite 1050, Miami, FL 33131;
☎ **800-707-4911; www.seadream.com**

SeaDream I/SeaDream II (**56/112 SCANDINAVIAN/INTERNATIONAL/89; 344 FEET/4,260 TONS**)

SeaDream Yacht Club, a venture of Norwegian entrepreneur Atle Brynestad (who founded Seabourn Cruise Line) and other cruise veterans, began operating in late 2001 and early 2002, offering seven-day summer Mediterranean and winter Caribbean cruises on the luxury twin ships *SeaDream I* and *II* (formerly *Sea Goddess I* and *II*). The twin megayachts, as the line calls them, were redesigned and refitted at Lloyd Werft's shipyard in Bremerhaven, Germany, prior to their entering service.

The handsome twins are meant to provide a totally different experience from today's typical cruise, one that more closely resembles yachting. Like yachts, the ships offer an open and unstructured ambience and provide passengers the ability to move at their own pace and to make personal choices. "No clocks, no crowds, no lines, no stress" could be the company's motto.

These are the SeaDream differences the owners cite:

- FLEXIBLE SCHEDULES AND ITINERARIES SeaDream yachts depart their first port and arrive at their last port as scheduled, but frequently, the port calls in between are not run by a strict timetable. Captains have the authority to adjust for local opportunities. If they want to visit a small island fish market so the chef can pick up the catch of the day, that's fine. If the weather and the snorkeling are perfect in a small, secluded bay and passengers want to remain longer, that's okay too.

- OVERNIGHT IN KEY PORTS Most cruise ships arrive at ports of call at about 8 a.m. and sail at 5 or 6 p.m. of the same day. SeaDream yachts overnight at such ports as Monte Carlo and St. Tropez, where the action doesn't even get started until late in the evening.

- OFFICERS AND STAFF AS GUIDES Passengers might visit a small-town pastry shop with the chef; go snorkeling with the captain; or go hiking, biking, or golfing with the officers. What better guides to have, SeaDream says, than those who know their sailing regions like the backs of their hands?

- NO TUXEDOS OR GALA GOWNS SeaDream has no dress code; rather it stresses the casual nature of yachting.

The outdoor features of *SeaDream I* and *II* include alcoves for sunning on double Balinese sun beds, a private massage tent on deck, a large-screen golf simulator, movies on deck by the outdoor swimming pool, and a water sports marina at the stern where there is equipment for kayaking, waterskiing, windsurfing, wave running, snorkeling, and Sunfish sailing. Tai chi, yoga, and aerobics classes are also offered. The Balinese beds are elevated so that you can see over the railing. We are told the beds are so dreamy, some passengers even spend the night outside under the stars on them.

Indoors, passengers have an Asian-style spa and fitness center with elliptical treadmills mounted with flat-screen televisions, as well as free weights and recumbent bikes. A personal trainer is available. Spa treatment can now be booked online at **www.seadreamspa.com.** The spa, open from 8 a.m. to 8 p.m. daily, offers an extensive range of Asian treatments such as traditional Thai massage, shiatsu massage, and Japanese body scrub. All spa offerings are for men as well as women. The spa also operates a salon for manicures, pedicures, and other beauty treatments.

The ships also have a **Main Lounge** with a 61-inch flat-screen television; a piano bar; casino; and a library with books, CDs, DVDs, and computer outlets. Laptop computers are available. Passengers are given their own onboard e-mail address.

Each ship accommodates up to 112 passengers, depending on the configuration. Of the 56 cabins, all but two are Yacht Club category with 195 square feet. Sixteen of these are convertible to Commodore Club cabins of 390 square feet, with his-and-her bathroom facilities and a dining area accommodating four. The 450-square-foot Owner's Suite has a bedroom, a bathroom with a tub and separate shower with a view of the sea, a living room and dining area, and a guest bathroom.

Both ships sport a new accommodation called The Admiral Suite, created in the space that had a boutique, which was moved elsewhere. The sumptuous 375-square-foot suite with three panorama windows looking out to the sea is bathed in light. It has an open living-dining area with a dining table that seats four, a master bedroom, and one-and-a-half bathrooms. The entertainment center has a wall-mounted flat-screen television, a refreshment center, and a writing desk. The separate master bedroom is furnished with a queen-size bed and an adjustable flat-screen television. The master bathroom with marble walls and floor has multijet, massage showerheads, a tub, and vanity area. The decor of the suite favors neutral tones and blond woodwork.

All cabins are Internet-ready and have an entertainment center with a flat-screen television, CD and DVD systems with an extensive selection of movies, and other offerings. A personal jukebox with more than 100 digital music programs is also available. All bathrooms have multiple-jet massage showers and lighted magnifying mirrors.

The cuisine is guaranteed to be top rate, with such luxuries as having all the bread baked aboard and including specialty breads such as multigrain, sourdough, pumpernickel, and focaccia.

Staff and crew number 89; most have been sailing on their respective ships for several years. The yachts, suitable for small meetings and incentive groups, are very popular for charter.

SeaDream makes a specialty of calling at new ports and ports where large ships cannot go, as well as unusual shore excursions that only a small ship can create. When SeaDream first made an irresistible offer to its passengers sailing on voyages out of Rome—an opportunity to drive a Ferrari—the adventure got such heavy response that there weren't enough Ferraris available. Not to worry. SeaDream continues to offer the program.

ITINERARIES *See* Itinerary Index.

Swan Hellenic Cruises
1800 SE Tenth Avenue, Suite 205, Fort Lauderdale, FL 33316;
☎ **866-623-2689; fax 954-761-7768; www.swanhellenic.us**

Minerva **(111 CABINS, 12 BALCONY SUITES/394;**
BRITISH, INTERNATIONAL/160 CREW; 436 FEET/12,500 TONS)

After a brief hiatus, Swan Hellenic Cruises, which had been owned by the Carnival Corporation as a result of its purchase of P&O/Princess Cruises, was allowed to go out of business. Fortunately, it was rescued by U.K.-based All-Leisure Holidays (a group headed by Lord Sterling), to the delight of its large loyal following in the United Kingdom as well as the United States, Australia, and Canada. The line caters to travelers (most ages 50 or older) who are intellectually curious and interested in the art and culture of destinations they visit.

Launched in 1996, *Minerva* is a stylish yet unpretentious ship that has been likened to a country-house inn, with gleaming brass, polished wood, fresh flowers, and original art decorating the walls. Passengers enjoy modern, well-appointed, and comfortable accommodations and public rooms on a ship with many facilities and great flexibility. But beneath these amenities, *Minerva* is comprised of strong steel, an ice-strengthened hull, stabilizers, and bow thrusters, which give her the power, stability, and agility to handle open-water cruising and icy seas.

The Lounge on the Main Deck forward is a favorite place for passengers to congregate before the day's excursion, listen to talks by onboard naturalists and other experts, or join friends for after-dinner coffee. Two bars—**Shackleton** and **South Cape**—provide additional corners in which to relax. The ship's library is exceptional, with a wide range of books, as well as newspapers, games, and puzzles. The Main Deck has the dining room aft and a beauty salon (which also offers massage) at midship. On the Bridge Deck is the swimming pool, a bar and informal restaurant, card room, cinema, library, exercise room, and sauna. The ship also has a gift shop, medical center, launderette, and two elevators.

The atmosphere on board *Minerva* is informal and unregimented and sports an easy camaraderie among the passengers and the experts (naturalists, geologists, zoologists, historians, and ornithologists) who accompany every cruise. Each day, passengers gather for informal pre-excursion briefings or post-trip wrap-ups in the ship's lounge or auditorium. Throughout the trip, they interact with the experts to exchange ideas and ask questions—at dinner, at the rail, or on a Zodiac. Staff and crew add to the experience with their informal talks and entertainment. Days are packed with intellectual and physical activities and the day's recap before dinner. Lectures are well attended but are also broadcast in cabins. Most talks are accompanied by audiovisuals.

A pianist might offer light entertainment in the Shackleton Lounge, and a *Minerva* quartet performs on selected evenings in the Main Lounge. Socializing resumes after dinner, sometimes continuing into the wee hours. A passenger may tickle the ivories or sing, but guests generally just converse. Slides or a film might be shown. The library is popular at any hour.

Minerva offers spacious and comfortable accommodations, some with private balconies. All cabins have a vanity table/writing desk and chair, television and radio, refrigerator, direct-dial telephone, hair dryer, and binoculars. There are two Owner's Suites and ten outside suites on Bridge Deck forward with floor-to-ceiling patio doors leading to a balcony; they are furnished with a queen or twin beds, a bathroom with a tub, a large double wardrobe, ample drawer space, and a separate sitting area with a sofa, chair, and table.

The 12 outside deluxe cabins on Promenade Deck forward have twin beds or a queen bed (some have a pull-out sofa for triple occupancy), a bathroom with a tub, a separate sitting area with a sofa, chair, and table, and a large picture window mirrored for privacy. Promenade Deck, midship and aft, also has 20 outside superior cabins with twin beds or a queen bed, bathroom with a tub, walk-in closet, armchair, and large picture window.

The standard categories are spread over two decks: 54 on A Deck and 26 on B Deck. All are outside and have twin beds or a queen bed, a bathroom with a shower, single and double wardrobes, a love seat, and a picture window or porthole. Four cabins are wheelchair accessible, and four are single cabins. Laundry service is available on Deck A. *Minerva* staff and crew provide a high level of warm, personal service.

The ship's two dining rooms afford open seatings and indoor and outdoor service. The menus offer international cuisine as well as selections of light fare and vegetarian dishes. Special diets can be accommodated with sufficient advance notice. "Smart casual" wear is the evening attire. Smoking is not permitted in most areas of the ship, but there is a dedicated smoking room on the Bridge Deck and designated areas on the outer decks.

In addition to accommodations and meals, the all-inclusive cruise prices include all bar drinks and house wines, onboard gratuities, and sightseeing. *Minerva* sails on diverse itineraries. In 2010–2011, the ship returns to India and the Far East with new itineraries that include Oman, India, Sri Lanka, Malaysia, Vietnam, Cambodia, Thailand, and the Philippines. Swan Hellenic's planning team aims to strike a balance of retaining world-class destinations while introducing new ports of call never visited by *Minerva*. In spring, a series of fly-cruises heads to the Mediterranean and Black Sea, while in summer, the ship will operate a series of cruises from Dover in the U.K. that call at ports in northern Europe, including Iceland. The line also offers European river cruises on the Danube that depart from Vienna, as well as cruises on the Rhone and Saone rivers, which take in Burgundy, Provence, and the Camargue in France.

In November 2009, the All-Leisure group acquired the 15,271-ton *Alexander von Humboldt* at auction. After the ship with 250 passenger cabins (90% are outside) undergoes an extensive $20-million upgrade and refurbishment, she will be put in service in summer 2011.

ITINERARIES *See* Itinerary Index.

Travel Dynamics International
132 East 70th Street, New York, NY 10021; ☎ 212-517-7555 or 800-257-5767; fax 212-774-1545; www.traveldynamicsinternational.com

Travel Dynamics International specializes in educational and cultural cruises aboard small deluxe ships. The customized programs are designed for well-traveled, destination-oriented individuals who want a learning experience but don't want to forgo their comfort. Itineraries span the globe and include exotic as well as familiar destinations. Lecturers and academics knowledgeable about the destinations accompany the cruises. The company currently operates two small ships described below.

Callisto **(17/34; GREEK/EUROPEAN/18; 164 FEET/435 TONS)**

This small luxury yacht, built in Germany, underwent comprehensive renovation and refurbishment prior to her debut in 2000. The ship has 17 outside cabins, 11 with large panoramic windows, and 6 on Daphne Deck with three large portholes each. Public areas include a spacious lounge, a library, and a dining room accommodating all passengers at one open seating. There are two broad decks for sunbathing and dining alfresco and a swimming platform at the vessel's stern.

All cabins are air-conditioned with generous storage space and have full- or queen-size beds, marble bathroom with shower radio, telephone, refrigerator, and television with VCR/DVD. The four-deck ship has a draft of eight feet and a speed of 14 knots. It is equipped with Zodiac landing craft. The bridge is outfitted with state-of-the-art navigational and communications equipment.

Callisto flies the Greek flag and is equipped with the latest navigational instruments, including satellite communication systems. The ship offers e-mail service. She sails to the Adriatic, Greek Islands, the Mediterranean, Turkey, and West Africa.

Corinthian II **(57/114; EUROPEAN/75; 297 FEET/4,200 TONS)**

The deluxe, all-suite *Corinthian II* offers a classic yachtlike atmosphere and fine accommodations. Originally built in 1992, the ship was redecorated and refurbished in 2005. *Corinthian II* accommodates all guests in 57 outside suites, each affording sea views. Suites have a sitting area, television/DVD, minifridge, safe, and other amenities, as well as a marble-appointed bathroom. Several suites include private balconies accessed via sliding glass doors. Fresh flowers and fruit provide a bright touch in every suite.

The *Corinthian II*'s spacious and finely decorated public areas include a library stocked with books related to the itinerary and other volumes. Four computer terminals with Internet access are available for e-mail. The ship has an elegant lounge as well as **The Club,** a space with picture windows for panoramic views and a relaxing place to enjoy musical arrangements by the ship's pianist. The restaurant serves fine cuisine prepared by European chefs and can accommodate all guests at a single unassigned seating or alfresco on the wide Sun Deck, which is specially equipped for outdoor dining. Other facilities on board include a gym, beauty salon, Sun Deck with whirlpool, and elevator serving all passenger decks. *Corinthian II* has an ice-strengthened hull for voyages into Antarctic waters and is equipped with a fleet of Zodiac inflatable craft for excursions ashore.

Clelia II **(50 SUITES/100; EUROPEAN/60; 290 FEET/4,077 TONS)**

Travel Dynamics' latest addition, *Clelia II*, entered service in 2009, after being refurbished extensively and having other improvements made. The all-suite ship offers a private yachtlike cruise experience, with 50 spacious, air-conditioned suites, all with ocean views, measuring 215 square feet or more. Each suite is furnished with twin or queen-size beds, a television and DVD/CD player, a telephone, a mini-refrigerator, fresh flowers, and a fruit basket, and has a sitting area or separate living room and spacious closets. In the marble bathroom with teak floors, passengers find fine toiletries, plush terry robes, and slippers. The 12 Deluxe Veranda Suites (245 square feet) on the Cleo Deck and the four Deluxe Penthouse Suites (260 square feet) on the Phoebe Deck have private balconies and sitting areas. There is 24-hour room service as well.

The decor of rich fabrics, handsome wood, polished brass, antiques, and fine works of art provides a warm and inviting ambience. The public facilities include the dining room and an outdoor cafe, a library with Internet access, two lounges with audiovisual facilities, a gym, a spa and beauty salon, a boutique, and a medical center. Outdoors are two sun decks, a Jacuzzi, and a swimming platform. An elevator serves all five passenger decks.

Clelia II complies with the latest international and U.S. Coast Guard safety regulations and is outfitted with the most current navigational and communications technology as well as with retractable fin stabilizers. She has an ice-strengthened hull and a fleet of Zodiacs.

The Malta-flagged ship with a 12-foot draft sails on a variety of cultural and expedition voyages, including a summer series in the Great Lakes, which was introduced in 2009; Atlantic Canada in the fall and her first Arctic cruises in 2010; South America, the Amazon, and Antarctica in the winter.

ITINERARIES *See* Itinerary Index.

Voyages of Discovery
1800 SE Tenth Avenue, Suite 205, Fort Lauderdale, FL 33316;
☎ **866-623-2689; fax 954-761-7768; www.voyagesofdiscovery.com**

Discovery **(351/650; SCANDINAVIAN, BRITISH, DUTCH/AMERICAN, EUROPEAN, FILIPINO; 553 FEET/20,186 TONS)**

In 2002, well-known travel industry entrepreneur Gerry Herrod (former chairman of Orient Lines, Ocean Cruise Lines, and Pearl Cruises) founded Discovery World Cruises to provide four-star cruises to less-traveled destinations at affordable prices, much like other niche-market companies that Herrod headed in the past. The cruises focus on giving passengers in-depth exposure to their destinations, while providing the traditional comforts of its deluxe ocean liner. In 2005, Discovery World Cruises was acquired by the United Kingdom–based All Leisure Group, the holding company of All Leisure Holidays Limited, an established cruise holiday company that also owns Swan Hellenic Cruises and Hebridean International Cruises, another company it pulled back from the brink.

Before entering service in 2003, *Discovery* (built as the *Island Venture* in 1972 in Germany and best known as Princess Cruises' *Island Princess*) underwent extensive, multimillion-dollar renovations that, in effect, created a new ship. She retained her handsome, classic profile and grand ocean liner ambience but now boasts modern safety features and amenities. During 2008–2009, more than $3.5 million was spent refurbishing the public areas, the **Seven Continents** restaurant, and some cabins to further improve the onboard facilities. An additional $3.5 million has been earmarked for more refurbishment of cabins and improvements to the Yacht Club over the next year. At 20,000 tons—small compared with today's megaliners—*Discovery* is large enough for cruising to faraway places, yet small enough to enter remote harbors that larger vessels must bypass.

Facilities on the eight-deck *Discovery* include three restaurants, five lounges, a lecture theater/cinema, a well-stocked library, a bridge room, modern gym, spa and beauty center, two swimming pools (one with a retractable dome), two Jacuzzis, a card room, an Internet center and wireless access, boutiques, and four elevators. There are nightly entertainment, classical music concerts, and folkloric performances by local groups.

All the ship's cabins and suites are equipped with private facilities, air-conditioning, televisions, hair dryers, and safes. Cabins on the Bridge and Promenade decks have a bathtub and a shower; those on other decks have showers. Cabins have two lower beds or a double bed. Some cabins have one or two upper berths or a sofa bed, allowing for a third or fourth person. Most beds in twin cabins are arranged parallel to each other, although some are arranged in an L shape. A small number of cabins have an interconnecting door and can be booked as adjoining cabins. Outside cabins on the Bridge and Promenade decks have picture windows; those on the Pacific Deck have two windows; those on the Bali and Coral decks have two portholes. Outside and inside standard cabins measure 135 square feet; outside superior cabins have 194 square feet.

A hallmark of Voyages of Discovery is its enrichment program of lectures and workshops at sea, area experts on each voyage who provide detailed briefings on each port of call, and local cultural performances on board. Most itineraries are marketed as cruise-tour vacation packages, which include extended stays and sightseeing in embarkation and/or disembarkation cities. *Discovery* also runs an unusual lecture series sponsored by the Mayo Clinic that features a comprehensive team of distinguished medical professionals aboard select cruises.

During the winter season, *Discovery* sails to the Red Sea, India, Southeast Asia, Far East, Indian Ocean Islands, South Africa, East Africa, Black Sea, and Mediterranean. In summer, she visits Scandinavia, Russia and the Baltic, Greenland, Iceland, Faroe Islands, British Islands and Ireland, Mediterranean and Adriatic, Aegean, Black Sea, and North Africa. New for winter 2010 are 12- to 72-night cruises with extensive overland tours and stays, plus 27 maiden calls. Special single rates and past-passenger savings are available.

Voyages to Antiquity

1800 SE Tenth Street, Suite 230, Fort Lauderdale, FL 33316;
☎ **954-302-6340; reservations 1-877-398-1460**
8 South Parade, Oxford, OX2 7JL, U.K.; office ☎ 01865 302 550;
reservations 0845 437 9737; www.voyagestoantiquity.com

Aegean Odyssey **(198/378; GREEK/INTERNATIONAL; 461 FEET/11,563 TONS)**

Well-known cruise entrepreneur Gerry Herrod (founder of Ocean Cruise Lines and Orient Lines) has launched a brand-new, destination-oriented cruise line called Voyages to Antiquity. The new venture is designed in the same spirit as Orient Lines itineraries for the *Marco Polo,* but it now is focused on the Mediterranean, North Africa, and Red Sea. Voyages to Antiquity is designed to provide passengers with a very up-close and personal experience, learning about the cultures of the "cradle of civilizations" in the shadows of the megaships that can only visit larger, more congested ports.

Inspired by the book *The Middle Sea* by Lord John Julius Norwich, and scheduled to begin in May of 2010, Voyages to Antiquity will travel to Rome, Egypt, and Greece and trace the development and impact of their prominent ancient cultures, with nine itineraries and 16 departures on the recently renovated *Aegean Odyssey.* The cruises combine cultural travel, enrichment with expert lecturers, and special destination-based events, including a private evening in St. Mark's Basilica in Venice and a cocktail reception at the Palazzo Gangi in Palermo, Sicily. In 2010, complimentary shore experiences are being offered at each port of call. Several itineraries have overnight stays.

On board *Aegean Odyssey,* the ambience will be smart casual and relaxed, with no formal nights. Dining will feature Continental cuisine augmented by regional foods with open seating in **Marco Polo,** the main restaurant for lunch and dinner (when wine is included). Two alternative dining venues are **Terrace Café,** for breakfast, lunch, and dinner, and **Tapas on the Terrace,** for a bistro-style dinner. Both dining venues, as well as the spa area, were enhanced in recent renovations. A late-night snack in the Lido and Rendezvous bars and a room-service menu will be available until midnight. Gratuities for cabin stewards and the restaurant staff are included in the cruise price.

After her extensive refurbishment, *Aegean Odyssey* now has more than 80 brand-new suites with balcony and deluxe cabins. All 40 suites and 158 cabins have a bathtub and/or shower, flat-screen television, safe, hair dryer, and are air-conditioned. Beds may be fixed double/queen size, separate twin beds, or twins that can be converted into a double. All accommodations are outside with a balcony or window, except for those in K category, which have portholes. There are 12 singles, eight for a third or fourth person, and two wheelchair-accessible cabins.

Concierge Class (the top 7 of 14 categories) has additional amenities, including a welcome bottle of Champagne, minibar, bottled water, robe and slippers, deluxe bathroom toiletries, DVD selection, and the service of a concierge. On the Lido Deck, the Owner's Suites (550 square feet) have convertible twin beds, separate sitting areas and balconies, marble bathrooms, and dressing areas; and Junior Balcony Suites (310 square feet) and Deluxe Balcony Suites (275 square feet) on the Bridge and Belvedere decks are similar, with sitting areas and balconies, walk-in showers or bathtubs, and fixed double beds, separate twin beds, or converted twins. Some cabins in this group are smaller and do not have a sitting area.

Deluxe cabins (200 to 215 square feet) on the Bridge and Belvedere decks have convertible twin beds and bathtubs/showers or walk-in showers; some cabins in this group are smaller but have a balcony. Premium outside cabins (130 square feet) on the Bridge, Belvedere, and Columbus decks have fixed twin beds with showers; some have views obstructed by lifeboats. Standard cabins are similar in size and layout but have portholes. Premium inside and standard inside cabins (130 square feet) on the Belvedere and Columbus decks have fixed twin beds and showers; some are singles.

Among the ship's other facilities are the nicely appointed and well-stocked library, an Internet room, an **Observation Lounge** where afternoon tea is served, an equipped gym with lockers and showers, and a spa with treatment rooms, saunas, beauty salon, and early-morning yoga.

Value will be a hallmark of Voyages to Antiquity. In 2010, in addition to a shore experience at each port of call, wine at dinner, and gratuities being included in the price, free airfare will be offered from select East Coast gateways and low air add-ons ($99 or $199) from additional gateways throughout North America. A handsome and informative brochure is available from the cruise line or travel agents.

ITINERARIES *See* Itinerary Index.

The World/ResidenSea, Ltd.
14471 Miramar Parkway, Miramar, FL 33027; ☎ 800-970-6601
(North America rentals); 954-538-8400; fax 954-431-7151;
www.aboardtheworld.com

The World **(165 RESIDENCES: 106 APARTMENTS; 19 ONE- AND TWO-BEDROOM APARTMENTS; 40 VERANDA STUDIOS; NORWEGIAN/320; 644 FEET/43,188 TONS)**

The World, the first residential cruise ship ever built, was launched from Oslo in March 2002 to begin her cruising odyssey and confounded the skeptics (us included), who said it would never happen. Five weeks later, she sailed to America on her maiden voyage.

Billed as the world's first residential resort community at sea continuously circumnavigating the globe, *The World* has 165 residences, many available for rent. A staff of about 250 attends them.

Here's what she offers on her 12 decks: two- and three-bedroom private apartments ranging from 1,106 to 3,242 square feet, with decor by top designers and fully furnished down to the Christofle flatware and Wedgewood china; four theme restaurants featuring French, Mediterranean, and Asian cuisine, plus a delicatessen; enrichment activities such as lectures and seminars; full-size tennis court; a retractable marina for water activities; two pools; a top-deck, open-air, full-shot driving range, 40-course golf simulators, real grass putting greens, two artificial greens, a sand bunker, and a PGA-certified golf director;

a fitness center; Banyan Tree's first spa at sea; and an art gallery, casino, Internet cafe, library, two conference rooms, nightclub, meditation chapel, and several boutiques. Oh, yes, and three emergency wards, full-time doctor and nurse, as well as a telemedicine hookup with Mount Sinai-Cedars Hospital in Miami Beach. Activities on board are deliberately kept to a minimum, but there are some typical cruise pastimes such as bridge and other games, trivia, lectures, movies, afternoon tea, and enrichment programs.

Passengers enjoy all this while traveling the world—140 ports in more than 40 countries with planned itineraries of 6 to 17 days—and attending such special events as the America's Cup and a New Year's Eve gala. One of their most thrilling experiences took place in summer of 2009, when *The World* made maritime history during a voyage to the Russian Arctic region and provided passengers with an uncommon opportunity to explore remote communities and observe rare wildlife. When the ship navigated the Bering Strait, which separates the easternmost point of Russia from Alaska, *The World* became the first foreign-flagged cruise ship to sail between the islands on the Russian side since World War II. On approach to Wrangel Island, renowned for its wildlife, passengers spotted 104 polar bears—more than most ships see in an entire summer—and even watched an inquisitive mother and cub bear swim to the ship to greet them. *The World* was the first foreign-flagged cruise ship to visit Wrangel Island since 1924. When *The World* reached the ice cap's edge, which extends to the North Pole, and while the ship was at anchor, the captain lowered the ship's retractable marina, enabling 35 adventurers to take the "Polar Plunge," into 33.3 °F water.

On tap for 2010 is an Iceland to Quebec via Greenland voyage in September and two Antarctica Expeditions in December 2010 and January 2011, among other trips.

And the price (ah, yes, if you have to ask): apartments range from $1.2 million to $6.5 million, with an average price of $2.8 million. And then there's the annual maintenance fee, which includes housekeeping, and varies based upon square footage. As of June 2006, all of the apartments in the ship's original inventory had been sold.

Who, you ask, bought these apartments? According to its management company, they are home owners who have two or three residences, are age 55, and are first-generation entrepreneurs who have built their worth as computer-chip makers, real-estate developers, and the like. They are very active, have an affinity for the sea, maybe own a yacht or have cruised a lot, and they guard their privacy. North Americans constitute the largest number of buyers, followed by Norwegians, Brits, Germans, Australians, and Swiss. Some owners stay aboard for three months a year, just as they would, say, at their condo in Aspen or their villa in the south of France.

The World's management says the ship is for people who hate having to pack a suitcase to travel, who really miss sleeping in their own beds when they're away, and who long to see the world without ever having to leave the comforts of home. It seems such a simple idea that it's surprising no one ever floated it before.

The residents bought out the original developers in 2006, and they now own the ship. ResidenSea, Ltd., remains the managing company of *The World*.

Rentals can be booked through travel agents or ResidenSea. Rentals are for a minimum of six nights; rates begin at approximately $1,600 per person per night, double occupancy. The rate includes all onboard dining, beverages, port charges, gratuities, and taxes. The ship also offers a regular selection of expeditions.

ITINERARIES *See* Itinerary Index.

PART THREE

CRUISING ALTERNATIVES

▌ RIVER *and* BARGE CRUISES

A RIVER CRUISE IS NOT ONLY A DIFFERENT WAY TO SEE A COUNTRY, it's a different country you will see. Whether you sail down the Danube or the Yangtze, up the Hudson or the Nile, or float on European channels or the Erie Canal, the cruise will be a new travel experience, even if you have visited the same area by land.

The river cruise most familiar to U.S. travelers is probably steamboating on the Mississippi, but there are many kinds of river cruises, their character shaped by the location and nature of the waterway. An adventure cruise on the Amazon, for example, is quite different from barging in Burgundy. Nonetheless, river cruises share certain characteristics, and all are light-years from an ocean cruise.

To begin with, boats (a vessel is a ship on the ocean but a boat on a river) offering river cruises are small. Most boats carry 100 to 200 passengers, although some of the new riverboats accommodate 250 or more, and Majestic America's *American Queen* takes 436 passengers. Barges that glide along small canals and waterways are much smaller, taking as few as 6 and never more than 24 passengers.

The small size of vessels and the nature of the waterways provide an intimate look at the cruise locale, heightening the sense of place and history in a way ocean liners never can. The destination, not the boat, is the main attraction on a river cruise.

Cabins are small but comfortable. The ambience is informal, the dress casual. Except on some large riverboats, nightly entertainment is absent. Passengers are left to their own devices, and many rediscover the pleasure of conversation and friendship.

RIVER AND BARGE CRUISES IN EUROPE

RIVER CRUISES ARE AVAILABLE on major rivers worldwide, but the largest selection—an estimated 400 passenger riverboats—is in

Europe on the Danube, Rhine, Rhône, Seine, and Volga, where rivers have been thoroughfares of commerce and culture for centuries. The growth in recent years has been phenomenal.

European cruises—most between April and November—take you to the Continent's great cities through beautiful scenery laced with ancient forts, mighty cathedrals, and storybook castles. They dock in the heart of a different town each day. Some river cruise lines include sightseeing tours in their cruise fare. If not, passengers may book optional tours for a fee, or they can easily sightsee on their own.

River cruises reveal Europe the way it was meant to be seen. Almost all historic buildings were built facing the river, so when the boat docks in front of Pillnitz Palace on the Elbe, for example, passengers enter the way guests of Augustus the Strong did centuries ago.

Some itineraries overnight in port, allowing passengers to attend local shows or dine ashore. Others sail at night, so passengers wake refreshed for the next day of sightseeing.

More than a dozen companies offer such cruises; the largest, Viking River Cruises, is typical in its itineraries. Its fleet of 25 ships sails the length of the Rhine, as well as the Elbe, Moselle, Rhône, Saône, and Seine. The Danube and Rhine-Main-Danube Canal were added in 1994, when the North and Black seas were linked for the first time.

Riverboats and barges have completely different styles. Canals and smaller rivers deep in the countryside are traversed by barges, which glide gently through some of the most beautiful and historic areas of England and Europe. The pace is so leisurely (three or four knots per hour) that passengers can get off to walk in the woods or bike in the village and not be left behind. The tortoiselike pace, the utter peace and relaxation, are for some the best vacation they ever had. For others, it's like watching grass grow.

By day, passengers lounge on deck, play cards, read, and watch the boat navigate the locks. They can walk or bike, discovering interesting places and friendly people, and reboard at the next lock. The price usually includes a choice of guided tours by minibus or bicycle to nearby castles, wineries, and medieval towns.

Hotel barges, as they are known, are like floating country inns. They vary in size, carrying from 6 to 51 passengers on cruises of 3, 6, or 13 days. Cabins are small and bathrooms tiny, but the barges, such as those of French Country Waterways, are luxurious. Many serve outstanding gourmet cuisine prepared by Le Cordon Bleu chefs. Regional wines, normally included in the cruise price, flow generously. The atmosphere is very informal—and very romantic.

The following is a sampling of the offerings from companies with U.S. offices or representatives. Note that several companies offer the same boats; agreements may not be exclusive.

Note: In parentheses after each boat name is information (where available) about the number of cabins and passengers; officers and crew; and the boat's length (cabins/passengers; officers/crew; boat length).

Abercrombie & Kent USA, LLC

1411 Opus Place, Executive Towers West II, Suite 300, Downers Grove, IL 60515; ☎ 800-652-7963 or 630-725-3400; fax 630-725-3401; www.abercrombiekent.com

(*Also see* Abercrombie & Kent under Yangtze River Cruises and Nile River Cruises, all later in this chapter.)

Alouette **(2/4; FRENCH/BRITISH/4; 98 FEET)**
Converted 1987, renovated 1999. Six nights on the Canal du Midi in France. Charter only.

Amaryllis **(4/8; FRENCH/BRITISH/6; 129 FEET)**
Entered service 2002. Heated saltwater pool. Six-night charters in Burgundy, Franche-Comte, Beaujolais, and Vallée du Rhône. Special "Wines of Burgundy" cruise in July 2010.

Anjodi **(4/8; FRENCH/BRITISH/4; 100 FEET)**
Entered service 1983; refurbished 2006. On-deck spa. Six nights on the Canal du Midi, in Provence, and the Camargue in France. Family, golf, wine, and other theme charters available.

Elisabeth **(3/6; BRITISH/FRENCH; 100 FEET)**
Converted 1988; refurbished 2007. Six-night cruises in Burgundy. Family and other theme charters available.

Fleur de Lys **(3/6; FRENCH/BRITISH/6; 129 FEET)**
Entered service 1986; refurbished 2000. Six nights in Burgundy and Beaujolais.

Hirondelle **(4/8; FRENCH/BRITISH/4; 128 FEET)**
Entered service 1992; refurbished 2002. Six nights in Loire Valley, Burgundy, and Beaujolais. L'Art de Vivre (4/8; French/British/4; 100 feet) Converted 1998; renovated 2008. One double, three twin beds. Six nights in Burgundy and Chablis. Family, walking, wine, and other theme charters available. La Belle Époque (7/13; French/British/5; 126 feet) Converted 1995; refurbished 2006. Outdoor spa and pool, plus fitness area. Six nights in Burgundy and Chablis. Theme charters available. For charters, can accommodate 13 passengers.

La Nouvelle Etoile **(4/8; FRENCH/DUTCH/5; 129 FEET)**
Entered service 2002; refurbished 2008. Six nights in Holland or France (Northern Burgundy, Champagne, Alsace-Lorraine, Upper Loire) or Moselle region in Germany.

L'Impressionniste **(6/12; FRENCH/BRITISH/5; 126 FEET)**
Converted 1996; refurbished 2007. Six nights in central Burgundy. Theme charters available. For charters, can accommodate 13 passengers.

Lorraine **(11/22; FRENCH/7; 128 FEET)**
Converted 1985; refurbished 2007. Six nights in Burgundy, Alsace-Lorraine, and Vosges Mountains in France.

Magna Carta **(4/8; BRITISH/4; 117 FEET)**
Converted 2002. Six nights on the River Thames in England. Theme charters available. For charters, can accommodate up to ten passengers.

Marjorie II **(6/12; FLEMISH/5 TO 6; 129 FEET)**
Converted 1998; refurbished in 2007. Six nights in Holland and Belgium in the spring; southern Belgium, May to June and October; northern Burgundy, July to September. Family charters available July to September.

Meanderer **(3/6; 5; 123 FEET)**
Converted 1992; refurbished 2008. Jacuzzi spa and pool; Internet access. Six nights in Upper Loire. Charters available.

Napoleon **(6/12; FRENCH/BRITISH/6 TO 7; 129 FEET)**
Converted 1992; refurbished 2001. Six nights in the Vallée du Rhône and Beaujolais.

Le Phénicien **(9/18; FRENCH/5 TO 6; 127 FEET)**
Entered service 1959; refurbished 2008. Six nights in Provence, the Camargue, and Languedoc. Cooking, cycling, golf, wine, and other theme charters and departures available.

Prospérité **(4/8; FRENCH/5; 128 FEET)**
Entered service 2003. Cabins with full tub and shower; on-deck hot tub. Six nights in central Burgundy. Charters available.

Renaissance **(4/8; BRITISH/FRENCH/5; 126 FEET)**
Converted 1997; refurbished 2006. Six-night cruise in western Burgundy and Upper Loire. Theme charters available.

River Cloud II **(44/88; INTERNATIONAL/35; 338 FEET)**
Entered service late spring 2001. Seven-night cruises in central Europe, including the Danube River. (*See descriptions later in this section.*)

Roi Soleil **(3/6; FRENCH/4; 98 FEET)**
Converted 1999; refurbished 2008. Six nights in Provence, the Camargue, Languedoc, and Canal du Midi. Charter only.

Saroche **(3/6; FRENCH/4; 128 FEET)**
Refurbished 2007. Owner operated. Spa pool. Six nights in central Burgundy, Provence, and the Camargue. Charters available.

Scottish Highlander **(4/8; BRITISH/4; 117 FEET)**
Built 1931; converted 2000; renovated 2006. Six nights on the Caledonian Canal in the Scottish Highlands. Cycling, family, fishing, golf, walking, and other theme charters available.

Shannon Princess II **(5/10; IRISH/5; 105 FEET)**
Entered service 2003; refurbished 2008. Six nights on the River Shannon and Lough Derg in Ireland. Golf, walking, and other theme charters available.

Volga Dream **(59/109; INTERNATIONAL/60; 314 FEET)**
Refurbished 2007. Seven nights on the Volga River from Moscow to St. Petersburg, Russia.

AMAWaterways
21625 Prairie Street, Chatsworth, California 91311;
☎ **800-626-0126; fax 818-772-7335; www.amawaterways.com**

Amacello/Amadagio/Amadante/Amadolce/Amalegro/Amalyra **(71 CABINS/ 4 JUNIOR SUITES/148; 41; 360 FEET)**

Amabella **(DEBUT 2010)**

Amadouro **(65/130; PORTUGESE/30; 255 FEET)**

La Marguerite **(46/92; VIETNAMESE/40; 235 FEET)**

Swiss Pearl **(59 CABINS/2 JUNIOR SUITES/123; SWISS/30; 360 FEET)**

Tolstoy **(66 CABINS/13 SUITES/6 SINGLES/160; RUSSIAN/105; 353 FEET)**

Founded in 2002 by three cruise-industry veterans (Rudi Schreiner, Kristin Karst, and Jimmy Murphy, former Brendan Worldwide Vacations owner), AMAWaterways is one of the fastest-growing cruise lines and newest fleets in European river cruising. Formerly known as Amadeus Waterways, the name was changed to AMAWaterways in 2008. Beginning with *MS Amadagio* in 2006, the line has steadily expanded its AMA fleet at the rate of two new boats a year and sails primarily on the Danube, Rhine, Main, and Mosel rivers.

All eight AMA ships were built in Holland, have the same dimensions, and represent an investment of more than $200 million. The line's cruising season lasts ten months, from mid-March until New Year's week, offering 7-, 14- and 21-night programs, often combined with pre- and post-tours.

Each of the AMA ships has four decks, including a Sun Deck, and spacious cabins (170 square feet) and junior suites (255 square feet), 82% with French balconies. Accommodations have premium bedding with plush, down duvets; terry bathrobes and slippers; as well as bottled water replenished daily. Marble-appointed bathrooms have a multi-jet shower system and spa-quality toiletries. Flat-panel televisions provide an infotainment system with Internet access and an array of satellite channels and movies. The vessels also have a fitness center, beauty salon, whirlpool, walking track on the Sun Deck, and bicycles for passengers to explore towns and villages on their own.

AMAWaterways vessels offer a host of complimentary amenities such as Wi-Fi in the public lounges, local wines at dinner, and a specialty coffee/tea station. A professional cruise director accompanies each cruise, and experienced tour guides lead complimentary shore excursions at every destination.

The line also sails in the Porto River Valley in Portugal (a UNESCO World Heritage Site), the Rhône River in France, and the waterways of Russia. In 2009, AMAWaterways took an unusual turn into Southeast Asia, with a new Vietnam, Cambodia, and Mekong River program. In 2010, it is introducing new itineraries on the Rhine and new land programs in Lucerne, Zurich,

Basel, Dresden, and Berlin. The romantic Danube program, which was introduced in 2009 and features three nights in Prague, followed by a cruise from Vilshofen to Budapest, is being repeated in 2010.

Amadolce, Amalyra, Amadante, Amacello, Amalegro, and *Amadagio* sail mostly on the Danube, Main, Rhine, and Mosel rivers. *The Tolstoy,* which the line charters, is one of the most luxurious and comfortable cruise ships ever built for Russian rivers. The *Swiss Pearl,* built in 1993 and renovated in 2006, is also a charter and sails in Spain and Provence. *Amadouro,* built in 2005, cruises on the Douro River in Portugal and in Spain.

The new *La Marguerite,* specifically built for the Mekong River, offers spacious outside accommodations, including 38 cabins (226 square feet), six Sadec Suites (284 square feet), and two Indochina Suites (443 square feet); 82% of accommodations have balconies. All accommodations have large windows or balconies, except for eight cabins on the lower Mekong Deck, which have portholes. The Indochina Suites also have whirlpool tubs. All cabins are air-conditioned and furnished with a wardrobe, writing desk, sofa, television, minibar, safe, bathroom with shower, hair dryer, bathrobe, and slippers. Bottled water in cabins is replenished daily. The ship has a gym, spa, main lounge, second panorama lounge with library, restaurant with bar, a business center, and a Sun Deck with a bar and a large hot tub and pool. Meals in the main restaurant include unlimited local beer and house-brand spirits. Smoking is allowed only on the Sun Deck. The seven-night cruises are included in a 15-day Vietnam and Cambodia package.

Avalon Waterways
5301 South Federal Circle, Littleton, CO 80123;
☎ 877-380-1540 or 877-797-8791; www.avalonwaterways.com

Avalon Affinity/Avalon Scenery **(65/138, 4 JUNIOR SUITES; CREW OF 39; 361 FEET)**

Avalon Artistry/Avalon Poetry **(87/84, 2/4 SUITES; 178/176 PASSENGERS; CREW OF 43; 426 FEET)**

Avalon Creativity **(68/140, 2 JUNIOR SUITES; CREW OF 39; 361 FEET)**

Avalon Imagery/Avalon Tranquility **(81/170, 4 JUNIOR SUITES; CREW OF 43; 443 FEET)**

Avalon Felicity/Avalon Luminary **(65/138, 4 JUNIOR SUITES; CREW OF 39; 361 FEET)**

Avalon Tapestry **(80/164, 2 JUNIOR SUITES; CREW OF 43; 443 FEET**

Avalon Waterways, a division of Globus Tours, offers a new generation of eight river cruise boats built specifically for the North American market, with nonsmoking interiors and English-speaking crews. The boats feature some of the largest cabins and suites available on river cruises, with comfortable beds and large floor-to-ceiling windows and sliding-glass doors to view the passing scenery. European cuisine tailored to North American tastes is served at an open, single seating in a spacious restaurant; wine is included with all onboard dinners; coffee and tea are available throughout the day. The company says its enrichment program is "geared for the way North Americans like to travel, with lively itineraries, time for individual discovery, and onboard entertainment."

The well-appointed boats have a two-story lobby, lit by a central glass skylight, and both the dining room and lounge have floor-to-ceiling windows with panoramic views. The boats are equipped with state-of-the-art technology and have a **Sky Bar, Club Lounge** exercise room with fitness equipment, walking track, whirlpool, hair salon, massage service, and gift shop. The Sky Deck is fitted with newly developed shade systems, which are lowered when passing under a bridge and then promptly raised again.

All cabins are outside ones. Some have picture windows, while 70% have floor-to-ceiling sliding glass doors to enjoy the passing scenery. The *Poetry* has four junior suites (two on the *Artistry*), each 258 square feet, and standard cabins of 172 square feet. On the *Artistry*, for example, all cabins have a granite bathroom, ample closet, radio, telephone, satellite flat-screen television, minibar, safe, and hair dryer. Beds may be configured as twins or one queen; connecting cabins are available. Other amenities include large cabin closets, Egyptian cotton linens, and laundry and ironing services. The cruise-tour itineraries range from 9 days in Holland and Belgium, to 12 days on the Lower Danube/Black Sea cruising from Budapest to Bucharest (with two nights in Budapest), to a cruise from Nuremberg to Budapest with a three-night stay in Prague. *Avalon Affinity* began her maiden season on the "Windmills, Vineyards, and Paris" itinerary to France, Luxembourg, Germany, Belgium, and Holland, sailing on eight itineraries. *Avalon Scenery* inaugurated the "Flavors of Burgundy and Provence" journey with frequent departures between April and November, beginning with a stay in Paris. In 2010, the new *Avalon Creativity* will cruise on new "Grand France" and "Paris to Normandy's Landing Beaches" itineraries.

Samplers of four- and five-day cruises on the Danube River, designed for first-timers and time-starved vacationers, are being offered in 2010. These cruises stop in small towns as well as capital cities, including Budapest, Vienna, and Bratislava, Slovakia. Other cruise-and-land combinations from 9 to 20 days are available with time spent in places such as Paris or Berlin. Discounts for AARP members are available.

The company also offers Nile and Yangtze river and Galápagos cruises.

The Barge Lady
101 West Grand Avenue, Suite 200, Chicago, IL 60654;
☎ **312-245-0900 or 800-880-0071; fax 312-245-0952;**
www.bargelady.com

A variety of barges on the canals of Belgium, France, Germany, Great Britain, Holland, Ireland, and Scotland; multigenerational, small-group, and wine-tasting cruises featured. More recently, the company also offers European river cruises, as well as cruises in Alaska, the Pacific Northwest, and Mexico (American Safari Cruises).

Crown Blue Line
980 Awald Road, Suite 302, Annapolis, MD 21403;
☎ **888-355-9491; fax 410-280-2406; www.crownblueline.com**

Specializes in self-drive boats with a large fleet of small boats operating in England, Ireland, Scotland; extensively in France; and others in Belgium, Italy, Germany, and Holland. The fleet consists of three dozen types of boats and more than 600 vessels. The company Le Boat, Inc., is part of Crown Blue Line.

Les Etoiles
c/o Karen Bull Associates, 3355 Lenox Road, Suite 750, Atlanta, GA 30326;
☎ **800-280-1492 or 770-394-6565; fax 404-237-1841**

La Nouvelle Etoiles **(4 SUITES/8; FRENCH; 128 FEET)**

Seven- and 13-day trips to Belgium, France, Germany, and Holland, April through September.

European Waterways/Go Barging
c/o 35 Wharf Road, Wraysbury, Staines, Middlesex, TW19 5JQ, England;
☎ **44-0-1784-482-439 or 800-394-8630; fax 44-0-1784 483-072;**
www.gobarging.com

Alouette/Anjodi/Athos/Enchante/Hirondelle/L'Arte de Vivre, La Belle Epoque/La Dolce Vita/La Nouvelle Etoile/La Reine Pedauque/L'Impressionniste/Magna Carta/ Nymphea/Renaissance/Savoir Faire/Scottish Highlander/Shannon Princess
(3 TO 6/6 TO 12; FRENCH/FRENCH AND ENGLISH; 80 TO 128 FEET)

The company offers six-night cruises on the rivers and canals of Belgium, the Czech Republic, England, France, Germany, Holland, Ireland, Italy, and Scotland. European Waterways also owns a medley of barges and riverboats for 6 to 12 passengers in Scotland and France. All cruises can be geared to special interests, such as golf, sportfishing, horseback riding, fine dining, cycling, wildlife, poetry, and more.

The company has an extensive Web site with pictures and descriptions of its boats, itineraries, and virtual tours, as well as links to its theme cruises and newsletter.

French Country Waterways
P.O. Box 2195, Duxbury, MA 02331; ☎ **781-934-2454 or 800-222-1236;**
fax 781-934-9048; www.fcwl.com

As its name implies, French Country Waterways' four boats, or hotel barges, as they are known, concentrate on the small rivers and canals that crisscross France, through a navigational system that began in the early 17th century. Unlike many barge and riverboat operators, French Country Waterways owns and operates all its fleet. Lunches and dinners are accompanied by Grand Cru and Premier Cru wines, and most cruises include a dinner ashore in a Michelin-starred restaurant. The line's handsome brochure details each of the barges and its itineraries with descriptions and photographs that convey an accurate and inviting look at its cruises.

A new "Casual Cruising" program for 2010 offers as much as 50% fare savings aboard the *Esprit,* with only some adjustments to its usual all-inclusive offerings. Guests enjoy three dinners on their own ashore, and there is no Michelin-starred restaurant dinner.

Adrienne **(6 SUITES/12; FRENCH/ENGLISH; 128 FEET)**
Champagne region.

Esprit **(9/18; FRENCH/ENGLISH/7; 128 FEET)**
Cote d'Or wine region (Burgundy Canal, Saône River, Canal du Centre between St. Leger-sur-Dheune and Pontailler-sur-Saône).

Horizon II **(4/8; FRENCH/ENGLISH/6; 128 FEET)**
Historic Burgundy itineraries (Canal de Bourgogne between Tanley and Veneray-les-Laumes).

Nenuphar **(6/12; FRENCH/ENGLISH/6; 128 FEET)**
Cote d'Or wine region (Burgundy Canal, Saône River, Canal du Centre). The boat was relaunched in 2007 after being renovated.

Gota Canal
AB Göta kanalbolag, Box 3, SE-591 21, Motala, Sweden;
☎ **+46 141-20 20 50; fax +46 141-21 55 50; www.gotakanal.se;**
e-mail info@gotakanal.se; www.vastsverige.com

Three vintage ships—M/S *Juno,* M/S *Wilhelm Tham,* and M/S *Diana*—were built in 1874, 1912, and 1931, respectively, and are lovingly maintained to preserve their classic interiors. They ply the historic Gota Canal between Stockholm and Göteborg, Sweden's largest port, from May to September. The 118-mile canal, an engineering landmark, hand-excavated from 1809 to 1832, provides a journey back in time—through lush countryside to medieval castles, ancient towns, and a Viking city. The unusual route links the Baltic and North seas via three canals, eight lakes, and a river.

Designed to fit the narrowest canal locks, the recently renovated vessels sail across Sweden at a leisurely five to ten knots on tree-lined canals bordered by fields and forests, the 11-lock Berg staircase, lakes Vanern and Vattern, and by many islands. Sightseeing, which varies according to cruise length and direction, may include Lacko and Stegeborg castles, the Birka Viking city on Bjorko Island, medieval towns of Vadstena and Soderkoping, seaside resort of Trosa, and the Royal Hunting, Trollhatten Canal, and Motala Motor museums.

The ships retain their stylish Art Nouveau decor, reminiscent of the heyday of upper-class sailings, with mahogany paneling, brass fittings, and paisley fabrics. Each has a lounge with a bar and small library, a dining room featuring French cuisine with a Swedish twist, and a large wine selection. There are 25 to 29 cozy cabins with bunk beds, washbasin and shared toilets, and showers with privacy locks.

Seven- and nine-day air-inclusive cruise tours are scheduled from mid-May to mid-September; a 15% discount applies to cabin rates at certain times during the season. Packages including round-trip flights from New York are available. Rates are lowest in May and September.

Unless you are fluent in Swedish, we suggest you deal with a travel company in the U.S. that handles Gota Canal cruises. Among them are Borton Overseas, 5412 Lyndale Avenue South, Minneapolis, MN 55419, ☎ 800-843-0602; Euro River Cruises, 365 Route 304, Suite 206, Nanuet, NY 10954, ☎ 800-543-4504, **www.eurorivercruisess.com;** and Scantours Inc. USA, ☎ 310-636-4656, or U.S. and Canada 800-223-7226, fax 310-390-0493, **www.scantours.com,** e-mail info@scantours.com. (*Note:* Vasts Verige in the Web site's address **www.vastsverige.com** means "West Sweden" and is the English language version of the Gota Canal Web site.)

Le Boat, Inc. (*See* Crown Blue Line earlier in Part Three)

Sea Cloud Cruises
32–40 North Dean Street, Englewood, NJ 07631; ☎ 201-227-9404 or 888-732-2568; fax 201-227-9424; www.seacloud.com

River Cloud II (**44/88; EUROPEAN/35; 338 FEET**)

Launched in late spring 2001, the splendidly appointed *River Cloud II* is one of the finest boats on European waterways. Her public rooms include a lounge and library, restaurant, boutique, and hair salon. The air-conditioned ship has 13 junior suites with windows, 20 double-bed cabins with portholes, and 10 twin-bed cabins. All have a direct-dial telephone, television with DVD player, radio and music channels, minibar, emergency button, and bath with shower, hair dryer, bathrobes, and toiletries. A fruit basket, half bottle of Champagne, bottled water, and soft drinks are replenished daily. She offers the impeccable service and fine cuisine for which her famous sister ship, *Sea Cloud*, is known.

River Cloud II's elegant dining room serves meals in a single, open seating in a relaxed, friendly atmosphere. Breakfast and lunch are buffet style; dinner is served at tables. Menus feature Continental specialties and complimentary fine wines, beer, and soft drinks. The centerpiece of the handsome lounge—encircled by windows at the bow—is a grand piano. It's much in use during afternoon tea and music cruises, when renowned pianists and opera stars are aboard. All cabins have a safe and a marble bathroom with shower and hair dryer.

River Cloud II operates on the Upper Danube and Lower Danube to the Danube Delta and the Black Sea, Main, Moselle, and Rhine rivers from April through October. The cruises are also sold through Dailey-Thorp Travel of New York, ☎ 212-307-1555; Abercrombie & Kent, ☎ 800-323-7308; EuroRiver Cruises ☎ 800-543-4504; and other U.S. companies. Her sister boat, *River Cloud,* is on charter to a Dutch company for a year or longer.

Uniworld River Cruises, Inc.
17323 Ventura Boulevard, Los Angeles, CA 91316; ☎ 818-382-7820 or 800-733-7820; www.uniworld.com; e-mail info@uniworld.com

Douro Queen **(63/126; EUROPEAN; 254 FEET)**

River Ambassador/River Baroness **(64/128; 361 FEET)**

River Beatrice **(80/160; 410 FEET)**

River Countess/River Duchess/River Empress **(67/134; 360 FEET)**

River Princess/River Queen/River Royale **(66/132; 360 FEET)**

River Tosca **(41 SUITES/82; 236 FEET)**

Los Angeles–based Uniworld Boutique River Cruise Collection is a premier river cruise and tour company, offering more than 35 itineraries on 12 rivers in 17 countries throughout Europe, Egypt, and China in winter; and Europe, Russia, Egypt, and China in spring through fall. Uniworld's boutique hotel-style cruise ships are designed for the experienced traveler. Uniworld's passengers are mainly educated and experienced travelers along with a growing number of younger couples and individuals interested in culture, history, food and wine, and the arts.

Uniworld owns and operates ten ships in Europe, two in Egypt, and partners with Victoria Cruises to operate four river ships on the Yangtze River in China. All its riverboats have English-speaking crews and river-view cabins, as well as most of the amenities found on ocean cruise ships, but they are not wheelchair accessible and do not have facilities for children. Meals are in the main dining room or alfresco on the Sun Deck. Breakfast is a full buffet; lunch includes salads, seasonal vegetables, cheeses, homemade soups and bread, and hearty sandwiches. Dinner menus change nightly and focus on the region being visited and the season. Desserts are made on board. Onboard activities and entertainment are often linked to the itinerary and might include local musicians or artists. Shore excursions are included in the fare. Uniworld's company-owned ships in Europe offer wireless Internet access.

In 2009, Uniworld added two new ships: *River Beatrice*, launched on the Danube River, with more junior suites than most comparable ships and a dazzling Owner's Suite. Eighty percent of her cabins have French balconies. All *River Beatrice* suites have butler service, including packing/unpacking assistance, in-room breakfast, daily fruit and cookie plate, and more.

River Tosca, Uniworld's newest ship on the Nile River, is a luxurious all-suite ship with rich wood paneling, original Egyptian artwork, handcrafted brass lanterns, and linen curtains. Most of *River Tosca*'s suites measure more than 300 square feet; Presidential Suites (650 square feet) have large, private terraces. The boat has a swimming pool lined with cabanas, a Jacuzzi on the Sun Deck, a gym, spa, hairdresser, library, boutique, and rooftop bar. Marble floors are heated (in winter). Leather night tables with brass-stud accents sit next to beds fitted with Egyptian cotton sheets and duvets. Tiled bathrooms are stocked with toiletries, plush robes, and slippers. The vessel supplies fine wine during dinner, bottled water in cabins, portable audio headsets for onshore sightseeing, and bicycles. All suites have flat-screen televisions with DVD players, iPod docking stations, morning coffee, shoeshine, free laundry services, and a bottle of wine upon arrival.

Uniworld cruises the Danube, Main, Rhine, and Moselle rivers of Central Europe; Seine, Saône, and Rhône of France; Douro of Portugal; Neva, Svir, Volga, and Don of Russia; Dnieper of Ukraine; Yangtze of China; and Nile of Egypt. Among the new itineraries Uniworld introduced in 2009 are 11 days from Paris to Nuremberg; 18 days from Paris to Vienna; 32 days from Paris to Bucharest; 11 days from Cairo to Cairo; and 18 days from Shanghai to Beijing. For 2010, a 9-day "Springtime along the Rhine from Amsterdam to Frankfurt" is a new itinerary; and in China, Uniworld is offering six all-inclusive excursions, ranging from 9 to 19 days.

Viking River Cruises

5700 Canoga Avenue, Suite 200, Woodland Hills, CA 91367;
☎ **818-227-1234 or 877-66VIKING (877-668-4546); fax 818-227-1237;**
www.vikingrivercruises.com

Viking River Cruises, a global company with U.S. headquarters in Los Angeles, California, offers Europe, Russia, Ukraine, Egypt, and China cruises. Since its inception in 1997, the company has grown to a fleet of 18 vessels. In Europe, the line has a variety of itineraries, ranging from 7 to 15 days on the Danube, Dnieper, Elbe, Main, Rhine, Rhône, Saône, Seine, Moselle, and Volga rivers. Those sold in North America cover inclusive programs created specifically for English-speaking passengers. (See the China cruises section later in this chapter for the line's Yangtze River program.) The following is a sampling of the fleet in Europe that caters to North Americans.

Viking Legend **(97/189; 443 FEET)**
In July 2009, *Viking Legend* sailed on her inaugural voyage as the newest and most eco-friendly vessel in the Viking fleet. One of the first boats to be certified under new European Union guidelines regulating greenhouse emissions, the cruise line sees *Viking Legend* as a harbinger for a new era of European river cruising. Her new diesel-electric hybrid engines use an estimated 20% less fuel. The two engine rooms, one fore and one aft, are noise-insulated. Another green feature is her membrane water treatment plant that helps reduce her impact on the environment. *Viking Legend*'s interiors were designed by the well-known Norwegian firm of Yran & Storbraaten, noted for their warm neutral colors, fine wood, and Scandinavian-inspired design. The boat has two suites, 90 deluxe doubles and five singles, most with a French balcony. Cabins are furnished with flat-screen televisions, refrigerators, hair dryers, and safes. The restaurant features seasonal menus and local specialties. The boat has a library, Sun Deck with panoramic views, boutique, and an observation lounge. She sails mostly from Amsterdam to Budapest along the Rhine, Main, and Danube rivers.

Viking Neptune/Viking Spirit **(75/150; FRENCH/INTERNATIONAL/40; 365 FEET)**
Launched in 2001, the sister ships cruise the best of France. The seven-night cruise traces the Rhône and Saône rivers through Burgundy, Provence, and the scenery of the Ardèche region as well as Paris. A 14-night cruise, France's Finest, combines Paris and the heart of Normandy with Burgundy and Provence.

Viking Kirov/Viking Pakhomov/Viking Surkov **(110/212; 430 FEET)**
Built between 1979 and 1990 and refurbished in 2003 and 2009, the boats sail the Volga and Svir rivers in Russia. From May to October, these boats sail on 10- and 11-day Waterways of the Czars cruises between St. Petersburg and Moscow.

Viking Europe/Viking Pride/Viking Spirit **(75/150; 40; 365 FEET)**
These sister ships sail a variety of European destinations, including France, Austria, Eastern Europe, Germany, and Hungary. An example is the seven-night Danube between Budapest and Nuremberg (or reverse) itinerary.

Viking Schumann **(60/124; 311 FEET)**
Built in 1991 and refurbished in 2001, this boat has all outside cabins. She sails on ten-night cruises with seven nights on the Elbe from Magdeburg to Melnik, plus overnights in both Berlin and Prague.

Viking Sky **(75/150; 360 FEET)**
Built in 1999, the deluxe ship has all outside cabins. She embarks on the 14-night cruise from Passau to Budapest (or reverse) or the 14-night from Amsterdam to Budapest (or reverse).

Viking Helvetia/Viking Sun **(99/198; 44; 433 FEET)**
Built in 2005–2006, the ships have an observation lounge, restaurant, sauna, Sun Deck, bar, massage room, beauty salon, Internet bar, and two elevators. All cabins are air-conditioned and have private bathrooms with showers and balconies. Both ships sail on the Rhine, including the seven-night Rhine cruise from Amsterdam to Basel (or reverse).

YANGTZE RIVER CRUISES IN CHINA

THE CHINESE APTLY CALL THE YANGTZE "Changjiang" (long river). Rising from the Tibetan plateau, it plunges through mountain passes into Sichuan to form a border between Hubei and Hunan before reaching the fertile plains of Jiangsu and Shanghai, a journey of almost 4,000 miles.

The Yangtze (a local name) is more than a scenic wonder. It was the site of epic battles in the second century BC, and archaeological excavations suggest that the area was a cradle of Chinese civilization.

The river remains the great highway of central China, carrying passenger ferries, patrol boats, and barges piled with coal, limestone, timber, and cement. Small freighters deliver supplies to towns built into the cliffs and collect the fruit grown in terraced orchards. The river is always busy, especially as it narrows into gorges. There, traffic control is essential, and cruise ship captains are in telephone contact with shore pilot stations as they steer the shallow-draft vessels between gravel shoals.

The Three Gorges: Qutang, Wu, Xiling

Qutang Gorge, also known as Wind Box Gorge, is five miles long but never wider than 490 feet. Limestone cliffs erupt on each side in sheer walls up to 4,000 feet tall. The cliff face is pitted with caves, and there remains visible an old towpath—the only way through the gorge before the biggest boulders were cleared from the river.

Less than an hour after leaving the Qutang Gorge, cruise-ship passengers enter 25-mile-long **Wu Gorge**. Its cliffs are so high and steep that the sun rarely touches the water. Twelve peaks dominate the skyline. According to myth, they're a goddess and her handmaidens who chose to be turned to stone to stand sentinel over the river.

Midway through the gorge is the border between Sichuan and Hubei provinces. The exit from the gorge is only 164 feet across, the narrowest part of the river.

It takes another day for cruise ships to reach **Xiling Gorge,** the longest canyon, which winds 47 miles through small gorges amid fierce rapids. On each side are examples of the mountains beyond mountains of classic Chinese scenery.

Three Gorges Dam

The Three Gorges Dam, located in Sandouping, at the eastern mouth of the gorges, is nearly completed. It's massive. The dam wall is almost two miles long and 607 feet tall. Behind it, a lake is filling that will eventually stretch 373 miles and cover 418 square miles, raising the water level of Xiling Gorge and a portion of the Wu Gorge. A million or more people were evacuated prior to the dam's completion in 2009.

Supporters say the multibillion-dollar dam will control flooding and generate 84.7 billion kilowatt hours of electricity a year for Shanghai and the Lower Yangtze Basin. Opponents say it will destroy the environment and build a reservoir of toxic silt in an earthquake-prone region. Either way, it adds poignancy to a Yangtze cruise.

With the construction completed, the reservoir continues to fill. The lake behind the dam will raise water levels in the Xiling and Wu gorges. Cruise boats journey through a new, five-stage lock to go around the dam wall.

The first Westerners to sail up the Yangtze River were British colonial administrators who established the inland port of Hankow (now part of Wuhan) in the 1840s. The most adventurous continued into the sparsely populated wilderness upstream and found the Three Gorges.

Transport was by sailing ships, which were hauled by teams of trackers through raging rapids and over great boulders, until English trader Archibald Little pioneered steamship service from Wuhan, finally reaching Chongqing (formerly Chungking) in 1898. The voyage remained extremely hazardous until the 1950s, when the Chinese blasted away the largest boulders.

Regular cruises through the gorges were introduced in the early 1980s and became an established part of many all-China itineraries. The gorges are on the 120-mile (192-kilometer) stretch of river between Baidicheng and Yichang. Some itineraries between Chongqing and Yichang reduce the trip by a day and night. However, it has often proven difficult to arrange air or land passage to or from Yichang. Many cruises cover the full 850-mile (1,370-kilometer) section between Chongqing and Wuhan.

Shore Excursions (Upstream or Downstream)

SHENNONG STREAM/DANING RIVER GORGES All cruises offer a side trip up one of the Yangtze's tributaries for a closer look at its natural grandeur. Excursions feature fast-flowing, crystal-clear streams with shifting, pebbled shoals and sheer cliffs pocked with caves, clad in waterfalls, and encrusted with ferns. With the rising waters of the river, some of the lesser gorges are also now fully accessible by larger boats, and tributaries previously difficult to navigate are now readily available to visitors.

Shennong Stream is a better option than Daning River, partly because the journey is taken in wooden longboats, which are steered, pushed, and sometimes hauled by husky young men of the Tujia minority. Shennong Stream is also a good option because it is one of the shallower tributaries. The half-day excursion includes a visit to a Tujia-style house, where local dance is performed and worthwhile souvenirs are sold.

ZIGUI This historic town, poised on the cliffs at the entrance to Xiling Gorge, exudes an air of ancient certainty, but it will be swallowed by the dam's reservoir. Only one building will be preserved: The temple dedicated to Chu Yuan, the scholar and statesman who drowned himself in 278 BC in protest of his government's policy, is being moved downstream with the population. Travelers will lose a town whose main street was packed with sidewalk kitchens, vegetable stalls, alfresco hairdressers, one-room tailors, and an alley of pool tables.

SHASHI/JINGZHOU Upstream from Wuhan, this bustling port contains the remains of a royal capitol from the seventh century BC. Some original walls are maintained, and the museum contains a 2,000-year-old mummy.

YUEYANG TOWER This gold-tiled pavilion on the Hunan banks of the river, upstream from Wuhan, was built in 716 AD as a military lookout. It was later expanded to provide a belvedere over scenic Dongting Lake.

FENGDU Near the western entrance of Qutang Gorge, this ancient cliff town is reputed to be where people's spirits go after death. To placate unhappy and potentially dangerous phantoms, a temple sells "passports to hell" and other souvenirs.

SHIBAOZHAI This cliffside temple complex, between Chongqing and the first gorge, has a 12-story red pagoda and hilltop temple. Built right into the cliff and called the Pearl of the Yangtze, the temple is an architectural treasure from the Ming Dynasty, dating to the mid-16th century. Some excursions visit it.

Cruise Lines and Ships

Dozens of ships offer cruises through the Yangtze gorges. Many are Chinese-owned and marketed internationally by Changjiang Cruise Overseas Travel Company **(www.ccotc.com)**, with offices throughout Asia.

A new generation of vessels caters to travelers whose interest has been fueled by reports that the gorges' days were numbered. These ships operate on regular itineraries designed to allow passage through the gorges during daylight. The timing concerns produce shore excursions that are conveniently located, interesting, varied, and appropriate to the area's history. The season lasts from late February to early December. Summer is extremely hot; in winter, the water level is low and temperatures are colder, often below freezing. There are almost weekly departures of the four-day, three-night downstream cruise from Chongqing and the five-day, four-night upstream trip from Wuhan.

However, those reports that the gorges' days are numbered are a bit exaggerated. Overall, the river will rise some 575 feet in total, but the gorges themselves are so deep that they will be less affected than some have claimed. While the landscape will change, the reality is that the water will not submerge the gorges. In fact, after completion of Stage Two of the dam, the river will rise only about another 131 feet. In addition, the deeper water opens even newer vistas to cruisers because the lesser gorges, which previously held little water, are now navigable, and visitors have the opportunity to explore previously inaccessible areas of the river.

Abercrombie & Kent USA

1411 Opus Place, Executive Towers West II, Suite 300, Downers Grove, IL 60515; ☎ 800-652-7963 or 630-725-3400; fax 630-725-3401; www.abercrombiekent.com

---

Yangzi Explorer **(38 CABINS/24SUITES/124; CHINESE; 300 FEET/6,733 TONS)**

The modern riverboat, *Yangzi Explorer*, launched in 2008, has brought a new level of comfort and luxury to Yangtze River cruises, with the largest accommodations of any other boat and a host of facilities. As one of the smallest luxury cruise boats on Chinese waters, the *Yangzi Explorer* provides a certain exclusivity and personalized service to her passengers in a relaxed and friendly atmosphere.

Designed for a maximum of 124 passengers, the ship has 38 deluxe cabins (each 333 square feet) and 24 spacious suites (each 420 square feet), all with private balconies. Among the most opulent suites, the Mandarin and the Jade suites each have 871 square feet; the Imperial and Celestial suites each measure 1,183 square feet. Several accommodations are interconnecting and suitable for families. All are nicely appointed with distinct Chinese touches and equipped with a safe, minibar, hair dryer, large television with satellite channels and video on demand, and 24-hour room service. Electricity is 220 volts; transformers are available on request.

The Dynasty Palace dining room can accommodate all passengers in a single seating and offers à la carte menus of Chinese and Western cuisine overseen by an onboard executive chef and a team of internationally trained chefs. Complimentary house wines are served at lunch and dinner, and there's a well-stocked wine cellar. Other facilities include a luxurious spa with six treatment rooms, a beauty salon, a gym with exercise equipment, a top deck observation lounge and bar, a two-deck theater and bar, library, coffee shop, and Internet access. A doctor travels on board.

Two private rooms on the ship can handle small groups for special dinners with family and friends, or they can serve as a venue with audiovisual equipment for meetings or lectures. The theater serves as an auditorium for a guest speaker, film presentation, or meetings.

The five-deck *Yangzi Explorer* claims to be the most environmentally friendly ship on the river, with up-to-date sewage disposal systems, recycling facilities, and other measures designed to ensure that the ship operates in the most environmentally sustainable manner. Her draft is 9.2 feet.

Shipboard programs such as tai chi, Chinese cooking, calligraphy and silk embroidery classes, and innovative shore excursions are intended to educate passengers about China's lifeline, the Yangtze River, and its historic role in China's history and traditions. Four-night upstream cruises depart Yichang on Sundays and arrive in Chongqing on Thursdays. Three-night downstream sailings depart Chongqing on Thursdays and arrive in Yichang on Sundays. Abercrombe & Kent has almost weekly departures between April and November. Cruises on the Yangzi Explorer are included in China programs by other U.S. tour companies as well. (See **www.sanctuary-cruising.com/china/yangziexplorer.html**)

Victoria Cruises
57-08 39th Avenue, Woodside, NY 11377; ☎ 212-818-1680 or 800-348-8084; fax 212-818-9889; www.victoriacruises.com

Victoria Jenna **(208 CABINS/40 SUITES/416; CHINESE/180; 439 FEET/10,000 TONS)**

Victoria Anna **(137 CABINS/48 SUITES/274; CHINESE/138; 348 FEET/6,200 TONS)**

Victoria Empress **(99 CABINS/8 SUITES/198; CHINESE/117; 281 FEET/3,868 TONS)**

Victoria Katarina **(126 CABINS/42 SUITES/2252; CHINESE/128; 324 FEET/ 5,780 TONS)**

Victoria Prince **(104 CABINS/11 SUITES/208; CHINESE/121; 293 FEET/4,587 TONS)**

Victoria Queen/Victoria Star **(103 CABINS/10 SUITES/206; CHINESE/121; 293 FEET/4,587 TONS)**

Victoria Rose **(63 CABINS/2 SUITES/130; CHINESE/110; 240 FEET/2,428 TONS)**

Victoria Cruises, a New York–based Sino-American joint venture, with American management, operates vessels with the wedding-cake look and character of Mississippi riverboats. Each boat has four decks (*Victoria Anna* and *Victoria Jenna,* five decks) and an observation area and offers single-seating dining with Chinese and Western cuisine.

Ships come in two categories: premier and classic. In September 2009, the luxurious *Victoria Jenna,* which claims to be the world's largest river cruise ship, was launched. She is also the first Yangtze River vessel with four elevators, two full-service kitchens, wireless CDMA Internet, full bathtubs, and dual-flush toilets in each stateroom. The eighth ship in the fleet, *Jenna* has 168 superior cabins, 35 executive suites, three deluxe suites, and two Shangri-La Suites. All cabins have private balconies, marble-top bathroom counters, refrigerators and safes, flat-screen televisions with HBO and CNN, and advanced-cooling air-conditioning systems. Suites have large televisions with DVD players. The new ship has an executive suite deck with an exclusive lounge area; a private, à la carte restaurant; and concierge service.

The boat's Dynasty Dining Room serves all passengers at one seating. The kitchens can provide kosher, gluten-free, and vegetarian cuisine. The smaller, upper-deck VIP Club offers à la carte dining with omelet and egg stations for breakfast, noodle and sandwich stations for lunch, and carving and Peking duck stations for lunch or dinner. All food on the ship is freshly made and baked, including handmade pastries, breads, and desserts.

The five-passenger-deck *Victoria Jenna,* with a draft of 8.8 feet, has two conference rooms with audiovisual-ready equipment: The Yangtze Club and a lecture room for talks on the river's history and lessons in tai chi, Mandarin language, and Mahjong. The ship boasts a library/reading room, cocktail lounge, beauty parlor and mini-spa, gift shop, observation deck, business center, health clinic, fitness center, and atrium lobby.

Additional premier ships include all of the other vessels listed above, except *Victoria Rose,* a classic ship that is smaller than the others; it was rebuilt in 2001 and maintains the same high-quality standards on board. The premier ships are new or newly rebuilt vessels and have a higher level of comfort and decor as well as private balconies for every cabin. Introduced in 2004, *Victoria Katarina* has floor-to-ceiling windows and a mix of modern and traditional architecture.

Victoria Anna and *Victoria Katarina* are being renovated to upgrade and enhance the vessels shipwide and will include the same executive suite decks offered on the new *Victoria Jenna,* with suite accommodations; an exclusive lounge area and private, à la carte restaurant; and concierge service.

All cruises have professional, multilingual Western cruise directors and trained local staff. Meals on all boats are served in a single-seating **Dynasty** dining room. Western and Chinese buffets are offered at breakfast and lunch; dinners are served banquet style. The company hired internationally known chef Walter Staib, who traveled to China to equip the ships and train its culinary teams with skills and recipes to prepare high-quality Western dishes. Passengers can enjoy cultural immersion both ashore and on board; tai chi is offered mornings on the boats, as are lectures in Chinese culture and history and live traditional performing arts. An onboard boutique sells Chinese gifts and souvenirs. The boats have cocktail lounges, game rooms, business centers, health, and other facilities.

Victoria Anna, another premier vessel, made her scheduled debut in 2006. She is the second largest ship in the company's fleet, with 89 standard cabins, 44 executive suites, 2 deluxe suites, and 2 Shangri-La Suites. The cabins have bathrooms with a shower and bathtub, television with HBO and CNN broadcasts, and private balconies. There is a single-seating main restaurant and an à la carte restaurant on the top deck. The boat has a three-story atrium lobby, two lounges, three bars, a fitness room, lecture room, reading room, beauty salon, mini-spa, gift shop, observation deck, Internet access, and two elevators.

Four- to nine-day itineraries are operated round-trip from Chongqing, between Chongqing and Yichang, and between Chongqing and Shanghai. Victoria Cruises provides cruises on the Yangtze exclusively for such tour operator partners as Avalon Waterways, Pacific Delight Tours, Travcoa, Uniworld, and a host of others that are listed on Victoria Cruises' Web site.

Viking River Cruises, Inc.
5700 Canoga Avenue, Suite 200, Woodland Hills, CA 91367;
☎ **877-66-VIKING (877-668-4546) or 818-227-1234; fax 818-227-1237;**
www.vikingrivercruises.com

Viking Century Sun **(153/306; EUROPEAN/CHINESE/168; 415 FEET)**

Europe's largest river-cruising company launched its first boat in China on the Yangtze River in March 2004. With local branch offices in Beijing and Chongqing, Viking River Cruises is headquartered in Los Angeles, California, and oversees all its cruise-tour components, from ship operations and shore excursions to land programs, tours, hotel selections, meals, and cultural performances. Each program has English-speaking escorts and guides.

Viking's Swiss hotel-management staff oversees all food and beverage service and a crew of 168. A variety of food, from the traditional family-style Chinese cuisine to Western selections and even an on-deck barbecue, is available. English is the primary language on board as well as during shore excursions and tours.

Included as part of all Yangtze cruises is an excursion on a local ferry along the scenic Lesser Three Gorges, a tributary of the Yangtze formerly difficult to navigate. One itinerary includes a three-night stay in Lhasa, Tibet. Pre- and postcruise land extensions are available for Hong Kong and Guilin. All cruise tours include Yangtze River cruises of varying duration, in addition to land stays in Beijing, Xian (home of the terra-cotta warriors), and Shanghai.

Itineraries range from 9 to 15 nights and include all shore excursions and tours, meals, deluxe hotels, intra-Asia flights, and English-speaking escorts. With its policy of contributing to the regions in which it sails, Viking River Cruises has helped rebuild three elementary schools in the Hubei province. Passengers on all China itineraries have the opportunity to visit one of the schools and meet the local children.

Other Yangtze River Cruises

Many other U.S.-based companies offer Yangtze cruises. All include the cruises as part of longer China itineraries ranging from 12 to 24 days and often use the boats of Victoria Cruises or Viking River Cruises. The following is a small sample:

China Vacation	☎ 888-285-8933	www.china-vacation.com
General Tours	☎ 800-221-2216	www.generaltours.com
Maupintour	☎ 800-255-4266	www.maupintour.com
Orient Flexi-pax Tours	☎ 800-223-7460	www.orientflexipax.com
Pacific Bestours	☎ 800-688-3288	www.bestour.com
Pacific Delight Tours	☎ 800-221-7179	www.pacificdelighttours.com
SITA World Travel	☎ 800-421-5643	www.sitatours.com
Travcoa	☎ 800-992-2003	www.travcoa.com
Uniworld	☎ 800-733-7820	www.uniworld.com
Vacations To Go	☎ 800-338-4962	www.vacationstogo.com
Visits Plus	☎ 800-321-3235	www.visitsplus.com

OTHER ASIAN RIVER CRUISES

Orient Express Hotels, Trains, and Cruises
1114 Avenue of the Americas, 38th Floor, New York, NY 10036;
☎ 800-524-2420; fax 401-351-7220; www.orient-express.com

Road to Mandalay **(66/118; EUROPEAN/BURMESE; 305 FEET)**

Unusual cruises in Myanmar (formerly Burma) are offered by Orient Express Hotels, Trains, and Cruises, the company that operates the famous Orient Express. The boat sails from February to April and July to December on three- to seven-night itineraries on the Irrawaddy (Ayeyarwady) River between Mandalay and Bagan and round-trip from Mandalay. Generally, the cruises are part of a package departing from Bangkok, Thailand, with round-trip flights to Yangon.

Two even more exotic journeys: One seven-night cruise sails round-trip from Bagan, while an 11-night adventure visits a little-known region north of Mandalay to beyond Bhamo, stopping just short of the Chinese border. Unlike the tranquil flood plains surrounding the lower Irrawaddy, the northern landscape changes as the ship enters the Three Narrows region, marked with lush forests and towering cliffs.

The German-built *Road to Mandalay*, a deluxe cruiser, previously sailed the Rhine and Elbe rivers. Before starting these cruises in 1996, the boat was renovated. More recently, after an absence of more than 12 months, the boat was relaunched in August 2009, following a complete remodel and refurbishment. Facilities include a pool, large Sun Deck, observation lounge, and several bars. The dining room accommodates all passengers in a single seating and serves international and Asian cuisine. The five cabin types include some singles. All have a private bath and air-conditioning. Doubles have twin beds; larger cabins have a sitting area.

Pandaw River Cruises
23 Mitchell Street, Edinburgh, Midlothian EH6 7BD, United Kingdom;
from US and Canada toll-free ☎ 800-798-4223;
other countries ☎ +44 131 514 1037; www.pandaw.com

Begun in 1995 by reviving the old Irrawaddy Flotilla Company, Pandaw River Cruises pioneered the exploration of the great rivers and their tributaries in Southeast Asia: The Irrawaddy and Chindwin rivers in Burma, the Mekong and Tonle rivers in Cambodia, and the backwaters of the Mekong Delta in Vietnam. (The Irrawaddy Flotilla Company was established by Scottish merchants in 1865. By the 1920s, the company ran more than 650 vessels on the rivers of Burma and had become the largest privately owned fleet of ships in the world. The entire fleet was scuppered in 1942 as an act of denial when the Japanese invaded.)

Today, Pandaw is one of the largest river cruise companies in the region. Its six riverboats, built new, were designed and finished as replicas of colonial river steamers (similar to Mississippi River steamers). The company takes its name from a steamer called the *Pandaw,* which it restored. The small vessels have very shallow drafts, enabling them to penetrate remote and inaccessible areas and to moor where larger ships could not stop. Inland water navigation in these regions is challenging, and the Pandaw vessels have been specially designed to cope with constantly changing river conditions.

The spacious, beautifully crafted ships have been hand-finished in brass and teak by traditional craftsmen and offer real adventure in comfort with fine dining, choice wines, and a high level of service. Dining is single seating in smart-casual dress. Pandaw Cruises says its steamers are more like being on a 1920s private yacht party than a cruise ship. All cruises feature once or twice daily shore excursions led by expert local guides to explore Buddhist temples, historical sites, markets, and handicraft workshops.

Each steamer, about 182 feet in length, has 28 to 30 cabins, which measure about 162 square feet. They are finished in traditional marine brass and teak with modern conveniences, such as air-conditioning and hot showers. All cabins on the main and upper decks open onto promenade decks with their own seating.

In September 2009, the cruise line inaugurated new itineraries on the Ganges River in India, sailing between Calcutta and Benares, and the Rajang River in Borneo, becoming the first passenger ship to ply the river since 1942.

NILE RIVER CRUISES

NO TRIP TO EGYPT IS COMPLETE without a cruise on the Nile. It is the perfect way to enjoy the Egyptian countryside, as well as to see ancient temples and monuments, because the most famous sites are clustered along the great river. Your first view of the Nile snaking through the desert will illustrate dramatically why the river has been so important throughout Egypt's history. Quite literally, Egyptian civilization would not exist without the Nile. Beyond the green ribbon—the land irrigated by the Nile—the desert stretches endlessly into the horizon. The Nile flows so gently that ships glide as though unmoving. Riverbanks, always near, give passengers an intimate view of rural life in Upper Egypt. Along the riverbanks and in the fields of the green valley, Egyptians live today much as they have for thousands of years. Life and land have a continuity bridging the centuries, as visitors will see in the ancient drawings on temple and tomb walls and the present scenes of the countryside. The sense of tranquility is an overwhelming sensation throughout a Nile cruise and is a total contrast from the roar and clamor of Cairo—the juxtaposition makes the pastoral setting of the Nile Valley all the more remote.

Nile Itineraries

Those beginning their cruise in Upper Egypt may travel from Cairo to Luxor or Aswan by plane or train. They can begin their trip in Aswan and cruise to Luxor or do the reverse. We recommend the former, as the trip then saves the best for last: climaxing with sightseeing at **Karnak** and the **Valley of the Kings** at Luxor.

Aswan was the capital of Nubia in ancient times and an important trading place. Today, it's primarily a winter resort and the administrative center for the **High Dam** and surrounding region. Aswan is dotted with antiquities. The most important is the **Temple of Philae**—one of many temples saved from the High Dam's reservoir—on an island in the river. The botanical gardens, also on an island, and a view of the Aga Khan's mausoleum (not open to the public) are standard stops on the popular excursion made by local felucca, the graceful sailboats of the Nile.

From Aswan, Nile steamers sail downstream (north) to Luxor, stopping at **Kom Ombo, Edfu,** and **Esna**—sites of temples dating from the Ptolemaic, or Greek, period. One temple has a wall carving bearing the only known likeness of Queen Cleopatra. Luxor is the modern town next to the ancient city of Thebes, capital of Egypt for most of its illustrious early history. Most boats dock on the east bank near the Luxor Museum or the **Sofitel Winter Palace Luxor** hotel, which are walking distance from **Luxor Temple** and a short carriage ride from the colossal **Karnak Temple.** A full-day excursion visits the west bank's **Valley of the Kings,** where tombs of Tutankhamen and other pharaohs were found; the **Valley of the Queens;** and the **Tombs of the Nobles,** which contain important art.

Longer cruises of six nights sail north from Luxor to Qena to visit the **Temples of Dendera** and **Abydos,** considered the most important temple in Egypt for its artwork. Visits beyond Abydos to **Tel al Amarna,** capital of revolutionary pharaoh Akhenaton and his wife, Nefertiti; Minya, central Egypt's largest town; and **Beni Hassan,** site of tombs containing drawings showing ancient Egyptians at play, must be made by road or rail from Cairo.

Lake Nasser and Abu Simbel

Construction of the Aswan High Dam created Lake Nasser, which stretches more than 300 miles south from Aswan to the Sudanese border. As waters rose, the famous temple of **Abu Simbel** would have been inundated had it not been moved to higher ground in a colossal 1950s international project. For decades while the waters rose, visitors flew or drove to the site of Abu Simbel. Now, they can go by Nile steamer, departing from the south side of the dam. (See Misr Travel on pages 540–541.)

Nile River Journeys

Nile riverboats range from cozy, friendly, and clubby to very luxurious. Some accommodate as few as 20 passengers; the largest carry 150 or more passengers. Cabins, smaller than those on standard cruise ships, are well-appointed and comfortable; on many new ships, suites are available. Most have twin lower beds (some have pull-down bunks for a third person), a dressing table or nightstand, closet, and private bathroom with shower. Boats holding 80 or more passengers have lounges for reading and relaxing, a bar, Sun Deck, dining room with table service, and evening entertainment. Laundry service is available. Some offer table tennis or a tiny swimming pool.

The boat's small size limits its recreational and entertainment facilities, but these aren't important on a Nile cruise, where antiquities and scenery are the attractions. Roaming room is surprisingly ample. Deck chairs invite lounging and watching history float by.

Newer four- and five-star vessels offer four- and six-night cruises between Luxor and Aswan. Some add **Dendera** and feature cruises of six or seven nights.

Nile cruises are divided into three seasons (prices include all meals, service, taxes, and guided sightseeing).

HIGH SEASON (*October to April*) Five-star boats range from $200 to $450 per person per night; four-star, approximately $150 to $210.

SHOULDER SEASON (*May and September*) 10% to 15% off high-season rates.

LOW SEASON (*June to August*) 15% to 50% off high-season rates. Generally, U.S. tour companies do not visit Upper Egypt during this period.

Although prices are lower in summer and many of the boats are air-conditioned, the heat in sightseeing areas can be intense. Large groups walking generate dust in which it's difficult to breathe; a dust mask or handkerchief over the mouth is helpful. Boat food usually is quite good. Be very careful to eat only fruits and vegetables that can be peeled.

More than 300 boats sail on Nile cruises. Unless you have the opportunity to inspect a vessel yourself, book only with established companies. Five-star boats operated by Mena House Oberoi, Movenpick, Sheraton, and Sonesta are among those used by major U.S. tour companies.

If you arrive in Egypt without reservations and decide to cruise, make inquiries and reservations through the managing company's office in Cairo, where cabin space is controlled. If you wait until you arrive in Luxor or Aswan to find space, you might have to walk among ships and ask the boat manager if a cabin is available.

If you have ample time, however, the latter method lets you see the ship, its cabins, and cleanliness (important, especially on boats of less than five stars) before booking. And if you're good at bargaining, you may negotiate a price better than you would have received in Cairo.

A selected list of companies and Nile river boats marketed in the United States follows.

Note: In parentheses after each boat name is information (where available) about the number of cabins and passengers; officers and crew; and the boat's length (cabins/passengers; officers/crew; boat length).

Abercrombie & Kent USA, LLC
1411 Opus Place, Executive Towers West II, Suite 300, Downers Grove, IL 60515; ☎ 800-652-7963 or 630-725-3400; fax 630-725-3401; www.abercrombiekent.com

---

Sun Boat III **(18 CABINS AND SUITES)**
The four-deck boat has a restaurant, upper Sun Deck with heated swimming pool, lower Sun Deck with lounge and bar. Cabins have a direct-dial phone, safe, minibar, and CD player. *Sun Boat III* was renovated in 2005.

Sun Boat IV (**40 CABINS AND SUITES; 220 FEET**)

The five-deck boat has a restaurant, upper Sun Deck with small pool, gift shop, lounge and bar, library, and lower Sun Deck. Cabins have a direct-dial phone, safe, minibar, and CD player. Renovated in 2006, the Art Deco interiors by Egyptian designer Mohammed Noaman used bold colors and Egyptian motifs. Floor-to-ceiling windows were added in the cabins on the Main Deck, the Bridge Deck, and the Promenade Deck, and teak flooring laid in all the outdoor areas and teak and Egyptian marble on the Sun Deck.

Cruises of four to eight days between Luxor and Aswan (or reverse) are normally included in the tour company's various small group and independent itineraries in Egypt. There are year-round twice-monthly and monthly departures. The *Sun Boat IV* has eight or more departures monthly, sailing every Saturday for three-night cruises and Tuesday on four-night ones.

Esplanade Tours

160 Commonwealth Avenue, Suite U-1A, Boston, MA 02116; ☎ 617-266-7465 or 800-426-5492; fax 617-262-9829; www.esplanadetours.com

Regency/Regina/Royale (**30 TO 70/50 TO 102; EGYPTIAN; 238 FEET**)

This luxury group's boats, owned and operated by Travcotels of Egypt, are fully air-conditioned. Each has lounges, bars, panoramic windows, single-seating dining, two Sun Decks, a swimming pool, gift shop, beauty salon, and laundry facilities. Cabins measure 230 square feet; suites have 380 square feet. All have a television, DVD player, minifridge, and bathroom with a shower, toilet, bidet, and hair dryer. The boats offer three-, four-, and seven-night cruises between Luxor and Aswan or a Lake Nasser cruise between Aswan and Abu Simbel. These destinations are included in Esplanade's 14-day Egypt package and in customized trips that are the company's specialty. Information on Esplanade's other destinations is available on its Web site.

Mena House Oberoi Hotels

Pyramids Road, Giza, Cairo, Egypt 12556; ☎ 20-+ 2 3377 3222; fax 20-2 3376 0518; www.oberoihotels.com; www.oberoizahra.com; e-mail centralreservation@oberoi.com.eg

Oberoi Philae (**50 DOUBLE CABINS, 4 SINGLES, 4 SUITES**)

The boat is operated by Oberoi Hotels, an international chain with hotels in Cairo. The *Oberoi Philae* resembles a paddle wheeler. Each cabin has floor-to-ceiling sliding-glass doors leading to a private balcony. Jacket and tie are preferred for men at dinner. The ship sails on three- to seven-night cruises between Luxor and Aswan. Oberoi also operates the twin boats, *Shehrayar/ Shehrazah* (59 cabins and suites).

Oberoi Zahra (**25 CABINS, 2 SUITES**)

The *Oberoi Zahra*, a Nile cruiser launched in 2007, is one of the most luxurious boats sailing on the Nile River. The boat has 25 luxury cabins, each with more than 98 square feet, and two luxury suites of 164 square feet with large windows overlooking expansive river views. The elegant interiors of the cabins are furnished with natural materials and colors—silk, leather, and wood in beige, champagne, and caramel tones; artwork and floral arrangements add bursts of color. The cabins have either a king-size or twin bed, flanked by large bedside tables and two lounge chairs with a coffee table, a 26-inch HD television and CD/DVD player, high-speed Internet access, a two-line speaker phone, data port, a well-stocked minibar, and tea/coffeemaker. The bathroom, finished in marble and mosaic tile, has a vanity counter and separate glass-enclosed steam and shower stall. The luxury suites have similar furnishings with the additional amenity of a separate living room, a 42-inch HD television mounted on the wall, and an attached terrace with a Jacuzzi. There are interconnecting cabins and nonsmoking cabins.

All cabins have bathrobes and slippers, down or foam pillows, hair dryer, tea/coffeemaker, basket of fresh fruit, daily newspapers, desk and bedside telephone with voice mail and international direct dialing, electronic safe, complimentary wireless Internet connection, 24-hour private butler service, and a welcome drink on arrival. The *Oberoi Zahra* is the only boat on the Nile with a full-service spa with four massage suites (each with a steam and shower stall), offering a wide range of treatments and a beauty salon. Other facilities include a theater, library, cigar lounge, boutique, outdoor swimming pool, and gym. The restaurant serves international and Egyptian cuisine with a new menu daily, as well as à la carte service. The ship provides complimentary shoeshine services and airport/railway station transfers. The boat sails on a seven-day itinerary from Luxor to Aswan (and vice versa) and enjoys private docking facilities in most ports.

Misr Travel
1279 Avenue of the Americas, Suite 604, New York, NY 10020;
☎ **212-332-2600 or 800-223-4978; fax 212-332-2609;**
www.misrtravel.org; e-mail info@misrtravel.org

Misr Travel has been taking tourists to Egypt for more than 70 years, and its network of 29 local offices at all major Egyptian tourist sites and in many of Egypt's leading hotels can be comforting to travelers. Misr offers a myriad of packages in Egypt and neighboring countries, with different cruise options. Packages can be customized with add-ons as well.

Misr offers several cruise tours that include a Nile cruise. For example, a nine-day Classic Egyptian Tour with year-round departures includes four nights at a Hilton, Marriott, or Sheraton Hotel in Cairo with full breakfast buffet and a four-night cruise on a Sonesta-, Movenpick-, or Oberoi-managed Nile cruise boat. Also included are air transportation between Cairo and the ship, transfers, and sightseeing. During the cruise portion of the journey, passengers visit the Valley of the Kings and Queens, the Colossi of Memnon, the Temples of Karnak, Luxor, Edfu, Kom Ombo, and Philae and Aswan.

For those short on time and low on funds, Misr also offers a lower-cost option on their Extraordinary Egypt package and Budget Cruncher packages. Passengers spend several nights in Cairo and three nights on board a Movenpick Nile cruiser, and also get local flights, transfers, a full-day guided tour of Cairo, and round-trip air from New York. An optional excursion to Abu Simbel by air from Aswan is available for an additional cost.

Misr Travel offers programs using the boats—*Eugenie* (50 cabins/100 passengers), *Nubian Sea* (60/120), *Kasr Ibrim* (60/120), and *Prince Abbas* (60/120)—that make three- and four-night cruises on Lake Nasser between Aswan and Abu Simbel. All the boats have outside cabins with private baths. The four-night program sails south from Aswan on Monday and ends at Abu Simbel on Friday; three-night cruises sail north on Friday from Abu Simbel to Aswan. The highlight is a daylight visit to Abu Simbel, and a special feature is a candlelight dinner on deck in front of the floodlit temple of Ramses II and a performance of the son et lumiere. The price is about $220 per person per night, double occupancy in winter; it is lower in off-season. All meals and shore excursions are included.

Sonesta Hotels, Resorts, and Nile Cruises

116 Huntington Avenue, Ninth Floor, Boston, MA 02116;
☎ **800-SONESTA (766-3782); www.sonesta.com;**
Sonesta Nile Cruises, 4 El Tayaran Street, Nasser City, Cairo, Egypt;
☎ **20-2-2628111; fax 20-2-2628765; www.sonesta.com/nilecruises**

Sonesta Amirat Dahabeya **(6 CABINS/2 SUITES; EGYPTIAN)**

Sonesta Moon Goddess **(48 CABINS/2 SUITES; EGYPTIAN)**

Sonesta Nile Goddess **(63 CABINS/2 SUITES/136; EGYPTIAN)**

Sonesta St. George I **(47 CABINS/10 SUITES; EGYPTIAN)**

Sonesta Star Goddess **(33 SUITES/66; EGYPTIAN)**

Sonesta Sun Goddess **(58 CABINS/4 SUITES; EGYPTIAN)**

Three four- to seven-night cruises between Luxor and Aswan are offered on the larger ships. The all-suite, five-star *Sonesta Star Goddess* is one of the company's newest, most luxurious boats. Designed and built in Cairo, the ship has four decks and measures 237 feet in length and 46 feet in width. It has 33 suites, each with a private terrace and elegant, sophisticated modern decor. There are three sizes of suites, each category named for a famous composer: 27 deluxe Beethoven Suites; four slightly smaller Mozart Suites; and two larger, superior Chopin Suites.

The *Sonesta Amirat Dahabeya*, launched in 2009, offers a cruise experience like no other on the Nile. The small boat will take you back to yesteryear, to a gentler, more gracious era on the Nile during a seven-night cruise between Luxor and Aswan. Facilities include an open-air Jacuzzi, spacious Sun Deck, and stylish common lounge. All accommodations have private direct-dial telephones, individual climate control, hair dryers, mini-bars, safe deposit boxes, plasma televisions and movie channels. Each suite has a private terrace. The small cruiser combines comfort and beauty and offers an unusual opportunity for an extended family or small group to discover the Nile on a private cruise.

UNITED STATES AND CANADIAN RIVER CRUISES

UNFORTUNATELY, SINCE THE DEMISE of the two cruise lines that sailed regularly on the Mississippi, there have been none to replace them, although there is a seasonal line. There are also seasonal cruises on some Pacific Northwest rivers and the Hudson River in the Northeast in autumn, when the main attraction is brilliant foliage.

American Canadian Caribbean Line (See Part Two.)

American Cruise Lines (See Part Two, under European and Smaller Cruise Lines.)

Cruise West (See Part Two.)

St. Lawrence Cruise Lines/
Canadian River Cruise Vacations
253 Ontario Street, Kingston, Ontario, Canada K7L 2Z4; ☎ 613-549-8091 or 800-267-7868; fax 613-549-8410; www.stlawrencecruiselines.com

Canadian Empress (32/66; CANADIAN; 108 FEET)

Canadian Empress is a replica of a steamboat but with modern conveniences and amenities. Built in 1981, she was designed to reflect the classic style of North American turn-of-the-century riverboats, with brass handrails and ornate metal ceilings, recapturing the grace of a turn-of-the-century lifestyle. Her size and shallow draft allow her to navigate the islands and through locks, some of which are inaccessible to larger vessels, and provide an up-close experience. A congenial Canadian crew provides good service in a comfortable atmosphere.

The boat sails on two-, three-, five-, and six-night cruises between May and October on the St. Lawrence and Ottawa rivers. Boarding ports include Kingston, Ottawa, and Quebec City. Cruise fares include most sightseeing tours and attractions.

AMAZON RIVER CRUISES

MANY MAINSTREAM SHIPS with South American itineraries include an Amazon River cruise. They enter on the Atlantic delta and sail upriver to Manaus. The river is very wide; any intimate view must be obtained aboard small crafts on tributaries. More exotic regions of the Upper Amazon are reached mainly from Iquitos, Peru, or via Ecuador.

Note: In parentheses after each boat name is information (where available) about the number of cabins and passengers; officers and crew; and the boat's length (cabins/passengers; officers/crew; boat length). Many companies offering tours from the United States use the same boats on the Amazon; these include the following:

Amazon Clipper **(8/16; PERUVIAN; 65 FEET)**

Three-night cruises explore the tributaries to bird-watch, fish for piranha, and visit Amazon Ecopark, a nature reserve and wildlife rehabilitation sanctuary. *Clipper's* cabins have private bathrooms, bunk berths, as well as nighttime air-conditioning. Facilities include a covered salon, bar, dining area, library, and fully equipped kitchen with freezer. Local cuisine is served—mainly fresh fish. Mineral water is provided.

Amazon Explorer **(8/16; PERUVIAN; 85 FEET)**

Three- or six-night round-trip cruises upriver from Iquitos. The steel-constructed boat has a small air-conditioned lounge, dining room/bar, and Sun Deck. Cabins are outside doubles with bunk beds; all are air-conditioned and have private bath/shower.

Arca **(13/31; PERUVIAN; 98 FEET)**

Three- to six-night trips on the Upper Amazon. The air-conditioned, steel-hull riverboat operates between Iquitos and the twin cities of Tabatinga, Brazil, and Leticia, Colombia. She offers ten twin-bedded cabins with upper/lower berths and three triples with lower beds. All cabins have private bathroom and shower. The boat has a lounge/bar and covered and uncovered deck areas.

Rio Amazonas **(21/44; PERUVIAN; 146 FEET)**

Three- to six-night explorations of the Upper Amazon, sailing downriver on Sunday from Iquitos to the twin cities of Tabatinga, Brazil, and Leticia, Colombia; upriver on Wednesday from Leticia. Itineraries can be combined. The ship has an air-conditioned dining room and library, covered and uncovered deck areas, and hot tub. Upper-deck cabins have picture windows and private bathrooms with shower. Sun Deck cabins are larger, offering three twin beds, a closet, and a chair.

MOST OF THE FOLLOWING COMPANIES also offer Galápagos cruises as well as Amazon ones. See listings in the next section, Adventure and Cultural Cruises.

Ecotour Expeditions

P.O. Box 128, Jamestown, RI 02835-0128; ☎ 800-688-1822 or 401-423-3377; fax 401-423-9630; www.naturetours.com

---

Tucano **(9/18; PERUVIAN/7; 82 FEET)**

The *Tucano*, built in 1997 and extensively renovated and refurbished in 2008, is designed in the tradition of the steamboats that navigated the Amazon in the late 19th century, giving her a shallow draft and a large volume of interior space. She is very wide at the base and has a flat bottom, drawing only five feet, enabling her to explore small rivers, where wildlife is abundant but which are closed to most other passenger vessels, and to venture far into the interior of the Amazon.

Due to the typical calm Amazon waters, *Tucano* is able to have three decks, resulting in her large interior space and the all-important large windows—70—all of which are three feet high and can be opened. Every cabin has at least four of these windows, making the cabins bright and airy. All cabins have private bathrooms with shower, toilet, and sink. The boat is air-conditioned and has wood-paneled walls, a large Observation Deck, a living room, a wide balcony around the front of the vessel, and a collection of science and nature reference books.

Seven-night cruises depart year-round. Air transportation can be arranged from Miami or Atlanta. The trips on the Amazon and tributaries are accompanied by naturalists. The company also offers Galápagos cruises.

Iberostar Grand Amazon Cruises
2566 Le Jeune Road, Coral Gables, FL 33134; ☎ 888-923-2722 or 305-774-9225; fax 305-774-4810; www.iberostar.com

Iberostar Grand Amazon **(72/148; BRAZILIAN; 270 FEET)**

In 2005, the Spanish hotel company, Iberostar, launched Its first cruise ship on the Amazon River in Brazil. Built in Manaus at a cost of $12 million and styled like Nile River boats after the owner and architects made several trips to Egypt for that purpose, the *Iberostar Grand Amazon* is the most deluxe riverboat on the Amazon.

The four-deck vessel has 72 spacious cabins and two suites, all with air-conditioning, small private balcony, private bathroom with a countertop of Brazilian marble, a large glass-enclosed shower (only suites have tubs), hair dryer, and an ingenious light sensor that turns the lights on/off when you step inside.

The cabins, each measuring 240 square feet—unusually large for riverboats—are identical in size and layout and are very comfortable. They are furnished with a queen or twin beds, a dressing table that can double as a desk, leather easy chair, night tables, mini-bar, television monitor for movies, safe, phone, and generous closet space and drawers. There is good lighting with bedside switches for all lights. The two suites have almost 500 square feet with a separate bedroom and sitting/dining room and a veranda that extends around both rooms.

Two dining venues serve local and international cuisine, offer fresh fruit and vegetables, and feature local fish from the Amazon, along with excellent lamb, pork, and beef from Brazil. The main dining room on the lower deck, accommodating all passengers at one time, has open seating for three meals with flexible times. It serves a buffet for breakfast and lunch, but at dinner passengers have a choice of the buffet or a menu with two selections for four courses, or they can take from both. All tables seat 8 people, except the Captain's table, which seats 12. A second dining venue for light breakfast and lunch and a bar are in the covered area of the top open-air deck. Another section of the deck has a swimming pool surrounded by comfortable wooden deck lounges and a hot tub (with lukewarm water).

The riverboat's other facilities include a large lounge with a bar that does duty as the lecture room, show lounge, and disco; a small gym with exercise equipment; one elevator; a boutique; a clinic with nurse available 24/7; and laundry service. Internet access is planned.

Decor throughout the vessel is low-key and pleasant and features generous use of Brazilian hardwoods and crafts. In the cabins, for example, several walls are faced with golden blond Brazilian hardwoods and artwork reflecting Amazonian traditions; several public rooms have lovely parquet floors.

The boat has an expedition staff of five to eight men, depending on the number of passengers. All come from the Manaus region and are knowledgeable about the flora and fauna of the Amazon. Daily excursions of two to three hours are scheduled for 8 a.m. and 4 p.m.; special outings for birding are offered at 6 a.m. at least twice during the week. The boat carries four launches, each holding up to 22 people; more launches are added as needed. Normally, passengers are divided by language—Portugese, Spanish, English, French, German, Italian—as necessary. At least two guides accompany every expedition.

Departing from Manaus, the *Iberostar Grand Amazon* sails on two itineraries: a four-night cruise (Sunday–Thursday) along the Rio Negro, the main tributary of the thousand tributaries that spill into the Amazon River; and a three-night one (Thursday–Sunday) along the Solimoes River, the name given to the Amazon prior to its arrival at Manaus. A third option combines the two itineraries into a seven-day cruise. The boat stops at several points along the Amazon jungle, offering excursions on small boats to explore certain areas up close.

Back on the ship after an excursion, passengers can attend lectures on Amazon history, flowers, fish, birds, and more with audiovisual accompaniment. During the week, two evening shows are performed by a lively folklore group from Manaus. And we particularly appreciate that there are none of the endless announcements heard on many cruise ships.

In addition to the standard inclusion of all meals and entertainment on the boat, all beverages and excursions are also included in the price. Dress throughout the cruise is casual.

For many people, a cruise on the Amazon is reason enough to take this trip, but when they can combine it with stylish accommodations, good food, and outstanding service, it's truly a winner.

International Expeditions
1 Environs Park, Helena, AL 35080; ☎ 800-633-4734; fax 205-428-1714; www.ietravel.com

---

La Amatista **(15/28; 127 FEET)**

This 30-year-old company uses exploratory vessels sailing from Nauta, past the start of the Amazon, to explore its tributaries. These include the Ucayali, Maranon, and Tapiche rivers and the Pacaya-Samiria National Reserve, all viewed from excursion craft and on foot along jungle trails. Naturalists/guides accompany the outings. All cabins have private facilities and air-conditioning. Nine-day cruises make weekly departures throughout the year. The company also offers Galápagos cruises and other expeditions in Central and South America.

Ladatco Tours
3006 Aviation Avenue, Suite 3A , Coconut Grove, FL 33133;
☎ **305-854- 8422 or 800-327-6162; fax 305-285-0504; www.ladatco.com**

Ladatco is a tour company that promotes and sells cruises on the following boats:

Amazon Clipper Premium **(16/32; BRAZILIAN; 106 FEET)**

Aqua **(12/24; PERUVIAN; 130 FEET)**

Delfin I **(6/12; PERUVIAN; 67 FEET)**

Delfin II **(14/28; PERUVIAN; 120 FEET)**

Tucano **(9/16; 80 FEET)**

Amazon Clipper Premium has all outside cabins, with lower beds, private bathroom facilities with hot showers, individual air-conditioning, and a safe. Three- to four-day cruises depart on Wednesday from Manaus on the Amazon and Negro rivers; a six-day cruise combines the two. A multilingual local guide accompanies all cruises.

Tucano sails year-round from Manaus on seven-night Heart of Amazonia cruises. (See Ecotour Expeditions earlier in this section.)

Tara Tours
12002 SW 128 Court, , Suite 209, Miami, FL 33186; ☎ **305-278-4464 or 800-327-0080; fax 305-278-4454; www.taratours.com**

The tour company utilizes a variety of vessels and offers Amazon cruises from both Iquitos and Manaus. Among its vessels are:

Rio Amazonas **(21/44; PERUVIAN; 146 FEET),**

La Amastista, La Esmeralda, La Turmalina **(11 TO 15/22 TO 30; PERUVIAN; 90 TO 125 FEET)**

Amazon Clipper **(8/16; PERUVIAN; 65 FEET)**

Eight-night Amazon packages offered year-round from Miami to Iquitos include boat trips and one night at a hotel in Lima, Peru, plus jungle walks, visits to native villages, and English-speaking naturalists. The company also offers cruises of the Galápagos.

ADVENTURE *and* CULTURAL CRUISES

THE DIFFERENCE BETWEEN AN ADVENTURE or expedition cruise and an educational or cultural cruise is often a matter of semantics or marketing. And although there are differences, there are also similarities, particularly in the type of person to whom they appeal—namely, experienced travelers who prefer an intellectually stimulating or educational environment when they travel and do not need (or want) the activities and entertainment typical of mainstream cruises. They prefer the hands-on learning that adventure and educational cruises provide, as well as the companionship of like-minded travelers.

Ships offering adventures or expeditions generally are informal and small, accommodating fewer than 150 passengers. Their small size enables them to visit places large ships cannot go. Vessels providing educational or cultural cruises might be larger and more formal. In all cases, the itineraries (which tend to be two weeks or longer) and the opportunity to learn from experts are the main attractions.

In the last two or three years, more deluxe ships have been added in the adventure and cultural cruises category, bringing with them a new level of comfort and expanded facilities. But the majority are still comfortable workhorses that safely ply icy waters or jungle rivers. They have cozy, functional cabins, friendly service, and good food, served at one open seating, often family-style. Dress is casual. Most ships maintain an open bridge.

Cruises are almost always seasonal, to take advantage of optimum weather and wildlife conditions. On board, passengers attend lectures by specialists and have time to enjoy fellow shipmates. Ports are likely to be remote, and passengers travel by Zodiac boats to the most inaccessible areas, often making wet landings where no docks are available.

On shore, participants view wildlife and scenery, hike into coastal forests, or encounter remote cultures. Not all cruises require heavy exertion—many are light adventure, nothing more than a short walk. In the evening, staff naturalists and guest lecturers recap the day's excursion in well-attended sessions. On educational or cultural cruises, lecturers are likely to be historians, anthropologists, museum authorities, and area specialists. Many such trips are sponsored by universities and museum groups, often as an alumni fund-raiser.

Destinations might be world-renowned sites visited by general tours, but participants on cultural cruises get in-depth information and excursions led by experts, rather than the commercial guides that regular cruise lines use. Participants also are likely to attend cultural and folklore events. It isn't unusual for adventure and cultural cruises to overlap in their activities, particularly those offering light adventure (or soft adventure, the unappealing term the travel trade uses). Not only do these cruises appeal to the same type of people—they may appeal to the same exact people.

If you've never tried an adventure/expedition cruise, there are a few things you need to consider. Adventure cruises are not exactly laid-back affairs. You might be rousted out of bed at 5:30 a.m. to see a whale, a penguin, or nearly anything else within the purview of the cruise's educational program. Even if you're not rolled out at 5:30 a.m., you'll probably have to rise by 6:30 or 7 a.m. to dress and have breakfast before the day's activities commence. If you try to sleep in, you can often count on some announcements over the public address speaker that can be heard in your cabin. Such cruises tend to pack a lot into a day. On some ships, you scarcely have time for a shower and a change of clothes before dinner is served, except on days at sea.

Before you book an adventure/expedition cruise, carefully scrutinize the itinerary and make some inquiries about the likelihood of rough seas. An Antarctic cruise, for example, must traverse the Drake Passage for two days southbound and two days northbound from South America. The Drake Passage can be one of the roughest seas on the planet—perhaps not the place to be if you've never cruised before or if your experience is limited to the calm waters of the Caribbean. But if you're lucky, the passage can be as smooth as a lake.

Because many adventure/expedition cruises are at the ends of the earth or halfway around the world, you need to pay attention to all aspects of your travel plans. We recommend an intermediate layover both coming and going, as well as an extra day in the port of embarkation. If you're going to the Far East or Australia, try to arrange a night in Hawaii or California before continuing to your final destination. If you're headed to Antarctica, you might want to spend a night in Santiago or Buenos Aires on the return.

If your cruise package includes a stopover (and many do), it pays to check out the city where you'll be stopping. A Galápagos Islands adventure cruise included an overnight in Quito, Ecuador. Those folks who didn't check out Quito before leaving home were astonished to learn upon arrival that it sits in the Andes at an elevation of 9,350 feet. Not only did most not have warm clothing—they were heading for the equator and sea level, after all—but they discovered it was quite impossible to acclimate to that altitude in one day. An equally compelling reason for an overnight stopover and an extra night in the port city is the opportunity to deal with lost luggage. The worst time to have your luggage disappear is when you're about to embark on an adventure/expedition cruise. Chances are you've spent weeks rounding up the specialized clothing and gear required for the cruise, but if you have a day or more prior to boarding for your luggage to catch up with you, you'll be fine 90% of the time. In a worst-case scenario, when your lost luggage stays lost, you'll still have time to re-equip in local stores before sailing.

Another precaution we take is to avoid luggage transfers between airlines. On an itinerary from Fort Lauderdale to Iceland for an expedition cruise out of Reykjavik, for example, we took an early Delta flight to New York's JFK International Airport, where we claimed our bags and then personally rechecked them with Icelandair. We were perfectly happy to suffer an extra hour or two at JFK for the peace of mind of knowing that our bags were safely checked with Icelandair to Reykjavik.

Adventure/expedition cruises don't require physical training, but participants should be in good condition and able to endure some exertion. More importantly, they need to be flexible in temperament as well as body. They should be good sports, keep a sense of humor, and be ready to forgo comforts occasionally. Adventure or expedition cruises take participants off the beaten path worldwide. They tend to be more expensive than mainstream cruises because fewer people share the cost and because it costs more to operate a ship in remote areas. Also, shore excursions are usually included, and lecturers must be accommodated in cabins that otherwise draw revenue.

Participants tend to be strong environmentalists who expect fellow travelers to share their views. They like to be outdoors, are active, well traveled, well educated, intellectually curious, affluent, and perhaps semiretired professionals ages 50 or older. They often belong to a museum or natural history group. They probably read *Audubon*, *National Geographic*, or *Smithsonian* magazines and watch public television.

Following is a representative list of companies offering adventure/ expedition or educational/cultural cruises. They provide brochures, usually with deck plans of vessels they use, and descriptions of itineraries. Being specialists, they usually can answer questions with more firsthand authority than a travel agent—unless it's an adventure travel specialist—or a mainstream cruise line can.

Regarding Galápagos cruises, in an effort to prevent overcrowding at certain visitor sites, the Galápagos National Park Service has revised the itineraries of many tour boats. Check with the tour company for the latest information.

Note: In parentheses after each boat name is information (where available) about the number of cabins and passengers; officers and crew; and the boat's length (cabins/passengers; officers/crew; boat length/tonnage).

Abercrombie & Kent USA, LLC (*See* Part Two.)

Small boats are chartered for Galápagos cruises, including *Eclipse* (27/48; Ecuadoran; 210 feet), among others. In Antarctica, the company uses the new *Le Boreal*.

Adventure Canada

Lochburn Landing, 14 Front Street South, Mississauga, Ontario, Canada L5H 2C4; ☎ 905-271-4000; fax 905-271-5595; www.adventurecanada.com; e-mail info@adventurecanada.com

Founded in 1987, Adventure Canada was created to bring travelers to "Canada's areas whose remoteness alone made them special." Over the last 22 years, the tour company has expanded and now offers expeditions worldwide, motivated by "there is so much to see 'beyond the binoculars' [we are driven] to delve deeper into our favourite places with every expedition and continually seek out new destinations."

The company offers a great variety of cruises as far afield as the Canadian Arctic, Greenland and Iceland, and Antarctica on small expedition ships carrying between 45 and 100 passengers, as well as a fleet of Zodiacs enabling them to visit remote places not accessible by larger vessels. In 2010, Adventure Canada will take the *Clipper Adventurer* on two expeditions through the famous Northwest Passage and another circumnavigating Newfoundland. On *Ocean Nova,* it will offer a "Birding the High Arctic and Northwest Territory" cruise; and on *National Geographic Islander,* a cruise to the Galápagos. In addition, Adventure Canada offers a series of specialized departures with a focus on art and culture or photography in its Art is Adventure and PhotoWild! programs.

This line extensively researches each offering, and its ships travel with topnotch teams of ten or more scientists, historians, naturalists, and other experts and expeditionary staff. The teams often include artists, writers, musicians, and photographers to provide balance to the scientific side of the group. Most important, the staff on every departure is supplemented by local inhabitants of the places to be visited. The company also promotes a two-way cultural exchange so that the people visited benefit as much as passengers do.

Adventure Canada works with international cultural, historical, and natural history organizations and arranges expeditions with some of the groups each year. These have included the Art Gallery of Ontario, Royal Ontario Museum, McGill University, National Wildlife Federation, Royal Canadian Geographical Society, and more. Adventure Canada has won a number of awards, including being named one of the "Best Adventure Travel Companies on Earth" by *National Geographic Adventure Magazine* for 2007 and 2008, among others.

American Safari Cruises
(*See* Part Two under European and Smaller Cruise Lines.)

Canodros, S.A.
Canodros 2735, P.O. Box 59-9000, Miami, FL 33159-9000;
☎ **800-613-6026; www.canodros.com**

Galápagos Explorer II **(50/100; ECUADORIAN; 295 FEET)**

The luxury, all-suite ship sails on three-, four-, and seven-night cruises weekly in the Galápagos Islands. Ecuadorian-owned and -operated, the ship has classic lines and interiors throughout. Suites, all with sitting rooms, are air-conditioned and have queen or two twin beds, telephone, television, refrigerator-bar, full-length wardrobe, marble bath, and 110-volt electrical outlets. Also on board are two whirlpools, a boutique, a library, an observation deck, a karaoke bar, and a massage suite. The vessel has satellite communications, Wi-Fi, and an onboard doctor.

The elegant, nonsmoking restaurant offers one informal open seating. International and Ecuadorian cuisine is served; special diets can be accommodated. A lunch buffet is served on deck. Staff will prepare additional dishes on request. Cruise price also includes twice-daily tours escorted by naturalists.

The ship always anchors offshore, and passengers are tendered on dinghies for dry or wet landings. In keeping with the company's environmental commitment, all soaps, detergents, and shampoo used on board are biodegradable. The ship produces its own fresh water and is equipped with a sewage treatment system to minimize environmental impact. Chlorine isn't used on board. Paper and nontoxic solids are incinerated, metal cans are compacted for recycling, and nonbiodegradable trash is returned to port.

The ship is used extensively by tour companies offering Galápagos–South America tour programs and Canodros can combine Ecuador, the Amazon, and the Andes with the Galápagos as destinations.

Compagnie Polynesienne de Transport Maritime
2028 El Camino Real South, Suite B, San Mateo, CA 94403;
☎ **650-574-2575 or 800-972-7268; www.aranui.com**

Aranui III **(85/200; MARQUESAN; 386 FEET)**

Most places on earth can be reached by air, but there are a few exceptions, such as the French Polynesian Marquesas and Tuamotu (or Tuomotu) islands in the South Pacific. These islands have been accessible by passenger freighters named *Aranui* (meaning "great highway" in the Maori language) since 1959. In 2003, a brand-new one arrived, the 200-passenger *Aranui III,* to take over the 14-day round-trips from Papeete, Tahiti. She carries all manner of cargo and 20-foot containers to the remote archipelago and is crewed mostly by Marquesans.

The passengers' quarters are of a high standard and include a main lounge, library, video room, gym, small shop, laundry, and outdoor swimming pool with a bar. The dining room can accommodate all passengers at one seating. The food is both international and Polynesian, with ingredients such as pork, poultry, fish, fruits and vegetables, and imported beef. French wines are included with lunch and dinner, which are served family-style, while breakfast is a buffet. Many passengers are French (French Polynesia is still part of France), and others are European, Australian, Canadian, and American.

The ship has a total of 85 cabins and suites. They include 63 standard, moderate-size cabins that are plainly appointed with light wood furnishings and have portholes, twin beds, showers, and toilets; 8 larger deluxe cabins with windows, more colorful decor, darker wood furnishings, a refrigerator, and a bathtub; and 14 suites,12 with private balconies. Some cabins will accommodate a third person.

The ship sails year-round from Papeete, about every two weeks, on a 14-day voyage, calling at two Tuamotu and six Marquesas islands, all with spectacular scenery and some with beautiful volcanic peaks. Most days are spent at anchor off an island, while the ship loads and unloads cargo; two days are spent at sea. Time in port varies from a few hours to a full day. The *Aranui*'s arrival is a major event for each of these islands.

Activities include watching locals harvest black pearls, swimming from fine sandy beaches, snorkeling over coral reefs, exploring archaeological ruins by jeep and on foot, buying handicrafts, and enjoying barbecues. Shore excursions are included in the fare. Scuba diving, horseback riding, fishing, and helicopter tours are extra. A 14-day voyage on *Aranui III* starts at about $3,675 per person, double occupancy.

Although assistance is provided, passengers need to be able to negotiate ladders into whale boats and disembark through the surf. April to October is the dry season, with an occasional shower. November to March is the rainy season. Daytime temperatures hover in the 80s and fall into the 60s and 70s after dark.

Cruise North Expeditions, Inc.
111 Peter Street, Suite 200, Toronto, Canada, M5V 2H1; ☎ 866-263-3220 or 416-789-3752; fax 416-955-9869; www.cruisenorthexpeditions.com

Lyubov Orlova **(59 CABINS, 2 SUITES/122; RUSSIAN, CANADIAN, INUIT/64; 328 FEET/4,251 TONS)**

Cruise North Expeditions, the Inuit-owned cruise line launched in July 2005, has revolutionized travel to the remote Canadian Arctic, a virtually undiscovered part of the world, by making it affordable, accessible, and authentic. The Inuit are the indigenous people of the Canadian Arctic, popularly known as the Eskimo.

The *Lyubov Orlova*, a Russian vessel with an ice-strengthened hull, a Russian captain and crew, was built in Yugoslavia in 1976, refurbished in 1999, and further upgraded in 2002. She is the only passenger ship docked in the Canadian Arctic with cruises starting in Kuujjuaq, at the northern limit of the great Boreal Forest. That's a clear advantage over other cruise ships that must sail into the region from distant locations, such as Greenland, requiring extra travel days at sea. Cruise North Expeditions chartered the ship in 2006 for five summer seasons from Quark Expeditions (see entry later in this chapter), which takes the ship on Antarctic voyages during the winter months.

The Cruise North package includes a short two-hour flight from Montreal to Kuujjuaq on its sister company, First Air, a Canadian airline that has served the northern region for more than 50 years. Kuujjuaq (population 2,500) is the main town and commercial center of Nunavik, the northernmost district of Quebec Province. It sits on the Koksoak River at the tree line, 914 miles north of Montreal and a few hundred miles below the North Pole. Arriving passengers will be surprised to see soft green hills and wide valleys covered with evergreen forests interspersed with lakes where the winter snows have melted. There are no buildings, no houses, and no roads in the landscape until a few minutes before the plane begins its landing. Any idea that the Arctic is similar to Antarctica will be quickly dispelled.

Cruise North is making a determined effort to have the local Inuit inhabitants actively involved in the cruise operation. At the same time, this venture is helping the Inuit preserve their culture by sharing their traditions and customs with passengers. By being in direct contact with Cruise North passengers and welcoming them to their homeland, Inuit hosts help passengers appreciate the indigenous people's deep reverence for the natural world, its scenic wonders, and wildlife.

Cruise North operates a series of 7- to 12-night Arctic cruises from June through September. Normally during that time, the average daily temperature is about 50 degrees and can even reach 70 degrees. The Arctic wildlife and scenery are certain to delight passengers when they see magnificent polar bears, walrus, Beluga whales, bearded seals, musk oxen, and up to 22 species of birds, including huge colonies of the indigenous thick-billed murre against the awesome backdrop of icebergs, towering cliffs, mountains, and fjords.

The cruises feature an experienced expedition team and daily lectures by naturalists, ornithologists, and historians who review the region's history, particularly the impact of European traders and the explorers who searched for the Northwest Passage. The Inuit members talk about their culture with insights into their society—a society in transition, adjusting from the traditional life of Eskimos to life in modern Canada. On several nights, passengers can watch some excellent films, including *Nanook of the North*, the classic, award-winning feature that vividly portrays the difficult life and extreme hardship that Inuits faced early in the last century, and *Climate On The Edge*, a documentary on the effects of climate change in the Arctic by the National Film Board of Canada.

In small settlements like Kimmirut (population 400) on the coast of Baffin Island, passengers are met by townspeople, who act as their guides, and a bevy of children, often shyly selling their soapstone carvings, an art for which the Inuit are famous. Kimmirut, once an important trading post, has a new promise of wealth—rubies and sapphires being mined only two miles from town. Sample gems are on display, along with a fine collection of soapstone carvings at the Sopher Gallery in town. Next to the Kimmirut Information Centre, with exhibits on the region's history and culture, a tent invites passengers inside to watch women making traditional bannock (a staple similar to doughnuts) and removing the blubber from a seal skin using an *uluk*, the traditional Inuit working knife.

The daily pattern of the voyage is typical of expedition cruises: awaken at 6:30 a.m. with a weather report, breakfast at 7 a.m., and board the Zodiacs to depart for the day's outing by 8 a.m. Passengers are advised to dress in layers, always prepared for a wet landing with waterproof boots, rain pants, and windbreaker, and, on some days, a parka. Cruise North Expeditions sends useful information, including maps, to passengers in advance of their cruise.

Cruise North's itineraries—Arctic Explorer, Baffin Adventure, High Arctic, Hudson's Wake, Labrador North, and Newfoundland and Labrador—include visits to ancient Inuit archaeological sites and entertainment by the Inuit community of traditional Inuit drum dancing and throat singing. Prices start at $2,995 per person, double occupancy, for a seven-night package. Generally, air transportation and taxes are extra. Pre- and postcruise options in the Arctic for small groups are offered and include kayaking, hiking, and a stay at a wilderness lodge.

Cruise North embarked on its inaugural trip through the Inuit homeland of the Northwest Passage in August 2009—made possible by the melting ice as a result of climate change—and will repeat the voyage in 2010. The voyage on the *Lyubov Orlova* traces the legendary trading route first navigated by Roald Amundsen in 1903–1906. Cruise North's Northwest Passage begins in the High Arctic's Resolute Bay and travels through the Canadian Arctic Archipelago, along with historic sites abandoned more than a hundred years ago, including Beechey Island, Victory Point, Cambridge Bay, Gjoa Haven, Bellot Strait, and Prince Leopold Island. A first-rate expedition team and historians, naturalists, ornithologists, and Inuit guides and elders accompany the voyage.

Another new destination for 2010 is Greenland, with two departures: one from Iqaluit, Nunavut, on July 23, the other from Kuujjuaq, Quebec, on August 6, with Inuit guides on board. The itinerary includes Baffin Island's Auyuittuq National Park and stops at communities on Greenland's west coast. There are two new Arctic cruise photo workshops: one on the Arctic Safari and the other on the High Arctic trip, which departs September 6.

Most cabins on the *Lyubov Orlova* have two lower berths and a porthole, a small private bath with shower, and are furnished with a chest of drawers and ample closet space. Upper-deck cabins open onto the deck. The ice-strengthened ship has four decks. Public rooms, situated on one deck, include a forward lounge, small bar, and library stocked with Arctic-related literature, a window-lined dining room that accommodates all passengers at one seating, an aft Observation Deck, and wide promenades, excellent for viewing wildlife and passing scenery.

Cruise North Expeditions is owned by the Makivik Corporation of Quebec, a successful investment corporation born of the first modern-day Aboriginal land claim settlement agreement in Canada (the JBNQA of 1975). Makivik also owns First Air and Air Inuit. The cruise line is headed by Adamie Alaku, the Inuk chairman, and Dugald Wells, a professional engineer and expedition cruise veteran, who began his career in the Arctic 20 years ago as a research scientist on board Canadian icebreakers. The deck staff and engine crew are Russian, who stage a great show of Russian folk songs and dances on one evening during the cruise. The expedition leader, guides, lecturers, chef, and bartender are mostly Canadian, including some Inuit. Cruise North Expeditions reservations and travel arrangements are handled by Exclusive Tours, 111 Peter Street, Suite 200, Toronto, Canada, M5V 2H1; **www.exclusivetours.ca**; ☎ 800-268-1820 or 416-368-8558; e-mail info@exclusivetours.ca. The Canadian-owned cruise tour wholesaler specializes in niche travel products and small-ship cruising to destinations around the world. Reservations can also be made through travel agents.

Cruceros Australis/USA

4014 Chase Avenue, Suite 215, Miami Beach, FL 33140; ☎ 305-695-9618 or 877-678-3772; fax 305-534-9276; www.australis.com

Mare Australis **(63/129; CHILEAN; 236 FEET)**

Via Australis (64/136; CHILEAN; 236 FEET)

Stella Australis (100/200; CHILEAN)

October to April, the two virtually identical expedition ships of Cruceros Australis sail the Magellan Strait and Beagle Channel, exploring Chilean-Argentinean Patagonia and Tierra del Fuego, one of the most beautiful and unexplored regions of the world at the tip of continental South America. While the departure ports are sizable and interesting, once the cruises are underway, the accent is on nature on a grand scale, with ships cruising deep into fjords for close-up experiences of crackling ice fields and wildlife encounters or scenery viewing at a leisurely pace.

The company launched operations on this routing in 1990 with the *Terra Australis*, which was replaced by the more luxurious *Mare Australis* in 2002, with the *Via Australis* added in 2005. Both ships were custom-built in a ship-yard in Valdivia, Chile, and carry Chilean officers and crew. Cruceros Australis is currently building a third ship, the *Stella Australis,* which will start operations at the end of 2010 and have a capacity of 200 passengers.

Cruises ply the waters between Punta Arenas, Chile, and Ushuaia, Argentina, on two different three- and four-night itineraries. With two ships crossing back and forth, the cruise line can offer passengers the option of weekly sailings on three-night or four-night cruises from either port; however, 5% of those cruising opt for the seven-night journey, cruising round-trip from either Punta Arenas or Ushuaia.

All cruises have daily Zodiac excursions that differ with the itinerary. Passengers taking the full cruise will sail along magnificent Glacier Alley, observe colonies of elephant seals and sea lions, walk among colonies of Magellanic penguins, visit Cape Horn National Park, and hike along the glacier of Pia Fjord and Wulaia Bay in Navarino Island. Weather can affect some shore excursions. Many passengers opt to explore more of Patagonia with land tours, combining Torres del Paine National Park in Chile with El Calafate and its impressive Glacier Perito Moreno in Argentina, with their three- or four-night sailings. These land/sea circuits are not operated by Cruceros Australis but can be requested at the time of the cruise booking.

Activities schedules are issued daily, and briefings are held prior to all disembarkations for Zodiac excursions. In this rather unknown corner of the world, lectures by knowledgeable naturalists are an important part of the cruise experience. They are held daily, introducing passengers to the flora and fauna of the Magellanic forest; marine mammals and birds of Patagonia; history and navigation in the Beagle Channel, Strait of Magellan, or Cape Horn; and history and customs of the native peoples.

The ships have four enclosed decks, with spacious, inviting public areas; the top Observation Deck is totally open, affording grand vistas of the passing scene. The views are almost as panoramic in the **Sky Lounge** on Deck Four, which has an open bar; here, most night activities take place, and in addition to the **Game Room,** it's the only place on board where smoking is permitted. The **Yamana Lounge** on Deck Three has a bar, small library, video and audio equipment, as well as wide-window views. Both lounges are used for lectures and light evening entertainment from a folklore show to bingo, special films, or a tango performance. The bridge is open to passengers, and also on board is a shop and first aid service from the resident doctor.

The **Patagonia dining room** is on Deck One, and the food on board the *Cruceros Australis* ships is very good—a mix of regional and international cuisine. For early risers, coffee and sweet rolls are available. Both breakfast and lunch are buffet service; breakfast has a full range of choices, from juice and fruits to cereal, cheeses, and cold cuts, to hot dishes prepared to order; lunch includes cold and hot choice dishes, salads, and a table of various desserts. Each evening, canapés (including Latin specialties such as empanadas) and trays of pisco sours are served in the lounge before dinner. For dinner, along with the first course, soup course, and dessert choice, two or three entrees are offered, including excellent beef and lamb, fish, and seafood. All beverages, including beer, Chilean and Argentine wines, and liquors are included in the ships' tariff.

There is a ship-wide equality in all cabins, measuring 161 square feet with outside positions and windows. These are nicely decorated and well-appointed cabins with two low twin beds (that can be moved together for queen-size sleeping), bathroom with shower, reasonable storage and closet space, independently controlled heater, safety box, closet, and 110-/220-volt power outlets. The *Mare Australis* has three triples with pull-down beds, and the *Via Australis* has seven.

Passengers are mostly mature, well-seasoned travelers, the majority a mix of North Americans and Europeans; lectures and excursions cater to various language groups aboard, although most passengers seem to speak some English. This is an informal ship, requiring that passengers bring warm and waterproof clothing rather than dressy outfits. The atmosphere is friendly, and passengers are generally committed to enjoying the adventure of cruising in the wakes of Darwin, Fitz Roy, and Magellan.

Ecotour Expeditions
P.O. Box 128, Jamestown, RI 02835-0128; ☎ 800-688-1822 or 401-423-3377; fax 401-423-9630; www.naturetours.com

This operator uses three small sister ships, *Eric, Flamingo*, and *Letty* (10/20; 83 feet), as well as the *Beluga* (8/16; 110 feet). All cabins and dining rooms are air-conditioned, and all cabins have private bathrooms with showers. The vessels are comfortable but not luxurious. On the upper Dolphin Deck, cabins have two twin lower beds and picture windows, except one cabin that has one double bed. Booby Deck cabins have one double bed and picture windows; while the lower Iguana Deck cabins have two twin lower beds and portholes. Two Iguana cabins have an upper berth and can be used as triples. The *Beluga* has a large dining room, salon, and a full Sun Deck. Of its eight cabins, two have queen-size beds, three bunk beds, and three have two twin beds. The cruises depart on Fridays; on each island passengers visit two to three different sites.

Ecoventura S.A. (*See* entry for Galápagos Network.)

Esplanade Tours (*See* Nile River Cruises earlier in Part Three.)

Expedition Cruises to the North Pole
15 Artisan Avenue, Huntington, NY 11743; ☎ 877-692-5701 (toll-free) or
631-692-5700 or 516-302-0782; www.expedition-cruises.com;
e-mail cruises@expedition-cruises.com or cruises@northpolecruises.us.com

50 Years of Victory **(64/128; RUSSIAN/140; 525 FEET)**

Expedition Cruises, the North American division of PAV (Poseidon Arctic Voyages), has been leading expeditions into the Russian Arctic on chartered icebreakers and expedition cruise ships since its first North Pole icebreaker expedition cruise in 2001, becoming a leader in Arctic-bound adventure tourism and helping to open up Russia's magnificent Arctic territories, much of which are still virgin and unexplored.

Today, Expedition Cruises is said to operate the only expedition cruises to Franz Josef Land archipelago, and the line opened and developed the spectacular Transpolar Bridge route from Murmansk to Pevek by way of the North Pole. Expert guides have led expeditions to such faraway places as the archipelagos of Novaya Zemlya and Severnaya Zemlya, as well as to the islands of Vaigach, Oranskiye, and Vise. They have taken expedition ships to the edge of Kamchatka and on to the Commander Islands and even ventured out to the Ring of Fire to lead expeditions to the Kuril Islands. The organization of such experiences has helped to establish Expedition Cruises as one of the most authoritative lines in adventure cruises to destinations in the Russian Arctic and beyond.

The unconventionally named *50 Years of Victory* is the largest and most modern nuclear-powered icebreaker in the world. She is a new-generation ship, an upgrade of the Arktika-class, the most powerful icebreakers in the world. As property of the Russian Federation, the ship received maritime registration under the name *50 Let Pobedy* (which translates to *50 Years of Victory*).

Combining state-of-the-art technology and comfort, *Victory*'s power plant is comprised of two nuclear reactors and two steam turbines rotating six generators. Among her state-of-the-art features are a spoon-shaped bow designed for greater icebreaking ability; an automated, digitalized control system; and the most up-to-date nuclear safeguards and protection systems. The powerful Russia-registered *50 Years of Victory* has a 36-foot draft and a cruising speed of 21 knots.

As a working icebreaker, *Victory* is more suitable to shipboard life than her predecessor, *Yamal,* an earlier Russian icebreaker, and offers passengers more room for socializing and get-togethers, in addition to comfortable cabins and suites.

All passenger cabins have exterior views and windows that open, a television, and a DVD player; suites also have a refrigerator and a coffeemaker. Cabin categories include standard twin (46) with one lower berth, one sofa bed, and private facilities with a shower; and mini-suites (6) furnished with a sitting area with sofa bed, a bed separated from the sitting area, and private facilities with a shower. Suites (6) have a bedroom, sitting area with a sofa bed, and private facilities with a bathtub or shower. The Victory Suite (1) has a large bedroom, sitting room with sofa bed, and private facilities with a bathtub. Arktika Suites (5) have a very spacious bedroom, sitting room with a sofa bed, safe, and private facilities with a bathtub. Cabin amenities include a selection of fresh fruit, drinks, and snacks.

Expedition Cruises voyages are bilingual. The expedition team and lecturers speak fluent English. Passengers are primarily North American, German, and Japanese. The cuisine has a European flair, with selections that appeal to North Americans.

Expedition Cruises says, "An expedition voyage to the Arctic or beyond is a sense-arousing, heart-opening experience that touches the very soul of all who have ever ventured into this unique domain where beauty, silence, and awe all intermingle to create an image so intense it brands itself into the mind forever."

Galápagos Cruises

c/o Adventure Associates, 7920 Belt Line Road, Suite 720, Dallas, TX 75254; ☎ 972-907-0414 or 800-527-2500; fax 972-783-1286; www.metropolitantouring.com or www.adventure-associates.com; e-mail info@adventure-associates.com

Adventure Associates is the U.S. division of Quito-based Metropolitan Touring, Ecuador's leading tour company, and the oldest company offering Galápagos cruises. Ships are well run and have excellent guides.

Isabela II **(21/40; ECUADORIAN; 166 FEET)**
Completely renovated in February 2000, this ship's new look includes an enlarged reception area, a redesigned library, and a new multimedia system for briefings and lectures. The mahogany-paneled dining room and library were totally refurbished, along with the lounge and cabins. The redesigned Sun Deck now has a bar, observation area for whale and dolphin watching, and a solarium. The air-conditioned ship offers satellite telephone, e-mail, and fax service. She sails from Baltra on Fridays on seven-night cruises of the Galápagos Islands; shorter cruises are offered on Tuesday departures. Children under age 12 who share a cabin with adults get a 25% discount off the regular price. Prices do not include Ecuador/Baltra flights or national park entrance fee.

Santa Cruz **(46/90; ECUADORIAN; 237 FEET)**
Offering three-, four-, and seven-night Galápagos cruises, this ship, renovated in 1998, is one of the largest and most comfortable sailing in Galápagos waters. Food and service are good, and the ship is well run. All cabins were refitted, and passengers can choose singles, doubles, or suites. The air-conditioned ship is mostly carpeted and has a large dining room, cocktail lounge, bar, library, Jacuzzi, and spacious decks. Three-night cruises visit the southern islands; four-night tours visit the central and northern groups. The two can be combined. Naturalist guides, trained and licensed by Galápagos National Park, give nightly briefings on the next day's visit and accompany passengers on excursions. Passengers are divided into groups of 20 people or fewer. In 2005, the company introduced enhancements to its established routes with visits to Sante Fe Island, home to endemic land

iguanas, a large sea lion colony, and the Galápagos' oldest rocks; Dragon Hill on Santa Cruz, where marine iguanas bask on black lava and a lagoon attracts flamingos; La Galapaguera, the giant-tortoise breeding station; and Stephen's Bay on San Cristobal, with indigenous Chatham mockingbirds, lava lizards, and a white coral beach.

La Pinta (24/48; ECUADORIAN; 207 FEET)

Completely refurbished in 2008, La Pinta is the newest addition to the fleet. All cabins are doubles or triples and located on the same deck; some cabins interconnect. The public areas include a cozy dining room, cocktail lounge, a well-stocked library, Jacuzzi, and spacious open decks. The ship carries three permanent naturalists on board who are trained and licensed by the Galápagos National Park. They lead groups (with no more than 16 persons) on their visits ashore or during water activities that include swimming, snorkeling, kayaking, and glass-bottom boat excursions. The ship sails on seven-night cruises, Friday to Friday, that include the islands of Bartolome, Hood, North Seymour, Isabela, Fernandina, Santa Cruz, San Cristobal, Floreana, and Rabida.

Adventure Associates offers other ships in the Galápagos and also has Upper Amazon cruises on the 26-passenger Manatee Amazon Explorer.

Galapagos Network (Ecoventura)

5805 Blue Lagoon Drive, Suite 160, Miami, FL 33126; ☎ 305-262-6264 or 800-633-7972; fax 305-262-9609; www.ecoventura.com; e-mail info@galapagosnetwork.com

Galapagos Network is the U.S.-based sales and reservation office for Ecoventura, a family-owned company based in Guayaquil, Ecuador, in operation since 1990. This tour company offers year-round, five- to ten-night cruises in the Galápagos Islands on its fleet of small vessels. Cruises are designed for the well educated, well traveled, and those eager to learn about nature, ecology, and environmental issues. The boats' size allows them to visit remote islands. Naturalist guides lecture and lead walks. Passengers are ferried to the islands by Zodiac-style dinghies.

In 2009, the Eric became the first hybrid-energy tour boat in the Galápagos following a $100,000 installation of 40 solar panels and two wind turbines on the upper deck. This work that began in October 2008 also included replacing canvas awnings with a hard fiberglass top for structural support. The initial goal is for the solar panels and wind-powered generators to provide approximately 17% of the energy formerly produced by two carbon fuel-based generators. This project was financed through a partnership with Toyota, a supporter of the World Wildlife Fund. The target goal is to have full fleet implementation by 2011.

Life aboard a Galapagos Network cruise, especially on the Letty, Eric, and Flamingo I, is, well, familial. The small number of passengers and Ecuadorian crew connect almost immediately in a friendship that only ripens over the duration of the cruise. The whole crew—from the captain to the cook—is invested in sharing the rugged beauty and abundant wildlife of the Galápagos, and their enthusiasm is impossible to resist.

Dining features Ecuadorian specialties, which in spice, aroma, and taste are always a surprise. Some dishes exhibit characteristics of provincial Mexican cuisine; others, remarkably, would be at home in an Indian (as in Mumbai) restaurant. But it's all good, even if it keeps you guessing.

One of the Galapagos Network's greatest strengths is its land support. From the time you step off your international flight, there is someone to watch over you. Most itineraries include an overnight in either Quito or Guayaquil in quirky but totally wonderful (and totally Ecuadorian) local hotels. Following an overnight, passengers continue on by plane the next day to the Galápagos.

Sky Dancer (8/16; **ECUADORIAN; 100 FEET**)

Built in the United States, this live-aboard dive vessel has a spacious dining area that serves both Ecuadorian and international cuisine, fully stocked bar, main salon with entertainment center, allocated personal dive storage, and Sun Deck. Cabins are air-conditioned and have private bathrooms. *Sky Dancer* attracts hard-core divers who can take as many as four dives per day on a preplanned, seven-night itinerary, Sunday to Sunday. Dive in the Northern Islands of Wolf and Darwin, famous for hammerhead sharks, giant manta rays, and whale sharks.

Eric/Flamingo I/Letty (10/20; **ECUADORAN; 83 FEET**)

Built in 1993, *Letty* is an air-conditioned luxury yacht. Cabins have private bathrooms. *Letty* departs on Sunday. Approximately four hours per day are spent on each island. The boats are well suited for families or groups. Five- to seven-night itineraries include the western islands of Fernandina and Isabela, as well as Española, Tower, Santa Cruz, Bartolome, North Seymour, Santiago, and San Cristobal. The ships depart from San Cristobal every Sunday for the week's cruise.

Galapagos Yacht Cruises

c/o Galapagos, Inc., 7800 Red Road, Suite 112, South Miami, FL 33143;
☎ 305-665-0841 or 800-327-9854; fax 305-661-1457;
www.galapagoscruises.net

Three-, four-, and seven-night cruises of the Galápagos on a dozen ships as different as the deluxe 100-passenger *Galapagos Explorer II* and the 16-passenger catamaran M/V *Millenium*, which has air-conditioned cabins, each with a private balcony, some with Jacuzzis, Sun Decks, and large social areas.

Skorpios III (49/125)

This is one of several companies that use the ship for their Chile program. *Skorpios III* was constructed in 1994 and 1995 to international standards for SOLAS and A-1 Ice, among others. She is equipped with fire, navigational, security, and lifesaving equipment and satellite phone service. The ship sails every Sunday from Puerto Natales, about 153 miles north of Punta Arenas, on a five-day cruise through the channels and fjords that border the Southern Ice Field in the Chilean Patagonia, considered the third largest reserve of freshwater on the planet and home to the most spectacular glaciers in the Southern Hemisphere.

Hurtigruten

(*See* Norwegian Coastal Cruises and Cruise Ferries later in Part Three.)

International Expeditions

One Environs Park, Helena, AL 35080; ☎ 800-633-4734; fax 205-428-1714; www.ietravel.com

---

Evolution **(16/32)**

The four-deck expedition ship is fully air-conditioned and has 13 cabins and 3 suites that measure about 190 square feet each, including a generous-size bath with shower and hair dryer. There is an Observation Deck, a Sun Deck with a Jacuzzi, a canopied bar on the roof deck, a library/video room, and an infirmary with a doctor aboard every voyage. Meals are served in the dining room in one seating or outdoors, weather permitting. In addition to daily hikes, swimming, and interpretive walks, the ship carries kayaks, snorkeling equipment, and wet suits. All cruises are accompanied by two level three-licensed naturalist guides. Ten-day Galápagos itineraries are offered year-round.

Kleintours

Avenue Eloy Alfaro N 34–151 and Catalina Aldaz, Quito, Ecuador; U.S. ☎ 888-50-KLEIN or 593-2-2267-000; fax 593-2-2442-389; www.kleintours.com; www.gogalapagos.com

---

Coral I **(16/36; 131 FEET)**

Coral II **(20/36; 112.7 FEET)**

These two vessels offer three-, four-, and seven-night cruises. Three-night cruises depart on Sunday; four-night cruises on Wednesday. *Coral I* has eight Junior and eight Moon cabins; *Coral II* has six Junior, four Moon, and two standard cabins.

Galapagos Legend **(57/100; ECUADORIAN/68; 301 FEET)**

Built in Germany in 2002 and refurbished in 2007, this ship has 57 cabins, of which 17 are superior and 4 are inside cabins, 4 are large suites, 8 are balcony suites, and 24 are junior suites; some are interconnected. All cabins are air-conditioned and have a private bathroom, hair dryer, and television. The ship has a dining room—where Continental cuisine and Ecuadorian specialties are served—and a bar, pool, and conference room for up to 70 persons. The ship has a lounge, library, 24-hour coffee bar, meeting room, observatory, jogging track, boutique, and clinic. This boat offers three-, four-, and seven-day cruises. Three-day cruises depart on Monday; four-day cruises depart on Thursday. Seven-night cruises depart on Monday or Thursday. The ship sails year-round from Baltra, accompanied by naturalist guides. Longer itineraries can include stay-overs in Quito, Ecuador.

Lindblad Expeditions
96 Morton Street, Ninth Floor, New York, NY 10014; ☎ 212-765-7740 or 800-397-3348; fax 212-265-3770; www.expeditions.com

Lindblad Expeditions describes its mission as "providing travelers with a more thoughtful way to see the world, avoiding crowded destinations, and seeking out natural ones." The company offers a wide selection of expedition cruises on small ships in various offbeat destinations around the world. The globe-roaming company was founded in 1979 by Sven-Olof Lindblad, son of the late Lars-Eric Lindblad, who pioneered modern expedition cruising. Each cruise is designed to take travelers to remote areas in comfort and safety. Lindblad Expeditions frequently operates cruises for universities or groups.

In 2004, Lindblad took a major step by joining forces with the National Geographic Society to combine their travel and expedition strengths in three broad areas:

1. Creating an education program to enhance passengers' expedition experience and bring the findings to an audience far beyond expedition participants.

2. Adding technological innovations across the Lindblad fleet, with a particular focus on the *National Geographic Explorer*, where state-of-the-art equipment allows for more extensive underwater exploration.

3. Establishing an expert advisory panel of researchers, scientists, and explorers, including oceanographer and National Geographic Society explorer-in-residence Sylvia Earle, to help shape the alliance's conservation, research, and education initiatives. The best part for Lindblad passengers is the opportunity to interact with the National Geographic Society team, as well as Lindblad's expedition leaders and naturalists.

More recently, the two companies moved even closer, with Lindblad adding "National Geographic" to the name of four of its ships.

National Geographic Explorer **(81/148; AMERICAN, EUROPEAN, FILIPINO; 356 FEET)**
The newest addition to the Lindblad fleet, *National Geographic Explorer* (formerly *Lyngen* of Hurtigruten) is a fully stabilized, ice-class 1A expedition ship, enabling it to navigate polar waters while providing onboard comfort. It carries kayaks and a fleet of Zodiacs. An undersea specialist operates a remotely operated vehicle (ROV) and sophisticated video equipment, extending access to the underwater world.

All the ship's cabins are outside ones with windows or portholes, private bathrooms, and climate controls. Accommodations come in ten categories, including 11 cabins with balconies. Most cabins are situated on the Main and Upper decks, the lower two of four passenger decks, and are furnished with twin beds. Some cabins have queen-size beds, and about a dozen can be sold as singles. The cabins have HD video screens on which passengers can watch real-time footage broadcasts of the remote-controlled camera on the crow's nest.

In the restaurant on the Upper Deck, meals are served in single seatings with unassigned tables for an informal atmosphere and easy camaraderie.

Menus are international with a local flair. The Bistro Bar and Global Gallery are also on the Upper Deck.

The ship's other facilities include the glass-lined Observation Lounge and the library next door on the Bridge Deck; a chart room with nautical information and maps forward and the main lounge and bar with facilities for films, slide shows, and presentations; and a Sun Deck aft on the Veranda Deck. One deck up, the Wellness Deck has a small spa with two treatment rooms and a sauna, as well as two wellness specialists and a glass-enclosed fitness center with exercise equipment. The ship has an Internet Cafe, laundry facilities, and a mud room with lockers for expedition gear.

Lindblad's "open bridge" policy provides passengers the opportunity to meet the ship's officers and captain and learn about navigation. In addition to the Zodiacs and kayaks, the ship's expedition equipment includes a remotely operated vehicle (ROV) that can explore the ocean's depth to 1,000 feet, a hydrophone, SplashCam underwater video camera, video microscope, and snorkeling gear. The ship sails on a great variety of cruises from the Arctic and Antarctica to Europe and Asia and places in between.

National Geographic Endeavour (61/96; ECUADORIAN; 295 FEET)

The *Endeavour*, after being renamed, sailed on its inaugural voyage in April 2005. Throughout the year, the ship operates in the Galápagos.The five-deck ship has a lounge with a bar and facilities for films and lectures, a library, small swimming pool, fitness center, sauna, hair salon, gift shop, and Observation Deck. Meals are served in one seating with unassigned tables in an informal setting. All cabins are outside above the waterline and have windows or portholes and private baths; there are a few singles. The ship provides a passenger e-mail station and laundry services. A doctor and massage therapist are on board. From time to time, the company offers cruises geared to families and others designed for travel photography buffs. Meals offer an international menu with Ecuadorian specialties. The ship carries Zodiac landing craft, snorkeling gear, and wet suits.

National Geographic Islander (24/48; ECUADORIAN; 164 FEET)

Put into Galápagos service in 2004, this fully air-conditioned ship has a lounge with a bar and facilities for films and lectures, a library, small gift shop, doctor's office, and deck space for lounging in the sun or shade. All meals are served in one seating and offer an international menu with Ecuadorian specialties. All cabins on the three-deck ship are outside and have windows and private baths. The ship carries Zodiac landing craft, snorkeling gear, and wet suits. The ship sails in the Galápagos year-round, departing Saturdays, and underscores Lindblad's 40 years of exploration in the region.

Lord of the Glens (29/54; SCOTTISH; 150 FEET)

A classic luxury yacht with rich mahogany finishes and teak decks, the vessel has two lounges, a small library and bar, and two open-air viewing areas. The cabins are outside with large windows (some have portholes), bathrooms with shower, bathrobes, hair dryer, phone, television, and safe. Meals that stress local fare and fresh products are served in a single seating in the room-with-a-view dining room. From May to September, the vessel offers ten-night or longer cruises in the heart of the Scottish Highlands, visiting historic places and extraordinary scenery. For a 14-day trip, the Heart of the Highlands cruise is combined with a Royal Scotsman train ride through countryside between Edinburgh and Inverness.

National Geographic Sea Bird/ National Geographic Sea Lion
(31/62; AMERICAN; 152 FEET)
The twin ships have a lounge with bar and facilities for films and lectures, a library, and outside deck with chairs. All meals, prepared by American chefs, are served in one seating. All cabins on the four-deck ship are outside and have windows (except four on the lower deck that have portlights) and private bath. The ship carries Zodiac landing craft, kayaks, snorkeling gear, and wet suits, and has an e-mail station. From May to September, the ships sail on 7- and 11-night Alaska cruises; in autumn and spring, they move to the Columbia and Snake rivers to Hells Canyon and Lewis and Clark sites, as well as Idaho and Montana. In winter, they offer a series of cruises to Baja California and the Gulf of California, timed for optimum whale watching.

MTS (Melanesian Tourist Services)
**P.O. Box 707, Coastwatchers Avenue, Madang, Papua New Guinea;
or USA Sales Office, MTS, P.O. Box 65515, Tucson, AZ 85728; ☎ 310-809-6700; fax 310-785-0314; www.mtspng.com; e-mail: mtsusa@cox.net**

MTS Discoverer **(21/42; NEW GUINEAN; 117 FEET)**
The *MTS Discoverer* was built exclusively for expeditionary cruising up the mighty Sepik River and around the Bismarck and Trobriand islands. She can cruise for 30 days without the need to take on fuel and water. She is fast, comfortable, and equipped with five tenders and a helicopter (subject to conditions). The vessel is air-conditioned; her facilities include a restaurant, library, in-house television system, bar, lounge, covered deck space, dive shop, laundry, and gift shop. All cabins have private bathroom, satellite phones, and public address system.

The ship meets international safety requirements and is the only vessel of its kind in Papua New Guinea. She sails on four- and five-night cruises on the Sepik River, in addition to seven-night cruises of the Trobriands and the remote islands of Bismarck and North Solomon. The cruises remain flexible to take advantage of the opportunity to witness an authentic local ceremony that may occur along the way or ensure maximum shore time in the villages.

MY Kalibobo Spirit **(10/20; QUEENSLANDER/6–8; 99 FEET)**
Launched in 2008, the *Kalibobo Spirit*, a luxury motor yacht, is the only vessel of her kind in Papua New Guinea, offering charters and scheduled departures of the Sepik River, Bismarck Sea, and Trobriand Islands. The air-conditioned vessel is comprised of four decks with ten cabins. Her facilities include a separate dining room, bar, lounge, satellite telephones, state-of-the-art hydraulic-lift dive platform, dive gear for hire, covered deck space, library, speedboat and Zodiac tenders, and rooftop helipad. She offers five-night cruises on the Sepik and seven- to ten-night cruises of the Trobriands and the

remote islands of the Bismarck and North Solomon seas. Each cruise is flexible and offers passengers the opportunity to witness authentic local events en route and to enjoy maximum shore time in the villages.

MTS, a Papua New Guinea–owned and –operated company, was founded in 1975 to develop the country's tourism in a sustainable manner. MTS operates full inbound services and is based in Madang with offices in Port Moresby, Japan, and North America.

Metropolitan Touring
(*See* entry for Galápagos Cruises.)

National Geographic Expeditions
1145 17th Street NW, Washington, D.C. 20036; ☎ 888-966-8687; www.nationalgeographicexpeditions.com

National Geographic Expeditions offers a wide selection of worldwide programs, including more than 20 cruises or journeys in which a cruise is part of the itinerary. The programs use a total of 16 ships as different as the 227-passenger *Royal Clipper* along the Dalmatian coast and the 64-passenger riverboat *Mekong Pandaw* in Vietnam and Cambodia; five of the ships are operated by Lindblad Expeditions. In 2004, the National Geographic Society and Lindblad Expeditions joined to offer excursions that combine the expertise of both. (See Lindblad Expeditions, page 562, for details.)

Oceanwide Expeditions
15710 JFK Boulevard, Suite 285, Houston, TX 77032;
☎ 800-453-7245 or 281-987-9600; fax 281-987-1140;
www.oceanwide-expeditions.com; e-mail usa@oceanwide-expeditions.com
Oceanwide Expeditions, Bellamypark 9, 4381 CG Vlissingen,
The Netherlands; ☎ +31 (118) 410 410; fax +31 (118) 410 417;
e-mail info@oceanwide-expeditions.com

Antarctic Dream **(42/84; CHILEAN/36; 274 FEET/ PANAMA REGISTRY)**

Noorderlicht **(10/20; DUTCH; 153 FEET/300 TONS)**

Plancius **(53/110; DUTCH/45; 293 FEET/3,175 TONS)**

Professor Multanovskiy/Professor Molchanov **(26/53; RUSSIAN/20; 236 FEET/ 2,140 TONS)**

Netherlands-headquartered Oceanwide Expeditions (OE) specializes in ship-based expeditions to the high northern and southern latitudes, that is, polar voyages and expedition cruises to the Arctic and Antarctica regions. OE is primarily defined by an exploratory educational travel program that allows its participants to spend as much time ashore as possible. OE has had a U.S. and Canada reservations office since 1995. In addition to the polar regions, the line offers expeditions to several remote North and mid-Atlantic islands, such as Ascension and Cape Verde. Even more unusual are its diving expeditions—yes, diving in polar waters—but the line hastens to say that these voyages are not for beginners. You must be a very experienced diver familiar with cold-water diving and dry-suit diving, having completed at least 20 such dives. Before departure, you must show an acceptable diving certificate, logbook, and doctor's current health evaluation. There are two Polar Circle/Antarctic Peninsula voyages with scuba diving options scheduled in 2010.

The onboard language is English, with the exception of special charters that could be in different languages. Some voyages are bilingual. The expedition and hotel personnel speak English, and the onboard programs are presented in English.

Oceanwide Expeditions uses five ships, including its newest polar expedition vessel, *Plancius*, scheduled to make her maiden Antarctic voyage in January 2010, after being completely renovated, renamed, and relaunched. Originally built in 1976 as an oceanographic research vessel for the Royal Dutch Navy named *Hr. Ms. Tydeman*, the ship sailed for the Dutch Navy until June 2004, when she was purchased by Oceanwide Expeditions. The ice-strengthened ice-class-1D ship with a 16-foot draft complies with the latest SOLAS (Safety Of Life At Sea) regulations. With a speed of 10–12 knots and flying the Dutch flag, the vessel is equipped with a diesel-electric propulsion system, which reduces the noise and vibration of its engines.

Plancius is a comfortable, nicely decorated, but not luxurious, vessel with a restaurant/lecture room on Deck 3 and a spacious observation lounge and bar with large windows looking out on full panoramic views on Deck 5. Its large open-deck spaces include a promenade that encircles the vessel on Deck 3, giving passengers excellent opportunities to enjoy the scenery and wildlife. She is equipped with 10 Mark V Zodiacs with 40-horsepower four-stroke outboard engines and has two gangways on her starboard side, ensuring a swift Zodiac operation. The vessel is manned by 17 nautical crew, 19 hotel staff (6 chefs, 1 hotel manager, 1 steward-barman, and 11 cabin stewards), 8 expedition staff (1 expedition leader and 7 guides-lecturers), and 1 doctor.

All of *Plancius*'s 53 passenger cabins have private toilets and showers and are comprised of 4 triple cabins, 39 twin cabins, and 10 twin superior cabins, ranging from 50 to 69 square feet. All cabins are furnished with either two single beds or one queen-size bed, except for the triple cabins, which have bunk beds and a lower bed.

The ice-class 100-A1 *Antarctic Dream*, a Dutch-built ice-reinforced vessel, served the Chilean Navy under the name *Piloto Pardo*. In 2005, she was rebuilt, completely refurbished as an unrestricted, worldwide passenger vessel, and renamed. The Panama-registered vessel with a 15-foot draft has a spacious dining room/observation lounge, bar, lecture room, fitness room plus sauna, boutique, and passenger bridge.

The vessel accommodates 84 passengers in 42 cabins with private toilets and showers. The four suites, 16 superior cabins, and 20 twin cabins located outside have portholes or windows and are furnished with either two separate lower beds or queen beds. Two twin cabins are inside. All cabins have a desk, closed-circuit television, and inter-cabin phone service. Satellite e-mail and phone service are available on the bridge. The vessel is manned by 18 Chilean crew members. The staff consists of a hotel manager, barman, doctor, four chefs and seven waitresses/cabin attendants, an expedition leader, and four guides/lecturers.

Antarctic Dream sails to Spitsbergen and Greenland, departing and ending at Longyearbyen. The captain and expedition leader assess conditions daily to maximize shore time, taking advantage of opportunities to land passengers via Zodiacs and making the best use of the sunlight on long summer days. Onboard lectures are offered by geologists, historians, naturalists, and expedition leaders. Oceanwide Expeditions operates *Antarctic Dream* only in the Arctic.

The ice-class *Noorderlicht* was originally built in 1910 in Flensburg, Germany, as a three-masted schooner. For most of her life she served as a light vessel on the Baltic. In 1991, the present owners purchased the hull and rerigged and refitted her thoroughly, under the rules of "Register Holland." The *Noorderlicht*, with an 11-foot draft and a cruising speed of seven knots, now has a well-balanced two-masted schooner rig and is capable of sailing the seven seas. Her captains have a great deal of ocean sailing experience.

Built in 1983 in Finland, *Professor Multanovskiy* and her twin *Professor Molchanov* (ice class: KM*UL(1)A2) are comfortable oceanographic research vessels. The vessels with a 15-foot draft were strongly built of steel with ice-strengthened hulls (from the bow to about a quarter of the ship's length), which makes them good for cruising polar seas. Their Russian ice-class notation LU(1) is identical with Lloyds Register 1D. They have a good anti-roll system and a range of 70 days of independent operation. The ships (with a speed of 10 to 12 knots) are manned by Russian crews of around 20 each, who are all experienced in ice navigation. Russian captains are recognized experts in polar navigation, and the ships' international expedition leaders and lecturers are highly knowledgeable and dedicated to the protection of the environment.

The ships have a large bridge (where passengers are almost always welcome) and good open deck-viewing areas. They carry full complements of Zodiacs for landings and wildlife viewing in otherwise inaccessible areas. Meals, prepared by international chefs, are served in the dining room, which is also used as the lecture room. Other public areas include a lounge and bar, small library, infirmary, and sauna. After a long-term contract, the ships are scheduled to leave Oceanwide Expeditions at the end of their Antarctic season. These itineraries will be taken over by OE's new *Plancius*.

All Oceanwide Expeditions cruises require that deposits are nonrefundable; emergency medical evacuation insurance is mandatory; passenger names must be as they appear on their passport; passengers must possess a passport with at least six months' validity from the date of departure; and it is the passenger's responsibility to meet visa requirements.

Orion Expeditions Cruises
(*See* Part Two, European, Asian, and Smaller Cruise Lines.)

Quark Expeditions
1019 Boston Post Road, Darien, CT 06820; ☎ 203-656-0499,
203-803-2888 or 800-356-5699; 888-961-2961; fax 203-655-6623;
www.quarkexpeditions.com

This expedition operator, a pioneer in Arctic and Antarctic expedition cruises, handles a large fleet of Russian- and Yugoslavian-built ships for polar travel, all with Russian officers and crew. The fleet includes icebreakers, adventure ships, and expedition ships. All ships are equipped with Zodiacs. Some icebreakers have helicopters. Each voyage is accompanied by an expedition leader, assistant expedition leader, lecturers, and Zodiac pilots who may be from the United States, Europe, Australia, or South America, depending on the destinations and staff expertise. Antarctica departures are varied and include the Antarctic Peninsula, Weddell Sea, South Georgia, Falkland Islands, Ross Sea, New Zealand, and Australian sub-Antarctic islands. Most cruises depart from Ushuaia, Argentina, but some depart from Auckland, New Zealand, or Hobart, Tasmania. The icebreakers sail on various itineraries in the High Arctic and to the North Pole.

In May 2007, Quark Expeditions was acquired by UK-based First Choice Holidays PLC, and has joined First Choice's Activity Holidays sector, a growing international collection of adventure travel companies.

Akademik Shokalskiy **(30/48; RUSSIAN; 213 FEET)**
The *Akademik Shokalskiy*, built in Finland in 1982 for polar and oceanographic research and converted to a passenger ship, was upgraded in 2006. She has two dining rooms, a lounge, bar, library, lecture room, sauna, and infirmary. There are twin and triple cabins; some with private baths and others with shared baths. From November to March, the ice-strengthened adventure ship sails to the Antarctic Peninsula, South Shetlands, South Georgia, and the Falklands round-trip to Ushuaia.

Lyubov Orlova **(59/110; RUSSIAN/70; 295 FEET)**
Built in 1976, refurbished in 1999, and upgraded in 2002 and 2006, this expedition ship is fully equipped with a lounge for lectures and entertainment, library, bar, and a dining room. Accommodations include twin and triple cabins and suites, all with a lower berth, private bathroom, porthole or window, and ample storage. Meals, prepared by international chefs, are served at a single seating in a window-lined dining room. *Orlova* operates cruises to the Antarctic Peninsula and South Georgia during the winter season and is chartered in summer by Cruise North Expeditions for cruises in the Canadian Arctic. (See Cruise North Expeditions earlier in this chapter for information on Canadian Arctic voyages.)

Clipper Adventurer **(61/122; FILIPINO; 330 FEET)**
The *Clipper Adventurer* (the former *Alla Tarasova*), a Russian expedition vessel, was built in 1975 in Yugoslavia. In 1998, the ship received a $15-million renovation, which transformed her into one of the most comfortable and stylish expedition ships afloat. The renovations added a window-lined observation

lounge, library/card room and bar, small gym, beauty salon, covered promenade, observation platform directly below the bridge, and stabilizers. The ship's public rooms are paneled in mahogany and the furnishings upholstered in attractive colors of deep blue, red, and aquamarine. The handsome four-deck vessel with upgraded amenities is well suited for exploration with an A-1 super ice–class rating, great maneuverability, and a shallow draft of 16 feet, enabling her to sail near shorelines, in polar waters, or along scenic riverbanks.

All cabins are outside with large windows or portholes, and average 130 square feet. Twin lower beds are in an L shape or parallel (no queen-size beds). Bathrooms with showers are tiled. Closet and storage space is ample. The ship's three suites have separate seating areas with desks and chairs. There are no elevators.

A window-lined dining room accommodates all passengers at one seating. Service is provided by a cheerful and attentive Filipino staff. The main lounge and bar is the center for talks by naturalists, historians, and other specialists. The Clipper Club lounge near the dining room is the favorite spot for cocktails. One of the ship's best features is a large observation platform directly below the bridge, which is ideal for viewing wildlife or scenery. Promenades on two decks provide additional viewing venues. The ship is equipped with Zodiacs for exploring hard-to-reach places.

The popular *Clipper Adventurer* is used by several other tour companies that offer adventure cruises. She is considered a sister ship of the *Orlova;* however, from personal experience, I can report that the *Clipper Adventurer* is much more comfortable and attractive.

Kapitan Khlebnikov (54/108; RUSSIAN/70; 369 FEET)

This Antarctic icebreaker, built in 1980 and refurbished in 1992 and 2006, became the first ship to circumnavigate Antarctica with passengers in 1997. All cabins and suites are outside ones and have two lower berths, private bath, desk, and large closet. There are two dining rooms, a lounge and bar, conference room, indoor swimming pool, gym and sauna, library of polar books and videos, shop, and small clinic with a doctor. The ship's satellite communication system provides phone, fax, and e-mail facilities when conditions permit.

The icebreaker sails a variety of itineraries in both polar regions. In the Arctic, the ship sails either west to east from Russia to Greenland or east to west from Scandinavia to Greenland. In the Antarctic, the ship sails to the Weddell Sea to visit an emperor penguin rookery and from the Antarctic peninsula to the Ross Sea or from the Weddell Sea to Prydz Bay. The icebreaker is equipped with a helicopter and Zodiacs.

The *Kapitan Khlebnikov* will be retired as an expedition vessel in March 2012 and will return to duty as an escort ship in the Russian Arctic. Quark Expeditions is marking the ship's retirement with an "End of an Era" series of unusual itineraries and special guests. The series begins with a Northwest Passage trip in 2010 and ends with an Antarctica's Far East itinerary from December 6, 2011, to January 5, 2012. In between these cruises, *Khlebnikov* will circumnavigate the Arctic, celebrate the Amundsen and Scott centennials, and return to Tanquary Fjord for the final time.

Ocean Nova **(42/82; RUSSIA/38; 239 FEET)**
Owned by Arctic Umiaq Line, a Greenland-based shipping company, the expedition ship was built in Denmark in 1992, renovated in 1999, and underwent a multimillion-dollar refurbishment in 2006 before joining the Quark fleet in November of that year. The latest renovation enhanced the ship's expedition facilities, added a glass-enclosed observation lounge, and refitted all passenger cabins with new beds, furniture, and fixtures. Her sister ship is expected to debut for the 2008 season. Accommodations include twin, triple, and dedicated single cabins, all with private facilities. Berths can be lower, or a combination of upper and lower. Meals, prepared by international chefs, are served in the dining room at a single seating. The ship also has a lounge/library. *Ocean Nova* sails on ten-day voyages of Antarctica, Falkland Islands, and South Georgia during the winter season.

Akademik Ioffe **(55/109; 53; 386 FEET)**

Akademik Sergey Vavilov **(50/104; 53; 386 FEET)**
Both ships are Finnish, built for the Russian Academy of Sciences and designed to travel quietly during hydro-acoustic research. External stabilizers and a built-in trimming system provide exceptional stability, yet the ships are very maneuverable. Russia-registered *Akademik Ioffe* and *Akademik Sergey Vavilov* have ice-strengthened hulls and a cruising speed in open water of 14.5 knots.

The ships' facilities include a gym, sauna, swimming pool, and one elevator. There is one dining room with unreserved seating, a theater-style presentation room, and a lounge. The bar, which opens in the late afternoon and evening, has a wide selection of wines and spirits. The library stocks a collection of polar-themed books. The clinic is staffed by a licensed doctor.

All cabins have exterior views and either shared, semi-private, or private facilities. Twin cabins have one upper and one lower berth, a writing desk, porthole, washbasin in the cabin, and shared bath facilities. Triples are similar but also include a sofa bed. Other twin cabins with a window and semi-private or private facilities are furnished with one lower berth, one sofa bed, and a desk. Superior cabins have two lower berths, a writing desk, and a window. Suites are furnished with one double berth in a separate sleeping area, one sofa bed, a television and DVD player, and have windows and private facilities. Certain twin cabins are available for single occupancy.

Akademik Ioffe sails to Spitsbergen, Eastern Greenland, Iceland, and the Arctic, while both ships offer voyages to Antarctica, the Falkland Islands, and South Georgia.

St. Helena Line
Andrew Weir Shipping, Ltd., Dexter House, 2 Royal Mint Court, London EC3N 4XX, England; ☎ 44-020-7575-6480; fax 44-020-7575-6200; www.rms-st-helena.com

St. Helena **(49/128; BRITISH, ST. HELENIAN/65)**
The island of St. Helena, a British South Atlantic territory located 1,200 miles off the coast of Africa, may be the world's most significant place with no

airport. For the mountainous island's 4,000 inhabitants, the 6,767-ton Royal Mail Ship (RMS) *St. Helena* provides the sole link to the outside world (at least until the island's new airport opens in 2010). For visitors, the voyage is one of the last true ocean liner experiences, plus it gives passengers the bonus of a full week on the island. The trips begin either at Cape Town, South Africa, and sail via Namibian ports to St. Helena and Ascension islands and return south (about three weeks) or, less frequently, sail from England and call at Las Palmas, Ascension, St. Helena, and on to Cape Town (about four weeks). The 31-day voyage from the U.K. to Capetown costs from £3,299.

The passenger, mail, and cargo service began in 1978 and operates under a contract with the British government. The present ship was purpose-built in a Scottish shipyard in 1989 to serve the islands, offering the comfortable facilities of a small liner for 128 passengers and a British and St. Helenian crew of 65. The 22-day round-trip voyage between Cape Town and St. Helena costs from £1,663.

The homey public rooms include a two-section forward observation lounge with a bar, and a video lounge for screening films and reading. The **Sun Lounge** looks onto the outdoor pool. Here, a light breakfast and lunch are served daily. The dining room, on a lower deck, operates with two reserved sittings at dinner. The food is good British fare, such as tasty soups, curries, roasts, and well-prepared fish.

All plainly furnished cabins are outside, with windows or portholes, twin beds, and upper and lower berths. Most have a private shower and toilet. Budget accommodations, reserved for the Saints, as the St. Helenians are called, are sometimes available for non-island passengers.

The local passengers are Saints—a people of mixed British, South Asian, East Indian, and Malagasy origin—and visitors from Britain, France, Germany, South Africa, and the United States. Cargo includes mail and parcels, refrigerated and frozen food, medical equipment and drugs, construction materials, textbooks, and vehicles. In short, the ship carries everything the islanders require.

During the daily cycle, passengers establish a routine of reading, socializing on deck, visiting the bridge or engine room, and taking a swim or playing deck tennis with the officers. In the evening, the purser hosts games, quizzes, and pantomime, all old-fashioned shipboard fun. There's also a captain's cocktail party.

St. Helena, the principal destination, spreads across the horizon beneath a low cloud clinging to the mountain peaks. The ship anchors off Jamestown, a pastel-colored 19th-century Georgian town sandwiched into a deep valley. Through and round-trip passengers get the bonus of a week on the island while the cargo is discharged and the ship makes a passenger run to Ascension and back. Most visitors stay at two small hotels in Jamestown, while others choose self-catering cottages up in the hills. Jamestown offers a small museum, a pretty Anglican church, a few shops, and a couple of restaurants, but the principal attraction is Main Street, the island's social center where everyone gathers to talk.

Napoleon spent six years here, from 1815 until his death in 1821; Longwood, his permanent residence and gardens, is open to visitors. Nearby,

Deadwood Plain is home to the island's indigenous wire bird. The governor's house, a handsome 1791 Georgian mansion, is home to a giant Seychellois tortoise named Jonathan, reputed to be about 175 years old. There are miles of walking trails around the coast and down to secluded bays. After a week, the ship returns to the island and embarks passengers for a continuation of the voyage. Once a year, the *St. Helena* also makes a three-week round-trip voyage to the even more remote island of Tristan da Cunha, located about halfway between South Africa and South America. This one sells out well in advance.

Voyages of Discovery

(*See* Part Two, European, Asian, and Smaller Cruise Lines.)

Wilderness Travel

1102 Ninth Street, Berkeley, CA 94710; ☎ 510-558-2488 or 800-368-2794; fax 510-558-2489; www.wildernesstravel.com

This adventure tour company offers Galápagos programs almost year-round, some with up to three departures monthly. The company combines cruises on small yachts with hiking in areas not usually covered by conventional excursions. As an example, the *Sagitta* (10/16; 120 feet), a sailing yacht, boasts three full masts; two decks; cabins with private bathrooms, hot showers, and air-conditioning; a library; dining room; salon; and conference room with video. The crew is made up of the captain, first mate, engineer, two sailors, a cook and assistant, cabin attendant, and naturalist guide.

The *Diamante* (6/12; 112 feet), a brigantine schooner motor sailer, is a modern, scaled-down version of the great naval training ships. She has an airy deckhouse that includes the main salon/dining room. The beamed salon is decorated with beautiful mahogany and teak and offers 360-degree visibility onto the passing scenery. It is also possible to dine outside, around a teak table aft of the pilothouse. The six cabins have upper and lower berths, private facilities with fresh hot- and cold-water showers.

The company also has a combination cruise of the Galápagos and the haciendas of Ecuador, with an optional extension to the Amazon rain forest; and a full program of expedition cruises to Antarctica and the South Pacific.

NORWEGIAN COASTAL CRUISES *and* CRUISE FERRIES

THE CRAGGY COAST OF NORWAY, deeply indented like the fingers on your hand, was carved eons ago by massive glaciers. Crevasses, which we call fjords, can be ten miles long. From their dark, mirror-like waters rise almost vertical cliffs, and awesome mountains climb to several thousand feet on each side.

Often at the head of fjords are snow-capped peaks. In some places, glaciers inch toward the North Sea. Along the shores are tiny fishing villages and isolated farmhouses. Farther up the mountains are lodges where hikers bed down in summer and Olympic hopefuls fine-tune their skiing in winter.

The setting is beautiful; late May through early autumn is ideal for cruising, although the other months are popular with some for the unusual experience those times offer. Most major lines with ships in Europe offer Norwegian fjord cruises, mostly in May and June. Itineraries differ slightly, but the program is essentially the same: departing from Bergen, Copenhagen, Dover, Harwich, or Oslo and going as far north as Trondheim, Norway's original capital and third-largest city, or Tromso, the largest town north of the Arctic Circle. Others continue to the North Cape, the northernmost point in Europe, and to Spitsbergen, a group of islands studded with massive glaciers. Another way to cruise the coast—the way Norwegians do—is on the Hurtigruten (formerly known in the U.S. market as Norwegian Coastal Express).

On the Coastal Express

Billed as the world's most beautiful voyage, especially when the weather cooperates, the Coastal Express offers relaxed and informal adventure. Aboard the *Kong Harald*, the feeling is that of a small, modern floating hotel. On the first morning at sea, a sheer mountain wall plunges into the narrow channel, and, to port, Norwegian Sea breakers pile up against low-lying islands. At a briefing, the courier reminds everyone that this is a working ship and that local passengers will be boarding and leaving at each port. The diesel engine throbs rhythmically in the background. At Bodo, a city at the northern end of Norway's main rail line, about 100 passengers typically board for the six-hour crossing to the Lofoten Islands. Automobiles come aboard, and forklifts maneuver whole fish, bundles of evergreen saplings, and building materials.

During brief port calls, you can walk briskly to the main shopping street to buy souvenirs and newspapers. On one excursion, during the stop at Harstad, passengers attend a short worship service in a fortress church. There are visits to the North Cape promontory; an excursion from Kirkenes, the voyage's turnaround port, to the Russian border; and a cruise into the **Trollfjord,** a one-mile passage between sheer rock cliffs bubbling with falling water. The moon reflects in the turning basin as the captain revolves his ship in a tight half circle. During the warmer months, the ship sails well inland to take in the spectacular **Geirangerfjord.** By voyage's end, round-trip passengers have shared a 2,500-mile feast of dramatic scenery, shore visits, fresh—if somewhat repetitious—food, and constantly changing weather.

Hurtigruten
5100 NW 33rd Avenue, Suite 256, Fort Lauderdale, FL 33309;
☎ **866-552-0371; fax 954-486-9340; www.hurtigruten.us**

Eleven passenger-cargo ships, known as Hurtigruten ("fast route" in Norwegian), operate a daily passenger and cargo service from Bergen to 35 ports on Norway's coast, well beyond the North Cape to Kirkenes, near the Russian border. A Norwegian institution since 1893, the ships operate year-round through all weather and are a lifeline for the people in small, often isolated communities along the way. The vessels, while increasingly cruise-oriented, provide transportation for locals and haul cargo ranging from automobiles and farm equipment to frozen fish.

The ships also carry tourists who may board and disembark at any port. Many visitors, however, take the 2,500-mile round-trip voyage as a 12-day cruise. Others sail one-way and return by road or air. (Some open-water passages can be rough; passengers should come prepared.)

Time in port varies from as little as 15 minutes to several hours. There are shore excursions that start at about $40 for a simple town tour and go up to $200 or more for dog sledding or a snowmobile safari. A few trips leave the ship at one port, travel inland, and rejoin it at another.

The best time to make the trip is mid-May to July, the period with 24 hours of daylight. Some travelers prefer the quieter months of early spring and fall. Summer sailings fill quickly, although space is often available at short notice. During the off-season, cabins usually are plentiful.

In the height of summer, some stretches are crowded with deck passengers, especially between the mainland and islands. Generally, about half of the passengers are local commuters or those attending an onboard conference; the balance is an international mix. There are usually quite a few English-speaking people, and always many Germans. Announcements are made in the languages required by passenger makeup. Meals are served at two seatings when traffic warrants. Breakfast and lunch are buffet-style. Dinner is from a set menu; tables are reserved. Dietary requests should be made when booking. Continental and Norwegian dishes are served. Lunch offers the widest selection of hot and cold foods. Because of hefty taxes, alcoholic beverages are expensive—$7 or more for a beer is common. Entertainment is limited to the gorgeous scenery, enlivened by commentary, good conversation, cargo handling, and the festive occasion of crossing the Arctic Circle. The line provides an excellent guidebook. In summer, the newest ships might have a band for dancing.

Hurtigruten markets the service in North America. The service has 11 ships in four classifications: Millennium, Contemporary, Midgeneration, and Traditional. In addition, the newly built exploration ship, MS *Fram* was launched in April 2007.

Millennium Ships

The *Finnmarken* and *Trollfjord*, completed in spring 2002, and the *Midnatsol*, completed in 2003, are 15,000 tons and take 643, 674, and

674 passengers, respectively. Of the three new ships, the *Finnmarken* appears to be the more innovative, with features such a Jugend-style (Art Nouveau) interiors, an indoor/outdoor cafe, wine bar, two panoramic lounges, an indoor pool, a racquet court and gym, four conference rooms, and 14 suites with private balconies. The *Trollfjord* has 21 suites (8 with balconies), glass elevators, a sauna and fitness room, and eight conference rooms. The cargo is handled via ramps through the side doors. The standard amenities are the same as the new ships. The *Midnatsol*, meaning "the midnight sun," has its interiors dedicated to the Norwegian summer, and natural light pours in through the big glass windows. Like the *Trollfjord*, the ship has some suites with balconies, as well as such amenities as a sauna, gym, and library. All three Millennium vessels have an Internet cafe.

Contemporary Ships

The *Kong Harald, Nordkapp, Nordlys, Polarlys*, and *Richard With*, all completed since 1993, add to the Hurtigruten the concept of the cruise ferry, with its greater comfort (well established and popular in Baltic waters). Large and boxy (390 feet long and 63 feet wide), the ships take as many as 490 passengers in relatively roomy accommodations. Cargo is handled via ramps.

The modern cabins are mostly outside. They have foldaway beds and two lower berths, audio channels, automated wake-up calls, tiled baths with showers, and hair dryers.

Public rooms have the fashionable look of modern cruise ships, with rich fabrics, thick carpets, and ample use of brass, glass, and veneers. Norwegian sculptures and painted seascapes are attractive features. A top-deck wraparound observation lounge is for viewing. A middle deck offers a cocktail lounge, library/card room, conference rooms, a souvenir shop, playroom, video arcade, 24-hour cafeteria, 240-seat restaurant, and private dining room. Also aboard are a sauna, small gym, and passenger laundry.

Midgeneration Ships

The *Vesteraalen*, built in 1983, then rebuilt and enlarged later in the same decade and refurbished in 1995, carry up to 320 passengers. Cabins are smaller and decidedly plainer, but most are outside, and all have private bathrooms with showers. The ship has a forward-facing observation lounge and glass-enclosed top-deck lounge. Freight and vehicles are handled via a roll-on ramp.

Traditional Ships

The 114-passenger *Nordstjernen*, built in 1956, is one of two remaining Traditional ships. She has very small outside and inside cabins, some without private facilities. The best cabins sell out fast. The ship possesses rich character, teak decks, and a battered hull from thousands of dockings. There are two lounges (the forward facing one is nonsmoking), a restaurant, and a cafeteria, the latter used by short-run passengers. Cargo and vehicles are loaded by crane. This ship is no longer in year-round service.

Hurtigruten also sells the 100-passenger *Polar Star*, an expedition ship rebuilt from a Swedish icebreaker, on eight-day Spitsbergen circumnavigation packages from Longyearbyen. *Polar Star* sails along Spitsbergen's northwest coast to the Russian mining town of Barentsburg, Prins Karl Forland Island, the Ny-Alesund research center, old whaling sites, spectacular fjords, and, weather and ice permitting, cross the 80° N.L. line. The more comprehensive *Polar Star* voyages continue along the coast to fjords in the archipelago's isolated northern and eastern regions. The ship's route and landing sites depend on weather and ice conditions, adding Hinlopen Strait and glacier-covered Nordaustlandet Island. The ship also offers cruises to Greenland, Iceland, Labrador, and Newfoundland.

The *Lofoten*, the second of the classic ships, was completed in 1964 and given a major refit in 2003. Her maritime character and paneled interiors are a well-maintained delight. With berths for 171 passengers, her cabins are small, with the majority having upper and lower berths; about half have private facilities. There are two forward observation lounges from which to watch the cargo handling, a dining room spanning the width of the ship, a cafeteria, and a bar aft. In the summer, the *Lofoten* is used on a fjords cruise program, including the 11-day Lofoten Islands and Western Fjords and 10-day Fjords to the North cruises.

In 2009, Hurtigruten introduced a layaway payment program, which enables passengers to make monthly, no-interest payments for voyages on any of its ships.

Fram Expedition Ship

Hurtigruten became even more active in expedition cruises to Greenland and Antarctica, with the addition of its deluxe expedition ship, the 12,700-ton MS *Fram* (136 cabins/318 berths). Launched in April 2007, the ship was built especially for cruising the iceberg-laden waters around Greenland and in Antarctica.

The eight-deck *Fram*, built at the Italian shipyard Fincantieri, was named after the polar ship built and used by Norwegian explorer Fridtjof Nansen on a three-year expedition around Greenland in the late 1800s. Greenland's culture inspired the ship's interior design, while at the same time incorporating a Scandinavian feel with the extensive use of wool, leather, and oak.

Continuing Hurtigruten's tradition of having original artwork as a theme on all its ships, Ane Birthe Hove from Nuuk, Greenland, was chosen as the ship's main artist, and several other artists from Greenland and Norway were given commissions. The ship's architect, Arne Johansen, made use of concept terms from the Inuit language in describing the design philosophy: **Imaq,** or "sea," describes the ship's main dining room, situated aft and close to the sea; **Nunami** means "ashore," and refers to the forward areas where the main reception and lobby are situated; and **Qilak,** or "sky," is the term for the ship's glass-enclosed observation salon, offering panoramic views of the outside scenery—from the sea to the sky. Additional highlights include meeting facilities; a wellness center with saunas, workout room, and two glass-screened heated outdoor whirlpools; a bistro; a passenger bridge viewing selected data from the ship's bridge; and her library. The ship carries Polarcirkels, similar to Zodiacs, for up-close viewing.

Accommodations vary, sometimes within the same category, in size and location. The suites range from about 194 square feet for mini-suites to 484 square feet for Grand Suites, some with a balcony. Suites and outside cabins on higher decks usually have picture windows, while cabins on lower decks have portholes. Of the ship's 136 cabins, six of the seven Grand Suites are aft on Decks 5 and 6, overlooking the wake. Also on these decks are 32 suites and mini-suites that are the most desirable of the ship's accommodations. All suites have a sitting area and are attractively furnished with a double bed (some suites have two beds), shower and toilet, hair dryer, and mini-bar. All suites and cabins have a television.

The 69 standard and 24 inside cabins are comfortable but considerably smaller and differ mostly in location and size. All are furnished with a bed or sofa bed, fridge, shower and toilet, and hair dryer. The cabins that can accommodate third and fourth persons have bunk beds. Two cabins (172 square feet to 215 square feet) are equipped for disabled passengers and are located on Deck 3 near the elevator. The ship's gangway accommodates wheelchairs.

In 2010, from early June to early July, the MS *Fram* sails on five itineraries in the Spitsbergen region; these are followed by six Greenland voyages of 8 to 15 days from mid-July to late September, departing from Copenhagen or Kangerlussuaq. Two itineraries explore the island's west and east coasts above the Arctic Circle. Two itineraries visit the southern area of Greenland, including Nuuk (the largest, oldest town), and the island's capital, as well as Iceland.

The *Fram*'s Antarctic cruises begin November 1, 2010, from Buenos Aires or Ushuaia and continue to mid-March 2011. There are seven itineraries, ranging from 10 to 19 days, which combine trips to Argentina and Antarctica or the Chilean fjords or the Falklands, South Georgia, and Antarctica.

For the first time, the *Fram* departs from Britain to Norway in April 2010. Also new are the Fram's springtime itineraries in Europe to Spain, Portugal, Germany, Sweden, Russia, and Finland.

Due to the growing popularity of Arctic cruises, Hurtigruten has added the 120-passenger *MS Expedition* to join the *Polar Star* on three Spitsbergen itineraries that range from 9 to 16 days. The *MS Expedition*, built in 1972, was completely rebuilt and modernized in 2008 and has a panorama lounge, restaurant, library, bar, fitness room, sauna, and a fleet of Zodiacs. All cabins are outside with a window or porthole and private facilities.

If you need polar expedition gear, Hurtigruten recently launched Hurti-Gear, an online logo-apparel shop at **www.hurti-gear.com**. The comprehensive collection has apparel for almost any outdoor activity, including windproof, waterproof, insulating, and quick-drying items, as well as waterproof binoculars, backpacks, and a bug- and sun-protection kit.

EUROPEAN CRUISE FERRIES

"CRUISE FERRY" IS AN INADEQUATE TERM for a sophisticated breed of ships that take passengers on overnight sea voyages but provide most of the comforts and amenities of a deluxe liner. Still, that's the name. And cars, recreational vehicles, and large trucks are indeed below deck.

Operating throughout Northern Europe, the ferries crisscross the Baltic and North seas, linking cities such as Copenhagen and Oslo, Stockholm and Helsinki, and Newcastle and Amsterdam. Creative train-ferry itineraries often include the Eurail Pass network. Most passengers are Scandinavians (Danish, Finnish, Norwegian, Swedish), traveling to visit Scandinavian friends and relatives or simply cruising. Germans are second-most numerous among passengers. North Sea sailings also attract Britons.

Larger, newer ships offer varied restaurants. Options include à la carte dining of high quality; a 60-item smorgasbord; and simpler, cheaper cafeteria meals. After-dinner entertainment includes cabarets, dancing, gambling, and films. There are playrooms, video arcades, saunas, and on some ships, duty-free shopping (purchases can be rolled to checkout in supermarket carts). English is widely spoken.

Cabins vary from well-appointed rooms with windows and cruise-ship amenities to large family cabins with private showers. Most accommodations are away from the activity and noise of public rooms. Young Scandinavians come aboard to party on weekend sailings, so be prepared for some public drunkenness.

The following lines are represented in North America. They offer the most extensive routes and some of the newest and most sophisticated ships. However, they're only a sampling of a wider network spanning all European seas, including the Mediterranean. Most major intercity services operate year-round. Ships occasionally may change routes or be sold.

Color Line

Norwegian-based Color Line operates four international cruise ferry lines between seven ports in Norway, Germany, Denmark, and Sweden. For example, it sails between Oslo, Norway, and Kiel, Germany; and between Kristiansand and Hirtshals in northern Denmark. The largest and most impressive of its ships are *Color Fantasy* and *Color Magic,* which are an amazing 75,000 tons and can carry up to 2,700 passengers—more than twice the size of the former *Kronprins Harald.* Both of these vessels operate the Oslo-to-Kiel route and leave daily from either port for the 20-hour overnight run. The ships enter and leave Oslo via the scenic Oslofjord, a two-hour stretch. Most passengers are German or Norwegian. Ship details, timetables, and prices are available on the Web site, **www.colorline.com.**

THE FLEET	BUILT/RENOVATED	TONNAGE	PASSENGERS
Bohus	1971	8,772	1,422
Color Fantasy	2004	76,600	2,770
Color Magic	2007	75,100	2,700
Color Viking	1985	19,763	1,720
Superspeed	2008	34,231	1,929

DFDS Seaways

Danish-owned DFDS Seaways operates cruise ferries between England and Denmark, England and the Netherlands, and Denmark and Norway.

The largest ships operate between Copenhagen and Oslo, with scenic departures from both cities at 5 p.m. and arrival about 9 a.m. the next day. The northbound route from Copenhagen passes Hamlet's Castle at Helsingor and enters the Oslofjord at dawn. Two-night round-trip cruises are popular from Oslo and Copenhagen. They give passengers time ashore between the morning arrival and late-afternoon departure. The Copenhagen pier is adjacent to the central business district, and the Oslo pier is a short walk from the city's center.

DFDS departs year-round from Harwich, England, which can be reached by boat or train from London. It has year-round, overnight services three to

THE FLEET	BUILT/RENOVATED	TONNAGE	PASSENGERS
Crown of Scandinavia	1994	35,498	2,026
Dana Sirena	2002	22,400	600
King of Scandinavia	1987	31,395	2053
Pearl of Scandinavia	1989/2001	40,039	2,166
Princess of Scandinavia	1986/2006	31,360	1,300

four times a week to Esbjerg on the Danish west coast. Additional sailings operate from Newcastle to Ijmuiden (Amsterdam). See the Web site for more information: **www.dfdsseaways.com.**

Silja Line

Operating some of the largest cruise ferries, Silja Line is the best-known Scandinavian ferry company. The ships are cities at sea; some carry as many as 3,000 passengers. In 2007, Silja Line was acquired by Tallink Line (see section that follows), and the three vessels above maintain the two overnight Finland-to-Sweden routes: Helsinki to Stockholm and Turku to Stockholm.

THE FLEET	BUILT/RENOVATED	TONNAGE	PASSENGERS
Silja Europa	1993	59,914	3,013
Silja Serenade	1990	58,376	2,852
Silja Symphony	1991	58,377	2,852

Although busy, the ships are designed to avert crowding and long queues. Cruise ship–style atriums are the centerpiece; nearby are eateries, lounges, and bars for all incomes. The prestige route is Stockholm to Helsinki. A ship leaves each port at 5 every night year-round (the sun shines until 10 p.m. or later in summer, this being the Land of the Midnight Sun) and arrives the next day at 9:30 a.m. The extended passage time includes a middle-of-the-night call in the Aland Islands that permits the continuation of duty-free shopping, a major attraction for high-taxed Scandinavians. The two-hour passage through the Stockholm archipelago is a highlight; to enjoy the entire transit, be up before 7 a.m. The ship docks conveniently next to central Helsinki; passengers on the two-night round-trip have the day ashore. Extended stopovers are easily arranged. Arrival in Stockholm is slightly less convenient, with a subway connection to the city center.

The Stockholm to Turku, Finland, route is offered twice daily, with overnight and daylight taking about 11 hours.

Tallink Silja Line

Tallink Silja Oy is one of the leading passenger and cargo shipping companies in the Baltic. The Tallink brand began in 1989, as a Finnish-Soviet joint venture with one chartered vessel, the Tallink ferry, primarily to transport tourists on the 48-mile route between Helsinki and Tallinn. Over the next decade, the company grew, always with chartered vessels, until 1997, when a new management team acquired three vessels. The following year, the company hit a milestone of 2 million passengers. Between 2002 and 2004, Tallink acquired two high-class cruise ferries, *Romantika* and her sister vessel, *Victoria I,* and added two new high-speed ships in 2007 and 2008. The same year, Tallink was listed on the Tallinn Stock Exchange.

In 2006, Tallink introduced its new 48,915-ton cruise vessel *Galaxy* to operate between Helsinki and Tallinn, acquired three *Superfast* ferries, started operating between Finland and Rostok, Germany, and in 2007, finalized the

THE FLEET	BUILT/RENOVATED	TONNAGE	PASSENGERS
Baltic Princess	2008	48,915	2,800
Baltic Queen	2009	28,900	2,800
Silja Festival	1986/92	34,414	1,916
Star	2007	33,000	1,900
SuperFast VII, VIII, IX	2001	30,285	676/728
Superstar	2008	36,400	2,080
Tallink Romantika	2002	40,000	2,500
Tallink Victoria I	2004	40,000	2,500

acquisition of Silja Line, one of the largest, best-known Scandinavian ferry companies. It also launched a new service, the Tallink Shuttle, providing scheduled service year-round in all weather conditions between Helsinki and Tallinn. The Shuttle has four restaurants, two bars and more than 1,500 square meters of shopping area, and a business class where one can relax in a quiet setting, enjoy a meal, and use the fax and Internet. *Baltic Princess* and *Baltic Queen*, similar to *Galaxy*, were added in 2008 and 2009. **www.tallinksilja.com/en**

Viking Line

The red-hulled ships of Viking Line, Silja Line's main competitor, cruise similar routes. The Stockholm-to-Turku daylight voyage calls at Mariehamn in the beautiful Aland Islands, about halfway between Sweden and Finland. The Stockholm-to-Helsinki route may be taken as a two-night round-trip cruise that includes two dinners and two breakfasts. The berth in Stockholm is closer to the city center than Silja's, while the Helsinki location is similar—just on the opposite side of South Harbor. The Web site has ship details, timetables, and prices: **www.vikingline.fi**. Viking Line has a ship under construction. The 1,500-passenger *Viking ADCC*, slated for 2010, will sail on the Mariehamn-to-Kapellskär route.

THE FLEET	BUILT/RENOVATED	TONNAGE	PASSENGERS
Amorella	1988	34,384	2,450
Cinderella	1989	46,398	2,500
Gabriella	1992	35,492	2,420
Isabella	1989	35,154	2,450
Mariella	1985	37,860	2,500
Rosella	1980	16,850	1,700
Viking ADCC	2009	15,600	1,500
Viking XPRS	2008	34,000	2,500

INFORMATION AND RESERVATIONS

Borton Overseas (for Viking Line)
5412 Lyndale Avenue South
Minneapolis, MN 55419
☎ 612-822-4640 or 800-843-0602; FAX 612-822-4755
www.bortonoverseas.com or www.vikingline.fi

DFDS Seaways (USA) Inc. and **Silja Line**
6801 Lake Worth Road, Suite 107
Lake Worth, FL 33567
☎ 800-533-3755 ext. 114; FAX 561-432-2550
www.seaeurope.com; www.silja.com; www.tallinkusa.com

Nordic Saga Tours (for Color Line)
303 Fifth Avenue South, Suite 109
Edmonds, WA 98020
☎ 800-848-6449 or 425-673-4800; FAX 425-673-2600
www.nordicsaga.com or www.colorline.com

The tour operator also represents Scandinavian Seaways, Fjord Line, and other European cruise ferries.

Traghettionline S.r.l.
Via Brigata Liguria 4, 16121
Genoa, Italy
www.traghettionline.net

Traghettionline, an Italian company with years of experience in sea transportation, provides information on some 90 ferry companies in Europe, North America, Australia, and Asia on its Web site. The Internet service enables users to book a ferry, receive the ticket directly at home, and pay with a credit card or bank transfer.

SAILING SHIPS

PEOPLE CHOOSE TO CRUISE FOR REASONS as diverse as the amazingly wide range of ships, itineraries, and services available. For many, however, there is a longing that transcends midnight buffets, luxurious cabins, and myriad ports of call. These are individuals who are transfixed and enchanted by the lure of the sea itself. The feeling of being underway, the buffeting wind, the salt sea spray over the bow, and the twinkling phosphorescent wake are to them the stuff of dreams. There is no bingo, afternoon tea, or stylish air-conditioned lounge for these folks. Rather, you'll find them on deck leaning on the starboard rail, taking in every white-capped wave.

Almost all are landlubbers—individuals whose imagination draws them to the sea—and many of them first experience the sea aboard a large, modern cruise ship. It doesn't take long for them to realize, however, that no matter how grand a particular floating resort might be, they desire a much more intimate relationship with the sea. Opting for a smaller cruise ship does the trick for some, but for others it's not enough. Sooner or later, these folks discover the wonderful world of cruising under sail.

Cruising under sail is cruising in concert with the sea. By definition, sailing uses currents, tides, and winds to the advantage of the sailor, always working with natural forces and never against them. Pursuing this harmony precipitates any number of outcomes (the elements are not always cooperative, you know), but it's always an adventure. Bringing home the reality of weather and sea conditions, sailing is for many a life-changing experience—an epiphany.

If you want to try sailing, you have a wide selection of alternatives. Choices range from medium-size cruise ships with computer-controlled sails and powerful, supplemental engines to tiny schooners with no motor at all, where every passenger must help work the boat. Accommodations range from conventional cruise-ship staterooms to tiny cabins accessible only by descending a ladder through a hatch. Some voyages are veritable courses in sailing and seamanship; others demand nothing beyond normal cruise ship passenger passivity.

If you've not sailed before, if you enjoy the amenities of a larger cruise ship, or you're uncertain how much of an adventure you want, consider sailing with either **Star Clippers** or **Windstar Cruises** (both described in detail in Part Two, Cruise Lines and Their Ships). Star Clippers operates four- and five-masted, square-rigged ships with small (by cruise ship standards), air-conditioned cabins with private baths. You'll find a small pool, a library, and even a piano lounge. Star Clippers vessels carry a maximum of 170 or 227 passengers, depending on the vessel.

Windstar, which operates three four-masted ships with triangular sails, costs about $350 to $550 per day before any applicable discounts, compared with an average non-discounted per diem of about $268 on Star Clippers. Two Windstar ships carry about 150 passengers, and one ship, *Wind Surf*, accommodates 308. Cabins on these ships approximate the size of those on mainstream cruise ships, and there's even a casino and a disco. Whereas a crew sets the sails in the traditional way aboard Star Clippers ships (you can pitch in if you want), sails on Windstar are computer-controlled. Ships of both lines have powerful diesel-electric engines. Windstar uses its engines for propulsion up to 50% of the time, whereas Star Clippers employs its engines primarily to get into and out of port.

Similar to Windstar's *Wind Surf* is **Club Med's** five-masted, computer-controlled sailing ship *Club Med 2*. The length of two football fields, *Club Med 2* carries almost 400 passengers with a per diem ranging from $130 to more than $350, depending on season and itinerary. Smaller, luxury ships with large cabins and many mainline cruise ship amenities are **Sea Cloud's Cruises'** *Sea Cloud* (64 passengers) and *Sea Cloud II* (94 passengers). The sailing cruise lines mentioned in this section offer itineraries that can take you all over the world.

Less expensive, but offering a more authentic, hands-on experience are the **Maine Windjammer Association** cruises and **Windjammer Barefoot Cruises.** The Maine Windjammer Association is the marketing arm for 12 individually owned and operated traditional tall ships, all schooners, ranging in size from 46 to 132 feet. The fleet operates exclusively along the midcoast region of Maine, with the majority of itineraries in the verdant, island-studded waters of Penobscot Bay. Most of the schooners were built between 1871 and 1945 as working boats for hauling cargo or fishing and were converted to passenger-carrying ships within the last 20 years or so. Nine of the 12 schooners are designated National Historic Landmarks.

Cruises depart Camden, Rockland, or Rockport from May through October for three- to six-day itineraries that include short ports of call at small islands and at historic Maine coastal villages. Days, for the most part, are spent sailing. The schooners anchor in protected coves or tie up at small, picturesque maritime communities at night. Meals are served family-style, sometimes in the galley and sometimes on deck, and feature local produce and seafood, among other selections. A lobster bake on a forested island is a highlight of many cruises. While most of the schooners accommodate 12 to 29 guests, the 46-foot *Mistress* carries only 6, and the *Victory Chimes*, the largest sailing vessel flying American colors, carries 40.

About 1,000 miles south, the Caribbean is home water to Windjammer Barefoot Cruises. Although the names are similar ("windjammer" is nautical slang for a seaman on a sailing ship), Windjammer Barefoot Cruises is related to the Maine Windjammers in concept only. Windjammer Barefoot Cruises operates four sailing vessels and one motorized vessel year-round, on a variety of 6- to 13-day Caribbean and Bahamas itineraries, particularly the Eastern Caribbean, including the Grenadines, and farther south to Aruba, Bonaire, Curaçao, and occasionally Panama and Costa Rica.

All of its sailing craft are larger than those of the Maine fleet, with the largest carrying 122 passengers and the smallest 64. Facilities are not as extensive as those of the *Sea Clouds, Club Med 2*, or Clipper and Windstar ships described earlier, but are more luxurious than those of the relatively spartan Maine fleet. Most Windjammer Barefoot cabins are air-conditioned and offer a private bath. Air-conditioning isn't generally needed in Maine, and schooner passengers usually share toilet and bathing facilities. Dining is of comparable quality in both fleets, with meals distinguished by fresh, locally available meat, seafood, vegetables, and fruit. On both Maine Windjammer and Windjammer Barefoot vessels, you can help the crew sail the ship. On the Barefoot cruises, however, such activity is take-it-or-leave-it, while Maine schooner captains frequently count on passengers to help out. On ships of either fleet, you can avail yourself of a fairly extensive sailing education during your time aboard.

For all the similarities, however, there are likewise some striking differences. The Maine experience is all about sailing, while the Barefoot ships spend most of the day in port or anchored in a secluded cove, where diving, water sports, or sunning are the main attractions. In fact, on a Barefoot cruise, most of the sailing is done between the hours of dinner and breakfast—the exact opposite of a Maine schooner.

If you think this type of cruising will appeal to you, take a moment to check out the respective Windjammer Web sites (**www.sailmaine coast.com** and **www.windjammer.com**). Potentially critical differences will become immediately apparent. The Caribbean cruise line's site screams fun, sun, and warm-weather delights. The Maine Windjammers' site, in contrast, emphasizes the peace and serenity of sailing, rugged Maine coastline scenery, and maritime skills and history. On Barefoot cruises, morning Bloody Marys, afternoon rum swizzles, and wine with dinner are provided in the price of the cruise. On a Maine schooner, no alcohol at all is served or sold, except at lobster bake events, though passengers are invited to bring their own private stock. Days start early in Maine, while in the Caribbean, sleeping in is definitely an option.

Climate additionally differentiates the two sail cruise options. The Caribbean is a perfect destination during the cold-weather months of the year, while Maine offers a great escape from the heat during the summer and early fall.

Finally, regardless which cruise line you choose, you should know that seasickness is rare on sailing ships. This is because the wind stabilizes the ship in the water and prevents almost all of the side-to-side rolling motion that is the primary cause of seasickness.

Note: In parentheses after each boat name is information about the number of cabins and passengers; officers and crew; and the boat's length (cabins/passengers; officers/crew; boat length).

Atlantic Stars Hotels and Cruises
Christie's Landing, Newport, RI 02840; ☎ 800-395-1343;
www.atlanticstars.com

Arabella **(20/40; AMERICAN; 160 FEET)**

Favored by sailing enthusiasts, romance seekers, and travelers who enjoy soft adventure, *Arabella*, a luxury schooner, offers cruises from late December through early May throughout the British and U.S. Virgin Islands, as well as St. Maarten, which the ship uses as a home port for part of the winter when she visits St. Kitt's and Nevis.

The Caribbean excursions, combining sailing, swimming, kayaking, and snorkeling with day trips and island dining, depart from St. Thomas on six-night sails. One sample itinerary might include St. John, U.S.V.I., and Norman Island; Jost Van Dyke, Tortola, Virgin Gorda, and Peter Island, B.V.I.; and Culebra and Vieques, Puerto Rico.

Arabella has 20 air-conditioned cabins, each with satellite television, viewing portholes, private bath, and communications capabilities that allow guests to conduct business while at sea. She also houses an on-deck hot water spa, a lounge and bar, and water sports equipment for passenger use.

Rates for Caribbean cruises range from $1,050 to $2,395 per person, based on double occupancy, and include all daytime meals, four dinners ashore, and optional excursions. The cruise departs Sunday afternoon and returns to St. Thomas on Saturday at or before noon. At the end of her Caribbean season, *Arabella* sails north in the spring (and south in the fall) and spends June through October along the eastern seaboard. Summer and fall cruises of five nights from Newport stop in Nantucket, Martha's Vineyard, Cuttyhunk, and Provincetown. Those cruises start at $1,100 per person, double occupancy. In October, she is in Chesapeake Bay for a cruise and is a part of the Annapolis Sailboat Show. She also participates with guests in the annual Great Chesapeake Bay Schooner Race.

Arabella is part of the Newport-based Atlantic Stars Hospitality Group, which has hotels in New York City, Newport, Miami Beach, and Martha's Vineyard; a restaurant in South Beach, Miami; and cruise vessels on day trips around Newport Harbor and Narragansett Bay.

Club Med
75 Valencia Avenue, Coral Gables, FL 33134; ☎ 800-CLUB MED or 800-258-2633; fax 305-443-0562; www.clubmed2.com

Club Med 2 **(190/392; FRENCH/200; 637 FEET/1,400 TONS)**
One of the world's largest cruise ships with sails offers casual, sports-oriented, all-inclusive vacations with an easy lifestyle for active, upscale vacationers. The ship sails on seven-day Caribbean cruises in winter, Mediterranean cruises in summer, and transatlantic voyages in spring and fall.

After two decades of spreading the gospel of all-inclusive resort vacations, Club Med applied its resort formula to a cruise ship, *Club Med 2*. Built in 1992, the 14,000-ton vessel marries today's technology to yesteryear's seafaring. She is as long as two football fields and rigged with five 164-foot masts and seven computer-monitored sails; there's no listing or heeling and no officers on deck—they are on the bridge monitoring computers.

Club Med 2 has an open, nautical feeling and is glitz-free, but she loses some of the intimacy that makes the Windstar line's smaller version so appealing. She is spacious and has multiple Burmese teak decks. Interiors by the well-known European designer Albert Pinto evoke understated luxury through meticulous craftsmanship and the use of fine mahogany, quality fabrics, and leather, reminiscent of classic sailing ships. Walls of windows afford sea and shore views. Recently, the ship was renovated with new decor by Eric Gizard, which earned her a 5-trident ranking and upgraded her category among Club Med's resorts.

The cabins are large, comfortable, and handsomely decorated with hand-rubbed mahogany cabinetwork. All cabins are outside and have twin portholes. They're fitted with twin or queen-size beds, a mahogany desk, large mirrors, ample closets, a television, radio, safe, refrigerator, minibar, and satellite telephone, which is also used to order room service. The teak-floored baths have showers, hair dryers, and fluffy bathrobes. Electrical outlets are 110/220 AC. In all, there are 190 outside cabins, 10 of which are suites of 380 square feet. Standard dimensions are 188 square feet. There are no single cabins, but you can book a cabin as a single by paying a supplement of 40% on the Deck C price.

Club Med 2 cruises are basically a French—Club Med says "international"—product with the same informal, carefree ambience of Club Med villages, but in deluxe surroundings with cruise ship amenities. Integral to both operations are GOs—*gentiles organisateurs*—the social hosts and hostesses who keep the action and smiles going day and night. Most GOs are Mauritian, French, and other Europeans, or Americans who speak very good French. Their first task when you board is to familiarize you with the ship and answer questions. They organize shipboard activities and can usually give valuable tips on the best bars and restaurants in ports of call.

The ship has two ocean-view dining rooms, each with a different menu featuring French cuisine. The **Méditerranée,** an open-air veranda cafe on the top deck, serves a casual breakfast, luncheon buffets, and theme dinners featuring cuisine from around the world. In the evening, the restaurant serves food choices à la carte; for a more intimate dinner, you can reserve a table for two at the reception desk. **The Magellan** is a more intimate, formal dining room with waiter service. The à la carte menu offers several choices for each course.

Dinner is a serious affair, lasting up to two hours or longer. Complimentary wine from Club Med's private label, beer, and bottled water accompany lunch and dinner. Smokers are in the majority on board and have the run of the ship. Restaurants have nonsmoking sections, but smoking is allowed in all public areas. Unlike at Club Med villages, breakfast can be enjoyed in your cabin. There is 24-hour room service, and laundry service is available for an extra charge.

Both restaurants have waiters and unreserved, unassigned seating at tables for two or more, with continuous service during dining hours. Officers and staff dine with passengers. Most seven-night Caribbean itineraries offer a lobster beach picnic.

The ship has several lounges, a nightclub, piano bar, and disco. The **Moby Dick Piano Bar,** one of several bars, is the most popular for afternoon tea with French pastries and music and for after-dinner drinks (at prices higher than average). A lounge that doubles as a theater has a bar, stage, bandstand, and dance floor. A different show or program is presented here each evening by GOs—some more entertaining than others and all amateur. Some passengers find this fun, while others say the luxury prices they pay merit more professional entertainers.

There's a small library, card tables and chairs in a lounge, and a boutique. Party seekers make their way to the disco with its lighted dance floor. One night of the cruise in the Caribbean is Carnival.

Sports facilities include a teak sports platform at the stern that unfolds into the sea to become a marina when the ship is at anchor. The vessel carries sailboards, sailboats, snorkels, fins, and masks and provides free lessons in waterskiing, windsurfing, sailing, and snorkeling. Two ski boats with scuba equipment take certified divers on diving trips. The scuba program is a good value.

The less ambitious can retire to a chaise lounge around the two outdoor, saltwater swimming pools. Even when the ship is full, space to lounge is ample. The supervised fitness center has exercise equipment that passengers use while enjoying a panoramic view from the top deck. Aerobics and water exercise in the pool are offered daily. Several decks below are a sauna and massage room. *Club Med 2* also has a beauty salon and spa with massage therapists and treatments—all at additional cost.

The Club Med imprint is obvious. Officers and crew are Mauritian; the staff, dressed in impeccable white shirts, shorts, and socks, handle dining and hotel duties and earn praise for their friendly, professional service. The energetic, attractive GOs are managed by the chef du village, the cruise director. These cheery camp counselors do it all: helm the reception desk, run activities, teach sports, and entertain. In the Caribbean, the ship visits a port each day and sails at night. Unfortunately for those who love sailing, passengers get very little opportunity to experience the pleasure of sailing under canvas.

The ship attracts a range of passengers that changes with the cruise, season, and location. Typically, passengers are 30 to 60 years old. The majority are couples. Children younger than age 8 are not accepted. Most passengers like the informality and sociability of the GO concept. On the other hand, the constant interaction between the young, bouncy GOs and passengers creates a summer camp atmosphere that is not for everyone.

The GO team is bilingual in English and French, but French is the ship's primary language. That could be a problem for English speakers who aren't up to the language challenge, or who might feel there's unequal treatment. Club Med's attitude is: This is a French-European or international product. The cruise is, after all, an experience in which Americans might lunch with people from Normandy, snorkel with Italians, and have cocktails with Austrians. That's part of the attraction.

Per diems start around $350 per person but may vary by season, cabin, and cruise areas. Tips, wine and beer at lunch and dinner, and most water sports are included in the fare; port charges are additional. Club Med offers specially priced cruises occasionally, but it does not discount prices.

Coastal Cruises
P.O. Box 798, Camden, ME 04843; ☎ 207-785-5670 or 800-992-2218; www.schoonermaryday.com

---

Mary Day (15/30; AMERICAN; 90 FEET)

This two-masted schooner sails on three- to six-day cruises along the Maine coast. Some cruises are themed ones, such as Lighthouses or Audubon Naturalist, while others focus on special events like the Great Schooner Race or a folk festival.

Maine Windjammer Association

P.O. Box 1144P, Blue Hill, ME 04614; ☎ 800-807-WIND; www.sailmainecoast.com

Formed in 1977, the Maine Windjammer Association is made up of 12 privately owned and operated traditional tall ships that once belonged to commercial fleets. They delivered everything from fish and granite to coal and Christmas trees along U.S. coasts. The two- and three-masted schooners range from 46 to 132 feet long. Seven are National Historic Landmarks, some older than 100 years.

The windjammers offer three- to six-day cruises from mid-May to October, departing Rockland and Camden on scenic Penobscot Bay, Maine. With more than 3,000 islands, the Maine coast is one of the best and most beautiful sailing areas anywhere. Ships sail by day, about 10 a.m. to 4 p.m., and anchor each night at a deserted inlet or quiet port or village where passengers can go ashore. Passengers may participate in all aspects of sailing, from hoisting sails and taking the wheel to helping in the galley.

Meals are served family-style and include fresh seafood, roasts, garden salads, chowder, and homemade breads and desserts. A lobster bake on an island is featured on every six-day trip and most three-day cruises. Accommodations are simple: single, double, or triple cabins with comfortable mattresses, fresh linens, and plenty of blankets. Shipboard life is relaxed and informal.

Each windjammer carries 6 to 40 passengers and a crew of two to ten. Cruises are ideal family vacations, appropriate for most ages. (Check with individual captains regarding children. Teens ages 12 years and up are accepted on most boats. However, because of an increasing demand for family cruises, two of the vessels are now offering cruises with a minimum age of 5 and 6, respectively. Some windjammers have theme cruises ranging from photography and lighthouse cruises to wine tasting and whale watching. The tall ships gather annually for an all-day race in which passengers can participate.

Three- to six-day cruises range from $400 to $950 per person. Charter rates are available. All vessels undergo rigorous U.S. Coast Guard inspections and carry ship-to-shore radios and electronic navigational devices.

Air transportation is available to departure ports via Portland International Jetport, with limousine service to the Rockland/Camden area. Commuter air service is available from Boston, and buses run from Boston and Portland. All vessels offer free parking.

Member vessels are *American Eagle, Angelique, Grace Bailey, Heritage, Isaac H. Evans, Lewis R. French, Mary Day, Mercantile, Mistress, Nathaniel Bowditch, Stephen Taber,* and *Victory Chimes.* The association provides descriptive brochures as well as a short DVD.

Although all are windjammers, each boat is different and special in its own way. *Angelique,* for example, has a deck house salon—a passenger lounge above deck. This gives passengers a warm, cozy alternative to the galley on rainy days. The *Grace Bailey* offers a combination lounge/galley below deck large enough to accommodate an upright piano. Most toilet and bath facilities are shared. Some schooners, like the *American Eagle*, with hallways running fore and aft below decks, offer toilets and hot showers situated adjacent to passenger cabins. On other ships, the communal heads are accessed from the Main Deck. A few vessels, including *Victory Chimes*, may have some cabins with private toilets in the cabin.

Cabins for the most part are very small—a place to sleep or change clothes but not a place to hang out. Most cabins include a reading light and private sink, sometimes with hot and cold fresh running water, sometimes just with cold water. Storage space in the cabins is minimal, sometimes problematic when two or more share a cabin. A few ships offer 110-volt electrical outlets for hair dryers and such, but this is more the exception than the rule.

During fair weather, almost everyone hangs out on deck, where lunch and sometimes other meals are served. Some ships have built-in benches on deck, while others provide collapsible chairs. On rainy days, a galley with a wood stove affords refuge from the elements during and between meals. While anchored, both in dry and wet weather, a canvas tarp is deployed over much of the deck.

Passengers should be reasonably agile. Access to lower decks is almost always by ladder, with the exception of the *Victory Chimes* and the *Heritage*, which substitute rather steep stairs.

Music, in the form of informal jam sessions or sing-alongs, is a favorite evening's entertainment on many schooners, including the *Stephen Taber*, *Grace Bailey*, *Victory Chimes*, *Angelique*, and *Mary Day*. The *Grace Bailey* and *Angelique* carry upright pianos, and the *Mary Day* carries an organ. Passengers are strongly encouraged to bring any sort of acoustic (that is, nonelectrical) instrument. On ships without captain or crew of a musical bent, storytelling is a preferred pastime. Regardless of the activity, it's a rare night when festivities go beyond 11 p.m.

In a rather marked departure from the rest of the cruise industry, no alcoholic beverages are sold or served on Maine Windjammer schooners (with the exception of educational wine tasting events or on some vessels, a lobster bake). Although guests are invited to bring their own stash, most precruise instructional material makes it clear that excessive imbibing will not be tolerated.

Itineraries are quite flexible, with no particular urgency to be at a certain place at a particular time. Many captains ad-lib their itineraries en route, responding to the weather and the stated preferences of the passengers. And, speaking of captains, they are as diverse as the ships. There are several husband-and-wife teams, some partnering gentlemen captains, and on the *Isaac H. Evans*, the fleet's only solo female captain. Some of the couple-captains bring their children along (amazingly socially acclimated and well behaved).

Summer weather in Maine is all over the map, although you can usually count on good wind. May and June are very unpredictable both in terms of temperature and rainfall. July is almost always warm but with more rain than the predictably dry and warm August and September. Regardless of the time of year, good rain gear is essential.

Sea Cloud Cruises
32–40 North Dean Street, Englewood, NJ 07631; ☎ 201-227-9404 or 888-732-2568; fax 201-227-9424; www.seacloud.com

Sea Cloud **(32/64; INTERNATIONAL; 360 FEET)**

One of the world's most luxurious sailing ships, the *Sea Cloud* was built in 1931 as a wedding present from financier E. F. Hutton for his bride, Marjorie Merriweather Post. The ship has 32 air-conditioned cabins with phone, safe, hair dryer, and bathrobes. The elegant dining room accommodates all passengers at one seating; complimentary wines are served at lunch and dinner. A library and boutique are available.

The four-masted bark sails on different itineraries year-round. She plies the Eastern Caribbean in winter and the Mediterranean during the remainder of the year, and she is marketed by several U.S. companies. Sea Cloud Cruises also owns the luxurious *River Cloud* sisters, which sail European rivers (*see* River and Barge Cruises in Europe, earlier in Part Three).

Sea Cloud II **(47/94; INTERNATIONAL; 384 FEET)**

The legendary *Sea Cloud* got a sibling in 2001. The 384-foot, $40 million vessel is square-rigged with three masts (rather than *Sea Cloud*'s four), and her 29,687 square feet of sail are manually operated, with the crew climbing the masts and clambering along the spars to set the square-rigged sails. Modern with the highest safety standards, the vessel is traditional in appearance and offers opulent 1930s decor. Forty-seven luxurious cabins range from 129 to 236 square feet, those on the Promenade Deck with ornate marble bathtubs and marble mantels; two Owner's Suites each contain 290 square feet, with separate shower stalls and four-poster beds. Large deck areas and a swimming platform provide plentiful outside space for jogging, walking, lounging, sunning, and dining. The ship has an alfresco bar, an attractive restaurant, an elegant lounge with large arched windows, an inviting sauna and gymnasium, and a sunny, well-stocked library with windows overlooking the foredeck. The European/Asian crew is attentive and efficient—you could almost be on a private yacht—and the cuisine, predominantly French and German, is outstanding. Many of the cruises are chartered to museum and alumni groups (but there are normally cabins available for nonmembers). Nightlife tends to consist of lectures, wine tastings, and recitals by soloists or chamber groups.

Sea Cloud II's all-weather cruising ability sets her apart from *Sea Cloud*, which is generally restricted to sunny climes. *Sea Cloud II* cruises through the North Sea and Baltic in summer, the Mediterranean in autumn, and the Caribbean in winter.

Sea Cloud Hussar **(69/136; GERMAN/90; 449 FEET)**

Scheduled to debut in October 2010, *Sea Cloud Hussar*, constructed at Factoria de Naval Marin shipyard in Vigo, Spain, is said to be the largest full-rigged, three-mast passenger ship ever built and has more than 44,920 square feet of sail surface. To supplement the sails, the Malta-registered ship is powered by an eco-friendly diesel-electric propulsion system with MAN-Siemens engines. Her draft is 18.5 feet.

With her elegant white hull, 28 white sails, and the classic gold Sea Cloud eagle at its bow, her kinship to her sister ships is obvious at first sight. And like them, *Sea Cloud Hussar* will be sailed in the traditional way—by hand. Yet, the new ship sets new standards in luxury for this kind of vessel.

Her interiors—classic and elegant—were designed by Partnership Design, a Hamburg-based company that created the interiors of *Sea Cloud II, River Cloud*, and *River Cloud II*. Her facilities include elaborate teak decks, a Lido bar and bistro, main restaurant with a 180-degree panoramic view, lounge with a bar, library, boutique, medical center, and an elevator. The spa on Cabin Deck has a sauna (also with a panoramic view), Rasul steam bath, relaxing area, massage room, beauty parlor, and a swim platform next to the spa. There's a Jacuzzi and sun beds on the Sun Deck. The fitness area is equipped with the latest cardio machines and enjoys an ocean view.

The 69 outside cabins include 43 deluxe cabins with a bath and shower; 23 Junior Suites and 3 Owner's Suites have a veranda, panoramic windows, walk-in closet, and bath with a tub. All accommodations are furnished with a queen-size bed or two singles (except single cabins), a sitting corner with a chair or couch and table, dressing table, closet with safe, hair dryer, secretary, minibar, television with movie and music channels, and a sophisticated info-tainment system that includes direct e-mail access.

The 35 deluxe outside cabins (183 to 226 square feet) on the Cabin Deck have portholes. Four cabins connect. The two deluxe singles (172 square feet) have similar amenities, except they are furnished with a single bed. The six deluxe outside cabins (161 to 205 square feet) on the Lido Deck are similar but with panoramic windows. The Verandah Deck houses 23 Junior Suites with 313 to 356 square feet, one Owner's Suite with 388 square feet, and two Owner's Suites with 420 square feet with verandas and panoramic windows. The Owner's Suite interiors are more luxurious, the bathrooms more spacious, and the sitting areas have couches.

Sea Cloud Hussar is being built by a Hamburg-based Hansa Treuhand Holding AG subsidiary and marketed by Sea Cloud Cruises GmbH, also part of Hansa Treuhand Holding AG. In her maiden year, the new ship is scheduled to cruise the eastern Mediterranean, including Syria, Egypt, Jordan, and the Red Sea, and the Persian Gulf between Muscat and Bahrain through April 2011, while based in Dubai. One cruise will call on Iran.

The Sea Cloud New Jersey office also handles the *River Cloud II*, which is described earlier in Part Three in the section entitled European River Cruises. *River Cloud I* has been chartered by a Dutch company for a year or longer.

Star Clippers, Inc. (See Part Two.)

Windstar Cruises (See Part Two.)

Zeus Tours and Yacht Cruises

c/o Tourlite International, 120 Sylvan Avenue, Englewood Cliffs, NJ 07632;
☎ 201-242-1770; 800-272-7600; fax 201-242-8085;
www.varietycruises.com

The Zeus Group, which has been in operation for almost a half-century, offers Greek Isles, eastern Mediterranean, and Central and South American cruises in its own and chartered vessels. The cruises are sold in the United States through Tourlite International.

Among their wide range of offerings are several set itineraries with frequent sailing dates on the following vessels.

Diogenis V **(24/49; GREEK; 165 FEET)**
From April to October, this vessel operates seven-night Aegean Mosaic cruises round-trip from Heraklion, Crete, visiting such destinations as Aghios Astypalea, Karpathos, Nicolaos, Rhodes, Santorini, and Simi. The vessel offers air-conditioned cabins with private facilities, a dining room, lounge bar with stereo music/TV, and a Sun Deck equipped with sun chairs.

Viking Star **(24/42; GREEK; 106 FEET)**
The vessel operates seven-night Ionian Odyssey cruises round-trip from Corfu, with port calls at Albania and such Greek Isles as Scorpios and Parga. The vessel was constructed in the mid-1990s and has 24 outside cabins, 19 on the main deck, and 5 on the lower deck; one dining room and adjacent bar/lounge; and a Sun Deck with sun beds and chairs.

▌ FREIGHTERS

FREIGHTER TRAVEL MAY BE THE LEAST-UNDERSTOOD segment of the cruise industry. You don't read or hear much about it, and cargo lines that offer passenger service rarely advertise in the mainstream media. Most travel agents, too, lack experience and expertise in booking freighter cruises.

Freighters roam the globe, visiting ports famous and exotic but usually industrial and removed from city centers and tourism attractions. They offer a carefree, informal environment conducive to total relaxation, and they may cost less than conventional cruise ships on a per diem basis.

Before the post–World War II boom in air travel and cruises, freighters were a significant mode of international travel. Expanding air routes, lower fares, and the growth of the cruise industry gradually relegated freighter travel to a minor niche in the cruise market.

Cargo lines have since recognized a revival of interest and the economics inherent in carrying passengers. Ten passengers at roughly $100 a day each adds up to good found money over the course of a year, and at the small cost of perhaps providing one extra steward and additional food. A few companies operate combined container and passenger vessels that can accommodate large numbers of passengers. But more typical are the 300 or more traditional freighters currently in service—mostly container ships—that accommodate from 2 to 12 passengers. Many enjoy brisk bookings and operate at capacity during peak seasons. However, extra regulations since 9/11 have caused several freight lines to reconsider the practicality of passenger service. Always call to confirm all information before making travel plans or reservations, and then deal with a freighter travel specialist who can keep you apprised of departure, embarkation time, and arrangements.

FREIGHTERS: DEFINING THE BREED

WHAT EXACTLY IS A FREIGHTER? First, let's say what it is not. A modern freighter isn't a rusty tramp steamer sailing on a mission of intrigue or romance as popularized in movies and novels. The vast majority of cargo vessels today are less than 20 years old. Imposing and boxy, they're loaded with sophisticated navigation and communication equipment. Most are containerized, that is, their freight is carried in large metal containers resembling railway box cars systematically stacked below and above decks. Some carry bulk items in holds such as iron ore, steel, or grain.

The International Conventions and Conferences on Marine Safety define the passenger-carrying freighter as a vessel principally engaged in transporting goods that is licensed to carry a maximum of 12 passengers. Those licensed to carry more than 12 are defined as combination passenger-cargo ships. The latter must meet stricter safety standards and carry more staff, including a doctor. Nowadays, most cargo ships run on fixed schedules along established routes, except for those in so-called tramp service. Tramps don't sail regular routes or schedules and can be hired to haul almost anything, anywhere, anytime. Only one tramp line, the Polish Steamship Company, now takes passengers; she loads grain from the Great Lakes. Also, many of today's freighters are often chartered for specific periods of time, so their fixed schedules and routes may change from time to time.

Note: The worldwide recession that began in 2007 hit cargo companies particularly hard, and, at last count, more than 500 vessels had been pulled out of service for lack of business. Added to this, the pirate menace in the Gulf of Aden area has caused some ships to be rerouted from their usual course. As we have said, it is important to deal with travel agencies that specialize in passenger freighter travel, but now that piece of advice is all the more important. The travel companies named later in this chapter deal with passenger freighter travel full time and have the resources to provide timely, accurate information.

Why People Choose Freighters

Traveling by freighter offers a rare opportunity to truly get away from it all. There are no crowds, no planned activities, no lines, no dress code, and no hoopla. The atmosphere aboard a freighter is relaxed and unstructured. Passengers can be as active or as lazy as they choose.

Freighters are for travelers who want to see the world on their own terms and are flexible about schedule changes and port substitutions. Most are veteran travelers who have become bored or disillusioned with conventional tours, cruises, and popular vacation destinations. Their sense of adventure and yearning for discovery demand something different.

A glance at freighter itineraries often reveals ports that would be impractical or prohibitively expensive to visit any other way. While some ships will dock in ports close to places you will want to visit, others may be berthed at a sprawling container terminal miles from the city. Often the ship and/or its port agents will help with hiring taxis or provide some basic touring information. But veteran freighter travelers know to come prepared with some knowledge of what they want to see, then perhaps ask local residents to suggest how to get there and back by their vessel's posted all-aboard notice. Time ashore is often limited, as modern ships can load or unload hundreds of containers in only a few hours; a long stay rarely exceeds 24 hours.

Freighter travelers recognize good value—on a per diem basis, there are few better travel values than freighters. With careful research and planning, you can roam the world for months aboard a freighter for roughly $90 to $250 per day. Unlike cruise ships with their large assortment of pay-as-you-go activities and amenities, there are few opportunities to spend money on board a freighter beyond the fare.

Some people are attracted by the camaraderie they enjoy with fellow passengers. Sailing with usually no more than a dozen like-minded, well-informed veteran travelers in a low-key, relaxing atmosphere is their ideal travel environment and often leads to lasting friendships. On the other hand, if you have a list of books that you have been eager to read, here's your chance. Be aware, some passengers are avid bridge players, and others can't wait to bend an elbow when the sun is over the yardarm.

Is Freighter Travel for You?

Judging from the high rate of repeat bookings, once a freighter traveler, always a freighter traveler. If you haven't tried it but you've read this far, you may be a good candidate.

You must usually have plenty of time, as most trips are long, although voyages of one to two weeks also exist. Most folks just can't get away for a 30-, 60-, or 90-day trip. For that reason alone, the majority of freighter travelers are retirees, teachers and professors, self-employed professionals, and the occasional artist or writer. Common characteristics include an extensive travel background, love of the sea, preference for independent travel, and a general dislike of formality.

Wherever on this planet your imagination might roam, chances are you can go there on a freighter. Some of the more exotic and popular routes (round-trip from the United States) include the East or West Coast to New Zealand and Australia (38 to 66 days), around the world from New York (90 days or longer; although if you are prepared to take a train across the U.S. for one segment, you can cut the trip to under 50 days), Marquesas Islands from Tahiti (16 days), Mediterranean from the East or West Coast (42 to 60 days), and South America from the East or Gulf Coast (42 to 70 days). Shorter one-way transatlantic trips, such as Chester, Pennsylvania, or Montreal to England, France, or Belgium, are an average of 8 to 11 days, and trips from the U.S. East Coast to the Mediterranean, some ranging from 10 to 20 days, are available.

Accommodations and Facilities

The majority of cargo liners have spacious, comfortable accommodations equal to, and often better than, those found on cruise ships. Normally they are located in a multistory superstructure at the stern. The cabins and public spaces may be on two to four different decks, so vertical movement is often the norm. Cabins have showers and sometimes bathtubs. In most cases they're air-conditioned and have a tastefully furnished lounge area. Often, they have taped music, service phones, VCRs or DVD players, minifridges, and picture windows rather than portholes.

Comfy, smartly decorated public lounges invite card games, conversation, and evening cocktails. Most vessels have large-screen televisions and an extensive library of videos and DVDs. The lounge may be shared with the officers, or there may be a separate one for passengers. Smoking policies will vary too. Many cargo liners have small pools, exercise rooms, and saunas for officer and passenger use, and plenty of deck space for walks.

Some lines offer single cabins; others charge a single supplement, usually less than 50%. You should ask if your assigned cabin window is likely to be blocked by a container during any part of the voyage. Because freighters are working vessels, most lines won't accept preteen children for passage. Those that do usually charge the adult fare for children. Pets aren't permitted.

An open-bridge policy prevailed among freighters in the past; some freighters may still have one, others may not. Policies on bridge access are stricter since 9/11. Some lines and governments in port destinations may prohibit noncrew passengers from gaining bridge access. When the vessel does have an open bridge, you're welcome to watch officers and crew in action, except during critical maneuvers such as docking. On some freighters, passengers are free to go almost anywhere, while on others there are sensible security and safety rules. Obviously during rough weather, the container decks are off-limits. Pampering is not part of the program, although the crew may be very attentive. Basic services are handled by stewards who usually double as cabin attendants and waiters. A washer and dryer are generally available for passenger use. Phone and fax services are always available in emergencies, but policies on casual use vary.

Ships carrying more than 12 passengers have a doctor on board and generally have a small hospital or treatment center. But medical services aboard freighters carrying 12 or fewer passengers are limited. All, however, carry basic medical supplies and someone aboard will be trained in first aid. In case of serious illness, the captain will contact the nearest ship or shore station with a doctor available for advice. In a grave emergency, the victim will be transferred to a ship with appropriate medical facilities or be put ashore at the nearest port. Costs incurred in medical evacuation and treatment are the passenger's responsibility. All freighters taking fewer than 12 passengers have age limits; many will not take passengers over age 79, and some have a cutoff as low as 70 years of age.

In view of this, you're advised to take out travel health insurance with medical evacuation coverage and to carry more than enough of any medications you require. (See Part One of this book for insurance information.)

Dining and Food

Every freighter has a comfortable dining room shared by officers and passengers. On some ships, the officers share their tables with passengers; on others, they eat at separate tables. Dining is the day's special event and an opportunity to socialize. Most officers are congenial, eager to please, and happy to share their knowledge of the ship, the sea, and the world. Most freighter food is of good restaurant quality, well-prepared, and plentiful. Menus often feature the national cuisine of the ship's and/or officers' origin, which are as wide-ranging as French, German, Italian, Polish, Ukrainian, or Indian. The deck crew's nationality may be entirely different.

Breakfast and lunch are often presented buffet-style, while dinners are served at tables, sometimes in four or five courses. Coffee and tea are usually available anytime, and between-meal snacks are provided. While beer, wine, and liquor are available on most ships, it may be necessary for you to BYOB. On French and Italian ships, complimentary table wine is provided with lunch and dinner.

PLANNING YOUR FREIGHTER VOYAGE

THE MAJORITY OF FREIGHTERS BOOK UP EARLY, especially for peak summer months and on voyages to tropical climes during northern winters. Start early yourself—six months or more—to get your choice of ship and routing, and a year ahead is not unusual on popular voyages. Planning, booking, and confirming your voyage can take much longer than you imagined. Depending on itinerary, you may have to obtain travel documents, such as visas, make arrangements concerning your home or business, get a physical check-up and inoculations, and decide on trip and travel health insurance options. Fewer than 40 nations require U.S. citizens to carry visas, but those that do will require some planning to avoid a potentially nasty situation. These are all reasons to engage a freighter travel specialist, especially when it is your first trip on a freighter.

Ford's Freighter Travel Guide
19448 Londelius Street
Northridge, CA 91324
☎ 818-701-7414

You might start by consulting a current issue of **Ford's Freighter Travel Guide,** a comprehensive quarterly guide listing almost all passenger-carrying freighter itineraries. Your local university library may have a copy. A subscription costs $24 (plus $1.98 sales tax for California residents). Single copies are $15.95.

A smart move would be to join **TravLtips Cruise and Freighter Association;** membership costs $20 per year per couple or $35 for two years, when paid by credit card; $35/$50 by check). You'll connect with this loose-knit group of thousands of freighter and offbeat cruising buffs and receive bimonthly issues of *TravLtips,* the association magazine, periodic issues of *Roam the World by Freighter,* which includes members' reports of voyages, access to the association's travel planning and reservation services, and member-only invitations on special and unusual cruises.

TravLtips Cruise and
Freighter Association
P.O. Box 580188
Flushing, NY 11358-0188
☎ 718-224-0435 or
800-872-8584
FAX 718-224-3247
www.travltips.com
e-mail info@travltips.com

Another very useful resource is California-based **Freighter World Cruises.** [3] Printed twice monthly, The *Freighter Space Advisory* reports cabin availability, descriptions, departure dates from the U.S. and foreign ports, en route ports of call, and fares. You can subscribe online at **www.freighterworld.com;** a one-year subscription costs $29. Both of these resources can help you select a vessel or voyage and book it, plus handle air and other travel arrangements.

Freighter World Cruises
180 South Lake Avenue, Ste. 335
Pasadena, CA 91101-2655
☎ 626-449-3106 or
800-531-7774
FAX 626-449-9573
www.freighterworld.com
e-mail info@freighterworld.com

Canada-based **The Cruise People**[4] has been in business since 1972 and employs a full-time freighter travel specialist. Access the Web site, **www.thecruisepeople.ca,** to get on the e-mail list for promotions on freighter voyages and cruises. In 1992, The Cruise People opened a second office in Europe, closer to the freighter lines. They also employ a full-time freighter travel specialist, and their freighter Web page can be found at **www.cruisepeople.co.uk/ freighters.htm.** All these companies' Web sites list the ever-changing freighter voyage opportunities, and access is free.

> The Cruise People
> 1252 Lawrence Ave. East
> Suite 210
> Don Mills, Ontario
> Canada M3A 1C3
> ☎ 416-444-2410 or
> 800-268-6523
> FAX 416-447-2628
> www.thecruisepeople.ca

Many cargo lines are represented by the above (or similar) specialized agents. These services can be a real blessing, particularly to first-timers, because booking passage on a freighter is neither quick nor easy.

You need lead time. Because freighter schedules are prone to change, some lines require wait-listing (no charge) until firm schedules are released. Only then will waiting passengers be given an option on a cabin. A deposit—usually 10–25%—is required only after a cabin option is accepted. Final payment is usually due 45 to 60 days before sailing.

During the months before sailing, the departure date may shift a few days, and the routing may change. (For example, you may be going to Wellington rather than Auckland.) This proves the value of having an experienced agent to keep you informed of changes and to help deal with them, as well as your need for flexibility in schedule and attitude.

Every freighter company has its own policies affecting passengers. Most have literature outlining these policies and describing their ships and itineraries. Obtain such materials through your travel agent or freighter travel specialist or directly from the line, and read everything thoroughly—including the fine print. Pay particular attention to the company's cancellation policy, and take it into account when you consider trip cancellation insurance. Also, it may be wise to take out deviation insurance, in case a voyage suddenly becomes longer by a week or more, because some lines will charge you for the extra days.

Your Health and Safety

Cargo lines require passengers ages 65 or older to present a certificate of good health from their doctor before booking can be completed. Review your itinerary with your physician regarding potential risk of disease or infection and any immunizations or protective medicines needed. Up-to-the-minute immunization recommendations are available from the **U.S. Centers for Disease Control**'s 24-hour hotline in Atlanta: ☎ 877-394-8747. You'll need a touch-tone phone and fax machine to receive faxed messages. You may also check for information on the CDC Web site at **www.cdc.gov.** You may also want to stay informed about potential unrest in the countries you are visiting. The U.S. State Department publishes travel advisories at **travel.state.gov.**

If something happens en route, the shipping line may change the itinerary. Or, if it is safe to call for handling cargo, you may be advised or even required to stay aboard.

Clothing and Essentials

Packing for a 90-day freighter voyage should be no different from selecting your gear and garments for a 10-day trip. Nor should it weigh more; cargo lines, unlike cruise lines, aren't obligated to provide baggage service. Don't bring more than you can handle, although crewmembers are likely to help you carry your luggage up a steep gangway.

Casual attire is the rule. It's possible there might be a special occasion calling for slightly dressier clothes or that restaurants ashore may require them. For everyday wear, bring low-heeled, nonskid, rubber-soled shoes. They are essential for safe maneuvering aboard ship in rough seas and during normal rolling conditions. Be prepared for just about any kind of climate. Light wraps (even in the tropics) and rain gear are essential.

Foul weather is almost a certainty during any long voyage, and many freighter veterans pack a lightweight, two-piece rain suit (parka and pants) and rubber boots. They also are handy for wading through the dust and residue that cakes bulk-loading docks. Bring binoculars, some reading material (don't overdo; most ships have extensive libraries), washcloths, and facial tissue.

Electrical current on most foreign-flagged freighters is 220/250 AC. You'll need a voltage converter and plug adapter to use your appliances. Funds for shipboard expenses should be in U.S. currency. Traveler's checks are generally accepted, but very few lines take credit cards or personal checks.

Some lines say they have no policy on tipping. A few say that their stewards who serve passengers get extra pay and suggest that tipping be reserved for exceptional or special service. The norm seems to be $1.50 per passenger per day to the room steward and an equal amount to the dining steward.

Smoking is allowed on nearly all freighters because many officers and crew members smoke. A few lines bar smoking in dining rooms. The majority of officers and crew who smoke are courteous around nonsmoking guests, and most passengers say smoking is not a big problem.

FREIGHTER TRAVEL RESOURCES

TODAY, THE MAJOR PLAYERS in the freighter travel world are French-, German-, and Italian-owned ships, with contributions as well from the U.K. and Poland.

The French ships are run by **CMA CGM The French Line,** with a large fleet of modern passenger-carrying container ships serving the Far

East, Australia and New Zealand, the French West Indies, India, and South America, and **Compagnie Polynésienne de Transport Maritime (CPTM),** which operates the 180-passenger *Aranui 3* from Tahiti. CMA CGM ships often carry 10 or 12 passengers, as the company chairman feels that the passenger service commemorates the long passenger lineage of the old French Line.

The German owners include **F Laeisz, Hamburg-Süd,** and **Rickmers,** all of Hamburg, and **NSB Freighter Cruises** of Bremen, as well as a number of others. German owners often operate ships on charter to the large worldwide container lines such as Evergreen, Hanjin, MSC, and Zim, whose own ships do not carry passengers, and also to CMA CGM, many of whose own ships do. Rickmers operates ships on its own routes, including the twice-monthly Rickmers Pearl String round-the-world service, while Hamburg-Süd also charters ships from other owners.

Italy is represented by Naples-based **Grimaldi Lines,** with a large and growing fleet of roll on–roll off container ships that serve northern Europe, the Mediterranean, the eastern coast of South America, and West Africa. Grimaldi ships have Owner's Cabins and outside staterooms, but they also operate the only passenger-carrying freighters with inside cabins, although all are en suite.

The sole remaining "British" ship, since the shutdown of the P&O Nedlloyd and Bank Line round-the-world passenger services, is the 124-passenger *St Helena,* which supplies that island from Cape Town and makes two voyages a year to the U.K. Although some CMA CGM and Evergreen ships are registered in the U.K., their officers are not British. The 131,332-ton passenger-carrying CMA CGM *Andromeda,* for example, is now the second largest ship under the U.K. flag after the 148,528-ton *Queen Mary 2,* but she has French officers.

Meanwhile, the **Polish Steamship Company** serves the Great Lakes from Amsterdam and IJmuiden and then tramps back to Europe or the Mediterranean with grain; it can be booked as a 60-day round-trip voyage. All of these companies can be booked through the specialized freighter agents named above. As noted previously, these agents are able to supply detailed information on these and other freighter companies and ships with the facilities to carry passengers.

ITINERARY INDEX

Abercrombie & Kent, Inc.

Eclipse **HOME PORT** Baltra

Year-round, 11–16 days: Peru/Galapagos, includes 5- or 7-night cruise of the Galapagos Islands.

Le Boreal **HOME PORT** Ushuaia

December 7, 14 days, Antarctica, from Buenos Aires and Ushuaia-m-round-trip to Drake Passage, Antarctic Peninsula, Paradise Bay and Lemaire Channel, Palmer Station. December 17, January 2, 2011, 20 days: Buenos Aires and Ushuaia-m-round-trip to Falkland Islands, South Georgia, Scotia Sea, Antarctica, Drake Passage; research station on the Antarctic Peninsula.

Adventure Canada

Clipper Adventurer **HOME PORTS** Varies with ship and itineraries

August 14, 15 days: Into Northwest Passage, from Kangerlussuaq to Kugluktuk via Sisimiut Coast, Ilulissat, Karrat Fjord, Upernavik, Mattimatalik, Dundas Harbour, Roker Bay, Beechey, Port Leopold Islands, Fort Ross, Bellot Strait, Pasley Bay, Uqsuqtuuq, Queen Maud Gulf, Bathurst Inlet, Coronation Gulf. August 28, 15 days: Out of Northwest Passage, from Kugluktuk to Ilulissat via Kangiryuar, Banks Island, Prince of Wales Strait, Winter Harbour, Parry Channel, Bathurst Island, Beechey Island, Radstock Bay, Dundas Harbour, Croker Bay, Aujuittuq, Smith Sound, Cape Alexander, Kap York, Upernavik, Karrat Fjord.

September 25, 8 days: Islands of the Gulf (St. Lawrence) from Corner Brook to Cape St. Mary's/St. Johns via Iles de la Madeleine, Gaspe/Bonaventure Island.

National Geographic Islander **HOME PORTS** Varies with ship and itineraries

October 21, March 31, 2011, 12 day: Galapagos round-trip from Baltra to Bartolome/ Santiago Islands, Puerto Ayora, Puerto Villamil, Isla Fernandina, Southern Isabela, Champion, Punta Cormorant, Gardner Bay, Punta Suarez.

Ocean Nova **HOME PORTS** Varies with ship and itineraries

September 18, 11 days: Newfoundland Circumnavigation, round-trip from St. John's to Fogo Town, Battle Harbour, L'Anse aux Meadows, Red Bay, Gros Morne National Park, Bay of Islands, Garia Bay/Francois & Ramea, Conne River/Miawpukek, St. Pierre Island, Cape St. Mary's.

Polar Star **HOME PORTS** Varies with ship and itineraries

November 21, 20 days, round-trip from Ushuaia to Terra del Fuego (embark Polar Star), Falkland Islands, South Georgia, Elephant Island, South Shetland Islands, Antarctic

Peninsula, Drake Passage, Beagle Channel. December 9, 11 days, Drake Passage, Antarctic Peninsula, South Shetland Islands, Beagle Channel.

American Canadian Caribbean Line

Grande Caribe **HOME PORTS** Belize, Charleston, Nassau, Warren (RI), and others

April, May, 7 nights, Charleston to Jacksonville via Beaufort, Savannah, Brunswick, Jekyll Island, St. Marys, Fernandina Beach. May, 14 nights, Atlantic coastal waterways between Jacksonville and Warren and reverse.

June, 7 nights, round-trip from Warren to New Bedford, Provincetown, Salem, Boston, Plymouth Newport. July, 7 nights, Coast of Maine, round-trip from Portland. July, August, 15 nights, Warren to Quebec City. August, 5 nights, round-trip from Warren to Cuttyhunk, Nantucket, Martha's Vineyard, Block Island, Newport.

September, October, 12 nights, Erie Canal/Saguenay and Fall Foliage between Warren and Quebec City.

Grande Mariner **HOME PORTS** Chicago, Warren

May–August, 15 nights, between Chicago and Warren via Manistee, Manitowoc, Mackinac Island, Wyandotte, Cleveland, Erie, Buffalo, Rochester, Oswego, Erie Canal Stops, Troy, Kingston, West Point. June–July, 6 nights, Lake Michigan, round-trip from Chicago.

August, September, 5 nights, round-trip from Warren to Cuttyhunk, Nantucket, Martha's Vineyard, Block Island, Newport. September, October, 12 nights, Erie Canal/Saguenay and Fall Foliage between Warren and Quebec City.

Niagara Prince **HOME PORT** New Orleans, Chicago, Knoxville, Warren; others vary with itinerary

April–May, 9 nights, Leg 2, Knoxville to Nashville via Chattanooga, Decator, Pickwick Dam, Kuttawa, Clarksville. May, 11 nights, Leg 3, Nashville to Chicago via Clarksville, Kuttawa, St. Genevieve, Alton, Havana, Peoria, Joliet. May–June, 14 nights, Chicago to New Orleans via Joliet, Peoria, Havana, Alton, St. Genvive, Kuttawa, Pickwick Dam, Rankin Lock/Montgomery Lock, Columbus, Demopolis, Mobile.

June–July, 15 nights, Chicago to Warren. July, 5 nights, round-trip from Warren. August, 7 nights, round-trip from Portland. August, September, 7 nights, round-trip from Warren. Ports similar to Grand Caribe above.

September–October, 11 nights, Warren to Burlington via Newport, New York City, Bear Mountain, West Point, Kingston, Catskill, Troy, Waterford, Champlain, Whitehall, Vergennes.

American Cruise Lines

American Eagle **HOME PORTS** Baltimore, Charleston

June–November, 7 nights, Chesapeake Bay, round-trip from Baltimore to Williamsburg/Yorktown, Tangier Island/Solomons Island, Cambridge, Oxford, St. Michaels, Annapolis.

November, 7 nights, Antebellum South between Charleston and Jacksonville; 7 nights, Mid-Atlantic Inland Passage, between Baltimore and Charleston; or 14 nights, between Baltimore and Jacksonville.

American Glory **HOME PORTS** Baltimore, Bangor, Charleston, and others

May, November–December, Charleston to Jacksonville and reverse. May 8, November 6, 7 nights, Charleston to Baltimore; or 14 nights, between Baltimore and Jacksonville. May, October, 7 nights, Chesapeake Bay, round-trip from Baltimore.

June, 7 nights, round-trip from Providence. June, July, 7 nights, round-trip from Bangor. July, September, 10 nights, Providence to Bangor and reverse via Nantucket Island, Martha's Vineyard, Glouscester, Portland, Boothbay Harbor, Bar Harbor, Camden, Belfast.

September–October, 6 or 7 nights, Hudson River Fall Foliage, round-trip from New York. November, December, 7 nights, round-trip from Jacksonville.

American Spirit **HOME PORTS** Baltimore, Charleston, Providence

May, November–December, 7 nights, Charleston to Jacksonville. May 8, 14 nights, Jacksonville to Baltimore and reverse. May, November, 7 nights, Charleston to Baltimore; or 14 nights, Baltimore to Jacksonville.

May–June, November, 6 or 7 nights, Chesapeake Bay, round-trip from Baltimore; or New England Islands, round-trip from Providence; or Alexandria to Philadelphia.

American Star **HOME PORTS** Baltimore, Charleston, Jacksonville, Providence

April–May, November–December, 7 nights, Jacksonville to Charleston and reverse.

May 15, November 6, 7 nights, Baltimore to Charleston; or 14 nights, Baltimore to Jacksonville. May–June, October, 6 or 7 nights, Chesapeake Bay, round-trip from Baltimore. May, November, 7 nights, Baltimore to Charleston.

June–September, 6 or 7 nights, round-trip from Providence to New Bedford, Nantucket Island, Martha's Vineyard, Bristol/Fall River, Newport, Block Island.

October, 7 nights, Hudson River round-trip from New York. December, 7 nights, Rivers of Florida, round-trip from St. Augustine.

Independence **HOME PORTS** Baltimore, Bangor, Charleston

June, October, 6 or 7 nights, round-trip from Baltimore. June, 10 nights, Providence to Bangor. July–September, 6 or 7 nights, Maine Coast, round-trip from Bangor.

October, 6 or 7 nights, Hudson River Fall Foliage, round-trip from New York to Catskill; or 14 nights, Baltimore to Jacksonville. November–December, 7 nights, Charleston to Jacksonville and reverse.

Queen of the West **HOME PORTS** Portland, Oregon and Clarkston, Washington

Summer 2010, 7 nights, Columbia and Snake rivers.

American Safari Cruises

Safari Explorer **HOME PORT** Lewiston, Portland, Juneau, Seattle, Wenatchee

April 30, September 10, 14 nights, Seattle to Juneau via San Juan Islands, Inside Passage, Prince Rupert, Ketchikan, Canoe Pass, Petersburg, Glacier Bay National Park. May–September, 7 nights, Alaska, round-trip from Juneau.

October 2, 7 nights, Columbia and Snake rivers, from Lewiston to Portland or reverse. October–November, 7 nights, Wenatchee to Portland via North Columbia Valley, Walla Walla, Red Mountain and Yakima Valley Appellation, Maryhill Museum/Columbia Gorge, Columbia River Gorge/Bonneville Dam.

Safari Quest **HOME PORTS** Juneau, Seattle

May 7, September 10, 14 nights, Alaska, between Seattle and Juneau; similar itinerary to Safari Explorer above. May–September, 7 nights, round-trip from Juneau to Glacier Bay, Icy Strait, Frederick Sound, Admirality Island, Ford's Terror, Endicott Arm.

Safari Spirit **HOME PORTS** Seattle, Juneau, Friday Harbor, La Paz, and others

April 30, September 3, 14 nights, Seattle to Juneau; similar itinerary to *Safari Explorer* above. May–August, 7 nights, round-trip from Juneau to Glacier Bay, Icy Strait, Frederick Sound, Admiralty Island, Ford's Terror, Endicott Arm. September–October, 7 nights, round-trip from Friday Harbor via Victoria, Harmony Islands, Pricess Louisa Inlet, Vancouver, Roche Harbor, Jones Island.

Azamara Club Cruises

Azamara Journey **HOME PORTS** San Diego, Miami, Barcelona, Venice, and others

April–May, 7 nights, Barcelona to Venice via Sorrento, Taormina, Corfu, Dubrovnik, Zadar;

Venice to Athens via Split, Kotor, Santorini, Nauplion; Athens to Rome via Ephesus, Bodrum, Rhodes, Mykonos, Katakolon; Rome to Barcelona via Bastia, Florence, Portofino, Monte Carlo, St. Tropez. May 23, 14 nights, Barcelona to Copenhagen via Gibraltar, Lisbon, St. Malo, Antwerp, London, Amsterdam, Kiel Canal.

June–August, 12 nights, round-trip from Copenhagen to Berlin, Helsinki, St. Petersburg, Tallinn, Stockholm. June–July, 12 nights, to Oslo, Eidfjord, Bergen, Olden, Geiranger, Molde, Ålesund, Flam, Stavanger; or Iceland and Fjords, round-trip from Copenhagen to Geiranger, Lerwick/Shetland, Akureyri, Isafjordur, Reykjavik, Torshavn, Faroe Islands, Kirkwall.

August, 12 nights, round-trip from Copenhagen to Kiel Canal, Germany, Amsterdam, Waterford, Liverpool, Dublin, Edinburgh, Oslo. August, 14 nights, from Copenhagen to Barcelona.

September–October, 7 nights, Barcelona to Rome via St. Tropez, Nice, Portofino, Florence, Bastia. Rome and Venice via Sorrento, Kotor, Montenegro, Dubrovnik. Venice to Istanbul via Koper, Slovenia, Korcula, Santorini, Ephesus. Istanbul to Athens via Rhodes, Bodrum, Mykonos, Nauplion. From Rome to Athens via Amalfi, Crete, Bodrum, Istanbul, Ephesus, Santorini.

October–November, 7 nights, Holy Land, Athens to Rome via Mykonos, Rhodes, Haifa, Jerusalem, Port Said, Alexandria, Sorrento. November 15, 14 nights, transatlantic, Rome to Miami via Cartagena, Gibraltar, Tenerife, Nassau.

November–December 2010, February–March 2011, 12 nights, round-trip from Miami to St. John, St. Martin, St. Kitts, St. Lucia, Guadeloupe, St. Barts, Virgin Gorda; or St. Croix, St. Martin, St. Barts, Dominica, St. Lucia, Antigua, Virgin Gorda; or St. John, St. Barts, Martinique, Bequia, Dominica, St. Kitts, Virgin Gorda. December 23, 16 nights, Miami to San Diego via Cartagena, Panama Canal, Puntarenas, San Juan Del Sur, Huatulco, Acapulco, Cabo San Lucas. January 30, 2011, 16 nights, similar itinerary in reverse.

January 2011, 11 nights, Sea of Cortez, round-trip from San Diego.

Azamara Quest **HOME PORTS** Hong Kong, Shanghai, Singapore, Athens, and others
May, 12 nights, Athens to Rome or reverse via Rhodes, Haifa, Jerusalem, Port Said, Alexandria, Mykonos, Sorrento. May, October, 14 nights, Rome to Sorrento, Taormina, Ravenna, Trieste, Venice, Dubrovnik, Florence.

June–July, 10 nights, Athens to Istanbul via Nauplion, Mykonos, Santorini, Rhodes, Bodrum, Ephesus. June 12, August 3, 12 nights, Istanbul to Athens via Yalta, Sevastopol, Odessa, Varna, Volos, Skiathos, Ephesus, Mykonos.

August 15, 12 nights, Athens to Venice via Santorini, Ephesus, Zakynthos, Delphi, Corfu, Bari, Split, Ravenna, Koper. August–September, 12 nights, Venice to Barcelona and reverse via Zadar, Dubrovnik, Kotor, Sorrento, Rome, Florence/Pisa, Monte Carlo, St. Tropez; Venice to Rome via Koper, Split, Kotor, Corfu, Delphi, Valletta, Malta, Sicily, Sorrento.

October–November, 14 nights, Rome to Athens and reverse via Sorrento, Chios, Istanbul, Ephesus, Bodrum, Fethiye, Antalya, Limassol, Alexandria. December 21, 18 nights, Singapore to Hong Kong via Bangkok, Sihanoukville, Ho Chi Minh City, Hue, Hanoi.

January 2, 2011, 14 nights, Singapore to Hong Kong. January–March 2011, 14 nights, Hong Kong to Bangkok via Hue, Ho Chi Minh City, Sihanoukville; or Singapore to Hong Kong via Bangkok, Ho Chi Minh City, Hue, Hanoi;

March 2011, 12 nights, Hong Kong to Shanghai via Xiamen, Kagoshima, Nagasaki, Kyoto, Busan; or Hong Kong to Shanghai via Taipei, Nagasaki, Seoul, Tianjin; or 12 nights, Shanghai to Hong Kong via Qingdao, Tianjin, Seoul, Jeju.

Carnival Cruise Lines

Carnival Conquest **HOME PORT** Galveston
September, November 7, December 5, January–April 2011, 7 days, round-trip from Galveston and reverse to Nassau, Freeport, Key West.

Carnival Destiny **HOME PORT** Miami

Year-round 2010, January–April 2011, 5 days, Caribbean, round-trip from Miami to Grand Turk, Half Moon Cay, Nassau; or 5 days, round-trip from Miami to Jamaica, Grand Cayman; or 4 days, round-trip from Miami to Key West, Cozumel.

Carnival Dream **HOME PORT** Port Canaveral

Year-round, 7 days, round-trip from Port Canaveral to Nassau, St. Thomas, St. Maarten; or Cozumel, Isla Roatan, Belize, Costa Maya.

Carnival Ecstasy **HOME PORT** Galveston

Year-round, 4 days, alternate Thursdays, Galveston to Cozumel; 5 days, alternate Mondays and Saturdays to Progresso (Yucatan) and Cozumel.

Carnival Elation **HOME PORTS** San Diego, Mobile

April 30, 15 days, San Diego to Mobile via Cabo San Lucas, Acapulco, Puntarenas, Panama Canal, Cartagena, Grand Cayman, Tampa.

May 15, July 3, July 10, October 23 and 30, 7 days, round-trip from Mobile to Montego Bay, Grand Cayman, Cozumel. May 2010–April 2011, 4–5 days, round-trip from Mobile, Mondays to Cozumel, Calica; Thursdays to Cozumel; alternate Saturdays to Progreso (Yucatan), Cozumel.

Carnival Fantasy **HOME PORTS** Charleston, Mobile

May, 4 or 5 days, round-trip from Mobile, alternate Mondays to Cozumel, Calica; alternate Thursdays to Cozumel; alternate Saturdays to Progreso (Yucatan), Cozumel. May 8, 7 days, round-trip from Mobile to Jamaica, Grand Cayman, Cozumel. May 23, 7 days, round-trip from Charleston to Nassau, Half Moon Cay, Grand Turk.

June 2010–April 2011, 5 days, Bahamas, round-trip from Charleston to Freeport, Nassau, or reverse. May 30, March 6, 6 days, add Key West. June 5, 26, July 24, 2010–April 23, 2011, 6 days, monthly, round-trip from Charleston to Key West, Freeport, Nassau; or July 17, August 14, September 11, 7 days, to Grand Turk, Half Moon Cay, Nassau.

Carnival Fascination **HOME PORT** Jacksonville

Year-round, 4 or 5 days, Bahamas, round-trip from Jacksonville, alternate Mondays via Key West, Nassau; 4 days, alternate Thursdays via Freeport, Nassau; alternate Saturdays via Half Moon Cay, Nassau.

Carnival Freedom **HOME PORT** Fort Lauderdale

Year-round, Sunday, 6 days, Western Caribbean, round-trip from Fort Lauderdale to Key West, Grand Cayman, Jamaica; or Saturday, 8 days, to Cozumel, Limon, Colon; or to Puerto Rico, St. Thomas, Antigua, Tortola, Nassau.

Carnival Glory **HOME PORTS** Miami, New York, Norfolk

Winter/spring, 7 days, round-trip from Miami to Nassau, St. Thomas, Puerto Rico, Grand Turk or reverse; or Grand Cayman, Isla Roatan, Belize, Cozumel.

May 24, November 1, 5 days, round-trip from Charleston to Freeport, Nassau. May 30, October 17, October 25, 6 days, Bahamas, round-trip from Norfolk to Nassau, Freeport.

June–September, Thursday, 4 days; Monday and Saturday, 5 days; round-trip from New York to St. John (4 days); or Saint John, Halifax. September–October, 7 days, to Boston, St. John, Halifax. October 23, 2 days, round-trip from Norfolk.

Carnival Imagination **HOME PORT** Miami

Year-round, Friday, 3 days, round-trip from Miami to Nassau; or Monday, 4 days, round-trip from Miami to Key West, Cozumel.

Carnival Inspiration **HOME PORT** Tampa

Year-round, round-trip from Tampa, 4 days, alternate Thursdays to Cozumel; 5 days, alternate Mondays to Grand Cayman and Cozumel; 5 days, alternate Saturdays to Grand Cayman and Cozumel.

Carnival Legend **HOME PORT** Tampa

Year-round, 7 days, round-trip from Tampa to Grand Cayman, Cozumel, Belize, Isla Roatan, Honduras.

Carnival Liberty **HOME PORTS** Fort Lauderdale, Miami

Year-round, 7 days, round-trip from Miami to Half Moon Cay, St. Thomas, Puerto Rico, Grand Turk; or Cozumel, Grand Cayman, Jamaica.

October 30, November 13, December 25, 7 days, to Nassau, St. Thomas, Nassau, Grand Turk.

Carnival Miracle **HOME PORTS** Fort Lauderdale, New York

April, October 2010–April 2011, 8 days, round-trip from Fort Lauderdale to St. Maarten, St. Lucia, St. Kitts; or Colon, Limon, Belize. April–October, 8 days, round-trip from New York to Grand Turk, Half Moon Cay, Nassau; or Puerto Rico, St. Thomas, Grand Turk. April 15, 2010, April 14, 2011, 6 days, to King's Wharf.

October 14, 2 days, cruise to nowhere, round-trip from New York. October 18, November 3, 19, December 5, 21, January 6, 22, 2011, February 23, March 27, 8 days, round-trip from Fort Lauderdale to Grand Turk, La Romana, Aruba, Curaçao; or Grand Turk, Catalina Island, Aruba, Curaçao.

January 30, 8 days, to St. Lucia, St. Kitts, St. Maarten.

Carnival Paradise **HOME PORT** Long Beach

Year-round, Mexico, round-trip from Long Beach, 3 days, Friday to Ensenada; 4 days, Monday to Catalina Island, Ensenada.

Carnival Pride **HOME PORT** Baltimore

Winter–spring, 7 days, round-trip from Baltimore to Port Canaveral, Nassau, Freeport.

May–September, 7 days, round-trip from Baltimore to Grand Turk, Half Moon Cay, Freeport.

Carnival Sensation **HOME PORT** Port Canaveral

Year-round, round-trip from Port Canaveral, 3 days, Thursdays to Nassau; 4 days, Sundays to Freeport and Nassau.

Carnival Spirit **HOME PORTS** Ensenada, Honolulu, San Diego, Seattle, Vancouver

May 5, 6 days, Vancouver to Seattle via Inside Passage, Juneau, Skagway, Ketchikan. May–August, 7 days, round-trip from Seattle via Tracy Arm Fjord, Skagway, Juneau, Ketchikan, Victoria.

September 7, 7 days, Seattle to Vancouver via Glacier Bay, Skagway, Ketchikan, Inside Passage. September 14, 12 days, Vancouver to Honolulu via Kona, Kauai, Hilo, Maui; September 26, 12 days, Honolulu to Ensenada via Kauai, Kona, Hilo, Maui.

October 2010, April 5, 2011, 4 or 5days, round-trip from San Diego to Cabo San Lucas.

October–December, 8 days, round-trip from San Diego to Acapulco, Zihuatanejo/Ixtapa, and Manzanillo.

Carnival Splendor **HOME PORT** Long Beach, Califronia

Year-round, 7 days, Mexico, round-trip from Long Beach to Puerto Vallarta, Mazatlan, Cabo San Lucas.

Carnival Triumph **HOME PORT** New Orleans

Year-round, 7 days, round-trip from New Orleans to Key West, Freeport, Nassau; or Progreso, Cozumel; or Nassau, Freeport, Key West; or Belize, Isla Roatan, Cozumel; or 4 or 5 days, or Cozumel (Thursday); or Progreso, Cozumel (Monday). December 20, 7 days, to Key West, Freeport, Nassau; December 27, 7 days, to Belize, Isla Roatan, Cozumel.

Carnival Valor **HOME PORT** Miami

Year-round, Sunday, 7 days, Western Caribbean, round-trip from Miami to Grand Cayman, Isla Roatan, Belize, Cozumel.

Carnival Victory **HOME PORTS** Barbados, Puerto Rico
Year-round, Sunday, 7 days, round-trip from Puerto Rico to St. Thomas, Dominica, Barbados, St. Lucia, St. Maarten, St. Kitts; or Wednesday, round-trip from Barbados to St. Lucia, St. Maarten, St. Kitts, Puerto Rico, St. Thomas, Dominica. November 21, 3 days, to St. Thomas, Dominica.

Celebration Cruise Line

MS Bahamas Celebration **HOME PORT** Palm Beach
Year-round, 2 nights, round-trip from Palm Beach to Grand Bahama Island.

Celebrity Cruises

Celebrity Century **HOME PORT** Miami
May 3, 7 nights, round-trip from Miami to George Town, Cozumel, Playa Del Carmen, Cococay. May 10, November 2010–April 2011, 5 nights, to Roatan, Cozumel; or Jamaica, Grand Cayman. May 20, 14 nights, transatlantic, Miami to Barcelona via Ponta Delgada, Lisbon, Cadiz, Malaga.

June 3–October 13, 12 nights, round-trip from Barcelona to Villefranche, Livorno, Rome (Civitavecchia), Messina, Mykonos, Kusadasi, Piraeus, Salerno; or Villefranche, Livorno, Rome (Civitavecchia), Dubrovnik, Venice, Split, Salerno; or Messina, Mykonos, Kusadasi, Piraeus, Salerno, Rome, Livorno, Toulon.

October 25, 14 nights, transatlantic, from Barcelona to Miami via Malaga, Funchal, Tenerife, La Palma. November 4, 4 nights, round-trip from Miami to Cozumel. December 24, Miami to Nassau, Cococay, Key West.

Celebrity Constellation **HOME PORTS** Miami, San Diego, Amsterdam, Barcelona
May 9, 7 nights, round-trip from Amsterdam to Oslo, Stavanger, Ålesund, Bergen. May–August, 12 nights, round-trip from Amsterdam to Berlin, Stockholm, Helsinki, St. Petersburg, Tallinn, Copenhagen.

June 21, 12 nights, Arctic Circle, round-trip from Amsterdam to Ålesund, Arctic Circle, Tromso, Honningsvag, Molde, Geiranger, Olden, Bergen.

September 3, 8 nights, Amsterdam to Barcelona via Brugges, Cherbourg, Vigo, Lisbon, Gibraltar. September–October, 7 nights, round-trip from Barcelona to Nice, Genoa, Florence/Pisa, Rome, Naples/Capri.

November 6, 14 nights, transatlantic, Barcelona to Fort Lauderdale via Palma De Mallorca, Alicante, Malaga, Madeira (Funchal), Tenerife, Canary Islands. November 2010, January–April 2011, 14 nights, round-trip from Fort Lauderdale to St. Maarten, Antigua, St. Lucia, Barbados, Grenada, Aruba, Curaçao, Bonaire. December 18, 15 nights, Fort Lauderdale to San Diego via Cartagena, Puerto Limon, Panama Canal, Huatulco, Acapulco, Puerto Vallarta, Cabo San Lucas.

January 2, 2011, 13 nights, San Diego to Fort Lauderdale via Cabo San Lucas, Acapulco, Huatulco, Puntarenas, Panama Canal, Cristobal Pier, George Town.

Celebrity Eclipse **HOME PORTS** Southampton, Miami
May–June, 11 nights, to Madeira, Tenerife, Gran Canaria, Lanzarote, Lisbon, Vigo, Spain.

May–July, 14 nights, to Brugges, Berlin (Warnemude), Stockholm, Helsinki, St. Petersburg, Tallinn, Copenhagen or Amsterdam.

July–September, 14 nights, to Vigo, Lisbon, Gibraltar, Barcelona, Provence (Toulon), Palma De Mallorca, Seville (Cadiz). September–October, 16 nights, to Cadiz, Sardinia, Split, Venice, Dubrovnik, Sicily, Malaga. October 20, to Madeira, Tenerife, Gran Canaria, Lanzarote, Lisbon, Vigo. October 31, 13 nights, transatlantic, Southampton to Miami via Paris, Cherbourg, Vigo, Azores. November 15, 5 nights, round-trip from Miami to George Town, Cozumel. November 2010–April 2011, 7 nights, round-trip from Miami to Puerto

Rico, St. Maarten, St. Kitts; or to Grand Cayman, Cozumel, Costa Maya, Roatan.

December 4, 2010, February 2011, 14 nights, alternating round-trip from Miami or Fort Lauderdale to St. Thomas, Antigua, St. Lucia, Barbados, Tobago, Grenada, Aruba, Curaçao. December 18, 8 nights, Miami to Puerto Rico, St. Thomas, St. Maarten, Labadee (Haiti).

January 2, 2011, 6 nights, round-trip from Miami to Jamaica, Grand Cayman, Cozumel.

Celebrity Equinox **HOME PORTS** Fort Lauderdale, Rome, Barcelona

May–August, 10 or 11 nights, round-trip from Rome to Santorini, Mykonos, Istanbul, Ephesus, Athens, Naples/Capri; or Sicily, Athens, Mykonos, Ephesus, Rhodes, Santorini, Naples/Capri.

August 6, 10 nights, to Venice via Naples/Capri, Santorini, Ephesus, Athens, Corfu, Dubrovnik.

September 2, 7 nights, Barcelona to Roma via Nice, Corsica, Naples/Capri, Dubrovnik.

September 9, 13 nights, round-trip from Rome to Athens, Rhodes, Ephesus, Haifa, Jerusalem, Alexandria, Naples/Capri; or September 22, Rome to Naples/Capri, Haifa, Jerusalem, Alexandria, Athens, Corfu, Sicily; or, October 5, Rome to Athens, Ephesus, Haifa, Jerusalem, Alexandria, Sicily, Naples/Capri; or, October 18, Rome to Naples/Capri, Sicily, Corfu, Alexandria, Jerusalem, Haifa.

October 31, 15 nights, transatlantic, from Rome to Fort Lauderdale via Florence/Pisa, Nice, Barcelona, Cartagena, Seville, Tenerife.

November–December, January–April 2011, 11 nights, Caribbean, round-trip from Fort Lauderdale to Grand Cayman, Cartagena, Colon, Puerto Limon, Roatan, Cozumel, or reverse. November–December, January–April 2011, 10 nights, to St. Thomas, St. Kitts, Barbados, Dominica, St. Maarten; or St. Maarten, St. Lucia, Barbados, St. Kitts, St. Thomas.

Celebrity Infinity **HOME PORTS** Buenos Aires, Fort Lauderdale, and others

May 10, 11 nights, San Francisco to Vancouver via Ketchikan, Juneau, Skagway, Icy Strait Point, Hubbard Glacier, Sitka, Victoria. May–September, 7 nights, round-trip from Seattle to Ketchikan, Tracy Arm Fjord, Juneau, Skagway, Inside Passage, Victoria. September 24, 16 nights, Seattle to Fort Lauderdale via San Diego, Cabo San Lucas, Acapulco, Huatulco, Puntarenas, Panama Canal (cruising), Cristobal Pier, Cartagena.

October–November, 14 nights, alternating, Fort Lauderdale to Los Angeles via Grand Cayman, Cartagena, Panama Canal, Puntarenas, Huatulco, Acapulco, Cabo San Lucas (westbound); or Cabo San Lucas, Acapulco, Huatulco, Puntarenas, Panama Canal, Cristobal Pier, Cartagena.

December 5, Fort Lauderdale to Valparaiso via Cartagena, Panama Canal, Manta, Lima, Arica, La Serena. December 2010–February 2011, 14 nights, Buenos Aires to Valparaiso and reverse via Puerto Montt, Chilean Fjords, Strait of Magellan, Punta Arenas, Ushuaia, Cape Horn, Puerto Madryn, Punta Del Este, Montevideo; or Antarctic, round-trip from Buenos Aires to Port Stanley, Falkland Islands, Elephant Island, Gerlache Straight, Paradise Bay, Ushuaia, Cape Horn, Puerto Madryn, Montevideo.

Celebrity Mercury **HOME PORTS** Charleston, Vancouver, Baltimore

May 5, 12 nights, Alaska, round-trip from Los Angeles to Juneau, Skagway, Tracy Arm Fjord, Ketchikan, Victoria. May 17, 13 nights, Los Angeles to Vancouver via Seattle, Ketchikan, Juneau, Skagway, Hubbard Glacier, Icy Strait Point, Victoria. May–September, 7 nights, round-trip from Vancouver to Inside Passage, Icy Strait Point, Hubbard Glacier, Juneau, Ketchikan. September 19, 12 nights, Vancouver to San Diego via Sitka, Hubbard Glacier, Juneau, Skagway, Ketchikan, San Francisco.

October 1, 17 nights, San Diego to Baltimore via Cabo San Lucas, Acapulco, Huatulco, Puntarenas, Costa Rica, Panama Canal, Cartagena, Santo Domingo. October 18, 11 nights, round-trip from Baltimore to Labadee, Puerto Rico, St. Thomas, St. Kitts, St. Maarten. October 29, 10 nights, round-trip from Baltimore to Charleston, Nassau, Cococay, Key West, Miami. November 2010–February 2011, 9 nights, Baltimore to Charleston, Key West, Nassau, Cococay.

January–February 2011, 12 nights, round-trip from Baltimore to St. Thomas, St. Croix, St. Kitts, Antigua, St. Maarten.

February–April 2011, 11 nights, round-trip from Charleston to Puerto Rico, St. Thomas, St. Maarten, St. Kitts, Tortola.

Celebrity Millennium **HOME PORTS** San Juan, San Diego, Vancouver

April, October 2010–April 2011, 10 or 11 nights, from San Juan to Tortola, St. Maarten, St. Lucia, Barbados, Grenada, Curaçao, Aruba (10 nights); or St. Croix, St. Kitts, Dominica, St. Lucia, Barbados, Grenada, Curaçao, Aruba.

May–September, 7 nights, Vancouver to Seward and reverse via Inside Passage, Ketchikan, Icy Strait Point, Juneau, Skagway, Hubbard Glacier.

September 17, 10 nights, Wine Cruise, Vancouver to San Diego via Nanaimo, Victoria, Seattle, San Francisco, Monterey, Catalina Island. September 27, San Diego to San Juan via Cabo San Lucas, Acapulco, Huatulco, Puntarenas, Panama Canal, Cristobal Pier, Aruba, Curaçao.

Celebrity Solstice **HOME PORT** Fort Lauderdale

April–November, January–April 2011, 7 nights, round-trip from Fort Lauderdale to Puerto Rico, St. Thomas, St. Maarten; or Grand Cayman, Cozumel, Costa Maya, Roatan.

Celebrity Summit **HOME PORTS** San Juan, Cape Liberty

April–September, 7 nights, round-trip from Cape Liberty to Bermuda; May–June, 7 nights, to Newport, Bermuda. May 16, to Newport, Boston, Bermuda.

July–August, 7 nights, round-trip from Cape Liberty to Portland, Bar Harbor, St. John, Halifax.

September–October, 14 nights, to Newport, Boston, Portland, Bar Harbor, Halifax, Quebec City, Charlottetown.

October 24, 6 nights, Cape Liberty to San Juan via Bermuda, St. Thomas.

October 2010–April, 2011, 7 nights, round-trip from San Juan to St. Croix, St. Kitts, Dominica, Grenada, Tobago; or St. Thomas, St. Maarten, Antigua, St. Lucia, Barbados. December, 8 nights, add Grenada; or St. Thomas, St. Croix, St. Kitts, Antigua, St. Lucia, St. Maarten.

Celebrity Xpedition **HOME PORT** Baltra (Galápagos Islands)

Year-round, 7, 11, or 13 nights, Galápagos Islands, round-trip from Baltra to North Seymour, San Cristobal, Punta Suarez, Cormorant Point, Baroness Outlook, Las Bachas, Bartolome, Elizabeth Bay, Punta Espinoza, Puerto Egas, Dragon Hill, Puerto Ayora.

Costa Cruises

Costa Atlantica **HOME PORTS** Fort Lauderdale, New York, Quebec, Copenhagen

May 5, reverse September 4, 17 nights, transatlantic, New York to Copenhagen via Boston, Bar Harbor, Halifax, Sydney, Le Havre, Dover, Bremerhaven.

May–August, 7 nights, round-trip from Copenhagen to Stockholm, Tallinn, St. Petersburg, Warnemunde; or Hellesylt, Geiranger, Flam, Stavanger, Oslo, Warnemunde.

October 24, 14 nights, Quebec to Fort Lauderdale via Charlottetown, Bar Harbor, Boston, New York, King's Wharf, Port Canaveral.

Costa Classica **HOME PORTS** Hong Kong, Singapore, Shanghai

May, August 26, 30, September–October, 3–5 nights, or Fukuoka, Cheju (4 nights); or Cheju, Fukuoka, Nagasaki (5 nights). June 4, 10, 16 nights, to Cheju, Nagasaki, Yokohama, Kobe, Keelung; July–August, 6 nights, to Pusan, Fukuoka, Kagoshima. October 18, 5 nights, Shanghai to Hong Kong via Kagoshima, Naha.

October 23, November 6, 14 nights, round-trip from Hong Kong to Manila, Kotakinabulu, Bandar Seri Begawan, Singapore, Ho Chi Minh City, Da Nang, Sanya.

November 20, 14 nights, Hong Kong to Singapore via Sanya, Halong Bay, Da Nang, Nha Trang, Ho Chi Minh City, Bangkok.

Costa Concordia **HOME PORTS** Santos, Savona, Barcelona

April–October, 7 nights, round-trip from Barcelona to Marseille, Savona, Naples, Palermo, Tunis, Palma de Mallorca.

November 24, 4 nights, round-trip from Savona to Barcelona, Palma de Mallorca, Ajaccio.

Costa Deliziosa **HOME PORTS** Savona, Dubai, Copenhagen

April, May 2, Inaugural season, 7 nights, to Muscat, Fujairah, Abu Dhabi, Bahrain.

May 9, 18 nights, repositioning, Dubai to Savona via Fujairah, Muscat, Salalah, Aden, Safaga, Sharm el Sheik, Alexandria, Rome; May 27, 10 nights, Savona to Copenhagen via Malaga, Cadiz, Lisbon, Vigo, Le Havre, Harwich.

June–August, September 5, 7 nights, alternate, round-trip from Copenhagen to Flam, Hellesylt, Geiranger, Bergen, Stavanger, Olso; or Tallinn, St. Petersburg, Helsinki, Stockholm. September 12, 10 nights, Copenhagen to Savona via Dover, Le Havre, Vigo, Lisbon, Cadiz, Malaga. September 22, October–November, 10 nights, Savona to Naples, Messina, Alexandria, Limassol, Marmaris, Santorini, Katakolon.

Costa Fortuna **HOME PORTS** Fort Lauderdale, Savona, Venice

April–November, 7 nights, round-trip Venice to Bari, Katakolon, Santorini, Mykonos, Rhodes, Dubrovnik.

November 29, 5 nights, Venice to Savona via Bari, Corfu, La Valletta, Naples.

Costa Luminosa **HOME PORTS** Dubai, Savona, Amsterdam,

May–June, August 21, 11 nights, round-trip from Amsterdam to Copenhagen, Stockholm, Helsinki, St. Petersburg, Tallinn; or Hellesylt, Geiranger, Honningsvag, Tromso, Gravdal, Trondheim, Andalsnes, Bergen.

July 7, 13 nights, round-trip from Amsterdam to Hellesylt, Geiranger, Trondheim, Gravdal, Honningsavag, Akureyri, Reykjavik, Lerwick. July 20, 12 nights, to Hellesylt, Geiranger, Honningsvag, Tromso, Gravdal, Trondheim, Andalsnes, Flam, Bergen. August 1, 20 nights, to Bergen, Akureyri, Nuuk, Ilulissat, Reykjavik, Thorshavn, Invergordon.

September 1, 9 nights, Amsterdam to Savona via Cork, Vigo, Lisbon, Cadiz, Barcelona.

Costa Magica **HOME PORTS** Santos, Savona, Kiel

May 19, 30, August 22, 11 nights, round-trip from Kiel to Stockholm, Helsinki, St. Petersburg, Tallinn, Riga, Klaipeda, Gdynia, Ronne/Bornholm. June 10, 17 nights, to Lerwick, Reykjavik, Isafjord, Akureyri, Ny Ålesund, Longyearbyen, Honningsvag, Hammerfest, Molde, Andalsnes, Bergen. June 27, 14 nights, to Geiranger, Tromso, Magdalene Fjord, Ny Ålesund, Longyearbyen, Honningsvag, Hammerfest, Molde, Andalsnes, Bergen. July 11, August 8, 6 nights, to Hellesylt, Geiranger, Bergen, Stavanger, Aarhus. July 17, 28, 11 nights, to Hellesylt, Geiranger, Honningsvag, Tromso, Gravdal, Trondheim, Andalsnes, Bergen. August 14, 8 nights, to Stockholm, Helsinki, St. Petersburg, Tallinn.

September 2, 11 nights, Kiel to Savona via Dover, Guernsey, Vigo, Lisbon, Valencia, Barcelona, Monte Carlo.

September–October, November 6, 9 nights, round-trip from Savona to Malaga, Casablanca, Cadiz, Lisbon, Valencia, Barcelona.

Costa Marina **HOME PORTS** Barcelona, Savona

May 31, June–September, 7 nights, round-trip from Barcelona to Monte Carlo, Livorno, Olbia, Capri, Tunis, Port Mahon. September 27, 7 nights, to Villefranche, Livorno, Olbia, Capri, Tunis, Port Mahon. November 4, 8 nights, to Villefranche, Livorno, Olbia, Capri, Tunis, Port Mahon, Monte Carlo.

Costa Mediterranea **HOME PORT** Savona

May 4, June 8, September 17, October 20, 11 nights, round-trip from Savona to Rome, Alexandria, Limassol, Rhodes, Izmir, Piraeus, Katakolon; or May 15, July, August 13, September 28, November 11, 11 nights, to Barcelona, Casablanca, Arrecife, Santa Curz de Tenerife, Funchal, Malaga. May 26, August 24, 13 nights, to Rome, Mykonos, Izmir, Istanbul,

Costanza, Odessa, Yalta, Piraeus, Katakolon. June 19, September 6, 11 nights, to Rome, Alexandria, Port Said, Ashdod, Limassol, Rhodes, Piraeus, Katakolon. October 9, 11 nights, to Rome, Alexandria, Limassol, Rhodes, La Valletta, Tripoli.

Costa Pacifica **HOME PORT** Rome

May–November, 7 nights, round-trip from Rome to Savona, Barcelona, Palma de Mallorca, Tunis, La Valletta, Catania.

Costa Serena **HOME PORTS** Savona, Venice

May–November, 7 nights, round-trip from Venice to Bari, Katakolon, Izmir, Istanbul, Dubrovnik. November 21, 5 nights, Venice to Savona via Bari, Corfu, La Valletta, Naples.

Costa Victoria **HOME PORTS** Buenos Aires, Savona, Venice

May–October, November 6, 7 nights, round-trip from Venice to Ancona, Santorini, Mykonos, Piraeus, Corfu, Dubrovnik. November 13, 5 nights, Venice to Savona via Bari, Corfu, La Valletta, Naples.

Cruise North Expeditions, Inc.

Lyubov Orlova **HOME PORT** Kuujjuaq

Weather, drifting ice, sea tides, and other conditions dictate itinerary and excursions; routes and landing sites will vary from one expedition to the next.

July 2, 11 nights, Spirit Mountains, round-trip from St. John's to L'Anse aux Meadows, Red Bay, Battle Harbour, The Wonderstrands, Rigolet, Nain, Hebron, Torngat Mountains National Park Reserve, Killiniq, Kuujjuaq.

July 13, 10 nights, Artic Safari (Photo Life Arctic Cruise Workshop), Kuujjuaq to Iqaluit via Akpatok Island, Quaqtag and Diana Island, Kangiqsujuaq, Digges Island and Mansel Island, Walrus Island, Cape Dorset and Mallikjuak Territorial Park, Kimmirut for Katannilik Territorial Park (Soper Heritage River), Nannuk Harbour, Lower Savage Island.

July 23, August 6, 13 or 14 nights, Baffin & Greenland Adventure, round-trip from Kuujjuaq or from Iqaliut to Kuujjuaq via Akpatok Island, Monumental Island, Sisimiut, Ilulissat, Jokobshaven Glacer and Icefiord, Uummannaq, Isabella Bay, Qikiqtarjuaq, Auyuittuq National Park.

August 19, September 6,10 nights, High Arctic (Photo Workshop), Kuujjuaq to Resolute Bay via Akpatok Island, Qikiqtarjuaq, Baffin Island, North Arm Fiord, Pond Inlet, Bylot Island, Lancaster Sound, Beechey Island.

August 29, 8 nights, Northwest Passage, round-trip from Resolute to Beechey Island, Victory Point, Cambridge Bay, Gjoa Haven, Bellot Strait, Prince Leopold Island.

Cruise West

Pacific Explorer **HOME PORTS** Colon, Los Sueños, Panama City

April, October 30, November 8, December 18, 27, 9 nights, Costa Rica and Panama, Colon, Portobelo, Panama Canal, Darién Jungle, Isla de Coiba, Coiba National Park, Golfo Dulce, Corcovado National Park, Manuel Antonio National Park, Los Suenos.

Spirit of Columbia **HOME PORTS** Whittier, Juneau

May 29, September 3, 10 nights, Juneau to Seattle via Skagway, Glacier Bay National Park, Sitka, Frederick Sound and Tracy Arm, Petersburg, Metlakatla, Strait of Georgia, cruising San Juan Islands, Friday Harbor.

June–August, 4 nights, Prince William Sound, round-trip from Whittier to College Fjord, Cordova, Chenega Glacier, Knight Island.

Spirit of Discovery **HOME PORTS** Juneau, Portland

May 14, May 24, June 3, August 28, 10 nights, Juneau to Seattle, same itinerary as Spirit of Columbia.

June–August, 4 nights, round-trip from Juneau to Skagway, Haines, wilderness cruising, Sitka,Glacier Bay National Park.

September–October, 7 nights, Columbia and Snake rivers, round-trip from Portland to Columbia River Gorge, Pendleton, Clarkston, Snake River, Hells Canyon, Walla Walla, Beacon Rock, Multnomah Falls, Cape Horn, Rooster Rock, The Dalles, Maryhill Museum, Astoria, Fort Clatsop.

Spirit of Endeavour **HOME PORTS** Cabo San Lucas, Juneau, Seattle

May–August, 7 nights, round-trip from Juneau to Tracy Arm, Frederick Sound, Wrangell/Wrangell Narrows/Petersburg, wilderness cruising, Peril Strait, Sergius Narrows, Sitka, Icy Strait, Glacer Bay National Park and Preserve.

May 9, September 1, 10 nights to Seattle via Skagway, Glacier Bay National Park, Sitka, Frederick Sound and Tracy Arm, Petersburg, Metlakatla, cruising Northern British Columbia, Strait of Georgia, cruising San Juan Islands and Friday Harbor.

May 2, September, 7 nights, round-trip from Seattle to Vancouver, Desolation Sound, Desolation Sound Marine Provincial Park, Nanaimo, Victoria/Butchart Gardens, Friday Harbor, San Juan Islands, Port Townsend.

January–March, round-trip from Cabo San Lucas to Isla Espiritu Santo, whale watching Sea of Cortes, Isla San Francisco, Isla San Jose, Loreto, Los Islotes, Isla Partida, La Paz.

Spirit of '98 **HOME PORT** Portland

April–October, 7 nights, round-trip from Portland to Columbia River Gorge, Pendleton, Clarkston, Snake River, Hells Canyon, Walla Walla, Beacon Rock, Multnomah Falls, Cape Horn, Rooster Rock, The Dalles, Maryhill Museum, Astoria, Fort Clatsop.

Spirit of Oceanus **HOME PORTS** Singapore; others vary with itineraries

March 6, 335 days, World Cruise Voyage of the Great Explorers, round-trip from Singapore, 242 ports of call in 59 countries. 10- to 18-night segments, Singapore to Chennai, Mumbai, Muscat, to Alexandria, Istanbul, Venice, Malta Rome, Barcelona, Honfleur, Oslo, London, St. John's, Halifax, Palm Beach, Panama, Guayaquil, Easter Island, Papeete, Lautoka, Auckland, Sydney, Darwin, Singapore.

Spirit of Yorktown **HOME PORT** Juneau

May 27, August 15, 25, September 4, 10 nights, Juneau to Seattle via Skagway, Glacier Bay, Sitka, Frederick Sound/Tracy Arm, Petersburg, Metlakatla, Strait of Georgia, San Juan Islands, Friday Harbor.

June–August, 7 nights, round-trip from Juneau to Tracy Arm, Frederick Sound, Wrangell/Wrangell Narrows/Petersburg, wilderness cruising, Peril Strait, Sergius Narrows, Sitka, Icy Strait, Glacier Bay National Park and Preserve.

Crystal Cruises

Crystal Serenity **HOME PORT** Varies with itinerary

May 11, 7 days, Rome to Piraeus via Sorrento, Sicily, Crete, Kusadasi, Mykonos. May 18, 7 days, from Piraeus to Venice via Santorini, Bodrum, Corfu, Dubrovnik. May 25, 12 days, Venice to Barcelona via Dubrovnik, Sicily, Sorrento, Rome, Florence, Cannes. June 6, 12 days, Barcelona to Athens via Monte Carlo, Porto Venere, Rome, Sorrento, Sicily, Kusadasi, Mykonos. June 18, 7 days, Athens to Venice via Mykonos, Kusadasi, Corfu, Split. June 25, 12 days, Venice to Athens via Ravenna, Corfu, Rhodes, Bodrum, Mykonos, Istanbul. July 7, 12 days, Athens to Venice via Kusadasi, Santorini, Patmos, Crete, Kotor, Split. July 19, August 24, 12 days, to Istanbul via Katakolon, Navplion, Nesebur, Yalta, Sevastopol, Odessa.

July 31, September 5, 12 days, Istanbul to Barcelona via Kusadasi, Santorini, Sorrento, Rome, Florence, St. Tropez, Monte Carlo. August 12, 12 days, Barcelona to Venice via Monte Carlo, Florence, Porto Venere, Rome, Sorrento, Trogir, Trieste. September 17, 12 days, via Monte Carlo, Florence, Elba, Rome, Sorrento, Corfu, Dubrovnik. September 29, 9 days, Venice to Monte Carlo via Dubrovnik, Sorrento, Rome, Porto Venere, Florence. October 8, 11 days, Monte Carlo to Piraeus via Portofino, Florence, Rome, Sorrento, Sicily, Kusadasi, Mykonos.

October 19, 12 days, Piraeus to Rome via Ashdod, Alexandria, Valletta, Sicily, Naples.

October 31, 11 days, Rome to Barcelona via Naples, Sicily, Valletta, Tunis, Malaga, Almeria, Valencia. November 11, 11 days, Barcelona to Lisbon via Malaga, Cadiz, Casablanca, Gran Canaria, Santa Cruz de Tenerife, Madeira. November 22, 9 days, Lisbon to Cadiz, Casablanca, Agadir, Gran Canaria, Santa Cruz de Tenerife, Madeira.

December 1, 10 days, transatlantic, Lisbon to Miami via Azores/Ponta Delgada, Grand Turk. December 11, 10 days, Caribbean, round-trip from Miami to St. Thomas, Antigua, St. Barts, St. Maarten, Grand Turk. December 21, 14 days, to St. Thomas, Barbados, St. Lucia, Antigua, St. Maarten, Curaçao, Grand Turk.

January 4, 2011, 13 days, Panama Canal, Miami to Los Angeles via Grand Cayman, Cartagena, Panama Canal, Huatulco, Puerto Vallarta.

January 17, 110 days, World Cruise, 13 days, Los Angeles, Oahu/Honolulu, Mooréa, Papeete; January 30, 12 days, Papeete, Bora Bora, Rarotonga, Nuku'alofa, Lautoka, Auckland; February 12, 16 days, Auckland, Tauranga, Napier, Wellington, Christchurch, Picton, Dunedin, cruising Dusky, Doubtful & Milford Sounds, Hobart, Melbourne, Sydney; February 28, 15 days, Sydney, Brisbane, Cairns, Darwin, Komodo, Bali, Singapore; March 15, 14 days, Singapore, Kuala Lumpur/Port Kelang, Phuket, Colombo, Cochin, Mumbai, Dubai; March 29, 19 days, Dubai, Al Fujairah, Mahé/Victoria, Mombasa, Durban, Cape Town; April 17, 21 days, Cape Town, Walvis Bay, Bom Bom Island, Lomé, Takoradi, Dakar, Lisbon, Dover.

May 22, 11 days, Hamburg to Stockholm via Copenhagen, Helsinki, St. Petersburg, Tallinn. June 2, 27, 11 days, Stockholm to Copenhagen via Tallinn, St. Petersburg, Helsinki, Warnemünde.

June 13, 14 days, Copenhagen to Stockholm via Hellesylt/Geiranger, Honningsvåg, North Cape, Bear Island, Sørkapp/Spitsbergen, Polar Ice Cap, Longyearbyen/Longyear City/ Svalbard, Ålesund, Bergen. July 8, 2011, 14 days, to Dover via Hellesylt/Geiranger, Honningsvåg, North Cape, Bear Island, Sørkapp/Spitsbergen, Polar Ice Cap, Longyearbyen/ Longyear City/Svalbard, Ålesund, Flåm/Gudvangen, Bergen.

July 22, 11 days, round-trip from Dover to Edinburgh, Belfast, Liverpool, Dublin, Waterford, Guernsey. August 2, 12 days, Dover to Rome via Oporto, Lisbon, Gibraltar, Valencia, Barcelona, Cannes, Florence/Livorno. August 14, 12 days, Rome to Barcelona via Porto Venere, Florence/Livorno, Portofino, St-Tropez, Monte Carlo, Palma de Mallorca, Valencia. August 26, 12 days, from Barcelona to Venice via Cannes, Florence/ Livorno, Rome, Sorrento, Dubrovnik.

September 7, 12 days, Venice to Istanbul via Katakolon, Navplion, Dardanelles/Bosporus Straits, Constanta, Odessa, Yalta, Trabzon. September 19, 12 days, Istanbul to Venice via Dardanelles, Kusadasi, Mykonos, Santorini/Thíra, Fethiye, Argostoli, Kotor, Dubrovnik. October 1, 12 days, Venice to Barcelona via Dubrovnik, Sicily/Taormina, Sorrento, Rome, Florence/Livorno, Monte Carlo. October 13, 11 days, Barcelona to Piraeus via Monte Carlo, Florence/Livorno, Rome, Sorrento, Kusadasi, Mykonos. October 24, 12 days, Piraeus to Istanbul via Santorini/Thíra, Ashdod, Alexandria/Cairo, Kusadasi, cruising the Dardanelles Strait.

November 5, 11 days, Istanbul to Venice via Dardanelles Strait, Kusadasi, Mykonos, Piraeus, Santorini/Thíra, Kotor, Dubrovnik. November 16, 11 days, Venice to Barcelona via Koper, Dubrovnik, Sicily/Catania, Naples, Rome, Florence/ Livorno. November 27, 11 days, Barcelona to Lisbon via Valencia, Málaga, Cádiz/Seville, Casablanca, Gran Canaria/ Las Palmas, Santa Cruz de Tenerife, Madeira/Funchal, Lisbon.

December 8, 13 days, transatlantic, from Lisbon to Miami via Casablanca, Santa Cruz de Tenerife, St. Maarten. December 21, 2011, 14 days, round-trip from Miami to St. Thomas, Barbados, St. Lucia, Antigua, St. Maarten, Curaçao, Grand Turk.

Crystal Symphony **HOME PORT** Varies with itinerary
June 14, 7 days, Northern Europe from Dover to Liverpool via Guernsey, Waterford, Dublin, Belfast. June 21, 11 days, to Stockholm via Oslo, Copenhagen, Visby, St. Petersburg,

Helsinki. July 2, 11 days, Stockholm to Copenhagen via St. Petersburg, Helsinki, Warnemünde, Kiel. July 13, 15 days, Copenhagen to Stockholm via Hellesylt/Geiranger, Trondheim. Honningsvåg, Longyearbyen/Longyear City/Svalbard, Ålesund, Flåm, Bergen. July 28, 10 days, to Copenhagen via St. Petersburg, Tallinn, Warnemünde, Helsinki. August 7, 7 days, to Stockholm via St. Petersburg, Tallinn. August 14, 11 days, Stockholm to Dover via Helsinki, St. Petersburg, Copenhagen, Tallinn, Oslo. August 25, 11 days, round-trip from London to Edinburgh, Belfast, Dublin Holyhead, Waterford, Portland, Guernsey.

September 5, 14 days, transatlantic, Dover to New York via Dublin, Reykjavik, Nuuk, Greenland, Halifax. September–October, 19 days, New England/Canada, New York to Montreal via Newport, Boston, Bar Harbor, Saint John, Halifax, Quebec City, and reverse.

November 2, 19 days, New York to Los Angeles via Philadelphia, Charleston, Miami, George Town, Cartagena, Panama Canal, Caldera, Acapulco, Cabo San Lucas. November 21, 28, December 5, 7 days, Mexican Riviera, roundtrip from Los Angeles to Cabo San Lucas, Mazatlan, Puerto Vallarta; or December 12, 10 days, to Cabo San Lucas, La Paz, Topolobampo, Loreto, Mazatlan, Puerto Vallarta. December 22, 14 days, roundtrip from Los Angeles to Hilo, Honolulu, Kauai/Nawiliwili, Lahaina, Ensenada.

January 5, 2011, 15 nights, Los Angeles to Valparaíso via Cabo San Lucas, Golfo de Papagayo, Guayaquil, Lima/Callao. January 20, 18 nights, Valparaiso to Buenos Aires via Puerto Montt, Punta Arenas, cruising Cape Horn, Ushuaia, Antarctica, Port Stanley, Puerto Madryn, Montevideo. February 7, 16 nights, Buenos Aires to Miami via Rio de Janeiro, Devil's Island, Barbados, Grand Turk. February 23, 11 nights, return March 6, Panama Canal, from Miami to Costa Rica/Caldera via Tortola, St. Martin, St. Barts, Aruba, Panama Canal.

March 17, 14 nights, Miami to Los Angeles via Grand Cayman/George Town, Cartagena, Panama Canal, Huatulco, Puerto Vallarta, Cabo San Lucas, San Diego. March 31, 10 nights, round-trip from Los Angeles to Puerto Vallarta, Mazatlán, Loreto, La Paz, Cabo San Lucas, San Diego; or April 10, 17, 7 nights, to Cabo San Lucas, Mazatlán, Puerto Vallarta. April 24, 14 nights, Hawaiian Islands, round-trip from Los Angeles to Hawaii/ Hilo, Oahu/Honolulu, Kauai/Nawiliwili, Maui/Lahaina, Ensenada.

May 9–August 13, 12 nights, Alaska round-trip from San Francisco to Victoria, Vancouver, Inside Passage, Sitka, Glacier Bay, Skagway, Juneau, Ketchikan. August 25, 19 nights, San Francisco to New York via Los Angeles, Cabo San Lucas, Caldera, Panama Canal, Aruba, Grand Cayman, Miami, Charleston.

September 13, 11 nights, New England/Canada, New York to Newport, Boston, Bar Harbor, Halifax, Québec City, Montréal. September 24, October 15, 10–11 nights, return October 5, New England/Canada, Montréal to New York via Québec City, Halifax, Saint John, Bar Harbor, Boston, Newport. October 25, 12 nights New York to Miami via Bermuda, St. Maarten, Antigua, Aruba, Grand Cayman.

November 6, 14 nights, Miami to Los Angeles via Grand Cayman, Cartagena, Panama Canal, Huatulco, Puerto Vallarta, Cabo San Lucas, San Diego. November 20, 27, December 4, 7 nights, round-trip from Los Angeles to Cabo San Lucas, Mazatlán, Puerto Vallarta, Los Angeles; or December 11, 10 nights, to Cabo San Lucas, La Paz, Topolobampo, Loreto, Mazatlán, Puerto Vallarta; or December 21, 2011, 14 nights, to San Diego, Cabo San Lucas, Acapulco, Zihuatanejo, Puerto Vallarta, Mazatlán, La Paz, San Diego.

Cunard Line

Queen Elizabeth **HOME PORT** Southampton

October 12, 13 nights, Maiden Voyage, round-trip from Southampton to Vigo, Lisbon, Cadiz, Gran Canaria, Tenerife, La Palma, Madeira. October 25, 14 nights, to Barcelona, Monte Carlo, Livorno, Rome, Naples, Cartagena, Gibraltar. November 8, 18 nights, to Malaga, Valletta, Venice, Dubrovnik, Kusadasi, Athens, Alicante, Gibraltar. November 26, 5 nights, to Amsterdam, Zebrugge, Cherbourg. December 1, 13 nights, to Vigo, Lisbon, Cadiz, Gran Canaria, Tenerife, La Palma, Madeira. December 14, 22 nights, to Madeira, Tortola, Dominica, Barbados, St. Lucia, Antigua, Ponta Delgada.

January 5, 2011, 103 nights, World Voyage, round-trip from Southampton via New York, Fort Lauderdale, Panama Canal, Acapulco, Cabo San Lucas, Los Angeles, Honolulu, Pago Pago, New Zealand, Australia, Bali, Hong Kong, Nha Trang/Phu My (Vietnam), Laem Chabang/Ko Samui (Thailand), Singapore, Kuala Lumpur, Penang, Langkawi, Cochin, Bombay, Muscat, Dubai, Aqaba, Suez Canal, Port Said, Athens, Rome, Lisbon; segments available.

Queen Mary 2 **HOME PORTS** New York, Southampton

May 15, 13 nights, from Southampton to New York. May 21, 17 nights, transatlantic, from New York to Southampton via Zeebrugge, Rotterdam, Cherbourg. June 1, 13 nights, round-trip transatlantic crossing from Southampton via New York. June 7, 24 nights, round-trip from New York to Southampton, Stavanger, Geiranger, Honningsvag, North Cape, Tromso, Olden, Bergen, Southampton. July 1, October 7, 5 nights, round-trip from New York via Halifax, Boston. July 8, 13 nights, round-trip transatlantic from New York via Southampton, available in westbound/eastbound segments. July 13, 13 nights, round-trip transatlantic crossing from Southampton to New York. July 20, 20 nights, round-trip from New York to Southampton, Stavanger, Flaam, Geiranger, Bergen, Southampton. All available in segments.

August 2, 12 nights, transatlantic Southampton to New York; October 12, 13 nights, New York to Southampton. August 8, 26 nights, Norway, round-trip from New York to Southampton via Hamburg, Ålesund, Trondheim, Lofoten Is No, Honningsvag, North Cape, Tromso, Bergen, Hamburg. August 26, 24 nights, transatlantic, Hamburg to Southampton via Newport, Boston, Bar Harbor, Halifax, Quebec, New York. September 29, 25 nights, round-trip from New York to Southampton, via Barcelona, Monte Carlo, Rome, Naples, Gibraltar, Lisbon. October 20, 20 nights, round-trip transatlantic from Southampton via New York, Newport, Boston, Bar Harbor, St. John, Halifax. All available in segments.

November 1, 8 nights, transatlantic, New York to Cherbourg via Southampton. November 9, transatlantic, reverse. November 19, Southampton to New York via St. Thomas, St. Lucia, Grenada, Barbados, Grand Turk. December 8, 11 nights, round-trip from New York to St. Thomas, St. Lucia, Grenada, Barbados, Grand Turk. December 19, 15 nights, to Grand Turk, St. Maarten, Curaçao, Grenada, Barbados, St. Lucia, St. Kitts, St. Thomas.

January 3, 2011, 10 nights, round-trip from New York to St. Thomas, St. Lucia, Barbados, Barbados, Grand Turk. January 13, 103 nights, World Voyage, round-trip from New York to Fort Lauderdale, Barbados, Salvador, Rio de Janeiro, Montevideo, Cape Town, Durban, Mauritius, Fremantle, Australia, New Zealand, Guam, Yokohama, Nagasaki, Xingang, Shanghai, Hong Kong, Nha Trang, Laem Chabang, Singapore, Phuket, Bombay, Dubai, Egypt, Rome, Monte Carlo, Barcelona, Southampton.

Queen Victoria **HOME PORTS** Southampton, Venice, and others

May 3, 11 nights, to Vigo, Lisbon, Tenerife, Gran Canaria, La Palma, Madeira. May 14, August 15, 12 nights, to Barcelona, Cannes, Livorno Rome, Gibraltar. May 26, August 27, 5 nights, to Amsterdam, Zebrugge, Le Havre. May 31, July 8, August 1, 14 nights, to Copenhagen, Stockholm, Tallinn, St. Petersburg, Helsinki, Oslo, Kristiansand. June 14, 17 nights, to Malaga, Dubrovnik, Venice, Messina, Naples, Rome, Ajaccio, Cadiz. July 1, 7 nights, to Bergen, Geiranger, Stavanger. July 22, 10 nights, to Cherbourg, Cork, Dublin, Liverpool, Belfast, Greenock, Rosyth.

September 1, 12 nights, to Venice via Barcelona, Cannes, Livorno, Rome, Messina, Corfu, Dubrovnik. September 13, 12 nights, Venice to Rome via Katakolon, Athens, Istanbul, Yalta, Odessa, Kusadasi, Naples. September 25, 12 nights, Rome to Venice via Naples, Santorini, Kusadasi, Istanbul, Samos, Athens, Zakynthos, Dubrovnik. October 7, 12 nights, Venice to Barcelona via Dubrovnik, Katakolon, Mykonos, Istanbul, Kusadasi, Messina, Rome, Livorno, Marseille. October 19, 12 nights, Barcelona to Venice via Monte Carlo, Livorno, Naples, La Goulette, Valletta, Athens, Katakolon, Dubrovnik. October 31, 12 nights, Venice to Rome via Split, Corfu, Athens, Kusadasi, Istanbul, Rhodes, Santorini, Naples. November 12, 12 nights, round-trip from Rome to Messina, Valletta, Port Said, Limassol, Rhodes, Kusadasi, Athens, Naples. November 24, 7 nights, Rome to Southampton via Monte Carlo, Barcelona, Cartagena, Gibraltar.

December 15, 5 nights, round-trip from Southampton to Amsterdam, Zebrugge, Le Havre. December 20, 16 nights, Canary Islands, round-trip from Southampton to La Coruna, Lisbon, Gibraltar, Lanzarote, Gran Canaria, Tenerife, La Palma, Madeira, Cadiz.

January 5, 2011, 39 nights, Southampton to Los Angeles via Port Everglade, Panama Canal, Puntarenas, Huatulco, Acapulco, Manzanillo Los Angeles, Hilo, Honolulu, Nawiliwili, La Haina, Ensenada; segments available.

Disney Cruise Line

Disney Dream **HOME PORTS** Bahamas, Port Canaveral. Launch 2011
January 26–May 26, 2011, August 25–December 29, 2011, 3 or 4 nights, round-trip from Port Canaveral to Nassau, Castaway Cay. May 29–August 21, 2011, 4 or 5 nights, round-trip from Port Canaveral to Nassau, Castaway Cay; or Castaway Cay, Nassau, Castaway Cay.

Disney Magic **HOME PORTS** Port Canaveral, Barcelona, Dover
June 12–July 18, 12 nights, round-trip from Dover to Oslo, Copenhagen, Warnemunde, St. Petersburg, Helsinki or Tallinn, Stockholm. July 30, 8 nights, repositioning, Dover to Barcelona via Cherbourg, Vigo, Lisbon, Cadiz, Gibraltar.

September 18, 14 nights, transatlantic, Barcelona to Port Canaveral via Gibraltar, Madeira, St. Maarten, Tortola. October 16–December 11, 7 nights, round-trip from Port Canaveral to St. Maarten, St. Thomas/St. John, Castaway Cay; or Key West, Grand Cayman, Cozumel, Castaway Cay. December 18, 11 nights, round-trip from Port Canaveral to St. Maarten, Guadeloupe, Barbados, St. Lucia, Martinique, Castaway Cay. December 29, 10 nights, to Nassau, St. Maarten, Antigua, Tortola, St. Thomas, Castaway Cay.

January–May 2011, September–December, 7 nights, round-trip from Port Canaveral to St. Maarten, St. Thomas/St. John, Castaway Cay or Key West, Grand Cayman and Cozumel, Castaway Cay.

May 14, 2011, 14 nights, Transatlantic, Port Canaveral to Barcelona. May 28–August 31, 10–11 nights, round-trip from Barcelona to Malta, Tunis, Naples, Rome, La Spezia, Ajaccio, Villefranche.

September 10, transatlantic, Barcelona to Port Canaveral.

December 17, 7 nights, round-trip from Port Canaveral to St. Maarten, St. Thomas/St. John, Castaway Cay. December 24, 6 nights, round-trip from Port Canaveral to Cozumel, Key West, Castaway Cay. December 30, 8 nights, round-trip from Port Canaveral to St. Maarten, Tortola, St. Thomas/St. John, Castaway Cay.

Disney Wonder **HOME PORTS** Los Angeles, Port Canaveral, Vancouver
May 30–August 17, 4–5 nights, round-trip from Port Canaveral to Nassau, Castaway Cay or Key West, Castaway Cay. December 23, 7 nights, to Key West, Grand Cayman, Cozumel, Castaway Cay. December 30, to St. Maarten, St. Thomas, Castaway Cay.

January 6, 2011, 15 nights, Port Canaveral to Los Angeles via Aruba, Panama Canal, Costa Rica, Manzanillo, Puerto Vallarta, Cabo San Lucas. January–April, September–December, 7 nights, round-trip from Los Angeles to Puerto Vallarta, Mazatlán, Cabo San Lucas. April 17, 10 nights, to Puerto Vallarta, Manzanillo, Mazatlán, Cabo San Lucas.

May–August, 7 nights, round-trip from Vancouver to Tracy Arm, Skagway, Juneau, Ketchikan.

September–December, 7 nights, round-trip from Los Angeles to Puerto Vallarta, Mazatlán, Cabo San Lucas.

easyCruise

easyCruise Life **HOME PORT** Varies with itinerary
April–October, 3–4 nights, round-trip from Piraeus to Mykonos, Kusadasi, Patmos, (4 nights add Rhodes), Heraklion, Santorini; or round-trip from Kusadasi to Patmos, (4 nights add Rhodes), Heraklion, Santorini, Piraeus, Mykonos.

Fred Olsen Cruise Lines

Balmoral **HOME PORTS** Dover, Southampton

May 3, 12 nights, round-trip from Dover to Funchal, Santa Cruz de la Palma, Santa Cruz de Tenerife, Las Palmas de Gran Canaria, Lisbon. May 15, 7 nights, round-trip from Dover to Oslo, Gredrikstad, Kristiansand, Stavanger. May 22, 22 nights, round-trip from Dover to Gibraltar, Cagliari, Messina, Piraeus, Volos, Thessaloniki, Kavala, Malta, Ibiza, La Coruna. June 13, August 21, 7 nights, Norway, round-trip from Dover to Bergen, Olden, Flam, Vik, Farsund. June 20, 12 nights, Baltic, round-trip from Dover to Kiel Canal Transit, Kiel, Tallinn, St. Petersburg, Helsinki, Stockholm, Copenhagen.

July 2, 15 nights, roundtrip from Dover to Narvik, Honningsvag, Bear Island (Svalbard), Ny Ålesund, Magdalenefjord, Longyearbyen, Tromso, Bergen. July 17, 9 nights, from Dover to Guernsey, Dublin, Isle of Man, Greenock (Scotland), Kirkwall (Orkney), Invergordon. July 26, September 9, 12 nights, round-trip from Dover to Kiel Canal Transit, Warnemunde, Ronne (Denmark), Gdynia (Poland), St. Petersburg, Tallinn, Copenhagen.

August 7, 14 nights, round-trop from Dover to Gibraltar, Cartagena, Livorno, Corsica, Ibiza, Lisbon. August 28, 2 nights, to Antwerp. August 30, 10 nights, to Stavanger (Norway), Eidfjord, Skjolden, Olden, Molde, Andalsnes, Bergen, Antwerp. September 21, 21 nights, to Gibraltar, Sardinia, Aeolian Islands, Strait of Messina, Brindisi, Venice, Croatia, Montenegro, Palma de Mallorca, Cadiz. October 12, 14 nights, to Gibraltar, Menorca, Marseille, Barcelona, Alicante, Malaga. October 26, 23 nights, to Gibraltar, Sardinia, Kalamata, Piraeus, Volos, Izmir, Marmaris, Antalya, Rhodes, Malta, Cadiz, Lisbon.

November 18, 11 nights, round-trip from Southampton to Leixoes (Portugal), Casablanca, Gibraltar, Cadiz, La Coruna. November 29, 8 nights, to Gothenburg (Sweden), Copenhagen, Kiel Canal, Hamburg, Amsterdam. December 7, 14 nights, to Casablanca, Arrecife, Las Palmas de Gran Canaria, Santa Cruz de Tenerife, Santa Cruz La Palma, Funchal. December 21, 15 nights, to Lisbon, Arrecife, Fuerteventura, Las Palmas de Gran Canaria, Santa Cruz de Tenerife, Santa Cruz La Palma, Funchal.

January 5, 2011, 108 nights, World Cruise, round-trip from Southampton to Santa Cruz de Tenerife, Barbados, Grenada, Curaçao, Manta, Callo, Marquesas, Rangiroa, Papeete, Rarotonga, New Zealand, Australia, Great Barrier Reef, Bitung (Indonesia), Kota Kinabalu, Brunei, Laem Chabang, Sihanoukville, Kuantan, Singapore, Phuket, Cochin, Goa, Mumbai, Dubai, Salalah, Egypt, Malta, Gibraltar; segments available.

Black Watch **HOME PORT** Southampton

May 1, 4 nights, to Guernsey, Honfleur, Antwerp. May 5, 13 nights, to Gibraltar, Cartagena, Castellon de la Plana, Barcelona, Tangier, Lisbon. May 18, 21 nights, to Gibraltar, Cagliari, Aeolian Islands, Strait of Messina, Brindisi, Venice, Sibenik, Kotor, Palma de Mallorca, Seville.

June 8, 14 nights, round-trip from Southampton to Kiel Canal, Szczecin (Poland), Tallinn, St. Petersburg, Karlskrona (Sweden), Lorsor, Kristiansand. June 22, 8 nights, to Bergen, Flam, Gudvangen, Olden, Ålesund, Stavanger. June 30, 16 nights, Lapland/Baltic, to Skagen, Stockholm, Sundsvall, Lulea, Kemi (Finland), Helsinki, St. Petersburg, Gdynia, Kiel Canal. July 16, 14 nights, North Cape, to Molde, Andalsnes, Tromso, Honningsvag, Alta, Narvik, Olden, Bergen. July 30, 8 nights, to La Coruna, Gibraltar, Lisbon, Vigo.

August 7, 15 nights, round-trip from Southampton to Qaqortoq (Greenland), Narsarsuaq, Nanotalik, Cape Farewell, Isafjordur, Reykjavik. August 22, 9 nights, to Guernsey, Harwich, Kirkwall (Orkney), Stornoway (Lewis), Dublin, Fowey. August 31, 5 nights, to Rouen, Guernsey, St. Malo. September 5, 12 nights, to Heimaey, Reykjavik, Isafjordur, Akureyri, Ålesund, Bergen, Farsund.

September 17, round-trip from Southampton to Almeria, Cagliari, Valletta, Piraeus, Nessebar (Bulgaria), Odessa, Sevastopol, Yalta, Istanbul, Canakkale, Iraklion, Palma de Mallorca, Gibraltar. October 15, 14 nights, to Gibraltar, Mahon, Monte Carlo, Barcelona, Ibiza, Almeria. October 29, 14 nights, to Casablanca, Las Palmas de Gran Canaria, Santa Cruz de Tenerife, San Sebastian la Gomera, Santa Cruz de la Palma, Funchal.

November 12, 28 nights, round-trip from Southampton to Santa Cruz de Tenerife, Barbados, Grenada, St. Lucia, St. Kitts, Tortola, Antigua, St. Maarten, Azores. December 10, 7 nights, to Ijmuiden, Kiel Canal, Copenhagen, Ostend. December 17, 3 nights, to Antwerp. December 20, 16 nights, to La Coruna, Funchal, Arrecife, Puerto del Rosario, Las Palmas de Gran Canaria, Santa Cruz de la Palma, San Sebastian la Gomera, Santa Cruz de Tenerife.

January 5, 2011, 77 nights, Round South America round-trip from Southampton to Santa Cruz de Tenerife, Mindelo, Recife, Salvador, Rio de Janeiro, Montevideo, Buenos Aires, Puerto Madryn, West Point Island, Port Stanley, Ushuaia, Punta Arenas, Puerto Chacabuco, Puerto Montt, Valparaiso, Arica, General San Martin, Callao, Salaverry, Manta, Balboa, Panama Canal, Puerto Limon, Aruba, Curaçao, Barbados, St. Lucia, St. Kitts, Antigua, St. Maarten, Ponta Delgada; segments available.

Boudicca **HOME PORTS** Liverpool, Greenock, Southampton, and others

May 13, 8 nights, to Bergen, Flam, Gudvangen, Olden, Ålesund, Kirkwall. May 21, 14 nights, to Skagen, Ystad, St. Petersburg, Tallinn, Warnemunde, Kiel Canal Transit, Zeebrugge. June 4, 2 nights, to Greenock via Dublin.

June 6, 14 nights, Canary Islands/West Africa, round-trip from Greenock to Leixoes, Arrecife, Santa Cruz de Tenerife, San Sebastian la Gomera, Santa Cruz de la Palma, Funchal, Vigo. June 20, 16 nights, to Gibraltar, Cagliari, Capri, Naples, Rome, Livorno, Portoferraio (Elba), Almeria. July 6, 7 nights, to Bergen, Flam, Gudvangen, Floro, Stavanger.

July 13, 14 nights, Spitsbergen, round-trip from Rosyth to Narvik, Honningsvag, Bear Island, Ny Ålesund, Moffen, Magdalenefjord, Longyearbyen, Tromso. July 27, 12 nights, Baltic, to Gothenburg, Helsinki, St. Petersburg, Tallinn, Warnemunde, Kalundborg. August 8, 7 nights, to Molde, Andalsnes, Trondheim, Olden, Bergen. August 15, 4 nights, to Newcastle via Bergen, Flekkefjord.

August 19, 13 nights, roundtrip from Newcastle to Olden, Molde, Andalsnes, Tromso, Honningsvag, Narvik, Geiranger, Bergen. September 1, 6 nights, roundtrip from Newcastle to Oslo, Gothenburg, Copenhagen. September 7, 12 nights, to Gothenburg, Helsinki, St. Petersburg, Tallinn, Warnemunde, Kalundborg. September 19, 7 nights, to Molde, Andalsnes, Trondheim, Olden, Bergen. September 26, 9 nights, to Portland, Guernsey, Milford Haven, Dublin, Tobermory, Invergordon. October 5, 14 nights, to Leixoes, Lisbon, Cartagena, Almeria, Gibraltar, Cadiz, La Coruna. October 19, 23 nights, to Liverpool via Lisbon, Almeria, Ibiza, Valletta, Kusadasi, Volos, Piraeus, Gythion, La Goulette, Cartagena, Gibraltar.

November 20, 18 nights, round-trip from Liverpool to Funchal, Santa Cruz de Tenerife, Mindelo, Praia, San Sebastian de Gomera, Santa Cruz de la Palma, Lisbon. December 8, 13 nights to Funchal, Santa Cruz de la Palma, Santa Cruz de Tenerife, Las Palmas de Gran Canaria, Arricife, Lisbon. December 21, 14 nights, to Leixoes, Arricife, Las Palmas de Gran Canaria, San Sebastian, Santa Cruz de Tenerife, Santa Cruz de la Palma, Funchal.

January 16, March 6, 2011, 14 nights, Canary Islands, round-trip from Southampton to Leixoes, Arricife, Santa Cruz de Tenerife, San Sebastian, Santa Cruz de la Palma, Funchal, Vigo. January 30, 35 nights, to Funchal, Mindelo, Santarem, Boca do Valeria, Manaus, Parintins, Trinidad, Tobago, Barbados, St. Lucia, Antigua, Ponta Delgada. March 20, 18 nights, to Funchal, Santa Cruz de Tenerife, Mindelo, Praia, San Sebastian de Gomera, Santa Cruz de la Palma, Lisbon. April 7, 3 nights, to Liverpool via Tresco, Dublin.

Braemar **HOME PORTS** Barbados, Dover, Malaga, Montego Bay, Rome, Southampton

May 20, 9 nights, round-trip from Dover to Dartmouth, Tresco, Dublin, Belfast, Stornoway, Kirkwall, Invergordon.

May 29, 13 nights, round-trip from Dover to Copenhagen, Visby, Turku, Helsinki, St. Petersburg, Szczecin, Sassnitz, Kiel Canal Transit. June 18, 13 nights, round-trip from

Dover to Molde, Andalsnes, Tromso, Honningsvag, Narvik, Olden, Stavanger. July 8, 13 nights, to Kiel Canal, Warnemunde, Riga, Tallinn, St. Petersburg, Helsinki, Stockholm, Copenhagen. July 21, 8 nights, to Amsterdam, Antwerp, L'Orient, St. Malo, Guernsey, Honfleur. July 29, 14 nights, to Leixoes, Arricife, Santa Cruz de Tenerife, San Sebastian la Gomera, Santa Cruz de la Palma, Funchal, Vigo. August 12, 7 nights, to Bergen, Eidfjord, Kristiansand, Oslo. August 19, 8 nights, to Fowey, Leixoes, La Coruna, Bilbao, La Pallice. August 27, 3 nights, to Guernsey, Honfleur. August 30, 7 nights, to Bergen, Olden, Flam, Gudvangen, Stavanger. September 22, 13 nights to Copenhagen, Visby, Turku, Helsinki, St. Petersburg, Szczecin, Sassnitz, Kiel Canal Transit.

September 6, 16 nights, Italy, round-trip Dover to Gibraltar, Cagliari, Capri, Naples, Rome, Livorno, Portoferraio, Almeria. October 5, 13 nights, to Funchal, Santa Cruz de la Palma, Santa Cruz de Tenerife, Las Palmas, Arrecife, Lisbon. October 18, 8 nights, to Lisbon, Portimao Leixoes, La Coruna. October 26, 17 nights, Caribbean, from Dover to Barbados via Funchal, Santa Cruze de Tenerife, St. Maarten, Tortola, St. Kitts, St. Lucia.

November 11–December 23, 2010, March 31, 2011, 15 nights, Barbados to Montego Bay via Curaçao, Aruba, Ocho Rios, Costa Maya, Cozumel, Havana, Grand Cayman; or Montego Bay to Bridgetown via Santo Domingo, Tortola, St. Maarten, St. Kitts or Dominica, Antigua, St. Lucia, Trinidad, Tobago, Grenada or St. Vincent.

January 6, March 17, 2011, 15 nights, Barbados to Montego Bay via Grenada, Isla Margarita, Cartagena, Colon, Puerto Limon, Roatan, Belize, Cozumel. February 3, 15 nights, to Santarem, Parintins, Manaus, Boca de Valeria, Alter do Chao. April 14, 16 nights, to Dover via Grenada, St. Lucia, St. Kitts, Antigua, St. Maarten, Ponta Delgada.

Hapag-Lloyd Cruises

Bremen **HOME PORT** Varies with itinerary

June 27, 16 days, Spitsbergen, from Travemuende to Tromsoe via Bergen, Gudvangen/ Naeroeyfjord, Flam/Aurlandsfjord, Geiranger/Geirangerfjord, Hammerfest, Honningsvag, circumnavigation of Spitsbergen (Longyearbyen, Ny-Ålesund, Magdalenefjord, Smeeren-burgfjord, Liefdefjord, Hinlopen Strait, Freemansund), cruising Bear Island.

November 15, 14 days, Seychelles and Comores, from Mahe to Mauritius via Seychelles (Praslin, La Digue, Desroches), Comores (Moroni, Mayotte), Madagascar (Nosy-Bé, Nosy Lakandava, Nosy-Mangabe), Le Port/Reunion.

January 3, 2011, 22 days, Antarctica, round-trip from Ushuaia to Falkland Islands, South Georgia, South Orkney Islands, South Shetland Islands, Antarctic Peninsula, Drake Passage.

Europa **HOME PORT** Varies with itinerary

August 24, 15 days, Britannia, round-trip from Kiel to Leith, Invergordon, Kirkwall, Gairloch, Ayr, Dublin, Holyhead, Cobh, Tresco, Falmouth, Cowes, Kiel Canal passage. On board: Ocean Sun Festival, lecturer Wolfgang Peters.

September 26, 10 days, Lisbon to Monte Carlo via Marbella, Palma de Mallorca, Barcelona, Sète, Marseille, Cannes, Calvi, cruise Gulf of Girolata. October 6, 4 days, Monte Carlo to Bonifacio, Capri, Cinque Terre, Portofino.

October 24, 13 days, Black Sea, Piraeus to Istanbul via Marmaris, Dardanelles/Bosporus, Trabzon, Sotschi, Yalta, Sevastopol, Odessa, Varna, Nesebur.

November 6, 20 days, Istanbul to Dubai via Dardanelles, Antalya, Paphos, Tartus, Port Said, Suez Canal, Hurghada, Aqaba, Sharm el Sheikh, Hodeidah, Salalah, Muscat, Khasab. November 25, 8 days, round-trip from Dubai to Manama, Doha, Sir Bani Yas, Abu Dhabi. On board: lecturer Dr Reinhard Laszig.

Hanseatic **HOME PORT** Varies with itinerary

May 29, 16 days, Newfoundland, round-trip from Halifax to Canso Strait/Charlottetown/ Prince Edward Island, St Lawrence-River, Baie d'Eternité/Saguenay, Québec, Newfound-land, St. Pierre/Saint Pierre et Miquelon, Louisbourg/Nova Scotia.

July 13, 14 days, Arctic, round-trip from Kangerlussuaq to Aasiaat/Greenland, Uummannaq, Canadian Arctic (Pond Inlet, Beechey Island, Dundas Harbor, cruising in Jones Sound and off Ellesmere Island), Qaanaaq, Upernavik, Qeqertarsuaq, Sisimiut. August 16, 26 days, Kangerlussuaq to Nome via Aasiaat/Greenland, Qeqertarsuaq, Upernavik, cruising Disko Bay, Baffin Island, Devon Island, Barrow Strait, Northwest Passage from Lancaster Sound to the Beaufort Sea, Alaska (Barrow, Point Hope).

September 8, 21 days, Kamchatka, from Nome to Yokohama via Chukchi Peninsula (Provideniya, Yittigran Islands, Janrakynnot, Uelen, Cape Deschnjow, Achen Lagoon), Chukotka (Cape Navarin, Meynipilgino Village), Kamchatka (Natalii Bay, Tymlat, Zhupanova, Petropavlovsk, Vestnik Bay), Kuril Islands (Ptichiy Islands, Atlasova), Sakhalin (Tyuleniy, Korsakov), Kushiro/Hokkaido.

January 5, 2011, 23 days, Antarctica, round-trip from Ushuaia to Falkland Islands, South Georgia, South Orkney Islands, South Shetland Islands, Antarctic Peninsula, Drake Passage.

Hebridean Island Cruises

Hebridean Princess **HOME PORT** Fairlie, Oban

April–November, 4–9 nights, Scotland, various itineraries, round-trip from Fairlie or Oban, including the Inner and Outer Hebrides, mainland Scotland, Northern Islands, Firth of Clyde Islands, Lochs of Argyll.

Holland America Line

Amsterdam **HOME PORTS** Fort Lauderdale, Seattle; others vary with itinerary

May 3 and 10, 7 days, round-trip from Seattle to Glacier Bay, Juneau, Sitka, Ketchikan, Victoria. May–September, 14 days, to Inside Passage, Ketchikan, Sitka, Skagway, Glacier Bay, Anchorage, Homer, Kodiak, Hubbard Glacier, Juneau, Victoria. July 12, add Tracy Arm.

September 24, 69 days, from Seattle to San Diego via Petropavlovsk, Sendai, Yokohama, Shimizu, Kobe, Xingang (Beijing), Shanghai, Hong Kong, Phu My, Bangkok, Sihanoukville, Singapore, Semarang, Komodo Island, Darwin, Torres Strait, Sherrard Island, Cairns, Brisbane, Sydney, Noumea, Suva, Apia, Honolulu, Oahu. 34–35-day segments available.

December 2 and 8, 6 days, round-trip from San Diego to Puerto Vallarta, Cabo San Lucas. December 22, 14 days, from Los Angeles to Fort Lauderdale via Cabo San Lucas, Acapulco, Puerto Quetzal, Puntarenas, Golfo Dulce, Panama Canal, Cartagena.

January 5, 2011, 110 days, World Voyage, round-trip from Fort Lauderdale to Georgetown, Puerto Limon, Panama Canal, Manta, Callao, Easter Island, Papeete, Bora Bora, Rarotonga, Alofi, Nuku' Alofa, Auckland, Tauranga, Napier, Wellington, Christchurch, Dunedin, Oban, Fiordland National Park Hobart, Port Arthur, Sydney, Cairns, Madang, Koror, Manila, Hong Kong, Phu My, Singapore, Cochin, Mumbai, Dubai, Muscat, Safaga, Sharm el Sheik, Aqaba, Suez Canal , Port Said, Alexandria, Kusadasi, Piraeus, Naples, Rome, Cartagena, Cadiz, Funchal. 16–48-day segments available.

Eurodam **HOME PORTS** Copenhagen, Dover, Fort Lauderdale, Rome

May 9, 20 days, to Dover via Dubrovnik, Corfu, Katakolon, Santorini, Kusadasi, Piraeus, Messina, Santa Margherita, Marseille, Barcelona, Cadiz, Lisbon, Guernsey, Le Havre. May 19, 21 days, via Santa Margherita, Marseille, Barcelona, Cadiz, Lisbon, Guernsey, Le Havre, Dover, Copenhagen, Tallinn, St. Petersburg, Helsinki, Stockholm.

June 9, 20 days, round-trip from Dover to Copenhagen, Warnemunde, Tallinn, St. Petersburg, Helsinki, Stockholm, Geiranger, Hellesylt, Ålesund, Bergen, Invergordon, S Queensferry. June 21, 18 days, to Copenhagen via Geiranger, Hellesylt, Ålesund, Bergen, Invergordon, S Queensferry, Kiel, Tallinn, St. Petersburg, Helsinki, Stockholm. June 29, 10 days, via Kiel, Tallinn, St. Petersburg, Helsinki, Stockholm. July 9, 19, 10 days, round-trip from Copenhagen to Warnemunde, Tallinn, St. Petersburg, Helsinki, Stockholm, Kiel.

August 8, 29 days, transatlantic, Amsterdam to New York via Copenhagen, Tallinn, St.

Petersburg, Helsinki, Stockholm, S Queensferry, Kirkwall, Torshavn, Reykjavik, Qaqortoq, St Anthony, St. Johns, Sydney, Halifax. September 6, 26, reverse. September 16, 10 days, New York to Quebec via Newport, Gloucester, Bar Harbor, Halifax, Sydney, Charlottetown, Saguenay, Saguenay Fjord. October 6, 10 days, Quebec to Fort Lauderdale via Baie-Comeau, Gaspe, Charlottetown, Sydney, Halifax, Bar Harbor, Gloucester.

October–December, 7 days, alternating reverse, round-trip from Fort Lauderdale to Grand Turk, San Juan, St. Thomas, Half Moon Cay. December 18, 8 days, to Half Moon Cay, St. Thomas, St. Maarten, San Juan, Nassau. December 26, 7 days, to Belize City, Santo Tomas, Mahogany Bay (Roatan), Costa Maya.

Maasdam **HOME PORTS** Boston, Fort Lauderdale, San Diego; others vary with itinerary

May 14, 15 days, Fort Lauderdale to Montreal via Charleston, Newport, Bar Harbor, Halifax, Sydney, Charlottetown, Gaspe, Sept-Iles, Saguenay Fjord, Saguenay, Quebec City. May–October, 7 or 14 days, Boston to Montreal and reverse via Bar Harbor, Halifax, Sydney, Charlottetown, Prince Edward, Quebec City.

July, 17, 35 days, transatlantic, Boston to Bar Harbor, St. Pierre, St. Johns, Qaqortoq (Greenland), Isafjord (Iceland), Akureyri (Iceland), Ålesund (Norway), Bergen, Oslo, Copenhagen, Dover, Amsterdam, Dunmore East, Waterford, Liverpool, Dublin, Heimaey, Westman Islands (Iceland), Reykjavik, Nanortalik (Greenland), St Anthony, Corner Brook, Bar Harbor. October 9, 3 days, Montreal to Fort Lauderdale via Quebec City, Saguenay Fjord, Baie-Comeau, Gaspe, Charlottetown, Sydney, Halifax, St. John, Bar Harbor.

October 22, December 6, 11 days, round-trip from Fort Lauderdale to Half Moon Cay, St. Croix, St. Kitts, St. Vincent, Barbados, St. Lucia, St. Maarten. November 2 and 26, 10 days to Nassau, San Juan, St. Barts, Dominica, Antigua, St. Thomas, Half Moon Cay. December 17, 10 days, to Cozumel, Costa Maya, Belize City, Santo Tomas, Roatan, Half Moon Cay. December 27, 11 days, to Grand Turk, St. Thomas, St. Maarten, Antigua, St. Croix, Santo Domingo, Half Moon Cay.

Nieuw Amsterdam **HOME PORTS** Venice, Barcelona

July 4, 7 or 10 days, Mediterranean Inaugural, Venice to Ravenna via Dubrovnik, Katakolon, Corfu, Kotor, Split; 7 days from Katakolon to Ravenna. July 14, 12 or 24 days, Venice to Barcelona via Split, Piraeus, Istanbul, Mykonos, Kusadasi, Santorini, Katakolon, Dubrovnik, Corfu, Argostoli, Catania, Naples, Rome, Livorno; 12 days from Dubrovnik to Barcelona. August 7, September 12, 12 or 24 days, Barcelona to Santorini via Monte Carlo, Livorno, Rome, Messina, Navplion, Katakolon, Corfu, Dubrovnik, Venice, Split, Piraeus, Istanbul, Mykonos, Kusadasi; 12 days from Barcelona to Venice. July 14, August 19, September 24, 24 days, Venice to Barcelona via Split, Piraeus, Istanbul, Mykonos, Kusadasi, Santorini, Katakolon, Dubrovnik, Corfu, Argostoli, Catania, Naples, Rome, Livorno; July 26, August 31, 12 or 24 days, Venice to Katakolon via Dubrovnik, Corfu, Argostoli, Santorini, Catania, Naples, Rome, Livorno, Barcelona, Monte Carlo, Messina, Navplion.

October 6, 12, 20 or 32 days, Transatlantic Inaugural, Venice to Fort Lauderdale via Dubrovnik, Croatia, Corfu, Argostoli, Santorini, Catania, Naples, Rome, Livorno, Barcelona (12 days), Monte Carlo, Valencia, Cartegena, Almeria, Cadiz, Portimao, Lisbon, Half Moon Cay.

November–December, 7 days, round-trip from Fort Lauderdale to Grand Turk, San Juan, St. Maarten, Half Moon Cay; or Half Moon Cay, Grand Turk, Georgetown, Costa Maya. November 14, Cozumel in place of Costa Maya. December 19, 7 days, to Half Moon Cay, Aruba, Curaçao.

Noordam **HOME PORTS** Fort Lauderdale, Barcelona, Rome

May 14, 13 days, transatlantic, Fort Lauderdale to Barcelona via Funchal, Cadiz, Malaga, Alicante. July 26, 7 or 17 days, Barcelona to Naples via Cannes, Santa Margherita, Rome, Trapani, Carthage/Tunis, Ajaccio, Monte Carlo, Livorno, Valletta, Mgarr (Victoria), Gozo; 7 days from Barcelona to Carthage/Tunis. August 2, 10 or 17 days, Barcelona to Trapani via Ajaccio, Monte Carlo, Livorno, Carthage/Tunis, Valletta, Mgarr (Victoria), Gozo, Naples, Rome (10 days), Cannes, Mallorca.

August 12, 7 or 17 days, Rome to Messina via Cannes, Barcelona, Mallorca, Carthage/ Tunis, Trapani (7 days), Dubrovnik, Corfu, Katakolon, Santorini, Kusadasi, Piraeus; 7 days from Rome to Trapani. August 19, 10 or 20 days, Rome to Naples via Dubrovnik, Corfu, Katakolon, Santorini, Kusadasi, Piraeus, Messina (10 days), Livorno, Monte Carlo, Barcelona, Mallorca, Carthage/Tunis, Trapani. August 29, 10 or 20 days, Rome to Sicily via Livorno, Monte Carlo, Barcelona, Mallorca, Carthage/Tunis, Trapani, Naples (10 days), Dubrovnik, Corfu, Katakolon, Santorini, Kusadasi, Piraeus.

September 8, 10 or 20 days, Rome to Naples via Dubrovnik, Corfu, Katakolon, Santorini, Kusadasi, Piraeus, Messina (10 days), Livorno, Monte Carlo, Barcelona, Mallorca, Carthage/Tunis, Trapani. September 18, 10 or 20 days, Rome to Messina via Livorno, Monte Carlo, Barcelona, Mallorca, Carthage/Tunis, Trapani, Naples (10 days), Dubrovnik, Corfu, Katakolon, Santorini, Kusadasi, Piraeus. September 28, 10 or 20 days, Rome to Naples via Dubrovnik, Corfu, Katakolon, Santorini, Kusadasi, Piraeus, Messina (10 days) Rome, Livorno, Monte Carlo, Barcelona, Mallorca, Carthage/Tunis, Trapani.

October 18, 16 days, transatlantic, Rome to Fort Lauderdale via Livorno, Monte Carlo, Barcelona, Cartagena, Malaga, Cadiz, Funchal. November–December, 10 days, round-trip from Fort Lauderdale to St. Maarten, St. Lucia, Barbados, Martinique, St. Thomas, Half Moon Cay; or Half Moon Cay, Grand Turk, Samana, Bonaire, Curaçao, Aruba. December 23, 7 days, to Half Moon Cay, Montego Bay, Georgetown, Cozumel. December 30, 7 days to Nassau, San Juan, St. Thomas, Half Moon Cay.

Oosterdam **HOME PORTS** San Diego, Seattle, Vancouver

April, October 2010–April 2011, 7 days, Mexican Riviera, round-trip from San Diego to Mazatlan, Puerto Vallarta, Cabo San Lucas.

April 24, 10 or 14 days, Sea of Cortez, San Diego to Vancouver via Cabo San Lucas, La Paz, Topolobampo, Loreto, Mazatlan, Puerto Vallarta (10 days), Victoria.

May–September, 7 days, round-trip from Seattle to Glacier Bay, Juneau, Sitka, Ketchikan, Victoria.

September 27, 5 to 12 days, round-trip from Vancouver to San Diego via Astoria, Avalon (5 days), San Diego, Mazatlan, Puerto Vallarta, Cabo San Lucas (7 days).

Prinsendam **HOME PORT** Amsterdam, Fort Lauderdale, Rome; others vary with itinerary

May 17, 39 days, Fort Lauderdale to London via Horta, Ponta Delgada, Cadiz, Portimao, Lisbon, La Coruna, Bilbao, Falmouth, Le Havre, Dover, Amsterdam, Kiel Canal, Lubeck, Copenhagen, Skagen, Oslo, Molde, Crossing the Artic Circle; Tromso, Honningsvag, Kristiansund, Ålesund, Bergen; segments available.

June 23, July 23, 36 days, Arctic and Kiel Canal, round-trip from Amsterdam to Lorient, Bordeaux, La Coruna, Bilbao, St Peter Port, Le Havre, Vlissingen, Brussels, London, Rosyth, Scrabster, Runavik, Reykjavik, Isafjord, Akureyri, Longyearbyen, Ny Ålesund, Bergen, Kristiansand, Oslo, Amsterdam, Kiel Canal, Tallinn, St. Petersburg, Helsinki, Stockholm, Berlin, Copenhagen; segments available.

July 9, 36 days, round-trip from Amsterdam to Lorient, Bordeaux, La Coruna, Bilbao, St Peter Port, Le Havre, Vlissingen, Brussels, Greenwich, Rosyth, Scrabster, Runavik, Reykjavik, Isafjord, Akureyri, Longyearbyen, Ny Ålesund, Bergen, Kristiansand, Oslo; segments available. August 14, 28 days, Amsterdam to Greenwich via Kiel Canal, Tallinn, St. Petersburg, Helsinki, Stockholm, Warnemunde, Copenhagen, Oslo, Greenwich, St Peter Port, Brest, Falmouth, Dublin, Holyhead, Belfast, Peel, Fort William, Portree, Scrabster, Rosyth; 14-day segments available. August 28, 29 days, Greenwich to Rome via St Peter Port, Brest, Falmouth, Dublin, Holyhead, Belfast, Peel, Fort William, Portree, Scrabster, Rosyth, Zeebrugge, Le Havre, A Coruna, Leixoes, Lisbon, Portimao, Cadiz, Melilla, Barcelona; segments available.

September 11, 29 days, round-trip from Greenwich to Piraeus via Zeebrugge, Le Havre, A Coruna, Leixoes, Lisbon, Portimao, Cadiz, Melilla, Barcelona, Rome, Katakolon, Larnaca, Alexandria, Port Said, Ashdod, Haifa, Bodrum, Kusadasi, Santorini; segments available.

September 26, 28 days, Black Sea, round-trip from Rome to Katakolon, Larnaca, Alexandria, Port Said, Ashdod, Haifa, Bodrum, Kusadasi, Santorini, Piraeus, Istanbul, Sochi, Batumi, Trabzon, Sinop, Sevastopol, Mykonos, Monemvasia; 14-day segments available. October 10, 29 days, round-trip from Piraeus to Istanbul, Sochi, Batumi, Trabzon, Sinop, Sevastopol, Kusadasi, Mykonos, Monemvasia, Rome, Dubrovnik, Kerkira, Katakolon, Alexandria, Ashdod, Haifa, Antalya, Bodrum; segments available.

October 24, 36 days, transatlantic, Rome to Fort Lauderdale via Dubrovnik, Kerkira, Katakolon, Alexandria, Ashdod, Haifa, Antalya, Bodrum, Kusadasi, Piraeus, Naples, Livorno, Calvi, Alghero, Barcelona, Cartagena, Malaga, Cadiz, Funchal; segments available. November 29, 23 days, Amazon, round-trip from Fort Lauderdale to St. Lucia, Devil's Island, Macapa, Santarem, Boca da Valeria, Manaus, Parintins, Alter Do Chao, Barbados, Aruba. December 22, 14 days, round-trip from Fort Lauderdale to Half Moon Cay, St. Barts, Guadeloupe, Barbados, Port of Spain, St. Vincent, Grenada, Mayaguez, Grand Turk.

January 5, 2011, 66 days, South America and Antarctica, round-trip from Fort Lauderdale to Half Moon Cay, Barbados, Devil's Island, Macapa, Santarem, Boca da Valeria, Manaus, Parintins, Alter Do Chao, Belem, Fortaleza, Fernando de Noronha, Recife, Salvador, Rio de Janeiro, Paraty, Montevideo, Buenos Aires, Pt. Stanley, Antarctic Sound, South Shetland Islands, Wilhelm Archipelago, Cape Horn and Drake Passage, Ushuaia, Punta Arenas, Chilean Fjords, Puerto Montt, Isla Robinson Crusoe, Santiago, General San Martin, Callao, Manta, Fuerte Amador, Panama Canal transit, Aruba; segments available.

Rotterdam **HOME PORTS** Fort Lauderdale, San Diego, Seattle; others vary with itinerary
May 15–September 11, 7 days, round-trip from Seattle to Juneau, Hubbard Glacier, Sitka, Ketchikan, Victoria. September 18, November 22, 35 days, Seattle to San Diego via Vancouver, San Diego, Hilo, Lahaina, Maui, Honolulu, Nawiliwili Kauai, Cross International Dateline, Kiribati, Rarotonga, Raiatea, Bora Bora, Papeete, Moorea, Rangiroa, Nuku Hiva; 15-, 31-, 34-day segments available.

October 23, February 2, 2011, 30 days, round-trip from San Diego to Cabo San Lucas, Puerto Vallarta, Puerto Quetzal, Corinto, Fuerte Amador, Salaverry, Callao, Guayaquil, Manta, Puerto Caldera, Puerto Chiapas, Huatulco, Acapulco, Zihuatanejo, Manzanillo; 15-day segments available. December 22, 12 days, round-trip from San Diego to Cabo San Lucas, Manzanillo, Acapulco, Huatulco, Puerto Vallarta, Mazatlan.

January 3, March 4, 2011, 30 days, round-trip from San Diego to Hilo, Lahaina, Honolulu, Nawiliwili, Fanning Island, Rarotonga, Raiatea, Bora Bora, Papeete, Moorea, Rangiroa, Nuku Hiva. April 3, 14 days, San Diego to Fort Lauderdale via Puerto Vallarta, Huatulco, Puerto Chiapas, Puerto Quetzal, Fuerte Amador, Panama Canal, Cartagena. April 17, 30 days, round-trip from Santa Marta, San Blas Islands, Panama Canal, Puntarenas, Corinto, Puerto Quetzal, Manta, Callao, Salaverry, Guayaquil, Fuerte Amador, Panama Canal, Puerto Limon, Mahogany Bay, Costa Maya, Cozumel; segments available.

Ryndam **HOME PORTS** Anchorage, San Diego, Tampa, Vancouver
May–September, 7 days, Vancouver to Seward via Inside Passage, Ketchikan, Juneau, Skagway, Glacier Bay, College Fjord; return Haines replaces Skagway. September 12, 7 days, round-trip from Vancouver to Inside Passage, Juneau, Sitka, Tracy Arm, Ketchikan.

April 11, 2011, 17 or 21 days, Tampa to Vancouver via Grand Cayman, Santa Marta, San Blas Islands, Panama Canal, Fuerte Amador, Puerto Caldera, Puerto Chiapas, Huatulco, Acapulco, Cabo San Lucas, San Diego (17 days), Victoria. September 19, 17 or 21 days, Vancouver to Tampa via San Diego, Cabo San Lucas, Acapulco, Puerto Quetzal, Puerto Caldera, Panama Canal, Curaçao, Aruba, Grand Cayman. October–December, 7 days, round-trip from Tampa to Key West, Belize City, Mahogany Bay, Costa Maya; or Key West, Falmouth, Georgetown, Cozumel.

Statendam **HOME PORTS** Fort Lauderdale, Vancouver, Anchorage, and others
April 25, 17 or 21 days, to Vancouver via Aruba, Panama Canal, Puerto Caldera, Corinto, Puerto Quetzal, Puerto Chiapas, Huatulco, Acapulco, Cabo San Lucas, San Diego (17 days), Los Angeles. May–September, 7 days, alternating, Wednesdays from Vancouver to Seward

via Inside Passage, Ketchikan, Juneau, Skagway, Glacier Bay, College Fjord; return Sundays Haines replaces Skagway. September 19, 7 days, Vancouver to Ketchikan via Inside Passage, Juneau, Skagway, Glacier Bay. September 26, 15 or 19 days, Vancouver to Fort Lauderdale via Victoria, San Diego, Puerto Vallarta, Huatulco, Puerto Chiapas, Puerto Quetzal, Corinto, Fuerte Amador, Panama Canal, Cartagena.

October 2010–April 2011, 14 days, Fort Lauderdale to San Diego via Aruba, Panama Canal, Puerto Caldera, Huatulco, Acapulco, Cabo San Lucas; return via Puerto Vallarta, Huatulco, Puerto Chiapas, Puerto Quetzal, Fuerte Amador, Panama Canal, Cartagena. April 29, 2011, 18 days, Fort Lauderdale to Vancouver via Aruba, Panama Canal, Puerto Caldera, Huatulco, Acapulco, Cabo San Lucas, San Diego (14 days), Victoria.

***Veendam* HOME PORTS** Rio de Janeiro, Santiago, New York
April–October, 7 days, round-trip from New York to St. Georges, Hamilton (Bermuda). October 10, 20 or 23 days, New York to Santiago via Fort Lauderdale, Half Moon Cay, Santa Marta, San Blas Islands, Panama Canal, Fuerte Amador, Manta, Guayaquil, Salaverry, Trujillo, Lima, Pisco, Arica, Coquimbo. November 14, December 8, January 23, 2011, February 4, 2011, 12 days, Buenos Aires to Santiago via Montevideo, Port Stanley, Cape Horn, Ushuaia, Romanche/Alemania Glaciers, Cockburn/Beagle Channels, Punta Arenas, Strait of Magellan, Amalia Glacier Canal Sarmiento, Darwin Channel/Chilean Fjords, Puerto Montt. December 20, January 6, 2011 reverse, 17 days, Santiago to Buenos Aires via Puerto Montt, Puerto Chacabuco, Darwin Channel/Chilean Fjords, Amalia Glacier Canal, Strait of Magellan, Punta Arenas, Cockburn and Beagle Channels, Romanche and Alemania Glaciers, Francia and Italia Glaciers, Ushuaia, Cape Horn, Drake Passage, Wilhelm Archipelago, South Shetland Islands, Antarctic Sound, Port Stanley, Montevideo.

February 16, 2011, 16 days, Santiago to Rio de Janeiro via Puerto Montt, Darwin Channel/ Chilean Fjords, Amalia Glacier Canal Sarmiento, Strait Of Magellan, Punta Arenas, Cockburn/Beagle Channels, Romanche/Alemania Glaciers, Ushuaia, Cape Horn, Port Stanley, Falkland Islands, Montevideo, Buenos Aires. March 4, 2011, 14 days, Rio de Janeiro to Paraty via Armacao dos Buzio, Ilha Grande, Santos, Montevideo, Buenos Aires, Punta del Este, Paranagua, Ilhabela. March 18, 2011, 28 days, Rio de Janeiro to Fort Lauderdale via Salvador, Recife, Fortaleza, Belem, Macapa, Santarem, Boca da Valeria, Manaus, Parintins, Alter do Chao, Devil's Island, Barbados, Aruba, Grand Turk, Half Moon Cay.

***Volendam* HOME PORTS** Auckland, Singapore, Sydney, Vancouver
May–September, 7 days, round-trip from Vancouver to Tracy Arm, Juneau, Skagway, Glacier Bay, Ketchikan. September 22, 28–29 days, Vancouver to Auckland via Seattle, Lahaina, Maui, Nawiliwili Kauai, Honolulu, Oahu, Kona, Pago Pago, Levuka, Ovalau, Suva, Luganville/Port Vila (Vanuatu), Ile Des Pins, Noumea, Bay of Islands, Tauranga (Rotorua). October 22, December 3, 14 days, Auckland to Sydney via Tauranga (Rotorua), Napier, Wellington, Picton, Christchurch, Dunedin, Hobart, Canberra.

November 2010, January 2011, 14 or 28 days, round-trip from Sydney to Noumea, Mouli, Ouvea, Port Vila/Luganville (Vanuatu), Fiji, Levuka, Ovalau, Ile Des Pins, Milford Sound, Dunedin, Christchurch, Wellington, Napier, Tauranga (Rotorua), Auckland, Bay of Islands. November 19, 2010, reverse February 13, 2011, 14 days, Sydney to Auckland via Melbourne, Burnie, Milford Sound, Fiordland National Park, Dunedin, Christchurch, Picton, Wellington, Napier, Tauranga. December 17, 16 days, round-trip from Sydney to Canberra, Milford Sound, Dunedin, Christchurch, Wellington, Napier, Tauranga, Auckland, Bay of Islands.

***Westerdam* HOME PORTS** Fort Lauderdale, Rotterdam, Venice; others vary
May 4, 12 or 24 days, Venice to Barcelona via Split, Piraeus, Istanbul, Mykonos, Kusadasi, Santorini, Katakolon, (12 days) Venice, Dubrovnik, Corfu, Argostoli, Cephalonia, Catania, Naples, Rome, Livorno.

July 26, 12 or 19 days, Rotterdam to Stavanger, Ålesund, Hellesylt, Geiranger, Vik, Flam (12 days), Rotterdam, Portland, Guernsey, Waterford, Dublin, Holyhead, Greenock (Glasgow),

Belfast, S Queensferry (Edinburgh), Newcastle upon Tyne. August 14, 12 or 24 days, round-trip from Rotterdam to Guernsey, Dublin, Liverpool, Glasgow, Portree, Isle of Skye, Invergordon, S Queensferry, Newcastle (12 days), Bergen, Hellesylt, Geiranger, Trondheim, Crossing Artic Circle, Honningsvag, Tromso, Ålesund, Stavanger. August 26, 12 or 24 days, Rotterdam to Piraeus via Bergen, Hellesylt, Geiranger, Trondheim, Crossing Artic Circle, Honningsvag, Tromso, Ålesund, Stavanger (12 days), Rotterdam, Guernsey, Brest, Lisbon, Cartagena, Barcelona, Monte Carlo, Rome, Katakolon.

September 7, 24 days, Rotterdam to Kusadasi via Guernsey, Brest, Lisbon, Cartagena, Barcelona, Monte Carlo, Rome, Katakolon (12 days), Piraeus, Istanbul, Antalya, Iskenderun, Haifa, Ashdod, Alexandria. October 1, 24 days, Piraeus to Rome via Kusadasi, Naxos, Thessaloniki, Istanbul, Sochi, Trabzon, Sinop, Sevastopol, Katakolon, Venice, Dubrovnik, Kotor, Corfu, Valletta, Trapani, Naples; 12 days to Sevastopol.

October 13, 12 to 30 days, transatlantic, Piraeus to Fort Lauderdale via Katakolon, Venice, Dubrovnik, Kotor, Corfu, Valletta, Trapani, Naples, Rome (12 days), Livorno, Monte Carlo, Barcelona, Cartagena, Malaga, Cadiz, Lisbon, Funchal, Madeira.

November–December, 7 or 14 days, round-trip from Fort Lauderdale to Half Moon Cay, Aruba, Curaçao; or to Half Moon Cay, Grand Turk, Grand Cayman, Cozumel; or to Grand Turk, Puerto Rico, St. Maarten, Half Moon Cay; 14 days combines eastern/southern or western.

Zaandam **HOME PORTS** San Diego, Seattle, Vancouver

May–September, 7 days, round-trip from Seattle to Juneau, Glacier Bay or Hubbard Glacier, Sitka, Ketchikan, Victoria. October 1, 16 days, Vancouver to San Diego via Hilo, Lahaina, Honolulu, Nawiliwili Kauai, Kona. October–December, February 27, 2011, March 2011, 14 days, round-trip from San Diego to Hilo, Honolulu, Nawiliwili Kauai, Lahaina, Maui, Ensenada.

January 2, February 6, 2011, 9–11 days, round-trip San Diego to Cabo San Lucas, La Paz, Loreto, Guaymas, Sonora (10 days), Topolobampo, Mazatlan, Puerto Vallarta. January 12, February 16, 2011, 11 days, round-trip from San Diego to Puerto Vallarta, Manzanillo, Acapulco, Huatulco, Zihuatanejo, Cabo San Lucas. April 10, 14 days, San Diego to Vancouver via Cabo San Lucas, Loreto, Guaymas, Topolobampo, Mazatlan, Puerto Vallarta, San Diego, Victoria. April 24, 18 days, Vancouver to Hilo, Kona, Honolulu, Nawiliwili, Lahaina, Seattle.

Zuiderdam **HOME PORTS** Fort Lauderdale, Vancouver

May–September, 7 days, round-trip from Vancouver to Tracy Arm, Juneau, Skagway, Glacier Bay, Ketchikan. September 25, 16 or 19 days, Vancouver to Fort Lauderdale via San Francisco, Puerto Vallarta, Huatulco, Puerto Chiapas, Puerto Quetzal, Corinto, Fuerte Amador, Panama Canal, Cartagena.

October–December, 10 days, round-trip from Fort Lauderdale to Half Moon Cay, Aruba, Curaçao, Panama Canal, Cristobal, Limon Bay, Puerto Limon.

Hurtigruten (formerly Norwegian Coastal Voyage)

Kong Harald, Lofoten, Midnatsol, Nordkapp, Nordlys, Nordstjernen, Polarlys, Richard With, Trollfjord, Vesteraalen **HOME PORT** Bergen

Year-round, 12 days, Hurtigruten round-trip from Bergen northbound to Kirkenes stopping at 34 ports and returning southbound visiting the same ports, but those visited in the day northbound are visited during the night southbound and vice versa. One-way, 7-day segments, northbound (Bergen to Kirkenes) and 6-day segments, southbound (Kirkenes to Bergen) available. April–October, 14 nights, Reykjavik to Oslo, Bergen, Norwegian Coastal Voyage, Kirkenes; 18 nights, Oslo to Bergen via Ulvik, Gudvangen, Bergen, Kirkensbergen. May–September, 15 nights, Bergen to Oslo via land tour of Lofthus, Balestrand, Bergen, embark Norwegian Coastal Voyage, Vadso, Karasjok, Alta; or 13 nights, Oslo to Bergen via Alta, Karasjok, Kirkenes, Bergen, Ulvik, Flam.

January–March 2011, 11 nights, Arctic from Bergen to Kirkenes (overnight in Snow Hotel) via Maloy, Torvik, Ålesund, Molde, Kristiansund, Trondheim, Rorvik, Ornes, Bodo, Stamsund, Svolvaer, Harstad, Finnsnes, Tromso, Skjervoy, Hammerfest, Havoysund, Honningsvag, Kjollefjord, Mehamn, Berlevag. March 6, 7 nights, round-trip from Tromso to Honningsvag.

Fram **HOME PORTS** Oslo, Reykjavik, Santiago, Ushuaia; varies with itinerary

May 29, 10 nights, Tromso to Longyearbyen via Honningsvag, North Cape and Gjesvaerstappan, Bjornoya, Hornsund, Bellsund, Ny Alesund, 80th parallel, Isfjorden. June, 8 nights, round-trip from Longyearbyen to Gashama, Gnalodden, Calypsobyen, Magdalenefjord, Moffen Island, Krossfjord–Ny-Alesund, Forlandssund–Skansbukta. July 7, 5 nights, to Magdalenefjord–Raudfjord, Woodfjord–Moffen Island, Ny-Alesund–Blomstrand.

July 16, 13 nights, Reykjavik to Kangerlussuaq via Grundarfjordur, Prins Christian Sund, South Greenland, Nuuk, Qeqertarsuaq, Uummannaq/ Ukkusissat, Eqip Sermia, Ilulissat, Sisimiut, Itilleq. July–August, 7 nights, round-trip from Kangerlussuaq to Sisimiut, Qeqertarsuaq, Uummannaq, Ukkusissat, Eqip Sermia, Ilulissat, Itilleq. August 19, 14 nights, to Sisimiut, Qeqertarsuaq, Uummannaq, Dundas, Siorapaluk, Ice Edge, Qaanaaq, Upernavik, Eqip Sermia, Ilulissat, Itilleq.

September 2, 11 nights, Kangerlussuaq to Reykjavik via Evighedsfjorden, Nuuk, South Greenland, Prins Christian Sund, East Greenland. September 13, 10 nights, Wild Coast/ Northeast Greenland, round-trip from Reykjavik to Ammassalik, Kangerlussuaq Fjord, Mikis Fjord, Scoresby Sund, Ittoqqortoormiit, Northeast Greenland National Park. September 26, 13 nights, Reykjavik to Halifax via East Greenland, South Greenland, St. Anthony, Red Bay, Bonne Bay, Baddeck.

November 1, 2010, February 25, 2011, 21 nights, Ushuaia to Buenos Aires via Drake Passage, Antarctica, Deception Island, Cuverville Island, Neko Harbour, Paradise Harbour, Lemaire Channel, Petermann Island, Port Lockroy, Wilhelmina Bay, Antarctic Sound, Brown Bluff, South Orkneys/Scotia Sea, Falkland Islands/Islas Malvinas. November 19, December 3, round-trip from Ushuaia to Drake Passage, Antarctica, Tierra del Fuego/Chilean Fjords (Diego Ramirez, Cape Horn, Puerto Williams, Beagle Channel, Magellan Strait, Magdalena Island, Punta Arenas). December 17, 16 nights, round-trip from Ushuaia to Falkland Islands/ Islas Malvinas, South Georgia, South Orkneys, Antarctica, Deception Island, Half Moon Island, Paradise Harbour, Petermann Island, Port Lockroy, Lemaire Channel, Drake Passage.

January–February 2011, 9–14 nights, round-trip from Ushuaia to Drake Passage, Antarctica. Schedules vary; highlights include Deception Island, Half Moon Island, Yankee Harbour, Snow Hill Island, James Ross Island, Vega Island, Trinity Peninsula, Prince Gustav Channel, Cuverville Island, Neko Harbour, Paradise Harbour, Lemaire Channel, Petermann Island, Port Lockroy, Wilhelmina Bay, Antarctic Sound, Brown Bluff.

Polar Star **HOME PORT** Longyearbyen

June–August, 8 nights, Spitsbergen, round-trip from Longyearbyen to Ny-Alesund, Woodfjord–Moffen Island, Hinlopen Strait, Lomfjord/Austfonna, Nordaustlandet– Wahlenbergfjord–Murchinsonfjord–Sorkapp, Hornsund, Icefjord; or to Ny-Alesund, Hinlopen Strait–Nordauslandet, Kvitoya, Barentsoya–Edgeoya–South Cape, Hornsund, Icefjord.

Kristina Cruises

Kristina Brahe **HOME PORTS** Helsinki, Kotka; others vary with itinerary

June–August, 4 days, Sunday, Archipelago Sea and Åland Archipelago, round-trip from Helsinki to Jussarö, Tammisaari, Jurmo, Utö, Kökar, Nauvo. Wednesday, Czars Route, round-trip from Helsinki to Kotka, Lappeenranta, Savonlinna, Puumala, Lappeenranta, Kotka. 2 days, Thursday, Lake Saimaa, round-trip from Lappeenranta to Savonlinna, Puumala; Friday, Southern Carelia, from Helsinki to Lappeenranta via Kotak, Mälkiä; or from Lappeenranta to Helsinki.

Kristina Regina **HOME PORTS** Helsinki, Sharm el Sheikh; others vary with itinerary

May 1, 7 nights, Heraklion to Malta via Kusadasi, Santorini, Piraeus, Messina. May 8, 7 nights, Malta to Gibraltar via Trapani, La Goulette/Tunis, Ibiza, Cartagena. May 15, 12 nights, Gibraltar to Helsinki via Lisbon, Vigo, Brest, Oostende, Amsterdam, Kiel Canal. May 29, 7 nights, round-trip from Helsinki to Visby, Kaliningrad, Gdynia, Klaipeda, Riga. June 8, 8 nights, round-trip from Helsinki to Copenhagen, Skagen, Oslo, Goteborg, Sassnitz.

June–August, 3 to 7 nights, round-trip from Helsinki to St. Petersburg; round-trip from Helsinki (3 nights); Norwegian Fjords; Baltic Sea; Greenland, Iceland, Faroe Islands, Shetland Islands.

Lindblad Expeditions

Islander **HOME PORT** Guayaquil

Year-round, alternating 10 or 15 nights, Galápagos Islands/Peru, 15 nights from Guayaquil to Lima with 7-day cruise of Galapagos Islands; 10 nights, round-trip from Guayaquil to Galapagos/Baltra, Bartolome/Santiago, Santa Cruz, Isabela/Fernandina, Fioreana, Espanola.

Lord of the Glens **HOME PORTS** Inverness, Portsmouth

June–August, 7 nights, round-trip from Inverness to Culloden, Loch Ness, Fort Augustus, Caledonian, Canal, Laggan Locks, Neptune's Staircase, Tobermory, Isles of Eigg and Skye, Inverie, Kyle of Lochalsh.

National Geographic Endeavour **HOME PORTS** Guayaquil

Year-round, alternating 10 or 15 nights, Galápagos Islands/Peru, 15 nights from Guayaquil to Lima with 7-day cruise of Galapagos Islands; 10 nights, round-trip from Guayaquil to Galapagos/Baltra, Gloreana/Isabela/Fernandina, Santa Cruz, Espanol.

National Geographic Explorer **HOME PORTS** Bergen, Copenhagen, Oslo, Portsmouth, Seville, Ushuaia

May 11, May 24, 14 nights, Bergen to Reykjavik via Orkney Islands, Shetland Islands, Vestmanna, Torshavn, Mykines, Djupivogur, Langanes Peninsula, Husavik/Lake Myvatn, Isafjordur, Westman Islands.

June 6, August 13, 16 nights, Bergen to Oslo via Nordfjord, fjords of Norway, Lofoten Islands, Tysfjorden, Tromso, Bear Island, Svalbard, Longyearbyen. June–July, 10 nights, round-trip from Oslo to Longyearbyen, Svalbard. August 29, September 6, reverse, 16 nights, Copenhagen to St. Petersburg via Lubeck, Christianso and Bornholm Islands, Gdansk, Riga, Visby, Stockholm, Swedish Archipelago, Tallinn, Helsinki. September 20, 16 nights, Copenhagen to Lisbon via Lubeck, Kiel Canal transit, Amsterdam, Oostende, Bayeux, Normandy/ Cherbourg, St. Malo/Mont St. Michel, Ile d'Aix/La Rochelle, La Cote Basque, Bilbao, La Coruna/Santiago de Compostela, Islas Cies/Bayona, Oporto. October 22, 19 nights, round-trip from Ushuaia to Falkland Islands via South Georgia Island.

November 2010–February 2011, 14 nights, round-trip from Ushuaia to Antarctica. November 7, 2010, February 15, 2011, 24 nights, round-trip from Ushuaia to Antarctica, Elephant Island, South Orkney Island, South Georgia, Port Stanley, Falkland Islands.

Sea Bird/Sea Lion **HOME PORTS** Seattle, Juneau, Portland, La Paz, and others

May–August, 7 nights, Juneau to Sitka via Tracy Arm, Petersburg, Frederick Sound/ Chatham Strait, Glacier Bay National Park, Point Adolphus/Inian Pass, Southeast Alaska's Islands, Bays, and Fjords.

September 5 (reverse), 11 nights, Seattle to Juneau via San Juan Islands, Alert Bay/Johnstone Strait, Inside Passage, Misty Fiords, Frederick Sound/Chatham Strait, Sitka, Southeast Alaska's Islands, Bays and Fjords, Glacier Bay Nat'l Park, Point Adolphus/Chichagof Island.

September–October, 6 nights, Columbia and Snake rivers, round-trip from Portland to Eastern Washington's wine country, Clarkston, Palouse River, Columbia River Gorge/Hood River, Astoria. September 30, October 8, 4 nights, round-trip from Portland to Astoria/Fort Clatsop, Mount St. Helens, Columbia River Gorge. October, 4 nights, round-trip from San Francisco to Angel Island, Sausalito, Muir Woods, Suisun Bay, Napa River, Napa Valley.

December, 4 nights, Los Angeles to La Paz via Islas Los Islotes/Espiritu Santo, Isla Santa Catalina, Sea of Cortez; or 7 nights via Isla San Jose, Isla Ildefonso, Isla Catalina, Isla San Francisco, Sea of Cortez, Islas Los Islotes/Espiritu Santo.

Louis Cruise Lines

Aegean Pearl HOME PORT Piraeus

April–November, 3 nights, Aegean, round-trip from Piraeus to Mykonos, Kusadasi, Patmos, Heraklion, Santorini.

Aquamarine HOME PORT Piraeus

April–November, 4 nights, Aegean, round-trip from Piraeus to Mykonos, Kusadasi, Patmos, Rhodes, Heraklion, Santorini.

Coral HOME PORTS Genoa, Marseilles

April–November, 10 nights, round-trip from Genoa or Marseille to Katakolon, Santorini, Istanbul, Mykonos, Piraeus, Corinth Canal, Messina, Ajaccio.

Louis Cristal HOME PORT Piraeus

April–October, 7 nights, round-trip from Piraeus to Istanbul, Mykonos, Patmos, Kusadasi, Rhodes, Ay Nikolaos, Santorini; or Istanbul, Mykonos, Ashdod, Port Said, Alexandria, Ay Nikolaos.

Louis Majesty HOME PORTS Genoa, Marseille

April–October, March 24 or 25, 2011, 6–8 nights, round-trip from Genoa or Marseille to Port Mahon, Tunis, La Valletta, Trapani (6 nights); or Palma de Mallorca, Almeria, Malaga, Tangier, Ibiza, Barcelona (7 nights); or Olbia, Messina, Katakolon, Zante, Corinthos, Saranda, Corfu (8 nights).

October 30 or 31, March 4 or 5, 2011, 8 nights, round-trip from Genoa or Marseille to Ajaccio, Tunia Sousse, La Valletta, Palermo, Rome. November 19 or 20, February 2 or 3, 2011, 10 nights, round-trip from Genoa or Marseille to Tangier, Lisbon, Cadiz, Casablanca, Malaga, Almeria, Alicante, Barcelona.

November 7 or 8, February 20 or 21, 2011, March 12 or 13, 2011, 12 nights, round-trip from Genoa or Marseille to La Valletta, Alexandria, Port Said, Ashdod, Limassol, Heraklion, Naples. December 2, 2010, 8 nights, round-trip from Marseille to Tangier, Casablanca, Malaga, Barcelona, Genoa. December 7 or 8, January 13 or 14, 2011, 12 nights, round-trip from Genoa or Marseille to Tangier, Casablanca, Funchal, Lanzarote, Cadiz, Cartagena, Barcelona. December 19, 8 nights, round-trip from Genoa to Marseille, Tangier, Casablanca, Malaga. December 27 or 28, 9 nights, round-trip from Genoa or Marseille to Tangier, Casablanca, Malaga, Alicante, Barcelona.

November 29 or 30, January 5 or 6, 2011, February 12 or 13, 2011, 8 nights, Iberian Coast, round-trip from Genoa or Marseille to Barcelona, Alicante, Gibraltar, Tangier, Casablanca, Malaga, Almeria. January 25 or 26, 2011, 8 or 9 nights, round-trip from Genoa or Marseille to Tangier, Casablanca, Cadiz, Cartagena, Barcelona.

Orient Queen HOME PORTS Marseille, Venice

April–October, 10 nights, round-trip from Marseille to Messina, Kotor, Split, Venice, Dubrovnik, Corfu Lipari, Rome or Livorno; or round-trip from Venice to Dubrovnik, Corfu, Lipari, Rome, Marseille, Messina, Kotor, Split.

MSC Cruises

MSC Armonia HOME PORTS Buenos Aires, Venice

May–August, September 6, 13, 7 nights, round-trip from Venice to Dubrovnik, Corfu, Piraeus, Argostoli, Kefalonia, Kotor, Ancona.

MSC Fantasia HOME PORTS Genoa

April–October, 7 nights, Mediterranean, round-trip from Genoa to Naples, Palermo, La Goulette (Tunis), Palma de Mallorca, Marseille.

MSC Lirica HOME PORTS Genoa, Rio de Janeiro
April–October, 7 nights, round-trip from Genoa to Ajaccio, Rome, Salerno, La Goulette (Tunis), Palma de Mallorca, Toulon.

MSC Magnifica HOME PORTS Hamburg, St. Nazaire, Venice
April–November, 7 nights, round-trip from Venice to Bari, Katakolon, Izmir, Istanbul, Dubrovnik.

MSC Melody HOME PORTS Genoa, Salvador de Bahia
April–October, 11 nights, round-trip from Genoa to Rome, Piraeus, Yalta, Odessa, Istanbul, Messina, Sorrento; or Almeria, Cadiz, Lisbon, Casablanca, Palma de Mallorca, Villefranche; or Sorrento, Alexandria, Limassol, Antalya, Rhodes, Messina, Olbia; or Almeria, Funchal, Tenerife, Tangier, Palma de Mallorca, Villefranche.

MSC Musica HOME PORTS Santos, Venice
April–September, October 3, 7 nights, round-trip from Venice to Bari, Katakolon, Santorini, Mykonos, Corfu, Dubrovnik.

MSC Opera HOME PORTS Santos, Amsterdam, Rio de Janeiro, Venice
May 3, 19 nights, positioning from Santos to Amsterdam via Rio de Janeiro, Salvador De Bahia, Recife, Mindelo, Las Palmas, Cadiz, Lisbon, Vigo, La Coruna, Dover. June, 11 nights, round-trip from Amsterdam to Dover, Bergen, Hellesylt, Honningsvag, Honningsvag, Ålesund. July–August, 11 nights, to Dover, Oslo, Stavanger, Flåm, Molde, Hellesylt, Bergen, Kristiansand; or Dover, Rostock, Stockholm, Helsinki, St. Petersburg, Copenhagen.

September 9, 10 or 11 nights, positioning from Amsterdam or Dover to Venice via La Coruna, Lisbon, Malaga, La Goulette (Tunis), Dubrovnik. September 20, October, 11 nights, round-trip from Venice to Kotor, Piraeus, Yalta, Odessa, Istanbul, Katakolon, Dubrovnik.

MSC Orchestra HOME PORTS Copenhagen, Genoa, Santos
May–August, 7 nights, round-trip from Copenhagen to Kiel, Stockholm, Tallinn, St. Petersburg; or Kiel, Hellesylt, Flåm, Stavanger, Oslo. August 28, 10 or 11 nights, positioning, Copenhagen to Barcelona or Genoa via Kiel, Dover, La Coruna, Lisbon, Gibraltar, Malaga. September–October, 8 nights, round-trip from Genoa to Malaga, Cadiz, Lisbon, Gibraltar, Alicante, Barcelona.

MSC Poesia HOME PORTS Fort Lauderdale, Hamburg, Kiel, New York, Quebec
May 30, 2 nights, Hamburg to Kiel. June 1, 3 nights, round-trip from Kiel to Oslo, Copenhagen; or June 4, 11 nights, to Bergen, Torshavn, Akureyri, Isafjordur, Hafnarfjordur, Lerwick; or June 15, 11 nights, to Copenhagen, Trondheim, Honningsvag, Honningsvag, Hellesylt, Bergen; or June 26, July–August, 7 nights, to Copenhagen, Oslo, Stavanger, Bergen, Hellesylt; or Stockholm, Tallinn, St. Petersburg. September 4, 18 nights, positioning, from Kiel to New York via Copenhagen, Southampton, Le Havre, Vigo, Lisbon, Ponta Delgada, Azores Islands, Bermuda.

September 22, 10 or 17 nights, New York to Quebec via Halifax, Charlottetown, Quebec, Sydney, Newport, New York (10 nights), Halifax, Sydney, Charlottetown. October 2, 7or 14 nights, round-trip from New York to Halifax, Charlottetown, Corner Brook, Quebec, Sydney, Bar Harbor, Boston, Newport; or 7 nights to Quebec. October 9, 7 or 14 nights, round-trip from Quebec to Sydney, Bar Harbor, Boston, Newport, New York, Halifax, Sydney, Charlottetown. October 16, 7 nights, New York to Quebec via Halifax, Sydney, Charlottetown. October 23, 9 nights, positioning from Quebec to Fort Lauderdale via Sydney, Boston, Newport, New York.

MSC Sinfonia HOME PORTS Durban, Livorno
May–September, 7 nights, round-trip from Livorno to Montecarlo, Valencia, Ibiza, La Goulette (Tunis), Catania, Naples.

MSC Splendida HOME PORT Genoa
April–October, November 6, 7 nights, round-trip from Genoa to Marseille, Barcelona, La

Goulette (Tunis), Malta, Messina, Rome. November 13, 24, December 5, 11 nights, to Katakolon, Piraeus, Rhodes, Alexandria, Heraklion, La Valletta, Messina, Naples; or to Katakolon, Ashdod, Alexandria, Heraklion, La Goulette, Naples.

Nomade Yachting

Tu Moana/Ti'a Moana **HOME PORT** Bora Bora

Year-round, 6 nights, Monday, Society Islands round-trip from Bora Bora to Taha'a, Raiatea (2 days), Huanine, overnight in Bora Bora.

Norwegian Cruise Line

Norwegian Dawn **HOME PORTS** Miami, New York

April–September, 7 days, round-trip from New York to Bermuda. September–October, 7 days round-trip from New York to Halifax, Saint John (Bay of Fundy), Bar Harbor, Boston, Newport. October 10, 12 days, New York to Miami via Samana, Curaçao, Aruba, Roatan, Belize City.

October 2010–April 2011, 5–14 days, round-trip from Miami to Samana, Tortola, Antigua, Barbados, St. Kitts, (9 days); or Grand Cayman, Cozumel (5 days); combine for 14 days; or Grand Cayman, Cozumel, Miami, Samana, Tortola, Antigua, Barbados, St. Kitts (14 days).

Norwegian Epic **HOME PORT** Miami

June 24, 7 days, Inaugural transatlantic, Southampton to New York.

July 2010–April 2011, 7 or 14 days, round-trip from Miami to St. Maarten, St. Thomas, Nassau; or Costa Maya, Roatan, Cozumel; combine for 14 days.

Norwegian Gem **HOME PORTS** New York, Venice

April 2010/2011, November–December 2010, 7 days, round-trip from New York to Port Canaveral, Great Stirrup Cay, Nassau.

April 10, reverse October 30, 14–21 days, transatlantic, New York to Venice via Ponta Delgada, Lisbon, Cadiz, Malaga (14 days), Venice, Split, Corfu, Santorini, Mykonos, Iraklion (21 days). April–October, 7 or 14 days, alternating round-trip from Venice to Split, Corfu, Santorini, Mykonos, Kraklion; or Dubrovnik, Piraeus, Izmir, Nafplion; combine for 14 days.

July 10, 14 days, round-trip from Venice to Dubrovnik, Piraeus, Izmir, Nafplion, Venice (7 days), Split, Corfu, Koper (14 days). July 17, 14 days, to Split, Corfu, Koper, Venice (7 days), Dubrovnik, Piraeus, Izmir, Nafplion, Venice (14 days).

Norwegian Jade **HOME PORT** Barcelona

April–November, 7 days, round-trip from Barcelona to Monte Carlo, Livorno, Rome, Naples, Palma. April 2010, December 2010–April 2011, 9–21 days, round-trip from Barcelona to Casablanca, Agadir, Las Palmas, Funchal, Malaga (9 days), Rome, Piraeus, Izmir, Alexandria, Malta (12 days); combine for 21 days.

Norwegian Jewel **HOME PORTS** Miami, New York

April–December 2010, February–April 2011, 7 days, round-trip from New York to Port Canaveral, Great Stirrup Cay, Nassau. February 2, 2011, 10 days, round-trip from New York to San Juan, St. Thomas, Antigua, St. Maarten, Tortola. January 22, February 12, 2011, weekend cruise, 1 day, round-trip from New York.

Norwegian Pearl **HOME PORTS** Miami, Vancouver

May 1, 8 days, Vancouver to Seattle via Inside Passage, Sawyer Glacier, Juneau, Skagway, Icy Strait Point Bay, Ketchikan, Victoria.

May–August, September 5, 7 days, round-trip from Seattle to Inside Passage, Juneau, Skagway, Glacier Bay, Ketchikan, Victoria. September 12, 7 days, Seattle to Vancouver via Inside Passage, Juneau, Skagway, Glacier Bay, Ketchikan, Victoria. September 19, 5 days, Vancouver to Los Angeles via Astoria, San Francisco. October–December 2010, January–April 2011, 7 days, round-trip Miami to Samana, St. Thomas, Tortola, Great Stirrup Cay; or Roatan, Belize City, Costa Maya, Key West; combine for 14 days.

Norwegian Sky **HOME PORT** Miami
March 2010–April 2011, round-trip from Miami to Nassau, Great Stirrup Cay (3 days); or
Grand Bahama Island, Nassau, Great Stirrup Cay (4 days). April 17, 2 days, weekend cruise,
round-trip from Miami to Great Stirrup Cay.

Norwegian Spirit **HOME PORTS** Boston, New Orleans
September 25, October 9, return October 2, 16, 7 or 14 days, Boston to Quebec City via Bar
Harbor, Saint John (Bay of Fundy), Halifax, Sydney, Corner Brook; or return Saguenay
Fjord, Sept-iles, Charlottetown, Halifax, Portland; or combine for 14 days round-trip
Boston. October 23, 15 days, Boston to New Orleans via Samana, Tortola, St. Kitts,
Barbados, Curaçao, Aruba, Roatan, Cozumel.
November–December 2010, January–April 2011, 7 days, round-trip from New Orleans to
Costa Maya, Santo Tomas de Castilla, Belize City, Cozumel. April 11, 12 days, New Orleans
to Boston via Costa Maya, Santo Tomas de Castilla, Aruba, Curaçao, Hamilton. April–
September, 7 days, Bermuda, round-trip from Boston to King's Wharf. September 24, 1
day, round-trip from Boston.

Norwegian Star **HOME PORTS** Los Angeles, Seattle
May 1, 7 days, Los Angeles to Vancouver via Juneau, Ketchikan, Inside Passage. May 8, 7
days, Vancouver to Seattle via Inside Passage, Ketchikan, Juneau, Skagway, Prince Rupert;
reverse September 25.
May–September, 7 days, round-trip from Seattle to Inside Passage, Ketchikan, Juneau,
Skagway, Prince Rupert. October 2, 6 days, Vancouver to Los Angeles via Victoria,
Astoria, San Francisco.
October 8, 13 days, Los Angeles to Miami via Cabo San Lucas, Acapulco, Huatulco,
Puntarenas, Panama Canal transit, Cartagena. November 4, 15 days, Miami to Los
Angeles via Roatan, Cartagena, Panama Canal, Puntarenas, Puerto Quetzal, Huatulco,
Acapulco, Cabo San Lucas. November 19, 1 day, round-trip from Los Angeles. November
20, 2010, January 1, 2011, 15 days, Los Angeles to Miami via Cabo San Lucas, Acapulco,
Huatulco, Puerto Quetzal, Puntarenas, Panama Canal, Cartagena, Key West. December 5,
13 days, Miami to Los Angeles via Cartagena, Panama Canal, Puntarenas, Huatulco,
Acapulco, Cabo San Lucas.
December 18, 25; January 29, 2011, February–April 2011, 7 days, round-trip from Los
Angeles to Cabo San Lucas, Mazatlan, Puerto Vallarta. April 25, 6 days, round-trip from
Los Angeles to Puerto Vallarta, Cabo San Lucas.

Norwegian Sun **HOME PORTS** Buenos Aires, Dover, Miami
May–August, September 8, 12 days, Dover to Copenhagen, Warnemuende, Tallinn, St.
Petersburg, Helsinki, Stockholm.
October 4, 12 or 19 days, transatlantic, Dover to Port Canaveral via Lisbon, Ponta Delgada (12
days), Port Canaveral, Cozumel, Santo Tomas de Castilla, Belize City, Key West (19 days).
October 2010–April 2011, 7 days, round-trip from Port Canaveral to Nassau, St. Thomas, St.
Maarten; or Cozumel, Santo Tomas de Castilla, Belize City, Key West; combine for 14 days.

NCL America
Pride of America **HOME PORT** Honolulu
Year-round, 7 days, round-trip from Honolulu to Kahului (2 days), Hilo, Kona, Kauai (2 days).

Oceania Cruises
Insignia **HOME PORT** Varies with itinerary
June 5, 12 days, Venice to Rome via Dubrovnik, Kotor, Corfu, Taormina, Sorrento, Amalfi,
Livorno, Monte Carlo, La Spezia, Portofino; reverse September 5. June 17, 10 days, Rome to
Barcelona via Bonifacio, Porto Venere, Provence, Cannes, Portofino, Olbia/Porto Cervo,
Saint-Tropez, Sanary-Sur-Mer, Sete. June 27, 14 days, to Amsterdam via Valencia, Gibraltar,
Seville, Lisbon, Bilbao, Biarritz, Bordeaux, Lorient, Saint-Malo, Honfleur, Zeebrugge.

July 11, 12 days, Amsterdam to Dover via Zeebrugge, Rotterdam, Kiel Canal transit, Copenhagen, Gothenburg, Oslo, Antwerp, Le Havre, Saint-Malo, Portland. July 23, 18 days, Dover to Copenhagen via Oslo, Stavanger, Hellesylt, Geiranger, Honningsvaag, Murmansk, Hammerfest, Polar Ice Barrier, Magdalene Bay, Spitzbergen, Harstad, Bergen, Kristiansand. August 10, 14 days, Copenhagen to Lisbon via Oslo, Amsterdam, Zeebrugge, Le Havre, Brest, La Rochelle, Bordeaux, Biarritz, Bilbao, La Coruna, Oporto.

August 24, 12 days, Lisbon to Rome via Tangier, Seville, Malaga, Alicante, Ibiza, Barcelona, Saint-Tropez, Cannes, Monte Carlo, Portofino, Livorno.

September 17, 14 days, Venice to Barcelona via Dubrovnik, Corfu, Taormina, Sorrento, Amalfi, Rome, Livorno, La Spezia, Portofino, Monte Carlo, Provence, Palma de Mallorca. October 1, 14 days, Barcelona to Istanbul via Malta, Aghios Nikolaos, Alexandria, Port Said, Ashdod, Haifa, Limassol, Marmaris, Kusadasi. October 15, 14 days, Istanbul to Monte Carlo via Mykonos, Kusadasi, Santorini, Messina, Sorrento, Amalfi, Rome, Livorno, La Spezia, Toulon, Barcelona. October 29, 12 days, Monte Carlo to Venice via Cannes, La Spezia, Livorno, Rome, Sorrento, Taormina, Corfu, Kotor, Dubrovnik, Koper. November 10, 14 days, Venice to Barcelona via Hvar, Dubrovnik, Corfu, Messina, Naples/Capri, Rome, La Spezia, Livorno, Monte Carlo, Provence, Palma de Mallorca, Valencia. December 6, 15 days, transatlantic, Barcelona to Rio de Janeiro via Gibraltar, Porto Grande, Recife, Salvador. December 21, March 3, 2011, 12 days, Rio de Janeiro to Buenos Aires via Buzios, Ilha Grande, Parati, Santos, Itajai, Punta del Este, Montevideo; return January 2, February 22.

January 14, 2011, 22 days, Antarctica, Rio de Janeiro to Valparaiso via Santos, Montevideo, Buenos Aires, Punta del Este, Port Stanley, Drake Passage, Deception Island, Paradise Bay, Half Moon Island, Ushuaia, Punta Arenas, Chilean Fjords, Puerto Chacabuco, Puerto Montt. February 5, 14 days, Valparaiso to Buenos Aires via Puerto Montt, Puerto Chacabuco, Laguna San Rafael, Chilean Fjords, Ushuaia, Port Stanley, Montevideo.

March 15, 19 days, transatlantic, Buenos Aires to Barcelona via Montevideo, Rio de Janeiro, Salvador, Recife, Porto Grande, Santa Cruz de Tenerife, Valencia.

Nautica **HOME PORT** Varies with itinerary

May–October, 10–14 days, Athens to Barcelona, Istanbul, Athens; Barcelona to Venice, Rome, Barcelona; Athens to Istanbul, Athens, Rome, Venice, Istanbul.

November 11, 30 days, Istanbul to Cape Town via Heraklion, Valletta, La Goulette, Valencia, Casablanca, Santa Cruz de Tenerife, Dakar, Banjul, Abidjan, Takoradi, Lome, Cotonou, Walvis Bay. December 11, 35 days, Cape Town to Singapore via East London, Durban, Richard's Bay, Maputo, Mayotte, Nosy Be, Dar Es Salaam, Zanzibar, Mombasa, Victoria, Male, Colombo, Rangoon, Phuket, Penang, Kuala Lumpur.

January–March 2011, 15–24 days, Singapore to Hong Kong, Bangkok, Beijing, Hong Kong. March 26, 25 days, Hong Kong to Dubai via Da Nang, Saigon, Singapore, Phuket, Rangoon, Cochin, Mumbai, Port Qaboos. April 20, 20 days, Dubai to Athens via Fujairah, Port Qaboos, Port Raysut, Aqaba, Luxor/Safaga, Sharm el Sheikh, Suez Canal, Port Said, Ashdod, Haifa.

Marina Launch Late 2010

Caribbean, Amazon, and Panama Canal in winter; Western Mediterranean in spring and fall; Scandinavia and Russia in summer.

Regatta **HOME PORT** Miami; others vary with itinerary

May 19, 14 days, Barcelona to London via Valencia, Gibraltar, Seville, Lisbon, Oporto, La Coruna, Bilbao, Bordeaux, Lorient, Guernsey, Rouen.

June 2, July 12, 14 days, Dover to Stockholm via Zeebrugge, Amsterdam, Kiel Canal, Warnemunde, Copenhagen, Visby, Riga, Tallinn, St. Petersburg, Helsinki; reverse June 16. June 30, 12 days, round-trip from Dover to Edinburgh, Invergordon, Lerwick, Ålesund, Geiranger, Hellesylt, Belfast, Dublin, Waterford, Fowey. July 26, 10 days, Stockholm to Copenhagen via Helsinki, St. Petersburg, Tallinn, Riga, Visby, Gdansk, Ronne, Rostock.

August 5, 14 days, Copenhagen to Tilbury via Kristiansand, Bergen, Flaam, Gudvangen, Lerwick, Torshavn, Isafjordur, Reykjavik, Portree, Belfast, Dublin. August 19, Tilbury to Stockholm via Zeebrugge, Amsterdam, Kiel Canal, Rostock, Copenhagen, Visby, Riga, Tallinn, St. Petersburg, Helsinki; reverse September 2.

September 16, 14 days, Dover to Monte Carlo via Honfleur, Saint-Malo, Lorient, La Rochelle, Bordeaux, Bilbao, La Coruna, Oporto, Lisbon, Seville, Port-Vendres. September 30, 12 days, Monte Carlo to Venice via Cannes, La Spezia, Livorno, Rome, Sorrento, Taormina, Corfu, Kotor, Dubrovnik, Koper. October 12, 12 days, Venice to Athens via Dubrovnik, Kotor, Corfu, Itea, Zakinthos, Monemvasia, Aghios Nikolaos, Santorini, Kusadasi, Delos, Mykonos. October 24, 10 days, Athens to Rome via Kusadasi, Rhodes, Santorini, Katakolon, Messina, Amalfi, Olbia/Porto Cervo, Ajaccio, Livorno. November 3, 10 days, Civitavecchia to Barcelona via Naples/Capri, Olbia/Porto Cervo, La Spezia, Livorno, Ajaccio, Monte Carlo, Provence, Sete, Palma de Mallorca.

November 13, 14 days, transatlantic, Barcelona to Miami via Tangier, Funchal, Bermuda.

November 27, March 19, 2011, 24 days, Amazon, round-trip from Miami to St. Barts, Scarborough, Santarem, Boca de Valeria, Manaus, Parintins, Devil's Island, Barbados, Dominica, Virgin Gorda, Samana, Grand Turk. December 21, 12 days, round-trip from Miami to Grand Turk, Samana, Tortola, Antigua, Barbados, Martinique, St. Barts, St Croix.

January 2, 2011, round-trip from Miami to Virgin Gorda, St. Barts, Antigua, Tortola, Samana, Grand Turk. January 12, February 15, March 9, 10 days, to Grand Cayman, Cozumel, Belize City, Santo Tomas, Roatan, Costa Maya, Key West. January 22, February 3, February 25, 12 days, to Virgin Gorda, St. Barts, Dominica, St. Lucia, Cruz Bay, Tortola, Samana, Grand Turk. April 26, 16 days, Miami to San Francisco via Key West, Cartagena, Panama Canal, Puntarenas, Puerto Chiapas, Huatulco, Acapulco, Cabo San Lucas.

Oceanwide Expeditions

Antarctic Dream **HOME PORT** Longyearbyen

June, 5 to 7 nights, Spitsbergen, round-trip from Longyearbyen. August 24, 12 nights, Northeast Greenland from Longyearbyen to Akureyri via Tryghamna, Shannon Island, Sabine Island, Kaiser Franz Joseph Fjord, Alpefjord, Scoresby Sund, Cape Hoffmann Halvo, Danmarks, Illoqqortoormiut. September 5, 9 nights, Scoresby Sund/Aurora Borealis, from Akureyri to Keflavik.

Noorderlicht **HOME PORT** Longyearbyen

June–August, 11 to 15 nights, Spitsbergen, round-trip from Longyearbyen. October 1, October 22, 7 nights, South Spitsbergen/Aurora Borealis, round-trip from Longyearbyen. November 10, November 17, November 24, 7 nights, Lofoten/Aurora Borealis.

Professor Molchanov **HOME PORT** Ushuaia

April 22, 7 nights, Ascension Island to Praia via Fogo. 10 nights, round-trip from Ushuaia to Beagle Channel, Drake Passage, Paulet Island, Seymout Island, Snow Hill Island, Devil and Vega islands, Hope Bay, Half Moon Island, Deception Island, Drake Passage.

Plancius **HOME PORT** Ushuaia

May 28, 7 nights, Scottish Islands, Aberdeen to Oban via Fair Islle, Moussa, Foula, Papa Stour, North Rona, Sula Sgeir, Callanish, Flannans, St. Kilda, Mungulay, Berneray, Canna. June 4, 10 nights, Faroes/Spitsbergen, from Oban to Longyearben via St. Iilda Islands, Thorshavn, Jan Mayen, Raudfjord, Fuglehuken. June–August, 7 or 10 nights, Spitsbergen, round-trip from Longyearbyen. October 18, November 4, November 22, January 7, 2011, February 4, 2011, 17 or 18 nights, round-trip from Ushuaia to Beagle Channel, Falkland Islands/Port Stanley, South Georgia/Grytviken, Orcadas Station, Wedell Sea, Brown Bluff, Deception Island, Cuverville Island, Drake Passage. December 10, 10 nights, Antarctic Peninsula/South Shetlands.

January 25, February 22, 2011, 10 nights, round-trip from Ushuaia to Beagle Channel, Drake Passage, Antarctic Peninsula, Petermann/Pleneau Island, Port Lockroy, Melchoir

Islands, Drake Passage. March 4, 11 nights, Wedell Sea/Antarctic Peninsula. March 15, 11 nights, Polar Circle/Antarctic Peninsula. March 26, 2011, 30 nights, from Ushuaia to Ascension Island via Drak Passage, Hope Bay, Brown Bluff, Devil Island, South Orkneys, South Georgia, Gough Island, Tristan da Cunha, St. Helena. April 25, 2011, 7 nights, from Ascension Island to Praia via Fogo.

Orion Expedition Cruises

Orion   **HOME PORTS**   Cairns; others vary with itinerary

May 4, 7 nights, round-trip from Thursday Island to Darwain via Yirrkala, Jensen Bay/Hole in the Wall, Elcho Island, Maningrida, Pirlangimpi (Melville Island).

May–September, 10 nights, Darwin to Broome via King George River and Falls, Vansittart Bay, Bigge Island, Hunter River/Mitchell Falls, Montgomery Reef/Raft Point, Talbot Bay/Horizontal Waterfalls, Cape Leveqae and The Lacepedes; alternating reverse. May 31, 10 nights, Darwin to Broome via Wyndham/Kununurra and Warmun, King George River and Falls, Vansittart Bay, Bigge Island, Hunter River/Mitchell Falls, Montgomery Reef/Raft Point, The Lacepedes.

July 10, 10 nights, round-trip from Darwin to Kisar (Maluku), Alor (East Nusa Tenggara), Maumere (Flores), Komodo, Waitgapu (Sumba Island), Savu, Nusa Manuk (Rote). August 19, 8 nights, Kimberly, round-trip from Broome to Rowley Shoals, One Arm Point, Nares Point, Montgomery Reef/Raft Point, Kuri Bay, Camden Harbour. August 27, 10 nights, Broome to Darwin via Talbot Bay/Horizontal Waterfalls, Montgomery Reef/Raft Point, Hunter River/Mitchell Falls, Bigge Island, Vansittart Bay, King George River and Falls.

September 26, 10 nights, Darwin to Cairns via Kisar (Maluku), Sangliat Dol and Weluan Beach, Aru, Agats (Asmat), Thursday Island/Torres Strait, Orion Reef, Lizard Island. October 11, 11 nights, New Guinea Islands, round-trip from Cairns to Alotau, Deboyne Lagoon, Egum Atoll, Kitava Island, Lambom, Lamassa Islands, Duke of York Islands, Rabaul.

November 2, 7 nights, Great Barrier Reef, Cairns to Sydney via Coonanglebah, Hayman Island, Percy Island. November 9, 7 nights, Sydney to Melbourne via Huskisson and Hyams Beach (Jervis Bay), Montague Island, Eden, Sealers Cove/Wilsons Promontory, Phillip Island. November 16, 7 nights, round-trip from Melbourne to Limestone Coast, Kangaroo Island, Port Lincoln, Flerieu Peninsula. November 24, 7 nights, Tasmania National Parks, Melbourne to Hobart via Flinders Island, Wineglass and Coles bays, Maria Island, Port Arthur.

December 1, 7 nights, Wild Tasmania, round-trip from Hobart to Port Davey (Southwest National Park), Port Huon, South Bruny Island, Maria Island, Wineglass and Coles bays, Port Arthur. December 8, 13 nights, Sub-Antarctic, Hobart to Dunedin via Macquarie Island, Campbell Island, Auckland Islands, Snares Island, Stewart Island, Milford Sound, Dusky and Doubtful sounds. December 21, 7 nights, Fjordland, round-trip from Dunedin to Jackson Bay, Milford Sound, Dusky and Doubtful sounds, Stewart Island. December 28, 18 nights, Mawson's Antarctica, round-trip from Dunedin to Snares Islands, Auckland Islands, Macquarie Island, Commonwealth Bay Region.

Orion II   **HOME PORT**   Singapore. Debut 2011

Tentatively, Circumnavigation of Borneo, including Indonesian Borneo, Malaysian Borneo, and Brunei.

Paul Gaugin Cruises

Paul Gaugin   **HOME PORT**   Papeete

July–October, 7 nights, Tahiti/Society Islands, round-trip from Papeete to Raiatea, Taha'a, Bora Bora, Moorea. July 13, August, 24, October 12, 11 nights, Cook Islands/Society Islands, round-trip from Papeete to Huahine, Aitutaki, Rarotonga, Bora Bora, Taha'a, Moorea. August 14, October 2, 10 nights, Society Islands/Tuamotus, round-trip from Papeete to Huahine, Raiatea, Rangiroa, Bora Bora, Taha'a, Moorea.

September 4, December 4, 14 nights, Marquesas/Tuamotus/Society Islands, round-trip from Papeete to Fakarava, Hanavave, Atuona, Vaipaee, Tiaohae, Huahine, Bora Bora, Taha'a, Moorea. November 6, 21, 14 nights, New Zealand/Tonga/Cook Islands/Society Islands, from Papeete to Auckland via Moorea, Taha'a, Bora Bora, Aitutaki, Rarotonga, Nuku'Alofa, Bay of Islands, Tauranga. December 18, 27, 9 nights, Tahiti, Society Islands, Tuamotus, round-trip from Papeete to Fakarava, Huahine, Bora Bora, Taha'a, Moorea.

P&O Cruises

Arcadia HOME PORT Southampton

May 9, August 1, 14 nights, round-trip from Southampton to Copenhagen, Stockholm, Helsinki, St. Petersburg, Tallinn, Oslo, Kristiansand. May 23, 7 nights, to Stavanger, Olden, Ålesund, Bergen. May 30, September 17, 3 nights, to Bruges, Le Havre.

June 2, July 18, September 3, November 2, December 19, 13–17 nights, round-trip from Southampton to Gibraltar, Ajaccio, Rome, Santa Margherita, Florence/Pisa, Villefranche, Barcelona; or Barcelona, Villefranche, Calvi, Rome, Naples, Cartagena, Gibraltar; or Malaga, Zakinthos, Corfu, Dubrovnik, Venice, Malta, Cadiz; or Barcelona, Monte Carlo, Florence/Pisa, Rome, Alicante, Gibraltar; or Lisbon, Cadiz, Cartagena, Malta, Naples, Rome, Cannes, Barcelona, Gibraltar.

June 19, 15 nights, round-trip from Southampton to Bruges, Amsterdam, Oslo, Stavanger, Flaam, Olden, Trondheim, Akureyri, Reykjavik. July 4, 12 nights, to Madeira, Gran Canaria, Tenerife, La Palma, Lisbon, Vigo. July 16, 2 nights, to Bruges. July 18, 14 nights, to Cadiz, Barcelona, Marseille, Santa Margherita, Rome, Palau, Gibraltar. August 15, 22, 7 or 12 nights, to Stavanger, Ålesund, Geiranger, Bergen; or Eidfjord, Andalsnes, Honningsvaag, Tromso, Trondheim, Olden, Bergen.

September 20, 23 nights, transatlantic, round-trip from Southampton to New York, Newport, Boston, Portland, St. John, NB, Halifax, Quebec, St. John's. November 15, 23 nights, to Ponta Delgada, Antigua, St. Maarten, St. Kitts, St. Lucia, Barbados, Madeira. December 8, 11 nights, to Madeira, La Palma, Tenerife, Lanzarote, Vigo.

January 5, 2011, 82 nights, World Cruise, round-trip from Southampton via Ponta Delgada, Barbados, Aruba, Acapulco, San Francisco, Honolulu, Oahu, Pago Pago, Port Denarau, Auckland, Sydney, Brisbane, Whitsunday Islands, Cairns, Hong Kong, Halong Bay (Vietnam), Bangkok, Ko Samuk, Singapore, Kuala Lumpur, Mumbai, Safaga, Sharm el Sheikh, Suez, Suez Canal transit, Piraeus, Rome; segments available.

Artemis HOME PORTS Barbados, Southampton

May, July–August, 14 nights, round-trip from Southampton to Oslo, Copenhagen, Visby, Stockholm, Helsinki, St. Petersburg, Warnemunde, Bruges; or Kristiansand, Oslo, Stavanger, Ålesund, Honningsvaag, Hammerfest, Tromso, Olden, Bergen; or Stavanger, Molde, Trondheim, Honningsvaag, Hammerfest, Tromso, Lofoten Islands, Bergen, Eidfjord; or Riga, Stockholm, Helsinki, St. Petersburg, Bornholm, Copenhagen, Oslo; or Stavanger, Eidfjord, Bergen, Ålesund, Akureyri, Isafjordur, Reykjavik, Greencastle, Dublin. August 16, 11 nights, to Newcastle, Edinburgh, Lerwick, Stornoway, Douglas, Dublin, Milford Haven, St. Peter Port.

September 27, November 18, 24 or 26 nights, round-trip from Southampton to Palma, Athens, Istanbul, Trabzon, Yalta, Odessa, Ephesus, Heraklion, Malta, Cadiz; or Palma, Athens , Istanbul, Ephesus, Rhodes, Limassol, Cairo/Giza, Katakolon, Messina, Rome, Valencia, Cadiz, Lisbon. November 7, 11 nights, to Madeira, Tenerife, Gran Canaria, Lisbon, Vigo. December 14, 7 nights, Baltic, to Oslo, Copenhagen, Amsterdam, Bruges. December 21, 14 nights, Canary Islands, to Lisbon, Casablanca, La Palma, Tenerife, Gran Canaria, Madeira.

January 4, 2011, Grand Voyage, round-trip from Southampton to Lisbon, Tripoli, Port Said, Suez Canal, Aqaba, Salalah, Muscat, Dubai, Mumbai, Cochin, Kuala Lumpur, Singapore, Vung Tau/Nha Trang (Vietnam), Hong Kong, Tokyo, Hiroshima, Pusan, Xingang, Shanghai, Hong Kong, Manila, Kota Kinabalu, Bandar Seri Begawan, Bali, Ujung Pandang,

Serarang, Singapore, Phuket, Port Victoria, Mauritius, Reunion, Port Elizabeth, Cape Town, Walvis Bay, Cape Verde Islands, Tenerife, Madeira; segments available.

Aurora **HOME PORT** Southampton

May–September, 14–17 nights, round-trip from Southampton to Malaga, Dubrovnik, Venice, Split, Corfu, Malta, Palma; or Gibraltar, Palau, Naples, Rome, Elba, Villefranche, Barcelona; or Malaga, Dubrovnik, Venice, Split, Kotor, Corfu, Gibraltar; or Palma, Naples, Dubrovnik, Venice, Split, Corfu, Cadiz; or Malaga, Athens, Dikili, Istanbul, Mytilene, Naples, Almeria; or Cadiz, Corfu, Dubrovnik, Venice, Split, Naples, Palma.

June 18, 18 nights, round-trip from Southampton, to Cork, Dublin, Julianehab, Nuuk, Reykjavik, Akureyri, Ålesund, Geiranger, Bergen, Stavanger. August 8, 12 nights, to Copenhagen, Stockholm, Helsinki, St. Petersburg, Tallinn, Bruges.

September 5, 24 nights, transatlantic, round-trip from Southampton to New York, Newport, Boston, Portland, Bar Harbour, St. John, New Brunswick, Halifax, Quebec, St. John's. October 16, 30 nights, to Ponta Delgada, Orlando, Port Everglades, Key West, New Orleans, Cozumel, Grand Cayman, Catalina Island, Tortola, Madeira. November 15, 12 nights, to Madeira, La Palma, Gran Canaria, Tenerife, Lisbon, Vigo. November 29, 18 nights, to Malaga, Cairo/Giza, Limassol, Rhodes, Ephesus, Athens, Tunis, Gibraltar. December 17, 23 nights, to Madeira, Antigua, St. Maarten, St. Kitts, St. Lucia, Barbados, Ponta Delgada.

January 9, 2011, 95 nights, round-trip from Southampton to Madeira, Recife, Rio de Janeiro, Montevideo, Buenos Aires, Port Stanley, Ushuaia, Punta Arenas, Puerto Montt, Valparaiso, Easter Island, Papeete, Bora Bora, Pago Pago, Noumea, Brisbane, Sydney, Milford Sound, Dunedin, Christchurch, Wellington, Napier, Auckland, Apia, Christmas Island, Honolulu, San Francisco, Acapulco, Huatulco, Panama Canal, Aruba, St. Lucia, Ponta Delgada; segments available.

Azura **HOME PORT** Southampton, Barbados,

April–September, 16 nights, round-trip from Southampton to Malaga, Katakolon, Corfu, Dubrovnik, Venice, Korcula, Gibraltar. April 28, August 8, October 17, 12 nights, to Madeira, La Palma, Gran Canaria, Tenerife, Lisbon, Vigo. May 26, July 2, 14 nights, round-trip from Southampton to Kristiansand, Stockholm, Tallinn, St. Petersburg, Helsinki, Copenhagen, Oslo. June 25, 7 nights to Stavanger, Olden, Geiranger, Bergen. July 16, September 21, 7 nights, to Dublin, Cork, Bilbao, Brest. October 14, 3 nights, to Bruges, Le Havre.

October 29, 15 nights, transatlantic, from Southampton to Barbados via Tenerife, St. Kitts, Antigua, St. Lucia, Grenada. November 2010–March 2011, 15 nights, round-trip from Barbados to Curaçao, Aruba, Catalina Island, Tortola, St. Maarten, St. Kitts, St. Lucia, Grenada. December 11, 29 nights, to Antigua, St. Thomas, San Juan, Orlando, Key West, New Orleans, Grand Cayman, Montego Bay, Catalina Island, Tortola, St. Lucia, St. Maarten, Dominica, Grenada. March 18, 2011, 14 nights, transatlantic, from Barbados to Southampton via St. Lucia, St. Maarten, Tortola, Tenerife.

Oceana **HOME PORTS** Barbados, Southampton

April–September, October 2, 14 nights, to Gibraltar, Cartagena, Rome, Florence/Pisa, Monte Carlo, Barcelona, Cadiz. August 21, 7 nights, Norway, round-trip from Southampton to Stavanger, Geiranger, Olden, Bergen. August 28, 7 nights, round-trip from Southampton to Dublin, Cobh, Bilbao, Brest. October 16, 9 nights, to Vigo, Lisbon, Cadiz, Casablanca, Gibraltar. October 25, 14 nights, to Barbados via Madeira, Antigua, St. Maarten, Dominica, St. Lucia.

November 2010–February 2011, 14 nights, Barbados to Acapulco via St. Lucia, Grenada, Bonaire, Aruba, Puntarenas, Zihuatanejo; return Huatulco, San Juan del Sur, Curaçao, Catalina Island, Tortola, Antigua.

February 28, 2011, 14 nights, Caribbean, round-trip from Barbados to Curaçao, Aruba, Grand Cayman, Cozumel, Costa Maya, Ocho Rios, Tortola, St. Maarten, St. Lucia. March 14, 2011, 14 nights, from Barbados to Southampton via St. Lucia, St. Maarten, Tortola, Antigua, Madeira.

Oriana **HOME PORTS** Southampton; others vary with itinerary

May 17, June 30, 17 nights, to Malaga, Dubrovnik, Venice, Split, Kotor, Corfu, Gibraltar; or Malaga, Corfu, Dubrovnik, Naples, Rome, Ajaccio, Vigo. May 5, December 17, December 28, 11 or 12 nights, to Madeira, La Palma, Tenerife, Cadiz, Lisbon, Vigo; or Ponta Delgada, Horta, Madeira, Tenerife, Lisbon, Vigo.

June 2, 14 nights, Spitsbergen, round-trip from Southampton to Stavanger, Andalsnes, Trondheim, Ny Ålesund, Tromso, Bergen, Eidfjord. June 16, July 11, 12 or 14 nights, to Copenhagen, Travemunde, Stockholm, Helsinki, St. Petersburg, Oslo, Bruges; or from Copenhagen, Stockholm, Helsinki, St. Petersburg, Tallinn, Bruges. June 30, 11 nights, to Edinburgh, Invergordon, Kirkwall, Belfast, Glasgow, Dublin, Cork, St. Peter Port. July 23, 7 nights, to Stavanger, Olden, Ålesund, Bergen.

August 27, 7 nights, round-trip from Southampton to Coruna, Bilbao, Le Verdon, Brest, St. Peter Port. September 3, 20 nights, to Palma, Istanbul, Yalta, Odessa, Rhodes, Athens, Lisbon.

September 23, 84 nights, World Cruise, round-trip from Southampton to Madeira, St. Lucia, Margarita Island, Curaçao, Acapulco, San Francisco, Kahalui, Maui, Honolulu, Oahu, Apia, Auckland, Tauranga, Wellington, Brisbane, Whitsunday Islands, Cairns, Manila, Hong Kong, Phu My, Bangkok, Ko Samui, Singapore, Kuala Lumpur, Mumbai, Sharm el Sheik, Suez, Suez Canal transit, Port Said, Piraeus, Lisbon; segments available.

January 8, 2011, 35 nights, round-trip from Southampton to Vigo, Madeira, St. Lucia, St. Maarten, Tortola, Ocho Rios, Grand Cayman, Cozumel, New Orleans, Tampa, Port Everglades, Princess Cays, Ponta Delgada. February 12, 2011, 36 nights, to Ponta Delgada, Antigua, St. Lucia, Barbados, Grenada, Curaçao, Limon, Aruba, Margarita Island, Dominica, St. Kitts, St. Maarten, Tortola, Madeira.

Ventura **HOME PORTS** Barbados, Southampton

May 22, June 19, July 3, September 11, October 8, 14 nights, to Lisbon, Palma, Barcelona, Cannes, Florence/Pisa, Rome, Gibraltar; or Barcelona, Cannes, Florence/Pisa, Elba, Rome, Valencia, Gibraltar.

May 8, 7 nights, round-trip from Southampton to Bergen, Flaam, Olden, Stavanger. May 15, 7 nights, to Vigo, Lisbon, Bilbao, Brest. June 5, 7 nights, to Corunna, Bilbao, La Rochelle, Brest, St. Peter Port. June 12, August 28, 7 nights, to Bergen, Flaam, Olden, Stavanger. September 4, 7 nights, to Vigo, Lisbon, La Rochelle, Brest.

October 22, 15 nights, transatlantic, Southampton to Barbados via Tenerife, Tortola, St. Maarten, St. Lucia, St. Vincent. November 2010–February 2011, 14 nights, round-trip from Barbados to Bonaire, Aruba, Ocho Rios, Grand Turk, St. Maarten, Antigua, Dominica, St. Lucia; or Bonaire, Aruba, Ocho Rios, Catalina Island, St. Maarten, Antigua, Dominica, St. Lucia. December 18, 29 nights, to Dominica, Antigua, Bonaire, Aruba, Catalina Island, Montego Bay, Grand Cayman, Cozumel, New Orleans, Key West, Port Everglades, Orlando, San Juan, St. Thomas, St. Maarten, St. Kitts, St. Lucia, Grenada; segments available. March 11, 2011, 14 nights, transatlantic, to Southampton via St. Lucia, Antigua, St. Kitts, Tenerife.

Peter Deilmann Cruises

Deutschland **HOME PORTS** Hamburg, Travelmunde, Barbados, and others.

April–June, 12 nights, Rome to Kiel via Valencia, Cartagena, Lisbon, La Pallice, Honfleur, Kiel Canal; 12 nights, Kiel to Hamburg via Gdynia, St. Petersburg, Helsinki, Stockholm, Kiel Canal, Helgoland; round-trip from Hamburg to Bergen, Hellesylt, Geiranger, Flam, Eidfjord; to London, Leith, Belfast, Liverpool, Holyhead, Milford Haven, Falmouth; from Hamburg to Travemunde via Kiel Canal, Gdynia, Visby, Riga, Tallinn, St. Petersburg, Stockholm, Copenhagen, Flensburg.

June–August, 12 nights, Travemunde to Reykjavik via Bergen, Kingsford, Longyearbyen, Mollerhaven, Ny Alesund, Magdalenefjord, Jan Mayen, Akureyri; 16 nights, Reykjavik to

Travemunde via Prince Christian Sound, Nanortalik, Holsteinborg, Jacobshaven, Egedsminde, Godthab, Julianehab, Cape Farbel, Torshavn, Kirkwall; 12 nights to Hamburg via Oslo, Geirangerfjord, Trondheim, Gravdal, Ålesund, Bergen; 12 nights, Russia, Kiel to Travemunde, Riga, St. Petersburg, Helsinki, Stockholm, Wismar; round-trip from Travemunde to Neustadt, Kiel Canal, List, Arendal, Oslo, Kalundborg, Ronne, Danzig; 12 nights, Travemunde to Hamburg via Heringsdorf, Pilau, St. Petersburg, Tallinn, Stockholm, Kiel Canal transit.

September, 8 nights, Hamburg to Cobh via London, Portland, Falmouth, St. Mary's; 8 nights, Cobh to Hamburg via Dublin, Belfast, Ullapool, Invergordon, Leith, Hull.

October–December, 13 nights, Hamburg to Nice via Portland Harbour, Hendays, Leixoes, Lisbon, Malaga, Barcelona, Monte Carlo; 11 nights, Nice to Monte Carlo via Livorno, Sorrento, Ischia, Trapani, Cagliari, Ponza, Rome, Portoferraio; from Monte Carlo to Istanbul via Catania, Mykonos, Nessebar, Odessa, Yalta; Istanbul to Rome via Rhodes, Limassol, Alexandria, Katakolon, Salerno; Monte Carlo to Funchal and Barcelona via Valencia, Malaga, Casablanca.

December 18, 18 nights, Barbados to Los Angeles via Martinique, Islas los Roques, Cartagena, Cristobal, Balboa, Punta Arenas, Puerto Quetzal, Acapulco, Cabo San Lucas.

January–March 2011, 11 nights, French Polynesia/New Zealand/Australia, Honolulu to Papeete via Nawiliwili, Kailua, Christmas Island, Bora Bora, Uturoa, Moorea; from Papeete to Auckland via Aitutaki, Apia, Nukualofa, Bay of Island; Auckland to Sydney via Tauranga, Napier, Wellington, Lyttelton, Port Chalmers, Fiordland cruise, Hobart; 19 nights, Sydney to Singapore via Hamilton Island, Townsville, Cairns, Lizard Island, Darwin, Denpasar; 15 nights, Singapore to Male via Port Klang, Langkawi, Phi Phi Island, Rangoon, Colombo.

April 1, 18 nights, from Male to Sharm el Sheikh via Kadmat, Dubai, Bander Abbas, Salalah, Hodeidah. April 19, 11 nights, Sharm el Sheikh to Monte Carlo via Suez Canal, Limassol, Rhodes, Messina, Rome, Portoferraio, Marina de Carrara.

Ponant Cruises/Compagnie des Iles du Ponant

Le Boreal **HOME PORTS** Vary with itineraries

May 6, 8 days, Maiden Voyage, Marseilles to Nice via Monaco, Bonifacio, Naples, Ischia, Capri, Portoferraio, Sailing Cinqueterre, Portofino. May 13, 5 days, round-trip from Nice to Venice via St. Tropez, Cannes, Monaco, Nice. May 20, 27, October 4, 11, 18, 8 days, round-trip from Venice to Sibenik, Split, Korcula, Kotor, Dubrovnik, Hvar, Pula, Rovinj. June 8, 8 days, Jazz and Gospel, Venice to Nice via Split, Dubrovnik, Taormina, cruising Stromboli, Naples, Bonifacio. June 18, 10 days, Nice to Honfleur via Barcelona, Almeria, Malaga Cadix, Lisbon, Porto, Dartmouth.

June 27, 8 days, Honfleur to Copenhagen via Zeebrugge, Amsterdam, Bremerhaven, Hamburg, Kiel Canal, Holtenau, Lubeck. July 4, 8 reverse. July 11, Copenhagen to Stockholm via Tallin, St. Petersburg (2 nights), Helsinki. July 22, July 29, 8 days, round-trip from Reykjavik to Grundarfjordur, Grimsey Island, Akureri, Isafjordur, cruise fjords, Heimaey.

August 16, September 20, 8 days, round-trip from Istanbul to Nessebar, Constantza, Odessa, Sebastopol, Yalta. August 23, 8 days, Istanbul to Antalya via Dikili, Chios, Patmos, Bodrum, Rhodes, Marmaris. August 30, 8 days, Symphony at Sea, Antalya to Istanbul via Fethiye, Rhodes, Bodrum, Patmos, Kusadasi, Dikili. September 13, 8 days, Athens to Istanbul via Delos, Mykonos, Santorini, Rhodes, Symi, Kusadasi, Dikili. September 27, 8 days, Istanbul to Venice via Dikili, Delos, Mykonos, cruise Corinth Canal, Itea, Parga, Kotor, Dubrovnik, Split, cruise Kornati Islands. October 25, 8 days, Venice to Nice via Split, Dubrovnik, Taormina, Stromboli, Naples, Bonifacio.

Le Diamant **HOME PORTS** Vary with itineraries

May 26, 13 days, Honfleur to Copenhagen via Scilly Isles, Cobh, Dublin, Holyhead, Iona disembark, Tobermory re-embark, Portree, Kirkwall, Leith/Edinburgh, Stavanger, Goteborg.

June 7, 11 days, Copenhagen to Stockholm via Turku, Rauma, Pori, Lulea, Umea, Sundsvall, Nudiksvall, Mariehamm, cruise Aland Islands. June 17, 8 days, Chopin's Bicentennial, Stockholm to Copenhagen via Visby, Gdansk, Rugen Island, Rostock/Warnemunde, Lubeck. June 24, 9 days, Copenhagen to Bodo via Bergen, Olden, Hellesylt, Geiranger, Ålesund, Trondheim, Svartisen.

July 2, 14 days, Bodo to Reykjavik via Liknes, Tromso, cruise North Cape, Honningsvag, Hornsund, Templefjord, Ny Alesund/King's Bay, cruise Jan Mayen Island, Akureyri, Grundarfjordur. July 15, August 8, 13 days, Family Cruise, Reykjavik to Kangerlussuaq via cruising Farwell Cape, Narsasuaq, Qaqortoq, Nuuk Godthaab, Eqi Glacier/Paul Emile Victor Base, Ilulissat, Sisimiut Holsteinborg.

July 27, 13 days, Baffin Sea, round-trip from Kangerlussuaq to Ilulissat, Eqi, Upernavik fjords, Melville Bay, Savissivik, Inlet Pond, North Arm Fjord, Isabella Bay, Kivitoo, Qikiqtarjuaq, Davis Strait. August 20, 12 days, Reykjavik to St. Malo via Heimaey, Lerwick, Scrabster, Portree, Belfast, Isle of Man, Pembroke/Milford Haven, Scilly Isles. August 31, 8 days, round-trip from St. Malo to Dartmouth, Cobh, Dublin, Holyhead, Waterford, Scilly Isles.

October 10, 9 days, Marseilles to Athens via Portovenere, Livorno, Rome, Naples, Lipari, sailing the Stromboli, Itea, Corinth Canal crossing. October 18, 9 days, Athens to Aqaba via Rhodes, Antalya, Latakia, Tartus, Port Said, Suez Canal, Sharm el Sheik.

Le Levant **HOME PORTS** Vary with itineraries

May 4, May 11, September 2, 8 days, round-trip from Istanbul to Nessebar, Constantza, Odessa, Sebastopol, Yalta. May 18, September 9, 8 days, Istanbul to Rome via Dikili, Mykonos, Corinth Canal crossing, Itea, Lipari, Stromboli. May 25, June 4, June 14, September 27, October 7, 11 days, Rome to Livorno, Monaco, Barcelona, Palma de Majorca, Tunia, Palermo, Naples.

June 24, 8 days, Rome to Athens via Capri, Stromboli, Taormina, Itea, Corinth Canal crossing, Santorini, Delos, Mykonos. July 1, reverse July 8, August 19, 8 days, Athens to Istanbul via Santorini, Paros, Naxos, Delos, Mykonos, Patmos, Chios, Limnos. July 15, reverse August 12, 8 days, Athens to Venice via Corinth Canal, Itea, Otranto, Kotor, Dubrovnik, Trogir, Kornati Archipelago, Rovinj, Piran. July 22, July 29, August 5, 8 days, Venice to Kornati Archipelago, Sibenik, Kotor, Dubrovnik, Hvar, Split, Zadar, Rab, Rovinj, Piran.

September 16, 7 days, Bridge Tournaments, round-trip from Rome to Portofino, Portoferraio, Bonifacio, Amalfi, Naples. October 17, 8 days, Rome to Nice via Lipari, Stromboli, Taormina, Palermo, Amalfi, Bonifacio, Portoferraio. October 24, 8 days, round-trip from Nice to Portoferraio, Ventotene, Ischia, Palermo, Naples, Rome, Portovenere.

Le Ponant **HOME PORTS** Vary with itineraries

May 2, 7, 6 days, Mellow Islands/Liguria, round-trip from Nice to cruise Piana Calanches, Ajaccio, Bonifacio, Portoferraio, Portovenere. May 17, 8 days, round-trip from Nice to Ile Rousse, Porto, Girolata, Bonifacio, Rome, Portoferraio, Lerici.

May 24, reverse May 31, October 10, 8 days, Nice to Malta via Portoferraio, Bonifacio, Ponza, Amalfi, Lipari, cruising Stromboli, Taormina. June 12–July 4, 8 days, alternating return, Nice to Barcelona via Porquerolles, Port St. Louis du Rhome, Port la Mouvelle, Palamos, Cuitadella Minorca, Mahon, Palma de Majorca. July 10, July 17, 8 days, round-trip from Nice to Viareggio, Portoferraio, Portisco, Bonivacio, Calvi, Cannes. July 24, 10 days, Nice to Venice via Portoferraio, Rome, Amalfi, Taormina, Hvar, Split, cruise Kornati Archipelago, Rovinj, Piran.

August 2, 8 days, round-trip from Venice to Zadar, Trofir, Hvar, Dubrovnik, Kotor, Mljet, Korkula, Sibenik, Kornati Archipelago. August 9, 11 days, Venice to Malta via Sibenik, Split, Hvar, Mljet, Korkula, Dubrovnik, Kotor, Otranto, Taormina, Gozo, Valletta. August 19, reverse August 26, September 25, reverse October 3, 8 days, Sicily and the Mezzogiorno, from Malta to Naples via Syracuse, Taormina, Palermo, Castellamare, Lipari, Stromboli, Amalfi, Naples. October 17, 23, 7 days, round-trip from Nice to Portofino, cruising Cinque Terre, Portovenere, Viareggio, Portoferraio, Monaco.

Princess Cruises

Caribbean Princess **HOME PORTS** New York, San Juan

May–July, 9 days, round-trip from New York to Bermuda, San Juan, St. Thomas, Grand Turk; or San Juan, St. Maarten, St. Thomas, Grand Turk; or Grand Turk, San Juan, St. Thomas, Bermuda.

August–October, 7 days, round-trip from New York to Newport, Boston, Bar Harbor, Saint John, Halifax. October 23, 8 days, New York to San Juan via Bermuda, Antigua, St. Thomas. December 12, 7 days, round-trip from San Juan to Barbados, St. Lucia, Antigua, Tortola, St. Thomas.

October 2010–May 2011, Sunday, 7 nights, round-trip from San Juan to St. Thomas, Tortola, Antigua, St. Lucia, Barbados; or St. Thomas, Dominica, Grenada, Bonaire, Aruba, or reverse; or combine for 14-night cruise. May 2, 7 days, San Juan to New York via St. Thomas, Antigua, Bermuda.

Coral Princess **HOME PORTS** Fort Lauderdale, Los Angeles, Vancouver

May 6, 4 days, Los Angeles to Vancouver via Victoria. May 10, 5 days, round-trip from Vancouver to Juneau, Ketchikan.

May–September, 7 days, Vancouver to Whittier and reverse via Ketchikan, Juneau, Skagway, Glacier Bay, College Fjord, and reverse (Hubbard Glacier replaces College Fjord).

September 18, 18 days, Vancouver to Fort Lauderdale via Los Angeles, Cabo San Lucas, Acapulco, Costa Rica, Fuerte Amador, Panama Canal, Cartagena, Aruba; or 3 days, Vancouver to Los Angeles. September 21, December 15, reverse, December 30, January 24, 2011 reverse, February 8, 15 days, Los Angeles to Fort Lauderdale to Cabo San Lucas, Acapulco, Costa Rica (Puntarenas), Fuerte Amador, Panama Canal, Cartagena, Aruba.

October 6, October 16, reverse, February 23, March 5, 2011, reverse, April 14, 2011, April 24, reverse, 10 days, Fort Lauderdale to Acapulco via Ocho Rios, Panama Canal full transit, Fuerte Amador, Costa Rica, Nicaragua, Huatulco, Acapulco. Cristobal replaces Fuerte Amador on reverse. October, 26, November 5, November 15, November 25 (Montego Bay replaces Ocho Rios), December 5, January 14, 2011, March 15, March 25, April 4, 10 days, Panama Canal, round-trip from Fort Lauderdale to Aruba, Cartagena, Panama Canal, Cristobal, Costa Rica (Límon), Ocho Rios.

May 4, 2011, 15 or 19 days, Panama Canal, Fort Lauderdale to Vancouver via Aruba, Cartegena, Panama Canal, Cristobal, Costa Rica, Cabo San Lucas, San Francisco (15 days), Astoria, Victoria; May 19, 4 days, San Francisco to Victoria, Vancouver.

Crown Princess **HOME PORTS** Fort Lauderdale, New York, Rome, Southampton

May 1, 14 or 26 days, transatlantic, Fort Lauderdale to Gibraltar via Alicante, Barcelona, Marseille/Provence, Florence/Pisa, Rome (14 days), Monte Carlo, Florence/Pisa, Naples, Santorini, Kusadasi, Mykonos, Athens (Piraeus), Katakolon, Corfu, Venice.

May 15, 12 days, Rome to Venice via Monte Carlo, Florence/Pisa, Naples, Santorini, Kusadasi, Mykonos, Athens (Piraeus), Katakolon, Corfu. May 27, 12 or 27 days, Venice to Southampton via Dubrovnik, Corfu, Katakolon, Athens, Mykonos, Kusadasi, Rhodes, Santorini, Naples, Rome (12 days), Florence/Pisa, Genoa, Cannes, Barcelona, Gibraltar, Lisbon, Dublin, Glasgow, Paris/Normandy, Brussels. June 8, 15 days, Rome to Southampton via Florence/Pisa, Genoa, Cannes, Barcelona, Gibraltar, Lisbon, Dublin, Glasgow/ Edinburgh, Paris/Normandy, Brussels.

June 23, July 17, August 10, August 22, 12 days, round-trip from Southampton to Guernsey, Cork, Dublin, Liverpool, Belfast, Glasgow, Inverness/Loch Ness, Edinburgh, Paris/Normandy. July 5, 12 days, to Stavanger, Hellesylt/Geiranger Fjord, Geiranger, Trondheim, Honningsvag/ North Cape, Tromso, Flaam/Sognefjord, Bergen. July 29, 12 days, to Reykjavik, Akureyri, Ålesund, Hellesylt/Geiranger Fjord, Geiranger, Olden/Nordfjord, Bergen.

August 22, transatlantic, 14 to 26 days, Southampton to New York via Guernsey, Cork,

Dublin, Liverpool, Belfast, Glasgow, Inverness/Loch Ness, Edinburgh, Paris/Normandy, London, Cornwall, Dublin, Belfast, Reykjavik, Qaqortoq, St. Johns; 12 days, London to Cornwall; 14 days, London to New York.

September 17, reverse September 27, October 7, 10 days, New York to Quebec via Newport, Boston, Bar Harbor, St. John, Halifax, Sydney, Charlottetown. October 17, 13 days, Quebec to Fort Lauderdale via Saguenay, Halifax, Bar Harbor, Boston, Newport, New York, Norfolk, Charleston.

October 2010–April 2011, 7 days, round-trip from Fort Lauderdale to Grand Cayman, Roatan, Cozumel, Princess Cays.

December 18, 5 days, round-trip from Fort Lauderdale to Grand Turk, Princess Cays. December 23, 7 days, to Princess Cays, Grand Cayman, Roatan, Cozumel. December 30, 9 days, to Antigua, Barbados, Dominica, St. Thomas, Princess Cays.

Dawn Princess HOME PORTS Melbourne, Sydney

May 8, 13 days, to Noumea, Fiji, Port Denarau, Dravuni Island, Vanuatu, Lifou.

May 21, 104 days, World Cruise, round-trip from Sydney to Darwin, Bali, Singapore, Kuala Lumpur, Langkawi, Cochin, Mumbai, Muscat, Dubai, Safaga, Suez Canal, Port Said, Kusadasi, Istanbul, Anzac Cove, Santorini, Athens, Venice, Dubrovnik, Rome, Florence/Pisa, Cannes, Barcelona, Gibraltar, Paris/Normandy, London, Dublin, Boston, Newport, New York, Antigua, Barbados, Curaçao, Panama Canal Transit, Acapulco, Manzanillo, Los Angeles, Honolulu, Tahiti Moorea, Pago Pago, Auckland; segments available.

September 3, November 10 (round-trip from Melbourne), March 11, 2011, 28 days, round-trip from Sydney to Brisbane, Port Douglas, Darwin, Broome, Bali, Perth, Bunbury, Albany, Adelaide, Melbourne, Burnie, Hobart. October 1, October 26, 13 days, to Nouméa, Ouvéa, Vanuatu, Dravuni Island, Port Denarau, Suva. October 14, 12 days, to Airlie Beach, Townsville, Yorky's, Port Douglas, Cooktown, Willis Island, Brisbane. November 7, 3 days, positioning, Sydney to Melbourne via Tasmania.

December 2010–February 2011, 13 days, New Zealand, round-trip from Melbourne to Fjordland National Park, Dunedin, Christchurch, Wellington, Gisborne, Tauranga, Auckland; or reverse. April 8, 2011, 35 days; Hawaii, Tahiti, and South Pacific; round-trip from Sydney to Suva, Port Denarau, Tin Can Island, Cross International Dateline, Apia, Pago Pago, Hilo, Maui, Honolulu, Kona, Tahiti, Moorea, Raiatea, Bora Bora, Vava'u, Nuku' Alofa.

December 22, January 3, 2011 reverse, January 15, 2011, January 27, 2011 reverse, 12 days, Australia and New Zealand, from Sydney to Auckland via Melbourne, Hobart, Fjordland National Park, Dunedin, Christchurch, Tauranga.

Diamond Princess HOME PORTS Bangkok, Anchorage, Beijing, Vancouver, and others

May–September, Saturday, 7 days, Whittier to Vancouver via Hubbard Glacier, Glacier Bay National Park, Skagway, Juneau, Ketchikan, and reverse.

September 11, 2010, May 6, 2011, 22 or 23 days, Vancouver to Beijing via Ketchikan, Juneau, Skagway, Glacier Bay National Park, College Fjord, Anchorage (Whittier), Sapporo, Vladivostok, Pusan, Qingdao, Dalian, Beijing. September 18, 2010, 15 or 31 days, Anchorage to Singapore via Sapporo, Vladivostok, Busan, Qingdao, Dalian, Beijing, Pusan, Nagasaki, Shanghai, Hong Kong, Nha Trang, Ho Chi Minh City (Phu My), Bangkok (Laem Chabang), Ko Samui; 15 days from Anchorage to Beijing.

October 4, November 3, reverse, 16 days, Southeast Asia and China, Beijing to Singapore via Pusan, Nagasaki, Shanghai, Hong Kong, Nha Trang, Ho Chi Minh City, Bangkok, Ko Samui. November 19, March 3, 2011, March 19, reverse, April 4, April 20, reverse, 16 days, Beijing to Bangkok via Shanghai, Okinawa, Taipei, Hong Kong, Nha Trang, Ho Chi Minh City, Singapore.

December 5, 17 or 29 days, Bangkok to Auckland via Ho Chi Minh City, Singapore, Bali, Darwin, Port Douglas (for Cairns), Airlie Beach (Great Barrier Reef), Sydney (17 days),

Melbourne, Hobart, Fjordland National Park, Dunedin, Christchurch, Tauranga.

January 27, 2011, 35 days, from Auckland to Beijing via Tauranga, Christchurch, Dunedin (Port Chalmers), Fjordland National Park scenic cruising, Hobart, Melbourne, Sydney, Port Douglas (Great Barrier Reef and Cairns), Darwin, Bali, Hong Kong, Taipei, Nagasaki, Shanghai, Dalian. February 8, 2011, 23 or 39 days, Sydney to Bangkok via Port Douglas, Darwin, Padang Bay, Hong Kong, Taipei, Nagasaki, Shanghai, Dalian, Beijing (23 days), Shanghai, Okinawa, Taipei, Hong Kong, Nha Trang, Ho Chi Minh City, Singapore.

March 19, 2011, April 20, 16 or 32 days, from Bangkok to Singapore, Ho Chi Minh City, Nha Trang, Hong Kong, Taipei, Okinawa, Shanghai, Beijing (16 days), Dalian, Qingdao, Pusan, Vladivostok, Sapporo (Muroran), Anchorage.

Emerald Princess **HOME PORT** Fort Lauderdale

September 2010, 7 or 14 days, round-trip from Fort Lauderdale alternating to Princess Cays, St. Maarten, St. Thomas, Grand Turk; 7 days to Princess Cays, Ocho Rios, Grand Cayman, Cozumel; 14-day round-trip option May–September.

September 2010–April 2011, 10 days, round-trip from Fort Lauderdale to Princess Cays, St. Thomas, Dominica, Grenada, Bonaire, Aruba; or to Antigua, St. Lucia, Barbados, St. Kitts, St. Thomas, Princess Cays.

September 19, October 9, December 8, January 17, 2011, February 26, March 8, April 27, 10 days, round-trip from Fort Lauderdale to Princess Cays, St. Thomas, Dominica, Grenada, Bonaire, Aruba; or 20 days, add Fort Lauderdale, Antigua, St. Lucia, Barbados, St. Kitts, St. Thomas, Princess Cays. September–November 2010, January–April 2011, 10 or 20 days, Eastern Caribbean, round-trip from Fort Lauderdale to Antigua, St. Lucia, Barbados, St. Kitts, St. Thomas, Princess Cays, Fort Lauderdale, Princess Cays, St. Thomas, Dominica, Grenada, Bonaire, Aruba. October 2010–April 2011, 10 or 20 days, reverse.

December 8, 20 days, round-trip from Fort Lauderdale to Princess Cays, St. Thomas, Dominica, Grenada, Bonaire, Aruba, Fort Lauderdale, Princess Cays, St. Thomas, Antigua, St. Kitts, Barbados, St. Lucia. December 18, 10 or 20 days, reverse.

February 6, 2011, 20 days, round-trip from Fort Lauderdale to Bonaire, Grenada, Dominica, St. Thomas, Princess Cays, Fort Lauderdale, Princess Cays, St. Thomas, Antigua, St. Lucia, Barbados, St. Kitts. February 16, 2011, 10 or 20 days, similar ports plus Barbados, Bonaire, Aruba.

Golden Princess **HOME PORTS** Los Angeles, Seattle

May–September 2010, 7 days, Inside Passage, round-trip from Seattle to Juneau, Skagway, Tracy Arm Fjord, Ketchikan, Victoria. September 25, 1 day, Seattle to Vancouver. September 26, 3 days, Vancouver to Los Angeles. May 11, 2011, Coastal, 3 days, from Los Angeles to Vancouver.

October 2010–April 2011, 14 days, round-trip from Los Angeles to Hilo, Honolulu, Kauai, Maui, Ensenada. May 9, 2010, 5 days, Los Angeles to Vancouver via Catalina Island, San Francisco, Victoria. May 14, 2010 and 2011, 1 day, Los Angeles to Seattle.

Grand Princess **HOME PORTS** Fort Lauderdale, London

June 19, July 24, August 21, 14 days, round-trip from Southampton to Seville, Sardinia, Rome, Florence/Pisa, Cannes, Barcelona, Gibraltar. May 8, June 5, August 7, September 4, 14 days, to Malaga, Barcelona, Monte Carlo, Rome, Naples/Capri, Corsica, Gibraltar.

May 22, July 3, 7 days, round-trip from Southampton to Brussels/Bruges, Copenhagen, Helsingbørg, Oslo. May 29, September 18, 7 days, to Vigo, Lisbon, La Rochelle, Guernsey. September 18, 16 or 23 days, transatlantic, from Southampton to Fort Lauderdale via Vigo, Lisbon, La Rochelle, Guernsey, London, Bergen, Shetland Islands, Faroe Islands, Akureyri, Reykjavik, Sydney; 16 days from London to Sydney.

October 2010–April 2011, 14 days, round-trip from Fort Lauderdale to Aruba, Curaçao, Grenada, Barbados, St. Vincent, St. Kitts, St. Thomas, Santo Domingo, Princess Cays.

October 25, December 20, 14 days, round-trip from Fort Lauderdale to Aruba, Curaçao, Grenada, Barbados, St. Vincent, Antigua, St. Thomas, Santo Domingo, Grand Turk. February 28, 2011, 14 days, round-trip from Fort Lauderdale to Curaçao, Aruba, Grenada, Barbados, St. Vincent, St. Kitts, St. Thomas, Santo Domingo, Princess Cays.

Island Princess **HOME PORTS** Fort Lauderdale, Los Angeles, Vancouver
May–September, 7 days, Vancouver to Whittier via Juneau, Skagway, Glacier Bay National Park, College Fjord; or return.

October 4, 17 days, Vancouver to Fort Lauderdale via San Francisco, Cabo San Lucas, Puntarenas, Panama City, Panama Canal, Cartagena, Aruba. October 6, 2010, April 29, 2011 reverse, 15 days, San Francisco to Fort Lauderdale via Cabo San Lucas, Costa Rica, Fuerte Amador, Panama Canal, Cartagena, Aruba.

October 21, reverse, November 5, November 20, reverse, December 5, February 28, 2011 reverse, March 15, March 30, reverse, April 14, 15 days, Los Angeles to Fort Lauderdale via Cabo San Lucas, Acapulco, Costa Rica, Fuerte Amador, Panama Canal, Cartagena, Aruba, Fort Lauderdale; Cristobal replaces Fuerte Amador on reverse.

December 2010–February 2011, 10 days, round-trip from Fort Lauderdale to Cartegena, Panama Canal, Colon, Limon, Ocho Rios. March 10, March 20, 2010 (reverse), 10 days, to Acapulco via Ocho Rios, Panama Canal, Panama City, Puntarenas, San Juan del Sur, Puerto Quetzal, Huatulco. April 29, 15 days, to Los Angeles via Cartegena, Panama Canal, Fuerto Amador, Puntarenas, Huatulco, Acapulco, Cabo San Lucas. May 14, 3 days, Los Angeles to Vancouver.

Ocean Princess **HOME PORTS** Bangkok, London, Shanghai, Singapore
June 7, 18 days, round-trip from London to Stavanger, Flaam/Sognefjord, Tromso, Magdalenafjord, Ny Alesund, Honningsvag, Murmansk, Lofoten Islands, Trondheim, Hellesylt, Geiranger Fjord, Geiranger, Bergen. June 25, 18 or 36 days, to Newcastle, Edinburgh (Rosyth), Faroe Islands (Tórshavn), Seydisfjordur, Reykjavik, Prins Christian Sund, Qaqortoq, St. John's (Newfoundland), St. Pierre Et Miquelon, New York (18 days), Halifax, St. Anthony, Qaqortoq, Nanortalik, Grundarfjordur, Isafjordur, Akureyri, Shetland Islands, Bergen, Eidfjord.

July 13, 18 days, transatlantic, New York to London via Halifax, St. Anthony (Newfoundland), Qaqortoq, Nanortalik (Greenland), Grundarfjordur, Isafjordur, Akureyri, Shetland Islands (Lerwick), Bergen, Eidfjord. July 31, 7 days, round-trip from London to Stavanger, Olden/ Nordfjord, Hellesylt, Geiranger Fjord, Geiranger, Bergen. August 7, 7 days, to Dartmouth, Waterford, Dublin, Edinburgh. August 14, 7 days, to Amsterdam, Kiel Canal transit, Lübeck (Travemünde), Copenhagen, Oslo. August 21, 11 or 18 days, London to Athens via Paris/Normandy, Lisbon, Algarve Coast (Portimão), Gibraltar, Barcelona, Cannes, Florence/Pisa, Rome (11 days), Itea, Argostoli, Santorini, Kusadasi, Mykonos. September 1, 7 days, Rome to Athens via Itea, Cephalonia (Argostoli), Santorini, Kusadasi, Mykonos. September 8, 7 or 14 days, Athens to Rome via Mykonos, Kusadasi, Santorini, Argostoli, Itea, Rome (7 days), Florence/Pisa, Portofino, Villefranche, Barcelona, Sorrento.

September–October, 7 days, round-trip from Rome to Florence/Pisa, Portofino, Villefranche, Barcelona, Sorrento/Capri.

October 27, 56 days, Rome to Singapore via Florence/Pisa, Rome, Cannes, Barcelona, Tangier, Casablanca, Dakar, Tema, Lomé, Cotonou, Walvis Bay, Lüderitz, Cape Town, East London, Durban, Maputo, Réunion, Mauritius, Seychelles, Muscat (Mina Qaboos), Dubai, Mumbai, Kuala Lumpur; segments available.

November 21, 47 days, Cape Town to Bangkok via East London, Durban, Maputo, Réunion, Mauritius, Seychelles, Muscat, Dubai, Mumbai, Kuala Lumpur, Singapore, Manila, Xiamen, Shanghai, Hong Kong, Nha Trang, Ho Chi Minh City, Bangkok; 31 days, Cape Town to Singapore. December 22, 16 days, Singapore to Bangkok via Manila, Xiamen, Shanghai, Hong Kong, Nha Trang, Ho Chi Minh City. January 7, 2011, 16 days, Bangkok to Shanghai,

Ko Samui, Singapore, Ho Chi Minh City, Da Nang, Hong Kong, Taipei, Okinawa. January 23, 2011, 16 days, Shanghai to Bangkok via Okinawa, Taipei, Hong Kong, Da Nang, Ho Chi Minh City, Singapore, Ko Samui.

February 8, 2011, 28 days, Bangkok to Osaka via Ko Samui, Singapore, Ho Chi Minh City, Da Nang, Hong Kong, Taipei, Okinawa, Shanghai, Dalian, Beijing, Inchon, Vladivostok, Hakata, Hiroshima. February 24, March 20, reverse March 8, April 1,12 days, Shanghai to Osaka via Dalian, Beijing, Inchon, Vladivostok, Hakata, Hiroshima.

Pacific Princess **HOME PORTS** Athens, Fort Lauderdale, Rome

May 15, August 31, October 18, 12 days, Holy Land, Rome to Athens via Sorrento, Patmos, Kusadasi, Ashdod, Haifa, Port Said, Alexandria, Santorini. May 27, July 2, October 6, 12 days, Athens to Rome, same ports. June 8, July 14, reverse August 19, 12 days, Rome to Venice via Portofino, Monte Carlo, Corsica, Sorrento, Messina, Valletta, Corfu, Kotor, Split, Koper. June 20, July 26, September 24, November 11, 12 days, Venice to Athens via Ravenna, Dubrovnik, Patmos, Haifa, Ashdod, Port Said, Alexandria, Kusadasi.

August 7, September 12, 12 days, Athens to Venice via Volos, Varna, Constanta, Odessa, Yalta, Istanbul. October 30, 12 days, Athens to Venice via Patmos, Kusadasi, Haifa, Ashdod, Port Said, Alexandria, Dubrovnik, Ravenna. November 23, 29 days, Athens to Fort Lauderdale via Santorini, Patmos, Kusadasi, Haifa, Ashdod, Port Said, Alexandria, Sorrento, Rome, Florence/Pisa, Monte Carlo, Barcelona, Ceuta, Casablanca, Ponta Delgada, Bermuda.

December 5, 17 days, transatlantic, Rome to Fort Lauderdale via Florence/Pisa, Monte Carlo, Barcelona, Ceuta, Casablanca, Ponta Delgada, Bermuda. December 22, 14 days, Amazon River, from Fort Lauderdale to Manaus via St. Thomas, St. Lucia, Tobago, Devil's Island, Santarém, Boca da Valéria, Parintins. January 5, 2011, Manaus to Fort Lauderdale via Parintins, Boca da Valeria, Santarem, Devil's Island, Trinidad, St. Lucia, St. Maarten.

January 19, 2011, 107 days, World Cruise, from Fort Lauderdale to Rome via Grand Cayman, Panama Canal, Quito, Lima, Easter Island, Pitcairn Island, Tahiti, Moorea, Auckland, Sydney, Adelaide, Bunbury, Perth, Bali, Sihanoukville, Bangkok, Ko Samui, Singapore, Kuala Lumpur, Andaman Islands, Cochin, Mumbai, Muscat, Dubai, Seychelles, Maputo, Durban, East London, Cape Town, Lüderitz, Walvis Bay Lomé (Togo), Tema, Dakar, Madeira, Casablanca, Gibraltar, Barcelona, Toulon, Monte Carlo, Portofino; segments available.

Royal Princess **HOME PORTS** Fort Lauderdale, Seattle, Tahiti

May–August, Monday, 14 days, round-trip from Seattle to Ketchikan, Juneau, Icy Strait Point, Glacier Bay, Seward, Kodiak, Skagway, Tracy Arm Fjord, Victoria. September 13, 2010, May 18, 2011 reverse, 1 day, Seattle to Vancouver. September 14, 2010, May 8, 2011 reverse, 10 days, Vancouver to Honolulu via Hilo, Kona, Maui, Kauai.

September 14, 22 days, Vancouver to Tahiti via Hilo, Kona, Maui, Kauai, Honolulu, Kauai, Maui, Hilo, Bora Bora, Raiatea. September 24, November 5, reverse, November 17, January 28, 2011 reverse, February 9, March 13, reverse, March 25, April 26, reverse, 12 days, Hawaii/Tahiti, from Honolulu to Tahiti via Kauai, Maui, Hilo, Bora Bora, Raiatea, Moorea.

October 2010–April 2011, 10 days, Tahiti/Polynesia, round-trip from Tahiti to Huahine, Rangiroa, Raiatea, Bora Bora, Moorea. April 26, 2011, 22 days, Tahiti to Vancouver via Moorea, Raiatea, Bora Bora, Hilo, Maui, Kauai, Honolulu, Hilo, Kona, Maui, Kauai.

Ruby Princess **HOME PORTS** Barcelona, Fort Lauderdale, Venice

Year-round to April 2011, 10 days, round-trip from Fort Lauderdale, alternating to Aruba, Bonaire, Grenada, Dominica, St. Thomas, Princess Cays; Princess Cays; St. Thomas, St. Kitts, Barbados, St. Lucia, Antigua.

May, July–September, 12 days, Venice to Barcelona via Athens, Kusadasi, Istanbul, Mykonos, Naples/Capri, Rome, Florence/Pisa, Monte Carlo, or reverse. June 10, July 28, 12 days, Venice to Rome via Dubrovnik (Split, June 10), Corfu, Katakolon, Piraeus, Mykonos, Kusadasi, Rhodes, Santorini, Naples/Capri. June 22, August 9, 12 days, Rome to Venice via Monte Carlo, Florence/Pisa, Naples (for Capri and Pompeii), Santorini, Kusadasi, Mykonos, Piraeus, Katakolon, Corfu.

September 26, 16 or 28 days, Barcelona to Fort Lauderdale via Monte Carlo, Florence/Pisa, Rome, Naples/Capri, Mykonos, Istanbul, Kusadasi, Athens, Venice, Naples/Capri, Rome, Cannes, Barcelona, Azores Islands; 16 days from Venice. October 2010–May 2011, Sunday, 7 days, round-trip from Fort Lauderdale to Princess Cays, St. Maarten, St. Thomas, Grand Turk.

Sapphire Princess **HOME PORTS** Los Angeles, Seattle, Vancouver

April–May 2010, November 2010–April 2011, 7 days, round-trip from Los Angeles to Puerto Vallarta, Mazatlán, Cabo San Lucas. May 8, 2010, May 7, 2011, 7 days, Los Angeles to Vancouver via Santa Barbara, San Francisco, Astoria, Seattle, Victoria. May 15, 1 day, Vancouver to Seattle.

May–September, 7 days, Inside Passage, round-trip from Seattle to Ketchikan, Tracy Arm Fjord, Juneau, Skagway, Victoria. September 19, 1 night, Coastal, from Seattle to Vancouver. September 20, 2 days, Vancouver to San Francisco.

September 22, 30–33 days, San Francisco to Sydney via Honolulu, Maui, Moorea, Papeete, Bora Bora, Pago Pago, Apia, Fiji, Auckland, Wellington, Christchurch, Dunedin, cruising Fjordland National Park. Departures available from Seattle (33 days) and Vancouver (32 days).

October 23, 29 days, Sydney to Los Angeles via cruising Fjordland National Park, Dunedin, Akaroa, Wellington, Auckland, Fiji, Pago Pago, Moorea, Papeete, Bora Bora, Honolulu, Maui. December 18, 4 days, Baja, round-trip from Los Angeles to Santa Barbara, Ensenada.

January 5, 2011, 10 days, Mexico, round-trip from Los Angeles to Acapulco, Ixtapa, Puerto Vallarta, Mazatlan, Cabo San Lucas. January 29, February 26, March 26, 14 days, round-trip from Los Angeles to Hilo, Honolulu, Kauai, Maui, Ensenada.

Sea Princess **HOME PORTS** Barbados, San Francisco

May 1, 6 to 21 days, Barbados to San Francisco via Grenada, Bonaire, Aruba, Fort Lauderdale, Aruba, Cartagena, Panama Canal, Panama City, Puntarenas, Huatulco, Acapulco; 6 days, Barbados/Fort Lauderdale; 15 days, Fort Lauderdale/San Francisco.

May–September, 10 days, round-trip from San Francisco to Ketchikan, Juneau, Skagway (or Haines), Tracy Arm Fjord, Victoria; or return Victoria, Juneau, Skagway (or Haines), Glacier Bay, Ketchikan.

September 29, 10 days, round-trip from San Francisco to Catalina Island, Puerto Vallarta, Mazatlan, Cabo San Lucas, San Diego. October 9, 7 or 23 days, San Francisco to Barbados via Cabo San Lucas, Costa Rica, Nicaragua (San Juan del Sur), Fuerte Amador, Panama Canal, Cartagena, Aruba, Fort Lauderdale, Princess Cays, Tortola, St. Maarten, Martinique, St Lucia; 16 days, San Francisco/Fort Lauderdale; or 7 days, Fort Lauderdale/Barbados.

November–December 2010, January–April 2011, alternating, 14 days, Caribbean, round-trip from Barbados to Grenada, Trinidad, Bonaire, Aruba, Grand Cayman, Ocho Rios, Tortola, St. Kitts, Antigua, Dominica; or Grenada, Bonaire, Curaçao, Grand Turk Tortola, St. Maarten, Antigua, St. Lucia, St. Vincent, Trinidad. April 18, 2011, 7 days, Barbados to Fort Lauderdale via Martinique, Dominica, St. Kitts, Tortola, Princess Cays. April 25, 15 days, Fort Lauderdale to Aruba, Cartagena, Panama Canal, Cristobal, Costa Rica, Cabo San Lucas, San Francisco.

Star Princess **HOME PORTS** Buenos Aires, Copenhagen, Fort Lauderdale, Rio de Janeiro, Rome, Venice

May–August, 10 days, round-trip from Copenhagen to Stockholm, Helsinki, St. Petersburg, Tallinn, Gdansk, Oslo. June 11, July 11, August, 10, 10 days, to Stockholm, Helsinki, St. Petersburg, Tallinn, Gdansk, Berlin, Helsingbørg.

August 30, 24 days, Copenhagen to Rome via Stockholm, Helsinki, St. Petersburg, Tallinn, Gdansk, Oslo, Copenhagen, Oslo, Rotterdam, London, Paris/Normandy, Lisbon, Barcelona, Cannes, Genoa, Florence/Pisa. September 9, 12–26 days, Copenhagen to Venice via Oslo, Rotterdam, London, Paris/Normandy, Lisbon, Gibraltar, Barcelona,

Cannes, Florence/Pisa, Rome, Naples/Capri, Santorini, Rhodes, Kusadasi, Mykonos, Athens, Katakolon, Corfu, Split; 14 days, Copenhagen/Rome; 12 days, Rome/Venice.

October 5, November 10, 12 days, Venice to Rome via Katakolon, Athens, Istanbul, Kusadasi, Santorini, Naples, Florence/Pisa, Monte Carlo; reverse October 29. October 17, November 22, 12 days, round-trip from Rome to Alexandria, Khios, Istanbul, Kusadasi, Athens, Naples. November 22, 16 or 28 days, Rome to Rio de Janeiro via Alexandria, Khios, Istanbul, Kusadasi, Athens, Naples, Rome, Florence/Pisa, Cannes, Barcelona, Casablanca, Agadir, Recife; 16 days, Rome/Rio de Janeiro.

December 20, 20 days, Rio de Janeiro to Buenos Aires via Port Stanley, Antarctic Peninsula (Elephant Island, Antarctic Sound, Hope Bay, South Shetland Island, Admiralty Bay, Gerlache Strait, Neumayer Channel, and Deception Island), Cape Horn, Beagle Channel, Ushuaia, Punta Arenas, Puerto Madryn, Montevideo.

January 9, 2011, 17 days, Buenos Aires to Santiago via Port Stanley, Antarctica Peninsula, Cape Horn, Ushuaia, Punta Arenas, Puerto Montt, La Serena. January 26, 2011, February 9, return, February 23, March 9, return, 14 days, Santiago to Rio de Janeiro via Chilean Fjords, Punta Arenas, Ushuaia, Cape Horn, Port Stanley, Buenos Aires, Montevideo.

March 9, 2011, 16 or 30 days, Rio de Janeiro to San Francisco via Montevideo, Buenos Aires, Port Stanley, Cape Horn, Ushuaia, Punta Arenas, Santiago, La Serena, Lima, Quito, Puntarenas, San Juan del Sur, Acapulco, Cabo San Lucas; 16 days, Santiago/San Francisco.

April 2011, 11 days, San Francisco to Acapulco, Zihuatanejo/Ixtapa, Puerto Vallarta, Cabo San Lucas. May 11, 2 days, San Francisco to Vancouver. May 13, 2011, 1 day, Vancouver to Seattle.

Sun Princess   **HOME PORTS**   Freemantle, Sydney

May 14, June 21, July 29, 17 days, round-trip from Fremantle to Geraldton, Penang, Phuket, Langkawi, Kuala Lumpur, Singapore. May 31, July 8, 21 days, to Geraldton, Bali, Ho Chi Minh City, Sihanoukville, Bangkok, Kuala Lumpur, Singapore. August 15, 30 days, to Singapore, Ko Samui, Bangkok, Sihanoukville, Ho Chi Minh City, Nha Trang, Da Nang/Hue, Halong Bay/Hanoi, Hong Kong, Bandar Seri Begawan, Kota Kinabalu, Bali. September 14, 17 days, to Sydney via Geraldton, Bali, Broome, Kimberley Coast, Darwin, Port Douglas, Townsville, Brisbane.

October 1, 12 days, New Caledonia/Vanuatu, round-trip from Sydney to Isles of Pines, Aneiyum Island, Vila, Wala, Champagne Bay, Nouméa (New Caledonia). October 2010–February 2011, 13 days, New Zealand, round-trip from Sydney to Bay of Islands, Auckland, Tauranga, Napier, Wellington, Christchurch, Dunedin, Fiordland National Park. March 5, 2011, 42 days, China/Japan, round-trip from Sydney to Airlie Beach, Darwin, Brunei, Kota Kinabalu, Hong Kong, Shanghai, Busan, Nagasaki, Osaka, Tokyo, Iwo Jima, Saipan, Guam, Rabaul, Brisbane.

Quark Expeditions

All visits to research stations are subject to permission and can only be confirmed locally. Itineraries are flexible and up to two or three Zodiac landings are attempted in a day based on sea and weather conditions.

Akademik Ioffe   **HOME PORTS**   Longyearbyen, Ushuaia

June 14, 21, 8 nights, Introduction to Spitsbergen, round-trip from Longyearbyen to Alkhornet, Smeerenburg, Alkefjellet, Monacobreen, Hamiltonbreen, Ny Alesund. June 28, 11 nights, to Western Spitsbergen, Smeerenburg, Phippsoya, Thousand Islands, Bournbonhamna. July 8, 15 nights, to Western Spitsbergen, Smeerenburg, Phippsoya, Thousand Islands, Sundneset, Diskobutka, Isbukta, Brepollen, Bournbonhamna, Alhornet.

July 22, 14 nights, Spitsbergen/Eastern Greenland/Iceland, from Longyearbyen to Reykjavik via Spitsbergen, Greenland Sea, Eastern Greenland, Westman Islands. August 3, 18 nights, Iceland/Greenland/Canadian Arctic, from Reykjavik to Iqaluit via Tasiilaq, Bernstorfs Isfjord; southern tip of Greenland, Sisimiut, Ilulissat; Uummannaq, Qilaqitsoq;

Baffin Bay, Clyde Inlet, Isabella Bay; Pangnirtung, Kerkerton; Monumental Island.

November–December 2010, January 16, 2011, 12 nights, Antarctic Explorer, round-trip from Ushuaia to Drake Passage, Antarctic Peninsula. December 29, February 8, 2011, 20 nights, round-trip from Ushuaia to Falkland Islands, Southern Ocean, South Georgia, South Shetland Islands, Antarctic Peninsula, Drake Passage. January 26, 2011, 15 nights, Antarctic Circle, round-trip from Ushuaia.

Akademik Sergey Vavilov **HOME PORTS** Longyearbyen, Ushuaia

July–August, 11 nights, Spitsbergen Explorer, round-trip from Longyearbyen to Western Spitsbergen, Smeerenburg, Phippsoya, Thousand Islands, Bournbonhamna.

November 16, February 8, 2011, 20 nights, Antarctic Peninsula/Falklands/South Georgia, round-trip from Ushuaia to Falkland Islands, Southern Ocean, South Georgia, South Shetland Islands, Antarctic Peninsula, Drake Passage. December 4, 2010, January 1, 11, 2011, 12 nights, Antarctic Explorer, round-trip from Ushuaia to Drake Passage, Antarctic Peninsula. January 21, February 13, 26, 15 nights, Antarctic Circle, round-trip from Ushuaia.

Akademik Shokalskiy **HOME PORT** Kangerlussuaq

June 17–July 7, 11 nights, Spitsbergen Explorer. July 17, 14 days, Spitsbergen/Eastern Greenland/Iceland. August 6, 9 days, West Greenland Explorer, round-trip from Kangerlussuaq to Sisimiut, Qeqetarsuaq, Uumannaq/Ukkusissat, Eqip Sermia, Ilulissat, Itilleq.

Clipper Adventurer **HOME PORT** Ushuaia

November–December, 10 or 20 nights, Antarctic Peninsula/Falklands/South Georgia or Antarctic Explorer, round-trip from Ushuaia.

Kapitan Khlebnikov **HOME PORT** Ushuaia; others vary with itinerary

July 18, 19 nights, Northwest Passage, from Andyr to Resolute via Russia's Chukotka Peninsula, Beaufort Sea, Canadian Arctic, Amundsen Gulf, Victoria Strait to Lancaster Sound. August 3, 17 nights, Tanquary Fjord, from Devon Island/Coburg Island to Resolute via Tanquary Fjord, Axel Heilberg Island, Amunsen Gulf, Norwegian Bay, Lancaster Sound, Beechey Island. August 16, 16 nights, High Arctic, from Devon Island to Beechey Island via Coburg Island National Wildlife Area, Grise Fjord, Smith Sound, Kane Basin, Fort Conger Dobbin Bay, Qaanaaq, Melville Bay, Baffin Island.

October, 14 nights, round-trip from Ushuaia to Drake Passage, Snow Hill Island, Antarctic Peninsula; helicopter flights to Emperor Penguin Show Hill Rookery. November 6, 30 nights, Ushuaia to Stanley via Drake Passage, Elephant Island, Brown Bluff, Paulet Island, the Weddell Sea, South Sandwich Islands, Drygalski Fjord, Gold Harbour, Grytviken. December 3, 32 nights, Stanley to Lyttelton (Hobart in 2011) via South Shetland Islands, Antarctic Peninsula, Amundsen Sea, Ross Sea, Southern Ocean, Campbell and Enderby islands.

July 10, 2011, 66 nights, Arctic Circumnavigation, round-trip from Anadyr to Bering Strait, Wrangel Island, New Siberian Islands, Severnaya Zemlya, Franz Josef Land, Murmansk, Spitsbergen, Murmansk, Greenland, Baffin Bay, Northwest Passage, Chukotka Peninsula; segments available.

November 8, December 6, 2011, 29 or 31 nights, Antarctica's Far East, from Christchurch to Hobart via Southern Ocean and South Georgia, the Snares, Auckland Islands, Campbell Island, Cape Adare, Ross Sea, Balleny Islands, Macquarie Island.

Lyubov Orlova **HOME PORT** Ushuaia

November 2010–January 2011, February 10, 2011, 11 or 12 nights, round-trip from Ushuaia to Drake Passage, Antarctic Peninsula. February 29, 2011, 20 nights, round-trip from Ushuaia to Falkland Islands, Southern Ocean, South Georgia, South Shetland Islands, Antarctic Peninsula, Drake Passage.

Ocean Nova **HOME PORT** Ushuaia

November 21, January 21, 2011, 20 nights, round-trip from Ushuaia to Falkland Islands, Southern Ocean, South Georgia, South Shetland Islands, Antarctic Peninsula, Drake Passage. November 11, 2010, February 21, 2011, 12 nights, round-trip from Ushuaia to Drake Passage, Antarctic Peninsula.

Regent Seven Seas Cruises

Seven Seas Mariner **HOME PORTS** Fort Lauderdale, Monte Carlo

April–July, 7–14 nights, Monte Carlo to Venice, Venice to Rome, Istanbul to Venice, Venice to Piraeus, Venice to Istanbul, Istanbul to Piraeus, Piraeus to Istanbul, Istanbul to Rome, Rome to Venice, Venice to Barcelona, Barcelona to Rome, Istanbul to Monte Carlo, Monte Carlo to Rome.

October 21, 75 nights, Istanbul to Fort Lauderdale via Limassol, Haifa, Ashdod, Port Said, Suez Canal, Luxor, Aqaba, Salalah, Muscat, Dubai, Fujairah, Bombay, Goa, Mangalore, Cochin, Port Victoria, Praslin Island, Port Louis, Ponte des Galets, Richard's Bay, Durban, Cape Town, Walvis Bay, St. Helena, Vitoria, Rio de Janeiro, Buzios, Salvador de Bahia, Recife, Belem, Devil's Island, Barbados, Dominica, St. Barts; segments available.

January 4, 2011, 7 nights, round-trip from Fort Lauderdale via Key West, Cozumel, Belize City, Santo Tomas, Costa Maya. January 11, 71 nights, Circle South America, round-trip from Fort Lauderdale to Curaçao, Aruba, Cartagena, Panama Canal transit, Manta, Guayaquil, Salaverry, Callao, Pisco, Coquimbo, Valparaiso, Puerto Montt, Puerto Chacabuco, Laguna San Rafael, Punta Arenas, Ushuaia, cruise Drake Passage/Deception Island/Paradise Bay/Half Moon Island, Port Stanley, Puerto Madryn, Montevideo, Buenos Aires, Montevideo, Punta del Este, Rio Grande, Santos, Parati, Ilha Grande, Buzios, Rio de Janeiro, Salvador de Bahia, Fortaleza, Macapa, Alter do Chao, Boca da Valeria, Manaus, Parintins, Santarem, Devil's Island, Antigua, St. Thomas; segments available.

March 23, 15 nights, transatlantic, Fort Lauderdale to Barcelona via Hamilton, Funchal, Casablanca, Malaga, Cartagena, Palma de Mallorca.

Seven Seas Navigator **HOME PORTS** Fort Lauderdale, Vancouver

May 6, 20 nights, Fort Lauderdale to San Francisco via George Town, Cartagena, Puerto Limon, Panama Canal, Puntarenas, Puerto Chiapas, Huatulco, Acapulco, Puerto Vallarta, Cabo San Lucas, San Diego. May 26, 14 nights, San Francisco to Vancouver via Astoria, Ketchikan, Juneau, Hubbard Glacier, Valdez, Skagway, Sitka, Victoria.

June 9, 7 nights, round-trip from Vancouver to Inside Passage, Ketchikan, Juneau, Skagway, Wrangell. June–September, 7 nights, Vancouver to Seward via Inside Passage, Ketchikan, Tracy Arm, Juneau, Skagway, Sitka, Hubbard Glacier, and reverse. September 8, 103 nights, from Vancouver to San Francisco via Inside Passage, Ketchikan, Tracy Arm, Juneau, Skagway, Sitka, Hubbard Glacier, Seward, Kodiak, Dutch Harbor, Petropavlovsk, Hakodate, Sendai, Yokohama, Nagoya, Kyoto, Beijing, Dalian, Shanghai, Okinawa, Taipei, Hong Kong, Halong Bay/Hong Gai, Da Nang, Saigon, Bangkok, Ko Samui, Singapore, Semarang, Benoa, Komodo Island, Darwin, Thursday Island, Cairns, Whitsunday Islands, Brisbane, Sydney, Geelong, Melbourne, Hobart, Milford Sound, Dunedin, Christchurch, Wellington, Napier, Tauranga, Auckland, Bay of Islands, Nuku'alofa, Vavau, Apia, Honolulu, Hilo; segments available.

December 20, 18 nights, San Francisco to Fort Lauderdale via San Diego, Cabo San Lucas, Zihuatanejo, Acapulco, Huatulco, Puerto Chiapas, Puntarenas, Cartagena, George Town.

January–April 2011, 7 or 10 nights, Fort Lauderdale to Key West, Cozumel, Belize City, Santo Tomas, Costa Maya (7 nights); or Princess Cays, San Juan, Virgin Gorda, St. Barts, Tortola, Cayo Levantado, Grand Turk; or reverse.

April 25, 2011, 18 nights, Fort Lauderdale to San Francisco via George Town, Cartagena, Panama Canal, Puntarenas, Puerto Chiapas, Huatulco, Acapulco, Mazatlan, Cabo San Lucas, San Diego. May 13, 12 nights, San Francisco to Vancouver via Astoria, Ketchikan, Juneau, Skagway, Glacier Bay, Sitka, Victoria.

Seven Seas Voyager **HOME PORTS** Copenhagen, Fort Lauderdale, Horta, Stockholm; others vary with itinerary

May 12, 24 nights, transatlantic, Fort Lauderdale to Southampton via Newport, Boston, Bar Harbor, Halifax, Corner Brook, L'anse Aux Meadows, Reykjavik, Heimaey, Torshavn, Kirkwall, Portree, Belfast, Dublin, Waterford, Cobh, Falmouth; segments available.

June 5, 14 nights, Southampton to Copenhagen via Amsterdam, Rostock, Visby, Stockholm, Helsinki, St. Petersburg, Tallinn, Riga. June 19, 15 nights, to Bergen, Hellesylt, Geiranger, Spitsbergen, Magdalena Bay, Ice Barrier, Honningsvag, Harstad, Gudvangen, Flaam, Stavanger, Oslo. July 4, August 4, 21, reverse July 11, 28, 7 nights, to Stockholm via Visby, Tallinn, St. Petersburg, Helsinki. July 18, reverse August 11, 10 nights, via Rostock, Gdansk, Visby, Riga, Tallinn, St. Petersburg, Helsinki. August 28, 12 nights, Stockholm to Dover via Helsinki, St. Petersburg, Tallinn, Visby, Copenhagen, Oslo, Amsterdam.

September–October, 10–14 nights, Dover to Monte Carlo, Piraeus, Venice, Athens, Barcelona.

November 8, 15 nights, transatlantic, Barcelona to Ft. Lauderdale via Valencia, Cartagena, Malaga, Funchal, Bermuda. November 23, December 10, 7 nights, Fort Lauderdale to Key West, Cozumel, Belize City, Santo Tomas, Costa Maya. November 30, December 17, 10 nights, round-trip from Fort Lauderdale to Princess Cays, San Juan, St. Maarten, St. Barts, Virgin Gorda, Cayo Levantado, Grand Turk.

December 27, 161 nights, World Cruise, Fort Lauderdale to Southampton via George Town, Cartagena, Panama Canal, Puntarenas, Puerto Chiapas, Huatulco, Acapulco, Cabo San Lucas, San Diego, San Francisco, Hilo, Honolulu, Lahaina, Christmas Island (Kiribati), Papeete, Moorea, Bora Bora, Nuku'alofa (Tonga), Bay of Islands, Auckland, Tauranga, cruise by White Island, Christchurch, Dunedin, Milford Sound, Hobart, Melbourne, Sydney, Brisbane, Townsville, Cairns, Thursday Island, Darwin, Bali, Lawi Lawi, Manila, Taipei, Seoul, Beijing, Shanghai, Fuzhou, Hong Kong, Da Nang, Saigon, Sihanoukville, Bangkok (Laem Chabang), Singapore, Kuala Lumpur, Penang, Phuket, Yangon, Colombo, Cochin, Bombay, Fujairah, Dubai, Muscat, Salalah, Aqaba, Luxor, Sharm el Sheikh, Port Said, Ashdod, Haifa, Sorrento, Rome, Porto Venere, Monte Carlo, Barcelona, Malaga, Cadiz, Lisbon, Bilbao, Bordeaux, Honfleur; segments available.

Royal Caribbean International

Adventure of the Seas **HOME PORTS** Barcelona, Malaga, San Juan

April, December, 7 nights, round-trip from San Juan to Barbados, St. Lucia, Antigua, St. Maarten, St. Croix; or Aruba, Curaçao, Dominica, St. Thomas.

May 2, 13 nights, transatlantic, San Juan to Barcelona. May–June, 4 or 5 nights, round-trip from Barcelona to Nice, Sardinia, Palermo; or Cannes, Livorno, Civitacchia; 4 nights, Provence, Ibiza. June 21, 5 nights, Barcelona to Malaga via Cannes, Rome, Corsica. June 26–October 16, 7 nights, round-trip from Malaga to Sardinia, Rome, Ajaccio, Palma de Mallorca. October 23, 6 nights, to Sardinia, Rome, Ajaccio. October 29, November 8, 18, 5 nights, to Corsica, Toulon. November 3, 5 nights, to Tenerife, Funchal. November 23, 5 nights, to Barcelona via Palma de Mallorca, Corsica, Toulon.

November 28, 14 nights, transatlantic, Barcelona to San Juan. December 19, 7 nights, San Juan to St. Thomas, St. Maarten, St. Kitts, Grenada, St. Lucia; December 26, to St. Thomas, St. Croix, St. Kitts, Dominica, Barbados.

January–April 2011, 7 nights, round-trip from San Juan to Barbados, St. Lucia, Antigua, St. Maarten, St. Croix; or Curaçao, Aruba, Dominica, St. Thomas.

Allure of the Seas **HOME PORT** Fort Lauderdale

December 12, 2010, 7 nights, Fort Lauderdale to Nassau, St. Thomas, St. Maarten.

January–October 2011, 7 nights, round-trip from Fort Lauderdale to Nassau, St. Thomas, St. Maarten; or Labadee, Falmouth, Cozumel.

Brilliance of the Seas **HOME PORTS** Barcelona, Miami, Southampton

May–November, 12 nights, round-trip from Barcelona to Nice or Toulon, Livorno, Rome, Piraeus, Kusadasi, Santorini, Naples; or Cannes, Livorno, Rome, Naples, Venice, Dubrovnik, Corfu. November–December, 12 nights, to Palermo, Piraeus, Rhodes, Alexandria, Valletta, Malta.

January 10, 2011, 14 nights, repositioning, Barcelona to Dubai via Alexandria, Suez Canal,

Aqaba, Safaga. January–March, 7 nights, Dubai, round-trip from Dubai to Muscat, Fujairah, Abu Dhabi, Mina Sulman. March 28, April 9, 12 nights, to Muscat, Cochin, Goa, Bombay.

April 21, 16 nights, repositioning, Dubai to Barcelona via Muscat, Safaga, Aqaba, Sharm El Sheikh, Suez Canal, Alexandria.

Enchantment of the Seas   **HOME PORTS**   Baltimore, Colon, Norfolk

May–November, 5 or 9 nights, round-trip from Norfolk or Baltimore to Bermuda; or San Juan, St. Thomas, Samana, Labadee (9 nights); or round-trip from Baltimore to Portland, Bar Harbor, St. John, Halifax, Boston (9 nights, August–October). June 18, 8 nights, Baltimore to Portland.

November 2010–May 2011, 9 or 12 nights, round-trip from Baltimore to Port Canaveral, Key West, Nassau, Cococay; or Labadee, Samana, San Juan, St. Thomas, St. Maarten, Tortola (12 nights).

Explorer of the Seas   **HOME PORT**   Cape Liberty (New Jersey)

April–October, 5 or 9 nights, round-trip from Cape Liberty to Bermuda (5 nights); or Bermuda, Nassau, Cococay; or St. Maarten, St. Thomas, San Juan; or Portland, Bar Harbor, Saint John, Halifax, Boston (September–October). October 28, 10 nights, round-trip from Cape Liberty to Labadee, Samana, St. Thomas, St. Kitts.

November–December, January–March 2011, 9 or 12 nights, alternating, round-trip from Cape Liberty to San Juan, St. Thomas, Samana, Labadee (9 nights); or Labadee, Samana, St. Thomas, St. Kitts, Antigua, St. Maarten. December 19, January 2, 2011, 14 nights, Cape Liberty to Labadee, Samana, St. Thomas, Barbados, Antigua, St. Maarten. March 20, 11 nights, to Labadee, Samana, St. Thomas, St. Kitts, Antigua. April–May, alternating to Bermuda (5 nights); or Bermuda, St. Maarten, St. Thomas, San Juan; or Kings Wharf, Nassau, Cococay (9 nights).

Freedom of the Seas   **HOME PORT**   Port Canaveral

Year-round, 7 nights, round-trip from Port Canaveral to Cococay, St. Thomas, St. Maarten; or Labadee, Ocho Rios, Grand Cayman, Cozumel. November 2010–May 2011, Falmouth in place of Ocho Rios.

Grandeur of the Seas   **HOME PORTS**   Tampa, Fort Lauderdale, Colon

April–October, 4 or 5 nights, round-trip from Fort Lauderdale to Key West, Cozumel, Costa Maya; or Key West, Cozumel, Cococay; Grand Cayman, Cozumel; or Key West, Cozumel (4 nights). November 1, 6 nights, repositioning, Fort Lauderdale to Colon.

November 2010–April 2011, 7 nights, round-trip from Colon to Cartagena, Santa Marta, Aruba, Curaçao, Bonaire; or Cartagena, Montego Bay, Grand Cayman, Roatan.

Independence of the Seas   **HOME PORTS**   Fort Lauderdale, Southampton

May–September, 14 nights, round-trip from Southampton to Gibraltar, Toulon or Nice, Livorno, Rome, Cagliari, Cadiz, Lisbon, Vigo; or Gibraltar, Corsica, Cannes, Barcelona, Ibiza, Malaga, Lisbon, Vigo. May 29, August 28, 4 nights, to Cork. November 18, 29, March–April 2011, 11 nights, to Vigo, Lisbon, Tenerife, Las Palmas, Funchal, La Coruna. December 10, 11 nights, to Vigo, Lisbon, Funchal, Las Palmas, Tenerife. December 21, January 8, 2011, 18 nights, to Lisbon, Palma de Mallorca, Barcelona, Livorno, Rome, Naples, Cagliari, Gibraltar, Cadiz.

Jewel of the Seas   **HOME PORTS**   Miami, Harwich

April, 10 or 11 nights, round-trip from Miami to Labadee, Cartagena, Colon, Puerto Limon, Grand Cayman (10 nights); or Aruba, Cartagena, Colon, Puerto Limon, Grand Cayman. May 6, 13 nights, transatlantic, Miami to Harwich. May–August, 12 nights, round-trip from Harwich to Copenhagen, Stockholm, Helsinki, St. Petersburg, Tallinn, Gothenburg. September 4, 14 nights, transatlantic, Harwich to Boston via Le Havre, Cherbourg, Cork, Akureyri, St. John's, Sydney. September–October, 7 nights, round-trip from Boston to

Portland, Bar Harbor, Saint John, Halifax. October 20, 13 nights, to Fort Lauderdale via St. Thomas, St. Maarten, Dominica, Barbados, Aruba, Curaçao.

November 2010–April 2011, 10 or 11 nights, round-trip from Fort Lauderdale to Labadee, Cartagena, Colon, Puerto Limon, Grand Cayman; or Aruba, Cartagena, Colon, Puerto Limon, Grand Cayman.

Legend of the Seas **HOME PORTS** Shanghai, Tianjin, Hong Kong, and others

May 2, 10, 8 nights, round-trip from Tokyo to Shanghai, Jeju, Busan. May 18, 8 nights, to Shanghai via Hakodate, Otaru, Vladivostok. June 20, July 4, 7 nights, Shanghai to Miyazaki, Kobe, Fukuoka, Busan. June 27, July 11, 7 nights, to Nagasaki, Kagoshima, Fukuoka, Busan.

May 26, 31, June 5, 10, 15, July 18, 5 nights, round-trip from Shanghai to Fukuoka, Busan. July 25, 6 nights, to Tianjin via Kagoshima, Fukuoka, Busan.

July–August, 7 nights, Japan/Korea, round-trip from Tianjin to Fukuoka, Kagoshima, Nagasaki, Busan. September 4, 13 nights, Tianjin to Hong Kong via Seoul, Shanghai, Naha, Taipei; September 17, reverse. September 30, 7 nights, Tianjin to Nagasaki, Kagoshima, Fukuoka, Busan. October 7, 14 nights, to Hong Kong via Seoul, Shanghai, Nagasaki, Kagoshima, Naha, Taipei.

October 21, 4 nights, round-trip from Hong Kong to Sanya, Hanoi. October 25, November 4, 5 nights, to Kaohsiung, Hualien, Taipei. October 30, 5 nights, to Sanya, Hue/Danang, Hanoi. November 9, 13 nights, Hong Kong to Singapore.

Liberty of the Seas **HOME PORT** Miami

November 2010–January 2011, round-trip from Miami to St. Maarten, San Juan, Labadee; or Costa Maya, Belize, Cozumel. January–April, to St. Thomas, St. Maarten, San Juan, Labadee (8 nights); or Belize, Costa Maya, Cozumel (6 nights).

Majesty of the Seas **HOME PORT** Miami

May 2010–April 2011, 3 or 4 nights, to Key West, Nassau, Cococay (4 nights); or Cococay, Nassau.

Mariner of the Seas **HOME PORT** Los Angeles

Year-round, 7 nights, Mexican Riviera, round-trip from Los Angeles to Cabo San Lucas, Mazatlan, Puerto Vallarta.

Monarch of the Seas **HOME PORT** Port Canaveral

Year-round, 3 or 4 nights, Bahamas, round-trip from Port Canaveral to Cococay, Nassau, or reverse.

Navigator of the Seas **HOME PORTS** Miami, Rome, Fort Lauderdale

April 24, May 6, 18, September 5, 17, 29, 12 nights, round-trip from Rome to Naples, Piraeus, Rhodes, Kusadasi, Alexandria, Messina.

November 15, 29, 4 nights, round-trip from Fort Lauderdale to Labadee, Ocho Rios.

November 2010–April 2011, 4 or 5 nights, round-trip from Fort Lauderdale to Grand Cayman, Cozumel; Labadee, Falmouth; or Cozumel (4 nights). December 23, 5 nights, to Nassau, Falmouth. December 28, 5 nights, to Cozumel, Belize.

Oasis of the Seas **HOME PORT** Fort Lauderdale

Year-round, 7 nights, round-trip from Fort Lauderdale to St. Thomas, St. Maarten, Nassau; or Labadee, Costa Maya, Cozumel. December 2010–October 2011, Falmouth replaces Costa Maya. December 18, 5 nights, to Labadee, Falmouth. December 23, 7 nights, to Labadee, Falmouth, Cozumel. December 30, 9 nights, to Labadee, St. Thomas, St. Maarten, Falmouth.

Radiance of the Seas **HOME PORTS** San Diego, Tampa, Vancouver

May 3, 5 nights, to Ensenada, Cabo San Lucas. May 8, 13 nights, San Diego to Vancouver via San Francisco, Ketchikan, Juneau, Skagway, Hubbard Glacier, Sitka, Nanaimo, Victoria. May–August, 7 nights, Vancouver to Seward via Inside Passage, Ketchikan, Icy Strait

Point, Juneau, Skagway, Hubbard Glacier; reverse. September 10, 14 nights, Vancouver to San Diego via Ketchikan, Icy Strait Point, Juneau, Skagway, Hubbard Glacier, Sitka, Victoria, San Francisco.

September 24, 15 nights, San Diego to Tampa via Cabo San Lucas, Acapulco, Huatulco, Puntarenas, Panama Canal, Cristobal Pier, Cartagena, Grand Cayman. October 9, 7 nights, round-trip from Tampa to Grand Cayman, Costa Maya, Belize, Cozumel. October 2010–April 2011, 4 or 5 nights, round-trip from Tampa to Cozumel, Costa Maya, or reverse; Cozumel (4 nights).

Rhapsody of the Seas **HOME PORTS** Perth, Sydney, Honolulu, Seattle, Vancouver

May 7, 7 nights, Vancouver to Seattle via Inside Passage, Juneau, Skagway, Tracy Arm Fjord, Ketchikan. May–September, 7 nights, round-trip from Seattle to Inside Passage, Juneau, Skagway, Tracy Arm Fjord, Victoria. September 10, 7 nights, to Vancouver via Skagway, Tracy Arm Fjord, Ketchikan, Inside Passage. September 17, 12 nights, Vancouver to Honolulu via Hilo, Mount Kilauea, Kailua Kona, Maui, Kauai. September 29, 2010, return April 14, 2011, 16 nights, Honolulu to Sydney via Moorea, Papeete, Tahiti, Bora Bora, Raiatea.

October 16, 2010, March 24, 2011, 11 nights, round-trip from Sydney to Newcastle, Willis Island, Port Douglas, Cairns, Airlie Beach, Brisbane. Octobert 27, 12 nights, to Isle of Pines, Suva, Lautoka, Vila, Lifou. November 8, 12 nights, to Noumea, Mystery Island, Lugannville, Champagne Bay, Vila, Ouvea, Ise of Pines. November 27, 7 nights, to Noumea, Isle of Pines.

December 4, 14 nights, round-trip from Sydney to Milford Sound, Doubtful Sound, Dusky Sound, Dunedin, Christchurch, Wellington, Napier, Volcanic White Island, Tauranga, Auckland, Bay of Islands. December 18, January 13, 2011, 9 nights, to Isle of Pines, Ouvea, Vila, Noumea. December 27, 2010, April 4, 2011, 10 nights, to Noumea, Lifou, Vila, Ouvea, Isle of Pines.

January 22, 2011, 14 nights, round-trip from Sydney to Bay of Islands, Auckland, Tauranga, Volcanic White Island, Wellington, Christchurch, Dunedin, Dusky Sound, Doubtful Sound, Milford Sound. February 5, 12 nights, to Lifou, Vila, Lautoka, Suva, Isle of Pines. February 17, 17 nights, to Perth via Brisbane, Airlie Beach, Qld, Cairns, Port Moresby, Darwin, Broome, Exmouth.

April 30, 2011, 13 nights, Hawaii, round-trip from Honolulu to Vancouver via Nawiliwili, Lahaina, Kailua Kona, Hilo, Seattle.

Serenade of the Seas **HOME PORT** San Juan

May 8, 8 nights, to Barbados, St. Lucia, Antigua, St. Maarten, St. Croix. May–November, to Curaçao, Aruba, Dominica, St. Thomas, Barbados.

December 5, January 2, 2011, 6 nights, round-trip from San Juan to St. Croix, Antigua, St. Lucia, St. Kitts. December 11, March 19, 2011, 7 nights, to St. Thomas, St. Croix, Antigua, Dominica, Grenada. December 18, 5 nights, to St. Croix, Antigua, St. Lucia. December 23, 10 nights, to St. Maarten, St. Kitts, Antigua, Dominica, St. Lucia, Barbados, Grenada.

January–April 2011, 7 nights, round-trip from San Juan to St. Thomas, St. Croix, Antigua, St. Lucia, Grenada; or Tortola, St. Maarten, St. Kitts, Dominica, Barbados.

Splendour of the Seas **HOME PORTS** Sao Paulo (Santos), Barcelona, Venice

April–November, 7 nights, round-trip from Venice to Split, Corfu, Piraeus, Mykonos, Katakolon; or Dubrovnik, Kusadasi, Santorini, Corfu. July 10, 6 nights, to Dubrovnik, Piraeus, Katakolon. July 16, 8 nights, to Dubrovnik, Mykonos, Kusadasi, Santorini, Corfu.

Vision of the Seas **HOME PORTS** Sao Paulo, Lisbon, Copenhagen, Oslo, and others

May, 5 nights, to Zeebrugge, Amsterdam; or Normandy, Cherbourg, Dublin, Edinburgh, Inverness/Loch Ness (9 nights). June, 7 nights, to Copenhagen, Tallinn, St. Petersburg. June 19, 4 nights, to Stockholm via Copenhagen, Talinn.

June 23, 27, July 1, 4 nights, round-trip from Stockholm to Tallinn, St. Petersburg. July 5, 6 nights, to Helsinki, St. Petersburg, Gdansk, Visby. July–August, 7 nights, to Helsinki, St. Petersburg, Riga, Gdansk, Visby. August 8, 4 nights, to Copenhagen via Gothenburg, Oslo.

August 12, 11 nights, round-trip from Copenhagen to Ålesund, Arctic Circle, Honningsvag, Tromso, Geiranger, Olden, Bergen. August 23, 5 nights, to Bergen, Geiranger. August 28, September 4, to Tallinn, St. Petersburg, Helsinki, Stockholm. September 11, 13 nights, to Venice via Amsterdam, Zeebrugge, Le Havre, Malaga, Cartagena, Valletta, Split.

September 24, 12 nights, round-trip from Venice to Haifa, Ashdod, Port Said, Alexandria, Kusadasi. October, 12 nights, to Alexandria, Port Said, Ashdod, Haifa, Piraeus, Split. November 11, 9 nights, to Lisbon via Split, Naples, Rome, Venice, Barcelona, Cadiz.

Voyager of the Seas **HOME PORTS** Galveston, Barcelona
November 21, December 5, 7 nights, round-trip from Galveston to Cozumel, Grand Cayman, Montego Bay; or Roatan, Costa Maya, Cozumel.

November 2010–April 2011, 7 nights, round-trip from Galveston to Cozumel, Grand Cayman, Montego Bay or Falmouth; or Roatan, Belize, Cozumel.

Saga Cruises

Saga Ruby **HOME PORTS** Dover, Southampton
May 25, 7 nights, to Dover via Stavanger, Flam, Skjolden, Bergen. June 1, 14 nights, round-trip from Dover to Kiel Canal, Stockholm, Helsinki, St. Petersburg, Tallinn, Gdynia, Warnemunde, Copenhagen, Oslo. June 15, 15 nights, round-trip from Dover to Stavanger, Sognefjord, Trondheim, Svolvaer, Hammerfest, Hinningsvag, Tromso, Geiranger, Bergen, Eidfjord.

June 30, 19 nights, Greenland, round-trip from Dover to Cobh, Qaqortoq, Ilulissat, Nuuk, Reykjavik, Torshavn, Lerwick, Bergen. August 4, 7 nights, to Bergen, Skjolden, Flam, Stavanger. August 11, 13 nights, to Leith, Kirkwall, Portree, Greenock, Belfast, Holyhead, Dublin, Cobh, Falmouth, Guernsey. August 24, to Leith, Bremerhaven. August 31, 13 nights, to Kiel Canal, Stockholm, Helsinki, St. Petersburg, Tallinn, Warnemunde, Copenhagen, Oslo.

September 13, 15 nights, from Dover to Southampton via Lisbon, Gibraltar, Rome, Livorno, Marseilles, Barcelona, Vigo. September 28, 24 nights, to Vigo, Cadiz, Palma, Valletta, Rhodes, Marmaris, Patmos, Piraeus, Katakolon, Palermo, Mahon, Gibraltar, Lisbon. October 22, 14 nights, to Arrecife, Santa Cruz La Palma, Santa Cruz Tenerife, San Sebastian La Gomera, Las Palmas Gran Canaria, Agadir, Casablanca, Lisbon. November 5, 31 nights, West Africa, round-trip from Southampton to Funchal, Dakar, Freetown, San Pedro, Limbe, Port Gentil, Sao Tome, Lome, Tema/Accra, Takoradi, Porto Grande, Santa Cruz Tenerife.

Saga Pearl II **HOME PORTS** Dover, Southampton
May 4, 10 nights, to Dover via Stavanger, Eidfjord, Floro, Kristiansund, Ålesund, Olden, Bergen. May 14, 16 nights, to Kiel Canal, Travemunde, Copenhagen, Stockholm, Helsinki, St. Petersburg, Tallin, Visby, Klaipeda, Gdynia, Ronne, Kiel Canal.

May 29, June 13, 7 nights, France/Belgium/Holland, round-trip from Dover to Dunkirk, Rotterdam, Ghent, Boulogne, Cherbourg, Guernsey.

June 5, 8 nights, Dover to Guernsey, Falmouth, Cobh, Dublin, Derry/Londonderry, Greencastle, Belfast. July 12, 8 nights, round-trip from Dover to Kirkwall, Scrabster, Invergordon, Peterhead, St. Andrews. July 20, September 1, 7 nights, to Bergen, Geiranger, Floro, Stavanger. July 27, 14 nights, to Kiel Canal, Korsor, Stockholm, Helsinki, St. Petersburg, Tallinn, Visby, Warnemunde, Malmo. August 10, 15 nights, to Stavanger, Floro, Trondheim, Bronnoysund, Bodo, Narvik, Leknes, Tromso, Molde, Skjolden, Bergen. August 25, 7 nights, to Bergen, Gudvangen, Flam, Jondal, Stavanger. September 8, 14 nights, to Kiel Canal, Stockholm, Mariehamn, Helsinki, St. Petersburg, Tallinn, Szczecin, Copenhagen, Olslo.

September 22, 16 nights, Dover to Southampton via Ferrol, Gibraltar, Melilla, Barcelona, Marseilles, Sete, Mahon, Cadiz, Lisbon. November 1, 18 nights, round-trip from Southampton to Melilla, Tunis, Sousse, Valletta, Algiers, Cartagena, Ceuta, Casablanca, Lisbon. November 19, 18 nights, to Leixoes, Lisbon, Portimao, Seville, Funchal, Ponta Delgada, Horta, Praia da Vitoria. December 7, 9 nights, to Ghent, Rotterdam, Amsterdam, Hamburg, Bremerhaven. December 16, 19 nights, to Villagarcia de Arosa, Cadiz, Ceuta, Casablanca, Agadir, Arrecife, Las Palmas Gran Canaria, Santa Cruz Tenerife, San Sebastian La Gomera, Funchal.

Seabourn Cruise Line

Seabourn Legend   **HOME PORTS**   Fort Lauderdale, Barcelona, Monte Carlo; others vary with itinerary

May 2, 7 or 14 days, from Monte Carlo to Porquerolles, Sanary-sur-mer, Cannes, Calvi, Portovenere, Portoferraio, Rome (7 days), Monte Carlo return.

May–October, 7–28 days, monthly departures, Barcelona to Palamos, Port Vendres, Bandol, Marseille, Le Lavandou, St. Tropez, Monte Carlo (7 days), Porquerolles, Sanary-sur-mer, Cannes, Calvi, Portovenere, Portoferraio, Rome (14 days), cruising Golfo Stella, Porto Rotondo, Ajaccio, Livorno, Portofino, Nice, Monte Carlo (21 days), Porquerolles, Antibes, Mahon, Palma de Mallorca, Valencia, Barcelona (28 days). Or, from Monte Carlo, same itineraries repeated. June 12, 7 days, Rome to Monte Carlo via Golfo Stella, Porto Rotondo, Ajaccio, Livorno, Portofino, Nice. June 19, 7 days, Monte Carlo to Barcelona via Porquerolles, Antibes, Saint Raphael, Mahon, Palma de Mallorca, Valencia.

October 2, 7–28 days, Rome to Portoferraio, Porto Rotondo, Ajaccio, Livorno, Portofino, Nice, Monte Carlo, Porquerolles, Antibes, Saint Raphael, Mahon, Palma de Mallorca, Valencia, Barcelona, Palamos, Port Vendres, Bandol, Marseille, Le Lavandou, St. Tropez, Monte Carlo, Porquerolles, Sanary-sur-mer, Cannes, Calvi, Portovenere, Portoferraio, Rome; segments available. November 13, 7 days, Rome to Malaga via Livorno, Barcelona, Valencia, Palma de Mallorca.

November 20, 13 days, transatlantic, Malaga to Fort Lauderdale via Funchal.

December 3, 13, 10 days, round-trip from Fort Lauderdale to Nassau or Grand Turk, Samana, St. Barts, Prickly Pear Island, San Juan. December 23, 14 days, to San Juan, St. John, St. Kitts, Antigua, St. Maarten, St. Barts, Jost Van Dyke, Prickly Pear Island, Grand Turk. January 6, 17, 2011, 11 days, to Grand Turk, Samana, Antigua, St. Martin, Prickly Pear Island, San Juan. January 28, 7 days, to St. Thomas via San Juan, St. Croix, St. Kitts, Prickly Pear Island. February 2011, March 4, 2011, 7 days, round-trip from St. Thomas to St. Martin, Jost Van Dyke, St. Barts, Antigua, St. Kitts, Prickly Pear Island. March 11, 2011, 10 days, to Fort Lauderdale via St. Martin, Jost Van Dyke, St. Barts, Antigua, St. Kitts, Prickly Pear Island, Grand Turk.

Seabourn Odyssey   **HOME PORTS**   Fort Lauderdale; others vary with itinerary

May–November, 7 to 30 days, round-trip, Istanbul and Venice, from Piraeus to Istanbul, Istanbul to Piraeus, Venice to Piraeus, Piraeus to Venice, Venice to Piraeus, Venice to Istanbul, Piraeus to Rome.

December 6, 13 days, transatlantic, Nice to Fort Lauderdale via Las Palmas. December 19, 16 days, round-trip from Fort Lauderdale to Grand Turk, Jost van Dyke, St. Kitts, Mayreau, Barbados, St. Lucia, Guadeloupe, Antigua, St. Bart's, Prickly Pear Island.

January 4, 2011, 73 days, South America, round-trip from Fort Lauderdale to San Blas Islands, Panama Canal, Fuerte Amador, Guayquil, Salaverry, Callao, Arica, Iquique, Valparaiso, Puerto Montt, Puerto Chacabuco, Punta Arenas, Ushuaia, Port Stanley, Puerto Madryn, Buenos Aires, Montevideo, Punta del Este, Parati, Rio de Janeiro, Salvador de Bahia, Natal, Santarem, Anavilhanas, Manaus, Parintins, Alter do Chao, Curua Una River, Devil's Island, Barbados, Jost van Dyke; segments available.

March 18, 2011, 12 days, transatlantic, from Fort Lauderdale to Lisbon via Funchal.

Seabourn Pride **HOME PORTS** Hong Kong, Singapore; others vary with itinerary

April–October, 12 to 25 days, Hong Kong to Xingang, Hong Kong to Kobe, Xingang to Kobe, Kobe to Xingang, Kobe to Hong Kong, Kobe to Shanghai, Kobe to Hong Kong, Xingang to Hong Kong, Kobe to Bangkok, Shanghai to Bangkok, Bangkok to Shanghai, Bangkok to Kobe, Shanghai to Kobe.

November–December, 14 to 28 days, round-trip from Singapore to Hong Kong.

January–April 2011, 12 days, Hong Kong to Bangkok and reverse via Cai Lan, Da Nang, Ho Chi Minh City, Ko Kood.

Seabourn Sojourn **HOME PORT** Varies with itinerary

June 6, 2010, 28 days, Maiden Voyage from London to Dover via Invergordon, Torshavn, Reykjavik, Djupivogur, Olden, Bergen, Amsterdam, Dover, Kiel Canal, Lubeck, Tallinn, St. Petersburg, Helsinki, Stockholm, Kiel Canal; segments available.

July 4, 14 days, Dover to Copenhagen via Invergordon, Kirkwall, Lerwick, Trondheim, Geiranger, Olden, Flaam, Bergen, Stavanger, Oslo. July 27, August 22, 26 days, round-trip from Copenhagen to Stockholm, Helsinki, St. Petersburg, Tallinn, Szczecin, Warnemuende, Copenhagen, Flaam, Ålesund, Olden, Bergen, Lerwick, Kirkwall, Invergordon, Leith; segments available. September 15, 26 days, to Lisbon via Flaam, Ålesund, Molde, Olden, Bergen, Stavanger, Amsterdam, Dover, Rouen, Guernsey, St. Malo, Lorient, La Pallice/La Rochelle, Bordeaux, Santander, La Coruna.

October 11, 23 days, round-trip from Lisbon to Cartagena, Valencia, Palma de Mallorca, Mahon, Naples, Siracusa, Valletta, Trapani, Lipari, Rome, Livorno, Monte Carlo, Marseille, Barcelona, Malaga, Gibraltar.

November 3, 12 days, Maiden transatlantic, Lisbon to Fort Lauderdale via Funchal.

November 19, 21 days, round-trip from Fort Lauderdale to San Juan, St. Kitts, St. Barts, Prickly Pear Island, Grand Turk, Fort Lauderdale, San Juan, St. Barts, Prickly Pear, St. Kitts, Grand Turk. November 30, 20 days, to San Juan via same ports as November 19. December 10, 26 days, Fort Lauderdale to Los Angeles via Grand Turk, St. Kitts, St. Bart's, Prickly Pear Island, San Juan, Fort Lauderdale, Cartagena, Panama Canal, Puerto Caldera, Puerto Chiapas, Huatulco, Cabo San Lucas, San Diego; segments available.

January 5, 2011, 111 days, World Cruise, Los Angeles to Southampton via Nuku Hiva, Papeete, Moorea, Bora Bora, Rarotonga, Bay of Islands, Auckland, Wellington, Akaroa, Lyttleton, Port Chalmers, Hobart, Sydney, Melbourne, Adelaide, Freemantle, Padang Bay, Sandakan, Hong Kong, Cai Lan, Ho Chi Minh City, Sihanoukville, Laem Chabang, Singapore, Penang, Phuket Island, Cochin, Mangalore, Mumbai, Dubai, Khasab, Muscat, Salalah, Safaga, Aqaba, Sharm El Sheikh, Sokhna, Port Said, Ashdod, Heraklion, Sorrento, Rome, Barcelona, Valencia, Cartagena, Lisbon, Bordeaux.

Seabourn Spirit **HOME PORTS** Fort Lauderdale, Venice, Civitavecchia, and others

May 1, 14 days, from Rome to Piraeus via Ponza Island, Trapani, Malta, Taormina, Amalfi, Gaeta, Rome, Sorrento, Lipari, Katakolon, Itea, Navplien; segments available.

May 22, 28 days, Istanbul to Venice via Itea, Katakalon, Taormina, Sorrento, Rome, Trapani, Valletta, Siracusa, Amalfi, Gaeta, Rome, Lipari, Corfu, Bari, Korcula, Rovinj, Venice, Kotor, Dubrovnik, Zadar, Koper, Trieste. June 19, July 17, 28 days, round-trip from Venice to Hvar, Bari, Siracusa, Lipari, Sorrento, Rome, Ponza Island, Trapani, Valletta, Taormina, Amalfi, Gaeta, Rome, Lipari Island, Corfu, Bari, Korcula, Rovinj, Venice, Kotor, Dubrovnik, Zadar, Koper, Trieste; segments available. July 31, 28 days, Venice to Rome via Kotor, Dubrovnik, Zadar, Koper, Trieste, Venice, Hvar, Bari, Siracusa, Lipari, Sorrento, Rome, Ponza, Trapani, Valletta, Taormina, Amalfi, Gaeta. September 4, 28 days, round-trip from Venice to Kotor, Dubrovnik, Zadar, Koper, Trieste, Venice, Hvar, Bari, Siracusa, Lipari Island, Sorrento, Rome, Ponza Island, Trapani, Valletta, Taormina, Amalfi, Gaeta, Rome, Lipari Island, Corfu, Bari, Korcula, Rovinj; segments available.

September 18, 28 days, round-trip from Rome to Ponza Island, Trapani, Malta, Taormina, Amalfi, Gaeta, Rome, Lipari Island, Corfu, Bari, Korcula, Rovinj, Venice, Sibenik, Kotor,

Dubrovnik, Zadar, Koper, Trieste, Venice, Hvar, Bari, Siracusa, Lipari, Sorrento. October 2, 28 days, round-trip from Venice to Sibenik, Kotor, Dubrovnik, Zadar, Koper, Trieste, Venice, Hvar, Bari, Siracusa, Lipari, Sorrento, Ponza Island, Trapani, Valletta, Taormina, Amalfi, Gaeta, Rome, Lipari Island, Corfu, Bari, Korcula, Rovinj; segments available.

October 9, 28 days, Venice to Rome via Hvar, Bari, Siracusa, Lipari, Sorrento, Ponza Island, Trapani, Malta, Taormina, Amalfi, Gaeta, Rome, Lipari Island, Corfu, Bari, Korcula, Rovinj, Venice, Hvar, Bari, Siracusa, Lipari, Sorrento. October 30, 67 days, Venice to Singapore via Hvar, Bari, Siracusa, Lipari, Sorrento, Rome, Trapani, Valletta, Aghios Nikolaos, Haifa, Ashdod, Suez Canal transit, Sokhna, Aqaba, Safaga, Salalah, Khasab, Dubai, Muscat, Mumbai, Mangalore, Cochin, Phuket Island, Langkawi Island, Pulai, Penang, Port Kelong, Singapore, Semarang, Padang Bay, Komodo Island, Ujung Padang, Sandakan, Kota Kinabalu, Muara; segments available. January 12, 2011, 37 days, Singapore to Cairns via Kuching, Karimunjawa, Semerang, Lembar, Padang Bay, Benoa, Komodo Island, Palopo, Ujung Pandang, Sandakan, Kota Kinabalu, Muara, Singapore, Karimunjawa, Semarang, Padang Bay, Komodo Island, Kupang, Darwin, Cooktown. February 18, 2011, 49 days, Cairns to Rome via Cooktown, Darwin, Kupang, Komodo, Padang, Semarang, Karimunjawa, Singapore, Penang, Cochin, Mangalore, Mumbai, Muscat, Dubai, Khasab, Salalah, Safaga, Aqaba, Sokhna, Suez Canal transit; segments available.

SeaDream Yacht Club

SeaDream I **HOME PORTS** St. Thomas, San Juan; others vary with itinerary

April 30, 13 days, San Juan to Malaga via Funchal. May 13, 7 days, Malaga to Nice via Cartagena, Formentera, Ibiza, Mahon, St. Tropez, Monte Carlo. May–September, 7–12 days, from Rome to Piraeus, Istanbul, Dubrovnik, Monte Carlo, Venice. October 2, 12 days, Piraeus to Malaga via Aigina Island, Mykonos, Corinth Canal, Itea, Fiskardho, Taormina, Malta, Tunis, Palma de Mallorca, Ibiza, Motril. October 14, 12 days, Milaga to San Juan via Funchal.

October–December, 7 days, San Juan to St. Thomas via Cruz Bay, Norman Island, Virgin Gorda, Jost van Dyke; or St. Thomas to San Juan via Cruz Bay, Virgin Gorda, Gustavia, Nevis, Saba, Jost van Dyke.

SeaDream II **HOME PORTS** Malaga, San Juan; others vary with itinerary

May–October, 6 to 11 days, Malaga to Monte Carlo, Rome, Piraeus, Istanbul, Malta, Dubrovnik, Venice, Barcelona.

November–December, 7 or 9 days, round-trip from San Juan to Antigua; or San Juan to St. Thomas, St. Thomas to San Juan, San Jan to Antigua, Antigua to San Juan, San Juan to Barbados. February 7, 21 days, round-trip from San Juan to Culebrita, Esperanza, Cruz Bay, Virgin Gorda, St. Barts, St. Martin, Nevis, Antigua, Guadeloupe, Montserrat, St. Barts, Anguilla, St. Martin, Nevis, Antigua, Saba, St. Barts, St. Martin, Anguilla, Jost van Dyke.

November 8, 13 days, transatlantic, Barcelona to San Juan. December 21, 7 days, San Juan to St. Maarten via Norman Island, Jost van Dyke, Anguilla, Nevis, St. Barts.

Silversea Cruises

Prince Albert II **HOME PORT** Varies with itinerary

May 10, 11 days, Portsmouth to Leith via Alderney, Guernsey, Tresco, Waterford, Dublin, Gigha, Islay, Iona, Staffa, St. Kilda, Lock Ewe, Stromness, Aberdeen. May 21, 15 days, Leith to London via Stomness, Lock Ewe, Eriskay, Rum, Treshnish Isles, Tobermory, Portrush, Tory Island, Dublin, Holyhead, Tresco, Penzance, St. Malo, Guernsey, Sark Island.

June 5, 17 days, London to Longyearbyen via Newcastle, Aberdeen, Shetland Islands (2 days), Trondheim, Lofoten Islands, Andoya Island, Mageroy Island, Skarsvag, Bear Island, Hornsund, Svalbard. June 22, 7 days, Spitzbergen, round-trip from Longyearbyen via Svalbard. June 29, reverse August 2, August 12, 10 days, Longyearbyen to Tromso via Svalbard, Hornsund, Bear Island, Mageroy Island, Skarsvag. August 22, 16 days, Tromso to Reykjavik via Bear Island, Svalbard (5 days), Longyearbyen, Jan Mayen Island, Husavik, Vigur Island, Grundarfjordur. September 7, 18 days, Greenland/Canadian Arctic, from Reykjavik to St. Johns NF via Vestmannaeyjar, Skjoldungen Fjord, Prince Christian Sound, Qaqortoq, Hvalsey, Arsuk Brae, Iqaluit, Lower Savage Islands, Akpatok Island, Hopedale, Battle Harbour, L'Anse aux Meadows, Twillingate.

October 3, 10 days, La Romana to Puerto Caldera via Curaçao, San Blas Islands, Panama Canal, Darien Jungle, Isla de Coiba, Golfito. October 13, 17 days, Puerto Caldera to Valparaiso via Golfito, Isla de Coiba, Isla de la Plata, Guayaquil, Salaverry, Callao, Paracas, Arica, Iquique, Antofagasta, Isla Pan de Acuzar, Coquimbo. October 30, 11 days, Valparaiso to Ushuaia via Niebla, Castro, Puyuhuapi, Puerto Eden, Puerto Natales, Garabaldi Glacier.

November 2010–February 2011, 11 days, round-trip from Ushuaia to Drake Passage, Antarctic Peninsula. November 10, December 19, 17 days, to West Point Island, Carcass Island, Stanley, South Georgia, South Sandwich Islands, South Orkney, Elephant Island, Antarctic Peninsula, Drake Passage.

Silver Cloud HOME PORT Varies with itinerary

May, 7–10 days, Rome to Venice, Venice to Piraeus, Piraeus to Barcelona, Barcelona to Tilbury.

June–July, 8 or 15 days, round-trip from Tilbury to Stockholm; Stockholm to Copenhagen. July 23, 11 days, Copenhagen to London via Tallinn, St. Petersburg, Helsinki, Visby, Warnemunde, Kiel Canal. August 3, 10 days, round-trip from London to Leith, Invergordon, Kirkwall, Oban, Dublin, Waterford, Fowey, London/Pilot Station. August 13, 10 days, London to Reykjavik via Leith, Invergordon, Lerwick, Thorshavn, Akureyri, Isafjordur. August 23, 9 days, round-trip from Reykjavik to Isafjordur, Akureyri, Husavik, Seydisfjordur, Thorshavn, Heimaey. September 1, 10 days, Reykjavik to London via Kirkwall, Stornoway, Oban, Greenock, Dublin, Waterford, Fowey.

September 11, 12 days, London to Nice via St. Malo, Bordeaux, Bilbao, Lisbon, Cadiz, Port Mahon. September–October, 10 days, Nice to Istanbul, Istanbul to Venice, Venice to Piraeus, Piraeus to Barcelona. November 2, 15 days, Barcelona to Barbados via Malaga, Casablanca, Las Palmas, Tenerife, Dominica, St. Lucia.

November 17, reverse December 4, 17 days, Barbados to Los Angeles via Aruba, Cartagena, San Blas Islands, Panama Canal, Puntarenas, Puerto Quetzal, Acapulco, Puerto Vallarta, Cabo San Lucas, Ensenada. December 21, 28, 7 days, round-trip from Barbados to Dominica, St. Barts, Tortola, Grenada, Bequia; or Guadeloupe, St. Maarten, Antigua, Mayreau, St. Lucia, Kingstown.

January 29, 2011, March 5, 2011, 9 nights, Caribbean, from Bridgetown to Fort Lauderdale, via Bequie, Dominica, St. Kitts, St. Barts, St. Maarten, Grand Turk. February 7, March 14, 10 days, to St. Kitts, Antigua, St. Barts, Grand Turk. February 26, round-trip from Bridgetown to St. Barts, St. Maarten, Antigua, Guadeloupe, St. Lucia. March 24, reverse April 9, 16 days, Panama Canal, from Fort Lauderdale to San Diego via Cartagena, San Blas Islands, Panama Canal, Puntarenas, Puerto Quetzal, Acapulco, Zihuatanejo, Cabo San Lucas. April 25, 9 days, to Bridgetown via Tortola, St. Martin, Antigua, St. Lucia, Bequia, Grenada.

Silver Shadow HOME PORTS Fort Lauderdale, Los Angeles, Tokyo, and others

May 13, 12 days, Los Angeles to Vancouver via San Francisco, Ketchikan, Sitka, Juneau, Skagway, cruising Sawyer Glacier, Victoria.

May–September, 7–10 days, round-trip from Vancouver, Vancouver to Seward, Seward to Vancouver, Vancouver to San Francisco; round-trip from San Francisco, San Francisco to Vancouver. September 12, 16 days, Vancouver to Tokyo via Inside Passage, Ketchikan, Tracy Arm Fjord, Sawyer Glacier, Juneau, Skagway, Kodiak, Dutch harbour, Petropavlovsk, Hakodate, Sendai.

September–December, 9 to 15 days, Tokyo to Shanghai, Shanghai to Hong Kong, Hong Kong to Thailand, Thailand to Singapore, Singapore to Hong Kong; round-trip from Hong

Kong, Hong Kong to Singapore, Singapore to Sydney, Sydney to Auckland.

January 4, 2011, 15 days, from Auckland to Sydney via Bay of Islands, Picton, Wellington, Christchurch, Port Chalmers, Stewart Island, cruising Milford Sound, Hobart, Melbourne. January 19, 30 days, Australia, round-trip from Sydney to Brisbane, Whitsunday Islands, Willis Islets, Port Douglas, Cooktown, Darwin, Broome, Exmouth, Perth, Albany, Port Lincoln, Adelaide, Geelong, Melbourne, Hobart.

Silver Spirit **HOME PORTS** New York, Southampton, Barcelona, and others

May 8, 12 days, Southampton to Barcelona via St. Malo, Bordeaux, Bilbao, Lisbon, Cadiz, Gibraltar, Malaga.

May–October, 7–9 days, Barcelona to Rome, Rome to Venice, Venice to Piraeus, Piraeus to Istanbul; round-trip Istanbul, Istanbul to Piraeus, Piraeus to Rome, Rome to Barcelona, Barcelona to Monte Carlo, Monte Carlo to Rome, Rome to Venice, Venice to Piraeus, Istanbul to Piraeus, Piraeus to Venice, Venice to Rome, Rome to Barcelona, Barcelona to Lisbon, Lisbon to Nice, Nice to Rome.

October 23, 14 days, Lisbon to Barbados via Tangier, Casablanca, Arricife, Tenerife, Antigua, St. Lucia. November–December, 7–14 days, round-trip from Barbados to Fort Lauderdale.

January 3, 2011, 16 days, Panama Canal, from Fort Lauderdale to Los Angeles via Cartagena, San Blas Islands, Panama Canal, Puntarenas, Puerto Quetzal, Acapulco, Cabo San Lucas, San Diego. January 19, 1 day, round-trip from Los Angeles. January 20, 12 days, from Los Angeles to Papeete via Nuku Hiva, Atuona, Rangiroa, Moorea. February 1, 10 days, from Papeete to Auckland via Raiatea, Bora Bora, Rarotonga, Bay of Islands. February 12, 17 days, from Auckland to Sydney via Wellington, Christchurch, Port Chalmers, cruising Milford Sound, Hobart, Kangaroo Island, Adelaide, Geelong, Melbourne.

January 19, 2011, 119-day World Cruise (her first) from Los Angeles, visiting 60 destinations in 25 countries with 11 overnight port visits and ending in Southampton on May 19.

Silver Whisper **HOME PORT** Varies with itinerary

May 24, 7 days, Rome to Nice via Sorrento, Taormina, Palermo, Calvi, St. Tropez. May 31, 12 days, Nice to Southampton via Barcelona, Malaga, Gibraltar, Lisbon, Oporto, Bilbao, St. Malo, Honfleur. June–August, 7–11 days, Southampton to Stockholm, Stockholm to Copenhagen, Copenhagen to Stockholm, round-trip Copenhagen, Stockholm to Southampton.

September 2, 12 days, transatlantic, Southampton to New York via Fowey, Waterford, St. John, Halifax, Newport. September 14, return September 24, 10 days, New York to Montreal via Newport, Cape Cod Canal, Boston, Bar Harbour, Halifax (Lunenburg on return), Sydney, Prince Edward Island, St. Lawrence River, Quebec City; or reverse. October 4, 10 days, round-trip from New York to Halifax, Sydney, St. John, Bar Harbour, Portland, Boston, Cape Cod Canal, Newport.

October 14, 10 days, New York to Barbados via Bermuda, San Juan, St. Barts, Antigua, Bequia. October 24, 16 days, Barbados to Rio de Janeiro via St. Lucia, Grenada, Devil's Island, Belem, Natal, Recife, Salvador. November 9, 8 days, Rio de Janeiro to Buenos Aires via Santos, Rio Grande Do Sul, Punta del Este, Montevideo. November 17, 2010, December 3, 2010 reverse, December 19, 2010, January 4, 2011 reverse, January 20, 2011, 16 days, Buenos Aires to Valparaiso via Montevideo, Punta del Este, Puerto Madryn, Stanley, Chilean Fjords/Magellan Strait, Punta Arenas, cruising Chilean Fjords, Laguna San Rafael, Puerto Chacabuco, Puerto Montt.

Silver Wind **HOME PORT** Varies with itinerary

March 2010–October 2010, March 2011–September 2011, 7–12 days, Mediterranean/ Iberia/Canary Islands, Las Palmas to Lisbon, Lisbon to Rome, Rome to Piraeus, Piraeus to Istanbul, Istanbul to Venice, round-trip Venice, Venice to Rome, Barcelona to Monte Carlo, Monte Carlo to Piraeus, Venice to Monte Carlo, Monte Carlo to Venice, Rome to

Barcelona, Barcelona to Lisbon, Lisbon to Monte Carlo, Venice to Piraeus, round-trip to Istanbul, Istanbul to Monte Carlo, Monte Carlo to Istanbul, Istanbul to Piraeus.

November 9, 16 days, Piraeus to Dubai via Rhodes, Alexandria, Suez Canal transit, Suez, Sharm el Sheikh, Aqaba, Safaga, Muscat. November 25, 7 days, round-trip from Dubai to Abu Dhabi, Fujairah, Muscat, Bahrain. December 2, 9 days, Dubai to Mumbai via Fujairah, Bandar Abbas, Khasab, Muscat, Porbandar. December 11, 9 days, Mumbai to Dubai via Mormugao, Cochin, New Mangalore, Muscat. December 20, 14 days, round-trip from Dubai to Abu Dhabi, Fujairah, Muscat, Salalah, Bandar Abbas, Khasab, Bahrain.

January 10, 17 days, from Dubai to Mahe via Fujairah, Muscat, Mumbai, Cochin, Colombo, Male, Curieuse Island, La Dique, Praslin. Janury 27, 14 days, from Mahe to Port Louis via Praslin, La Dique, Silhouette Island, Mombasa, Zanzibar, Mosy Be/Nosy Komba, Pointe des Galets. February 10, 10 days, from Port Louis to Cape Town via Tulear, Richards Bay, Durban, Port Elizabeth. February 20, March 2, 10 days, round-trip from Cape Town to East London, Maputo, Richards Bay, Durban, Port Elizabeth, Mossel Bay.

Star Clippers, Inc.

Note: All ports may not be included on every Star Clipper cruise, as itineraries are subject to weather conditions and alterations by the captain, in search of calm sailing and best anchorage.

Royal Clipper **HOME PORTS** Barbados, Malaga, Rome, and others.

April 26, 12 nights, Malaga to Rome via Cadiz, Tangier, Gibraltar, Puerto Banus, Motril, Cartagena, Palma, Mallorca, Mahon, Menorca, Calvi, Portoferraio. May–June, September–October, 7 nights, round-trip from Rome to Ponza, Sorrento/Capri, Amalfi, Taormina, Lipari. June–August, 10 or 11 nights, between Rome and Venice, Ponza, Capri, Taormina, Corfu, Kotor, Dubrovnik, Korcula, Hvar, Rovinj, or reverse without Rovinj. October 16, 12 nights, Rome to Lisbon via Bonifacio, Mahon, Menorca, Ibiza, Motril, Safi, Casablanca, Tangier, Cadiz, Portimao. October 28, 16 nights, transatlantic, Lisbon to Barbados via Casablanca, Safi, Tenerife. December 18, 8 nights, round-trip from Barbados to Grenadines, Grenada, Tobago Cays, Young Island, Bequia, Martinique, Dominica, St. Lucia.

November–April 2011, 7 nights, round-trip from Barbados to St. Lucia, Dominica, Antigua, St. Kitts, Martinique; or Grenadines, Grenada, Tobago Cays, St. Vincent, Bequia, Martinique, St. Lucia.

January 2, 2011, 6 nights, round-trip from Barbados to Grenadines, Grenada, Tobago Cays, St. Vincent, Bequia, St. Lucia. March 12, 22, 2011, 10 or 11 nights, round-trip from Barbados to St. Barts, Norman Island, Sopers Hole, Jost Van Dyke, Virgin Gorda, Antigua, St. Kitts, Martinique, St. Lucia; or 11 nights with Dominica.

Star Clipper **HOME PORTS** Phuket, Singapore, Athens, Lisbon; others vary with itinerary

May–July, August–October, round-trip from Athens to Camlimani, Kusadasi, Patmos, Amorgos, Delos, Mykonos, Tinos; or Bodrum, Dalyan River, Santorini, Milos, Hydra. July 10, July 28 reverse, 10 or 11 nights, Athens to Venice via Mykonos, Santorini, Yithion, Corfu, Kotor, Dubrovnik, Korcula, Hvar, Mali Lusinj; reverse without Korcula. November 21, reverse November 28, 7 nights, Phuket to Singapore via Similan Islands, Phang Nga/Ko Hong, Ko Adang, Penang, Malacca; return Malacca, Langkawi, Butang Group, Phang Nga/Ko Hong, Ko Miang. October 14, reverse, 38 nights, Phuket to Athens via Simian Islands, Colombo, Cochin, Goa, Safaga, Sharm el Sheik, Suez Canal, Port Said, Alexandria, Rhodes, Mykonos; reverse includes Salalah.

November 2010–March 2011, 7 nights, alternating southern, northern, and Myanmar routes, round-trip from Phuket to Ko Adang, Penang, Ko Butang, Ko Rok Nok, Phang Nga, Ko Hong, Similan Islands; or Surin Islands, Similan Islands, Ko Rok Nok, Ko Muk, Langkawi, Ko Kradan, Phang Nga, Ko Hong; or Ko Surin, Mergui Archipelago, Bo Cho, Ko Phawt, Great Swinton Island, Shark Island, Nyaung Wee, Similan Islands.

Star Flyer **HOME PORTS** Cannes, Monte Carlo, Papeete; others vary with itinerary
April–October, 3–7 nights, alternating Ligurian and Tyrrhenian, Monte Carlo or Cannes to L'lle Rousse/St. Florent, East Corsica, Bastia, Portoferraio, Portofino, Hyeres Island, Sanary-sur-Mer, San Tropez; or Cannes to Monte Carlo via Calvi, Figari Beach, Bonifacio, Costa Smeralda, Giglio, Lerici, St. Tropez; 4 nights, round-trip from Cannes to Monte Carlo, Calvi, Portofino; 3 nights, Monte Carlo to L'lle Rousse/St. Florent, St. Tropez; Cannes to Monaco or reverse.

July 3, August 21, 14 nights, Monte Carlo to Rhodes via Calvi, Figari Beach, Bonifacio, Costa Smeralda, Ponza, Sorrento, Lipari, Stromboli, Taormina, Elafonisos, Santorini, Amorgos, Bodrum, Dalyan River; or Rhodes to Monte Carlo via Marmaris, Bodrum, Amorgos, Santorini, Elafonisos, Taormina, Lipari/Stromboli, Sorrento, Ponza, Giglio, Portoferraio, Lerici.

October 31, 14 nights, Barbados to Balboa via Grenadines, Grenada, Margarita Island, Blanquilla, Bonaire, Curaçao, Aruba, Cartagena, San Blas Islands, Panama Canal. November 14, 7 nights, Balboa to Puerto Caldera via Isla Iguana, Isla de Coiba, Golfito, Isla del Cano, Drake Bay, Quepos, National Reserve of Curu, Isla Tortugas.

November 2010–March 2011, 7 nights, Costa Rica, alternating Nicaragua and Panama, round-trip from Puerto Caldera to San Juan del Sur, Playas del Coco, National Park Santa Rosa, Samara, Puerto Carrillo, National Reserve of Curu, Isla Tortugas; or Isla Coiba, Golfito, Isla del Cano, Drake Bay, Quepos, National Reserve of Curu, Isla Tortugas.

Swan Hellenic Cruises

Minerva **HOME PORT** Dover
May, 13–16 days, South Africa, Mozambique, Madagascar, Tanzania, Kenya, Seychelles, Yemen, Egypt, Jordan, Greece, Turkey, Ukraine, Bulgaria, Malta, Libya, Tunisia, Spain, Portugal, England.

June–August, 15 or 16 days, round-trip from Dover to Norway, Netherlands, France, Isles of Scilly, Channel Islands, Germany, Denmark, Russia, Sweden, Scotland, Iceland, Faroe Islands, Ireland.

August 26–December 4, 15–43 days, Channel Islands, Spain, Portugal, Italy, Corsica, Sicily, Croatia, Albania, Greece, Greek Islands, Turkey, Bulgaria, Ukraine, Malta, Tunisia Libya, Cyprus, Syria, Egypt, Jordan, Saudi Arabia, Yemen, Oman, Dubai.

December 19, 2010–March 16, 2011, 15–44 days, India, Sri Lanka, Thailand, Malaysia, Singapore, Brunei, Philippines, Hong Kong, Vietnam, Cambodia.

Travel Dynamics International

Clelia II **HOME PORT** Buenos Aires; others vary with itinerary
June–September, 8 nights, Great Lakes, Toronto to Duluth via Port Weller, Welland Canal, Niagara Falls, Lake Erie, Lake Huron, Little Current, Lake Huron, Mackinac Island, Lake Michigan, Lake Huron, Soo Locks, Lake Superior, Houghton, Thunder Bay, from Torotno to Newfoundland via Thousand Islands/St. Lawrence Seaway, Montreal, Quebec City, Saguenay River, Gaspe/Perce/Ile Bonaventure, Charlottetown, Ingonish, St. Pierre.

September 25, October 4, 10 or 11 nights, Newfoundland to Gloucester via Louisbourg, Baddeck, Charlottetown, Halifax, Bar Harbor, Portland. October 13, Halifax to West Palm Beach via Lunenburg, Bar Harbor, Portland, Newport, Alexandria, Yorktown/Colonial Williamsburg, Charleston, Savannah

Corinthian II **HOME PORT** Ushuaia; others vary with itinerary
September 9, 13 nights, Tunis to Rome via Malta, Licata, Messina, Agropoli, Salerno, Gaeta. September 20, 9 nights, Music Cruise, Rome to Istanbul via Salerno/Pompeii or Ravello/ Amalfi, Syracuse, Santorini, Rhodes/Lindos, Kusadasi/Ephesus, Chios. September 27, 11 nights, round-trip from Istanbul to Thasos, Thessaloniki/Vergina, Volos/Pelion or Meteora/Volos, Canakkale/Troy, Mudanya/Bursa, Amasra, Nessebur.

October 5, 14 nights, Istanbul to Venice via Chios, Rhodes/Lindos, Heraklion/Knossos/ Rethymnon, Valletta, Roccella Ionica/Gerace, Nafpaktos, Otranto, Kotor. October 27, 14 nights, Istanbul to Alexandria via Chios, Delos, Kusadasi/Ephesus or Priene/Kusadasi, Heraklion/Knossos, Rhodes/Lindos, Paphos, Marsa Matruh/Siwa Oasis. November 5, 17 nights, Alexandria to Casablanca via Tubruq, Derna/Cyrene/Apollonia, Khoms/Leptis Magna, Tripoli/Sabratha, Sfax/El Djem, Tunis/Carthage, Annaba/Hippo Regius, Bejaia/ Djemila, Melilla, Tangier.

November 20, 35 nights, Casablanca to Ushuaia via Laayoune, Santo Antao, Sao Vicente, Recife/Olinda, Salvador, Rio de Janeiro, Santos/Sao Paolo/Itatinga, Paranagua/Curitiba, Montevideo, Mar del Plata, Puerto Madryn, Westpoint Island/Saunders Island/Stanley.

Voyages to Antiquity

Aegean Odyssey **HOME PORTS** Athens, Cairo, Istanbul, Rome, Venice
May 4, September 7, 15 days, round-trip from Athens to Mycenae, Epidaurus, Crete, Rhodes, Delos, Troy, Istanbul, Mount Athos. May 18, July 27, September 21, 15 days, Athens to Rome via Sicily, Palermo, Italy, Pompeii, Herculaneum, Capri.

June 1, August 10, October 5, 15 days, Rome to Venice via Pompeii, Amalfi, Aeolian Islands, Segesta, Vesuvius, Etna and Stromboli, Split. July 13, August 24, October 19, 15 days, Venice to Athens via Split, Kornati Islands, Greece, Osios Loùkas Monastery, Corinth Canal. June 15, 15 days, Venice to Istanbul via exclusive evening in St Mark's, Greek Islands. June 29, 15 days, Istanbul to Venice via Pátmos, monasteries of Metéora, Butrint, Ravenna.

November 2, 15 days, Athens and Cairo via Malta Mdina, Carthage, El-Jem, Leptis Magna, Cairo. November 13, 15 days, Cairo to Amman via Red Sea, Suez Canal, Luxor, Wadi Rum, Petra, Jerash. November 21, 15 days, Cairo and Athens via Egypt, Suez Canal, Lebanon, Syria, Cyprus, Antalya.

Voyages of Discovery

Discovery **HOME PORT** Varies with itinerary
May 8, 18 nights, Istanbul to Harwich (London) via Heraklion, Valletta, Messina, Sorrento Rome, Ajaccio, Almeria, Gibraltar, Lisbon, Harwich.

May 21, 10 nights, Harwich to Bergen, Ålesund, Geiranger, Hellesylt, Flam. May 28, 15 nights, to Copenhagen, Stockholm, St. Petersburg (overnight), Gdynia, Warnemunde, Kiel Canal. June 9, 13 nights, round-trip from Harwich to Ålesund, Honningsvag, Tromso, Leknes, Flam. June 19, 14 nights, Harwich to St. Peter Port, Tresco, Dublin, Liverpool Belfast, Oban, Invergordon, Dundee. June 30, 17 nights, Harwich to Ålesund, Honningsvag, Ny Alesund, Longyearbyen, Barentsburg, Tromso, Leknes, Flam. July 14, 15 nights, round-trip from Harwich to Copenhagen, Stockholm, Tallinn, Helsinki, Warnemunde, Kiel Canal transit. July 26, 11 nights, Harwich to Reykjavik via Flam, Ålesund, Torshavn, Akureyri. July 26, 25 nights, Iceland and Greenland. August 5, 17 nights, Iceland and Greenland, from Reykjavik to Harwich via Illulissat, Nuuk, Qaqortoq, Kirkwall.

August 17, 13 nights, round-trip from Harwich to St. Peter Port, La Rochelle, Bordeaux (overnight), St. Malo, Rouen (overnight). August 27, 10 nights, round-trip from Harwich Bergen, Ålesund, Geiranger, Hellesylt, Flam. September 3, 20 nights, Harwich to Malta via Lisbon, Gibraltar, Almeria, Nice (overnight), Santa Margherita, Livorno, Rome, Sorrento (overnight), Palermo, Catania. September 3, 52 nights, Iberia, Italy, and with Spain; Italy and Adriatic; Adriatic and Black Sea; 42 nights, Andalucia, Italy combined with Adriatic, continues on to Cephalonia, Nauplia, Santorini, Mykonos, Piraeus, Volos, Canakkale, Istanbul; 30 nights, combines Iberia and Italy, continues to Korcula, Zadar, Venice, Koper, Split, Hvar, Dubrovnik. September 12, 43 nights, Mediterranean, Adriatic and Black Sea to Trabzon, Sochi (overnight), Yalta, Sevastopol, Odessa, Nesebur,

Istanbul; 33 nights, Italy, Greece, and Croatia, continues on to Cephalonia, Nauplia, Santorini, Mykonos, Piraeus, Volos, Canakkale, Istanbul; 21 nights, Italy and Croatia, continues on to Korkula, Zadar, Venice (overnight), Koper, Split, Hvar, Dubrovnik; 11 nights, Nice (overnight) to Malta via Santa Margherita, Livorno, Rome, Sorrento (overnight), Palermo (overnight), Catania.

September 22, 11 nights, Malta to Dubrovnik via Korcula, Zadar, Venice (overnight), Koper, Split, Hvar; 23 nights, Balkans, Adriatic, and Aegean; 33 nights, Italy, Adriatic, Aegean and Black Sea.

October 2, 13 nights, Dubrovnik to Istanbul via Cephalonia, Nauplia, Santorini, Mykonos, Piraeus, Volos, Canakkale. October 14, 11 nights, round-trip from Istanbul to Trabzon, Sochi, Yalta, Sevastopol, Odessa, Nesebur. October 24, 15 nights, Istanbul to Cairo via Sea of Marmara, Heraklion, Malta, Tripoli, Al Khums, Gulf of Sirte, Benghazi, Alexandria (overnight). October 24, Libya and the Red Sea. November 3, 15 nights, Cairo to Malaga via Benghazi, Al Khums, Valletta, Trapani, La Goulette, Cagliari, Cartagena.

Windstar Cruises

Wind Spirit **HOME PORTS** Athens, Istanbul, Rome, St. Martin; others vary with itinerary
April–May, 7 days, Lisbon to Barcelona, Barcelona to Nice, Nice to Rome. May 22, 7 days, Rome to Athens via Ischia, Amalfi, Messina, Monemvasia, Milos. May–October, 7 days, Athens to Istanbul via Mykonos, Santorini, Rhodes, Bodrum, Kusadasi or reverse. July 10, reverse July 24, Athens to Venice via Monemvasia, Pylos, Kotor, Dubrovnik, Hvar; or Pula, Dubrovnik, Kotor, Pylos, Monemvasia. July 17, 7 days, round-trip from Venice to Rovinj, Opatija, Trogir, Dubrovnik. October–November, 7 days, round-trip from Rome to Barcelona, Lisbon. November 20, 14 days, transatlantic, Lisbon to St. Maarten.

December, 7 days, round-trip from St. Martin to St. Kitts, Tortola, Jost Van Dyke, Virgin Gorda, St. Barts.

Wind Star **HOME PORTS** Athens, Lisbon, Puerto Caldera, Rome; others vary with itinerary
May–October, 7 days, Rome to Athens, Athens to Istanbul or reverse.

December, 7 days, round-trip from Puerto Caldera to San Juan del Sur, Playas del Coco, Quepos, Bahia Drake, Curu, Tortuga Island.

Wind Surf **HOME PORTS** Barbados, Barcelona, Lisbon; others vary with itinerary
April–November, 7 days, Lisbon to Barcelona and reverse, Rome to Athens, Athens to Rome, Rome to Venice and reverse, Rome to Nice and reverse, round-trip from Rome, round-trip from Venice, Nice to Barcelona, Barcelona to Rome.

November 14, 14 days, transatlantic, from Lisbon to Barbados.

November–December, 7 days, round-trip from Barbados to Bequia, Dominica, St. Lucia, Mayreau, Grenada, Tobago.

The World/ResidenSea

The World **HOME PORT** Varies with itinerary as it continually sails around the world
2010, Austrialia, Indonesia/Bali, Singapore, Thailand, Yangon, Port Blair, Havelock Island, Male, Cochin, Dubai, Doha, Muscat, Egypt, Greece, Kotor, Rovinj, Venice, Rab, Novalja, Split, Korcula, Italy, France, Spain, Lisbon, Hendaye, Guernsey, Britain, Oban, Torshavn, Reykjavik, Greenland, St. Anthony, Quebec, Montreal, Halifax, Boston, Newport, New York, Bermuda, Baltimore, Charleston, Savannah, Port Canaveral, Nassau, Fort Lauderdale, San Juan, Gustavia, Barbados, Brazil, Parati, Punta del Este, Montevideo, Buenos Aires, Usuaia, Antarctica.

CRUISE SHIP INDEX

DESTINATION INDEX

SUBJECT INDEX

Unofficial Guide to Cruises Reader Survey 2010

If you would like to express an opinion about your cruise or this guidebook, complete the following survey and return to:

Unofficial Guide Reader Survey
P.O. Box 43673
Birmingham, AL 35243

Name of ship: _____

Today's date: _____

Date, duration, and destination of cruise: _____

Was this your ☐ 1st ☐ 2nd ☐ 3rd ☐ 4th ☐ 5th or more cruise?

Would you take another cruise on this ship? ☐ Yes ☐ No

Recommend it to a friend? ☐ Yes ☐ No

Do you plan to cruise ☐ within a year ☐ within next 3 years?

Your age: ☐ teens ☐ 20s ☐ 30s ☐ 40s ☐ 50s ☐ 60s ☐ 70s

☐ over 80

You are: | employed ☐ self-employed ☐ retired

Your line of work: _____

Please score items below from 1 to 10 with 10 being the highest or best. Feel free to add your comments.

Value for money: _____

Total cruise experience: _____

Your overall impression of the ship (*appearance, appeal, furnishings and decor, cleanliness, sports and recreation facilities, consistency, comfort, boarding/disembarking procedures*): _____

Cruise director (*available, helpful, friendly*): _____

Cruise staff: _____

Dining room food (*choices, quality, taste, presentation*): _____

Breakfast and lunch buffet: _____

Dining room service: _____

Bar service: _____

Cabin (*size, layout, soundproofing, cleanliness, appearance, condition*):

Bathroom: _____

Cabin attendant (*service, attitude*): _____

Enrichment programs, lectures, games *(variety and quality)*: _____

Entertainment in the main lounge: _____

Entertainment in other lounges: _____

Children's programs: _____

Youth counselors: _____

Shore excursions (guides, variety, advanced information, value): _____

MORE QUESTIONS:

Was the food quality better, worse, or about what you expected? _____

Were wine and bar prices low, moderate, or high? _____

Was the music level tolerable or too loud, especially by the pool? _____

Were you bothered by announcements over the public address system? _____

Was the promotion of shipboard shops low key, moderate, or hard sell? _____

Was the lifeboat drill well executed? _____

Did you choose your cruise for its itinerary? _____

Which ports of call did you like best? _____

Were port talks poor or helpful? _____

Did the speakers plug specific shops? _____

*Was passenger information available prior to the cruise? in your cabin?
during the cruise?* _____

YOUR HOMETOWN:

How did you learn about your cruise? _____

How did you learn about this book? _____

Where did you buy your cruise? _____

When and where did you buy this book? _____

If you are available for a telephone interview, please give us your name,
address, telephone number, and a convenient time to call.

_____

_____

_____

THANK YOU!